Contemporary Authors

NEW REVISION SERIES

Contemporary Authors
was named an
***"Outstanding
Reference Source"*** *by
the American Library
Association Reference
and Adult Services
Division after its 1962
inception.*
*In 1985 it was listed by
the same organization
as one of the
twenty-five most
distinguished reference
titles published in the
past twenty-five years.*

ISSN 0275-7176

Contemporary

Authors®

A Bio-Bibliographical Guide to
Current Writers in Fiction, General Nonfiction,
Poetry, Journalism, Drama, Motion Pictures,
Television, and Other Fields

SUSAN M. TROSKY
Editor

NEW REVISION SERIES *volume* **41**

 Gale Research Inc. • *DETROIT* • *WASHINGTON, D.C.* • *LONDON*

STAFF

Susan M. Trosky, *Editor, New Revision Series*

Bruce Ching, Elizabeth A. Des Chenes, Susan M. Reicha, Pamela L. Shelton, Kenneth R. Shepherd, Deborah A. Stanley, and Thomas Wiloch, *Associate Editors*

Pamela S. Dear, Margaret Mazurkiewicz, Thomas F. McMahon, Terrie M. Rooney, and Brandon Trenz, *Assistant Editors*

Joan Goldsworthy, Jeff Hill, Anne Janette Johnson, Elizabeth Judd, Charles F. Kennedy, Cornelia A. Pernik, Roger M. Valade III, and Michaela Swart Wilson, *Contributing Editors*

James G. Lesniak, *Senior Editor, Contemporary Authors*

Victoria B. Cariappa, *Research Manager*

Mary Rose Bonk, *Research Supervisor*

Reginald A. Carlton, Clare Collins, Andrew Guy Malonis, and Norma Sawaya, *Editorial Associates*

Rachel A. Dixon, Eva Marie Felts, Shirley Gates, and Sharon McGilvray, *Editorial Assistants*

♾ ™ This book is printed on acid-free paper that meets the minimum requirements of American National Standard for Information Sciences-Permanence Paper for Printed Library Materials, ANSI Z39.48-1984.

Library of Congress Catalog Card Number 81-640179

ISBN 0-8103-1972-1
ISSN 0275-7176

Printed in the United States of America.

Published simultaneously in the United Kingdom
by Gale Research International Limited
(An affiliated company of Gale Research Inc.)

I(T)P™

The trademark ITP is used under license.
10 9 8 7 6 5 4 3 2 1

Contents

Indexing note: All *Contemporary Authors New Revision Series*
entries are indexed in the *Contemporary Authors* cumulative
index, which is published separately and distributed with even-
numbered *Contemporary Authors* original volumes and odd-
numbered *Contemporary Authors New Revison Series* volumes.

**As always, the most recent *Contemporary Authors* cumulative
index continues to be the user's guide to the location of an
individual author's listing.**

Preface

The *Contemporary Authors New Revision Series* (*CANR*) provides completely updated information on authors listed in earlier volumes of *Contemporary Authors* (*CA*). Entries for individual authors from *any* volume of *CA* may be included in a volume of the *New Revision Series*. *CANR* updates only those sketches requiring significant change.

Authors are included on the basis of specific criteria that indicate the need for significant revision. These criteria include bibliographical additions, changes in addresses or career, major awards, and personal information such as name changes or death dates. All listings in this volume have been revised or augmented in various ways. Some sketches have been extensively rewritten, and many include informative new sidelights. As always, a *CANR* listing entails no charge or obligation.

How to Get the Most out of *CA*: Use the Index

The key to locating an author's most recent entry is the *CA* cumulative index, which is published separately and distributed with even-numbered original volumes and odd-numbered revision volumes. It provides access to *all* entries in *CA* and *CANR*. Always consult the latest index to find an author's most recent entry.

For the convenience of users, the *CA* cumulative index also includes references to all entries in these Gale literary series: *Authors and Artists for Young Adults, Authors in the News, Bestsellers, Black Literature Criticism, Black Writers, Children's Literature Review, Concise Dictionary of American Literary Biography, Concise Dictionary of British Literary Biography, Contemporary Authors Autobiography Series, Contemporary Authors Bibliographical Series, Contemporary Literary Criticism, Dictionary of Literary Biography, Drama Criticism, Hispanic Writers, Major Authors and Illustrators for Children and Young Adults, Major 20th-Century Writers, Poetry Criticism, Short Story Criticism, Something about the Author, Something about the Author Autobiography Series, Twentieth-Century Literary Criticism, World Literature Criticism,* and *Yesterday's Authors of Books for Children.*

A Sample Index Entry:

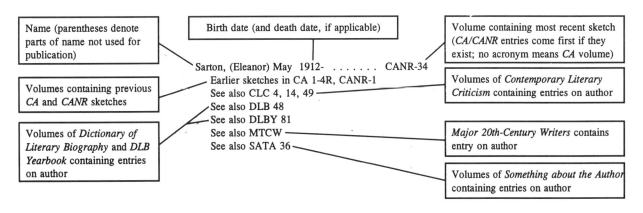

For the most recent *CA* information on Sarton, users should refer to Volume 34 of the *New Revision Series,* as designated by "CANR-34"; if that volume is unavailable, refer to CANR-1. And if CANR-1 is unavailable, refer to CA 1-4R, published in 1967, for Sarton's First Revision entry.

How Are Entries Compiled?

The editors make every effort to secure new information directly from the authors. Copies of all sketches in selected *CA* and *CANR* volumes previously published are routinely sent to listees at their last-known addresses, and returns from these authors are then assessed. For deceased writers, or those who fail to reply to requests for data, we consult other reliable biographical sources, such as those indexed in Gale's *Biography and Genealogy Master Index,* and bibliographical sources, such as *National Union Catalog, LC MARC,* and *British National Bibliography.* Further details come from published interviews, feature stories, and book reviews, and often the authors' publishers supply material.

* Indicates that a listing has been compiled from secondary sources believed to be reliable but has not been personally verified for this edition by the author sketched.

What Kinds of Information Does an Entry Provide?

Sketches in *CANR* contain the following biographical and bibliographical information:

- **Entry heading:** the most complete form of author's name, plus any pseudonyms or name variations used for writing

- **Personal information:** author's date and place of birth, family data, educational background, political and religious affiliations, and hobbies and leisure interests

- **Addresses:** author's home, office, or agent's addresses as available

- **Career summary:** name of employer, position, and dates held for each career post; résumé of other vocational achievements; military service

- **Membership information:** professional, civic, and other association memberships and any official posts held

- **Awards and honors:** military and civic citations, major prizes and nominations, fellowships, grants, and honorary degrees

- **Writings:** a comprehensive, chronological list of titles, publishers, dates of original publication and revised editions, and production information for plays, television scripts, and screenplays

- **Adaptations:** a list of films, plays, and other media which have been adapted from the author's work

- **Work in progress:** current or planned projects, with dates of completion and/or publication, and expected publisher, when known

- **Sidelights:** a biographical portrait of the author's development; information about the critical reception of the author's works; revealing comments, often by the author, on personal interests, aspirations, motivations, and thoughts on writing

- **Biographical and critical sources:** a list of books and periodicals in which additional information on an author's life and/or writings appears

Related Titles in the *CA* Series

Contemporary Authors Autobiography Series complements *CA* original and revised volumes with specially commissioned autobiographical essays by important current authors, illustrated with personal photographs they provide. Common topics include their motivations for writing, the people and experiences that shaped their careers, the rewards they derive from their work, and their impressions of the current literary scene.

Contemporary Authors Bibliographical Series surveys writings by and about important American authors since World War II. Each volume concentrates on a specific genre and features approximately ten writers; entries list works written by and about the author and contain a bibliographical essay discussing the merits and deficiencies of major critical and scholarly studies in detail.

Suggestions Are Welcome

The editors welcome comments and suggestions from users on any aspects of the *CA* series. If readers would like to recommend authors whose entries should appear in future volumes of the series, they are cordially invited to write: The Editors, *Contemporary Authors*, 835 Penobscot Bldg., Detroit, MI 48226-4094; call toll-free at 1-800-347-GALE; or fax to 1-313-961-6599.

CA Numbering System and Volume Update Chart

Occasionally questions arise about the *CA* numbering system and which volumes, if any, can be discarded. Despite numbers like "29-32R," "97-100" and "140," the entire *CA* series consists of only 108 physical volumes with the publication of *CA* New Revision Series Volume 41. The following charts note changes in the numbering system and cover design, and indicate which volumes are essential for the most complete, up-to-date coverage.

CA First Revision
- 1-4R through 41-44R (11 books)
  Cover: Brown with black and gold trim.
  There will be no further First Revision volumes because revised entries are now being handled exclusively through the more efficient *New Revision Series* mentioned below.

CA Original Volumes
- 45-48 through 97-100 (14 books)
  Cover: Brown with black and gold trim.
- 101 through 140 (40 books)
  Cover: Blue and black with orange bands.
  The same as previous *CA* original volumes but with a new, simplified numbering system and new cover design.

CA Permanent Series
- *CAP*-1 and *CAP*-2 (2 books)
  Cover: Brown with red and gold trim.
  There will be no further *Permanent Series* volumes because revised entries are now being handled exclusively through the more efficient *New Revision Series* mentioned below.

CA New Revision Series
- *CANR*-1 through *CANR*-41 (41 books)
  Cover: Blue and black with green bands.
  Includes only sketches requiring extensive changes; **sketches are taken from any previously published *CA, CAP,* or *CANR* volume.**

If You Have:	You May Discard:
CA First Revision Volumes 1-4R through 41-44R **and** *CA Permanent Series* Volumes 1 and 2	*CA* Original Volumes 1, 2, 3, 4 Volumes 5-6 through 41-44
CA Original Volumes 45-48 through 97-100 **and** 101 through 140	**NONE:** These volumes will not be superseded by corresponding revised volumes. Individual entries from these and all other volumes appearing in the left column of this chart may be revised and included in the various volumes of the *New Revision Series*.
CA New Revision Series Volumes *CANR*-1 through *CANR*-41	**NONE:** The *New Revision Series* does not replace any single volume of *CA*. Instead, volumes of *CANR* include entries from many previous *CA* series volumes. All *New Revision Series* volumes must be retained for full coverage.

A Sampling of Authors and Media People
Featured in This Volume

Robert Bly
One of America's most influential poets, Bly has also gained renown for the prose work *Iron John,* which explores contemporary men and masculinity.

Zbigniew K. Brzezinski
A former national security adviser, Brzezinski predicted the collapse of Soviet-style communism in *The Grand Failure.*

Robin Cook
In novels like the best-selling *Coma* and *Vital Signs,* eye surgeon Cook depicts mystery and mayhem in the medical establishment.

Peter De Vries
A long-time staff member at the *New Yorker,* De Vries brings a finely honed sense of wit and whimsy to works like *The Tunnel of Love.*

Robert J. Donovan
Donovan, a journalist and former White House correspondant, portrays twentieth-century American politics and politicians in *PT 109, Confidential Secretary,* and *Unsilent Revolution.*

T. S. Eliot
One of the most influential poets of the twentieth century, Eliot was also a respected critic and dramatist. His works include *Murder in the Cathedral* and *The Wasteland.*

Louise Erdrich
Erdrich's Native American heritage influences her short stories and novels such as *The Beet Queen* and *The Crown of Columbus,* the latter written with her husband, Michael Dorris.

Allen Ginsberg
Ginsberg remains to many critics the poet who epitomizes the "Beat" generation. His poem "Howl" is widely regarded as a modern classic.

Nikki Giovanni
Although Giovanni first gained fame as a poet, her more recent works are nonfiction: *Sacred Cows ... and Other Edibles* and *Conversations with Nikki Giovanni.*

Tom Hayden
Hayden's memoir, *Reunion,* describes the authors' evolution from radical activist to mainsteam politician.

Derek Humphry
A euthanasia rights advocate, Humphry gained much critical and popular attention for his controversial work *Final Exit,* which examines methods for committing suicide.

Susan Isaacs
Isaac's popular novels *Compromising Positions* and *Shining Through* feature ordinary people facing uncommon dilemmas and have been adapted as motion pictures.

Betty Bao Lord
Lord has chronicled modern Chinese life and politics in works such as the biographical *Eighth Moon* and *Legacies: A Chinese Mosaic,* which describes the Cultural Revolution in China during the 1960s and 1970s.

Robert Ludlum
Ludlum's bestselling suspense novels include *The Holcroft Covenant, The Icarus Agenda,* and *The Bourne Ultimatum.*

Edna O'Brien
O'Brien's stories, praised for their elegant prose, depict troubled and lonely women. Her story collection *Lantern Slides* won a *Los Angeles Times* book prize in 1990.

P. J. O'Rourke
Journalist O'Rourke demonstrates his wild sense of humor in his bestsellers *Parliament of Whores* and *Give War a Chance.*

Ellis Peters
The adventures of Medieval sleuth Brother Cadfael have put Peters on international bestseller lists and earned her the Crime Writers Association Silver Dagger.

John Sayles
Noted independent screenwriter and director Sayles has also acted in and edited many of his feature films, including *The Brother from Another Planet* and *Eight Men Out.*

Paul Schrader
Screenwriter Schrader has earned acclaim for such controversial films as *Taxi Driver, American Gigolo,* and *The Last Temptation of Christ.*

Hedrick Smith
A Pulitzer Prize-winning journalist, Smith depicts Russian life before and after the fall of communism in *The Russians* and its sequel, *The New Russians.*

Contemporary Authors®

NEW REVISION SERIES

*Indicates that a listing has been compiled from secondary sources believed to be reliable
but has not been personally verified for this edition by the author sketched.*

ABBEY, Edward   1927-1989

PERSONAL: Born January 29, 1927, in Home, PA; died
of internal bleeding due to a circulatory disorder, March
14, 1989, in Oracle, AZ; buried in a desert in the southwestern United States; son of Paul Revere (a farmer) and
Mildred (a teacher; maiden name, Postlewaite) Abbey;
married Judith Pepper, 1965 (died, 1970); married fifth
wife, Clarke; children: Joshua, Aaron, Suzi, one other son,
one other daughter. *Education:* University of New Mexico, B.A., 1951, M.A., 1956; attended University of Edinburgh. *Politics:* "Agrarian anarchist." *Religion:* Piute.

ADDRESSES: Home—P.O. Box 1690, Oracle, AZ 85623.
Agent—Don Congdon, Harold Matson Co., Inc., 22 East
40th St., New York, NY 10016.

CAREER: Writer. Park ranger and fire lookout for National Park Service in the southwest United States,
1956-71. *Military service:* U.S. Army, 1945-46.

AWARDS, HONORS: Fulbright fellow, 1951-52; Western
Heritage Award for Best Novel, 1963, for *Fire on the
Mountain;* Guggenheim fellow, 1975; American Academy
of Arts and Letters award, 1987 (declined).

WRITINGS:

NOVELS

Jonathan Troy, Dodd, 1956.
The Brave Cowboy, Dodd, 1958.
Fire on the Mountain, Dial, 1962.
Black Sun, Simon & Schuster, 1971, published in England
   as *Sunset Canyon,* Talmy, 1972.
The Monkey Wrench Gang, Lippincott, 1975.
Good News, Dutton, 1980.
Confessions of a Barbarian (bound with *Red Knife Valley,*
   by Jack Curtis), Capra, 1986.
The Fool's Progress, Holt, 1988.

Hayduke Lives!, Little, Brown, 1990.

NONFICTION

Desert Solitaire: A Season in the Wilderness, illustrated by
   Peter Parnall, McGraw, 1968.
Appalachian Wilderness: The Great Smoky Mountains,
   photographs by Eliot Porter, Dutton, 1970.
(With Philip Hyde) *Slickrock: The Canyon Country of
   Southeast Utah,* Sierra Club, 1971.
(With others) *Cactus Country,* Time-Life, 1973.
*The Journey Home: Some Words in Defense of the Ameri-
   can West,* illustrated by Jim Stiles, Dutton, 1977.
Back Roads of Arizona, photographs by Earl Thollander,
   Northland Press, 1978, published as *Arizona's Scenic
   Byways,* 1992.
The Hidden Canyon: A River Journey, photographs by
   John Blaustein, Viking, 1978.
(With David Muench) *Desert Images: An American Land-
   scape,* Chanticleer, 1979.
Abbey's Road: Take the Other, Dutton, 1979.
(Self-illustrated) *Down the River,* Dutton, 1982.
(With John Nichols) *In Praise of Mountain Lions,* Albu-
   querque Sierra Club, 1984.
Beyond the Wall: Essays from the Outside, Holt, 1984.
(Editor and illustrator) *Slumgullion Stew: An Edward
   Abbey Reader,* Dutton, 1984, published as *The Best
   of Edward Abbey,* Sierra Club, 1988.
One Life at a Time, Please, Holt, 1988.
*A Voice Crying in the Wilderness: Essays from a Secret
   Journal,* illustrated by Andrew Rush, St. Martin's,
   1990.

OTHER

Also author of introductions for books, including *The
Rain, Fire, and the Will of God,* by Donald Wetzel, Second
Chance, 1985; *Ecodefense: A Field Guide to Monkey-
wrenching,* edited by Dave Foreman, Ned Ludd Books,

1987; *Spinoza: Practical Philosophy,* by Gilles Deleuze, City Lights Books, 1988; *The Land of Little Rain,* by Mary Austin, Viking, 1988; and *Wilderness on the Rocks,* by Howie Wolke, Ned Ludd Books, 1991. Author of afterword of *Everett Ruess, Everett Ruess: A Vagabond for Beauty,* Smith, Gibbs, 1985. Contributor to books, including *Utah Wilderness Photography: An Exhibition,* Utah Arts Council, 1978; and *Images from the Great West,* Chaco, 1990. A collection of Abbey's manuscripts is housed at the University of Arizona, Tucson.

ADAPTATIONS: The Brave Cowboy was adapted for film and released as *Lonely Are the Brave,* 1962; *Fire on the Mountain* was adapted for film, 1981.

SIDELIGHTS: Edward Abbey was best known for his hard-hitting, frequently bitter, usually irreverent defense of the world's wilderness areas. Anarchistic and outspoken, he was called everything from America's crankiest citizen to the godfather of modern environmental activism. Abbey himself strenuously resisted any attempt to classify him as a naturalist, environmentalist, or anything else. "If a label is required," Burt A. Folkart quoted him as saying in the *Los Angeles Times,* "say that I am one who loves the unfenced country." His favorite places were the deserts and mountains of the American West, and the few people who won his respect were those who knew how to live on that land without spoiling it. The many targets of his venom ranged from government agencies and gigantic corporations responsible for the rape of the wild country, to cattlemen grazing their herds on public lands, to simple-minded tourists who, according to Abbey, defile the solitude with their very presence.

Born on a small farm in Appalachia, Abbey hitchhiked west in 1946, following one year in the U.S. Army. Captivated by the wide-open spaces of Arizona, New Mexico, and Utah, he stayed there, studying philosophy and English at the University of New Mexico. In the early years of his writing career Abbey worked a variety of odd jobs, including that of road inspector for the Forest Service and ranger for the National Park Service. The experiences he gained in those positions were the foundation of his first notably successful book, *Desert Solitaire,* which was published in 1968.

Desert Solitaire opens with a truculent preface, in which the author expresses his hope that serious critics, librarians, and professors will intensely dislike his book. In the body of the book, which compresses many of Abbey's experiences with the Park Service and Forest Service into the framework of one cycle of the seasons, readers find both harsh criticism and poetic description, all related to the landscape of the West and what mankind is doing to it. Freeman Tilden, reviewing *Desert Solitaire* in *National Parks,* recommended the book, "vehemence, egotism, bad

taste and all. Partly because we need angry young men to remind us that there is plenty we should be angry about. . . . Partly because Abbey is an artist with words. There are pages and pages of delicious prose, sometimes almost magical in their evocation of the desert scene. . . . How this man can write! But he can do more than write. His prehension of the natural environment—of raw nature—is so ingenuous, so implicit, that we wonder if the pre-Columbian aborigines didn't see their environment just that way."

In a review of *Desert Solitaire* for the *New York Times Book Review,* Pulitzer Prize-winning writer Edwin Way Teale noted that Abbey's work as a park ranger brought him to the wilderness before the invasion of "the parked trailers, their windows blue tinged at night while the inmates, instead of watching the desert stars, watch TV and listen to the canned laughter of Hollywood." Calling the book "a voice crying in the wilderness, *for* the wilderness," Teale warned that it is also "rough, tough and combative. The author is a rebel, an eloquent loner. In his introduction, he gives fair warning that the reader may find his pages 'coarse, rude, bad-tempered, violently prejudiced.' But if they are all these, they are many things besides. His is a passionately felt, deeply poetic book. It has philosophy. It has humor. It has sincerity and conviction. It has its share of nerve tingling adventure in what he describes as a land of surprises, some of them terrible." Teale concluded: "Abbey writes with a deep undercurrent of bitterness. But as is not infrequently the case, the bitter man may be the one who cares enough to be bitter and he often is the one who says things that need to be said. In *Desert Solitaire* those things are set down in lean, racing prose, in a close-knit style of power and beauty. Rather than a balanced book, judicially examining in turn all sides, it is a forceful presentation of one side. And that side needs presenting. It is a side too rarely presented. There will always be others to voice the other side, the side of pressure and power and profit."

While it never made the bestseller lists, *Desert Solitaire* is credited as being a key source of inspiration for the environmental movement that was growing in the late 1960s. Abbey's no-holds-barred book awakened many readers to just how much damage was being done by government and business interests to so-called "public" lands, as did the many other essay collections he published throughout his career. But an even greater influence may have come from his 1975 novel, *The Monkey Wrench Gang.* Receiving virtually no promotion, it nonetheless became an underground classic, selling half a million copies. Within the comic story, which follows the misadventures of four environmentalist terrorists, is a serious message: peaceful protest is inadequate; the ecology movement must become radicalized. The ultimate goal of the Monkey Wrench

Gang—blowing up the immense Glen Canyon Dam on the Colorado River—is one Abbey seemed to endorse, and his book provides fairly explicit instructions to anyone daring enough to carry it out. The novel is said to have inspired the formation of the real-life environmental group Earth First!, which impedes the progress of developers and loggers by sabotaging bulldozers and booby-trapping trees with chainsaw-destroying spikes. Their term for such tactics: monkeywrenching.

National Observer reviewer Sheldon Frank called *The Monkey Wrench Gang* a "sad, hilarious, exuberant, vulgar fairy tale filled with long chase sequences and careful conspiratorial scheming. As in all fairy tales, the characters are pure cardboard, unbelievable in every respect. But they are delightful." A contributor to the London *Times* observed that the book is "less a work of fiction . . . than an incitement to environmentalists to take the law into their own hands, often by means of vandalizing whatever they considered to be themselves examples of vandalism and overkill." A sequel to *The Monkey Wrench Gang,* completed shortly before Abbey's death, was published posthumously; *Hayduke Lives!* finds most of the cast of the earlier novel settled comfortably into middle-class lives, only to be galvanized into action again by the reappearance of their leader, thought to be long dead. Critical assessment of the sequel varied widely. Grace Lichtenstein, reviewing it in the *Washington Post Book World,* found "the entire theme of ecotage" to be "shopworn," while *Chicago Tribune* editor David E. Jones stated that "the fun-loving bawdiness [of the original] is still there, and the camaraderie and dedication," along with "an unexpected darker side."

Abbey's personal favorite of his more than twenty books was the bulky, largely autobiographical novel *The Fool's Progress.* "From the outset of this cross-country story it seems almost impossible to separate Edward Abbey from his narrator," observed Howard Coale in the *New York Times Book Review.* "The harsh, humorous, damn-it-all voice of Henry Lightcap is identical to the voice in the author's many essays." In Coale's opinion, the book was too "self-involved" to be a really successful work of fiction, although it contained some excellent descriptive passages. Other commentators agreed that the book was flawed. John Skow wrote in *Time,* "Abbey . . . is feeling sorry for his hero and probably for himself too. What saves the book is that he is skilled enough to pull sympathetic readers into his own mood of regret." "Abbey is not for everybody," summarized Kerry Luft in her *Chicago Tribune* assessment. "He's about as subtle as a wrecking ball. Some might call him sexist or downright misogynistic and point out that his female characters tend to be shallow stereotypes. I can only agree. But for those readers with the

gumption and the stomach to stay with him, Abbey is a delight."

Reviewing Abbey's body of work after his death, many environmentalists and critics concluded that his nonfiction works were his most powerful. "At his best" he was "the nonpareil 'nature writer' of recent decades," wrote Edward Hoagland in the *New York Times Book Review.* "He was uneven and self-indulgent as a writer and often scanted his talent by working too fast. But he had about him an authenticity that springs from the page and is beloved by a rising generation of readers." "*Desert Solitaire* stands among the towering works of American nature writing," stated Lichtenstein. "Abbey's polemic essays on such subjects as cattle subsidies and Mexican immigrants, scattered through a half-dozen volumes, remain so angry, so infuriating yet so relevant that they still provoke arguments among his followers. As for his outdoors explorations, no one wrote more melodic hymns to the red rocks and rivers of the Southwest; no one ever defended them with more elan. It is in those nonfiction odes to the wilderness, by turns cantankerous and lyrical . . . that Abbey lives, forever."

BIOGRAPHICAL/CRITICAL SOURCES:

BOOKS

Contemporary Literary Criticism, Gale, Volume 36, 1986, Volume 59, 1990.
Hepworth, James, and Gregory McNamee, editors, *Resist Much, Obey Little: Some Notes on Edward Abbey,* Dream Garden Press, 1985.
McCann, Garth, *Edward Abbey,* Boise State University, 1977.
Ronald, Ann, *The New West of Edward Abbey,* University of New Mexico Press, 1982.

PERIODICALS

Audubon, July, 1989, pp. 14, 16.
Best Sellers, June 15, 1971.
Chicago Tribune, February 14, 1988, Section 14, p. 3; November 29, 1988; February 12, 1990.
Chicago Tribune Book World, November 30, 1980, Section 7, p. 5.
Christian Science Monitor, July 27, 1977.
Harper's, August, 1971; February, 1988, pp. 42-44.
Library Journal, January 1, 1968; July, 1977.
Los Angeles Times, October 22, 1980; January 3, 1988.
Los Angeles Times Book Review, June 17, 1979; May 16, 1982, p. 1; November 29, 1987, p. 10; January 24, 1988, p. 12; May 15, 1988, p. 14; November 20, 1988, p. 3; September 2, 1989, p. 8; January 7, 1990, p. 1.
Nation, May 1, 1982, pp. 533-35.
National Observer, September 6, 1975, p. 17.
National Parks, February, 1968, pp. 22-23.

National Review, August 10, 1984, pp. 48-49.
New Yorker, July 17, 1971.
New York Times, June 19, 1979.
New York Times Book Review, January 28, 1968, p. 7; July 31, 1977, pp. 10-11; August 5, 1979, pp. 8, 21; December 14, 1980, p. 10; May 30, 1982, p. 6; April 15, 1984, p. 34; December 16, 1984, p. 27; February 28, 1988, p. 27; May 1, 1988; December 18, 1988, p. 22; May 7, 1989, pp. 44-45; February 4, 1990, p. 18; July 8, 1990, p. 28; January 27, 1991, p. 32.
Publishers Weekly, October 5, 1984, p. 85; August 12, 1988, p. 439; November 11, 1988, pp. 34-36.
Southwest Review, winter, 1976, pp. 108-11; winter, 1980, pp. 102-05.
Time, November 28, 1988, p. 98.
Washington Post, December 31, 1979; January 5, 1988.
Washington Post Book World, March 24, 1968; June 25, 1979; May 30, 1982, p. 3; April 1, 1984, p. 9; April 3, 1988, p. 12; December 31, 1989, p. 12; January 28, 1990, p. 5; April 1, 1990, p. 8; April 22, 1990, p. 12; June 10, 1990, p. 15.
Western American Literature, fall, 1966, pp. 197-207; May, 1989, pp. 37-43.

OBITUARIES:

PERIODICALS

Detroit Free Press, March 15, 1989.
Los Angeles Times, March 16, 1989, pp. 3, 34; May 22, 1989.
Los Angeles Times Book Review, April 2, 1989, p. 11.
New York Times, March 15, 1989, p. D19.
Times (London), March 28, 1989.
Washington Post, March 17, 1989.*

—Sketch by Joan Goldsworthy

*   *   *

AGASSI, Joseph   1927-

PERSONAL: Born May 7, 1927, in Jerusalem, Israel; son of Samuel M. and Fruma (Reichmann) Birnbaum; married Judith Buber (a university teacher), August 10, 1949; children: Tirzah, Aaron. *Education:* Hebrew University, Jerusalem, M.Sc., 1951; University of London, Ph.D., 1956. *Religion:* Jewish.

ADDRESSES: Home—37 Eshkol St., Herzlia 46745, Israel. *Office*—Department of Philosophy, York University, North York, Ontario, Canada M3J 1P3.

CAREER: University of London, London School of Economics and Political Science, London, England, lecturer in philosophy, 1957-60; University of Hong Kong, Hong Kong, reader in philosophy and head of department,

1960-63; University of Illinois at Urbana-Champaign, associate professor of philosophy, 1963-65; Boston University, Boston, MA, professor of philosophy, 1965-83; Tel Aviv University, Tel Aviv, Israel, professor of philosophy, 1971—; York University, North York, Ontario, professor of philosophy, 1982—. Visiting professor, Tel Aviv University, 1966, Hebrew University, Jerusalem, 1970-71, Goethe University, Frankfurt am Main, Germany, 1983, and Carleton College, Northfield, MN, 1989. Center for Advanced Studies in the Behavioral Sciences, Stanford, CA, research associate, 1956-57; University of Bielefeld, Bielefeld, Germany, resident, 1978-79. *Military service:* Israeli Defense Army, parachute instructor, 1948-49.

MEMBER: Israeli Philosophical Association, Canadian Philosophical Association, American Philosophical Association, Canadian Association of University Teachers, American Association of University Professors, Philosophy of Science Association, History of Science Society, Society for Philosophy and Technology.

AWARDS, HONORS: Alexander von Humboldt Stiftung Senior Fellow, 1978-79 and 1986-87; American Association for the Advancement of Science fellow.

WRITINGS:

Towards an Historiography of Science, Mouton, 1963.
The Continuing Revolution: A History of Physics from the Greeks to Einstein, McGraw, 1968.
Faraday as a Natural Philosopher, Chicago University Press, 1971.
Boston Studies in the Philosophy of Science, D. Reidel, Volume 28: *Science in Flux,* 1975, Volume 50: (with Yehuda Fried) *Paranoia: A Study in Diagnosis,* 1976, Volume 65: *Science and Society: Studies in the Sociology of Science,* 1981, Volume 67: (editor with Robert S. Cohen) *Scientific Philosophy Today: Essays in Honor of Mario Bunge,* 1982.
Letters to My Sister Concerning Contemporary Philosophy (written in Hebrew), Sarah Batz Publications, 1976.
Towards a Rational Philosophical Anthropology, Nijhoff, 1977.
(Editor) *Psychiatric Diagnosis: Proceedings of an International Interdisciplinary Interschool Symposium, Bielefeld University, 1978,* Balaban International, 1981.
(With Fried) *Psychiatry as Medicine: Contemporary Psychotherapies,* Nijhoff, 1983.
Between Faith and Nationality: Towards an Israeli National Identity (written in Hebrew), Tel-Aviv University, 1985, 2nd edition, 1993.
Technology: Philosophical and Social Aspects, Kluwer Academic, 1985.
(With I. C. Jarvie) *Rationality: The Critical View,* Nijhoff, 1987.

The Gentle Art of Philosophical Polemics: Selected Reviews and Comments, Open Court, 1988.

Albert Einstein: Ahdut ve-ribui, Matkal/Ketsin, 1989.

(With Nathaniel Laor) *Diagnosis: Philosophical and Medical Perspectives,* Kluwer Academic, 1990.

An Introduction to Philosophy: The Siblinghood of Humanity, Caravan Books, 1990, 2nd edition published as *The Siblinghood of Humanity: An Introduction to Philosophy,* 1991.

EDITOR WITH I. C. JARVIE

Hong Kong: A Society in Transition, Praeger, 1969.

Cause and Meaning in the Social Sciences (selected papers by Ernest Gellner), Routledge & Keegan Paul, 1973.

Contemporary Thought and Politics (selected papers by Ernest Gellner), Routledge & Keegan Paul, 1974.

The Devil in Modern Philosophy (selected papers by Ernest Gellner), Routledge & Keegan Paul, 1975.

Spectacles and Predicaments (selected papers by Ernest Gellner), Cambridge University Press, 1980.

Relativism and Social Sciences (selected papers by Ernest Gellner), Cambridge University Press, 1985.

OTHER

Author of *Radiation Theory and the Quantum Revolution,* 1993. Contributor to books, including *Studies in Bunge's Treatize,* edited by Paul Weingartner and Georg Dorn, Rodopi, 1990. Also contributor of numerous articles to philosophy, economic and science journals, including *Science and Society, Technology and Culture, Ratio, Philosophical Studies, Science, Philosophical Forum, New Scientist,* and *British Journal of Philosophy and Science.* Consulting editor, *Studies in the History and Philosophy of Science,* 1970, *Nature and Systems,* 1978, *Research in Philosophy and Technology,* 1978, *For the Learning of Mathematics,* 1981, *Philosophy and Social Action,* 1983, and *Methodology and Science,* 1984. Agassi's works have been translated into German, Italian, Finnish, Spanish, and Hebrew.

WORK IN PROGRESS: The Sociology of Science: A Collection of Essays; Academic Agonies and How to Avoid Them: Advice to Young People on Their Way to Academic Careers; numerous articles for scholarly journals and books.

SIDELIGHTS: Joseph Agassi once told *CA:* "At the time where most of what goes on under the rubric of philosophy, especially in universities, is academic, pompous and tired, a real revolution in philosophy is underway, which takes into account the many radical developments in social and political life, in science and culture and technology, which make our century the most turbulent ever. My writings attempt to capture the spirit of this revolution on its diverse aspects, always in the hope to contribute to the social and political reform of our world. As far as the life of the intellect is concerned, my dream is to see the walls of the university come down and learning integrate as much as possible with work and with play."

* * *

ALCOCK, Vivien 1924-

PERSONAL: Born September 23, 1924, in Worthing, England; daughter of John Forster (a research engineer and scientist) and Molly (Pulman) Alcock; married Leon Garfield (a writer), October 23, 1947; children: Jane Angela. *Education:* Attended Ruskin School of Drawing and of Fine Arts, Oxford, 1940-42, and Camden Art Centre. *Politics:* Liberal. *Religion:* Church of England. *Avocational interests:* Painting, patchwork, reading.

ADDRESSES: Home—59 Wood Lane, London N6 5UD, England. *Agent*—John Johnson Ltd., Clerkenwell House, 45-47 Clerkenwell Green, London EC1R 0HT, England.

CAREER: Writer of books for juveniles and young adults. Artist, Gestetner Ltd. (duplicating firm), London, England, 1947-53; manager of employment bureau, 1953-56; secretary, Whiltington Hospital, London, 1956-64. *Military service:* British Army, ambulance driver, 1942-46.

MEMBER: Authors Society.

AWARDS, HONORS: Travelers by Night was named to the *Horn Book* Honor List and named notable book of the year by the American Library Association, both 1985; *The Cuckoo Sister* was named notable book of the year by the American Library Association, 1986; *The Monster Garden* was named *Voice of Youth Advocate* best science fiction/fantasy book and named notable book of the year by the American Library Association, both 1988.

WRITINGS:

FOR YOUNG PEOPLE

The Haunting of Cassie Palmer, Delacorte, 1980.

The Stonewalkers, Delacorte, 1981.

The Sylvia Game: A Novel of the Supernatural, Delacorte, 1982.

Travellers by Night, Methuen, 1983, published as *Travelers by Night,* Delacorte, 1985.

Ghostly Companions: A Feast of Chilling Tales (collection of ten ghost stories), illustrated by Jane Lydbury, Methuen, 1984.

The Cuckoo Sister, Methuen, 1985.

The Mysterious Mr. Ross, Delacorte, 1987.

The Monster Garden, Delacorte, 1988.

The Thing in the Woods, illustrated by Sally Holmes, Hamish Hamilton, 1989.

The Trial of Anna Cotman, Delacorte, 1990.

A Kind of Thief, Delacorte, 1991.

The Dancing Bush, illustrated by Honey de Lacey, Delacorte, 1991.

Singer to the Sea God, Delacorte, 1993.

ADAPTATIONS: The Sylvia Game was adapted for television and broadcast on BBC-TV, 1983; *The Haunting of Cassie Palmer* was the basis of a television series produced by TVS (Television South), 1984; *Travellers by Night* was adapted for television and broadcast on BBC-TV, 1984, and was the basis of a television series produced by TVS, 1985.

SIDELIGHTS: Vivien Alcock is the author of ten action-packed books of mystery and fantasy that are very popular with teenage readers, especially in Alcock's native country of England. Reviewers have praised Alcock for creating gripping and suspenseful tales involving intriguing characters that sensitively reflect many of the emotions and experiences of her young readers. Alcock is also recognized as an author whose sense of humor is as evident in her books as her ability to captivate and entertain. Writing in the *Times Literary Supplement,* Elaine Moss describes Alcock as a "writer who can command plot, character, nuance, and dialogue with a precision and sensitivity that sets her firmly among the elite of English fantasy authors for the young."

Alcock started writing at a very early age. She found expressing her thoughts and feelings on paper was an effective way to deal with such tumultuous events as her parents' divorce, her mother's death when Alcock was ten years old, and the adjustment of moving from her home to live with a guardian in another city. She was thrilled to discover something that she loved and that was unique to her.

As Alcock explained to *CA:* "I wrote a lot of verse as a child and I also made up all kinds of stories. It is easy to be the hero of a story if you write it yourself. I started telling myself stories in which the heroines were always small and skinny and dark, like me. It was comforting to find out how well they got on, facing up to incredible adventures and danger—as long as I was writing the script. It was a form of escapism, I suppose, just as daydreams are. But I think it was a valuable one."

Although she spent much of her childhood and adolescence writing, it wasn't until after she was sparked by her young daughter's love of original stories that Alcock considered turning her hobby into a profession. So, inspired by her daughter's interest in her stories, Alcock started writing again, launching what would become a rewarding career for Alcock. Alcock told *CA:* "Careers often seem to happen almost by accident. When I left school, I wanted to be either a writer or an artist. Chance (in the form of an entrance exam needing more Latin than I pos-

sessed), sent me to art school rather than to the university. Chance (in the form of a small daughter who wanted to be told stories, rather than have them read to her), turned me back to the idea of writing. I like writing for children because I love telling stories of adventure and fantasy. I don't set out to instruct or preach, but it is impossible to write without one's own views showing. I can only hope my heart and my morals are in the right place."

Alcock's first book, *The Haunting of Cassie Palmer,* is a tale about the seventh child of a seventh child who has spiritual powers. Cassie Palmer has unhappily inherited her magical abilities from her mother and she longs to be a normal and average teenager—just like her friends. However, one day, on a dare, Cassie conjures up a ghost who refuses to leave her alone. A reviewer for the *Bulletin for the Center of Children's Books* described Alcock's *The Haunting of Cassie Palmer* as "an impressive first novel from a British writer, with a fusion of realism and fantasy that is remarkably smooth." Dudley Carlson remarked in *Horn Book* that in *The Haunting of Cassie Palmer* Alcock "achieves a good balance between family tensions and financial worries, on the one hand, and supernatural uncertainties, on the other; the result is a satisfying brew."

As in her first novel, all of Alcock's stories contain elements of fantasy and the supernatural. For example, in Alcock's second novel, *The Stonewalkers,* lonely and friendless Poppy Brown pours her feelings out to a statue that suddenly comes to life. Unfortunately, the statue is mean and destructive and Poppy struggles to stop the statue's trail of terror. Alcock explained her thoughts on writing about fantasy and the supernatural to Amanda Smith in an interview with *Publishers Weekly:* "Oddly enough, I've never had a supernatural experience, and I don't even think I quite believe in them, but I find a ghost or supernatural element is a marvelous catalyst. It can be a sort of an echo of a character, like a shadow thrown out before them, showing back part of their own image. Most ghosts are very pitiful objects, so a child can learn compassion. But it's also fun in a book. It gives a little chill—binds a book together."

In a *School Library Journal* review of *The Stonewalkers,* Anita C. Wilson wrote: "The author skillfully creates a sense of escalating horror. The blending of suspenseful fantasy and elements of the contemporary problem novel works remarkably well here, and may appeal to children not ordinarily attracted to fantasy literature."

Critics continued to praised Alcock's following books. Whether it be the suspenseful mystery involving the supernatural and art forgery in *The Sylvia Game: A Novel of the Supernatural,* the exciting attempt of two circus children to save an old elephant from the slaughterhouse in *Travellers by Night,* the exciting collection of stories found in

Ghostly Companions: A Feast of Chilling Tales, the fascinating tale of separated sisters in *The Cuckoo Sister,* the untold story dramatically revealed in *The Mysterious Mr. Ross,* the experiments in genetic engineering in *The Monster Garden,* or the evil and secrecy in *The Trial of Anna Cotman,* Alcock's books have been recognized for their intriguing stories and endearing characters. Geoffrey Trease commented in the *Times Literary Supplement* that "Alcock is unsentimental, but there is an unmistakable depth of feeling in her deft handling of her very human and imperfect characters. She is writing of fear and courage, exploring the ambivalent relationships of parent and child, boy and girl, boy and boy. The contemporary juvenile dialogue rings true, and there is felicity in the descriptive phrasing."

"Vivien Alcock has the uncanny ability to create stories of suspense with overtones of fantasy which are firmly grounded in reality," Mary M. Burns wrote in *Horn Book.* "Her timing is impeccable; her characters are unforgettable; her imagery is as subtle as it is precise." And finally George English remarked in *Books for Your Children:* "Vivien Alcock has always been a dramatic writer, with a strong sense of story. Her books begin with a bang almost on page one and they hurtle at breakneck pace to a thundering climax. Where other authors linger over physical descriptions of character and setting, Alcock is more concerned with keeping the action moving. Yet at the same time she's very aware of the inner, emotional life that her characters are leading."

Alcock shared some of her interesting and insightful thoughts on writing in this manner: "Although I have a liking for dramatic and sometimes fantastic plots, I try to make my characters as real as possible, and their relationships true. I suppose, like all writers, I am influenced to some extent by my own experience, though I do not draw on it consciously. My heroines are no longer always small and skinny and dark. I suspect there is a little of me still lurking at the bottom of all the characters I create, blown up out of all recognition. I find I tend to write about children who are facing some great change or difficulty in their lives, and who learn to grow through it to a greater understanding of themselves and other people. I do not apologize for having happy endings. I firmly believe that children are resilient and resourceful, and will make their own happiness somehow if given a chance. The end of childhood is not necessarily when the law decides it shall be."

BIOGRAPHICAL/CRITICAL SOURCES:

BOOKS

Children's Literature Review, Volume 26, Gale, 1992, pp. 1-8.

PERIODICALS

Books for Your Children, Number 1, spring, 1991, p. 22.
Bulletin for the Center of Children's Books, May, 1982, p. 161; October, 1982.
Horn Book, June, 1982, p. 294; July/ August, 1987, p. 460; November/December, 1988, p. 781.
New York Times Book Review, September 11, 1983, p. 57.
Publishers Weekly, September 30, 1988, pp. 28-30.
School Library Journal, May, 1983, p. 68.
Times Literary Supplement, November 20, 1981, p. 1354; July 23, 1982, p. 788; November 8, 1985, p. 1274; September 4, 1987, p. 964.

—*Sketch by Margaret Mazurkiewicz*

*   *   *

ALLEN, Robert C(lyde) 1950-

PERSONAL: Born August 13, 1950, in Charlotte, NC; son of Clyde Alexander (a bookkeeper) and Arzelia (a homemaker; maiden name, Crenshaw) Allen; married Allison Briggs Adams (a public relations executive), August 11, 1979. *Education:* Davidson College, B.A. (cum laude), 1972; University of Iowa, M.A., 1974, Ph.D., 1977.

ADDRESSES: Office—Department of Radio, Television, and Motion Pictures, University of North Carolina at Chapel Hill, Chapel Hill, NC 27514.

CAREER: Virginia Polytechnic Institute and State University, Blacksburg, assistant professor of communications, 1977-79; University of North Carolina at Chapel Hill, assistant professor, 1979-84, professor, 1984-91, Smith Professor of radio, television, and motion pictures, 1991—, Associate Dean, College of Arts and Science, 1987—.

MEMBER: Society for Cinema Studies (member of executive council, 1982-85).

AWARDS, HONORS: Outstanding Academic Book designation, *Choice,* 1987, for *Channels of Discourse: Television and Contemporary Criticism;* George Freedley Memorial Award, 1991, for *Horrible Prettiness: Burlesque and American Culture.*

WRITINGS:

Vaudeville and Film, 1895-1915, Arno, 1980.
(With Douglas Gomery) *Film History: Theory and Practice,* Knopf, 1985.
Speaking of Soap Operas, University of North Carolina Press, 1985.
Editor, *Channels of Discourse: Television and Contemporary Criticism,* University of North Carolina Press, 1987.
Horrible Prettiness: Burlesque and American Culture, University of North Carolina Press, 1991.

Editor, *Channels of Discourse, Reassembled,* University of North Carolina Press, 1992.

Contributor to film, theatre, and television journals. Associate editor of *Cinema Journal,* 1984-87.

WORK IN PROGRESS: Editing an anthology of essays on television serial narrative around the world for the University of North Carolina Press.

* * *

ANDREWS, John Malcolm 1936-
(John Malcolm)

PERSONAL: Born August 21, 1936, in Manchester, England; son of Ernest (an engineer) and May (Whiteley) Andrews; married Geraldine Lacey (a picture restorer), March 25, 1961; children: Simon Charles. *Education:* St. John's College, Cambridge, M.A., 1958.

ADDRESSES: Home—Carriers Oast, Northiam, East Sussex TN31 6NH, England. *Agent*—Teresa Chris, 15 Castellain Mansions, Castellain Rd., London W9 1HA, England.

CAREER: Design engineer, 1958-63; export manager, 1963-70; management consultant, 1970-76; international marketing manager, 1976-90; business consultant, 1990—.

MEMBER: Crime Writers Association, Society of Authors.

WRITINGS:

Price Guide to Antique Furniture, Antique Collectors Club, 1969, new edition published as *British Antique Furniture,* 1989.
Price Guide to Victorian, Edwardian, and 1920s Furniture, Antique Collectors Club, 1980, new edition published as *Victorian and Edwardian Furniture,* 1992.

NOVELS UNDER NAME JOHN MALCOLM

A Back Room in Somers Town, Collins, 1984, Scribner, 1985.
The Godwin Sideboard, Collins, 1984, Scribner, 1985.
The Gwen John Sculpture, Collins, 1985, Scribner, 1986.
Whistler in the Dark, Scribner, 1986.
Gothic Pursuit, Scribner, 1987.
Mortal Run, Scribner, 1988.
The Wrong Impression, Scribner, 1990.
Sheep Goats and Soap, Scribner, 1991.
A Deceptive Appearance, Scribner, 1992.
The Burning Ground, Collins, 1993.

OTHER

Also contributor of short stories, under name John Malcolm, to anthologies, including *A Suit of Diamonds,* Collins, 1990; *Midwinter Mysteries,* Scribner, 1991; and *Winters Crimes 24,* Macmillan, 1992.

BIOGRAPHICAL/CRITICAL SOURCES:

PERIODICALS

Listener, July 19, 1984.
Observer, August 26, 1984.
Punch, May 30, 1984.

* * *

APPERE, Guy 1923-

PERSONAL: Born October 1, 1923, in Bois-Colombes, France; son of Herve (an electrician) and Germaine (Vivier) Appere; married Claude Lemaire, September 9, 1950 (deceased); married Suzy Honegger, November 24, 1989; children: (first marriage) Paul, Jean, Claire. *Education:* Toronto Baptist Seminary, B.Th., 1950. *Religion:* Baptist.

ADDRESSES: Home—11 rue du Bosquet, F. 74240 Gaillard, France. *Office*—Eglise Baptiste, Cherbuliez 7, CH 1207 Geneva, Switzerland.

CAREER: Inspector with telephone company in Paris, France, 1942-46; Grace Baptist Church, Lavigne, Ontario, Canada, pastor, 1947-50; Evangelical Baptist Church, Geneva, Switzerland, pastor, 1951-92. *Military service:* French Resistance, 1943-44; French Army, served in France and Germany, 1944-46; received Croix de Guerre.

WRITINGS:

Pour un dialogue avec Dieu, Grace et Verite, 1974, translation published as *Dialogue with God,* Evangelical Press, 1979.
Le Mystere de Christ, Grace et Verite, 1980, translation by Alan Gibb and Simone Gibb published as *The Mystery of Christ,* Evangelical Press, 1984.
Saisissements, Jaillissements (poems), Grace et Verite, 1992.
(Translator into French) G. Bilezikian, *Homme-Femme, vers une autre relation* (title means "Beyond Sex Roles"), Grace et Verite, 1992.

Also co-translator from the Spanish of books, including *The Doctrines of Grace* and *Manual of Ethics.* Editor, *Lien fraternel* (a publication of the French Baptist Association, 1957-87.

WORK IN PROGRESS: Research on women in church and society; a book of meditations on the First Epistle of John.

SIDELIGHTS: Guy Appere once told *CA:* "Many of my writings have come out of Sunday morning sermons, which explains their pastoral perspective and style. I try to give a simple and clear exposition of books of scripture or doctrine, using simple language. But behind my books there is serious research. I have been very interested in interpreting Paul's writings in light of their place in history, including the social conditions of the time. For this study, I organized fourteen one-month trips with groups of young people, following the footsteps of Paul through Greece, Turkey, and Italy.

"I enjoy much contemporary writing, especially that of Greek Orthodox authors. But I have also gained a lot from nineteenth-century writers such as J. B. Lightfoot, A. B. Bruce, and W. M. Ramsey, and from many French writers as well."

BIOGRAPHICAL/CRITICAL SOURCES:

PERIODICALS

Christian Update, September, 1984.
Evangelical Times, June, 1980.

*   *   *

APTERYX
See ELIOT, T(homas) S(tearns)

*   *   *

ARMITAGE, Michael 1930-

PERSONAL: Born August 25, 1930, in Oldham, England; son of John and Annie Armitage; married Gretl Renate Steinig, 1970. *Education:* Attended Royal Air Force College, 1950-53, Royal Air Force Staff College, 1965, Joint Services Staff College, 1970, and Royal College of Defence Studies, 1975.

ADDRESSES: Home—c/o Lloyds Bank, 7 Pall Mall, London, England.

CAREER: Royal Air Force, career officer, 1953—, notable assignments include commanding officer of No. 17 Squadron in Wildemrath, Germany, 1967-70, Station Commander in Luqa, Malta, 1972-74, Director of Forward Policy for Ministry of Defence Air Force Department, London, England, 1976-78, and Deputy Commander in Germany, 1978-80; Royal College of Defence Studies, member of senior directing staff, 1980-82, Commandant, 1988-89; Ministry of Defence, London, Director of Service Intelligence, 1982, Deputy Chief of Defence Staff, 1983-84, Chief of Defence Intelligence, 1985, Air Member for Supply and Organization, 1986-87.

MEMBER: International Institute for Strategic Studies, Royal United Services Institute for Defence Studies.

AWARDS, HONORS: Commander of the Order of the British Empire, 1975; Knight Commander of the Order of Bath, 1983.

WRITINGS:

(With R. A. Mason) *Air Power in the Nuclear Age,* University of Illinois Press, 1983.
Unmanned Aircraft, Brusseys, 1988.
Illustrated History of the Royal Air Force, Arms and Armour Press, 1993.

Contributor of numerous articles to professional and military journals.

WORK IN PROGRESS: Research in the field of air power history.

SIDELIGHTS: Michael Armitage once told *CA:* "I have a keen interest in twentieth-century military history, particularly in the theory and practice of contemporary air power, and its military uses. I also have a deep interest in the history of intelligence and, in particular, how assessments can go wrong. I am a qualified interpreter in German, which is a great help in studying the literature of military and intelligence history, particularly in this century."

*   *   *

ATKINS, P(eter) W(illiam) 1940-

PERSONAL: Born August 10, 1940, in Amersham, England; son of William Henry and Ellen Louise (Edwards) Atkins; children: Juliet. *Education:* University of Leicester, B.Sc., 1961, Ph.D., 1964; University of Oxford, M.A., 1965.

ADDRESSES: Office—Lincoln College, Oxford OX1 3DR, England.

CAREER: University of Oxford, Oxford, England, lecturer in physical chemistry, 1965—; Lincoln College, Oxford, tutor and fellow, 1965; Harvey Mudd College, Dreyfus lecturer, 1979. Visiting professor at University of Tokyo, Japan, 1974, Technion, Israel, 1979, Fudan University, People's Republic of China, 1979, University of Sheffield, England, 1984, University of Grenoble, France, 1986, and Auckland University, New Zealand, 1993.

MEMBER: Royal Society of Chemistry.

AWARDS, HONORS: Harkness fellow, University of California, Los Angeles, 1964-65; Meldola Medal, Royal Society of Chemistry, 1969; honorary Doctorate of Science, University of Utrecht, 1992.

WRITINGS:

(With M. C. R. Symons) *The Structure of Inorganic Radicals: An Application of Electron Spin Resonance to the Study of Molecular Structure,* Elsevier, 1967.

Molecular Quantum Mechanics: An Introduction to Quantum Chemistry, Clarendon Press, 1970, 2nd edition, 1983.

(With M. S. Child and C. S. G. Phillips) *Tables for Group Theory,* Oxford University Press, 1970.

(Editor with L. T. Muus) *Electron Spin Relaxation in Liquids,* Plenum, 1972.

Quanta: A Handbook of Concepts, Clarendon Press, 1974, 2nd edition, 1991.

(Editor with Muus, K. A. McLauchlan, and J. B. Pedersen) *Chemically Induced Magnetic Polarization,* Reidel, 1977.

Physical Chemistry, W. H. Freeman, 1978, 4th edition, 1990.

Solutions Manual for Physical Chemistry, W. H. Freeman, 1978, 4th edition, 1990.

The Creation, W. H. Freeman, 1981.

Quantization (workbook and cassette), Royal Society of Chemistry, 1981.

(With M. J. Clugston) *Principles of Physical Chemistry,* Pitman, 1982.

Solutions Manual for Molecular Quantum Mechanics, Oxford University Press, 1983.

The Second Law, Scientific American Library, 1984.

Molecules, Scientific American Library, 1987.

General Chemistry, Scientific American Books, 1989, 2nd edition, 1991.

(With D. F. Shriver and C. H. Langford) *Inorganic Chemistry,* W. H. Freeman, 1990.

Atoms, Electrons, and Change, Scientific American Library, 1991.

Elements of Physical Chemistry, W. H. Freeman, 1992.

Creation Revisited, W. H. Freeman, 1992.

Editor of "Oxford Chemistry" series. Contributor to Proceedings of the Royal Society; contributor to scientific journals and other periodicals, including *Molecular Physics, Nature, Times Higher Education Supplement, New Scientist, Chemistry in Britain,* and *New Humanist.*

WORK IN PROGRESS: Several books.

SIDELIGHTS: In *The Creation* (and more recently in *Creation Revisited*) British physical chemist P. W. Atkins puts forth a comprehensive paradigm of the universe. According to Atkins, our universe emerged from nothing, independent of any creator, and follows its inherent laws of development. Although unable to accept "the notion of selfcreation from nothing," *Times Literary Supplement* reviewer J. L. Mackie called Atkins "an independent thinker" and praised *The Creation* as "a brilliant and challenging essay on a topic of the greatest significance." Atkins's books have been translated into numerous languages, including Russian, Japanese, Polish, French, German, Italian, Portuguese, and Spanish.

Atkins once told *CA:* "I am interested in the communication of science at all levels and to all audiences. Scientists have a responsibility to share the extraordinary insights their subject provides and to illuminate nature for others. I therefore write for all types of audiences—high school, college, lay—and try to develop people's minds. The area of contact between science and religion is of particular interest to me, and I try to dispel obfuscation by exposing the simplicity beneath apparent complexity.

"I try to expose the stark simplicity of nature at a number of different levels. In my textbooks, which are high school, college, and graduate texts on chemistry, I try to show that the broad canvas of nature can be expressed concisely, and that a great deal of science is constrained, systematic common sense. I believe that people lack confidence when confronted with science and that they should be helped to gain self-confidence. This is true of college students just as much as of lay audiences. I like to try to show in my textbooks that a few simple ideas, thoroughly and systematically pursued, can account for much of the phenomena of the world. Moreover, I like to try to dispel the expected dull-drabness of science by writing in an appealing way.

"*The Creation* went beyond my textbooks in many ways. Structurally it is unusual because it is written in two styles. The poetic vision (on right-hand pages) was written in a language that might induce the non-scientist to enter its pages, and the background to the vision (on left-hand pages) was written in the cool tones of conventional science. In *The Second Law* I pursue some of the points raised in *The Creation* and give a pictorial account of the Second Law of Thermodynamics, that awesome product of the nineteenth-century mind which in my view is the spring of much insight into the world, and perhaps is the scientific principle that does more to liberate the human spirit than any other. In *Molecules* and *Atoms, Electrons, and Change* I try to share with my readers some of the additions to joy that come from understanding the inner workings of nature. In *Molecules* I explore the molecules that we eat, breathe, wear, ride, and excrete; in *Atoms, Electrons, and Change,* I explore how these molecules go about their business in the everyday world.

"In my thinking on the conflict of science and religion, I take the view that there can be no reconciliation, that the tenacity of religion in people's minds is due to cultural conditioning, imposition for political control, and lust after immortality. I like to use Occam's razor down to the flesh, and I regard all nonscientific accretions to our description of the world as claptrap. This does not mean, however, that I have no ethical base nor does it mean that I am not fascinated by the deep structure of space, time and consciousness."

BIOGRAPHICAL/CRITICAL SOURCES:

PERIODICALS

Times Literary Supplement, February 5, 1982.

B

BAKER, Paul R(aymond) 1927-

PERSONAL: Born September 28, 1927, in Everett, WA; son of Loren R. (a factory manager) and Alma (Ball) Baker; married Elizabeth Kemp, 1972; children: one. *Education:* Stanford University, A.B., 1949; Columbia University, M.A., 1951; Harvard University, Ph.D., 1960. *Politics:* Independent.

ADDRESSES: Home—90 Hillside Ave., Glen Ridge, NJ 07028. *Office*—Department of History, New York University, 19 University Pl., Rm. 523, New York, NY 10003.

CAREER: Encyclopedia Americana, New York City, staff writer and editor, 1952-55; Harvard University, Cambridge, MA, history tutor, 1957-58, 1959-60; California Institute of Technology, Pasadena, 1960-63, began as instructor, became assistant professor of history; University of California, Riverside, lecturer in history, 1963-64; University of Oregon, Eugene, lecturer in history, 1964-65; New York University, New York City, 1954—, began as associate professor, became professor of history and director of American Civilization Program.

MEMBER: American Historical Association, American Studies Association (president of Metropolitan New York chapter, 1968-69), Organization of American Historians, Society of Architectural Historians (founding member and vice-president of New Jersey chapter), Victorian Society in America, New York Academy of Sciences, Phi Beta Kappa (vice-president and president of Beta of New York chapter, 1966-70).

WRITINGS:

(Editor) Frances Wright D'Arusmont, *Views of Society and Manners in America,* Harvard University Press, 1963.

The Fortunate Pilgrims: Americans in Italy, 1800-1860, Harvard University Press, 1964.

(Editor and author of introduction) *The Atomic Bomb: The Great Decision,* Holt, 1968, revised edition, 1976.

(With William Hall) *The American Experience,* Oxford Book Co., Volume 1: *The American People,* 1976, Volume 2: *Growth of a Nation,* 1976, Volume 3: *Organizing a Democracy,* 1979, Volume 4: *The American Economy,* 1979, Volume 5: *The United States in World Affairs,* 1979.

Richard Morris Hunt, MIT Press, 1980, revised edition, 1986.

Master Builders, Preservation Press, 1985.

The Architecture of Richard Morris Hunt, University of Chicago Press, 1986.

Stanny: The Gilded Life of Stanford White, Free Press, 1989.

Insight and Inspiration II: The Italian Presence in American Art, 1860-1920, Fordham University Press, 1992.

General editor, "The American Problem Studies" series, forty-one volumes, Dryden. Contributor to *Around the Square,* New York University Press, 1982. Contributor to *Encyclopedia Americana, Americana Annual, Notable American Women, Dictionary of American Biography, Harper's Encyclopedia of Notable Americans,* and *Macmillan Encyclopedia of Architects.* Contributor of numerous articles and reviews to periodicals, including *Keats-Shelley Journal.*

One of Baker's books has been published in a Spanish edition.

SIDELIGHTS: Paul R. Baker told *CA,* "My aim is always to bring meticulous scholarship to readable, insightful prose."

BAKER, Russell (Wayne) 1925-

PERSONAL: Born August 14, 1925, in Loudoun County, VA; son of Benjamin Rex (a stonemason) and Lucy Elizabeth (a schoolteacher; maiden name, Robinson) Baker; married Miriam Emily Nash, March 11, 1950; children: Kathleen Leland, Allen Nash, Michael Lee. *Education:* John Hopkins University, B.A., 1947.

ADDRESSES: Office—c/o *New York Times,* 229 West 43rd St., New York, NY 10036.

CAREER: Baltimore *Sun,* Baltimore, MD, member of staff, 1947-53, London bureau chief, 1953-54; *New York Times,* member of Washington, DC, bureau, 1954-62, author of "Observer" column, 1962—. *Military service:* U.S. Naval Reserve, 1943-45.

AWARDS, HONORS: Frank Sullivan Memorial Award, 1976; George Polk Award, 1979, for commentary; Pulitzer Prize, 1979, for distinguished commentary (in "Observer" column), and 1983, for *Growing Up;* Elmer Holmes Bobst prize, 1983, for nonfiction; American Academy and Institute of Arts and Letters, 1984; Fourth Estate Award, National Press Club, 1989; L.H.D., Hamilton College, Princeton University, Johns Hopkins University, and Franklin Pierce College; LL.D., Union College; D.Litt, Wake Forest University.

WRITINGS:

COLLECTIONS

No Cause for Panic, Lippincott, 1964.
Baker's Dozen, New York Times, 1964.
All Things Considered, Lippincott, 1965.
Poor Russell's Almanac, Doubleday, 1972.
So This Is Depravity, Congdon & Lattes, 1980.
The Rescue of Miss Yaskell and Other Pipe Dreams, Congdon & Weed, 1983.

AUTOBIOGRAPHY

Growing Up, Congdon & Weed, 1982.
The Good Times, Morrow, 1989.

OTHER

(Author of text) *Washington: City on the Potomac,* Arts, 1958.
An American in Washington, Knopf, 1961.
Our Next President: The Incredible Story of What Happened in the 1968 Elections (fiction), Atheneum, 1968.
The Upside Down Man (children's book), McGraw, 1977.
(Editor) *The Norton Book of Light Verse,* Norton, 1986.

Also co-author of musical play *Home Again,* 1979. Contributor to periodicals, including *Saturday Evening Post, New York Times Magazine, Sports Illustrated, Ladies Home Journal, Holiday, Theatre Arts, Mademoiselle, Life, Look,* and *McCalls.*

ADAPTATIONS: One of Baker's columns, "How to Hypnotize Yourself into Forgetting the Vietnam War," was dramatized and filmed by Eli Wallach for *The Great American Dream Machine,* PBS, 1971.

SIDELIGHTS: Noted humorist Russell Baker has charmed readers for years with his witty, literate observations of the foibles and follies of contemporary life. Baker began his career as a journalist for the Baltimore *Sun* and the *New York Times,* where he enjoyed a reputation as a skilled reporter and astute political commentator. The author is perhaps best known for his "Observer" column, which has appeared in the *New York Times* since 1962 and in syndication in hundreds of other papers across the country. Regarded by *Washington Post Book World* critic Robert Sherrill as "the supreme satirist of this half century," Baker has been credited with taking newspaper humor and turning it into "literature—funny, but full of the pain and absurdity of the age," according to *Time's* John Skow.

Armed with a sense of humor described by *Washington Post* writer Jim Naughton as "quick, dry, and accessibly cerebral," Baker has taken aim at a wide range of targets, including the presidency, the national economy, and the military. In one "Observer" column, Baker spoofed the government's MX-missile plan, a proposal to transport nuclear weapons around the country using the nation's railroads. Baker took the idea even further by proposing the MX-Pentagon plan, a system of mobile Pentagon replicas, complete with a phony president and secretary of defense, that would criss-cross the United States and confuse the nation's enemies. In another essay, Baker suggested that the reason Congress voted against a bill requiring truth-in-advertising labels on defective used cars was the politicians' fear that the same fate would someday befall them: "Put yourself in your Congressman's shoes. One of these days he is going to be put out of office. Defeated, old, tired, 120,000 miles on his smile and two pistons cracked in his best joke. They're going to put him out on the used-Congressman lot. Does he want to have a sticker on him stating that he gets only eight miles on a gallon of bourbon? That his rip-roaring anti-Communist speech hasn't had an overhaul since 1969? That his generator is so decomposed it hasn't sparked a fresh thought in 15 years?"

Though many of Baker's columns concern themselves with the dealings of pompous politicians and the muddled antics of government bureaucrats, not all of the author's essays are political in nature. All manner of human excesses, fads, and trendy behavior have come under Baker's scrutiny; among the topics he has satirized are Super Bowl Sunday, the Miss America pageant, television commercials, and the jogging craze. Other selections have touched on the author's anger over the physical and moral decay of urban America. In "Such Nice People," Baker examined his fellow New Yorkers' reactions to the deterioration of their city, finding a thin veneer of civility masking their barely-suppressed rage. "In a city like this," he wrote, "our self-control must be tight. Very tight. So we are gentle. Civilized. Quivering with self-control. So often so close to murder, but always so self-controlled. And gentle." *Spectator* critic Joe Mysak applauded this type of essay, judging its significance to be "closer to the grain of American life" than Baker's politically-tinged writings, and columns of this sort moved Sherrill to write: "when it comes to satire of a controlled but effervescent ferocity, nobody can touch Baker." In addition to having his column appear in newspapers, Baker has published several compilations of selected "Observer" columns.

Along with his writings in "Observer," Baker is also known for his memoirs, *Growing Up* and *The Good Times.* The former chronicles Baker's adventures as a youngster in Depression-era Virginia, New Jersey, and Baltimore, while the latter recounts his career as a journalist, from his early work on the crime beat at the Baltimore *Sun* to his days as a Washington correspondent with the *New York Times.* Both books earned critical and popular acclaim for their gentle humor and warm, retrospective narratives.

Described by Mary Lee Settle of the *Los Angeles Times Book Review* as "a wondrous book, funny, sad, and strong," *Growing Up* explores the often difficult circumstances of Baker's childhood with a mix of humor and sadness. His father, a gentle, blue-collar laborer fond of alcohol, died in an "acute diabetic coma" when Baker was five. Baker's mother, Lucy Elizabeth, suddenly widowed and impoverished, accepted her brother's offer to live with his family in New Jersey. Before moving, Lucy left her youngest daughter Audrey in the care of wealthier relatives who could provide the infant with a more comfortable existence than she. In *Growing Up,* Baker bore witness to his mother's pain and ambivalence over the decision: "It was the only deed of her entire life for which I ever heard her express guilt. Years later, in her old age, she was still saying, 'Maybe I made a terrible mistake when I gave up Audrey.' "

The family lived off the kindness of relatives for years, finally settling in Baltimore, where Lucy eventually remarried. Baker got his first taste of journalistic life at a young age when, at his mother's insistence, he began selling copies of *The Saturday Evening Post.* Lucy exerted a strong influence over Baker's life, serving as "goad, critic, and inspiration to her son," in the words of *New York Times Book Review* critic Ward Just. The loving but tempestuous relationship that existed between mother and son threaded

its way through the work, so that *Growing Up* becomes as much the mother's story as the son's. Baker portrays Lucy as a driven woman, haunted by her life of poverty and obsessed with the idea that her son would achieve success. "I would make something of myself," Baker wrote in *Growing Up,* "and if I lacked the grit to do it, well then she would make me make something of myself." *Spectator* critic Peter Paterson saw the work as "a tribute" to the women in Baker's life, first and foremost to Lucy, "who dominates the book as she dominated her son's existence."

Baker's fully-drawn portraits of his mother and other relatives were a result of his extensive research efforts. To gather information for his book, Baker interviewed dozens of family members, collecting a trove of facts about historical America in the process. In a *Washington Post* interview, Baker said, "I was writing about a world that seemed to have existed 200 years ago. I had one foot back there in this primitive countrylife where women did the laundry running their knuckles on scrub boards and heated irons on coal stoves. That was an America that was completely dead." In a review of *Growing Up, Washington Post Book World* reviewer Jonathan Yardley wrote that Baker "passed through rites that for our culture are now only memories, though cherished ones, from first exposure to the miracle of indoor plumbing to trying on his first pair of long pants," and Settle found Baker's descriptions of such scenes "as funny and as touching as Mark Twain's."

Many critics also lauded Baker's ability to translate his personal memories into a work of universal experience. *New Statesman* critic Brian Martin admired the author's "sharp eye for the details of ordinary life," while Yardley offered even stronger praise, affirming that Baker "has accomplished the memorialist's task: to find shape and meaning in his own life, and to make it interesting and pertinent to the reader. In lovely, haunting prose, he has told a story that is deeply in the American grain, one in which countless readers will find echoes of their own, yet in the end is very much his own."

The Good Times, the sequel to *Growing Up,* continued Baker's story, recounting the author's coming of age as a journalist during the 1950s and 1960s. Hired in 1947 as a writer for the Baltimore *Sun,* Baker developed a reputation as a fast, accurate reporter, eventually earning a promotion to the post of London bureau chief. In the opinion of *New York Times* reviewer Frank Conroy, the time spent in London made Baker a better reporter and a better writer. Conroy determined that Baker's "ability to take the best from the Brits—who in general write better than we do . . . was perhaps the key event in his growth as a writer." Though Baker enjoyed London, he moved on to become the *Sun*'s White House correspondent, a decision he soon regretted. Once in Washington, Baker found the work boring, the atmosphere stifling, and his writing style unappreciated. Writing in *The Good Times,* Baker acknowledged: "I had swapped the freedom to roam one of the world's great cities and report whatever struck my fancy. And what had I got in return? A glamorous job which entitled me to sit in a confined space, listening to my colleagues breathe."

Frustrated at the *Sun,* Baker jumped at an offer to write for the *New York Times* Washington bureau, although he insisted on covering the Senate, hoping to capture the human side of the country's leaders. But in time even Congress, with its fawning politicians and controlled press briefings, proved disappointing. Recalling his dissatisfaction with the work, Baker told *Time,* "I began to wonder why, at the age of thirty-seven, I was wearing out my hams waiting for somebody to come out and lie to me." When the *Sun* attempted to regain Baker's services with the promise of a column, the *Times* promptly countered the offer with its own column, a proposal which convinced Baker to stay.

The Good Times is filled with Baker's portrayals of political heavyweights like John Kennedy, Lyndon Johnson, and Richard Nixon. Baker also profiled some of his fellow journalists, saving his harshest criticisms for those reporters who compromised their professional integrity by letting themselves become seduced by savvy politicians. Complimenting Baker on his balanced characterizations, Just reported that the author's "level gaze is on full display here in the deft, edged portraits" of his Congressional contacts, while William French of the *Toronto Globe and Mail* stated that "Baker's thumbnail sketches of the Washington movers and shakers of his time are vivid."

Many critics viewed *The Good Times* favorably, including Just who wrote: "*The Good Times* is a superb autobiography, wonderfully told, often hilarious, always intelligent and unsparing." Some reviewers, however, felt that Baker's trademark sense of modesty was used to excess in the book. In Conroy's opinion, Baker took too little credit for his early success, "ascribing much to luck and his ability to touch-type." Naughton was more critical of Baker's style, asserting that "his humility weakens the book." Other reviewers observed that, because of its subject matter, *The Good Times* necessarily evoked different feelings than its predecessor, *Growing Up.* "Some readers may find that this sequel lacks the emotional tug of the original," Robert Shogan stated in the *Los Angeles Times Book Review,* "what *The Good Times* offers instead is an insider's view of modern American journalism that illuminates both the author and his trade." Along those lines, Yardley added that "Baker seems to understand that it is one thing to write for public consumption about the distant years of childhood, and quite another to write about the unfinished stories of marriage and parenthood. . . ." He concluded,

"In the end, though, *The Good Times* is every bit as much a personal document as was *Growing Up.*"

Describing his success to Naughton, Baker downplayed his talents, stating, "I've just had the good luck to escape the meaner reviewers." Readers of his work attribute Baker's success to things altogether different. Skow noted that while Baker most often uses humor to make his point, he "can also write with a haunting strain of melancholy, with delight, or . . . with shame and outrage." In addition, Baker's consistency and clarity are mentioned as strengths. "There is just a lucidity and a sanity about him that is so distinctive," U.S. Senator Daniel Patrick Moynihan told *Time,* "He writes clearly because he thinks clearly." Finally, summarizing the opinions of many critics, Mysak declared: "For a look at how we live now . . . Baker has no superiors, and few peers."

BIOGRAPHICAL/CRITICAL SOURCES:

BOOKS

Baker, Russell. *So This Is Depravity,* Congdon & Lattes, 1980.
Baker, R. *Growing Up,* Congdon & Weed, 1982.
Baker, R. *The Rescue of Miss Yaskell and Other Pipe Dreams,* Congdon & Weed, 1983.
Baker, R. *The Good Times,* Morrow, 1989.
Contemporary Literary Criticism, Volume 31, Gale, 1985.

PERIODICALS

Chicago Tribune, January 16, 1987.
Detroit Free Press, June 27, 1989.
Detroit News, November 7, 1982; July 9, 1989.
Globe and Mail (Toronto), January 19, 1985; June 24, 1989.
Library Journal, May 1, 1989.
Los Angeles Times, December 7, 1980; January 22, 1984; March 17, 1988.
Los Angeles Times Book Review, October 10, 1982; November 30, 1986; June 11, 1989.
New Statesman, March 16, 1984.
Newsweek, September 29, 1980; November 8, 1982.
New York Times, January 30, 1972; October 6, 1982; May 23, 1989.
New York Times Book Review, January 30, 1972; October 18, 1982; May 28, 1989; July 8, 1990.
New York Times Magazine, September 12, 1982.
People, December 20, 1982.
Publishers Weekly, January 24, 1972; April 28, 1989.
Spectator, February, 1984; March, 1984.
Time, January 19, 1968; January 17, 1972; June 4, 1979; November 1, 1982.
Times Literary Supplement, April 6, 1984.
Tribune Books (Chicago), January 16, 1987; May 21, 1989.

Washington Post, July 25, 1989.
Washington Post Book World, October 5, 1980; October 3, 1982; October 9, 1983; January 18, 1987; May 28, 1989.

* * *

BALAAM
See LAMB, G(eoffrey) F(rederick)

* * *

BARK, Dennis L(aistner) 1942-

PERSONAL: Born March 30, 1942, in Appleton, WI; son of William C. (a professor of history) and Eleanor (Carlton) Bark; married France de Sugny; children: (stepchildren) Dwight, Matthew, Samuel. *Education:* Stanford University, A.B., 1964; Free University of Berlin, Ph.D. (summa cum laude), 1970.

ADDRESSES: Office—Hoover Institution on War, Revolution, and Peace, Stanford University, Stanford, CA 94305-2323.

CAREER: Stanford University, Hoover Institution on War, Revolution, and Peace, Stanford, CA, national fellow, 1970-72, research fellow, 1972-76, senior research fellow, 1976-81, senior fellow, 1981—, assistant to director, 1972-73, executive secretary of National, Peace, and Public Affairs Program, 1973-84, assistant director of institution, 1975-78, associate director, 1978-81, deputy director, 1981-83, director of National Security Affairs Program, 1983-90. Lecturer at Free University of Berlin and Stanford University. Chairman of advisory committee of U.S. Coast Guard Academy, 1981-84; chairman of board of trustees of Earhart Foundation; member of President's Commission on White House Fellowships, 1981—; member board of directors, United States Institute of Peace, 1985-93. *Military service:* U.S. Coast Guard Reserve, 1964-68.

MEMBER: Mont Pelerin Society, Berlin Wissenschaltliche Gesellschaft (corresponding member).

AWARDS, HONORS: First prize in French poetry from French Consulate General, San Francisco, CA, 1966, for "Nectar et Ambroisie"; H. B. Earhart fellow in West Germany, 1966-68; fellow of Hoover Institution on War, Revolution, and Peace in West Germany, 1968-70; fellow of Alexander von Humboldt-Stiftung and Fritz Thyssen-Stiftung, 1968-70; Woodrow Wilson fellow, 1974; Meritorious Public Service Award from U.S. Coast Guard, 1984.

WRITINGS:

Die Berlin-Frage, 1949-1955 (title means "The Berlin Question, 1949 to 1955"), de Gruyter, 1972.

Agreement on Berlin: A Study of 1970-1972 Quadripartite Negotiations, American Enterprise Institute for Public Policy Research, 1974.
(Editor) *To Promote Peace: U.S. Foreign Policy in the Mid-1980's,* Hoover Institution, 1984.
(With Annelise Anderson) *Thinking About America: The United States in the 1990s,* Hoover Institution, 1988.
(Editor) *The Red Orchestra: The Case of Africa,* Hoover Institution, 1988.
(With David R. Gress) *A History of West Germany,* Basil Blackwell, Volume 1: *From Shadow to Substance, 1945-1963,* 1989, Volume 2: *Democracy and Its Discontents, 1963-1988,* 1989.
(With Gress and Robert Laffont) *Histoire de l'Allemagne Dupuis, 1945-1992,* [Paris], 1992.

OTHER

Contributor to *Great Issues of International Politics,* edited by Morton Kaplan, 2nd edition, Aldine, 1974. Also author of "Nectar et Ambroisie." Contributor to *Yearbook on International Communist Affairs.* Contributor to political science journals and newspapers. Associate editor for Western Europe, *Yearbook on International Communist Affairs,* 1972-91.

WORK IN PROGRESS: A contemporary history, *The Choice Is Unity,* with David R. Gress; *Europe 1992: America's Heritage?*

SIDELIGHTS: The title of Dennis L. Bark's 1984 book, *To Promote Peace: U.S. Foreign Policy in the Mid-1980's,* is derived from former President Herbert Hoover's 1941 dedication of the Tower Building of the Hoover Institution, the stated purpose of which was "to promote peace."

* * *

BARNES, Douglas 1927-

PERSONAL: Born July 1, 1927, in Twickenham, England; son of Arthur George (a teacher) and Margaret (Wing) Barnes; married Dorothy M. Raistrick (a researcher), December 30, 1954; children: Ursula, Richard Jeronym. *Education:* Received B.A., M.A., and certificate of education from Downing College, Cambridge.

ADDRESSES: Home—4 Harrowby Rd., Leeds LS16 5HN, England. *Office*—School of Education, University of Leeds, Leeds LS2 9JT, England.

CAREER: High school English teacher in Bradford, Yorkshire, England, 1950-53, Dartford, Kent, England, 1954-56, Ruabon, Denbighshire, Wales, 1956-59, and London, England, 1959-66; University of Leeds, Leeds, England, lecturer, 1966-73, senior lecturer in education, 1973-84, reader in education, 1984-89. Joint director of national evaluation project for curriculum aspects of the government-sponsored Technical and Vocational Education Initiative.

MEMBER: National Association for the Teaching of English (chairman, 1967-69).

AWARDS, HONORS: Awarded Order of the British Empire, 1984.

WRITINGS:

(With James Britten and Harold Rosen) *Language, the Learner, and the School,* Penguin, 1969, 4th edition (with Britten and Mike Torbe), Boynton/Cook, 1990.
Language in the Classroom, Open University Press, 1973.
From Communication to Curriculum, Penguin, 1976, 2nd edition, Boynton/Cook, 1992.
(With Frankie Todd) *Communication and Learning in Small Groups,* Routledge & Kegan Paul, 1977.
Practical Curriculum Study, Routledge & Kegan Paul, 1982.
(With wife, Dorothy Barnes and Stephen Clarke) *Versions of English,* Heinemann, 1984.
(With Ganina Sheeran) *School Writing: Discovering the Ground Rules,* Open University Press, 1991.

Contributor to education and language journals.

SIDELIGHTS: Douglas Barnes told *CA:* "Two major influences on my thinking have been the critic F. R. Leavis—though I have never accepted his elitism—and the educationist J. N. Britton. Leavis first made me realize that each of us has to recreate literature for himself. Britton helped me to apply this to the whole of our knowledge of the world and therefore to all education. Emphasis upon the active participation of the learner in learning has thus informed all my writing about 'language' in the classroom—which is really about increasing the learner's control of learning.

"During most of my seventeen years as a school teacher I had no intentions of leaving the classroom, and now after many years in a university I still feel a conflict between the priorities implicit in each of these contexts. I have always wanted my work to be useful to teachers, but as time has passed my perspective has insensibly moved away from theirs, as I have become aware of assumptions that I no longer hold and beliefs about education that I now question.

"In the classroom and in the education system as a whole I see a conflict between forces making for custodialism and social reproduction on the one hand and those which seek to turn education into an instrument and a power in the learner's hand. The latter has to colonize the crevices left by the massive inefficiency of the former."

BARRON, Fred

ADDRESSES: Agent—David Tenzer/Sally Wilcox, Creative Artists Agency, 9830 Wilshire Blvd., Beverly Hills, CA 90210.

CAREER: Screenwriter for motion pictures and television; Columbia Broadcasting Systems, Inc. (CBS-TV), executive script consultant, *Kate and Allie,* 1984; National Broadcasting Company, Inc. (NBC-TV), executive producer, *Seinfeld,* 1990; Home Box Office (HBO), co-executive producer, *Sessions,* 1991, and *The Larry Sanders Show,* 1992.

MEMBER: Writers Guild of America (West).

AWARDS, HONORS: Berliner Morganpost Legerjury Prize, Berlin Film Festival, 1977, for *Between the Lines;* Emmy Award, outstanding children's program, Academy of Television Arts and Sciences, 1984, for *Displaced Person;* Ace nominations (2), best comedy series, both 1992, for *Sessions,* and for *The Larry Sanders Show.*

WRITINGS:

Between the Lines (screenplay), Midwest Film Productions, 1977.
Something Short of Paradise (screenplay), Orion Pictures, 1979.
Displaced Person (teleplay), broadcast on *American Playhouse,* Public Broadcasting Service, 1985.
(With Billy Crystal) *Sessions* (television series), HBO, 1991.
(With Garry Shandling) *The Larry Sanders Show* (television series), HBO, 1992.

WORK IN PROGRESS: Trauma, a screenplay for Metro-Goldwyn-Mayer.

BIOGRAPHICAL/CRITICAL SOURCES:

PERIODICALS

New York Times, April 28, 1977.
Washington Post, October 26, 1979.

*   *   *

BARTLETT, Eric George 1920-

PERSONAL: Born August 25, 1920, in Llanbradach, Wales; son of William (a miner) and Elsie Ruth (Groves) Bartlett; married Pauline Nancy Lewis (an experimental officer at Cardiff University), 1974. *Education:* Attended secondary school in Newport, England. *Religion:* Quaker. *Avocational interests:* Travel.

ADDRESSES: Home—5 Bryngwyn Rd., Cyncoed, Cardiff CF2 6PQ, Wales.

CAREER: Duke Brothers, Builders Merchants, Newport, Isle of Wight, England, clerk, 1937-41; British Railways, clerk at Caerphilly, Glamorganshire, Wales, 1946-48, signalman at Pengam, Glamorganshire, 1948-64; Caerphilly Urban District Council, Caerphilly, refuse disposal worker, 1964; postal officer, 1974-84; writer, 1984—. Instructor in judo, Glamorgan County Youth Centre; instructor, Rhymney Valley Judo and Physical Recreation Society, 1955-74; instructor, Yudachi School of Judo, 1977—. *Wartime service:* British Army, 1941-46; conscientious objector in non-combatant service.

MEMBER: International Budo Council, Bushido Za-Zen International, Society of Authors.

AWARDS, HONORS: Black Belt for judo, British Judo Council, 1961; Orange Belt for karate; 2nd Dan Judo and teaching certificate, International Budo Council, 1981; 3rd Dan Judo, 1990, and 1st Dan Judo, Bushido Za-Zen International.

WRITINGS:

The Case of the Thirteenth Coach, Staples, 1958.
The Complete Body Builder, Thorsons, 1961.
Judo and Self Defense, Arco, 1962.
Self Defense in the Home, Thorsons, 1964.
New Ways in Self Defense, Hart, 1968.
Basic Judo, Arco, 1974.
Basic Fitness, David & Charles, 1976.
Smoking Flax (novel), Mitre Press, 1977.
Summer Day at Ajaccio, Skilton & Shaw, 1979.
Basic Karate, Faber, 1980.
Weight Training, David & Charles, 1984.
Healing without Harm: Pathways to Alternative Medicine, Elliot Right Way Books, 1985.
(With Mary Southall) *Weight Training for Women,* David & Charles, 1986.
(With Southall) *Weight Training for the Over 35s,* David & Charles, 1987.
Strangers in Eden (novel), R. Hale, 1989.
Mysterious Stranger (novel), R. Hale, 1990.
Jungle Nurse (novel), R. Hale, 1990.
Clouded Love (novel), R. Hale, 1991.
Beloved Hostage (novel), R. Hale, 1991.
Master of Kung Fu (novel), R. Hale, 1991.

Contributor of short stories and articles to periodicals.

Two of Bartlett's books have been translated into French and Hebrew.

WORK IN PROGRESS: Nonfiction; romantic novels.

SIDELIGHTS: Eric George Bartlett once told *CA:* "You may be interested to know that I have been greatly influenced in my philosophical thought by Leo Tolstoy's understanding of the Christian Gospel. I feel that a writer should attempt to communicate his faith, but not necessarily or even desirably by direct preaching. Rather, his books should enlarge the reader's understanding and deepen his sympathies. I believe the greatest challenge in the world today is to improve understanding not only between nations but between classes, races, and individuals, whatever their creed, so that genuine peaceful coexistence can become a reality, not only internationally but in the local and urban scene.

"My advice to young writers would be to read widely and never to give up. Just as a concert pianist must practice for many hours to give just one performance, so you must expect to write many pages which will be just practice for the one that is published."

Bartlett added: "I am learning the Russian language since my retirement. I am interested in travel and have visited the former Soviet Union a number of times, hence my study of the language, which I work at every day for an hour."

*   *   *

BARTOLOME de ROXAS, Juan
See RUBIA BARCIA, Jose

*   *   *

BAUGHMAN, James L(ewis) 1952-

PERSONAL: Born January 10, 1952, in Warren, OH; son of Lewis E. (a banker) and Ann (Buker) Baughman. *Education:* Harvard University, B.A., 1974; Columbia University, M.A., 1975, M.Phil., 1977, Ph.D., 1981. *Politics:* Republican. *Religion:* Presbyterian.

ADDRESSES: Office—School of Journalism, University of Wisconsin—Madison, 821 University Avenue, Room 5115, Madison, WI 53706.

CAREER: University of Wisconsin—Madison, lecturer, 1979-81, assistant professor, 1981-85, associate professor, 1985-90, professor of journalism, 1990—. Member of Wisconsin State Advisory Committee of U.S. Commission on Civil Rights, 1985-92, chairperson, 1990-92.

MEMBER: American Historical Association, Organization of American Historians, Association for Education in Journalism and Mass Communications, Business History Conference, Ohio Historical Society, State Historical Society of Wisconsin, Harvard Club of New York.

WRITINGS:

Television's Guardians: The FCC and the Politics of Programming, 1958-1967, University of Tennessee Press, 1985.

Henry R. Luce and the Rise of the American News Media, Twayne, 1987.

The Republic of Mass Culture: Journalism, Broadcasting, and Filmmaking in America since 1941, Johns Hopkins University Press, 1992.

Contributor to magazines, including *Historian, Journal of Popular Culture, Prospects, Mid-America,* and *Historical Journal of Film, Radio, and Television.*

WORK IN PROGRESS: A scholarly history of television in the 1950s.

SIDELIGHTS: James L. Baughman once told *CA:* "Forces shaping the modern American mass media have long engaged me. I am convinced that circumstances other than consumer preference, including technology and production costs, as well as the geographical location of production, help to shape our mass culture, especially in television and motion pictures. To what extent should these factors fashion our national culture?"

*   *   *

BEDAU, Hugo Adam   1926-

PERSONAL: Born September 23, 1926, in Portland, OR; married Jan Mastin, 1952 (divorced, 1988); married Constance Putnam, 1990; children: (first marriage) Lauren, Mark, Paul, Guy. *Education:* University of Redlands, B.A. (summa cum laude), 1949; Boston University, M.A., 1951; Harvard University, A.M., 1953, Ph.D., 1961. *Avocational interests:* Swimming, cycling, hiking.

ADDRESSES: Office—Department of Philosophy, Tufts University, Medford, MA, 02155.

CAREER: Dartmouth College, Hanover, NH, instructor, 1953-54; Princeton University, Princeton, NJ, lecturer, 1954-61; Reed College, Portland, OR, associate professor, 1962-66; Tufts University, Medford, MA, professor of philosophy, 1966—; Adjunct Lecturer, Harvard extension, 1969—. Visiting fellow, Clare Hall, Cambridge University, 1980, Wolfson College, Oxford University, 1988. *Military service:* U.S. Naval Reserve, 1944-46.

MEMBER: American League for Abolition of Capital Punishment (president, 1969-72), National Coalition to Abolish the Death Penalty (chairman, 1990—), American Civil Liberties Union, Civil Liberties Union of Massachusetts (board of directors, 1986—), American Philosophical Association, American Society of Political and Legal Philosophy (vice-president, 1981-83), American Association of University Professors (president of Tufts University chapter, 1977-79), Northwest Conference on Philosophy (president, 1965), Society for Philosophy and Public Affairs, Boston Atheneum, Phi Beta Kappa.

AWARDS, HONORS: Danforth teacher grant, 1957-58; Liberal Arts Fellow, Harvard Law School, 1961-62; National Endowment for the Humanities summer stipend, 1977.

WRITINGS:

Civil Disobedience: Theory and Practice, Macmillan, 1969.

The Courts, the Constitution, and Capital Punishment, Heath, 1977.

Death Is Different, Northeastern University Press, 1987.

(With Sylvan Barnet) *Current Issues and Enduring Questions,* Bedford Books, 1987.

EDITOR

The Death Penalty in America (anthology), Doubleday-Anchor, 1964.

Civil Disobedience: Theory and Practice, Pegasus, 1969.

Justice and Equality, Prentice-Hall, 1971.

(With Chester M. Pierce) *Capital Punishment in the United States,* AMS Press, 1976.

Civil Disobedience in Focus, Routledge, 1991.

OTHER

Contributor to numerous books including *The Concept of Academic Freedom,* University of Texas Press, 1972; *Human Rights and U.S. Foreign Policy,* Heath, 1979; *Matters of Life and Death,* Random House, 1980; *Environmental Decision Making,* edited by Richard A. Chechile, Van Nostrand, 1991; *The Mosaic of Contemporary Psychiatry in Perspective,* edited by A. Kales and M. Greenblatt, Springer-Verlag, 1992. Contributor to *Guide to American Law, Funk & Wagnalls New Encyclopedia, Encyclopedia of Crime and Justice,* and *Academic American Encyclopedia.* Contributor of essays and reviews to *Nation, New Leader, Christian Century, Philosophical Review, Journal of Philosophy, Philosophy of Science, Inquiry, Monist, Worldview, Juris Doctor, Hastings Center Report, American Behavioral Scientist, Criminal Justice Ethics, Crime and Delinquence, Social Philosophy and Policy, Ethics, Stanford Law Review, Michigan Law Review, Human Rights Quarterly,* and other periodicals.

WORK IN PROGRESS: A book on the theory of punishment.

*   *   *

BEERS, Burton F(loyd)   1927-

PERSONAL: Born September 13, 1927, in Chemung, NY; son of Franklin and Alice (Wood) Beers; married Pauline E. Cone, 1952; children: Martha Beers Williams, Burton F. *Education:* Hobart College, A.B., 1950; Duke University, M.A., 1952, Ph.D., 1956; Harvard University, postdoctoral fellow in East Asian studies, 1959-60. *Religion:* Baptist.

ADDRESSES: Home—629 South Lakeside Dr., Raleigh, NC 27606. *Office*—Department of History, Box 8108, North Carolina State University, Raleigh, NC 27695-8108.

CAREER: North Carolina State University at Raleigh, instructor, 1955-57, assistant professor, 1957-61, associate professor, 1961-66, professor, 1966-70, Alumni Distinguished Professor of History, 1970—, head of department, 1981-86. Fulbright lecturer, National Taiwan University, 1966-67. Director of Asian Materials Projects, North Carolina State University-National Endowment for the Humanities, 1974, 1976. Former member of national advisory council, Education Division, Asia Society, and of China Council.

MEMBER: World History Association, American Historical Association, Association of Asian Studies (chairman of southeastern regional conference, 1962-64), Southern Historical Association, North Carolina Literary and Historical Association, Historical Society of North Carolina, Association of Historians in North Carolina, Phi Beta Kappa, Phi Kappa Phi, Theta Delta Chi.

AWARDS, HONORS: First recipient, Alexander Holladay Medal, 1992; North Carolina State Board of Trustees Highest Award for Excellence in Teaching.

WRITINGS:

Vain Endeavor: Robert Lansing's Attempts to End the American-Japanese Rivalry, Duke University Press, 1962.
(With Paul H. Clyde) *The Far East: A History of Western Impacts and Eastern Responses,* Prentice-Hall, 4th edition, 1966, 6th edition, 1975.
(Contributor) Ernest R. May and James C. Thomson, Jr., editors, *American-East Asian Relations: A Survey,* Harvard University Press, 1972.
China in Old Photographs, 1860-1910, Scribner, 1978.
(Contributor) Alexander Deconde, editor, *Encyclopedia of American Foreign Policy: Studies of the Principal Movements and Ideas,* three volumes, Scribner, 1978.
(Editor with Barbara M. Parramore) *Chiliying: Life in a Rural Commune in China* (booklet), with teacher's guide, School of Education, North Carolina State University's Office of Publications, 1979.
(With Lawrence Kessler and Charles Lamonic) *North Carolina's China Connections,* North Carolina China Council, 1981.
(Senior writer) *World History: Patterns of Civilization,* Prentice-Hall, 1983, 6th edition, 1992.
(With Murray S. Downs) *N.C. State: A Pictorial History,* North Carolina State University, 1986.

(Contributor) Virginia Wilson and James Lytle, editors, *Teaching History and the Social Studies: Handbook of Trends, Issues, and Implications for the Future,* Greenwood Press, 1993.

Contributing writer of historical introductions, *Prentice-Hall Literature: World Masterpieces,* Prentice-Hall, 1991; consultant on East Asia, *World Cultures: A Global Mosaic,* Prentice-Hall, 1992; consultant on content, *Japan and Korea,* Globe Books, 1992. Contributor of articles and reviews to professional journals.

SIDELIGHTS: Burton F. Beers recently told *CA:* "As I approach forty years on the faculty at North Carolina State University at Raleigh, I'm increasingly conscious of how much my writing has been shaped by an evolving campus environment and a deep interest in teaching, both my own and the work of others in public schools. When I joined the faculty in 1955, N.C. State was a land grant college offering programs heavily weighted toward the technologies to about 4,000 students, mostly undergraduates; in 1992, it is a multifaceted university enrolling more than 26,000, a considerable portion of whom are in graduate school. Like other faculty of my generation, I have taught a broader range of courses than is common now in an era of narrow specialization. My job was to help expand course offerings in history and political science as the university's programs diversified.

"My interest in America-East Asian relations, an area addressed in my first book, has been sustained by ever enlarged opportunities to teach American foreign relations for advanced undergraduates and graduate students. My interests in the field, however, have shifted from pure diplomatic history to what might be called the impacts of Americans—missionaries, businessmen, the military—on Asia and the reverse impacts of East Asians on American society, especially in the South. Research has gone slowly, since the sources dealing with southerners in foreign areas have not been systematically collected, but I am now reaching the point of writing about what I have found.

"Meanwhile, as the only faculty in the late 1950s with some education in things Asian, I was asked to initiate undergraduate courses on China and Japan. I did so, while continuing to teach standard departmental offerings in American and European history. For these latter courses I was well-grounded from undergraduate and graduate studies. When Asia was added, the university encouraged post-doctoral studies at Duke and Harvard as well as time for residence and travel in Asia. More important, my Ph.D. mentor, who had retired from the Duke faculty, asked me to undertake the task of updating *The Far East: A History of Western Impacts and Eastern Responses,* a leading college text which had appeared in 1948 and was to remain in print until 1991. Both the teaching and text required systematic reading in Asian history.

"Quite unexpectedly these efforts to sustain my university teaching came into play in work with public schools. Like most historians in the late 1960s, I knew little about public education. That changed rapidly in the 1970s when I was asked by the Association for Asian Studies to help in North Carolina with the introduction of a pioneering world studies curriculum. Soon I was working with the Social Studies staff of the Department of Public Instruction, travelling the state and participating in workshops for teachers. My job was to provide teachers with the essentials for teaching about East Asia, a responsibility that entailed considerable adjustments in my own thinking both about the subject matter and how it might be taught. Again, my affiliations with N.C. State proved important in encouraging me to stick with work that I found intellectually stimulating and thought important. The university took deep pride in its mission to the people of the state. In keeping with this tradition, the administration saw my work with the schools as something to be encouraged.

"By the late 1970s I had begun to work with commercial textbook publishers. An early product of these efforts was *World History: Patterns of Civilization,* a tenth grade text which dominated the market during much of the 1980s. Since that publication, I have worked in a number of other capacities, chiefly shaping the content of other texts as they have dealt with East Asian history. These assignments have always presented intellectual challenges in that I have been confronted with tasks of translating complex materials into forms that young people can comprehend. At the same time the work challenges a writer's ego. No matter whether I'm listed as 'senior author' or 'consultant,' I'm engaged (as is anyone touching a text these days) with a host of editors in a collaborative effort that sometimes is as demanding of one's diplomatic as intellectual resources."

*   *   *

BENJAMIN, David
    See SLAVITT, David R(ytman)

*   *   *

BENNETT, John M(ichael) 1942-

PERSONAL: Born October 12, 1942, in Chicago, IL; son of John William (an anthropologist) and Kathryn (Goldsmith) Bennett. *Education:* Washington University, St. Louis, MO, B.A. (cum laude), 1964, M.A., 1966; University of California, Los Angeles, Ph.D., 1970; also studied

at Universidad de Puerto Rico, 1961, Universidad Internacional, Mexico, 1962, and Universidad de Guadalajara, 1962-63.

ADDRESSES: Home and office—Luna Bisonte Prods, 137 Leland Ave., Columbus, OH 43214.

CAREER: Ohio State University, Columbus, assistant professor of Hispanic literature, 1969-76, Ohio State University Libraries, Latin American bibliographic assistant and editor, 1976—; Luna Bisonte Prods (publisher of artists' books and poetry broadsides), Columbus, publisher and editor, 1974—. Certified poetry therapist, 1985. Has had numerous exhibitions of his art and participated in many invitational and judied group and one-man shows; also participated in poetry readings nationwide. Has conducted research in Santiago, Chile, and in Mexico.

MEMBER: National Association for Poetry Therapy (member of board of directors, 1983-84), Association for Applied Poetry (vice-president, 1984-86).

AWARDS, HONORS: Awards from San Francisco Poetry Film Festival and Ann Arbor Film Festival, 1979, for film *Time's T-Bone*; grants from Ohio Arts Council, 1979, 1980, 1982, 1985, 1988, and 1989; Ohio Governor's Award, 1984, for volunteer service as poetry therapist at Central Ohio Psychiatric Hospital.

WRITINGS:

Blank Blue Side of Chevy (pamphlet), Cuervo Press, 1970.
Found Objects (collage poems), New Rivers Press, 1973.
Works, New Rivers Press, 1973.
Freeway Gas Station (pamphlet), Frustration Press, 1973.
Seven Rituals (pamphlet), Frustration Press, 1973.
Copy: Early Death News (hand printed concrete poems), Luna Bisonte, 1974.
Image Standards, Luna Bisonte, 1975.
Six Portraits, Luna Bisonte, 1975.
Time's Dipstick, Luna Bisonte, 1976.
(With Pablo Virumbrales) *La Revolucion: A Reader in Spanish-American Revolutionary Thought,* Oxford University Press, 1976.
White Screen, New Rivers Press, 1976.
Meat Dip, Laughing Bear Press, 1976.
Do Not Cough, Luna Bisonte, 1976.
Meat Watch, Fireweed Press, 1977.
Contents, Luna Bisonte, 1978.
Time Release, Luna Bisonte, 1978.
Nips Poems, Luna Bisonte, 1980.
(With C. Mehrl Bennett) *Pumped Gravel,* Luna Bisonte, 1980.
Blank Wall, Laughing Bear Press, 1980.
Main Road, Luna Bisonte, 1980.
Motel Moods, Luna Bisonte, 1980.
(With Robin Crozier) *Meat Click,* Luna Bisonte, 1980.

Puking Horse, Luna Bisonte, 1980.

Jerks, Laughing Bear Press, 1980.

(With Bennett) *Applied Appliances,* Luna Bisonte, 1981.

(With Bennett) *Some Blood,* Luna Bisonte, 1982.

Blender, Ghost Dance, 1983.

Burning Dog, Luna Bisonte, 1983.

Antpath, Proper Tales, 1984.

Nose Death, Luna Bisonte, 1984.

No Boy, Laughing Bear Press, 1985.

13 Spits, Clarel Editions, 1986.

The Poems, Curvd H & Z, 1987.

Cascade, Luna Bisonte, 1987.

Stones in the Lake, Luna Bisonte, 1987.

Twitch, Sub Rosa Press, 1988.

Swelling, Runaway Spoon Press, 1988.

Regression, Luna Bisonte, 1988.

Lice, Grinding Wheels Enterprises, 1989.

Tide, Luna Bisonte, 1989.

Milk, Luna Bisonte, 1990.

(With Shelia E. Murphy) *Lens Rolled in a Heart,* Etymon Press, 1990.

(With others) *Woods Nymphs of the Sahara,* Musical Comedy Editions, 1990.

Tempid, Luna Bisonte, 1990.

Span, Runaway Spoon Press, 1990.

Bell-Nail, Modom, 1991.

Was Ah, Burning Press, 1991.

Fenestration. Luna Bisonte, 1991.

Consumed, Luna Bisonte, 1991.

Somation, Pneumatic Press, 1992.

Neuf Poemes, translation by Philippe Bille, Les Editions de Garenne, 1992.

Bleached, BGS Press, 1992.

Also author of screenplays with John McClintock, including *E Z Sleep,* 1978, *Time's T-Bone,* 1979, *Mail Art Romance,* 1982; and *Be Blank,* 1988. Contributor to numerous anthologies, including *The Sensuous President,* edited by C. W. Truesdale, New Rivers Press, 1972; *Correspondence Art,* Contemporary Arts Press, 1984; *A Good Day to Die,* Vagabond Press, 1985. Contributor of poetry, graphics, articles, reviews, and translations to magazines, including *Clown War, Porch, Quoz?, Scree, Generator, Rampike, High Performance, Underpass, White Wall, Texture, Lynx, Shattered Wig, Beef,* and *This Is Important.* Editor, *Lost and Found Times* (journal of experimental and avant-garde art and writing), 1974—.

Bennett's prose poems have been recorded on audio cassette, including *John M. Bennett Reads,* Luna Bisonte, 1982; *Hybernatin'* (with Eleanor Crockett), Laughing Bear Press, 1986; *Binary Reductions* (with Dick Metcalf), Zzaj Productions, 1991; and *Bag Talk* (with Dave Clark and Chris Culhane), Music You Can Almost See, 1992.

WORK IN PROGRESS: Several more books of poems; visual and conceptual poetry.

SIDELIGHTS: John M. Bennett told *CA:* "I am interested in the word, in language as a vehicle for containing or referring to the whole of my experience alive. My work has moved in several directions toward that goal: language in poetry, as conceptual object, as visual object, as somatic graph in handwriting. Usually I try to combine two or more of these aspects in my search for a total expression. The placing of experience or self into language is perhaps the most unique aspect of being human. It is sometimes a difficult, painful or joyful process. It is the self coming alive and leaving itself simultaneously.

"My motto: Be blank."

*   *   *

BENNETT, Neville 1937-

PERSONAL: Born July 25, 1937, in Bradford, England; son of Stanley (an engineer) and Gladys (Welch) Bennett; married Susan Gail Umney (a social worker), March 18, 1961; children: Neil Stephen, Louise Gail, Sara Jane. *Education:* University of Lancaster, B.Ed. (with first class honors), 1969, Ph.D., 1972. *Politics:* None. *Religion:* None. *Avocational interests:* Cycling, gardening, photography, painting, squash.

ADDRESSES: Office—Department of Education, University of Exeter, St. Luke's, Exeter, England.

CAREER: International Marine Radio Co., Croydon, England, radio officer, 1956-61; British Aerospace, Warton, England, radio and radar engineer, 1961-65; University of Lancaster, Bailrigg, England, research officer, 1969-70, lecturer, 1970-76, senior lecturer, 1977-78, professor of educational research and director of Centre for Educational Research and Development, 1978-85, head of department of educational research, 1981-85; University of Exeter, Exeter, England, professor of education, 1985—, director of Centre for Research on Teaching and Learning, 1987—.

MEMBER: European Association for Research on Learning and Instruction (founding member), British Educational Research Association (founding member; member of executive council, 1975-78 and 1981-85), British Psychological Society, American Educational Research Association.

WRITINGS:

Teaching Styles and Pupil Progress, Harvard University Press, 1976.

(With David McNamara) *Focus on Teaching,* Longman, 1979.

Open Plan Schools: Teaching, Curriculum, and Design, National Foundation for Educational Research, 1980.

(With Charles Desforges) *The Quality of Pupil Learning Experiences,* Lawrence Erlbaum, 1984.

Recent Advances in Classroom Research, Scottish Academic Press, 1985.

(With J. Kell) *A Good Start? Four-Year-Olds in School,* Basil Blackwell, 1989.

(With A. Cass) *From Special to Ordinary School,* Cassell, 1989.

(With E. Dunne) *Talking and Learning in Groups,* Macmillan, 1990.

(With Dunne) *Managing Classroom Groups,* Simon & Schuster, 1992.

(With C. Carre) *Learning to Teach,* Routledge & Kegan Paul, 1993.

Editor, *Teaching and Teacher Education,* 1992—; co-editor, *British Educational Research Journal,* 1975-85; assistant editor, *British Journal of Educational Psychology,* 1974-84.

WORK IN PROGRESS: Research on teaching/learning processes in schools with particular reference to classroom groupings and teacher education.

SIDELIGHTS: Neville Bennett once told *CA:* "I came to academic life late, after spells in the Merchant Navy and in industry. Recognition came from my research on educationally sensitive topics. The material covered in my book *Teaching Styles and Pupil Progress* is one such area. My work on teaching and learning processes in classrooms continues with the ultimate aim of improving teaching and learning in the nation's schools irrespective of pupil's age, sex, race, or ability. This work has now extended to considerations of the quality of teacher education programmes."

*   *   *

BETZ, Hans Dieter 1931-

PERSONAL: Born May 21, 1931, in Lemgo, Germany; emigrated to U.S., 1963, naturalized U.S. citizen, 1973; son of Ludwig (an educator) and Gertrude (Vietor) Betz; married Christel H. Wagner, November, 1958; children: Martin, Ludwig, Arnold. *Education:* Attended School of Theology, Bethel, Germany, 1951-52; Westminster College, Cambridge, graduate study, 1955-56; University of Mainz, Dr. Theol. habil, 1957, 1966.

ADDRESSES: Home—5630 South Blackstone Ave., Chicago, IL 60637. *Office*—School of Divinity, University of Chicago, 1025 East 58th St., Chicago, IL 60637.

CAREER: Ordained minister in the Reformed Church in Germany, 1961, recognized as ordained minister in the United Presbyterian Church in the United States, 1963; School of Theology and Claremont Graduate School, Claremont, CA, assistant professor, 1963-65, associate professor, 1965-67, professor of New Testament, 1967-78; University of Chicago, Chicago, IL, professor of New Testament, 1978—, chairman of department of New Testament and early Christian literature, 1985—. Director of research project "Institute for Antiquity and Christianity," Claremont, CA, 1966-78; visiting professor, University of Mainz, 1967, University of Uppsala, 1973-74, University of Zurich, 1977, Oxford University, 1981, Cambridge University, 1984, University of Tuebingen, 1987-88, and Hebrew University, Jerusalem, 1990.

MEMBER: Studiorum Novi Testamenti Societas, Society of Biblical Literature, Chicago Society of Biblical Research.

AWARDS, HONORS: Alexander von Humboldt Research Award, 1986; Lady Davis Fellowship, Hebrew University, Jerusalem, 1990.

WRITINGS:

Lukian von Samosata und das Neue Testament (title means "Lucian of Samosata and the New Testament"), Akademie-Verlag (Berlin), 1961.

Nachfolge und Nachahmung Jesu Christi im Neuen Testament (title means "Discipleship and Imitation of Jesus Christ in the New Testament"), Mohr/Siebeck (Tuebingen, Germany), 1972.

Der Apostel Paulus und die sokratische Tradition (title means "The Apostle Paul and the Socratic Tradition"), Mohr/Siebeck, 1972.

(Editor with Luise Schottroff) *Neues Testament und Christliche Existenz: Festschrift fuer Herbert Braun* (title means "New Testament and Christian Existence: Essays in Honor of Herbert Braun"), Mohr/Siebeck, 1973.

(Editor) *Plutarch's Theological Writings and Early Christian Literature,* E. J. Brill, 1974.

(Editor) *Plutarch's Ethical Writings and Early Christian Literature,* E. J. Brill, 1978.

Galatians, Fortress, 1979.

(Editor) *The Bible as a Document in the University,* Scholars Press, 1981.

Second Corinthians Eight and Nine: A Commentary on Two Administrative Letters of the Apostle Paul, Fortress, 1985.

Essays on the Sermon on the Mount, Fortress, 1985.

(Editor) *The Greek Magical Papyri in Translation, Including the Demotic Spells,* University of Chicago Press, 1986, 2nd edition, 1992.

Hellenismus and Urchristen tum: Gesammelte Aufsaetze I, Mohr/Siebeck, 1990.

Synoptische Studien: Gesammelte Aufsaetze II, Mohr/Siebeck, 1992.

Also editor of *Christology and Modern Pilgrimage,* 1971, 2nd edition, 1974. Contributor of one hundred fifty articles and reviews to periodicals.

WORK IN PROGRESS: The Sermon on the Mount and on the Plain, a commentary; directing a research project on the Greek Magical Papyri with international scholars.

*   *   *

BIRKIN, Andrew (Timothy) 1945-

PERSONAL: Born December 9, 1945, in London, England; son of David Leslie (a naval commander) and Judy (an actress; maiden name, Campbell) Birkin; children: David Tristan, Alexander Kingdom, Edmund Xavier. *Education:* Attended Harrow School, England.

ADDRESSES: Home—81 Iverna Court, Kensington, London W8, England. *Agent*—William Morris Agency, 1350 Avenue of the Americas, New York, NY 10019.

CAREER: Twentieth Century-Fox Productions Ltd., London, England, runner, 1963, assistant in publicity department, 1964; worked as location scout and camera assistant, 1965; Metro-Goldwyn Mayer, Borehamwood, England, runner, 1965-66, special effects assistant director and location scout, 1966, location manager in Africa, 1967; screenwriter, producer, and director, 1967—.

MEMBER: Writers Guild of Great Britain, Society of Authors, Association of Cinema and Allied Television Technicians.

AWARDS, HONORS: Writer's Award, Royal Television Society, and television writing award, Writers Guild of Great Britain, both 1979, both for *The Lost Boys;* British Academy Award, 1981, and American Academy Award nomination, 1983, both for *Sredni Vashtar.*

WRITINGS:

J. M. Barrie and the Lost Boys: The Love Story That Gave Birth to Peter Pan (biography), Constable, 1979, revised edition, C. N. Potter, 1980.

SCREENPLAYS

The Pied Piper, Paramount, 1970.
Slade in Flame (also see below), Goodtimes, 1973.
(Coauthor) *Peter Pan* (musical adaptation of the play by J. M. Barrie), Associated Television, 1975.
The Lost Boys, British Broadcasting Corp., 1978, published as *The Lost Boys: A Television Trilogy,* BBC Publications, 1980.

The Thief of Baghdad, National Broadcasting Co. (NBC-TV), 1978.
The Final Conflict, Twentieth Century-Fox, 1981.
(And director) *Sredni Vashtar* (based on the short story by Saki), Twentieth Century-Fox, 1981.
(With James Costigan) *King David,* Paramount, 1985.
(With Gerard Brach, Howard Franklin, and Alain Godard) *The Name of the Rose* (based on the novel by Umberto Eco), Twentieth Century-Fox, 1985.
(And director) *The Burning Secret* (based on the novella *Brennendes Geheimnis,* by Stefan Zweig), Vestron Pictures, 1988.

Also screenwriter of *Jude the Obscure* (adapted from the novel by Thomas Hardy), 1967; *McTeague,* 1969; *Little Lord Fauntleroy* (adapted from the story by Frances Hodgson Burnett), 1971; *Inside the Third Reich,* 1971; *Wasp,* 1972; *The Silent People,* 1973; *The Secret Garden* (adapted from the novel by Burnett), 1973; *Madame Kitty,* 1973; *Saturday's Games,* 1975; *The Dhows,* 1980; *The Cement Garden* (based on the novel by Ian McEwan), 1983. Contributor to British and American newspapers.

ADAPTATIONS: Slade in Flame was adapted as the novel *Flame,* by John Pidgeon, St. Albans, 1975.

WORK IN PROGRESS: Writer/director of untitled ghost story for Walt Disney Productions.

SIDELIGHTS: Film director and writer Andrew Birkin is the author of many scripts for television and screenplays for full-length motion pictures. Among his writing credits are such notable films as *King David, The Name of the Rose, Sredni Vashtar,* and *The Burning Secret,* the latter two which he also directed. His successful projects for British television include a musical version of J. M. Barrie's *Peter Pan,* and *The Lost Boys,* a popular BBC-TV special presentation. Much of Birkin's television work, as well as his popular biography *J. M. Barrie and the Lost Boys,* centers on Barrie's classic childhood tale and the events that led up to its creation. Birkin once explained to *CA* that his continuing work on this subject was motivated by a quotation from Barrie himself: "Nothing that happens after we are twelve matters very much."

Birkin first became interested in the life of noted Scottish playwright and novelist Barrie in 1975, when he and a coauthor were in the process of adapting *Peter Pan* into a musical for BBC-TV. In 1978, Birkin wrote *The Lost Boys,* a three-part television script dramatizing the efforts of Barrie in winning over members of the family of Arthur and Sylvia Llewellyn Davies in an effort to develop a close relationship with the couple's five young sons. It was this relationship between the elderly author and the five Llewellyn Davies children that provided the inspiration for Barrie's play, *Peter Pan,* which was published in 1904. The television drama was re-broadcast by BBC-TV two years after its initial release, and was accompanied by the publication of Birkin's television script under the title *The Lost Boys: A Television Trilogy.* Benny Green praised the book in the *Spectator,* commenting that Birkin's three scripts comprise "a priceless addition to a corpus of literature which as yet hardly exists at all, the literature of coherent television drama."

Publication of *The Lost Boys* coincided with that of Birkin's biography, *J. M. Barrie and the Lost Boys: The Love Story That Gave Birth to Peter Pan.* Relying heavily on original documentation, including Barrie's diaries and an assortment of letters and photographs of the Llewellyn Davies family, the volume was well-received by critics. "The book that Mr. Birkin has written is as lucid and as gripping as was his television trilogy," writes Morton N. Cohen in the *New York Times Book Review,* adding that Birkin "writes well [and] has a good sense of balance and dramatic power." Reviewer Eve Auchincloss also expresses admiration for the research that went in to *J. M. Barrie and the Lost Boys.* Remarking on Birkin's ability to retain a biographer's neutrality, she comments that "photographs of these beautiful, doomed people thickly scattered through the text, many taken by Barrie, make the story the more deeply poignant."

"I loathe writing," Birkin once admitted to *CA,* "yet some masochistic urge—as well as a need to earn a living—drives me into making fresh commitments. Without a deadline I would write nothing. I work best in a state of semi-panic; this I ensure by not starting to write until within weeks—sometimes days—of a deadline. I didn't begin work on the Barrie biography until a week after the contractual date for delivery had expired." Birkin noted that these circumstances resulted in an "unpremeditated advantage": the book's publishers were forced by the lag in finished manuscript to put the book into print chapter by chapter. "By the time they realized I had written almost twice the length originally contracted, they had no time left in which to make any cuts."

"Write from your heart, not from your head," Birkin advises other writers. "Don't try and anticipate what other people want to read if it's not what you want to write. Set out to satisfy yourself, and just hope to God that it pleases others. Whether a writer or a bricklayer, you are unique, but the moment you try to imitate others (by not being yourself), you've lost that uniqueness and have joined the crowd."

BIOGRAPHICAL/CRITICAL SOURCES:

PERIODICALS

New York Times, November 30, 1979.
New York Times Book Review, January 13, 1980, pp. 3, 36.
Spectator, March 1, 1980, pp. 21-22.

Washington Post Book World, December 23, 1979, p. 5.

*   *   *

BLAKENEY, Jay D.
  See CHESTER, Deborah

*   *   *

BLY, Robert (Elwood) 1926-

PERSONAL: Born December 23, 1926, in Madison, MN; son of Jacob Thomas (a farmer) and Alice (Aws) Bly; married Carolyn McLean, June 24, 1955 (divorced, June, 1979); married Ruth Counsell, 1980; children: Mary, Bridget, Noah Matthew Jacob, Micah John Padma. *Education:* Attended St. Olaf College, 1946-47; Harvard University, A.B., 1950; University of Iowa, M.A., 1956. *Politics:* Democrat. *Religion:* Lutheran.

ADDRESSES: Home—308 First St., Moose Lake, MN 55767.

CAREER: Poet, translator, and editor. Fifties (became Sixties, Seventies, Eighties, then Nineties) Press, Moose Lake, MN, founder, publisher, and editor, 1958—. Conductor of writing workshops. *Military service:* U. S. Navy, 1944-46.

MEMBER: American Academy and Institute of Arts and Letters, Association of Literary Magazines of America (executive committee), American Poets Against the Vietnam War (founder member; co-chairman).

AWARDS, HONORS: Fulbright grant, 1956-57; Amy Lowell travelling fellowship, 1964; Guggenheim fellow, 1964, 1972; American Academy grant, 1965; Rockefeller Foundation fellowship, 1967; National Book Award, 1968, for *The Light Around the Body;* nomination for poetry award from *Los Angeles Times,* 1986, for *Selected Poems.*

WRITINGS:

POEMS

(With William Duffy and James Wright), *The Lion's Tail and Eyes: Poems Written Out of Laziness and Silence,* Sixties Press, 1962.
Silence in the Snowy Fields, Wesleyan University Press, 1962.
The Light Around the Body, Harper, 1967.
Chrysanthemums, Ox Head Press, 1967.
Ducks, Ox Head Press, 1968.
The Morning Glory: Another Thing That Will Never Be My Friend (12 prose poems), Kayak Books, 1969, revised edition, 1970, complete edition, Harper, 1975.

The Teeth Mother Naked at Last, City Lights, 1971.
(With William E. Stafford and William Matthews) *Poems for Tennessee,* Tennessee Poetry Press, 1971.
Christmas Eve Service at Midnight at St. Michael's, Sceptre Press, 1972.
Water under the Earth, Sceptre Press, 1972.
The Dead Seal Near McClure's Beach, Sceptre Press, 1973.
Sleepers Joining Hands, Harper, 1973.
Jumping Out of Bed, Barre, 1973.
The Hockey Poem, Knife River Press, 1974.
Point Reyes Poems, Mudra, 1974, new edition, Floating Island, 1989.
Old Man Rubbing His Eyes, Unicorn Press, 1975.
The Loon, Ox Head Press, 1977.
This Body Is Made of Camphor and Gopherwood (prose poems), Harper, 1977.
Visiting Emily Dickinson's Grave and Other Poems, Red Ozier Press, 1979.
This Tree Will Be Here for a Thousand Years, Harper, 1979.
The Man in the Black Coat Turns, Doubleday, 1981.
Finding an Old Ant Mansion, Martin Booth, 1981.
Four Ramages, Barnwood Press, 1983.
The Whole Moisty Night, Red Ozier Press, 1983.
Out of the Rolling Ocean, Dial Press, 1984.
Mirabai Versions, Red Ozier Press, 1984.
In the Month of May, Red Ozier Press, 1985.
A Love of Minute Particulars, Sceptre Press, 1985.
Selected Poems, Harper, 1986.
Loving a Woman in Two Worlds, Perennial/Harper, 1987.
The Moon on a Fencepost, Unicorn Press, 1988.
What Have I Ever Lost by Dying?: Collected Prose Poems, HarperCollins, 1992.
The Apple Found in the Plowing, Haw River Books, 1989.

EDITOR

The Sea and the Honeycomb, Sixties Press, 1966.
(With David Ray) *A Poetry Reading against the Viet Nam War,* Sixties Press, 1967.
Forty Poems Touching upon Recent History, Beacon Press, 1970.
News of the Universe: Poems of Twofold Consciousness, Sierra Books, 1980.
Ten Love Poems, Alley Press, 1981.
(With Duffy) *The Fifties and the Sixties* (ten volumes), Hobart and William Smith, 1982.
The Winged Life: The Poetic Voice of Henry David Thoreau, Sierra Books, 1986.
(With James Hillman and Michael Meade) *The Rag and Bone Shop of the Heart: Poems for Men,* HarperCollins, 1992.
Leaping Poetry, Beacon Press, 1975.

David Ignatow, *Selected Poems,* Wesleyan University Press, 1975.

TRANSLATOR

Hans Hvass, *Reptiles and Amphibians of the World,* Grosset, 1960.
(With J. Wright) Georg Trakl, *Twenty Poems,* Sixties Press, 1961.
Selma Lager, *The Story of Gosta Berling,* New American Library, 1962.
(With James Knoefle and Wright) Cesar Vallejo, *Twenty Poems,* Sixties Press, 1962.
Knut Hamson, *Hunger* (novel), Farrar, Straus, 1967.
(With Christina Paulston) Gunnar Ekeloef, *I Do Best Alone at Night,* Charioteer Press, 1967.
(With Paulston) Ekeloef, *Late Arrival on Earth: Selected Poems,* Rapp & Carroll, 1967.
(With Wright) Pablo Neruda, *Twenty Poems,* Sixties Press, 1968.
(With others) Yvan Goll, *Selected Poems,* Kayak, 1968.
Issa Kobayashi, *Ten Poems,* privately printed, 1969.
(And editor) Neruda and Vallejo, *Selected Poems,* Beacon Press, 1971.
Kabir, *The Fish in the Sea Is Not Thirsty: Versions of Kabir,* Lillabulero Press, 1971.
Tomas Transtroemer, *Night Vision,* Lillabulero Press, 1971.
Transtroemer, *Twenty Poems,* Seventies Press, 1972.
Rainer Maria Rilke, *Ten Sonnets to Orpheus,* Zephyrus Image, 1972.
Basho, *Basho,* Mudra, 1972.
Federico Garcia Lorca and Juan Ramon Jimenez, *Selected Poems,* Beacon Press, 1973.
Friends, You Drank Some Darkness: Three Swedish Poets—Martinson, Ekeloef, and Transtroemer, Seventies, 1975.
Kabir, *Grass from Two Years,* Ally Press, 1975.
Kabir, *Twenty-eight Poems,* Siddha Yoga Dham, 1975.
Kabir, *Try to Live to See This!,* Ally Press, 1976.
Rilke, *The Voices,* Ally Press, 1977.
Kabir, *The Kabir Book: Forty-Four of the Ecstatic Poems of Kabir,* Beacon Press, 1977.
Rolf Jacobsen, *Twenty Poems of Rolf Jacobsen,* Eighties Press, 1977.
Antonio Machado, *I Never Wanted Fame,* Ally Press, 1979.
Machado, *Canciones,* Coffee House Press, 1980.
Transtroemer, *Truth Barriers,* Sierra Books, 1980.
(And editor) Rilke, *Selected Poems of Rainer Maria Rilke: A Translation from the German, and Commentary,* Harper, 1981.
Rumi, *Night and Sleep,* Yellow Moon Press, 1981.
Goran Sonnevi, *The Economy Spinning Faster and Faster,* SUN, 1982.

Machado, *Times Alone: Selected Poems,* Wesleyan University Press, 1983.

Rumi Jelaluddin, *When Grapes Turn to Wine,* Yellow Moon Press, 1986.

Olav H. Hauge, *Trusting Your Life to Water and Eternity,* Milkweed Editions, 1987.

Also translator of such volumes as *Forty Poems of Juan Ramon Jimenez,* 1967, and, with Lewis Hyde, *Twenty Poems of Vincente Alexandre,* 1977.

OTHER

A Broadsheet against the New York Times Book Review, Sixties Press, 1961.

Talking All Morning: Collected Conversations and Interviews, University of Michigan Press, 1980.

The Eight Stages of Translation, Rowan Tree, 1983, 2nd edition, 1986.

The Pillow and the Key: Commentary on the Fairy Tale Iron John, Ally Press, 1987.

A Little Book on the Human Shadow, edited by William Booth, Harper, 1988.

American Poetry: Wildness and Domesticity, Harper, 1990.

Iron John: A Book about Men, Addison-Wesley, 1990.

Remembering James Wright, Ally Press, 1991.

ADAPTATIONS: Bly appears on the recordings *Today's Poets 5,* Folkways, and *For the Stomach: Selected Poems,* Watershed, 1974; Bly appears on the videocassettes *On Being a Man,* 1989, *A Gathering of Men,* 1990, and *Bly and Woodman on Men and Women,* 1992.

SIDELIGHTS: Robert Bly is one of America's most influential poets. Since the 1960s he has championed a nonacademic poetry of nature, the visionary and the irrational. The hidden connections between the natural world and the human mind, their surreal interactions, are the subjects of his poems. As Anthony Libby explains in the *Iowa Review,* "Bly is most explicitly [a] mystic of evolution, [a] poet of 'the other world' always contained in present reality but now about to burst forth in a period of destruction and transformation." Bly's poetry is often categorized as part of the deep image school of writing in which the poet employs a system of private imagery. But rather than express a private, even hermetic, vision, Bly wishes to describe modern American life through powerful metaphors and intense imagery, much in the manner of such Spanish-language writers as Cesar Vallejo and Garcia Lorca. Hugh Kenner, writing in the *New York Times Book Review,* finds that "Bly is attempting to write down what it's like to be alive, a state in which, he implies, not all readers find themselves all the time."

Bly has always chosen to be a kind of outsider, both in the larger society, which he sees as being dominated by a consumerist culture, and in the literary world, which he sees as being dominated by the academy. He has never taken the academic route favored by so many poets. Instead, he lives in a small town in rural Minnesota, venturing out several months a year to deliver poetry readings and conduct writing workshops. "I hear from a lot of universities that want me to become a poet in residence," Bly tells Joseph McLellan in the *Washington Post.* "My reaction is: Why bother? I'm already in residence in Moose Lake, Minnesota."

Writing in the *New York Times Book Review,* Bly explains how he first became interested in poetry. "As a Navy recruit in World War II," he states, "I met for the first time a person who wrote poetry, a man named Marcus Eisenstein. . . . I had somehow never understood that poems were written by human beings, and I still remember that moment with delight." Bly began writing poetry to impress a woman—an unsuccessful venture—and continued to write because of what poetry could do. "One day while studying a Yeats poem I decided to write poetry the rest of my life," he states in the *New York Times Book Review.* "I recognized that a single short poem has room for history, music, psychology, religious thought, mood, occult speculation, character and events of one's own life. I still feel surprised that such various substances can find shelter and nourishment in a poem."

Throughout Bly's career, Michiko Kakutani observes in the *New York Times,* "what has remained constant in his work, . . . is Mr. Bly's interest in man's relationship with nature, and his commitment to an idiom built upon simplified diction and the free associative processes of the unconscious mind." Peter Stitt of the *New York Times Book Review* also emphasizes the importance of free association in Bly's poetry. "Bly's method," Stitt writes, "is free association; the imagination is allowed to discover whatever images it deems appropriate to the poem, no matter the logical, literal demands of consciousness." M. L. Rosenberg, writing in *Tribune Books,* notes in Bly's work a blending of European and South American influences with a decidedly American sensibility: "Bly is a genius of the elevated 'high' style, in the European tradition of Rilke and Yeats, the lush magical realism of the South Americans like Lorca and Neruda. Yet Bly's work is truly American, taking its atmosphere of wide empty space from the Midwest, and its unabashed straightforward emotionalism and spiritualism." "The energy with which the Minnesota poet Robert Bly unreservedly gives himself to his ideas, or in some cases, his prejudices," James F. Mersmann comments in his *Out of the Vietnam Vortex: A Study of Poets and Poetry against the War,* "makes him both one of the most annoying and most exciting poets of his time."

"Bly's poetry," C. Michael Smith writes in the *Dictionary of Literary Biography,* "springs from his theories: he is in conscious rebellion against what he sees as the prevalent literary mode in the United States. The poetry championed by John Crowe Ransom and Allen Tate, according to Bly, is too intellectual, too rigid, too rhetorical, and too removed from life." In an interview with David Ossman, Bly explained: "I think that for about 20 or 25 years, American poetry has been out of touch with the current poetry being done in Europe. . . . This is not from a lack of experience so it must be from a lack of a way to approach this experience. My conviction is that poetry in the English and American languages has been tied down too much to the kind of poetry . . . which loses itself in forms and which is too conscious of the English tradition." Speaking at the 1966 Houston Festival of Contemporary Poetry, Bly added: "I think it is wrong to approach a poem by studying meter or form. . . . We turn away from content, and take refuge in technique, because we have a fear of content and a fear of experience, everyone shares it."

To a certain extent, Bly finds that the Beat poets have successfully countered this "stronghold of Academic poetry." "However," he told Ossman, "[the] poetry itself is old-fashioned. The way [the Beat poets] put together a poem is basically the way a poem was put together in the nineteenth century: making very direct statements and talking directly and specifically about the subject matter. . . . Unless English and American poetry can enter, really, an inward depth, through a kind of surrealism, it will continue to become dryer and dryer."

In his note on the jacket of *Silence in the Snowy Fields,* Bly states that he is "interested in the connection between poetry and simplicity. . . . The fundamental world of poetry is an inward world. We approach it through solitude." He adds that the poems in this volume "move toward that world." Frederick Nordell writes of this collection: "This is no casual rustic versifier but a poet who reaches from his midwestern center to a sophisticated circumference of interest and concern." Nordell noted, however, that Bly is "better at evocative surfaces than ambiguous depths," and a *Virginia Quarterly Review* writer introduced this further reservation: "Seen together, [these poems] reveal weaknesses which were not so apparent when the poems appeared separately. Bly's language is pared down to a bare minimum, and his poems are often repetitions of a series of pastoral scenes with little variation and less imagination. Bald statement is not poetry."

But Richard Howard believes that this restriction of language constitutes Bly's achievement: "Robert Bly's success in *Silence in the Snowy Fields* has been to confer upon even the simplest words a weight and consequence as of new things. It is not a difficult or even a structured poetry he writes; Bly is often content with only just enough. . . . But he manages to invest his seasons and spectacles, however dull or even dreary, with so much felt life that the simplest monosyllables speak to him, and to us." The

Times Literary Supplement reviewer was less kind, and referred to Bly's method as "heavy simplicity." He adds: "For years Mr. Bly has been writing poems so transparent that . . . they tend to go in one eye and out the other. . . . Mr Bly's vocabulary is drab. When he attempts a greater resonance the words fail him." Hayden Carruth, writing in *Harper's Magazine,* finds Bly to be a "poet I don't believe and never have" who writes "Swedenborgian nonsense, very dangerous." Despite this aversion, Carruth nonetheless admits that "in some poems he catches me, and I am not off my guard. . . . Sometimes it is good, better than good, to guard oneself and still be caught."

Although Bly's poetry has earned him a place among the foremost American poets of his generation, in 1990 he published an uncharacteristic book that brought him to the attention of a far wider audience. *Iron John: A Book about Men* concerns the ancient rituals and traditional myths which humanity has used to connect with the masculine side of nature. The book argues that contemporary men are out of touch with their own masculinity, an estrangement that causes tremendous grief and alienation. Bly posits a "Wild Man" inside of each male, an archetypical figure who leads men into their full manhood. Not an advocate of machoism or destructive behavior, Bly emphasizes that true masculinity contains such virtues as courage, strength, and wisdom.

Iron John was a national bestseller, while a related videocassette, *A Gathering of Men,* was an equally phenomenal success. For the ten years before the publication of *Iron John,* Bly had, with James Hillman and Michael Reade, been leading seminars for men, teaching poetry and ancient stories along with ideas about initiation. During these seminars, Bly tells *Newsweek,* the emotions can run high. "On the first night of a seminar," he explains, "I may simply put out a question like, 'Why are you having such trouble in relationships with women, or your father?' And the amount of grief and loneliness that pours out is tremendous. So sometimes by the third day there'll be a lot of weeping."

Critical reaction to *Iron John* was favorable and stressed the book's importance to contemporary culture's ongoing redefinition of sexuality. As Deborah Tannen puts it in the *Washington Post Book World,* "This rewarding book is an invaluable contribution to the gathering public conversation about what it means to be male—or female." Bly's poetic style comes through in his prose as well. "To be sure, Bly's quirky style of argumentation does not follow a linear model from Point A to Point B," Dan Cryer notes in the *Detroit News.* "When he uses poems to make a point, clarity sometimes suffers. And his metaphorical language no doubt will put off some readers. Once a reader catches on, though, the rewards are plentiful."

Gregory Orr, in his essay for *On Solitude and Silence: Writings on Robert Bly,* summarizes Bly's importance as poet, translator and critic. "In a time when poets seemed content to quietly or emphatically write their poems and keep on with business," he states, "Robert Bly was determined to think and write seriously about how important poetry is. . . . Bly didn't simply translate, he championed the poets and the ideas about poetry that their work embodied. . . . When, in conjunction with his translating, Bly affirmed what he called 'the image' (and which has since acquired the critical label, 'deep image'), he was attempting to reunite American poetry with the mainstream developments of Romantic poetry as it had evolved on the European mainland. . . . What Bly's talk of 'the image' accomplished was a naive and necessary affirmation of the symbolic imagination that structures lyric poetry. . . . Robert Bly has, in his time, changed American poetry: opened up new directions it might move in, inspired some poets to explore those directions, others to react strongly against such prospects. His role, stature, and style seem to me equivalent to that of Ezra Pound in the early decades of this century."

BIOGRAPHICAL/CRITICAL SOURCES:

BOOKS

Contemporary Literary Criticism, Gale, Volume 1, 1973, Volume 2, 1974, Volume 5, 1976, Volume 10, 1979, Volume 15, 1980, Volume 38, 1986.

Daniels, Kate and Richard Jones, editors, *On Solitude and Silence: Writings on Robert Bly,* Beacon Press, 1982, pp. 146-152.

Davis, William V., *Understanding Robert Bly,* University of South Carolina Press, 1989.

Dictionary of Literary Biography, Volume 5: *American Poets Since World War II,* Gale, 1980.

Friberg, Ingegard, *Moving Inward: A Study of Robert Bly's Poetry,* Acta University Gothoburgensis, 1977.

Howard, Richard, *Alone with America: Essays on the Art of Poetry in the United States since 1950,* Atheneum, 1969, revised edition, 1980.

Lacey, Paul A., *The Inner War: Forms and Themes in Recent American Poetry,* Fortress Press, 1972.

Lensing, George S., and Ronald Moran, *Four Poets and the Emotive Imagination: Robert Bly, James Wright, Louis Simpson, and William Stafford,* Louisiana State University Press, 1976.

Malkoff, Karl, *Escape from the Self: A Study in Contemporary American Poetry and Poetics,* Columbia University Press, 1977.

Mersmann, James F., *Out of the Vietnam Vortex: A Study of Poets and Poetry against the War,* University Press of Kansas, 1974, pp. 113-157.

Molesworth, Charles, *The Fierce Embrace: A Study of Contemporary American Poetry,* University of Missouri Press, 1979.

Nelson, Howard, *Robert Bly: An Introduction to the Poetry,* Columbia University Press, 1984.

Ossman, David, *The Sullen Art,* Corinth, 1963.

Peseroff, Joyce, editor, *Robert Bly: When Sleepers Awake,* University of Michigan Press, 1984.

Poems for Young Readers, National Council of Teachers of English, for the Houston Festival of Contemporary Poetry, 1966.

Roberson, William H., *Robert Bly: A Primary and Secondary Bibliography,* Scarecrow, 1986.

Shaw, Robert B., editor, *American Poetry since 1960: Some Critical Perspectives,* Dufour, 1974, pp. 55-67.

Smith, Thomas R., editor, *Walking Swiftly: Writings and Images on the Occasion of Robert Bly's 65th Birthday,* Ally Press, 1992.

Stepanchev, Stephen, *American Poetry Since 1945: A Critical Survey,* Harper, 1965, pp. 185-187.

Sugg, Richard P., *Robert Bly,* Twayne, 1986.

PERIODICALS

American Dialog, winter, 1968-69.

Boundary 2, spring, 1976, pp. 677-700, 707-725.

Carleton Miscellany, Volume XVIII, number 1, 1979-80, pp. 74-84.

Chicago Review, Volume 19, number 2, 1967.

Chicago Tribune Book World, May 3, 1981; February 28, 1982, p. 2.

Christian Science Monitor, January 23, 1963.

Commonweal, July 23, 1971, pp. 375-380.

Detroit News, December 5, 1990, p. 3D.

English Studies, April, 1970, pp. 112-137.

Far Point, fall/winter, 1969, pp. 42-47.

Globe and Mail (Toronto), April 4, 1987; December 8, 1990, p. C10.

Harper's Magazine, August, 1968, pp. 73-77; January, 1980, p. 79.

Hollins Critic, April, 1975, pp. 1-15.

Hudson Review, autumn, 1968, p. 553; spring, 1976; spring, 1978; summer, 1987.

Iowa Review, summer, 1972, pp. 78-91; spring, 1973, pp. 111-126; fall, 1976, pp. 135-153.

Lamp in the Spine, Number 3, 1972.

Listener, June 27, 1968.

London, December, 1968.

Los Angeles Times Book Review, May 18, 1980, p. 9; December 29, 1985, p. 11; October 26, 1986, p. 4; November 30, 1986, p. 11; December 2, 1990.

Michigan Quarterly Review, spring, 1981, pp. 144-154.

Modern Poetry Studies, winter, 1976, pp. 231-240.

Moons and Lion Tailes, Volume II, number 3, 1977, pp. 85-89.

Nation, March 25, 1968, pp. 413-414; November 17, 1979, pp. 503-504; October 31, 1981, pp. 447-448.

New Republic, November 14, 1970, pp. 26-27.

Newsweek, November 26, 1990, pp. 66-68.

New York Review of Books, June 20, 1968.

New York Times, May 3, 1986.

New York Times Book Review, September 7, 1975; January 1, 1978; March 9, 1980, p. 8; April 26, 1981; February 14, 1982, p. 15; January 22, 1984, p. 1; October 13, 1985, p. 15; May 25, 1986, p. 2; February 22, 1987, p. 34; September 30, 1990, p. 29; December 9, 1990, p. 15.

New York Times Magazine, February 3, 1980, p. 16.

Ohio Review, fall, 1978.

Partisan Review, Volume XLIV, number 2, 1977.

Poetry, June, 1963.

Prairie Schooner, summer, 1968, pp. 176-178.

Publishers Weekly, May 9, 1980, pp. 10-11; October 12, 1990.

Rocky Mountain Review of Language and Literature, Number 29, 1975, pp. 95-117.

San Francisco Review of Books, July-August, 1983, pp. 22-23.

Schist I, fall, 1973.

Sewanee Review, spring, 1974.

Shenandoah, spring, 1968, p. 70.

Texas Quarterly, Number 19, 1976, pp. 80-94.

Times Literary Supplement, March 16, 1967; February 20, 1981, p. 208.

Tribune Books (Chicago), April 12, 1987, p. 5.

TWA Ambassador, December, 1980.

Virginia Quarterly Review, winter, 1963.

Washington Post, October 23, 1980; February 3, 1991, p. F1.

Washington Post Book World, April 1, 1973, p. 13; January 5, 1986, p. 6; December 14, 1986, p. 9; November 18, 1990, p. 1.

Western American Literature, spring, 1982, pp. 66-68; fall, 1982, pp. 282-284.

Win, January 15, 1973.

Windless Orchard, Number 18, 1974, pp. 30-34.

World Literature Today, autumn, 1981, p. 680.

*   *   *

BLYTH, John
See HIBBS, John

*   *   *

BOLLER, Paul Franklin, Jr. 1916-

PERSONAL: Born December 31, 1916, in Spring Lake, NJ; son of Paul Franklin (a clergyman) and Grace (Hall) Boller. *Education:* Yale University, B.A., 1939, Ph.D., 1947. *Politics:* Liberal Democrat. *Religion:* "Seeker." *Avocational interests:* Music, reading, films, beer parties, jogging, surf-bathing, hiking, and bicycling.

ADDRESSES: Office—Department of History, Texas Christian University, Fort Worth, TX 76129.

CAREER: U.S. Navy Department, Washington, DC, civilian analyst, 1947-48; Southern Methodist University, Dallas, TX, 1948-66, began as assistant professor, became professor of history; University of Massachusetts—Boston, professor of history, 1966-76; Texas Christian University, Fort Worth, L.B.J. Professor of History, 1976-83. Visiting professor, University of Texas at Austin, 1963-64. *Military service:* U.S. Navy, 1942-46; became lieutenant junior grade.

MEMBER: Authors Guild, Authors League of America, De Golyer Institute of American Studies, Phi Beta Kappa.

WRITINGS:

This Is Our Nation, McGraw, 1961.

George Washington and Religion, Southern Methodist University Press, 1963.

(Contributor) H. Wayne Morgan, editor, *The Gilded Age,* Syracuse University Press, 1963.

Quotemanship, Southern Methodist University Press, 1966.

American Thought in Transition, 1865-1900, Rand McNally, 1969.

American Transcendentalism, 1830-1860, Putnam, 1974.

Freedom and Fate in American Thought: From Edwards to Dewey, Southern Methodist University Press, 1978.

Presidential Anecdotes, Oxford University Press, 1981.

Presidential Campaigns, Oxford University Press, 1984.

(With Ronald Story) *A More Perfect Union,* two volumes, Houghton, 1984.

Contributor to professional journals.

SIDELIGHTS: In *Presidential Anecdotes* and *Presidential Campaigns,* Paul Franklin Boller, Jr., has written essays and recounted stories about American presidential campaigns and the presidents' lives. In these books, Boller provides new information about and new insights into the presidents and the presidency. Paul Gray maintains in *Time* that in *Presidential Anecdotes,* "the material that Boller has culled is fascinating even when the Presidents are not." Similarly, Richard E. Meyer comments in the *Los Angeles Times Book Review* that in *Presidential Campaigns,* "Boller has larded chapter after chapter with anecdotes and vignettes, to build a collection of lore about those who were and who *would* have been President that is unrivaled anywhere."

Boller provides interesting details about the presidents' lives in *Presidential Anecdotes*. For example, he chronicles the problems-all presidents have had with the handshake, as Gray reports: "[James K.] Polk and William McKinley both developed extensive theories about the best way to shake many hands without pain or injury; Lyndon Johnson could extend a normal greeting into something like a mugging. [But] some Presidents failed handshaking. Benjamin Harrison's grip was likened to 'a wilted petunia,' while one newsman described Woodrow Wilson's as 'a ten-cent pickled mackerel in brown paper." Boller also presents a new side to the presidents. George Washington, often considered to be severe and conservative, was really quite different. "In fact," writes Elizabeth Peer in *Newsweek,* Boller finds that Washington "told ribald jokes, admired a well-turned ankle, indulged a sulfurous temper, relished card playing and took a puerile delight in chasing fire wagons." Peer concludes that the book is a "stylish smorgasbord of anecdotes."

In *Presidential Campaigns,* Boller challenges the belief that elections are more corrupt in recent years than they were in the past. Lynne Cheney remarks in the *Washington Post* that the book "makes clear that American presidential campaigns have always been affairs where winning is at least partly a function of making sure the other guy loses." Gene Lyons agrees with this assessment in *Newsweek,* stating that "it's tempting to imagine that the Founding Fathers, in their powdered wigs, did the job of electing a president with dignity. Not so, says historian Paul F. Boller Jr. . . . In fact, Boiler writes, 'presidential campaigns are a lot nicer today than they used to be.' " Despite problems with campaigning, "Boller sees no threat to the democratic process in the extravagant, exuberant, often emotional way in which we go about selecting leaders," Cheney points out.

Critics also praise Boller's skill in relating his information. Gray finds that "the presidency has stumbled through its ribbon cuttings, receiving lines and mumbled gaffes. *Presidential Anecdotes* is an entertaining thumbnail history of how this survival occurred." George E. Reedy reports in the *New York Times Book Review* that Boller "has a good eye for the offbeat and the ludicrous, and he spins the anecdotes together with the skill of the old-fashioned Yankee yarn master." Reedy thinks that Boller's journalistic style "helps eliminate tedium" but it also "may involve considerable oversimplification." Cheney also notes Boller's skill at writing these stories, but criticizes his editing; "He has a wonderful ear for anecdotes, a clear love for them; in fact, he likes them so much, he refuses to leave any of them out." Reedy concludes that *Presidential Campaign*'s "panoramic view . . . affords an opportunity to look at the whole thing in one reading and reflect upon it."

Boller commented to *CA* on his reasons for writing about history: "My work in the history of American ideas, like all scholarly work, involves fun and games; but it is also motivated by my wish to learn what unusually gifted people have had to say about the Big Questions in religion, science, philosophy, and ethics. In my books on American thought I have tried to pass on something of what I have learned about these things to other people."

BIOGRAPHICAL/CRITICAL SOURCES:

BOOKS

Boller, Paul Franklin, Jr., *Presidential Anecdotes,* Oxford University Press, 1981.
Boller, Paul Franklin, Jr., *Presidential Campaigns,* Oxford University Press, 1984.

PERIODICALS

Chicago Tribune Book World, September 20, 1981.
Los Angeles Times Book Review, June 3, 1984.
Newsweek, September 21, 1981; September 3, 1984.
New York Times, May 31, 1967.
New York Times Book Review, July 15, 1984.
Saturday Review, June 10, 1967.
Time, August 24, 1981.
Washington Post, May 22, 1984.
Washington Post Book World, December 15, 1985.

* * *

BORNEMAN, Ernest 1915-
(Cameron McCabe)

PERSONAL: Born April 12, 1915, in Berlin, Germany; son of Curt and Hertha (Blochert) Borneman; married Eva Geisel (an editor and translator); children: Stephen. *Education:* Studied at University of Berlin, 1931-33, School of Oriental and African Studies, 1933-35, and Emmanuel College, Cambridge, 1935-37. *Politics:* Liberal. *Avocational interests:* Painting, music.

ADDRESSES: Home—A 4612, Scharten, Austria.

CAREER: National Film Board of Canada, Ottawa, Ontario, head of foreign language production, 1941-45, head of international distribution, 1945-47; UNESCO, Paris, France, head of films division, 1947-49; Granada Television Network, London and Manchester, England, head of script department, 1955-58; British Film Institute, London, head of programming, 1959-60; Freies Fernsehen, Frankfurt, Germany, controller of programs and productions, 1960-62; currently teaching at the Universities of Salzburg, Klagenfurt, Bremen, and Marburg.

WRITINGS:

(Under pseudonym Cameron McCabe) *The Face on the Cutting Room Floor,* Gollancz, 1937.

A Love Story, Jarrolds, 1941.

A Critic Looks at Jazz (originally published as a serial, "An Anthropologist Looks at Jazz" in *Record Changer*), JazzMusic Books, 1946.

Tremolo (also see below) Harper, 1948.

Tomorrow Is Now: The Adventures of Welfare Willy in Search of a Soul, Neville Spearman, 1959.

Something Wrong, Four Square, 1961.

The Compromisers, Deutsch, 1962.

The Man Who Loved Women, Coward, 1968.

IN GERMAN

Lexikon der Liebe, two volumes, List, 1968, four volume edition, Ullstein, 1979.

Landschaft mit Figuren, Bertelsmann, 1971.

Sex im Volksmund, Rowohlt, 1971, two volume pocket edition, 1974.

Psychoanalyse des Geldes, Suhrkamp, 1973, Urizen Books, 1976.

Unsere Kinder, Walter, 1973.

Die Umwelt des Kindes, Walter, 1974.

Das Patriarchat, S. Fischer, 1975.

Die Welt der Erwachsenen, Walter, 1976.

Die Ur-Szene, S. Fischer, 1977.

Sexualitaet, Beltz, 1979.

Wir machen keinen grossen Mist, Ullstein, 1980.

Lehrbuch der sexuellen Entwicklungspsychologie, Volume I, Jugend & Volk, 1981.

Arbeiterbewegung und Feminismus, Ullstein, 1982.

Der Neanderberg, Ullstein, 1983.

Rot-weiss-rote Herzen, Hannibal, 1984.

Das Geschlechtsleben des Kindes, Urban & Schwarzenberg, 1985.

Die Neue Eifersucht, Heyne, 1986.

Ausgewaehlte Texte, Goldmann, 1990.

Ullstein Enzyklopaedie der Sexualitaet, Ullstein, 1990.

Sexuelle Marktwirtschaft, ProMedia, 1992.

Aus! Nachruf auf die Sexualitaet, Hoffmann & Campe, 1993.

FILM SCRIPTS

Ulysses, 1949.

(With Guy Elmes) *The Flanagan Boy* (based upon novel by Max Catto), 1950, released by Lippert as *Bad Blonde,* 1953.

(With Elmes) *Bang! You're Dead* (also known as *Game of Danger*), British Lion, 1954.

Face the Music (musical), 1954.

Double Jeopardy, Republic, 1956.

(With others) *The Long Duel* (based upon story by Ranveer Singh), 1959, released by J. Arthur Rank (Britain) and Paramount (USA), 1967.

Contributor, in one capacity or another, to about two hundred other features, documentaries, and shorts filmed in Canada, the United States, and Europe.

TELEVISION SCRIPTS

Tremolo (based on his novel of same title), 1950.

Four O'Clock in the Morning Blues, 1954.

(Translator and adapter) *Hedda Gabler,* 1957.

(Adapter from radio play) *Sorry, Wrong Number,* 1957.

(Adapter) *Break-Up,* 1957.

(Adapter) *Don't Destroy Me,* 1957.

(Adapter) *The Lie,* 1957.

(With John Hopkins) *After the Party,* 1957.

Contributor, in one capacity or another, to about seventy other television and radio shows.

OTHER

Also author of stage plays, *The Girl on the Highway* and *The Windows of Heaven.* Contributor of more than one thousand articles to magazines, including *Reader's Digest, Harper's Bazaar, Holiday, Esquire, Playboy,* and *Times Literary Supplement.*

SIDELIGHTS: Ernest Borneman worked his way through school playing in a jazz band and has collected folk music and jazz on four continents.

BIOGRAPHICAL/CRITICAL SOURCES:

PERIODICALS

Maledicta, summer, 1979.
New York Times Book Review, June 9, 1968.

*   *   *

BOWLER, Jan Brett
    See BRETT, Jan (Churchill)

*   *   *

BOWMAN, John S(tewart) 1931-

PERSONAL: Born May 30, 1931, in Cambridge, MA; son of John Russell (a teacher) and Anne (a church administrator; maiden name, Stewart) Bowman; married second wife, Francesca Di Pietro (a federal probation officer), February 11, 1967; children: (second marriage) Michela Ann, Alexander Russell. *Education:* Harvard University, B.A., 1953; attended Trinity College, Cambridge, 1953-54, and University of Munich, 1958-59. *Avocational interests:* Archeology, particularly of the Mediterranean; the theatre, particularly the commedia dell'arte; baseball, both as a game to watch and as a reflection of American social history.

ADDRESSES: Home—53 Massasoit St., Northampton, MA 01060.

CAREER: New England Opera Theatre, Boston, MA, production assistant, 1957; University of Maryland overseas program, Athens and Crete, Greece, English instructor, 1959-60; *Story* (magazine), staff member, 1960; *Natural History,* New York City, associate editor, 1961-62; Grolier, Inc. (encyclopedia publisher), New York City, associate editor, 1962-63; free-lance writer and editor, 1963—; University of Massachusetts—Amherst, teacher, 1978—. *Military service:* U.S. Army, 1954-56.

MEMBER: National Association of Science Writers, Society for American Baseball Research, Phi Beta Kappa.

WRITINGS:

Crete, Secker & Warburg, 1962, published as *A Guide to Crete,* Pantheon, 1963, revised and expanded edition published as *The Travellers' Guide to Crete,* 7th edition, J. Cape, 1990.
Early Civilizations, Golden Press, 1966.
The Age of Enlightenment, Golden Press, 1966.
On Guard: Living Things Defend Themselves, Doubleday, 1969.
The Quest for Atlantis, Doubleday, 1971.
Imperial Greece, HBJ Press, 1980.
(With Joel Zoss) *Diamonds in the Rough: The Untold History of Baseball,* Macmillan, 1989.
(With Zoss) *The Pictorial History of Baseball,* fifth edition, W. H. Smith, 1993.

EDITOR

A Book of Islands (anthology), Doubleday, 1971.
The Civil War Almanac, World Almanac, 1983.
The Twentieth Century: An Almanac, World Almanac, 1984.
The American West: An Almanac, World Almanac, 1986.
Encyclopedia of the Civil War, Dorset, 1992.
Chronicle of 20th Century History, Bison Group, 1993.
Almanac of American History, Brompton, 1993.

OTHER

Also author of guides to Santorini and Iraklion/Knossos, Efstathiadis, 1974. Author of librettos for operas "The Face," composed by Henry Mollicone, "Young Goodman Brown," and "Emperor Norton." Contributor to *New Yorker, Drama Survey, Parents' Magazine, Athenian, International History, Nature and Science, Interplay,* and *Hampshire Daily Life.*

WORK IN PROGRESS: The Cambridge University Press Dictionary of American Biography, 1994; a travel book about Crete; guides to Greece; various magazine articles.

SIDELIGHTS: John S. Bowman's *Diamonds in the Rough: The Untold History of Baseball* "may be to baseball trivia what 'Late Night with David Letterman' is to talk shows," Wes Lukowsky commented in *Booklist.* The book, co-authored with Joel Zoss and described as "pleasurable fan reading" by *Library Journal* contributor Morey Berger, features topics beyond the usual statistics and hero stories and chronicles the impacts of racism, art, literature, and war on America's favorite pastime. A *Washington Post Book World* reviewer noted that *Diamonds in the Rough* "can serve to remind us of the game's true joys."

BIOGRAPHICAL/CRITICAL SOURCES:

PERIODICALS

Booklist, December 1, 1989, p. 718.
Library Journal, December, 1989, p. 129.
Washington Post Book World, December 10, 1989, p. 17.
Wilson Library Bulletin, June, 1992, p. 149.

*   *   *

BOYER, Paul Samuel 1935-

PERSONAL: Born August 2, 1935, in Dayton, OH. *Education:* Harvard University, A.B. (magna cum laude), 1960, M.A., 1961, Ph.D., 1966.

ADDRESSES: Office—Department of History, University of Wisconsin, 500 Lincoln Dr., Madison, WI 53706.

CAREER: Harvard University Press, Cambridge, MA, assistant editor, "Notable American Women" series, 1964-67; University of Massachusetts—Amherst, assistant professor, 1967-70, associate professor, 1970-75, professor of history, 1975-80, chairman of department, 1978; University of Wisconsin—Madison, professor of history, 1980—, Merle Curti Professor of History, 1985—. Visiting lecturer, Smith College, spring, 1969, fall, 1975, and Mount Holyoke College, spring, 1977. Visiting professor, University of California, Los Angeles, 1987-88, and Northwestern University, Evanston, IL, 1988-89.

MEMBER: American Antiquarian Society, Society of American Historians, Phi Beta Kappa.

AWARDS, HONORS: American Philosophical Society grant, 1969; Guggenheim fellowship, 1973-74; John H. Dunning Prize, American Historical Association, 1974, and National Book Award nomination, 1975, both for *Salem Possessed;* Rockefeller Foundation humanities fellowship, 1982-83.

WRITINGS:

Purity in Print: Book Censorship in America, Scribner, 1968.
Urban Masses and Moral Order in America, 1820-1920, Harvard University Press, 1978.
By the Bomb's Early Light: American Thought and Culture at the Dawn of the Atomic Age, Pantheon, 1985.
(Co-author) *The Enduring Vision: A History of the American People,* Heath, 1989.
When Time Shall Be No More: Prophecy Belief in Modern American Culture, Harvard University Press, 1992.

EDITOR

(With E. T. James and J. W. James) *Notable American Women: 1607-1950,* three volumes, Harvard University Press, 1971.
(With Stephen Nissenbaum) *Salem Village Witchcraft: A Documentary Record of Local Conflict in Colonial New England,* Wadsworth, 1972.
(With S. Nissenbaum) *Salem Possessed: The Social Origins of Witchcraft,* Harvard University Press, 1974.
(With S. Nissenbaum) *The Salem Witchcraft Papers,* three volumes, Da Capo Press, 1977.
Reagan as President: Contemporary Views of the Man, His Politics, and His Policies, Ivan R. Dee, 1990.

Also general editor of the "Wisconsin" volumes in the history of American thought and culture series, University of Wisconsin Press. Contributor to *Dictionary of American History, Dictionary of American Biography, Encyclopedia Americana, World Book Encyclopedia,* and *Encyclopedia of American History;* contributor of articles and reviews to *William and Mary Quarterly, American Quarterly, New Republic, American Historical Review, Journal of American History,* and *Historian.*

WORK IN PROGRESS: A history of the United States since 1945, Heath, 1993; editor, *Oxford Companion to American History,* Oxford University Press, expected 1995.

SIDELIGHTS: Paul Samuel Boyer's *Salem Possessed: The Social Origins of Witchcraft* has been praised for presenting new information and theories behind the witchhunt that occurred in this Massachusetts village. Boyer and his coauthor, Stephen Nissenbaum, examined such legal documents as tax records and land holdings and uncovered social and economic rivalries among the villagers. Boyer and Nissenbaum then proceeded to show how this friction might have been one of the causes of the Salem witchhunt.

Phoebe Adams writes in *Atlantic* that *Salem Possessed* demonstrates "that witchcraft charges . . . were brought principally by members and friends of the tribe with cause for envy, and directed principally against minor members or peripheral connections of the enviable group." Adams goes on to state that "the recent history and practical circumstances which permitted such action are explored, and the whole approach to the Salem disaster is canny, rewarding, and sure to fascinate readers interested in that aberrant affair."

Keith Thomas comments in the *New York Review of Books* that *Salem Possessed* "offers an illuminating and imaginative interpretation . . . of the social and moral state of Salem Village in 1692. . . . It has the extra recommendation of telling a gripping story which builds up to a horrifying climax." And finally, Robin Briggs remarks in a *Times Literary Supplement* review of *Salem Possessed:* "The authors have produced an explanatory scheme which accounts fully for the events of 1692, renders them significant in a much wider context of social and economic change, and yet allows room for the operation of personalities and accidental influences. . . . *Salem Possessed* reinterprets a world-famous episode so completely and convincingly that virtually all the previous treatment can be consigned to the historical lumber-room."

Another of Boyer's books to capture the attention of reviewers is his historical study, *Urban Masses and Moral Order in America, 1820-1920.* Thomas Bender writes in *Nation:* "Boyer's theme is the search for a particular moral order in America's cities. The multiplicity of urban reforms that he describes derives from a vision or, better, a misty memory of the unified moral order of the village. A century of urban reform turns out to be a succession of attempts to contrive some 'artifice' for reproducing in the city the 'natural' order of a village life that was receding irretrievably into the past."

BIOGRAPHICAL/CRITICAL SOURCES:

PERIODICALS

Atlantic, April, 1974.
Library Journal, August, 1974.
Nation, September 8, 1979.
Newsweek, November 25, 1985.
New York Review of Books, August 8, 1974.
New York Times Book Review, November 10, 1985.
Times Literary Supplement, January 3, 1975.
Virginia Quarterly Review, autumn, 1974.

*   *   *

BRAHAM, Randolph L(ewis) 1922-

PERSONAL: Born in 1922, in Romania; married Elizabeth Sommer, 1954; two children. *Education:* City College (now City College of the City University of New York), M.S., 1949; New School for Social Research, Ph.D., 1952.

ADDRESSES: Home—114-07 Union Turnpike, Forest Hills, NY 11375. *Office*—Graduate Center of the City University of New York, 33 West 42nd St., New York, NY 10036.

CAREER: Mid-European Studies Center, New York City, research associate, 1952-53; YIVO Institute for Jewish Research, New York City, research associate, 1954-61; Fairleigh Dickinson University, Teaneck, NJ, instructor, 1956-62; researcher, Publication Research Service, 1957; City College of the City University of New York, New York City, lecturer, 1959-64, assistant professor, 1964-67, associate professor, 1967-70, professor, 1970-86, then distinguished professor of political science, 1986—, department chairman, 1970-1980, director, Institute for Holocaust Studies. Visiting assistant professor, Hofstra College (now University), 1962; guest lecturer.

MEMBER: American Political Science Association, Association for the Advancement of Slavic Studies.

AWARDS, HONORS: Leon Jolson Award, National Jewish Book Council, 1981, for *The Politics of Genocide.*

WRITINGS:

Education in Romania (two volumes), U.S. Joint Publications Research Service, 1958.

(With M. M. Hauer) *Jews in the Communist World: A Bibliography, 1945-60,* Twayne, 1961, enlarged edition, Pro Arte, 1963.

Eichmann and the Destruction of Hungarian Jewry, Twayne, 1961.

The Hungarian-Jewish Catastrophe: A Selected and Annotated Bibliography, YIVO Institute for Jewish Research, 1962, 2nd edition, Columbia University Press, 1984.

Jews in the Communist World: A Non-English Source Book, Pro Arte, 1963.

Education in the People's Republic of Rumania, Office of Education, U.S. Department of Health, Education & Welfare, 1964.

Israel: A Modern Education System, Office of Education, U.S. Department of Health, Education & Welfare, 1966.

(With Samuel Hendel) *The U.S.S.R. after Fifty Years: Promise and Reality,* Knopf, 1967.

The Eichmann Case: A Source Book, World Federation of Hungarian Jews, 1969.

Education in the Hungarian People's Republic, Institute of International Studies, U.S. Office of Education, 1970.

Education in Romania: A Decade of Change, Institute of International Studies, U.S. Office of Education, 1972.

The Politics of Genocide: The Holocaust in Hungary (two volumes), Columbia University Press, 1981, 2nd edition, Institution for Holocaust Studies, 1993.

Perspectives on the Holocaust, Kluwer-Nijhoff, 1983.

Genocide and Retribution: The Holocaust in Northern Transylvania, Kluwer-Nijhoff, 1983.

Contemporary Views on the Holocaust, Kluwer-Nijhoff, 1983.

Jewish Leadership in the Nazi Era: Patterns of Behavior in the Free World, Institute for Holocaust Studies, 1985.

The Holocaust in Hungary: Forty Years Later, Institute for Holocaust Studies, 1985.

The Tragedy of Hungarian Jewry: Essays and Document, Institute for Holocaust Studies, 1986.

The Origins of the Holocaust: Christian Anti-Semitism, Institute for Holocaust Studies, 1986.

The Treatment of the Holocaust in Textbooks, Institute for Holocaust Studies, 1987.

The Psychological Perspectives of the Holocaust and of Its Aftermath, Institute for Holocaust Studies, 1988.

The Holocaust: Reflections in Art and Literature, Institute for Holocaust Studies, 1990.

Studies on the Holocaust in Hungary, Institute for Holocaust Studies, 1990.

Anti-Semitism and the Treatment of the Holocaust in Post-Communist East Central Europe, Institute for Holocaust Studies, 1993.

Studies on the Tragedy of Rumanian Jewry, Institute for Holocaust Studies, 1993.

Author's works have been translated into Hungarian.

EDITOR

The Destruction of Hungarian Jewry: A Documentary Account (two volumes), World Federation of Hungarian Jews, 1963.

Soviet Politics and Government: A Reader, Knopf, 1965.

Documents on Major European Governments, Knopf, 1966.

Hungarian-Jewish Studies (three volumes), World Federation of Hungarian Jews, 1966-73.

Human Rights: Contemporary Domestic and International Issues and Conflicts, Irvington, 1980.

Social Justice, Nijhoff, 1981.

CONTRIBUTOR

Hungary, Praeger, 1957.
Romania, Praeger, 1957.
European Political Systems, Knopf, 1959.

Contributor to *Grolier Encyclopedia, Encyclopedia of Zionism and Israel, Yad Vashem Studies,* and to numerous scientific books and journals.

WORK IN PROGRESS: Reflections on the Hungarian Labor Service System, Institute for Holocaust Studies.

SIDELIGHTS: Professor Randolph L. Braham, a specialist in comparative politics, is a recognized authority on the Holocaust. His interest in this tragic period in world history is personal: his study *The Politics of Genocide: The Holocaust in Hungary* is dedicated to his parents who met their deaths at Auschwitz during World War II. In a review of the book for the *New York Times Book Review*, Elenore Lester claims that *The Politics of Genocide* "now joins the most important works of Holocaust history." Lester adds that the book's "comprehensive presentation provides insights into how the Jews were able to survive until the German occupation and why the end came with such catastrophic impact." The two-volume work, concentrating on the Holocaust as it affected Hungarian Jews, places that tragedy within the context of Hungarian political history. Lester concludes of Braham's efforts: "At a time when quack 'history' books maintaining that the Holocaust was all in the fevered Zionist imagination reach library shelves all over the world, it is a comfort that this book will stand there, too, in its immense and meticulous documentation." Reflecting the credibility of his sources and the meticulous documentation of his research, Braham's works have been used as sourcebooks in litigation involving restitution and war crimes in the U.S., Canada, Germany, and Israel.

BIOGRAPHICAL/CRITICAL SOURCES:

PERIODICALS

American Historical Review, October, 1981.
Choice, May, 1981.
Jewish Social Studies, summer-fall, 1981.
New York Times Book Review, October 4, 1981.

*   *   *

BRAIN, J(oy) B(lundell) 1926-

PERSONAL: Born January 17, 1926, in Transvaal, South Africa; daughter of William Kenneth and Kathleen Beatrice (Blundell) Brown; married Peter Brain (a pathologist), December 29, 1948; children: Elizabeth, Richard, Phillippa Brain Beckerling, Robert, Helen Brain Stubbs. *Education:* University of the Witwatersrand, Diploma in Librarianship, 1946; University of South Africa, B.A., 1969, B.A. (with honors), 1971, M.A., 1974, Ph.D., 1979; University of Natal, Diploma in Education, 1971. *Religion:* Roman Catholic.

ADDRESSES: Home—14 Richmond Ave., Kloof 3610, South Africa. *Office*—Department of History, University of Durban-Westville, Durban, South Africa.

CAREER: Johannesburg Public Library, Johannesburg, South Africa, reference librarian, 1943-48; South African Library, Cape Town, librarian in charge of Africana Department, 1949, 1954-58; Edgewood College of Educaton, Pinetown, South Africa, librarian in charge, 1970-76; University of Durban-Westville, Durban, South Africa, lecturer, 1976-79, senior lecturer, 1980-83, associate professor, 1984-87, professor and head of department of history, 1988-91, professor emeritus, 1992—. South African representative to Pontifical Council on Culture, Rome, Italy, 1985—.

MEMBER: South African Historical Society, South African National Society, South African Archives Society, Ecclesiastical History Society (United Kingdom), Catholic Archives Society (United Kingdom), Friends of the South African Library.

WRITINGS:

Catholic Beginnings in Natal, Griggs, 1975.
Catholics in Natal II, Roman Catholic Archdiocese of Durban, 1982.
Christian Indians in Natal, 1860-1911, Oxford University Press (South Africa), 1983.
(Contributor) *Enterprise and Exploitation*, University of Natal Press, 1985.
(Editor) Patrick Raymond Griffith, *The Cape Diary of Patrick Raymond Griffith, 1837-39*, Southern Africa Catholic Bishops Conference, 1988.
The Catholic Church in the Transvaal, Missionary Oblates of Mary Immaculate, 1991.
(Contributor) *Essays on Indentured Indians in Natal*, Peepal Tree Press, 1992.

Contributor to history, religious studies, and medical history journals.

WORK IN PROGRESS: Revising *The Catholic Church in South Africa* by W. E. Brown; working on *The Orange Free State;* researching the height, caste and health of indentured Indians in Natal, as compared with those in Fiji.

SIDELIGHTS: J. B. Brain told *CA:* "Minority groups, their problems, the animosity they arouse, and their efforts to come to terms with these difficulties have interested me since I grew up and began to think about such things. As a Roman Catholic in a predominantly Calvinist country I became aware very early that Catholics were a small and far from popular group; yet the very antagonism they experienced revealed an influence out of proportion to their numbers, which at the time was less than 4 percent of the population.

"The questions that I began to ask concerned the religious loyalty of Catholics to their church, which seemed to ignore racial and social barriers and attracted members from every racial and economic group. Had the first missionaries exerted an influence so strong that ordinary Catholics had developed attitudes substantially different for those of the white population as a whole? How had such a numerically insignificant group established the prominent educational and social institutions to be found in the towns, cities, and other locations? These questions led me to the study of church history in general and South African Catholic church history in particular.

"In the case of Christian Indians, of whom I made a detailed study in later work, the minority problem was twofold. Not only are Indians a minority group in South Africa but Indian Christians made up a minute section of the Indian population in the nineteenth and early twentieth centuries and are still numerically insignificant compared with Muslims and Hindus. Yet they have played an important part in the educational, social, and political life of their community.

"The question asked, then, is whether minority groups, by closing ranks and defending their beliefs, often at the cost of personal sacrifice, are able to develop successful means of adaptation.

"The belief that the people of the past faced problems just as real and as urgent as our own has persuaded me that in no circumstances should one attempt to judge them and their actions by our present-day standards. In many ways we have much to learn from the nineteenth century!"

*   *   *

BRETT, Jan (Churchill) 1949-
(Jan Brett Bowler)

PERSONAL: Born December 1, 1949, in Hingham, MA; daughter of George (a sales engineer) and Jean (Thaxter) Brett; married Daniel Bowler, February 27, 1970 (divorced, 1979); married Joseph Hearne (a musician), August 18, 1980; children: (first marriage) Lia. *Education:* Attended New London Academy (now Colby-Sawyer College), 1968-69, and Boston Museum of Fine Arts School, 1970.

ADDRESSES: Home—132 Pleasant St., Norwell, MA 02061.

CAREER: Painter; author and illustrator of books for young people. Has exhibited art work at galleries and museums throughout New York, Massachusetts, Michigan, and Ohio, 1981—.

AWARDS, HONORS: Parent's Choice Award for illustration in children's books, Parent's Choice Foundation, 1981, for *Fritz and the Beautiful Horses* and *St. Patrick's Day in the Morning,* 1988, for *Mother's Day Mice,* and 1990, for *Goldilocks and the Three Bears;* Ambassador of Honor, English-Speaking Union of the United States, 1983, for *Some Birds Have Funny Names;* Best of the Year Award, NBC-TV critic Gene Shalit, 1983 and 1984, both for Sunrise calendar; Outstanding Science Trade Book for Children, National Science Teachers Association, 1984,

for *Some Plants Have Funny Names;* Children's Book Award, University of Nebraska, 1984, for *Fritz and the Beautiful Horses;* Top Ten Children's Books of the Year citation, *Redbook,* 1985, for *Annie and the Wild Animals;* American Library Association, *Booklist* Editor's Choice Award, 1986, for *The Twelve Days of Christmas,* and 1987, for *Goldilocks and the Three Bears,* and Best Children's Books of the 1980s citation, 1989, for *The Mitten.*

Best Books of the Year citation, *Parent's* and *Newsweek,* both 1987, both for *Goldilocks and the Three Bears;* Best Children's Books citation, *New Yorker,* 1988, for *The First Dog,* 1989, for *The Mitten,* 1990, for *The Wild Christmas Reindeer,* and 1991, for *Berlioz the Bear;* artist selected to paint "Easter at the White House," 1988; Best Children's Books citation, *Parent's,* Best Children's Book Honor Award, Waldenbooks, and American Library Association Notable Book, all 1991, all for *The Owl and the Pussycat;* Best Children's Book, *Newsweek,* 1991, for *Berlioz the Bear.*

WRITINGS:

SELF-ILLUSTRATED JUVENILES

Fritz and the Beautiful Horses, Houghton, 1981.
Good Luck Sneakers, Houghton, 1981.
Annie and the Wild Animals, Houghton, 1985.
(Reteller) *Goldilocks and the Three Bears,* Putnam, 1987.
The First Dog, Harcourt, 1988.
(Reteller) *The Mitten,* Putnam, 1989.
(Reteller) *Beauty and the Beast,* Clarion Books, 1989.
The Wild Christmas Reindeer, Putnam, 1990.
Berlioz the Bear, Putnam, 1991.
Trouble with Trolls, Putnam, 1992.

ILLUSTRATOR; JUVENILES

(Under name Jan Brett Bowler) Stephen Krensky, *Woodland Crossings,* Atheneum, 1978.
Mary Louise Cuneo, *Inside a Sand Castle and Other Secrets,* Houghton, 1979.
Simon Seymour, *The Secret Clocks Time Senses of Living Things,* Viking, 1979.
Eve Bunting, *St. Patrick's Day in the Morning,* Clarion Books, 1980.
Mark Taylor, *Young Melvin and Bulger,* Doubleday, 1981.
Betty Boegehold, *In the Castle of the Cats,* Dutton, 1981.
Diana Harding Cross, *Some Birds Have Funny Names,* Crown, 1981.
Ruth Krauss, *I Can Fly,* Golden Press, 1981.
Jeanette Groth, *Prayer,* Concordia, 1983.
Bunting, *The Valentine Bears,* Clarion Books, 1983.
Cross, *Some Plants Have Funny Names,* Crown, 1983.
Jennifer Perryman, *Where Are All the Kittens?,* Random House, 1984.

Dorothy Van Woerkom, *Old Devil Is Waiting,* Harcourt, 1985.
Bunting, *The Mother's Day Mice,* Clarion Books, 1986.
Noelle of the Nutcracker, Houghton, 1986.
Scary, Scary Halloween, Clarion Books, 1986.
The Twelve Days of Christmas, Putnam, 1986.
Look at the Kittens, Random House, 1987.
The Enchanted Book, Harcourt, 1987.
Happy Birthday Dear Duck, Clarion Books, 1988.
The Owl and the Pussycat, Putnam, 1991.

OTHER

Illustrator of a calendar for Sunrise Publications, 1983, 1984. Many of Brett's books have been published in foreign languages, including Norwegian, German, and French.

ADAPTATIONS: Berlioz the Bear was adapted for television and broadcast on "Reading Rainbow," PBS, 1992.

SIDELIGHTS: Jan Brett lives in a seacoast town in Massachusetts close to the place where she grew up. During the summer her family moves to a cabin in the Berkshire Mountains, where her husband performs with the Boston Symphony at Tanglewood and Brett paints. She finds the beautiful music, birds, wild animals, and the shimmering lake a perfect place to work.

As a child, Brett decided upon a career as an illustrator and spent many hours reading and drawing. She once told *CA:* "I remember the special quiet of rainy days when I felt that I could enter the pages of my beautiful picture books. Now I try to recreate that feeling of believing that the imaginary place I'm drawing really exists. The detail in my work helps to convince me, and I hope others as well, that such places might be real."

Brett commented that all her ideas come from her memory. As a student at the Boston Museum School she spent many hours in the Museum of Fine Arts. "It was overwhelming to see roomsize landscapes and towering stone sculpture, and then moments later to refocus on delicately embroidered kimonos and ancient porcelain," she added. "I'm delighted and surprised when fragments of these beautiful images come back to me in my painting."

*   *   *

BRODSKY, Michael Mark 1948-

PERSONAL: Born August 2, 1948, in New York, NY; son of Martin (an executive) and Marian (a clerical worker; maiden name, Simon) Brodsky; married Laurence Lacoste, November 28, 1976; children: Joseph Matthew, Matthew Daniel. *Education:* Columbia College, Columbia

University, B.A., 1969; attended Case Western Reserve University, School of Medicine, 1970-72.

ADDRESSES: Home—560 Main St., Apt. 1010, New York, NY 10044. *Office*—United Nations, Editorial Section/ECOSOC Affairs and Inter-agency Coordination Division, New York, NY 10017.

CAREER: Teacher of mathematics and science in New York City, 1969-70; teacher of French and English in Cleveland, OH, 1972-75; Institute for Research on Rheumatic Diseases, New York City, editor of arthritis newsletter, 1976-85; College Board, editor, 1985; Springer-Verlag Publishers, New York City, editor, 1985-1991; United Nations, editor, 1991—.

AWARDS, HONORS: Citation, Ernest Hemingway Foundation, 1979, for *Detour.*

WRITINGS:

Detour (novel), Urizen Books, 1977.
Wedding Feast and Two Novellas, Urizen Books, 1980.
Project and Other Short Pieces, Guignol, 1980.
The Envelope of the Given, Suhrkamp Verlag, 1982.
Circuits (novel), Guignol, 1985.
Xman (novel), Four Walls Eight Windows, 1987.
X in Paris (short fiction), Four Walls Eight Windows, 1988.
Dyad (novel), Four Walls Eight Windows, 1989.
Three Goat Songs (short fiction), Four Walls Eight Windows, 1991.

PLAYS

Terrible Sunlight (four-act), produced in New York City at South Street Theater, 1980.
Dose Center, produced in New York City at Theater for the New City, 1990.
Night of the Chair, produced in New York City at Theater Club Funambules, 1990, 1991.

OTHER

Contributor to periodicals and newspapers, including *Partisan Review, Journal of Existential Psychology and Psychiatry,* and *Santa Monica Review.*

WORK IN PROGRESS: A novel; plays.

SIDELIGHTS: Michael Brodsky's "brilliant but grotesque first effort [his novel *Detour*] reveals a very real talent and a very real commitment to experimental writing," asserts a *Virginia Quarterly Review* writer. The novel has been compared to Philip Roth's *Portnoy's Complaint* by reviewers such as Daphne Merkin, who notes in *Partisan Review* that *Detour* features a Jewish narrator/protagonist who is "swamped in the same anguished self-consciousness" as Alexander Portnoy. "But most *unlike* Roth, Brodsky has dallied in recent literary pyrotechnics of the academy, with rather unfortunate results," continues Merkin. "[Brodsky] *shows* nothing and narrates everything." The narration is heavily laced with allusions to classic works of literature and the films of Antonioni, Bergman, Fellini, Godard, Truffaut, and others, prompting Robert Towers to write in the *New York Review of Books,* "Up to a point one can enjoy the virtuosity with which Brodsky loads every [page]. . . . But the pleasures of recognition pall, and what had once been welcomed as an enlivening device becomes ultimately tiresome, a mere tic or fashionable reflex. Brodsky too often seems less a novelist than the brightest graduate student in the room." Merkin agrees that *Detour* "reeks of its own talent; it is uneasily ahead of itself, racked by an off-putting discrepancy between intellectual savviness and emotional naivete. Too often Brodsky's precocity fails to rise to the occasion it sets itself and totters into mere showing off; see how many books I've read, movies I've seen, paintings I've studied, records I've carefully listened to. One pays attention at such moments the way one would to a feverish, brainy child—wearily indulgent of its assumption that *every* permutation of thought, *every* vacillation of emotion is of supreme concern." Despite such criticism, Towers characterizes the book as "an extremely dense, ambitious, and stylistically accomplished first novel," and Merkin concludes that "it has taken a compelling, valiant stab at liberation."

Brodsky's *Xman,* published in 1987, received similar reviews. The story of an unemployed man newly arrived in New York City, *Xman* concerns the protagonist's quest to be unique as well as employed. An Everyman character, Xman struggles through one job interview after another, until he is hospitalized after being hit by a truck. At the hospital he meets and joins a group of terrorists, then, as disillusion overwhelms him, he ends both his life and that of his fellow terrorists. "Xman is the grand inquisitor of meaning. He is also its chief victim," comments Stewart Lindh in the *Los Angeles Times Book Review.* John Mutter in *Publishers Weekly* comments: "Although most readers' eyes are likely to glaze over early on, those devoted to serious writing will find many rewards." Harry Marten in the *New York Times Book Review* concludes that "at its best, *Xman* brings the reader to reflect anew on ways of knowing and truths of being in an uncertain world."

Brodsky once described his own stance on literature in a letter to *CA:* "My interest in contemporary writing remains minimal. I find immersion in film, dance and painting/sculpture much more to the point for fueling exploration in a realm where the concrete becomes abstract and vice-versa. The void at the heart of the current literary scene has been exacerbated by the alarming transformation of large-scale, middle-scale and even small-scale publishing into the computerized fantasy of marketers and ed-itors (either without crucial clout or intent on apotheosizing the slick, the vacant, the mediocre—the old story well told, well told one thousand times before). There is no interest in reexamining worn forms, turning them inside out on behalf of thought hungrily traversing, colonizing the outermost reaches of perception.

"*There is not enough rage, disgust, indignation at the injustices of this world, all the unspeakable doings in procrustean beds.* People flaunt their conformity with a vengeance, with a shamelessness, a drugged defiance that recalls the worst crowd mentality. Writing is more than ever big business, a poor relation of technology. The true artist must continue to take his quantum leap, no matter how excruciating, out of the common plane, making himself or herself available to collision with the events that strain thought to the breaking point. This is my aim, and the applause of imbeciles be damned."

BIOGRAPHICAL/CRITICAL SOURCES:

BOOKS

Contemporary Literary Criticism, Volume 19, Gale, 1981.

PERIODICALS

Library Journal, October 1, 1977.
Los Angeles Times Book Review, November 22, 1987, p. 10.
New York Review of Books, June 15, 1978.
New York Times Book Review, November 15, 1987, p. 31; February 12, 1989, p. 18.
Partisan Review, Volume 46, number 3, 1979.
Publishers Weekly, September 11, 1987, p. 83.
Virginia Quarterly Review, spring, 1979.

*   *   *

BROWN, Mary Ellen 1939-

PERSONAL: Born January 6, 1939, in Vicksburg, MS; daughter of Samuel Evans (a minister) and Janie (Stevens) Brown; divorced, 1976; children: Perrin Wardlaw Rubin (daughter), Torrence Evans Lewis. *Education:* Mary Baldwin College, B.A. (with honors), 1960; University of Pennsylvania, M.A., 1963, Ph.D., 1968.

ADDRESSES: Home—Bloomington, IN. *Office*—Folklore Institute, Indiana University—Bloomington, Bloomington, IN 47405.

CAREER: Indiana University—Bloomington, visiting assistant professor, 1972-73, assistant professor, 1974-79, associate professor, 1979-85, professor of folklore, 1985, professor of women's studies, 1988, adjunct professor of English, 1989, director of women's studies, 1985-91. University of Edinburgh, visiting tutor, 1973-74, research fellow at Institute for Advanced Studies in the Humanities, 1978, 1979.

MEMBER: Modern Language Association of America (member of executive committee of Division of Anthropological Approaches to Literature, 1977-82), American Folklore Society (member of executive board, 1979-82).

AWARDS, HONORS: American Council of Learned Societies grants, 1979, 1984; Horizons of Knowledge grants, 1979, 1984; Indiana University graduate school grants, 1975, 1976, 1982, 1984, 1987, 1988, 1989, 1991.

WRITINGS:

Burns and Tradition, University of Illinois Press, 1984.
(With Silvia Arrom and Darlene Sadlier) *New Research: Latin American Women's Studies,* Number 5, Women's Studies Occasional Series, 1991.
(With Michal Rozbicki) *Cross-Currents: East-West Dialogues on Women and Work,* Number 6, Women's Studies Occasional Series, 1991.

Advisory editor, *Folklore and Literature: An Encyclopedia,* Garland Publishing. Contributor to *Narrative Folksong: New Directions,* 1985; *The Dictionary of Literary Biography,* Volume 109, Gale, 1991; and *Creativity and Tradition,* Utah State University Press, 1992. Contributor of more than thirty-five articles to literature and folklore journals. Special editor, *Journal of the Folklore Institute,* 1976; editor, *Journal of Folklore Research,* 1992—.

WORK IN PROGRESS: Alienation, Appropriation, Recuperation: William Motherwell.

SIDELIGHTS: Mary Ellen Brown once told *CA:* "My goal—as teacher, researcher, and participant in university life—is to understand people and culture by focusing on the various traditions available in a cultural context for individual/group adoption or rejection. Thus, all of my research has dealt with *tradition*—the implicit and explicit forms, styles, themes, and behaviors which recur dynamically in and through time, sustaining culture. In my Scottish studies I have looked at a total culture but particularly at the oral and written literary traditions; in my general work on ballads and folksongs, I have sought a means of quantifying continuities in form and content, in performance, in repertoire; and in my work on women I am seeking to identify as well as evaluate repetitive activities which transmit cultural values."

She added: "My active research today deals with William Motherwell (1797-1835)—journalist, poet, cultural nationalist—whose life and activities offer unparalleled insight into early nineteenth-century Scottish life. Resident of Paisley and then Glasgow during the Industrial Revolution, a member himself of the rising middle class, he was staunchly and vocally against reform or any change—the

very principles of the Enlightenment, which prevailed and thus dominate the historical record. Virtually all of his professional or avocational involvements—as poet, ballad collector and editor, participant in the periodical press, journalist—affirm either implicitly or explicitly a Scottish nation and traditional patterns of life and status."

*   *   *

BROWN, Terence 1944-

PERSONAL: Born January 17, 1944, in Loping, China; son of Henry Montgomery (a minister) and Elizabeth (a teacher; maiden name, Cully) Brown; married Suzanne Marie Krochalis (a teacher), 1969; children: Michael, Carolyn. *Education:* Trinity College, Dublin, B.A., 1966, Ph.D., 1970. *Avocational interests:* Collecting Irish paintings, the arts in general, travel, most sports, wine.

ADDRESSES: Office—School of English, Trinity College, University of Dublin, Dublin 2, Ireland.

CAREER: University of Dublin, Trinity College, Dublin, Ireland, lecturer, 1968-82, fellow, 1976-86, associate professor of English, 1982—, director of modern English, 1976-83, registrar, 1980-81.

MEMBER: International Association for the Study of Anglo-Irish Literature (vice-chairman, 1988—), Royal Irish Academy (member of sub-committee of Anglo-Irish literature).

WRITINGS:

(Editor with Alec Reid) *Time Was Away: The World of Louis MacNeice,* Humanities Press, 1974.
Louis MacNeice: Sceptical Vision, Harper, 1975.
Northern Voices: Poets from Northern Ulster, Roman & Littlefield, 1975.
(Editor with Patrick Rafroidi) *The Irish Short Story,* Humanities Press, 1979.
Ireland: A Social and Cultural History, 1922-79, Fontana, 1981, new edition with postscript published as *Ireland: A Social and Cultural History, 1922 to the Present,* Cornell University Press, 1985.
The Whole Protestant Community: The Making of a Historical Myth, Field Day Theatre Co., 1985.
Hemathena, T. C. D., 1986.
(Editor with B. Hayley) *Samuel Ferguson: A Centenary Tribute,* Royal Irish Academy, 1987.
Ireland's Literature: Selected Essays, Barnes & Noble, 1988.
(Editor with N. Grene) *Traditions and Influence in Anglo-Irish Literature,* Macmillan, 1989.
(Contributing editor) *The Field Day Anthology of Irish Writing,* [Derry], 1991.
(Editor) James Joyce, *Dubliners,* Penguin Books, 1992.

Also editor, with Grene, of *Beckett at Eighty: A Trinity Tribute.* Contributor to books. Contributor to scholarly journals. Editor, *Poetry Ireland Review,* 1985-86.

WORK IN PROGRESS: A critical biography of W. B. Yeats; various literary essays.

SIDELIGHTS: The Irish Short Story, a collection of essays edited by Terence Brown and Patrick Rafroidi, praises Gaelic short stories as "a characteristically Irish alternative to the confident and cosmopolitan English novel," notes Richard Brown in the *Times Literary Supplement.* "The editors should be congratulated for providing a tribute to the continued production of excellent short stories in Ireland. The contributors to the volume are Irish, French and American and perhaps for this reason have been able to treat the Anglo-Irish short story as an autonomous form, and not merely as an offshoot of English literature."

BIOGRAPHICAL/CRITICAL SOURCES:

PERIODICALS

Times Literary Supplement, July 4, 1980.

* * *

BRUCE, F(rederick) F(yvie) 1910-1990

PERSONAL: Born October 12, 1910, in Elgin, Scotland; died, 1990; son of Peter Fyvie and Mary (MacLennan) Bruce; married Betty Davidson, 1936; children: Iain Anthony Fyvie, Sheila Davidson. *Education:* University of Aberdeen, M.A., 1932; Cambridge University, B.A., 1934, M.A., 1945; University of Vienna, graduate study, 1934-35.

CAREER: University of Edinburgh, Edinburgh, Scotland, lecturer in Greek, 1934-38; University of Leeds, Leeds, England, lecturer in Greek, 1938-47; University of Sheffield, Sheffield, England, professor of Biblical history and literature, 1947-59; University of Manchester, Manchester, England, Rylands Professor of Biblical Criticism and Exegesis, 1959-78, professor emeritus, 1978-90.

MEMBER: Society for Old Testament Study (president, 1965), Studiorum Novi Testamenti Societas (president, 1975), Victoria Institute (president, 1958-65), British Academy (fellow).

AWARDS, HONORS: D.D., University of Aberdeen, 1957; Burkitt Medal for Biblical Studies, British Academy, 1979; Litt.D., University of Sheffield, 1988.

WRITINGS:

The Books and the Parchments, Pickering & Inglis, 1950.
Second Thoughts on the Dead Sea Scrolls, Paternoster, 1956.

The Spreading Flame, Paternoster, 1958.
The English Bible, Lutterworth, 1961.
Israel and the Nations, Paternoster, 1963.
An Expanded Paraphrase of the Epistles of Paul, Paternoster, 1965.
New Testament History, Doubleday, 1971.
Paul: Apostle of the Heart Set Free, Eerdmans, 1978.
Men and Movements in the Primitive Church, Paternoster, 1979.
In Retrospect: Remembrance of Things Past, Pickering & Inglis, 1980.
The Hard Sayings of Jesus, Hodder & Stoughton, 1983.
The Work of Jesus, Kingsway, 1984.
The Real Jesus, Hodder & Stoughton, 1985.
Paul and His Converts, Highland Books, 1985.
A Mind for What Matters, Eerdmans, 1990.

Also author of *The Pauline Circle,* 1985; also author of commentaries on various books of the Bible. Contributor of articles to philology and theology journals. Editor of *Evangelical Quarterly,* 1949-80, and *Palestine Exploration Quarterly,* 1957-71.

WORK IN PROGRESS: Further Biblical commentaries.*

* * *

BRYANT, Dorothy 1930-

PERSONAL: Born February 8, 1930, in San Francisco, CA; daughter of Joseph (a mechanic) and Judith (a bookkeeper; maiden name, Chiarle) Calvetti; married Louis Ungaretti, June 11, 1949 (divorced, 1963); married Robert K. Bryant (a photographer), October 18, 1968; children: (first marriage) John, Lorri; (stepchildren) Evan, Victoria. *Education:* San Francisco State College (now University), B.A., 1950, M.A., 1964.

ADDRESSES: Home—1928 Stuart St., Berkeley, CA 94703.

CAREER: High school English teacher in public schools of San Francisco, CA, 1953-56, and at Lick-Wilmerding High School, San Francisco, 1956-61; San Francisco State College (now University), San Francisco, instructor in English, 1962; Golden Gate College, San Francisco, instructor in English, 1963; Contra Costa College, San Pablo, CA, instructor in English and creative writing, 1964-76; Ata Books, Berkeley, CA, founder and president, 1978—. Teacher of music, 1953-76.

AWARDS, HONORS: American Book Award, Before Columbus Foundation, 1987, for *Confessions of Madame Psyche;* Best Play Awards, Bay Area Drama Critics Circle, and Best Play Award, Drama Logue, both 1991, both for *Dear Master.*

WRITINGS:

NOVELS

Ella Price's Journal, Lippincott, 1972.
The Comforter, privately printed, c. 1973, published as *The Kin of Ata Are Waiting for You,* Random House, 1976.
Miss Giardino, Ata Books, 1978.
The Garden of Eros, Ata Books, 1979.
Prisoners, Ata Books, 1980.
Killing Wonder, Ata Books, 1981.
A Day in San Francisco, Ata Books, 1982.
Confessions of Madame Psyche, Ata Books, 1986.
The Test, Ata Books, 1991.

PLAYS

Dear Master, produced in Berkeley, CA, 1991.
Tea with Mrs. Hardy, produced in Lafayette, CA, 1992.

NONFICTION

Writing a Novel, Ata Books, 1979.

OTHER

Also contributor to anthologies, including *Myths to Lie By,* Ata Books, 1984; *The Dream Book: Writing by Italian American Women,* edited Helen Barolini, Schocken, 1985; and *The Graywolf Annual Eight—The New Family,* Graywolf, 1991.

WORK IN PROGRESS: Anita, Anita, a novel about Giuseppe Garibaldi's years in South America; and *The Panel,* a play about Simone Weil.

SIDELIGHTS: Dorothy Bryant once told *CA:* "From the age of four I read omnivorously and constantly, but I started writing late, at thirty. I write every weekday morning. The longer I write, the less I feel qualified to say about the process, except to note that it gets harder, but that accepting the inevitability of difficulty makes it also, paradoxically, easier. I guess I agonize less about the difficulty. . . . If I don't write for a week or two, I begin to come unraveled. This does not mean I am driven by some sort of compulsive if artistic madness. It simply means that I am one of those lucky people who have found their work.

"My readers say that all my novels are so different from each other in subject and form that they can hardly believe the same person wrote them all. I can only say that a story chooses me and demands its only possible form. I write in obedience to these intuitive promptings, then rewrite and rewrite with all the craft I can muster."

Bryant more recently added, "In 1990 I began writing plays and was fortunate to have my first two plays produced in the Bay Area, to excellent reviews. My first play

seemed to just happen—because two of my literary heroes (George Sand and Gustave Flaubert) provided a subject for a vehicle for a friend and favorite actress of mine. I think I've found a natural form for me. Dialogue has always been one of my strengths, so the transition to drama was quite natural. The subjects of my plays have so far been literary-historical. Is that because the ex-teacher in me pops up to present history this way? Is it because, now that I'm over sixty, I feel more in touch with previous generations than with contemporary youth? I don't know why my work has taken this turn, any more than I know how I started writing in the first place."

*   *   *

BRZEZINSKI, Zbigniew K(azimierz)   1928-

PERSONAL: Born March 28, 1928, in Warsaw, Poland; immigrated to Canada in 1938, came to United States in 1953, naturalized in 1958; son of Tadeusz (a diplomat; former consul general in Montreal) and Leonia (Roman) Brzezinski; married Emilie Ann Benes (a painter and sculptress); children: Ian, Mark, Mika. *Education:* McGill University, B.A. (first class honors in economics and political science), 1949, M.A., 1950; Harvard University, Ph.D., 1953.

ADDRESSES: Office—Center for Strategic and International Studies, 1800 K St. NW, Washington, DC, 20006.

CAREER: Harvard University, Cambridge, MA, instructor and research fellow, Russian Research Center, 1953-56, assistant professor of government and research associate, Russian Research Center and Center for International Affairs, 1956-60; Columbia University, New York, NY, associate professor, 1960-62, professor of public law and government and director of Research Institute on International Change, 1962-77; special assistant to President Jimmy Carter for national security affairs, 1977-81; Columbia University, professor of public law and government and director of Research Institute on International Change, 1981-89; Robert E. Osgood Professor of American Foreign Policy, Paul Nitze School of Advanced International Studies, Johns Hopkins University, Washington, DC, 1989—. Official, National Security Council, 1977-81. Director, Trilateral Commission, 1973-76. Counselor, Center for Strategic and International Studies, 1981—. Member of Policy Planning Council, Department of State, 1966-68; member of board of trustees, Freedom House, Amnesty International, and Institute for Defense Analysis. Guest lecturer to numerous private and governmental institutions in the U.S. and abroad, 1953—; participant in international conferences and meetings, 1955—. Consultant to RAND Corp.

MEMBER: American Academy of Arts and Sciences (fellow), National Association for the Advancement of Colored People, Century Club (New York), Federal City Club (Washington, DC).

AWARDS, HONORS: Guggenheim fellowship, 1960; named one of the ten outstanding young men in America, U.S. Junior Chamber of Commerce, 1963; Ford fellowship, 1970, to study Japan's role in international politics.

WRITINGS:

(Editor and contributor) *Political Controls in the Soviet Army,* Praeger, 1954.

The Permanent Purge: Politics in Soviet Totalitarianism, Harvard University Press, 1956.

(Principal author) *Ideology and Foreign Affairs,* Center for International Affairs, Harvard University, 1959.

The Soviet Bloc: Unity and Conflict, Harvard University Press, 1960, revised and enlarged edition, 1967.

(With Carl Joachim Friedrich) *Totalitarian Dictatorship and Autocracy,* Praeger, 1961, 2nd edition, Harvard University Press, 1965.

Ideology and Power in Soviet Politics (collected essays), Praeger, 1962, revised edition, 1967.

(Editor) *Africa and the Communist World,* Stanford University Press, 1963.

(With Samuel P. Huntington) *Political Power: USA/USSR,* Viking, 1964, 2nd edition, 1977.

Alternative to Partition: For a Broader Conception of America's Role in Europe, Viking, 1965.

(Editor and compiler) *Dilemmas of Change in Soviet Politics,* Columbia University Press, 1969.

The Fragile Blossom: Crisis and Change in Japan, Harper, 1972.

Between Two Ages: America's Role in the Technetronic Era, Harper, 1972.

The Relevance of Liberalism, Westview, 1977.

Power and Principle: Memoirs of the National Security Advisor, 1977-1981, Farrar, Straus, 1983.

(With David Owen, Saburo Okita, and members of the Trilateral Commission) *Democracy Must Work: A Trilateral Agenda for the Decade; A Task Force Report to the Trilateral Commission,* New York University Press, 1984.

Game Plan: A Geostrategic Framework for the Conduct of the U.S.-Soviet Contest, Atlantic Monthly Press, 1986.

(Editor with Richard Sincere, Marin Strmecki, and Peter Wehner) *Promise or Peril, the Strategic Defense Initiative: Thirty-Five Essays by Statesmen, Scholars, and Strategic Analysts,* Ethics and Public Policy Center, Washington, DC, 1986.

(With others) *American Security in an Interdependent World: A Collection of Papers Presented at the Atlantic Council's 1987 Annual Conference,* University Press of America, 1988.

In Quest of National Security, edited and annotated by Marin Strmecki, Westview Press, 1988.

The Grand Failure: The Birth and Death of Communism in the Twentieth Century, Scribner, 1989.

Mysl i dzialanie w polityce miedzynarodowej, Katolickiego Uniwersytetu Lubelskiego, 1990.

Out of Control: Global Turmoil on the Eve of the Twenty-First Century, Scribner, 1993.

Also author of studies, reports, and papers on U.S. foreign policy and foreign relations. Contributor of numerous articles on comparative government, international politics, and current affairs to journals and other periodicals, including *American Political Science Review, Der Monat, Journal of Politics, Annals of the American Academy of Political and Social Science, Polish Review,* and *World Politics.* Member of international advisory committee, *Survey;* member of editorial board, *Foreign Policy.*

SIDELIGHTS: Zbigniew Brzezinski's past helps explain his preoccupation with communism. His father, a man of aristocratic descent, served as the Polish consul-general in Montreal during the Second World War, and helped Jewish refugees flee Nazi and Soviet persecution. When the communists seized control of the Polish government in 1945, Tadeusz Brzezinski retired and remained with his family in Canada. Zbigniew attended Roman Catholic schools in Montreal. He moved to the United States in order to attend Harvard and after receiving his Ph.D., joined the university's faculty. His doctoral thesis, published by Harvard University Press in 1956 under the title *The Permanent Purge: Politics in Soviet Totalitarianism,* attracted attention as an important new synthesis of Soviet politics.

During the 1960s Brzezinski left Harvard for Columbia University, where he was named director of the new Institute on Communist Affairs. He served as an advisor to President Kennedy on foreign affairs and worked under President Johnson's administration as a member of the Department of State's Policy Planning Council. Although Brzezinski originally supported America's presence in Vietnam, believing that it would help deter further unrest in Southeast Asia, he came to see that the war was politically unjustifiable, and left the Council position in protest in 1968. He later worked as a foreign policy advisor to presidential hopeful Hubert Humphrey during the 1968 campaign. Among his writings during this period was *The Soviet Bloc: Unity and Conflict,* in which, over thirty years before the dissolution of the Soviet Union, Brzezinski saw the beginnings of disunity in Soviet-bloc countries.

In 1976 Brzezinski served as foreign affairs advisor to Democratic candidate Jimmy Carter and was appointed head of the National Security Council after Carter's election. Articulate and energetic in expressing his views, in the opinion of the press Brzezinski sometimes overwhelmed Carter's soft-spoken Secretary of State, Cyrus Vance. He gained influence and, in some corners, notoriety, as President Carter's idea man, tutor, and coach on foreign policy. By arguing that a powerful Chinese government could help deter Soviet intervention in Southeast Asia, he helped set the Carter administration's policy toward the People's Republic of China. In *Of Power and Principle: Memoirs of the National Security Advisor, 1977-81,* Brzezinski further details the story of the Carter Administration's foreign policy.

Brzezinski's career is often compared with that of Henry Kissinger. Both are academics—the two were in fact competitors for a tenured position at Harvard in the late 1950s, a position Brzezinski lost to Kissinger. Both served as advisors on national security to presidents, and both held influential positions in the administrations in which they served. But there are significant differences, especially in their respective world views; critics agree that Brzezinski has a more optimistic outlook than Kissinger. His first bestseller, *The Grand Failure,* was based on his many years of experience in observing Soviet politics and society. Written just before the collapse of the Soviet Union, the book expressed his optimism that the totalitarianism and repression of Soviet-style communism had failed at last.

The Grand Failure was structured as a schematic expose of the communist plight. Each of the book's six sections focused on a different aspect of "the grand failure." Brzezinski suggested that communism's overall failure as a doctrine was due mainly to the political, social, and economic failure of the Leninist prototype, the model on which most communist states are based. Reforms proposed by Premier Gorbachev, he felt, would be largely unsuccessful, and would result in frustration, turmoil, and the abandonment of the Soviet model by the Eastern European communist states—a process that took place in Poland soon after the book was published. On the other hand, Brzezinski believes that communist China is liable to succeed with its reforms because of its leaders' willingness to abandon Marxist and Leninist doctrines and experiment with capitalist economics.

Because of the economic and social success of the Western democracies, communism has lost its attractiveness to many potential revolutionaries, and Brzezinski envisions a post-communist world in which democracy, not communism, is the guiding light. "Communism cannot be revived by a reform program and still be communism," states a reviewer for the *Economist.* "The world is on the edge of the post-communist era—certainly in Eastern Europe, in a different way in China too, and probably even in Mr. Gorbachev's Russia. . . . This is a stark proposition, too stark for many people besides Mr. Gorbachev. It

carries the notion of 'irreversibility' well beyond what . . . others mean by the word. This is the irreversibility of the man who has leapt over a cliff."

"The national problem is clearly the Achilles' heel of *perestroika,*" Brzezinski writes in *The Grand Failure.* "By the spring of 1988, the Soviet mass media were finally conceding that the national problem was far from having been resolved. At the same time, the increasing Great Russian awareness of anti-Muscovite national sentiments has been further inhibiting the chances of genuine decentralization, one that could perhaps promote a constructive evolution of the system. It has been reinforcing the vested stake of the Great Russians in the continued exercise by them of central rule, even at the price of economic inefficiency."

"To decentralize a state-owned economy," he continues, "one has to decentralize the political system as well; but to decentralize the political system of a multinational empire means yielding power to previously subordinated nations. Accordingly, to be successful economically, *perestroika* must involve the restructuring of the Soviet 'Union' into a genuine confederation, thereby ending the Muscovite rule. In effect, that is tantamount to the dissolution of the empire. It is doubtful that the Russian political elite would be prepared to trade the effective loss of their imperial power for the benefits of economic decentralization." The events of August 1991—the attempted coup that marked the effective end of President Gorbachev's rule and the beginning of Boris Yeltsin's rise to power—confirmed the latter view: the Soviet politicos were not prepared to relinquish power.

In *Out of Control: Global Turmoil on the Eve of the Twenty-First Century,* Brzezinski turns his attention to post-Cold War international politics. The political future, he feels, will be dominated by global "power clusters" rather than superpowered individual nation-states. In order to preserve its place at the forefront of the global hegemony, the United States must correct the impact its lax morality—including the proliferation of sex and violence in the mass media, inadequate health care and education for its citizens, excessive consumption by wealthy citizens who are opposed to tax reforms—has had on its global partners. Brzezinski suggests that the United Nations must play a greater role in politics worldwide, and that the United States be prepared to share responsibilities with its neighbors in Europe, the Americas, and East Asia.

BIOGRAPHICAL/CRITICAL SOURCES:

BOOKS

Brzezinski, Zbigniew, *The Grand Failure: The Birth and Death of Communism in the Twentieth Century,* Scribner, 1989.

PERIODICALS

Canadian Forum, March, 1971.
Economist, March 11, 1989.
Los Angeles Times Book Review, April 2, 1989.
New Leader, June 19, 1967; October 19, 1970.
New Republic, January 1, 1977; October 22, 1977; March 11, 1978.
Newsweek, December 27, 1976; May 9, 1977; January 30, 1978; June 12, 1978; July 6, 1981; November 22, 1982; September 22, 1986.
New Yorker, May 1, 1978.
New York Times, May 23, 1976; April 18, 1982.
New York Times Book Review, March 26, 1989.
People, March 14, 1977.
Publishers Weekly, February 3, 1989; March 8, 1993.
Time, December 27, 1976; August 8, 1977; June 12, 1978.
U. S. News, November 15, 1976; April 17, 1978.
Virginia Quarterly Review, winter, 1971.
Washington Post Book World, March 12, 1989.

*   *   *

BUCHANAN, Laura
See KING, Florence

*   *   *

BULLOCK, Alan (Louis Charles), Lord 1914-

PERSONAL: Born December 13, 1914, in England; son of Frank Allen Bullock; married Hilda Yates Handy, 1940; children: Nicholas, Adrian, Rachel, Matthew. *Education:* Wadham College, Oxford, Lit. Hum. (first class honours), 1936, M.A. (modern history; first class honours), 1938.

ADDRESSES: Home and office—St. Catherine's College, Oxford University, Oxford OX1 34J, England.

CAREER: British Broadcasting Corporation (BBC) European Service, diplomatic correspondent, 1940-45; Oxford University, Oxford, England, fellow, dean, and tutor in modern history, New College, 1945-52, censor, St. Catherine's Society, 1952-62, founding Master of St. Catherine's College, 1961-80, vice-chancellor of the university, 1969-73. Director, London *Observer,* 1977-81; general editor, with F. W. Deakin, *Oxford History of Modern Europe.* Member: Arts Council of Great Britain, 1961-64; Advisory Council on the Public Records; Social Science Research Council, 1966; committee of vice-chancellors and principals, 1969-73. Chairman: committee of enquiry on industrial democracy, 1976; British National Advisory Council on the Training and Supply of Teachers, 1963-65; British Schools Council, 1966-69; committee on reading and other uses of the English language, 1972-74; board of trustees, Tate Gallery, London, 1973-80. Trustee and fellow, Aspen Institute for Humanistic Studies; trustee, *Observer,* 1957-69.

MEMBER: Academia Europa.

AWARDS, HONORS: Honorary doctorate, University of Marseilles; fellow, British Academy; chevalier, Legion d'Honneur; created Baron (life peer) of Leafield, 1976; honorary fellow, Royal Institute of British Architects; honorary fellow, Wadham College, Merton College, and Linacre College, Oxford.

WRITINGS:

(Editor) *Germany's Colonial Demands,* Oxford University Press, 1939.
Hitler, A Study in Tyranny, Odhams, 1952, revised, Penguin, 1962, Harper, 1964.
(With M. Shock) *The Liberal Tradition,* Clarendon Press, 1956.
The Life and Times of Ernest Bevin, Volume I: *Trade Union Leader,* Heineman, 1960, Volume II: *Minister of Labour and National Service, 1940-1945,* Heineman, 1967, Volume III: *Foreign Secretary, 1945-1951,* Oxford University Press, 1983.
(Editor) *The Doubleday Pictorial Library of World History,* Doubleday, 1962.
Die Grossen Stroeme Europas, R. Loewit (Germany), 1966.
(Editor) *The Twentieth Century,* Thames & Hudson, 1971.
(With Oliver Stallybrass) *The Harper Dictionary of Modern Thought,* Harper, 1977, published as *The Fontana Dictionary of Modern Thought,* Fontana, revised, with Stephen Trombly and Bruce Eadie, 1988.
(Editor) *The Faces of Europe,* Phaidon Press, 1980.
Twentieth-Century Genius: 250 Biographies of the People Who Shaped the Greatest Period in Human History, Exeter Books, 1981.
(Editor) *Rime: Vittoria Colonna,* G. Laterza (Rome), 1982.
(Editor) *Le voci della sera: Natalia Ginzburg,* Manchester University Press, 1982.
(Editor, with R. B. Woodings and John Cummings) *Twentieth-Century Culture: A Biographical Companion,* Harper, 1983, published as *The Fontana Biographical Companion to Modern Thought,* Fontana.
The Humanist Tradition in the West (lectures), Norton, 1985.
Domenico Tordi e il carteggio colonnese della Biblioteca nazionale di Firenze (biography), L. S. Olschki (Italy), 1986.
Biblioteca nazionale centrale di Firenze (archives), L. S. Olschki, 1991.

Natalia Ginzburg: Human Relationships in a Changing World, St. Martin's, 1991.
Hitler and Stalin: Parallel Lives, Knopf, 1991.

Lord Bullock is also the author of *Hitler and the Origins of the Second World War,* 1967; *A Language for Life* (also known as the "Bullock Report"), Committee on Reading and Other Uses of the English Language, 1975; *John Wheeler Wheeler-Bennett, 1902-1975,* British Academy; author of reports for various government committees in Great Britain.

Lord Bullock's works have been translated into other languages, including German and Italian.

SIDELIGHTS: Lord Alan Bullock, distinguished historian and founding Master of Oxford University's St. Catherine's College, is the author of several notable books on twentieth-century European history. His most highly regarded work is *Hitler: A Study in Tyranny,* published in 1952 and long considered a definitive work on the life of the Nazi leader. Viewing the volume in retrospect, John Campbell notes in the London *Times* that "despite a steady flow of fresh evidence and reinterpretation, it has not been surpassed in nearly forty years." And critic Norman Davies states in the *New York Times Book Review* that Bullock's "knowledge of Germany and the Nazi Reich is formidable, and his evaluation of Hitler stands largely undented." In addition to his work on Adolph Hitler, Lord Bullock is also noted for his exhaustive political biography of British Foreign Secretary Ernest Bevin as well as the 1975 report *A Language for Life*—commonly referred to as the "Bullock Report," it proved greatly influential in reforming the English language curriculum within the British educational system.

Bullock published the first of three volumes comprising *The Life and Times of Ernest Bevin* in 1960. In this unprecedented work, Bullock explores the life of Ernest Bevin, whose pioneering efforts within Britain's trade unions propelled him to a position, first, as minister of labour under Winston Churchill during World War II and, later, to British foreign secretary from 1945 until Bevin's death in 1951. "Bullock marshals the mass of material—of circulars, orders, memoranda, reports, bills and speeches—which might easily have made so dull a story, into a truly absorbing whole," notes a reviewer in the *Listener,* adding that "it is very difficult to fault him on the most minor point of detail, and the shape of the whole is maintained throughout." With the publication of *Ernest Bevin, Foreign Secretary, 1945-1951* in 1983, Bullock's massive work was complete. "Long in coming, it arrives triumphantly," proclaims Stephen Koss in the *New York Times Book Review,* "and stands as a major landmark in the crowded field of modern political biography. Like Bevin

himself, it is large in girth, forthright in its judgements and disarmingly unconventional."

While Bullock's *Hitler: A Study of Tyranny* has stood the test of time as a comprehensive biography of that controversial figure, the historian again returned to the subject in *Hitler and Stalin: Parallel Lives,* published in 1992. Interweaving the life of the German dictator with a detailed biography of Josef Stalin, Bullock incorporates the wealth of scholarship that has been generated over the past decades into a panorama that encompasses not only these two men, but also much of twentieth-century Europe: the Russian Revolution, the growing Nazi movement, World War II, and the growth of Communism in the newly-formed Soviet Union. Reviewing the 1,100-page *Parallel Lives,* Campbell writes: "Serious historians do not often tackle such huge themes. . . . It sounds like a recipe for confusion, irritation and indigestion. In fact, it works brilliantly. The book is a triumph of organisation, lucidity, and perspective." However, Paul Johnson criticizes the work in the *Times Literary Supplement,* commenting that although the history is heavily documented with biography and narrative accounts, there is little analysis of the influence of each man on the other, nor of the effect of the epoch within which they lived on their rise to power. "With less description and more elucidation," Johnson writes, "Lord Bullock might have given us a more valuable and certainly less unwieldy book."

Johnson also questions the assumption underlying Bullock's work: that Stalin's "right-wing" Marxism and the fascist philosophies of Hitler stood in political opposition. Johnson describes Stalin and Hitler as "pseudo-intellectuals" familiar both with nineteenth- and twentieth-century political philosophy: "It is vital to grasp that they shared much of the same ideological genealogy," he notes, "and worth while going back a bit to see exactly what it was." While praising the revisionist viewpoint that allows Bullock to view Stalin in the same "rogues' gallery" as Hitler, Davies cautions against the historian's overall conservative perspective. "He belongs by temperament to the cautious, common-sense school of history," notes Davies, "with a touch of his native Yorkshire's obstinacy thrown in; he is reluctant to enter the war of ideas." However, Ronald Spector praises Bullock's "monumental" work in the *Washington Post Book World.* "The writing is invariably interesting and informed and there are new insights and cogent analysis in every chapter," Spector writes of *Parallel Lives.* "Altogether, it is an impressive literary and scholarly achievement."

BIOGRAPHICAL/CRITICAL SOURCES:

PERIODICALS

Illustrated London News, April 29, 1967.
Listener, April 27, 1967, pp. 563-4.

New York Times Book Review, May 6, 1984, pp. 13-14;
    March 22, 1992, pp. 3, 31.
Observer, April 16, 1967.
Punch, May 3, 1967, p. 655.
Times, November 10, 1983; June 22, 1991, p. 21.
Times Literary Supplement, April 20, 1967; July 5, 1991,
    pp. 4-6.
Washington Post Book World, May 3, 1992, p. 4.*

*   *   *

BURGESS, Thornton Waldo   1874-1965
(W. B. Thornton)

PERSONAL: Born January 14, 1874, in Sandwich, MA;
died of lung cancer, June 5, 1965, in Hampden, MA; son
of Thornton Waldo and Caroline F. (Hayward) Burgess;
married Nina E. Osborne, June 30, 1905 (died, 1906);
married Fannie P. Johnson, April 30, 1911 (died, 1950);
children: (first marriage) Thornton Waldo; (second marriage) two stepchildren. *Education:* Graduated from Sandwich High School, Sandwich, MA, in 1891; attended business college in Boston for one year.

CAREER: Editor and author of books for children. Held
early jobs as a cashier and assistant bookkeeper in a shoe
store; began working for the Phelps Publishing Company,
as an office boy, 1895, becoming a reporter for one of the
firm's weekly magazines, 1895-1911, and literary and
household editor for Orange Judd weeklies, 1901-11.
Founder and director of the Burgess Radio Nature
League, where for six years he gave weekly talks.

AWARDS, HONORS: Litt.D., Northeastern University,
1938.

WRITINGS:

"OLD MOTHER WEST WIND" SERIES

Old Mother West Wind, illustrated by George Kerr, Little,
    Brown, 1910.
Mother West Wind's Children, illustrated by Kerr, Little,
    Brown, 1911, new edition illustrated by Harrison
    Cady, 1962.
Mother West Wind's Animal Friends, illustrated by Kerr,
    Little, Brown, 1912.
Mother West Wind's Neighbors, illustrated by Kerr, Little,
    Brown, 1913, new edition illustrated by Cady, 1968.]
Mother West Wind "Why" Stories, illustrated by Cady,
    Little, Brown, 1915.
Mother West Wind "How" Stories, illustrated by Cady,
    Little, Brown, 1916.
Mother West Wind "When" Stories, illustrated by Cady,
    Little, Brown, 1917.
Mother West Wind "Where" Stories, illustrated by Cady,
    Little, Brown, 1918.

"BOY SCOUTS" SERIES

The Boy Scouts of Woodcraft Camp, illustrated by C. S.
    Corson, Penn, 1912.
The Boy Scouts on Swift River, illustrated by Corson,
    Penn, 1913.
The Boy Scouts on Lost Trail, illustrated by Corson, Penn,
    1914.
The Boy Scouts in a Trapper's Camp, illustrated by F. A.
    Anderson, Penn, 1915.

*"BEDTIME STORY-BOOKS" SERIES; ILLUSTRATED BY
HARRISON CADY, EXCEPT AS NOTED*

The Adventures of Johnny Chuck, Little, Brown, 1913.
The Adventures of Reddy Fox, Little, Brown, 1913.
The Adventures of Unc' Billy Possum, Little, Brown, 1914.
The Adventures of Mr. Mocker, Little, Brown, 1914.
The Adventures of Jerry Muskrat, Little, Brown, 1914.
The Adventures of Peter Cottontail, Little, Brown, 1914,
    abridged edition illustrated by Phoebe Erickson,
    Grosset & Dunlap, 1967.
The Adventures of Grandfather Frog, Little, Brown, 1915.
The Adventures of Chatterer, the Red Squirrel, Little,
    Brown, 1915.
The Adventures of Danny Meadow Mouse, Little, Brown,
    1915.
The Adventures of Sammy Jay, Little, Brown, 1915.
The Adventures of Old Mr. Toad, Little, Brown, 1916.
The Adventures of Old Man Coyote, Little, Brown, 1916.
The Adventures of Buster Bear, Little, Brown, 1916.
The Adventures of Prickly Porky, Little, Brown, 1916.
The Adventures of Poor Mrs. Quack, Little, Brown, 1917.
The Adventures of Paddy the Beaver, Little, Brown, 1917.
The Adventures of Jimmy Skunk, Little, Brown, 1918.
The Adventures of Bobby Coon, Little, Brown, 1918.
The Adventures of Ol' Mistah Buzzard, Little, Brown,
    1919.
The Adventures of Bob White, Little, Brown, 1919.

*"WISHING STONE" SERIES; ILLUSTRATED BY HARRISON
CADY*

Tommy and the Wishing Stone, Century, 1915.
Tommy's Change of Heart, Little, Brown, 1921.
Tommy's Wishes Come True, Little, Brown, 1921.

*"GREEN MEADOW" SERIES; ILLUSTRATED BY HARRISON
CADY*

Happy Jack, Little, Brown, 1918.
Mrs. Peter Rabbit, Little, Brown, 1919.
Old Granny Fox, Little, Brown, 1920.
Bowser the Hound, Little, Brown, 1920.

*"GREEN FOREST" SERIES; ILLUSTRATED BY HARRISON
CADY*

Lightfoot the Deer, Little, Brown, 1921.
Whitefoot, the Wood Mouse, Little, Brown, 1922.

Blacky the Crow, Little, Brown, 1922.
Buster Bear's Twins, Little, Brown, 1923.

"SMILING POOL" SERIES; ILLUSTRATED BY HARRISON CADY

Billy Mink, Little, Brown, 1924.
Little Joe Otter, Little, Brown, 1925.
Jerry Muskrat at Home, Little, Brown, 1926.
Longlegs the Heron, Little, Brown, 1927.

"LITTLE COLOR CLASSICS" SERIES; ILLUSTRATED BY HARRISON CADY

Little Pete's Adventure, McLoughlin, 1941.
Little Red's Adventure, McLoughlin, 1942.
Little Chuck's Adventure, McLoughlin, 1942.

ANIMAL STORIES; ILLUSTRATED BY HARRISON CADY, EXCEPT AS NOTED

The Burgess Animal Book for Children, illustrated by Louis Agassiz Fuertes, Little, Brown, 1920.
Animal Folk, Saalfield, 1925.
Friendly Animals, Saalfield, 1925.
The Christmas Reindeer, illustrated by Rhoda Chase, Macmillan, 1926.
Happy Jack Squirrel Helps Unc' Billy, Stoll & Edwards, 1928.
Grandfather Frog Gets a Ride, Stoll & Edwards, 1928.
A Great Joke in Jimmy Skunk, Stoll & Edwards, 1928.
The Neatness of Bobby Coon, Stoll & Edwards, 1928.
Baby Possum's Queer Voyage, Stoll & Edwards, 1928.
Digger the Badger Decides to Stay, Stoll & Edwards, 1928.
Cubby Bear Books (contains *A Frightened Baby, Farmer Brown's Boy Becomes Curious, What Farmer Brown's Boy Did, Cubby Bear Has a Mind of His Own, An Imp of Mischief, Cubby in Mother Brown's Pantry, A Woe-Begone Little Bear, Cubby Gets a Bath, Milk and Honey,* and *Cubby Finds an Open Door*), illustrated by Nina Jordan, Whitman, 1929.
Wee Little Books (contains *Little Joe Otter's Slide, Betty Bear's Lesson, Unc' Billy Gets Even, Whitefoot's Secret, Jimmy Skunk's Justice,* and *Peter Rabbit's Carrots*), Whitman, 1929-33.
Tales from the Storyteller's House, illustrated by Lemuel Palmer, Little, Brown, 1937.
While the Story-Log Burns, illustrated by Palmer, Little, Brown, 1938.
The Three Little Bears, Platt & Munk, 1940, published as *A Bear Scare,* 1961.
Reddy Fox's Sudden Engagement, Platt & Munk, 1940, published as *Reddy Fox Leaves in a Hurry,* 1961.
Peter Rabbit Proves a Friend, Platt & Munk, 1940, published as *Peter Rabbit Goes Scouting,* 1961.
Paddy's Surprise Visitor, Platt & Munk, 1940, published as *Paddy the Beaver's Visitor,* 1961.

Bobby Coon's Mistake, Platt & Munk, 1940, published as *Bobby Coon's Surprise,* 1961.
Young Flash, the Deer, Platt & Munk, 1940, published as *Flash the Young Deer,* 1961.
A Merry Coasting Party, Platt & Munk, 1940, published as *Fun on the Queer Trail,* 1961.
A Robber Meets His Match, Platt & Munk, 1940, published as *Robber the Rat Loses Out,* 1961.
Animal Stories, Platt & Munk, 1942, published as *The Animal World of Thornton Burgess,* 1961.
Baby Animal Stories, illustrated by Erickson, Grosset & Dunlap, 1949.
Peter Rabbit and Reddy Fox, illustrated by Mary and Carl Hauge, Wonder Books, 1954.

VERSE; ILLUSTRATED BY CADY, EXCEPT AS NOTED

Animal Paint Book, Saalfield, 1925.
Peter Cottontail's Own Paint Book, Saalfield, 1925.
Animal Pictures, Saalfield, 1925.
Mother Nature's Song and Story Book, music by Rebecca Richards, illustrated by Henry Johnson and Lemuel Palmer, Worley, 1938.

NATURE STORIES

The Burgess Bird Book for Children, illustrated by Fuertes, Little, Brown, 1919.
The Burgess Flower Book for Children, Little, Brown, 1923.
The Burgess Seashore Book for Children, illustrated by W. H. Southwick and George Sutton, Little, Brown, 1929.
Wild Flowers We Know, Whitman, 1929.
On the Green Meadows: A Book of Nature Stories, illustrated by Cady, Little, Brown, 1944.
At the Smiling Pool: A Book of Nature Stories, illustrated by Cady, Little Brown, 1945.
The Crooked Little Path: A Book of Nature Stories, illustrated by Cady, Little, Brown, 1946.
The Dear Old Briar Patch: A Book of Nature Stories, illustrated by Cady, Little, Brown, 1947.
Along Laughing Brook: A Book of Nature Stories, illustrated by Cady, Little, Brown, 1949.
Nature Almanac, illustrated by Erickson, Grosset & Dunlap, 1949.
At Paddy Beaver's Pond: A Book of Nature Stories, illustrated by Cady, Little, Brown, 1950.
The Littlest Christmas Tree, illustrated by M. and C. Hauge, Wonder Books, 1954.
The Burgess Book of Nature Lore: Adventures of Tommy, Sue, and Sammy with Their Friends of Meadow, Pool, and Forest, illustrated by Robert Candy, Little, Brown, 1965.

OTHER

(Author of text with others) *The Bride's Primer: Being a Series of Quaint Parodies on the Ways of Brides and Their Misadventures Interlarded with Useful Hints for Their Advantage,* illustrated by F. Strothmann, Phelps Publishing, 1905.

Picture Book, illustrated by Cady, Saalfield, 1925.

The Burgess Big Book of Green Meadow Stories, illustrated by Cady, Little, Brown, 1932.

Birds You Should Know, illustrated by Fuertes, Little, Brown, 1933.

The Wishing-Stone Stories, illustrated by Cady, Little, Brown, 1935.

(With Thora Stowell) *The Book of Animal Life,* Little, Brown, 1937.

The Little Burgess Animal Book for Children, illustrated by Fuertes, Rand McNally, 1941.

The Little Burgess Bird Book for Children, illustrated by Fuertes, Rand McNally, 1941.

A Thornton Burgess Picture Book, illustrated by Nino Carbe, Garden City Publishing, 1950.

Aunt Sally's Friends in Fur; or, The Woodhouse Night Club, photographs by the author, Little, Brown, 1955.

Stories around the Year, illustrated by Erickson, Grosset & Dunlap, 1955.

50 Favorite Burgess Stories: On the Green Meadows [and] *The Crooked Little Path,* illustrated by Harrison Cady, Grosset & Dunlap, 1956.

Bedtime Stories, illustrated by C. and M. Hauge, Grosset & Dunlap, 1959.

Now I Remember: Autobiography of an Amateur Naturalist, Little, Brown, 1960.

The Million Little Sunbeams, illustrated by Cady, Six Oaks Press, 1963.

Contributor to magazines, including *Country Life in America,* under pseudonym W. B. Thornton, and *Good Housekeeping.* Associate editor, *Good Housekeeping,* 1904-11. The Burgess manuscript collections are included at the Sandwich Public Library and the Burgess Society, Sandwich, Massachusetts.

ADAPTATIONS: The Adventures of Jimmy Skunk was adapted as a phonotape, Taped Books Project, 1973.

SIDELIGHTS: Thornton Waldo Burgess was one of the most prolific and best-loved authors of children's stories in the twentieth century. "His radio broadcasts and public lectures and readings," declared Lucien L. Agosta in the *Dictionary of Literary Biography,* "brought the antics of Peter Rabbit, Johnny Chuck, Jimmy Skunk, and all the other denizens of the Green Meadow, the Smiling Pool, and the Green Forest before countless numbers of children and adults alike." Many of Burgess's animal fables and stories, first introduced through the story columns he

wrote for the Associated News and the New York Herald Tribune syndicates, remained in print more than 75 years after their first publication.

Burgess was raised by his semi-invalid mother because his father died when the future writer was nine months old. He had to sell the candy his mother made to make ends meet, but still found time for hunting, fishing, and collecting wild flowers along the Cape Cod coast. He explained in his autobiography, *Now I Remember,* "It was my very good fortune to be born minus the proverbial silver spoon and to spend my formative years in a lovely small village before the era of too much and too fast. For this I have long been thankful."

After he graduated from high school, Burgess found work in a grocery store. He dreamed of attending college, but his mother's candy business did not provide enough income for higher education. However, his grandfather, a successful merchant, provided money for business training courses at a Boston school. Although Burgess completed the training, he found the business world not to his liking; he stated in his autobiography, "In short, the unpleasant fact that I was a misfit in the business world was rubbed into me rather painfully every day, and there seemed to be nothing I could do about it."

Eventually Burgess found himself working for a magazine publisher as janitor and office boy. "At that time publishing agricultural journals," wrote Agosta, "the Phelps Company soon took over *Good Housekeeping* magazine." Over the next several years Burgess worked his way up to become associate editor of *Good Housekeeping,* and contributor to *Country Life in America*—according to Agosta, "perhaps the most beautiful pictorial magazine of its day." "By 1905," Agosta continued, "Burgess was earning forty dollars a week—enough, he felt, to support himself, his mother, and a wife." He married Nina Osborne of West Springfield, Massachusetts, but she died in 1906, of complications while giving birth to their son, Thornton Waldo Burgess III.

Griefstricken by the loss of his wife, Burgess sought relief in his work. He formed a habit of making up stories to tell his motherless son at bedtime. In 1910, he received a visit from a representative of the Boston publisher Little, Brown and Company, who had read some of these stories that Burgess had published in *Good Housekeeping.* "Within a week or two," declared Agosta, "Burgess had signed a contract to provide a total of sixteen stories for a volume to be called *Old Mother West Wind.* . . . Over 15,000 similar stories were to appear in Burgess's newspaper story-column during his long career, and Little, Brown continued to publish his books for over half a century."

Although Burgess's style evolved over the years, he generally pursued three goals in his work: to instruct children in moral behavior; to provide examples of nature lore; and to entertain. He explained in his autobiography that he wanted to teach "the facts about the forms of animal life most familiar to American children. I endeavored to do this by stimulating the imagination, which is the birthright of every child." Burgess's earliest stories, stated Agosta, presented his animals wearing clothes and socializing among themselves, and suppressed elements of animal life—such as Reddy Fox's predatory habits—that might frighten children. Instead, Burgess used animals as characters to teach children proper behavior. "Nature study," Burgess wrote in his autobiography, "is unequaled as a vehicle for conveying information of all kinds. The direst of facts if embedded in a nature story written so as to appeal to the imagination will not only be unhesitatingly accepted but will be permanently retained."

However, Burgess never regarded his animals as merely people in fur. His work promoted a genuine interest in animal life in general, and in conservation in particular. The "Wishing Stone" series of books show how Farmer Brown's boy Tommy is converted from a menace to the animals into a friend and conservationist. In *The Burgess Bird Book for Children, The Burgess Animal Book for Children,* and *The Burgess Flower Book for Children,* Peter Rabbit and his friends learn about the habits and life cycles of the wild plants and animals that surround them, while *The Adventures of Poor Mrs. Quack* promotes control on waterfowl hunting. In 1924, Burgess founded the Radio Nature League, the purpose of which, he stated in his autobiography, was "to preserve and conserve American wild life, including birds, animals, flowers, trees and other living things, and also the natural beauty spots and scenic wonders of all America." The League proved immensely popular, reaching "an international audience of children and adults alike," stated Agosta.

Burgess continued to write his animal stories for many years. "The story," he declared in his autobiography, "is the most acceptable and effective way of conveying knowledge and guidance to the child mind and establishing them therein. The animal story, because of the psychological factor involved . . . is the most effective form of story. Thus I much, much prefer to write for children. In so doing I feel a greater sense of real power than could ever be mine were I a writer for adults or in high political office."

BIOGRAPHICAL/CRITICAL SOURCES:

BOOKS

Burgess, Thornton Waldo, *Now I Remember: Autobiography of an Amateur Naturalist,* Little, Brown, 1960.

Dictionary of Literary Biography, Volume 22: *American Writers for Children, 1900-1960,* Gale, 1983.
Twentieth-Century Children's Writers, 3rd edition, St. James Press, 1989.

PERIODICALS

Life, November 14, 1960.
Nature, January, 1956.
Reader's Digest, October, 1967.

OBITUARIES:

PERIODICALS

Library Journal, September 15, 1965.
Newsweek, June 21, 1965.
New York Times, June 6, 1965.
Publishers Weekly, June 14, 1965.
Time, June 18, 1965.

*   *   *

BURGHARDT, Walter J(ohn) 1914-

PERSONAL: Born July 10, 1914, in New York, NY; son of John A. and Mary (Krupp) Burghardt. *Education:* Woodstock College, M.A., 1937, Ph.L., 1938, S.T.L., 1942; Catholic University of America, S.T.D., 1957.

ADDRESSES: Home and office—Manresa-on-Severn, P.O. Box 9, Annapolis, MD 21404.

CAREER: Entered Society of Jesus (Jesuits), 1931, ordained priest, 1941; Woodstock College, professor of patristic theology, Woodstock, MD, 1946-70, and New York City, 1970-74; Union Theological Seminary, New York City, lecturer in patristic theology, 1971-74; Catholic University of America, Washington, DC, professor of patristic theology, 1974-78; Georgetown University, Washington, theologian in residence, 1978-90; "Preaching the Just Word," founder and director, 1990—. Visiting lecturer in theology, Princeton Theological Seminary, 1972-73. Research associate, Woodstock Theological Center, 1974—. Host of bi-weekly radio program, WWIN, Baltimore, MD, 1951-59. Member of Baltimore Archdiocesan Commission for Christian Unity, 1962-70, Lutheran-Roman Catholic Dialogue, 1965-76, and International Papal Theological Commission, 1968-80. Consultant to (Vatican) Secretariat for Christian Unity, 1968-73.

MEMBER: World Council of Churches (member of faith and order commission, 1968-76), Catholic Commission on Intellectual and Cultural Affairs, National Council of Churches (member of faith and order commission, 1971-75), American Theological Society (president, 1974-75), Catholic Theological Society of America (president, 1967-68), Mariological Society of America (president, 1961-62), North American Academy of Ecumenists (president, 1967-70), Association Internationale d'Etudes Patristiques.

AWARDS, HONORS: Mariological Award, 1958; Cardinal Spellman Award, 1962; LL.D., University of Notre Dame, 1966, St. Thomas University, 1991, and Gonzaga University, 1992; D.H.L., University of Scranton, 1966, Canisius College, 1974, St. Joseph's College, 1977, Loyola College, 1977, Christ the King Seminary, 1989, John Carroll University, 1989, University of San Francisco, 1990, and St. Peter's College, 1991; Andrew White Medal, Loyola College, 1968; Litt.D., St. Bonaventure University, 1968, Wheeling College, 1970, Spring Hill College, 1974, and St. Mary's College, Notre Dame, 1978; St. Francis de Sales Award, Catholic Press Association, 1979; D.D., Jesuit School of Theology at Berkeley, 1980, and Colgate University, 1987; D.R.S., Marquette University, 1981; President's Medal, Catholic University of America, 1982; William Toohey Award for Distinguished Preaching, University of Notre Dame, 1984; D.Min., Holy Cross College, 1984; Order of the Keeper of the Lamp, United Theological Seminary, 1986; Catholic Hospital Administrative Personnel Award, 1987; Sollicitudo rei socialis Award, Christ the King Center for Social Concern, 1988; Distinguished Catholic Leadership Award, Foundations and Donors Interested in Catholic Activities, 1991.

WRITINGS:

The Image of God in Man According to Cyril of Alexandria, Woodstock College Press, 1957.
The Testimony of the Patristic Age Concerning Mary's Death, Newman, 1957.
All Lost in Wonder: Sermons on Theology and Life, Newman, 1960.
(With William F. Lynch) *The Idea of Catholicism,* Meridian, 1960, revised edition, 1964.
Saints and Sanctity, Prentice-Hall, 1965.
Towards Reconciliation, U.S. Catholic Conference, 1974.
Seven Hungers of the Human Family, U.S. Catholic Conference, 1976.
(Editor) *Woman: New Dimensions,* Paulist Press, 1977.
(Editor) *Religious Freedom: 1965 and 1975,* Paulist Press, 1977.
(Editor with William G. Thompson) *Why the Church?,* Paulist Press, 1977.
Tell the Next Generation: Homilies and Near Homilies, Paulist Press, 1979.
Sir, We Would Like to See Jesus: Homilies from a Hilltop, Paulist Press, 1982.
Seasons That Laugh or Weep: Musings on the Human Journey, Paulist Press, 1983.
Still Proclaiming Your Wonders: Homilies for the Eighties, Paulist Press, 1984.

Grace on Crutches: Homilies for Fellow Travelers, Paulist Press, 1986.
Preaching: The Art and the Craft, Paulist Press, 1987.
Lovely in Eyes Not His: Homilies for an Imaging of Christ, Paulist Press, 1988.
To Christ I Look: Homilies at Twilight, Paulist Press, 1989.
Dare To Be Christ: Homilies for the Nineties, Paulist Press, 1991.
When Christ Meets Christ: Homilies for the Just Word, Paulist Press, 1993.

Contributor to books, including *Encyclopaedia Britannica* and *World Book Encyclopedia. Theological Studies,* managing editor, 1946-67, editor-in-chief, 1967—; *Woodstock Papers,* co-editor, 1957-67; *Ancient Christian Writers,* co-editor, 1958; American Heritage dictionaries, Catholic consultant, 1967-70; *Living Pulpit,* editor and president, 1991; *New Catholic Encyclopedia,* sub-editor for patrology; *Encyclopedia of Bioethics,* advisory editor. Contributor to religion and theology journals.

SIDELIGHTS: Walter J. Burghardt once told *CA:* "My life as a historian and theologian has been a ceaseless effort to wed the past and the present, the old and the new, tradition and reform. It is summed up in a sentence from an old editorial in *Life:* 'Anyone who wants to know who he is should begin by finding out where he comes from and where he's been.' This is true not only of an individual but of a nation, even a church. Tradition is often misunderstood, as if it were a musty relic buried in the past, of interest to graying antiquarians. No, genuine tradition is the best of the past, invigorated by insights of the present, with a view to a more fruitful future.

"Together with history, I would urge on the educators of the nineties a concern for contemplation. For contemplation is not some unreal abstraction; contemplation is a long loving look at the real. Our schooling is still excessively absorbed with facts and figures, with argument and analysis; we do not learn loving awareness—to let the real delight us—a blade of grass, a sparkling glass of Burgundy, a child licking an ice-cream cone, a striding woman with wind-blown hair, a summer breeze caressing our cheeks, yes, a God who smiles. Without contemplation the people perish."

*   *   *

BURKE, James Lee 1936-

PERSONAL: Born December 5, 1936, in Houston, TX; son of James Lee (a natural gas engineer) and Frances (Benbow) Burke; married Pearl Pai, January 22, 1960; children: James, Andree, Pamela, Alafair. *Education:* Attended University of Southwest Louisiana, 1955-57; University of Missouri, B.A., 1959, M.A., 1960. *Politics:* "Jeffersonian Democrat." *Religion:* Roman Catholic. *Avocational interests:* Fishing, tennis, baseball, bluegrass music.

ADDRESSES: Home—Louisiana and Montana.

CAREER: Writer. Worked variously as a surveyor, social worker in Los Angeles, CA, 1962-64, newspaper reporter in Lafayette, LA, 1964, and English instructor at colleges and universities, including University of Southern Illinois, University of Montana, Miami-Dade Community College, and Wichita State University; U.S. Forest Service, Job Corps Conservation Center, Frenchburg, KY, instructor, 1965-66.

AWARDS, HONORS: Breadloaf fellow, 1970; Southern Federation of State Arts Agencies grant, 1977; Pulitzer Prize nomination, 1987, for *The Lost Get-Back Boogie;* Guggenheim fellow, 1989; Edgar Allan Poe Award, Mystery Writers of America, 1989, for *Black Cherry Blues.*

WRITINGS:

NOVELS

Half of Paradise, Houghton, 1965.
To the Bright and Shining Sun, Scribner, 1970.
Lay Down My Sword and Shield, Crowell, 1971.
Two for Texas, Pocket Books, 1983, published as *Sabine Spring,* Watermark Press, 1989.
The Lost Get-Back Boogie, Louisiana State University Press, 1986.

"DAVE ROBICHEAUX" CRIME NOVELS

The Neon Rain, Holt, 1987.
Heaven's Prisoners, Holt, 1988.
Black Cherry Blues, Little, Brown, 1989.
A Morning for Flamingos, Little, Brown, 1990.
A Stained White Radiance, Hyperion, 1992.
In the Electric Mist with Confederate Dead, Hyperion, 1993.

OTHER

The Convict and Other Stories, Louisiana State University Press, 1985.
(With Kenneth E. Davison) *Ohio's Heritage,* Peregrine Smith Books, 1989.
Texas City, Nineteen Forty-Seven, Lord John Press, 1992.

Short story anthologized in *Best American Short Stories of 1986.* Also contributor of short stories to periodicals, including *Atlantic, Quarterly West, Antioch Review, Kenyon Review, New England Review,* and *Southern Review.*

ADAPTATIONS: To the Bright and Shining Sun has been optioned for film; actor Alec Baldwin holds movie rights to three "Dave Robicheaux" crime novels.

SIDELIGHTS: James Lee Burke poetically evokes New Orleans and its rural bayous in his series of detective novels featuring Dave Robicheaux. An ex-New Orleans police officer, Vietnam veteran, and recovering alcoholic, Robicheaux is a human character, possessing as many faults as virtues. "Burke has created, in Dave Robicheaux, a complex and convincing protagonist, a deeply moral, but troubled and self-divided man who strikes us as the antithesis of the stereotypical macho detective of popular culture," describes Joyce Carol Oates in the *Washington Post Book World.* In addition to creating such an extraordinary character, Burke also fills his novels with a rich and fertile setting. "No one captures current Louisiana culture, or the feel of that very particular *place,* as well as James Lee Burke," maintains *Washington Post Book World* contributor James Sallis. "Again and again Burke brings you the diversity of parallel Louisiana cultures—Cajun, black, criminal—and gives you a sense of how they manage to coexist, how they've always managed to coexist here. . . . And again and again Burke makes you feel the humid, laden air pressing close, smell the particular sweetness of banana trees and stagnant water, taste *boudin* and fried shrimp and cayenne pepper and thyme, watch pelicans rising against crimson sunsets. It is also possible that no one writes better detective novels."

Born in Houston, Burke grew up on the Texas and Louisiana coast, writing his first short stories while attending the University of Southwestern Louisiana. It was when one of these stories won an honorable mention in a contest that Burke "got hooked" on writing. Following graduate school, where he earned a teaching degree, Burke worked for the Sinclair Oil Company, but soon returned to the University of Southwestern Louisiana to teach. And in 1965, four years after its completion, Burke's first novel was published. *Half of Paradise,* written when Burke was twenty-four, interweaves three stories that are linked by time and geography. The three protagonists are from varying characteristic situations in the South, but they all begin and end in tragic circumstances. Wirt Williams, writing in the *New York Times Book Review,* points out that Burke's writing could be sharper, but concludes that "no reservations alter the important things about the book: it is an exciting piece of writing and a solid debut for a writer to be taken absolutely seriously."

Burke, who had given up hope for *Half of Paradise,* was surprised by the critical acclaim the novel received, but still felt restless with his life. "I guess it happens to a lot of guys who go from grad school into university teaching," explains Burke in an interview with W. C. Stroby for *Writer's Digest.* "You feel you're missing something. So I went from job to job. We bounced all over the country, literally." By the mid-1960s, Burke was teaching at the University of Montana, and his next novel, *To the Bright and*

Shining Sun, was published in 1970. Set in a mining town in Kentucky, this work is narrated by sixteen-year-old Perry Woodson Hatfield James, a loyal member of the union who knows nothing of the world outside his small town. Offered the chance to learn a trade, Perry's hopes are dashed when his father is killed in an explosion set by non-union miners. "Burke takes these harsh facts and brings them to life in a surging, bitter novel as authentic as moonshine," relates Martin Levin in the *New York Times Book Review.* And a *Publishers Weekly* contributor asserts that Burke "has presented a powerful and cruel picture of the Appalachia many Americans would like to forget."

Around the same time *To the Bright and Shining Sun* was published, Burke had a falling out with the agent who negotiated the sales of his first two books. Confident from his early success, Burke quickly signed with the William Morris Agency and published his third book, *Lay Down My Sword and Shield,* to less enthusiastic reviews. Angered over the advertising for this work, Burke elected to take his next novel, *The Lost Get-Back Boogie,* to a new publisher. Things then began to go downhill for him. "I found out I couldn't publish *The Lost Get-Back Boogie* anywhere," recalls Burke in his interview with Stroby. "I stayed with William Morris for six more years, but I couldn't sell a thing. After that, the agency returned all my material, cut me loose, and suddenly it was ground zero again."

It was not until thirteen years later that Burke published another novel. "I fell onto bad days," he says in his *Writer's Digest* interview. "By the time I was 34, I had published three novels, and I thought I was home free. I discovered I was just starting to pay dues." These dues came mostly in the form of short stories and unpublished novels, which Burke spent the next several years writing. Eventually meeting New York agent Philip G. Spitzer, Burke finally sold another novel in 1983—*Two for Texas,* a paperback original. While his other manuscripts, including *The Lost Get-Back Boogie,* continued to circulate, Burke proceeded with his teaching career. And in 1986, a year after publishing a collection of his short stories, the Louisiana State University Press finally published a revised version of *The Lost Get-Back Boogie,* a book which earned Burke a Pulitzer Prize nomination. "I owe those people at LSU Press a lot," Burke tells Stroby. "They resurrected my whole career. Suddenly I was back in business."

Ironically, *The Lost Get-Back Boogie,* which racked up ninety-three rejection slips and went unpublished for more than a decade, became one of Burke's most successful books. The novel opens on the day its protagonist, Iry Paret, gets out of a Louisiana prison after spending two years inside for manslaughter. A Korean War veteran and country musician, Paret ends up in Montana ranch coun-

try with the family of one of his prison friends, Buddy Riordan. Attempting to write a song which captures his life before the war and prison, Paret finds himself unwillingly drawn into a feud between Riordan's father and his neighbors. Set in the 1960s, the novel is filled with flashbacks, dreams, and drunken meditations that show a glimpse of Paret's past and point to the novel's tragic climax. Regina Weinreich, writing in the *New York Times Book Review,* finds the language in *The Lost Get-Back Boogie* "exceptionally poetic: a muscular prose enlivened by lyric descriptions of the landscape and the lingo of the roughnecks Paret encounters in the American hinterland." A *Washington Post Book World* contributor similarly concludes that "Burke's prose is by turns taut and poetic and his portrait of a fundamentally decent man trying to do right—but too often only able to do wrong—is riveting."

It was before *The Lost Get-Back Boogie* was published that Burke first decided to try his hand at a crime novel. With the encouragement of fellow writers, he combined elements of two of his unpublished novels to create *The Neon Rain,* the first book in the "Dave Robicheaux" crime series. Burke got three offers for the novel almost immediately, and has since written several books featuring Robicheaux. In his debut, *The Neon Rain,* Robicheaux is a New Orleans Police homicide detective investigating the murder of a prostitute whose body is discovered in the bayou. The case ends up encompassing everything from a contract on Robicheaux's life to encounters with the Nicaraguan mafia. Eventually framed and suspended from his job, Robicheaux must clear his name, and his ability to do so is made difficult when he gives up and returns to drinking. "Mr. Burke has created a real character in Dave Robicheaux," points out Newgate Callendar in the *New York Times Book Review.* "This is a detective who is more than a lethal man of action." Alan Ryan, writing in the *Washington Post Book World,* also sees Robicheaux as a "human" character, concluding: "Burke's writing is masterful, catching the violence of words and attitudes as well as the dizzying action, the pain and the blood. I love this book."

Robicheaux's life is significantly changed in his next adventure, *Heaven's Prisoners.* No longer working for the police, he now runs a bait shop on the rural bayou and is happily married to Annie, the woman who helped pull him out of his depression in *The Neon Rain.* The couple's peaceful life is interrupted when they watch a plane crash into the sea. Going down to investigate, Robicheaux discovers four bodies and a little Latina girl who has managed to survive the crash (he eventually adopts her). When the newspaper accounts of the accident report only three bodies, Robicheaux tries to find out why. Discovering that there is a drug connection, he is warned off the case and severely beaten by two thugs. A tragic turn of events prompts Robicheaux to start drinking again, but in the end a form of justice is done. The *Los Angeles Times Book Review*'s Charles Champlin observes that in *Heaven's Prisoners* Burke mixes "hard-line action and terse dialogue with lyrical evocations of the bayou country and explorations of the deepest feelings of anger, revenge, love, compassion and understanding." Callendar, in his review of the book, similarly relates that Burke "has the knack of combining action with reflection; he has pity for the human condition, and even his villains can have some sympathetic and redeeming qualities. . . . *Heaven's Prisoners* is a long way from your average action novel."

After his wife is killed by hired killers and he makes a trip to Montana to help out an old friend in *Black Cherry Blues,* Robicheaux finds himself in debt and joins the small New Iberia police force in his fourth adventure, *A Morning for Flamingos*. While transferring prisoners for execution—Jimmy Lee Boggs, a cold-blooded killer, and Tante Lemon, the grandson of an old Creole woman—Robicheaux finds himself shot and lying in a ditch after the two prisoners escape. Once recovered, he agrees to go undercover to infiltrate a mafia gang in New Orleans, the same gang for which Boggs is a hit-man. Along the way, Robicheaux also meets up with an old sweetheart and undergoes an interior battle with his own fears. *A Morning for Flamingos,* maintains Champlin in his review of the book, is "a poetically expressed merging of melodramatic events and sensitive problems of character and relationship." Kevin Moore, writing in Chicago *Tribune Books,* relates that in *A Morning for Flamingos* "the air always seems heavy with static electricity—and there is no telling when, or why, things may reach a flash point. This is gumshoe gumbo at its tastiest."

Robicheaux remains a member of the New Iberia sheriff's department for his 1992 adventure, *A Stained White Radiance.* Having recently married his childhood sweetheart, he finds himself drawn into the affairs of the Sonnier family, which is made up of a wealthy oilman, a politician with Klan connections, a television evangelist, and another of Robicheaux's old girlfriends. After a cop is killed while investigating a break-in at one of the Sonniers' homes, the other members of the secretive family are attacked one by one and Robicheaux must find the killer. Chicago *Tribune Books* contributor John Fink asserts: "Burke can write. He drops in local color and vibrant characters with masterly precision. His action scenes crackle." And a *Los Angeles Times Book Review* contributor observes that Burke "is an intricate plotter with all the narrative gifts of the born storyteller. Yet he is uncommonly concerned with and eloquent about the textures and stresses of his times."

Speaking of the "Robicheaux" series in general, Stroby points out that "the Robicheaux books are often as much explorations of faith and fear as they are tightly crafted thrillers about crime and punishment in southern Louisiana." Burke relates to Stroby that he believes the books in the series "are all different, at least in my opinion. There are certain elements (of plotting and action) in any novel that are fictive devices, I guess, but I don't think I've ever put anything into a book that I didn't believe organically belonged there. When the books have trouble with reviewers, it's usually because they see them as being too introspective, too much about the inner struggle of a man. And they're correct in that sense. The books are mysteries about the psychology of Dave Robicheaux."

No matter how the books in the "Robicheaux" series are perceived, they, and Burke himself, are both critically acclaimed and popular with the public. "James Lee Burke is one of the ablest crime novelists of the day, a remarkable combination of poetic sensibility and hard-muscled storyteller," contends Champlin. And Sallis maintains that "few other writers have ever obtained the delicate balance between action and contemplation that's a given in any James Lee Burke book. The sensuousness of descriptive and lyric passages would be remarkable in any novel, and in the context of thrillers, becomes truly astonishing. There simply aren't many writers who look this closely at things, who open themselves so fully to the sensual world; fewer still who so richly recreate such moments for the reader."

BIOGRAPHICAL/CRITICAL SOURCES:

PERIODICALS

Armchair Detective, winter, 1989, p. 22.

Los Angeles Times Book Review, April 10, 1988, p. 10; October 8, 1989; November 11, 1990, p. 15; April 12, 1992, p. 12.

New York Times Book Review, March 14, 1965; August 9, 1970; January 16, 1972; January 11, 1987; June 21, 1987; June 26, 1988, p. 43; October 8, 1989, p. 20; November 4, 1990, p. 30; April 5, 1992, p. 14.

Publishers Weekly, June 1, 1970, p. 63; November 8, 1971, p. 47.

Tribune Books (Chicago), April 3, 1988; September 10, 1989; October 14, 1990; April 12, 1992.

Washington Post Book World, May 17, 1987; October 4, 1987; September 10, 1989, p. 5; December 16, 1990, pp. 1, 8; April 5, 1992.

Writer's Digest, January, 1993, pp. 38-40.*

—*Sketch by Susan M. Reicha*

BURKHOLZ, Herbert 1932-
(John Luckless, a joint pseudonym)

PERSONAL: Born December 9, 1932, in New York, NY; son of Sidney and Eva (Margolin) Burkholz; married Yvonne Schwartz, December 9, 1948 (divorced, 1962); married Susan Blaine, November 1, 1962; children: (first marriage) Howard, Matthew. *Education:* New York University, A.B., 1950. *Avocational interests:* Sailing and skin diving.

ADDRESSES: Agent—Georges Borchardt Inc., 136 East 57th St., New York, NY 10022.

CAREER: Writer. College of William and Mary, Williamsburg, VA, visiting professor and writer-in-residence, 1975-76; Hofstra University, Hempstead, NY, lecturer, 1977-78.

MEMBER: PEN International.

WRITINGS:

Sister Bear, Simon & Schuster, 1969.
(With Clifford Irving) *Spy: History of Modern Espionage* (nonfiction), Macmillan, 1969.
The Spanish Soldier, Charterhouse, 1973.
Mulligan's Seed, Harcourt, 1975.
(With Irving, under joint pseudonym John Luckless) *The Death Freak,* Summit Books, 1978, published under real names, Sphere Books, 1979.
(With Irving) *The Sleeping Spy,* Atheneum, 1983.
The Snow Gods, Poseidon, 1984, Atheneum, 1985.
The Sensitives, Atheneum, 1987.
Strange Bedfellows, Atheneum, 1988.
Brain Damage (sequel to *The Sensitives*), Macmillan, 1992.
Writer in Residence, Permanent Press, 1992.

Contributor of short stories to numerous magazines including *New York Times Magazine* and *Playboy.*

SIDELIGHTS: "[Herbert] Burkholz is a writer of considerable skill and more than considerable versatility," comments L. J. Davis in the *Washington Post Book World.* Known for his inventiveness and humor, the author chooses themes ranging from incest, in *Sister Bear,* to international intrigue in *The Sleeping Spy.*

Davis describes Burkholz's widely reviewed work *The Spanish Soldier* as an "extraordinarily ingenious, refreshingly intricate, and beautifully worked out" novel. The book's central character, Matthew Mendelsohn, lives two lives: that of a widowed ex-politician from New York who resides with his beautiful mistress on a Spanish island and that of the title's "Spanish soldier." The latter existence is purely one of imagination—a fantasy life where Mendelsohn is variously a Carlist soldier in the 1835 Spanish civil war, a member of the Abraham Lincoln Brigade in 1939,

or an Israeli intelligence officer in the 1970s. Writes Davis, "Whatever [Mendelsohn's] identity of the moment, in the realms of both fantasy and reality, he is searching ceaselessly for the Unholy Grail, the battered pewter cup Judas drank from at the Last Supper." While "this may sound like a lot of romantic hokum . . . *The Spanish Soldier* is considerably more than that," Davis contends.

Sara Blackburn, however, notes in her *New York Times Book Review* article that she "had the eerie feeling . . . that the author is a writer of talent who, somehow lacking material, has settled for concerns considerably beneath either his skills or his real interests." Calling *The Spanish Soldier* "well-written," Blackburn nonetheless feels its central character is a shallow, decadent person, a fact that "seems to go unrecognized by the author, . . . [and that] just doesn't mesh with Burkholz's very apparent abilities at character, dimension, humor and setting." "Yet," maintains Davis, "even in its flaws *The Spanish Soldier* is . . . an achievement of considerable proportions and much more than passing interest. It is a well-wrought novel boldly conceived and boldly executed, with a breadth and audacity of vision that is all too rare."

Burkholz later teamed up with Clifford Irving, the author of the hoax autobiography of Howard Hughes, to produce two spy thrillers, the first of which, *The Death Freak,* was published in 1978 under the joint pseudonym John Luckless. Described by Michael Demarest of *Time* as "clever, cynical, and compelling," *The Death Freak* tells of two Cold War operatives, Eddie Mancuso of the CIA and Vasily Borgneff of the KGB, who have decided to leave the spy business. The problem, of course, is that "retirement" is not allowed, for the agents know far too much to be allowed to live. Marked for "extraction," Mancuso and Borgneff join forces to strike back at their former employers, targeting the chiefs of the two organizations. Both agents are masters of UKDs (Unusual Killing Devices), utilizing such weapons as flame-throwing hair dryers and exploding tennis balls to dispatch their targets. Ultimately, the CIA and KGB must also cooperate in an attempt to halt the assassins' spree. The *Virginia Quarterly Review* compares *The Death Freak* to the adventures of James Bond, calling it "a slam-bam spoof of the spy novel." Though the novel is definitely written with tongue placed firmly in cheek, Demarest still pronounces *The Death Freak* "a suavely persuasive, anti-Establishment thriller with the bitter aftertaste of Campari and vodka."

BIOGRAPHICAL/CRITICAL SOURCES:

PERIODICALS

New York Times Book Review, January 28, 1973; February 13, 1983; June 16, 1985, p. 24; August 30, 1987, p. 29; April 19, 1992, p. 12.
Time, November 20, 1978, p. 124.

Times Literary Supplement, January 29, 1970.
Tribune Books (Chicago), August 30, 1992, p. 7.
Virginia Quarterly Review, winter, 1979, p. 20; autumn, 1988, p. 128.
Washington Post Book World, March 18, 1973; June 2, 1985, p. 8; July 26, 1992, p. 1.
West Coast Review of Books, November, 1978, p. 37; Volume 13, number 3, 1987, p. 33.

*   *   *

BURNETT, Alfred David 1937-

PERSONAL: Born August 15, 1937, in Edinburgh, Scotland; son of Alfred Harding (a railway superintendent) and Jessica Millar (a teacher; maiden name, Scott) Burnett. *Education:* University of Edinburgh, M.A. (with honors), 1959; University of Strathclyde, A.L.A., 1964. *Religion:* Presbyterian.

ADDRESSES: Home—33 Hastings Ave., Merry Oaks, Durham DH1 3QG, England.

CAREER: University of Glasgow, Glasgow, Scotland, library assistant, 1959-64; University of Durham, Durham, England, assistant librarian, 1964-90. Guest of Soviet Union of Writers, 1984.

MEMBER: International Academy of Poets, Amnesty International, Bibliographical Society, Library Association, Private Libraries Association, National Council for Civil Liberties, Colpitts Poetry.

AWARDS, HONORS: Patterson Bursary in Anglo-Saxon from University of Edinburgh, 1958; Kelso Memorial Prize in bibliography from University of Strathclyde, 1964; essay prize from Library Association, 1966, for "Problems of Older Material in British University Libraries and Some Suggested Solutions"; Sevensma Prize from International Federation of Library Associations, 1971, for *Studies in Comparative Librarianship;* Hawthornden fellowships, 1984 and 1992; Panizzi Medal of the British Library, 1991.

WRITINGS:

POETRY

Mandala, Magpie Press, 1967.
Diversities, Magpie Press, 1968.
A Ballad upon a Wedding, Magpie Press, 1969.
Columbaria, London Literary Editions, 1971.
Shimabara, Pointing Finger Press, 1972.
Thirty Snow Poems, North Gate Press, 1973.
Fescennines, Tragara Press, 1973.
Hero and Leader: A Poem, privately printed, 1975.
The True Vine, Hedgehog Press, 1975.
He and She, Tragara Press, 1976.

The Heart's Undesign, Tragara Press, 1977.
Figures and Spaces, Pointing Finger Press, 1978.
Jackdaw, Tragara Press, 1980.
Thais, Black Cygnet Press, 1981.
Romans, Tragara Press, 1983.
Vines, Rocket Press, 1984.
Kantharos, Tragara Press, 1989.
Lesbos, Tragara Press, 1990.
Root and Flower, Snake River Press, 1990.

NONFICTION

Cataloguing Policy Objectives and the Computer, [Durham], 1966.
Report of the North-East Libraries and Computers Group Working Party on the Operational Data Requirements of Different Kinds of Library, [Durham], 1968.
(With R. K. Gupta and S. Simsova) *Studies in Comparative Librarianship: Three Essays Presented for the Sevensma Prize, 1971,* Library Association, 1973.
Wood and Type: An Exhibition of Books, [Durham], 1977.
Five Hundred Years of Science: Descriptive Catalogue of an Exhibition in the University Library, Palace Green, Durham, Durham University Library, 1978.
(Editor with E. E. Cumming) *International Library and Information Programmes: Proceedings of the Tenth Anniversary Conference of the International and Comparative Librarianship Group of the Library Association,* Library Association, 1979.
(Editor and author of introduction, with D. F. C. Surman) *Henri Gaudier-Brzeska and Ezra Pound: A Display of Printed Material and Related Items Arranged to Accompany the Fourth International Ezra Pound Conference,* [Durham], 1979.
(Editor with S. P. Green) *The British Commitment Overseas: A Transcript of Seminar Discussions Held at the Library Association Study School and National Conference, Brighton,* International and Comparative Librarianship Group (London), 1979.
(Editor with A. Whatley) *Language and Literacy: The Public Library Role* (proceedings), International and Comparative Librarianship Group, 1981.
Arabic Resources: Acquisition and Management in British Libraries, Mansell, 1986.
(Editor) *Technology for Information in Development: Proceedings of the Sixth Conference of the International and Comparative Librarianship Group of the Library Association, Falmer, Sussex, 1987,* International and Comparative Librarianship Group, 1988.
Pharos: Two Essays upon Thais, Tragara Press, 1989.
The Presence of Japan: Lafcadio Hearn, 1890-1990, Durham University Library, 1991.

OTHER

(Translator with J. Cayley) *Mirror and Pool: Translations from the Chinese,* Wellsweep, 1991.

Also contributor of numerous articles, poems, and reviews to scholarly journals and literary magazines, including *Journal of Librarianship, Universities Quarterly, Northern Notes, Annals of Science, Notes and Queries, Libri,* and *Focus.*

Several of Burnett's poems have been translated into Russian and Lithuanian.

WORK IN PROGRESS: Poems and articles.

SIDELIGHTS: Alfred David Burnett wrote: " 'Homo sum; humani nil a me alienum puto.' ['I am a man; I consider nothing human foreign to me.']—Terence (*Heauton Timarumenos,* 77)."

*   *   *

BURNS, Olive Ann   1924-1990
(Amy Larkin)

PERSONAL: Born July 17, 1924, in Banks County, GA; died of heart failure (some sources say lymphoma), July 4, 1990, in Atlanta, GA; daughter of William Arnold (a farmers' cooperative executive) and Ruby (a homemaker; maiden name, Hight) Burns; married Andrew H. Sparks (an editor), August 11, 1956 (deceased, 1989); children: Rebecca Marie, John Andrew. *Education:* Attended Mercer University, 1942-44; University of North Carolina at Chapel Hill, A.B., 1946. *Politics:* Democrat. *Religion:* Methodist. *Avocational interests:* Reading, walking, camping, swimming, art, classical music, conversation, dancing to rock music, museums of all kinds, travel, public speaking ("not necessarily in that order").

ADDRESSES: Agent—c/o Mitch Douglas, International Creative Management, 40 West 57th St., New York, NY 10019.

CAREER: Writer and free lance journalist. *Coca Cola Bottler* and *Laundryman's Guide,* Atlanta, GA, staff writer, 1946-47; *Atlanta Journal and Constitution* Sunday magazine, Atlanta, staff writer, 1947-57; author of local newspaper advice column "Ask Amy" under pseudonym Amy Larkin, 1960-67.

MEMBER: Authors Guild, Atlanta Historical Society, University of North Carolina Alumni Association.

WRITINGS:

NOVELS

Cold Sassy Tree, Ticknor & Fields, 1984.

Leaving Cold Sassy Tree: The Unfinished Sequel to Cold Sassy Tree, with a reminiscence by Katrina Kenison, Ticknor & Fields, 1992.

OTHER

Also contributor of numerous articles to the *Atlanta Constitution. Cold Sassy Tree* has been translated into German.

ADAPTATIONS: Cold Sassy Tree was adapted as a teleplay starring Richard Widmark and Faye Dunaway by TNT, 1990, and as an audio cassette by Books on Tape.

SIDELIGHTS: Olive Ann Burns once told *CA* that "it has been said that growing up in the South and becoming a writer is like spending your life riding in a wagon, seated in a chair that is always facing backwards. I don't face life looking backwards, but I have written about past times and past people." Some of these "past times and past peoples" formed the basis for Burns's bestselling novel *Cold Sassy Tree* and its unfinished sequel, *Leaving Cold Sassy Tree.* Burns began her writing career as a journalist; it was only after being diagnosed with cancer that she decided to try her hand at penning a novel. *Cold Sassy Tree*—the tale of a rather unorthodox marriage as seen through the eyes of a fourteen-year-old boy—took eight and one-half years to complete, during which time the author battled the side effects of chemotherapy. Despite the physical difficulties she encountered while working on both of the "Cold Sassy Tree" novels, Burns concluded that the "one thing I've learned is that whatever it is you want to write, you must decide what you will give up in order to have the time and energy to do it. . . . You have to give up some things or you'll end up being one of those people who would like to have written a novel."

Burns drew on the colorful history of her father's family in order to write *Cold Sassy Tree.* The author once recalled that her great grandfather Power—a recent widower—decided "he had to git him another wife or hire a housekeeper . . . and it would jest be cheaper to git married." Power's ensuing marriage to a younger woman served as the inspiration for the controversial fictional nuptials of Grandpa Blakeslee and Miss Love Simpson. This May-December union is observed and commented on by Blakeslee's grandson Will Tweedy, who quickly realizes that what initially appeared to be a marriage of financial convenience is really a love match. In a review of the novel for *Washington Post Book World,* Jeanne McManus wrote that "the characters of this gossipy, small southern haven, captured at the turn of the century, are summoned forth from an imagination so fertile . . . that the very force of the prose could put Cold Sassy on the map."

Burns continued the story of Will Tweedy and his family in *Leaving Cold Sassy Tree.* Packaged with biographical notes by Burns's editor, this unfinished novel presents Tweedy as a young man of twenty-five facing both the onslaught of World War I and the prospect of marriage to a young schoolteacher. Unfortunately, the author's untimely death left most of *Leaving Cold Sassy Tree*'s plot lines and character development incomplete. While praising the vivid, small-town imagery found in the fifteen published chapters, *Publishers Weekly* critic Sybil Steinberg warned readers against expecting too much from the text. "The knowledge that the narrative will abruptly end . . . dictates a cautious approach," she noted, adding that "readers should prepare for an interrupted work-in-process."

Although Burns's literary output was limited to two works, her colorful characters, detail-driven use of setting, and humor-laced plots endeared her to readers of all ages. In large part because she was inspired by what she knew best—the idiosyncracies of her own family history—Burns was able to bring a region and an era to life. "What I was after was not just names and dates," the author once commented. "I wanted stories and details that would bring the dead to life."

BIOGRAPHICAL/CRITICAL SOURCES:

PERIODICALS

Atlanta Weekly, October 14, 1984.
Horn Book, January, 1987, p. 102.
New York Times Book Review, January 1, 1989, p. 20.
Publishers Weekly, November 9, 1984.
Washington Post Book World, November 25, 1984, pp. 3, 11.

OBITUARIES:

PERIODICALS

Chicago Tribune, July 6, 1990.
Los Angeles Times, July 6, 1990.
New York Times, July 6, 1990.
Washington Post, July 8, 1990.*

* * *

BUSH, (John Nash) Douglas 1896-1983

PERSONAL: Born March 21, 1896, in Morrisburg, Ontario, Canada; died of pneumonia, March 2, 1983, in Boston, MA; became U.S. citizen in 1940; son of Dexter Calvin (a businessman) and Mary Evelina (Nash) Bush; married Hazel Cleaver, September 3, 1927; children: Geoffrey Douglas. *Education:* University of Toronto, B.A., 1920, M.A., 1921; Harvard University, Ph.D., 1923. *Politics:* Democrat. *Religion:* Protestant.

CAREER: Harvard University, Cambridge, MA, instructor and tutor in English, 1924-27; University of Minnesota, Minneapolis, assistant professor, 1927-28, associate professor, 1928-31, professor of English, 1931-36; Harvard University, associate professor, 1936-37; professor, 1937-57, Gurney Professor of English, 1957-66.

MEMBER: Modern Language Association of America, Modern Humanities Research Association (president, 1955), American Philosophical Society, British Academy (corresponding fellow), Cambridge Scientific Club, Signet Society, Phi Beta Kappa.

AWARDS, HONORS: Sheldon Travelling Fellow, Harvard University, 1923-24; Guggenheim fellow, 1934-35; Society for Libraries Medal, New York University, 1947; humanities award, American Council of Learned Societies, 1957; Litt.D., Tufts University, 1952, Princeton University, 1958, University of Toronto, 1958, Oberlin College, 1959, Harvard University, 1959, Swarthmore College, 1960, Boston College, 1965, Michigan State University, 1968, Merrimack College, 1969; L.H.D., Southern Illinois University, 1962, and Marlboro College, 1966.

WRITINGS:

(Editor with Cecil A. Moore) *English Prose, 1600-1660*, Doubleday, 1930.
Mythology and the Renaissance Tradition in English Poetry, University of Minnesota Press, 1932, revised edition, Norton, 1963.
Mythology and the Romantic Tradition in English Poetry, Harvard University Press, 1937, revised edition, 1965.
The Renaissance and English Humanism, University of Toronto Press, 1939, revised edition, 1956.
"Paradise Lost" in Our Time, Oxford University Press, 1945.
English Literature in the Earlier Seventeenth Century, 1600-1660, Clarendon Press, 1945, 2nd revised edition, Oxford University Press, 1973.
(Editor) John Milton, *The Portable Milton*, Viking, 1949.
Science and English Poetry: A Historical Sketch, 1590-1950, Oxford University Press, 1950.
(Editor) Alfred Tennyson, *Tennyson: Selected Poetry*, Random House, 1951.
Classical Influences in Renaissance Literature, Harvard University Press, 1952.
English Poetry: The Main Currents from Chaucer to the Present, Oxford University Press, 1952.
(Editor) John Keats, *John Keats: Selected Poems and Letters*, Houghton, 1959.
(Editor with Alfred Harbage) William Shakespeare, *Shakespeare's Sonnets*, Penguin, 1961.
John Milton: A Sketch of His Life and Writing, Macmillan, 1964.
Prefaces to Renaissance Literature, Harvard University Press, 1965.

(Editor) John Milton, *The Complete Poetical Works of John Milton,* Houghton, 1965.
John Keats, Macmillan, 1966.
Engaged and Disengaged, Harvard University Press, 1966.
Pagan Myth and Christian Tradition in English Poetry, American Philosophical Society, 1968.
(Editor) *Variorum Commentary on the Poems of Milton,* Columbia University Press, Volume 1 (with J. E. Shaw and A. B. Giametti): *Latin and Greek Poems,* 1970, Volume 2 (with A. S. P. Woodhouse and Edward Weismiller): *Minor English Poems,* 1972.
Matthew Arnold: A Survey of His Poetry and Prose, Macmillan, 1971.
Jane Austen, Macmillan, 1975.
Themes and Variations in English Poetry of the Renaissance: Two Lectures, R. West, 1977.
(Editor) Baptista Mantuanus, *The Eclogues of Mantuan,* Scholars' Facsimiles & Reprints, 1977.

Contributor to *Milton Encyclopedia,* Bucknell University Press, 1978, and to *Encyclopaedia Britannica.* Contributor of articles to literary journals, including *American Scholar, Kenyon Review,* and *Sewanee Review.*

BIOGRAPHICAL/CRITICAL SOURCES:

PERIODICALS

Times Literary Supplement, February 2, 1967.
Virginia Quarterly Review, spring, 1969.

OBITUARIES:

PERIODICALS

AB Bookman's Weekly, April 11, 1983.
New York Times, March 8, 1983.*

[Date of death provided by son, Geoffrey Bush.]

*   *   *

BUTLER, (Frederick) Guy 1918-

PERSONAL: Born January 21, 1918, in Cradock, Cape Province, South Africa; son of Ernest Collett and Alice E. (Stringer) Butler; married Jean Murray Satchwell, 1940; children: three sons, one daughter. *Education:* Rhodes University, M.A., 1939; Brasenose College, Oxford, M.A., 1947. *Avocational interests:* Producing plays, restoring old houses.

ADDRESSES: Home—"High Corner," 122 High St., Grahamstown 6140, South Africa. *Office*—Institute for the Study of English in Africa, Rhodes University, Grahamstown, Cape Province, South Africa.

CAREER: University of the Witwatersrand, Johannesburg, South Africa, lecturer in English, 1948-50; Rhodes University, Grahamstown, Cape Province, South Africa, professor of English, 1952-86, professor emeritus and honorary research fellow, 1987—. *Military Service:* South African Army, 1940-45; served in Egypt, Lebanon, Italy, and England.

MEMBER: English Academy of Southern Africa, 1820 Settler Monument Foundation, Shakespeare Society of Southern Africa (president, 1985; honorary life president, 1991), Shakespeare Birthplace Trust.

AWARDS, HONORS: D.Litt., University of Natal, 1970, and University of Witwatersrand, 1984; C.N.A. award (literature), 1975; D.Litt. and Phil., University of South Africa, 1989; Lady Usher Award for Literature, 1992.

WRITINGS:

An Aspect of Tragedy (literary criticism), Rhodes University, 1953.
The Republic and the Arts, Witwatersrand University Press, 1964.
A Rackety Colt: The Adventures of Thomas Stubbs (novel), Tafelberg, 1989.
Tales from the Old Karoo, Donker, 1989.
(With Herman Potgieter) *South Africa, Landshapes, Landscapes, Manscapes,* Struik, 1990.

POETRY

Stranger to Europe, Balkema, 1952, enlarged edition, 1960.
South of the Zambesi: Poems from South Africa, Abelard, 1966.
On First Seeing Florence, Rhodes University, 1968.
Selected Poems, Donker, 1975.
Songs and Ballads, David Philip, 1978.
Pilgrimage to Dias Cross: A narrative poem by Guy Butler, woodcuts and engravings by Cecil Skotnes, David Philip, 1987.
(With David Butler) *Out of the African Ark: Anthology of Animal Poems,* Donker, 1988.
(With Jeff Opland) *The Magic Tree: South African Stories in Verse,* Donker, 1989.

EDITOR

A Book of South African Verse, Oxford University Press, 1959.
When Boys Were Men, Oxford University Press, 1969.
The 1820 Settlers, Human & Rousseau, 1974.
(With Chris Mann) *A New Book of South African Verse in English,* Oxford University Press, 1979.
(With N. Visser) *The Re-Internment on Buffelskop, S.C. Cronwright-Schreiner, My Diary, 7-15 June 1921 and 8 to 29 August 1921,* I.S.E.A., Rhodes University, 1983.

PLAYS

The Dam (three-act; produced in Cape Town, South Africa, at Little Theatre, 1953), Balkema, 1953.

The Dove Returns (three-act; produced in Pretoria, South Africa, at National Theatre, 1954), Fortune Press, 1956.

Cape Charade (three-act; produced in Cape Town, at Labia Theatre, 1967), Balkema, 1968.

Take Root or Die (produced in Grahamstown, South Africa, at University Theatre), Balkema, 1970.

Richard Gush of Salem (produced in Grahamstown and Cape Town, 1970), Maskew Miller, 1982.

Demea (produced at National Arts Festival, Grahamstown, 1990), David Philip, 1990.

AUTOBIOGRAPHY

Karoo Morning: An Autobiography, 1918-35, Volume I, David Philip, 1978.

Bursting World: An Autobiography, 1936-45, Volume II, David Philip, 1983.

A Local Habitation: An Autobiography, 1945-90, Volume III, David Philip, 1991.

Also sometime editor of *New Coin;* sometime English editor of *Standpunte;* advisory editor of *Contrast;* founder and editor of *Shakespeare in Southern Africa,* 1987-90.

ADAPTATIONS: Richard Gush of Salem was broadcast on S.A.T.V., 1984.

WORK IN PROGRESS: Critical work on Shakespeare and South African literature; new poems.

SIDELIGHTS: Guy Butler told *CA:* "I have spent much thought and time on the promotion of English literature in southern Africa, and have attempted to encourage the use of English as a creative medium for South African writers whatever their racial origins. I have also tried to get works by South African authors into schools and universities. Although English is now an African language, it remains our world-contact language, and South African literature is influenced by and contributes to English world literature. I believe profoundly in the greatness of certain authors (Shakespeare, for example) and their importance to all writers, wherever they may be."

BIOGRAPHICAL/CRITICAL SOURCES:

BOOKS

Butler, Guy, *Karoo Morning: An Autobiography, 1918-35,* Volume I, David Philip, 1978.

Butler, G., *Bursting World: An Autobiography, 1936-1945,* Volume II, David Philip, 1983.

Butler, G., *A Local Habitation: An Autobiography, 1945-90,* Volume III, David Philip, 1991.

Read, John, compiler, *Guy Butler: A Bibliography,* National English Literary Museum, 1992.

Van Wyk Smith, Malvern, and Don Maclennan, editors, *Olive Schreiner and After: Essays on Southern African Literature in Honour of Guy Butler,* David Philip, 1983.

C

CALISTRO, Paddy
See CALISTRO McAULEY, Patricia Ann

*   *   *

CALISTRO McAULEY, Patricia Ann   1948-
(Paddy Calistro)

PERSONAL: Surname is pronounced Ca-*lis*-tro; born March 24, 1948, in Alameda, CA; daughter of George and Ann (Spikula) Calistro; married Scott McAuley (a computer scientist), January 5, 1980; children: David George, Genevieve Grace. *Education:* University of California, Santa Barbara, B.A., 1970; University of Southern California, M.S., 1972.

ADDRESSES: Agent—Benderoff-Galtman Agency, 1120 Park Ave., New York, NY 10128.

CAREER: Los Angeles Times, Los Angeles, CA, staff writer, 1979-81; *American Style,* Los Angeles, editor, 1981-83; writer and free-lance journalist, 1983—. President, Angel City Press.

WRITINGS:

UNDER NAME PADDY CALISTRO

(With Edith Head) *Edith Head's Hollywood,* Dutton, 1983.
(With Michael Maron) *Michael Maron's Instant Makeover Magic,* Rawson, 1983.
(With Franco Columbu and Anita Columbu) *Redesign Your Body,* Dutton, 1985.
(With Betty Goodwin) *L.A. Inside Out: The Architecture and Interiors of America's Most Colorful City,* Viking Studio, 1992.
(With Victoria Jackson) *Victoria Jackson: Redefining Beauty,* Warner, 1993.

Contributor to *Los Angeles Times,* and to magazines, including *Allure, Longevity, House Beautiful,* and *Woman's Day.* Interior design editor of *Los Angeles.*

*   *   *

CAMILLERI, Joseph A.   1944-

PERSONAL: Born November 21, 1944, in Egypt; son of Lorenzo (a fitter and musician) and Polixeni (a homemaker; maiden name, Orfanides) Camilleri; married Rita Rotin (a teacher), May 19, 1973; children: Kristian, Emil. *Education:* University of Melbourne, B.A. (with honors), 1966; Monash University, M.A., 1969; London School of Economics and Political Science, Ph.D., 1972.

ADDRESSES: Home—13 Mascoma St., Strathmore, Victoria 3041, Australia. *Office*—Department of Politics, La Trobe University, Bundoora, Victoria 3083, Australia.

CAREER: La Trobe University, Bundoora, Australia, 1973—, began as lecturer, became reader in politics, 1986—. President of Pax Christi Australia, 1973—. Convener of Action for Aboriginal Rights, 1973-81, Movement against Uranium Mining, 1976-81, and of People for Nuclear Disarmament, 1982-84. National spokesperson for Rainbow Alliance, 1990—.

MEMBER: International Peace Research Association, International Political Science Association, Australian Political Studies Association.

WRITINGS:

An Introduction to Australian Foreign Policy, Jacaranda Press, 1973, 4th edition, Jacaranda Wiley, 1979.
Civilization in Crisis: Human Prospects in a Changing World, Cambridge University Press, 1976.
Australian-American Relations, Macmillan Australia, 1980.

Chinese Foreign Policy: The Maoist Era and Its Aftermath, Martin Robertson, 1980.

The State and Nuclear Power: Conflict and Control in the Western World, University of Washington Press, 1984.

The Australia-New Zealand-U.S. Alliance: Regional Security in the Nuclear Age, Westview, 1987.

The End of Sovereignty? Politics in a Shrinking and Fragmenting World, Edward Elgar, 1992.

WORK IN PROGRESS: Two research projects: "Alliances in the Post-Cold War Era" and "Political Community and World Society: Evolution in Theory and Practice."

SIDELIGHTS: In his 1984 book, *The State and Nuclear Power: Conflict and Control in the Western World,* Joseph A. Camilleri discusses the reasons for public opposition to the use—and misuse—of nuclear power. *New York Times* reviewer John C. Sawhill notes Camilleri's conclusion that "the underlying cause of the public's disaffection with nuclear power has been the nature and extent of government intervention in its development and use, rather than the ostensible issues around which the debate has raged—weapons proliferation, waste disposal, reactor safety." In his book Camilleri supports his proposition by studying the relationship between the various approaches taken by the governments of six countries regarding the development, use, and regulation of nuclear power and the public response to nuclear power in each nation. According to Sawhill, who describes *The State and Nuclear Power* as "well-documented," Camilleri also "helps us to understand the relationship between governments and the scientific and industrial communities." The critic concludes, "If he [Camilleri] fails to offer guidance for the future, he has set the stage for others to do so."

BIOGRAPHICAL/CRITICAL SOURCES:

PERIODICALS

New York Times Book Review, February 17, 1985.

*   *   *

CAMP, Roderic (Ai) 1945-

PERSONAL: Born February 19, 1945, in Colfax, WA; son of Ortho O. (in small business) and Helen (a counselor; maiden name, Eknoyan) Camp; married Emily Ellen Morse (a librarian), October 1, 1966; children: Christopher, Alexander. *Education:* George Washington University, B.A., 1966, M.A., 1967; University of Arizona, Ph.D., 1970. *Avocational interests:* Reading, sailing.

ADDRESSES: Home—333 State St., New Orleans, LA 70118. *Office*—Department of Political Science, Tulane University, New Orleans, LA 70118.

CAREER: Central College, Pella, IA, assistant professor, 1970-75, associate professor, 1975-80, professor of political science, 1980-91, chairman of department, 1973-76, 1980-83, 1985-91, director of study program in Yucatan, Mexico, 1973, chairman of Council on International Programs, 1975-76, director of Latin American studies, 1976-91, assistant to academic dean and director of institutional research, 1978-79, chairman of cross-cultural division, 1984-85, chairman of behavioral science division, 1985-90; Tulane University, New Orleans, LA, professor of Latin American studies and political science, 1991—. Visiting professor at Grand Valley State Colleges (now Grand Valley State University), Allendale, MI, 1974-75; visiting researcher at Centro de Estudios Internacionales, Colegio de Mexico, 1978; professor at University of Arizona's program in Guadalajara, Mexico, summer, 1980, visiting professor at university, spring, 1981. Scholar in residence, Center for the Study of Foreign Affairs, Foreign Service Institute, Washington, DC, 1983; visiting scholar, Woodrow Wilson Center, Smithsonian Institution, Washington, DC, 1984. *Military service:* U.S. Marine Corps, 1970; became sergeant.

MEMBER: Latin American Studies Association, American Historical Association (Conference on Latin America), American Political Science Association, Midwest Association of Latin American Studies, Midwest Political Science Association (member of executive council, 1978-81), Rocky Mountain Council of Latin American Studies, North Central Council of Latin Americanists.

AWARDS, HONORS: U.S. State Department scholar, 1971; National Science Foundation grant, 1974-75; American Philosophical Society grants for Mexico, 1974, 1975, 1980; National Endowment for the Humanities fellow, 1977, 1981; Earthwatch fellow in Peru, 1977; Fulbright-Hays grant for Mexico, 1978; grant from National Endowment for the Humanities and Iowa Humanities Board, 1979, 1982; University House fellow at University of Iowa, 1980; Distinguished Professor Award, Central College, 1980-81, 1983-84; Woodrow Wilson fellow, 1984; State Department grant on Mexico, 1984-85; Fulbright-Hays fellow to South America, 1985; Howard Heinz Foundation fellow, 1990-91.

WRITINGS:

IN ENGLISH

Latin American Civilization (textbook), Grand Valley State Colleges, 1975.

Mexican Political Biographies, 1935-1975, University of Arizona Press, 1976, revised edition, 1981.

The Role of Economists in Policy-Making: A Comparative Study of Mexico and the United States, University of Arizona Press, 1977.

Mexico's Leaders: Their Education and Recruitment, University of Arizona Press, 1980.

The Making of a Government: Political Leaders in Modern Mexico, University of Arizona Press, 1984.

Intellectuals and the State in Twentieth-Century Mexico, University of Texas Press, 1985.

Mexico's Political Stability, Westview, 1986.

Who's Who in Mexico Today, Westview, 1988, revised edition, 1993.

Memoirs of a Mexican Politician, University of New Mexico Press, 1988.

Entrepreneurs and Politics in Twentieth Century Mexico, Oxford University Press, 1989.

Mexican Political Biographies, 1884-1935, University of Texas Press, 1991.

Generals in the Palacio: The Military in Modern Mexico, Oxford University Press, 1992.

Politics in Mexico, Oxford University Press, 1993.

Contributor to numerous books, including *Quantitative Latin American Studies: Methods and Findings,* Volume 4, edited by James W. Wilkie and Kenneth R. Ruddle, Latin American Center, University of California, Los Angeles, 1977; *Statistical Abstract of Latin American Supplement Series,* Volume 10, edited by Wilkie and Peter Reich, Latin American Center, University of California, Los Angeles, 1980; *Handbook of Latin American Studies,* edited by Dolores Martin, University of Texas Press, Volume 45, 1983, Volume 46, 1985, Volume 47, 1989, Volume 49, 1991; *Latin America and Caribbean Contemporary Record,* edited by Jack W. Hopkins, Holmes & Meier, Volume 2, 1984, Volume 4, 1986, Volume 7, 1990; *Proceedings of the Role of the Military in Mexican Politics and Society: A Reassessment,* edited by David Ronfeldt, U.S.-Mexican Studies Center, University of California, San Diego, 1984; *Mexican Politics in Transition,* edited by Judith Gentleman, Westview, 1986; *Government and Private Sector in Mexico,* edited by Sylvia Maxfield, U.S.-Mexican Studies Center, University of California, San Diego, 1987; *Prospects for Mexico,* edited by George Grayson, Transaction Books, 1990; *Handbook of Political Science and Research on Latin America,* edited by David Dent, Greenwood Press, 1990; *From Military to Civilian Rule,* edited by Constantine Danopoulous, Routledge & Kegan Paul, 1992; and *Intellectuals in the Twentieth-Century Caribbean,* edited by Alistair Hennessy, Macmillan, 1992.

IN SPANISH

La Formacion de un Politico: La Socializacion de los Functionarios Publicos en Mexico Post-Revolucionario (title means: "The Formation of a Politician: The Socialization of Public Men in Post Revolutionary Mexico"), Fondo de Cultura Economica, 1980.

Los Lideres en Mexico (title means "Mexico's Leaders"), Fondo de Cultura Economica, 1983.

Los Intelectuales y el Estado en Mexico (title means "Intellectuals and the State in Mexico"), Fondo de Cultura Economica, 1988.

Memorias de un Politico Mexicano (title means "Memoirs of a Mexican Politician"), Fondo de Cultura Economica, 1989.

Los Empresarios y la Politica en Mexico (title means "Entrepreneurs and Politics in Mexico"), Fondo de Cultura Economica, 1991.

Biograficos Politicos Mexicanos, 1935-1992 (title means "Mexican Political Biographies, 1935-1992"), 3rd edition, Fondo de Cultura Economica, 1993.

Contributor to *Sociologia de la Paz y de la Guerra* (title means "The Sociology of Peace and War"), edited by Lucio Mendieta Nunez, 1979; *Perspectivas del Sistema Politico Mexicano* (title means "Perspectives of the Mexican Political System"), Comite Ejecutivo Nacional del PRI, 1982; and *Sucesion Presidencial,* edited by Edgar Butler, Westview, 1991.

OTHER

Contributing editor, *Handbook of Latin American Studies* and *World Book Encyclopedia.* Contributor of more than 150 articles, photographs, and reviews to education and Latin American studies journals.

WORK IN PROGRESS: A book on a theory of political recruitment; a book on church-state relations in Mexico.

SIDELIGHTS: Roderic Camp once told *CA:* "I am interested in directing scholarly work to a much larger, nonscholarly audience. I have published numerous black-and-white photographs, and recently have begun to combine scholarly writing with photography." Camp more recently added, "I have turned to fiction, writing an autobiography of a Mexican politician, and more recently, a thriller set in 1999, focusing on Mexico and the U.S."

BIOGRAPHICAL/CRITICAL SOURCES:

PERIODICALS

El Sol de Mexico, April 29, 1977.
Excelsior, December 10, 1976; December 11, 1976.
Proceso, May 15, 1978.

* * *

CAVES, Richard E(arl) 1931-

PERSONAL: Born November 1, 1931, in Akron, OH; son of Earl Leroy (a teacher) and Verna (Jobes) Caves. *Education:* Oberlin College, B.A., 1953; Harvard University, M.A., 1956, Ph.D., 1958.

ADDRESSES: Home—24 Agassiz St., Cambridge, MA 02140. *Office*—Department of Economics, Harvard University, Cambridge, MA 02138.

CAREER: University of California, Berkeley, 1957-62, began as assistant, became associate professor of economics; U.S. Government, Washington, D.C., deputy to special assistant to the president for foreign trade policy, 1961; Harvard University, Cambridge, MA, professor of economics, 1962—. Member, U.S. Budget Bureau Review Committee for Balance of Payments Statistics, 1964, and White House Task Force on Foreign Economic Policy, 1964. Consultant, U.S. Treasury Department, Council of Economic Advisers, 1960-61.

MEMBER: American Economic Association.

AWARDS, HONORS: Wells Prize, 1957-58, for *Trade and Economic Structure;* Kenan Enterprise Award, 1990.

WRITINGS:

(With Richard H. Holton) *The Canadian Economy: Prospect and Retrospect,* Harvard University Press, 1959.

Trade and Economic Structure, Harvard University Press, 1960.

Air Transport and Its Regulators, Harvard University Press, 1962.

American Industry: Structure, Conduct, Performance, Prentice-Hall, 1964, 7th revised edition, 1992.

(Co-editor and contributor) *Trade, Growth, and the Balance of Payments,* Rand McNally, 1965.

(With J. S. Bain and J. Margolis) *Northern California's Water Industry,* Johns Hopkins University Press, 1966.

(With others) *Britain's Economic Prospects,* Brookings Institution, 1968.

(With G. L. Reuber) *Capital Transfers and Economic Policy,* Harvard University Press, 1971.

(With J. A. Frankel and R. W. Jones) *World Trade and Payments,* Little, Brown, 1973, 6th revised edition, 1993.

(Co-editor and contributor) *Regulating the Product,* Ballinger, 1974.

(With M. Uekusa) *Industrial Organization in Japan,* Brookings Institution, 1976.

(With M. E. Porter and M. Spence) *Competition in the Open Economy,* Harvard University Press, 1980.

(Co-editor and contributor) *Britain's Economic Performance,* Brookings Institution, 1980.

Multinational Enterprise and Economic Analysis, Cambridge University Press, 1982.

(Co-editor and contributor) *The Australian Economy: A View from the North,* Brookings Institution, 1984.

(With S. W. Davies) *Britain's Productivity Gap,* Cambridge University Press, 1987.

(With D. R. Barton) *Efficiency in U.S. Manufacturing Industries,* MIT Press, 1990.

(With others) *Industrial Efficiency in Six Nations,* MIT Press, 1992.

Contributor to professional journals.

*   *   *

CHADWICK, (William) Owen 1916-

PERSONAL: Born May 20, 1916, in Bromley, Kent, England; son of John (a lawyer) and Edith Mary (Horrocks) Chadwick; married Ruth Hallward, December 28, 1949; children: Charles, Stephen, Helen, Andre. *Education:* St. John's College, Cambridge, B.A., 1939. *Religion:* Church of England.

ADDRESSES: Home—67 Grantchester St., Cambridge, England.

CAREER: Cambridge University, Cambridge, England, dean of Trinity Hall, 1949-56, master of Selwyn College, 1956-83, Dixie Professor of Ecclesiastical History, 1958-68, Regius Professor of Modern History, 1968-83.

MEMBER: British Academy (fellow), Royal Historical Society (fellow).

AWARDS, HONORS: D.D., University of St. Andrews, Oxford University, and University of Wales; D.L., University of Kent, Columbia University, University of East Anglia, University of Bristol, and University of Leeds; LL.D., University of Aberdeen; Wolfson Prize for history, 1981, for *The Popes and European Revolution.*

WRITINGS:

John Cassian, Cambridge University Press, 1959, revised edition, 1968.

The Founding of Cuddesdon, Oxford University Press, for Cuddesdon College, 1954, revised edition, 1990.

From Bossuet to Newman, Cambridge University Press, 1957.

(Editor) *Western Asceticism,* S.C.M. Press, 1958, Westminster, 1979.

Creighton on Luther, Cambridge University Press, 1959.

Mackenzie's Grave, Hodder & Stoughton, 1959.

Victorian Miniature, Hodder & Stoughton, 1960, Cambridge University Press, 1991.

(Editor) *The Mind of the Oxford Movement,* A. & C. Black, 1960, Stanford University Press, 1961, revised edition published as *The Spirit of the Oxford Movement: Tractarian Essays,* Cambridge University Press, 1990.

(Editor with G. Nuttall) *From Uniformity to Unity, 1662-1962,* S.P.C.K., 1962.

Westcott and the University, Cambridge University Press, 1962.

The Reformation, Penguin, 1964.

The Victorian Church, A. & C. Black, Volume I, 1966, 3rd edition, Barnes & Noble, 1979, Volume II, 1970, 2nd edition, Barnes & Noble, 1979.

Acton and Gladstone, Athlone Press, 1976.

The Secularization of the European Mind, Cambridge University Press, 1977.

Catholicism and History, Cambridge University Press, 1977.

The Popes and European Revolution, Clarendon Press (of Oxford University), 1981.

Newman, Clarendon Press (of Oxford University), 1983.

Hensley Henson: A Study in the Friction between Church and State, Clarendon Press (of Oxford University), 1983.

History, Society and the Churches, edited by Derek Beales and Geoffrey Best, Cambridge University Press, 1985.

Britain and the Vatican during the Second World War, Cambridge University Press, 1986.

Michael Ramsey: A Life, Clarendon Press (of Oxford University), 1990.

The Christian Church in the Cold War, Penguin, 1992.

Editor, with brother Henry Chadwick, of "The Oxford History of the Christian Church" series, 1981—. Contributor to *Times* (London), *New Statesman, Spectator, Manchester Guardian, Sunday Times, Observer, Independent,* and to history and ecclesiastical history journals.

Several of Chadwick's works have been translated into French, Italian, Portuguese, Serbo-Croatian, Dutch, and Polish.

ADAPTATIONS: Mackenzie's Grave was adapted for a radio drama.

WORK IN PROGRESS: Studies in modern church history.

SIDELIGHTS: "Nobody in England is better equipped to write 'a study in the friction between Church and State' than Professor Owen Chadwick," writes Eric James in a London *Times* review of *Hensley Henson: A Study in the Friction between Church and State.* Chadwick, a scholar of European religious history, is widely recognized by British critics as being among the leaders in his field. In a London *Times* review of *The Popes and European Revolution,* Earnon Duffy notes that Chadwick's "eye for significant detail is unerring, his enjoyment of a good story manifest, his knowledge of primary and secondary sources in Italian, German and Spanish unrivalled. . . . Chadwick the historian is neither preacher nor judge, but a confessor, not a lion but a lamb." Derek Beales also praises *The Popes and European Revolution* in a *Times Literary*

Supplement review: "This is a long book, and so concisely written that any summary of its argument or indication of its contents is sure to seem unsatisfactory to a reader. The theme is a great one, and the novelty of the author's perspective . . . makes it original in conception as well as material." While Ian Ker notes in a *Times Literary Supplement* review of *Newman* that the book is "on the whole balanced and reliable," he finds the short work disappointing because, among other reasons, the study "is . . . too narrowly religious and theological." Chadwick's biography of Hensley Henson, conversely, has drawn a warm reception from *Times Literary Supplement* contributor Michael Ramsey, who writes: "There cannot be many biographies in which the story of the man and the history of his times more fascinatingly illustrate one another."

BIOGRAPHICAL/CRITICAL SOURCES:

PERIODICALS

Times (London), March 26, 1981; August 11, 1983.
Times Literary Supplement, August 28, 1982; April 1, 1983; August 19, 1983.

*   *   *

CHARLES, Nicholas J.
See KUSKIN, Karla (Seidman)

*   *   *

CHESTER, Deborah   1957-
(Jay D. Blakeney, Sean Dalton)

PERSONAL: Born April 25, 1957, in Chicago, IL; daughter of Kern E. (a chiropractor) and Ann (an image consultant; maiden name, Hatcher) Chester. *Education:* University of Oklahoma, B.A. (with honors), 1978, M.A., 1986. *Religion:* Church of Christ. *Avocational interests:* Gardening, needlework.

ADDRESSES: Home—Norman, OK.

CAREER: Writer, 1978—.

AWARDS, HONORS: The Sign of the Owl was named to the Best Books for Young Adults list, American Library Association, 1981; named Oklahoma Writer of the Year, 1985.

WRITINGS:

The Sign of the Owl (juvenile), Four Winds, 1981.

NOVELS

A Love So Wild, Coward, 1980.
French Slippers, Coward, 1981.
Royal Intrigue, Dell, 1982.

Heart's Desire, Avon, 1983.
Captured Hearts, Harlequin, 1989.

UNDER PSEUDONYM JAY D. BLAKENEY

The Children of Anthi, Ace Books, 1985.
The Omcri Matrix, Ace Books, 1986.
The Goda War, Ace Books, 1989.
Requiem for Anthi, Ace Books, 1990.

UNDER PSEUDONYM SEAN DALTON

Space Hawks, Ace Books, 1990.
Code Name Peregrine, Ace Books, 1990.
Beyond the Void, Ace Books, 1990.
The Rostma Lure, Ace Books, 1991.
Destination Mutiny, Ace Books, 1991.
The Salukan Gambit, Ace Books, 1991.
Time Trap, Ace Books, 1992.
Showdown, Ace Books, 1992.
Pieces of Eight, Ace Books, 1992.

OTHER

Also author of other books. Contributor to *Good Housekeeping. A Love So Wild* has been published in German; *Heart's Desire* has been published in Italian.

WORK IN PROGRESS: A medical thriller; a science fiction novel.

SIDELIGHTS: Deborah Chester told *CA:* "Several of my books have been published in foreign editions. *A Love So Wild* was published in Great Britain and Germany. *French Slippers* was published in Great Britain. It also was condensed in *Good Housekeeping* magazine. *Royal Intrigue* was published in Great Britain. *Heart's Desire* was published in Italy.

"The three authors who had the greatest impact on my early development as a writer were Andre Norton, Alastair MacLean, and Georgette Heyer. They are no longer my favorites, but during my formative years, they provided me with hours of enjoyment, and I credit their work with helping shape my desire to become a writer. Andre Norton's tales of science fiction and fantasy spurred my childhood imagination. Her vivid style and original viewpoint taught me how to look at the world around me through different, even multiple perspectives. Alastair Maclean's adventure novels held excitement, danger on every page, riveting suspense, and fast pace. Even to this day, I am happiest writing stories that incorporate as many of those elements as possible. Georgette Heyer's Regency romances opened a whole new world to me, a world of elegance, style, and wit. The first novel I published was a Regency, written from my fascination with an era brought to life through Heyer's work. So in part, I must attribute that breakthrough in my early career to her influence.

"In the past ten years, one writer who has influenced me a great deal has been Dean Koontz. I admire the way he has built his career from category to mainstream. Of course I have many other favorite writers. I read constantly; being a bookworm is what got me into the writing business in the first place. As Flaubert said, 'Reading is to the mind what exercise is to the body.'

"I started writing at an early age, but even a nine-year-old writer can find it hard to get published. I discovered that talent and story ideas weren't enough. I needed knowledge of the writing craft if I was ever going to get anywhere, and I started learning all I could. By the time I'd finished high school, I'd written a few novels, countless short stories, and a bit of bad poetry, none of which sold. Going to the University of Oklahoma to major in professional writing was the smartest thing I ever did. The intense training in craft which I received there finally enabled me to harness my spark of talent and do something salable with it. The instructors were published novelists who knew what they were talking about. And it was through contacts made at the university that I got my first agent, wrote my first publishable manuscripts, and began to sell at age 21.

"I am not a 'literary' writer in the sense that I attempt to create a heavily thematic book awash in symbolism and designed to be read and understood only by an erudite few. My purpose in writing is to entertain myself and my readers. I want to give people their money's worth by providing them with a story that is fun to read. To me, the highest compliment I can receive from a reader is, 'I stayed up all night to finish your book because I couldn't put it down.'

"My work habits have changed over the years. I used to write one book a year, taking off about three months between projects. Then I started writing on a computer, and my productivity has increased steadily ever since. Writing nine series novels (the 'Operation Starhawks' series and 'Time Trap' series) in three years really forced me to exercise self-discipline. With a book deadline every four months, I couldn't write at a leisurely pace. I set myself a strict daily page quota to be sure I met my deadlines. My ideal schedule, however, is where I produce about 50 pages a week. No matter what, I think it's very important that I always work steadily on a book, because that keeps my momentum going. It also keeps my mind on the novel, and that helps me avoid mistakes with plot or characterization. I prefer to write an entire chapter at a sitting. If that's not possible, then I make sure I at least complete the scene I'm working on before I leave the keyboard. That keeps my emotional involvement with the characters and story at an optimum level.

"Every few years, I somehow find myself writing two books at once. *A Love So Wild* and *The Sign of the Owl* were written at the same time. Both books were successful. While I was writing the historical romance *Captured Hearts,* I found myself lured away by a science fiction idea. I ended up writing both of those at the same time. *Captured Hearts* sold; the sf book did not. I think one book at a time is best, although if the ideas are crowding too hard I'll usually give in. Letting a good idea grow cold is a shame, but splitting your attention too much between two demanding projects may or may not work.

"Although I have written several books sold on the basis of proposal or outline, I prefer to write on speculation. I have learned the necessity of outlining, but I would rather let a book grow in my mind, taking shape bit by bit. Whenever I get a piece of it grown, I outline that portion to see if the plot is going to hold together, then I let it grow some more. If the book is complex, I may revamp the whole synopsis several times over the course of the project. But to sit down cold and outline a book from start to finish, then stick with that to the letter—no, that's not for me. I'm usually halfway through the book before I begin to feel like I'm definitely on the right track. I figure my subconscious always knows how the book is going to turn out. What's important is for me to catch up with it, stick to story principles, and not get in its way.

"Who can say what motivates me to write? The story idea is the temptress, luring me out into the darkness, step by step, away from familiar ground. But without discipline, pride, professionalism, and the need to earn a living at this business, art alone won't bring it together. For me, writing is a profession, not a hobby."

*   *   *

CHITHAM, Edward (Harry Gordon) 1932-

PERSONAL: Born May 16, 1932, in Birmingham, England; son of Norman E. (an export official in steel tubing) and Elaine (Newman) Chitham; married Mary Tilley (in adult education), December 29, 1962; children: Eleanor M. E., John W. H., Rachel J. W. *Education:* Jesus College, Cambridge, B.A., 1955, M.A., 1959; University of Birmingham, Certificate in Education, 1956; University of Warwick, M.A., 1978; University of Sheffield, Ph.D., 1984. *Politics:* Liberal. *Religion:* Church of England.

ADDRESSES: Home—11 Victoria Rd., Harborne, Birmingham B17 0AG, England. *Office*—Education Consultant, National Association for Gifted Children, Park Campus, Boughton Green Road, Northampton NN2 7AL, England.

CAREER: Master in charge of Latin at grammar school, Old Hill, England, 1956-61, head of library department,

1961-67; Dudley College of Education, Dudley, England, lecturer, 1967-73, senior lecturer in English, 1973-77; Polytechnic Wolverhampton, Wolverhampton, England, senior lecturer in education, 1977-88; Newman College, Birmingham, England, part-time tutor, 1988—; University of Warwick, England, part-time tutor, 1991-92; tutor and counselor at Open University.

WRITINGS:

The Black Country (local history), Longman, 1972.
Ghost in the Water (children's novel), Longman, 1973.
The Poems of Anne Bronte, Macmillan, 1979.
(With Tom Winnifrith) *Bronte Facts and Bronte Problems,* Macmillan, 1983.
(With Winnifrith) *Selected Bronte Poems,* Basil Blackwell, 1985.
The Brontes' Irish Background, Macmillan, 1986.
A Life of Emily Bronte, Basil Blackwell, 1987.
A Life of Anne Bronte, Basil Blackwell, 1991.

Contributor to *Black Countryman.*

WORK IN PROGRESS: Poems of Emily Jane Bronte, with Derek Roper, for Oxford University Press; a project on gifted children under the age of six; a work on *Wuthering Heights.*

SIDELIGHTS: Edward Chitham once told *CA:* "I often find myself passionately defending 'lost' causes. To take two: Latin is a most fascinating language, and if you can be patient, it rewards you by giving an accurate and painstaking turn of mind, as well as access to wild and extraordinary mythology; Liberalism in Great Britain must be renewed. It may have an overoptimistic strand, but it is only by ending 'confrontation' politics that Britain can survive as a positive force into the twenty-first century.

"Although I work in education, I think teaching is an art where you need to throw away the textbooks and use your own God-given common sense."

*   *   *

CLARK, Eleanor 1913-

PERSONAL: Born July 6, 1913, in Los Angeles, CA; raised in Roxbury, CT; daughter of Frederick Huntington (a mining engineer) and Eleanor (Phelps) Clark; married Robert Penn Warren (Pulitzer Prize-winning author and poet), December 7, 1952 (deceased, 1989); children: Rosanna, Gabriel Penn. *Education:* Vassar College, B.A., 1934. *Avocational interests:* Skiing, tennis, gardening, music, theatre, travelling.

ADDRESSES: Home—2495 Redding Road, Fairfield, CT 06430.

CAREER: Writer. Worked as a free-lance writer and ghostwriter/editor for German refugee scholars, 1934-36; W. W. Norton & Co., New York City, editor, 1936-1939; U.S. Office of Strategic Services, Washington, DC, 1943-45.

MEMBER: National Institute of Arts and Letters, Corporation of Yaddo.

AWARDS, HONORS: Guggenheim fellowship for fiction, 1946, 1949; grant, National Institute of Arts and Letters, 1947, for literature; National Book Award, 1965, for *The Oysters of Locmariaquer.*

WRITINGS:

FICTION

The Bitter Box, Doubleday, 1946.
Baldur's Gate (Book-of-the-Month-Club selection), Pantheon, 1970.
Dr. Heart: A Novella, and Other Stories, Pantheon, 1974.
Gloria Mundi, Pantheon, 1979.
Camping Out, Putnam, 1986.

OTHER

(Editor, with Horace Gregory) *New Letters in America,* Norton, 1937.
(Translator) Ramon Jose Sender, *Dark Wedding,* Doubleday, Doran, 1943.
Rome and a Villa, Doubleday, 1952, expanded edition, Pantheon, 1975, with illustrations by Eugene German, Atheneum, 1980.
The Song of Roland (for children; part of "Legacy" series), Random House, 1960.
The Oysters of Locmariaquer, Pantheon, 1964.
Eyes, Etc.: A Memoir, Pantheon, 1977.
Tamrart: 13 Days in the Sahara, illustrated by Lucy Hamlin, Palaemon Press, 1984.

Also author of two plays performed at Yale University. Contributor of stories, plays, essays, and book reviews to anthologies and periodicals, including *Georgia Review, Kenyon Review, Nation, New England Review, New Republic, New Yorker, Partisan Review, Sewanee Review,* and *Southern Review.*

SIDELIGHTS: Although her name is unfamiliar to the general reading public, writer Eleanor Clark has received consistently high critical praise for both her novels and works of nonfiction. Winner of the 1965 National Book Award for *The Oysters of Locmariaquer,* Clark has been described by Stanley W. Lindberg in *Dictionary of Literary Biography* as "an original and serious artist . . . [demonstrating] an uncompromising avoidance of the formulaic best-seller approach, producing instead a relatively small but solidly impressive body of fiction and nonfiction that continues to merit attentive reading and

appreciation." Her inspiring descriptions of the people, places, and impressions gained through travels with her late husband, poet and fellow-novelist Robert Penn Warren, along with such notable novels as *Baldur's Gate* and *Gloria Mundi,* have proved Clark to be an uncompromising witness of the decline of both the moral and physical American landscape.

Clark's love for the land and culture of her native New England illuminates much of her work. Although born in California, she was raised in Roxbury, a small Connecticut town to which her family returned shortly after her birth. During her childhood, Clark was introduced to a variety of worlds: The provinciality of the one-room schoolhouse in her rural hometown was eventually replaced by a wholly different experience when she went abroad to attend convent schools in Italy and France. Returning eventually to New England, Clark finished her preparatory education at a private girl's school in affluent Greenwich, Connecticut. From there she moved to New York City to attend Vassar College where she wrote poetry and worked on literary magazines with fellow students Elizabeth Bishop and Muriel Rukeyser.

After graduating from Vassar in 1934, Clark spent several years as a free-lance writer, editor, and translator, and successfully publishing several short stories while working on a longer work of fiction. In 1946, she published her first novel, *The Bitter Box,* a reflection of the political consciousness she had gained during college as a witness to the economically unstable, war-torn 1930s. Called "a serious, funny, and truthful picture of Communist doings in this country, and therefore a work of courage" by reviewer Diana Trilling in the *Nation,* Clark's story of a innocent bank teller whose life and career are destroyed as a result of his naive involvement in the activities of a radical political group was praised by critics. Reviewer Kenneth Pitchford "delighted" in the novel's "perfect fictive technique," writing in the *New England Review* that "Clark succeeds here so brilliantly . . . at the detailed and striking depiction of a quotidian world that we recognize with a shock as our own."

After World War II, Clark made several extended trips to Italy which provided the inspiration for *Rome and a Villa,* sketches and essays about both the architectural monuments to Rome's historic past and the writer's impressions of the busy streets, commerce, and people that would carry it into the future. The book was widely praised by critics: Pearl K. Bell noted in the *New Leader* that "rarely has the love affair between a modern sensibility and an ancient locale—consummated in every glance, with every step—been more exuberantly recorded." After her marriage to Warren in 1952, Clark and her family traveled to Europe, a trip that inspired her award-winning account of a fishing community in Brittany, *The Oysters of Loc-mariaquer.*

Clark's works have always had a strong grounding in time and place, whether they be nonfictional accounts of her travels or novels. "I do not approach any place with the idea of writing about it. The place approaches me really," she once told Barbara Bannon in *Publishers Weekly.* "Both *Rome and a Villa* and *The Oysters of Locmariaquer* were as much about America as they are about Rome and Brittany. When you get that much of a wallop from other places you are really writing a kind of negative of your own place." Unlike these two earlier works, *Tamrart: 13 Days in the Sahara,* which Clark published in 1985, is a pure travelogue combining regional tales and useful information with details of the author's trip across the Sahara Desert. Although not as fictional a narrative as *Rome and a Villa* or *The Oysters, Tamrart* continues Clark's inspirational look at foreign lands: As Stephen Arkin noted of her travel writing in *New England Review,* "What rises so beautifully from her pages is a sense that lives are defined by a search for order and that home is the name we give to the place where, finally, we do not struggle to prevail but are simply accepted by ourselves and others as Odysseus was after many years away by his old dog. . . . [Clark] values pride in what one can do, deep feeling for where one settles, and she praises the strength that comes from having worked long and hard in a kind of cooperative opposition to the world."

In 1970, Clark published her second novel, *Baldur's Gate.* In what has been considered by critics to her major novel, the author examines the changing perspective of a woman who lives with her husband and young son in a manner much beneath that in which her once affluent family once lived. The struggle of the novel's protagonist to accept her situation is paralleled by her small New England town's inspired effort to break its identification with the relics of its colonial past and move towards a changing future. Published nine years after *Baldur's Gate,* Clark's *Gloria Mundi* depicts another small "paradise," a town in the Green Mountains of the author's beloved New England, and its fall under the bulldozers and earth-movers of a group of ruthless land developers. "If the portrait of the small town, seen through the varied lives of its inhabitants and its visitors, is one of Eleanor Clark's aims, her real aim is to communicate to us how she feels about the loss of rural values," noted Doris Grumbach in the *Chicago Tribune Book World.* Through its complex cast of many characters, *Gloria Mundi* depicts the transfer of the evils of urban "progress"—congestion, noise, violence, greed—to the simple Vermont countryside where the serenity of a way of life is destroyed. Praising Clark for her "elegant prose style [and] richly lyrical gift," reviewer Annalyn Swan nonetheless commented in *Time* that nonfiction

"better serves her discerning eye." Swan added that "Readers of [Clark's travel narratives] *Oysters* or *Rome and a Villa* will not be surprised to find that the best thing in *Gloria Mundi* is her evocation of New England's character and countryside." F.D. Reeve agreed, noting of Clark that the "countryside of her vision is so clear and distinct that we know that she has seen and felt and what its loss means," in *New England Quarterly.* "Oddly, there's a second glory—the glory that the glory of the earth *keeps* passing—as self-regenerating, after all, as the faith which bore this book and houses all her work."

In *Camping Out,* a novel published in 1986, Clark's beloved Vermont wilderness becomes "as malevolent as anything a woman from the city could imagine, and then some," according to Nancy Wigston in the Toronto *Globe & Mail.* Two female acquaintances go on an overnight camping trip only to cross paths with "Fred," an eloquent criminal whose violence towards the two women have an ironic impact upon their lives. A complex novel, *Camping Out* "continues to develop the themes that have obsessed her for so long," Carolyn Kizer wrote of author Clark in the *New York Times Book Review,* praising the energy with which the author invests her multi-level story: "As if [Clark] had summoned all her considerable powers to emit one pure Maenad shriek of fury at the masters of civilization and their degenerate get, who foul our world."

In addition to her novels and works of nonfiction, Clark has collected several short fictional works written over four decades into *Dr. Heart: A Novella, and Other Stories,* published in 1974 to mixed critical review. While Karen Durbin found the author's irony towards her characters "smug" in a review of the collection for *Ms.,* noting that "this tendency to adopt a superior stance toward her characters . . . badly mars *Dr. Heart,*" Peter Sourian noted in the *New York Times* that Clark's "cultivation . . . is an integral element in her art, an art which invites if it does not require a reciprocal cultivation on the part of her reader."

Eyes, Etc. is a memoir of Clark's experience dealing with macular degeneration, a condition of the eye that struck the writer in 1976, leaving her unable to see clearly. As an author and avid reader, the loss of her ability to read even large type without the use of a magnifying glass was difficult for Clark to bear. As she told Bannon, "I had no idea of any sort about *Eyes, Etc.* when I began writing it, except self-preservation. I, who had typed all my life, just began scribbling on huge drawing pads, using a series of Magic Marker pens." The book, completed in three months, begins "Try to write a page a day this way. Get used to it. Other people have." Lindberg commented on the "elliptically spontaneous flow" of the personal account and the challenge it poses to the reader. The voice running through Clark's diatribe on the arbitrary cruelties dealt out by life—not only to Clark, but to friends and acquaintances as well—is described by Joyce Carol Oates in the *New York Times Book Review* as "hardly meek and passive: stoic perhaps, but hardly 'accepting' of her fate in the usual sense of the word. . . . Her condition, at the start of the memoir, is simply defined: 'This is HELL.' " As with all her work, Clark's attitude in *Eyes, Etc.* is a reflection of her strong opinions and Yankee pragmatism. As Lindberg noted, "all of her writing—fictional and nonfictional—presents a wealth of visual detail as captured by a fiercely independent and perceptive observer."

BIOGRAPHICAL/CRITICAL SOURCES:

BOOKS

Clark, Eleanor, *Eyes, Etc.,* Pantheon, 1977.
Doepke, Dale K., "Eleanor Clark," *Contemporary Novelists,* St. James Press, 1986, pp. 183-84.
Lindberg, Stanley W., "Eleanor Clark," *Dictionary of Literary Biography,* Volume 6: *American Novelists since World War II,* Gale, 1980, pp. 48-54.

PERIODICALS

Chicago Tribute Book World, October 14, 1979.
Globe & Mail (Toronto), August 9, 1986.
Los Angeles Times Book Review, May 11, 1986, p. 3.
Ms., June, 1975, pp. 46, 83-85.
Nation, April 27, 1946; October 13, 1979, pp. 346-47.
New England Review, autumn, 1978, pp. 49-70; (special "Eleanor Clark" edition), winter, 1979, pp. 233-271.
New Leader, February 17, 1975, pp. 16-17.
New Republic, January 4, 1975, pp. 30-31; October 13, 1979, pp. 38-40.
Newsweek, October 17, 1977, pp. 114-116.
New York Times Book Review, January 12, 1975, p. 7; October 16, 1977, pp. 11, 40-41; September 16, 1979; May 5, 1985; May 4, 1986, p. 11.
Publishers Weekly, October 24, 1977, p. 6.
Time, September 4, 1979; July 7, 1986, pp. 61-62.
Washington Post Book World, January 26, 1975, p. 3; October 28, 1979, p. 4.*

—*Sketch by Pamela L. Shelton*

*   *   *

CLARKE, Hugh Vincent 1919-

PERSONAL: Born November 27, 1919, in Brisbane, Queensland, Australia; son of Patrick John (a publican) and Catherine (a secretary; maiden name, Goggin) Clarke; married Mary Patricia Ryan (a journalist), June 6, 1961; children: David, Bryan, John, Justin, Brigid. *Education:* Attended Teachers Training College, Brisbane, Australia, 1937, and Melbourne Technical College, 1947-48.

ADDRESSES: Home and office—14 Chermside St., Deakin, Australian Capital Territory, Australia.

CAREER: Worked as assistant surveyor for Old Main Roads Commission, 1945-46; Department of the Interior, Australia, senior survey computer, 1947-56; Department of External Territories, Canberra, Australian Capital Territory, Australia, director of information and publicity, 1966-73; Department of Aboriginal Affairs, Canberra, director of information and public relations, 1973-75; writer, 1975—. *Military service:* Australian Imperial Forces, bombardier, 1940-45; served in Malaya and Singapore; prisoner of war, 1942-45, in Singapore, Thailand, and Japan.

MEMBER: Australian Journalists Association, Society of Australian Authors, Canberra Historical Society.

WRITINGS:

The Tub (novel), Jacaranda, 1963.
(With Takeo Yamashita) *Breakout* (nonfiction; also see below), Horwitz, 1965.
(With Yamashita) *To Sydney by Stealth* (nonfiction; also see below), Horwitz, 1966.
The Long Arm (biography), J. S. Cumpston, 1974.
Fire One! (includes *Breakout* and *To Sydney by Stealth*), Angus & Robertson, 1978.
The Broke and the Broken, Boolarong Publications, 1982.
Last Stop Nagasaki, Allen & Unwin, 1984.
Twilight Liberation, Allen & Unwin, 1985.
A Life for Every Sleeper, Allen & Unwin, 1986.
(With Colin Burgess and Russell Braddon) *Prisoners of War,* Time-Life, 1988.
When the Balloon Went Up, Allen & Unwin, 1990.
(With Burgess) *Barbed Wire and Bamboo,* Allen & Unwin, 1992.

Also contributor to anthologies, including *Australia Writes,* 1953, and *Australia at Arms,* 1955. Contributor of articles and stories to periodicals.

Some of Clarke's books have been published in Japanese.

SIDELIGHTS: Hugh Vincent Clarke once described *The Tub* for *CA* readers as a "factual novel about P.O.W. life in Singapore, Thailand, and Japan." About some of his other earlier books, he added: "*Breakout* is the story of the biggest mass escape of P.O.W.s in British military history. Some one thousand Japanese prisoners broke out of a camp at Cowra, New South Wales, Australia, on August 5, 1944, and by morning, 231 of the escapees were shot dead. My next book, *To Sydney by Stealth,* details the episode of the Japanese midget submarine raid on Sydney Harbor on May 31, 1942. Three submarines entered the harbor and fired on the U.S.S. Chicago, but missed. Two of the enemy subs were then sink, while one escaped, although it was never seen again. *The Long Arm* is the biography of a mounted policeman in Arnhem Land and elsewhere in the Northern Territory before World War II. *The Broke and the Broken* is the story of a family living in the country towns of Owensland and Brisbane between 1926 and 1939."

* * *

COE, Michael Douglas 1929-

PERSONAL: Born May 14, 1929, in New York, NY; son of William Rogers and Clover (Simonton) Coe; married Sophie Dobzhansky, June 5, 1955; children: Nicholas, Andrew, Sarah, Peter, Natalie. *Education:* Harvard University, A.B., 1950, Ph.D., 1959.

ADDRESSES: Home—376 St. Ronan St., New Haven, CT 06511. *Office*—Peabody Museum, Yale University, New Haven, CT 06511-8161.

CAREER: University of Tennessee, Knoxville, assistant professor of anthropology, 1958-60; Yale University, New Haven, CT, 1960—, began as instructor, currently Charles J. MacCurdy Professor of Anthropology.

MEMBER: Royal Anthropological Institute, National Academy of Sciences, Sociedad Mexicana de Antropologia, Society for Historical Archaeology, Society for American Archaeology, Connecticut Academy of Arts and Sciences.

WRITINGS:

Mexico, Praeger, 1962, revised edition, Thames & Hudson, 1984.
The Jaguar's Children: Pre-Classical Central Mexico, Museum of Primitive Art, 1965.
The Maya, Praeger, 1966, 5th revised edition, Thames & Hudson, 1993.
An Early Stone Pectoral from Southeastern Mexico, Dumbarton Oaks, 1966.
(With Elizabeth P. Benson) *Three Maya Relief Panels at Dumbarton Oaks,* Dumbarton Oaks, 1966.
(With Kent V. Flannery) *Early Cultures and Human Ecology in South Coastal Guatemala,* Smithsonian Press, 1967.
America's First Civilization: Discovering the Olmec, American Heritage Press, 1968.
(Author of introductory text) *Pre-Columbian Mexican Miniatures,* Praeger, 1970.
The Maya Scribe and His World, Grolier Club, 1973.
Classic Maya Pottery at Dumbarton Oaks, Dumbarton Oaks, 1975.
The Lords of the Underworld: Masterpieces of Classical Maya Ceramics, Princeton University Press, 1978.
(With Richard A. Diehl) *In the Land of the Olmec,* University of Texas Press, 1980.

Old Gods and Young Heroes: The Pearlman Collection of Maya Ceramics, Israel Museum, 1982.
(With Gordon Whittaker) *Aztec Sorcerers in Seventeenth-Century Mexico,* Institute for Mesoamerican Studies, 1982.
(With Dean Snow and Benson) *Atlas of Ancient America,* Facts on File, 1986.
Breaking the Maya Code, Thames & Hudson, 1992.

Contributor to professional journals.

* * *

COETZEE, J(ohn) M(ichael) 1940-

PERSONAL: Born February 9, 1940, in Cape Town, South Africa; son of a sheep farmer; married, 1963 (divorced, 1980); children: Nicholas, Gisela. *Education:* University of Cape Town, B.A. 1960, M.A., 1963; University of Texas, Austin, Ph.D., 1969.

ADDRESSES: Home—P.O. Box 92, Rondebosch, Cape Province 7700, South Africa. *Agent*—Peter Lampack, 551 Fifth Ave., New York, NY 10017.

CAREER: International Business Machines (IBM), London, England, applications programmer, 1962-63; International Computers, Bracknell, Berkshire, England, systems programmer, 1964-65; State University of New York at Buffalo, assistant professor, 1968-71, Butler Professor of English, 1984, 1986; University of Cape Town, Cape Town, South Africa, lecturer in English, 1972-82, professor of general literature, 1983—; Johns Hopkins University, Hinkley Professor of English, 1986, 1989.

MEMBER: International Comparative Literature Association, Modern Language Association of America.

AWARDS, HONORS: CNA Literary Award, 1977, for *In the Heart of the Country;* CNA Literary Award, James Tait Black Memorial Prize, and Geoffrey Faber Award, all 1980, all for *Waiting for the Barbarians;* CNA Literary Award, Booker-McConnell Prize, and Prix Femina Etranger, all 1984, all for *The Life and Times of Michael K;* Jerusalem Prize for the Freedom of the Individual in Society, 1987. D. Litt., University of Strathclyde, Glasgow, 1985. Life Fellow, University of Cape Town.

WRITINGS:

Dusklands (two novellas), Ravan Press (Johannesburg), 1974, Penguin Books, 1985.
(Translator) Marcellus Emants, *A Posthumous Confession,* Twayne, 1976.
From the Heart of the Country (novel), Harper, 1977, published in England as *In the Heart of the Country,*

Secker & Warburg, 1977, reprinted as *In the Heart of the Country,* Penguin Books, 1982.

Waiting for the Barbarians (novel), Secker & Warburg, 1980, Penguin Books, 1982.

The Life and Times of Michael K (novel), Secker & Warburg, 1983, Viking, 1984.

(Translator) Wilma Stockenstroem, *The Expedition to the Baobab Tree,* Faber, 1983.

(Editor with Andre Brink) *A Land Apart: A Contemporary South African Reader,* Viking, 1987.

Foe (novel), Viking, 1987.

White Writing: On the Culture of Letters in South Africa (essays), Yale University Press, 1988.

Age of Iron, Random House, 1990.

Doubling the Point: Essays and Interviews, edited by David Attwell, Harvard University Press, 1992.

ADAPTATIONS: An adaptation of *In the Heart of the Country* was filmed as "Dust," by ICA (Great Britain), 1986.

SIDELIGHTS: Using his native South Africa as a backdrop, J. M. Coetzee explores the implications of oppressive societies on the lives of their inhabitants. As a South African, however, Coetzee is "too intelligent a novelist to cater for moralistic voyeurs," Peter Lewis declared in *Times Literary Supplement.* "This does not mean that he avoids the social and political crises edging his country towards catastrophe. But he chooses not to handle such themes in the direct, realistic way that writers of older generations, such as Alan Paton, preferred to employ. Instead, Coetzee has developed a symbolic and even allegorical mode of fiction—not to escape the living nightmare of South Africa but to define the psychopathological underlying the sociological, and in doing so to locate the archetypal in the particular."

Though his stories are set in South Africa, Coetzee's lessons are relevant to all countries, as *Books Abroad*'s Ursula A. Barnett wrote of *Dusklands,* which contains the novellas *The Vietnam Project* and *The Narrative of Jacobus Coetzee.* "By publishing the two stories side by side," Barnett remarked, "Coetzee has deliberately given a wider horizon to his South African subject. Left on its own, *The Narrative of Jacobus Coetzee* would immediately have suggested yet another tale of African black-white confrontation to the reader." Although each is a complete story, "their nature and design are such that the book can and should be read as a single work," Roger Owen commented in *Times Literary Supplement. Dusklands* "is a kind of diptych, carefully hinged and aligned, and of a texture so glassy and mirror-like that each story throws light on the other." Together the tales present two very different outcomes in confrontations between the individual and society.

The Vietnam Project introduces Eugene Dawn, employed to help the Americans win the Vietnam War through psychological warfare. The assignment eventually costs Dawn his sanity. The title character of *The Narrative of Jacobus Coetzee,* a fictionalized ancestor of the author, is an explorer and conqueror in the 1760s who destroys an entire South African tribe over his perception that the people have humiliated him through their indifference and lack of fear. H. M. Tiffin, writing in *Contemporary Novelists,* found that the novellas in *Dusklands* are "juxtaposed to offer a scarifying account of the fear and paranoia of imperialists and aggressors and the horrifying ways in which dominant regimes, 'empires,' commit violence against 'the other' through repression, torture, and genocide."

Coetzee's second novel, *In the Heart of the Country,* also explores racial conflict and mental deterioration. A spinster daughter, Magda, tells the story in diary form, recalling the consequences of her father's seduction of his African workman's wife. Both jealous of and repulsed by the relationship, Magda murders her father, then begins her own affair with the workman. The integrity of Magda's story eventually proves questionable. "The reader soon realizes that these are the untrustworthy ravings of a hysterical, demented individual consumed by loneliness and her love/hate relationship with her patriarchal father," Barend J. Toerien reported in *World Literature Today.* Magda's "thoughts range widely, merging reality with fantasy, composing and recomposing domestic dramas for herself to act in and, eventually introducing voices . . . to speak to her from the skies," Sheila Roberts noted in *World Literature Written in English.* "She imagines that the voices accuse her, among other things, of transforming her uneventful life into a fiction." *World Literature Today*'s Charles R. Larson, found *In the Heart of the Country* "a perplexing novel, to be sure, but also a fascinating novelistic exercise in the use of cinematic techniques in prose fiction," describing the book as reminiscent of an overlapping "series of stills extracted from a motion picture."

Coetzee followed *In the Heart of the Country* with *Waiting for the Barbarians,* in which the author, "with laconic brilliance, articulates one of the basic problems of our time—how to *understand* the mentality behind the brutality and injustice," Anthony Burgess wrote in *New York.* In the novel, a magistrate attempting to protect the peaceful nomad people of his district is imprisoned and tortured by the army that arrives at the frontier town to destroy the "barbarians" on behalf of the Empire. The horror of what he has seen and experienced affects the magistrate in inalterable ways, bringing changes in his personality that he cannot understand. Doris Grumbach, writing in *Los Angeles Times Book Review,* found *Waiting for the Barbar-*

ians a book with "universal reference," an allegory which can be applied to innumerable historical and contemporary situations. "Very soon it is apparent that the story, terrifying and unforgettable, is about injustice and barbarism inflicted everywhere by 'civilized' people upon those it invades, occupies, governs." "The intelligence Coetzee brings us in *Waiting for the Barbarians* comes straight from Scripture and Dostoevsky," Webster Schott asserted in *Washington Post Book World.* "We possess the devil. We are all barbarians."

In *Waiting for the Barbarians* Coetzee "succeeded in creating a tragic fable of colonialism that surpassed the boundaries of his native South Africa and made universal the agony of its conscience-stricken European protagonist," Christopher Lehmann-Haupt remarked in the *New York Times.* "In . . . *The Life and Times of Michael K,* Mr. Coetzee goes even further in the same direction." The story follows the title character as he helps his dying mother on a journey to her childhood home. She dies along the way, leaving Michael, a disfigured and supposedly slow-witted young man, to fend for himself in a country at war. "Mr. Coetzee's landscapes of suffering are defined by the little by little art of moral disclosure—his stories might be about anyone and anyplace," Cynthia Ozick commented in *New York Times Book Review.* "At the same time they defy the vice of abstraction; they are engrossed in the minute and the concrete. It would be possible, following Mr. Coetzee's dazzlingly precise illuminations, to learn how to sow, or use a pump, or make a house of earth." In a review for *Maclean's,* Mark Abley found that the book "begins as a study of an apparently ordinary man; it develops into a portrait of an exceptional human being, written with unusual power and beauty."

Coetzee's work is often compared to that of Franz Kafka, a reference that appears in many reviews of *The Life and Times of Michael K.* In *Chicago Tribune Book World,* Charles R. Larson described the author as "writing from a tradition that might be identified as Kafkaesque," noting that Michael K. "shares the same initial as Kafka's heroes. Moreover, the world in which he tries to operate is unknowable in many of the same ways as Kafka's inexplicable reality. South Africa, one concludes, has become the reality of Kafka's nightmares."

Foe, a retelling of Daniel Defoe's *Robinson Crusoe,* marked a transitional stage for Coetzee, according to Maureen Nicholson in *West Coast Review.* Nicholson found many areas in which *Foe* differs from Coetzee's previous work. "Coetzee initially appeared to me to have all but abandoned his usual concerns and literary techniques" in *Foe,* Nicholson commented. "I was mistaken. More importantly, though, I was worried about why he has chosen *now* to write this kind of book; I found his shift of focus and technique ominous. Could he no longer sustain the

courage he had demonstrated [in *Waiting for the Barbarians* and *The Life and Times of Michael K*], turning instead to a radically interiorized narrative?" Nicholson concluded, "Perhaps *Foe* is best viewed as a pause for recapitulation and evaluation, transitional in Coetzee's development as a writer." Ashton Nichols, however, writing in *Southern Humanities Review,* found that Coetzee had not strayed far from his usual topics. "Like all of Coetzee's earlier works, *Foe* retains a strong sense of its specifically South African origins, a sociopolitical subtext that runs along just below the surface of the narrative," Nichols remarked. The reviewer emphasized Coetzee's role as "an archeologist of the imagination, an excavator of language who testifies to the powers and weaknesses of the words he discovers," a role Coetzee has performed in each of his novels, including *Foe.* Central to this idea are the mute Friday, whose tongue was cut out by slavers, and Susan Barton, the castaway who struggles to communicate with him. Daniel Foe, the author who endeavors to tell Barton's story, is also affected by Friday's speechlessness. Both recognize their duty to provide a means by which Friday can relate the story of his escape from the fate of his fellow slaves who drowned, still shackled, when their ship sank, but also question their right to speak for him. "The author, whether Foe or Coetzee, . . . wonders if he has any right to speak for the one person whose story most needs to be told," Nichols noted. "Friday is . . . the tongueless voice of millions."

While he found *Foe* somewhat lighthearted in places, *Tribune Books*'s John Blades also recognized the serious element embedded in the story. Noting that readers familiar with *Robinson Crusoe* will enjoy Coetzee's "mischievous little touches," such as replacing the goats on the island with apes, thereby forcing Cruso (Coetzee's spelling) to wear "apeskin" clothing, Blades remarked that the author "is not simply an exalted mischief maker," and concluded that in *Foe* "what is now considered a preadolescent classic is transformed into an infinitely intriguing adult conundrum, a vessel that overflows with mystery and allusion, a novel that is both a funhouse and a madhouse." In a *New York Times* review, Michiko Kakutani asserted that in *Foe* "the operative forces are not so much history or politics as art and imagination—how can one individual's story be apprehended and translated through language by another?" Kakutani concluded that *Foe* "—which remains somewhat solipsistically concerned with literature and its consequences—lacks the fierceness and moral resonance of *Barbarians* and *Michael K,* and yet it stands, nonetheless, as a finely honed testament to its author's intelligence, imagination, and skill."

In *Age of Iron* Coetzee at last addresses the crisis of South Africa in direct, rather than allegorical, form. The story of Mrs. Curren, a retired professor dying of cancer and attempting to deal with the realities of apartheid in Cape Town, *Age of Iron* is "an unrelenting yet gorgeously written parable of modern South Africa, . . . a story filled with foreboding and violence about a land where even the ability of children to love is too great a luxury," Michael Dorris wrote in *Tribune Books.* As her disease and the chaos of her homeland progress, Mrs. Curren feels the effects her society has had on its black members; her realization that "now my eyes are open and I can never close them again" forms the basis for her growing rage against the system. After her housekeeper's son and his friend are murdered in her home, Mrs. Curren runs away and hides beneath an overpass, leaving her vulnerable to attack by a gang. She is rescued by Vercueil, a street person she has gradually allowed into her house and her life, who returns her to her home and tends to her needs as the cancer continues its destruction. The book takes the form of a letter from Mrs. Curren to her daughter, living in the United States because she cannot tolerate apartheid. "Dying is traditionally a process of withdrawal from the world," Sean French commented in *New Statesman and Society.* "Coetzee tellingly reverses this and it is in her last weeks that [Mrs. Curren] first truly goes out in the baffling society she has lived in." As her life ends, Mrs. Curren's urgency to correct the wrongs she never before questioned intensifies. "In this chronicle of an aged white woman coming to understand, and of the unavoidable claims of her country's black youth, Mr. Coetzee has created a superbly realized novel whose truths cut to the bone," Lawrence Thornton declared in *New York Times Book Review.* In a *Washington Post Book World* review, Michael Heyward found that *Age of Iron,* "like Coetzee's other novels, leaves an indelible image of the South Africa it is set in— but it is not simply a novel about politics or nationality. The detail with which Coetzee inscribes Mrs. Curren's inner life makes this an absorbing book, a powerful account of an old woman's descent into death."

Coetzee's nonfiction works include *White Writing: On the Culture of Letters in South Africa* and *Doubling the Point: Essays and Interviews.* In *White Writing,* the author "collects his critical reflections on the mixed fortunes of 'white writing' in South Africa, 'a body of writing [not] different in nature from black writing,' but 'generated by the concerns of people no longer European, yet not African,'" Shaun Irlam observed in *MLN.* The seven essays included in the book discuss writings from the late seventeenth century to the present, through which Coetzee examines the foundations of modern South African writers' attitudes. Irlam described the strength of *White Writing* as its ability "to interrogate succinctly and lucidly the presuppositions inhabiting the language with which 'white writers' have addressed and presumed to ventriloquize Africa." In *Rocky Mountain Review of Language and Literature,* Barbara Temple-Thurston noted, "Coetzee's book reiterates

impressively how cultural ideas and language bind and limit the way in which we interpret our world." In *Doubling the Point: Essays and Interviews,* a collection of critical essays on Samuel Beckett, Franz Kafka, D. H. Lawrence, Nadine Gordimer, and others, Coetzee presents a "literary autobiography," according to Ann Irvine in a *Library Journal* review. Discussions of issues including censorship and popular culture and interviews with the author preceding each section round out the collection.

In addition to his writing, Coetzee produces translations of works in Dutch, German, French, and Afrikaans, serves as editor for others' work, and teaches at the University of Cape Town. "He's a rare phenomenon, a writer-scholar," Ian Glenn, a colleague of Coetzee's, told *Washington Post's* Allister Sparks. "Even if he hadn't had a career as a novelist he would have had a very considerable one as an academic." Coetzee told Sparks that he finds writing burdensome. "I don't like writing so I have to push myself," he said. "It's bad if I write but it's worse if I don't." Coetzee hesitates to discuss his works in progress, and views his opinion of his published works as no more important than that of anyone else. "The writer is simply another reader when it is a matter of discussing the books he has already written," he told Sparks. "They don't belong to him any more and he has nothing privileged to say about them—while the book he is engaged in writing is far too private and important a matter to be talked about."

BIOGRAPHICAL/CRITICAL SOURCES:

BOOKS

Contemporary Literary Criticism, Gale, Volume 23, 1983, Volume 33, 1985, Volume 66, 1991.
Contemporary Novelists, fourth edition, St. James Press, 1986, pp. 190-191.

PERIODICALS

Africa Today, third quarter, 1980.
America, September 25, 1982.
Books Abroad, spring, 1976.
Books in Canada, August/September, 1982.
British Book News, April, 1981.
Chicago Tribune Book World, April 25, 1982; January 22, 1984, section 14, p. 27.
Christian Science Monitor, December 12, 1983.
Encounter, October, 1977; January, 1984.
Globe and Mail (Toronto), August 30, 1986.
Library Journal, June 1, 1992, p. 124.
Listener, August 18, 1977.
Los Angeles Times Book Review, May 23, 1982, p. 4; January 15, 1984; February 22, 1987.
Maclean's, January 30, 1984, p. 49.
MLN, December, 1988, pp. 1147-1150.

New Republic, December 19, 1983.
New Statesman and Society, September 21, 1990, p. 40.
Newsweek, May 31, 1982; January 2, 1984; February 23, 1987.
New York, April 26, 1982, pp. 88, 90.
New Yorker, July 12, 1982.
New York Review of Books, December 2, 1982; February 2, 1984.
New York Times, December 6, 1983, p. C22; February 11, 1987; April 11, 1987.
New York Times Book Review, April 18, 1982; December 11, 1983, pp. 1, 26; February 22, 1987; September 23, 1990, p. 7.
Rocky Mountain Review of Language and Literature, Volume 53, Nos. 1-2, 1989, pp. 85-87.
Southern Humanities Review, fall, 1987, pp. 384-386.
Spectator, December 13, 1980; September 20, 1986.
Time, March 23, 1987.
Times (London), September 29, 1983; September 11, 1986; May 28, 1988.
Times Literary Supplement, July 22, 1977; November 7, 1980, p. 1270; January 14, 1983; September 30, 1983; September 23, 1988.
Tribune Books (Chicago), February 15, 1987, pp. 3, 11; September 16, 1990, section 14, p. 3.
Village Voice, March 20, 1984.
Voice Literary Supplement, April, 1982.
Washington Post, October 29, 1983.
Washington Post Book World, May 2, 1982, pp. 1-2, 12; December 11, 1983; March 8, 1987; September 23, 1990, pp. 1, 10.
West Coast Review, spring, 1987, pp. 52-58.
World Literature Today, spring, 1978, pp. 245-247; summer, 1978, p. 510; autumn, 1981.
World Literature Written in English, spring, 1980, pp. 19-36.*

—*Sketch by Deborah A. Stanley*

*   *   *

COHEN, Sharleen Cooper

PERSONAL: Born in Los Angeles, CA; daughter of Sam (a film producer and director) and Claretta (a teacher and artist; maiden name, Ellis) White; married R. Gary Cooper, December 18, 1960 (died February, 1971); married Martin L. Cohen (a psychiatrist and corporate management consultant), August 27, 1972; children: (first marriage) Cambria Lee, Dalisa Robin. *Education:* Attended University of California, Berkeley, 1957-58, University of California, Los Angeles, 1958-61, and Los Angeles Valley College, 1973-75.

ADDRESSES: Home—16170 Clear Valley Pl., Encino, CA 91436. *Agent*—Elaine Markson Literary Agency, Inc., 44 Greenwich Ave., New York, NY 10011.

CAREER: Designs on You (interior design firm), Los Angeles, CA, owner, 1965-77; writer, 1977—. United Jewish Appeal, member of Women of Distinction and executive committee; member of California State Council of the Humanities, 1991-92.

MEMBER: Authors Guild, Authors League of America, Screen Writers Guild of America, American Film Institute, National Gaucher Foundation (member of board; chairperson of Los Angeles chapter), PEN Los Angeles.

AWARDS, HONORS: Certificates of merit, Santa Barbara Writers Conference, 1977, for story "A Touch of Kindness," and 1978, for story "The Sculpture."

WRITINGS:

NOVELS

The Day after Tomorrow, Dell, 1979.
Regina's Song, Dell, 1980.
The Ladies of Beverly Hills, Delacorte, 1983.
Marital Affairs, Macmillan, 1985.
Love, Sex, and Money, Dutton, 1988.
Lives of Value, Warner Books, 1991.

OTHER

Writer for television series *Corbin and Corbin.* Contributor of interior designs to magazines, including *Architectural Digest, House and Garden,* and *House Beautiful.*

Many of Cohen's novels have been translated into Norwegian, Spanish, and Italian.

WORK IN PROGRESS: A novel, *Innocent Gestures;* a full-length play, *Solomon and Sheba.*

SIDELIGHTS: Sharleen Cooper Cohen grew up in California in a family of motion picture pioneers. She once told *CA:* "The single most important factor in my becoming a writer was the death of my first husband of cancer, at age thirty-three. I turned to writing as a source of expression for my grief. My daughters, both young women now, have made the adjustment to their new adopted father, and I place family unity and solidarity above all else in my life."

She later added: "As I continue writing, the path of my career has been crossed by many and varied experiences, and much rejection. It never gets easy, the business of writing, but I cannot do anything else; it compels me. One of my novels, *The Ladies of Beverly Hills,* was optioned by a producer for television, but it has not been produced. Having something of mine produced on screen or television is only the icing on the cake. Having my readers say they loved my book, or it made them cry is the ultimate compliment. That is why I write, not only to express and reveal myself, but to move others, to make them feel, and reflect on their lives, and perhaps be entertained, but most of all to share the universal experience of living in my own particular way. If my readers identify with my characters it is because my characters express truths or emotions understandable by all of us."

BIOGRAPHICAL/CRITICAL SOURCES:

PERIODICALS

Arizona Daily Star, April 10, 1983.
Bethlehem Globe, July 19, 1979.
Beverly Hills People, July 18, 1979.
Complete Woman, December, 1988.
Derby Evening Telegraph, December 6, 1979.
Evening Post (Reading, England), January 2, 1980.
Good Housekeeping, October, 1990.
Jewish Journal, May 29, 1992.
Lancaster Sunday News, July 15, 1979.
Northshore, November, 1988.
Tennessean, May 18, 1979.*

*   *   *

COLE, J. P.
See COLE, John P(eter)

*   *   *

COLE, John P(eter) 1928-
(J. P. Cole)

PERSONAL: Born December 9, 1928, in Sydney, New South Wales, Australia; son of Philip (an artist) and Marjorie (Pickford) Cole; married Isabel Urrunaga, June 21, 1952; children: Francis John, Richard Philip. *Education:* University of Nottingham, B.A., M.A., Ph.D.; additional study, Pavia University, 1950-51.

ADDRESSES: Home—10, Ranmore Close, Beeston, Nottingham NG9 3FR, England. *Office*—Department of Geography, University of Nottingham, Nottingham NG7 2RD, England.

CAREER: University of Reading, Reading, England, assistant lecturer in geography, 1955-56; University of Nottingham, Nottingham, England, lecturer, 1956-69, reader, 1969-75, professor of regional geography, 1975—. *Military service:* Royal Navy, two years; became lieutenant commander in the reserve.

MEMBER: Royal Geographical Society.

AWARDS, HONORS: Honorary D.Litt. from University of Nottingham.

WRITINGS:

Gli squilibri territoriali, Franco Angeli, 1984.

UNDER NAME J. P. COLE

La geografia urbana de la Gran Lima, National Planning Office of Peru, 1957.
Geography of World Affairs, Penguin, 1959, 6th edition, Butterworth, 1983.
(With F. C. German) *A Geography of the U.S.S.R.,* Butterworth, 1961, 2nd edition published as *A Geography of the U.S.S.R.: The Background of a Planned Economy,* 1970.
Italy, Chatto & Windus, 1964, published as *Italy: An Introductory Geography,* Praeger, 1966.
Latin America: An Economic and Social Geography, Butterworth, 1965, 2nd revised edition, 1975.
(With C. A. M. King) *Qualitative Geography: Techniques and Theories in Geography,* Wiley, 1968.
(With N. J. Beynon) *New Ways in Geography,* Blackwell, 1968.
Situations in Human Geography: A Practical Approach, Blackwell, 1975.
(With P. M. Mather) *Peru, 1940-2000: Performance and Prospects,* Department of Geography, University of Nottingham, 1978.
The Development Gap, Wiley, 1981.
Geography of the Soviet Union, Butterworth, 1984.
China, 1950-2000: Performance and Prospects, Department of Geography, Nottingham University, 1985.
Development and Underdevelopment: A Profile of the Third World, Methuen, 1986.
(With T. Buck) *Soviet Economic Performance,* Blackwell, 1987.
(With son, Francis John Cole) *The Geography of the European Community,* Routlege, 1993.

*   *   *

COLE, John Y(oung), Jr. 1940-

PERSONAL: Born July 30, 1940, in Ellensburg, WA; son of John Y. (a banker) and Alice (Van Leuven) Cole; married Nancy E. Gwinn (a librarian), April 28, 1973. *Education:* University of Washington, Seattle, B.A., 1962, M.L.S., 1963; Johns Hopkins University, M.L.A., 1966; George Washington University, Ph.D., 1971.

ADDRESSES: Home—7206 Lenhart Dr., Chevy Chase, MD 20815. *Office*—Center for the Book, Library of Congress, Washington, DC 20540.

CAREER: Library of Congress, Washington, D.C., librarian and library administrator, 1966-75, chairman of Librarian's Task Force on Goals, Organization, and Planning, 1976, executive director of Center for the Book, 1977—. Associate professorial lecturer at George Washington University, 1977. *Military service:* U.S. Army, 1963-66; became first lieutenant.

MEMBER: American Library Association, Organization of American Historians.

WRITINGS:

For Congress and the Nation: A Chronological History of the Library of Congress, Library of Congress, 1979.

EDITOR

Ainsworth Rand Spofford: Bookman and Librarian, Libraries Unlimited, 1975.
Television, the Book, and the Classroom, Library of Congress, 1978.
The Library of Congress in Perspective, Bowker, 1978.
Responsibilities of the American Book Community, Library of Congress, 1981.
Books in Action: The Armed Services Editions, Library of Congress, 1984.
The Community of the Book: A Directory of Selected Organizations and Programs, Library of Congress, 1986.
Biography and Books, Library of Congress, 1986.
Book Collectors of Stanford, California State Library, 1991.
Jefferson's Legacy: A Brief History of the Library of Congress, Library of Congress, 1993.

WORK IN PROGRESS: Research on history of books and libraries in American society, with emphasis on the Library of Congress.

*   *   *

CONYBEARE, Charles Augustus
   See ELIOT, T(homas) S(tearns)

*   *   *

COOK, Robin   1940-

PERSONAL: Born May 4, 1940, in New York, NY; son of Edgar Lee (an artist) and Audrey (Koons) Cook; married Barbara Ellen Mougin (an actress), July 18, 1979. *Education:* Wesleyan University, B.A., 1962; Columbia University, M.D., 1966; postgraduate study at Harvard University. *Avocational interests:* Skiing, surfing, painting, cooking.

ADDRESSES: Home—6001 Pelican Bay Blvd., Naples, FL 33963-8166. *Office*—c/o G. P. Putnam's Sons, 51 Madison Ave., New York, NY 10010-1603. *Agent*—

William Morris Agency, 1350 Avenue of the Americas, New York, NY 10019.

CAREER: Queen's Hospital, Honolulu, HI, resident in general surgery, 1966-68; Massachusetts Eye and Ear Infirmary, Boston, resident in ophthalmology, 1971-75, staff member, 1975—. Clinical instructor at Harvard Medical School, 1972. *Military service:* U.S. Navy, 1969-71; became lieutenant commander.

WRITINGS:

NOVELS

The Year of the Intern, Harcourt, 1972.
Coma, Little, Brown, 1977.
Sphinx (also see below), Putnam, 1979.
Brain, Putnam, 1981.
Fever, Putnam, 1982.
Godplayer, Putnam, 1983.
Mindbend, Putnam, 1985.
Outbreak, Putnam, 1987.
Mortal Fear, Putnam, 1988.
Mutation, Putnam, 1989.
Harmful Intent, Putnam, 1990.
Vital Signs, Putnam, 1990.
Blindsight, Putnam, 1991.
Terminal, Putnam, 1992.

OTHER

(Adaptor) *Sphinx: Movie Edition,* New American Library, 1981.

Cook's works have been translated into Spanish.

ADAPTATIONS: Coma was adapted for film and released by United Artists, 1978; *Sphinx* was adapted for film by John Byrum and released by Orion, 1981; *Mutation* was adapted for film and released by Warner Brothers, 1990; *Brain* and *Fever* are both scheduled for production as motion pictures.

WORK IN PROGRESS: Another medically oriented novel.

SIDELIGHTS: Eye surgeon Robin Cook writes best selling medical mystery thrillers that are admired for their topical themes and technical facts concerning the medical world. It is important to Cook to be able to relay information about the moral and social issues in the medical profession to the general public through his stories. "Practically nobody, including most doctors, pays attention to the problem or reads the editorials in the *New England Journal of Medicine,*" explains Cook in an interview with Sandy Rovner for the *Washington Post.* "I decided early on that I would couch my stories as thrillers. It was an opportunity to get the public interested in things about medicine they didn't seem to know about." Cook's novels typically place a good doctor in a struggle against people who are abusing the medical establishment. The abusers include other doctors selfishly protecting their businesses, lawyers greedily pursuing malpractice cases, and pharmaceutical firms illicitly ensuring the use of their product. "Cook's technique," writes Rovner, "is to take a particular issue and weave it into a suspenseful, mildly sexual, occasionally gory story that requires little more than a two-hour investment and takes his medical 'problem' to a logical if fanciful conclusion."

Cook had not fully developed this technique in his first book, *The Year of the Intern.* He began writing this story on a submarine in the Pacific, just after being drafted into the military. When the book failed to make the best seller list, Cook set out to discover why. He read dozens of successful novels, studying plots and characterizations, trying to tap the elements that most appealed to the reading public. Concentrating particularly on suspense fiction, Cook decided on a formula that combined medicine and murder, focusing on the macabre side of the healing arts.

Cook's subsequent novel, *Coma,* proved a huge success. In it, he weaves a suspense tale revealing a black market in human organs. Intern Susan Wheeler encounters mysterious deaths at her first day on the job at Boston Memorial; she spends the rest of the novel trying to convince unbelieving police and hospital officials of the conspiracy while being chased by the criminals. Charles J. Keffer, in *Best Sellers,* pronounces *Coma* "an absolutely fascinating story" whose descriptions of technical terms and medical procedures lead to deep reader involvement. "I do not think anyone can beat the suspense and the story line developed throughout this novel," he adds. *New York Times* contributor Mel Watkins reiterates the compliment, admiring Cook's skillful plot development, which thrusts the protagonist "into an escalating cycle of terrifying events that keep the action moving." *Coma* is, he continues, "a gripping, scarifying novel." Watkins also notes that Cook makes "unusual and entertaining use" of our enthrallment with the world of human medicine, portent of our own mortality. David Brudnoy expresses a similar observation in the *National Review:* "[*Coma*] strikes to the core of many people's queasiness about the current debate as to when death occurs," he comments. "By and large this is a horror story of the first order" and "a splendid read."

In another novel, *Brain,* Cook again uses his suspense formula. This time his hero is a neuroradiologist who discovers abnormalities in the brain scans of several young women who mysteriously disappear. The evidence eventually points to medical researchers run amok. "Shall I say, 'I couldn't put the book down'?," ventures William A. Nolen in the *Washington Post Book World.* "Why not? It's true. Even though *Brain* is low-grade formula fiction . . . [it's] a damn fast read" and "[has] a plot with enough

twists and turns to satisfy any reader." The *New York Times'* Christopher Lehmann-Haupt concurs, declaring the novel "very cleverly plotted." And Rosalind Smith, writing in the *Los Angeles Times Book Review,* notes that *Brain* "is unnervingly plausible, deeply frightening—and possibly prophetic." "The milieu of a large university medical center is rendered with exquisite accuracy, from the bureaucratic regulations victimizing both patients and personnel to the atmosphere of the operating rooms and the laboratories," she comments. "Like any good mystery writer, Cook drops hints and clues throughout, albeit hidden in a maze of technical jargon. . . . Medical procedure assumes the importance of character."

Fever, Cook's third medical thriller, "once again pits an individual against a corrupt and incredulous establishment," relates Watkins. Medical researcher Dr. Charles Martel is being forced to work on a questionable cancer drug, his young daughter is dying of the disease, the factory upstream from his house is dumping benzene into a nearby river, and he is fighting to complete his own cancer research in time to save his child. Add bureaucratic stalling, company thugs, a kidnapping, and a siege. "Can an intelligent reader possibly believe all this stress and turmoil?," Lehmann-Haupt queries. He answers: "Dr. Cook . . . has the storytelling skill to seduce us away from intelligence. . . . By the time *Fever* began to deteriorate into absolute absurdity, I was having too good a time to be willing to notice." Watkins concurs that the story suffers from "immoderately coincidental circumstances," but counters that "Dr. Cook's medical knowledge stands him in good stead and somewhat alleviates this novel's credibility problem. His descriptions of the interaction between doctors and patients are vivid and believable, as is his depiction of doctors' attitudes about cancer and its treatment. Not as tightly written as *Coma, Fever* is nonetheless gripping."

In the *Washington Post Book World,* Joseph McLellan contemplates the vast appeal of Cook's medical thrillers, proposing that "the horrible revelations about the medical establishment . . . are the real payoff for reading his books." "What makes you start reading Cook," he assesses, "is the expectation of horror and a glimpse behind the scenes at the medical establishment. Cook discovered some time ago that for the average person an active, well-lit modern hospital is infinitely spookier than a dark old abandoned house." McLellan adds that "it will be hard for all but the most dedicated literary purist to put [*Fever*] down once they have begun."

Boston Memorial Hospital is the familiar setting for Cook's fourth medical mystery, *Godplayer.* Amidst a hospital power struggle that pits resident doctors against private practitioners, eighteen cardiac surgery patients mysteriously die. Doctors Cassandra Kingsley and Robert Seibert investigate the deaths, uncovering such disturbing things as a drug-taking, knife-happy surgeon and lethal IV's. "There is enough going on here to engage one until the end," Jonathan Coleman writes in the *New York Times Book Review*. "Dr. Cook is marvelous when he reveals the mysterious workings of the medical world." Lehmann-Haupt observes that "Robin Cook will grab any medical device he can to get a reader's attention. . . . What [he] knows—and all he needs to know—is the latest thing in medicine, be it technology or syndrome. But he also knows the shortcomings of doctors." Lehmann-Haupt also comments that while the author's prose may be "cliche," his clues obvious, and his characters wooden, "you get the feeling that . . . you are never going to be bored. You are willing to keep watching the cards even if you know they are going to drop from the performer's hand." *Detroit News* writer Leola Floren finds *Godplayer* a suspenseful story "guaranteed to keep medical-mystery lovers poised on the sleek points of steel pins and flashing hypodermic needles."

A subversive plot to take over "the entire medical profession" by the pharmaceutical industry is the subject of Cook's book *Mindbend*. Adam Schonberg, a third-year medical student already 20,000 dollars in debt, feels forced to take a job with Arolin Pharmaceutical when he learns his wife is pregnant and has quit her job. Adam unwittingly discovers that the medical seminars sponsored by his firm are a coverup to brainwash physicians into prescribing Arolin's drugs. Furthermore, he learns that these physicians have begun working for a health maintenance clinic backed by the firm—the same clinic that his pregnant wife is using. Cook admits to Rovner that although the story is a fictional account of the pharmaceutical industries influence on doctors, in reality many doctors rely heavily on pharmaceutical representatives' knowledge. Referring to a scene in the book illustrating the interaction between a busy physician and a persuasive pharmaceutical representative Cook contends, it "is just the way it happens. Don't think it isn't because the scene is faintly humorous. Some of the doctors are that stupid about drugs." Michael A. Morrison of the *Washington Post Book World*, acknowledging the importance of examining the affects of business on medicine, credits Cook for writing on such "an important and timely subject," but believes in the end that the book fails to convey the message effectively because Cook "retreats from this issue." The *Chicago Tribune*'s Clarence Petersen, however, claims the thrilling story line in *Mindbend* "is apt to keep you up reading all . . . night."

According to *Washington Post Book World* contributor Marjorie Williams, Cook's next mystery, *Outbreak*, includes a message about the potential power and danger in "the organized political clout of traditional medicine."

Marissa Blumenthal, M.D., has been assigned to uncover the cause of the spreading of a deadly virus across the United States. What she discovers is the mad plan of a group of doctors to undermine health maintenance organization (HMO) facilities by infecting unknowing HMO practitioners with the virus. The practitioners in turn pass the fatal and incurable disease on to their patients. Marissa is chased by several hit men while trying to find enough evidence to convince the authorities of the deadly scheme and stop the looming epidemic. Noting stylistic errors in *Outbreak, New York Times Book Review* contributor Donovan Fitzpatrick nevertheless asserts that "Mr. Cook is nimble at stitching together the ingredients of terror, suspense, intrigue and medical expertise." In a similar vein, *Los Angeles Times Book Review*'s Jonathan Kellerman points out Cook's weakness in style and stiff dialogue, but also predicts that "*Outbreak* will undoubtedly be a best seller."

Cook tackles the abuses of medical research in his ninth novel, *Mortal Fear*. Free-lance medical researcher Dr. Alvin Hayes, on assignment with a Boston health clinic, accidently discovers a death hormone. After the discovery he becomes convinced someone is trying to kill him. Seeking aid, Hayes confides in Dr. Jason Howard, the acting chief of medicine at the clinic, but abruptly dies before he finishes divulging the information. At the same time, many previously healthy patients at the Boston health clinic have been aging rapidly and dying. Howard begins investigating Hayes' research, connects the discovery to the recent death of healthy patients, and is subsequently chased by a psychopathic hit man. "This is Cook's best book since his first novel, *Coma*," declares Susan Toepfer in *People*. Chicago *Tribune Books* writer Randall K. Packer praises Cook's "flare for description," adding that his writing is "rich in powerful imagery, and medical definitions are detailed yet easily understandable." "While the author's passion for detail provides some of the most engrossing passages in *Mortal Fear*," continues Packer, "it's also responsible for some dull repetition." Larry Thompson of the *Washington Post* criticizes Cook's flaws in logic and stiff characters, but hails his "clean, economical writing style that holds the reader's attention and clearly explains complex science without taxing the mind."

The 1989 novel *Harmful Intent* exposes Cook's feelings concerning malpractice issues in the field of medicine. Jeffrey Rhodes, an anesthesiologist, is sued and then convicted of murder when one of his patients dies after a routine anesthetic injection. Determined to clear his record, Rhode jumps bail, disguises himself, and takes a position as a janitor in the hospital to investigate the death. With the aid of a nurse, he discovers that he and other doctors have been framed for the deaths. The killer is benefiting from the court cases and pursues Rhodes, attempting to eliminate him too. In an interview for *Bestsellers 90,* Cook explains the purpose of this book: "I wanted the public to view this medical malpractice situation from a different perspective, because the public has a gross misconception about what this medical malpractice problem is." While the critics were less impressed with this book, it fared well with the public; *Harmful Intent* stayed on the *New York Times* best seller list for more than a month.

Cook's subsequent novels, including *Vital Signs, Blind Sight,* and *Terminal,* follow the same basic format as his previous books and have been criticized for many of the same weaknesses—underdeveloped characters, incredulous story line, blatant clues, and stiff dialogue. Yet these books continue to remain consistently popular with the public. Critics often allow that Cook's weaknesses as a writer are overcome by the subject matter and medical expertise he shares. "The key to Cook's success," claims Kellerman, "is his ability to tap the love-hate-terror relationship that exists between dispensers and recipients of health care—dredging up the helplessness that we feel when confronted by disease and disability." Describing the writer's appeal, Williams states that Cook "so energetically and lovingly strokes our phobias," and furthermore "has the knack, common to all good popular writers, of taking his subjects seriously." Keeping in mind some of the criticism he receives, Cook works to improve his writing skills; however, he is not concerned with meeting the literary standards of a all reviewers. He once stated in a *CA* interview with Jean W. Ross: "My books are written as mystery thrillers and not written to be compared with Henry James or any other more literary writer. They're written more or less as current-day entertainment-type novels. . . . I like my books to be enjoyed by someone who might be the chief of surgery here at the Massachusetts General Hospital as well as by a bus driver in Indiana."

BIOGRAPHICAL/CRITICAL SOURCES:

BOOKS

Bestsellers 90, Issue 2, Gale, 1990, pp. 24-27.
Contemporary Literary Criticism, Volume 14, Gale, 1980.
Cook, Robin, in an interview with Jean W. Ross for *Contemporary Authors,* Volume 111, Gale, 1984.
Cook, Robin, *Mindbend,* Putnam, 1985.

PERIODICALS

Best Sellers, June, 1977.
Chicago Tribune, January 12, 1986, Section 14, p. 39.
Detroit News, July 10, 1983.
Los Angeles Times Book Review, February 1, 1981; August 28, 1983, p. 9; February 15, 1987 p. 4.
National Review, August 5, 1977.

New York Times, May 14, 1977; February 17, 1981; February 12, 1982; July 11, 1983; February 5, 1987.
New York Times Book Review, May 8, 1977; May 13, 1979; March 1, 1981; March 7, 1982; July 24, 1983; February 22, 1987, p. 28; April 10, 1988, p. 32; February 11, 1990, p. 15; December 16, 1990, p. 12.
People, January 11, 1988.
Publishers Weekly, November 10, 1989; November 23, 1990, p. 55; November 15, 1991, pp. 62-63; November 9, 1992, p. 72.
Time, March 30, 1987, p. 73.
Tribune Books (Chicago), January 10, 1988, p. 4.
Washington Post, April 29, 1985, pp. C1-C2; January 8, 1988.
Washington Post Book World, May 18, 1979; March 8, 1981; February 20, 1982; July 3, 1983; March 26, 1985; February 15, 1989, p. 5.*

*   *   *

COOMBS, Robert H(olman)   1934-

PERSONAL: Born September 16, 1934, in Salt Lake City, UT; son of Morgan S. (a physician) and Vivian (Holman) Coombs; married Carol Jean Cook, May 29, 1958; children: Robert S., Kathryn, Lorraine, Holly Ann, David Jeremy. *Education:* University of Utah, B.S., 1958, M.S., 1959; Washington State University, Ph.D., 1964; Wake Forest University, postdoctoral study in medicine, summer, 1966. *Religion:* Church of Jesus Christ of Latter-day Saints (Mormon).

ADDRESSES: Home—29439 Green Grass Ct., Agoura Hills, CA 91301. *Office*—School of Medicine, University of California, 760 Westwood Plaza, Los Angeles, CA 90024.

CAREER: Iowa State University, Ames, instructor, 1963-64, assistant professor of sociology, 1964-66; Wake Forest University, Bowman Gray School of Medicine, Winston-Salem, NC, assistant professor, 1966-68, associate professor of sociology at Behavioral Sciences Center, 1968-70; California Department of Mental Hygiene, Sacramento, chief of research, Camarillo State Hospital, 1970-73; University of California, Los Angeles, chief of Camarillo-Neuropsychiatric Institute Research Program, Medical School, 1970-77, associate research sociologist in Department of Psychiatry, 1970-73, associate adjunct professor, 1977-78, adjunct professor of biobehavioral sciences, 1978-87, professor of biobehavioral sciences in residence, 1987—, assistant director for research at Neuropsychiatric Institute, 1978-84, director of Office of Education at Neuropsychiatric Institute, 1980—. Member of adjunct faculty, University without Walls, Antioch College—West, 1971-74. Delegate to White House Conference on Children, 1970. University of California, Los Angeles, member of executive council, Alcohol Research Center, 1977-82, member of executive committee, Biobehavioral Sciences Program, and director of Family Learning Center. Director of White House Conference on Families. Licensed marriage, family, and child counselor in California. Counselor on drug abuse, family health, and family and marriage relations for public service organizations; substance abuse counselor. *Military service:* U.S. Army, Military Police, 1958-64.

MEMBER: International Scientific Commission on the Family, International Sociological Association, International Family Therapy Association, World Federation for Mental Health, World Federation for Medical Education, Conference on Social Science and Health, Association for the Behavioral Sciences and Medical Education, American Association for the Advancement of Science (fellow), American Sociological Association, American Association of Marriage and Therapists, American Psychological Association (fellow), American Medical Student Association, National Council on Family Relations (member of executive committee, 1967-68, 1969-71), Association of American Medical Colleges, Association for Medical Education and Research in Substance Abuse, Society of Psychologists in Addictive Behavior, Clinical Sociology Association, Pacific Sociological Association, Alpha Kappa Delta (chapter president, 1961), Phi Kappa Phi, Sigma Xi, Kappa Delta Pi, Kappa Delta Pi.

AWARDS, HONORS: National Science Foundation fellowship, 1962, 1963; National Institute of Mental Health grant to study marital and socialization stresses in medical training, 1968-73; lectureship award, Southern Medical Association, 1969; National Fund for Medical Education grant to study psychosocial adjustment of medical students, 1969-71; California Council on Criminal Justice grant to conduct Camarillo Resocialization Program for Drug Abusers, 1971-74; U.S. Congress citation for exemplary project, 1975, 1976; National Institute on Drug Abuse grant to study techniques for reducing youth problems by strengthening families, 1977-79; California Department of Alcohol and Drug Abuse grant to study family and peer influences on polydrug use; awarded numerous research and training grants.

WRITINGS:

Marriage, the Family, and Human Sexuality in Medical Education, Bowman Gray School of Medicine, Wake Forest University, 1966.

(Editor with H. T. Christensen, D. M. Fulcomer, J. C. Green, R. N. Hey, D. F. Hobbs, R. H. Klemer, E. B. Luckey, M. H. McCaulley, and J. H. Meyerowitz, and contributor) *Human Sexuality in Medical Education and Practice,* C. C Thomas, 1968.

(Editor with C. E. Vincent, and contributor) *Psychosocial Aspects of Medical Training,* C. C Thomas, 1971.

(Editor) *Junkies and Straights: The Camarillo Experience,* Lexington Books, 1975.

(Editor with L. J. Fry and P. G. Lewis) *Socialization in Drug Abuse,* Schenkman, 1976.

Mastering Medication in Drug Abuse, Schenkman, 1976.

Mastering Medicine: Professional Socialization in Medical School, Spectrum, 1979.

(With J. St. John) *Making It in Medical School,* Spectrum, 1979.

(With D. S. May and G. W. Small) *Inside Doctoring: Stages and Outcomes in the Professional Development of Physicians,* Praeger, 1986.

The Family Context of Adolescent Drug Use, Haworth Press, 1988.

(Editor with L. S. West) *Drug Testing: Issues and Options,* Oxford University Press, in press.

Preventing Adolescent Drug Abuse: A Family Strengthening Approach, Government Printing Office, in press.

(With D. Ziedonis) *Handbook of Drug Abuse Prevention: A Comprehensive Strategy to Prevent the Abuse of Alcohol and Other Drugs,* Prentice-Hall, in press.

Contributor to over twenty books, including *Selected Readings in Marriage and Family Relationships for L.D.S.,* edited by K. L. Cannon, Brigham Young University Press, 1966; *Sex Differences in Personality: Readings,* Brooks/Cole, 1971; *Sociological Stuff,* edited by H. P. Chalfant, D. W. Curry, and C. E. Palmer, Kendall/Hunt, 1977; *Drug Problems of the Seventies: Solutions for the Eighties,* edited by R. M. Faulkinberry, National Drug Abuse Conference, 1980; and *Advances in Therapies for Adolescents,* edited by Carol Shaw Avstad and Nina M. Steefel, Jossey-Bass, in press.

Also author of technical reports and numerous papers presented at conferences. Contributor to social science journals, including *Journal of Medical Education, Medical Aspects of Human Sexuality, Social Psychology, Journal of Educational Research, American Journal of Psychiatry, Journal of Marriage and the Family,* and *Sociology and Social Research. Family Relations: Journal of Applied Family and Child Studies,* associate editor, 1970-80, contributing editor and member of editorial board, 1977—. Editor of *International Newsletter on Substance Abuse,* 1990—. Associate editor of *Journal of Drug Issues, Clinical Sociology Review, Qualitative Health Research,* and *Journal of Marriage and the Family.* Member of editorial board, *Family Dynamics of Addiction Quarterly,* 1990—.

SIDELIGHTS: Robert H. Coombs told *CA:* "One of my greatest pleasures is to analyze complex problems and then explain them simply. Simplicity, in my view, is always the goal of rigorous analysis, effective teaching, and powerful writing. But, when after much labor one has managed to accomplish this, others are prone to think: 'It's all so simple; I could have easily explained it as well myself.' "

*　　　*　　　*

COOPER, (Brenda) Clare 1935-

PERSONAL: Born January 21, 1935, in Falmouth, England; daughter of Robert (a ship's plater) and Lillian (a housewife; maiden name, Waight) Payne; married Bill Cooper (a civil servant), April 6, 1953; children: Steven, Robert, Sarah.

ADDRESSES: Home—Tyrhibin Newydd, Newport, Dyfed, SA42 0NT, Wales.

CAREER: Writer. South Devon Health Authority, Devonshire, England, student nurse, 1952-53; volunteer worker with the elderly.

MEMBER: Society of Authors, Greenpeace, Friends of the Earth, Irish Wolfhound Club of Great Britain and Northern Ireland, PEN, Welsh Academy.

AWARDS, HONORS: The Black Horn was named a Children's Book of the Year, National Book League, 1981; *David's Ghost* was runner-up for the Ty'r na Nog Award, 1981.

WRITINGS:

FOR CHILDREN

David's Ghost, Hodder & Stoughton, 1980.
The Black Horn, Hodder & Stoughton, 1981.
Andrew and the Gargoyle, Hodder & Stoughton, 1983.
A Wizard Called Jones, Hodder & Stoughton, 1984.
Earthchange, Hodder & Stoughton, 1985, Lerner, 1986.
The Kings of the Mountain, Hodder & Stoughton, 1986.
Children of the Camps, Hodder & Stoughton, 1988.
Ashar of Qarius, Simon & Schuster, 1988.
The Skyrifters, Simon & Schuster, 1989.
Miracles and Rubies, Gomer, 1992.

Contributor to magazines, including *Nursery World, Irish Wolfhound,* and *Cornishman.*

WORK IN PROGRESS: A crime series for adults; *The Settlement on Planet B,* a science fiction book for children; a sequel to *Earthchange;* research on medieval history for a historical novel about pilgrims.

SIDELIGHTS: "In spite of all the many and varied things which have happened since then," Clare Cooper told *CA,* "probably the one decision which has had the most effect on my life was the one taken by my parents when they decided against the school in town and sent me instead to the small, Cornish village school which had a headmaster who actively encouraged his pupils to read and to write poetry. This meant that from the age of about five, not only was I made very aware of the countryside around me and the fact that I was Cornish, but I was also experiencing the pleasure of writing creatively. Even though later I loathed the competitiveness of high school, I never lost these three things gained at Budock Church of England School.

"In spite of my loathing for school, however, I did well academically, and it was suggested that I should sit for a scholarship for Oxford. I wasn't interested. I had other plans for my life, and it wasn't until I became involved with the education of my children that I realized what a chance I had thrown away. I set about re-educating myself, intending, eventually, to take a degree with our Open University.

"My country school background caught up with me here. Shakespeare, Charlotte Bronte, George Eliot, and, above all, Chaucer, revived all the early love of beautiful writing and a great desire to try to write like that myself. What an ambition! What was I going to write about? My whole life, it seemed, had been one long childhood—my own and then my children's, so I had better write for children.

"We had left Cornwall for the London area long ago, but I had never lost my love for the countryside. Now we moved to Wales, and all the old delight in being Cornish was revived in this other Celtic land with its ancient history, legends, and sense of mystery. I began to write, just for fun, for my daughter, nothing really serious.

"Then I was forty. The new life we are all led to expect obviously needed assistance at its birth—assistance in the form of a little determination by me. I got down seriously to writing. The result was *David's Ghost.*"

*　　　*　　　*

COPELAND, Ann
　　See FURTWANGLER, Virginia W(alsh)

*　　　*　　　*

CORSO, (Nunzio) Gregory 1930-

PERSONAL: Born March 26, 1930, in New York, NY; son of Fortunato Samuel and Michelina (Colonni) Corso; married Sally November (a teacher), May 7, 1963 (divorced); married Belle Carpenter, 1968; children: (first marriage) Mirandia; (second marriage) Cybelle Nuncia, Max-Orphe. *Education:* Attended grammar school. *Politics:* "Individualism and freedom." *Religion:* "God."

ADDRESSES: Home—100 Sullivan St., New York, NY. *Agent*—c/o Thunder's Mouth Press, P.O. Box 780, New York, NY, 10025.

CAREER: Writer. Manual laborer in New York City, 1950-51; employee of *Los Angeles Examiner,* Los Angeles, CA, 1951-52; merchant seaman on Norwegian vessels, 1952-53. Appeared in Peter Whitehead's film, *Wholly Communion,* and in Andy Warhol's *Couch.*

AWARDS, HONORS: Longview Award for poem, "Marriage"; $1,000 Poetry Foundation award; Jean Stein Award for Poetry, American Academy and Institute of Arts and Letters, 1986.

WRITINGS:

The Vestal Lady on Brattle, and Other Poems, R. Brukenfeld (Cambridge, MA), 1955.

This Hung-Up Age (play) produced at Harvard University, 1955.

Bomb (poem; broadside), [San Francisco], 1958.

Gasoline (poems), introduction by Allen Ginsberg, City Lights, 1958, new edition, 1992.

(With Henk Marsman) *A Pulp Magazine for the Dead Generation: Poems,* Dead Language, 1959.

(With William S. Burroughs, Brion Gysin, and Sinclair Beiles) *Minutes to Go,* Two Cities Editions (Paris, France), 1960.

Happy Birthday of Death (poems), New Directions, 1960.

(Editor with Walter Hollerer) *Junge Amerikanische Lyrik* (anthology), Carl Hansen Verlag, 1961.

The American Express (novel), Olympia Press, 1961.

(With Anselm Hollo and Tom Raworth) *The Minicab War,* Matrix Press, 1961.

Find It So Hard to Write the How Why & What . . . , Paterson Society, 1961.

Long Live Man (poems), New Directions, 1962.

Selected Poems, Eyre & Spottiswoode, 1962.

(With Lawrence Ferlinghetti and Allen Ginsberg) *Penguin Modern Poets 5,* Penguin, 1963.

The Mutation of the Spirit: A Shuffle Poem, Death Press, 1964.

There Is Yet Time to Run Back through Life and Expiate All That's Been Sadly Done (poems), New Directions, 1965.

(Contributor) Paris Leary and Robert Kelly, editors, *A Controversy of Poets,* Doubleday Anchor, 1965.

The Geometric Poem: A Long Experimental Poem, Composite of Many Lines and Angles Selective, [Milan, Italy], 1966.

(Contributor) Bob Booker and George Foster, editors, *Pardon Me, Sir, But Is My Eye Hurting Your Elbow?* (screenplays), Bernard Geis, 1967.

10 Times a Poem: Collected at Random From 2 Suitcases Filled With Poems—the Gathering of 5 Years, Poets Press, 1967.

Elegiac Feelings American, New Directions, 1970.

Gregory Corso, Phoenix Book Shop, 1971.

Egyptian Cross, Phoenix Book Shop, 1971.

The Night Last Night Was at Its Nightest . . . , Phoenix Book Shop, 1972.

Earth Egg, Unmuzzled Ox, 1974.

Way Out: A Poem in Discord (play), Bardo Matrix (Kathmandu, Nepal), 1974.

The Japanese Notebook Ox, Unmuzzled Ox, 1974.

Collected Plays, City Lights, 1980.

Writings from Ox, edited by Michael Andre, Unmuzzled Ox, 1981.

Herald of the Autochthonic Spirit, New Directions, 1981.

Mindfield: New and Selected Poems, Thunder's Mouth, 1989.

Also co-author of screenplay *Happy Death,* 1965; contributor to periodicals, including *Evergreen Review* and *Litterair Paspoort.*

SIDELIGHTS: Gregory Corso is a key member of the Beats, a group of convention-breaking writers who are generally credited with sparking much of the social and political change that transformed America in the 1960s. Corso's spontaneous, insightful, and inspirational verse once prompted fellow Beat poet Allen Ginsberg to describe him as an "awakener of youth." Although Corso enjoyed his greatest level of popularity during the 1960s and 1970s, he continues to influence contemporary readers and critics today. Writing in the *American Book Review,* Dennis Barone remarked that Corso's 1990 volume of new and selected poems was a sign that "despite doubt, uncertainty, the American way, death all around, Gregory Corso will continue, and I am glad he will."

Born in 1930 to teenaged parents who separated a year after his birth, Corso spent his early childhood in foster homes and orphanages. At the age of eleven, he went to live with his natural father, who had remarried. A troubled youth, Corso repeatedly ran away and was eventually sent to a boys' home. One year later, he was caught selling a stolen radio and was forced to testify in court against the dealer who purchased the illegal merchandise. While he was held as a material witness in the trial, the twelve-year-old boy spent several months in prison where, as he wrote in a biographical sketch for *The New American Poetry,* the other prisoners "abused me terribly, and I was indeed like an angel then because when they stole my food and beat me up and threw pee in my cell, I . . . would come out and tell them my beautiful dream about a floating girl who landed before a deep pit and just stared." He later spent three months under observation at Bellevue Hospital.

When Corso was sixteen, he returned to jail to serve a three-year sentence for theft. There he read widely in the classics, including Fyodor Dostoevsky, Stendahl, Percy Bysshe Shelley, Thomas Chatterton, and Christopher Marlowe. "When I left [prison], I left there a young man, educated in the ways of men at their worst and at their best," he once told *CA*. "Sometimes hell is a good place—if it proves to one that because it exists, so must its opposite, heaven exist. And what was heaven? Poetry," Corso declared. He has never written poems about his time in prison, however: "If one must climb a ladder to reach a height and from that height see, then it were best to write about what you see and not about how you climbed. Prison to me was such a ladder."

After his release in 1950, Corso worked as a laborer in New York City, a newspaper reporter in Los Angeles, and a sailor on a boat to Africa and South America. It was in New York City that he first met Allen Ginsberg, the Beat poet with whom he is most closely associated. The pair met in a Greenwich Village bar in 1950 while Corso was working on his first poems. Until then he had read only traditional poetry, and Ginsberg introduced him to contemporary, experimental work. Within a few years Corso was writing in long Whitmanesque lines similar to those Ginsberg had developed in his own work. The surreal word combinations that began to appear in Ginsberg's work about the same time may in turn suggest Corso's reciprocal influence.

In 1954, Corso moved to Boston, where several important poets, including Edward Marshall and John Wieners, were experimenting with the poetics of voice. But the center for Corso's life there was not "the School of Boston," as these poets were called, but Harvard and particularly the Harvard library, where he spent his days reading the great works of poetry. His first published poems appeared in the *Harvard Advocate* in 1954, and his play, *In This Hung-Up Age* (concerning a group of Americans who, after their bus breaks down midway across the continent, are trampled by buffalo), was performed by students at the university the following year.

Harvard and Radcliffe students also underwrote the expenses of Corso's first book, *The Vestal Lady on Brattle, and Other Poems*. The poems featured in the volume are usually considered apprentice works heavily indebted to Corso's reading. They are, however, unique in their innovative use of jazz rhythms (notably in "Requiem for 'Bird' Parker, Musician," which many call the strongest poem in the book), cadences of spoken English, and hipster jargon. Corso explained his use of rhythm and meter in an interview with Gavin Salerie for *Riverside Interviews:* "My music is built in—it's already natural. I don't play with the meter." In other words, Corso believes the meter must arise naturally from the poet's voice; it is never consciously chosen.

In a review of Corso's first book for *Poetry,* Reuel Denney asked whether "a small group jargon" such as bop language would "sound interesting" to those who were not part of that culture. Corso, he concluded, "cannot balance

the richness of the bebop group jargon . . . with the clarity he needs to make his work meaningful to a wider-than-clique audience." Ironically, within a few years, that "small group jargon" became, of course, a national idiom.

As it continued to develop, Corso's work became a unique example of the poetics of voice. Unlike many of his contemporaries, he never abandoned completely his interest in older conventions of rhyme, meter, and stanzaic pattern. He trained himself in an immense range of poetries from German Romanticism to seventeenth-century lyricism and from the Babylonian epic *Gilgamesh* to Walt Whitman's *Leaves of Grass.* Even when Beat Generation writers with whom he was associated, particularly Ginsberg and Jack Kerouac, were talking about poetry as immediate expression or utterance, Corso continued to consider his own works as crafted objects.

Corso's vocabulary is as eclectic as his sense of form, borrowing as freely from words heard in the street as from the archaic diction of seventeenth-century English poetry. Corso, who studied a dictionary extensively while still in his teens, once told Michael Andre in an *Unmuzzled Ox* interview that he "got that whole book in me, all the obsolete and archaic words. And through that I knew that I was in love with language and vocabulary, because the words and the way they looked to me, the way they sounded, and what they meant, how they were defined and all that, I tried to revive them, and I did."

Despite Corso's reliance on traditional forms and archaic diction, he remains a street-wise poet, described by Bruce Cook in *The Beat Generation* as "an urchin Shelley." Gaiser suggested that Corso adopts "the mask of the sophisticated child whose every display of mad spontaneity and bizarre perception is consciously and effectively designed"—as if he is in some way deceiving his audience. But the poems at their best are controlled by an authentic, distinctive, and enormously effective voice that can range from sentimental affection and pathos to exuberance and dadaist irreverence toward almost anything except poetry itself.

When Corso moved to San Francisco in 1956, he was too late to participate in the famous reading at the Six Gallery, at which Ginsberg read "Howl" and which, since it was widely noted in newspapers and popular magazines, is conventionally cited as the first major public event in the rise of the Beat movement. However, Corso was soon identified as one of the major figures of the movement and that celebrity status or notoriety undoubtedly contributed much to the fame of his poetry in the late 1950s and early 1960s. With Ginsberg, he also co-authored "The Literary Revolution in America" (originally published in *Litterair Paspoort*), an article in which they declared that America now had poets who "have taken it upon themselves, with angelic clarions in hand, to announce their discontent, their demands, their hope, their final wondrous unimaginable dream."

From 1957 to 1958, Corso lived in Paris, where, he told Andre, "things burst and opened, and I said, 'I will just let the lines go. . . .'" Poems that resulted were published in *Gasoline*, his first major book. *Gasoline* also contains poems written while Corso was traveling with Ginsberg in Mexico, and Ginsberg's influence is evident in much of the work. Here Whitman's long poetic line has become Corso's much as it had become Ginsberg's, and the diction is occasionally reminiscent of Ginsberg as well. "Ode to Coit Tower," for example, echoes "In the Baggage Room at Greyhound," on which Ginsberg recently had been working, and "Sun" utilizes structural devices and incantatory effects used in "Howl." But however influential Ginsberg may have been, Corso always maintained his own distinctive voice. In an essay collected in *The Beats: Essays in Criticism*, Geoffrey Thurley summarized some of the principal characteristics that differentiate Corso from Ginsberg: "Where Ginsberg is all expression and voice, Corso is calm and quick, whimsical often, witty rather than humourous, semantically swift rather than prophetically incantatory."

The influence of bop is far more evident in *Gasoline* than in *The Vestal Lady on Brattle*. In his introduction, Ginsberg quotes Corso as saying that his poems were written the way Charlie Parker and Miles Davis played music. He would start with standard diction and rhythm but then be "intentionally distracted diversed [sic] into my own sound." The result is an intricate linguistic pattern involving extremely subtle modulations of sound and rhythm. "For Corso," Neeli Cherkovski wrote in *Whitman's Wild Children: Profiles of Ten Contemporary American Poets*, "poetry is at its best when it can create a totally unexpected expression," and many of these linguistic fusions suggest the pleasure in invention for its own sake.

In the 1960s, though Beats such as Ginsberg and Kerouac became cult figures for the counterculture, Corso was generally overlooked. He taught for a short time at the University of New York at Buffalo, but his appointment was terminated when he refused to sign a loyalty oath required of all university employees by the state of New York. Then in 1969, Kerouac died, and Corso responded with "Elegiac Feelings American," a major poem that became the title work in the collection published the following year. Corso had never been as politically motivated a poet as Ginsberg, but "Elegiac Feelings American" is a profound statement of his frustration at the apparent collapse of the revolution of the spirit that he and other Beat writers had once thought would alter America irrevocably. But the promise is not gone absolutely, and if America, as the poem contends, destroyed Kerouac, there are still those who followed him: "the children of flowers."

Corso shaped his poems from 1970 to 1974 into a book that he planned to call *Who Am I—Who I Am*, but the manuscript was stolen, and there were no other copies. Aside from chapbooks and a few miscellaneous publications, he did not issue other work until 1981 when *Herald of the Autochthonic Spirit* appeared. Shorter than any of his major books since *Gasoline*, it contains some critically acclaimed poems, many of them written in clipped, almost prosaic lines more reminiscent of William Carlos Williams than of Whitman. "Return" deals with barren times in which there had been no poems but also asserts that the poet can now write again and that "the past [is] my future." The new poems, however, are generally more subdued than the earlier ones, though there are surreal flights, as in "The Whole Mess . . . Almost," in which the poet cleans his apartment of Truth, God, Beauty, Death, and essentially everything but Humor.

By the early 1980s, when Corso's *Herald of the Autochthonic Spirit* was published, language-centered writing, in which the conventions of language themselves become the subjects of poems, had long since surpassed the poetics of voice as the center of attention for many younger poets working outside academic traditions. Thus the book was not widely reviewed, even though it contains some of Corso's best work. But if the voice that shaped these poems is often quieter than it had been a generation before, it nonetheless continues to affirm Kenneth Rexroth's characterization of Corso as "a real wildman." "At his worst," Rexroth added, "he is an amusing literary curiosity; at his best, his poems are metaphysical hotfoots and poetic cannon crackers."

In 1991, Corso published a volume entitled *Mindfield: New and Selected Poems*. The book consists of selections from five previously published books and close to sixty pages of previously unpublished poems, including one almost thirty pages long. Barone declared that the volume "provides for new readers the opportunity to be awakened and for those familiar with Corso's work a chance to be reawakened."

Although Corso has greatly reduced the number of poems he publishes in recent years, he continues to believe in the power of poetry to bring about change. He once explained his Utopian vision in a letter to *CA:* "I feel that in the future many many poets will blossom forth—the poetic spirit will spread and reach toward all; it will show itself not in words—the written poem—but rather in man's being and in the deeds he enacts. . . . A handful of poets in every country in the world can and have always been able to live in the world as well as in their own world; . . . [and] when such humankind becomes manifold, when all are embraced by the poetic spirit, by a world of poets, not by the written word but by deed and thought and beauty, then society will have no recourse but to become suitable for them and for itself. I feel man is headed in such a direction; he is fated and due to become aware of and knowledgeable about his time; his good intelligence and compassion will enable him to cope with almost all the bothersome, distracting difficulties that may arise—and when he becomes so, 'poet' will not be his name, but it will be his victory."

BIOGRAPHICAL/CRITICAL SOURCES:

BOOKS

Allen, Donald M., editor, *The New American Poetry,* Grove Press, 1960.

Allen, and Warren Tallman, *The Poetics of the New American Poetry,* Grove Press, 1973.

Bartlett, Lee, *The Beats: Essays in Criticism,* McFarland, 1981.

Chassman, Neil A., editor, *Poets of the Cities: New York and San Francisco, 1950-1965,* Dutton, 1974.

Cherkovski, Neeli, *Whitman's Wild Children: Profiles of Ten Contemporary American Poets,* Lapis Press, 1988.

Contemporary Literary Criticism, Gale, Volume 1, 1973, Volume 11, 1979.

Cook, Bruce, *The Beat Generation,* Scribner, 1971.

Corso, Gregory, *Gasoline,* introduction by Allen Ginsberg, City Lights, 1958.

Corso, *Herald of the Autochthonic Spirit,* New Directions, 1981.

Dictionary of Literary Biography, Gale, Volume 5: *American Poets since World War II,* 1980, Volume 16: *The Beats: Literary Bohemianism in Postwar America,* 1983.

Gifford, Barry, and Lawrence Lee, *Jack's Book: An Oral Biography of Jack Kerouac,* St. Martin's, 1978.

Knight, Arthur, and Kit Knight, editors, *The Beat Vision: A Primary Sourcebook,* Paragon House, 1987.

Leary, Paris, and Robert Kelly, editors, *A Controversy of Poets,* Doubleday Anchor, 1965.

Nemerov, Howard, editor, *Poets on Poetry,* Basic Books, 1966.

Parkinson, Thomas, editor, *A Casebook on the Beat,* Crowell, 1961.

Rexroth, Kenneth, *Assays,* New Directions, 1961.

Selerie, Gavin, *Riverside Interviews 3: Gregory Corso,* Binnacle Press, 1982.

Tytell, John, *Naked Angels: The Lives and Literature of the Beat Generation,* McGraw, 1976.

Wilson, Robert A., *A Bibliography of Works by Gregory Corso, 1954-1965,* Phoenix Book Shop, 1966.

PERIODICALS

American Book Review, September, 1990, p. 17.

Hudson Review, spring, 1963.

Kenyon Review, spring, 1963.

North Dakota Quarterly, spring, 1982.

Partisan Review, fall, 1960.

Poetry, October, 1956.

Thoth, winter, 1971.

Unmuzzled Ox, winter, 1981.*

*   *   *

COURSEN, Herbert R(andolph), Jr. 1932-

PERSONAL: Born March 28, 1932, in Newark, NJ; son of Herbert R. (in life insurance) and Mildred (Huntoon) Coursen; married Susan Kirkconnell (a teacher), February 15, 1957 (divorced, 1970); children: Elizabeth, Susan Leigh, Virginia. *Education:* Amherst College, B.A., 1954; Wesleyan University, M.A., 1962; University of Connecticut, Ph.D., 1965. *Politics:* Liberal. *Religion:* Episcopalian.

ADDRESSES: Home—RR 2, Box 5210, Brunswick, ME 04011.

CAREER: Choate School, Wallingford, CT, English teacher, 1958-62; Bowdoin College, Brunswick, ME, instructor, 1964-65, assistant professor, 1965-69, associate professor, 1969-74, professor of creative writing and Shakespeare, 1974-91. Visiting professor at New Hampshire College, 1974-76, Westfield College, summers, 1975-78, and Washington and Jefferson College, fall, 1990; lecturer at Globe Centre, London, England, 1992. Bowdoin College, squash coach, 1965-68, teacher in Upward Bound program, 1965-70, 1977, 1980. Director of poetry, New England Writer's Conference, 1973-74, 1980; director of National Endowment for the Humanities summer seminars, 1985-90. Delegate, Shakespeare Institute, 1978, 1980, 1992. Consulting editor in Shakespeare, Princeton University, Bucknell University, and University of Georgia. *Military service:* U.S. Air Force, fighter pilot, 1954-58; became captain.

MEMBER: Conference on Christianity and Literature (chairman of book awards, 1979).

AWARDS, HONORS: Ford Foundation fellowship, 1969-71; Folger Library fellowship, 1970-71; Percy Bysshe Shelley Lifetime Achievement Award, 1991; Poet Chapbook award, 1991; Chester Jones Foundation award, 1992.

WRITINGS:

"The Rarer Action": Hamlet's Mousetrap, University of Wisconsin Press, 1969.

As up They Grew: Autobiographical Essays, Scott, Foresman, 1970.

(Editor) William Shakespeare, *Henry V, Part II,* W. C. Brown, 1971.

Shaping the Self: Style and Technique in the Narrative, Harper, 1975.

Christian Ritual and the World of Shakespeare's Tragedies, Bucknell University Press, 1976.

After the War (novel), Heidelberg Graphics, 1980.

The Leasing out of England: Shakespeare's Second Henriad, University Press of America, 1982.

The Compensatory Psyche: A Jungian Approach to Shakespeare, University Press of America, 1986.

(Editor, with James Bulman) *Shakespeare on Television,* University Press of New England, 1988.

The Outfielder (novel), Heidelberg, 1992.

Shakespeare Performance as Interpretation, Delaware University Press, 1992.

Watching Shakespeare on Television, Fairleigh, Dickinson University Press, 1993.

POETRY

Storm in April, Arco Multi-Media, 1973.

Survivor, Ktaadn Poetry Press, 1974.

Lookout Point, Samisdat, 1974.

Inside the Piano Bench, Samisdat, 1975.

Fears in the Night, Samisdat, 1976.

Walking Away, Samisdat, 1977.

Hope Farm: New and Selected Poems, Cider Mill Press, 1979.

Winter Dreams, Cider Mill Press, 1982.

War Stories, Cider Mill Press, 1985.

Rewriting the Book, Cider Mill Press, 1987.

Rewinding the Reel, Cider Mill Press, 1988.

Songs and Sonnets, Magic Circle, 1991.

Five Minutes after "Mayday," Skywriters, 1992.

Lament for the Players, Magic Circle, 1992.

Love Poem (sort of), Cooper House, 1993.

OTHER

Editor of four Upward Bound student anthologies, 1968-80. Contributor of articles, reviews, and poems to periodicals, including *Shakespeare Quarterly, Studies in Philology, New England Quarterly, New Republic, Change, New York Times, Washington Post, Nation, Sports Illustrated, Poetry Now,* and *Studies in English Literature.* Assistant editor, *British Studies Monitor,* 1970-78; poetry editor, *Maine Sunday Telegram,* 1980-86; consulting editor, *Poet,* 1991—; editor, *Shakespeare and the Classroom.*

WORK IN PROGRESS: Reading Shakespeare on Stage.

SIDELIGHTS: Herbert R. Coursen, Jr., wrote *CA:* "I am enjoying retirement, but still writing—on the computer which I have recently learned to use. I resisted the process, but recommend it for those who are still holding out."

COVEY, Stephen R. 1932-

PERSONAL: Born October 24, 1932, in Salt Lake City, UT; son of Stephen Glenn and Louise (Richards) Covey; married Sandra Merrill, August 14, 1956; children: Cynthia, Maria, Stephen, Michael Sean, David, Catherine, Colleen, Jenny, Joshua. *Education:* University of Utah, B.S., 1952; Harvard University, M.B.A., 1957; Brigham Young University, D.R.E., 1976. *Religion:* Church of Jesus Christ of Latter-day Saints.

ADDRESSES: Office—3507 North University Ave., Suite 100, Provo, UT 84604.

CAREER: Brigham Young University, Provo, UT, administrative posts, 1965-69, associate professor, 1970-83, adjunct professor of organizational behavior, 1983—; consultant in leadership. Founder and chairman, Covey Leadership Center, 1983; publisher, *Executive Excellence* (periodical), 1984—; founder of Institute for Principle-Centered Leadership. Guest lecturer, Brookings Institution, Washington, DC, 1961—.

AWARDS, HONORS: Thomas More College Medallion, 1990, for continued service to humanity; Utah Symphony Fiftieth Anniversary Award, 1990, for outstanding national and international contribution; McFeely Award, International Management Council, 1991, for significant contributions to management and education.

WRITINGS:

Spiritual Roots of Human Relations, Deseret, 1970.

How to Succeed with People, Deseret, 1971.

The Divine Center, Bookcraft, 1982.

(With Truman Madsen) *Marriage and Family,* Bookcraft, 1983.

The Seven Habits of Highly Effective People, Simon & Schuster, 1989.

Principle-Centered Leadership, Summit Books, 1991.

Contributor to numerous periodicals, including *Modern Office Technology.*

Author's works have been translated into numerous languages, including Chinese, French, German, Japanese, and Spanish.

WORK IN PROGRESS: (With A. Roger and Rebecca Merrill) *First Things First,* in press; *The Seven Habits of Highly Effective Families; The Seven Habits of Highly Effective Organizations.*

SIDELIGHTS: Stephen R. Covey is the author of several books and numerous articles on leadership, personal and organizational effectiveness, and family and interpersonal relationships. *The Seven Habits of Highly Effective People,* published in 1989, reached bestseller status with sales of over two and a half million copies worldwide.

BIOGRAPHICAL/CRITICAL SOURCES:

PERIODICALS

Entrepreneur, May, 1993.
Equity, March, 1993.
Industry Week, June, 1992.
Library Journal, March 15, 1990, p. 46; November 1, 1991, p. 124.
Public Management, July, 1990, p. 21.

*   *   *

CRANE, Caroline 1930-

PERSONAL: Born October 30, 1030, in Chicago, IL; daughter of Roger Alan (a foundation executive) and Jessie Louise (a social worker; maiden name, Taft) Crane; married Yoshio Kiyabu (a travel agent), July 11, 1959; children: James Ryo, Laurel Rei. *Education:* Bennington College, A.B., 1952; Columbia University, graduate study, 1952-53. *Politics:* Democrat. *Avocational interests:* Travel, history, ballet, opera, reading suspense novels.

ADDRESSES: Home—34 Beech St., Westwood, NJ 07675.

CAREER: United Nations Children's Fund, U.S. Committee, New York City, writer, 1957-60; writer.

MEMBER: Authors Guild, Authors League of America.

WRITINGS:

YOUNG ADULT NOVELS

Pink Sky at Night, Doubleday, 1963.
Lights down the River, Doubleday, 1964.
A Girl like Tracy, McKay, 1966.
Wedding Song, McKay, 1967.
Don't Look at Me That Way, Random House, 1970.
Stranger on the Road, Random House, 1971.

ADULT NOVELS

Summer Girl, Dodd, 1979.
The Girls Are Missing, Dodd, 1980.
Coast of Fear, Dodd, 1981.
Wife Found Slain, Dodd, 1981.
The Foretelling, Dodd, 1982.
The Third Passenger, Dodd, 1983.
Trick or Treat, Dodd, 1983.
Woman Vanishes, Dodd, 1984.
Something Evil, Dodd, 1984.
Someone at the Door, Dodd, 1985.
Circus Day, Dodd, 1986.
Man in the Shadows, Dodd, 1987.
The People Next Door, Dodd, 1988.
Whispers from Oracle Falls, Avalon, 1991.

WORK IN PROGRESS: A contemporary adult suspense novel; a biographical novel.

SIDELIGHTS: Caroline Crane once told *CA:* " It seems sometimes as though I have had not one, but two or three writing careers. As a stagestruck teenager, I wrote plays for the sole purpose of producing and acting in them. Years later, when I turned to novels, enough of the teenager must have been left in me so that she was the one who defined my writing. The first six books I wrote, which spanned a publication period of eight years, are novels for young adults. Of those, the first two deal with the theatre. The rest are 'problem' novels, that is, they are concerned with the subjects of teenage marriage, alcoholic parents, and mental retardation.

"Suddenly, everything changed; I was no longer interested in writing for young people. The transition, however, was long and painful. Apparently, my writing style and way of thinking had not caught up with my interests. It was another eight years, and almost as many unpublished manuscripts, before I finally broke through with my first adult suspense novel, *Summer Girl.*

"The only things that kept me going during that discouraging era were the knowledge that I had published before and, therefore, could probably do it again and the fact that, no matter what else I tried, from office work to running a home typing service, I could not stop writing. It is an addiction. It colors my whole life. Whatever I do, whatever places I visit, always seem to bear a tag that reads: How can I use this in my writing? In 1978, a friend persuaded me to join her on a train trip through France. I took notes along the way and used that trip as chapter one of *Coast of Fear.*

"*Summer Girl* was inspired by a magazine article about women who summer at the Long Island beaches, taking with them live-in teenage babysitters to share the work load. A nubile adolescent, a harried mother perhaps lacking in self-confidence, a susceptible husband—what a dynamite situation. *The Girls Are Missing* was born of reflections on the case of Jack the Ripper. Didn't the man have a family, friends, neighbors? Did any of them have any idea of his double identity? What *would* it be like to wonder?

"For me, writing is a kind of sharing of emotions, experiences, and ideas. I love reading other people's suspense novels and hope I can bring the same pleasure and excitement to my own readers."

BIOGRAPHICAL/CRITICAL SOURCES:

PERIODICALS

Chicago Tribune Book World, April 27, 1986.

CRUMP, Fred H., Jr. 1931-

PERSONAL: Born June 7, 1931, in Houston, TX; son of Fred H. and Carol Crump. *Education:* Sam Houston State Teachers College, B.S., 1953, M.S., 1961.

ADDRESSES: Home—94 Santa Anita, Rancho Mirage, CA 92270.

CAREER: Junior high school art teacher, Orange, TX, then Palm Springs, CA, 1960-1990. Author and illustrator of children's books.

WRITINGS:

JUVENILES; SELF ILLUSTRATED

Marigold and the Dragon, Steck, 1964.
The Teeny Weeny Genie, Steck, 1966.
Missy and the Duke, Blaine Ethridge, 1977.
Ringo and the Raccoon, Children's Press, 1982.
Petipois le panda, Harlequin Publishers (France), 1982.
Doc le coq, Harlequin Publishers, 1982.
Tetenlair le ver, Harlequin Publishers, 1982.
Pluche La Truche, Harlequin Publishers, 1982.
Fripon le raton-laveur, Harlequin Publishers, 1982.
Floc le phoque, Harlequin Publishers, 1982.
Sacha le petit rat, Harlequin Publishers, 1982.
A Rose for Zemira, Winston-Derek, 1987.
Thumbelina, Winston-Derek, 1988.
Little Red Riding Hood, Winston-Derek, 1989.
Mother Goose, Winston-Derek, 1990.
Cinderella, Winston-Derek, 1990.
Jamako and the Beanstalk, Winston-Derek, 1990.
Afrotina and the Three Bears, Winston-Derek, 1991.
Hakim and Grenita, Winston-Derek, 1991.
Rapunzel, Winston-Derek, 1991.
Mgambo and the Tigers, Winston-Derek, 1992.
Sleeping Beauty, Winston-Derek, 1992.
Rumpelstiltskin, Winston-Derek, 1992.
The Ebony Duckling, Winston-Derek, 1992.
Beauty and the Beast, Winston-Derek, 1992.
The Mouse Opera House, Winston-Derek, 1992.
The Mouse Ballet, Winston-Derek, 1993.

Also author of *Trigger the Trucker Mouse, and Other Stories.*

ILLUSTRATOR; JUVENILES BY GARRY AND VESTA SMITH

Creepy Caterpillar, Steck, 1961.
Flagon the Dragon, Steck, 1962.
Mitzi, Steck, 1963.
Jumping Julius, Steck, 1964.
Leander Lion, Steck, 1966.
Florabelle, Steck, 1968.
Crickety Cricket, Steck, 1969.
Poco, Prism Press, 1975.

OTHER

Contributor of illustrations to magazines, including *Turtle* and *Playmate.*

WORK IN PROGRESS: "A cartoon coloring book, a reluctant angel, a singing hippo, and some more fairy tales."

SIDELIGHTS: Fred H. Crump told *CA:* "I am still scribbling stories and splashing ink and paint. And I go to lots of movies, take naps and visit a dog named 'Blue.' I have a lot of projects planned and *so* far am living 'happily ever after'."

*   *   *

CUMMINGS, Jack
See CUMMINGS, John W(illiam), Jr.

*   *   *

CUMMINGS, John W(illiam), Jr. 1940-
(Jack Cummings)

PERSONAL: Born March 30, 1940, in Fort Lauderdale, FL; son of John William (a realtor) and Jeanne (a realtor; maiden name, Jones) Cummings; married Gloria Lopez (a travel agent), October 31, 1963; children: Robert, Anne Marie. *Education:* University of Florida, A.A., 1959; attended Wofford College, 1960; Drake College, B.S./B.A., 1962; graduate studies at University of Liege and University of Madrid. *Religion:* Methodist.

ADDRESSES: Home—3111 Northeast 22nd St., Fort Lauderdale, FL 33305.

CAREER: Realtor, 1964——. President of Investment Division of Fort Lauderdale Board of Realtors, 1966, 1972; member of board of directors of Fort Lauderdale Symphony Orchestra, 1974; director of Fort Lauderdale Junior Achievement, 1976. *Military service:* U.S. Air Force, 1961.

MEMBER: National Association of Realtors, National Association of Real Estate Editors, Fort Lauderdale Toastmasters Club (president, 1973).

WRITINGS:

The Ultimate Game (novel), Major Books, 1976.

UNDER NAME JACK CUMMINGS

The Venture (novel), Charter House Publishers, 1978.
Complete Guide to Real Estate Financing, Prentice-Hall, 1978, revised edition, 1979.
Lauderdale Run (novel), Manor Books, 1979.
Complete Handbook of How to "Farm" Real Estate Listings and Sales, Prentice-Hall, 1979.

Successful Real Estate Investing for the Single Person, Playboy Press, 1980.

Cashless Investing in Real Estate, Playboy Press, 1982, revised edition published as *$1,000 Down Can Make You Rich,* Prentice-Hall, 1985.

Creative Investing in Real Estate, H. Pierce & Co., 1982.

Real Estate Financing Manual, Prentice-Hall, 1986.

The Guide to Real Estate Exchanging, Wiley, 1991.

The Business Travel Survival Guide, Wiley, 1991.

The 36-Hour Real Estate Investing Course, McGraw, 1992.

OTHER

Also author of *This Condo'll Kill Ya,* a two-act play, and *Cocaine Alley,* a screenplay.

WORK IN PROGRESS: A book for McGraw; a novel.

SIDELIGHTS: In *Successful Real Estate Investing for the Single Person,* Jack Cummings advises unmarried persons of all ages and circumstances on the many advantages of real estate ownership. He recommends particularly the tax advantage and inflation protection offered single people by such investment. Convinced that neither lack of money nor lack of spouse ought to prevent home ownership, Cummings offers a wide range of investment opportunities for unmarried people, including condominiums, houses, apartment complexes, vacant land, and commercial and recreational property. Alan Wolfe, member of *Nation*'s editorial board, describes *Successful Real Estate Investing for the Single Person* as "a guidebook to the illicit, a set of rules about how to procreate and multiply in a world of ever-changing real estate transactions," and, in his examination of five other real estate investment titles which appeared in the expanding economy of the early 1980s, judged Cummings's book "the most interesting of the lot."

In *Cashless Investing in Real Estate,* Cummings presents forty techniques which allow a buyer to purchase property without using any of his own money. Cummings explains the advantages and pitfalls of each method he suggests and illustrates them with case histories.

Cummings once told *CA:* "My motivation has been to express things as I feel them and to allow my mind to be visible on paper in as structured and clear a form as possible. My past has allowed me to travel extensively and to have had many varied experiences on which to draw as a temper and backdrop for my work. I believe that no matter the kind of writing, it must be entertaining.

"I speak Spanish, understand French, and am conversant in English, although I was once nearly deterred from being a writer by a mindless university professor who said that since I couldn't spell worth a 'dam,' I should consider a non-writing profession. Editors have since told me that

a writer's gift isn't the properly spelled word but the picture the words placed on paper depict."

Cummings adds that he lectures frequently throughout the world and spends eight to ten weeks each year on board cruise lines as a speaker on numerous topics. He told *CA* that on one cruise he "provided several lectures that combined the history of wine development with wine tastings of Spanish wine and brandy."

BIOGRAPHICAL/CRITICAL SOURCES:

PERIODICALS

Nation, May 16, 1981.

*   *   *

CUTLER, Bruce 1930-

PERSONAL: Born October 8, 1930, in Evanston, IL; son of Richard S. and Dorothea (Wales) Cutler; married Tina Cirelli, July 3, 1954; children: David, John, Ann. *Education:* Attended Northwestern University, 1947-49; University of Iowa, B.A. (with highest distinction), 1951; Kansas State College of Agriculture and Applied Science (now Kansas State University), M.S., 1957; Universita degli Studi, graduate study, 1957-58. *Religion:* Society of Friends (Quaker).

ADDRESSES: Home—11 Summit Ct., #11, St. Paul, MN 55102.

CAREER: American Friends Service Committee, Philadelphia, PA, social worker, 1951-55; Kansas State University, Manhattan, instructor in English, 1958-60; Wichita State University, Wichita, KS, instructor, 1960-61, assistant professor, 1961-64, associate professor, 1964-67, professor of English, beginning 1967, Distinguished Professor of Humanities, 1973-78, Adele M. Davis Distinguished Professor of Humanities, beginning 1978, coordinator of creative writing program, beginning 1967.

Fulbright lecturer and chairman of faculty, Institute of Languages, Universidad Nacional de Asuncion, Paraguay, 1965; visiting lecturer under Fulbright Exchange Program, Argentina, 1965, and Ecuador, 1965 and 1967; Fulbright professor of American literature, Universidad de Zaragoza, Spain, 1968-69; visiting professor of American literature, University of Bern, Switzerland, 1975-76. Visiting short-term American grantee, U.S. Department of State, Peru, Chile, and Paraguay, 1974, and Bolivia, Honduras, and Panama, 1975. Member of guild, American Poets series, 1971—. Contest judge for Devins Awards, 1971 and 1972. Vice-chairman of editorial committee, University Press of Kansas, 1967-71.

MEMBER: Society for Values in Higher Education (fellow), Phi Beta Kappa.

AWARDS, HONORS: First prize in poetry competition, *Kansas City Star,* 1964; Outstanding Educators of America Award, 1973; First Book Poetry Award, University of Nebraska Press, for *The Year of the Green Wave;* Octave Thanet Award (Iowa Writers Prize); Carr Scholar; D.H.L., Southwestern College, 1975; creative writing fellowship in poetry, National Endowment for the Arts, 1989; Bush artist fellowship, 1990-91.

WRITINGS:

The Year of the Green Wave, University of Nebraska Press, 1960.
A West Wind Rises, University of Nebraska Press, 1962.
Sun City, University of Nebraska Press, 1964.
A Voyage to America, University of Nebraska Press, 1967.
(Editor) *The Arts at the Grass Roots,* University Press of Kansas, 1968.
(Editor) *In That Day,* University Press of Kansas, 1969.
(With others) *Developing Awareness through Poetry,* Center for Twentieth-Century Studies, University of Wisconsin—Milwaukee, 1972.
The Doctrine of Selective Depravity, Juniper Press, 1980.
The Maker's Name, Juniper Press, 1980.
Nectar in a Sieve, Juniper Press, 1983.
Dark Fire, BkMk Press, 1985.
The Massacre at Sand Creek, Clark City Press, 1993.

Contributor to *Two Long Poems,* Juniper Press, 1991. Contributor to numerous anthologies, including *Midland,* edited by Paul Engle and others, Random House, 1961; *Bear Crossings,* edited by Anne Newman and Julie Suk, New South, 1978; and *As Far as I Can See,* edited by Charles Woodard, Windflower, 1989. Translator of poetry written by Octavio Paz, J. A. Rauskin, Pier Paolo Pasolini, and Luigi Compagnone. Contributor of over 125 poems, articles, and reviews to periodicals, including *Poetry, Prairie Schooner, Canadian Forum, Steppenwolf,* and *New York Times.* Advisory editor, *Kansas Quarterly,* 1968-87; member of advisory board, *Nimrod,* 1972-79.

WORK IN PROGRESS: The Book of Naples; three works for theatre, *A Brave Man's Part, The Keats of Comedy,* and *East Lynne,* a new play.

SIDELIGHTS: Bruce Cutler worked with migrants in a United Nations Demonstration Area in Health and Education in El Salvador, 1952-53, and in Texas, 1953-55. He speaks and writes Spanish and Italian.

BIOGRAPHICAL/CRITICAL SOURCES:

PERIODICALS

Eagle (Wichita, KS), February 18, 1962; October 5, 1962; May 24, 1981.
Kansas City Star, February 18, 1963.
Pioneer Press (St. Paul, MN), February 12, 1989.

*   *   *

CYNTHIA
See KING, Florence

D

DALTON, Sean
See CHESTER, Deborah

*   *   *

DAVEY, Cyril J(ames) 1911-

PERSONAL: Born May 31, 1911, in Liverpool, England; son of William Edward Gerrish and Margaret Boyd (Thom) Davey; married Gwendolen Mary Toone, August 19, 1937; children: Gillian Davey Allen, Susan Davey Donaldson, Paul. *Education:* Attended Handsworth Theological College, Birmingham, England, 1930-33. *Avocational interests:* Overseas travel, youth work, mental health studies, Methodist history, and drama.

ADDRESSES: Home—17 Yeomead, Nailsea, Bristol BS19 1JA, England.

CAREER: Methodist minister in England, 1933-39, in Nottingham, Bristol, and Tonbridge; garrison chaplain in India, 1939-46, in North-West Frontier, Madras, New Delhi, and Poona; Methodist minister in England, 1947-65, in Rickmansworth, Liverpool, Epsom, and Reigate, 1962-65; general secretary of Methodist Missionary Society, 1965-76; Methodist minister in Bristol, 1976-79. Has served on many Methodist and inter-church committees dealing with missionary activities, youth work, and inter-church relations, and as a mental hospital chaplain.

MEMBER: Society of Authors.

WRITINGS:

Handbook to the North-West Frontier, Ray, 1941.
A Book about India, Ray, 1943.
The Man Who Wanted the World, Cargate, 1947.
Indian Airmail, Edinburgh House Press, 1948.
The Yellow Robe, S.C.M. Press, 1951.

Mallory Kent's Secret Mission, Edinburgh House Press, 1955.
Talking round the Calendar, Lutterworth, 1955.
Lady with a Lamp, Lutterworth, 1956, published as *Lady with the Lamp: Florence Nightingale,* 1965.
Horseman of the Kings, Lutterworth, 1957, published as *Horseman of the King: John Wesley,* 1975.
Samuel Marsden, Oliphants, 1957.
The Monk Who Shook the World, Lutterworth, 1960, published as *Monk Who Shook the World: Martin Luther,* 1975.
Makers of the English Bible, Lutterworth, 1961.
On the Clouds to China, Lutterworth, 1964, published as *On the Clouds to China: Hudson Taylor,* 1975.
Never Say Die, Lutterworth, 1964.
Lights That Shine (also see below), Cargate, 1965.
Into Action, Edinburgh House Press, 1965.
Fifty Lives for God, Oliphants, 1973.
The Glory Man, Hodder & Stoughton, 1979.
Sadhu Sundar Singh, Send the Light Trust, 1980.
West Country Place Names and What They Mean, Abson Books, 1983.
Mad about Mission (biography of Thomas Coke), Marshall Pickering, 1985.
John Wesley and the Methodists, Marshall Pickering, 1985.
(Contributor) *Great Leaders of the Christian Church,* Moody, 1986.
Caring Comes First (history of Leprosy Mission International), Marshall Pickering, 1987.
Changing Places, Marshall Pickering, 1988.
Martin Luther, Hunt and Thorpe, 1992.
Mother Teresa, Hunt and Thorpe, 1992.

PUBLISHED BY EPWORTH

Maharajahs: Misery and Magic, 1948.
The March of Methodism, 1951.

The Methodist Story, 1955.
The Golden Arrow, 1957.
God and the Beanstalk, 1959.
Kagawa of Japan, 1960.
Silver Skates, 1961.
John Wesley (pamphlet), 1961.
Methodism: What It Is and How It Works, 1961.
A Story before We Sing, 1962.
Cornish Holiday, 1964.
The Santi Story, 1966.
Oberammergau Holiday, 1969.
Home from Home: Story of the Methodist Homes for the Aged, 1976.

PLAYS

Flying Pillar Box (juvenile), Methodist Missionary Society, 1947.
Thomas Coke (juvenile), Methodist Missionary Society, 1948.
Sister Grace (adult), Epworth, 1950.
Seat of Judgement (adult), Epworth, 1955.
The Five Pound Note (juvenile), Methodist Missionary Society, 1955.
The Penny that Worked (juvenile), Methodist Missionary Society, 1956.
Flame in the Forest (adult), Epworth, 1956.
Bananas for Breakfast (juvenile), Methodist Missionary Society, 1957.
The Curtain Line (adult), Epworth, 1958.
Take Your Pick (juvenile), Methodist Missionary Society, 1959.
Mr. Nodding's Nightmare (juvenile), Methodist Missionary Society, 1961.
Tune on the White Notes (adult), Methodist Missionary Society, 1961.
Television Trouble (juvenile), Methodist Missionary Society, 1963.
Coffee Morning (adult), Edinburgh House Press, 1963.

OTHER

Also author of *Home for Good,* 1983. Editor of "Heroes of the Faith" series. Also author of film scripts *Hello, Children,* for Methodist Missionary Society, *Lights That Shine,* 1965, and *Man in My Skin,* 1972, and of numerous stories for BBC's "Five to Ten" television series. Contributor to *Encyclopedia of World Methodism;* contributor to *Methodist Recorder, British Weekly, Christian World, Liverpool Evening Press,* and other publications. Contributor of short stories and features to local and national radio shows.

SIDELIGHTS: Cyril J. Davey's works have been translated into German, Swedish, Danish, Norwegian, Dutch, Italian, French, Spanish, Indonesian, Hindi, Burmese, and Arabic.

DAVIDSON, Jeffrey P(hilip) 1951-

PERSONAL: Born January 13, 1951, in Hartford, CT; son of Emanuel (a teacher and school vice-principal) and Shirley (a sales representative; maiden name, Leader) Davidson; married Susan Millard (a nurse manager), December 9, 1989; children: Valerie Ann. *Education:* University of Connecticut, B.S., 1973, M.B.A., 1974.

ADDRESSES: Home—2417 Honeysuckle Road, Suite 2A, Chapel Hill, NC 27514.

CAREER: Burroughs Corp., East Hartford, CT, marketing representative, 1974-75; Profiles, Inc. (management consulting firm), Vernon, CT, project manager, 1975-77; EMAY Corp., (management consulting firm), Washington, DC, senior project manager, 1977-80; IMR Systems, Inc. (management consulting firm), Falls Church, VA, vice-president of marketing, 1980-84; writer and lecturer, 1984—. Has appeared on numerous television and radio talk shows, including *CBS Nightwatch* and *America in the Morning.*

MEMBER: American Marketing Association, Institute of Management Consultants, National Speakers Association, Washington Independent Writers, Washington Area Writers.

AWARDS, HONORS: State winner, Small Business Media Advocate of the Year, Small Business Administration, 1983-87, for books and articles; Executive of Distinction designation, American Institute of Management, 1984; selected one of Outstanding Young Men in America, 1982, 1986; Professional Insurance Communicator's Association award, 1986, for outstanding feature article; *The Domino Effect* was among Best Business Books of 1992, *Library Journal.*

WRITINGS:

(With Richard A. Connor, Jr.) *Marketing Your Consulting and Professional Services,* Wiley, 1985.
Checklist Management: The Eight-Hour Manager, National Press, 1986, published in England as *Essential Management Checklists.*
Marketing Your Community, Public Technology, 1986.
Marketing to the Fortune 500 and Other Corporations, Dow Jones-Irwin, 1987.
Blow Your Own Horn: How to Get Ahead and Get Noticed, American Management Association, 1987.
(With Connor) *Getting New Clients,* Wiley, 1987.
(With Don Beveridge, Jr.) *The Achievement Challenge: How to Be a "10" in Business,* Dow Jones-Irwin, 1987.
Marketing on a Shoestring, Wiley, 1988.
Avoiding the Pitfalls of Starting Your Own Business, Walker, 1988.
The Marketing Sourcebook for Small Business, Wiley, 1989.

Marketing for the Home-Based Business, Bob Adams, 1990, as *Marketing to Home-Based Businesses,* Business One Irwin, 1991.
(With Dave Yoho) *How to Have a Good Year Every Year,* Berkley Books, 1991.
Power and Protocol for Getting to the Top, Shapolsky Publishers, 1991.
Selling to the Giants, Liberty Hall Press, 1991.
Breathing Space: Living and Working at a Comfortable Pace in a Sped-up Society, Mastermedia, 1991.
Cash Traps, Wiley, 1992.
(With Donald J. Vlcek) *The Domino Effect,* Business One Irwin, 1992.

Also author of numerous articles to periodicals, including *Business Horizons, Business and Society Review, Entrepreneur, Executive Female, Leaders, New Englander, Personnel, Rotarian, Supervisory Management, Today's Office, Unity, Washington Business Journal, World Executive Digest,* and *Working Woman.*

Davidson's work has been published in Italian, Spanish, Portuguese, Hebrew, Dutch, and Indonesian.

SIDELIGHTS: In *Breathing Space: Living and Working at a Comfortable Pace in a Sped-Up Society,* author Jeffrey P. Davidson addresses one of his major concerns: How to live and work at a comfortable pace while remaining competitive, balanced, and happy. While his previous books have focused on career enhancement, entrepreneurism, and personal achievement, Davidson now focuses his writing and lecturing on what he sees as today's fundamental challenges to individuals.

Davidson told *CA:* "Today everybody is under pressure both on and off the job. We exist with an overabundance of people, choices, and information. Yet, because modern technology enables us to gain new information faster, we have greater expectations about what we need to accomplish in our lives.

"Nearly every aspect of American society has become more complex even since the mid-1980s. Learning new ways to manage and new ways to increase productivity takes its toll. *Merely living* in America today and participating as a functioning member of society guarantees that your day, week, month, year, and *life*—and your physical, emotional, and spiritual energy—will easily be depleted without the proper vantage point from which to approach each day.

"Right now, keen focus on a handful of priorities has never been more important for each of us. Yes, some compelling issues must be given short shrift. Otherwise you run the risk of being overwhelmed by more demanding issues, and feeling overwhelmed always intensifies the feeling of being overworked. *This is not how it has to be.* As

an author, I have a vision. I see Americans leading balanced lives, with rewarding careers, happy home lives, and the ability to enjoy themselves. Our ticket to living and working at a comfortable pace is to not accommodate a way of being that doesn't support us."

BIOGRAPHICAL/CRITICAL SOURCES:

PERIODICALS

ABA Journal, December, 1985.
Boston Herald, January 5, 1992.
Chicago Tribune, June 23, 1991.
Christian Science Monitor, May 17, 1984.
Harvard Courant, July 31, 1985.
Los Angeles Times, June 15, 1985.
Miami Herald, June 17, 1985.
Washington Post, May 20, 1985; December 14, 1989.

*   *   *

DAVIS, Harley
See GREEN, Kay

*   *   *

DAVIS, James Robert   1945-
(Jim Davis)

PERSONAL: Born July 28, 1945, in Marion, IN; son of James William (a farmer) and Anna Catherine (Carter) Davis; married Carolyn L. Altekruse (formerly an elementary school teacher), July 26, 1969; children: James Alexander. *Education:* Attended Ball State University, 1963-67, B.S., 1986.

ADDRESSES: Home—Muncie, IN. *Office*—Paws, Inc., R.R. 1, Box 98-A, Albany, IN 47320. *Contact*—United Feature Syndicate, Inc., 200 Park Ave., New York, NY 10166.

CAREER: Groves & Associates, Muncie, IN, artist, 1968-69; free-lance advertising artist, 1969-78; assistant to "Tumbleweeds" comic strip author Tom Ryan, 1969-78; writer and cartoonist of "Garfield," and later "U.S. Acres," cartoon strips, syndicated internationally by United Feature Syndicate, 1978—; Paws, Inc. (art base for Garfield merchandising), Albany, IN, founder, 1981.

MEMBER: National Cartoonists Society, Newspaper Features Council, Screen Actors Guild, American Federation of Television and Radio Artists, Newspaper Features Council, Cartoon Art Museum of California (member of board of directors), Museum of Cartoon Art, Ball State Alumni Association, Muncie Civic Theatre (member of board of directors, 1974-76).

AWARDS, HONORS: Outstanding Young Men of America Award, 1972; National Cartoonists Society, Reuben Award for best humor strip, 1982, 1986, and 1990, Segar Award, 1985, Cartoonist of the Year, 1990; Golden Plate, American Academy of Achievement, 1983; Marketing Hall of Fame award, American Marketing Association (southern California chapter), 1983; Sagamore of the Wabash Award, State of Indiana, 1984; Emmy Award for outstanding animated program, National Academy of Television Arts and Sciences, 1984, for *Garfield on the Town*, 1985, for *Garfield in the Rough*, and 1986, for *Garfield's Hallowe'en Adventure;* Volunteer of the Year designation, Indiana Council of Fund Raising Executives, 1985; Forest Conservationist of the Year designation, Indiana Wildlife Federation, 1990; Hoosier Pride Award, 1990; Arbor Day Award, National Arbor Day Foundation, 1990; Distinguished Alumnus Award, American Association of State Colleges and Universities. Honorary doctorates from Ball State University and Purdue University, both 1991.

WRITINGS:

"GARFIELD" COMIC STRIP COLLECTIONS; UNDER NAME JIM DAVIS

Garfield at Large, Ballantine, 1980.
Garfield Gains Weight, Ballantine, 1981.
Garfield, Bigger than Life: His Third Book, Ballantine, 1981.
Garfield Weighs In, Ballantine, 1982.
Garfield Treasury, Ballantine, 1982.
Here Comes Garfield (based on the television special; also see below), Ballantine, 1982.
Garfield Takes the Cake, Ballantine, 1982.
Garfield Sits around the House, Ballantine, 1983.
Garfield on the Town (based on the television special; also see below), Ballantine, 1983.
Garfield Eats His Heart Out, Ballantine, 1983.
The Second Garfield Treasury, Ballantine, 1984.
Garfield Tips the Scales, Ballantine, 1984.
Garfield Loses His Feet, Ballantine, 1984.
Garfield: His Nine Lives, Ballantine, 1984.
Garfield Makes It Big, Ballantine, 1985.
Garfield Rolls On, Ballantine, 1985.
Garfield in Disguise, Ballantine, 1985.
The Third Garfield Treasury, Ballantine, 1985.
Garfield Out to Lunch, Ballantine, 1986.
The Unabridged, Uncensored, Unbelievable Garfield Book, Ballantine, 1986.
Garfield Food for Thought, Ballantine, 1987.
The Fourth Garfield Treasury, Ballantine, 1987.
A Garfield Christmas (based on the television special; also see below), Ballantine, 1987.
Garfield Swallows His Pride, Ballantine, 1987.

Garfield Goes Hollywood (based on the television special; also see below), Ballantine, 1987.
Garfield Rounds Out, Ballantine, 1988.
Garfield's Thanksgiving (based on the television special; also see below), Ballantine, 1988.
The Garfield How to Party Book, Ballantine, 1988.
Garfield World-wide, Ballantine, 1988.
Garfield Chews the Fat, Ballantine, 1989.
Garfield Presents: Babes and Bullets, story adapted by Ron Tuthill, Ballantine, 1989.
The Fifth Garfield Treasury, Ballantine, 1989.
Garfield Goes to Waist, Ballantine, 1990.
Garfield Hangs Out, Ballantine, 1990.
Garfield on the Farm, Ballantine, 1990.
Garfield's Feline Fantasies, Ballantine, 1990.
Garfield's Judgment Day, story adapted by Kim Campbell, illustrated by Mike Fentz and others, Ballantine, 1990.
Garfield Takes Up Space, Ballantine, 1991.
Garfield by the Pound, Ballantine, 1991.
Garfield: The Truth about Cats, Ballantine, 1991.
Garfield Takes his Licks, Ballantine Books, 1993.

"U.S. ACRES" COMIC STRIP COLLECTIONS; UNDER NAME JIM DAVIS

U.S. Acres Counts Its Chickens, Pharos Books/Ballantine, 1987.
U.S. Acres Goes Half Hog!, Pharos Books, 1987.
U.S. Acres Rules the Roost, Pharos Books, 1988.
U.S. Acres I: I Wasn't Hatched Yesterday, Berkley Publishing, 1989.
U.S. Acres Runs Amuck, Pharos Books, 1989.
(Creator) Jim Kraft, *U.S. Acres: The Big Camp Out,* designed and illustrated by Betsy Brackett and others, Bantam, 1989.
(Creator) Kraft, *U.S. Acres: Wade Dives In,* designed and illustrated by Brackett and others, Bantam, 1989.
U.S. Acres: It's a Pig's Life, Berkley Publishing, 1989.
U.S. Acres: Hold That Duck, Berkley Publishing, 1989.
(Creator) Kraft, *U.S. Acres: Beware! Rooster at Work,* designed and illustrated by Brett Koth and others, Bantam, 1989.
U.S. Acres Hams It Up, Topper Books, 1989.
(Creator) Kraft, *U.S. Acres: Sir Orson to the Rescue,* designed and illustrated by Koth and others, Bantam, 1989.
U.S. Acres, Berkley Publishing, 1990.
U.S. Acres: Take This Rooster, Berkley Publishing, 1990.
(Creator) Kraft, *U.S. Acres: Happy Birthday Sheldon!,* designed and illustrated by Koth, Larry Fentz, and Dwight Ferris, Bantam, 1990.
Wade's Haunted Halloween, Bantam, 1990.
Counting Sheep, Berkley Publishing, 1990.

JUVENILES; UNDER NAME JIM DAVIS

(Illustrator) Shep Steneman, *Garfield: The Complete Cat Book,* Random House, 1981.

(Illustrator) Emily P. Kingsley, *Garfield the Pirate,* 1982.

Garfield Mix and Match Storybook, Random House, 1982.

(Illustrator) *Garfield the Knight in Shining Armor,* Random House, 1982.

Garfield Counts to Ten, Random House, 1983.

Garfield in Space, Random House, 1983.

Garfield Goes Underground, Random House, 1983.

(Illustrator) Jack Harris, *Garfield Goes to a Picnic,* Random House, 1983, published as *Garfield's Picnic Adventure* (also see below), Western Publishing, 1988.

(With M. Fentz and Dave Kuhn) *Garfield A to Z Zoo,* Random House, 1984.

(With M. Fentz and Kuhn) *Garfield Book of the Seasons,* Random House, 1984.

(Illustrator) *Garfield Water Fun,* Random House, 1985.

(With L. Fentz and M. Fentz) *Garfield Goes to the Farm,* Random House, 1985.

My Little Pony through the Seasons, illustrated by Kathy Allert, Random House, 1985.

(Illustrator) Kate Klimo, editor, *Garfield Touch-&-Go-Seek: Things to Touch, See, & Smell,* Random House, 1986.

(Creator) Norma Simone, *Garfield, the Fussy Cat,* Western Publishing, 1988.

Garfield's Night before Christmas, Putnam, 1988.

(Creator) Kraft, *U.S. Acres: The Great Christmas Contest,* illustrated by Paws, Inc., Bantam, 1988.

(Creator) Leslie McGuire, *Garfield and the Space Cat* (also see below), Western Publishing, 1988.

Garfield and the Haunted Diner: A Lift-the-Flap Book, Putnam, 1989.

(Creator) Kraft, *Garfield and the Tiger,* Western Publishing, 1989.

Garfield in the Park, Western Publishing, 1989.

(Creator) Simone, *Garfield the Big Star* (also see below), Western Publishing, 1989.

(Creator) Diane Namm, *Happy Birthday, Garfield,* Western Publishing, 1989.

Garfield's Furry Tales, Putnam, 1989.

(Creator) Kraft, *Garfield, the Easter Bunny?,* Putnam, 1989.

(Creator) Jack C. Harris, *Garfield's Longest Catnap,* Western Publishing, 1989.

(Creator) Kraft, *U.S. Acres: A Most Special Easter Egg: From the Creator of Garfield,* illustrated by Paws, Inc., Bantam, 1989.

(Creator) Kraft, *U.S. Acres: Let's Play Ball!,* Bantam, 1989.

(Creator) Simone, Harris, and McGuire, *Garfield Stories: Including The Big Star, Garfield's Picnic Adventure,*

Garfield and the Space Cat, Western Publishing, 1990.

(Creator) Kraft, *Garfield: Mini-Mysteries,* illustrated by Kuhn and M. Fentz, Western Publishing, 1990.

Scary Tales, Grosset & Dunlap, 1990.

Garfield's Tales of Mystery, Putnam, 1991.

Garfield at the Gym, Western Publishing, 1991.

"GARFIELD LEARNS ABOUT" SERIES; JUVENILE

Garfield Learns about Cooking: Any Cat Can Cook, Western Publishing, 1992.

Garfield Learns about Fire Safety: Where's the Fire?, Western Publishing, 1992.

Garfield Learns about Money: Money Madness!, Western Publishing, 1992.

Garfield Learns about Planning: Surprise Party, Western Publishing, 1992.

Garfield Learns about Thoughtfulness: Don't Be Late!, Western Publishing, 1992.

ANIMATED TELEVISION SPECIALS; UNDER NAME JIM DAVIS

Here Comes Garfield, Columbia Broadcasting System (CBS-TV), 1982.

Garfield on the Town, CBS-TV, 1983.

Garfield in the Rough, CBS-TV, 1984.

The Garfield Hallowe'en Special, CBS-TV, 1985.

Garfield in Paradise, CBS-TV, 1986.

Garfield Goes Hollywood, CBS-TV, 1987.

The Garfield Christmas Special, CBS-TV, 1987.

Garfield's Thanksgiving Special, CBS-TV, 1988.

Garfield—His Nine Lives, CBS-TV, 1988.

Babes and Bullets, CBS-TV, 1989.

Garfield's Feline Fantasies, CBS-TV, 1990.

Garfield Gets a Life, CBS-TV, 1991.

OTHER "GARFIELD" BOOKS; UNDER NAME JIM DAVIS

(With Bill Tornquist) *The Garfield Trivia Book,* Ballantine, 1986.

(With Carol Wallace) *The Garfield Book of Cat Names,* Ballantine, 1988, also published as *The Garfield Cat Naming Book,* 1988.

(Creator) Kraft, *Garfield: The Me Book: A Guide to Superiority, How to Get It, Use It, and Keep It,* illustrated by Koth, Ballantine, 1990.

Also the creator of postcard books published by Ballentine, including *Garfield Postcard: Birthday,* 1990; *Garfield Birthday Greetings,* 1992; *Garfield Postcard Book: Be My Valentine,* 1992; and *Garfield's Thank You Postcard Book,* 1993.

SIDELIGHTS: A fat, lazy, bad-tempered cat named Garfield has made James Robert Davis, known professionally as Jim Davis, one of today's most successful cartoonists. Appearing in newspapers across the United States and in dozens of countries around the world, Garfield's familiar face appears on book jackets, in the starring role of animated television specials, and decorates merchandise ranging from t-shirts to bookmarks. But even though he has become a millionaire, the creative talent behind Garfield has not allowed his celebrity status to alter his lifestyle. "Everything I did cannot erase the fact that I am an Indiana farm boy," Davis told Mary Vespa in an interview for *People.* "Except for the media attention, precious little has changed."

The origin of Davis's love for cartooning can be traced back to his childhood in rural Indiana. As a young boy, much of his time was spent sick in bed, for when Davis was less than a year old he developed severe asthma. The condition kept him inside where, to alleviate young Davis's boredom, his mother encouraged him to draw. "She's the one who got me started," the cartoonist explained. "She'd give me a paper and pencil and make me try to draw. I'd draw someone, and as soon as I learned to spell, I'd have them saying something. Then I started drawing boxes and in second or third grade, it was cartooning."

Continuing his hobby into high school, Davis created a cartoon strip he called "Herman." A few years later, when he entered college, he decided to add practicality to creativity. He majored in both art and business but ended up not doing very well in either. Low grades persuaded Davis to leave school and seek gainful employment, which turned out to be an entry level job at an advertising agency where he earned $1.60 per hour. Even so, he told John Heins in an article for *Forbes,* "I liked advertising . . . , but my ulcer didn't." After working in the art department for a year and a half, he quit his job to work for cartoonist Tom Ryan. Davis drew backgrounds for "Tumbleweeds," Ryan's humorous look at Westerns, and Ryan served as mentor to the young artist by instructing him in many of the basics of writing and drawing cartoon strips.

With Ryan's encouragement, Davis created his own strip, "Gnorm the Gnat." He described the strip to *Los Angeles Times* contributor Paul Galloway: "Some of the characters were fruit flies. They have a life expectancy of about three weeks, and they are very nervous and insecure, as you can imagine. They never worried about long engagements. Freddy Fruit Fly would say 'Bill me' when he bought something." The concept did not appeal much to the cartoon syndicates—Davis tried to sell "Gnorm the Gnat" for five years before finally giving up on it.

Despite this setback, Davis kept up his resolve and set out to create a new strip idea. "I wanted to keep working with animals because they have the advantage of not being either white or black, male or female, young or old," he told Galloway. "I didn't want . . . to be controversial." Davis

noticed the predominance of dogs in cartoons: "There was Snoopy, Marmaduke, Fred Basset—a lot of dogs but hardly any cats." So Davis created a cat character, borrowing the name and much of the personality from his grandfather, John Garfield Davis. Although the central character of Davis's strip was intended to be Jon Arbuckle, Garfield's bumbling owner and the object of the cat's surly temper and needle-sharp claws, Davis soon realized that Garfield was the real star of the cartoon. He shifted his attention to developing the feline's distinctive personality and visual characteristics. Davis altered Garfield's appearance; his body became smaller, his arms and legs longer, and the eyes larger and more expressive. Garfield's unapologetically rude and self-indulgent personality produced the strip's most memorable lines: "I'm not fat, I'm undertall"; "Cats don't ask. Cats take"; "I never met a lasagna I didn't like"; "Big, fat, hairy deal"; and many others. As a contrast to Garfield's surly temperament, Davis would eventually introduce Nermal, "the world's cutest kitten," and Odie, a good-natured but extremely slobbery mutt.

After fine-tuning "Garfield" for about a year, Davis felt he was ready to propose it to the syndicates. The first two, Chicago Tribune-New York News and King Features, turned Davis down. But United Feature Syndicate liked the cartoonist's idea and signed Davis to a ten-year contract. "Garfield" was immediately distributed to forty-one newspapers but the success of the new strip initially seemed in jeopardy. Newspapers in Chicago, Salt Lake City, and Little Rock canceled "Garfield" after test runs. But readers of each of the papers quickly petitioned for the strip's reinstallment. United Features capitalized on this incident by using it to promote the popularity of "Garfield"—it soon became the fastest-growing comic-strip in the country.

Davis's break into national recognition was the comic-strip collection *Garfield at Large.* He created a rough book dummy, using six month's worth of strips, and took it to United Feature to see if they could get a publisher interested in it. When he returned home to Indiana there was a letter awaiting him from Ballantine. Then editor-in-chief Nancy Coffey had seen the strip in Philadelphia newspapers and was already a fan of the feline curmudgeon. She eagerly accepted the idea and published the comic collection in 1980. The book sold hundreds of thousands of copies—somewhat ironically, *Garfield at Large* appeared on the *New York Times* best-seller list even before the strip "Garfield" ever appeared in a New York City newspaper. Several years after the success of *Garfield at Large,* Davis was the first author to have more than two of his books on the *New York Times* trade-paperback best-seller list concurrently. At one point, seven of his books were on the list in one week. Since then, the popularity of "Garfield" has spread across the globe, with translations appearing in Europe, Africa, Australia, and Asia.

Davis's main goal in writing has always been to be entertaining. "I feel a responsibility to keep 'Garfield' good and fluffy," he told Jean W. Ross in an interview for *CA*. "I feel like we're balancing the scales just a bit with some of the very real, very depressing things going on. In fact, the harder the times, the more popular the comics page, from what I've noticed. They were very, very popular during the Great Depression; that was their heyday. And even today, with the economic recession or the military conflicts, it seems like people come back to the comics page again and again. I feel someday comics will take their rightful place as a piece of Americana. It's not exactly art, it's not exactly writing, it's *cartooning*. We invented it, and even now nobody does it better. If you look at a comics page in a foreign newspaper, by and large it will be American strips. Cartooning will come into its own. Its getting more and more attention, and that's good."

"Some newspapers have been shrinking the size of comics," Davis told Ross in a discussion of his artistic approach. "There simply isn't the room for the detail that there used to be. I also like to draw a cartoon as one would tell a joke. I keep the characters in the same position; I use very little background if any—usually I use the table top. That allows the eye to travel through the strip without having to stop and start and look at any art work or tricky variation on character angle. I use as few words as possible so that people can read through a strip smoothly in three frames and laugh as if they were being told a joke. It's timing; it's bomp, bomp, ta-*domp*. If the eye doesn't stop, if it doesn't have to linger over a lot of words, you can get the spontaneous laugh. Otherwise you've lost your timing, you've lost your humor in a way. So I like to keep the art simple."

As more "Garfield" books came out and the strip's popularity continued to soar, the cartoon character began to diversify. Davis designed several television specials for CBS; the first one, *Here Comes Garfield*, was initially broadcast in 1982. The voice-over for Garfield was provided by Lorenzo Music, whose sleepy, low-key utterances reflect the cat's laid-back personality. In addition to television appearances, "Garfield" has branched out into a long list of books for children, including *Garfield: The Complete Cat Book*, a book instructing children how to take care of their pet cat, and a counting book, *Garfield Counts to Ten*. Davis feels that his ability to write a joke outweighs his artistic talents. "My strong point is, frankly, the writing," he told Ross, "Writing the strip, writing for some of the books, and also writing the TV shows. Since I know the character so well, since I've been doing the Garfield gags for so many years, he really does exist in my mind. There-

fore it's very easy for me to anticipate what he'll do in given situations."

On the heels of "Garfield"'s popularity, Davis went on to create a new strip called "U.S. Acres." Inspired by his own experience growing up in rural Indiana, the strip is set on a farm and involves the shenanigans of barnyard animals. The central character is Orson the Pig; other characters include a baby chick named Sheldon who refuses to come out of his shell and a paranoid duck named Wade who—because of his fear of water—insists on wearing an inner tube at all times. Although not nearly as popular as "Garfield," "U.S. Acres" has had some success and a number of comic strip collections have been published over the last few years.

"The best part of [my success]," Davis confided to Ross, "is getting to draw cartoon strips. That's all I've ever wanted to do. And I think if I do anything in the service of the readers, it's to provide some humor, make them feel a little better. That's the reason I started the whole thing anyway. My favorite fan letters are those that say I brightened that reader's day a little bit. If I can make someone laugh, smile, or just think a nice thought, then I've accomplished my job. Cartooning is entertainment, and if 'Garfield' serves that purpose, then I've accomplished what I wanted to do. That, for me, is the biggest thrill."

For a previously published interview, see entry in *Contemporary Authors New Revisions*, Volume 16, Gale, 1985, pp. 77-81.

BIOGRAPHICAL/CRITICAL SOURCES:

PERIODICALS

Cartoonist Profiles, December, 1978.
Chicago Sun-Times, November 2, 1978.
Forbes, November 21, 1983, pp. 326, 328.
Los Angeles Times, November 14, 1982.
New York Times Book Review, July 27, 1980.
People, November 17, 1980, pp. 106-109; November 1, 1982, pp. 88-92.
Publishers Weekly, March 13, 1981, pp. 6-7.
Sunday Record (New Jersey), February 20, 1983.
Time, December 7, 1981, pp. 72-79.

[Sketch verified by Kim Campbell, secretary to Jim Davis]

*   *   *

DAVIS, Jim
See DAVIS, James Robert

DAVIS-FRIEDMANN, Deborah 1945-

PERSONAL: Born August 25, 1945; daughter of William Shippen and Deborah (Wood) Davis; married Michael Friedmann; children: Eli. *Education:* Wellesley College, B.A., 1967; Harvard University, M.A., 1970; Boston University, Ph.D., 1978.

ADDRESSES: Office—Department of Sociology, P.O. Box 1965, Yale University, New Haven, CT 06520.

CAREER: Chinese University of Hong Kong, Hong Kong, lecturer in sociology, 1967-69; Tunghai University, Taichung, Taiwan, lecturer in English, 1970-71; Yale University, New Haven, CT, assistant professor, 1978-83, associate professor, 1984-88, professor of sociology, 1989—.

MEMBER: American Sociological Association, Gerontological Society, Association of Asian Studies, Yale China Association (vice-president of board of trustees, 1983-86).

AWARDS, HONORS: Grants from Social Science Research Council, 1975 and 1979, National Academy of Sciences, 1979, 1987, National Institute on Aging, 1981-82, and American Council of Learned Societies, 1985-86, 1989.

WRITINGS:

Long Lives: Chinese Elderly and the Communist Revolution, (nonfiction), Harvard University Press, 1983, expanded edition, Stanford University Press, 1991.
(With Ezra Vogel) *Chinese Society on the Eve of Tiananmen: The Impact of Reform,* Harvard University Press, 1990.
(With Steven Hancel) *Chinese Family in the Post-Mao Era,* Calyuma, 1993.

WORK IN PROGRESS: Getting Ahead, Falling Behind: Occupational Mobility in China, and *Chinese Urban Living.*

*   *   *

DeCHANCIE, John 1946-

PERSONAL: Born August 3, 1946, in Pittsburgh, PA; son of Gene (in construction business) and Fannie (a librarian; maiden name, DiNardo) DeChancie; married Holly Marie Seliy (a nurse), July 31, 1976; children: Jason, Gene. *Education:* University of Pittsburgh, B.A., 1968.

ADDRESSES: Home—6002 Squires Manor Lane, Library, PA 15129.

CAREER: WQED Public Television, Pittsburgh, PA, engineer, 1970-75; self-employed film and videotape producer and director of short dramatic films, including *The Lightning Rod Man,* based on a short story by Herman

Melville, Pyramid Films, 1975-84; Broadcast Music, Inc., New York City, field representative, 1984-86; writer, 1986—.

MEMBER: Science Fiction Writers of America

WRITINGS:

"SKYWAY" SCIENCE FICTION SERIES

Starrigger, Ace Books, 1983.
Red Limit Freeway, Ace Books, 1984.
Paradox Alley, Ace Books, 1986.

"CASTLE" FANTASY SERIES

Castle Perilous, Ace Books, 1987.
Castle for Rent, Ace Books, 1989.
Castle Kidnapped, Ace Books, 1989.
Castle War!, Ace Books, 1990.
Castle Murders, Ace Books, 1991.
Castle Dreams, •Ace Books, 1992.
Castle Spellbound, Ace Books, 1992.
Bride of the Castle, Ace Books, in press.

OTHER

(With Thomas F. Monteleone) *Crooked House* (novel), Tor Books, 1987.
Peron (nonfiction), Chelsea House, 1987.
Nasser (nonfiction), Chelsea House, 1987.
(With David Bischoff) *Dr. Dimension* (novel), Roc Books, 1993.
The Kruton Interface (novel), Ace Books, 1993.
Magicnet (novel), Avon/Morrow, 1993.

Contributor of short stories to books, including "The Grass of Remembrance," *Borderlands,* Avon Books, 1991; "Murder On-Line," *Whatdunits,* edited by Mike Resnick, DAW Books, 1992; "Hitler Clone in Argentina Plots Falklands Reprise," *Alien Pregnant by Elvis,* edited by Esther Friesner, DAW Books, 1993; and "Tu Quoque," *Larger Than Life,* edited by John Varley, Ace Putnam, in press. Also contributor of short stories and poetry to periodicals, including *Pittsburgh Quarterly, Bulletin of Science Fiction Writers of America,* and *Magazine of Fantasy and Science Fiction.*

SIDELIGHTS: John DeChancie once told *CA:* "The first few books I sold were science fiction, and I'm sure I'll continue to write it, but probably not exclusively. In the past, science fiction writers have been confined to a ghetto. I want to range wide and free. I've sold [several] books so far, the last two being related to science fiction but not squarely within the genre. I can't say now what I'll do next, but eventually I want to swim in mainstream waters. Those back creeks can get brackish and stagnant.

"All of the above notwithstanding, the ideas and concerns of science fiction are still of abiding interest to me. We live in a world that was once science fiction. Space travel has been reduced to bus schedules; ray guns appear on government appropriation bills. My science fiction, however, doesn't deal with these headline realities. I am attracted to archetypal images which long have been associated with the genre: domed cities on the plain, the road that winds through space and time, alien ruins in starlight, the otherworldly landscape, and more; images which I suspect are etched deep within the uncreated consciousness of humankind. Mythology fascinates me. Science fiction is latter-day mythology, and the entire corpus of science fiction may be looked at as a mythos concerning man's future. I don't mean to imply, though, that my writings are collections of disconnected images; on the contrary, I think of myself primarily as a storyteller. I people my stories with beings—human and nonhuman—who act and react, think and do, triumph and fail. Without them a story would be an empty shell, like a building stripped to the girders, revealing the machinery in the basement clanking and grinding away to no purpose."

BIOGRAPHICAL/CRITICAL SOURCES:

PERIODICALS

New York Times Book Review, December 11, 1983.

*   *   *

DELANY, Paul   1937-

PERSONAL: Born July 1, 1937, in London, England; son of George F. and Clare (Parfait) Delany; children: Nicholas, Lev, Katherine. *Education:* McGill University, B.Comm., 1957; Stanford University, A.M., 1958; University of California, Berkeley, M.A., 1961, Ph.D., 1965. *Politics:* New Democratic Party (Canada).

ADDRESSES: Home—3478 W. 35th Ave., Vancouver, British Columbia, Canada. *Office*—English Department, Simon Fraser University, Burnaby, British Columbia.

CAREER: Columbia University, New York City, assistant professor of English, 1964-70; Simon Fraser University, Burnaby, British Columbia, associate professor, 1970-76, professor of English, 1977—. Visiting professor, University of Waterloo, Ontario, 1985-86.

MEMBER: Royal Society of Literature (fellow), D. H. Lawrence Society of North America (president, 1991-92), Modern Language Association of America.

AWARDS, HONORS: Fellowships from Guggenheim Foundation, 1975-76, and Killam Society, 1992-93; *D. H. Lawrence's Nightmare* was named one of the best books of the year by the *New York Times,* 1979.

WRITINGS:

British Autobiography in the Seventeenth Century, Columbia University Press, 1969.
D. H. Lawrence's Nightmare, Basic Books, 1978.
The Neo-Pagans, Free Press, 1987.

Contributor of articles to periodicals, including *Chaucer Review, New York Times Books Review,* and *London Review of Books.*

EDITOR

(With R. W. Hanning and J. Ford) *Sixteenth-Century English Literature: A Selective Anthology,* Holt, 1976.
(With George Landow) *Hypermedia and Literary Studies,* MIT Press, 1991.
(With Landow) *The Digital Word,* MIT Press, 1992.

SIDELIGHTS: Paul Delany's book *D. H. Lawrence's Nightmare* examines the author's life during the time that he and his German wife Freda stayed in England after traveling from Italy for a brief visit in 1914 and become trapped there after the war broke out. The couple was placed under surveillance by British authorities, who suspected them of spying. Lawrence, broke and in ill health, was forced to rely on the charity of friends; the Lawrences lived in a succession of borrowed cottages during their stay, which lasted until 1919. The "nightmare" of Delany's title is a specific reference to a chapter in Lawrence's *Kangaroo* in which the author details how he had to live with the constant threat of conscription and was forced to undergo three military physical examinations.

It was while he was in England that the author formulated his eccentric political philosophy which, as Stanley Weintraub explains it in the *New Republic,* consisted of a utopian dream "of a future intellectual and agrarian community in Florida or Samoa, where his followers would live by the visionary phallic philosophy of 'the great male and female duality and unity.'" As Lawrence's "mood darkened," John Gross explains in the *New York Review of Books,* "he swung round and began to preach the need for fixed hierarchies, a strong leader, a state run on authoritarian lines and the more estranged from England he felt, the harsher his contempt for the liberal-democratic virtues. They were part of the rationalism that he saw as the ruin of Europe, with its denial of instinct and impulse—and with mechanized warfare as its natural culmination."

Despite these facts, Lawrence produced some of his best work during this period, completing the major part of *Women in Love* and all of *The Rainbow,* which was suppressed by the police in 1915 as pornography. According to Irving Howe in the *New York Times Book Review,* although Lawrence himself referred to these years as a "nightmare," "in retrospect, it seems clear that they formed a time of crisis and renewal as fruitful as it was painful."

Delany's book about these years, *D. H. Lawrence's Nightmare,* has been widely praised by reviewers. Gross indicates that Delany "follows Lawrence's zigzag progress from cottage to cottage, from book to book, from crisis to crisis, always setting the scene clearly, reconstructing the story with admirable sympathy and objectivity. And detail, with such a story, counts for as much as it would in a novel." David Gordon adds in the *Washington Post Book World* that "the particular success of Paul Delany's chronicle is due to its narrative energy, sharp yet balanced insights, and to the focus provided by a detailed and nuanced account of the personal experience that went into the making of Lawrence's most strenuous novel, *Women in Love.*" Yet, he writes, "it is Delany's purpose to show us that the artist could probably not have written with such force if the man had not tried to actualize the vision, to find real alternatives to the grim reality of wartime England."

Howe adds that Delany "is admirably sympathetic, but critical too, in describing the tragicomedy of Lawrence's swings from hunger for a new fraternity to heated bullying of those who hesitated to join with him. Lawrence can easily be made to look ridiculous—indeed he was; but Mr. Delany writes with the assurance that Lawrence was also seeing into the decay of bourgeois civilization as none of the more sane and balanced liberals did." As a reviewer for the *New Yorker* explains, "this is a distressing and chilling . . . chronicle of a fine mind in a purgatory of, for the most part, its own making, but the book has its brighter aspects. . . . As a contribution to a fuller understanding of one of the great flawed writers of our time, it is indispensable."

BIOGRAPHICAL/CRITICAL SOURCES:

PERIODICALS

New Republic, January 27, 1979.
New Yorker, January 15, 1979.
New York Review of Books, September 27, 1979.
New York Times Book Review, January 28, 1979.
Times Literary Supplement, October 2, 1969; December 7, 1979.
Washington Post Book World, March 25, 1979.

*   *   *

DEVERAUX, Jude
See WHITE, Jude Gilliam

De VRIES, Peter 1910-

PERSONAL: Born February 27, 1910, in Chicago, IL; son of Joost (a furniture warehouse owner) and Henrietta (Eldersveld) De Vries; married Katinka Loeser (a writer), October 16, 1943; children: Jan, Peter Jon, Emily (deceased), Derek. *Education:* Calvin College, A.B., 1931; attended Northwestern University, summer, 1931. *Politics:* Democrat.

ADDRESSES: Home—170 Cross Hwy., Westport, CT 06880.

CAREER: Writer and editor. Editor of community newspapers, Chicago, IL, 1931; candy vending machine operator, taffy apple peddler, lecturer, and radio actor, Chicago, 1931-38; free-lance writer, 1931—; *Poetry* magazine, Chicago, associate editor, 1938-42, co-editor, 1942-44; *The New Yorker,* staff member, 1944—. Balch Lecturer, University of Virginia, Charlottesville, 1962; lecturer, 1968 Sophomore National Literary Festival, University of Notre Dame; lecturer during 1960s at several universities in Germany as part of a U.S. State Department-sponsored program.

MEMBER: National Institute of Arts and Letters, American Academy of Arts and Letters.

AWARDS, HONORS: American Academy of Arts and Letters grant, 1946; D.H.L., University of Bridgeport, CT, 1968, University of Michigan, and Susquehanna University, PA; Arts Award, Connecticut Commission on the Arts, 1991.

WRITINGS:

NOVELS

But Who Wakes the Bugler?, Houghton, 1940.
The Handsome Heart, Coward, 1943.
Angels Can't Do Better, Coward, 1944.
The Tunnel of Love (also see below), Little, Brown, 1954.
Comfort Me with Apples (also see below), Little, Brown, 1956.
The Mackerel Plaza, Little, Brown, 1958.
The Tents of Wickedness (sequel to *Comfort Me with Apples*), Little, Brown, 1959.
Through the Fields of Clover, Little, Brown, 1961.
The Blood of the Lamb, Little, Brown, 1962.
Reuben, Reuben, Little, Brown, 1964.
Let Me Count the Ways, Little, Brown, 1965.
The Vale of Laughter, Little, Brown, 1967.
The Cat's Pajamas and Witch's Milk (novellas), Little, Brown, 1968.
Mrs. Wallop, Little, Brown, 1970.
Into Your Tent I'll Creep, Little, Brown, 1971.
Forever Panting, Little, Brown, 1973.
The Glory of the Hummingbird, Little, Brown, 1974.

I Hear America Swinging, Little, Brown, 1976.

Madder Music, Little, Brown, 1977.

Consenting Adults; or, The Duchess Will Be Furious, Little, Brown, 1980.

Sauce for the Goose, Little, Brown, 1981.

Slouching towards Kalamazoo, Little, Brown, 1983.

The Prick of Noon, Little, Brown, 1985.

Peckham's Marbles, Putnam, 1986.

SHORT STORIES

No, But I Saw the Movie, Little, Brown, 1952.

Without a Stitch in Time: A Selection of the Best Humorous Short Pieces, Little, Brown, 1972.

OTHER

(With Joseph Fields) *The Tunnel of Love* (dramatization of the novel; produced on Broadway by Theatre Guild and in London, 1957), Little, Brown, 1957.

Contributor of short stories to *The New Yorker.*

De Vries's manuscript collection is housed at the Boston University Library.

ADAPTATIONS: The Tunnel of Love was filmed by Metro-Goldwyn-Mayer, 1958; *Reuben, Reuben* was adapted by Herman Shumlin and produced on Broadway at ANTA Theatre as *Spofford,* 1967, and filmed by Twentieth Century-Fox, 1983; *Let Me Count the Ways* was filmed by American Broadcasting Co. as *How Do I Love Thee?,* 1970; *Witch's Milk* was adapted by Julius J. Epstein and filmed by Universal as *Pete 'n' Tillie,* 1972.

SIDELIGHTS: Author Peter De Vries, described by Sybil S. Steinberg in *Publishers Weekly* as "something of a national humorist laureate," has made a career of satirizing society's shortcomings with wit, irony, and plenty of puns. "He is a serious man whose comic cast of mind developed as a defense against the severe Dutch Calvinist indoctrination of his formative years," Steinberg noted. Indeed, De Vries's background is reflected in his recurring themes of love, lust, marriage and its alternatives, and the unholy battles aroused by the topic of religion.

De Vries began his lucrative and long-lasting partnership with *The New Yorker* magazine in 1944, while working as editor of *Poetry* magazine in Chicago. De Vries invited humorist James Thurber to speak at a lecture to benefit his financially strapped publication, and Thurber in turn persuaded De Vries to contribute to *The New Yorker.* De Vries was soon offered the position of poetry editor. His affiliation with *Poetry* brought him another rewarding partnership—he met his wife, Katinka Loeser, also an author, when she won the magazine's Young Poet's Prize in 1942. Over the years, beyond his editorial duties, De Vries has contributed numerous short stories to *The New Yorker* which were later published in collected volumes. The mag-

azine has served as a forum for his wife's work as well. "Often the coterie of loyal De Vries fans are the same ones who savor Katinka Loeser's memorable stories in *The New Yorker* and other magazines . . . , unaware that in private life Loeser is Mrs. De Vries," Steinberg reflected.

De Vries chose to disown his first three novels. "For a while I tried to buy up extant copies and burn them, but now it costs too much," he told Steinberg. The irony of a rare book catalog's listing of *But Who Wakes the Bugler?* at an exorbitant price was not lost on the author. *The Tunnel of Love,* the first novel De Vries acknowledges, sets his pattern of including at least one pun-addicted character in each work and introduces a favorite topic: marriage and its accompanying problems and delights. *Comfort Me with Apples* and *Tents of Wickedness* both follow Chick Swallow through his marital discomforts and infidelities. "Typically, the overall movement of De Vries' novels is first a reaction against and then a comic acceptance of the adult community of marriage, and Swallow ends the second book by refusing the tempting offer of a tryst with an old girlfriend, 'Thanks just the same . . . but I don't want any pleasures interfering with my happiness,'" T. Jeff Evans observed in *American Humor: An Interdisciplinary Newsletter.*

The Mackerel Plaza, published between *Comfort Me with Apples* and *The Tents of Wickedness,* introduces the now-familiar discord wrought by religion in De Vries's novels. The story follows the plight of the Reverend Andrew (Holy) Mackerel, who faces opposition from his congregation when he expresses his wish to remarry after his saintly wife dies. Again his characters provide abundant De Vriesian commentary. "Some of De Vries's aphorisms are worthy of Oscar Wilde, and his characters are never short of repartee," Stuart Sutherland observed in *Times Literary Supplement.* "The ultramodern young clergyman of *Mackerel Plaza* is caught staring at a girl's legs; 'Stop looking at my legs,' she says, to which he replies, 'Don't worry, ma'am, my thoughts were on higher things.' Of twentieth-century novelists, only P. G. Wodehouse and Evelyn Waugh have De Vries's capacity to make the reader laugh out loud."

The Blood of the Lamb, which many critics consider his most important work, marked a turning point in De Vries's writing. His youngest daughter's death from leukemia in 1960 brought a deepening cynicism and somberness to De Vries's novels during the following decade, most noticeably to *The Blood of the Lamb,* in which a father wrestles with questions of religion and comes to terms with the tragic death of his child. The seemingly incongruous combination of comedy, always present in De Vries's work, and tragedy is successful; De Vries proves that "comedy is not the opposite of tragedy but its Siamese twin," *Time's* R. Z. Sheppard noted. The author returned to farcical religious figures in *Let Me Count the Ways,* featuring agnostic Tom Waltz, the product of an evangelical mother and atheistic father who agreed to compromise on his spiritual upbringing. A pilgrimage to the healing shrine at Lourdes provides Tom with the disease that reunites him with his estranged wife.

"Integral to De Vries' structures is a plot where the individual moves away from conformity and institutions in order to discover the repressed self," Evans remarked in *American Humor.* "What he typically discovers, however, is that the self is false or distorted outside its community; the novels generally then return the individual to society through reconciliation. But not so *Cat's Pajamas,* which may be De Vries' most radical vision while still positing a comic world." Published together with *Witch's Milk, Cat's Pajamas* reveals the fate of Hank Tattersall, who "resists communal responsibility," Evans noted, and dies of exposure when his head gets stuck in a doggie door. A child's death in *Witch's Milk* holds very different consequences for each of his parents—the father recognizes the event as part of a universal order, while the mother finds only bitterness.

De Vries's novels of the 1970s begin his exploration of the sociological phenomena of feminism, gender identity, and the sexual revolution. Here De Vries defends marriage in earnest, pointing up the shortcomings of excessive sexual freedom but also illuminating the difficulties of maintaining the necessary degree of wedded bliss. Critics remarked on the black humor and cynicism still evident in De Vries's work of this period, but generally agreed that *Consenting Adults; Or, The Duchess Will Be Furious* marked the author's return to a lighter, more humourous style. While still exploring the seamier sides of human existence, De Vries seemed once again able to embrace life and its myriad unknowns. "Question: Is it possible to cram into a novel every joke the theme and plot will allow, then add a couple of hundred more for good measure, and still maintain, from first page to last, a graceful, elegant and, above all, seemingly effortless prose style?," Christopher Cerf queried in the *New York Times Book Review.* "Answer: Absolutely—but probably only if you're Peter De Vries. And in [*Consenting Adults*] Mr. De Vries once again demonstrates his unique ability to blend a motley array of absurd aphorisms, one-sentence character sketches, running gags, cosmological musings and inspired word games into a coherent—well, almost coherent—and hugely enjoyable book."

Washington Post Book World's Joseph McLellan summarizes *Consenting Adults* as a chronicle of the "social and sexual aspirations and misadventures of Ted Peachum of Pocock, Ill., who is 16 years old when we first meet him and grows up (but not too much) in the course of the next 200 pages." McLellan finds the book's subject "of some

interest but not really crucial, because in a De Vries novel the important point is not what he writes about but the way he writes about it." "*Consenting Adults* is rarely serious and only occasionally does it evoke pathos," Sutherland wrote in *Times Literary Supplement.* "It is more of a fun novel than a funny one—a literary romp." A young man's sexual awakening and subsequent troubles is again the subject in *Slouching towards Kalamazoo.* Anthony Thrasher, an underachieving fifteen-year-old, finds himself a father-to-be after an indiscretion with his teacher during a tutoring session. The teacher, who shocked the small burg of Ulalume, North Dakota, by assigning *The Scarlet Letter* to her eighth-grade English class of 1961, leaves town to have the baby. Anthony follows, planning to make an honest woman of her, but falls for the baby's sitter, the nubile Bubbles Breedlove. *Slouching towards Kalamazoo* is "vintage De Vries, a perfect example of the sort of hilarious and expertly crafted comic novel that he amazingly seems to be able to turn out annually," Thomas Meehan declared in the *New York Times Book Review.*

De Vries's use of puns and one-liners, staples in his pantry of literary devices, often finds favor with reviewers such as Meehan who described him as "America's master of comic wordplay." The *New York Times*'s Michiko Kakutani, however, criticized his jokes in *Slouching towards Kalamazoo,* some of which "have a nasty, prejudicial edge" and "simply tend to sit there on the page as lumpy, unalloyed one-liners; they serve no larger comic vision and are never integrated into the drama." Yet De Vries's trademark tendency to sketch scenes simply as vehicles for his quips is also one of the most often admired qualities of his writing.

De Vries employed a particularly thought-provoking double entendre as the title of *The Prick of Noon,* in which pornographer Eddie Teeters, known as Monty Carlo to his clientele, attempts to fit in with the society crowd while concealing his identity. "*The Prick of Noon* is in every respect a thoroughly characteristic De Vries novel," Jonathan Yardley commented in the *Washington Post.* "Its people have odd names and do odd things, but where it counts they are as human as any to be found in contemporary American literature; its commentary is in equal measures perceptive and irreverent; its prose is facile and its puns outrageous. Not merely is De Vries the funniest of living American novelists, he is also one of the best." Among the book's memorable passages is "one of the most imaginative accounts of delirium in contemporary fiction," Elaine Kendall observed in the *Los Angeles Times Book Review,* "in which Teeters imagines himself going naked through a car wash, lathered by the rotary brushes, slapped by the hanging strips, blasted with suds like mad dog saliva, dried with powerful jets of hot air and finally waxed and finished off by avaricious attendants who expect a lavish tip for their attentions." Kendall concluded, "Like the preceding 21, this novel is well supplied with redeeming social value masquerading as risque frivolity." Sheppard remarked in *Time* that *The Prick of Noon* "may not be his strongest performance. But . . . De Vries still projects a vision that is fresh and sensuous. His is a comedy that does not reduce character with sociology and psychology but sees instincts and folly through the eyes of a naturalist."

In *Peckham's Marbles,* Earl Peckham, fresh out of a sanitarium after recovering from a case of hepatitis that forced him to "look on the world with a jaundiced eye," sets out to revive his literary career. Three copies of his book were sold to bookstores; he hopes to find and autograph them so they can't be returned to the publisher. Unfortunately for him, though, "Peckham tries to make things happen, but he is ultimately the sort of person to whom things happen," Christopher Buckley observed in *Washington Post Book World.* Remarking on Peckham's constant recitation of lines from the works of Mark Twain, F. Scott Fitzgerald, T. S. Eliot, Willa Cather, and a host of other literary icons, Buckley noted, "At times it seems as if the book has been crossbred with one of the tonier Writers on Writers quotebooks. But this is a book about writers and the lit'ry life, after all, and anyway, the sheer felicity of watching Peter De Vries handle the language vaporizes that objection like a blue neon Bug Zapper."

To those who have yet to read a De Vries novel, the *Observer's* Julian Barnes offers this suggestion: "Samuel Butler advised us to eat a bunch of grapes downwards, so that each grape gets bigger and sweeter. Perhaps you should read Mr De Vries backwards, so that each book will seem funnier and truer." The *New York Times Book Review's* Meehan advised, "If you've somehow never read Mr. De Vries, you should, starting . . . with *Slouching towards Kalamazoo* and working your way back to *The Tunnel of Love* and *Comfort Me with Apples,* for such highly intelligent literary pleasures as he has to offer are rare indeed to come upon these days."

BIOGRAPHICAL/CRITICAL SOURCES:

BOOKS

Bowden, Edwin T., *Peter De Vries: A Bibliography 1934-1977,* University of Texas Humanities Research Center, 1978.
Bowden, J. H., *Peter De Vries,* Twayne, 1983.
Jellema, Roderick, *Peter De Vries,* Eerdmans, 1967.

PERIODICALS

American Humor: An Interdisciplinary Newsletter, fall, 1980, pp. 13-16.
Chicago Tribune, February 21, 1984; April 14, 1985.

Chicago Tribune Book World, August 10, 1980, sec. 7, p. 1; September 6, 1981, sec. 7, p. 1; June 6, 1982, p. 2; November 7, 1982, p. 7; July 17, 1983, p. 29.
Christian Century, November 26, 1975.
Detroit News, May 19, 1985.
Encounter, January, 1973.
Globe and Mail (Toronto), October 18, 1986.
Los Angeles Times, September 25, 1986.
Los Angeles Times Book Review, September 21, 1980, p. 1; September 13, 1981, p. 4; August 28, 1983, p. 7; May 8, 1985.
New Republic, October 23, 1976.
Newsweek, October 5, 1981, p. 82; August 1, 1983, p. 68.
New Yorker, March 11, 1974; March 26, 1979.
New York Times, July 31, 1980, p. C18; September 18, 1981; July 22, 1983; April 5, 1985; October 3, 1986; October 6, 1986.
New York Times Book Review, August 17, 1980, pp. 1, 22; September 20, 1981, p. 14; August 14, 1983, pp. 7, 20; May 19, 1985, p. 16; April 20, 1986, p. 38; November 2, 1986, p. 26.
Observer, January 26, 1986, p. 51.
Publishers Weekly, October 16, 1981, pp. 6-8.
Studies in American Humor, April, 1974.
Theology Today, April, 1975.
Time, September 21, 1981, p. 81; April 22, 1985, p. 69; October 13, 1986, p. 102.
Times (London), February 26, 1981.
Times Literary Supplement, January 30, 1981, p. 107; January 22, 1982, p. 76; August 26, 1983, p. 898; January 24, 1986, p. 82.
Tribune Books (Chicago), October 19, 1986, p. 6.
Washington Post, May 18, 1984; April 17, 1985.
Washington Post Book World, August 7, 1980; September 6, 1981, p. 3; March 14, 1982, p. 16; June 6, 1982, p. 12; July 17, 1983, p. 3; October 5, 1986, p. 5.

—*Sketch by Deborah A. Stanley*

*   *   *

DONOVAN, Robert J(ohn) 1912-

PERSONAL: Born August 21, 1912, in Buffalo, NY; son of Michael Joseph (an interior decorator) and Katherine (Sullivan) Donovan; married Martha Fisher, May 9, 1941 (deceased); married Gerry Van der Heuvel (a writer), March 17, 1978; children: (first marriage) Patricia, Peter, Amy.

ADDRESSES: Home and office—3031 Beechwood Ln., Falls Church, VA 22042. *Agent*—Sterling Lord, One Madison Ave., New York, NY 10010.

CAREER: Buffalo Courier-Express, Buffalo, NY, reporter, 1933-37; *New York Herald Tribune,* New York

City, reporter, 1937-63, member of Washington bureau, 1947-63, chief of Washington bureau, 1957-63; *Los Angeles Times,* Los Angeles, CA, chief of Washington bureau, 1963-70, associate editor, 1970-77; Woodrow Wilson International Center for Scholars, Washington, DC, fellow, 1978-79; Princeton University, Princeton, NJ, senior fellow at the Woodrow Wilson School of Public and International Affairs, 1979-80, Ferris Professor of Journalism, 1980-81. *Military service:* U.S. Army, 1943-45; became sergeant; awarded Bronze Star.

MEMBER: White House Correspondent's Association (president, 1954), Gridiron Club.

WRITINGS:

The Assassins, Harper, 1955.
Eisenhower: The Inside Story, Harper, 1956.
(With Joseph W. Martin, Jr.) *My First Fifty Years in Politics, as Told to Robert J. Donovan,* McGraw, 1960.
PT 109: John F. Kennedy in World War II, McGraw, 1961.
The Future of the Republican Party, New American Library, 1964.
Six Days in June: Israel's Fight for Survival, New American Library, 1967.
Conflict and Crisis: The Presidency of Harry S. Truman, 1945-48, Norton, 1977.
Tumultuous Years: The Presidency of Harry S. Truman, 1949-53, Norton, 1982.
Nemesis: Truman and Johnson in the Coils of War in Asia, St. Martin's, 1984.
The Second Victory: The Marshall Plan and the Postwar Revival of Europe, Madison Books, 1987.
Confidential Secretary: Ann Whitman's Twenty Years with Eisenhower and Rockefeller, Dutton, 1988.
(With Ray Scherer) *Unsilent Revolution: Television News and American Public Life, 1948-1991,* Cambridge University Press, 1992.

ADAPTATIONS: PT 109: John F. Kennedy in World War II was the basis for the motion picture *PT 109,* released by Warner Bros. in 1963.

WORK IN PROGRESS: Speaking of Congress: How About the Good-for-Nothing Eightieth, a Political Extravaganza?, completion expected in 1993.

SIDELIGHTS: Robert J. Donovan, a respected journalist and former White House correspondent, has received critical acclaim for his nonfiction books which portray the lives of political figures and assess political events. He has examined the lives of presidents, the dealings of the Republican party, and the influence of broadcast journalism on American society, earning a reputation for his scrupulous attention to detail and his objective approach to his subject matter. A *Foreign Affairs* contributor described

Eisenhower: The Inside Story as "responsibly handled and written" and "a surprisingly intimate picture of the inner workings of the Eisenhower administration," two qualities which are mentioned repeatedly by reviewers of Donovan's later books. In *Book Week,* R. K. Price identified Donovan as "a thorough professional with an intimate knowledge of politics and the ways of politicians," and named "brevity, lucidity, objectivity, and a sharp focus on the essentials" as the strengths of Donovan's *The Future of the Republican Party.*

Donovan's ability to tell an engrossing story in *PT 109: John F. Kennedy in World War II* was commended by John Toland in the *New York Times Book Review:* "Even if the leading character had remained an ordinary citizen, this saga . . . would be a thriller." In *New York Herald Tribune Books,* W. S. White also mentioned the power of the narrative, but suggested that the importance of the book was not limited to the story: "For its value only as a good and bracing tale of adventure under cordite, [*PT 109*] would be well worth reading. But there is a great deal more here than that. . . . Mr. Donovan sheds, through recalled incident and anecdote, much light upon the whole character, the whole personality, of John F. Kennedy."

Conflict and Crisis: The Presidency of Harry S. Truman, 1945-48 and *Tumultuous Years: The Presidency of Harry S. Truman, 1949-53* received numerous commendations for their attention to detail and objective perspective. According to Roscoe Drummond in the *Christian Science Monitor, Conflict and Crisis* "gives us a faithful portrait of Harry Truman, the man. . . . [Donovan] tells us so much we didn't know. . . . The resulting account adds new insight, perspective, and depth to our understanding of what really happened. . . . [Donovan] leaves it to the reader to reach his own judgment of the Truman presidency, but the record is all there in trustworthy detail." A. H. Raskin, writing in the *New York Times,* praised Donovan's approach: "The Donovan achievement . . . is particularly admirable because he marshals his material with scrupulous endeavor to exclude personal judgement. He writes without idolatry or malice, leaving to the reader the privilege, rare in contemporary biography, of arriving at his own assessment." This absence of judgement evoked the opposite reaction from another critic, however. In the *Nation,* Richard J. Walton noted: "It seems a terrible waste that Donovan's knowledge of the Truman years should have resulted in just another journalistic account that, no matter how full and how skilled, adds little to our understanding of one of the most consequential periods of American history."

Despite these disparate reviews, most critics agree that *Conflict and Crisis* and *Tumultuous Years* are thorough and definitive accounts of the Truman era. "We are likely to get no better chronicle of the years 1945-48," *New York*

Review of Books contributor H. Stuart Hughes wrote of the first volume. "It is all there—everything you have ever wanted to know (and possibly more) about the first Truman administration." In the *New York Times Book Review,* Merle Miller stated that the two studies "are among the best books on the Presidency ever written." Beschloss agreed: "Together, the two volumes should stand as the central source on the Truman presidency."

Critical response to Donovan's *Nemesis: Truman and Johnson in the Coils of War in Asia* was highly positive. "*Nemesis* is an excellent study in tandem of both [the Korean War and the Vietnam War] and of the devastating effect they had on the lives of presidents Truman and Johnson," wrote Archimedes L.A. Patti in the *Washington Post Book World.* "It skillfully and unambiguously compares the causes and effects, the pressures and commitments, the traps and pitfalls that led to tragic and inconclusive results. . . . *Nemesis* is rich with anecdotes about the two presidents and the men around them." In the *New York Times Book Review,* Drew Middleton called Donovan's work "a closely reasoned, well-researched commentary on troubles that convulsed the United States for a quarter of a century," and further noted that Donovan "excels in recounting the criticism that fell on Truman and Johnson during their war years."

Apart from his books on specific aspects of politics, Donovan wrote *Unsilent Revolution: Television News and American Public Life, 1948-1991* with Ray Scherer, a former White House correspondent for NBC. The book attempts to describe how television news has influenced American social life and politics by discussing the most dramatic events television news broadcast during the four decades under consideration, moments which include the assassination of President Kennedy in 1963 and the explosion of the space shuttle Challenger in 1986. The authors also discuss how the advent of broadcast journalism edged newspapers out of the business of announcing headlines and instead into the analysis of the news they present. "As a compilation of images and episodes," wrote Richard Wightman Fox in the *New York Times Book Review,* "this book is a feast."

Donovan told *CANR:* "I began writing for the *Buffalo-Courier Express* as a cub reporter in 1934. Now, a month short of my eightieth birthday, I am deep in a book on Congress. The reading is voluminous beyond any previous experience I have had. But the satisfaction and pleasure of getting it all on paper is a wonderful antidote to octogenarian ennui I have observed in others over the years. No time for that now. On the other hand, the lingering worry is that I'll labor through three quarters of the manuscript only to have some goofy artery break in two somewhere. But there's not an hour to dwell on that now. On to chapter fourteen!"

BIOGRAPHICAL/CRITICAL SOURCES:

PERIODICALS

Atlantic, February, 1978.
Bookmark, October, 1956.
Book Week, February 14, 1965.
Chicago Sunday Tribune, July 1, 1956.
Christian Science Monitor, November 16, 1961; December 13, 1977.
Contemporary Review, May, 1983.
Foreign Affairs, October, 1956.
Los Angeles Times Book Review, September 5, 1982; January 6, 1985.
Nation, August 4, 1956; November 27, 1982.
National Review, March 9, 1965.
New Republic, July 30, 1956; January 2, 1965; November 26, 1977.
New Yorker, January 30, 1965; November 7, 1977.
New York Herald Tribune Book Review, July 1, 1956.
New York Herald Tribune Books, November 19, 1961.
New York Review of Books, April 20, 1978.
New York Times, July 1, 1956; December 5, 1977.
New York Times Book Review, November 19, 1961; October 16, 1977; September 5, 1982; October 3, 1982; November 4, 1984; May 3, 1992, pp. 7, 9.
Political Science Quarterly, spring, 1978.
San Francisco Chronicle, July 8, 1956; November 13, 1961.
Saturday Review, October 1, 1960; August 26, 1967.
Spectator, May 14, 1983.
Springfield Republican, July 15, 1956.
Washington Post Book World, October 30, 1977; January 6, 1985.

*   *   *

DOUGLAS, Ellen
   See HAXTON, Josephine Ayres

*   *   *

du BOIS, William (Sherman) Pene
   See PENE du BOIS, William (Sherman)

E

EARLY, Jack
See SCOPPETTONE, Sandra

* * *

EASTMAN, John 1935-

PERSONAL: Born April 23, 1935, in Reed City, MI; son of Alva W. (a clergyman) and Blanche (Bassett) Eastman. *Education:* Attended University of Michigan, 1963; Western Michigan University, B.S., 1965. *Politics:* "Left of center."

ADDRESSES: Home and office—4424 Moonlite, Kalamazoo, MI 49009. *Agent*—Peter L. Ginsberg, Curtis Brown Ltd., 10 Astor Pl., New York, NY 10003.

CAREER: Illinois Natural History Survey, Champaign-Urbana, research associate, 1966, held various positions, 1966-73; NUS Corp., Pittsburgh, PA, environmental consultant, 1973-74; Illinois Natural History Survey, staff member, 1974-76; free-lance writer, 1974-76; Nelson-Hall Publishing Co., Chicago, IL, free-lance copy editor, 1976-80; Wadsworth Publishing Co., Belmont, CA, free-lance copy editor, 1977-82; free-lance writer, 1982—; Turner Network Television, Atlanta, GA, factoid writer, 1991—. Researcher for *Reflections on the Silver Screen* interview program, American Movie Classics television channel, 1991—. Member of Kalamazoo Nature Center. *Military service:* U.S. Army, 1958-60.

MEMBER: American Civil Liberties Union.

WRITINGS:

(With Susan Woolley Stoddard) *Kalama-Who?: A Kalamazoo Quiz Book,* privately printed, 1982.
Who Lived Where: A Biographical Guide to Homes and Museums, Facts on File, 1983.
Who Lived Where in Europe: A Biographical Guide to Homes and Museums, Facts on File, 1985.
Retakes: Behind the Scenes of 500 Classical Movies, Ballantine, 1989.
(Editor) *Enjoying Birds in Michigan,* 4th edition, Center for Environmental Study, 1989.
The Book of Forest and Thicket: Trees, Shrubs, and Wildflowers of Eastern North America, Stackpole, 1992.

Contributor to books, including *The Intimate Sex Lives of Famous People,* by Irving Wallace and others, Delacorte, 1981; *People's Almanac 2* and *People's Almanac 3;* and *The Atlas of Breeding Birds of Michigan,* Michigan State University Press, 1991. Contributor to periodicals, including *Natural History, Bird Watcher's Digest, National Wildlife,* and *Michigan Out-of-Doors.*

WORK IN PROGRESS: The Book of Swamp and Bog, for Stackpole.

SIDELIGHTS: John Eastman, a long-time student of Zen Buddhism, once told *CA:* "My literary work focuses on two main areas of interest: biology and natural history, and history and biography, with the aim of popularizing specific subjects in these areas for the general reader. I am attracted to the guidebook or gazetteer format because it offers the chance of gathering and exhibiting a great deal of useful information in a concise, interesting fashion. I consider *Who Lived Where* to be my most important work to date, because it contains much original research from unpublished sources."

BIOGRAPHICAL/CRITICAL SOURCES:

PERIODICALS

Chicago Tribune, July 9, 1989.

EICHNER, Hans 1921-

PERSONAL: Born October 30, 1921, in Vienna, Austria; son of Alexander (a merchant) and Valerie (Ungar) Eichner; children: Elizabeth Jane, James Alexander. *Education:* University of London, B.A., 1944, Ph.D., 1949. *Avocational interests:* Music, aesthetics, sailing.

ADDRESSES: Home—Box 41, Rockwood, Ontario, Canada N0B 2K0. *Office*—Department of German, University of Toronto, Toronto, Ontario, Canada.

CAREER: Bedford College, University of London, London, England, assistant lecturer in German, 1948-50; Queen's University at Kingston, Kingston, Ontario, assistant professor, 1950-57, associate professor, 1957-62, professor of German and head of department, 1962-67; University of Toronto, Toronto, Ontario, professor of German, 1967-88, chairman of department, 1967-72 and 1975-84.

MEMBER: Royal Society of Canada (fellow), Modern Language Association of America.

AWARDS, HONORS: Nuffield Foundation fellowship, 1952; Canada Council fellowship, 1959; Gold Medal, Goethe Institute, 1973; LL.D., Queen's University, 1974; honorary professor, University of Calgary, 1978; Hermann Boeschenstein Medal, 1988; J. G. Robertson Prize; William Riley Parker Prize.

WRITINGS:

IN ENGLISH

(Editor and author of introduction and commentary) Friedrich Schlegel, *Literary Notebooks, 1797-1801,* Athlone Press, 1957.
(With Hans Hein) *Reading German for Scientists,* Wiley, 1959.
Four Modern German Authors: Mann, Rilke, Kafka, Brecht, Canadian Broadcasting Corp., 1964.
Friedrich Schlegel, Twayne, 1970.
(Editor, with Lisa Kahn and Ernst Behler) *Studies in German in Memory of Robert L. Kahn,* Rice University Studies, 1971.
(Editor) *"Romantic" and Its Cognates: The European History of a Word,* University of Toronto Press, 1972.

IN GERMAN

Thomas Mann: Eine Einfuehrung in sein Werk, Francke, 1953, 2nd edition, 1962.
(Editor) *Kritische Friedrich Schlegel-Ausgabe,* Schoeningh, Volume 4: *Ansichten und Ideen von der christlichen Kunst,* 1959, Volume 6: *Geschichte der alten und neuen Literatur,* 1961, Volume 5: *Dichtungen,* 1962, Volume 2: *Charakteristiken und Kritiken I,* 1966, Volume 3: *Charakteristiken und Kritiken II,* 1974,

Volume 16: *Fragmtente zur Poesie und Literatur I,* 1981.
(Editor and contributor) *Schlegel, Gespraech ueber die Poesie,* Metzler, 1968.
(Editor and contributor, with Norma Lelless, of epilogue) Friedrich Schlegel, *Gemaelde alter Meister,* Wissenschaftliche Buchges., 1984.
(Editor and contributor) *Friedrich Schlegel, Ueber Goethes Meister, Gespraech ueber die Poesie,* Uni-Taschenbuecher, 1985.
Deutsche Literatur im klassisch-romantischen Zeitalter, 1795-1805, Peter Lang, 1990.
(Editor and contributor) *E. T. A. Hoffmann: Der Artushof und andere Erzaehlungen,* [Berlin], 1991.

OTHER

Contributor to books, including *Verbannung: Aufzeichnungen deutscher Schriftsteller im Exil,* Christian Wegner, 1964; *The Romantic Period in Germany: Essays by Members of the London University Institute of Germanic Studies,* edited by S. Prawer, Weidenfeld & Nicolson, 1970; and *Goethe's Narrative Fiction: The Irving Goethe Symposium,* edited by William J. Lillyman, De Gruyter, 1983. Contributor to professional journals in England, Germany, and the United States.

WORK IN PROGRESS: Friedrich Schlegel as Seen by His Contemporaries: A Documentation.

*   *   *

EITZEN, D(avid) Stanley 1934-

PERSONAL: Born August 4, 1934, in Glendale, CA; son of David D. (a psychologist) and Amanda (Heidebrecht) Eitzen; married Florine Kay Voran, May 29, 1956; children: Keith, Michael, Kelly. *Education:* Bethel College, Newton, KS, A.B., 1956; College of Emporia, M.S., 1962; University of Kansas, M.A., 1966, Ph.D., 1968. *Politics:* Democrat. *Religion:* Mennonite.

ADDRESSES: Home—924 Breakwater, Fort Collins, CO 80525. *Office*—Department of Sociology, Colorado State University, Fort Collins, CO 80523.

CAREER: Menninger Foundation, Topeka, KS, recreational therapist, 1956-58; public school teacher of social science in Galva, KS, 1958-60, and in Turner, KS, 1960-65; University of Kansas, Lawrence, instructor, 1967-68, assistant professor, 1968-72, associate professor of sociology, 1972-74; Colorado State University, Fort Collins, professor of sociology, 1974—. *Military service:* Alternative service in lieu of military, 1956-58.

MEMBER: International Sociological Association, International Committee for the Sociology of Sport, American

Sociological Association, Society for the Study of Social Problems, Southwestern Social Science Association, Midwest Sociological Society, Western Social Science Association.

WRITINGS:

Social Structure and Social Problems in America, Allyn & Bacon, 1974.
In Conflict and Order, Allyn & Bacon, 1978.
Sociology of American Sport, W. C. Brown, 1978.
Sport in Contemporary America, St. Martin's, 1979.
Social Problems, Allyn & Bacon, 1980.
Elite Deviance, Allyn & Bacon, 1982.
Criminology, Wiley, 1985.
Diversity in Families, Harper/Collins, 1987.
Crime in the Streets and Crime in the Suites, Allyn & Bacon, 1989.
The Reshaping of America, Prentice-Hall, 1989.
Society's Problems, Allyn & Bacon, 1989.

Contributor of more than one hundred articles to professional journals. Editor of *Social Science Journal,* 1978-84.

WORK IN PROGRESS: Paths to Homelessness, for Westview.

*   *   *

ELIOT, T(homas) S(tearns)   1888-1965
(Apteryx, Charles Augustus Conybeare,
Reverend Charles James Grimble, Gus Krutzch,
Muriel A. Schwartz, J. A. D. Spence, Helen B.
Trundlett)

PERSONAL: Born September 26, 1888, in St. Louis, MO; moved to England, 1914, naturalized British subject, 1927; died January 4, 1965, in London, England; cremated; his ashes are entombed at St. Michael's Church in East Coker, England; son of Henry Ware (president of Hydraulic Press Brick Co.) and Charlotte Chauncey (a teacher, social worker and writer; maiden name Stearns) Eliot; married Vivienne Haigh-Wood (a dancer), June 26, 1915 (divorced c. 1930; died, 1947); married Esme Valerie Fletcher (his private secretary before their marriage), January 10, 1957. *Education:* Attended Smith Academy (of Washington University), St. Louis, 1898-1905; Milton Academy, Milton, MA, graduated, 1906; Harvard University, B.A. (philosophy), 1909, M.A. (philosophy), 1910, graduate study, 1911-14; attended University of Paris (Sorbonne), 1910-11; studied in Munich, 1914; read philosophy at Merton, Oxford, 1914-15; also studied under Edward Kennard Rand, Irving Babbitt, and Alain Fournier, and attended courses given by Henri Bergson. *Politics:* Conservative ("royalist"). *Religion:* Church of

England (Anglo-Catholic wing; confirmed, 1927; served as vestryman in a London church).

CAREER: Harvard University, Cambridge, Mass., assistant in philosophy department, 1913-14; teacher of French, Latin, mathematics, drawing, geography, and history at High Wycombe Grammar School, London, then at Highgate School, London, 1915-17; Lloyds Bank Ltd., London, clerk in the Colonial and Foreign Department, 1917-25; *The Egoist,* London, assistant editor, 1917-19; *The Criterion* (literary quarterly), London, founder, 1922, editor, 1922-39 (ceased publication, at Eliot's decision, in 1939 because of the paper shortage of World War II); Faber & Faber Ltd. (publishers), London, literary editor, director, and member of the advisory hoard, 1925-65. Clark Lecturer at Trinity College, Cambridge, 1926; Charles Eliot Norton Professor of Poetry at Harvard University, six months, 1932-33; Page-Barbour Lecturer at University of Virginia, 1933; resident at Institute for Advanced Study at Princeton, 1948; Theodore Spencer Memorial Lecturer at Harvard University, 1950; lecturer at University of Chicago during the 1950s; lecturer at the Library of Congress, University of Texas, University of Minnesota, and before many other groups. President of London Library, 1952-65.

MEMBER: Classical Association (president, 1941), Virgil Society (president, 1943), Books Across the Sea (president, 1943-46), American Academy of Arts and Sciences (honorary member), Accademia dei Lincei (Rome; foreign member), Bayerische Akademie der Schoenen Kuenste (Munich; foreign member), Athenaeum, Garrick Club, Oxford and Cambridge Club.

AWARDS, HONORS: Sheldon Travelling Fellowship for study in Munich, 1914; *Dial* magazine award, 1922, for *The Waste Land;* Nobel Prize in Literature, 1948; Order of Merit, 1948; Commander, Ordre des Arts et des Lettres; Officier de la Legion d'Honneur; New York Drama Critics Circle Award, 1950, for *The Cocktail Party* as best foreign play; Hanseatic Goethe Prize of Hamburg University, 1954; Dante Gold Medal (Florence), 1956; Ordre pour le Merite (West Germany), 1959; Emerson-Thoreau Medal of the American Academy of Arts and Sciences, 1959; honorary fellow of Merton College, Oxford, and of Magdalene College, Cambridge; honorary citizen of Dallas, TX; honorary deputy sheriff of Dallas County, TX; Campion Medal of the Catholic Book Club, 1963, for "long and distinguished service to Christian letters"; Eliot is remembered with a large memorial tablet in the Poet's Corner of Westminster Abbey; Medal of Freedom for distinguished contribution to American literature and public life; a T. S. Eliot College was created at the University of Kent in 1969; the United States government issued a T. S. Eliot stamp, the fifth in the "Literary Arts" series, on September 26, 1986; a T. S. Eliot Centenary Fund was established at the London Library in 1988. Honorary degrees: Litt.D., Columbia University, 1933, Cambridge University, 1938, University of Bristol, 1938, University of Leeds, 1939, Harvard University, 1947, Yale University, 1947, Princeton University, 1947, Washington University, 1953, University of Rome, 1958, and University of Sheffield, 1959; LL.D., University of Edinburgh, 1937, and St. Andrews' University, 1953; D.Litt., Oxford University, 1948, and University of London, 1950; D.Philos., University of Munich, 1959; D. es L., University of Paris, 1959, Universite d'Aix-Marseille, 1959, and University of Rennet, 1959.

WRITINGS:

POETRY

Prufrock, and Other Observations, The Egoist (London), 1917.

Poems, Hogarth, 1919.

Ara Vos Prec, Ovid Press (London), 1920, published as *Poems,* Knopf, 1920.

The Waste Land (first published in *Criterion,* first issue, October, 1922), Boni & Liveright, 1922.

Poems, 1909-1925, Faber, 1925, Harcourt, 1932.

Journey of the Magi, Rudge, 1927.

A Song for Simeon, Faber, 1928.

Animula, Faber, 1929.

Ash-Wednesday, Putnam, 1930.

Marina, Faber, 1930.

Triumphal March, Faber, 1931.

Words for Music, [Bryn Mawr], 1934.

Two Poems, Cambridge University Press, 1935.

Collected Poems, 1909-1935, Harcourt, 1936.

(With Geoffrey Faber, Frank Morley, and John Hayward) *Noctes Binanianae* (limited edition of 25 copies for the authors and friends; never reprinted), privately printed (London), 1939.

Old Possum's Book of Practical Cats, Harcourt, 1939.

The Waste Land, and Other Poems, Faber, 1940, Harcourt, 1955.

East Coker, Faber, 1940.

Burnt Norton, Faber, 1941.

The Dry Salvages, Faber, 1941.

Later Poems, 1925-1935, Faber 1941.

Little Gidding, Faber, 1942.

Four Quartets (consists of *Burnt Norton, East Coker, The Dry Salvages,* and *Little Gidding*), Harcourt, 1943.

A Practical Possum, Harvard Printing Office, 1947.

Selected Poems, Penguin, 1948, Harcourt, 1967.

The Undergraduate Poems of T. S. Eliot Published While He Was in College in "The Harvard Advocate," Harvard Advocate (unauthorized reprint), 1949.

Poems Written in Early Youth, privately printed by Bonniers (Stockholm), 1950, new edition prepared by Valerie Eliot and John Hayward, Farrar, Straus, 1967.

The Cultivation of Christmas Trees, Faber, 1954, Farrar, Straus, 1956.

Collected Poems, 1909-1962, Harcourt, 1963.

The Waste Land: A Facsimile and Transcript of the Original Drafts, Including the Annotations of Ezra Pound, edited and with introduction by Valerie Eliot, Harcourt, 1971.

Growltiger's Last Stand and Other Poems, Farrar, Straus, 1987.

Poetry also represented in numerous anthologies.

PLAYS

Fragment of a Prologue, [London], 1926.

Fragment of the Agon, [London], 1927.

Sweeney Agonistes: Fragments of an Aristophanic Melodrama (first produced at Vassar College, May, 1933; first produced in New York at Cherry Lane Theater, March 2, 1952), Faber, 1932.

The Rock: A Pageant Play (a revue with scenario by E. Martin Browne and music by Martin Shaw; first produced in London at Sadler's Wells Theatre, May 28, 1934), Faber, 1934.

Murder in the Cathedral (first produced in an abbreviated form for the Canterbury Festival in the Chapter House of Canterbury Cathedral, June 15, 1935; produced in London at Mercury Theatre, November 1, 1935; first produced in America at Yale University, January, 1936; first produced in New York at Manhattan Theater, March 20, 1936), Harcourt, 1935.

The Family Reunion (first produced in London at Westminster Theatre, March 21, 1939; first produced in New York at Phoenix Theater, October 20, 1958), Harcourt, 1939.

The Cocktail Party (first produced for the Edinburgh Festival, Scotland, August 22, 1949; first produced in New York at Henry Miller's Theater, January 21, 1950), Harcourt, 1950.

The Confidential Clerk (first produced for the Edinburgh Festival, August 25, 1953; first produced in London at Lyric Theatre, September 16, 1953; first produced in New York at Morosco Theater, February 11, 1954), Harcourt, 1954.

The Elder Statesman (first produced for the Edinburgh Festival, August, 1958; produced in London at Cambridge Theatre, September 25, 1958), Farrar, Straus, 1959.

Collected Plays, Faber, 1962.

Plays also represented in numerous anthologies.

PROSE

Ezra Pound: His Metric and Poetry (published anonymously) Knopf, 1918.

The Sacred Wood: Essays on Poetry and Criticism, Methuen, 1920, 7th edition, 1950, Barnes & Noble, 1960.

Homage to John Dryden: Three Essays on Poetry of the Seventeenth Century, Leonard and Virginia Woolf at Hogarth Press, 1924, Doubleday, 1928.

Shakespeare and the Stoicism of Seneca (an address), Oxford University Press, for the Shakespeare Association, 1927.

For Lancelot Andrewes: Essays on Style and Order, Faber, 1928, Doubleday, 1929.

Dante, Faber, 1929.

Thoughts After Lambeth, (a criticism of the *Report* of the Lambeth Conference, 1930), Faber, 1931.

Charles Whibley: A Memoir, Oxford University Press, for the English Association, 1931.

Selected Essays, 1917-1932, Harcourt, 1932, 2nd edition published as *Selected Essays,* Harcourt, 1950, 3rd edition, Faber, 1951.

John Dryden: The Poet, the Dramatist, the Critic (three essays), Terence & Elsa Holliday (New York), 1932.

The Use of Poetry and the Use of Criticism: Studies in the Relation of Criticism to Poetry in England (the Charles Eliot Norton lectures), Harvard University Press, 1933, 2nd edition, Faber, 1964.

Elizabethan Essays (includes *Shakespeare and the Stoicism of Seneca*), Faber, 1934, abbreviated edition published as *Essays on Elizabethan Drama,* Harcourt, 1956, published as *Elizabethan Dramatists,* Faber, 1963.

After Strange Gods: A Primer of Modern Heresy (the Page-Barbour lectures), Harcourt, 1934.

Essays, Ancient and Modern, Harcourt, 1936.

The Idea of a Christian Society (three lectures), Faber, 1939, Harcourt, 1940.

Christianity and Culture (contains *The Idea of a Christian Society* and *Notes Towards the Definition of Culture*), Harcourt, 1940.

Points of View (selected criticism), edited by John Hayward, Faber, 1941.

The Classics and the Man of Letters (an address), Oxford University Press, 1942.

The Music of Poetry (lecture), Jackson (Glasgow), 1942.

Reunion by Destruction: Reflections on a Scheme for Church Union in South India (an address), Council for the Defence of Church Principles (London), 1943.

What Is a Classic? (an address), Faber, 1945.

Die Einheit der Europaischen Kultur, Carl Havel (Berlin), 1946.

On Poetry, Concord Academy, 1947.

Milton (lecture), Geoffrey Cumberlege (London), 1947.

A Sermon Preached in the Magdalene College, Cambridge University Press, 1948.

From Poe to Valery (first published in *Hudson Review,* 1948), privately printed for friends by Harcourt, 1948.

Notes Towards the Definition of Culture (seven essays), Faber, 1948, Harcourt, 1949.

The Aims of Poetic Drama, Poets' Theatre Guild, 1949.

Poetry by T. S. Eliot: An NBC Radio Discussion, [Chicago], 1950.

Poetry and Drama (the Theodore Spencer lecture), Harvard University Press, 1951.

The Value and Use of Cathedrals in England Today, Friends of Chichester Cathedral, 1952.

An Address to Members of the London Library, London Library, 1952, Providence Athenaeum, 1953.

American Literature and the American Language (an address and an appendix entitled "The Eliot Family and St. Louis," the latter prepared by the English Department at Washington University), Washington University Press, 1953.

The Three Voices of Poetry (lecture), Cambridge University Press, for the National Book League, 1953, Cambridge University Press (New York), 1954.

Selected Prose, edited by John Hayward, Penguin, 1953.

Religious Drama: Mediaeval and Modern, House of Books (New York), 1954.

The Literature of Politics (lecture), foreword by Sir Anthony Eden, Conservative Political Centre, 1955.

The Frontiers of Criticism (lecture), University of Minnesota Press, 1956.

On Poetry and Poets (essays), Farrar, Straus, 1957.

Essays on Poetry and Criticism, introduction and notes in Japanese by Kazumi Yano, Shohakusha (Tokyo), 1959.

William Collin Brooks (an address), The Statist (London), 1959.

Geoffrey Faber, 1889-1961, Faber, 1961.

George Herbert, Longmans, Green, for the British Council and the National Book League, 1962.

Knowledge and Experience in the Philosophy of F. H. Bradley (doctoral dissertation), Farrar, Straus, 1964.

To Criticize the Critic, and Other Writings (includes *From Poe to Valery; American Literature and the American Language; The Literature of Politics; The Classics and the Man of Letters; Ezra Pound, His Metric and Poetry*), Farrar, Straus, 1965.

Selected Prose of T. S. Eliot, edited by Frank Kermode, Harcourt, 1975.

The Literary Criticism of T. S. Eliot: New Essays, Athlone Press, 1977.

Prose also represented in numerous anthologies.

OMNIBUS VOLUMES

The Complete Poems and Plays, 1909-1950, Harcourt, 1952.

AUTHOR OF INTRODUCTION

Charlotte Chauncey Eliot, *Savonarola: A Dramatic Poem,* Cobden-Sanderson (London), 1926.

Seneca His Tenne Tragedies, Knopf, 1927.

Wilkie Collins, *The Moonstone* (novel), Oxford University Press, 1928.

James B. Connolly, *Fishermen of the Banks,* Faber, 1928.

Edgar Ansel Mowrer, *This American World,* Faber, 1928.

(And editor) Ezra Pound, *Selected Poems,* Faber, 1928.

Samuel Johnson, *London, a Poem [and] The Vanity of Human Wishes,* Etchells & Macdonald, 1930.

G. Wilson Knight, *The Wheel of Fire: Essays in Interpretation of Shakespeare's Sombre Tragedies,* Oxford University Press, 1930.

Charles Baudelaire, *Intimate Journals,* translation by Christopher Isherwood, Random House, 1930.

(And translator) St. J. Perse, *Anabasis a Poem,* Faber, 1930, Harcourt, 1938, revised edition, Harcourt, 1949, Faber, 1959.

Pascal's Pensees, translation by W. F. Trotter, Dutton, 1931.

(And editor) Marianne Moore, *Selected Poems,* Macmillan, 1935.

Poems of Tennyson, Nelson, 1936.

Djuna Barnes, *Nightwood* (novel), Harcourt, 1937, 2nd edition, Faber, 1950.

(And compiler) *A Choice of Kipling's Verse,* Faber, 1941.

Charles-Louis Philippe, *Bubu of Montparnasse,* translation by Laurence Vail and others, 2nd edition (not associated with first edition), Avalon, 1945.

Samuel L. Clemens, *The Adventures of Huckleberry Finn,* Cresset Press, 1950.

Simone Weil, *The Need for Roots,* Putnam, 1952.

(And editor) *Literary Essays of Ezra Pound,* New Directions, 1954.

Stanislaus Joyce, *My Brother's Keeper,* edited by Richard Ellmann, Viking, 1958.

Paul Valery, *The Art of Poetry,* translation by Denise Folliot, Pantheon, 1958.

Hugo von Hofmannsthal, *Poems and Verse Plays,* edited by Michael Hamburger, Pantheon, 1961.

David Jones, *In Parenthesis* (novel), Viking, 1961.

John Davidson: A Selection of His Poems, edited by Maurice Lindsay, Hutchinson, 1961.

(Editor and author of introduction) *Introducing James Joyce* (selected prose), Faber, 1962.

Also author of introductions to books of poems by Harry Crosby and Abraham Cowley.

RECORDINGS

Harvard University recorded Eliot's readings of the poems "The Hollow Men," "Gerontion," "The Love Song of J. Alfred Prufrock," "Journey of the Magi," "A Song for Simeon," "Triumphal March," "Difficulties of a Statesman," "Fragment of an Agon," and "Four Quartets"; Eliot's readings of "The Waste Land," "Landscapes I and II," and "Sweeney Among the Nightingales" were recorded by the Library of Congress.

OTHER

(Translator) St. John Perse (pseudonym of Alexis Saint-Leger Leger) *Anabasis* (poem; published in a bilingual edition with the original French), Faber, 1930, revised edition, Harcourt, 1949.

(With George Hoellering) *Murder in the Cathedral* (screenplay based on Eliot's play), Harcourt, 1952.

(Editor) *The Criterion, 1922-1939,* 18 volumes, Barnes & Noble, 1967.

The Letters of T. S. Eliot, Volume 1: *1898-1922,* edited by Valerie Eliot, Harcourt, 1988.

Also lyricist for songs "For An Old Man," [New York], 1951, and "The Greater Light," [London], 1956, with music by David Diamond and Martine Shaw. Also published humorous letters in *The Egoist* under the pseudonyms Charles Augustus Conybeare, Reverend Charles James Grimble, Gus Krutzch, Muriel A. Schwartz, J. A. D. Spence, and Helen B. Trundlett. Editor of the *Harvard Advocate,* 1909-1910. Member of the editorial boards of *New English Weekly, Inventario, Christian News-Letter,* and other periodicals. Contributor to *Dial, Bookman, Little Review, Athenaeum, Cambridge Review, Enemy, Times Literary Supplement, Harvard Advocate, Norseman, Daedalus,* and other periodicals.

ADAPTATIONS: The poem "The Hollow Men" was set for baritone solo, male voice chorus, and orchestra, and published by Oxford University Press, 1951; Igor Stravinsky set sections of the poem *Little Gidding* to music; *Murder in the Cathedral* was filmed in 1952, and Eliot wrote some new lines for the script and himself read the part of The Fourth Tempter, who is never seen: The Old Vic issued a recording of *Murder in the Cathedral* in 1953; *Sweeney Agonistes* was adapted as a jazz musical by John Dankworth for "Homage to T. S. Eliot"; *Old Possum's Book of Practical Cats* was adapted by Andrew Lloyd Webber as the stage musical *Cats* in 1981; *Cats* has been seen by over 25 million people in 15 countries.

SIDELIGHTS: A major figure in twentieth century literature, T. S. Eliot was renowned as a poet, dramatist, and critic. His poem *The Waste Land,* a long, sweeping, multi-voiced work published in 1922, is one of the masterpieces of modernist poetry. His critical essays on literature were instrumental in creating the New Criticism, "the most influential school of literary criticism in this century," as Jewel Spears Brooker defined it in the *Dictionary of Literary Biography.* George Steiner pointed out in the *New Yorker* that "much of the current syllabus in the study of

English literature is the direct product of his essays and pronouncements." Eliot's plays, written to revitalize poetic drama, include *Murder in the Cathedral* and *The Cocktail Party,* winner of the New York Drama Critics Circle Award in 1950. In addition to his written work, Eliot also played an important role as editor and publisher of *The Criterion,* a literary review, and as an editor with the British publishing firm of Faber and Faber. As Harold Bloom stated in *Modern Critical Views: T. S. Eliot,* "Eliot is a central figure in the Western literary culture of this century." Echoing this opinion is Joseph Schwartz in *Renascence,* who called Eliot the "greatest literary figure of the English-speaking world in this century. Poetry and criticism were permanently changed and enriched by his work." Northrop Frye claimed in his *T. S. Eliot:* "A thorough knowledge of Eliot is compulsory for anyone interested in contemporary literature. Whether he is liked or disliked is of no importance, but he must be read."

Eliot began writing poetry while still in college, producing his first major work, "The Love Song of J. Alfred Prufrock," in 1911. His first collection appeared in 1917. With these early poems, Eliot "virtually invented modern English poetry," as Brooker stated. Drawing from earlier classics of Western literature, Eliot combined these traditional models with a unique, present-day sensibility, creating poems which pay homage to their forerunners while reflecting the contemporary world. In the essay "Tradition and the Individual Talent," written in 1917, Eliot presented his view of how a new literary work interacted with the existing body of literature. "No poet, no artist of any sort, has his complete meaning alone," Eliot wrote. "His significance, his appreciation is the appreciation of his relation to the dead poets and artists. . . . What happens when a new work of art is created is something that happens simultaneously to all the works of art which preceded it. The existing monuments form an ideal order among themselves, which is modified by the introduction of the new (the really new) work of art among them. The existing order is complete before the new work arrives; for order to persist after the supervention of novelty, the *whole* existing order must be, if ever so slightly, altered." "A poet," Eliot wrote in 1945, "must take as his material his own language as it is actually spoken around him." Correlatively, the duty of the poet, as Eliot emphasized in a 1943 lecture, "is only indirectly to the people: his direct duty is to his language, first to preserve, and second to extend and improve."

"The Love Song of J. Alfred Prufrock" begins with the lines "Let us go then, you and I,/When the evening is spread out against the sky." According to John Berryman in *The Freedom of the Poet,* "that sounds very pretty—lyrical . . . there is a nice rhyme—it sounds like other dim romantic verse. Then comes the third line: 'Like a patient etherised upon a table.' With this line, modern poetry begins." "Its hero," James F. Knapp said of "Prufrock" in the *Arizona Quarterly,* "is not defined according to the familiar conventions of thought and action. Prufrock is not a man, but a mind, a mind shaped by Eliot along the lines of modern depth psychology and metaphysical uncertainty. The world we witness in the poem is a world which reveals only the dynamics of Prufrock's mind, not any verifiable fact of his physical existence." Karl Shapiro, writing in his collection *In Defense of Ignorance,* found "Prufrock" to be "a poem *about* self-consciousness. . . . Prufrock as a character is of no intrinsic interest but he is of high *literary* interest to all. In this poem Eliot has remained close enough to a human footing to make poetry out of a personal complex of crises, private, social, and intellectual. Had he written nothing else he would be remembered for this masterly little poem." In an article for *Sewanee Review* Vincent Miller wrote: "By 1911, when he finished 'Prufrock,' [Eliot] had already abandoned as had no previous poet the mode of writing which creates, out of words on a page, a 'point of view' from which the world can be judged; and he had done so in an effort to seek objective correlatives of word and rhythm that would allow the quite unheroic feelings he shared with his contemporaries to reveal themselves as the feelings they actually were."

Another early poem, "Gerontion," illuminates some of the poetic ideas which Eliot later developed. "Gerontion," Gabriel Pearson wrote in *Eliot in Perspective: A Symposium,* "must be seen as central to Eliot's poetic practice; here he initiates and exhaustively explores permanent features of his basic idiom." One such feature, Pearson continued, is that " 'Gerontion' by common agreement is a dramatic monologue in which the drama has collapsed into incoherence and the monologuist has disintegrated into fragments of his own memory. . . . Eliot's words and cadences are memories, largely memories of literature. Eliot's world is itself constructed as a huge, sounding memory in search of a contemporary identity to attach itself to. . . . Memory, and with it necessarily personal identity, ricochet back, as it were, off the blankness of the present." Conversely, Jack Behar, writing in *Twentieth Century Literature,* found that in "Gerontion" "no sense of a person living through, or recreating, an intimate memory can be forthcoming; the poem contrives a voice without a body, a purely mental universe."

"After three slim volumes of poems," Philip R. Headings wrote in his *T. S. Eliot,* "had greatly extended his reputation, Eliot published in 1922 *The Waste Land,* a poem which many writers have called the most influential poem of the twentieth century." In *The Waste Land,* Eliot best embodied his early poetic intentions. *The Waste Land* is a complex work in which are interspliced a host of narrative voices, quotations taken from classical literature, cultural, religious, and historical allusions, and a variety of contemporary references. With little but the poet's voice to link its diverse elements into a coherent whole, *The Waste Land* captures and embodies the meaningless emptiness of contemporary society. Some critics have compared the poem to a kaleidoscope; others to a verbal collage. "These fragments I have shored against my ruins," Eliot writes near poem's end.

The ancient myth of the quest for the Holy Grail provides the framework for the poem. In the myth, the Waste Land is the barren realm of the Fisher King, who guards the Holy Grail. The sterility of the Waste Land is tied to the Fisher King's own sterility. Eliot sets his Waste Land in the modern world, and equates its barrenness with the decadence and spiritual malaise of the twentieth century. According to Cleanth Brooks in his *Modern Poetry and the Tradition,* in the waste land, "men have lost the knowledge of good and evil." This "keeps them from being alive, and is the justification for viewing the modern waste land as a realm in which the inhabitants do not even exist."

The Waste Land is composed of five parts: "The Burial of the Dead," "A Game of Chess," "The Fire Sermon," "Death by Water," and "What the Thunder Said." "The Burial of the Dead" introduces the primary concerns of the poem. It "develops the theme of the attractiveness of death, or of the difficulty in rousing oneself from the death in life in which the people of the waste land live," as Brooks stated. The section begins with the phrase "April is the cruelest month," a phrase voiced by the inhabitants of the waste land in response to the rebirth of spring and their own reluctance to come fully alive. Allusions to ancient fertility myths, to the waste land of the biblical character Ezekiel, and to Dante's depiction of Limbo follow. Eliot also incorporates quotes from Wagner's opera *Tristan und Isolde* and a sequence about the allegorical figures of the Tarot cards, ending the section with a quote from the French poet Baudelaire.

The composition of the first section of *The Waste Land*— its mixing of elements from many sources into a new whole made comprehensible by the poet's consciousness—is typical of the entire poem. Writing in his *New Bearings in English Poetry: A Study of the Contemporary Situation,* F. R. Leavis related the structure of the poem to its theme of a modern spiritual waste land. "The seeming disjointedness [of the poem]," Leavis wrote, "is intimately related to the erudition that has annoyed so many readers and to the wealth of literary borrowings and allusions. These characteristics reflect the present state of civilization. The traditions and cultures have mingled, and the historical imagination makes the past contemporary; no one tradition can digest so great a variety of materials, and the result is a break-down of forms and the irrevocable loss

of that sense of absoluteness which seems necessary to a robust culture."

Eliot wrote *The Waste Land* while recuperating from an illness. The forced rest gave him the necessary leisure to pursue a project he had been contemplating for almost two years. As he explained to George Seferis: "I'd been sick and the doctors recommended rest. I went to Margate . . . in November [1921]. There I wrote the first part. Then I went to Switzerland on vacation and finished the poem. It was double its present length. I sent it to Pound; he cut out half of it."

Ezra Pound's contribution to the shaping of *The Waste Land* consisted of drastically cutting the manuscript (eliminating in the process several smaller poems which were at first meant to form a part of the work), rearranging certain passages, and suggesting a number of word changes. Some of the cuts were extensive. Pound eliminated Eliot's fifty-four-line opening to *The Waste Land.* Written in a prosaic style and telling of a working-class night on the town, the opening was intended by Eliot as a way to ease the reader into the poem. Pound felt it was inappropriate and irrelevant to the body of the text. In Part 3, Eliot had included forty-three couplets in the satirical manner of Pope. Pound argued that Pope had already done satirical couplets well enough, and cut them. In Part 4, Pound cut three quatrains and a seventy-one line blank verse segment about a sea voyage and shipwreck. The poem's title was also eliminated. Eliot's original title was a quotation from Dickens' *Our Mutual Friend,* "He Do the Police in Different Voices," a reference to the many voices to be found in *The Waste Land.*

"The poem which resulted from the Eliot-Pound collaboration was in some respects quite different from that which Eliot had had in mind," Donald Gallup wrote in the *Atlantic.* Pound's editing had condensed *The Waste Land* significantly, intensifying the poem's kaleidoscopic effect. Writing in his *The Invisible Poet: T. S. Eliot,* Hugh Kenner stated that *The Waste Land*'s "self-sufficient juxtaposition without copulae of themes and passages in a dense mosaic, had at first a novelty which troubled even the author." Gallup believed that "at least part of what the central poem gained in concentration, intensity, and general effectiveness through Pound's editing was at the sacrifice of some of its experimental character." Nonetheless, Gallup continued, "By clearing away this material and demonstrating that it was not essential, Pound allowed the central long poem to emerge." Steiner believed that in his role as editor, Pound "elicited from Eliot excellences that were latent in Eliot himself—in himself alone and in his vision of the poem. Pound has never claimed more." Eliot acknowledged Pound's contribution to *The Waste Land* in the poem's dedication: "For Ezra Pound, *il miglior fabbro* [the better craftsman]."

Initial reaction to *The Wasteland* was overwhelmingly negative. Louis Untermeyer, for example, wrote in the *Freeman* that the poem was "a kaleidoscopic movement in which the bright-coloured pieces fail to atone for the absence of an integrated design." The poem raised so much controversy that Herbert S. Gorman was moved to write in the *Literary Digest International Book Review:* "*The Waste Land* has become a battle-field. . . . No poem since the advent of the *Spoon River Anthology* has aroused so much infuriated discussion, and no book, not even James Joyce's *Ulysses,* has been approached more blindly. Its adherents see nothing but its virtues; its detractors see nothing but its faults." The premiere issue of *Time* magazine (March 3, 1923) even reported the rumor that *The Waste Land* was nothing but a hoax.

But *The Waste Land* has withstood the test of time to become a signal achievement in the history of twentieth-century literature and one of the outstanding masterpieces of Modernist writing. Richard Ellmann, in the *New York Review of Books,* quoted James Joyce on the significance of *The Waste Land.* The poem, Joyce believed, "ended the idea of poetry for ladies. Whether admired or detested, it became, like *Lyrical Ballads* in 1798, a traffic signal." Schwartz claimed that "*The Waste Land* remains (and probably will remain) the most famous poem of this century." In an article for *Time,* Paul Gray called it "the single most influential poem in English of the 20th century." So influential was *The Waste Land* that it changed the tone and approach of much serious poetry which followed it. The poem's collage structure, its erudite and ironic tone, and most importantly, its depiction of a world without faith or values can be found echoed in the work of many later poets.

The spiritual despair Eliot expressed in *The Waste Land* led him in 1927 to join the Anglican Church. This decision was reflected in *Four Quartets,* a poem cycle with a religious theme. Breaking drastically with the style of *The Waste Land, Four Quartets* is written in a more conventional verse. "The archetype of this cycle is the Bible," Frye commented, "which begins with the story of man in a garden." So *Four Quartets* begins and ends at the same point, "with the Word as the circumference of reality, containing within itself time, space, and poetry viewed in the light of the conception of poetry as a living whole of all the poetry that has ever been written." "The triumphant achievement of the *Four Quartets,*" Alvarez writes, "is in the peculiar wholeness and isolation of their poetic world. . . . Eliot has always worked obliquely, by suggestion and by his penetrating personal rhythms. His power is in his sureness and mastery of subject and expression. And this sense of inviolable purpose seems to remove his verse from the ordinary realm of human interchange. He has created a world of formal perfection. It lacks the di-

mension of human error." Neville Braybrooke writes in his *T. S. Eliot:* "It is . . . generally agreed . . . that in his *Four Quartets* [Eliot] attempted . . . to achieve a poetry so transparent that in concentrating on it attention would not fall so much on the words, but on what the words pointed to. And in his rigorous stripping away of the poetic, such a pure poetry is sustained." *Four Quartets* was, as Robert Giroux noted in the *Washington Post Book World,* Eliot's "last major poem" and "will doubtless stand as his greatest."

Eliot's religious conversion also found expression in a new genre for the author, that of verse drama. He modeled his plays after medieval religious theatre. Eliot's "primary goal," Nancy Duvall Hargrove wrote in the *Dictionary of Literary Biography,* "is to portray the presence and the significance of the spiritual in the human experience by means of *poetic* drama. . . . By poetic drama Eliot means not only drama written in poetry but also drama with a spiritual design or pattern, an intrinsic order." In the *Aims of Poetic Drama* Eliot wrote: "What I should like to do is this: that the people on the stage should seem to the audience so like themselves that they would find themselves thinking: 'I could talk in poetry too!' Then they are not transported into an unaccustomed, artificial world; but their ordinary, sordid world is suddenly illuminated and transfigured. And if poetry cannot do that for people, it is merely superfluous decoration."

Of the seven plays Eliot wrote, *Murder in the Cathedral, The Family Reunion,* and *The Cocktail Party* were his most successful, both in terms of fulfilling his dramatic intentions and entertaining an audience. Eliot himself believed that *The Family Reunion,* at least poetically, was the best of all his plays. Helen Gardner, writing in *T. S. Eliot and the English Poetic Tradition,* believes that *The Cocktail Party* and *The Confidential Clerk* are his finest. She says of these works: "No other plays of our generation present with equal force, sympathy, wisdom, and wit the classic subject of comedy: our almost, but mercifully not wholly, unlimited powers of self-deception, and the shocks and surprises that life gives to our poses and pretences." Hargrove noted that "A most telling fact is that each of the plays is the favorite of at least one critic." But history will almost certainly endow *Murder in the Cathedral* with the longest life and the greatest fame. John Gross argued: "Whether or not *Murder in the Cathedral* augments our ability to live, it is certainly a remarkable piece of work. It is Eliot's one indubitable theatrical triumph, and the one English addition to the classic repertoire since [George Bernard] Shaw."

In addition to his roles as poet and dramatist, Eliot achieved prominence—some would say domination—as a literary critic and theorist. The eminent historian of criticism Rene Wellek wrote in the *Sewanee Review:* "T. S.

Eliot is by far the most important critic of the twentieth century in the English-speaking world." Writing in the *Dictionary of Literary Biography,* Michael Beehler defined Eliot's position as a literary critic: "No name is more closely associated with the course of modern poetry and literary criticism than that of T. S. Eliot, for no writer has had a greater hand in shaping the sensibilities, expectations, and projects of modern critical and creative letters. . . . [It] is in his role as theorist, critic, reviewer, editor, and public man of letters that Eliot's influence has most profoundly and enduringly affected modern thinking about literature. This influence had a particularly direct impact upon New Criticism, the most important American literary theory of the first half of the twentieth century."

Eliot's criticism stressed the impersonality of literature, the independence of the work of art from the artist's personal life, the author's intentions, or the historical situation in which it was created. Eliot, Beehler wrote, "envisions texts as autotelic, self-sufficient objects whose meanings inhere in their own internal structures and organizations." As objects, works of literature can be examined by critics in much the same way as scientists examine physical objects. "Eliot," Beehler concluded, "asserts the standards and authority of a literary tradition within which a work must be set in order to be evaluated. . . . [Literary criticism] is de-subjectivized and de-historicized, and poetic meaning becomes impersonal, public, and objective."

In addition to his influence on how literary critics viewed literature, Eliot also helped to set the established canon of literary works. Eliot's "influence as a critic," George Steiner remarked in the *New Yorker,* "remains formidable in the academic world; much of the current syllabus in the study of English literature is the direct product of his essays and pronouncements." As Bloom complained in his *Modern Critical Views: T. S. Eliot:* "An obsessive reader of poetry growing up in the nineteen thirties and forties entered a critical world dominated by the opinions and example of Eliot. . . . Anyone adopting the profession of teaching literature in the early nineteen fifties entered a discipline virtually enslaved not only by Eliot's insights but by the entire span of his preferences and prejudices." Such was Eliot's influence that during the 1940s and 1950s the phrase "the Age of Eliot" was commonly used to refer to contemporary literary criticism. In his summary of Eliot's critical stance, A. Alvarez wrote in his *Stewards of Excellence:* "Our interest and standards in literature are Eliot's creation."

Particularly for his work as a poet, Eliot has earned a lasting place in the pantheon of twentieth century literature. Paul Roche, writing in *Poetry Review,* believed that "with Yeats and Pound [Eliot] will undoubtedly live in history

as one of the most important poets of this century." Similarly, Martin Scofield, in his *T. S. Eliot: The Poems,* found that "it seems certain that Eliot will retain his place, with W. B. Yeats, as one of the two greatest poets of the first half of this century." Edwin M. Yoder, Jr., in the *Washington Post* observed that Eliot "wielded more power than any other 20th century poet. . . . It is impossible to write poetry today without hearing in some inner ear the echoes of those wonderfully dry, melancholy, cryptic, melodic and haunting poems." Speaking of Eliot's place in contemporary letters, Shapiro claimed: "Eliot is untouchable; he is Modern Literature incarnate and an institution unto himself. One is permitted to disagree with him on a point here or a doctrine there, but no more."

Shortly after Eliot's death in 1965, a program entitled "Homage to T. S. Eliot" was presented at the Globe Theatre in London. To the program Igor Stravinsky contributed "Introitus," a new choral work written in Eliot's memory, and Henry Moore presented a huge sculpture entitled "The Archer." Andrei Voznesensky, Peter O'Toole, Laurence Olivier, and Paul Scofield recited. Poems read during the program were selected by W. H. Auden, and Cleanth Brooks contributed a brief narration.

To celebrate the centenary of Eliot's birth in 1988, a number of events were organized around the world. Conferences were held at Washington University in Eliot's hometown of St. Louis, at the University of Maine, at the Dali Museum and Poynter Institute in St. Petersburg, Florida, the University of Arkansas at Little Rock, the University of New Hampshire at Durham, Miami University of Ohio, the California Institute of Technology, at meetings of the Modern Language Association and similar organizations, and in Japan. The T. S. Eliot Society, headquartered in St. Louis, held a four-day celebration which included performances of several Eliot plays, readings from his works, and a symposium. In England, the British Council organized an exhibition celebrating Eliot's career, while the London Library established the T. S. Eliot Centenary Fund to provide students and scholars free access to library resources. Among other celebrations, a dinner party was held at Eliot's favorite restaurant, L'Ecu de France in Paris, the Bishop of London presided at a memorial "Mass of Thanksgiving" for Eliot's life at St. Stephen's Church in Gloucester Road, a reception was held at Lloyd's Bank, where Eliot once worked as a clerk, and memorial services were held at Westminster Abbey, St. Michael's Church in East Coker, Little Gidding, and at St. Edmundsbury Cathedral.

BIOGRAPHICAL/CRITICAL SOURCES:

BOOKS

Ackroyd, Peter, *T. S. Eliot: A Life,* Simon & Schuster, 1984.

Adams, Robert Martin, *AfterJoyce: Studies in Fiction after 'Ulysses,'* Oxford University Press, 1977.

Aiken, Conrad, *A Reviewer's ABC,* World Publishing, 1958.

Allan, Mowbray, *T. S. Eliot's Impersonal Theory of Poetry,* Bucknell University Press, 1974.

Alldritt, Keith, *Eliot's Four Quartets: Poetry as Chamber Music,* Woburn Press, 1978.

Alvarez, A., *Stewards of Excellence,* Scribner, 1958.

Baybrooke, Neville, editor, *T.S. Eliot: A Symposium for His Seventieth Birthday,* Farrar, Straus, 1958.

Bedient, Calvin, *He Do the Police in Different Voices: 'The Waste Land' and Its Protagonist,* University of Chicago Press, 1986.

Behr, Caroline, *T. S. Eliot: A Chronology of His Life and Works,* St. Martin's, 1983.

Bergonzi, Bernard, editor, *T. S. Eliot, Four Quartets: A Casebook,* Macmillan, 1969.

Bergonzi, Bernard, *T. S. Eliot,* Macmillan, 1972.

Bergsten, Staffan, *Time and Eternity: A Study in the Structure and Symbolism of T. S. Eliot's Four Quartets,* Bonniers, 1960.

Berryman, John, *The Freedom of the Poet,* Farrar, Straus, 1976, pp. 270-278.

Blamires, Harry, *Word Unheard: A Guide Through Eliot's Four Quartets,* Methuen, 1969.

Bolgan, Anne C., *What the Thunder Really Said: A Retrospective Essay on the Making of The Waste Land,* Queen's University Press (Montreal), 1973.

Bloom, Harold, editor, *Modern Critical Views: T. S. Eliot,* Chelsea House, 1985.

Bloom, Harold, *T. S. Eliot's 'The Waste Land,'* Chelsea House, 1986.

Bogard, Travis, and William I. Oliver, editors, *Modern Drama: Essays in Criticism,* Oxford University Press, 1965.

Bornstein, George, *Transformations of Romanticism in Yeats, Eliot, and Stevens,* University of Chicago Press, 1977.

Bradbrook, Muriel, *T. S. Eliot,* revised edition, Longmans, Green, 1963.

Brady, Ann P., *Lyricism in the Poetry of T. S. Eliot,* Kennikat, 1978.

Braybrooke, Neville, editor, *T. S. Eliot: A Symposium for His Seventieth Birthday,* Farrar, Straus, 1958.

Braybrooke, Neville, *T. S. Eliot,* Eerdmans, 1967.

Breit, Harvey, *The Writer Observed,* World Publishing, 1956.

Brooker, Jewel Spears, editor, *Approaches to Teaching T. S. Eliot's Poetry and Plays,* Modern Language Association of America, 1988.

Brooks, Cleanth, *Modern Poetry and the Tradition,* University of North Carolina Press, 1939, pp. 136-172.

Browne, E. Martin, *The Making of T. S. Eliot's Plays,* Cambridge University Press, 1969.

Bush, Ronald, *T. S. Eliot: A Study in Character and Style,* Oxford University Press, 1984.

Calder, Angus, *T. S. Eliot,* Humanities Press, 1987.

Canary, Robert, *T. S. Eliot: The Poet and His Critics,* American Library Association, 1982.

Chace, William M., *The Political Identities of Ezra Pound and T. S. Eliot,* Stanford University Press, 1973.

Chiari, Joseph, *T. S. Eliot: A Memoir,* Enitharmon Press, 1982.

Concise Dictionary of American Literary Biography: The New Maturity, 1929-1941, Gale, 1989.

Contemporary Literary Criticism, Gale, Volume 1, 1973, Volume 2, 1974, Volume 3, 1975, Volume 6, 1976, Volume 9, 1978, Volume 10, 1979, Volume 13, 1980, Volume 15, 1980, Volume 24, 1983, Volume 34, 1985, Volume 41, 1987, Volume 55, 1989, Volume 57, 1990.

Cooper, John Xiros, *T. S. Eliot and the Politics of Voice: The Argument of 'The Waste Land,'* UMI Research Press, 1987.

Cox, C. B. and A. P. Hinchcliffe, editors, *T. S. Eliot: 'The Waste Land,' A Casebook,* Macmillan, 1968.

Craig, Cairns, *Yeats, Eliot, Pound, and the Politics of Poetry,* University of Pittsburgh Press, 1982.

Crawford, Robert, *The Savage and the City in the Works of T. S. Eliot,* Oxford at the Clarendon Press, 1987.

Dale, Alzina S., *T. S. Eliot: The Philosopher Poet,* Shaw Publications, 1988.

Dictionary of Literary Biography, Gale, Volume 7: *Twentieth-Century American Dramatists,* 1981, Volume 10: *Modern British Dramatists, 1940-1945,* 1982, Volume 45: *American Poets, 1880-1945, First Series,* 1986, Volume 63: *Modern American Criticism, 1920-1955,* 1988.

Dictionary of Literary Biography Yearbook, 1988, Gale, 1989.

Donoghue, Denis, *Modern British and American Verse Drama,* Princeton University Press, 1959.

Drew, Elizabeth, *T. S. Eliot: The Design of His Poetry,* Eyre & Spottiswoode, 1950.

Eder, Doris L., *Three Writers in Exile: Pound, Eliot, and Joyce,* Whitson, 1984.

Forster, E. M., *Abinger Harvest,* Harcourt, 1936, pp. 89-96.

Freed, Lewis, *T. S. Eliot: The Critic as Philosopher,* Purdue University Press, 1979.

French, Warren G., *The Twenties: Fiction, Poetry, Drama,* Everett/Edwards, 1975, pp. 1-26.

Frye, Northrop, *T. S. Eliot,* Oliver & Boyd, 1963.

Gallup, Donald C., *T. S. Eliot: A Bibliography,* Harcourt, 1969.

Gardner, Helen, *The Art of T. S. Eliot,* Cresset Press (London), 1949, Dutton, 1959.

Gardner, Helen, *The Composition of Four Quartets,* Oxford University Press, 1978.

Gardner, Helen, *T. S. Eliot and the English Poetic Tradition,* University of Nottingham Press, 1966.

Gish, Nancy K., *Time in the Poetry of T. S. Eliot: A Study in Structure and Theme,* Barnes & Noble, 1981.

Gordon, Lyndall, *Eliot's Early Years,* Oxford University Press, 1977.

Gordon, Lyndall, *Eliot's New Life,* Farrar, Straus, 1988.

Grant, Michael, *T. S. Eliot: The Critical Heritage,* two volumes, Routledge & Kegan Paul, 1982.

Gray, Piers, *T. S. Eliot's Intellectual and Poetic Development, 1909-1922,* Humanities Press, 1982.

Gunther, Bradley, *The Merrill Checklist of T. S. Eliot,* Merrill, 1970.

Hargrove, Nancy Duvall, *Landscape as Symbol in the Poetry of T. S. Eliot,* University Press of Mississippi, 1978.

Headings, Philip R., *T. S. Eliot,* Twayne, 1964, revised edition, G. K. Hall, 1982.

Hinchliffe, Arnold P., *British Theatre, 1950-70,* Rowman & Littlefield, 1974.

Howarth, Herbert, *Notes on Some Figures Behind T. S. Eliot,* Houghton, 1964.

Howe, Irving, editor, *Modern Literary Criticism,* Beacon, 1958.

Hyman, Stanley Edgar, editor, *The Critical Performance,* Vintage, 1956.

Hynes, Samuel, *The Auden Generation: Literature and Politics in England in the 1930s,* Viking, 1977.

Ishak, Fayek M., *The Mystical Philosophy of T. S. Eliot,* New College University Press, 1970.

Jones, Genesius, *Approach to the Purpose: A Study of the Poetry of T. S. Eliot,* Hodder & Stoughton, 1964.

Kearns, Cleo M., *T. S. Eliot and Indic Traditions: A Study in Poetry and Belief,* Cambridge University Press, 1987.

Kenner, Hugh, *T. S. Eliot: The Invisible Poet,* McDowell, Obolensky, 1959, published as *"The Invisible Poet": T. S. Eliot,* Harcourt, 1969.

Kenner, Hugh, editor, *T. S. Eliot: A Collection of Critical Essays,* Prentice-Hall, 1962.

Kenner, Hugh, *The Pound Era,* University of California Press, 1971.

Kermode, Frank, *Continuities,* Random House, 1968, pp. 67-77.

Kirk, Russell, *Eliot and His Age: T. S. Eliot's Moral Imagination in the Twentieth Century,* Random House, 1971.

Knoll, Robert E., editor, *Storm Over The Waste Land,* Scott, Foresman, 1964.

Leavis, F. R., *New Bearings in English Poetry: A Study of the Contemporary Situation,* AMS Press, 1978, pp. 75-132.

Levin, Harry, *Ezra Pound, T. S. Eliot, and the European Horizon,* Oxford University Press, 1975.

Levy, William Turner and Victor Scherle, *Affectionately, T. S. Eliot: The Story of a Friendship, 1947-1965,* Lippincott, 1968.

Litz, A. Walton, editor, *Eliot in His Time: Essays on the Occasion of the Fiftieth Anniversary of The Waste Land,* Princeton University Press, 1973.

Lobb, Edward, *T. S. Eliot and the Romantic Critical Tradition,* Routledge & Kegan Paul, 1981.

Lumley, Frederick, *New Trends in 20th Century Drama,* Oxford University Press, 1967.

MacCarthy, Desmond, *Humanities,* MacGibbon & Kee, 1953, pp. 126-132.

March, Richard and Thurairajah Tambimuttu, editors, *T. S. Eliot: A Symposium from Conrad Aiken and Others,* Editions Poetry (London), 1948, Regnery, 1949.

Margolis, John D., *T. S. Eliot's Intellectual Development,* University of Chicago Press, 1972.

Martin, Graham, editor, *Eliot in Perspective: A Symposium,* Macmillan, 1970.

Martin, Jay, editor, *A Collection of Critical Essays on "The Waste Land,"* Prentice-Hall, 1968.

Martin, Mildred, *A Half-Century of Eliot Criticism: Annotated Bibliography of Books and Articles in English, 1916-1965,* Bucknell University Press, 1972.

Materer, Timothy, *Vortex: Pound, Eliot, and Lewis,* Cornell University Press, 1979.

Matthews, Thomas S., *Great Tom: Notes Toward the Definition of T. S. Eliot,* Harper, 1974.

Matthiessen, F. O., *The Achievement of T.S. Eliot: An Essay on the Nature of Poetry,* Oxford University Press, 1935, third edition, 1958.

Maxwell, D. E. S., *The Poetry of T. S. Eliot,* Routledge & Kegan Paul, 1952.

Mesterton, Eric, *The Waste Land: Some Commentaries,* Haskell Booksellers, 1975.

Miller, James E., Jr., *T. S. Eliot's Personal Waste Land: Exorcism of the Demons,* Pennsylvania State University Press, 1977.

Moody, A. D., *Thomas Stearns Eliot: Poet,* Cambridge University Press, 1979.

Moody, A. D., editor, *The Waste Land in Different Voices,* St. Martin's, 1974.

Newton-De Molina, David, editor, *The Literary Criticism of T. S. Eliot,* Athlone Press, 1977.

Order of Service in Memory of Thomas Stearns Eliot, Hove Shirley Press (London), 1965.

Patterson, Gertrude, *T. S. Eliot: Poems in the Making,* Barnes & Noble, 1971.

Pinkney, Tony, *Women in the Poetry of T. S. Eliot: A Psychoanalytic Approach,* Macmillan, 1984.

Poetry Criticism, Volume 5, Gale, 1992.

Preston, Raymond, *Four Quartets Rehearsed,* Sheed & Ward, 1946.

Pritchard, John Paul, *Criticism in America,* University of Oklahoma Press, 1956.

Raffel, Burton, *T. S. Eliot,* Ungar, 1982.

Raffel, Burton, *Possum and Ole Ez in the Public Eye: Contemporaries and Peers on T. S. Eliot and Ezra Pound, 1892-1972,* Archon, 1985.

Rajan, Balachandra, *The Overwhelming Question: A Study of the Poetry of T. S. Eliot,* University of Toronto Press, 1976.

Rajan, Balachandra, editor, *T. S. Eliot: A Study of His Writing by Several Hands,* Dobson, 1947.

Ransom, John Crowe, *The New Criticism,* New Directions, 1941.

Remembering Poets: Reminiscences and Opinions, Harper, 1978, pp. 203-221.

Rexroth, Kenneth, *Assays,* New Directions, 1961.

Ricks, Beatrice, *T. S. Eliot: A Bibliography of Secondary Works,* Scarecrow, 1980.

Ricks, Christopher, *T. S. Eliot and Prejudice,* Faber, 1988.

Riddel, Joseph N., *The Inverted Bell: Modernism and the Counterpoetics of William Carlos Williams,* Louisiana State University, 1974.

Roby, Kinley E., editor, *Critical Essays on T. S. Eliot: The Sweeney Motif,* G. K. Hall, 1985.

Rosenthal, M. L., *The Modern Poets: A Critical Introduction,* Oxford University Press, 1960, pp. 75-103.

Rosenthal, M. L., *Sailing into the Unknown: Yeats, Pound, and Eliot,* Oxford University Press, 1978.

Schneider, Elisabeth W., *T. S. Eliot: The Pattern in the Carpet,* University of California Press, 1975.

Schwartz, Sanford, *The Matrix of Modernism: Pound, Eliot, and Early Twentieth Century Thought,* Princeton University Press, 1985.

Scofield, Martin, *T. S. Eliot: The Poems,* Cambridge University Press, 1988.

Scott-James, R. A., *Fifty Years of English Literature, 1900-1950,* Longmans, Green, 1951.

Sencourt, Robert, *T. S. Eliot: A Memoir,* edited by Donald Adamson, Dodd, Mead, 1971.

Shapiro, Karl, *In Defense of Ignorance,* Random House, 1960, pp. 35-60.

Shapiro, Karl, *The Poetry Wreck: Selected Essays, 1950-1970,* Random House, 1975, pp. 3-28.

Shaw, Ramesh Chandra, *Yeats and Eliot: Perspectives on India,* Humanities Press, 1983.

Skaff, William, *The Philosophy of T. S. Eliot,* University of Pennsylvania Press, 1986.

Smidt, Kristian, *Poetry and Belief in the Work of T. S. Eliot,* Dybwad (Oslo), 1949, revised edition, Humanities Press, 1961.

Smidt, Kristian, *The Importance of Recognition: Six Chapters on T. S. Eliot,* Peter Norbye (Tromso), 1973.

Smith, Grover, *T. S. Eliot's Poetry and Plays: A Study in Sources and Meanings,* University of Chicago Press, 1974.

Smith, Grover, *The Waste Land,* Allen & Unwin, 1983.

Southam, B. C., *A Guide to the Selected Poems of T. S. Eliot,* Harcourt, 1970.

Spender, Stephen, *The Destructive Element: A Study of Modern Writers and Beliefs,* J. Cape, 1935, pp. 132-175.

Spender, Stephen, *T. S. Eliot,* Viking, 1975.

Spurr, David, *Conflicts in Consciousness: T. S. Eliot's Poetry and Criticism,* University of Illinois Press, 1984.

Sullivan, Sheila, editor, *Critics on T. S. Eliot,* Allen & Unwin, 1973.

Tate, Allen, editor, *T. S. Eliot, the Man and His Work: A Critical Evaluation by Twenty-Six Distinguished Writers,* Dell, 1966.

Thompson, Eric, *T. S. Eliot: The Metaphysical Perspective,* Southern Illinois University Press, 1963.

Thomrahlen, Marianne, *The Waste Land: A Fragmentary Wholeness,* C. W. K. Gleerup, 1978.

Traversi, Derek, *T. S. Eliot: The Longer Poems,* Bodley Head, 1976.

Tynan, Kenneth, *Curtains,* Atheneum, 1961.

Ungar, Leonard, editor, *T.S. Eliot: A Selected Critique,* Rinehart, 1948.

Ungar, Leonard, *T. S. Eliot,* University of Minnesota Press, 1961.

Ungar, Leonard, *T. S. Eliot: Movements and Patterns,* University of Minnesota Press, 1966.

Untermeyer, Louis, *Lives of the Poets,* Simon & Schuster, 1959.

Wagner, Linda, editor, *T. S. Eliot: A Collection of Criticism,* McGraw, 1974.

Warren, Austin, *Connections,* University of Michigan Press, 1970, pp. 152-183.

Watson, George, *The Literary Critics: A Study of English Descriptive Criticism,* Rowman & Littlefield, 1973.

Weales, Gerald, *Religion in Modern English Drama,* University of Pennsylvania Press, 1961.

Williams, Helen, *T. S. Eliot: The Waste Land,* Edward Arnold, 1968.

Williamson, George, *A Reader's Guide to T. S. Eliot,* Noonday Press, 1966.

Wilson, Edmund, *Axel's Castle: A Study in the Imaginative Literature of 1870-1930,* Scribner, 1931.

PERIODICALS

Agenda, spring-summer, 1985, pp. 82-86.

American Literature, May, 1943, pp. 101-126; January, 1962.

American Quarterly, summer, 1961.

American Scholar, winter, 1960-61, pp. 43-55.

Ariel, January, 1971, pp. 26-42.

Arizona Quarterly, spring, 1966.

Atlantic Monthly, May, 1965; January, 1970.

Book Week, February 13, 1966.

Bucknell Review, Volume 22, number 2, 1976, pp. 180-207.

Cambridge Quarterly, Volume XVIII, number 1, 1989, pp. 34-62.

Canadian Forum, February, 1965.

Centennial Review, summer, 1981, pp. 225-228.

College English, February, 1951, pp. 269-275.

Commentary, November, 1958.

Contemporary Literature, winter, 1968.

Critical Quarterly, spring-summer, 1986, pp. 145-153.

Criticism, fall, 1966; winter, 1967.

Daily Express (London), September 20, 1957, p. 6.

Dial, December, 1922, pp. 611-616.

Drama, summer, 1967.

Dublin Magazine, April-June, 1933, pp. 11-19.

Encounter, March, 1965; April, 1965; November, 1965; April, 1972, pp. 80-83.

Esquire, August, 1965.

Explicator, winter, 1978, pp. 8-10.

Freeman, January 17, 1923, p. 453.

Granite Review, Volume 24, number 3, 1962, pp. 16-20.

Guardian, August 19, 1988, p. 21.

Horizon IX, winter, 1972, pp. 105-109.

The Hound and Horn, March, 1928, pp. 187-213; June, 1928, pp. 281-319.

Jewish Quarterly, summer, 1969.

John O'London's Weekly, August 19, 1949, pp. 497-498.

Kenyon Review, winter, 1965, pp. 11-21.

Listener, November 28, 1940, pp. 773-774; June 25, 1967; September 29, 1988, p. 37.

Literary Digest International, April, 1923, p. 46.

Little Review, December, 1917, pp. 8-14.

London Review of Books, September 29, 1988, pp. 3-6; November 24, 1988, p. 26.

Los Angeles Times, October 2, 1988; October 6, 1988.

Midwest Quarterly, winter, 1979.

Nation, August 5, 1925, pp. 162-164; October 3, 1966; November 8, 1971, pp. 470-472.

New England Quarterly, June, 1971, pp. 179-196.

New Leader, November 6, 1967.

New Republic, February 7, 1923, pp. 294-295; May 20, 1967; November 13, 1971, pp. 25-26.

New Statesman, November 3, 1923, p. 116; October 11, 1963; March 13 1964.

New Yorker, April 22, 1972, p. 134.

New York Herald Tribune, February 7, 1954.

New York Review of Books, March 3, 1966; November 18, 1971, p. 10; May 13, 1976, pp. 15-18; February 9, 1978, pp. 3-4; November 10, 1988, pp. 3-4.

New York Times, January 5, 1965; June 14, 1965; November 23, 1968; November 3, 1971; September 28, 1986; August 9, 1988; August 22, 1989.

New York Times Book Review, November 29, 1953, p. 5; November 19, 1967; October 20, 1985, p. 3; October 16, 1988, p. 1.

New York Times Magazine, September 21, 1958.

Observer, June 11, 1967; September 25, 1988, p. 44.

Paris Review, spring-summer, 1959, pp. 47-70.

Partisan Review, spring, 1945, pp. 199-206; February, 1949, pp. 119-137; spring, 1966.

PN Review, Volume 4, number 1, 1976.

Poetry Review, spring, 1968.

Publishers Weekly, December 10, 1962.

Quagga, Volume 2, number 1, 1962, pp. 31-33.

Quarterly Review of Literature, numbers 1-2 (double issue), 1967.

Renascence, spring, 1988, p. 158.

St. Louis Post-Dispatch, October 5, 1930.

Saturday Review, September 13, 1958; October 19, 1963; February 8, 1964.

Sewanee Review, summer, 1934, pp. 365-371; winter, 1948, pp. 69-81; winter, 1962; spring, 1967; summer, 1976; summer, 1984, pp. 432-441.

South Atlantic Quarterly, winter, 1969.

Southern Review, summer, 1937, pp. 106-136; autumn, 1985, pp. 914-923.

Southwest Review, summer, 1965.

Studies in American Humor, January, 1975, pp. 167-171.

Time, March 3, 1923; June 7, 1943; November 22, 1968, p. 96; September 26, 1988, p. 88.

Times (London), September 29, 1958; August 9, 1988; August 15, 1988.

Times Educational Supplement, September 26, 1958.

Times Literary Supplement, September 20, 1923, p. 616; June 1, 1967; November 18, 1988, p. 1279.

transition, Number 27, April/May, 1938, p. 236.

Twentieth Century Literature, December, 1977, pp. 487-497.

Virginia Quarterly Review, autumn, 1967.

Washington Post, October 8, 1988, p. A27.

Washington Post Book World, September 25, 1988, p. 1; December 18, 1988, p. 1.

Yorkshire Post, August 29, 1961.*

—*Sketch by Thomas Wiloch*

*   *   *

ELKIN, Judith Laikin   1928-

PERSONAL: Born June 7, 1928, in Baltimore, MD; daughter of Benjamin (a manufacturer) and Anna (Golomb) Laikin; married Sol Elkin (a labor arbitrator), August 5, 1960; children: Alissa, Susannah. *Education:* University of Michigan, B.A., 1948, Ph.D., 1976; Columbia University, M.A., 1950; London School of Economics and Political Science, graduate study, 1957.

ADDRESSES: Home—2104 Georgetown Blvd., Ann Arbor, MI 48105. *Office*—Frankel Center for Judaic Studies, University of Michigan, Ann Arbor, MI 48109.

CAREER: Foreign Service Officer with U.S. Department of State, served as third secretary of embassy in New Delhi, India, 1952-54, and as vice-consul in London, England, 1954- 56; Wayne State University, Detroit, MI, assistant professor of political science, 1964-68; Albion College, Albion, MI, associate professor of history, 1969-79; Great Lakes Colleges Association, Ann Arbor, MI, program officer, 1980-84; visiting associate professor of history at University of Michigan, Ann Arbor, 1984-85, and Ohio State University, Columbus, 1985-86; currently research scientist, University of Michigan.

MEMBER: American Historical Association, Latin American Jewish Studies Association (founding president), Conference on Latin American History.

AWARDS, HONORS: Avery Hopwood Literary Awards, 1947, 1948; Phi Alpha Theta award in history, 1974; Minnie Cumnock Blodgett Fellow, American Association of University Women, 1974; senior archives fellow, *American Jewish Archives,* 1980; Fulbright fellowship for work in Argentina, and American Council of Learned Societies grant, both 1984; National Endowment for the Humanities, fellowship, 1988, grants, 1989 and 1990.

WRITINGS:

Background: Indochina (pamphlet), U.S. Department of State, 1951.

Background: Iran (pamphlet), U.S. Department of State, 1951.

Report on the United Nations (pamphlet), U.S. Department of State, 1952.

The United States in the United Nations (pamphlet), North Central Association of Colleges and Secondary Schools, 1960.

Understanding Israel, Laidlaw Brothers, 1962.

A People-to-People School and Classroom Exchange (pamphlet), North Central Association of Colleges and Secondary Schools, 1962.

Krishna Smiled: Assignment to Southeast Asia, Wayne State University Press, 1972.

Jews of the Latin American Republics, University of North Carolina Press, 1980.

Great Lakes Colleges: Twenty Years of Leadership in Higher Education, Great Lakes Colleges Association, 1984.

(Editor) Thomas Niehaus and others, *Resources for Latin American Jewish Studies,* Latin American Jewish Studies Association, 1984.

(Editor with Gilbert W. Merkx) *The Jewish Presence in Latin America,* Allen & Unwin, 1987.

(With Analya Sater) *Latin American Jewish Studies: An Annotated Guide to the Literature,* Greenwood Press, 1990.

Contributor to *Latin American and Caribbean Contemporary Record,* 1984, and *American Jewish Yearbook,* 1985. Also contributor of reviews to *Choice, Americas, American Jewish Archives,* and *Hispanic American Historical Review.* Editor of *Latin American Jewish Studies Newsletter.*

SIDELIGHTS: Mark Falcoff of *Commentary* calls Judith Laikin Elkin's *Jews of the Latin American Republics* "a formidable undertaking, not embarked upon lightly," but notes that Elkin "has managed it all—with grace, insight, and really astonishing erudition. *Jews of the Latin American Republics* is even—rarest of things—a scholarly monograph that is a genuine pleasure to read."

Elkin told *CA:* "With the publication of my book *Jews of the Latin American Republics,* I began the process of rendering visible this community which has hitherto been neglected by Latin Americanists and by Jewish scholars alike. This was also an integrating experience for me, as I am able to combine my interests in Jewish and in Latin American studies in a way that has not been done before.

"My dream of establishing Latin American Jewish Studies as an academic discipline was accomplished with formation of LAJSA (Latin American Jewish Studies Association), which joins four hundred scholars and one hundred institutions in twenty-two countries, all of whom share the same research interest. The result has been a tremendous increase in scholarship, and its integration into the two cognate fields of Latin American and Jewish studies."

"With the sponsorship of National Endowment for the Humanities, I was able to project a series of conferences, concerts, and exhibits on the theme, 'Jews and the Encounter with the New World, 1492-1992.' Based at the University of Michigan, these events enriched public understanding of the complex events underlying the 'discovery' of America. 1992 was a year in which we all 'discovered' new elements of our heritage.

"The lasting quality of my work was confirmed for me when a German publisher requested translation rights for *Jews of the Latin American Republics,* now out of print in the United States."

BIOGRAPHICAL/CRITICAL SOURCES:

PERIODICALS

Choice, October 20, 1986; June, 1991.

Commentary, September, 1980.

*   *   *

ENGBERG, (Johanna) Susan 1940-

PERSONAL: Born June 12, 1940, in Dubuque, IA; daughter of King G. (a banker) and Julia M. (a teacher; maiden name, Hansen) Herr; married Charles Martin Engberg (an architect), August 17, 1963; children: Siri Johanna, Gillian Louisa. *Education:* Lawrence College (now Lawrence University), A.B. (cum laude), 1962; graduate study at University of Iowa, 1972-74.

ADDRESSES: Home—Milwaukee, WI. *Agent*—Lisa Bankoff, International Creative Management, 40 West 57th St., New York, NY 10019.

CAREER: American Field Service International Scholarships, New York City, correspondent, 1962-63; Metropolitan Museum of Modern Art, Department of Publications, New York City, 1963-64; Yale University, New Haven, CT, secretary and manuscript transcriber to Thomas More Project, 1964-66; New Haven Public Library, New Haven, library assistant and teacher, 1966-67; *Iowa Review,* University of Iowa, Iowa City, fiction reader, 1972-74; part-time teacher of creative writing, Iowa Writer's Workshop, Iowa City, 1978; Maharishi International University, Fairfield, IA, 1979; University of Wisconsin-Milwaukee, 1984-86; Warren Wilson College M.F.A. program in creative writing, 1989, 1991.

AWARDS, HONORS: Fiction award, Society of Midland Authors, and Banta Award, Wisconsin Library Association, both 1983; fellowship, National Endowment for the Arts, 1987.

WRITINGS:

SHORT STORIES

Pastorale, University of Illinois Press, 1982.
A Stay by the River, Viking, 1985.
Sarah's Laughter, and Other Stories (novella and stories), Knopf, 1991.

Work represented in anthologies, including *Prize Stories 1969: The O. Henry Awards,* edited by William Abrahams, Doubleday, 1969; *Prize Stories 1977: The O. Henry Awards,* edited by Abrahams, Doubleday, 1977; *Prize Stories 1978: The O. Henry Awards,* edited by Abrahams, Doubleday, 1978; *Pushcart Prize VI: Best of the Small Presses,* edited by Bill Henderson, Avon, 1982; *The Ploughshares Reader: New Fiction for the Eighties,* 1985; *Prime Number: 17 Stories from Illinois Short Fiction,* 1988; and *A Good Deal: Selected Stories from the Massachusetts Review,* 1988.

SIDELIGHTS: Susan Engberg's collections of short stories have been widely praised by reviewers and her works have been anthologized in several volumes of new short fiction. *Pastorale,* the first of several volumes of Engberg's short fiction, was published in 1982. The book was praised by *Village Voice Literary Supplement* reviewer M. Mark. "*Pastorale* gave me back the tastes and smells of childhood," Mark noted, adding that "the descriptions of what it's like to be half-formed, groping toward adulthood, are vivid, precise—true. I think Engberg knows something important about needing to leave the past behind but not wanting to obliterate it." Poet and fiction writer Tess Gallagher agreed, commenting in the *New York Times Book Review* that in both *Pastorale* and Engberg's 1985 story collection, *A Stay by the River,* the author's "pervasive concerns are with the ways in which our identities and visions of each other often complement, merge, or crucially impinge upon one another."

Critic James Idema stated in the *Chicago Tribune* that the author of *A Stay by the River* has "an affinity for themes [concerning] the joys and anxieties of relationships within domestic situations." Gallagher, proclaiming the collection "excellent" and "intriguing," concluded that "Engberg's is a subtle and impressive talent.. The stories in *A Stay by the River* deeply nourish our will to discover how to love and trust in a world where these invitations seem increasingly compromised." "Sarah's Laughter," the title novella of Engberg's third collection of short fiction, was praised by Michiko Kakutani in the *New York Times* as "a small gem." While noting that the author's overlying thematic concern about her characters' inner consciousness causes the stories in *Sarah's Laughter* to lose their uniqueness when read in an unbroken sequence, Kakutani praised Engberg for her "uncanny understanding of the darting, itchy paths taken by the introspective mind," and her ability to "translate these emotional states into lyrical, meticulous prose, granting to the reader privileged admission into her characters' hearts and minds."

BIOGRAPHICAL/CRITICAL SOURCES:

PERIODICALS

Chicago Tribune, October 27, 1985.
Los Angeles Times Book Review, November 3, 1985.
New York Times, November 15, 1991.
New York Times Book Review, November 3, 1985.
Village Voice Literary Supplement, December, 1982.

*   *   *

ENSLIN, Theodore (Vernon) 1925-

PERSONAL: Born March 25, 1925, in Chester, PA; son of Morton Scott (a professor) and Ruth May (a teacher;

maiden name, Tuttle) Enslin; married Mildred Marie Stout, August 1, 1945 (divorced June 6, 1961); married Alison Jane Jose, September 14, 1969; children: (first marriage) Deirdre, Jonathan Morton; (second marriage) Jacob Hezekiah. *Education:* Private study of musical composition with Nadia Boulanger and Francis Judd Cooke.

ADDRESSES: Home—R.F.D. Box 289, Kansas Rd., Milbridge, ME 04658.

CAREER: Full-time writer.

MEMBER: American Foundation for Homeopathy.

AWARDS, HONORS: Niemann Award, 1955, for weekly newspaper column, "Six Miles Square," in *Cape Codder;* Hart Crane Award, 1969, for *To Come, to Have Become;* National Endowment for the Arts fellowship, 1976-77.

WRITINGS:

POETRY

The Work Proposed, Origin Press, 1958.
New Sharon's Prospect (also see below), Origin Press, 1962.
The Place Where I Am Standing, Elizabeth Press, 1964.
This Do [and] *The Talents,* El Corno Emplumado (Mexico), 1966.
New Sharon's Prospect [and] *Journals,* Coyote's Journal, 1966.
To Come, to Have Become, Elizabeth Press, 1966.
The Dependencies, Caterpillar, 1966.
Characters in Certain Places, Wine Press, 1967.
The Diabelli Variations, and Other Poems, Matter Books, 1968.
2/30-6/31: Poems, 1967, Vermont Stoveside Press, 1968.
Agreement and Back: Sequences, Elizabeth Press, 1969.
Forms, Elizabeth Press, Part 1: *The First Dimensions,* 1970, Part 2: *The Tessaract,* 1971, Part 3: *The Experiences,* 1972, Part 4: *The Fusion,* 1972, Part 5: *Coda,* 1973.
The Poems, Elizabeth Press, 1970.
Views 1-7, Maya, 1970.
The Country of Our Consciousness: Selected Poems, Sand Dollar, 1971.
Etudes, Elizabeth Press, 1972.
With Light Reflected: Poems, 1970-1972, Sumac Press, 1973.
Views, Elizabeth Press, 1973.
In the Keeper's House, Salt-Works, 1973.
The Swamp Fox, Salt-Works, 1973.
Fever Poems, Blackberry Press, 1974.
The Last Days of October, Salt-Works, 1974.
The Mornings, Shaman Drum Press, 1974.
Sitio, Granite Publications, 1974.
The Median Flow: Poems, 1943-1973, Black Sparrow Press, 1975.

Synthesis 1-24, North Atlantic Books, 1975.
Laendler, Elizabeth Press, 1975.
Some Pastorals: A New Year's Cycle for Jake, Salt-Works 1975.
Carmina, Salt-Works, 1976.
Papers, Elizabeth Press, 1976.
Ascensions, Black Sparrow Press, 1977.
Concentrations, Salt-Works, 1977.
The Further Regions, Pentagram, 1977.
Tailings, Pentagram, 1978.
Ranger, North Atlantic Books, Volume 1, 1978, 2nd revised edition, 1980, Volume 2, 1980.
May Fault, Great Raven, 1979.
Opus 31 #3, Pentagram, 1979.
A Root in March, University of Maine Press, 1979.
16 Blossoms in February, Blackberry Press, 1979.
The Flare of Beginning Is in November, Jordan Davies, 1980.
Star Anise, Pentagram, 1980.
The Fifth Direction, Pentagram, 1980.
Two Geese, Pentagram, 1980.
Axes 52, Ziesing Bros., 1981.
In Duo Concertante, Pentagram, 1981.
Markings, Membrane Press, 1981.
Opus O, Membrane Press, 1981.
(With others) *Knee Deep in the Atlantic,* Pentagram, 1981.
Processionals, Salt-Works, 1981.
September's Bonfire, Potes and Poets Press, 1981.
(Translator from the Greek) Pindar and Calimachus, *Fragments/Epigrammata,* Salt-Works, 1982.
(Editor) *F.P.,* Ziesing Bros., 1982.
A Man in Stir, Pentagram, 1983.
To Come Home (To), Great Raven, 1983.
Meditations, Potes and Poets Press, 1983.
Passacaglia, Beehive Press, 1983.
Grey Days, Last Straw Press, 1984.
Songs w/out Notes, Salt-Works, 1984.
(With Keith Wilson) *Meeting at Jal,* Southwestern American Literature Association, 1985.
Music for Several Occasions, Membrane Press, 1985.
Case Book, Potes and Poets Press, 1988.
From Near the Great Pine, Spoon River, 1989.
Love and Science, Light and Dust, 1990.
Gamma UT, Tel-Let, 1992.

Also author of *The Weather Within,* 1986, and *Circles,* Great Raven.

PROSE

Mahler, Black Sparrow Press, 1975.
The July Book, Sand Dollar Press, 1976.
Two Plus Twelve (short stories), Salt-Works, 1979.

OTHER

Author of play, "Barometric Pressure 29.83 and Steady," first produced in New York at Hardware Poets Theatre, October, 1965. Author of weekly newspaper column, "Six Miles Square," in *Cape Codder,* 1949-56. Contributor of poems to periodicals.

SIDELIGHTS: Theodore Enslin told *CA:* "It is always very tempting to say more than one should concerning those things that are dearest and closest. I will try to avoid that, and simply hope that the record is in the work itself. In the past few years I have found myself drawn more and more to the musical possibilities of the poem, and I mean this in quite literal terms. For me, poetry and music are one art. The greatest compliment that anyone could pay me: 'He was a composer who happened to use words.' "

BIOGRAPHICAL/CRITICAL SOURCES:

BOOKS

Contemporary Authors Autobiography Series, Volume 3, Gale, 1986.

*   *   *

ERDRICH, Louise   1954-
(Heidi Louise, Milou North)

PERSONAL: Born Karen Louise Erdrich June 7 (one source says July 6), 1954, in Little Falls, MN; daughter of Ralph Louis (a teacher with the Bureau of Indian Affairs) and Rita Joanne (affiliated with the Bureau of Indian Affairs; maiden name, Gourneau) Erdrich; married Michael Anthony Dorris (a writer and professor of Native American studies), October 10, 1981; children: Abel, Jeffrey, Sava, Madeline, Persia, Pallas, Aza. *Education:* Dartmouth College, B.A., 1976; Johns Hopkins University, M.A., 1979. *Politics:* Democrat. *Religion:* "Antireligion." *Avocational interests:* Quilling, running, drawing, "playing chess with daughters and losing, playing piano badly, speaking terrible French."

ADDRESSES: Home—Hanover, NH.

CAREER: Writer. North Dakota State Arts Council, visiting poet and teacher, 1977-78; Johns Hopkins University, Baltimore, MD, writing instructor, 1978-79; Boston Indian Council, Boston, MA, communications director and editor of *Circle,* 1979-80; Charles-Merrill Co., textbook writer, 1980. Previously employed as a beet weeder in Wahpeton, ND; waitress in Wahpeton, Boston, and Syracuse, NY; psychiatric aide in a Vermont hospital; poetry teacher at prisons; lifeguard; and construction flag signaler. Has judged writing contests.

MEMBER: International Writers, PEN (member of executive board, 1985-88), Authors Guild, Authors League of America.

AWARDS, HONORS: Johns Hopkins University teaching fellow, 1979; MacDowell Colony fellow, 1980; Yaddo Colony fellow, 1981; Dartmouth College visiting fellow, 1981; First Prize, *Chicago* magazine's Nelson Algren fiction competition, 1982, for "The World's Greatest Fisherman"; Pushcart Prize, 1983; National Magazine Fiction awards, 1983 and 1987; *Love Medicine* received the National Book Critics Circle Award for best work of fiction, and the Virginia McCormick Scully Prize for best book of the year, both 1984, the *Los Angeles Times* Award for best novel, the best first fiction award from the American Academy and Institute of Arts and Letters, the Sue Kaufman Prize, and was named one of the best eleven books of 1985 by the *New York Times Book Review;* Guggenheim fellow, 1985-86; *The Beet Queen* was named one of *Publishers Weekly*'s best books, 1986; First Prize, O. Henry awards, 1987; National Book Critics Circle Award nomination.

WRITINGS:

NOVELS

Love Medicine, Holt, 1984, expanded edition, 1993.
The Beet Queen, Holt, 1986.
Tracks, Harper, 1988.
(With husband, Michael Dorris) *The Crown of Columbus,* HarperCollins, 1991.

POETRY

Jacklight, Holt, 1984.
Baptism of Desire, Harper, 1989.

OTHER

Imagination (textbook), C. E. Merrill, 1980.
(Author of preface) Michael Dorris, *The Broken Cord: A Family's Ongoing Struggle with Fetal Alcohol Syndrome,* Harper, 1989.
(Author of preface) Desmond Hogan, *A Link with the River,* Farrar, Straus, 1989.

Author of short story, "The World's Greatest Fisherman"; contributor to anthologies, including the *Norton Anthology of Poetry; Best American Short Stories* of 1981-83, 1983, and 1988; and *Prize Stories: The O. Henry Awards,* in 1985 and 1987. Contributor of stories, poems, essays, and book reviews to periodicals, including *New Yorker, New England Review, Chicago, American Indian Quarterly, Frontiers, Atlantic, Kenyon Review, North American Review, New York Times Book Review, Ms., Redbook* (with her sister Heidi, under the joint pseudonym Heidi Louise), and *Woman* (with Dorris, under the joint pseudonym Milou North).

ADAPTATIONS: The Crown of Columbus has been optioned for film production.

WORK IN PROGRESS: The Bingo Palace, a novel.

SIDELIGHTS: Award-winning author Louise Erdrich published her first two books—*Jacklight,* a volume of poetry, and *Love Medicine,* a novel—at the age of thirty. The daughter of a Chippewa Indian mother and a German-American father, the author explores Native American themes in her works, with major characters representing both sides of her heritage. *Love Medicine,* which traces two Native American families from 1934 to 1984 in a unique seven-narrator format, was extremely well-received, earning its author numerous awards, including the National Book Critics Circle Award in 1984. Since then, Erdrich has gone on to publish *The Beet Queen* and *Tracks*—two more novels in what she plans to be a four-part series—which explore the roots of *Love Medicine*'s characters, as well as those of their white neighbors. These three novels, which are related through recurring characters and themes, all became national best-sellers.

Erdrich's interest in writing can be traced to her childhood and her heritage. She told *Writer's Digest* contributor Michael Schumacher, "People in [Native American] families make everything into a story. . . . People just sit and the stories start coming, one after another. I suppose that when you grow up constantly hearing the stories rise, break, and fall, it gets into you somehow." The oldest in a family of seven children, Erdrich was raised in Wahpeton, North Dakota. Her Chippewa grandfather had been the tribal chair of the nearby Turtle Mountain Reservation, and her parents worked at the Bureau of Indian Falls boarding school. Erdrich once told *CA* of the way in which her parents encouraged her writing: "My father used to give me a nickel for every story I wrote, and my mother wove strips of construction paper together and stapled them into book covers. So at an early age I felt myself to be a published author earning substantial royalties."

Erdrich's first year at Dartmouth, 1972, was the year the college began admitting women, as well as the year the Native American studies department was established. The author's future husband and collaborator, anthropologist Michael Dorris, was hired to chair the department. In his class, Erdrich began the exploration of her own ancestry that would eventually inspire her novels. Intent on balancing her academic training with a broad range of practical knowledge, Erdrich told Miriam Berkley in an interview with *Publishers Weekly,* "I ended up taking some really crazy jobs, and I'm glad I did. They turned out to have been very useful experiences, although I never would have believed it at the time." In addition to working as a lifeguard, waitress, poetry teacher at prisons, and construction flag signaler, Erdrich became an editor for the *Circle,*

a Boston Indian Council newspaper. She told Schumacher, "Settling into that job and becoming comfortable with an urban community—which is very different from the reservation community—gave me another reference point. There were lots of people with mixed blood, lots of people who had their own confusions. I realized that this was part of my life—it wasn't something that I was making up—and that it was something I *wanted* to write about." In 1978, the author enrolled in an M.A. program at Johns Hopkins University, where she wrote poems and stories incorporating her heritage, many of which would later become part of her books. She also began sending her work to publishers, most of whom sent back rejection slips.

After receiving her master's degree, Erdrich returned to Dartmouth as a writer-in-residence. Dorris—with whom she had remained in touch—attended a reading of Erdrich's poetry there, and was impressed. A writer himself—Dorris would later publish the best-selling novel *A Yellow Raft in Blue Water* and receive the 1989 National Book Critics Circle Award for his nonfiction work *The Broken Cord*—he decided then that he was interested in working with Erdrich and getting to know her better. When he left for New Zealand to do field research and Erdrich went to Boston to work on a textbook, the two began sending their poetry and fiction back and forth with their letters, laying a groundwork for a literary relationship. Dorris returned to New Hampshire in 1980, and Erdrich moved back there as well. The two began collaborating on short stories, including one titled "The World's Greatest Fisherman." When this story won five thousand dollars in the Nelson Algren fiction competition, Erdrich and Dorris decided to expand it into a novel—*Love Medicine.* At the same time, their literary relationship led to a romantic one. In 1981 they were married.

The titles Erdrich and Dorris have chosen for their novels—such as *Love Medicine* and *A Yellow Raft in Blue Water*—tend to be rich poetic or visual images. The title is often the initial inspiration from which their novels are drawn. Erdrich told Schumacher, "I think a title is like a magnet: It begins to draw these scraps of experience or conversation or memory to it. Eventually, it collects a book." Erdrich and Dorris's collaboration process begins with a first draft, usually written by whoever had the original idea for the book, the one who will ultimately be considered the official author. After the draft is written, the other person edits it, and then another draft is written; often five or six drafts will be written in all. Finally, the two read the work aloud until they can agree on each word. Although the author has the original voice and the final say, ultimately, both collaborators are responsible for what the work becomes.

Erdrich's novels *Love Medicine, The Beet Queen,* and *Tracks* encompass the stories of three interrelated families living in and around a reservation in the fictional town of Argus, North Dakota, from 1912 through the 1980s. The novels have been compared to those of William Faulkner, mainly due to the multi-voice narration and non-chronological storytelling which he employed in works such as *As I Lay Dying.* Erdrich's works, linked by recurring characters who are victims of fate and the patterns set by their elders, are structured like intricate puzzles in which bits of information about individuals and their relations to one another are slowly released in a seemingly random order, until three-dimensional characters—with a future and a past—are revealed. Through her characters' antics, Erdrich explores universal family life cycles while also communicating a sense of the changes and loss involved in the twentieth-century Native American experience.

Poet Robert Bly, describing Erdrich's nonlinear storytelling approach in the *New York Times Book Review,* emphasized her tendency to "choose a few minutes or a day in 1932, let one character talk, let another talk, and a third, then leap to 1941 and then to 1950 or 1964." The novels' circular format is a reflection of the way in which the works are constructed. Although Erdrich is dealing with a specific and extensive time period, "The writing doesn't start out and proceed chronologically. It never seems to start in the beginning. Rather, it's as though we're building something around a center, but that center can be anywhere."

Erdrich published her first novel, *Love Medicine,* in 1984. "With this impressive debut," stated *New York Times Book Review* contributor Marco Portales, "Louise Erdrich enters the company of America's better novelists." *Love Medicine* was named for the belief in love potions which is a part of Chippewa folklore. The novel explores the bonds of family and faith which preserve both the Chippewa tribal community and the individuals that comprise it.

The novel begins at a family gathering following the death of June Kashpaw, a prostitute. The characters introduce one another, sharing stories about June which reveal their family history and their cultural beliefs. Albertine Johnson, June's niece, introduces her grandmother, Marie, her grandfather, Nector, and Nector's twin brother, Eli. Eli represents the old way—the Native American who never integrated into the white culture. He also plays a major role in *Tracks,* in which he appears as a young man. The story of Marie and Nector brings together many of the important images in the novel, including the notion of "love medicine." As a teenager in a convent, Marie is nearly burned to death by a nun who, in an attempt to exorcise the devil from within her, pours boiling water on Marie.

Immediately following this incident, Marie is sexually assaulted by Nector. Marie and Nector are later married, but in middle age, Nector begins an affair with Lulu Lamartine, a married woman. In an attempt to rekindle Nector and Marie's passion, their grandson Lipsha prepares "love medicine" for Nector. But Lipsha has difficulty obtaining a wild goose heart for the potion. He substitutes a frozen turkey heart, which causes Nector to choke to death.

Reviewers responded positively to Erdrich's debut novel, citing its lyrical qualities as well as the rich characters who inhabit it. *New York Times* contributor D. J. R. Bruckner was impressed with Erdrich's "mastery of words," as well as the "vividly drawn" characters who "will not leave the mind once they are let in." Portales, who called *Love Medicine* "an engrossing book," applauded the unique narration technique which produces what he termed "a wondrous prose song."

After the publication of *Love Medicine,* Erdrich told reviewers that her next novel would focus less exclusively on her mother's side, embracing the author's mixed heritage and the mixed community in which she grew up. Her 1986 novel, *The Beet Queen,* deals with whites and half-breeds, as well as American Indians, and explores the interactions between these worlds. The story begins in 1932, during the Depression. *The Beet Queen* begins when Mary and Karl Adare's recently-widowed mother flies off with a carnival pilot, abandoning the two children and their newborn brother. The baby is taken by a young couple who have just lost their child. Karl and eleven-year-old Mary ride a freight train to Argus, seeking refuge with their aunt and uncle. When they arrive in the town, however, Karl, frightened by a dog, runs back onto the train and winds up at an orphanage. Mary grows up with her aunt and uncle, and the novel follows her life—as well as those of her jealous, self-centered cousin Sita and their part-Chippewa friend Celestine James—for the next forty years, tracing the themes of separation and loss that began with Mary's father's death and her mother's grand departure.

The Beet Queen was well-received by critics, some of whom found it even more impressive than *Love Medicine.* Many noted the novel's poetic language and symbolism; Bly noted that Erdrich's "genius is in metaphor," and that the characters "show a convincing ability to feel an image with their whole bodies." Josh Rubins, writing in *New York Review of Books,* called *The Beet Queen* "a rare second novel, one that makes it seem as if the first, impressive as it was, promised too little, not too much."

Other reviewers had problems with *The Beet Queen,* but they tended to dismiss the novel's flaws in light of its positive qualities. *New Republic* contributor Dorothy Wickenden considered the characters unrealistic and the ending contrived, but she lauded *The Beet Queen*'s "ringing clarity and lyricism," as well as the "assured, polished quality" which she felt was missing in *Love Medicine.* Although Michiko Kakutani found the ending artificial, the *New York Times* reviewer called Erdrich "an immensely gifted young writer." "Even with its weaknesses," proclaimed Linda Simon in *Commonweal,* "*The Beet Queen* stands as a product of enormous talent."

After Erdrich completed *The Beet Queen,* she was uncertain as to what her next project should be. The four-hundred-page manuscript that would eventually become *Tracks* had remained untouched for ten years; the author referred to it as her "burden." She and Dorris took a fresh look at it, and decided that they could relate it to *Love Medicine* and *The Beet Queen.* While more political than her previous novels, *Tracks,* Erdrich's 1989 work, also deals with spiritual themes, exploring the tension between the Native Americans' ancient beliefs and the Christian notions of the Europeans. *Tracks* takes place between 1912 and 1924, before the settings of Erdrich's other novels, and reveals the roots of *Love Medicine*'s characters and their hardships. One of the narrators, Nanapush, is the leader of a tribe that is suffering on account of the white government's exploitation. He feels pressured to give up their land in order to avoid starvation. While Nanapush represents the old way, Pauline, the other narrator, represents change. The future mother of *Love Medicine*'s Marie Lazarre, Pauline is a young half-breed from a mixed-blood tribe "for which the name was lost." She feels torn between her Indian faith and the white people's religion, and is considering leaving the reservation. But at the center of *Tracks* is Fleur, a character whom *Los Angeles Times Book Review* contributor Terry Tempest Williams called "one of the most haunting presences in contemporary American literature." Nanapush discovers this young woman—the last survivor of a family killed by consumption—in a cabin in the woods, starving and mad. Nanapush adopts Fleur and nurses her back to health.

Reviewers found *Tracks* distinctly different from Erdrich's earlier novels, and some felt that her third novel lacked the characteristics that made *Love Medicine* and *The Beet Queen* so outstanding. *Washington Post Book World* critic Jonathan Yardley felt that, on account of its more political focus, the work has a "labored quality." Robert Towers stated in *New York Review of Books* that he found the characters too melodramatic and the tone too intense. Katherine Dieckmann, writing in the *Voice Literary Supplement,* affirmed that she "missed [Erdrich's] skilled multiplications of voice," and called the relationship between Pauline and Nanapush "symptomatic of the overall lack of grand orchestration and perspectival interplay that made Erdrich's first two novels polyphonic mas-

terpieces." According to *Commonweal* contributor Christopher Vecsey, however, although "a reviewer might find some of the prose overwrought, and the two narrative voices indistinguishable . . . readers will appreciate and applaud the vigor and inventiveness of the author."

Other reviewers enjoyed *Tracks* even more than the earlier novels. Williams stated that Erdrich's writing "has never appeared more polished and grounded," and added, "*Tracks* may be the story of our time." Thomas M. Disch lauded the novel's plot, with its surprising twists and turns, in the *Chicago Tribune.* The critic added, "Louise Erdrich is like one of those rumored drugs that are instantly and forever addictive. Fortunately in her case you can *just say yes.*"

Erdrich and Dorris's jointly-authored novel, *The Crown of Columbus,* explores Native American issues from the standpoint of the authors' current experience, rather than the world of their ancestors. Marking the quincentennial anniversary of Spanish explorer Christopher Columbus's voyage in a not-so-celebratory fashion, Erdrich and Dorris raise important questions about the meaning of that voyage for both Europeans and Native Americans today. The story is narrated by the two central characters, both Dartmouth professors involved in projects concerning Columbus. Vivian Twostar is a Native American single mother with eclectic tastes and a teenage son, Nash. Vivian is asked to write an academic article on Columbus from a Native American perspective and is researching Columbus's diaries. Roger Williams, a stuffy New England Protestant poet, is writing an epic work about the explorer's voyage. Vivian and Roger become lovers—parenting a girl named Violet—but have little in common. Ultimately acknowledging the destructive impact of Columbus's voyage on the Native American people, Vivian and Roger vow to redress the political wrongs symbolically by changing the power structure in their relationship. In the end, as Vivian and Roger rediscover themselves, they rediscover America.

Some reviewers found *The Crown of Columbus* unbelievable and inconsistent, and considered it less praiseworthy than the individual authors' earlier works. However, *New York Times Book Review* contributor Robert Houston appreciated the work's timely political relevance. He also stated, "There are moments of genuine humor and compassion, of real insight and sound satire." Other critics also considered Vivian and Roger's adventures amusing, vibrant, and charming.

Although Erdrich has planned a final sequel to her three related novels, in which the younger characters from *Love Medicine* will interact with those from *The Beet Queen,* her involvement with *The Crown of Columbus* represents a significant departure from that world. Although *The*

Crown of Columbus involves interpreting and finding new meaning in history, the Argus characters are themselves living out history and guiding the reader through its changes. It is unlikely that Erdrich will be able to avoid returning to the series for very long. As she once told the *New York Times Book Review,* "I can't stand not knowing what's happening . . . [because] there's an ongoing conversation with these fictional people. Events suggest themselves. You have no choice."

BIOGRAPHICAL/CRITICAL SOURCES:

BOOKS

Erdrich, Louise, *Tracks,* Harper, 1988.
Erdrich, Louise, *Baptism of Desire,* Harper, 1989.

PERIODICALS

Chicago Tribune, September 4, 1988, pp. 1, 6.
Commonweal, October 24, 1986, pp. 565, 567; November 4, 1988, p. 596.
Los Angeles Times Book Review, October 5, 1986, pp. 3, 10; September 11, 1988, p. 2.
New Republic, October 6, 1986, pp. 46-48.
Newsday, November 30, 1986.
New York Review of Books, January 15, 1987, pp. 14-15; November 19, 1988, pp. 40-41.
New York Times, December 20, 1984, p. C21; August 20, 1986, p. C21; August 24, 1988, p. 41.
New York Times Book Review, August 31, 1982, p. 2; December 23, 1984, p. 6; October 2, 1988, pp. 1, 41-42; April 28, 1991, p. 10.
People, June 10, 1991, pp. 26-27.
Publishers Weekly, August 15, 1986, pp. 58-59.
Voice Literary Supplement, October, 1988, p. 37.
Washington Post Book World, August 31, 1986, pp. 1, 6; September 18, 1988, p. 3.
Writer's Digest, June, 1991, pp. 28-31.

*   *   *

ESSICK, Robert N(ewman) 1942-

PERSONAL: Born October 19, 1942, in Los Angeles, CA; son of Bryant (a business executive) and Jeanette M. (a secretary; maiden name, Quinn) Essick. *Education:* Attended Williams College, 1961-64; University of California, Los Angeles, B.A. (with honors), 1965; University of California, San Diego, Ph.D., 1969. *Avocational interests:* Book and print collecting, oriental rugs, eighteenth-century English furniture.

ADDRESSES: Home—1379 La Solana Dr., Altadena, CA 91001. *Office*—Department of English, University of California, Riverside, CA 92521.

CAREER: California State University, Northridge, assistant professor, 1970-73, associate professor of English, 1973-77; University of California, Riverside, professor of English, 1979—. American Blake Foundation, member of advisory board of directors, 1971-80; Essick Investment Co., vice-president and member of board of directors, 1973—; Huntington Library, member of board of overseers and chair of the art committee, 1991—. Essick Foundation Inc., treasurer, 1973—; Friends of the Huntington Library, treasurer, 1984-90. Center for Ideas and Society, University of California, Riverside, fellow, 1991.

MEMBER: Modern Language Association of America, Grolier Club, Blake Trust (American patron).

AWARDS, HONORS: Woodrow Wilson fellowships, 1965, 1969; National Endowment for the Humanities grant, 1972, senior fellowship, 1986; Guggenheim fellowship, 1979; President's Research Fellowship in the Humanities, University of California, 1989-90.

WRITINGS:

(With Roger R. Easson) *William Blake: Book Illustrator,* American Blake Foundation, Volume 1, 1972, Volume 2, 1979.
(Editor) *The Visionary Hand,* Hennessey & Ingalls, 1973.
(Editor and author of introduction with Jenijoy LaBelle) Edward Young, *Night Thoughts; or, The Complaint and the Consolation,* Dover, 1975.
(Editor with Donald Pearce) *Blake in His Time,* Indiana University Press, 1978.
William Blake: Printmaker, Princeton University Press, 1980.
(With Morton Paley) *Robert Blair's "The Grave" Illustrated by William Blake,* Scolar Press, 1982.
The Separate Plates of William Blake: A Catalogue, Princeton University Press, 1983.
The Works of William Blake in the Huntington Collections, Huntington Library, 1985.
William Blake and the Language of Adam, Clarendon Press, 1989.
William Blake's Commercial Book Illustrations, Clarendon Press, 1991.

Also author of *William Blake's Relief Inventions,* 1978. Regular contributor to *Blake Newsletter.*

WORK IN PROGRESS: Editions of Blake's early illuminated books and of *Milton* for the Blake Trust.

SIDELIGHTS: Robert N. Essick's works on William Blake have focused especially on the poet's illustrations, both for his own and for others' works. In the *Times Literary Supplement,* Michael Mason describes *William Blake: Printmaker* as "an extraordinary book, manifesting a grasp of the subject and a degree of knowledgeable, discerning examination of the material quite remarkable for one man to have achieved." A *Choice* reviewer finds the same book "meticulously researched and well written," asserting, "Essick's arguments gain authority through his own efforts to duplicate Blake's visual effects by duplicating Blake's techniques."

In another *Times Literary Supplement* review, Raymond Lister considers Essick's *Robert Blair's "The Grave" Illustrated by William Blake* "beautifully produced," adding, "Blake and the authors have been served well." About *Blake and the Language of Adam,* Brian Wilkie claims in *Modern Language Review* that it is "among the half-dozen or so most essential books on Blake." Another *Choice* critic applauds *Blake's Commercial Book Illustration,* labelling it "a superb piece of scholarship."

BIOGRAPHICAL/CRITICAL SOURCES:

PERIODICALS

Choice, December, 1980; April, 1992.
Modern Language Review, July, 1991.
Times Literary Supplement, February 13, 1981; June 11, 1982.

* * *

ESTES, Richard J. 1942-

PERSONAL: Born June 20, 1942, in Philadelphia, PA; son of Lebert L. and Marguerite (DeSequin) Estes; divorced; children: Lynn, Vicki, Jennifer. *Education:* La Salle College, A.B., 1965; University of Pennsylvania, M.S.W., 1967; Menninger Foundation, Ph.D., 1968; University of California, Berkeley, D.S.W., 1973.

ADDRESSES: Home—311 Woodside Ave., Narberth, PA 19072. *Office*—School of Social Work, University of Pennsylvania, 3701 Locust Walk, Philadelphia, PA 19104.

CAREER: University of Pennsylvania, Philadelphia, assistant professor, 1973-77, associate professor, 1977-85, professor of social work, 1985—, chairman of health specialization, 1974-77; director of Lazarus-Goldman Center, 1977-83, director of doctoral education, 1983-90. Fulbright lecturer at University of Teheran, 1978, and University of Trondheim, 1979; visiting professor at University of Hawaii at Manoa, 1982-83, Shanghai Jiao Tong University of the People's Republic of China, 1986-87, King Mohammed V University, 1987, Washington University, 1991, 1992, Soong Sil University, 1992, and University of Malaysia, 1992. Member of board of directors and executive committee of West Philadelphia Mental Health Consortium, 1976-78; member of Pennsylvania governor's Committee for the Physically Disabled, 1977-78; member of research advisory board of J. F. Kapnek Charitable Trust, 1985-90. Guest on radio and television programs; consultant to numerous organizations and agencies, including National Institutes of Health, U.S. Department of Health and Human Services, Big Brothers Association, U. S. Veterans Administration, and Canadian Office of Manpower and Immigration. Lecturer at conferences and workshops.

MEMBER: International Council on Social Welfare (member of board of directors, U.S. Committee, 1986-88, 1988-91), Consortium for International Social Development, International Association of Schools of Social Work, World Futurist Society, National Association of Social Workers, Academy of Certified Social Workers, American Orthopsychiatric Association (fellow), American Association of University Professors, American Public Health Association (member of council, 1976-79), Fulbright Association, Council on Social Work Education (member of House of Delegates, 1986-89), Society for International Development (president of Delaware Valley chapter, 1985-87; member of executive committee, 1989—), Group for the Advancement of Doctoral Education (president, 1988-90), World Affairs Council of Philadelphia, Phi Beta Delta (founding member).

AWARDS, HONORS: Summer research awards from University of Pennsylvania, 1974 and 1985; Fulbright-Hays Awards to Iran, 1978, and to Norway, spring, 1979; social development fellow at Adelphi University, 1985; named Social Worker of the Year, Pennsylvania chapter of National Association of Social Workers; distinguished Fulbright scholar to Indonesia, spring, 1994.

WRITINGS:

Directory of Social Welfare Research Capabilities, Dorrance, 1981.
The Social Progress of Nations, Praeger, 1984.
(Editor and contributor) *Health Care and the Social Services: Handbook of Social Work Practice in Health Settings,* Warren Green, 1984.
Trends in World Social Development: The Social Progress of Nations, 1970-1987, Praeger, 1988.
Internationalizing Social Work Education: A Guide to Resources for a New Century, School of Social Work, University of Pennsylvania, 1992.
(With Edward Van Roy) *Towards a Social Development Strategy for the ESCAP Region,* United Nations Economic and Social Commission for Asia and the Pacific, 1992.
At the Crossroads: Development Dilemmas to the Year 200 and Beyond, Praeger, 1993.

Also author of numerous research monographs, data bases, and conference notes and papers. Contributor of chapters to many books, including *Management in Social Welfare: Casebook Studies,* edited by Elizabeth Schaub, School of Social Work, University of Pennsylvania, 1977; *Social Work and Mental Health,* edited by Joseph Bevilacqua and A. Levond Jones, Free Press, 1983; and *Working from Strengths: The Essence of Group Work,* Barry University Center for Group Work Studies, 1992. Also contributor of articles to journals and periodicals, including *Philadelphia Inquirer, Jewish Social Welfare Forum, Social Development Issues, Journal of International and Comparative Social Welfare,* and *Journal of the American College Health Association.*

Guest editor of *Social Development Issues,* summer, 1985; member of editorial review board of *Social Development Issues,* 1984—, *Journal of International and Comparative Social Welfare,* 1984—, *Journal of Social Service Research,* 1985—, and *Foundations: An International Journal for the Philosophical Foundations of Social Knowledge and Social Practice,* 1989—.

WORK IN PROGRESS: Social Development Trends among the Newly Industrializing Countries of Asia; Social Development Trends in Morocco and North Africa; Social Development Trends in Central and Latin America.

SIDELIGHTS: Richard J. Estes later told *CA:* "My current research and writings focus on two areas: the widening gap in social development that is occurring between the world's richest and poorest nations, and the discovery of international solutions that promote increased social justice among the world's most impoverished nations to these ends. My writing reflects an empirical approach to assessing changes that occur over time in the capacity of nations to provide for the most basic social and material needs of their populations. Current data predict global social cataclysms of the worst sort, should present-day trends continue into the future."

F

FERGUSON, William M(cDonald) 1917-

PERSONAL: Born December 2, 1917, in Wellington, KS; son of William McDonald (a stockman) and May (a homemaker; maiden name, Deems) Ferguson; married Harriet Shelden (a homemaker), September 5, 1939; children: Joan Ferguson Peck, William McDonald III. *Education:* Attended College of William and Mary, 1934-35; University of Kansas, B.A., 1938; Harvard University, LL.B., 1941; attended Universidad de las Americas, 1974. *Politics:* Republican.

ADDRESSES: Home—1023 South Washington, Wellington, KS 67152; Ferguson Ranch, Cambridge, KS 67203; and 312 County Rd. 243, Durango, CO 81301. *Office*— Ferguson & Doctor, 123 North Jefferson, Wellington, KS 67152.

CAREER: Private practice of law, 1946—; City of Wellington, KS, attorney, 1948-57; Security State Bank, Wellington, president, 1959-71, chairman of board, 1971-85, chairman emeritus, 1985—. Member of Kansas House of Representatives, 1949-57; attorney general of State of Kansas, 1961-65. Managing partner of Ferguson Ranch. *Military service:* U.S. Naval Reserve, 1942-46; became lieutenant senior grade.

MEMBER: American Bar Association (member of House of Delegates, 1961-62), Kansas Bar Association (member of executive council, 1952-61; vice-president, 1961; president, 1963), Sigma Alpha Epsilon, American Legion, Elks.

AWARDS, HONORS: Gasper de Perez Award for Outstanding Publication by an Individual or Individuals, Historical Society of New Mexico, 1987, for *Anasazi Ruins of the Southwest in Color.*

WRITINGS:

(WIth John Q. Royce) *Maya Ruins of Mexico in Color: Palenque, Uxmal, Kabah, Sayil, Xlapac, Lobna, ChichenItza, Coba, Tulum* (Book-of-the-Month Club alternate selection), University of Oklahoma Press, 1977.

(With Royce) *Maya Ruins in Central America in Color,* University of New Mexico Press, 1984.

(With Arthur H. Rohn) *Anasazi Ruins of the Southwest in Color,* University of New Mexico Press, 1986.

(With Rohn and Royce) *Mesoamerica's Ancient Cities* (Book-of-the-Month Club alternate selection; Natural Science Book Club selection), University Press of Colorado, 1990.

WORK IN PROGRESS: Anasazi Ruins of Mesa Verde and the Northern San Juan, for University Press of Colorado.

SIDELIGHTS: William McDonald Ferguson once told *CA:* "After I completed two terms as Kansas attorney general and an abortive run for governor of Kansas, my old friend John Q. Royce and I began a series of small plane visits to Mexico and Central American to see and photograph Maya sites—just for the fun of it. I had owned a plane since 1948 for use in the cattle business, and Royce had been a squadron commander in World War II. We were both amateur photographers.

"In preparation for these trips we read most of the literature on the Maya that had been written for the general public and much of the technical data. We found that much of it was long outdated, particularly the popular books, articles, and guide books. We decided to do a book on the Maya of Mexico combining our aerial and site photographs so that, with the help of young Mayanists such as Linda Schele, we could produce a book bringing the

Maya up to date for the general reader: *Maya Ruins of Mexico in Color.*

"Royce and I followed the Mexican book with a more ambitious volume: *Maya Ruins in Central America in Color.* For this one we used a Cessna 185 bush plane so that we could get into small jungle fields. We had auxiliary fuel tanks that enabled us to operate for several days without refueling.

"I am now just completing *Anasazi Ruins of the Southwest in Color* with a new colleague, Arthur H. Rohn. For this book we took about four thousand photographs to get the three hundred fifty we will use in the book. This one has been a four-year effort.

"The photography, both on the ground and from the air, was a learn-by-doing process. The key to the aerials is to get the plane in position low enough to take an oblique photograph that is aesthetically good and also displays the ruins.

"When I began to put together the first Maya book in 1975, I was 57. I had enjoyed a reasonable success as a rancher and cattleman (a family business), as a lawyer, and as a banker so I could take the time to do what I wanted to do—put together books on pre-Columbian ruins that combined photographs of visible sites and the last word on the discipline."

Ferguson later added: "*Mesoamerica's Ancient Cities* combined the sites John Q. Royce (deceased December 7, 1991) and I had visited and photographed over a twenty-five year period. The new book, *Anasazi Ruins of Mesa Verde and the Northern San Juan* will focus on the cliff dwellings, rock art, and artifacts of the Anasazi from Mesa Verde to Comb Ridge in Southeastern Utah."

*   *   *

FERLING, Lawrence
See FERLINGHETTI, Lawrence (Monsanto)

*   *   *

FERLINGHETTI, Lawrence (Monsanto) 1919(?)-
(Lawrence Ferling)

PERSONAL: Born Lawrence Ferling, March 24, c. 1919, in Yonkers, NY; original family name of Ferlinghetti restored, 1954; son of Charles S. (an auctioneer) and Clemency (Monsanto) Ferling; married Selden Kirby-Smith, April, 1951 (divorced); children: Julie, Lorenzo. *Education:* University of North Carolina, A.B., 1941; Columbia

University, M.A., 1948; Sorbonne, University of Paris, Doctorat de l'Universite (with honors), 1951. *Politics:* "Now an enemy of the State." *Religion:* "Catholique manque."

ADDRESSES: Home—San Francisco, CA. *Office*—City Lights Books, 261 Columbus Ave., San Francisco, CA 94133.

CAREER: Poet, playwright, editor, and painter; worked for *Time,* New York City, post-World-War-II; taught French in a adult education program, San Francisco, CA, 1951-52; City Lights Pocket Bookshop (now City Lights Books), San Francisco, co-owner, 1953—, founder and editor of City Lights Books (publisher), 1955—. Participant in numerous national and international literary conferences and poetry readings. *Military service:* U.S. Naval Reserve, 1941-45; became lieutenant commander; was commanding officer during Normandy invasion.

AWARDS, HONORS: National Book Award nomination, 1970, for *The Secret Meaning of Things;* Notable Book of 1979 citation, *Library Journal,* 1980, for *Landscapes of Living & Dying;* Silver Medal for poetry, Commonwealth Club of California, 1986, for *Over All the Obscene Boundaries.*

WRITINGS:

(Translator) Jacques Prevert, *Selections From Paroles,* City Lights, 1958.
Her (novel), New Directions, 1960.
Howl of the Censor (trial proceedings), edited by J. W. Ehrlich, Nourse Publishing, 1961.
(With Jack Spicer) *Dear Ferlinghetti,* White Rabbit Press, 1962.
The Mexican Night: Travel Journal, New Directions, 1970.
Northwest Ecolog, City Lights, 1978.
(With Nancy J. Peters) *Literary San Francisco: A Pictorial History from the Beginning to the Present,* Harper, 1980.
The Populist Manifestos, Grey Fox Press, 1983.
Seven Days in Nicaragua Libre (journal), City Lights, 1985.
Leaves of Life: Fifty Drawings From the Model, City Lights, 1985.
(Translator with others) Nicanor Parra, *Antipoems: New & Selected,* New Directions, 1985.
(Translator with Francesca Valente) Pier Paolo Pasolini, *Roman Poems,* City Lights, 1986.
Love in the Days of Rage (novel), Dutton, 1988.

POETRY

Pictures of the Gone World, City Lights, 1955.

Tentative Description of a Dinner Given to Promote the Impeachment of President Eisenhower, Golden Mountain Press, 1958.

A Coney Island of the Mind, New Directions, 1958.

Berlin, Golden Mountain Press, 1961.

One Thousand Fearful Words for Fidel Castro, City Lights, 1961.

Starting From San Francisco, with recording of poems, New Directions, 1961, revised edition without recording, 1967.

(With Gregory Corso and Allen Ginsberg) *Penguin Modern Poets 5,* Penguin, 1963.

Thoughts of a Concerto of Telemann, Four Seasons Foundation, 1963.

Where Is Vietnam?, City Lights, 1965.

To F--- Is to Love Again, Kyrie Eleison Kerista; or, The Situation in the West, Followed by a Holy Proposal, F--- You Press, 1965.

Christ Climbed Down, Syracuse University, 1965.

An Eye On the World: Selected Poems, MacGibbon & Kee, 1967.

Moscow in the Wilderness, Segovia in the Snow, Beach Books, 1967.

After the Cries of the Birds, Dave Haselwood Books, 1967.

Fuclock, Fire Publications, 1968.

The Secret Meaning of Things, New Directions, 1969.

Tyrannus Nix?, New Directions, 1969.

Back Roads to Far Places, New Directions, 1971.

Love Is No Stone on the Moon, ARIF Press, 1971.

The Illustrated Wilfred Funk, City Lights, 1971.

Open Eye, Open Heart, New Directions, 1973.

Who Are We Now? (also see below), City Lights, 1976.

Landscapes of Living and Dying (also see below), New Directions, 1979.

A Trip to Italy and France, New Directions, 1980.

Endless Life: Selected Poems, New Directions, 1984.

Over All the Obscene Boundaries: European Poems and Transitions, New Directions, 1985.

Inside the Trojan Horse, Lexikos, 1987.

Wild Dreams of a New Beginning: Including "Landscapes of Living & Dying" and "Who Are We Now?", New Directions, 1988.

When I Look at Pictures, Peregrine Smith Books, 1990.

PLAYS

Unfair Arguments with Existence: Seven Plays for a New Theatre (contains "The Soldiers of No Country" [produced in London, 1969], "Three Thousand Red Ants" [produced in New York City, 1970; also see below], "The Alligation" [produced in San Francisco, 1962; also see below], "The Victims of Amnesia" [produced in New York City, 1970; also see below], "Motherlode," "The Customs Collector in Baggy

Pants" [produced in New York City, 1964], and "The Nose of Sisyphus"), New Directions, 1963.

Routines (contains thirteen short plays, including "The Jig Is Up," "His Head," "Ha-Ha," and "Non-Objection"), New Directions, 1964.

3 by Ferlinghetti: Three Thousand Red Ants, The Alligation, [and] The Victims of Amnesia, produced in New York City, 1970.

EDITOR

Beatitude Anthology, City Lights, 1960.

Pablo Picasso, *Hunk of Skin,* City Lights, 1969.

Charles Upton, *Panic Grass,* City Lights, 1969.

City Lights Anthology, City Lights, 1974.

(With Peters) *City Lights Review, No. 1,* City Lights, 1987.

(With Peters) *City Lights Review, No. 2,* City Lights, 1988.

AUTHOR OF INTRODUCTION

Diane Di Prima, *This Kind of Bird Flies Backward,* Totem Press, 1958.

Michael McClure, *Meat Science Essays,* City Lights, 1963.

Bob Kaufmann, *Solitudes,* Union General d'Editions (Paris), 1966.

Ray Bremser, *Angel,* Tompkins Square Press, 1967.

Tom Picard, *High on the Walls,* Fulcrum, 1967.

Ralph T. Cook, *The City Lights Pocket Poets Series: A Descriptive Bibliography,* Laurence McGilvery, 1982.

Dick McBride, *Cometh with Clouds,* Cherry Valley Editions, 1982.

CONTRIBUTOR

New Directions in Prose and Poetry 16, New Directions, 1957.

Ralph J. Gleason, editor, *Jam Session: An Anthology of Jazz,* Putnam, 1958.

Seymour Krim, editor, *The Beats,* Fawcett, 1960.

Elias Wilentz, *The Beat Scene,* Corinth, 1960.

Donald M. Allen, editor, *The New American Poetry: 1945-1960,* Grove, 1960.

Lyle E. Linville, editor, *Tiger,* Linville-Hansen Associates, 1961.

Ursule Spier Erickson and Robert Pearsall, editors, *The Californians,* Hesperian House, 1961.

Thomas Parkinson, editor, *A Casebook on the Beat,* Crowell, 1961.

Gene Baro, editor, *Beat Poets,* Vista Books (London), 1961.

J. Laughlin, editor, *New Directions in Prose and Poetry 17,* New Directions, 1961.

Laughlin, editor, *New Directions in Prose and Poetry 18,* New Directions, 1964.

Paris Leary and Robert Kelly, editors, *A Controversy of Poets,* Doubleday, 1965.

Chad Walsh, editor, *Garlands for Christmas,* Macmillan, 1965.
Louis Dudek, editor, *Poetry of Our Time,* Macmillan (Toronto), 1965.
Harriet W. Sheridan, *Structure and Style,* Harcourt, 1966.
Walter Lowenfels, editor, *Where Is Vietnam?,* Doubleday, 1967.
Judith Clancy, *Paris Alive, the Point of View of an American,* Synergistic Press, 1986.

RECORDINGS

(With Kenneth Rexroth) *Poetry Readings in "The Cellar,"* Fantasy, 1958.
Tentative Description of a Dinner To Impeach President Eisenhower, and Other Poems, Fantasy, 1959.
Tyrannus Nix? and Assassination Raga, Fantasy, 1971.
(With Corso and Ginsberg) *The World's Greatest Poets 1,* CMS, 1971.

OTHER

Author of narration, *Have You Sold Your Dozen Roses?* (film), California School of Fine Arts Film Workshop, 1957. Contributor to numerous periodicals, including *San Francisco Chronicle, Nation, Evergreen Review, Liberation, Chicago Review, Transatlantic Review,* and *New Statesman.* Editor, *Journal for the Protection of All Beings, Interim Pad,* and *City Lights Journal.*

Ferlinghetti's manuscripts are collected at Columbia University, New York City.

ADAPTATIONS: Ferlinghetti's poem "Autobiography" was choreographed by Sophie Maslow, 1964. *A Coney Island of the Mind* was adapted for the stage by Steven Kyle Kent, Charles R. Blaker, and Carol Brown and produced at the Edinburgh Festival, Scotland, 1966; poem was adapted for television by Ted Post on *Second Experiment in Television,* 1967.

SIDELIGHTS: As poet, playwright, publisher, and spokesman, Lawrence Ferlinghetti helped to spark the San Francisco literary renaissance of the 1950s and the subsequent Beat movement in American poetry. Ferlinghetti was one of a group of writers—later labeled the "Beat Generation"—who felt strongly that art should be accessible to all people, not just a handful of highly-educated intellectuals. Ferlinghetti's career, now spanning four decades, has been marked by a constant challenge to the status quo in art. His poetry engages readers, defies popular political movements, and reflects the influence of American idiom and modern jazz. In *Lawrence Ferlinghetti: Poet-At-Large,* Larry Smith notes that the author "writes truly memorable poetry, poems that lodge themselves in the consciousness of the reader and generate awareness and change. And his writing sings, with the sad and comic music of the streets."

Ferlinghetti performed numerous functions essential to the establishment of the Beat movement while also creating his own substantial body of work. His City Lights bookstore provided a gathering place for the fertile talents of the San Francisco literary renaissance, and his City Lights press offered a forum for publication of Beat writings. As Smith puts it in the *Dictionary of Literary Biography,* "What emerges from the historical panorama of Ferlinghetti's involvement is a pattern of social engagement and literary experimentation as he sought to expand the goals of the Beat movement." Smith adds, however, that Ferlinghetti's contribution far surpasses his tasks as a publisher and organizer. "Besides molding an image of the poet in the world," the critic writes, "he created a poetic form that is at once rhetorically functional and socially vital." *Dictionary of Literary Biography* essayist Thomas McClanahan likewise contends that Ferlinghetti "became the most important force in developing and publicizing antiestablishment poetics."

In his book entitled *Poets, Poems, Movements,* Thomas Parkinson suggests that what the Beats did in the history of modern American poetry "was to challenge the stiff ornateness of the poetry then dominant and bring poetry back to the realities of experience. They expanded the possibilities of the medium. . . . And they served to remind us that life is the origin and purpose of poetry. In that general set of aims, Ferlinghetti was, and remains, an important figure." According to Smith in the *Dictionary of Literary Biography,* Ferlinghetti has persisted as an important writer for decades through the "engaged stance of his life and work and by the powerful and popular art he has wrought."

Ferlinghetti was born Lawrence Monsanto Ferling, the youngest of five sons of Charles and Clemency Ferling. His father, an Italian immigrant, had shortened the family name upon arrival in America. Only years later, when he was a grown man, did Ferlinghetti discover the lengthier name and restore it as his own.

A series of disasters struck Ferlinghetti as a youngster. Even before he was born, his father died suddenly. When he was only two, his mother suffered a nervous breakdown that required lengthy hospitalization. Separated from his brothers, Lawrence went to live with his maternal uncle, Ludovic Monsanto, a language instructor, and his French-speaking wife, Emily. The marriage disintegrated, and Emily Monsanto returned to France, taking Lawrence with her. During the following four years, the youngster lived in Strasbourg and spoke only French.

Ferlinghetti's return to America began with a stay in a state orphanage in New York. His aunt placed him there while she sought work in Manhattan. Eventually the pair were reunited when the aunt found a position as governess to the wealthy Bisland family in Bronxville. The youngster endeared himself to the Bislands to such an extent that when his aunt disappeared suddenly, he was allowed to stay. Surrounded by fine books and educated people, he was encouraged to read and learn fine passages of literature by heart. His formal education proceeded first in the elite Riverdale Country Day School and later in Bronxville public schools. As a teenager he was sent to Mount Hermon, a preparatory academy in Massachusetts.

Calling himself Lawrence Monsanto Ferling, Ferlinghetti enrolled at the University of North Carolina in 1937. There he majored in journalism and worked with the student staff of the *Daily Tarheel.* He earned his bachelor's degree in the spring of 1941 and joined the United States Navy that fall. His wartime service included patrolling the Atlantic coast on submarine watch and commanding a ship during the Normandy invasion. After his discharge he took advantage of the G.I. Bill to continue his education. He did graduate study at Columbia University, receiving his master's degree in 1948, and he completed his doctoral degree at the University of Paris in 1951. Throughout this period Ferlinghetti experimented with creative writing, drawing, and painting. Parkinson claims that the author's "youth in New York, his university days there and in Paris, and his maturity in San Francisco gave him urban settings and tones that he thrived on."

Ferlinghetti returned from Paris in 1951 and moved to San Francisco. For a short time he supported himself by teaching languages at an adult education school and by doing free-lance writing for art journals and the *San Francisco Chronicle.* In 1953 he joined with Peter D. Martin to publish a magazine, *City Lights,* named after a Charlie Chaplin silent film. In order to subsidize the magazine, Martin and Ferlinghetti opened the City Lights Pocket Book Shop in a neighborhood on the edge of Chinatown. McClanahan writes: "When Ferlinghetti opened his bookstore it was the only bookstore in the country specializing in paperback books. The atmosphere of the Chinatown district was conducive to the success of his store, which also specialized in extremist political magazines that were difficult to secure in more traditional outlets."

Before long the City Lights Book Shop was a popular gathering place for San Francisco's avant-garde writers, poets, and painters. "We were filling a big need," Ferlinghetti told the *New York Times Book Review.* "City Lights became about the only place around where you could go in, sit down, and read books without being pestered to buy something. That's one of the things it was supposed to be. Also, I had this idea that a bookstore should be a center of intellectual activity; and I knew it was a natural for a publishing company too." Not only was the store a successful business venture, it also proved to be a launching ground for experimental poetry readings and other literary activities. McClanahan, among others, notes that the City Lights bookstore became "an unofficial headquarters for the continuation of a developing poetic movement."

Ferlinghetti was busy creating his own poetry, and in 1955 he launched the City Lights Pocket Poets publishing venture. First in the "Pocket Poets" series was a slim volume of his work, *Pictures of the Gone World.* In *Lawrence Ferlinghetti,* Smith observes that from his earliest poems onwards, the author became "the contemporary man of the streets speaking out the truths of common experience, often to the reflective beat of the jazz musician. As much as any poet today he . . . sought to make poetry an engaging oral art." McClanahan writes: "The underlying theme of Ferlinghetti's first book is the poet's desire to subvert and destroy the capitalist economic system. Yet this rather straightforward political aim is accompanied by a romantic vision of Eden, a mirror reflecting the Whitmanesque attempts to be free from social and political restraints."

These sentiments found an appreciative audience among young people agonizing over the nuclear arms race and Cold War politics. By 1955 Ferlinghetti counted among his friends such poets as Kenneth Rexroth, Allen Ginsberg, and Philip Whalen, as well as the novelist Jack Kerouac. Ferlinghetti was in the audience at the watershed 1955 poetry reading "Six Poets at the Six Gallery," at which Ginsberg unveiled his poem *Howl.* Ferlinghetti immediately recognized *Howl* as a classic work of art and offered to publish it in the "Pocket Poets" series. The first edition of *Howl and Other Poems* appeared in 1956 and sold out quickly. A second shipment was ordered from the British printer, but United States customs authorities seized it on the grounds of alleged obscenity. When federal authorities declined to pursue the case and released the books, the San Francisco Police Department arrested Ferlinghetti on charges of printing and selling lewd and indecent material.

Ferlinghetti engaged the American Civil Liberties Union for his defense and welcomed his court case as a test of the limits to freedom of speech. Not only did he win the suit on October 3, 1957, he also benefitted from the publicity generated by the case. In the *Dictionary of Literary Biography,* Smith writes: "The importance of this court case to the life and career of Ferlinghetti as well as to the whole blossoming of the San Francisco renaissance in poetry and the West Coast Beat movement is difficult to overestimate. Ferlinghetti and Ginsberg became national as well as international public figures leading a revolution in thinking as well as writing. The case solidified the writing into a movement with definite principles yet an openness of form."

For Ferlinghetti, the "principles" included redeeming poetry from the ivory towers of academia and offering it as a shared experience with ordinary people. He began reading his poems to the accompaniment of experimental jazz and reveled in an almost forgotten oral tradition in poetry. In 1958, New Directions press published Ferlinghetti's *A Coney Island of the Mind,* a work that has since sold well over one million copies in America and abroad. In his *Dictionary of Literary Biography* piece, Smith contends that *A Coney Island of the Mind* "is one of the key works of the Beat period and one of the most popular books of contemporary poetry. . . . It launched Ferlinghetti as a poet of humor and satire, who achieves an open-form expressionism and a personal lyricism." Walter Sutton offers a similar assessment in *American Free Verse: The Modern Revolution in Poetry.* Sutton feels that the general effect of the book "is of a kaleidoscopic view of the world and of life as an absurd carnival of discontinuous sensory impressions and conscious reflections, each with a ragged shape of its own but without any underlying thematic unity or interrelationship." Sutton adds: "To this extent the collection suggests a Surrealistic vision. But it differs in that meanings and easily definable themes can be found in most of the individual poems, even when the idea of meaninglessness is the central concern."

In *Lawrence Ferlinghetti,* Smith suggests that the poems in *A Coney Island of the Mind* demonstrate the direction Ferlinghetti intended to go with his art. Ferlinghetti "enlarged his stance and developed major themes of anarchy, mass corruption, engagement, and a belief in the surreality and wonder of life," to quote Smith. "It was a revolutionary art of dissent and contemporary application which jointly drew a lyric poetry into new realms of social- and self-expression. It sparkles, sings, goes flat, and generates anger or love out of that flatness as it follows a basic motive of getting down to reality and making of it what we can." Smith concludes: "Loosely, the book forms a type of 'Portrait of the Artist as a Young Poet of Dissent.' There are some classic contemporary statements in this Ferlinghetti's—and possibly America's—most popular book of modern poetry. The work is remarkable for its skill, depth, and daring."

Ferlinghetti developed into a social poet-observer of life at large, a reporter, so to speak, from the streets. His rejection of academic pretense was particularly compelling because he had earned the highest degrees with honors and therefore knew firsthand the weaknesses of the system. "Ferlinghetti's disdain for academia is not a rejection of intellectuals," observes McClanahan. "Surely the most erudite of the Beats, he publicly affirms his love of reading. . . . The poet's hostility is not to learning *per se* (even traditional learning encouraged in the universities); rather, his distress is with the cloistered atmosphere created by those scholars who would keep truth 'the secret of a few.' In the poet's analysis, this sort of intellectual elit-

ism translates into political elitism, and the long-term result is a governmental system unresponsive to those it should serve." Smith notes in *Lawrence Ferlinghetti* that the academic community responded to the poet's challenge by attacking his work as "simplistic, sentimental, undisciplined, and in open violation of the conventional form."

If certain academics grumbled about Ferlinghetti's work, others found it refreshing for its engagement in current social and political issues and its indebtedness to a bardic tradition. "Ferlinghetti has cultivated a style of writing visibly his own," claims Linda Hamalian in the *American Book Review.* "He often writes his line so that it approximates the rhythm and meaning of the line. He also has William Carlos Williams' gift of turning unlikely subjects into witty poems. . . . He introduces the unexpected, catching his readers open for his frequently sarcastic yet humorous observations." *Poetry* magazine contributor Alan Dugan maintains that the poet "has the usual American obsession, asking, 'What is going on in America and how does one survive it?' His answer might be: By being half a committed outsider and half an innocent Fool. He makes jokes and chants seriously with equal gusto and surreal inventiveness, using spoken American in a romantic, flamboyant manner."

As the 1960s progressed, Ferlinghetti's radicalism deepened and his poetry offered blatant tirades against the destructive tendencies of America's political leadership. McClanahan writes: "Ferlinghetti views nationalism as a fundamental destructive agent, and his polemics against what he considers to be a dangerous expression of nationalism represent a substantial portion of his canon. . . .[Ferlinghetti] alienates himself from the political left and right in an effort at stating the need for fundamental individuality amidst a culture that must, in his eyes, crush the individual to maintain national security." Not surprisingly, the poet was arrested and jailed during a protest of the Vietnam War in Oakland, and the Federal Bureau of Investigation kept a file on his activities throughout the 1960s. In an interview reprinted in *Poetry Criticism,* Ferlinghetti said: "It's not cool to write about politics or make impassioned political statements. But I think a poet has to do that."

Drama also proved a fertile ground for Ferlinghetti. He carried his political philosophies and social criticisms into experimental plays, many of them short and surrealistic. In *Lawrence Ferlinghetti,* Smith contends that the writer's stint as an experimental dramatist "reflects his stronger attention to irrational and intuitive analogy as a means of suggesting the 'secret meaning' behind life's surface. Though the works are provocative, public, and oral, they are also more cosmic in reference, revealing a stronger influence from Buddhist philosophy." In *Dialogue in Ameri-*

can Drama, Ruby Cohn comments that the plays "are brief sardonic comments on our contemporary lifestyle. . . . The themes may perhaps be resolved into a single theme—the unfairness of industrial, consumer-oriented, establishment-dominated existence—and the plays are arguments against submission to such existence."

The Beat movement passed into history decades ago, but Ferlinghetti continues to produce poetry, fiction, and even paintings that testify to his continued commitment to engaged art. Parkinson contends that the author's work "reminds us that he and his contemporaries among the Beat writers have been consistently productive and responsible writers and human beings." *Georgia Review* contributor Diane Wakoski claims that in his more recent poetry, Ferlinghetti "paints with a broad Dionysian stroke which encompasses a dream of natural processes restored to their natural cycles, with human beings speaking out in love or in engaged attention to the burlesque of civilized life. . . . No amount of anger at hypocrisy or absurdity can finally dull his exuberance and celebratory joy for life." Hamalian expresses a similar view. "Instead of becoming cynical," the critic concludes, "[Ferlinghetti] seems to be telling us that although life endures at the price of considerable pain, at the same time it joyfully perpetuates itself. He has no choice but to affirm it, to celebrate it."

Ferlinghetti continues to operate the City Lights bookstore, and he travels frequently to give poetry readings. His paintings and drawings have been exhibited in San Francisco galleries; his plays have been performed in experimental theatres. Smith observes in the *Dictionary of Literary Biography* that Ferlinghetti's life and writing "stand as models of the existentially authentic and engaged. . . . His work exists as a vital challenge and a living presence to the contemporary artist, as an embodiment of the strong, anticool, compassionate commitment to life in an absurd time." *New York Times Book Review* correspondent Joel Oppenheimer cites Ferlinghetti's work for "a legitimate revisionism which is perhaps our best heritage from those raucous [Beat] days—the poet daring to see a different vision from that which the guardians of culture had allowed us." *New Pages* contributor John Gill concludes that reading the works of Lawrence Ferlinghetti "will make you feel good about poetry and about the world—no matter how mucked-up the world may be."

BIOGRAPHICAL/CRITICAL SOURCES:

BOOKS

Allen, David M., editor, *The New American Poetry: 1945-1960,* Grove, 1960.
Charters, Samuel, *Some Poems/Poets: Studies in American Underground Poetry since 1945,* Oyez, 1971.

Cherkovski, Neeli, *Ferlinghetti: A Biography,* Doubleday, 1979.
Cohn, Ruby, *Dialogue in American Drama,* Indiana University Press, 1971.
Concise Dictionary of American Literary Biography: The New Consciousness, 1941-1968, Gale, 1987.
Contemporary Literary Criticism, Gale, Volume 2, 1974, Volume 6, 1976, Volume 10, 1979, Volume 27, 1984.
Dictionary of Literary Biography, Gale, Volume 5: *American Poets since World War II,* 1980, Volume 16: *The Beats: Literary Bohemians in Postwar America,* 1983.
Kherdian, David, *Six Poets of the San Francisco Renaissance: Portraits and Checklists,* Giligia Press, 1967.
Morgan, Bill, *Lawrence Ferlinghetti: A Descriptive Bibliography,* Garland, 1981.
Parkinson, Thomas, *Poets, Poems, Movements,* UMI Research Press, 1987.
Poetry Criticism, Volume 1, Gale, 1991.
Rexroth, Kenneth, *American Poetry in the Twentieth Century,* Herder & Herder, 1971.
Rexroth, *Assays,* New Directions, 1961.
Smith, Larry, *Lawrence Ferlinghetti: Poet-At-Large,* Southern Illinois University Press, 1983.
Stanford, Donald E., editor, *Nine Essays in Modern Literature,* Louisiana State University Press, 1965.
Sutton, Walter, *American Free Verse: The Modern Revolution in Poetry,* New Directions, 1973.

PERIODICALS

America, August 20, 1977.
American Book Review, March/April, 1984.
American Poetry Review, September/October, 1977.
Arizona Quarterly, autumn, 1982.
Books and Bookmen, November, 1967.
Carleton Miscellany, spring, 1965.
Chicago Tribune, May 19, 1986; September 13, 1988.
Chicago Tribune Book World, February 28, 1982.
Cite, October 3, 1970.
Commentary, December, 1957.
Commonweal, February 3, 1961.
Critique: Studies in Modern Fiction, Volume 19, number 3, 1978.
Georgia Review, winter, 1989.
Italian Americana, autumn, 1974.
Liberation, June, 1959.
Library Journal, November 15, 1960.
Life, September 9, 1957.
Listener, February 1, 1968.
Los Angeles Times, July 20, 1969; March 18, 1980; September 27, 1985.
Los Angeles Times Book Review, August 24, 1980; October 19, 1980; March 24, 1985; September 4, 1988.
Midwest Quarterly, autumn, 1974.
Minnesota Review, July, 1961.

Nation, October 11, 1958.
New Pages, spring/summer, 1985.
New Republic, February 22, 1975.
New Statesman, April 14, 1967.
New York, October 5, 1970.
New York Times, April 14, 1960; April 15, 1960; April 16, 1960; April 17, 1960; February 6, 1967; February 27, 1967; September 13, 1970.
New York Times Book Review, September 2, 1956; September 7, 1958; April 29, 1962; July 21, 1968; September 8, 1968; September 21, 1980; November 1, 1981; November 6, 1988.
Observer, November 1, 1959; April 9, 1967.
Parnassus: Poetry in Review, spring/summer, 1974.
Poetry, November, 1958; July, 1964; May, 1966.
Prairie Schooner, fall, 1974; summer, 1978.
Punch, April 19, 1967.
Ramparts, March, 1968.
Reporter, December 12, 1957.
San Francisco Bay Guardian, October 6, 1977.
San Francisco Chronicle, March 5, 1961.
San Francisco Oracle, February, 1967.
San Francisco Review of Books, September, 1977.
Saturday Review, October 5, 1957; September 4, 1965.
Sewanee Review, fall, 1974.
Sunday Times (London), June 20, 1965.
Times (London), October 27, 1968.
Times Literary Supplement, April 27, 1967; November 25, 1988.
Virginia Quarterly Review, autumn, 1969; spring, 1974.
Washington Post Book World, August 2, 1981.
West Coast Review, winter, 1981.
Western American Literature, May, 1982.
Wilson Library Bulletin, June, 1958.
Wisconsin Studies in Contemporary Literature, summer, 1967.
World Literature Today, summer, 1977.

—*Sketch by Anne Janette Johnson*

*   *   *

FICHTER, Joseph 1908-

PERSONAL: Born June 10, 1908, in Union City, NJ; son of Charles J. and Victoria (Weiss) Fichter. *Education:* St. Louis University, B.A., 1935, M.A., 1939; Harvard University, Ph.D., 1947.

ADDRESSES: Home—6363 St. Charles Ave., New Orleans, LA 70118.

CAREER: Entered Roman Catholic order Society of Jesuits, 1930, ordained priest, 1942; Loyola University, New Orleans, LA, professor of sociology and chairman of department, 1947-64; Harvard University, Cambridge, MA,

held Chauncey Stillman Chair, 1965-70; State University of New York at Albany, professor, 1971-72; Loyola University, professor of sociology, beginning 1972, now professor emeritus. Held Favrot Chair of Human Relations, Tulane University, 1973-74. Visiting professor at University of Muenster, 1953-54, University of Notre Dame, 1956-57, Fordham University, 1959, Universidad Catolica de Santiago, 1961, Universidad Ibero-Americana, 1963, Sir George Williams University, 1964, and University of Chicago, 1964-65. Visiting fellow, Princeton Theological Seminary, 1970; scholar-in-residence, Southern Methodist University, 1971, and Notre Dame University, 1979. Founder of New Orleans Commission on Human Rights, 1948. Member of board of trustees, University of Bridgeport.

MEMBER: American Sociological Association (member of executive council), Society for the Scientific Study of Religion (former president), Association for the Sociology of Religion, Religious Research Association, American Association of University Professors, National Urban League, National Association for the Advancement of Colored People, National Organization for Women, Southern Sociological Society (past president).

AWARDS, HONORS: D.Litt., Spring Hill College; Doctor of Laws, Marquette University; D.Hum., Rockhurst College.

WRITINGS:

Roots of Change, Appleton, 1939.
Man of Spain: Francis Suarez, Macmillan, 1940.
Saint Cecil Cyprian, B. Herder, 1942.
James Laynez, Jesuit, B. Herder, 1944.
Christianity, B. Herder, 1946.
Textbook in Apologetics, Bruce, 1947.
Southern Parish, Volume 1: *Dynamics of a City Church,* University of Chicago Press, 1951, reprinted, Arno, 1978.
Social Relations in the Urban Parish, University of Chicago Press, 1954.
Sociology, University of Chicago Press, 1957, 2nd edition, 1971.
Parochial School, University of Notre Dame Press, 1958.
Religion as an Occupation, University of Notre Dame Press, 1961.
Cambio Social en Chile, University of Santiago, 1962.
Priests and People, Sheed & Ward, 1964.
(Editor) *Dimensions of Authority in the Religious Life,* University of Notre Same Press, 1966.
Send Us a Boy, Get Back a Man, Jesuit Educational Association, 1966.
Graduates of Predominantly Negro Colleges, U.S. Government Printing Office, 1967.
America's Forgotten Priests, Harper, 1968.

Jesuit High School Revisited, Jesuit Educational Association, 1969.

Organization Man in the Church, Schenkman, 1973.

One-Man Research (autobiographical), Wiley, 1974.

The Catholic Cult of the Paraclete, Sheed & Ward, 1975.

Rehabilitation of Clergy Alcoholics, Human Sciences Press, 1979.

Religion and Pain, Crossroad Publishing, 1981.

(Editor) *Alternatives to American Mainline Churches,* Rose of Sharon, 1983.

The Holy Family of Father Moon, Leaven, 1985.

The Health of American Catholic Priests, U.S. Catholic Conference, 1985.

A Sociologist Looks at Religion, Michael Glazier, 1988.

The Pastoral Provisions, Sheed & Ward, 1989.

Wives of Catholic Clergy, Sheed & Ward, 1992.

Sociology of Good News, Loyola University Press, 1993.

Also author of *Police Handling of Arrestees,* 1964, and *The Guest House Experience,* 1975. Member of editorial board, Association for the Sociology of Religion and Religious Research Association; member of board of directors, *National Catholic Reporter.*

WORK IN PROGRESS: Research on bigotry and discrimination against religious cults.

SIDELIGHTS: Joseph H. Fichter once told *CA:* "The themes about which I write are almost exclusively sociological and therefore often considered 'controversial.' A humanistic author with a belief in the sacred dignity of persons is impelled to write about injustice and inequality, about pain and suffering, and about the ways in which we try to alleviate these problems. I think the serious and intelligent reader wants to know whether and how a better world is in the making. My autobiographical *One-Man Research* tells some of this story."

BIOGRAPHICAL/CRITICAL SOURCES:

BOOKS

Fichter, Joseph H., *One-Man Reader* (autobiographical), Wiley, 1974.

*   *   *

FISKE, Edward B(ogardus) 1937-

PERSONAL: Born June 4, 1937, in Philadelphia, PA; son of Edward R., Jr., and Jean (Bogardus) Fiske; married Dale Alden Woodruff (a travel consultant), July 12, 1963; children: Julia Fiske Hogan, Suzanna Rawson. *Education:* Wesleyan University, B.A. (summa cum laude), 1959; attended Graduate School of International Relations, Geneva, Switzerland, 1961-62; Princeton Theological Seminary, M.A. (theology), 1963; Columbia University, M.A.

(political science), 1965. *Avocational interests:* Playing squash, travel.

ADDRESSES: Home and office—45 South Turkey Hill Rd., Greens Farms, CT 06436. *Agent*—Sterling Lord Literistic, 1 Madison Ave., New York, NY 10010.

CAREER: John Knox House, Geneva, Switzerland, assistant director, 1961-62; *Trentonian,* Trenton, NJ, journalist, 1962-63; *Packet,* Princeton, NJ, journalist, 1962-63; ordained United Presbyterian minister, 1963; Church of the Master, New York City, assistant minister, 1963-64; *New York Times,* New York City, news clerk and metropolitan reporter, 1964-65, religion reporter, 1965-68, acting chief of Rome bureau, 1967, religion editor, 1968-74, education news editor and editor of quarterly education supplement, 1974-91; writer. Visiting scholar, School of Education, Stanford University, 1991—. Affiliated with Family Services—Woodfield. Lecturer at colleges and universities, including Rice University, University of Houston, Lewis and Clark College, University of Puget Sound, Dartmouth College, University of Missouri, University of Kansas, and Trinity University. Education commentator on radio and television programs, including *The Today Show, Good Morning America, Meet the Press,* and the *Larry King Show;* co-moderator of Presidential debate over education policy, University of North Carolina at Chapel Hill, 1987. Member of board of directors, Wesleyan University, 1968-72, and New Canaan Country School, 1977-83; member of board, Forum for World Affairs, 1987—, and South-North News Service. Consultant, Pew Forum on Education Reform, Palo Alto, CA, 1991—; editorial consultant, Business Roundtable and Scholastic, Inc.

MEMBER: Education Writers Association, Phi Beta Kappa.

AWARDS, HONORS: LL.D. from Beaver College, 1980; honorary doctorates from Occidental College, 1990 and Wheeling Jesuit College, 1992; honored for education series on Japanese schools by Education Writers Association, 1983; Wolynsky-Joukowsky Fellow, Brown University, 1990; Montgomery Fellow, Dartmouth College, 1991; awards for education reporting from Education Writers Association, American Association of University Professors, and other groups.

WRITINGS:

(Editor and compiler with others) *The New York Times Selective Guide to Colleges, 1982-83,* Times Books, 1982, 2nd edition published as *Selective Guide to Colleges, 1984-85,* 1983.

Fiske Guide to Colleges, Times Books, 1982—.

(With Joseph M. Michalak) *The Best Buys in College Education,* Times Books, 1985, revised edition, 1988.

How to Get into the Right College: Secrets of College Admissions Officers, Times Books, 1988.
Get Organized!: Fiske's Unbeatable System for Applying to College, Peterson's Guides, 1990.
Smart Schools, Smart Kids: Why Do Some Schools Work?, Simon & Schuster, 1991.

Contributor of articles and book reviews to periodicals, including *Redbook, Saturday Review, Atlantic Monthly, New Republic, New York Times Book Review, Seventeen, Popular Computing, Christian Herald,* and *Reader's Digest.* Member of editorial board, *Theology Today.*

SIDELIGHTS: Former *New York Times* education editor Edward B. Fiske is well known for his guides to selecting and applying to colleges and universities, including his best-selling *Fiske Guide to Colleges,* as well as his reports on educational reform, such as his 1991 *Smart Schools, Smart Kids: Why Do Some Schools Work?.* However, the twenty-six-year veteran of the *Times* found himself specializing in education only after more than a decade of diversified professional experience. Following studies at the Graduate School of International Relations in the early 1960s, Fiske worked briefly for the John Knox House in Geneva, then returned to the United States to write for local papers and later serve as a United Presbyterian minister at a New York City church. He moved to the *Times* as a news clerk in 1964 and rose through the paper's ranks during the late 1960s and early 1970s to become a religion reporter, then religion editor, and finally education news editor in 1974. Through his sixteen-year stint as education editor, Fiske's expertise in the field expanded to include co-moderating a 1987 Presidential debate on education policy, appearing as an education commentator on well-known programs such as *The Today Show* and *Good Morning America,* writing informative books like *How to Get into the Right College: Secrets of College Admissions Officers* and *Get Organized!: Fiske's Unbeatable System for Applying to College,* and lecturing at colleges and universities. In 1991 he left his position at the *Times,* he said "to concentrate my writing and research on the structural revolution now sweeping through American elementary and secondary schools."

Among his more popular works are *The Best Buys in College Education* and *Smart Schools, Smart Kids.* The former, written with Joseph M. Michalak, lists about two hundred "bargain" colleges—those that meld high quality with affordable costs. Based on research as well as on student and faculty polls, *Best Buys* profiles institutions ranging from small, private colleges, to large, state-run universities. Factual information about academic standards, admissions policies, and physical locales is complemented by brief essays that describe each school's particular atmosphere, including its housing conditions, extracurricular activities, and student makeup. The latter, *Smart Schools,*

Smart Kids, grew out of Fiske's nationwide tour of restructured public schools. Reviewers pointed out that Fiske's conclusion is an encouraging one: He believes that American schools are slowly turning from assembly-line-like institutions into "smart" machines that produce individual thinkers. He notes such advancements as innovative teaching techniques focused on "active" learning, enhanced technology, and improved associations between schools and communities. Although Jeannie Oakes, reviewing *Smart Schools* in the *New York Times,* found that the types of reforms Fiske witnessed can be expensive (many of the schools he visited had obtained additional financing), she generally praised the volume and its findings. "Chapters of fascinating examples," she concluded, "argue that educators and policymakers are making impressive grass-roots changes that, if combined into systemic reforms, could transform the whole of American education."

Fiske shared his view concerning public education reform with *CA:* "Most major institutions—from large corporations, the military, and the health care system to the political structure of Eastern Europe—are undergoing massive, fundamental restructuring. So it's no surprise that our public education system, a $240 billion a year enterprise, should be going through similar upheavals. It's an exciting time to be a journalist writing about education in the United States. It's the best domestic story going."

BIOGRAPHICAL/CRITICAL SOURCES:

PERIODICALS

Booklist, October 1, 1985, p. 214; March 1, 1988, p. 1128.
Los Angeles Times Book Review, April 4, 1982; October 6, 1985, p. 17.
Newsweek, March 1, 1982, p. 69.
New York Times, October 24, 1991, p. C21.
New York Times Book Review, August 21, 1983, p. 27.
Publishers Weekly, June 28, 1991, p. 92.
School Library Journal, February, 1986, p. 104; April, 1989, p. 129.
Voyager, June, 1988, p. 107; June, 1989, p. 122.
Washington Post Book World, March 7, 1982; September 18, 1983.

*   *   *

FORD, R(obert) A(rthur) D(ouglass) 1915-
(Robert A. D. Ford)

PERSONAL: Born January 8, 1915, in Ottawa, Ontario, Canada; son of Arthur Rutherford (a journalist) and May Lavinia (Scott) Ford; married Maria Thereza Gomes, June 27, 1946 (deceased). *Education:* University of Western Ontario, B.A., 1938; Cornell University, M.A., 1939.

ADDRESSES: Home—La Poivriere, Randan 63310, France.

CAREER: Gazette, Montreal, Quebec, reporter, 1938; Cornell University, Ithaca, NY, instructor in history, 1938-40; Canadian Department of External Affairs, Ottawa, Ontario, third secretary, 1940-41; Canadian Embassy, Rio de Janeiro, Brazil, third secretary, 1941-45; Canada House, London, England, second secretary, 1945-46, first secretary, 1947-49; Canadian Embassy, Moscow, Soviet Union, second secretary, 1946-47; Canadian Department of External Affairs, Ottawa, first secretary for United Nations Affairs, 1949-51; Canadian Embassy, Moscow, charge d'affaires, 1951-54; Canadian Department of External Affairs, Ottawa, head of European division, 1954-57; ambassador to Columbia, 1957-58, ambassador to Yugoslavia, 1959-61, ambassador to United Arab Republic (now Arab Republic of Egypt) and the Sudan, 1961-63, ambassador to the Soviet Union in Moscow, 1964-80, dean of diplomatic corps in Moscow, 1971-80, and ambassador to Mongolia, 1974-80. Special advisor to the Canadian Government on East-West relations, 1980-84; member of the Independent Commission on Disarmament and Security Issues (Palme Commission), 1980; board member, International Institute of Geopolitics; advisor, Canadian Institute for Global Security.

MEMBER: League of Canadian Poets, France-Canada Association, Cercle des Ecrivains Bourbonnais.

AWARDS, HONORS: Governor General's Award, 1957, for *A Window on the North;* D.Litt. from University of Western Ontario, 1965; Companion of Order of Canada, 1971; gold medal from Professional Institute of Public Service of Canada, 1971; LL.D. from University of Toronto, 1987.

WRITINGS:

POETRY

A Window on the North, Ryerson, 1956.
The Solitary City: Poems and Translations, McClelland & Stewart, 1969.
Holes in Space, Hounslow Press, 1979.
Needle in the Eye: Poems New and Selected, Mosaic, 1983.
Doors, Words and Silence, Mosaic, 1985.
Dostoyevsky and Other Poems, Mosaic, 1989.
Coming from Afar: Selected Poems, McClelland & Stewart, 1990.

CONTRIBUTOR TO ANTHOLOGIES

Canadian Poetry in English, Ryerson, 1954.
Penguin Book of Canadian Verse, Penguin (London), 1958.

Also contributor to *The Oxford Book of Canadian Verse in English and French, Twentieth-Century Canadian Poetry,* and *Modern Canadian Verse.*

UNDER NAME ROBERT A. D. FORD

Our Man in Moscow: A Diplomat's Reflections on the Soviet Union, University of Toronto Press, 1989.
Diplomate et Poete a Moscou, Editions Collignon, 1990.

Contributor to *Encounter, Malahat Review, Maryland Quarterly, Canadian Forum, Montreal Gazette, Financial Post,* and *Foreign Affairs.* Works have been translated into Russian, French, Spanish, and Portuguese.

OTHER

(Translator) *Russian Poetry: A Personal Anthology,* Mosaic, 1986.

WORK IN PROGRESS: A Moscow literary notebook.

SIDELIGHTS: R. A. D. Ford considers himself a diplomat first and a poet second. Having spent much of his life outside the borders of his Canadian homeland, he is not easily grouped with other contemporary Canadian poets. He told *CA:* "A very active diplomatic career limited the amount of time I had for poetry, but it also extended my horizons, exposing me to the misery of the world— Columbia, Yugoslavia, Egypt, Sudan, what was then the USSR. This had the effect of creating a pessimistic view of the world and mankind, and is reflected in my verse." Also reflected in his poetry is Ford's lifelong battle with "a form of muscular atrophy which has helped to shape a rather somber view of the world," according to Ford. This sadness permeates Ford's poems, which are often set in the arctic wastes of Canada and Russia.

In addition to his original verse, Ford has also published a number of translated poems, many of which are included in his volume *Russian Poetry: A Personal Anthology.* "I was completely bilingual in French and had learned Latin, German, and Russian at school," he told *CA.* "I subsequently added Serbo-Croation, Portuguese, Spanish, and Italian." In the author's note included in his book *A Window on the North,* he explains that his goal in translating poetry is "to make of each adaptation as fine or even finer a poem in his (the translator's) own language," a goal which often requires the taking of "considerable liberties with the verse form and rhyme in order to transmit the spirit of the original."

Russian verse, in particular, has often been the subject of Ford's interpretation. He once told *CA:* "The richness of Russian literature, and above all Russian poetry . . . is so little appreciated because of the difficulty of the language." He later told *CA:* "The 20th century poets who have most influenced me are Eliot, Auden, William Carlos

Williams, Garcia Lorca, Rilke, Eluard, and the great Russians—Pasternak, Akhmatova, Tsvetaeva, and Esenin."

BIOGRAPHICAL/CRITICAL SOURCES:

BOOKS

Dictionary of Literary Biography, Gale, Volume 88: *Canadian Writers, 1920-1959,* Second Series, 1989.
Ford, R. A. D., *A Window on the North,* Ryerson, 1956.
Ford, *Needle in the Eye,* Mosaic, 1983.

PERIODICALS

Globe and Mail (Toronto), October 13, 1984.

*   *   *

FORD, Robert A. D.
   See FORD, R(obert) A(rthur) D(ouglass)

*   *   *

FOREYT, John P(aul) 1943-

PERSONAL: Surname is pronounced For-et; born April 6, 1943, in Manitowoc, WI; son of John Otto and Ann Rose (Hynek) Foreyt. *Education:* University of Wisconsin—Madison, B.S., 1965; Florida State University, M.S., 1967, Ph.D., 1969.

ADDRESSES: Home—7708 Nairn, Houston, TX 77074. *Office*—Nutrition Research Clinic, Baylor College of Medicine, 6535 Fannin, MS F700, Houston, TX 77030.

CAREER: University of Southern California Medical Center, Los Angeles, intern, 1968-69; Florida State University, Tallahassee, assistant professor of psychology, 1969-74; Baylor College of Medicine, Houston, TX, associate professor and director of Diet Modification Center, beginning 1974, currently professor of medicine and psychiatry and director of Nutrition Research Clinic. Private practice of clinical psychology, 1975—.

MEMBER: American Psychological Association, Academy for Behavioral Medicine Research, Association for the Advancement of Behavior Therapy, Behavior Therapy and Research (fellow), American Institute of Nutrition, American Dietetic Association (honorary member).

WRITINGS:

(With Julian C. Davis) *Medical Examiner's Source Book,* C. C. Thomas, 1975.
(Editor with Ben J. Williams and Sander Martin) *Obesity,* Brunner, 1976.
(Editor) *Behavioral Treatments of Obesity,* Pergamon, 1977.
(Editor with Diana P. Rathjen) *Cognitive-Behavior Therapy: Research and Application,* Plenum, 1978.

(Editor with Rathjen) *Social Competence,* Pergamon, 1982.
(Editor with Williams and G. Ken Goodrick) *Pediatric Behavioral Medicine,* Praeger, 1983.
(With Michael De Bakey, Antonio Gotto, Jr., and Lynne Scott) *The Living Heart Diet,* Simon & Schuster, 1984.
(Editor with Kelly Brownell) *Handbook of Eating Disorders,* Basic Books, 1986.
(With G. Terence Wilson, Cyril M. Franks, and Philip C. Kendall) *Review of Behavior Therapy,* Volume 11, Guilford, 1987.
(With Wilson, Franks, and Kendall) *Review of Behavior Therapy,* Volume 12, Guilford, 1990.
(With Goodrick) *Living without Dieting,* Harrison, 1992.
(With De Bakey, Gotto, and Scott) *The Living Heart Brand Name Shoppers Guide,* Mastermedia, 1992.

SIDELIGHTS: John P. Foreyt commented: "*The Living Heart Diet* required seven years of research. Hopefully it will help readers reduce some of the cardiovascular risk factors associated with heart disease."

*   *   *

FOSTER, Frederick
   See GODWIN, John (Frederick)

*   *   *

FRIEDMANN, John 1926-

PERSONAL: Born in 1926, in Vienna, Austria; immigrated to the United States, 1940, naturalized citizen, 1944; son of Robert (a professor) and Susanne (a pianist; maiden name, Martinz) Friedmann; children: Manuela Christine. *Education:* University of Chicago, M.A., 1952, Ph.D., 1955.

ADDRESSES: Home—Los Angeles, CA. *Office*—Graduate School of Architecture and Urban Planning, University of California, 405 Hilgard Ave., Los Angeles, CA 90024.

CAREER: Tennessee Valley Authority, Knoxville, industrial economist, 1952-55; Brazilian School of Public Administration, Rio de Janeiro, regional planning adviser and visiting professor of public administration, 1955-58; U.S. Operations Mission in Korea, Seoul, head of economic development section, 1958-61; Massachusetts Institute of Technology, Cambridge, associate professor of city and regional planning, 1961-65; Catholic University of Chile, Santiago, professor of urban development, 1966-69; University of California, Los Angeles, professor of planning, 1969—, head of urban planning program, 1969-75, 1983-87, 1991—.

Visiting professor at University of Bahia, 1955-58, University of Lund, summer, 1966, Hebrew University of Jerusalem, 1969, United Nations African Institute for Economic Development and Planning, 1971, Japan Center for Area Development Research, 1972, Institute of Social Studies (The Hague, Netherlands), 1973, Centre for Environmental Studies (London, England), 1976, University of California, Berkeley, 1980 and 1990, and University of Witwatersrand, 1983; lecturer at universities all over the world; keynote speaker at professional meetings. Founding member of INTERPLAN, 1963-66; director of Ford Foundation urban and regional development advisory program in Chile, 1965-69; member of board of directors of Urban Innovation Group, 1972-75. Consultant to Organization of American States, United Nations, U.S. Agency for International Development, and World Bank. *Military service:* U.S. Army, 1944-47; became first lieutenant.

MEMBER: Interamerican Planning Society (director, 1982-86), Phi Beta Kappa.

AWARDS, HONORS: Honorary degree, Catholic University of Chile, 1969; Order of Bernardo O'Higgins in rank of Commander (Chile), 1969; Guggenheim fellow, 1975-76; honorary professorship, East China Normal University, Shanghai, 1985; honorary doctorate, University of Dortmund, Germany, 1988; Distinguished Planning Education Award, Association of Collegiate Schools of Planning, 1988.

WRITINGS:

The Spatial Structure of Economic Development in the Tennessee Valley (monograph), Department of Geography, University of Chicago, 1955.

Introducao ao planejamento democratico (title means "Introduction to Democratic Planning"), Getulio Vargas Foundation (Rio de Janeiro), 1959.

(Editor with William Alonso; and contributor) *Regional Development and Planning: A Reader,* MIT Press, 1964, revised edition published as *Regional Policy: Readings in Theory and Applications,* 1975.

Venezuela: From Doctrine to Dialogue, Syracuse University Press, 1965.

Regional Development Study: A Case Study of Venezuela, MIT Press, 1966.

(Editor and contributor) *Chile: Contribuciones a las politicas urbana, regional y habitacional* (title means "Chile: Contributions to Urban, Regional, and Housing Policies"), Centro de Desarrollo Urbana y Regional, 1970.

Retracking America: A Theory of Transactive Planning, Doubleday, 1973.

Urbanization, Planning, and National Development, Sage Publications, 1973.

(With Robert Wulff) *The Urban Transition: Comparative Studies of Newly Industrializing Societies,* Edward Arnold, 1975.

(With Clyde Weaver) *Territory and Function: The Evolution of Regional Planning,* University of California Press, 1979.

The Good Society, MIT Press, 1979.

Planning in the Public Domain: From Knowledge to Action, Princeton University Press, 1987.

Life Space and Economic Space: Essays in Third World Planning, Transaction Books, 1988.

Empowerment: The Politics of Alternative Development, Blackwell, 1992.

(With Haripriya Rangan) *In Defense of Livelihood: Comparative Studies in Environmental Action,* Kumarian Press, 1993.

OTHER

Contributor to books, including *Research and Education for Regional and Area Development,* edited by W. R. Maki and B. J. L. Berry, Iowa State University Press, 1966; *Action under Planning,* edited by Bertram Gross, McGraw, 1967; *Perspectives on Regional Transportation Planning,* edited by Joseph S. DeSalvo, Heath, 1973; *Progress in Geography: International Reviews of Current Research,* Volume 8, edited by Christopher Board, Edward Arnold, 1975; *Growth Strategy and Regional Development: Asian Experiences and Alternative Approaches,* edited by Fuchen Lo and Kamil Salih, Pergamon, 1978; *The Crises of European Regions,* edited by Dudley Seers and Kjell Ostrom, Macmillan (London), 1983; and *Regional Economic Development: Essays in Honour of Francois Perioux,* edited by Benjamin Higgins and Donald J. Savoie, Unwin Hyman, 1988. Also contributor of over 130 articles and reviews to professional journals and numerous reports. Editor of special issue of *Journal of the American Institute of Planners,* May, 1964, and *Development and Change* (Netherlands), 1985.

Member of editorial board of *Journal of the American Institute of Planners,* 1961-75, *Revista Latinoamericana de Estudios Urbano-Regionales,* 1969-76, *Journal of the Interamerican Planning Society, Growth and Change, Development and Change* (Netherlands), *Regional Studies* (United Kingdom), *Comparative Urban and Community Research, Journal of Planning Education and Research, Built Environment* (United Kingdom), *Journal of American Planning Association,* and *Revista Urbana* (Venezuela).

SIDELIGHTS: John Friedmann wrote to *CA:* "Writing for me is a necessity. I want to get things clear, and the only way I know how to do that is by writing, thinking, writing. Putting thoughts on paper forces me to be clear (I want to communicate!), coherent, and complete. As an academic writer, I sometimes envy 'real' writers who know how to put things simply in language ordinary folks can understand, and who can find drama in even the smallest event. I am continuously struggling against academic jargon, but in the end, jargon is unavoidable, because for our work, concepts are indispensable. And concepts, neatly delimited to single layers of meaning (so that they behave properly, and say exactly what you want them to mean), become part of the jargon. My thoughts never come out just the way I want them to. So I edit my texts repeatedly until I have the euphonious result for which I strive. A euphonious text is one that sounds good when you read it aloud."

*   *   *

FRIESNER, Esther M. 1951-

PERSONAL: Born July 16, 1951, in New York, NY; daughter of David R. (a teacher) and Beatrice (a teacher; maiden name, Richter) Friesner; married Walter Stutzman (a software engineer), December 22, 1974; children: Michael Jacob, Anne Elizabeth. *Education:* Vassar College, B.A. (cum laude), 1972; Yale University, M.A., 1975, Ph.D., 1977.

ADDRESSES: Home—53 Mendingwall Circle, Madison, CT 06443. *Agent*—Richard Curtis Literary Agency, 171 East 74th Street, New York, NY 10021.

CAREER: Writer. Yale University, New Haven, CT, instructor in Spanish, 1977-79, and 1983.

MEMBER: Science Fiction Writers of America.

AWARDS, HONORS: Named Outstanding New Fantasy Writer by *Romantic Times,* 1986; Best Science Fiction/Fantasy Titles citation, *Voice of Youth Advocates,* 1988, for *New York by Knight.*

WRITINGS:

FANTASY NOVELS

Harlot's Ruse, Popular Library, 1986.
New York by Knight, New American Library, 1986.
The Silver Mountain, Popular Library, 1986.
Elf Defense, New American Library, 1988.
Druid's Blood, New American Library, 1988.
Sphynxes Wild, New American Library, 1989.
Gnome Man's Land (first volume in trilogy), Ace, 1991.
Harpy High (second volume in trilogy), Ace, 1991.
Unicorn U (third volume in trilogy), Ace, 1992.
Yesterday We Saw Mermaids, Tor Books, 1992.
Wishing Season (young adult), Atheneum, 1993.
Majik by Accident, Ace, 1993.
(With Lawrence Watt-Evans) *Split Heirs,* Tor Books, 1993.

"CHRONICLES OF THE TWELVE KINGDOMS" SERIES; FANTASY NOVELS

Mustapha and His Wise Dog, Avon, 1985.
Spells of Mortal Weaving, Avon, 1986.
The Witchwood Cradle, Avon, 1987.
The Water King's Laughter, Avon, 1989.

"DEMONS" SERIES; FANTASY NOVELS

Here Be Demons, Ace, 1988.
Demon Blues, Ace, 1989.
Hooray for Hellywood, Ace, 1990.

SIDELIGHTS: "Esther M. Friesner," writes Fred Lerner in *Voice of Youth Advocates,* "has established herself as one of the most prolific writers of fantasy fiction, and one of the funniest." She overturns many of the conventions of modern and traditional fantasy in books ranging from *New York by Knight,* in which a dragon and his armored pursuer bring their ages-old battle to the streets of modern-day New York, and *Elf Defense,* in which a mortal woman seeks to escape her marriage to the king of Elfhame by hiring a divorce lawyer, to the "Gnome Man's Land" trilogy—where Tim Desmond, a high-school student from a single-parent home, must cope not only with adolescence but with successive invasions of "little people" from folklore, as well as exotic monsters and gods. Friesner's works, Lerner continues, "open new territory. She has made a specialty of ferreting out obscure creatures from the mythologies and demonologies of the world and turning them loose on unsuspecting places like Brooklyn, New Haven, and Hollywood."

Friesner herself was born and raised in Brooklyn, where she attended high school. She later went on to Vassar College, studying Spanish and drama, and Yale University, where she earned her Masters and doctoral degrees in classical Spanish literature, specializing in the works of playwright Lope de Vega. "I always knew that I wanted to write," Friesner told an interviewer for *Something about the Author* (*SATA*). "I was trying to get published while I was in college, but it wasn't until I was in grad school that I got very serious about it. . . . The first time I got an encouraging rejection slip (saying 'We are not buying this, but this is why') was from George Scithers of *Isaac Asimov's Science Fiction Magazine.* I continued to send to him and he continued to send me back rejection slips, but always telling me what was wrong. Finally I made my first sale to *IASFM* as a result of his encouragement. That was a short story, but I got into writing full-length fantasy thanks to a group at Yale." In the Yale grad school, Friesner relates, was a published science fiction author—Shariann Lewitt—who was working on a fantasy novel. "We saw her building a whole world," Friesner explains, "working out all the details on a big legal pad she had. This was quite different from writing a short story.

I thought, 'Oh, building a world. I get to be God! How nice. I'm going to try that.' And that was how I got started on fantasy novels.

"The novel I wrote from my first world-building was actually the second book I sold," Friesner relates. "It was *Spells of Mortal Weaving,* in the 'Chronicles of the Twelve Kingdoms' series." Friesner's first published book was *Mustapha and His Wise Dog,* an Arabian Nights-style adventure "enlivened by an exotic and evocative fantasy setting, and a pair of captivating characters," declares Don D'Ammassa in *Twentieth-Century Science-Fiction Writers.* The series, continued in *The Witchwood Cradle* and *The Water King's Laughter,* follows the struggles of various mortals through several generations to overthrow Morgeld, an evil demigod. "Although Friesner followed traditional forms for the most part in this series," D'Ammassa concludes, "her wry humor and gift for characterization marked her early as someone to watch."

Friesner originally conceived the "Chronicles of the Twelve Kingdoms" as a twelve-volume high fantasy series. But, she explains, she also wanted to try some ideas about characterization that were not traditional in the high fantasy genre. "I wanted to have characters that were not just good and evil," she tells the interviewer. "There are several villains in the series, but the main one is the demigod-type known as Morgeld. Morgeld was half god but he was also half of another kind of creature, a night spirit. I tried to explain why he was so horrible, to give a reason for him being so villainish and, in fact, give him a chance to redeem himself from his evil. Most people, unless they are really unbalanced mentally, do not do evil things without a reason. Their reasons seems perfectly good and perfectly justified to them, and they go ahead and do atrocious things in the belief that they are doing the right thing. In *The Witchwood Cradle,* the villain shows up as something other than villainish, while you actually get to see a hero that is not always perfectly sterling silver pure. There can be a lot of mercilessness behind being a hero, and by the end of that book I had pretty well established the point that *you can't just accept this guy is the good guy in the white hat.* I think that comes out of the real world too. A lot of people want to believe that so-and-so is our flawless leader, and if our flawless leader all of a sudden decides to do something that isn't right, they will follow it anyway: *our leader is good, therefore everything our leader does must be good, and we must do it; we must not question.*"

"I don't think that I have a particular cause in writing fantasy," Friesner states in her *SATA* interview. "I just try to make it interesting and also to say a few things that I feel need to be said. For instance, in *Gnome Man's Land* . . . I was speaking about the suppression of people's ethnic heritage. In fact, I pointed out how this could get a little dangerous, because every culture has its own domestic spirits. Now, America is a melting pot of ethnicity, so while you can have an American who is predominantly Irish, you often have people who really aren't predominantly anything, and then all the little spirits from their different ethnic backgrounds will fight over them. In America the only little domestic spirits kids ever learn about are in the story 'The Shoemaker and the Elves,' which draws on a British tradition. The kids don't realize that there are the *hinzelmaenner,* little people myths from Germany, and they don't know about the *duende* in the Hispanic culture. The little people of Hawaii are quite active even today—it's still an active belief."

In addition to the warring ethnic spirits, the protagonist, Tim Desmond, has to deal with his own personal problems: getting through high school, living in a single-parent family—his father disappeared one evening on his way to buy a paper—and stabilizing a relationship with his girlfriend. Tim also has to fend off the lusty attentions of his own personal spirit, the Desmond family banshee. "A lot of the modern American perception of the elfin community in general is very sanitized—you know, Santa's little helpers happily making toys and shoes and whatever—but traditionally most otherworldly sprites were incredibly sexy creatures," Friesner explains. "They did not invite the ladies to come and join them just to have a cup of tea. In addition, there's a whole history of changelings and elfin babies with mortal mothers, and on the other side, the women of Elfhame stealing men. I think the Irish hero Oisin was taken away to the Land of Youth by a woman, a female elf. The ballad of Tam Lyn tells of a mortal man who has been stolen away by the Queen of Elves. He takes a mortal lover who winds up pregnant by him and she saves him from becoming Elfland's tithe to hell, from being sacrificed by the elves to hell. These are not nice elves, so having an amorous banshee is pretty much in keeping with the spirit of the otherworldly creatures."

Friesner views humor as an important ingredient in her works, but necessarily the defining one. "Humor can make you think, and therefore can be very, very dangerous," she warns. "There is a long tradition of humorists being regarded as very dangerous people. I think that a country that can stand humorists has got an open mind and is willing to take chances, because humor can be devastating—it can make you stop and question things that you accepted before. But if the humor doesn't arise naturally out of the plot, the story's going to resemble one of the really bad sitcoms. Good humor, and good writing in general, should seem to be pretty natural. There is a lot of humor that does arise out of day to day situations; in fact, humor shows up in places that you wouldn't believe, in some of the most ghastly situations. In times like those laughter could be the saving of us."

Several of Friesner's works also use historical figures and settings. "I have always loved history," she tells the *SATA* interviewer. "History is full of incredible trashy gossip that has been legitimized, because it is history: great stories, the things that people did and how they got around to doing them, how they justified them, and some of the things that they actually said. I have learned from some of this. . . . In *Sphynxes Wild* I used the Roman Emperors from my old reading of Suetonius. With *Druid's Blood* . . . I had a perfectly justified way of getting some of my favorite characters from English history together. I finally got to use Spanish history for my first hardback, called *Yesterday We Saw Mermaids*. The title is a direct quote from the diary of the first voyage of Christopher Columbus. He wrote, 'Yesterday we saw mermaids. They are not as beautiful as we have been led to believe.' And you know what he saw—manatees (adorable animals but they have got a face that would make a train take a dirt road). I thought 'Well, what would happen if indeed they saw mermaids but it's not Christopher Columbus who sees it, it's the ship that got there ahead of him.' Now in history when Columbus got to the New World and discovered the native Americans, a whole chunk of years passed during which the Europeans were debating whether the natives were human or not. 'Do they have souls or not? Because if we decide they are not human and do not have souls, then we can do whatever we want to them without any fear.' Well, finally the Europeans published the *Dialogue of the Dignity of Man,* in which they decided 'Oh, well, I guess they do have souls.' They kept on being pretty awful to the natives anyway, in spite of the excellent work of a number of churchmen who kept saying, 'What are you doing? These are human beings, they have souls and we must save their souls.' (If they didn't have their souls saved, they were still semi-fair game.) So that was my little ax to grind with Columbus and the *are they human* people."

"When I write," Friesner concludes, "I try to make the story so interesting that I wouldn't mind rereading it myself. This is actually a very good thing. It's important to interest your readers because if you don't you won't have readers anymore. But if you don't interest yourself in what you're writing. . . . Well, the process of going from the first draft to the published book takes an awfully long time. You will have to look at that story and those characters a lot—you'll have to do another draft, perhaps even a third, then the editor will go over it, then the copy editor. Every time you're going to be reading the same words. If they aren't good words, you're going to get the feeling of being trapped at a party with people you don't like.

"Now my husband Walter is a published writer too. He is the person who pushed me to go from the typewriter to the computer for writing. Now whenever I have a problem with the computer I don't reach for the manual; I just say, 'Oh *hon*ey!' And a few years back, while we were sitting around just joking about these ads on TV—the ones for Ronco or Ginsu blades that will cut through anything, or for Elvis Presley's Greatest Hits—we started to write a fantasy parody titled 'But Wait, There's More,' which was later published. He contributed as much as I did. Again, recently I was asked to participate in an anthology called *Whatdunnit: Science Fiction Mysteries.* The editor gave me my choice of scenarios but I said, 'Could I please have Walter help me on this, because he's a mystery fan?' (I'm the one who looks at the last page to find out who done it and then decides if I'm going to read the book or not.) I did the actual writing but Walter was the plotter. Now I'm trying to drag him into writing a full length science mystery with me. I'm also going to try and drag our poor innocent thirteen-year-old son in. He's becoming a young computer expert and he likes to do computer gaming and I'd like to make the project a family thing. I may drag my daughter in at some point, too. The cat is still safe."

BIOGRAPHICAL/CRITICAL SOURCES:

BOOKS

Twentieth-Century Science-Fiction Writers, 3rd edition, St. James, 1991.
Something about the Author, Volume 71, Gale, 1993.

PERIODICALS

Analog, December, 1989, pp. 184-185; September, 1991, pp. 166-167.
Locus, April, 1989, pp. 25-27; January, 1990, p. 25.
Science Fiction Chronicles, June, 1990, p. 37; October, 1991, p. 41.
Voice of Youth Advocates, April, 1991, p. 42; December, 1991, p. 294.

* * *

FRITSCH, Bruno 1926-

PERSONAL: Born July 24, 1926, in Prague, Czechoslovakia; son of Josef (a civil servant) and Rosa Fritsch; married Jadwiga Przybyl, October 23, 1953; children: Martin, Caroline. *Education:* University of Basel, Dr.rer.pol., 1952, habilitation, 1958; attended University of Prague, 1964, and Harvard University.

ADDRESSES: Home—Aussichtsstrasse 13, Herrliberg 8704, Switzerland. *Office*—Eidgenoessiche Technische Hochschule-Institut fuer Wirtschaftsforschung, Zurich 8092, Switzerland.

CAREER: Basel Center for Economic and Financial Research, Basel, Switzerland, director, 1958; University of

Karlsruhe, Karlsruhe, Germany, professor of economics, 1959-63; University of Heidelberg, South Asia Institute, Heidelberg, Germany, professor of economics, 1963-65; Swiss Federal Institute of Technology, Zurich, professor of economics, 1965—. Visiting instructor, College of Europe, 1960-69, Harvard University, summers, 1963-74, and Australian National University, 1971. Advisor to various governments, missions in Asia, and Latin America.

MEMBER: World Future Studies Federation, Swiss Future Studies Association (president), Swiss Economic Association, Swiss Association for Environmental Protection, American Economic Association, German Economic Association.

AWARDS, HONORS: Institute for Advanced Studies, fellow, Berlin, 1982-83.

WRITINGS:

Die Geld-und Kredittheorie von Karl Marx: Eine Darstellung und kritische Wuerdigung (title means "Karl Marx's Theory of Money and Loanable Funds"), Polygraphischer Verlag, 1954.

(Translator from the English) K. William Kapp, *Volkswirtschaftliche Kosten der Privatwirtschaft* (title means "The Social Costs of Private Enterprise"), Polygraphischer Verlag, 1958.

Geschichte und Theorie ser amerikanischen Stabilisierungspolitik, 1933-1939/1946-1953 (title means "History and Theory of American Stabilization Policy, 1933-1939/1946-1953"), Polygraphischer Verlag, 1959.

(Editor) *Entwicklungslaender* (title means "Developing Countries"), Kiepenheuer & Witsch, 1968.

Die Vierte Welt: Modell einer neuen Wirklichkeit (title means "The Fourth World: The Model of a New Reality"), Deutsche Verlag (Stuttgart), 1970.

(With others) *World Trade Flows,* Polygraphischer Verlag, 1971.

Bildung, Luxus oder Ueberlebenschance? (title means "General Education: Luxury or Chance for Survival?"), Artemis, 1973.

Wachstumsbegrenzung als Machtinstrument, Deutsche Verlag, 1974, translation by Claire E. Reade published as *Growth Limitation and Political Power,* Ballinger, 1976.

(Editor with others) *Problems of World Modeling: Political and Social Implications,* Ballinger, 1977.

(Editor with Karl W. Deutsch) *Zur Theorie der Vereinfachung: Reduktion von Komplexitaet in der Datenverarbeitung fuer Weltmodelle* (title means "On the Theory of Simplification: Reduction of Complexity in Data Processing for World Models"), Athenaeum, 1980.

Wir werden ueberleben: Orientierungen und Hoffnungen in schwieriger Zeit (title means "We Shall Survive"), Olzog, 1981.

Das Prinzip Offenheit: Anmerkungen zum Verhaltnis von Wissen und Politik (title means "The Rule of Openness"), Olzog, 1985.

(With Georg Erdmann) *ASEAN and the EC: Trends in the Cost of Capital in Major EC Countries and Their Effects on the Production Structure,* Institute of Southeast Asian Studies, 1989.

(With others) *Dissipative Strukturen in Integrierten Systemen,* International Book Import Service, 1989.

(With Erdmann) *Zeitungsvielfalt im Vergleich: Das Angebot an Tageszeitungen in Europa,* Hase & Koehler, 1990.

Die Veraenderung der Atmosphaere: Physikalische Prozesse und politische Implikationen, Nomos, 1990.

Contributor to books, including *Zukunftsforschung in der Schweiz* (title means "Future Research in Switzerland"), edited by Gerhard Kocher, Paul Haupt, 1970.

WORK IN PROGRESS: Research on global modeling, the future of the world system, global energy models, the relationship between industrial and less-developed countries, and the future of the international system.*

* * *

FUCHS, Victor R(obert) 1924-

PERSONAL: Born January 31, 1924, in New York, NY; son of Alfred and Frances (Scheiber) Fuchs; married Beverly Beck, August 29, 1948; children: Nancy, Fred, Paula, Kenneth. *Education:* New York University, B.S. (cum laude), 1947; Columbia University, M.A., 1951, Ph.D., 1955.

ADDRESSES: Home—796 Cedro Way, Stanford, CA 94305. *Office*—National Bureau of Economic Research, 204 Junipero Serra Blvd., Stanford, CA 94305.

CAREER: Al Fuchs Company, Inc., New York City, international fur broker, 1946-50; Columbia University, New York City, lecturer, 1953-54, instructor, 1954-55, assistant professor of economics, 1955-59; New York University, New York City, associate professor of economics, 1959-60; affiliated with Ford Foundation program in economic development and administration, 1960-62; National Bureau of Economic Research, New York City and Stanford, CA, member of senior research staff, 1962—, vice-president of research, 1968-78; City University of New York, Graduate Center, New York City, professor of economics, 1968-74; Mt. Sinai School of Medicine, New York City, professor of community medicine, 1968-74; Stanford University, Stanford, CA, professor of economics, 1974—, Henry J. Kaiser, Jr., Professor, 1988—. Member of National Academy of Science Institute of Medicine, 1971—; member of board of directors, Bankers Life Company, 1981-90; member of research advisory board, Committee for Economic Development, 1984-88; currently on board of reviewing editors for *Science*. Fellow, Center for Advanced Study of Behavioral Sciences, 1972-73 and 1978-79; fellow, Northeast Asia Foundation. *Military service:* U.S. Army Air Forces, 1943-46; became first lieutenant.

MEMBER: American Economic Association (member of executive committee, 1984-87; distinguished fellow, 1990—), American Academy of Arts and Sciences (fellow, 1982—), National Academy of Social Insurance, American Philosophical Society, Beta Gamma Sigma, Alpha Epsilon Pi.

AWARDS, HONORS: Madden Distinguished Alumni Award, college of business and public administration, New York University, 1982; first economist to receive Distinguished Investigator Award, Association for Health Services Research, 1988; Baxter Foundation Health Services Research Prize, Association of University Programs in Health Administration, 1991.

WRITINGS:

The Economics of the Fur Industry, Columbia University Press, 1957.
(With Aaron Warner) *Concepts and Cases in Economic Analysis,* Harcourt, 1958.
Changes in the Location of Manufacturing in the United States since 1929, Yale University Press, 1962.
(With Irving F. Leveson) *The Service Economy,* National Bureau of Economic Research, 1968.
Who Shall Live? Health, Economics and Social Choice, Basic Books, 1974.
How We Live: An Economic Perspective on Americans from Birth to Death, Harvard University Press, 1983.
The Health Economy, Harvard University Press, 1986.
Women's Quest for Economic Equality, Harvard University Press, 1988.
No Pain, No Gain: The Future of Health Policy, Harvard University Press, 1993.

Also author of several monographs. Contributor to more than 100 books, anthologies, and professional journals.

EDITOR

Production and Productivity in the Service Industries, National Bureau of Economic Research, 1969.
Essays in the Economics of Health and Medical Care, National Bureau of Economic Research, 1972.
Policy Issues and Research Opportunities in Industrial Organization, National Bureau of Economic Research, 1972.

(With Joseph Newhouse) *The Economics of Physician and Patient Behavior,* University of Wisconsin Press, 1978.
Economic Aspects of Health, University of Chicago Press, 1982.

SIDELIGHTS: Victor R. Fuchs's book *How We Live: An Economic Perspective on Americans from Birth to Death* examines the effect income and the quality of public services have on Americans' lives at all stages of progress. As Harry S. Ashmore notes in the *Los Angeles Times Book Review:* "[Fuchs's] approach is to analyze such phenomena as marriage, divorce, fertility, education and health in terms usually applied to the market—price, quantity, demand, supply, and the like. But he abandons the jargon, and tempers the dehumanizing effect, as he goes on to discuss the implications for public policy." Peter Passell likewise writes favorably of Fuchs's book in the *New York Times Book Review*. Describing it as "a compendium of economic research" on the family, Passell observes that "this accessible little book is chock-full of fascinating facts and educated conjectures," some of the most interesting of which "are only marginally related to economics," providing "an economist's eye view on everything from why some women smoke during pregnancy, to whether it makes sense to send Junior to Harvard." Concludes the critic: "Larded between the obvious and the ridiculous in 'How We Live,' there is much insightful research. And Mr. Fuchs's compact style makes the book a pleasure to read."

BIOGRAPHICAL/CRITICAL SOURCES:

PERIODICALS

American Journal of Sociology, November, 1989, p. 801.
Boston Globe, October 16, 1988, p. A1.
Harvard Business Review, September 1989, p. 50.
Journal of Economic Literature, June, 1989, p. 737; March, 1990, p. 110.
Los Angeles Times Book Review, May 1, 1983.
New York Times Book Review, May 1, 1983.
Wall Street Journal, November 10, 1988, p. B1.

*   *   *

FURTWANGLER, Albert (J.) 1942-

PERSONAL: Born July 17, 1942, in Seattle, WA; son of Albert E. (a manager) and Lourice (Mowbray) Furtwangler; married Virginia Walsh (a writer under pseudonym Ann Copeland), August 17, 1968; children: Thomas Gavin, Andrew Edward. *Education:* Amherst College, B.A., 1964; Cornell University, M.A., 1967, Ph.D., 1968.

ADDRESSES: Home—P.O. Box 1450, Sackville, New Brunswick, Canada E0A 3C0. *Office*—Department of English, Mount Allison University, Sackville, New Brunswick, Canada E0A 3C0.

CAREER: University of Chicago, Chicago, IL, assistant professor of English and humanities, 1968-71; Mount Allison University, Sackville, New Brunswick, assistant professor, 1971-76, associate professor, 1976-83, professor of English, 1983—. Visiting fellow at Yale University, 1977-78; visiting professor of Linfield College, 1980-81; member of School of Historical Studies, Institute for Advanced Study, Princeton, NJ, 1984-85.

WRITINGS:

The Authority of Publius: A Reading of the Federalist Papers, Cornell University Press, 1984.
American Silhouettes: Rhetorical Identities of the Founders, Yale University Press, 1987.
Assassin on Stage: Brutus, Hamlet, and the Death of Lincoln, University of Illinois Press, 1991.
Acts of Discovery: Visions of America in the Lewis and Clark Journals, University of Illinois Press, 1993.

Contributor to journals, including *Modern Language Quarterly, New England Quarterly, English Studies in Canada, Dalhousie Review, Early American Literature,* and *University of Toronto Quarterly.*   •

SIDELIGHTS: Albert Furtwangler told *CA:* "I write about literary patterns in American history—the cunning formality of early constitutional debates, the resonant tragedy of Lincoln's assassination, the peculiar blend of poetry and science in the Lewis and Clark journals. My chapters often focus on dialogues, debates, or collaborations between strong but sharply different minds: Madison and Hamilton, Jefferson and Adams, Lincoln and Booth, Lewis and Clark. But they also unfold complex relations between such principals and other major figures: Hamilton and Madison as successive collaborators in Washington's Farewell Address; Lincoln and Booth as modern counterparts of Caesar and Brutus; Lewis and Clark as fresh agents of Washington and Jefferson's ambitious designs. I have tried to trace arguments worth pondering on many sides of some enduring American dilemmas. And I have tried to bring early leaders to life, by catching them in the act of answering or transcending forceful challenges."

*   *   *

FURTWANGLER, Virginia W(alsh) 1932-
(Ann Copeland)

PERSONAL: Born December 16, 1932, in Hartford, CT; daughter of William M. and Agnes (a homemaker; maiden name, Bresnahan) Walsh; married Albert J. Furtwangler (a professor of English), August 17,1968; children: Thomas Gavin, Andrew Edward. *Education:* College of New Rochelle, B.A. (cum laude), 1954; Catholic University of America, M.A., 1959; Cornell University, Ph.D., 1970.

ADDRESSES: Home and office—P. O. Box 1450, Sackville, New Brunswick, Canada E0A 3C0. *Agent*—Barbara Kouts, Philip G. Spitzer Literary Agency, 1465 Third Ave., New York, NY 10028.

CAREER: Writer. College of New Rochelle, New Rochelle, NY, instructor in English, 1963-66; Indiana University Northwest, Gary, assistant professor of English, 1970-71; Mount Allison University, Sackville, New Brunswick, part-time teacher of extension courses, 1971-76, assistant professor of English, 1976-77. Member of faculty at Universite de Moncton, 1971-72, and Dorchester Maximum Security Penitentiary, 1976-77. Visiting fiction writer, College of Idaho, Caldwell, Linfield College, 1980-81, Bemidji State University, 1987, Wichita State University, 1988, and Mt. Allison University, 1990-91. Lecturer in English, Extension Department, Mount Allison University, 1983-84. Distinguished visiting fiction writer at University of Idaho, 1983 and 1986. Gives readings of work at universities and on radio programs.

MEMBER: International Women's Writing Guild, Writers Union of Canada, Associated Writing Programs, New Brunswick Federation of Writers.

AWARDS, HONORS: Canada Council grants, 1977, 1980-81, 1982, and 1988; fellow of National Endowment for the Arts, 1978; Arts Award from New Brunswick Department of Youth, Recreation, and Culture, 1982; Governor General's Award, 1990; Ingram Merrill Award, 1990.

WRITINGS:

COLLECTIONS; UNDER PSEUDONYM ANN COPELAND

At Peace, Oberon, 1978.
The Back Room, Oberon, 1979.
Earthen Vessels, Oberon, 1984.
The Golden Thread, Harper/Collins, 1989.

Also author of songs. Work represented in numerous anthologies, including *Best Canadian Stories,* Oberon, 1982; *Easterly: Sixty Atlantic Writers,* Academic Press, 1983; and *The Atlantic Anthology,* Volume I, Ragweed Press, 1984. Contributor to magazines, including *English Journal, Toronto Life, Fiddlehead, Canadian Fiction, Southwest Review,* and *Texas Quarterly.*

WORK IN PROGRESS: Two novels, *Vigil* and *Gift;* short stories.

SIDELIGHTS: Virginia W. Furtwangler wrote: "My book *The Golden Thread* is a collection of convent stories based on my thirteen years as a member of the Ursuline order. I am an American citizen who has lived in Canada for twenty-one years, and I have written some stories about the dual identity that results from such an experience.

"For example, I have dramatized that double identity in my short story 'Remembrance Day' (a holiday that is the Canadian equivalent of the American 'Veteran's Day'), in which a man who came over to Canada during the sixties to escape the draft takes his young Canadian son to the Remembrance Day services in his small Canadian town.

"I often write about people finding ways to transcend the limits of their situations—whether these be convicts in a penitentiary, women in the home, older people facing mortality or, in *Gift,* the novel I am working on, the difficulties of being profoundly deaf in a hearing world. Quite a few stories are concerned with the problem of faith in our world today—what it means to believe—or not believe—in God, or in the possibility of transcendent reality.

"I am also a musician and am interested in the connections between music and writing—both the process of making music or writing and the product. One of the pieces I wrote and composed music for 'Why Eat Pot Roast When You Can Sing,' and this has been performed several times in Canada."

G

GANLEY, Gladys Dickens 1929-

PERSONAL: Born June 7, 1929, in Berryville, VA; daughter of Benjamin Franklin (a farmer) and Ocie (Bolt) Dickens; married Robert Hampton Hammill, Jr., August 27, 1950 (divorced October, 1953); married Oswald Harold Ganley (a researcher and writer), September 3, 1955; children: Robert Charles, Delia Anne. *Education:* Mediterranean Institute, Rome, Italy, Certificate for Studies in Politics and Economics, 1973; University of Maryland, B.A., 1974; Harvard University, A.L.M., 1987. *Religion:* Presbyterian.

ADDRESSES: Home and office—1572 Massachusetts Ave., Apt. 26, Cambridge, MA 02138.

CAREER: United States Industries, White Oak, MD, writer in publications division, 1965; National Institute of Allergy and Infectious Diseases, Bethesda, MD, writer and public relations officer, 1965-68, 1975-76, writer and researcher, 1977-78; National Institutes of Health, Division of Computer Research and Technology, Bethesda, information officer, 1968-69; free-lance writer in Rome, Italy, 1970-73; free-lance writer and researcher, 1977—. Acting executive director of the Program on Information Resources Policy, Harvard University, 1985.

WRITINGS:

(With husband, Oswald Harold Ganley) *International Implications of U.S. Communications and Information Resources,* Program on Information Resources Policy, Harvard University, 1981, revised edition published as *To Inform or to Control? The New Communications Networks,* McGraw, 1982, 2nd edition, Ablex, 1989.

(With Thomas White) *The "Death of a Princess" Controversy,* Program on Information Resources Policy, Harvard University, 1983.

(With O. H. Ganley) *Unexpected War in the Information Age: Communications and Information in the Falklands Conflict,* Program on Information Resources Policy, Harvard University, 1984.

(With O. H. Ganley) *The Political Implications of the Global Spread of the Videocassette Recorder and Videocassette Programming,* Program on Information Resources Policy, Harvard University, 1986, published as *Global Political Fallout: The VCR's First Decade, 1976-1985,* Ablex, 1987.

Political Significance of the Changing Media, Ablex, 1989.

The Exploding Political Power of Personal Media, Ablex, 1992.

Mikhail and the Multiplying Media, Program on Information Resources Policy, Harvard University, 1993.

Author of booklets, press releases, and newspaper articles on health. Author of articles on communication technologies for journals, including *Washington Quarterly.* Contributor to books with O. H. Ganley, including *Issues in New Information Technology,* edited by Benjamin M. Compaine, Ablex, 1988. Speech writer for health professionals.

SIDELIGHTS: Gladys Dickens Ganley told *CA:* "The 'information revolution' of the past few decades is among the most important happenings of the twentieth century. My books attempt to make this complicated subject understandable to decision makers and ordinary interested readers."

Ganley provided these descriptions of her books: "*To Inform or to Control?* discusses what electronic games, missile guidance systems, talking cash registers, videotapes, space shuttles, satellites, touch telephones, television, computer dating, weather forecasting, automatic bank tellers, and AWACS planes have in common. They are all part of the network of the information revolution that has been brought into being by computers and microchips. They are all rapidly changing the way we live, play, work, make war, and keep the peace—sometimes in a positive way and sometimes negatively. The book discusses the evolution of these various new electronic devices and what is being done with them. It discusses the alterations in domestic and global industries due to them, the changed role of the U.S. media abroad due to greater access, the effects of all these changes on U.S. foreign policy, the possible uses of these new devices to help developing countries, and the way they can be used for war and peace. The second edition updates the subject to the late 1980s, and describes the rise of Japan and the newly industrialized nations to economic power, changes in international telecommunications, and the rise in economic importance of the services sector.

"*The 'Death of a Princess' Controversy* describes an international confrontation between Saudi Arabia and a number of countries in spring of 1980, when a British-U.S.-made television docudrama was scheduled to be aired on the public television stations in about twenty-five nations. The film dealt with the execution of a Saudi Arabian princess and her lover for adultery, which is a crime under Islamic law. The Saudi Government made concerted attempts to block showing of the film in a host of countries, using its power to control world oil. The book discusses the political and legal fallout in a number of democracies, and the implications of one nation's attempt to control what people see in others.

"*Unexpected War in the Information Age* discusses all the new information-age equipment that was available to Great Britain and Argentina for waging the 1982 war in the Falklands and who supplied what sophisticated arms and communications equipment to whom. It discusses whether the arms worked or not (frequently they did not). The book describes the new vogue for commanding wars by satellite and talks about the restriction of the press in the Falklands and in Grenada due to lingering fears over Vietnam War coverage. It also describes the switch by world governments from traditional trenchcoated spies to electronic spying—the switch from 'humint' to 'sigint'—human intelligence to signals intelligence. It asks why nobody knew the war was going to happen, and whether we will be ready when such wars break out in the future.

"*Global Political Fallout: The VCR's First Decade* describes the global spread of the videocassette recorder and its political uses worldwide between 1976 and 1985. *The Exploding Political Power of Personal Media* extends the findings for the VCR to the personal computer, the facsimile machine, and other types of new electronic personal media. *Mikhail and the Multiplying Media* discusses the buildup of communications and information resources during the Gorbachev years and their uses during the at-

tempted coup d'etat of August 1991." Ganley once described her writings in general as portraying the advantages that the information revolution has contributed while acknowledging the numerous problems generated by it. She stressed that there are no quick fix solutions to these problems "because there aren't any or if there were, we probably couldn't predict them."

*   *   *

GANLEY, Oswald Harold 1929-

PERSONAL: Born January 28, 1929, in Amsterdam, Netherlands; immigrated to United States, 1947, naturalized citizen, 1952; son of Eric Harold (a musicologist) and Emily (Auerbach) Ganley; married Gladys Dickens (a writer), September 3, 1955; children: Robert Charles, Delia Anne. *Education:* Hope College, A.B., 1950; University of Michigan, M.S. and Ph.D., both 1953; Harvard University, M.P.A., 1965. *Religion:* Presbyterian.

ADDRESSES: Home—1572 Massachusetts Ave., Apt. 26, Cambridge, MA 02138. *Office*—Center for Information Policy Research, 200 Aiken, Harvard University, Cambridge, MA 02138.

CAREER: Walter Reed Army Medical Center, Washington, DC, research assistant, 1954-55; Merck Institute for Therapeutic Research, Rahway, NJ, research associate in allergy and immunology, 1955-60; Merck, Sharp & Dohme Research Laboratories, Rahway, assistant director of international relations, research, and development, 1955-64; U.S. Agency for International Development, Washington, DC, special assistant to science director, 1965-66; U.S. Department of State, Washington, DC, head of European Affairs Division in Office of General Science Affairs, 1966-67, chief of Technology Division, 1968-69, science counselor at American embassies in Rome, Italy and Bucharest, Romania, 1969-73, director of Office of Soviet and Eastern European Scientific and Technological Affairs, 1973-75, deputy assistant secretary of state for sciences and technology, 1975-78; Harvard University, Cambridge, MA, foreign affairs fellow at John F. Kennedy School of Government, 1978-80, lecturer in public policy at John F. Kennedy School of Government and executive director of Program on Information Resources Policy, 1980—. Lecturer at Georgetown University's Foreign Service Institute. Member of board of directors of New Jersey Jaycees, Plainfield, 1958-60, New Jersey Civil Defense Council, Plainfield, 1962-64, Fulbright Commission, Rome, Italy, 1969-73, and American Hospital, Rome, 1971-73; consultant to U.S. Department of Commerce, American Federation of Information Processing Societies, and undersecretary of state. *Military service:* U.S. Army, 1953-55.

MEMBER: American Physiological Society, American Society of Microbiology, American Academy of Microbiology (fellow), Association of Military Surgeons, Sigma Xi, Cosmos Club, Circolo Catoniere Teveremo.

AWARDS, HONORS: Science and public policy fellow, Harvard University, 1964-65.

WRITINGS:

The United States-Canadian Communications and Information Resources Relationship and Its Possible Significance for Worldwide Diplomacy, Center for Information Policy Research, Harvard University, 1981.

(With wife, Gladys Dickens Ganley) *International Implications of U.S. Communications and Information Resources,* Program on Information Resources Policy, Harvard University, 1981, revised edition published as *To Inform or to Control?: The New Communications Networks,* McGraw, 1982, 2nd edition, Ablex, 1989.

(With G. D. Ganley) *Unexpected War in the Information Age: Communications and Information in the Falklands Conflict,* Program on Information Resources Policy, Harvard University, 1984.

(With G. D. Ganley) *The Political Implications of the Global Spread of the Videocassette Recorder and Videocassette Programming,* Program on Information Resources Policy, Harvard University, 1986, published as *Global Political Fallout: The VCR's First Decade, 1976-1985,* Ablex, 1987.

Contributor to books with G. D. Ganley, including *Issues in New Information Technology,* edited by Benjamin M. Compaine, Ablex, 1988. Also contributor to scientific journals.

WORK IN PROGRESS: Research on U.S.-Japan trade relations in high-technology electronics.

SIDELIGHTS: Oswald Harold Ganley's writings frequently focus on the impact technology has on the world. He once told *CA:* "I am deeply interested in the effects of high technology on our U.S. domestic welfare and on our relationships with other nations. There is almost no private or public area in the world today that is not affected by satellites, electronic news, electronic arms, computers, videotapes, and the rest. The movement is global, and the good things far outweigh the bad. But new dynamics upset established equilibria. They need understanding. This—plus the insistence of my writer wife and co-author Gladys Ganley—impelled me to write *To Inform or to Control?.*" In this book the Ganleys discuss the evolution of electronic media and its positive and negative influences. *Los Angeles Times Book Review* critic Irwin R. Blacker stresses that in *To Inform or To Control?* the Ganleys have

revealed what are "dangerous developments in the use and misuse of mass-communications technology."

BIOGRAPHICAL/CRITICAL SOURCES:

PERIODICALS

Los Angeles Times Book Review, May 23, 1982, p. 8.*

*   *   *

GARFIELD, Leon 1921-

PERSONAL: Born July 14, 1921, in Brighton, Sussex, England; son of David Kalman (a businessman) and Rose (Blaustein) Garfield; married Vivien (Dolores) Alcock (a writer and artist), October 23, 1947; children: Jane Angela. *Education:* Attended grammar school in Brighton, England. *Politics:* "Somewhere between Labour and Liberal." *Religion:* Jewish. *Avocational interests:* Eighteenth-century music, snooker, collecting paintings and china, films theatre (mainly Shakespeare).

ADDRESSES: Home—59 Wood Lane, Highgate, London N6 5UD, England. *Agent*—John Johnson Ltd., Clerkenwell House, 45-47 Clerkenwell Green, London EC1R OHT, England; and International Creative Management, 40 West 57th St., New York, NY 10019.

CAREER: Writer of novels, short stories, and plays. Whittington Hospital, London, England, biochemical technician, 1946-66; part-time biochemical technician in various hospital laboratories in London, 1966-69. *Military service:* British Army, Medical Corps, 1940-46; served in Belgium and Germany.

MEMBER: Royal Society of Literature (fellow), International PEN.

AWARDS, HONORS: Gold medal from Boys Clubs of America, for *Jack Holborn; Guardian* Prize for children's fiction, 1967, for *Devil-in-the-Fog;* Carnegie commendation, 1967, for *Smith,* 1968, for *Black Jack,* and 1970, for *The Drummer Boy* and *The God beneath the Sea;* Arts Council of Great Britain Award for the best book for older children and Children's Literature Association Phoenix Award, both 1967, and *Boston Globe/Horn Book* Award, 1968, all for *Smith; New York Times* Best Illustrated Award, 1968, for *Mister Corbett's Ghost, and Other Stories;* Carnegie Medal for the most outstanding book of the year and Greenaway Award, both 1970, both for *The God beneath the Sea;* Greenaway Award, 1972, for *The Ghost Downstairs;* Child Study Association Children's Book of the Year, 1976, for *The House of Hanover: England in the Eighteenth Century;* Whitbread Literary Award, 1980, for *John Diamond; Boston Globe/Horn Book* Award, 1981, for *Footsteps;* Federation of Children's Book Groups

Award, 1981, for *Fair's Fair*; Prix de la Fondation de France, 1984; Maschler Award runner-up, 1985, for *Tales from Shakespeare* and *The Wedding Ghost*; Golden Cat Award from country of Sweden, 1985; Children's Literature Association Phoenix Award, 1987.

WRITINGS:

JUVENILE NOVELS

Jack Holborn, illustrated by Antony Maitland, Constable, 1964, Pantheon, 1965.

Devil-in-the-Fog, illustrated by Maitland, Pantheon, 1966.

Smith, illustrated by Maitland, Pantheon, 1967.

Black Jack, illustrated by Maitland, Longman, 1968, Pantheon, 1969.

The Drummer Boy, illustrated by Maitland, Pantheon, 1970.

(Adaptor with Edward Blishen) *The God beneath the Sea,* illustrated by Charles Keeping, Longman, 1970, published with illustrations by Zevi Blum, Pantheon, 1971.

The Ghost Downstairs, illustrated by Maitland, Longman, 1970, Pantheon, 1972.

The Strange Affair of Adelaide Harris, illustrated by Fritz Wegner, Pantheon, 1971.

The Captain's Watch, illustrated by Trevor Ridley, Heinemann, 1971.

Lucifer Wilkins, illustrated by Ridley, Heinemann, 1973.

(Adaptor with Blishen) *The Golden Shadow,* illustrated by Keeping, Pantheon, 1973.

(With Blishen) *The Sound of Coaches,* illustrated by John Lawrence, Viking, 1974.

The Prisoners of September, Viking, 1975.

The Pleasure Garden, illustrated by Wegner, Viking, 1976.

An Adelaide Ghost, Ward, Lock, 1977.

The Book Lovers, Ward, Lock, 1977, Avon, 1978.

The Confidence Man, Kestrel, 1978, Viking, 1979.

The Night of the Comet: A Comedy of Courtship Featuring Bostock and Harris, Delacorte, 1979, published in England as *Bostock and Harris; or, The Night of the Comet,* Kestrel, 1979.

Footsteps, Delacorte, 1980, published as *John Diamond,* illustrated by Maitland, G. K. Hall, 1988.

King Nimrod's Tower, illustrated by Michael Bragg, Lothrop, 1982.

Fair's Fair, Doubleday, 1982.

The Writing on the Wall, Methuen, 1982, Lothrop, 1983.

Guilt and Gingerbread, illustrated by Wegner, Viking, 1984.

The King in the Garden, Lothrop, 1984.

The December Rose, Viking, 1987.

The Wedding Ghost, Oxford University Press, 1987.

The Empty Sleeve, Delacorte, 1988.

Blewcoat Boy, Delacorte, 1988, published as *Young Nick and Jubilee,* illustrated by Ted Lewin, Delacorte, 1989.

Revolution!, Collins, 1989.

The Saracen Maid, illustrated by John Talbot, Simon & Schuster, 1991.

"APPRENTICES" SERIES

The Lamplighter's Funeral, illustrated by Maitland, Heinemann, 1976.

Mirror, Mirror, illustrated by Maitland, Heinemann, 1976.

Moss and Blister, illustrated by Faith Jaques, Heinemann, 1976.

The Cloak, illustrated by Jaques, Heinemann, 1976.

The Valentine, illustrated by Jaques, Heinemann, 1977.

Labour in Vain, illustrated by Jaques, Heinemann, 1977.

The Fool, illustrated by Jaques, Heinemann, 1977.

Rosy Starling, illustrated by Jaques, Heinemann, 1977.

The Dumb Cake, illustrated by Jaques, Heinemann, 1977.

Tom Titmarsh's Devil, illustrated by Jaques, Heinemann, 1977.

The Enemy, Heinemann, 1978.

The Filthy Beast, Heinemann, 1978.

The Apprentices (contains the twelve "Apprentices" series books), Viking, 1978.

ADULT NOVELS

The Mystery of Edwin Drood (completion of the novel begun by Charles Dickens), Deutsch, 1980, Pantheon, 1981.

The House of Cards, Bodley Head, 1982, St. Martin's, 1983.

ADAPTOR; "SHAKESPEARE: THE ANIMATED TALES" SERIES

Hamlet, Knopf, 1993.

Macbeth, Knopf, 1993.

A Midsummer Night's Dream, Knopf, 1993.

Romeo and Juliet, Knopf, 1993.

The Tempest, Knopf, 1993.

Twelfth Night, Knopf, 1993.

OTHER

The Restless Ghost: Three Stories by Leon Garfield, illustrated by Saul Lambert, Pantheon, 1969.

Mister Corbett's Ghost, and Other Stories, Longman, 1969.

The Boy and the Monkey (short stories), illustrated by Ridley, Heinemann, 1969, Watts, 1970.

(With David Proctor) *Child O'War: The True Story of a Sailor Boy in Nelson's Navy,* illustrated by Maitland, Holt, 1972.

(Editor) *Baker's Dozen: A Collection of Stories,* Ward, Lock, 1973, published as *Strange Fish and Other Stories,* Lothrop, 1974.

The House of Hanover: England in the Eighteenth Century, Seabury, 1976.

(Editor) *The Book Lovers: A Sequence of Love Scenes,* Ward, Lock, 1976.

(Editor) *A Swag of Stories: Australian Stories,* illustrated by Caroline Harrison, Ward, Lock, 1978.

(Editor with Blishen, and author of introduction) Charles Dickens, *Sketches from Bleak House,* illustrated by Mervyn Peake, Methuen, 1983.

(Adaptor) *Tales from Shakespeare,* illustrated by Michael Foreman, Gollancz, 1984.

(Adaptor) *Shakespeare Stories,* illustrated by Foreman, 1991.

Author with Patrick Hardy of play "The Cabbage and the Rose," published in *Miscellany Four,* edited by Blishen, Oxford University Press, 1967. Short stories published in anthologies, including *Winter's Tales for Children 4,* Macmillan, 1968.

ADAPTATIONS: Devil-in-the-Fog, Smith, and *The Strange Affair of Adelaide Harris* have been adapted as television serials for British Broadcasting Corp. (BBC-TV); *Black Jack* was adapted for film, produced by Tony Garnett and directed by Ken Loach, and won the International Jury Award at the Cannes Film Festival in 1979; *John Diamond* was adapted for television and broadcast on BBC-TV, 1981; *Jack Holborn* was adapted for film and released by Taurus Films, and was broadcast on German Television, 1982; *The Ghost Downstairs* was adapted for film, 1982; *The Restless Ghost: Three Stories by Leon Garfield* was adapted for film, 1983; *The December Rose* was adapted for television and broadcast on BBC-TV, 1986.

SIDELIGHTS: An internationally respected author of over fifty books for juvenile and older readers, Leon Garfield has been praised for producing fictional literature that is powerful, dramatic, and highly entertaining. Inspired by Greek myths, Bible stories, and Victorian novels like *Great Expectations* by Charles Dickens, British-born Garfield recalls the mystery and theatrics associated with the long-ago past in such books as *Smith, The Strange Affair of Adelaide Harris, The Prisoners of September,* and *The Night of the Comet: A Comedy of Courtship Featuring Bostock and Harris.* "Of all the talents that emerged in the field of British writing for children in the 1960s," proclaims John Rowe Townsend in *A Sense of Story: Essays on Contemporary Writers for Children,* "that of Leon Garfield seems to me to be the richest and strangest. I am tempted to go on and say that his stories are the tallest, the deepest, the wildest, the most spine-chilling, the most humorous, the most energetic, the most extravagant, the most searching, the most everything."

Although Garfield's interest in writing stories began when he was very young, his writing career did not formally begin until he was in his early forties. Garfield was studying to be an artist and writing in his spare time when World War II interrupted his schooling. He served six years in the British Army's Medical Corps and upon his release took a job as a biochemical technician at a London hospital. He held this full-time position for nearly twenty years and wrote in his free time.

Garfield's break into professional writing came in the early 1960s when he sent his completed manuscript for *Jack Holborn* to publishers. An editor for Constable thought the book, originally written for adults, would be more successful as a juvenile novel. "She suggested that, if I would be willing to cut it, then she'd publish it as a juvenile book," Garfield recalls to Justin Wintle and Emma Fisher in *The Pied Pipers.* "And of course, though I'd vowed I'd never alter a word, once the possibility of its being published became real, I cut it in about one week."

While the vast majority of his works are categorized as fiction for younger readers, many critics have described Garfield as one of the few contemporary writers whose works are closing the gap between literature for adults and the young. Garfield insists that he writes for all ages. As he told *CA,* "At no time did I ever think of writing for any particular audience, children or otherwise. I do not believe anybody ever does. . . . One does not write *for* children. One writes so that children can understand. Which means writing as clearly, vividly, and truthfully as possible."

Often set in the eighteenth century, most of Garfield's novels follow the main character's adventurous search for truth, identity, and purpose. Garfield's first novel, *Jack Holborn,* is a tale of piracy that follows a young orphan's journey back to his homeland to discover his roots. In *Devil-in-the-Fog,* a young boy who works in a traveling show may well be the real heir to a baronet. According to Roni Natov in *Lion and the Unicorn,* Garfield's adventure stories "are romances—sea stories, picaresque adventures, historical novels—which confront the same problems that all the 'relevant' adolescent novels hinge on: the quest for identity, coming to terms with one's roots and heritage, learning to distinguish between authenticity and artifice, and finding a place for oneself in the world. Yet the use of the 18th century . . . allows a fresh look at these essential themes."

Other Garfield books set in the eighteenth century include such novels as *The Sound of Coaches,* the story of a coachman's son who discovers his true identity, *The Prisoners of September,* set in grim and chillingly violent Revolutionary France, and *Blewcoat Boy,* in which two orphans convince a pickpocket to pose as their father so they can qualify for charity assistance. In an article for *Children's*

Literature in Education, Garfield talks about his use of historical settings in his novels, particularly eighteenth-century England. He reveals that in "spite of all my research and caution over detail, I don't really write historical novels. To me, the eighteenth century—or my idea of it—is more a locality than a time. And in this curious locality I find that I can represent quite contemporary characters more vividly than I could otherwise." The eighteenth century was not chosen "by caprice," Garfield insists. "I preferred the discipline of classicism to the freedom of romanticism. Just as Alan Gardner admits that he uses fantasy as a crutch, so I use the classical form."

Garfield's writing has frequently been compared to the works of such great authors as Charles Dickens, Jane Austen, Robert Louis Stevenson, and Henry Fielding. However, Garfield's literature is unique in its viewpoint and dramatic style. In such popular and award-winning historical adventure novels as *The God beneath the Sea, Footsteps,* and *The Wedding Ghost,* readers are treated to elaborate plots, fascinating and distinctive characters, and a blending of comic touches with serious topics. "Few present-day writers combine the attributes that seem so effortless in Mr. Garfield's work: well-built plots, suspense, a writing style suited to the mood of each book, and characters that come to life," stresses Ruth Hill Viguers in *A Critical History of Children's Literature.*

Garfield's distinctive and imaginative style is a well-known trademark of his fiction. He is generally considered one of the most innovative writers of historical fiction in the field of juvenile literature. "Leon Garfield's first book, *Jack Holborn,* marked him out at once as an historical novelist with an individual style," Gordon Parsons emphasizes in the *School Librarian and School Library Review.* "Mr. Garfield really knows the eighteenth-century scene and his background is impressively authentic. What gives this knowledge wings and makes him so readable is his command of a vivid, fast-moving prose." "The style Garfield uses also appeals to children. His language is highly coloured, full of imagery and humour, shot through with irony and ambiguity," writes Rhodri Jones in *Use of English.*

Absorbing and fascinating plots are additional reasons why many reviewers feel Garfield's books are so successful. Critics list Garfield's ability to capture and hold his readers' attention as possiby his greatest talent as a writer. "Few contemporary writers of children's fiction can tell a story as well as Leon Garfield," insists David Rees in the *School Librarian.* And Mary Wadsworth Sucher remarks in *English Journal* that "rich in atmosphere, character, and style, with the gusto of a Dickens or a Sterne, Garfield's elaborate and witty tales are full of surprises, courage of survival, and hope for the future."

While Garfield's books are packed with action and filled with authentic historical detail, the author sprinkles traces of comedy throughout his stories to add to his readers' enjoyment. Reviewers such as Sheila A. Egoff point to *Mirror, Mirror* and *The Enemy* as classic examples of Garfield's ability to smoothly combine exciting action with brief moments of humor. "Because the major writers of historical fiction deal with serious and profound themes, they very rarely indulge in the light touch," observes Egoff in *Thursday's Child: Trends and Patterns in Contemporary Children's Literature.* "There is one outstanding exception, Leon Garfield, whose works serve to remind us that the comic side of life persists, even amid portentous events."

Humor balances the drama in Garfield's literature, Natov points out in the *Lion and the Unicorn:* "While any Garfield novel uses all the conventional melodramatic devices, his sense of humor tempers, refines, and adds complexity, so his novels don't feel corny or staged. . . . Garfield seems to embrace humanity in all its pettiness and smugness, and is appreciative of man's ingenuity. . . . While Garfield takes us through slums, onto pirate ships, into prisons, his touch is always lightened by humor, and therein lies his chief debt to Dickens."

While he has used historical settings in many of his stories, Garfield has also written historical nonfiction. Examples of such work are *Child O'War: The True Story of a Boy Sailor in Nelson's Navy, The House of Hanover: England in the Eighteenth Century,* and the twelve volumes in his "Apprentices" series. In *The House of Hanover,* Garfield presents a look at the Georgian period of English history. "Taking the brilliant device of viewing the period through the portraits of its leading figures," explains Anne Wood in *Books for Your Children,* Garfield "proceeds to follow this through literally by making the entire book an account of a visit to the National Portrait Gallery. It is brilliantly done, never flagging for a second in breathless interest and amusement. . . . *The House of Hanover* must surely be one of the most entertaining introductions, not just to the artistic life of a particular period but to the relationship between art and life in any age, ever written."

In *Child O'War,* Garfield joined with David Proctor to present the story of the British Navy's youngest recruit ever, Sir John Theophilus Lee, who enlisted at the age of five and served in the Napoleonic wars. Based on Lee's own memoirs, Catherine Storr describes the book in *New Statesman* as "a compassionate and witty short book which should do more to illustrate to the young what horror lies behind the brave front of war than all the diatribes contrived by moralists and preachers."

In his "Apprentices" series, Garfield writes for a younger age group about boys and girls learning various trades in eighteenth-century England. Each book tells a brief tale of an apprentice who struggles toward maturity while gaining insight into the often deceptive nature of the world. "On one level," writes Egoff in *Thursday's Child,* "the stories are straightforward, exciting, and, at times, comic narratives. . . . There are as well other levels of meaning—highly symbolical, often allegorical—and these are sometimes elusive. . . . The motifs of light and dark, of friendship and love, not romantic love, but the divine love of compassion, forgiveness, and rebirth, are creatively varied and skillfully interwoven." Writing in the *Times Literary Supplement,* Lance Salway finds the "Apprentices" books to be a "remarkable combination of precise historical detail and timeless characterization. . . . The series as a whole is an achievement that matches the best of Leon Garfield's more prestigious work."

Seeming to sum up Garfield's impact and significance as an author, Neil Philip remarks in the *Times Literary Supplement* that "Garfield's virtues are clear; perhaps because that is so he has not always been fully valued for them. His books are exuberant, densely-plotted, robust, bravura performances. There is nothing anaemic or prissy about them, and nothing brutal. He is not afraid of romance, of sentiment, of adventure. He can deal with moral questions without becoming ponderous; he can provoke both laughter and tears. He can also be simply provoking. His is a rich talent." And writing in the *Children's Book Review,* C. S. Hannabuss contends that "the richly styled atmospherics of Leon Garfield form one of the salient literary features in the landscape of the last decade and a half of children's books. . . . [His] tales of misty derring-do, replete with coincidental encounters and nightmare villainies that work an insidious chemistry on the imagination of the reader, will remain on booklists for a long while."

BIOGRAPHICAL/CRITICAL SOURCES:

BOOKS

Authors and Artists for Young Adults, Volume 8, Gale, 1992, pp. 51-59.
Children's Literature Review, Volume 21, Gale, 1990, pp. 82-122.
Contemporary Literary Criticism, Volume 12, Gale, 1980, pp. 215-242.
Egoff, Sheila A., *Thursday's Child: Trends and Patterns in Contemporary Children's Literature,* American Library Association, 1981, pp. 159-192.
Fisher, Margery, *Classics for Children and Young People,* Thimble Press, 1986.
Major Authors and Illustrators for Children and Young Adults, Gale, 1993, pp. 919-923.
Townsend, John Rowe, *A Sense of Story: Essays on Contemporary Writers for Children,* Lippincott, 1971, pp. 97-107.

Viguers, Ruth Hill, *A Critical History of Children's Literature,* edited by Cornelia Meigs and others, revised edition, Macmillan, 1969, pp. 484-510.
Wintle, Justin, and Emma Fisher, *The Pied Pipers,* Paddington, 1974.

PERIODICALS

Books for Your Children, summer, 1976, pp. 2-3; spring, 1985, p. 17.
Children's Book Review, December, 1973, pp. 182-183; autumn, 1974, p. 110; summer, 1975, pp. 66-67.
Children's Literature in Education, July, 1970, pp. 56-63; November, 1970, pp. 66-67; March, 1973; Volume 9, number 4, 1978, pp. 159-172; Volume 21, number 1, 1990, pp. 23-36.
Contemporary Children's Literature, number 54, 1989.
English Journal, September, 1983, pp. 71-72.
Lion and the Unicorn, Volume 2, number 2, fall, 1978, pp. 44-71.
New Statesman, May 26, 1967, pp. 732-733; May 16, 1969, p. 700; June 2, 1972, pp. 758-759; May 25, 1973.
New York Times Book Review, January 26, 1986, p. 32; February 26, 1986, p. 32.
Publishers Weekly, September 30, 1988, p. 28.
School Librarian, May, 1988, pp. 43-47.
School Librarian and School Library Review, March, 1969, p. 84.
Times Educational Supplement, February 19, 1982, p. 23; November 25, 1988, p. 31.
Times Literary Supplement, November 26, 1964, p. 1072; May 25, 1967, p. 446; December 5, 1968, p. 1369; October 30, 1970, p. 1254; June 15, 1973; July 5, 1974, p. 713; July 7, 1978, p. 772; April 26, 1985, p. 478; June 24, 1988, p. 716.
Use of English, summer, 1972, pp. 293-299.

OTHER

Leon Garfield, Conn Films, Inc., 1969.*

—Sketch by Margaret Mazurkiewicz

*   *   *

GAY, Peter (Jack) 1923-

PERSONAL: Surname originally Froehlich; born June 20, 1923, in Berlin, Germany; emigrated to Cuba, April, 1939; came to the United States in 1941, naturalized in 1946; son of Morris Peter and Helga (Kohnke) Gay; married Ruth Slotkin (a writer), May 30, 1959; stepchildren: Sarah Khedouri, Sophie Glazer Cohen, Elizabeth Glazer. *Education:* University of Denver, A.B., 1946; Columbia University, M.A., 1947, Ph.D., 1951; psychoanalytic training at Western New England Institute for Psychoanalysis, 1976-83. *Politics:* Democrat. *Religion:* Atheist.

ADDRESSES: Home—105 Blue Trail, Hamden, CT 06518. *Office*—Department of History, Yale University, P.O. Box 1504-A, Yale Station, New Haven, CT 06520-7425.

CAREER: Columbia University, New York City, instructor, then assistant professor of government, 1947-56, associate professor, 1956-62, professor of history, 1962-69; Yale University, New Haven, CT, professor of comparative and intellectual European history, 1969—, Durfee Professor of History, 1970-84, Sterling Professor of History, 1984—.

MEMBER: American Historical Association, French Historical Association, American Psychoanalytic Association (honorary member), Phi Beta Kappa.

AWARDS, HONORS: Alfred Hodder, Jr. fellow, Princeton University, 1955-56; fellow, American Council of Learned Societies, 1959-60; fellow, Center for Advanced Study in the Behavioral Sciences, 1962-63; Frederic G. Melcher Book Award, 1967, for *The Party of Humanity: Essays in the Enlightenment;* National Book Award, 1967, for *The Enlightenment: An Interpretation,* Volume I: *The Rise of Modern Paganism;* Guggenheim fellow, 1967-68 and 1976-77; Ralph Waldo Emerson Award, Phi Beta Kappa, 1969, for *Weimar Culture: The Outsider as Insider;* D.H.L., University of Denver, 1970, University of Maryland, 1979, Hebrew Union College, 1983, Clark University, 1985, Suffolk University, 1987, and Tufts University, 1988; overseas fellow, Churchill College, Cambridge, 1970-71; Rockefeller Foundation fellow, 1979-80; *Los Angeles Times* Book Prize nomination, 1984, for *The Bourgeois Experience: Victoria to Freud,* Volume 1: *Education of the Senses;* visiting fellow, Institute for Advanced Study-Berlin, 1984; recipient of first awarded Amsterdam Prize for History, 1991.

WRITINGS:

The Dilemma of Democratic Socialism: Eduard Bernstein's Challenge to Marx, Columbia University Press, 1952.
Voltaire's Politics: The Poet as Realist, Princeton University Press, 1959, reprinted, Yale University Press, 1988.
The Party of Humanity: Essays in the French Enlightenment, Knopf, 1964.
(With editors of Time-Life Books) *Age of Enlightenment,* Time, 1966.
The Loss of Mastery: Puritan Historians in Colonial America, University of California Press, 1966.
The Enlightenment: An Interpretation, Knopf, Volume I: *The Rise of Modern Paganism,* 1966, Volume II: *The Science of Freedom,* 1969.
Weimar Culture: The Outsider as Insider, Harper, 1968.

The Bridge of Criticism: Dialogues among Lucian, Erasmus, and Voltaire on the Enlightenment—On History and Hope, Imagination and Reason, Constraint and Freedom—And on Its Meaning for Our Time, Harper, 1970.
Eighteenth-Century Studies, University Press of New England, 1972.
(With Robert K. Webb) *Modern Europe* (two volumes), Harper, 1973.
Style in History, Basic Books, 1974.
Art and Act: On Causes in History—Manet, Gropius, Mondrian, Harper, 1976.
Freud, Jews and Other Germans: Masters and Victims in Modernist Culture, Oxford University Press, 1978.
The Bourgeois Experience: Victoria to Freud, Oxford University Press, Volume I: *Education of the Senses,* 1984, Volume II, *The Tender Passion,* 1986, Volume III: *The Cultivation of Hatred,* 1993.
Freud for Historians, Oxford University Press, 1985.
A Godless Jew: Freud, Atheism, and the Making of Psychoanalysis, Yale University Press, 1987.
Freud: A Life for Our Time, Norton, 1988.
Reading Freud, Yale University Press, 1990.

EDITOR

(And translator) Ernst Cassirer, *The Question of Jean Jacques Rousseau,* Columbia University Press, 1954.
(And translator) Francois Marie Arouet de Voltaire, *Philosophical Dictionary* (two volumes), Basic Books, 1962.
(And translator) Voltaire, *Candide* (bilingual edition), St. Martin's, 1963.
(And author of introduction) John Locke, *John Locke on Education,* Columbia University Press, 1964.
(Compiler) *Deism: An Anthology,* Van Nostrand, 1968.
(With John Arthur Garraty) *The Columbia History of the World,* Harper, 1971, published as *A History of the World,* Harper, 1972.
Historians at Work, Harper, Volume I (with Gerald J. Cavanaugh): *Herodotus to Froissart,* 1972, Volume II (with Victor G. Wexler): *Valla to Gibbon,* 1972, Volume III (with Wexler), 1975, Volume IV (with Cavanaugh), 1975.
The Enlightenment: A Comprehensive Anthology, Simon & Schuster, 1973, revised edition, 1985.
A Freud Reader, Norton, 1989.

Contributor of articles to periodicals including *American Scholar* and *New Republic.* Author of introductions for books including *The German Dictatorship: The Origins, Structure, and Effects of National Socialism* by Karl Dietrich Bracher, Praeger, 1971; and *Memoirs of Madame de La Tour du Pin,* edited and translated by Felice Harcourt, McCall, 1971. Also author of *Eighteenth-Century Studies Presented to Arthur M. Wilson,* 1972.

Author's works have been translated into Dutch, Finnish, French, German, Italian, Japanese, Portuguese, Spanish, and Swedish.

WORK IN PROGRESS: Research on Volume IV of *The Bourgeois Experience: Victoria to Freud.*

SIDELIGHTS: The cultural historian Peter Gay has gained the respect of fellow educators and the regard of the general reading public with his detailed examination of modern history. From the philosophical movements of eighteenth-century France that ushered in the "modern" era to the artistic, scientific, and political movements characteristic of Germany early in this century, Gay draws on the traditions of both art and science in developing historical perspectives strongly grounded in a social/intellectual framework. The process by which Gay writes is painstaking in its thoroughness to detail. He conducts copious research, uncovering treatises, diaries, letters, literary works, artworks, and numerous other records of significance to the historical epoch. Through careful analysis, Gay determines the relative importance of his findings to his subject and reconstructs a comprehensive and objective image of the period and people under scrutiny, an image stripped of the alterations of previous historians and the obscuring effects of both time and cultural bias. The process of historical reconstruction is shaped by Gay's varied experience—an education that includes degrees in political science, history, and psychoanalysis, as well as an ongoing interest in the arts—and his interpretations of primary source material have continuously elicited the praise of critics for their insight and innovation. Gay's seminal works of history have helped to expose distortions in long-accepted accounts and establish new foundations for future study.

While still an undergraduate at the University of Denver, Gay became fascinated with the eighteenth-century Scottish philosopher David Hume. From Hume, Gay's interest in philosophy extended to the Enlightenment, a European movement that opposed religion by maintaining that a man's capacity to reason was his key to knowledge and understanding of the universe. When Gay became a professor of government at Columbia University, he found that existing secondary sources concentrating on this period were lacking in scope. In 1955 Gay began work on what would become one of the most in-depth treatments of the age and its epistemology. Often used as a text in college history classes since its publication, *The Enlightenment: An Interpretation* is divided into two parts. Volume I, *The Rise of Modern Paganism,* inquires into the origins of the philosophes' ideas; how such men as Voltaire, Diderot, and Montesquieu achieved intellectual freedom. Gay provides an explanation of how these new ideas were put into practice in Volume II, *The Science of Freedom.* A *Times Literary Supplement* reviewer praised the work,

commenting that "for a very long time to come the Enlightenment researcher will have to reckon with Professor Gay's two books, a monument of humane scholarship."

Although much has been written on this period of French history since *The Enlightenment* was first published in the mid to late 1960s, the book's perspective on the years preceeding the French Revolution is unique. "Ever since the fulminations of Burke and the denunciations of the German Romantics, the Enlightenment has been held responsible for the evils of the modern age, and much scorn has been directed at this supposed superficial rationalism, foolish optimism, and irresponsible Utopianism," Gay contends in the preface to Volume I. Even the period's defenders had done it no great service: "The amiable caricature drawn by liberal and radical admirers of the Enlightenment has been innocuous," he added, urging historians that "the time is ready and the demand urgent to move from polemics to synthesis."

"The picture that is painted is wide-ranging: evidence is drawn from writers in Italy and North America as well as France, Germany and Britain," states a reviewer for the *Times Literary Supplement* of Gay's *The Rise of Modern Paganism,* which received the National Book Award in 1967. The reviewer expressed admiration for the volume as "penetrating in its interpretive insight as well as sympathetic in its grasp of the historical situation of the eighteenth-century educated man." *The Science of Freedom* sets forth the social history that provided the intellectual and political climate in which new ideas could flourish. "With increasing secularization, man gains a true picture of his environment and sees how free his is," notes a *Times Literary Supplement* contributor; "the freedom encourages him toward inquiry, criticism, reform, a readiness to take risks, an awareness of his self-dependence." The American Revolution provided the European philosophes with the proof of their convictions. Gay writes in the book's "Finale": "the splendid conduct of the colonists, their brilliant victory, and their triumphant founding of a republic were convincing evidence, to the philosophes at least, that men had some capacity for self-improvement and self-government, that progress might be a reality instead of a fantasy, and that reason and humanity might become governing rather that merely critical principles." Thirteen years later, in 1789, the Enlightenment would face yet another test of its validity via the French Revolution. But the rallying cry of the street mobs—"Liberte, Egalite, Fraternite"—would reflect only a subversion of the philosophical principles that the revolutionary government professed to espouse.

After several years of scholarship on the Enlightenment, during which time he wrote *The Party of Humanity: Essays on the Enlightenment* and translated and edited both Voltaire's *Philosophical Dictionary* and *Candide,* Gay turned his attention to the study of late nineteenth- and early twentieth-century Germany. Born in Berlin and raised during this turbulent era, Gay brought many personal insights to his writing. *Weimar Culture: The Outsider as Insider,* examines Germany as it was during the author's youth, with a population disillusioned following a defeat in World War I and a government burdened, in 1921, with the repayment to the Allies of billions of dollars in war reparations. From the time it was established in 1918 for the purpose of rescuing the German people from the Empire's failure during the Great War, the Weimar Republic faced almost insolvable problems. Extremists from both the Right and Left generated political turmoil while the rubble-lined streets of German towns and cities and the cost of reparations abroad fueled inflation and fomented economic chaos. Nonetheless, out of this political and economic instability emerged a multitude of cultural activities that comprise the focus of Gay's book. Reviewers of *Weimar Culture* have praised Gay for his ability to communicate such a complex period to his reader. Peter Jacobsohn writes in the *New Republic* that the book is "a virtuoso performance, not least because it has captured, with the greatest economy, a culture whose origin and essence were closely intertwined with its politics." And Walter Laqueur notes in the *New York Times Book Review* that, while the book contains several "snap statements and characterizations, . . . [*Weimar Culture*] has clearly been a labor of love, and despite the difficulties of doing justice to so many disparate trends in various field, [Gay] has succeeded exceedingly well." Laqueur adds that the author has "recaptured the spirit of this exciting decade and he provides a reliable guide to it."

Gay further extended his examination of modern German history in a collection of essays published in 1978. *Freud, Jews, and Other Germans: Masters and Victims in Modernist Culture* reflects its author's concern that Nazi Germany's legacy had tarnished nineteenth- and twentieth-century German culture and distorted their dynamics. More specifically, *Freud, Jews, and Other Germans* offers readers a reappraisal of "deeply entrenched views about the nature of modernism, the role Jews have played in it, and the relations of Jews to recent German culture," according to reviewer Robert Alter in *Commentary.* Praising Gay for the balance of his approach, Alter notes that the author "helpfully points out that the great swarm of Jewish thinkers, artists and writers in the Germanic sphere had its healthy share of old-fashioned bourgeois conservatives, and the German Jewry as a whole was by no means predominantly intellectual, and even included appreciable numbers of that rarely mentioned species, the stupid Jew."

The essays in *Freud, Jews, and Other Germans* reflect Gay's interest in psychology as a means of uncovering the

motivation of the individual within a historical context. In the mid 1970s, Gay began seven years of training in psychoanalysis, a course of study that would aid him in his next major work, a projected six-volume history of nineteenth-century middle-class culture entitled *The Bourgeois Experience: Victoria to Freud.* Gay presents his case for a study of history informed by psychoanalysis in *Freud for Historians,* published in 1985: "The professional historian has always been a psychologist—an amateur psychologist," he writes. "Whether he knows it or not, he operates with a theory of human nature; he attributes motives, studies passion, analyzes irrationality, and constructs his work on the tacit conviction that human beings display certain stable and discernible traits, certain predictable, or at least discoverable, modes of coping with their experience. He discovers causes, and his discovery normally includes acts of the mind . . . . Among all his auxiliary sciences, psychology is the historian's unacknowledged principal aid."

Education of the Senses, published in 1984, and *The Tender Passion,* which followed two years later, together comprise Volumes I and II of *The Bourgeois Experience.* The two volumes paint a portrait of sexuality in middle-class England by illustrating the sexual attitudes and perceptions of men and women as they actually existed, dislodging the filter of stereotypes through which the period has often been viewed. Critics of the Victorians have blanketed the period with such adjectives as "stuffy," "hypocritical," "inhibited," and "prudish." "Good" Victorian women were believed to have no interest in sex—indeed, the sexual act itself was consented to solely for the purpose of procreation. At the same time, it is assumed that Victorian husbands typically squandered large portions of their income on frivolities for "kept" women or frequented the establishments of prostitutes. Gay, however, portrays the bourgeois in less extreme terms, in a manner described by Peter S. Prescott in *Newsweek* as "by no means uncritical, but he makes a plausible case that bourgeois life was both an appropriate response to a world in flux and richer in experience than is generally thought."

"Peter Gay's themes are the pangs of sex, the pressures of technology, the anxieties of physicians, the risks of pregnancy, the passion of privacy, and man's fear of women," points out novelist Robertson Davies in a review of *Education of the Senses* for the Toronto *Globe and Mail.* In his study of such topics, Gay rejects conclusions drawn in the 1800s by contemporary critics of nineteenth-century society and relies on journals, personal letters, forgotten novels, medical reports, and other sources that allow the Victorians to speak for themselves. In this way, reviewers note, his complex themes are distilled from those reflected by the society as a whole, through private family interactions, down to their core within the individual.

Education of the Senses received praise from reviewers for the quantity of resources and depth of analysis brought to bear on its subject by its author. Paul Robinson of the *New Republic* writes that Gay "traffics with equal comfort in literary works, medical treatises, and advice manuals, not to mention painting and sculpture." However, despite the thoroughness of his documentation, some reviewers have expressed disappointment that the work did not encompass such information as the role of Queen Victoria, the rising tide of homosexual movements, and society's toleration of prostitutes, all of which were major aspects of Victorian society. Noel Annan, reviewing *The Tender Passion* for the *New York Review of Books,* reflects a contrary criticism leveled at Gay's work when he comments that there will be "those who will shake their heads over attempts to encapsulate the experience of a social class not merely in one country but in Europe and America and not merely in one or two decades but over a period of seventy years." Although sometimes critical of Gay's Freudian approach, Elaine Showalter of the *Nation* commends the work, commenting that *Education of the Senses* is "a major work of cultural history, monumental in its ambitions, immensely readable, powerfully human. It is sure to change the way we think about our present as well as our past."

In adopting the Freudian perspective within his historical analysis, it was natural that Gay eventually turn his scrutiny to the father of psychoanalysis himself. This the historian did, publishing both *Freud: A Life for Our Time* and *A Godless Jew: Freud, Atheism, and the Making of Psychoanalysis* in 1988. "Gay seems intent on presenting Freud's development of psychoanalysis as the result of a purely scientific pursuit of truth, isolated from any external influences," William J. McGrath writes in the *New York Review of Books* of *A Godless Jew.* In support of his contention that Freud's science was not influenced by the cultural, political, or religious climate in which its creator lived, Gay counters arguments to the contrary in a series of well-documented essays. Although critical of the book for the position Gay espouses concerning Freud's early influences, McGrath concedes that "Gay's work on Freud has many strengths, and offers much that contributes to a deepened understanding of his life and personality."

Relying on archival materials far in excess of anything previously available to revisionist historians of the life of Freud, Gay imbues his biography of the great man, *Freud: A Life for Our Time,* with "a delightful freshness and assures it a wonderful transparency: you see straight through it to its subject," according to Richard Wollheim in the *New York Times Book Review.* Gay concludes his work with a bibliographic essay that Wollheim notes will be invaluable in scholarly research on this subject: "Mr. Gay nearly exhausts the Freud literature, interspersing lists of books and articles with comments that are judicious, witty and incisive."

Setting his examination of Freud's life and work under the shadow of war that constantly fell over Germany's political horizon, Gay examines the life, relationships, and thoughts of this noted twentieth-century thinker. "The great man, in Gay's eyes, was the product of a culture and period as well as of his upbringing," according to R. Z. Sheppard of *Time* magazine. The book covers a broad scope of material: it provides an account of Freud's daily life, details the history of the nascent psychoanalytic movement in early twentieth-century Vienna, provides a psychoanalytic view of Freud's relationship with both himself and with others, contains a chronology of the development of his psychoanalytic theories, and places both Freud's life and work within a cultural framework. Frances Partridge praises *Freud: A Life for Our Time* in the *Spectator:* "The professor's summaries and elucidations of Freud's works, including the case histories, are dazzling, and only a little less enjoyable than the books themselves." David Ingleby takes Gay to task in the *Times Literary Supplement* however, for not going into greater detail in his analysis of the components and contradictions inherent in Freud's theories themselves. "In fact," Ingleby comments, "apart from a few concessions in the direction of feminism, Gay's reading of Freudian theory is more or less that of the analytic institutes: many other ways of looking at the texts are simply ignored, or relegated to the bibliographical essay at the end of the book. In a work that claims to give 'the total Freud,' this will hardly do." However, Ingleby agrees that *Freud: A Life for Our Time* "is impressive not so much because of any new factual revelations about Freud but for the original way in which it weaves together what we already know," and reflects the estimation of critics by noting of Gay's style: "It is written with enormous vitality and insight; the language is colourful but precise, bringing to life a wealth of personal information with a novelist's eye for detail."

BIOGRAPHICAL/CRITICAL SOURCES:

BOOKS

Gay, Peter, *The Enlightenment: An Interpretation,* Knopf, Volume I: *The Rise of Modern Paganism,* 1966, Volume II: *The Science of Freedom,* 1969.

Gay, Peter, *The Bourgeois Experience: Victoria to Freud,* Volume I: *Education of the Senses,* Oxford University Press, 1984.

Gay, Peter, *Freud for Historians,* Oxford University Press, 1985.

PERIODICALS

America, February 25, 1984.
American Scholar, winter, 1976.

Antioch Review, winter, 1969-70.
Commentary, May, 1970; March, 1978.
Commonweal, January 19, 1979.
Globe and Mail (Toronto), March 17, 1984; September 28, 1985.
Harper's, December, 1983.
Los Angeles Times Book Review, February 26, 1984; September 28, 1985.
Nation, May 29, 1967; April 7, 1969; December 29, 1969; May 24, 1984.
New Leader, October 14, 1974; June 5, 1978; March 5, 1984.
New Republic, January 4, 1969; November 26, 1977; February 6, 1984.
New Statesman, May 30, 1975; May 19, 1978.
Newsweek, January 2, 1984.
New Yorker, July 15, 1974; February 21, 1977.
New York Review of Books, December 18, 1969; May 21, 1970; November 20, 1986, pp. 8-12; August 18, 1988, pp. 25-29.
New York Times, December 16, 1966; February 17, 1978; December 29, 1983; March 1, 1986.
New York Times Book Review, January 1, 1967; November 24, 1968; November 16, 1969; August 22, 1976; January 29, 1978; January 8, 1984; September 8, 1985; March 16, 1986; October 11, 1987, pp. 39, 68; April 24, 1988, pp. 3, 43, 47.
Publishers Weekly, January 6, 1984.
Saturday Review, November 26, 1966; November 15, 1969.
Spectator, January 3, 1976; June 11, 1988, pp. 35-36.
Time, January 23, 1984; April 18, 1988, pp. 85-86.
Times Literary Supplement, August 29, 1968; June 26, 1969; September 11, 1970; June 20, 1975; August 17, 1984; May 20, 1988, pp. 547-8.
Washington Post Book World, October 10, 1976; February 5, 1978; January 29, 1984; September 29, 1985; March 16, 1986.

* * *

GERBER, Dan(iel Frank) 1940-

PERSONAL: Born August 12, 1940, in Grand Rapids, MI; son of Daniel Frank (a businessman) and Dorothy (Scott) Gerber; married Virginia Elizabeth Hartjen, August 12, 1961; children: Wendy, Frank, Tamara. *Education:* Michigan State University, B.A., 1962. *Politics:* Anarchist. *Religion:* Buddhist. *Avocational interests:* Fishing, cooking, sailing, music, photography.

ADDRESSES: Home—P.O. Box 1106, Leland, MI 49654. *Agent*—Robert Dattila, 160 East 48th St., Apt. 12-U, New York, NY 10017.

CAREER: Writer. Worked as a professional race car driver for five years, and a high school teacher of English in Fremont, MI, for two years; Grand Valley State College, Thomas Jefferson College, Allendale, MI, poet-in-residence, 1969-70; Michigan State University, East Lansing, writer-in-residence, 1970.

MEMBER: PEN, Authors Guild, Poetry Society of America.

AWARDS, HONORS: Michigan Author Award, Michigan Center for the Book and Thunder Bay Literary Conference, 1992, "in recognition of an outstanding body of fiction work by a Michigan author."

WRITINGS:

(With Jim Harrison, Charles Simic, J. D. Reed, and George Quasha) *Five Blind Men* (poems), Sumac Press, 1969.
The Revenant (poems), Sumac Press, 1971.
Departure (poems), Sumac Press, 1973.
American Atlas (novel), Prentice-Hall, 1973.
Out of Control (novel), Prentice-Hall, 1974.
Indy: The World's Fastest Carnival Ride (nonfiction), Prentice-Hall, 1977.
The Chinese Poems: Letters to a Distant Friend, drawings by Jack Smith, Sumac Press, 1978.
Snow on the Backs of Animals: Poems, illustrated by Grant Wood, Winn Books, 1986.
Grass Fires: Stories, Winn Books, 1987.
A Voice from the River (novel), Clark City Press, 1990.
A Last Bridge Home: New and Selected Poems, illustrated by Russell Chatham, Clark City Press, 1992.

Contributor to anthologies, including *Heartland,* edited by L. Stryk, Northern Illinois University Press, 1967; *Inside Outer Space,* edited by R. Vas Dias, Anchor Books, 1971; *Keener Sounds: Selected Poems from the Georgia Review,* edited by Stanley W. Lindberg and Stephen Cory, University of Georgia Press, 1987; *Under a Single Moon: Buddhism in Contemporary American Poetry,* edited by Kent Johnson and Craig Paulenick, Shambala, 1991; and *From A to Z: 200 Contemporary American Poets,* edited by David Ray. Also contributed poems to *Young American Poets,* published in Japan. Contributor of poetry, essays, and stories to *New York, Playboy, Sports Illustrated, New Yorker, Nation, Partisan Review, Georgia Review, Tricycle, Wind Horse,* and other magazines.

WORK IN PROGRESS: Poems, a collection of essays, and a novel.

SIDELIGHTS: Dan Gerber's writing covers an array of topics and styles, including a nonfiction account of the Indianapolis 500, novels and stories that relate man's search for a sense of purpose and values, essays, and books of poetry. Gerber's personal experience is reflected in his writing; his years as a race car driver have provided detail and topic for part of his work. He once related to *CA*, "In poetry as well as prose, I feel less a creator than an instrument of experience. I write what presents itself to me as necessary."

Gerber's experiences are expressed in his novel *American Atlas*, as with later novels such as *Out of Control* and *A Voice from the River*, through the story of man's search for meaning and purpose in his life. In these works he dramatizes his characters' reevaluations of career, family life, and values. The career choice is questioned, the family separates while the main character examines his past and contemplates his future, and in the end reconciliation is considered. In his 1973 novel *American Atlas*, the man's journey for self-knowledge begins after his father dies and leaves him heir to the family business. James R. Frakes in the *New York Times Book Review* describes the main character as a contemporary Ishmael. He adds, "*American Atlas* is a book of places, food, things, objects . . . most of them functional, crisp, funny, sharply evocative." Gerber's 1974 novel *Out of Control* is about the chaotic and dangerous life of a race car driver. Joseph McLellan of the *Washington Post Book World* maintains that *Out of Control* is a "taut, vivid novel."

In addition to novels, Gerber's poetry is an integral part of his writing oeuvre. He once told *CA*, "Randall Jarrel's definition of a good poet, 'a man who, in a lifetime of standing out in thunderstorms, manages to be struck by lightning a half dozen times,' suits me. The active business of the poet is to keep his lightning rod polished and his ear tuned to the rumblings of distant thunder. . . . A man struck by lightning is seldom appeased by house current."

BIOGRAPHICAL/CRITICAL SOURCES:

PERIODICALS

Library Journal, March 15, 1977, p. 724.
New York Times Book Review, September 16, 1973, p. 4.
Publishers Weekly, July 2, 1973, pp. 77-78; January 21, 1974, p. 79; June 29, 1990, p. 96.
Washington Post Book World, May 12, 1974, p. 4.

*   *   *

GIBSON, James (Charles) 1919-
(James C. Gibson)

PERSONAL: Born July 8, 1919, in London, England; son of Lionel George (a soldier) and Phyllis (a seamstress; maiden name, Gann) Gibson; married May Joyce Neame (a secretary), October 30, 1954 (marriage terminated); married Helen Joy Taylor (a teacher), October 2, 1992; children: (first marriage) Christopher, Clare, Antony,

Theresa. *Education:* Queens' College, Cambridge, B.A., 1949, M.A., 1954; Birbeck College, London, Ph.D., 1978. *Politics:* "Right of center." *Religion:* Church of England.

ADDRESSES: Home and office—21 Abbot's Walk, Cerne Abbas, Dorchester, Dorset D72 7JN, England.

CAREER: Newton Chamber & Company, England, clerk, 1936-39; Dulwich College, London, England, English department head, 1949-62; Christ Church College, Canterbury, England, principal lecturer in English, 1962-82. Literary advisor to Macmillan, 1959—; literary adviser to Folkestone Arts Centre, 1976-82; member and chairman of South East Arts Literature panel, 1980-82. *Military service:* British Army, 1939-46; became captain; received Territorial Medal.

MEMBER: Society of Authors, Thomas Hardy Society (chairman, 1992—), Betjeman Society (first chairman, 1989-91).

AWARDS, HONORS: Honorary vice-president, Thomas Hardy Society, 1980; honorary vice-president, Betjeman Society, 1989-91.

WRITINGS:

(Under name James C. Gibson, with Nancy Jane Bowden) *Better Spelling*, St. Martin's, 1964.

Also author of *Tess of the D'Urbervilles: A Macmillan Master Guide to Literature*, Macmillan (London).

EDITOR

(And author of introduction and notes) *Selections From the Diaries of John Evelyn and Samuel Pepys*, Chatto & Windus, 1957.
Thomas Hardy: The Making of Poetry (audiovisual program), Macmillan Education, 1971.
Let the Poet Chose (anthology), Harrap, 1973.
William Shakespeare, *Romeo and Juliet*, Macmillan (London), 1974.
Chosen Poems of Thomas Hardy, Macmillan, 1975.
(And author of introduction and notes) Thomas Hardy, *Far From the Madding Crowd*, Macmillan, 1975.
(And author of introduction and notes) Hardy, *Tess of the D'Urbervilles: A Pure Woman*, Macmillan, 1975.
The Complete Poems of Thomas Hardy, Macmillan (London), 1976, Macmillan, 1978.
(With Trevor Johnson) *Thomas Hardy, Poems: A Casebook*, Macmillan (London), 1979.
The Variorum Edition of the Complete Poems of Thomas Hardy, Macmillan, 1979, published as *The Complete Poems of Thomas Hardy: Variorum Edition*, Macmillan (London), 1979.

Also editor of "Dent Everyman Library" editions of Thomas Hardy's *Far From the Madding Crowd, Tess of* the *D'Urbervilles,* and *Jude the Obscure,* 1984; editor of *Selected Short Stories and Poems of Thomas Hardy,* 1992. Editor of *Adventure, War, Detective, Science Fiction,* and *Animals* (short story anthologies), J. Murray, 1980-84. General editor of textbook series, novel series, and critical guides, including "Murray Short Story Series," "Macmillan Student' Novels," and "Macmillan Master Guides to Literature."

COMPILER

Poetry and Song (anthology), Books 1 and 2, St. Martin's, 1967, Books 3 and 4, Macmillan, 1971.
(With Christopher Copeman) *As Large as Alone: Recent Poems,* Macmillan, 1969, with Donald Murdoch, Macmillan (Australia), 1971.

COMPILER; WITH RAYMOND WILSON

(Under name James C. Gibson) *Reading Aloud,* St. Martin's, 1961.
Solo & Chorus, illustrated by A. R. Whitear, Volume I: *Red Book,* Volume II: *Blue Book,* St. Martin's, 1964.
(Under name James C. Gibson) *Rhyme and Rhythm,* Volume I: *Red Book,* illustrated by Violet Morgan, Volume II: *Blue Book,* illustrated by Victor Ambius, Volume III: *Green Book,* illustrated by A. R. Whitear, Volume IV: *Yellow Book,* illustrated by Ian Ribbons, St. Martin's, 1965.
The Red and Black Rhyme Book, illustrated by Gareth Adamson, St. Martin's, 1967.
Poetry Pack 1 & 2 (anthology), Macmillan, 1975.

OTHER

Contributor of reviews and articles to periodicals, including *English, New Blackfriar's, Out of Town, Speech and Drama, Tablet,* and *Use of English.* Founding editor of the *Thomas Hardy Journal,* 1985-1990; founder and editor of *The Betjemanian,* 1989.

WORK IN PROGRESS: A short life of Thomas Hardy for the "Macmillan Literary Lives" series and the Hardy volume in the "Macmillan Interviews and Recollections" series.

BIOGRAPHICAL/CRITICAL SOURCES:

PERIODICALS

Washington Post Book World, April 25, 1982.

*   *   *

GIBSON, James C.
See GIBSON, James (Charles)

GIFF, Patricia Reilly   1935-

PERSONAL: Born April 26, 1935, in Brooklyn, NY; daughter of William J. and Alice Tieman (Moeller) Reilly; married James A. Giff, January 31, 1959; children: James, William, Alice. *Education:* Marymount College, B.A., 1956; St. John's University, Jamaica, NY, M.A., 1958; Hofstra University, professional diploma in reading, 1975. *Religion:* Roman Catholic.

ADDRESSES: Home—15 Fresh Meadow Rd., Weston, CT 06883. *Agent*—Joyce Appelman, Dell Publishing Co., 245 E. 47th St., New York, NY 10017.

CAREER: Public school teacher in New York, NY, 1956-60; Elmont Public Schools, Elmont, NY, elementary teacher, 1964-71, reading consultant, 1971-84; writer of children's books, beginning in 1979.

MEMBER: Society of Children's Book Writers, Authors Guild, Authors League of America.

AWARDS, HONORS: D.H.L., Hofstra University, 1990.

WRITINGS:

JUVENILE

Fourth Grade Celebrity, illustrated by Leslie Morrill, Delacorte, 1979.
The Girl Who Knew It All, illustrated by Morrill, Delacorte, 1979.
Today Was a Terrible Day, Viking, 1980.
Next Year I'll Be Special, illustrated by Marylin Hafner, Dutton, 1980.
Left Handed Shortstop: A Novel, illustrated by Morrill, Delacorte, 1980.
Have You Seen Hyacinth Macaw?: A Mystery, illustrated by Anthony Kramer, Delacorte, 1981.
The Winter Worm Business: A Novel, illustrated by Morrill, Delacorte, 1981.
The Gift of the Pirate Queen, illustrated by Jenny Rutherford, Delacorte, 1982.
Suspect, Dutton, 1982.
Loretta P. Sweeny, Where Are You? A Mystery, illustrated by Kramer, Delacorte, 1983.
Kidnap in San Juan, Dell, 1983.
The Almost Awful Play, Viking, 1983.
Rat Teeth, Delacorte, 1984.
Watch out, Ronald Morgan, Viking, 1985.
Mother Teresa: A Sister to the Poor Viking, 1986.
Love, from the Fifth Grade Celebrity, Delacorte, 1986.
Happy Birthday, Ronald Morgan!, Viking, 1986.
Laura Ingalls Wilder: Growing Up in the Little House, Viking, 1987.
Tootsie Tanner, Why Don't You Talk? An Abby Jones Junior Detective Mystery, Delacorte, 1987.
Ronald Morgan Goes to Bat, Viking, 1988.

Poopsie Pomerantz, Pick up Your Feet!, Delacorte, 1989.
I Love Saturday, Viking, 1989.
Matthew Jackson Meets the Wall, Delacorte, 1990.
Emily Arrow Promises to Do Better This Year, Dell, 1990.
The War Begins at Supper: Letters to Miss Loria, Delacorte, 1991.
Monster Rabbit Runs, Dell, 1991.

"KIDS OF THE POLK STREET SCHOOL" SERIES

The Beast in Ms. Rooney's Room, Dell, 1984.
Fish Face, Dell, 1986.
The Candy Corn Contest, Dell, 1984.
December Secrets, Dell, 1984.
In the Dinosaur's Paw, Dell, 1985.
The Valentine Star, Dell, 1985.
Lazy Lions, Lucky Lambs, Dell, 1985.
Snaggle Doodles, Dell, 1985.
Purple Climbing Days, Dell, 1985.
Say "Cheese," Dell, 1985.
Sunny-Side Up, Dell, 1986.
Pickle Puss, Dell, 1986.

"NEW KIDS AT THE POLK STREET SCHOOL" SERIES

The Kids of the Polk Street School, Dell, 1988.
Watch Out! Man-Eating Snake!, Dell, 1988.
If the Shoe Fits, Dell, 1988.
All about Stacy, Dell, 1988.
Fancy Feet, Dell, 1988.
B-E-S-T Friends, Dell, 1988.
Spectacular Stone Soup, Dell, 1989.
Stacy Says Good-Bye, Dell, 1989.
Beast and the Halloween Horror, Dell, 1990.

"POLKA DOT, PRIVATE EYE" SERIES

The Mystery of the Blue Ring, Dell, 1987.
The Riddle of the Red Purse, Dell, 1987.
The Secret at the Polk Street School, Dell, 1987.
The Powder Puff Puzzle, Dell, 1987.
The Case of the Cool-Itch Kid, Dell, 1989.
Garbage Juice for Breakfast, Dell, 1989.
The Trail of the Screaming Teenager, Dell, 1990.
The Clue at the Zoo, Dell, 1990.

OTHER

Advent: Molly McGuire, Viking, 1991.

Also author of the "Lincoln Lions Band" series.

ADAPTATIONS: Happy Birthday, Ronald Morgan, Today Was a Terrible Day, and *The Almost Awful Play* have been recorded on audio cassette and released by Live Oak Media.

SIDELIGHTS: Patricia Reilly Giff once wrote *CA:* "While the rest of the kids were playing hide and seek, I sat under the cherry tree reading. On winter evenings, I shared an armchair with my father while he read *Hiawatha* and *Evangeline* to me. I read the stories of my mother's childhood and every book in our little library in St. Albans. I wanted to write. Always.

"But the people who wrote were dead . . . or important, far away and inaccessible. And who was I to dream about writing something like *Little Women,* or *The Secret Garden,* or *Jane Eyre?*

"In college, I studied Keats, Poe, Pope, and Dryden, and, overcome by their genius, switched from English to business, and then to history, where I listened to a marvelous man named Mullee spin tales about the past. I fell into teaching because my beloved dean, who had no idea I wanted to write, saw that it was a good place for me. I taught for almost twenty years before I wrote a story. I was married and had three children. I had a Master's in history, and a professional diploma in reading. I had started doctoral studies. Then suddenly I was forty. I hadn't written a story; 1 hadn't even tried.

"By this time I had worked with so many children who had terrible problems that I wanted to say things that would make them laugh. I wanted to tell them they were special. That we all are. Maybe I didn't have to be a Milton or a Longfellow to do that.

"I began to write. Early on dark cold mornings, fortified by innumerable cups of hot tea, I worked at it. It was hard. It was really so hard. But then I began to feel the joy of it, learning as I wrote, laughing . . .

"It's still hard. But I can't stop now. I'm still getting up early still trying to learn . . . still laughing. I wish I had started sooner."

BIOGRAPHICAL/CRITICAL SOURCES:

PERIODICALS

New York Times Book Review, September 2, 1984.

*   *   *

GILCHRIST, Ellen 1935-

PERSONAL: Born February 20, 1935, in Vicksburg, MS; daughter of William Garth (an engineer) and Aurora (Alford) Gilchrist; children: Marshall Peteet Walker, Jr., Garth Gilchrist Walker, Pierre Gautier Walker. *Education:* Millsaps College, B.A., 1967; University of Arkansas, postgraduate study, 1976. *Avocational interests:* Love affairs (mine or anyone else's), all sports, children, inventions, music, rivers, forts and tents, trees.

ADDRESSES: Home and office—Fayetteville, AK.

CAREER: Author and journalist. *Vieux Carre Courier,* contributing editor, 1976-79. National Public Radio,

Washington, DC, commentator on *Morning Edition* (news program), 1984-85.

MEMBER: Authors Guild, Authors League of America.

AWARDS, HONORS: Poetry award, Mississippi Arts Festival, 1968; poetry award, University of Arkansas, 1976; craft in poetry award, *New York Quarterly,* 1978; National Endowment for the Arts grant in fiction, 1979; Pushcart Prizes, Pushcart Press, 1979-80, for the story "Rich," and 1983, for the story "Summer, An Elegy"; fiction award, *Prairie Schooner,* 1981; Louisiana Library Association Honor book, 1981, for *In the Land of Dreamy Dreams;* fiction awards, Mississippi Academy of Arts and Science, 1982 and 1985; Saxifrage Award, 1983; American Book Award for fiction, Association of American Publishers, 1984, for *Victory over Japan;* J. William Fulbright Award for literature, University of Arkansas, 1985; literature award, Mississippi Institute of Arts and Letters, 1985; national scriptwriting award, National Educational Television Network, for the play *A Season of Dreams.*

WRITINGS:

SHORT STORIES

In the Land of Dreamy Dreams, University of Arkansas Press, 1981, reissued, Little, Brown, 1985.
Victory over Japan: A Book of Stories, Little, Brown, 1984.
Drunk with Love, Little, Brown, 1986.
Two Stories: "Some Blue Hills at Sundown" and "The Man Who Kicked Cancer's Ass," Albondocani Press, 1988.
Light Can Be Both Wave and Particle: A Book of Stories, Little, Brown, 1989.

NOVELS

The Annunciation, Little, Brown, 1983.
The Anna Papers, Little, Brown, 1988.
I Cannot Get You Close Enough (three novellas), Little, Brown, 1990.
Net of Jewels, Little, Brown, 1992.

OTHER

The Land Surveyor's Daughter (poetry), Lost Roads (Fayetteville, AK), 1979.
Riding out the Tropical Depression (poetry), Faust, 1986.
Falling through Space: The Journals of Ellen Gilchrist, Little, Brown, 1987.

Also author of *A Season of Dreams* (play; based on short stories by Eudora Welty), produced by the Mississippi Educational Network. Work represented in anthologies, including *The Pushcart Prize: Best of the Small Presses,* Pushcart, 1979-80, 1983. Contributor of poems, short stories, and articles to magazines and journals, including *Atlantic Monthly, California Quarterly, Cincinnati Poetry Review, Cosmopolitan, Iowa Review, Ironwood, Kayak, Mademoiselle, New Laurel Review, New Orleans Review, New York Quarterly, Poetry Northwest, Pontchartrain Review, Prairie Schooner,* and *Southern Living.*

WORK IN PROGRESS: A novel; short stories; a play; a screenplay.

SIDELIGHTS: The author of poems, numerous short stories, and several novels, Ellen Gilchrist opens for her readers a side door through which to view the world of the gracious, upscale South. With a prose steeped in the traditions of her native Mississippi, Gilchrist's fiction is unique: As Sabine Durrant commented in the London *Times,* her writing "swings between the familiar and the shocking, the everyday and the traumatic." "She writes about ordinary happenings in out of the way places, of meetings between recognizable characters from her other fiction and strangers, above all of domestic routine disrupted by violence." The world of her fiction is awry; the surprise ending, although characteristic of her works, can still shock the reader. "It is disorienting stuff," noted Durrant, "but controlled always by Gilchrist's wry tone and gentle insight."

With the publication of her first short story collection in 1981, Gilchrist gained the attention of literary critics, publishers, and, most importantly, the reading public. In its first few months in print, *In the Land of Dreamy Dreams* sold nearly ten thousand copies in the Southwest alone, a phenomenon particularly impressive since the book was published by a small university press, unaccompanied by major promotional campaigns. The book's popular appeal continued to spread, generating reviews in major newspapers, until it reached the attention of Little, Brown & Co. which offered Gilchrist a cash advance on both a novel and a second collection of short stories. In the meantime, the critical review of *In the Land of Dreamy Dreams* reflected that of the public. As Susan Wood remarked in a review for the *Washington Post Book World,* "Gilchrist may serve as prime evidence for the optimists among us who continue to believe that few truly gifted writers remain unknown forever. And Gilchrist is the real thing alright. In fact," added Wood, "it's difficult to review a first book as good as this without resorting to every known superlative cliche—there are, after all, just so many ways to say 'auspicious debut.'"

In the Land of Dreamy Dreams is a collection of fourteen short stories. Most are set in the city of New Orleans and many focus on the lives and concerns of young people. They are "traditional stories" according to Wood, "full of real people to whom things really happen—set, variously, over the last four decades among the rich of New Orleans, the surviving aristocracy of the Mississippi Delta, and Southerners transplanted . . . to southern Indiana." The main characters in the stories, many of them adolescents, exhibit such flaws of character as envy, lust, and avarice; however Wood noted that more positive motivations lay underneath the surface: "It is more accurate to say that *In the Land of Dreamy Dreams* is about the stratagems, both admirable and not so, by which we survive our lives." Jim Crace, in a *Times Literary Supplement* review of *In the Land of Dreamy Dreams,* indicated that Gilchrist's text "is obsessively signposted with street names and Louisiana landmarks . . . . But *In the Land of Dreamy Dreams* cannot be dismissed as little more than an anecdotal street plan . . . . The self-conscious parading of exact Southern locations is a protective screen beyond which an entirely different territory is explored and mapped. Gilchrist's 'Land of Dreamy Dreams' is Adolescence."

The adolescent struggle to come to terms with the way one's dreams and aspirations are limited by reality figures largely in these fourteen stories. Gilchrist introduces her readers to a variety of characters: an eight-year-old girl who delights in masquerading as an adult and commiserates with a newly widowed wartime bride; a girl who fantasizes about the disasters that could befall the brothers who have excluded her from their Olympic-training plans; a young woman who gains her father's help in obtaining an abortion; another girl who discovers the existence of her father's mistress; and an unruly teenager who disrupts the order of her adoptive father's world, challenges his self-esteem, and so aggravates him that he finally shoots her and then commits suicide. "Domestic life among the bored, purposeless, self-indulgent and self-absorbed rich" is the author's central focus, according to reviewer Jonathan Yardley in the *Washington Post Book World*. But domestic is not to be confused with tame. As Yardley observed, the "brutal realities that Gilchrist thrusts into these lives are chilling, and so too is the merciless candor with which she discloses the emptiness behind their glitter." And John Mellors similarly remarked in the *Listener:* "*In the Land of Dreamy Dreams* has many shocks. The author writes in a low, matter-of-fact tone of voice and then changes key in her dramatic, often-bloody endings."

Gilchrist completed her second collection of short stories, *Victory over Japan,* three years later. Winner of the 1984 American Book Award for fiction, *Victory over Japan* was hailed by reviewers as a return to the genre, style, and several of the characters of *In the Land of Dreamy Dreams.* Beverly Lowry, critiquing *Victory over Japan* in the *New York Times Book Review,* commented: "Those who loved *In the Land of Dreamy Dreams* will not be disappointed. Many of the same characters reappear . . . . Often new characters show up with old names . . . . These crossovers are neither distracting nor accidental . . . . Ellen

Gilchrist is only changing costumes, and she can 'do wonderful tricks with her voice.' " *Drunk with Love,* published in 1987, and *Light Can be Both Wave and Particle,* released two years later, expanded the author's exploration of her characters' many facets. While continuing to praise her voice, critics have found Gilchrist's later work to be of a more "uneven" quality than her early writing. Reviewing the volume in the *Chicago Tribune,* Greg Johnson noted that Gilchrist "seems to get carried away with her breezy style and verbal facility. The stories read quickly and are often enjoyable, but they lack the thought and craft that make for memorable fiction." However, Roy Hoffman praised the book in the *New York Times Book Review* as full of "new energy" and noted of the title story that "it brings together lovers from different cultures more spiritedly than any past Gilchrist story."

Indeed, the "voice" and characters that Gilchrist employs throughout her fiction are the hallmarks of her work. David Sexton remarked of her voice in a *Times Literary Supplement* review of *Victory over Japan* that it had its roots in the "talk of the Mississippi Delta," adding that "the drawly 'whyyyyy not' world of the modern South which she creates is a great pleasure to visit." Equally important within her prose are the characters who appear time and time again throughout her writing. "Without much authorial manicuring or explanation, [Gilchrist] allows her characters to emerge whole, in full possession of their considerable stores of eccentricities and passion," commented reviewer Lowry. The central characters in her works are usually women; whether they are young, as in *The Land of Dreamy Dreams,* or more mature, they are usually spirited, spoiled, and fighting their way out of poverty or out of a bad relationship. "Ms. Gilchrist's women . . . are unconventional, nervy, outspoken," noted Hoffman. "As grown-ups they are passionate to the point of recklessness, romantic in the midst of despair. As youngsters they vex adults."

In 1983, Gilchrist's first novel, *The Annunciation,* was published. It recounts the life of Amanda McCarney, from her childhood on a Mississippi Delta plantation where she falls in love with and, at the age of fourteen, has a child by her cousin Guy, to her marriage to a wealthy New Orleans man and a life of high society and heavy drinking. Eventually rejecting this lifestyle, Amanda returns to school where she discovers a gift for languages that has lain dormant during the forty-some years of her life and is offered the chance to translate the rediscovered poetry of an eighteenth-century Frenchwoman. She divorces her husband and moves to a university town in Arkansas to pursue her translating where, in addition to her work, Amanda finds love and friendship among a commune of hippie-type poets and philosophers in the Ozarks. *The Annunciation* received mixed reviews from critics. Yardley, critiquing the book in the *Washington Post Book World,* asserted that for most of its length "*The Annunciation* is a complex, interesting, occasionally startling novel; but as soon as Gilchrist moves Amanda away from the conflicts and discontents of New Orleans, the book falls to pieces." Yardley agreed, noting that once Amanda moves to the Ozarks *The Annunciation* "loses its toughness and irony. Amid the potters and the professors and the philosopher-poets of the Ozarks, Amanda McCarney turns into mush." However Frances Taliaferro, reviewing *The Annunciation* in *Harper's,* deemed Gilchrist's novel "'women's fiction' par excellence" and described the book as "a cheerful hodgepodge of the social and psychological fashions of the past three decades." Taliaferro explained that "Amanda is in some ways a receptacle for current romantic cliches, but she is also a vivid character of dash and humor. . . . Even a skeptical reader pays her the compliment of wondering what she will do next in this surprisingly likable novel." Taliaferro concluded that, despite some tragedy, the "presiding spirit of this novel is self-realization, and Amanda [in the end] has at last made her way to autonomy."

Gilchrist has gone on to write several more books in the novel or novella genre. *The Anna Papers* takes as its start the short story "Anna, Part I" that concluded *Drunk with Love.* Published in 1988, the novel begins with the suicide of 43-year-old Anna Hand, who decides to conclude her life after being diagnosed with cancer. The work deals with the aftermath of her death as family and friends are left to the influence of Anna's legacy; the recollection of her full and joyous, yet unconventional, life. Although the critical reception of the novel was mixed, *The Anna Papers* was praised for both the quality of its prose and the complexity of Gilchrist's fictional characters. Ann Vliet ascribed to its author "a stubborn dedication to the uncovering of human irony, a tendency, despite temptations toward glamour and comfort, to opt for the harder path, often using 'poorly disguised' autobiographical fiction, usually the short story, to dredge up the order in messy human relationships" in a review in the *Washington Post Book World. I Cannot Get You Close Enough,* published in 1991, is a continuation of *The Anna Papers* in the form of three novellas, each taking as its focus one of the characters of the previous book. Ilene Raymond of the *Washington Post Book World* praised the work. "Not since J. D. Salinger's Glass family has a writer lavished so much loving attention on the eccentricities and activities of an extended clan," Raymond commented, adding that the novellas were not "easy tales, but stories rich with acrimony, wisdom, courage and, finally, joy."

Gilchrist explained to Wendy Smith her evolution from short-story writer to novelist in an interview for *Publishers Weekly:* "The thing about the short story form is that in

order to do a good job with it you've got to concentrate on no more than two characters; you've got to pretend that nobody has any children or parents, that only this moment in these two characters" The novel provides her with a larger canvas on which to set forth her fictional world. "I think that in order to serve the vision I currently have of reality, I'm going to have to have at least five or six characters interplaying," she noted. However, Gilchrist has found that the novel format presents its own set of problems. As she told Walker, "You can't go back to the easy fix you learn as a short story writer, where you kill somebody off or get somebody laid to create a climax. What I'm trying to do now is make a study of existence—that's the high ground, but I perceive it as that. I want it to be as true to what I know about human beings as it can be." Commenting on her latest novel, *Net of Jewels,* Gilchrist explained that the more she writes about a character in a short story or a novel, the more she discovers about that character. She decided to "serve that knowledge" in *Net of Jewels,* an account of character Rhoda Manning's emotional growth in college and beyond, as her young protagonist becomes involved with a succession of other characters through situations that influence her, sometimes indulge her innate willfulness, and shape her personality. "This is the difference between writing novels and writing short stories," commented Gilchrist, "there aren't any tricks."

In 1987 Gilchrist published *Falling through Space,* a collection of brief journal excerpts. Originally intended as segments of her National Public Radio commentary, the book's segments reflect the life of a working writer. "I write to learn and to amuse myself and out of joy and because of mystery and in praise of everything that moves, breathes, gives, partakes, is," Gilchrist once told *CA.* "I like the feel of words in my mouth and the sound of them in my ears and the creation of them with my hands. If that sounds like a lot of talk, it is. What are we doing here anyway, all made out of stars and talking about everything and telling everything? The more one writes the clearer it all becomes and the simpler and more divine. A friend once wrote to me and ended the letter by saying: 'Dance in the fullness of time.' I write that in the books I sign. It may be all anyone needs to read."

Critics have repeatedly praised Gilchrist for her subtle perception, unique characters, and sure command of her writer's voice. Yardley remarked of *In the Land of Dreamy Dreams,* "Certainly it is easy to see why reviewers and readers have responded so strongly to Gilchrist; she tells home truths in these stories, and she tells them with style." Crace concluded that her "stories are perceptive, her manner is both stylish and idiomatic—a rare and potent combination." Miranda Seymour, reviewing her first short story collection for the London *Times,* noted that

"Gilchrist's stories are elegant little tragedies, memorable and cruel" and compared her writing to that of fellow southerners Carson McCullers and Tennessee Williams in that all three writers share "the curious gift for presenting characters as objects for pity and affection." And Wood observed: "Even the least attractive characters become known to us, and therefore human, because Gilchrist's voice is so sure, her tone so right, her details so apt."

BIOGRAPHICAL/CRITICAL SOURCES:

PERIODICALS

BOOKS

Contemporary Literary Criticism, Gale, Volume 34, 1985, Volume 48, 1988, pp. 114-122.

PERIODICALS

Chicago Tribune, October 14, 1986; October 9, 1987; October 2, 1988, p. 6; October 1, 1989, p. 6.
Harper's, June, 1985.
Listener, January 6, 1983.
Los Angeles Times Book World, September 14, 1986, p. 2; November 27, 1988, p. 8.
Ms., June, 1985.
New Statesman, March 16, 1984.
Newsweek, January 14, 1985; February 18, 1985.
New Yorker, November 19, 1984.
New York Times Book Review, September 23, 1984; October 5, 1986, p. 18; January 3, 1988, p. 19; January 15, 1989, p. 16; October 22, 1989, p. 13; November 4, 1990, pp. 4, 24; October 13, 1991, p. 34; April 12, 1992, p. 18.
Observer, November 24, 1991.
Publishers Weekly, March 2, 1992, pp. 46-47.
Times (London), November 25, 1982; June 7, 1990; November 21, 1991, p. 16.
Times Literary Supplement, October 15, 1982; April 6, 1984; May 24, 1985; March 6, 1987; p. 246; October 27, 1989, p. 1181; November 29, 1991, p. 22; September 7, 1990, p. 956.
Washington Post, September 12, 1984; September 28, 1986, p. 6; December 31, 1987; October 20, 1988; December 15, 1989.
Washington Post Book World, January 24, 1982; March 21, 1982, pp. 4, 13; May 29, 1983; December 31, 1987; December 16, 1990.

*   *   *

GILGUN, John F(rancis)   1935-

PERSONAL: Education: Attended Boston University, 1957; University of Iowa, M.A., 1959, M.F.A., 1970, Ph.D., 1972.

ADDRESSES: Home—P.O. Box 7152, St. Joseph, MO 64507. *Office*—Department of English and Modern Languages, Missouri Western State College, St. Joseph, MO 64507.

CAREER: Missouri Western State College, St. Joseph, professor of English, 1972—.

MEMBER: Modern Language Association of America.

AWARDS, HONORS: Chicago Book Clinic Award, American Institute of Graphic Arts Award, Midwestern Book Award from the University of Kentucky, and the Bumbershoot Award from the Seattle Arts Council, all 1981, all for *Everything That Has Been Shall Be Again; Music I Never Dreamed Of* was nominated for the Lambda Award for "best gay novel of 1990" and the American Library Association Gay and Lesbian Task Force Award; Western States Exhibit Award, for *The Dooley Poems,* 1991.

WRITINGS:

Everything That Has Been Shall Be Again: The Reincarnation Fables of John Gilgun, Bieler Press, 1981.
Music I Never Dreamed Of, Amethyst, 1989.
The Dooley Poems, Robin Price, 1991.
From the Inside Out, Three Phase, 1991.

BIOGRAPHICAL/CRITICAL SOURCES:

PERIODICALS

Bookways, fall, 1992.
Come-All-Ye, winter, 1984, p. 7.
Fine Print, July, 1982, p. 98.
James White Review, winter, 1991.
Lambda Book Report, August, 90, p. 24.
Librarian's Browser, fall 1982, p. 7.
Library Journal, December 15, 1982, p. 2305.
Remark, spring, 1992.

*   *   *

GINSBERG, Allen   1926-

PERSONAL: Born June 3, 1926, in Newark, NJ; son of Louis (a poet and teacher) and Naomi (Levy) Ginsberg. *Education:* Columbia University, A.B., 1948. *Politics:* "Space Age Anarchist." *Religion:* "Buddhist-Jewish."

ADDRESSES: Home—P. O. Box 582, Stuyvesant Station, New York, NY 10009.

CAREER: Poet. Brooklyn Naval Yard, Brooklyn, NY, spot welder, 1945; Bickford's Cafeteria, New York City, dishwasher, 1945; worked on various cargo ships, 1945-56; literary agent, reporter for New Jersey union newspaper, and copy boy for *New York World Telegram,*

1946; May Co., Denver, CO, night porter, 1946; *Newsweek*, New York City, book reviewer, 1950; market research consultant in New York City and San Francisco, CA, 1951-53; University of British Columbia, Vancouver, instructor, 1963; founder and treasurer, Committee on Poetry Foundation, 1966—; organizer, Gathering of the Tribes for a Human Be-In, San Francisco, 1967; Jack Kerouac School of Disembodied Poetics, Naropa Institute, Boulder, CO, co-founder, co-director, and teacher, 1974-83, director emeritus, 1983—; Brooklyn College, Brooklyn, NY, distinguished professor, 1986—. Resident Lecturer, Virginia Military Institute, 1991. Has given numerous poetry readings at universities, coffee houses, and art galleries in the United States, England, Russia, India, Peru, Chile, Poland, and Czechoslovakia; has addressed numerous conferences, including Group Advancement Psychiatry Conference, 1961, Dialectics of Liberation Conference, 1967, LSD Decade Conference, 1977, and World Conference on Humanity, 1979; has appeared in numerous films, including *Pull My Daisy*, 1960, *Guns of the Trees*, 1962, *Couch*, 1964, *Wholly Communion*, 1965, *Allen for Allen*, 1965, *U.S.A. Poetry: Allen Ginsberg and Lawrence Ferlinghetti* (TV film), 1966, *Joan of Arc*, 1966, *Galaxie*, 1966, *Herostratus*, 1967, *The Mind Alchemists*, 1967, *Chappaqua*, 1967, *Don't Look Back*, 1967, (narrator) *Kaddish* (TV film), 1977, *Renaldo and Clara*, 1978, *Fried Shoes, Cooked Diamonds*, 1978, and *This Is for You, Jack*, 1984; one-person exhibitions of photographs throughout the United States, including New York City, Washington, DC, and Boulder CO, and in foreign countries, including Poland, Denmark, Canada, Japan, Germany, France, and Scandinavia; also appears on performance videos and films.

MEMBER: American Institute of Arts and Letters, PEN (vice-president of American chapter, 1987-88), New York Eternal Committee for Conservation of Freedom in the Arts, Modern Language Association of America (honorary member).

AWARDS, HONORS: Received Woodbury Poetry Prize; Guggenheim fellow, 1963-64; National Endowment for the Arts grant, 1966; National Institute of Arts and Letters award, 1969; National Book Award for Poetry, 1974, for *The Fall of America;* National Arts Club Medal of Honor for Literature, 1979; *Los Angeles Times* Book Prize for poetry, 1982, for *Plutonian Ode and Other Poems, 1977-1980;* National Endowment for the Arts fellowship, 1986; Golden Wreath Prize, 1986; Poetry Society of America gold medal, 1986; Manhattan Borough President Dinkens' Award for Arts Excellence, 1989; Lifetime Achievement Award, Before Columbus Foundation, 1990; Harriet Monroe Poetry Award, University of Chicago, 1991; Chevalier de l'Ordre des Artes et des Lettres,

1992; fellow, American Academy of Arts and Sciences, 1992.

WRITINGS:

POEMS

Howl and Other Poems, introduction by William Carlos Williams, City Lights, 1956, expanded edition published as *Howl: Original Draft Facsimile, Transcript and Variant Versions, Fully Annotated by Author, with Contemporaneous Correspondence, Account of First Public Reading, Legal Skirmishes, Precursor Texts and Bibliography,* edited by Barry Miles, Harper, 1986.

Siesta in Xbalba and Return to the States, privately printed, 1956.

Kaddish and Other Poems, 1958-1960 (also see below), City Lights, 1961.

Empty Mirror: Early Poems, Corinth Books, 1961, new edition, 1970.

A Strange New Cottage in Berkeley, Grabhorn Press, 1963.

Reality Sandwiches: 1953-1960, City Lights, 1963.

The Change, Writer's Forum, 1963.

Kral Majales (title means "King of May"), Oyez, 1965.

Wichita Vortex Sutra, Housmans, 1966, Coyote Books, 1967.

TV Baby Poems, Cape Golliard Press, 1967, Grossman, 1968.

Airplane Dreams: Compositions From Journals, House of Anansi (Toronto), 1968, City Lights, 1969.

(With Alexandra Lawrence) *Ankor Wat,* Fulcrum Press, 1968.

Scrap Leaves, Hasty Scribbles, Poet's Press, 1968.

Wales—A Visitation, July 29, 1967, Cape Golliard Press, 1968, published as *Wales Visitation,* Five Seasons Press, 1979.

The Heart Is a Clock, Gallery Upstairs Press, 1968.

Message II, Gallery Upstairs Press, 1968.

Planet News, City Lights, 1968.

For the Soul of the Planet Is Wakening . . . . , Desert Review Press, 1970.

The Moments Return: A Poem, Grabhorn-Hoyem, 1970.

Ginsberg's Improvised Poetics, edited by Mark Robison, Anonym Books, 1971.

New Year Blues, Phoenix Book Shop, 1972.

Open Head, Sun Books (Melbourne), 1972.

Bixby Canyon Ocean Path Word Breeze, Gotham Book Mart, 1972.

Iron Horse, Coach House Press, 1972, City Lights, 1974.

The Fall of America: Poems of These States, 1965-1971, City Lights, 1973.

The Gates of Wrath: Rhymed Poems, 1948-1952, Grey Fox, 1973.

Sad Dust Glories: Poems during Work Summer in Woods, 1974, Workingman's Press, 1975.

First Blues: Rags, Ballads, and Harmonium Songs, 1971-1974, Full Court Press, 1975.

Mind Breaths: Poems, 1972-1977, City Lights, 1978.

Poems All Over the Place: Mostly Seventies, Cherry Valley, 1978.

Mostly Sitting Haiku, From Here Press, 1978, revised and expanded edition, 1979.

Careless Love: Two Rhymes, Red Ozier Press, 1978.

(With Peter Orlovsky) *Straight Hearts' Delight: Love Poems and Selected Letters,* edited by Winston Leyland, Gay Sunshine Press, 1980.

Plutonian Ode and Other Poems, 1977-1980, City Lights, 1982.

Collected Poems, 1947-1980, Harper, 1984.

Many Loves, Pequod Press, 1984.

Old Love Story, Lospecchio Press, 1986.

White Shroud: Poems, 1980-1985, Harper, 1986.

Snapshot Poetics, Chronicle Press, 1993.

OTHER

(Author of introduction) Gregory Corso, *Gasoline* (poems), City Lights, 1958.

(With William Burroughs) *The Yage Letters* (correspondence), City Lights, 1963.

(Contributor) David Solomon, editor, *The Marijuana Papers* (essays), Bobbs-Merrill, 1966.

Prose Contribution to Cuban Revolution, Artists Workshop Press (Detroit), 1966.

(Translator with others) Nicanor Parra, *Poems and Antipoems,* New Directions, 1967.

(Contributor) Charles Hollander, editor, *Background Papers on Student Drug Abuse,* U.S. National Student Association, 1967.

(Author of introduction) John A. Wood, *Orbs: A Portfolio of Nine Poems,* Apollyon Press, 1968.

(Contributor) Bob Booker and George Foster, editors, *Pardon Me, Sir, but Is My Eye Hurting Your Elbow?* (plays), Geis, 1968.

(Author of introduction) Louis Ginsberg, *Morning in Spring* (poems), Morrow, 1970.

(Compiler) *Documents on Police Bureaucracy's Conspiracy against Human Rights of Opiate Addicts and Constitutional Rights of Medical Profession Causing Mass Breakdown of Urban Law and Order,* privately printed, 1970.

(Contributor of commentary) Jean Genet, *May Day Speech,* City Lights, 1970.

Indian Journals: March 1962-May 1963; Notebooks, Diary, Blank Pages, Writings, City Lights, 1970.

Notes after an Evening with William Carlos Williams, Portents Press, 1970.

Improvised Poetics, edited by Mark Robison, Anonym Press, 1971.

Declaration of Independence for Dr. Timothy Leary, Hermes Free Press, 1971.

(Author of introduction) William Burroughs, Jr., *Speed* (novel), Sphere Books, 1971.

Kaddish (play; based on poem of same title), first produced at the Brooklyn Academy of Music, February 10, 1972.

(Author of foreword) Ann Charters, *Kerouac* (biography), Straight Arrow Books, 1973.

(Contributor of interview) Donald M. Allen, editor, *Robert Creeley, Contexts of Poetry: Interviews 1961-1971,* Four Seasons Foundation, 1973.

The Fall of America Wins a Prize (text of speech), Gotham Book Mart, 1974.

Gay Sunshine Interview: Allen Ginsberg with Allen Young, Grey Fox, 1974.

The Visions of the Great Rememberer (correspondence), Mulch Press, 1974.

Allen Verbatim: Lectures on Poetry, Politics, and Consciousness, edited by Gordon Ball, McGraw, 1975.

Chicago Trial Testimony, City Lights, 1975.

To Eberhart from Ginsberg: A Letter about Howl, 1956, Penmaen Press, 1976.

The Dream of Tibet (bound with *The Retreat Diaries* by William S. Burroughs), City Moon, 1976.

(With Jack Kerouac) *Take Care of My Ghost, Ghost* (correspondence), Ghost Press, 1977.

Journals: Early Fifties, Early Sixties, edited by Ball, Grove, 1977.

(With others) *Madeira and Toasts for Basil Bunting's 75th Birthday,* edited by Jonathan Williams, Jargon Society, 1977.

(With Neal Cassady and author of afterword) *As Ever: The Collected Correspondence of Allen Ginsberg and Neal Cassady,* Creative Arts, 1977.

(Author of introduction) Anne Waldman and Marilyn Webb, editors, *Talking Poetics from Naropa Institute: Annals of the Jack Kerouac School of Disembodied Poetics,* Volume I, Shambhala, 1978.

Composed on the Tongue: Literary Conversations, 1967-1977, edited by Donald Allen, Grey Fox Press, 1980.

(With others) *Nuke Chronicles,* Contact Two, 1980.

(Author of text) Ann Charters, *Scenes Along the Road: Photographs of the Desolation Angels, 1944-1960,* City Lights, 1984.

(Co-author of text with Pierre Restany) Karel Appel, *Street Art, Ceramics, Sculpture, Wood Reliefs, Tapestries, Murals,* H. J. W. Becht (Amsterdam), 1985.

Allen Ginsberg and Robert Frank (photographs), Galerie Watari (Tokyo), 1985.

Allen Ginsberg, Fotografier, 1947-87, Forlaget Klim (Arhus, Denmark), 1987.

Your Reason and Blake's System, Hanuman Books, 1989.

The Hydrogen Jukebox (play), music by Philip Glass, first produced in Spoleto, Italy, 1990.

Allen Ginsberg: Photographs, Twelvetrees Press, 1990.

Reality Sandwiches (photographs), Fotografien (Berlin), 1989.

Performer on numerous recordings, including *San Francisco Poets,* Evergreen Records, 1958, *Howl and Other Poems,* Fantasy, 1959, *Kaddish,* Atlantic Verbum, 1966, *William Blake's Songs of Innocence and Experience Tuned by Allen Ginsberg,* Metro-Goldwyn-Mayer, 1970, *Giono Poetry Systems,* G. P. S., 1975-80, *Gate: Two Evenings with Allen Ginsberg,* City Lights, 1980, *Birdbrain,* Wax Trax, 1981, *First Blues,* Hammond, 1983, *Made in Texas,* Paris Records, 1986, and *The Lion for Real,* Great Jones Records, 1989. Work appears in numerous anthologies, including *The Beat Generation and the Angry Young Men,* edited by Gene Feldman and Max Gartenberg, Citadel Press, 1958 (published in England as *Protest,* Panther Books, 1960); and *The New Oxford Book of American Verse,* edited by Richard Ellmann, Oxford University Press, 1976. Contributor of poetry and articles to periodicals, including *Evergreen Review, Journal for the Protection of All Beings, Playboy, New Age, Atlantic, Partisan Review,* and *Times Literary Supplement.* Correspondent, *Evergreen Review,* 1965; former contributing editor, *Black Mountain Review;* former advisory guru, *Marijuana Review.* Collections of Ginsberg's manuscripts are housed at Columbia University and at the Humanities Research Center of the University of Texas, Austin.

SIDELIGHTS: Although an influential figure in contemporary poetry, Allen Ginsberg is also known for his political activities, his outspoken homosexuality, and his interest in the visionary. A leading figure of the Beat movement of the 1950s, Ginsberg also played a part in the hippie and anti-war movements of the 1960s and the anti-nuclear movement of the 1970s. So identified is he with these protest movements that Ginsberg is perhaps as well known for his political activities as for his poetry. James F. Mresmann writes in his *Out of the Vietnam Vortex: A Study of Poets and Poetry against the War:* "Ginsberg is not a great poet, but he is a great figure in the history of poetry. We do not win from him many new insights or subtle understandings, but we do take from his poetry a simple intensity and a certain freedom."

Ginsberg first came to public attention in 1956 with the publication of *Howl and Other Poems.* "Howl," a long-line poem in the tradition of Walt Whitman, is an outcry of rage and despair against a destructive, abusive society. The poem's raw, honest language and its "Hebraic-Melvillian bardic breath," as Ginsberg calls it, stunned many traditional critics. Filled with flamboyant metaphors, wild indignation, graphic homosexuality, and lists of indictments against society, "Howl" is meant to stun its audience. James Dickey, for instance, refers to "Howl" as "a whipped-up state of excitement" and concludes that "it takes more than this to make poetry. It just does." Critic Walter Sutton dubs "Howl" "a tirade revealing an animus directed outward against those who do not share the poet's social and sexual orientation." Robert Richman, writing in *Commentary,* claims that "Howl" is "a document of social and spiritual liberation. If by liberation one means the willed celebration of depravity, dereliction, and obscenity, the poem certainly qualifies as one of the most liberated in American literature."

Other critics responded more positively to "Howl." Richard Eberhart, for example, calls the poem "a powerful work, cutting through to dynamic meaning. . . . It is a howl against everything in our mechanistic civilization which kills the spirit. . . . Its positive force and energy come from a redemptive quality of love." Paul Carroll judges it "one of the milestones of the generation." Appraising the impact of "Howl," Paul Zweig notes that it "almost singlehandedly dislocated the traditionalist poetry of the 1950's." Reed Whittemore, although noting that "Howl" is one of "a small number of earth-moving angry poems of this century, poems that poets (and people) who come after have been unable to ignore," nonetheless believes it to be "a sort of natural disaster" for American poetry. "Rightly or wrongly," he states, " 'Howl' knocked hell out of earlier images of what best minds say and do."

Ginsberg introduced "Howl" at a poetry reading, his first, at the Six Gallery in San Francisco in October of 1955. Following readings by five other San Francisco poets, Ginsberg read his new poem to a capacity audience. Reaction was immediate and enthusiastic. Inspired by the poem's reception, Martha Rexroth, poet Kenneth Rexroth's wife, assembled Ginsberg's available poems into a mimeographed edition of about fifty copies and gave them away to friends. By October of 1956, Lawrence Ferlinghetti of the City Lights Bookstore took this mimeograph edition of *Howl* and published it as number four in his new series of paperback poetry collections.

In addition to stunning many critics, *Howl* also stunned the San Francisco Police Department. Because of the graphic sexual language of the poem, particularly Ginsberg's blatant lines about homosexual oral and anal sex, they declared the book obscene and arrested Ferlinghetti. The ensuing trial attracted national attention as such prominent literary figures as Mark Schorer, Kenneth Rexroth, and Walter Van Tilberg Clark spoke in defense of the poem. Schorer testified that "Ginsberg uses the rhythms of ordinary speech and also the diction of ordinary speech. I would say the poem uses necessarily the language of vulgarity." Clark called *Howl* "the work of a thoroughly honest poet, who is also a highly competent technician." The testimony eventually persuaded Judge Clayton W. Horn to rule that *Howl* was not obscene.

Howl became the manifesto of the Beat literary movement, a small group of poets and novelists who wrote in the language of the street about previously forbidden and unliterary topics. Novelist Jack Kerouac coined the term "beat," using the word to signify a group of writers who were tired and worn-out by the increasingly centralized and bureaucratized American society of the 1940s and 1950s. He also coined the phrase "the Beat generation," an echo of Gertrude Stein's "lost generation," which described the expatriate writers of the 1920s. Ginsberg and such poets as Gregory Corso, Michael McClure, and Gary Snyder were prominent figures among the Beats.

In 1961, Ginsberg published *Kaddish and Other Poems.* "Kaddish," a poem similar in style and form to "Howl," is based on the traditional Hebrew prayer for the dead and tells the life story of Ginsberg's mother, Naomi. A lifelong Communist, Naomi suffered from severe paranoia and was eventually put into an asylum. "Kaddish" tells of Ginsberg's mixed feelings for this woman whom he loved even while she caused him so much anguish. Partly because of this personal theme, "Kaddish" is considered to be one of Ginsberg's better poems. Using and expanding upon the long lines of the earlier "Howl," "Kaddish" also includes prose sections and verse which accurately capture the poet's thought processes. "The whole of [part IV of 'Kaddish'] was composed under various hallucinogenic drugs—amphetamine injections, morphine, and dexadrine," as Paul Christensen states in the *Dictionary of Literary Biography.* Thomas F. Merrill dubs it "Ginsberg at his purest and perhaps at his best." Helen Vendler considers "Kaddish" Ginsberg's "great elegy for his mother." Louis Simpson simply refers to it as "a masterpiece."

Ginsberg's early poems were greatly influenced by fellow Paterson, New Jersey, resident William Carlos Williams. Ginsberg recalls being taught at school that Williams "was some kind of awkward crude provincial from New Jersey," but upon talking to Williams about his poetry, Ginsberg "suddenly realized [that Williams] was hearing with raw ears. The sound, pure sound and rhythm—as it was spoken around him, and he was trying to adapt his poetry rhythms out of the actual talk-rhythms he heard rather than metronome or sing-song archaic literary rhythms." Ginsberg acted immediately on his sudden understanding. "I went over my prose writings," he told an interviewer, "and I took out little four-or-five line fragments that were absolutely accurate to somebody's speak-talk-thinking and rearranged them in lines, according to the breath, according to how you'd break it up if you were actually to talk it out, and then I sent 'em over to Williams. He sent me back a note, almost immediately, and he said 'These are it! Do you have any more of these?' "

Another major influence was Ginsberg's friend Jack Kerouac, who wrote novels in a "spontaneous" style that Ginsberg admired and adapted in his own work. Kerouac had written some of his books by putting a roll of white paper into a typewriter and typing continuously in a "stream of consciousness" until the manuscript was completed. This spontaneity, a faith that the first word that comes to the writer will be the best possible to use, inspired Ginsberg. He began writing poems not, as he states, "by working on it in little pieces and fragments from different times, but remembering an idea in my head and writing it down on the spot and completing it there."

Both Williams and Kerouac also emphasized that a writer's emotions and natural mode of expression took precedence over traditional literary structures. Ginsberg has cited as historical precedents for this idea the works of poet Walt Whitman, novelist Herman Melville, and writers Henry David Thoreau and Ralph Waldo Emerson.

Yet another influence on Ginsberg's poetry has been the work of the nineteenth-century poet William Blake. His interest in the poet stems back to a series of visions he had while reading Blake's poetry. After finishing the poem "Ah! Sunflower," Ginsberg recalls hearing "a very deep earthen grave voice in the room, which I immediately assumed, I didn't think twice, was Blake's voice . . . the peculiar quality of the voice was something unforgettable because it was like God had a human voice, with all the infinite tenderness and anciency and mortal gravity of a living Creator speaking to his son." On several other occasions during the next few weeks, Blake's voice returned to speak to Ginsberg. These visits figure large in Ginsberg's development as a poet. From this time on, he saw himself as a poet of the visionary, one whose poems were prophetic orations.

Ginsberg's interest in the mystical, and his adoption of the role of prophetic poet, led him to experiments with various drugs like marijuana and Benzedrine for the mystical insights they seemed to provide. He has said that some of his best poetry was written under the influence of drugs: the second part of "Howl" with peyote, "Kaddish" with amphetamines, "I Hate America" with heroin, "On Neal's Ashes" with morphine and marijuana, "Denver Doldrums" with Benzedrine, and "Wales—A Visitation" with LSD. After a trip to India in 1962, however, during which he was introduced to meditation and yoga, Ginsberg changed his mind about drugs. He has since maintained that meditation and yoga are far superior to drugs in raising one's consciousness, although he still believes that psychedelics could prove helpful in writing poetry. Psychedelics, he has said, are "a variant of yoga and [the] exploration of consciousness."

Ginsberg's study of Eastern religions was spurred by his discovery of mantras, rhythmic chants used for spiritual effects. Their use of rhythm, breath, and elemental sounds seemed to him a kind of poetry. In a number of poems, he has incorporated mantras into the body of the text, transforming the work into a kind of poetic prayer. During poetry readings, he often begins by chanting a mantra in order to set the proper mood. Eastern mantras are similar, Ginsberg believes, to the long-line poetry of Whitman and Williams, both forms showing the same awareness of the poet's breath. When speaking to Kenneth Koch in the *New York Times Book Review,* Ginsberg explained that he liked best the "cranky music" of his poetry, it's "vowelic melodiousness, adjusted towards speech syncopation."

Ginsberg's interest in Eastern religions eventually led him to the Venerable Chogyam Trungpa, Rinpoche, a Buddhist abbot from Tibet who has had a strong influence on Ginsberg's writing. The early seventies found Ginsberg taking classes at Trungpa's Naropa Institute in Colorado as well as teaching poetry classes there. In 1972, Ginsberg took the Refuge and Boddhisattva vows, formally committing himself to the Buddhist faith.

A primary aspect of Trungpa's teaching is a form of meditation called shamatha in which one concentrates on one's own breathing. This meditation, Ginsberg says, "leads first to a calming of the mind, to a quieting of the mechanical production of fantasy and thought-forms; it leads to sharpened awareness of them and to taking an inventory of them." Ginsberg's book *Mind Breaths,* dedicated to Trungpa, contains several poems written with the help of shamatha meditation.

In 1974, Ginsberg and poet Anne Waldman co-founded the Jack Kerouac School of Disembodied Poetics as a branch of Trungpa's Naropa Institute. "The ultimate idea is to found a permanent arts college," Ginsberg says of the school, "sort of like they have in Tibetan tradition where you have teachers and students living together in a permanent building which would go on for hundreds of years. Sort of a center where you'd have a poet old enough to really be a teacher or guru poet." Ginsberg has attracted such prominent writers as Diane di Prima, Ron Padgett, and William Burroughs to speak and teach at the school. "Trungpa wants the presence of poets at Naropa," Ginsberg has said, "to inspire the Buddhists towards becoming articulate, and he also sees the advantage of having the large scale Buddhist background to inspire the poets to silence; to the appreciation of silent space in meditation and breath."

One poet who was drawn to the Naropa Institute was W. S. Merwin. In 1975, during a drunken Halloween party at the Institute, Merwin and a woman companion who refused to join the festivities were forcibly dragged from their room by Trungpa's guards. Merwin defended himself with a broken beer bottle. When finally subdued, the couple were brought before a group of one hundred Trungpa followers and forced to strip. "The Wisdom of the East was being unveiled," Ginsberg later said of the incident, "and [Merwin's companion]'s going, 'Call the police!' I mean, shit! F--- that shit! Strip 'em naked, break down the door!"

Relating his poetry to his interest in the spiritual, Ginsberg once said: "Writing poetry is a form of discovering who I am, and getting beyond who I am to free awakeness of consciousness, to a self that isn't who I am. It's a form of discovering my own nature, and my own identity, or my own ego, or outlining my own ego, and also seeing what part of me is beyond that."

A major theme in Ginsberg's poetry has been his politics. Kenneth Rexroth calls this aspect of Ginsberg' work "an almost perfect fulfillment of the long, Whitman, Populist, social revolutionary tradition in American poetry." In a number of poems, Ginsberg refers to the union struggles of the 1930's, popular radical figures, the McCarthy red hunts, and other leftist touchstones. In "Wichita Vortex Sutra," Ginsberg attempts to end the Vietnam War through a kind of magical, poetic evocation. In "Plutonian Ode," he attempts a similar feat—this time ending the dangers of nuclear power through the magic of a poet's breath. Many other poems are condemnations of American consumerism, its military, its middle class, and its system of government. As Bruce Bawer notes in the *New Criterion,* "Television and Nazi gas chambers, the mass media and Stalin's gulags: to Ginsberg, as far as one can tell, they are all equally horrible. He makes no distinctions at all—he is just *against, against, against*—and this is a significant failing, for perceptive, sensitive distinctions are the basis of all intelligent discourse and all worthwhile art." Other poems, such as "Howl," although not expressly political in nature, are nonetheless considered by many critics to contain strong social criticism.

Ginsberg's political activities have revolved around the various protest movements of the past thirty years. In the mid-sixties, he became publicly associated with the hippie and antiwar movements. He created and advocated "flower power," a strategy in which antiwar demonstrators would promote positive values like peace and love to dramatize their opposition to the death and destruction caused by the Vietnam War. The use of flowers, bells, smiles, and mantras (sacred chants) became common among demonstrators for some time. In 1967, Ginsberg was an organizer of the "Gathering of the Tribes for a Human Be-In," an event modeled after the Hindu mela, a religious festival. It was the first of the hippie festivals and served as an inspiration for hundreds of others. In 1969, when some antiwar activists staged an "exorcism of the Pentagon," Ginsberg composed the mantra they chanted. He testified for the defense in the Chicago 7 Conspiracy Trial in which antiwar activists were charged with "conspiracy to cross state lines to promote a riot."

Sometimes, Ginsberg's politics ran afoul of the authorities. He was arrested at an antiwar demonstration in New York City in 1967 and teargassed at the Democratic National Convention in Chicago in 1968. In 1972, he was jailed for demonstrating against President Richard Nixon at the Republican National Convention in Miami. In 1978, he and longtime companion Peter Orlovsky were arrested for sitting on train tracks in order to stop a trainload of radioactive waste coming from the Rocky Flats Nuclear Weapons Plant in Colorado.

Ginsberg's political activities have caused him problems in other countries as well. In 1965, he visited Cuba as a correspondent for *Evergreen Review*. After he complained about the treatment of gays at the University of Havana, the government asked Ginsberg to leave the country. In the same year, Ginsberg traveled to Czechoslovakia where he was elected "King of May" by thousands of Czech citizens. The next day, the Czech government requested that he leave, ostensibly because he was "sloppy and degenerate." Ginsberg attributes his expulsion to the Czech secret police who were embarrassed by the acclaim given to "a bearded American fairy dope poet." In 1990 Ginsberg visited post-communist Czechoslovakia, was greeted by President Havel, and recrowned King of May.

Ginsberg has lived a kind of literary "rags to riches"—from his early days as the feared, criticized, and "dirty" poet to his present position within what Richard Kostelanetz calls "the pantheon of American literature." Richman notes "the passage of Allen Ginsberg, radical scourge, hero of the counterculture, mystic, now the proud holder of a six-figure book deal and seemingly irrevocable status as a major American poet." Writing in the *Village Voice,* Ken Tucker claims that "Ginsberg may be the most uneven of great modern poets, given to garrulousness and cathartic rants, but he has no equal for narrative drive and emotional power—even when he's acting the addled asshole, his babble is frothy, compelling stuff." Paul Carroll has even speculated that Ginsberg "may become the first American poet to win the Nobel Prize."

But not all critics are so certain of Ginsberg's achievement. Bawer notes a strong Ginsberg influence on other writers. Ginsberg, he states, "has been the model for countless aspiring writers to whom the distinctive characteristics of a good contemporary poet are his disdain for literary tradition, his refusal (and often inability) to write in conventional forms, his lack of attention to matters of craft, his vulgar exhibitionism, and his preoccupation with knee-jerk political dissent. Ginsberg is, in short, the father

of a generation of Americans to whom 'culture' is a word most often used immediately following the word 'drug'—a generation to whom poetry is something marked not by intelligence, sensitivity, and an imaginatively expressed apperception of natural order, but by incoherent egoism, fashionable anarchistic platitudes, and put-on paranoia. This is the legacy of Allen Ginsberg. . . . It is not a legacy to celebrate."

Christensen explains that Ginsberg's "poetry is calculated to blast the controlling opposition with spell-binding celebrations of personal freedom and spiritual liberty. As might be expected of a large canon of such work," he goes on, "some of it now begins to fade with its fractious rhetoric and its passing topical importance, but there remains an imperishable core of major testaments to the ideals of self-fulfillment and communal well-being that assure Ginsberg his major status among modern writers."

In recent years, Ginsberg has presented himself in a slightly revised light during poetry readings. During a reading in New York City, as William A. Henry III reports in *Time* magazine, "Something has changed. This puckish little figure, this professorial imp with the loony grin, does not sound angry. He is not wailing about the wickedness of his time. He is mocking the past—mocking the angry radicals, mocking the dreamers, mocking the quest for visions. The audience is laughing with him. . . . [Many of the audience members] are reflecting on their own older-but-wiser bemusement about antiwar and anti-Establishment excesses of the 1960s."

How would Ginsberg like to be remembered? "As someone in the tradition of the oldtime American transcendentalist individualism," he has said, "from that old gnostic tradition . . . Thoreau, Emerson, Whitman . . . just carrying it on into the 20th century." Ginsberg told *CA* that among human faults he is most tolerant of anger; in his friends he most appreciates tranquillity and sexual tenderness; his ideal occupation would be "articulating feelings in company"; his favorite authors are William Burroughs, Hubert Selby, Jack Kerouac, and Jean Genet; he would like to die peacefully.

BIOGRAPHICAL/CRITICAL SOURCES:

BOOKS

Bertholf, Robert J. and Annette S. Levitt, editors, *William Blake and the Moderns,* State University of New York Press, 1982.

Breslin, James E. B., *From Modern to Contemporary: American Poetry, 1945-1965,* University of Chicago Press, 1984.

Burroughs, William S., *Letters to Allen Ginsberg, 1953-1957,* Full Court Press, 1982.

Carroll, Paul, *The Poem in Its Skin,* Follett, 1968.

Charters, Ann, *Scenes Along the Road,* Gotham Book Mart, 1971, published as *Scenes Along the Road: Photographs of the Desolation Angels, 1944-1960,* City Lights, 1984.

Charters, Ann, *Kerouac,* Straight Arrow Books, 1973.

Charters, Samuel, *Some Poems/Poets: Studies in American Underground Poetry Since 1945,* Oyez, 1971.

Clark, Thomas, *Writers at Work: The Paris Review Interviews,* third series, Viking, 1967, pp. 279-320.

Concise Dictionary of Literary Biography: 1941-1968, Gale, 1987.

Contemporary Literary Criticism, Gale, Volume 1, 1973, Volume 2, 1974, Volume 3, 1975, Volume 4, 1975, Volume 6, 1976, Volume 13, 1980, Volume 36, 1986, Volume 69, 1992.

Cook, Bruce, *The Beat Generation,* Scribner, 1971.

Davidson, Michael, *The San Francisco Renaissance: Poetics and Community at Mid-Century,* Cambridge University Press, 1989.

Dictionary of Literary Biography, Gale, Volume 5: *American Poets since World War II,* 1980, Volume 16: *The Beats: Literary Bohemians in Postwar America,* 1983.

Dowden, George, *A Bibliography of Works by Allen Ginsberg, October, 1943-July 1, 1967,* City Lights, 1970.

Ehrlich, J. W., editor, *Howl of the Censor,* Nourse Publishing, 1961.

Faas, Ekbert, editor, *Towards a New American Poetics: Essays and Interviews,* Black Sparrow Press, 1978.

Fielder, Leslie A., *Waiting for the End,* Stein & Day, 1964.

Gay Sunshine Interview: Allen Ginsberg with Allen Young, Grey Fox Press, 1974.

Gross, Theodore L., editor, *Representative Men,* Free Press, 1970.

Hyde, Lewis, editor, *On the Poetry of Allen Ginsberg,* University of Michigan Press, 1984.

Kramer, Jane, *Allen Ginsberg in America,* Random House, 1969.

Kraus, Michelle P., *Allen Ginsberg: An Annotated Bibliography, 1969-1977,* Scarecrow, 1980.

Lipton, Lawrence, *The Holy Barbarians,* Messner, 1959.

Lucie-Smith, Edward, *Mystery of the Universe: Notes on an Interview with Allen Ginsberg,* Turret Books, 1965.

McBride, Dick, *Cometh with Clouds (Memory: Allen Ginsberg),* Cherry Valley, 1983.

McNally, Dennis, *Desolate Angel: Jack Kerouac, the Beats, and America,* Random House, 1979.

Merrill, Thomas F., *Allen Ginsberg,* Twayne, 1969.

Mersmann, James F., *Out of the Vietnam Vortex: A Study of Poets and Poetry against the War,* University Press of Kansas, 1974.

Miles, Barry, *Allen Ginsberg: A Biography,* Simon and Schuster, 1989.

Morgan, Bill and Bob Rosenthal, editors, *Best Minds: A Tribute to Allen Ginsberg,* Lospecchio Press, 1986.

Mottram, Eric, *Allen Ginsberg in the Sixties,* Unicorn Bookshop, 1972.

Ossman, David, *The Sullen Art,* Corinth Books, 1963, pp. 87-95.

Packard, William, editor, *The Craft of Poetry: Interviews from the New York Quarterly,* Doubleday, 1974, pp. 53-78.

Parkinson, Thomas F., *A Casebook on the Beats,* Crowell, 1961.

Poetry Criticism, Gale, Volume 4, 1992.

Portuges, Paul, *The Visionary Poetics of Allen Ginsberg,* Ross-Erikson, 1978.

Rather, Lois, *Bohemians to Hippies: Waves of Rebellion,* Rather Press, 1977.

Rexroth, Kenneth, *American Poetry in the Twentieth Century,* Herder, 1971.

Rosenthal, Mocha L., *The Modern Poets: A Critical Introduction,* Oxford University Press, 1960.

Rosenthal, Mocha L., *The New Poets: American and British Poetry since World War II,* Oxford University Press, 1967.

Roszak, Theodore, *The Making of a Counter Culture,* Doubleday, 1969.

Selerie, Gavin, editor, *Allen Ginsberg* (interviews), Binnacle Press, 1980.

Shaw, Robert B., editor, *American Poetry since 1960: Some Critical Perspectives,* Dufour, 1974.

Simpson, Louis, *A Revolution in Taste,* Macmillan, 1978.

Stepanchev, Stephen, *American Poetry since 1945,* Harper, 1965.

Stephenson, Gregory, *The Daybreak Boys: Essays on the Literature of the Beat Generation,* Southern Illinois University Press, 1990.

Sutton, Walter, *American Free Verse: The Modern Revolution in Poetry,* New Directions, 1973.

Tytell, John, *Naked Angels: The Lives and Literature of the Beat Generation,* McGraw, 1976.

Widmer, Kingsley, *The Fifties: Fiction, Poetry, Drama,* Everett/Edwards, 1970.

Woods, Gregory, *Articulate Flesh: Male Homo-Eroticism and Modern Poetry,* Yale University Press, 1987, pp. 195-211.

PERIODICALS

American Poetry Review, September, 1977; September-October, 1982, pp. 10-14, 16-18.

Best Sellers, December 15, 1974.

Black Mountain Review, autumn, 1957.

Book World, May 25, 1969.

Carolina Quarterly, spring-summer, 1975.

Chicago Review, summer, 1975, pp. 27-35.

Commentary, July, 1985, pp. 50-55.

Denver Post, July 20, 1975.

East West Journal, February, 1978.

Encounter, February, 1970.
Esquire, April, 1973.
Evergreen Review, July-August, 1961.
Globe and Mail (Toronto), February 23, 1985.
Harper's, October, 1966.
Hudson Review, autumn, 1973.
Iowa Review, spring, 1977, pp. 82-108.
Journal of Popular Culture, winter, 1969, pp. 391-403.
Library Journal, June 15, 1958.
Life, May 27, 1966.
London Review of Books, November 7, 1985, p. 20; April 23, 1987, p. 22.
Los Angeles Times, May 2, 1983; April 18, 1985; January 28, 1989.
Los Angeles Times Book Review, February 15, 1987, p. 2.
Nation, February 25, 1957; November 11, 1961; March 10, 1969, pp. 311-313; November 12, 1977.
National Observer, December 9, 1968.
National Review, September 12, 1959; March 18, 1988, p. 52.
National Screw, June, 1977.
New Age, April, 1976.
New Criterion, February, 1985, pp. 1-14.
New Republic, July 25, 1970; October 12, 1974; October 22, 1977.
New Times, February 20, 1978.
New Yorker, August 17, 1968; August 24, 1968; May 28, 1979; January 13, 1986, pp. 77-84.
New York Times, February 6, 1972.
New York Times Book Review, September 2, 1956; May 11, 1969; August 31, 1969; April 15, 1973, p. 1; March 2, 1975; October 23, 1977; March 19, 1978; December 30, 1984, p. 5.
New York Times Magazine, July 11, 1965.
North Dakota Quarterly, spring, 1982, pp. 76-80.
Observer, March 15, 1987, p. 26.
Parnassus: Poetry in Review, spring-summer, 1974, pp. 128-135.
Partisan Review, Number 2, 1959; Number 3, 1967; Number 3, 1971; Number 2, 1974.
People, July 3, 1978.
Philadelphia Bulletin, May 19, 1974.
Playboy, April, 1969.
Plays and Players, April, 1972.
Poetry, September, 1957; July, 1969; September, 1969.
Poetry Review, summer, 1968, pp. 116-120.
Prospects: An Annual of American Cultural Studies, Number 2, 1976, pp. 527-567.
Salmagundi, spring-summer, 1973.
San Francisco Oracle, February, 1967.
Saturday Review, October 5, 1957.
Small Press Review, July-August, 1977.
Stand, spring, 1988, p. 73.
Thoth, winter, 1967, pp. 35-44.

Time, February 9, 1959; November 18, 1974; March 5, 1979; December 7, 1981, p. 8.
Times (London), January 9, 1988.
Times Literary Supplement, July 7, 1978; November 12, 1982, p. 1251; May 24, 1985, p. 574.
Tribune Books (Chicago), November 30, 1986, p. 1.
Unmuzzled Ox, Volume III, number 2, 1975.
Village Voice, April 18, 1974; January 29, 1985, pp. 42-43; October 31, 1989, p. 67.
Virginia Quarterly Review, spring, 1987, p. 66.
Washington Post, December 19, 1983; March 17, 1985.
Washington Post Book World, January 13, 1985, p. 1.
World Literature Today, autumn, 1987, p. 630.

* * *

GIOVANNI, Nikki 1943-

PERSONAL: Born Yolande Cornelia Giovanni, Jr., June 7, 1943, in Knoxville, TN; daughter of Jones (a probation officer) and Yolande Cornelia (a social worker; maiden name, Watson) Giovanni; children: Thomas Watson. *Education:* Fisk University, B.A. (with honors), 1967; postgraduate study at University of Pennsylvania and Columbia University.

ADDRESSES: Office—c/o William Morrow Inc., 105 Madison Ave., New York, NY 10016.

CAREER: Poet, writer, lecturer. Queens College, City University of New York, Flushing, NY, assistant professor of black studies, 1968-69; Rutgers University, Livingston College, New Brunswick, NJ, associate professor of English, 1969-70; Ohio State University, visiting professor of English, 1984; College of Mount St. Joseph, professor of creative writing, 1985-87; Virginia Polytechnic Institute and State University, Blacksburg, VA, professor of English, 1987—; Texas Christian University, Fort Worth, TX, Honors Week Visiting Professor of Humanities, 1991. Founder of publishing firm, Niktom Ltd., 1970; co-chair of Literary Arts Festival for State of Tennessee Homecoming, 1986; Duncanson Artist-in-Residence, Taft Museum, Cincinnati, OH, 1986; appointed to Ohio Humanities Council, 1987; director of Warm Hearth Writer's Workshop, 1988—; elected to board of directors, Virginia Foundation for the Humanities and Public Policy, 1990-93; participant in Appalachian Community Fund, 1991-93, and Volunteer Action Center, 1991-94; featured poet, International Poetry Festival, Utrecht, Holland, 1991. Has given numerous poetry readings and lectures at universities in the United States and Europe, including the University of Warsaw, Poland; has made numerous television and stage appearances.

MEMBER: National Council of Negro Women, Society of Magazine Writers, National Black Heroines for PUSH,

Winnie Mandela Children's Fund Committee, Delta Sigma Theta (honorary member).

AWARDS, HONORS: Grants from Ford Foundation, 1967, National Endowment for the Arts, 1968, and Harlem Cultural Council, 1969; named one of ten "Most Admired Black Women," *Amsterdam News,* 1969; "Woman of the Year" citation, *Mademoiselle,* 1971; Omega Psi Phi Fraternity Award, 1971, for outstanding contribution to arts and letters; Meritorious Plaque for Service, Cook County Jail, 1971; Prince Matchabelli Sun Shower Award, 1971; life membership and scroll, National Council of Negro Women, 1972; National Association of Radio and Television Announcers award for best spoken word album, 1972, for *Truth Is on Its Way;* Woman of the Year Youth Leadership Award, *Ladies Home Journal,* 1972; National Book Award nomination, 1973, for *Gemini;* "Best Books for Young Adults" citation, American Library Association, 1973, for *My House;* "Woman of the Year" citation, Cincinnati chapter of YWCA, 1983; elected to Ohio Women's Hall of Fame, 1985; "Outstanding Woman of Tennessee" citation, 1985; Post-Corbett Award, 1986; Distinguished Recognition Award, Detroit City Council, 1986; Ohioana Book Award, 1988, for *Sacred Cows . . . and Other Edibles*; Silver Apple Award, Oakland Museum Film Festival, 1988, for *Spirit to Spirit*; "Woman of the Year" citation, Lynchburg, VA, chapter of National Association for the Advancement of Colored People, 1989.

Doctorate of Humanities, Wilberforce University, 1972, and Fisk University; Doctorate of Literature, University of Maryland (Princess Anne Campus), 1974, Ripon University, 1974, Smith College, 1975, and College of Mount St. Joseph, 1983; Doctorate of Humane Letters, Mount St. Mary College and Indiana University. Keys to numerous cities, including Dallas, TX, New York, NY, Cincinnati, OH, Savannah, GA, Miami, FL, New Orleans, LA, and Los Angeles, CA.

WRITINGS:

POETRY

Black Feeling, Black Talk (also see below), Broadside Press, 1968, 3rd edition, 1970.

Black Judgement (also see below), Broadside Press, 1968.

Black Feeling, Black Talk/Black Judgement (contains *Black Feeling, Black Talk* and *Black Judgement*), Morrow, 1970.

Re: Creation, Broadside Press, 1970.

Poem of Angela Yvonne Davis, Afro Arts, 1970.

Spin a Soft Black Song: Poems for Children, illustrated by Charles Bible, Hill & Wang, 1971, illustrated by George Martin, Lawrence Hill, 1985, revised edition, Farrar, Straus, 1987.

My House, foreword by Ida Lewis, Morrow, 1972.

Ego Tripping and Other Poems for Young People, illustrated by George Ford, Lawrence Hill, 1973.

The Women and the Men, Morrow, 1975.

Cotton Candy on a Rainy Day (also see below), introduction by Paula Giddings, Morrow, 1978.

Vacation Time: Poems for Children, illustrated by Marisabina Russo, Morrow, 1980.

Those Who Ride the Night Winds, Morrow, 1983.

NONFICTION

Gemini: An Extended Autobiographical Statement on My First Twenty-five Years of Being a Black Poet, Bobbs-Merrill, 1971.

(With James Baldwin) *A Dialogue: James Baldwin and Nikki Giovanni,* Lippincott, 1973.

(With Margaret Walker) *A Poetic Equation: Conversations Between Nikki Giovanni and Margaret Walker,* Howard University Press, 1974.

(Editor with Jessie Carney Smith) *Images of Blacks in American Culture: A Reference Guide to Information Sources,* Greenwood, 1988.

(Editor with Cathee Dennison) *Appalachian Elders: A Warm Hearth Sampler,* Pocahontas Press, 1991.

Conversations with Nikki Giovanni, edited by Virginia C. Fowler, University Press of Mississippi, 1992.

SOUND RECORDINGS

Truth Is on Its Way, Right-On Records, 1971.

Like A Ripple on a Pond, Niktom, 1973.

The Way I Feel, Atlantic Records, 1974.

Legacies: The Poetry of Nikki Giovanni, Folkways Records, 1976.

The Reason I Like Chocolate, Folkways Records, 1976.

Cotton Candy on a Rainy Day, Folkways Records, 1978.

OTHER

(Editor) *Night Comes Softly: An Anthology of Black Female Voices,* Medic Press, 1970.

(Author of introduction) Adele Sebastian, *Intro to Fine* (poems), Woman in the Moon, 1985.

Sacred Cows . . . and Other Edibles (essays), Morrow, 1988.

Contributor to numerous anthologies. Author of columns "One Woman's Voice," for Anderson-Moberg Syndicate of the *New York Times,* and "The Root of the Matter," for *Encore American and Worldwide News.* Contributor to magazines, including *Black Creation, Black World, Ebony, Essence, Freedom Ways, Journal of Black Poetry, Negro Digest,* and *Umbra.* Editorial consultant, *Encore American and Worldwide News.*

A selection of Giovanni's public papers are held at Mugar Memorial Library of Boston University, Boston, Massachusetts.

ADAPTATIONS: Spirit to Spirit: The Poetry of Nikki Giovanni, featuring the poet reading from her published works, was produced by the Public Broadcasting Corporation, the Corporation for Public Broadcasting, and the Ohio Council on the Arts and first aired in 1986.

SIDELIGHTS: One of the most prominent poets to emerge from the black literary movement of the late 1960s, Nikki Giovanni is famous for strongly voiced poems that testify to her own evolving awareness and experience: as a daughter and young girl, a black woman, a revolutionary in the Civil Rights Movement, and a mother. Popular for her adult poetry and essays as well as her best-selling recordings, Giovanni has also published three books of acclaimed verse for children. As a child, Giovanni gained an intense admiration and appreciation for her race from her outspoken grandmother; other members of her close-knit family influenced her in the oral tradition of poetry. "I come from a long line of storytellers," she once told *CA.* "My grandfather was a Latin scholar and he loved the myths, and my mother is a big romanticist, so we heard a lot of stories growing up. . . . I appreciated the quality and the rhythm of the telling of the stories, and I know when I started to write that I wanted to retain that—I didn't want to become the kind of writer that was stilted or that used language in ways that could not be spoken."

When Giovanni was still young, she moved with her parents from Knoxville, Tennessee to a suburb of Cincinnati, Ohio, but remained close to her grandmother and spent several of her teen years with her in Knoxville. In 1960, at the age of seventeen, Giovanni enrolled in Nashville's all-black Fisk University, but eventually came into conflict with the school's dean of women and was asked to leave. She returned to Fisk in 1964, however, and became a leader in both political and literary activities. She served as editor of a campus literary magazine, *Elan,* and worked to restore Fisk's chapter of the Student Non-Violent Coordinating Committee (SNCC) at a time when the organization was pressing the concept of "black power" to bring about social and economic reform. In 1967, Giovanni graduated with an honors degree in history. As a teenager, Giovanni had been conservative in her outlook—a supporter of Republican presidential candidate Barry Goldwater and a follower of author Ayn Rand, famous for her philosophy of objectivism. In college, however, a roommate named Bertha succeeded in persuading Giovanni to adopt her revolutionary ideals. "Before I met [Bertha] I was Ayn Rand-Barry Goldwater all the way," Giovanni remarked in *Gemini: An Extended Autobiographical Statement on My First Twenty-five Years of Being a Black Poet.* "Bertha kept asking, how could Black people be conservative? What have they got to conserve? And after awhile (realizing that I had absolutely nothing, period) I came around."

Giovanni's first three books of poetry—*Black Feeling, Black Talk; Black Judgment;* and *Re: Creation*—display a strong black perspective as she recounts her growing political awareness. These early books quickly established Giovanni as a prominent new voice in black poetry; they sold numerous copies and she became an increasingly popular figure on the reading and speaking circuit. In *Dictionary of Literary Biography,* Mozella G. Mitchell described these poems, published between 1968 and 1970, as "a kind of ritualistic exorcism of former nonblack ways of thinking and an immersion in blackness. Not only are they directed at other black people whom [Giovanni] wanted to awaken to the beauty of blackness, but also at herself as a means of saturating her own consciousness." This poetic "immersion in blackness" becomes evident, Mitchell feels, in the "daring questions, interspersed with ironic allusions to violent actions blacks have committed for the nation against their own color across the world." Giovanni's vision, however, "goes beyond . . . violent change to a vision of rebuilding."

Critical reaction to Giovanni's early volumes centered upon her more revolutionary poems. "Nikki writes about the familiar: what she knows, sees, experiences," Don L. Lee observed in *Dynamite Voices I: Black Poets of the 1960s.* "It is clear why she conveys such urgency in expressing the need for Black awareness, unity, solidarity. . . . What is perhaps more important is that when the Black poet chooses to serve as political seer, he must display a keen sophistication. Sometimes Nikki oversimplifies and therefore sounds rather naive politically." Similarly, Mitchell remarked, "In this early stage of her commitment of her talent to the service of the black revolution, her creativity is bound by a great deal of narrowness and partiality from which her later work is freed." *Dictionary of Literary Biography* contributor Alex Batman recognized Giovanni's indebtedness to oral tradition. "The poems . . . reflect elements of black culture, particularly the lyrics of rhythm-and-blues music," Batman wrote. "Indeed the rhythms of her verse correspond so directly to the syncopations of black music that her poems begin to show a potential for becoming songs without accompaniment." Lee commented, "Nikki is at her best in the short, personal poem. . . . Her effectiveness is in the area of the 'fast rap.' She says the right thing at the right time." Batman concluded that in reaching to create "a blues without music," Giovanni "repeats the worst mistake of the songwriter—the use of language that has little appeal of its own in order to meet the demands of the rhythm."

Critical reservations notwithstanding, Giovanni's earliest works were enormously successful, given the relatively low public demand for modern poetry. In a *Mademoiselle* article, Sheila Weller noted that *Black Judgement* sold six thousand copies in three months, making that volume five to six times more sellable than the average. Mitchell suggested that Giovanni's poems of that period brought her prominence "as one of the three leading figures of the new black poetry between 1968 and 1971."

In 1969 Giovanni took a teaching position at Rutgers University and that summer gave birth to her son, Thomas. She explained her choice in *Ebony:* "I had a baby at 25 because I *wanted* to have a baby and I could *afford* to have a baby. I did not get married because I didn't *want* to get married and I could *afford* not to get married." The author's work through the mid-1970s reflected her changing priorities after her son's birth. She remarked to *Harper's Bazaar,* "To protect Tommy there is no question I would give my life. I just cannot imagine living without him. But I can live without the revolution." Describing this period in Giovanni's career, during which she produced a collection of autobiographical essays, two books of poetry for children, and two poetry collections for adults, Mitchell wrote, "We see evidence of a more developed individualism and greater introspection, and a sharpening of her creative and moral powers, as well as of her social and political focus and understanding." Reflecting on *The Women and the Men,* published in 1975, Batman noted, "The revolution is fading from the new poems, and in its place is a growing sense of frustration and a greater concern with the nature of poetry itself. Throughout these poems is a feeling of energy reaching out toward an object that remains perpetually beyond the grasp."

The themes of family love, loneliness, frustration, and introspection explored in Giovanni's earlier works find further expression in *My House* and *The Women and the Men.* In the foreword to *My House,* Ida Lewis described the key to understanding the poet's conviction: "The central core [of Giovanni's work] is always associated with her family: the family that produced her and the family she is producing. She has reached a simple philosophy more or less to the effect that a good family spirit is what produces healthy communities, which is what should produce a strong (Black) nation." Mitchell discussed *The Women and the Men* with emphasis upon Giovanni's heightened sense of self: "In this collection of poems, . . . she has permitted to flower fully portions of herself and her perception which have been evident only in subdued form or in incompletely worked-through fragments. Ideas concerning women and men, universal human relatedness, and the art of poetry are seen here as being in the process of fuller realization in the psyche of the author." Noting the aspects of personal discovery in *My House,* critic John W. Connor suggested in the *English Journal* that Giovanni "sees her world as an extension of herself . . . sees

problems in the world as an extension of her problems, and . . . sees herself existing amidst tensions, heartache, and marvelous expressions of love. . . . When a reader enters *My House,* he is invited to savor the poet's ideas about a meaningful existence in today's world." "*My House* is not just poems," Kalumu Ya Salaam commented in *Black World.* "*My House* is how it is, what it is to be a young, single, intelligent Black woman with a son and no man. Is what it is to be a woman who has failed and is now sentimental about some things, bitter about some things, and generally always frustrated, always feeling frustrated on one of various levels or another."

Concurrent with her poetry for adults, Giovanni has published three volumes of poetry for children, *Spin a Soft Black Song, Ego-Tripping and Other Poems for Young People,* and *Vacation Time.* According to Mitchell, the children's poems have "essentially the same impulse" as Giovanni's adult poetry; namely, "the creation of racial pride and the communication of individual love. These are the goals of all of Giovanni's poetry, here directed toward a younger and more impressionable audience." In a *New York Times Book Review* article on *Spin a Soft Black Song,* Nancy Klein noted, "Nikki Giovanni's poems for children, like her adult works, exhibit a combination of casual energy and sudden wit. No cheek-pinching auntie, she explores the contours of childhood with honest affection, sidestepping both nostalgia and condescension." A *Kirkus Reviews* contributor, commenting on *Ego-Tripping,* claimed: "When [Giovanni] grabs hold . . . it's a rare kid, certainly a rare black kid, who could resist being picked right up." Critics of *Vacation Time* suggested that some of the rhyme is forced or guilty of "an occasional contrivance to achieve scansion," in the words of Zena Sutherland for the *Bulletin of the Center for Children's Books,* but praise is still forthcoming for the theme of Giovanni's verses. "In her singing lines, Giovanni shows she hadn't forgotten childhood adventures in . . . exploring the world with a small person's sense of discovery," wrote a *Publishers Weekly* reviewer. Mitchell, too, claimed: "One may be dazzled by the smooth way [Giovanni] drops all political and personal concerns [in *Vacation Time*] and completely enters the world of the child and brings to it all the fanciful beauty, wonder, and lollipopping."

As early as 1971, Giovanni began to experiment with another medium for presenting her poetry—sound recording. Recalling how her first album, *Truth Is on Its Way,* came to be made, Giovanni told *Ebony:* "Friends had been bugging me about doing a tape but I am not too fond of the spoken word or of my voice, so I hesitated. Finally I decided to try it with gospel music, since I really dig the music." Giovanni also remarked in *Ebony* that she chose gospel music as background for her poetry because she wanted to make something her grandmother would listen to. *Truth Is on Its Way* was the best selling spoken-word album of 1971, contributing greatly to Giovanni's fame nationwide. "I have really been gratified with the response [to the album] of older people, who usually feel that black poets hate them and everything they stood for," Giovanni told *Ebony*. The popularity of *Truth Is on Its Way* encouraged Giovanni to make subsequent recordings of her poetry as well as audio- and videotapes of discussions about poetry and black issues with other prominent poets.

In 1978 Giovanni published *Cotton Candy on a Rainy Day,* which Mitchell described as "perhaps her most sobering book of verse. . . . It contains thoughtful and insightful lyrics on the emotions, fears, insecurities, realities, and responsibilities of living." Mitchell detected a sense of loneliness, boredom, and futility in the work, caused in part by the incompleteness of the black liberation movement. Batman, too, sensed a feeling of despair in the poems: "What distinguishes *Cotton Candy on a Rainy Day* is its poignancy. One feels throughout that here is a child of the 1960s mourning the passing of a decade of conflict, of violence, but most of all, of hope." In her introduction to the volume, Paula Giddings suggested that the emotional complacency of the 1970s is responsible for Giovanni's apparent sense of despondency: "Inevitably, the shining innocence that comes from feeling the ideal is possible is also gone, and one must learn to live with less. . . . The loneliness carries no blame, no bitterness, just the realization of a void. . . . Taken in the context of Nikki's work [*Cotton Candy on a Rainy Day*] completes the circle: of dealing with society, others, and finally oneself."

Those Who Ride the Night Winds, Giovanni's 1983 publication, represents a stylistic departure from her previous works. "In this book Giovanni has adopted a new and innovative form; and the poetry reflects her heightened self-knowledge and imagination," Mitchell commented. The subject matter of *Those Who Ride the Night Winds* tends once more to drift toward a subdued but persistent political activism, as Giovanni dedicates various pieces to Phillis Wheatley, Martin Luther King, Jr., Rosa Parks, and the children of Atlanta, Georgia, who were at the time of the writing living in fear of a serial murderer. Mitchell suggests that the paragraphs punctuated with ellipses characteristic of the volume make the poems "appear to be hot off the mind of the author. . . . In most cases the poems are meditation pieces that begin with some special quality in the life of the subject, and with thoughtful, clever, eloquent and delightful words amplify and reconstruct salient features of her or his character." In *Sacred Cows . . . and Other Edibles* Giovanni presents essays on such diverse topics as literary politics, game shows, black political leaders, termites, and national holiday celebrations, and explores them "with humor that is street and worldly wise, and with occasional insights that, in the best

Giovanni style, turn a neat phrase too," Marita Golden remarked in *Washington Post Book World.* Golden described the collection as "quintessential Nikki Giovanni—sometimes funny, nervy and unnerving with flashes of wisdom." *Library Journal* reviewer Nancy R. Ives found *Sacred Cows* "both amusing and enlightening" and "a joy to read."

Over the years Giovanni's work has evolved from the "open, aggressive, and explosive revolutionary tendencies that characterized her early verses" to "expressions of universal sensitivity, artistic beauty, tenderness, warmth, and depth," Mitchell wrote. She further noted that Giovanni has a deep concern "about her own identity as a person . . . and what her purpose in life should be." As Giddings noted in the introduction to *Cotton Candy on a Rainy Day,* "Nikki Giovanni is a witness. Her intelligent eye has caught the experience of a generation and dutifully recorded it. She has seen enough heroes, broken spirits, ironies, heartless minds and mindless hearts to fill several lifetimes." Giddings concluded, "I have never known anyone who cares so much and so intensely about the things she sees around her as Nikki. That speaks to her humanity and to her writing. Through the passion and the cynicism of the last two decades she has cared too much to have either a heartless mind or, just as importantly, a mindless heart."

BIOGRAPHICAL/CRITICAL SOURCES:

BOOKS

Authors in the News, Volume 1, Gale, 1976.
Children's Literature Review, Volume 6, Gale, 1984.
Contemporary Literary Criticism, Gale, Volume 2, 1974, Volume 4, 1975, Volume 9, 1981.
A Dialogue: James Baldwin and Nikki Giovanni, Lippincott, 1972.
Dictionary of Literary Biography, Gale, Volume 5: *American Poets Since World War II,* 1980, Volume 41: *Afro-American Poets Since 1955,* 1985.
Evans, Mari, editor, *Black Women Writers, 1950-1980: A Critical Evaluation,* Doubleday, 1984.
Fowler, Virginia C., editor, *Conversations with Nikki Giovanni,* University Press of Mississippi, 1992.
Fowler, Virginia C., editor, *Nikki Giovanni: An Introduction to Her Life and Work,* Macmillan, 1992.
Gibson, Donald B., editor, *Modern Black Poets: A Collection of Critical Essays,* Prentice-Hall, 1973.
Giovanni, Nikki, *Gemini: An Extended Autobiographical Statement on My First Twenty-five Years of Being a Black Poet,* Bobbs-Merrill, 1971.
Giovanni, Nikki, *My House,* foreword by Ida Lewis, Morrow, 1972.
Giovanni, Nikki, *Cotton Candy on a Rainy Day,* introduction by Paula Giddings, Morrow, 1978.

Henderson, Stephen, *Understanding the New Black Poetry: Black Speech and Black Music as Poetic References,* Morrow, 1973.

Lee, Don L., *Dynamite Voices I: Black Poets of the 1960s,* Broadside Press, 1971.

Noble, Jeanne, *Beautiful, Also, Are the Souls of My Black Sisters: A History of the Black Woman in America,* Prentice-Hall, 1978.

Tate, Claudia, *Black Women Writers at Work,* Crossroad Publishing, 1983.

PERIODICALS

Best Sellers, September 1, 1973; January, 1976.

Black World, December, 1970; January, 1971; February, 1971; April, 1971; August, 1971; August, 1972; July, 1974.

Bulletin of the Center for Children's Books, October, 1980.

Choice, May, 1972; March, 1973; September, 1974; January, 1976.

Christian Science Monitor, June 4, 1970; June 19, 1974.

CLA Journal, September, 1971.

Ebony, February, 1972; August, 1972.

Encore, spring, 1972.

English Journal, April, 1973; January, 1974.

Essence, August, 1981.

Harper's Bazaar, July, 1972.

Ingenue, February, 1973.

Jet, May 25, 1972.

Kirkus Reviews, January 1, 1974, p. 11.

Library Journal, February 15, 1988, p. 169.

Los Angeles Times, December 4, 1985.

Los Angeles Times Book Review, April 17, 1983.

Mademoiselle, May, 1973; December, 1973; September, 1975.

Milwaukee Journal, November 20, 1974.

New York Times, April 25, 1969; July 26, 1972.

New York Times Book Review, November 7, 1971; November 28, 1971; February 13, 1972; May 5, 1974.

Partisan Review, spring, 1972.

Publishers Weekly, November 13, 1972; May 23, 1980; December 18, 1987, p. 48.

Saturday Review, January 15, 1972.

Time, April 6, 1970; January 17, 1972.

Washington Post, January 30, 1987.

Washington Post Book World, May 19, 1974; March 8, 1981; February 14, 1988, p. 3.

OTHER

The Poet Today (sound recording), The Christophers, 1979.*

—*Sketch by Deborah A. Stanley*

GODWIN, John (Frederick) 1922-
(Frederick Foster)

PERSONAL: Born December 4, 1922, in Hednesford, England; son of Frederick John (a colliery purchases manager) and Grace (Foster) Godwin; married Elizabeth Walsh (a teacher), December 22, 1952; children: Helen Elizabeth, Philip John. *Education:* County of Stafford Training College, teaching certificate, 1946; Leicester College of Education, certificate in education of the handicapped, 1969. *Politics:* Conservative. *Religion:* Church of England. *Avocational interests:* Listening to short-wave radio.

ADDRESSES: Home—Lark Rise, 10 Church Lane, Etching Hill, Rugeley, Staffordshire, England.

CAREER: Midland Bank Ltd., Bloxwich, Hednesford, and Cannock, Staffordshire, England, clerk and cashier, 1940-46; residential school, Rugeley, Staffordshire, assistant teacher, 1948-55; village school, Mawnan, England, headmaster, 1955-58; residential school, Corley, England, deputy headmaster, 1958-61; primary school, Stamford, England, headmaster, 1961-69; St. Michael's Primary School, Lichfield, England, headmaster, 1970-81; writer and broadcaster of radio programs, 1981—. *Military service:* British Army, served in Radio Security Service, 1942-45; received Defence Medal.

MEMBER: National Association of Head Teachers.

WRITINGS:

Battling Parer (aviation history), Angus & Robertson, 1967.

Wings to the Cape (aviation history), Tafelberg Uitgewers Beperk (Cape Town, South Africa), 1970.

Give Your Child a Better Start: Manual of Information for Preschool Education, Cressrelles Publishing, 1973.

Lives to Inspire (religious education textbook), Moorley's Bible and Book Shop, 1978.

More Lives to Inspire, Moorley's Bible and Book Shop, 1980.

Lessons from Life and Legend, Moorley's Bible and Book Shop, 1981.

The Murder of Christina Collins, Staffordshire County Library, 1981, revised and illustrated edition, Godwin, 1990.

Some Staffordshire Characters, Staffordshire Education Committee, 1982.

Beaudesert and the Pagets, Staffordshire County Library, 1982, revised and illustrated edition published as *Beaudesert, the Pagets and Waterloo,* Godwin, 1992.

More Staffordshire Characters, Staffordshire Education Committee, 1983.

Some Notable Eighteenth Century Staffordshire M.P.'s, Staffordshire County Library, 1984.

Early Aeronautics in Staffordshire, Staffordshire County Library, 1986.

Still More Lives to Inspire, Moorley's Bible and Book Shop, 1986.

The Pocket Palmer—The Story of Rugeley's Most Infamous Character, Godwin, 1992.

Tom Coulthwaite, Wizard of the Chase, Godwin, 1993.

Contributor to history, education, and religious journals, including *Christian,* and newspapers; also contributor to *Mother* (magazine) under pseudonym Frederick Foster.

WORK IN PROGRESS: Staffordshire Quiz Book, for Steve Benz Publications; *Medical Personnel of Staffordshire;* research on Staffordshire history.

SIDELIGHTS: John Godwin once told *CA:* "My first and second books are factual accounts of early long-distance flights. 'Battling Parer' was the first man to fly in a single-engined airplane from England to Australia (1920). *Wings to the Cape* is a story of endeavor and adventure as several airplane crews from England tried to be first to reach the Cape of Good Hope (1920).

"Preschool education is the theme of my third book. It was published with a kit of apparatus and is designed to show parents (particularly mothers) how a child can be profitably employed at home in the important formative years before he comes to school.

"My four religious education books are for use in connection with Christian education. I see evidence around me, in many aspects of life, of moral and spiritual decadence while I read of the appalling rise in crime statistics. It seems reasonable to me to suppose that this decadence and the increasing crime figures are connected. In the course of my work as a teacher I see many children and young people who obviously have no standards of thought or of action set before them at home, and I suspect that even at school in some instances the standards set are little better. Many young people (and, indeed, grown ups) seem to be preoccupied much more about their rights rather than about their responsibilities and with what they can grab from life rather than with what they can give. I feel that adults must accept a large share of the blame for such attitudes in the younger people.

"From what I have seen, I believe that the education of many of our children lacks a spiritual dimension and is concerned exclusively (or nearly so) with material things and material values. Many who leave school find themselves adrift on the ocean of life without a pilot to show them the way. They seem to have little idea of right and wrong. Many are without any real purpose in life and, worst of all, without any hope for the future.

"I feel that children must be given anew a set of permanent, eternal values by which to live. They must be taught that true fulfillment does not come from the acquisition of material things. They must be given an appreciation of the Force which can take command of their lives and make them want to do things for the good of others rather than for themselves. They must be guided to see that in pursuing selflessness they will, not by deliberate searching but incidentally, achieve a happiness which transcends anything that comes from a life of selfseeking.

"What better way is there to teach children to think of others than to give them stories of inspiration of men and women who have given their lives, regardless of cost, to the service of God and their fellow men? Youth is a time when minds can be fired with ideas which can profoundly affect the hearts and minds of the rising generation. It was this consuming desire to give children a glimpse of the eternal that prompted me to write *Lives to Inspire, More Lives to Inspire, Lessons from Life and Legend,* and *Still More Lives to Inspire,* for use at school morning assemblies in schools where Christian teaching is given.

"Several of my publications relate to local history, and I broadcast quite frequently on this subject. To me, the relating of history to the locality brings the subject to life—it becomes no longer a matter of the study of distant people and places, with dull sets of dates to remember. Instead, the subject matter becomes closely related to the area in which the students live. They can see first hand the work of men and women of the past in the history of their area—men and women who have left their distinguishing mark in a particular field of human activity, and even men and women who have lived perfectly ordinary lives, in accordance with the state of knowledge of the age, and the practices of the times."

*   *   *

GOODWIN, Eugene D.
   See KAYE, Marvin (Nathan)

*   *   *

GOODYEAR, John H(enry) III 1941-

PERSONAL: Born February 5, 1941, in Mechanicsburg, PA; son of John H. II (a minister and teacher) and Ruthann (a teacher; maiden name, Stoner) Goodyear; married Carol L. Bistline (a teacher), June, 1964; children: Victoria Ann, John Henry IV, Heather Elizabeth. *Education:* Shippensburg University, B.S., 1963, M.Ed., 1966; Columbia Pacific University, Ph.D., 1985; graduate study at Temple University and Pennsylvania State University; further study at United Christian Bible Institute, 1983-85.

ADDRESSES: Home—21 Wooded Run Dr., Dillsburg, PA 17019-9116. *Office*—Division of Communicative

Arts, Harrisburg Area Community College, 3300 Cameron State Rd., Harrisburg, PA 17110.

CAREER: High school English teacher in Mechanicsburg, PA, 1963-66; Pennsylvania State University, Harrisburg, adjunct instructor, 1965-66, instructor in English, 1966-72, counselor, 1967-73; Harrisburg Area Community College, Harrisburg, associate professor, 1973-77, professor of English, 1977—, currently senior professor of English. Part-time instructor in biblical studies at Bethany Bible Institute, 1979-81.

WRITINGS:

Writings for a Purpose, Kendall/Hunt, 1974.
Theory-Example-Demonstration in Writing for a Purpose, Kendall/Hunt, 1977.
Principles and Practices of Applied Christianity, Plank Press, 1978.
A Writer's Workshop, Kendall/Hunt, 1986, 2nd edition published as *A Writer's Workshop: Individualized, Self-Paced Written Composition,* 1986.
(With Alden) *Intro to College Grammar and Writing Skills,* C.A.T., 1987.

WORK IN PROGRESS: The Principle of Revelation-Revolution-Reward, a booklet.

SIDELIGHTS: John H. Goodyear III once told *CA:* "The central focus of *Principles and Practices of Applied Christianity* centers on the explanation of how selected Old Testament and New Testament characters responded to the call of God the Father, God the Son, and God the Holy Spirit by developing a personal relationship with a living, triune Creator. The Holy Bible gives an elaborate record of human beings who have practiced the principles of fundamental Christian behavior. Specifically, there are three vital principles that function in total symmetry: the principle of promise-condition-choice; the principle of action-reaction-result; and the principle of symmetry and synthesis. Understood and practiced in harmony, these principles provide the basis of a balanced Christian life-style."

*   *   *

GOONERATNE, (Malini) Yasmine 1935-

PERSONAL: Born December 22, 1935, in Colombo, Ceylon (now Sri Lanka); daughter of Samuel James Felix (an estate owner and proprietor) and Esther Mary (Ramkeesoon) Dias Bandaranaike; married Brendon W. M. Gooneratne (a doctor, medical researcher, and university lecturer), December 31, 1962; children: Channa Brendon Randhiren (son), Esther Malathi Devika (daughter). *Education:* University of Ceylon, B.A. (with honors), 1959; Cambridge University, Ph.D., 1962.

ADDRESSES: Office—School of English and Linguistics, Macquarie University, North Ryde, New South Wales 2109, Australia.

CAREER: University of Ceylon, Peradeniya, assistant lecturer, 1962-65, lecturer, 1966-67, senior lecturer in English, 1968-72, acting head of Department of English, 1970-72; Macquarie University, North Ryde, New South Wales, Australia, 1972—, currently professor of English and holder of personal chair, became foundation director of Post-Colonial Literatures and Language Research Centre, 1988—. Visiting fellow of Indiana University's Institute for Advanced Study, Yale University, and Princeton University, all 1984; visiting professor of English, Edith Cowan University, Western Australia, spring, 1991, and University of Michigan, fall, 1991. Professional associate of the East-West Culture Learning Institute, Honolulu; research associate of the Centre for Research in the New Literature in English, Flinders University, Australia. Conductor of seminars and fiction and poetry readings at the Universities of Missouri-Kansas, Guelph, and New Brunswick.

MEMBER: Australian and Pacific Society for Eighteen-Century Studies, Australian Federation of University Women, Australian Association for the Conservation of the Cultural Heritage of Sri Lanka, South Asian Studies Association of Australian, National Trust of Australia, South Pacific Association for Commonwealth Literature and Language Studies, Jane Austen Society of Australia (patron), Macquarie University Staff Association.

AWARDS, HONORS: Senkadalaga Memorial Prize for Poetry, 1953; Pettah Library Prize for English Literature, 1955; Leigh Smith Prize for English Literature, 1958; Leon Foundation grant, University of London, 1968; Mary E. Woolley International Fellow for research in English literature, American Association of University Women, 1968; D.Litt., Macquarie University, 1981; Fulbright Senior Scholar Award, American-Australian Education Foundation, 1984; Order of Australia, 1990, for distinguished service to literature and education.

WRITINGS:

English Literature in Ceylon, 1815-1878: The Development of an Anglo-Ceylonese Literature, Tisara Press, 1968.
Jane Austen, Cambridge University Press, 1970.
(Editor and contributor) *New Ceylon Writing,* [Kandy], 1970.
Word, Bird, Motif (poetry), [Kandy], 1971.
The Lizard's Cry and Other Poems, [Kandy], 1972.
Alexander Pope, Cambridge University Press, 1976.
(Editor) *Stories from Sri Lanka,* Heinemann Educational, 1979.
(Editor) *Poems from India, Sri Lanka, Malaysia, and Singapore,* Heinemann Educational, 1979.

Diverse Inheritance: A Personal Perspective on Common-wealth Literature, Centre for Research in the New Literature in English, 1980.

Jane Austen: Sense and Sensibility, Longman, 1981.

Six-Thousand-Foot Death Dive: Poems, [Colombo], 1981.

Silence, Exile and Cunning: The Fiction of Ruth Prawer Jhabvala, Sangam, 1983, 2nd edition, 1992.

Relative Merits: A Personal View of the Bandaranaike Family of Sri Lanka, Hurst & Co., 1986.

A Change of Skies (novel), Picador Australia, 1991.

Celebrations and Departures, 1951-1991: Selected Poems, Wild and Woolley, 1991.

Contributor to over twenty books, including *The Commonwealth Pen: An Introduction to the Literature of the British Commonwealth,* Cornell University Press, 1961; *Australian Poems in Perspective: A Collection of Poems and Critical Commentaries,* edited by Peter Elkin, University of Queensland Press, 1978; *Essays in Contemporary Post-Colonial Fiction,* edited by Albert Werttheim, Max Hueber Verlag, 1985; and *International Literature in English: The Major Writers,* Gale, 1991.

Contributor of over 200 articles to literary and historical journals, including *Ariel, Cambridge Historical Journal, Journal of South Asian Literature, Ceylon Journal of Historical and Social Studies,* and *English.* Bibliographer for *Journal of Commonwealth Literature,* 1966-78; co-founder and editor of *New Ceylon Writing,* 1970—; member of editorial board of *Ceylon Journal of the Humanities, Ariel, Commonwealth Novel in English, CRNLE Reviews Journal* (Australia), *Kunapipi* (Denmark), *World Literature Written in English,* and *Southern Review* (Australia).

WORK IN PROGRESS: A second novel.

SIDELIGHTS: Yasmine Gooneratne told *CA:* "I have heard many academics who, like myself, are writers as well, wish they had more time to give to their creative work. This has never been my problem. In fact, teaching and research have always dovetailed happily with my writing of poetry (and, occasionally, of fiction). Writing of any kind is for me a kind of delicious self-indulgence—I feel guiltily that I should be doing something else of more obvious use to my family or friends—but the writing of a lecture is for me as enjoyable as writing a story or a poem. I've been extraordinarily lucky in some things—I was born into a very bookish family, and I married someone from whose interest in history I was able to learn a good deal. And then, I come from a country where wit and good writing have always been honoured, Sri Lanka. Moving to Australia in 1972 was not an easy decision to make, but it had to be done if our children were to have an English education. I'm very happy that *New Ceylon Writing,* a literary journal I co-founded in 1970, survived the move to a new country. I think it has done what I hoped it would

do: bring writers together and give them an audience worth having.

"I decided, quite some time ago, that I would never give a lot of time to writing that was second-rate. This decision, which I have been able to sustain, has paid unexpected dividends: a long-established admiration of Alexander Pope's poetry and a study of his techniques served me well when my father died in 1969 and I found myself writing poetry seriously for the first time. And again, my interest in the writing of Ruth Prawer Jhabvala made it easier for me to come to terms with some of the problems of expatriation, which include (for me) writing in and about a new country. I have been thinking I'd like to write a novel, a new form for me. Perhaps the years of enjoyable reading I put in on Jane Austen will be of use to me if I do. I think a writer needs to be able to know the world's best writing intimately—one's own work need never be even remotely like the great models, but the models need to be there."

*   *   *

GOTTSCHALK, Louis A(ugust) 1916-

PERSONAL: Born August 26, 1916, in St. Louis, MO; son of Max W. and Kelmie (Mutrvx) Gottschalk; married Helen Reller (a dermatologist), July 24, 1944; children: Guy, Claire Gottschalk Cable, Louise Gottschalk Clickner, Susan Gottschalk Smith. *Education:* Washington University, St. Louis, B.A., 1940, M.D., 1943; Southern California Psychoanalytic Institute, Ph.D., 1977; additional study at Chicago Institute for Psychoanalysis, 1948-51, and Washington Psychoanalytic Institute, 1952-53.

ADDRESSES: Home—4607 Perham Rd., Corona Del Mar, CA 92625. *Office*—College of Medicine, University of California, Irvine, CA 92717.

CAREER: Barnes & McMillan Hospitals, St. Louis, MO, intern, 1943-44, assistant resident, 1944-45, chief resident in neuropsychiatry, 1945-46; U.S. Public Health Service Hospital, Fort Worth, TX, clinical neuropsychiatrist, 1946-48; Southwestern Medical College, Dallas, TX, instructor in psychiatry, 1947-48; Michael Reese Hospital, Chicago, IL, research associate at Institute of Psychosomatic Research and Training and Child Psychiatry Clinic, 1948-51, assistant chief of Child Psychiatry Clinic, 1950-51; National Institute of Mental Health, Bethesda, MD, research psychiatrist, 1951-53; University of Cincinnati, College of Medicine, Cincinnati, OH, associate professor, 1953-61, research professor of psychiatry, 1961-67; University of California, College of Medicine, Irvine, professor of psychiatry and human behavior, 1967—, founding chairman of department, 1967-77, professor of social science and social ecology, Division of Social Science, 1969—, director of Psychiatric Consultation and Liaison Division, Medical Center, 1978—. Resident scholar, Rockefeller Conference Center, Bellagio, Italy, 1985. Visiting professor at several universities, including Johns Hopkins School of Medicine, Washington University Medical School, Albert Einstein Medical College, University of Pennsylvania, and University of California, Los Angeles; Herbert S. Ripley Lecturer, University of Washington, 1981. Attending physician, Cincinnati General Hospital, 1953-67, and Los Angeles County General Hospital, 1967-68; member of staff, Canyon General Hospital, Anaheim, 1974-79. Training and supervising analyst, Chicago Institute for Psychoanalysis, 1957-67, and Southern California Psychoanalytic Institute, Los Angeles, 1974—; director of psychiatric residency training, Orange County Medical Center, University of California, Irvine, 1967-78. Extramural research review committee chairman, National Institute on Drug Abuse and National Institute of Mental Health; originator and director, Laguna Beach Free Drug Abuse Clinic for Youth, 1968-71; scientific co-director, Alcohol Research Center, 1978—. Chief consultant in psychiatry, Veterans Administration Hospital, Long Beach, 1967-77; consultant to health departments, hospitals, and pharmaceutical companies; member of consultative or advisory committees at the local, state, and national levels. *Military service:* U.S. Public Health Service, 1946-53; became lieutenant commander. U.S. Public Health Service Reserve, medical director, 1979.

MEMBER: International College of Psychosomatic Medicine (fellow), International Psychoanalytical Association, American Psychiatric Association (life fellow), American Psychosomatic Society (member of council, 1967-80), Group for the Advancement of Psychiatry, American Association for the Advancement of Science (fellow), American Association of Psychoanalytic Physicians (fellow), American Psychoanalytic Association, American College of Neuropsychopharmacology (charter fellow), American College of Psychiatrists (charter fellow), American Association of Child Psychoanalysts, Association for Research in Nervous and Mental Diseases, Southern California Psychoanalytic Society, Southern California Psychiatric Society, Phi Beta Kappa, Sigma Xi, Alpha Omega Alpha, Omicron Delta Kappa, Cosmos Club (Washington, DC), Balboa Bay Club (Newport Beach, CA).

AWARDS, HONORS: Honorable mention, Hofheimer Award for Research in Psychiatry, American Psychiatric Association, 1955; U.S. Public Health Service Research Career Award, National Institute of Mental Health, 1961-67; Physicians Recognition Award in continuing medical education, American Medical Association, 1969, 1974, 1978, 1982, 1985, 1988, and 1991; Franz Alexander Essay Prize, Southern California Psychoanalytic Society,

1973; Distinguished Research Award, Alumni Association of University of California, Irvine, 1974; Foundations' Fund Prize for Research in Psychiatry, American Psychiatric Association, 1978; named distinguished practitioner, National Academy of Medical Practice, 1984; Daniel Aldrich Distinguished University Service Award, 1992.

WRITINGS:

(Editor and contributor) *Comparative Psycholinguistic Analysis of Two Psychotherapeutic Interviews,* International Universities Press, 1961.

(Editor with Arthur H. Auerbach, and contributor) *Methods of Research in Psychotherapy,* Appleton-Century-Crofts, 1966.

(With Goldine C. Gleser) *The Measurement of Psychological States through the Content Analysis of Verbal Behavior,* University of California Press, 1969.

(With Gleser and Carolyn N. Winget) *Manual of Instructions for Using the Gottschalk-Gleser Content Analysis Scales: Anxiety, Hostility, and Social Alienation-Personal Disorganization,* University of California Press, 1969.

(Editor with others, and contributor) *Psychosomatic Classics,* S. Karger, 1972.

How to Understand and Analyze Your Own Dreams, Vantage, 1975, new edition, Eder/Art Reproductions, 1987.

(Author of foreword and contributor) Gilbert C. Morrison, editor, *Emergencies in Child Psychiatry: Emotional Crises in Children, Youth and Their Families,* C. C Thomas, 1975.

(Editor and contributor) *Pharmacokinetics, Psychoactive Drug Blood Levels, and Clinical Response,* Spectrum Books, 1976.

(Editor with others) *Guide to the Investigation and Reportings of Drug Abuse Deaths,* U.S. Government Printing Office, 1977.

(Editor and contributor) *The Content Analysis of Verbal Behavior: Further Studies,* Spectrum Books, 1979.

(Editor and contributor) *Pharmacokinetics of Psychoactive Drugs: Further Studies,* Spectrum Books, 1979.

(With others) *Drug Abuse Deaths in Nine Cities: A Survey Report,* U.S. Government Printing Office, 1980.

(With R. H. Cravey) *Toxicological and Pathological Studies on Psychoactive Drug-Involved Deaths,* Biomedical Publications, 1980.

(With C. N. Winget, G. C. Gleser, and F. Lolas) *Analysis de la Conducta Verbal,* Editorial Universitaria, 1984.

The Tree of Knowledge (novel), Eden Press, 1985.

(Editor, and contributor with Lolas and L. Vineg) *The Content Analysis of Verbal Behavior: Significance in Clinical Medicine and Psychiatry,* Springer-Verlag, 1986.

(With Lolas) *Estudios Sobre Conducta Verbal,* Editorial Universitaria, 1987.

How to Do Self Analysis and Other Self-Psychotherapies, Aronson, 1989.

New Findings and Clinical Applications of the Content Analysis of Verbal Behavior in Adults and Children, Guilford, 1993.

OTHER

Contributor to over forty books, including *Life Stress and Bodily Disease,* Association for Research in Nervous and Mental Disease, 1950; *Psychoanalytic Study of the Child,* edited by Ruth S. Eissler and others, International Universities Press, 1956; *The Manipulation of Human Behavior,* edited by Albert D. Biderman and Herbert M. Zinner, Wiley, 1961; *Sensitivity Training and Group Encounter,* edited by Robert W. Siroka, Ellen E. Siroka, and Gilbert A. Schloss, Grosset, 1971; *Advances in B-blocker Therapy II,* edited by A. Zanchetti, Excerpta Medica, 1982; *Drugs in Psychiatry,* edited by G. T. Burrows, T. Norman, and B. Davies, Elsevier Science, 1984.

Contributor to annual publications and yearbooks. Contributor of over one hundred articles and occasional reviews and abstracts to journals, including *Brain Research, Comprehensive Psychiatry, Psychoanalytic Psychology, American Journal of Psychiatry, Psychiatry Research, Surgery, Gynecology and Obstetrics, Psychopharmacologic, General Practice,* and *Science.* Member of editorial board, *Psychosomatic Medicine,* 1958-70, *World Journal of Psychosynthesis,* 1960-76, *Psychiatry,* 1967—, *American Journal of Psychotherapy,* 1975—, *Psychiatric Journal of the University of Ottawa Faculty of Medicine,* 1976—, *Research Communications, Psychology, Psychiatry and Behavior,* 1976—, and *Methods and Findings in Experimental and Clinical Pharmacology,* 1980—. Consulting editor, *Science, New England Journal of Medicine,* and *Journal of the American Medical Association,* 1960—; member of publications committee, Group for the Advancement of Psychiatry, 1967-70.

WORK IN PROGRESS: More scientific books and articles for journals.

SIDELIGHTS: Louis A. Gottschalk once told *CA* that "my most enjoyable writing, lately, has been writing my first novel, *The Tree of Knowledge,* in 1985. I would have the characters in the novel say anything I wanted to, and I did not have to give any references or footnotes as is required in my scientific writings. Writing the novel gave me a sense of elation which I have rarely experienced with other writings. I hope to write a second novel in the near future."

Gottschalk recently wrote *CA:* "In the meantime, I have just completed a new scientific book, and I am actively publishing journal articles on the relationships between the arousal of anxiety and hostility in dreams and wakeful silent mentation and cerebral glucose metabolic rates measured by positron emission tomographic brain scans."

*   *   *

GRADIDGE, (John) Roderick (Warlow) 1929-

PERSONAL: Born January 3, 1929, in Old Hunstanton, Norfolk, England; son of John Henry (an Indian Calvary brigadier and O.B.E.) and Lorraine Beatrice (Warlow-Harry) Gradidge. *Education:* Architectural Association School of Architecture, Stowe, England, Royal Institute of British Architects (RIBA) certification, 1957. *Religion:* Church of England. *Avocational interests:* Early twentieth-century architecture.

ADDRESSES: Home and office—21 Elliott Rd., London W4 1PF, England. *Agent*—Andrew Best, 81 Knatchbull Road, London SE5, England.

CAREER: Ind Coope Brewery, London, England, pub architect, 1960-65; architect in private practice, 1965—. Specialist in pub alterations in Great Britain and Holland, with works including Markham Arms, Guilford Arms, Rose and Orange, and Whitbread Brewery; specialist in restoration of country houses, including Fulbrook House, Tancreds Ford, Cholmondeley Castle, Mount Stuart, and Bodelwyddan Castle. Architect to Tramway Museum, National Portrait Gallery entrance hall, St. Edmund's College, Cambridge, and to recreation of Victorian interiors, Northampton Guildhall. Architectural advisor, Lutyens Trust.

MEMBER: Victorian Society, Art Workers Guild (honorary secretary, 1976-84, master, 1987), Twentieth Century Society (vice-chairman, 1987-90).

AWARDS, HONORS: City Heritage Award, City Heritage Society and Worshipful Company of Paint Stainers, 1980, for Whitbread Brewery alterations; Best Newcomer to Property Journalism award, Incorporated Society of Valuers and Auctioneers, 1984; Heritage Museum of the Year designation, 1989, for Bodelwyddan Castle interior and National Portrait Gallery.

WRITINGS:

(Contributor) Jane Fawcett, editor, *Seven Victorian Architects,* Thames & Hudson, 1976.

Dream Houses: The Edwardian Ideal, Braziller, 1980.

Edwin Lutyens: Architect Laureate, Allen & Unwin, 1981.

(Contributor) *Edwin Lutyens* (catalog), Arts Council, 1981.

Architects of the Art Workers Guild, 1884-1984 (catalog), RIBA Heinz Gallery, 1984.

The Surrey Style: A House & Cottage Handbook, Surrey Historic Buildings Trust, 1991.

(Contributor) *Great Residences,* Michael Beazley, 1993.

(Contributor) *Victorian Style,* Michael Beazley, 1993.

Author of weekly architectural property column in *The Field,* 1984-87, and *Country Life,* 1988—. Contributor to *Guardian, Country Life,* and *London Times.*

WORK IN PROGRESS: Architectural projects.

SIDELIGHTS: In *Dream Houses: The Edwardian Ideal,* British architect Roderick Gradidge examines twenty country houses built in the 1890s—along with the architects who created them. Gradidge maintains that such "traditional" designers as Edwin Lutyens and Ernest Newton have been largely ignored by historians intent upon the advancing modern movement; he feels that their work exemplifies "the last period when English architecture was flourishing"—an era when "architects gave clients what they wanted." *Spectator* reviewer Gavin Stamp commented that "excellence . . . stemmed in part from . . . the right and honest use of building materials and . . . good craftsmanship," tenets of the Arts and Crafts movement from which they were, in part, inspired. "All of [these houses] aspire to a kind of Anglo-Saxon domestic idealism that is deeply rooted in the English soul," concurred Colin Amery in the *Times Literary Supplement.* "[This] is a romantic book that struggles to present to the reader a picture of a lost world, in which architect and client and craftsman were united in their vision and in their domestic dreams."

Because Gradidge "is a practicing architect and not an art historian his view of buildings is based on a feeling for materials and spaces that arises from his own experience," noted Amery. The critic found the author's descriptions "fresh and often eye-opening." Stamp agreed, describing *In Dream Houses* as a "remarkable and stimulating book. . . . Here are no carefully qualified assessments but forthright opinions, delivered with an authority which comes from practical knowledge of building and form a commitment to an ideal of what architecture should be." The reviewers also agreed that the author's strong convictions could amuse or anger. "Gradidge is a highly subjective writer, which makes him both interesting and infuriating to read," Amery stated. "No one can accuse him of rehearsing received opinions."

Gradidge once told *CA:* "Over the years I have been closely associated with the movement for the rejection of modern architecture and the return to more traditional forms, as exemplified in the work of the great Edwardian arts and crafts architects, such as Edwin Lutyens; the Arts Council Hayward Gallery exhibition of 1981-82 is now seen as the turning point in Britain of the public rejection of modern architecture. I have also been much involved with the conservation movement, being a committee member of the Victorian Society for nearly twenty years, and was closely concerned with the centenary of the Art Workers Guild, which took place in 1984."

BIOGRAPHICAL/CRITICAL SOURCES:

PERIODICALS

Architects Journal, April 10, 1991.
Country Life, November 17, 1983; November 24, 1983; April 11, 1991.
Daily Telegraph, April 24, 1991.
Guardian, March 16, 1983.
New York Times Book Review, November 30, 1980.
Observer (London), November 23, 1980.
Spectator, October 18, 1980.
Traditional Homes, July, 1991.
Times Literary Supplement, April 3, 1981; November 27, 1981.
World of Interiors, September, 1991.

*   *   *

GRANGER, Guy
See GREEN, Kay

*   *   *

GRASSI, Joseph A(ugustus) 1922-

PERSONAL: Born November 4, 1922, in New Rochelle, NY; son of Joseph (a plastering contractor) and Marie G. (DiNunzio) Grassi; married Carolyn M. Cook (a writer and poet), September 20, 1968; children: Edwin, Peter. *Education:* Attended Manhattan College, 1939-41; Maryknoll Seminary (now Maryknoll School of Theology), B.A., 1943, B.D., 1948; Angelicum, S.T.D., 1949; Pontifical Biblical Institute, S.S.L., 1951. *Avocational interests:* The ocean, hiking, rag-time jazz.

ADDRESSES: Home—1746 Emory St., San Jose, CA 95126. *Office*—Department of Religious Studies, University of Santa Clara, Santa Clara, CA 95053.

CAREER: Maryknoll Seminary (now Maryknoll School of Theology), Ossining, NY, assistant professor of Old Testament, 1951-57; served as missionary in Guatemala, 1957-60; Maryknoll Seminary, associate professor of New Testament, 1960-67; Drew University, Madison, NJ, associate professor of New Testament, 1968-70; University of Santa Clara, Santa Clara, CA, associate professor, 1971-74, professor of religious studies, 1975—, chairman of department, 1972-79. Visiting scholar at Union Theological Seminary, New York City, summer, 1968, and Columbia University, 1968-69. Presented summer workshops in Chile, Colombia, Peru, Bolivia, Mexico, and Guatemala, 1966; conducts classes in New Testament and in Christian origins.

MEMBER: Catholic Biblical Association.

WRITINGS:

A World to Win: The Missionary Methods of Paul the Apostle, Maryknoll Publications, 1965.
The Teacher in the Primitive Church and the Teacher Today, University of Santa Clara Press, 1973.
Underground Christians in the Earliest Church, Diakonia Press, 1975.
The Secret of Paul the Apostle, Orbis Books, 1978.
Jesus as Teacher: A New Testament Guide to Learning the Way, St. Mary's College Press, 1978.
Teaching the Way: Jesus, the Early Church, and Today, University Press of America, 1982.
Broken Bread and Broken Bodies: The Eucharist and World Hunger, Orbis Books, 1985.
God Makes Me Laugh, Michael Glazier, 1986.
Changing the World Within: The Dynamics of Personal and Spiritual Growth, Paulist Press, 1986.
Healing the Heart: The Power of Biblical Heart Imagery, Paulist Press, 1987.
Rediscovering the Impact of Jesus's Death, Sheed & Ward, 1987.
Mary: Mother and Disciple, Michael Glazier, 1988.
The Hidden Heroes of the Gospels: Female Counterparts of Jesus, Liturgical Press, 1989.
Loaves and Fishes: The Gospel Feeding Narratives, Liturgical Press, 1991.
The Secret Identity of the Beloved Disciple, Paulist Press, 1992.

Contributor to books, including *Jerome Biblical Commentary: Ephesians, Colossians,* edited by R. E. Brown, J. Fitzmyer, and R. E. Murphy, Prentice-Hall, 1968; and *Does Jesus Make a Difference?,* edited by T. M. McFallen, Seabury, 1974.

SIDELIGHTS: Joseph A. Grassi once told *CA:* "Teaching, studying, and writing in my special field of the New Testament and Christian origins are my main interests. In addition, my wife and I enjoy conducting groups and classes in meditation and personal growth. This has proved to be a rewarding personal experience for us. We also donate our services to coordinate 'Skip-a-Meal,' a nonprofit organization whose members skip a meal each week and send the savings directly to purchase food for starving and hungry people throughout the world."

GRAYSMITH, Robert 1942-

PERSONAL: Born Robert Gray Smith, September 17, 1942, in Pensacola, FL; name legally changed in 1976; son of Robert Gray (a lieutenant colonel in the U.S. Air Force) and Frances Jane (Scott) Smith; married Margaret Ann Womack (a nurse), November 8, 1963 (divorced June, 1973); married Melanie Krakower, November 26, 1975 (divorced September, 1980); children: David Martin, Aaron Vincent, Margot Alexandra. *Education:* California College of Arts and Crafts, B.F.A., 1965. *Politics:* Democrat. *Religion:* Jewish. *Avocational interests:* Collecting comic books and antique toys.

ADDRESSES: Home—1015 Lincoln Way, San Francisco, CA 94122. *Office*—San Francisco Chronicle, 901 Mission St., San Francisco, CA 94103. *Agent*—Dan Strone, William Morris Agency, 1350 Avenue of the Americas, New York, NY 10022.

CAREER: Oakland Tribune, Oakland, CA, sports department, 1964-65; *Stockton Record,* Stockton, CA, staff artist, 1965-68; *San Francisco Chronicle,* San Francisco, CA, editorial cartoonist, 1968-80, illustrator, 1980-83; freelance illustrator and writer, 1983—.

AWARDS, HONORS: Award from Foreign Press Club, 1973, for cartoons; award from World Population Contest, 1976, for "The Five Horsemen."

WRITINGS:

NONFICTION; SELF-ILLUSTRATED

Zodiac, St. Martin's, 1986, included in "Unsolved Mystery" series, Time-Life, 1993.
The Sleeping Lady: The Trailside Murders above the Golden Gate, E. P. Dutton, 1990.
The Murder of Bob Crane, Crown, 1992.

Zodiac has been translated into French.

WORK IN PROGRESS: The Bell-Tower, the "Crime of the Century," about the 1895 Durrant Case; *Melville and Gericault: Polished Shield, Dark Helmet,* the story of two great works of art and literature inspired by a shipwreck on the Equator; *Cape Disappointment,* a mystery novel; *Gluck,* a retelling of John Ruskin's *King of the Golden River* for children; illustrations for *I Didn't Know What to Get You,* a children's book by Penny Wallace.

SIDELIGHTS: "After Jack the Ripper and before the Green River Killer came the Zodiac, one of the most deadly, elusive, and mysterious mass murderers in U.S. history," Robert Graysmith told *CA.* His popular novel, *Zodiac,* is an account of the numerous murders which haunted San Francisco during the late 1960's and early 1970's and perpetrated by a person who called himself "Zodiac."

"Like a political cartoon, I wanted this book to accomplish something, to effect a change. Witchcraft, death threats, cryptograms, a hooded killer in consume, dedicated investigators, and a mysterious man in a white Chevy who is seen by all and known by no one are all parts of the Zodiac story—the scariest story I know. Slowly each arcane symbol and cipher broke away and I learned how the killer wrote the untraceable Zodiac letters (printed in their entirety for the first time in this book), why he killed when he did, and even the inspiration for his crossed-circle symbol and his executioner's costume.

"From my perspective as political cartoonist for the largest paper in northern California, the *San Francisco Chronicle,* I was there from the beginning as each cryptic letter, each coded message, each bloody swatch of victim's shirt came across the wood-grained editorial desk," recalled Graysmith. "At first the visual qualities of the Zodiac symbols drew me, but gradually a resolve grew within me to unravel the killer's clues and discover his true identity—and, failing that, to present every scrap of evidence available to ensure that someone, somewhere, might recognize the Zodiac and provide the missing piece to the puzzle."

The popularity of *Zodiac* pushed it on to national bestseller lists and ran it into thirteen printings and a French translation. Unfortunately, its popularity extended beyond mere readers. Graysmith told *CA* that in 1990, *Zodiac* again made the best-seller list after New York City officials announced that a mass-murderer dubbed 'Zodiac' appeared to be "going by the book" that described the details of the killings that had once terrorized San Francisco. Investigators on the New York City Zodiac task force believed the gunman stalking their city had possibly copied methods outlined in Graysmith's book. "*Zodiac* was referred to as a 'handbook for death' and a 'blueprint for the killer's astrological shootings,'" Graysmith noted. "I spent a week in New York telling what I knew about the original case. The East Coast killer was undoubtedly a copycat and since he knew the birth signs of his victims, all strangers, before he shot them I suspected he was a census taker."

The Murder of Bob Crane, published in 1992, is an investigation into the mysterious unsolved murder of the star of the popular television series, "Hogan's Heroes." "I have always been enormously lucky in obtaining confidential documents and exclusive photos for my books, and the Crane book is no exception. I returned from Scottsdale, Arizona, where Bob was murdered with over a thousand pages of police and D.A.'s documents." With a talent for both illustration and cartooning, Graysmith has provided the illustrations for each of his works of non-fiction: "*Crane* has twenty-nine illustrations and maps that I drew—it is my favorite part of the work." *Gluck,* a retelling of the Victorian classic, *King of the Golden River* by John Ruskin, along with *I Didn't Know What to Get You* by children's author Penny Wallace, have provided Graysmith with yet another outlet for his talent. As he told *CA:* "Children's book illustration is something I have dreamed of doing my entire life."

BIOGRAPHICAL/CRITICAL SOURCES:

PERIODICALS

Library Journal, March 1, 1986, p. 104; April 15, 1990, p. 108.

*   *   *

GREEN, Kay 1927-
(Harley Davis, Guy Granger, Katie Kent, Roumelia Lane, Florissa May)

PERSONAL: Born December 31, 1927, in Bradford, England; daughter of Wilfred (a trader) and May (a caterer; maiden name, Sidney) Sutton; married Gavin Green (a corporate adviser), October 1, 1949; children: Valerie Yvonne, Philip Ralph. *Education:* Educated in Bradford, England. *Politics:* Conservative. *Religion:* Methodist. *Avocational interests:* Walking, painting, photography, travel, animal care, gardens.

ADDRESSES: Home and office—Green Acres, Santa Eugenia, Mallorca Baleares, Spain 07142.

CAREER: Novelist and screenwriter.

MEMBER: Society of Authors, Authors Copyright Lending Society.

WRITINGS:

ROMANCE NOVELS UNDER PSEUDONYM ROUMELIA LANE

Rose of the Desert, Mills & Boon, 1967.
Hideaway Heart, Mills & Boon, 1967.
A Summer to Love, Mills & Boon, 1968.
House of the Winds, Mills & Boon, 1968.
Sea of Zanj, Mills & Boon, 1969.
Terminus Teheran, Mills & Boon, 1969.
The Scented Hills, Mills & Boon, 1970.
Cafe Mimosa, Mills & Boon, 1971.
In the Shade of the Palms, Mills & Boon, 1972.
Nurse at Noongwalla, Mills & Boon, 1973.
Stormy Encounter, Mills & Boon, 1974.
Across the Lagoon, Mills & Boon, 1974.
Where the Moonflower Weaves, Mills & Boon, 1974.
Harbour of Deceit, Mills & Boon, 1975.
The Tenant of San Mateo, Mills & Boon, 1976.
Himalayan Moonlight, Mills & Boon, 1977.
The Brightest Star, Mills & Boon, 1978.
Hidden Rapture, Mills & Boon, 1978.

Second Spring, Mills & Boon, 1980.
Dream Island, Mills & Boon, 1981, Harlequin, 1982.
Desert Haven, Mills & Boon, 1981, Harlequin, 1982.
Lupin Valley, Mills & Boon, 1982, Harlequin, 1983.
The Fire of Heaven, Mills & Boon, 1983.
Summer of Conflict, Mills & Boon, 1984.
Night of the Beguine, Mills & Boon, 1984.
Master of Marraxt, Mills & Boon, 1984.
Tempest in the Tropics, Mills & Boon, 1985.
Dear Brute, Mills & Boon, 1985.

OTHER

Also author of mainstream novels, including *Death from the Past, Killerwatch, The Nawindi Flyer, The Call of the Cobra, Where Are the Clowns?,* and *Heartbreak Island.* Author of children's books, under the pseudonyms Guy Granger and Katie Kent, including *The Adventures of Hugglemush, The Adventures of Hugglemush, No. Two,* and *The Tiddley-Wink Man.* Contributor to British newspapers.

WORK IN PROGRESS: Screenplays for *Death from the Past, Killerwatch, The Call of the Cobra, The Nawindi Flyer, Where Are the Clowns?,* and *Gilligan's Last Gamble.*

SIDELIGHTS: Kay Green told *CA:* "I ended the 1980s on the crest of a wave of optimism, with two of my works being optioned for film productions. They say that hubris is followed by nemesis, and this was the case at the beginning of the 1990s as far as my writing career was concerned." Because of the world wide recession, Green's producers were unable to come up with the necessary funds for the productions of the two films and their options ran out. "In the meantime I had been busy as usual, writing," continues Green. "I had plenty of adult fiction on the stockpile, both for books and films; what was needed was a new departure, to widen our market potential. I have for many years had an empathy with children, and was a lover of fantasy and nature; toying with a hazy idea one day I came up with a new character, which I named *Hugglemush.* Born out of nature's own materials, such as leaves and straw, flower petals, berries, moss and other items, he played with the friendly wind, and ended up living under an armchair in a big old empty house, deep in Farmer Millet countryside. Hugglemush became the friend of countless small animals, birds, insects and other creatures; including several fantasy characters. The old saying that 'As one door closes another opens' came true for me."

In addition to her first few children's books, Green also spent the end of 1992 and the beginning of 1993 working on a number of film projects. "1993 sees a new change in my work," explains Green. "Originally a romantic book author, I had experienced the work of the new editorial 'Wiz-kids' who had decreed that it was *sex* that sold

books, and authors were asked to be more sexually explicit in their novels. It was nothing more than soft porn, and I for one, along with many other established authors, simply refused to go along with this sordid practice; so we fell out of favour, and our books were no longer promoted as they used to be. The publishers lost many of their old-established authors, and replaced them with the new porn-writers who were willing to abandon good morals and ethics, for the satisfaction of seeing their work in print. This is a general trend, and not just confined to my own previous publishers; however it has its own built-in backlash! A lot of the new porn stuff simply hasn't sold as well as was predicted by the marketing 'Wiz-kids'! And more than one publisher has seen his profits suffer. Maybe in time they'll wake up to the fact that it's a good story with believable characters, plus an attractive front cover and a compelling synopsis of the story on the back cover that *really sells books!*

"I am now working on action/adventure novels, with a thread of romance running through the story. They are mainstream books suitable for readers of all ages and both sexes, and the romantic element is just that, *real romance,* not lust, voyeurism or vulgar titillation. I am not a prude, and can describe adult relationships as they would be in real life; but without causing moral damage by exposing young impressionable minds to false ideas od sexual conduct, as today's porn-merchants in books, the press, radio, T.V. and movies are doing to society today! It's time for a return to good ethics and high moral values by the media, to protect society from further damage via current attitudes to sex and family honour.

"Writing for me is a way of life; I couldn't imagine living *without* writing! There are so many stories to tell; so much of life's own drama, humour, romance, pathos, suspense and adventure observed every day through the press, T.V., the movies, and life in general, which I can draw on to weave fiction into pieces of literature, which hopefully will entertain my readers."

BIOGRAPHICAL/CRITICAL SOURCES:

BOOKS

Contemporary Authors Autobiography Series, Volume 11, Gale, 1990.

*   *   *

GREEN, Michael Frederick 1927-

PERSONAL: Born January 2, 1927, in Leicester, England; son of Jack (a store manager) and Winifred (a secretary; maiden name, Smeath) Green. *Education:* Open University, B.A. (with honors), 1978.

ADDRESSES: Home—78 Sandall Rd., London W5 1JB, England. *Agent*—Anthony Sheil Associates, Ltd., 43 Doughty St., London WC1N 2LF, England.

CAREER: Leicester Mercury, Leicester, England, reporter, 1943; *Northampton Chronicle and Echo*, Northampton, England, reporter, 1943-50; Birmingham *Gazette*, Birmingham, England, sub-editor, 1950-53; *Star*, London, England, sub-editor, 1953-56; free-lance writer, 1956—. *Military service:* British Army, 1944-48; became sergeant.

MEMBER: National Union of Journalists, Incorporated Society of Authors, Playwrights & Composers, Equity.

WRITINGS:

Stage Noises and Effects, Jenkins, 1958.

HUMOROUS BOOKS

The Art of Coarse Rugby, Hutchinson, 1960.
The Art of Coarse Sailing, Hutchinson, 1962.
Even Coarser Rugby, Hutchinson, 1963.
Don't Print My Name Upside Down (novel), Hutchinson, 1963.
The Art of Coarse Acting, Hutchinson, 1964, Drama Book Publishers, 1980.
The Art of Coarse Sport, Hutchinson, 1965.
The Art of Coarse Golf, Hutchinson, 1968.
The Art of Coarse Moving, Hutchinson, 1969.
Rugby Alphabet, Pelham, 1971.
The Art of Coarse Drinking, Hutchinson, 1973.
Squire Haggard's Journal (novel), Hutchinson, 1975.
The Art of Coarse Cruising, Hutchinson, 1976.
Even Coarser Sport, Hutchinson, 1978.
The Art of Coarse Sex, Hutchinson, 1980.
Tonight, Josephine, Secker and Warburg, 1981.
Don't Swing from the Balcony, Romeo, Secker and Warburg, 1983.
The Art of Coarse Office Life, Secker and Warburg, 1985.
The Boy Who Shot Down an Airship, Heinemann, 1988.
Nobody Hurt in Small Earthquake, Heinemann, 1990.

PLAYS

Four Plays for Coarse Actors (produced in Edinburgh, Scotland, at Cathedral Hall, August 22, 1977, under title *The Coarse Acting Show*; contains *Streuth, Il Fornicazione, A Collier's Tuesday Tea*, and *All's Well That Ends As You Like It*), Samuel French, 1978.
The Coarse Acting Show 2 (produced in Edinburgh at George Square Theatre, August 20, 1979; produced in London, England, at Shaftesbury Theatre, October 1, 1979; contains *Moby Dick, Last Call for Breakfast, The Cherry Sisters*, and *Henry the Tenth: Part Seven*), Samuel French, 1980.

The Third Coarse Acting Show (contains *A Fish in Her Kettle, Present Slaughter, The Vagabond Prince, Stalag 69*, and *Julius and Cleopatra*), Samuel French, 1985.

OTHER

Contributor of articles to periodicals, including *News Chronicle, Observer, Sunday Times, Daily Telegraph, Times* (London), *Punch*, and *Spectator*.

ADAPTATIONS: The Art of Coarse Moving was serialized by BBC-TV and broadcast as *A Roof Over My Head* in 1977; *Squire Haggard's Journal* was serialized by BBC-TV and broadcast as *Haggard* in 1990 and 1992.

SIDELIGHTS: Michael Frederick Green wrote *CA:* "My books, *The Art of Coarse . . .*, deal with various human activities (sports such as golf or sailing, or social affairs such as drinking and sex) and are largely devoted to the way things are done in reality as distinct from theory. In theory, for instance, yachtsmen are bold, alert experts, braving the storm and tempest. In *The Art of Coarse Sailing*, I pointed out that, in reality, most people who own small boats are suburban cowards who, in a crisis, forget all nautical language and shout, 'For God's sake, turn left before we're all killed!'

"From this there is a natural transition to a 'coarse' golfer, who goes from tee to green without touching the fairway; and a 'coarse' amateur actor, who is defined as one who can remember the lines but not in the order in which they come; not to mention the 'coarse' lover, who always hopes it will be better next time. In the desperately competitive modern world, my books are about those who don't quite measure up to the theoretical standards of achievement expected in life and in sport. The majority of us, in fact the vast army of sportsmen hacking their way around the great golf course of life, can never hope to break *100*, let alone reach par."

*   *   *

GREIDER, William (Harold) 1936-

PERSONAL: Surname is pronounced *Gry*-der; born August 6, 1936, in Cincinnati, OH; son of Harold William (a chemist) and Gladys (a teacher; maiden name, McClure); married Linda Furry (a writer), June 17, 1961; children: Cameron, Katharine. *Education:* Princeton University, A.B., 1958. *Politics:* Democrat. *Religion:* None.

ADDRESSES: Home—5931 Utah Ave., NW, Washington, DC 20015. *Office*—c/o *Rolling Stone*, 1901 L St., NW, Suite 330, Washington, DC 20036. *Agent*—Lynn Nesbit, Janklow and Nesbit, 598 Madison Ave., New York, NY 10022.

CAREER: Wheaton Daily Journal, Wheaton, IL, reporter, 1960-62; *Louisville Times and Courier-Journal,* Louisville, KY, reporter and Washington correspondent, 1962-68; *Washington Post,* Washington, DC, reporter and assistant managing editor of national news, 1968-82; *Rolling Stone,* Washington, DC, columnist and national affairs editor, 1982—.

AWARDS, HONORS: First prize award for economic understanding, Champion International Corp., and George Polk Award in Journalism, Long Island University, both 1982, both for *Atlantic Monthly* article "The Education of David Stockman"; named Pulitzer Prize runner-up, 1982, for commentary (in Washington Post column "Against the Grain"); Los Angeles Times Book Prize, 1988, for *Secrets of the Temple: How the Federal Reserve Runs the Country.*

WRITINGS:

The Education of David Stockman and Other Americans, Dutton, 1982.
Secrets of the Temple: How the Federal Reserve Runs the Country, Simon and Schuster, 1988.
The Trouble with Money: A Prescription for America's Financial Fever, illustrated by Jeffrey Smith, with photographs by George Lange and charts by Genigraphics Corp., Whittle Direct Books, 1989.
Who Will Tell the People: The Betrayal of American Democracy, Simon and Schuster, 1992.

Also contributor to periodicals, including *Ramparts, Today's Education, Washington Monthly, Atlantic Monthly, Esquire,* and *Washington Post Book World.*

SIDELIGHTS: When an article entitled "The Education of David Stockman" appeared in the *Atlantic Monthly* in 1981, its author, William Greider, found himself in the middle of a highly publicized controversy along with the subject of his article, the new director of the Office of Management and Budget (OMB) under President Ronald Reagan. Based on a series of interviews conducted over a nine-month period beginning when Stockman first assumed his post in 1981, Greider's article chronicled the events surrounding the new OMB director's formidable challenge: to balance the federal budget by 1984 while accommodating the president's fiscal plan—what became known as "Reaganomics"—to reduce income taxes and increase defense spending.

The *Atlantic Monthly* story, reprinted in Greider's 1982 book, *The Education of David Stockman and Other Americans,* created a national furor because it exposed the realities of managing the federal budget, sending "a deliciously shocking thrill across a nation that had begun to feel as ignorant as a hog and didn't dare to grunt," wrote Harold Evans in a *Washington Post Book World* commentary.

"From the beginning everyone knew, or should have known," noted Lester C. Thurow in the *New York Review of Books,* "that you could not put together huge tax cuts, gigantic increases in defense spending, a modest slowdown in the rate of growth of social welfare spending, and tight monetary policies without bringing on disaster."

Nevertheless, Stockman, a Republican and former U.S. congressman known for his staunch conservativism, was initially optimistic—despite what he called an "absolutely shocking" economic forecast—and sought to cut the budget by about $40 billion. Later, however, the thirty-four-year-old OMB director, whom the press had referred to as "the whiz kid" and "the boy wonder" of the Reagan administration, admitted to Greider that "none of us [in the OMB] really understands what's going on with all these numbers." The article created a public uproar, as Evans suggested, "because the proliferation of the daily [news] stories had splintered the reality: only [Greider's] comprehensive narrative, decoded, enabled people to understand what had been going on."

In addition to the reprinted article, *The Education of David Stockman and Other Americans* contains Greider's analysis of the public reaction to the *Atlantic Monthly* interviews as well as an examination of Reaganomics and its shortcomings. In a review in the *Chicago Tribune Book World,* Clarence Petersen described the latter section of the book as a "thoughtfully streetwise essay on the problems of supply-side economics and the effects of the political process" on the American economy. "Greider's narrative is now a piece of history," observed *New Republic* critic Bruce Mazlish, who added that the work is "destined to appear in future anthologies of politics, for it raises fundamental issues of faith, loyalty, betrayal, morality, and personality. . . . The 'Education of David Stockman' is not just the story of an ambitious and complicated young man learning more about himself and politics, but an education for all of us."

Greider became embroiled in a second controversy with the publication of *Secrets of the Temple: How the Federal Reserve Runs the Country,* a history and analysis of America's central bank. In *Secrets of the Temple,* Greider contends that the Federal Reserve Board, a seven-member governing body appointed by the President that determines the nation's money supply and lending interest rates, has often instituted measures which prove damaging to the economy. Much of the book is devoted to a study of the Fed under Paul Volcker, who served as chairman from 1979 to 1987 and pursued a tight money policy that helped control runaway inflation. In Greider's opinion, however, that policy also contributed to a severe recession, a massive debt burden, a trade deficit, and an inequitable distribution of the nation's wealth. In a *Rolling Stone* article, Greider stated, "During the 1980s, whenever the Federal Reserve erred, it nearly always erred on the side of hard money—sacrificing the real economy to protect prices." He described the consequences as "devastating, like deep body wounds still not healed. . . ." Greider further criticized the Fed for operating independently of other government organizations. Greider, declared Peter Cook in the *Toronto Globe and Mail*, "sees the existence of a bunch of unelected but powerful technocrats at the Fed as an affront to the U.S. political system."

Like the *Atlantic Monthly* article before it, *Secrets of the Temple* generated intense debate among politicians, economists, and bankers. For their part, Federal Reserve officials acknowledged that Greider was correct in his assertion that their efforts to control inflation hurt the poor disproportionately, but they denied that these efforts were a deliberate attempt to protect the moneyed classes. And though other critics also disputed Greider's arguments (especially his contention that some inflation is good for the economy), many praised his depth of research. "After this book," opined Adam Smith in the *New York Times Book Review*, "the Fed can scarcely be called secret and mysterious. Even experienced professionals can find something to learn."

Since the publication of *Secrets of the Temple*, Greider has written *The Trouble with Money*, a direct-mail book that caused a stir in the publishing world because it included eighteen pages of advertising, and *Who Will Tell the People: The Betrayal of American Democracy*, which explores the general decay of the political process. Reviewers found *Who Will Tell the People* to be a serious look at the problems plaguing democracy; Jefferson Morley of the *New York Times Book Review* called the work "an indispensable and comprehensive guide to the continuing meltdown of the American political system." In addition to his efforts on those books, Greider continues to serve as the national editor for *Rolling Stone*, and he writes a regular political column on national affairs for that magazine.

BIOGRAPHICAL/CRITICAL SOURCES:

PERIODICALS

Atlantic Monthly, February, 1982.
Chicago Tribune Book World, September 5, 1982.
Christian Science Monitor, September 10, 1982.
Detroit News, April 13, 1982.
Globe and Mail (Toronto), February 6, 1988.
Los Angeles Times Book Review, January 1, 1983; December 13, 1987, pp. 1, 12; January 29, 1989, p. 10; June 7, 1992, pp. 2, 7.
Nation, January 23, 1988, pp. 93-94.
New Republic, December 23, 1981; February 22, 1988, pp. 32-36.
New York Review of Books, October 7, 1982.
New York Times, January 21, 1988.
New York Times Book Review, January 17, 1988, p. 7; January 14, 1990, p. 10; May 24, 1992, p. 3.
Time, December 7, 1987, p. 80.
Tribune Books (Chicago), January 31, 1988, p. 3, 11.
Washington Post, March 1, 1982; May 19, 1982; January 17, 1988; January 21, 1988.
Washington Post Book World, October 3, 1982; January 3, 1988, p. 1; January 29, 1989, p. 12; February 25, 1990, p. 3; May 17, 1992, pp. 4-5.

* * *

GRIMBLE, Reverend Charles James
    See ELIOT, T(homas) S(tearns)

H

HACKER, Andrew 1929-

PERSONAL: Born August 30, 1929, in New York, NY; son of Louis Morton (a professor) and Lillian (Lewis) Hacker; married Lois Sheffield Wetherell (a librarian), June 17, 1955; children: Ann. *Education:* Amherst College, B.A., 1951; Oxford University, A.M., 1953; Princeton University, Ph.D., 1955. *Politics:* Republican. *Religion:* Jewish.

ADDRESSES: Home— West 64th St., Apt. 16-K, New York, NY 10023. *Office—*Department of Political Science, Queens College of the City University of New York, 65-30 Kissena Blvd., Flushing, NY 11367.

CAREER: Cornell University, Ithaca, NY, instructor, 1955-56, assistant professor, 1956-61, associate professor, 1961-66, professor of government, 1966-71; Queens College of the City University of New York, Flushing, NY, professor, 1971—. Visiting professor, Salzburg Seminar in American Studies, Salzburg, Austria. Consultant, Fund for the Republic, National Industrial Conference Board, National Broadcasting Company, Rockefeller Brothers Fund.

MEMBER: American Political Science Association, American Society for Legal and Political Philosophy, Phi Beta Kappa.

AWARDS, HONORS: Fellowships from Social Science Research Council, 1954-55, and Ford Foundation, 1962-63.

WRITINGS:

Political Theory: Philosophy, Ideology, Science, Macmillan, 1961.
(Co-author) *Social Theories of Talcott Parsons,* Prentice Hall, 1961.
(Co-author) *The Uses of Power,* Harcourt, 1962.

The Study of Politics, McGraw, 1963.
Congressional Districting: The Issue of Equal Representation, Brookings Institution, 1964.
(Editor) *The Corporation Take-Over,* Harper, 1964.
Politics and Government in the United States, Harcourt, 1965.
The End of the American Era, Atheneum, 1970.
The Study of Politics, McGraw, 1973.
The New Yorkers: A Profile of an American Metropolis, Mason/Charter, 1975.
Free Enterprise in America, Harcourt, 1977.
(Editor with Lorrie Millman) *U/S: A Statistical Portrait of the American People,* Viking, 1983.
Two Nations: Black and White, Separate, Hostile, Unequal, Scribner's, 1992.

Also contributor to numerous periodicals, including *Atlantic, Harper's,* and *New York Times Magazine.*

SIDELIGHTS: Political scientist Andrew Hacker is best known for a series of books that make the study of statistics both accessible and interesting. Whether examining political redistricting, statistical analysis, or race relations, Hacker imaginatively uses numbers to illustrate complex themes. In *Two Nations,* the author uses numbers to help define modern race relations. While some of the examples presented in *Two Nations* have been criticized by reviewers as being too simplistic, the book generally fares well with critics. "Andrew Hacker is a political scientist known for doing with statistics what Fred Astaire did with hats, canes, and chairs. . . . In . . . [Hacker's] new book on race relations in America, he doesn't crunch numbers: he makes them live and breathe," enthuses David Gates in *Newsweek.* "The real value of his book . . . is in Mr. Hacker's calm, analytical eye, his unblinking view of American history and his unwillingness to accept cant and 'common sense' as facts," notes Tom Wicker in the *New York Times Book Review,* adding that "equally important is his compassion for the plight and sensibilities of those from whom white Americans ask 'an extra patience and perseverance' that the same whites have never required of themselves."

BIOGRAPHICAL/CRITICAL SOURCES:

PERIODICALS

Los Angeles Times, February 7, 1983.
National Review, July 28, 1970.
Newsweek, June 6, 1970; March 22, 1992, p. 61.
New York Times Book Review, April 10, 1983, p. 7; March 8, 1992, p. 1.
Time, June 1, 1970.

*   *   *

HALPERIN, David M(artin) 1952-

PERSONAL: Born April 2, 1952, in Chicago, IL; son of S. William (a professor) and Elaine P. (a translator) Halperin. *Education:* Attended Intercollegiate Center for Classical Studies, Rome, Italy, 1972-73; Oberlin College, B.A., 1973; Stanford University, M.A., 1977, Ph.D., 1980.

ADDRESSES: Office—Literature Faculty, 14N-432, Massachusetts Institute of Technology, 77 Massachusetts Ave., Cambridge, MA 02139.

CAREER: Intercollegiate Center for Classical Studies, Rome, Italy, acting instructor in classics, 1977-78; Massachusetts Institute of Technology, Cambridge, assistant professor, 1979-83, associate professor, 1983-89, professor of literature, 1989—. Visiting professor of literature and the history of consciousness at the University of California, Santa Cruz, 1991.

MEMBER: American Philological Association, Modern Language Association, Women's Classical Caucus, Petronian Society, Joseph Conrad Society of America.

AWARDS, HONORS: Prix de Rome, American Academy in Rome, 1976; National Humanities Center fellow, 1985-86; Stanford Humanities Center fellow, 1987-88; Humanities Research Centre fellow, Australian National University, 1993.

WRITINGS:

Before Pastoral: Theocritus and the Ancient Tradition of Bucolic Poetry, Yale University Press, 1983.
One Hundred Years of Homosexuality and Other Essays on Greek Love, Routledge, 1990.
(Editor with John J. Winkler and Froma I. Zeitlin; and contributor) *Before Sexuality: The Construction of Erotic Experience in the Ancient Greek World,* Princeton University Press, 1990.

(Editor with Henry Abelove and Michele Aina Barale) *The Lesbian and Gay Studies Reader,* Routledge, 1993.
The Metaphysics of Desire: Studies in Plato's Erotic Theory, Yale University Press, in press.

Contributor to books, including *Aleksandr Solzhenitsyn: Critical Essays and Documentary Materials,* edited by John B. Dunlop, Richard Haugh, and Alexis Klimoff, 2nd edition, Collier Books, 1975; *Great Foreign Language Writers,* edited by James Vinson and Daniel Kirkpatrick, St. James Press, 1984; *Solzhenitsyn in Exile: Critical Essays and Documentary Materials,* edited by Dunlop, Klimoff, and Michael Nicholson, Hoover Institution Press, 1985; *Civilization of the Ancient Mediterranean: Greece and Rome,* edited by Michael Grant and Rachel Kitzinger, Scribner, 1988; *Hidden from History: Reclaiming the Gay and Lesbian Past,* edited by Martin Bauml Duberman, Martha Vicinus, and George Chauncey, Jr., New American Library, 1989; *Sexual Discourses: Aristotle to AIDS,* edited by Donna C. Stanton, University of Michigan Press, 1992; and *Foucault and the Writing of History,* edited by Jan Goldstein, Basil Blackwell, 1993. Also contributor to scholarly journals, including *Salmagundi, History and Theory, Diacritics, American Journal of Philology, Ancient Philosophy, Partisan Review, Classical Journal,* and *Virginia Quarterly Review.*

WORK IN PROGRESS: Queering the Canon: Oppositional Readings of Classical Texts, for Oxford University Press; *Ancient Greek Dialogues of Desire: Plato's SYMPOSIUM and Lucian's EROTES,* annotated translations, for Routledge.

SIDELIGHTS: David M. Halperin once told *CA:* "When we speak today of 'Platonic love,' we usually have a clear notion of what we mean: we use the phrase to refer to a personal feeling of great warmth and affection that, however powerful or intense it may be, is entirely undisturbed by sexual passion. The modern understanding of 'Platonic love' bears little more than an incidental resemblance to the theory of *eros* articulated by Socrates in the dialogues of Plato and it has long been in disgrace among those familiar with the original texts—among classical scholars and readers of Greek, that is, since accurate and unexpurgated English translations of these texts were not made available to the general public until after the Second World War. Although it is a well-known fact, then, that Plato did not expound the erotic doctrine we currently ascribe to him, few attempts have been made, until recently, to discover exactly what it was that Plato did believe and teach.

"Many factors have long combined to obscure the nature of Plato's contribution to Western thinking about love. The brilliant but highly tendentious interpretation of

Plato which accompanied his rediscovery by the Italian humanists eventuated, during the sixteenth century, in a controversy over the ethical and religious value of human love; the participants, in their enthusiasm, quickly left the terms of the original argument far behind them. The Romantics tried to reclaim Plato from the arid debates of the academicians, recognizing in his celebration of 'divine madness' and in his praise of Eros, the Great Daernon, an anticipation of their own 'natural supernaturalism.' Our historical understanding of Plato has not always been well served by these intellectual movements.

"Classical scholars, though hardly immune to the effects of contemporary intellectual currents, have been baffled in their study of Plato chiefly by a reluctance to investigate, or even to mention, the particular realities of ancient social relations on which Plato's inquiry into the nature of love is based. Specifically, classicists have been slow to investigate the extent, character, and conventions of homosexual behavior among the ancient Greeks. Since Plato's discussion of love is couched almost entirely in homo-erotic terms, and since much of what can be known about the sexual codes and practices of the ancient Athenians derives from Plato, such scholarly fastidiousness has led both to a neglect of Plato's individual doctrines and to a misleading tendency to identify Plato's views with the dominant ideology of his culture. It is only within the last two decades that new research into this previously forbidden scholarly preserve has uncovered a rich store of new evidence, making it possible for the first time to bring to bear on the study of Plato a largely independent knowledge of the moral conventions governing sexual behavior in classical Athens. It is finally becoming practicable to study Plato's ideas in their historical context, to identify the various social and emotional options confronting Plato in his own day, and thereby to understand why Plato selected from among those options his now famous, and to us perhaps bizarre, sexual ethic.

"If the current state of classical scholarship is congenial to a new study of Platonic love, the present topics of debate in continental philosophy made such a study indispensable. From its origins in German idealism, particularly in Hegel's meditation on the master/slave dialectic, to its important role in psychoanalysis and in what is called metapsychology, the concept of desire has achieved progressively greater prominence until it has become, in the work of Rene Girard and his followers, the key to an entire theory of human social relations. Plato can indeed be thought of as the founder, or at least the precursor, of the intellectual traditions and critical methodologies which are coming to maturity in our own time. Whoever succeeds, therefore, in bringing Plato's ideas into alignment with our own will not only enrich our appreciation of the power, relevance, and originality of ancient philoso-

phy but will also contribute significantly to our own ongoing process of cultural self-understanding.

"Much work, of course, has already been done on 'Platonic love,' but many details remain obscure. What exactly is the nature of the human relationship envisaged by Plato as conforming most closely to his erotic theory? How can such a relationship be justified both psychologically and ethically; that is, to what extent is Plato's theory grounded in the realities of human experience, and to what extent is it defensible as a coherent standard of behavior? What is the connection between Plato's descriptive analysis of human sexuality and his aesthetics, ontology, metaphysics, and soteriology? How do Plato's myths relate to modern ways of conceptualizing erotic experience? What contribution did Plato make to Greek thinking about eros in his own day, and what insights does he offer the modern reader? In an effort to answer these and other questions, I have been working on a series of articles about various aspects of Plato's erotic theory, and I have contracted with Yale University Press to write a book, based on those articles but incorporating other material and addressed to a more general audience, about Plato's relation to the tradition of erotic theory in the West.

"The primary purpose of that book is to dissolve the apparent paradox of Platonic eroticism. The paradox to which I refer arises from the wide application given to the term *eros* in Plato's writings and extends to the logical structure of his psychology and metaphysics. In many of the dialogues, but especially in the *Symposium* and *Phaedrus, eros* (or 'desire') signifies a force which operates in both the sexual and intellectual spheres of human activity. Commentators and scholars have traditionally assumed that *eros* cannot represent an equally valid, or applicable, concept in both realms of life and have tended accordingly to treat one version of eros as central to Plato's philosophical intent and to view the other as a logical or figural corollary to the first. Those who privilege the metaphysical function of desire in Plato's system regard his eloquent appeal to the data of sexual experience as a racy analogy, model, or metaphor for the erotics of philosophical inquiry. Those who consider sexuality a basic and irreducible element in human life treat philosophical eros as a redirected, sublimated form of sexual energy. Neither approach does justice I believe, to the psychological and philosophical unity of Platonic *eros*. Sexual desire, inasmuch as it is aroused by the presence in a human body of transcendental beauty (an object of metaphysical knowledge), is continuous, according to Plato, with the philosopher's desire to become immortal in the contemplation of the eternal forms. I hope to show what sense it makes for Plato to advance such a claim. I hope to demonstrate, in short, that a coherent account can be given of Platonic eroticism without collapsing either its sexual or its metaphysical dimension to the other."

*   *   *

HAMILTON, (Robert) Ian   1938-

PERSONAL: Born March 24, 1938, in King's Lynn, Norfolk, England; son of Robert Tough and Daisy (Mckay) Hamilton; married Gisela Dietzel, 1963; married Ahdaf Souief, 1981; children: (first marriage) one son; (second marriage) two sons. *Education:* Keble College, Oxford, B.A. (with honors), 1962.

ADDRESSES: Home—54 Queens Rd., London SW19, England.

CAREER: Tomorrow, Oxford, England, founder and editor, 1959-60; *Review,* London, England, founder and editor, 1962-72; *Times Literary Supplement,* London, poetry and fiction editor, 1965-73; University of Hull, Yorkshire, England, lecturer in poetry, 1971-72; *New Review,* London, editor, 1974-79; British Broadcasting Corp. (BBC), London, presenter of television program *Bookmark,* 1984-87.

AWARDS, HONORS: Eric Gregory Award, 1963; Malta Cultural Award, 1974; Melville Cane Award, Poetry Society of America, 1983; English-Speaking Union Award, 1984.

WRITINGS:

POEMS

Pretending Not to Sleep: Poems (pamphlet), Review, 1964.
The Visit: Poems, Faber, 1970.
Anniversary and Vigil, Poem-of-the-Month Club, 1971.
Returning, privately printed, 1976.
Fifty Poems, Faber, 1988.

EDITOR

The Poetry of War, 1939-45, Alan Ross, 1965.
Alun Lewis, *Selected Poetry and Prose,* Allen & Unwin, 1966.
The Modern Poet: Essays from 'The Review,' Macdonald & Co., 1968, Horizon Press, 1969.
Eight Poets, Poetry Book Society, 1968.
(And author of introduction) Robert Frost, *The Poetry of Robert Frost,* J. Cape, 1971, published as *Selected Poems,* Penguin, 1973.
(With Colin Falck) *Poems since 1900: An Anthology of British and American Verse in the Twentieth Century,* Macdonald & Jane's, 1974, published as *Poems since 1900: An Anthology,* Beekman, 1975.
Yorkshire in Verse, Secker & Warburg, 1984.
The 'New Review' Anthology, Heinemann, 1985.
Soho Square (2), Bloomsbury, 1989.

The Faber Book of Soccer, Faber, 1992.

OTHER

A Poetry Chronicle: Essays and Reviews, Barnes & Noble, 1973.
The Little Magazines: A Study of Six Editors, Weidenfeld & Nicolson, 1976.
Robert Lowell: A Biography, Random House, 1982.
In Search of J. D. Salinger, Random House, 1988.
Writers in Hollywood, 1915-1951, Harper, 1990.

Poetry reviewer, *London Magazine,* 1962-64; poetry critic, *Observer,* 1965-70.

SIDELIGHTS: For some thirty years, Ian Hamilton has been known as a critic, poet, biographer, and editor of anthologies, as well as the founder and editor of the *Review,* an influential British literary journal. His many roles have won Hamilton acclaim. He "is the best critic of modern verse we have had since G. S. Fraser," according to Derek Stanford in *Books and Bookmen.* Lachlan Mackinnon, writing in the *Times Literary Supplement,* notes that as editor of the *Review,* Hamilton "did much to foster new talent and to keep open an interest in American poetry in Britain." Much of Hamilton's criticism is found in *A Poetry Chronicle,* while his own poetry has been collected in *Fifty Poems.*

Hamilton first began publishing poetry in the 1960s, leaving that genre to edit magazines and anthologies and serve as a literary critic. His poems, and the poems he chose to publish in the *Review,* follow from the early Imagist work of Ezra Pound, "short, taut, 'minimalist' poems which at best showed a compacted and controlled energy," according to William Cookson in the *Dictionary of Literary Biography.* Cookson believes that in "his finest poems, Hamilton has found the right words for subject matter which he has lived and suffered directly; it is this honesty that will make his poetry last." Noting that Hamilton chose to pursue other forms of writing over poetry, Mackinnon opines: "It is a great pity that shunting poetry aside has left [Hamilton] so little work to show, for he could have been a larger poet and a more fruitful influence. The decision to live another kind of life may not have been easy, but it is not only Hamilton who has been impoverished by it." Cookson finds that "at least twelve [of Hamilton's poems] should survive among that small body of memorable work produced in the 1960s."

A Poetry Chronicle gathers together much of Hamilton's early poetry criticism, including his discussions of T. S. Eliot's *The Wasteland* and the works of William Carlos Williams. Hamilton argues that Eliot's landmark poem is blanketed in allusions because of Eliot's own inability to confront personal despair. Eliot would have written "more complex and affecting work," Hamilton writes, if he had been willing to pass judgment on his own "crippling refinement." In his criticism of Williams, Hamilton performs a "demolition" of the Williams cult, according to Stanford. He concentrates on the poet's "open syntax" technique, its drawbacks, and what Hamilton perceives as its utter failure as practiced by Williams' disciples, especially Robert Creely. Hamilton's critical analysis, Stanford believes, "by the operation of discrimination and intellectual scorn, proceeds to question, scale-down or explode current and fashionable reputations which lack an adequate validity."

As the editor of *Review* and then *New Review,* Hamilton was committed to raising the general level of English poetry, both by criticizing less-than-adequate work and by helping foundling poets publish their work. "Though limited in scope," Cookson says of the *Review,* "this periodical was usually worth reading because it had a clear editorial policy and stood for the poetic standards that Hamilton believes in and from which his finest poems have been made." Hamilton has also edited two anthologies of work first published in his magazines: *The Modern Poet: Essays from 'The Review'* and *The 'New Review' Anthology.*

In *Robert Lowell: A Biography,* Hamilton not only provides a summary of the poet's life but a critical analysis of his work. A longtime friend of the poet during his later years in England, "Hamilton writes with the authority of personal acquaintance and personal sympathy, as well as with a different authority (rare in literary biographers)—the authority of one who reads Lowell's work with accuracy, understanding, and a sense of technical interest," Helen Vendler states in the *New York Review of Books.* Jean Strouse of *Newsweek* praises "Hamilton's seamless weave of life story and literary criticism, his calm, sharp assessments and his refusal to idealize or 'explain' Lowell's genius or his pain." The book "in some ways," Vendler concludes, "will probably not be superseded."

To write his biography of the reclusive novelist J. D. Salinger, best known for his *The Catcher in the Rye,* Hamilton visited Salinger's old neighborhoods, spoke with his school friends, and even located some unpublished letters from the author. These letters, quoted in the original manuscript without authorization, moved Salinger to take legal action. After a protracted court battle, all quotations from these unpublished letters were removed from the book. Still, the remaining manuscript, focusing on Salinger's career as a writer rather than on his personal life, contains information unavailable elsewhere. Ironically, Hamilton was able to provide a close look at "Salinger's conduct during the legal battles," William Gargan writes in *Library Journal.* This insight, Gargan concludes, "actually reveals more of Salinger's character than the snippets of letters that appeared in the original work."

While researching a piece on F. Scott Fitzgerald for his television program *Bookmark,* Hamilton visited Hollywood where Fitzgerald had spent the last years of his life working for film studios. The visit perked Hamilton's interest in other writers who had worked in film. In his *Writers in Hollywood, 1915-1951,* Hamilton presents "an ably researched and entertaining" history of writers and film, according to Clancy Sigal in the *New York Times Book Review.* Beginning with the early silent films, Hamilton traces the history of screenwriting until the fall of the studio system in 1951. In particular he speaks of major authors who wrote for film, including Fitzgerald, William Faulkner, P. G. Wodehouse, and Aldous Huxley. Sigal finds that "Hamilton's brisk, no-nonsense approach to film writing—he respects craft and is suspicious of 'messages'—is a welcome antidote to the woozy ambiguities of the *auteur* theory." According to Zachary Leader in the *Times Literary Supplement,* Hamilton's account is "craftsmanlike and unassuming, and especially alert to pretension, a frequent failing of screenwriter and *cineaste* alike."

BIOGRAPHICAL/CRITICAL SOURCES:

BOOKS

Dictionary of Literary Biography, Volume 40: *Poets of Great Britain and Ireland since 1960,* Gale, 1985.

PERIODICALS

America, March 2, 1991, p. 252.
American Literature, October, 1989, p. 465.
American Spectator, October, 1988, p. 38.
Atlantic, February, 1983, p. 105.
Books, September, 1988, p. 19; October, 1988, p. 9; July, 1989, p. 11; February, 1990, p. 19; March, 1992, p. 19.
Books and Bookmen, June, 1973; August, 1976.
Books in Canada, October, 1988, p. 29.
British Book News, January, 1986, p. 50; December, 1987, p. 842.
Bulletin of the Poetry Book Society, summer, 1974.
Choice, February, 1989, p. 939.
Christian Science Monitor, May 21, 1990, p. 14.
Economist, September 17, 1988, p. 108.
Encounter, May, 1973; November, 1988, p. 63.
Film Quarterly, fall, 1991, p. 46.
Films in Review, November, 1990, p. 566.
Georgia Review, fall, 1988, p. 609.
Guardian Weekly, May 7, 1989, p. 29; June 24, 1990, p. 27.
Harper's, December, 1982, p. 52.
Illustrated London News, December 25, 1988, p. 72.
Library Journal, December 1, 1982, p. 2258; July, 1988, p. 81.
Listener, July 28, 1988, p. 32; September 22, 1988, p. 23; June 14, 1990, p. 29.

London Observer, January 14, 1973.

London Review of Books, March 3, 1988, p. 13; October 27, 1988, p. 3; June 14, 1990, p. 21.

Los Angeles Times Book Review, June 12, 1988, p. 3; August 20, 1989, p. 12; April 1, 1990, p. 1.

Maclean's, June 27, 1988, p. 56.

Magazine of Fantasy and Science Fiction, February, 1991, p. 28.

Modern Fiction Studies, summer, 1989, p. 299; summer, 1991, p. 259.

Modern Language Review, October, 1979.

Nation, February 26, 1983, p. 246.

National Review, March 18, 1983, p. 333; August 5, 1988, p. 48.

New Statesman, August 27, 1976; March 25, 1988, p. 28.

New Statesman and Society, September 23, 1988, p. 33; June 15, 1990, p. 33; February 21, 1992, p. 41.

Newsweek, November 15, 1982, p. 105; May 23, 1988, p. 73.

New York, May 23, 1988, p. 93.

New York Review of Books, December 2, 1982, p. 3; October 27, 1988, p. 35.

New York Times, May 20, 1988, p. C29; May 21, 1990, p. C14.

New York Times Book Review, November 28, 1982, p. 1; June 5, 1988, p. 7; August 13, 1989, p. 28; May 27, 1990, p. 2.

Observer, April 12, 1987, p. 23; January 31, 1988, p. 26; July 31, 1988, p. 43; September 18, 1988, p. 43; April 30, 1989, p. 47; July 16, 1989, p. 42; July 1, 1990, p. 57; July 22, 1990, p. 52; February 9, 1992, p. 63.

Poetry, June, 1961.

Poetry Review, autumn, 1970.

Punch, March 25, 1988, p. 46; September 23, 1988, p. 49; July 6, 1990, p. 48.

Reference and Research Book News, August, 1990, p. 23.

Sewanee Review, July, 1990, p. 515.

Spectator, September 4, 1976; December 20, 1986, p. 53; October 1, 1988, p. 33; June 23, 1990, p. 32; March 7, 1992, p. 27.

Stand, spring, 1990, p. 27.

Time, May 23, 1988, p. 74.

Times Educational Supplement, September 23, 1988, p. 28.

Times Literary Supplement, January 30, 1969; February 7, 1970; August 11, 1972; March 23, 1973; October 19, 1973; January 29, 1988, p. 115; September 30, 1988, p. 1066; July 15, 1990, p. 630; May 1, 1992, p. 32.

Tribune Books (Chicago), November 2, 1986, p. 3; May 8, 1988, p. 3; August 27, 1989, p. 4; June 30, 1991, p. 8.

Village Voice, July 5, 1988, p. 49.

Virginia Quarterly Review, summer, 1983, p. 516.

Washington Post Book World, August 27, 1989, p. 12; June 10, 1990, p. 4; May 26, 1991, p. 12.

World Literature Today, summer, 1983, p. 463.

—*Sketch by Thomas Wiloch*

*   *   *

HAMILTON, (Charles) Nigel 1944-

PERSONAL: Born February 16, 1944, in Alnmouth, England; son of Denis (a journalist) and Olive (a writer; maiden name, Wanless) Hamilton; married Hannelore Pfeifer, 1966 (died, 1973); married Outi Palovesi, July 31, 1976; children: Alexander, Sebastian, Nicholas. *Education:* Trinity College, Cambridge, B.A. (with honors), 1965, M.A., 1976.

ADDRESSES: Home—Heveningham House, Heveningham, Suffolk 1P19 0EA, England. *Agent*—Bruce Hunter, David Higham Associates, 5-8 Lower John St., London W1R 4HA, England.

CAREER: Writer. Employed by Andre Deutsch (publishers), London, England, 1965; secondary schoolteacher in London, 1966; Greenwich Bookshop, Greenwich, England, founder and proprietor, 1966-79; University of Massachusetts, John W. McCormack Institute, Boston, John F. Kennedy Scholar and visiting professor, late 1980s.

WRITINGS:

(With mother, Olive Hamilton) *Royal Greenwich,* privately printed, 1969.

Greenwich in Colour, Greenwich Bookshop, 1970.

Guide to Greenwich, Greenwich Bookshop, 1971.

America Began at Greenwich, Poseidon, 1976.

The Brothers Mann: The Lives of Heinrich and Thomas Mann, 1871-1950 and 1875-1955, Secker & Warburg, 1978, Yale University Press, 1979.

Monty: The Making of a General, 1887-1942, McGraw, 1981.

Master of the Battlefield: Monty's War Years, 1942-1944, McGraw, 1983.

Monty: Final Years of the Field-Marshal, 1944-1976, McGraw, 1987.

JFK: Reckless Youth, Random House, 1992, published in England as *JFK: Life and Death of an American President,* Volume 1: *Reckless Youth,* Century, 1992.

Also author of books under undisclosed pseudonyms.

SIDELIGHTS: Nigel Hamilton is a biographer who specializes in the lives of prominent men in politics and the arts. His *The Brothers Mann* tells of the relationship between German novelist Thomas Mann and his brother Heinrich, a relationship marked by their rivalry as writers.

Hamilton's three-volume biography of British Field-Marshall Montgomery follows the illustrious soldier's career from his childhood, through his triumphs during World War II, to his murder at the hands of Irish Republican terrorists in 1976. With *JFK: Reckless Youth* Hamilton begins a new multi-volume work on President John Kennedy, focusing on the president's youthful indiscretions, including a love affair with a Nazi spy.

The Brothers Mann, Jack Dierks writes in the *Chicago Tribune Book World,* "shows a conception imaginative enough and an execution absorbing enough to make one wonder why it has all taken so long" to write such a biography. Thomas, the younger of the two brothers, was the Nobel Prize-winning author of such works as *Buddenbrooks, The Magic Mountain,* and *Death in Venice.* Although Heinrich, also a writer, is well known in Europe, most of his writings remain untranslated into English. Today he is known principally as the author of the novel on which the Marlene Deitrich film *Blue Angel* is based.

If the younger brother eclipsed the elder as a writer, the elder was more involved in the political and social upheaval of modern Europe. Reviewers find the strength of *The Brothers Mann* to be in its portrayal of the Manns' life against this backdrop of societal conflict. Dierks comments that "the story of the Manns' productive life is the story of the capsizing of the cultural, intellectual, and social traditions into which they were born and attained maturity; and of their struggle to keep artistic heads above the undertow. . . . Hamilton plays on the right dramatic chord here as world conflict, economic and domestic chaos are used as backdrops to the literary growth and evolving political convictions of the brothers." Peter Gay of the *New York Times Book Review* writes that Hamilton has "an irresistible subject: the maturation of two immensely gifted brothers, their quarrel about World War I which, in miniature, reflected quarrels between cultures, and their moving reconciliation in the face of personal illness and the growing threat of Nazism. In general, Mr. Hamilton deals with his complex subject with effective and sober impartiality; he flags only toward the end—without significantly marring his book as a whole—in his inability to take distance from the Manns' embittered anti-American statements."

Hamilton's three-volume biography of British Field Marshal Bernard Law Montgomery, authorized by Montgomery's family and based in part on the general's personal diaries, "throws fresh light on matters around which controversy has raged unceasingly," according to Michael Carver in the *Times Literary Supplement.* Hamilton and Montgomery were friends, Robin Higham notes in the *New York Times Book Review,* "thus it is all the more surprising not only that this is a sound and sympathetic biography but also that its author has some very damning

things to say about its hero." Among the character flaws Hamilton finds in Montgomery are an enormous arrogance and a tendency to find fault with others.

Despite Montgomery's personal flaws, his career as England's leading general of World War II made him one of the most respected military leaders of the twentieth century. Montgomery played a pivotal role in the Allied invasion of Normandy—leading the British and American forces in the difficult landings on the beaches of northern France against overwhelming Nazi forces—and in the subsequent battle across France and into the heart of Germany. Although he was sometimes at odds with other Allied generals over strategy—favoring a bolder attack against the German heartland, for example, than was thought prudent by the High Command—Montgomery was beloved by those who served under him. Hamilton quotes General Dwight Eisenhower's observation of Montgomery, that he was able to inspire "an intense devotion and admiration" among his soldiers, "the greatest personal asset a commander can possess."

Although some critics believe Hamilton is ultimately too much an apologist for Montgomery, most find his biography to be of much value nonetheless. Despite finding several shortcomings in Hamilton's presentation of Montgomery, Russell F. Weigley admits in the *Washington Post Book World* that "no other work has approached Hamilton's as a portrayal of the man and his character." Carver calls Hamilton's biography "a notable contribution to history and to the psychological assessment of a man who, for all his grave defects of character, became Britain's greatest military commander of the twentieth century."

With *JFK: Reckless Youth,* Hamilton presents what Roger Morris in the *New York Times Book Review* calls "the gripping first volume of an ambitious full-scale life of John F. Kennedy." Covering Kennedy's life until he was first elected to Congress in 1946, *JFK: Reckless Youth* reveals much new material about the future president and his family. "Kennedyland, a theme park of family values, has flourished in the American imagination," Martin F. Nolan comments in the *Los Angeles Times Book Review.* "Hamilton has dismantled it."

According to Hamilton, John's father, Joe Kennedy, was a notorious philanderer who early in his marriage moved to a hotel where he could entertain showgirls without interference from his wife. His mother, Rose, was an emotionally distant woman who spent as much time away from her children as possible, leaving them in the care of a string of housekeepers. The young John Kennedy, sickly and scholarly, was bullied by his older brother Joe, Jr. In addition, Hamilton claims that Kennedy developed a fetish for cleanliness which moved him to shower five times a day. He suffered from Parkinson's Disease, venereal disease, and, while serving in the Navy during the Second World War, had an affair with a woman suspected of being a Nazi spy.

JFK: Reckless Youth became a bestseller in the United States. It also garnered critical praise for its incisive portrait of the troubled president. Hamilton's biography, Nolan comments, is an "investigative sweep of letters, school transcripts, books, newspapers and magazines, archives and oral history projects, all funneled into a narrative that neither demonizes nor sanctifies its subject." Morris concludes that "by the very detail and depth of the revelations, the flashes of brilliance and consistency of insight, 'JFK: Reckless Youth' easily takes its place beside the best of recent Presidential portraits. . . . By turns poignant and horrifying, but always awe-inspiring, the first volume gives us back a lost history."

BIOGRAPHICAL/CRITICAL SOURCES:

PERIODICALS

American Historical Review, December, 1982, p. 1412.
American Spectator, March, 1982, p. 34.
Atlantic Monthly, March, 1984, p. 125.
Books, August, 1987, p. 20.
Books and Bookmen, October, 1983, p. 16; August, 1986, p. 17.
British Book News, October, 1981, p. 602; February, 1984, p. 90; September, 1986, p. 529; May, 1987, p. 289; September, 1987, p. 594.
Business Week, September 28, 1981, p. 15; December 28, 1981, p. 9.
Chicago Tribune Book World, April 8, 1979.
Christian Science Monitor, March 17, 1987, p. 24.
Contemporary Review, February, 1984, p. 106.
Economist, June 13, 1981, p. 91; November 19, 1983, p. 109; September 27, 1986, p. 98; January 16, 1993, p. 88.
Encounter, June, 1985, p. 23.
Foreign Affairs, summer, 1984, p. 1257.
Guardian Weekly, June 21, 1981, p. 22; November 22, 1981, p. 18; November 6, 1983, p. 21; July 20, 1986, p. 21.
History Today, October, 1983, p. 64; March, 1985, p. 53; November, 1986, p. 36.
Illustrated London News, July, 1981, p. 58; December, 1983, p. 92; August, 1986, p. 69.
Listener, June 18, 1981, p. 780; October 27, 1983, p. 26.
London Review of Books, December 22, 1983, p. 7; September 4, 1986, p. 3; January 28, 1993, p. 22.
Los Angeles Times Book Review, March 22, 1987, p. 2; November 22, 1992, p. 1.
Maclean's, December 15, 1986, p. 62.

Nation, December 28, 1992, p. 813.
National Review, August 21, 1981, p. 965.
New Leader, December 14, 1992, p. 3.
New Statesman, June 12, 1981, p. 17.
Newsweek, September 14, 1981, p. 82; September 14, 1992, p. 70.
New York, September 14, 1992, p. 111.
New Yorker, July 9, 1979; April 23, 1984, p. 131; April 27, 1987, p. 105.
New York Review of Books, January 14, 1993, p. 3.
New York Times, May 3, 1979; April 16, 1984, p. 21.
New York Times Book Review, August 5, 1979; October 4, 1981, p. 14; March 11, 1984, p. 24; December 28, 1986, p. 11; November 22, 1992, p. 1.
Observer, June 7, 1981, p. 32; July 19, 1981, p. 29; December 6, 1981, p. 25; August 15, 1982, p. 31; November 6, 1983, p. 31; March 3, 1985, p. 27; July 21, 1985, p. 22; June 29, 1986, p. 22; July 20, 1986, p. 23; June 28, 1987, p. 22; July 19, 1987, p. 23; January 15, 1989, p. 49; July 16, 1989, p. 42; November 15, 1992, p. 64.
Punch, June 24, 1981, p. 1023.
Spectator, June 27, 1981, p. 20; December 31, 1983, p. 20; July 5, 1986, p. 28; December 12, 1992, p. 36.
Times Educational Supplement, November 23, 1984, p. 29; December 26, 1986, p. 11.
Times Literary Supplement, June 12, 1981, p. 657; July 18, 1986, p. 777.
Virginia Quarterly Review, spring, 1982, p. 51.
Washington Post Book World, April 15, 1979.

—*Sketch by Thomas Wiloch*

*   *   *

HARRIS, Errol E(ustace) 1908-

PERSONAL: Born February 19, 1908, in Kimberley, South Africa; son of Samuel J. (a merchant) and Dora (Gross) Harris; married Sylvia Mundahl, July 11, 1946 (died June 22, 1983); children: Jonathan, Nigel, Hermione, Martin. *Education:* Rhodes University, B.A., 1927, M.A., 1929; Magdalen College, Oxford, B.Litt., 1950. *Religion:* Episcopalian.

ADDRESSES: Home—High Wray House, Ambleside, Cumbria LA22 0JQ, England.

CAREER: Fort Hare University College (now University of Fort Hare), Fort Hare, South Africa, lecturer in philosophy, 1930; British Colonial Service, education officer in Basutoland and Zanzibar, 1937-42; University of the Witwatersrand, Johannesburg, South Africa, lecturer, 1946-50, senior lecturer, 1951-52, professor of philosophy, 1953-56; Connecticut College, New London, professor of philosophy, 1956-62; University of Kansas, Lawrence, Roy Roberts Distinguished Professor of Philosophy,

1962-66; Northwestern University, Evanston, IL, professor of philosophy, 1966-76, John Evans Professor of Moral and Intellectual Philosophy, 1973-76. Yale University, visiting lecturer, 1956-57, Terry Lecturer, 1957; visiting professor and acting head of department of logic and metaphysics, University of Edinburgh, 1959-60; Heinz Werner Lecturer, Clark University, 1973; Matchette Lecturer, Tulane University, 1975; Marquette University, visiting distinguished professor, 1976-77, Aquinas Lecturer, 1977; Cowling Professor, Carleton College, 1977-78; visiting distinguished professor of Christian philosophy, Villanova University, 1982; visiting professor, Emory University, 1983-84; Ryle Lecturer, Trent University, 1984. *Military service:* British Army, South African Information Service, 1942-46; became major.

MEMBER: American Philosophical Association, Metaphysical Society of America (president, 1968-69), Hegel Society of America (president, 1976-78), Vereniging het Spinozahuis, Mind Association, Aristotelian Society.

AWARDS, HONORS: Hugh Le May research fellow at Rhodes University, 1949; Bollingen research fellow, 1960-62; Ford Foundation research fellow, 1964; research fellow, Institute for Advanced Studies in the Humanities, University of Edinburgh, 1978; Paul Weiss Medal, Metaphysical Society of America, 1989, for distinguished work in metaphysics.

WRITINGS:

The Survival of Political Man: A Study in the Principles of International Order, Witwatersrand University Press, 1950.

"White" Civilization: How It Is Threatened and How It Can Be Preserved in South Africa, South African Institute of Race Relations, 1952.

Nature, Mind, and Modern Science, Macmillan, 1954.

Objectivity and Reason (inaugural lecture), Witwatersrand University Press, 1955.

(Editor) Harold H. Joachim, *Descartes's Rules for the Direction of the Mind* (reconstructed from notes), Allen & Unwin, 1957.

Revelation through Reason: Religion in the Light of Science and Philosophy, Yale University Press, 1958.

Analysis and Insight (inaugural lecture), University of Kansas, 1962.

The Foundations of Metaphysics in Science, Humanities Press, 1965.

Annihilation and Utopia: The Principles of International Politics, Humanities Press, 1966.

Fundamentals of Philosophy: A Study of Classical Texts, Holt, 1969.

Hypothesis and Perception: The Roots of Scientific Method, Humanities Press, 1970.

Salvation from Despair: A Reassessment of Spinoza's Philosophy, Nijhoff, 1973.

Perceptual Assurance and the Reality of the World, Clark University Press, 1974.

Atheism and Theism, Tulane University Press, 1977.

The Problem of Evil (Aquinas Lectures), Marquette University Press, 1977.

An Interpretation of the Logic of Hegel, University Press of America, 1983.

Formal Transcendental, and Dialectical Thinking, State University of New York Press, 1987.

Time and the World, State University of New York Press, 1988.

(Translator with Peter Heath) F. W. J. Schelling, *Ideas for a Philosophy of Nature,* Cambridge University Press, 1988.

Cosmos and Anthropos, Humanities Press, 1991.

Spinoza's Philosophy: An Outline, Humanities Press, 1992.

Cosmos and Theos, Humanities Press, 1992.

The Spirit of Hegel, Humanities Press, 1993.

Contributor to over thirty books, including *Theories of the Mind,* edited by J. Scher, Free Press of Glencoe, 1962; *The Personal Universe,* edited by Thomas E. Wren, *The Personal Universe,* Humanities Press, 1975; *Hegel's Philosophy of Action,* edited by L. Stepelevich and D. Lamb, Humanities Press, 1983; and *Philosophical Perspectives on Newtonian Science,* MIT Press, 1990.

WORK IN PROGRESS: One World or None.

SIDELIGHTS: Errol E. Harris told *CA:* "Three major concerns have motivated most, if not all, of the writing I have done: i. an intense desire for the emancipation of black South Africans, of whatever racial origin, from the white domination prevailing in the land of my birth. *'White' Civilization* was intended as a reasoned appeal to the white regime in that country to realize that their much vaunted civilization did not depend on colour but could be maintained and preserved only by observing its central principle of equal dignity for all persons, irrespective of race, colour or creed; ii. a deep anxiety for the establishment of world peace during an era in which the constant menace of nuclear war has threatened the final destruction of that civilization. This inspired the writing of *The Survival of Political Man* and *Annihilation and Utopia.* A similar concern about the destruction of the planetary environment with its terminal threat to life on Earth has moved me to write another book, *One World or None,* now in press; iii. a persistent urge to revitalize and restore the philosophical foundations of our civilization in epistemology, ethics and philosophy of religion, through recovery of a genuine speculative method of investigating fundamental principles, as against the prevalent positivistic, materialistic and formalistic empiricism of our age."

Reviewing *The Foundations of Metaphysics in Science,* W. H. Thorpe writes in the *British Journal for the Philosophy of Science:* "Professor Harris states that the aim of science is to produce a theory of the real and it is his intention as a philosopher to try to develop *ab initio* the metaphysical theory which the discoveries of science demand and for which they provide the empirical grounds. It is, of course, clear that individual scientists will find in this great work statements and points of emphasis about their specialties, with which they disagree. Similarly, philosophers will obviously find much to dispute. Nevertheless, that it is a great work is, I think, beyond doubt; and I feel that there are very few philosophers and philosophically-minded scientists who will not find reading it a great stimulus and even an inspiration."

A critic for *Choice* writes about *Cosmos and Anthropos:* "As one would expect from Harris, *Cosmos and Anthropos* is a model of erudition, great analytic clarity, and splendid stylistic elegance. Everyone interested in science, philosophy, religion, and theology will find this book truly rewarding."

BIOGRAPHICAL/CRITICAL SOURCES:

PERIODICALS

British Journal for the Philosophy of Science, November, 1966.
Choice, 1992.

* * *

HART, Carolyn G(impel) 1936-

PERSONAL: Born August 25, 1936, in Oklahoma City, OK; daughter of Roy William (an organ builder) and Doris (Akin) Gimpel; married Philip Donnell Hart (an attorney), June 10, 1958; children: Philip Donnell, Jr., Sarah Ann. *Education:* University of Oklahoma—Norman, B.A., 1958. *Religion:* Protestant.

ADDRESSES: Home—1705 Drakestone Ave., Oklahoma City, OK 73120. *Agent*—Deborah C. Schneider, Gelfman Schneiders Agents Inc., 250 West 57th St., New York, NY 10107.

CAREER: Norman Transcript, Norman, OK, reporter, 1958-59; *Sooner Newsmakers* (University of Oklahoma alumni newsletter), editor, 1959-60; free-lance writer, 1961-82; University of Oklahoma, School of Journalism and Mass Communications, assistant professor, 1982-85; full-time writer, 1986—.

MEMBER: Sisters in Crime (president, 1991-92), Mystery Writers of America (past national director), Authors Guild, Phi Beta Kappa, Theta Sigma Phi.

AWARDS, HONORS: Dodd, Mead-*Calling All Girls* Prize, 1964, for *The Secret of the Cellars;* Agatha Award, Malice Domestic, 1989, for *Something Wicked;* Anthony Award, Bouchercon, 1989, for *Something Wicked,* and 1990, for *Honeymoon with Murder;* Macavity Award, Mystery Readers International, 1990, for *A Little Class on Murder.*

WRITINGS:

"DEATH ON DEMAND" MYSTERIES

Death on Demand, Bantam, 1987.
Design for Murder, Bantam, 1988.
Something Wicked, Bantam, 1988.
Honeymoon with Murder, Bantam, 1989.
A Little Class on Murder, Doubleday, 1989.
Deadly Valentine, Doubleday, 1990.
The Christie Caper, Bantam, 1991.
Southern Ghost, Bantam, 1992.

JUVENILES

The Secret of the Cellars, Dodd, 1964.
Dangerous Summer, Fair Winds, 1968.
Rendezvous in Vera Cruz, M. Evans, 1970.
No Easy Answers, M. Evans, 1970.
Danger! High Explosives!, M. Evans, 1972.

OTHER

Flee from the Past, Bantam, 1975.
A Settling of Accounts, Doubleday, 1976.
(With Charles F. Long) *The Sooner Story, 1890-1980,* University of Oklahoma Foundation, 1980.
Escape from Paris, Hale, 1982, St. Martin's, 1983.
The Rich Die Young, Hale, 1983.
Death by Surprise, Hale, 1983.
Castle Rock, Hale, 1983.
Skulduggery, Hale, 1984.
The Devereaux Legacy, Harlequin, 1986.
Brave Hearts, Pocket Books, 1987.
Dead Man's Island, Bantam, 1993.

SIDELIGHTS: Carolyn G. Hart is best known as the award-winning author of the best-selling "Death on Demand" series of mystery novels. Set on fictional Broward's Rock Island, South Carolina, the series features Annie Laurance, proprietor of the mystery bookshop *Death on Demand.* With her handsome blond husband, consultant Max Darling, Laurance both sells and solves mysteries that come her way.

Inspired by a love of reading, Hart began her literary career as a reporter, and only later becoming an author of fiction. "I can't even remember when I started reading," she told *Something about the Author (SATA)* in a specially conducted interview. "It was always a part of my life. I read very widely when I was young; Robert Louis Stevenson and Charles Dickens were favorites. There were so many—Thomas Chastain, Pearl S. Buck. . . . And of course I adored Alexandre Dumas's *The Man in the Iron Mask* and *The Count of Monte Cristo* (that was my favorite). My parents were both readers: my father enjoyed Agatha Christie, and my mother was always interested in history. I don't remember ever not being involved with books.

"I always loved mysteries, especially the Nancy Drew stories. A lot of women mystery writers have talked about this at conferences, and to all of us she was a wonderful inspiration. At that time (the forties, before the independent female characters that characterize fiction today appeared) Nancy had her own roadster, and she was free to come and go as she wished. She solved the problems, not her boyfriend Ned. This was one of the few areas in which girls could read about a young woman who was in charge of her own destiny. So I think Nancy Drew had a tremendous effect, not only on me, but on many of the women who are writing mysteries today.

"I enjoyed the Hardy Boys thoroughly as well. I was especially fond of Joe—I thought he was very, very attractive. Another of my great favorites was the Beverly Gray Mysteries series, written by Clair Blank. I think it was wonderful that there was reading available for us young girls that truly gave us a feeling of freedom—a feeling that we didn't find in the rest of our society and environment at that time."

Hart's love of mysteries continues to this day. She still harbors a fondness for many of the great women mystery writers of the earlier part of the century. "It's wonderful how so many of the great mysteries of the past are being made available again," she remarks. "The Foul Play Press has reissued all of Phoebe Atwood Taylor's books, and a good many others as well. I just love Phoebe Atwood Taylor. Whenever I get really tired, I'll pick one of her books up and reread it. She was a wonderful writer. I have read all of Agatha Christie; in fact, one of the books in my 'Death on Demand' series is called *The Christie Caper.* In that book, Annie is hosting a conference on the island in honor of the hundredth anniversary of Christie's birth, and the entire book has to do (in addition to the mystery) with a celebration of Christie, her works and her life. If I thought of the three authors who have influenced me the most as a mystery writer, it would be Agatha Christie, and Phoebe Atwood Taylor, and Mary Roberts Rinehart. The three of them are my complete favorites, although I don't write in the style of any of them. Yet I have learned so much from all of them."

"I grew up in Oklahoma during World War II, and the war had a great effect upon my approach to life," Hart told *SATA.* "We waited so eagerly for the newspaper—of course you did get news on the radio, but this was still in the era of newspaper extras—when something very exciting or important happened in the war. I think my whole perspective as a child was affected by the war: the newspaper was very important, so obviously it was very important to produce newspapers. This formed my ambition to be a newspaper reporter. That's what I worked toward all the way through school and at the University of Oklahoma.

"It never occurred to me that I would write fiction, but as so often happens in life, different things affect the course of our lives. I met a young law student at the university, and we were married. When I had finished being a reporter and was starting to have a family (that was in the period before young women were expected to have full-time careers and full-time families at the same time) I was at home a lot. I wasn't happy not writing, and that was the first time it ever occurred to me to write fiction. I think I first tried juvenile mysteries because of my original love of Nancy Drew. That's the story of my transformation from a newspaper reporter to a writer of fiction."

Hart's first book, titled *The Secret of the Cellars,* appeared in 1964. She followed it with another mystery and several young-adult suspense novels, including *No Easy Answers,* about the Vietnam War, and *Danger! High Explosives!,* about a college torn over the question of a military presence on the campus. "There's a very definite distinction between mystery and suspense," Hart told *SATA.* "In a mystery novel the point of the book is to figure out who committed a crime. When you do that, what you're really exploring (especially in the case of murder, which is what mysteries are usually about) is what went wrong in the lives of these people. How did these relationships become so tortured that violence resulted? A suspense novel, on the other hand, tells the story of a person who is trying to accomplish something. It doesn't matter if it's getting to the top of the mountain, escaping from the Japanese during the war, or whatever—the suspense novel is built around a series of episodes where the character must continue to struggle to achieve a goal. It's a very different kind of story than a mystery.

"I rather doubt that I will ever write another juvenile. I believe that to write a successful juvenile you have to have a real understanding of what it is like to look at life without preconceptions—the difference between an adult and a child. At the point I wrote those books, I was much younger, and I had young children. Now I'm 56, I've just started a new series from the perspective of a retired newspaper woman about ten years older than I am (it's a very sardonic appraisal of life), and I don't think that I could ever go back and find the freshness you have to have to be a successful juvenile author, and that I so admire in the works of Joan Lowry Nixon and George Edward Stanley."

After finishing the last of her juveniles, Hart moved on to writing for adults. "*The Devereaux Legacy* was written during a very desperate period in my career," she explained. "I couldn't sell anything. I had seven manuscripts in New York—some of which ultimately sold in England, but have never been reprinted in the U.S. I was at a very low point, the point where I thought that maybe I should just give up writing. No one was buying mysteries by American women, but the romance novel was at the height of its popularity, and my agent said, 'There's just no point in writing mysteries. You've got to write romances.' I thought, 'Well, maybe I can do this. I suppose the question is not *Who Killed Roger Ackroyd?* but *Will she win the hero in the end?* So I tried my hand at it. Basically what I did with *The Devereaux Legacy* was to take a mystery that I had written and recast it as a romance. It has a very southern background, and that's why it was bought by the Harlequin Gothic arm.

"That was my foray into the romance field—I was not successful with it. It's not a bad book; it's just that (not to be derogatory to people who write romances) I see a lack in myself. As my daughter once told me, 'Mother, the reason you can't write romances is because you aren't romantic.' And I said, 'Honey, you are so right,' because I'm not—I'm a very analytical person. I think that is the kind of mind it takes to be successful in writing mysteries, but it's not the sort of mind a romance writer needs. You need an emotional response in good romance novels. I only know of two or three authors who have been very successful in both fields. I think it would be very difficult to do.

"*Southern Ghost* has elements of the gothic in it intentionally. My editor said 'Why don't you write a Southern Gothic?' and I said, 'Well, all right, I'll see what I can do with that.' It was a very fascinating and difficult book to write. I later realized that the reason why it was so stressful was because when you're writing a Southern Gothic you're writing about a family, and nothing is more distressing than destructive emotions in a family situation. In only one of my other books had there been a focus on a family rather than just a group of individuals. It was a challenge."

Hart recently completed a term as president of "Sisters in Crime"—an organization that, she explains, "is intended to provide information on women writers of crime and mystery fiction. We put out a catalogue twice a year which lists books by all of our members. The aim of the organization is to get the word out to libraries and bookstores about the enormous proliferation of mysteries by women. 'Sisters in Crime' came into existence because in 1986 Sara Paretsky went to the Bouchercon, one of the major mystery meetings that's held annually, and there were no books by American women mystery writers being discussed. There weren't even American women mystery writers on any of the panels. This did not sit well with Sara. So she talked to three or four other women who were attending the conference, and that was the start of 'Sisters in Crime.'

"Sue Grafton, Marsha Muller, and Sara Paretsky are the ones who opened the window of opportunity for women mystery writers. Before their books became popular, the market belonged primarily to American male hard-boiled writers and to dead British ladies. Nobody was very interested in books by American women until these three writers wrote the book that's considered the American mystery—the hard-boiled private eye book. But the characters were women, and the books were written by women. The enormous popularity of these books attracted the attention of publishers in New York, who thought 'Hey, people like books by American women, not just British women.' Frankly, my career would have gone nowhere had not these women broken through the barrier that American women mystery writers faced for a long time. So we're very grateful to all three of them."

Hart forsees a bright future for both writers and readers of the mystery genre. She told *SATA*, "My sense is that the current boom in the mystery genre will last because the caliber of the writing is so good—there are so many wonderful writers writing mysteries now. So as long as readers are happy I think that they will continue to buy mysteries, and I don't see how the readers could help but be extremely happy right now."

BIOGRAPHICAL/CRITICAL SOURCES:

BOOKS

Something about the Author, Volume 74, Gale, 1993.

PERIODICALS

Chattanooga Times, June 26, 1992, p. C6.
Clarion-Ledger (Jackson, MS), July 5, 1992.
Island Packet (Hilton Head Island, SC), June 14, 1992.
Nashville Banner, June 13, 1992.
Pioneer Press (St. Paul, MN), July 15, 1992.
Wilson Library Journal, March, 1987.

*   *   *

HASSAN, Ihab Habib 1925-

PERSONAL: Born October 17, 1925, in Cairo, Egypt; came to United States in 1946, naturalized in 1956; son of Habib and Faika (Hamdi) Hassan; married Alida Koten, April 18, 1949 (divorced); married Sarah Margaret

Greene, 1966; children: (first marriage) Geoffrey. *Education:* University of Cairo, B.Sc., 1946; University of Pennsylvania, M.S., 1948, M.A., 1950, Ph.D., 1953.

ADDRESSES: Home—2137 North Terrace Ave., Milwaukee, WI 53202. *Office*—University of Wisconsin—Milwaukee, P.O. Box 413, Milwaukee, WI 53201.

CAREER: Rensselaer Polytechnic Institute, Troy, NY, instructor in English, 1952-54; Wesleyan University, Middletown, CT, instructor, 1954-55, assistant professor, 1955-58, associate professor, 1958-62, professor of English, 1962-63, Benjamin L. Waite Professor of English, 1964-70, chairman of department, 1963-64, 1968-69, director of College of Letters, 1964-66, director of Center for Humanities, 1969-70; University of Wisconsin—Milwaukee, Vilas Research Professor, 1970—. Tutor, American Seminars at Salzburg, 1965 and 1975; member of faculty, Stuttgart Seminars; visiting professor, Seijo University, 1991. Director of National Endowment for the Humanities summer seminars for college teachers, 1982, 1984, and 1989. Fulbright lecturer, Grenoble, France, 1966-67, and Nice, France, 1974-75; distinguished Fulbright lecturer, Kyoto Seminars in American Studies, summer, 1974. Visiting fellow, Woodrow Wilson International Center for Scholars, 1972; senior fellow, Camargo Foundation, 1974-75; visiting scholar, Rockefeller Bellagio Study and Conference Center, 1978. Member of editorial board, Wesleyan University Press, 1963-66; member of divisional executive committee of Comparative Literature in the Twentieth Century, 1976-79, and American Literature in the Twentieth Century, 1984-89.

MEMBER: International Comparative Literature Association, International Association of University Professors of English, Modern Language Association of America, American Studies Association, Sigma Xi.

AWARDS, HONORS: Guggenheim fellow, 1958-59 and 1962-63; fellow, School of Letters, Indiana University, 1964, Humanities Research Institute, University of California, Irvine, 1990, and Humanities Research Center, 1990; Japan Foundation grant, 1979; honorary research fellow, Institute of United States Studies, University of London, 1988.

WRITINGS:

Radical Innocence: The Contemporary American Novel, Princeton University Press, 1961.
Aspects du Hero Americain Contemporain, Lettres Modernes, 1963.
The Literature of Silence: Henry Miller and Samuel Beckett, Knopf, 1967.
(Editor) *Liberations: New Essays on the Humanities in Revolution,* Wesleyan University Press, 1971.

The Dismemberment of Orpheus: Toward a Postmodern Literature, Oxford University Press, 1971, 2nd edition, University of Wisconsin Press, 1982.
Contemporary American Literature: 1945-1972, Ungar, 1973.
Paracriticisms: Seven Speculations of the Times, Illinois University Press, 1975.
The Right Promethean Fire: Imagination, Science, and Cultural Change, Illinois University Press, 1980.
(Editor with Sally Hassan) *Innovation/Renovation: New Perspectives on the Humanities,* University of Wisconsin Press, 1981.
Out of Egypt: Fragments of an Autobiography, Southern Illinois University Press, 1986.
The Postmodern Turn: Essays in Postmodern Theory and Culture, Ohio State University, 1987.
Selves at Risk: Patterns of Quest in Contemporary American Letters, University of Wisconsin Press, 1990.

OTHER

Contributor to journals and newspapers, including *Saturday Review, New York Times Book Review, American Scholar, Critique, Nation, Critical Inquiry, New Literary History, Salmagundi,* and *Book Week.* Member of editorial board, *American Quarterly,* 1965-67. Member of advisory board, *Diacritios,* 1973—, *Humanities in Society,* 1978—, and *PMLA,* 1979-83.

SIDELIGHTS: In her review of *The Literature of Silence: Henry Miller and Samuel Beckett,* Sue Wienhorst writes in *Encounter* of Ihab Habib Hassan's talent as a literary critic: "As a combination of cultural analysis and genre description that focuses upon the interior logic of the contemporary spirit and the literary form in which this logic is reflected, Mr. Hassan's criticism has great power. In his adept and sensitive hand, this approach convinces us of the seriousness and the integrity of anti-literature as an *avant-garde* genre and illumines a broad range of contemporary art and thought."

Hassan told *CA* that since his first work, *Radical Innocence: The Contemporary American Novel,* he "has concerned himself with *avant-garde* movements, the postmodern phenomenon, travel as quest, vision, and transgression, the collision and interanimation of cultures, especially Oriental and Occidental."

BIOGRAPHICAL/CRITICAL SOURCES:

PERIODICALS

Encounter, summer, 1968.
New York Review of Books, February 13, 1969.
Times Literary Supplement, February 17, 1984.

HAXTON, Josephine Ayres 1921-
(Ellen Douglas)

PERSONAL: Born July 12, 1921 in Natchez, MS; daughter of Richardson (an engineer) and Laura (a homemaker; maiden name, Davis) Ayres; married Kenneth Haxton, January 12, 1945 (divorced); children: Richard, Ayres, Brooks. *Education:* Attended Randolph Macon Women's College, 1938-39; University of Mississippi, B.A., 1942.

ADDRESSES: Home and office—1600 Pine St., Jackson, MS 39202. *Agent*—Robert L. Rosen Associates, 7 West 51st St., New York, NY 10019.

CAREER: Writer. Northeast Louisiana University, Monroe, writer-in-residence, 1976-79; University of Mississippi, Oxford, writer-in-residence, 1982—; University of Virginia, Charlottesville, writer-in-residence, spring, 1984. Faculty member of Faulkner Symposium, University of Mississippi, 1980. Welty Professor, Millsaps College, Jackson, spring, 1988. Guest reader and lecturer at University of Michigan, Louisiana State University, and other colleges and universities.

AWARDS, HONORS: Short story "On the Lake" included in O. Henry collection, 1961; Houghton Mifflin fellowship, 1961, and best novel of the year citation, *New York Times,* both for *A Family's Affairs;* five best works of fiction citation, *New York Times,* 1963, for *Black Cloud, White Cloud;* National Book Award finalist, National Book Committee, 1973, for *Apostles of Light;* National Endowment for the Humanities fellowship, 1976; Mississippi Institute of Arts and Letters Award (literature), 1979, for *The Rock Cried Out,* and 1983, for *A Lifetime Burning;* grants from National Educational Association for *The Rock Cried Out* and *Can't Quit You, Baby;* fiction award, The Fellowship of Southern Writers, 1989, for body of work.

WRITINGS:

COLLECTIONS; UNDER PSEUDONYM ELLEN DOUGLAS

Black Cloud, White Cloud: Two Novellas and Two Stories (fairy tales), Houghton, 1963.
The Magic Carpet, University Press of Mississippi, 1987.

NOVELS; UNDER PSEUDONYM ELLEN DOUGLAS

A Family's Affairs, Houghton, 1962.
Where the Dreams Cross, Houghton, 1968.
Apostles of Light, Houghton, 1973.
The Rock Cried Out, Harcourt, 1979.
A Lifetime Burning, Random House, 1982.
Can't Quit You, Baby, Atheneum, 1988.

Also contributor to periodicals, including *Harper's, New York Times Book Review, Esquire, New Yorker,* and *New Republic.*

SIDELIGHTS: Like William Faulkner, Ellen Douglas has created a fictional Mississippi county in which many of her novels and stories take place. Called Homochito County, it is the setting for Douglas's fourth novel, *The Rock Cried Out*—a tale that explores the southern staples of "secret love, unrevealed parentage, miscegenation, hatred, revenge and murder," reported Doris Grumbach in the *Washington Post Book World.* "Some of the elements are gothic," she continued, "but in Ellen Douglas's talented hands the story unfolds slowly, believably, without the piled-up, exclamatory haste of the gothic novel."

The narrator of *The Rock Cried Out* is an ex-hippie who returns to his native Chickasaw Ridge to reconnect with the land and his past. His serenity is shattered, however, when another native son returns and stirs up buried information about a gory car accident that took place several years ago, at the height of the town's civil rights and Ku Klux Klan activities. Jonathan Yardley wrote in the *New York Times Book Review* that it is Douglas's "admirably sensitive treatment" of "the corrosive effect upon whites and their families of massive, violent reaction to the civil-rights movement . . . that gives '*The Rock Cried Out*' its true distinction." Yardley further explained that "the author does not present this as an apology; it's an attempt, to me a persuasive one, at explanation."

A *New Yorker* critic noted that in *The Rock Cried Out* "Miss Douglas achieves . . . an illuminating portrait of an exceptionally troubled region and era." Grumbach concurred, calling the book "a valuable and impressive fictional portrait. Here we are brought to know, poignantly, a time, a young man's loss of innocence, a civilization's endurance despite the menace of outside forces and, most of all, a place," she added. And Yardley concluded: "Miss Douglas knows her fellow Mississippians well, and her exploration of their hearts and lives is at once passionate and clinical. She will have nothing of evasions and deceptions; she forces all of her characters to confront the legacy of their past head-on. She writes very well and thinks very clearly. '*The Rock Cried Out*' is powerful and disturbing. It should secure Ellen Douglas's place in the literature of the South."

In *A Lifetime Burning* Douglas takes a departure from her southern narratives, presenting her fifth novel in the form of a diary of a sixty-two year old Southern woman—a literature professor named Corinne—who bitterly tries to make sense of her life. Corinne's discovery of her husband's love affair has forced a lifetime of past hurts and confusions to resurface; she professes to write the diary for the illumination of her grown children but her real need is to piece together an existence that holds meaning for her. Susan Isaacs, writing in the *New York Times Book Review,* observed that "Corinne is engaging and credibly drawn. Because she is so intelligent and literate, Corinne can express her hurt eloquently. . . . It is fascinating to watch Corinne expose herself as she peels off layers of lies and facile explanation."

Because the diary shifts back and forth between dream and reality, invention and confession, the reader can never be sure of the "truth" of Corinne's revelations. "Lies, distortions, deceptions, evasions—these are essential to the maintenance of the delicate fabric of which family and society are made," explained Yardley in a second *Washington Post Book World* review. He continued: "This, as I interpret it, is the central theme of *A Lifetime Burning:* we are separate beings and cannot be otherwise, we are mysteries to each other and will always be. In order to keep the structure of our lives intact, it is necessary to withhold the full truth: we invent ourselves for others—and, perhaps, for ourselves." The critic deemed the book "a splendid piece of writing . . . [Douglas's] finest novel." Expressing similar praise, Isaacs stated that, while the book has "too literary" moments when "technique overpower[s] characterization," it "is for the most part a beautifully constructed work of fiction." She added that "Ellen Douglas has all the qualities a reader could ask of a novelist: depth, emotional range, wit, sensitivity and the gift of language. 'A Lifetime Burning' is a fine showcase for her talents."

BIOGRAPHICAL/CRITICAL SOURCES:

PERIODICALS

Esquire, May, 1973.
Observer (London), June 13, 1983.
New York Times Book Review, February 18, 1973; September 23, 1979; November 25, 1979; October 31, 1982.
New Yorker, March 3, 1973; October 8, 1979.
Newsweek, March 5, 1973.
Time, April 15, 1974.
Washington Post Book World, September 9, 1979; December 9, 1979; October 31, 1982; September 9, 1990.

*   *   *

HAYDEN, Thomas E(mmet) 1939-
(Tom Hayden)

PERSONAL: Born December 11, 1939, in Royal Oak, MI; son of Jack (an accountant) and Genevieve (a librarian; maiden name, Garity) Hayden; married Sandra Cason (a civil rights worker; divorced, 1963); married Jane Fonda (an actress), January 20, 1973 (divorced); children: Vanessa Vadim (stepdaughter), Troy Garity. *Education:* University of Michigan, B.A., 1960, and graduate study. *Politics:* Democrat. *Religion:* Roman Catholic.

ADDRESSES: Home—Santa Monica, CA. *Office*—State Capitol, Room 3091, Sacramento, CA 95814.

CAREER: Political activist. Member of Student Nonviolent Coordinating Committee; cofounder of Students for a Democratic Society, 1961, president, 1962-63; cofounder of Economic Research and Action Project, 1964; director of Newark Community Union Project, Newark, NJ, 1965-67; project director of National Mobilization Committee to End the War in Vietnam; national coordinator of Indochina Peace Campaign, 1973-75; candidate for United States Senate in California Democratic Primary, 1976; founder and chairman of Campaign for Economic Democracy (now known as Campaign California), 1977—; founder of Students for Economic Democracy; member of California state assembly, District 44, 1982—. Chairman of state of California's SolarCal Council, 1978-82; director of Western Solar Utilization Network, 1978-82; delegate to White House conference on economic development, 1978; governor's representative on Southwest Border Regional Commission, 1979-80; member of California Public Investment Task Force; cofounder of Toxics Responsibility Advisory Committee. Member of faculty of University of Southern California, Los Angeles, Pitzer College, Claremont, CA, and Immaculate Heart College, Los Angeles; lecturer at universities, including Rutgers University.

WRITINGS:

Radical Nomad: Essays on C. Wright Mills and His Times, Center for Research on Conflict Resolution, University of Michigan, 1964.
(With Staughton Lynd) *The Other Side,* New American Library, 1966.
Rebellion in Newark: Official Violence and Ghetto Response, Vintage Books, 1967.
Rebellion and Repression: Testimony by Tom Hayden before the National Commission on the Causes and Prevention of Violence, and the House Un-American Activities Committee, World Publishing, 1969.
Trial, Holt, 1970.
The Love of Possession Is a Disease with Them, Holt, 1972.
Vietnam: The Struggle for Peace, 1972-73, Indochina Peace Campaign (Santa Monica), 1973.
The American Future: New Visions beyond Old Frontiers, South End Press, 1980, revised edition published as *The American Future: New Visions beyond the Reagan Administration,* Washington Square Press, 1982.
(With J. H. Bunzel) *New Force on the Left,* Hoover Institution Press, 1983.
Reunion: A Memoir, Random House, 1988.
The Port Huron Statement: The Founding Manifesto of Students for a Democratic Society, Charles Kerr, 1990.

Contributor to *The Conspiracy,* edited by Bob Abel, Peter Babcox, and Deborah Babcox, Dell, 1969. Also contributor of articles to magazines and newspapers, including *New York Times, New York Review of Books, Los Angeles Times, Wall Street Journal, National Catholic Reporter, Rolling Stone, Ramparts,* and *Nation.*

SIDELIGHTS: Since the early 1960s, the political career of activist Thomas E. Hayden has paralleled the development of leftist politics in America. Hayden first became involved in politics while a student at Ann Arbor's University of Michigan, where he was exposed to the earliest stirrings of the student activist movement. He began attending student activist conferences and soon became involved in the Student Nonviolent Coordinating Committee (SNCC). He traveled to Georgia and Mississippi as a journalist for the university's *Michigan Daily,* covering the committee's activities in the South and the civil rights movement. He was arrested, along with ten other SNCC members, while organizing to desegregate public transportation facilities in Albany, Georgia, and was beaten during a voter-registration drive in McComb, Mississippi. Hayden recorded various aspects of his turbulent political career in such works as *Rebellion in Newark* and *Trial.* And in 1988 he reflected on his life and activities of his youth in *Reunion: A Memoir.* "If the outline of [Hayden's] autobiography could serve almost as a generational profile, however, the particulars are unique," asserts Elinor Langer in the *Los Angeles Times Book Review,* "for at virtually every point at which the events that gave the period its special character unfolded, he seemed to be naturally in the lead."

After graduating from college, Hayden became involved in Students for a Democratic Society (SDS). One of the SDS's founding members, Hayden wrote the initial draft of the SDS policy manifesto, which was entitled "The Port Huron Statement." This document, notes Joel Kotkin in *Esquire,* was "the first national declaration of the New Left." It contains "a declaration of potentialities which could flourish in a decent social context," explains Peter Clecak in *Nation,* and it calls for such changes as "reduced military spending, increased worker participation in government and business decisions, and a rejection of liberal 'trickle down' economics as the means of achieving social justice."

Hayden, who served as president of SDS from 1962 to 1963, also cofounded the Economic Research and Action Project (ERAP). The project was designed by SDS to aid the urban poor in the northern United States. Beginning in 1965 Hayden was in charge of the ERAP effort in Newark, New Jersey, where he helped organize the Newark Community Union Project. This effort supported the local poor by pressuring city government to respond to their grievances. The Newark project outlasted all other ERAP

ventures; it ended after the city's race riots in the summer of 1967. In his book that appeared later that year, Hayden reported on those riots, offering, as Dudley Randall notes in the *Negro Digest,* "the underside of the Newark uprising." Though Randall does not feel that *Rebellion in Newark* provides a definitive account of the riots, he urges that it be read, because "it tells the side which is usually untold." Eugene D. Genovese, writing for *Nation,* calls *Rebellion in Newark* a "brilliant little book, which is the more forceful for its understatement and economy of style." However, he finds the last chapter "blandly liberal," and adds that although "the omissions and the disingenuousness do not destroy the value of this fine piece of reporting, . . . they will, I fear, reduce its effectiveness among those who need it most."

In a similar effort to tell the "untold" side of a story, Hayden wrote, with Yale professor of history Staughton Lynd, a book called *The Other Side.* The "other side" is North Vietnam, which Hayden and Lynd, along with American Communist party member Herbert Aptheker, visited in 1965 at the invitation of North Vietnamese leaders. By traveling to North Vietnam, the trio hoped, as Christopher Lasch explains in the *New York Times Book Review,* "to see the 'enemy' as people." However admirable the authors' aims, their book "presents no new facts, nor even any new falsehoods," relates Joseph W. Bishop, Jr., in *Harper's.* "As an elucidation of a complex, tangled, obscure tragedy it is useless. Worse, it makes very hard reading." The *New Republic*'s Ronald Steel similarly remarks that the book is characterized by "dense syntax," but goes on to conclude, "we owe a great deal to the radicals of the left, and to such courageous men as Staughton Lynd and Tom Hayden for having forced us to come to terms with the shortcomings, indeed the staggering inadequacies and injustices, of our own society."

Hayden made a second trip to North Vietnam in 1967, following a meeting between antiwar activists and North Vietnamese leaders held in Bratislava, Czechoslovakia. At the meeting, it was suggested that the North Vietnamese release some prisoners of war (POWs) to demonstrate their solidarity with the antiwar movement in America. Shortly thereafter, they released three POWs into Hayden's custody (this was the first release of American POWs), and Hayden escorted them to the United States. Back in America, Hayden's involvement in the antiwar movement continued. Hayden and Rennie Davis, also a former SDS member, were project directors of the National Mobilization Committee to End the War in Vietnam. In 1968 the two helped organize the antiwar demonstrations that took place during the Democratic National Convention in Chicago, Illinois. They and six other activists were arrested for their activities during the convention. The highly publicized trial of the "Chicago Eight" (which became the "Chicago Seven" after one of the defendants, Black Panther leader Bobby Seale, was removed to stand trial on other charges in New Jersey) resulted in the sentencing of all seven defendants on contempt-of-court charges. In addition, Hayden, Davis, Jerry Rubin, Abbie Hoffman, and Dave Dellinger were convicted of crossing state lines to incite riot. In the appeals that followed, however, the initial decisions were overturned on the grounds that Julius Hoffman, the judge who presided at the trial, had antagonized the defense and had generally displayed improper conduct. Hayden's account of the Chicago courtroom proceedings is contained in his 1970 book entitled *Trial.*

After the trial Hayden traveled to Berkeley, California, where he helped organize a commune that Kotkin describes as a "great bastion of radicalism and experimental living." Hayden also spent much of his time traveling across the United States, attending rallies and denouncing both the war in Vietnam and the repression of the radical Left. On May 16, 1971, he participated in a demonstration to celebrate the second anniversary of People's Park, during which one student was shot and killed by state troopers. The park, a state-owned, two-and-a-half acre vacant lot that students and "street people" had transformed into a park, had, after being reclaimed by the state, become a celebrated point of controversy between radicals and police. Following the May 16 demonstrations, Hayden was arrested again, but was released shortly afterwards.

Later in 1971, while attending an antiwar rally in Ann Arbor, Hayden met actress and political activist Jane Fonda. The next year they traveled together, speaking out against the war and campaigning for presidential candidate Senator George McGovern. Hayden and Fonda were married in 1973, and together they organized and participated in Indochina Peace Campaign (IPC) tours. During one of the IPC's tours, Kotkin relates, they were "received with warm applause by an audience of students and middle-class family people." According to Hayden, the tour marked "the beginning of our turn to electoral politics."

Hayden's candidacy for a United States Senate seat in the 1976 California Democratic primaries reflects this "turn to electoral politics." One of his campaign slogans, reports a *Newsweek* writer, was: "The radicalism of the '60s is the common sense of the '70s." Hayden's opponent in the race, incumbent Senator John V. Tunney, was heavily favored. But Hayden, against great odds, made a dramatic showing. With the endorsements and financial support of such celebrities as Jackson Browne, Linda Rondstadt, Groucho Marx, James Taylor, and Jon Voight, as well as a well-organized campaign, Hayden managed to win forty percent of the vote. And although Tunney won the Democratic primary, he was ultimately unseated by Republican S. I. Hayakawa. "Hayden had proved his point," declares

Kotkin, "he could succeed in electoral politics; he could raise money, gather troops, destroy liberal leaders—even senators—if he had to."

In 1977, using the momentum gained during his race for the senate seat, Hayden organized the Campaign for Economic Democracy (CED). The CED platform, reports *National Review*'s Kevin Lynch, "called for control of corporations, full employment, public ownership of utilities, a restructuring of the tax system, and support for rent control." Hayden aide and former SDS member Sam Hurst explained the CED's focus on economics, saying: "The economic platform is the only thing that appeals to enough people. There is no single issue such as war or civil rights. But you can build around poverty or the threat of it." Apparently, such reasoning served Hayden and his CED well; by 1980 *Esquire* magazine would report the CED to be the "largest single organized force on the California Left."

In his 1980 book, *The American Future: New Visions beyond Old Frontiers,* Hayden further describes his plan for achieving economic democracy. "Though not without flaws," writes Michael Harrington in *Nation,* Hayden's book "is in the main serious, well-documented, and takes intellectual and political chances." The ingredients of Hayden's vision include "greater equality of income, particularly among the races and between the sexes, and the democratic control of production." *The American Future* questions "not only the possibility, but also the desirability, of continuing to increase the nation's output of goods and services," explains David Vogel in the *New York Review of Books.* "Instead of mindlessly seeking to restore the prosperity of the 1950s and 1960s, Hayden argues, we should regard the decline of America's economy as an opportunity to conceive a new vision of a good society. If the American public were no longer mesmerized by the prospect of ever increasing wealth, other values, such as equality, economic democracy, community, and a healthy physical environment would finally become the principal concerns of American politics."

In 1982 Hayden was elected to the California assembly. The win, however, came after an expensive and difficult campaign in which his opponents accused him of treason for his 1965 trip to Hanoi. The trip to Hanoi and other acts committed in his radical youth continued to haunt Hayden even though he had been working as part of the establishment in the Democratic party for over a decade; his anti-establishment image of the 1960s would not dissipate. Even in 1988 when his autobiography, *Reunion: A Memoir,* was released, graffiti denouncing his antiwar activity during the 1960s was scrawled across advertisements announcing his promotional tour for the new book. Hayden, noting people's difficulty in perceiving him as part of the system, pointed out to Paul Galloway during an interview for the *Chicago Times:* "Almost every reporter I meet says 'Hayden has joined the Establishment now.' I'll be in my grave, and they'll still be saying that Hayden is finally in the Establishment now."

Hayden's memoir, *Reunion,* outlines "how he got from one place [radical 60s activist] to the other [mainstream political spokesperson], and what it means socially and politically, as well as personally," explains Langer. In the book Hayden relates the inspirational moment following an interview with Martin Luther King when he decided to become a political participator instead of just a reporter. He reflects on what it was like to be the straight man in the cultural revolution—drug free, ambitious, and political, and he also reevaluates his judgements and actions during the Vietnam War, admitting errors and regrets. Qualifying his behavior in the 1960s, Hayden writes in his autobiography, "Our cause was both just and rational, even if all our methods were not. Our values were decent ones, even if we could not always live up to them." After describing his involvement in many of the rebellious acts of the 1960s, Hayden explains his transformation from working against and outside the political system to working within the political structures: "I had gone to the brink of breakdown, to the preliminary stages of civil strife, but now there were signs that working within the fabric of society was producing change." At this point Hayden reveals himself as "a 'born-again' middle American, emotionally charged by my reacceptance in the political mainstream."

While his book was well received overall, Hayden's controversial political activities during the 1960s and current involvement in mainstream politics spurred a variety of interpretations about his intent for writing the book. David J. Garrow, writing in *Washington Post Book World,* points out that Hayden "is far more at ease with his identity from these past 15 years than he is with his earlier, even more visible life as one of the 1960s' most controversial figures." Some critics view Hayden's reevaluation of his past as a sign of growth; other critics consider it merely another political ploy. "Hayden's memoir is obviously a carefully-crafted bid for complete rehabilitation," asserts Peter Brimelow in a London *Times* review, adding, "Hayden's basic method [for seeking absolution for his past behavior] is suppression" of information. Furthermore, Brimelow notes that some of Hayden's contemporaries feel he implies far more moderate beliefs and actions in his memoir than occurred in reality. In fact, Brimelow quotes former SDS member Abbie Hoffman as calling Hayden "the Stalinist of the group" and as accusing Hayden of using the book to appeal for votes. "Hayden was much closer to the edge than he admits," Brimelow maintains.

In contrast, other critics found Hayden's autobiography impressive rather than suppressive in its sharing of infor-

mation. Garrow finds *Reunion* "honest, impressive and at times quite moving," and sees Hayden as striving "with considerable success" to present his political and personal transformation. Garrow also believes that Hayden reveals himself in his autobiography as "an impressive individual whose turmoils and stresses, public and private, over three decades' time have made him a better human being." Similarly impressed, Paul Berman in the *New York Times Book Review* hails Hayden as "the single greatest figure of the 1960's student movement." With praise for Hayden and his memoirs, Berman concludes: "I turned the last page feeling a wary admiration for its author, hero of darkest Mississippi, brave and foolish champion, still philosophizing about values and visions, ever plucky, a man who was never afraid of plunging into the unknown. That was always his appeal."

BIOGRAPHICAL/CRITICAL SOURCES:

BOOKS

Hayden, Tom, *Reunion: A Memoir,* Random House, 1988.
Saïe, Kirkpatrick, *SDS: Ten Years toward a Revolution,* Random House, 1973.

PERIODICALS

Chicago Tribune, July 19, 1988.
Commonweal, January 12, 1967, p. 450; October 13, 1967.
Detroit Free Press, May 7, 1982.
Esquire, May, 1967; December, 1968; May, 1980.
Harper's, December, 1967.
Los Angeles Times, June 29, 1987.
Los Angeles Times Book Review, May 29, 1988, pp. 2, 6.
Nation, August 5, 1968, p. 86; January 12, 1970, p. 21; February 21, 1981; April 4, 1981, p. 405.
National Review, October 20, 1970, p. 1118; September 30, 1977; November 23, 1979; May 2, 1980.
Negro Digest, August, 1968, p. 86.
New Republic, April 8, 1967; November 17, 1979.
New Statesman, April 23, 1971, p. 567.
Newsweek, September 30, 1968; April 6, 1970; November 12, 1973; June 7, 1976; October 8, 1979.
New York Review of Books, June 11, 1981, p. 29.
New York Times, October 17, 1967, p. 45; December 10, 1969.
New York Times Book Review, April 23, 1967; June 12, 1988, p. 7.
People, October 15, 1979; May 24, 1982.
Time, January 5, 1970, p. 58; August 15, 1977; October 8, 1979.
Times (London), August 31, 1989.
Washington Post, September 23, 1971.
Washington Post Book World, May 22, 1988, p. 4.*

HAYDEN, Tom
see HAYDEN, Thomas E(mmet)

*   *   *

HECKLER, Jonellen (Beth) 1943-

PERSONAL: Born October 28, 1943, in Pittsburgh, PA; daughter of John Edward (a mechanical engineer) and Florence (an artist; maiden name, Milliken) Munn; married Louis Roy Heckler (a management consultant), August 17, 1968; children: Steven Louis. *Education:* University of Pittsburgh, B.A., 1965. *Avocational interests:* "Family and friends! Travel, speaking, swimming, walking, reading."

ADDRESSES: Home and office—5562 Pernod Dr. S.W., Fort Myers, FL 33919-3429. *Agent*—Cynthia A. Cannell, Janklow & Nesbit Associates, 598 Madison Ave., New York, NY 10022.

CAREER: United Fund of Allegheny County, Pittsburgh, PA, secretary to public relations director, 1965-67; United Fund of Broward County, Fort Lauderdale, FL, director of public relations, 1967-68; North Carolina Heart Association, Chapel Hill, NC, program planner, 1968-69; free-lance copy-writer, Charlotte, NC, 1969-70; Charlene Hillman Public Relations Associates, Indianapolis, IN, copy-writer, 1970-72; free-lance writer, 1972—.

MEMBER: Authors Guild, Broadcast Music International, Mystery Writers of America.

WRITINGS:

Safekeeping (novel; Literary Guild Selection), Putnam, 1983.
A Fragile Peace (novel; Literary Guild Selection), Putnam, 1986.
White Lies (novel; Literary Guild Selection), Putnam, 1989.
Circumstances Unknown (novel; Book-of-the-Month Club Selection), Pocket Books, 1993.

Also author of song lyrics. Contributor of poems and stories to *Ladies' Home Journal.*

WORK IN PROGRESS: Final Tour (novel), for Pocket Books.

SIDELIGHTS: Jonellen Heckler once told *CA:* "It has been my desire to reflect in my writing a very positive attitude about this wonderful life. I'm not trying to ignore its flaws and troubles, but I want to keep illuminating its joys. My novel, *Safekeeping,* was intended as a tribute to human love. For counterbalance I set it against one of the most tragic and perplexing eras in American History, the Vietnam war. It was my intent to record, in my own way, the confusion Americans felt about it."

Heckler recently told *CA:* "My first three novels were mainstream, but the next two are in the realm of suspense. I derive much enjoyment from writing a plot-driven novel, one in which the reader knows more than any individual character about what is going on in the story. In this way, I make the reader a participant. All of my novels are about families and the problems they face. *Safekeeping* concerns a prisoner of war. *A Fragile Peace* deals with alcoholism. *White Lies* is about honesty in family life. And *Circumstances Unknown* depicts the aftermath of a murder."

*   *   *

HEILBRON, J(ohn) L(ewis) 1934-

PERSONAL: Born March 17, 1934, in San Francisco, CA. *Education:* University of California, Berkeley, A.B., 1955, M.A., 1958, Ph.D., 1964.

ADDRESSES: Office—Department of History, University of California, Berkeley, CA 94720.

CAREER: Sources for History of Quantum Physics, Berkeley, CA, and Copenhagen, Denmark, assistant director, 1961-64; University of Pennsylvania, Philadelphia, assistant professor of history of science, 1964-67; University of California, Berkeley, assistant professor, 1967-71, associate professor, 1971-73, professor of history, 1973—, currently Class of 1936 Professor of History and the History of Science and director of Office for History of Science and Technology, chair of Academic Senate, 1988-90, Vice Chancellor, 1990—. Andrew Dickson White Professor at Large, Cornell University, 1985-91.

MEMBER: American Philosophical Society, American Academy of Arts and Sciences, History of Science Society, British Society for the History of Science, Royal Swedish Academy of Sciences.

WRITINGS:

(With Lini Allen, Paul Forman, and T. S. Kuhn) *Sources for History of Quantum Physics,* American Philosophical Society, 1967.
H. G. J. Mosely: The Life and Letters of an English Physicist, 1887-1914, University of California Press, 1974.
(With Forman and Spencer Weart) *Physics circa 1900: Personnel, Funding, and Productivity of the Academic Establishments,* Princeton University Press, 1975.
(With Wayne Shumaker) *John Dee on Astronomy,* University of California Press, 1978.
Electricity in the Seventeenth and Eighteenth Centuries: A Study of Early-Modern Physics, University of California Press, 1979.
Historical Studies in the Theory of Atomic Structure, Arno, 1981.

(With Bruce R. Wheaton) *Literature on the History of Twentieth-Century Physics,* Office for History of Science and Technology, University of California, 1981.

(With Robert W. Seidel and Wheaton) *Lawrence and His Laboratory: Nuclear Science at Berkeley,* Lawrence Berkeley Laboratory and Office for History of Science and Technology, University of California, 1981.

(With Wheaton) *An Inventory of Published Letters to and from Physicists,* Office for History of Science and Technology, University of California, 1982.

Elements of Early Modern Physics, University of California Press, 1982.

Physics at the Royal Society during Newton's Presidency, Clark Library, University of California, Los Angeles, 1983.

The Dilemmas of an Upright Man: Max Planck as Spokesman for German Science, University of California Press, 1986.

(With Elisabeth Crawford and Rebecca Ullrich) *The Nobel Population 1901-1937: A Census of the Nominators and Nominees for the Prizes of Physics and Chemistry,* Office for History of Science and Technology, University of California, 1987.

(With Seidel) *Lawrence and His Laboratory: A History of the Lawrence Berkeley Laboratory,* Volume 1, University of California Press, 1989.

(Editor with T. Frangsmyr and Robin E. Rider, and contributor) *The Quantifying Spirit in the Eighteenth Century,* University of California Press, 1990.

Quantitative Science around 1800, University of California Press, 1993.

Also contributor to *Physics in the Twentieth Century,* edited by C. Weiner, Academic Press, 1977; *Rutherford and Physics at the Turn of the Century,* edited by Mario Bunge and William R. Shea, Science History Publications, 1979; *The Ferment of Knowledge,* edited by G. S. Rousseau and Roy Porter, Cambridge University Press, 1980; *Conceptions of Ether: Studies in the History of Ether Theories, 1740-1900,* edited by Geoffrey Cantor and J. Hodge, Cambridge University Press, 1981; and *World Changes,* edited by Paul Horwich, MIT Press, 1993. Contributor to journals in the history of science. Editor of *Historical Studies in the Physical Sciences.*

WORK IN PROGRESS: The Institutionalization of Physics 1600-2000; Physics in the Twentieth Century; Physical Science and the Expert Witness.

BIOGRAPHICAL/CRITICAL SOURCES:

PERIODICALS

Los Angeles Times, June 11, 1986.
Times Literary Supplement, January 25, 1985.

HENLEY, Virginia   1935-

PERSONAL: Born December 5, 1935, in Bolton, Lancashire, England; daughter of Thomas (a steelworker) and Lillian (Bleakley) Syddall; married Arthur Howard Henley (an architect), July 7, 1956; children: Sean, Adam. *Education:* Attended University of Toronto, 1966-67. *Religion:* Anglican.

ADDRESSES: Home—Beamsville, Ontario, Canada.

CAREER: Steel Co. of Canada, Hamilton, Ontario, executive secretary, 1953-56; Labatts Brewery, London, Ontario, assistant buyer, 1956-61; writer, 1977—.

WRITINGS:

HISTORICAL ROMANCE NOVELS

The Irish Gypsy, Avon, 1982.
The Conquest, Avon, 1983.
A Skulk of Foxes, Avon, 1984.
The Raven and the Rose, Dell, 1987.
The Hawk and the Dove, Dell, 1988.
The Falcon and the Flower, Dell, 1989.
The Pirate and the Pagan, Dell, 1990.
The Dragon and the Jewel, Dell, 1991.
Wild Hearts, Avon, 1993.
Tempted, Dell, 1993.

SIDELIGHTS: Author Virginia Henley once commented: "After my mother died of cancer in 1976, I desperately needed an outlet. She had been deeply interested in the occult and was a voracious reader. The books I gave her had to become lighter in subject matter, and we both started to enjoy historical romances. I decided I could write them as well as read them.

"Women need a romantic escape from everyday realities. I don't want women to read me to raise their consciousness! I want them to derive pure pleasure and escape. A romantic novel is a small luxury, like chocolates or perfume, with which a woman can indulge herself. If just one woman can put her feet up after she puts the kids to bed and lose herself in a book I have written, I will be satisfied. All of us at times meet situations we think we cannot face, but somehow we manage to cope, as my heroines do. I hope that between the first and last pages of any of my novels my heroine grows as a woman and as a human being, but that is all I require of her."

BIOGRAPHICAL/CRITICAL SOURCES:

PERIODICALS

Publishers Weekly, June 25, 1982; July 22, 1988, p. 53; July 21, 1989, p. 54; October 26, 1990, p. 64.

HERMANN, Philip J(ay) 1916-

PERSONAL: Born September 17, 1916, in Cleveland, OH; son of Isodore (a tailor) and Gazella (a homemaker; maiden name, Gross) Hermann; married Cecilia Alexander (a Naval officer) December 31, 1945 (divorced, 1991); married Marj Hollingsworth (an interior decorator), October 15, 1992; children: (first marriage) Gary, Ann. *Education:* Attended Hiram College, 1935-37; Ohio State University, B.A., 1939; Western Reserve University (now Case Western Reserve University), J.D., 1942. *Avocational interests:* Traveling abroad (Africa, Europe, Mid-East, Far East, South America), golfing, exercising, reading, wine.

ADDRESSES: Home—615 Acadia Point, Aurora, OH 44202. *Office*—Legal Information Publications, Chagrin Plaza East Bldg., 23811 Chagrin Blvd., Beachwood, OH 44122.

CAREER: Founded and associated with Payne & Hermann, beginning 1946; Hermann, Cahn & Schneider (law firm), Cleveland, OH, partner, 1976-87. Served as president and chair of board of directors, Jury Verdict Research, Cleveland, 1960-91; chair of board, Lawyer to Lawyer Consultation Panel. *Military Service:* U.S. Naval Reserve, 1942-46; served in Pacific theater; became lieutenant commander.

MEMBER: American Law Firm Association (past chair of board of directors), American Bar Association (past chair of Use of Modern Technology Committee), Ohio Bar Association (past chair of Insurance Committee and Federal Court Committee; past member of House of Delegates), Cleveland Bar Association (past chair of membership), Walden Golf and Tennis Club.

WRITINGS:

Better Settlements through Leverage, Lawyers Co-Operative Publishing, 1965.
Do You Need a Lawyer?, Prentice-Hall, 1980.
Better, Earlier Settlements through Economic Leverage, Jury Verdict Research, 1989.
Injured? How to Get Every Dollar You Deserve, Legal Information Publications, 1990.
The Ninety-six Billion Dollar Game: You Are Losing, Legal Information Publications, 1993.
How to Select Competent Cost-Effective Counsel, Legal Information Publications, 1993.

Contributor to numerous law journals.

WORK IN PROGRESS: Getting Your Money's Worth from Your Lawyer, and *How to Avoid Going to Court.*

SIDELIGHTS: Philip J. Hermann once told *CA:* "Litigation is now an important item of cost to the businessperson—indirectly, through insurance, as well as directly.

This is why both of my forthcoming books are being written for businesspeople. *Getting Your Money's Worth from Your Lawyer,* for instance, tells them how to use lawyers efficiently—that is, 'managing' them. There are no similar books on the market from the businessperson's standpoint." He later added: "*Better Earlier Settlements through Economic Leverage* is revolutionizing the valuation of personal injury claims. Tables from it now appear on software. *The Ninety-six Billion Dollar Game: You Are Losing* is about the cost of litigation and how to control it."

*   *   *

HIBBS, John 1925-
(John Blyth)

PERSONAL: Born May 5, 1925, in Birmingham, England; son of Alfred Leonard (a minister) and Sylvia (Blyth) Hibbs; married Constance Tillyard, July 8, 1950 (divorced September, 1975); married Kathleen Patricia Macrae, 1986; children: (first marriage) Michael, Robin, Alison. *Education:* University of Birmingham, B.Com. Social Study, 1950, Ph.D., 1983; London School of Economics and Political Science, M.Sc., 1954. *Religion:* Congregationalist.

ADDRESSES: Home—Copper Beeches, 134 Wood End Rd., Erdington, Birmingham B24 8BN, England. *Office*—University of Central England in Birmingham, Perry Barr, Birmingham B42 2SU, England.

CAREER: Premier Travel Ltd., Cambridge, England, personal assistant to managing director, 1950-52; technical journalist and transport consultant, 1954-56; Corona Coaches Ltd., Sudbury, England, managing director, 1956-60; British Railways, Eastern Region, London, England, traffic survey officer and market research officer, 1961-67; City of London Polytechnic, London, senior lecturer, 1967-69, principal lecturer in transport, 1969-73; City of Birmingham Polytechnic (now University of Central England), Birmingham, principal lecturer in transport and business studies, 1973-83, director of transport studies, 1983—, professor of transport management, 1987-90, emeritus professor, 1990—. Adjunct scholar, Adam Smith Institute. Liberal Party, member of advisory panel on transport, 1969-84, chairman of panel, 1971-75. Member of Liberal Industrial Partnership Committee, 1968-70, and of transport board of Council for National Academic Awards, 1978-84. Personal members' representative, Congregational Federation Council, 1987—.

MEMBER: Liberal International, PEN International, Chartered Institute of Transport (fellow), Institute of Transport Administration, Organization of Teachers of

Transport Studies (former chairman), Transport Economists Group, Transport History Group, Railway and Canal Historical Society, Charles Williams Society.

WRITINGS:

Transport for Passengers, Institute of Economic Affairs, 1962, 2nd edition, 1971.
(Under pseudonym John Blyth) *New Found Land* (poetry), Outposts, 1963.
(Under pseudonym John Blyth) *Being a Patient* (poetry), Breakthru, 1965.
The History of British Bus Services, David & Charles, 1968, 2nd edition, 1989.
Transport Studies: An Introduction, John Baker, 1970, revised edition, Kogan Page, 1981.
(Editor) *The Omnibus,* David & Charles, 1971.
How to Run the Buses, John Baker, 1972.
People and Transport, Unservile State Group, 1973.
The Bus and Coach Industry: Its Economics and Organization, Dent, 1975.
(With Roger Seaton) *The Teaching of Transport Studies,* Organisation of Teachers of Transport Studies, 1976.
Transport without Politics . . . ?, Institute of Economic Affairs, 1982.
Bus and Coach Management, Chapman & Hall, 1985.
The Country Bus, David & Charles, 1986.
Regulation: An International Study of Bus and Coach Licensing, Coachex, 1985.
Bus and Coach Operator's Handbook, Kogan Page, 1987.
The Country Chapel, David & Charles, 1988.
Marketing Management in the Bus and Coach Industry, Croner, 1989.
Looking Upwards, Congregational Federation, 1991.
(With Gabriel Roth) *Tomorrow's Way: Managing Roads in a Free Society,* Adam Smith Institute, 1992.
A Market for Mobility, Institute of Economic Affairs, 1993.

Contributor to *The Omega File,* Adam Smith Institute, 1983. Editor, *Proceedings* of the Chartered Institute of Transport, 1992—. Contributor to transport, history, and banking journals.

WORK IN PROGRESS: Research projects on transport pricing policy and marketing strategies for bus companies; a brief history of transport in the U.K.

SIDELIGHTS: John Hibbs once told *CA:* "It is proper to pay tribute to those who have influenced me, notably Charles Williams. Two quotations underlie what I would want my work to be remembered by. Dante said, 'We are created for our function, not our function for us.' And Jakob Boehme said, 'If a man did only cast stones into the sea (if his brother be pleased with it, and that he get his living by it) then he is as acceptable to God as a preacher in a pulpit.' As I see it, neither in economics, nor in poli-

tics, nor in art, dare we tell other people what is good for them."

*   *   *

HOGAN, Robert (Goode) 1930-

PERSONAL: Born May 29, 1930, in Boonville, MO; son of Robert Goode and Helen (Sombart) Hogan; married Betty Matthews, December 1, 1950 (divorced, 1978); married Mary Rose Callaghan, December 21, 1979; children: (first marriage) Robert, Kathleen, Pamela (Mrs. Clifford Krause), Sean, Shivaun (Mrs. Richard Maisel). *Education:* University of Missouri, B.A., 1953, M.A., 1954, Ph.D., 1956. *Politics:* Shavian. *Religion:* Shavian.

ADDRESSES: Home—10 Gulistan Pl., Rathmines, Dublin 6, Ireland. *Office*—Department of English, University of Delaware, Newark, DE 19711.

CAREER: University of Missouri—Columbia, instructor in English, 1954-56; Ohio University, Athens, instructor in English, 1956-58; Purdue University, West Lafayette, IN, assistant professor of English, 1958-66; University of California, Davis, associate professor of English, 1966-70; University of Delaware, Newark, professor of English, 1970—. Visiting professor, University College Dublin, 1961-62, and University of Rochester, Rochester, NY, 1962-63. Publisher, Proscenium Press, 1965—. *Military service:* U.S. Army, 1950-52.

AWARDS, HONORS: Guggenheim fellowship for playwriting, 1961-62.

WRITINGS:

EDITOR

(With Sven E. Molin) *Drama: The Major Genres,* Dodd, 1962.
Feathers from the Green Crow: Sean O'Casey, 1905-1925, University of Missouri Press, 1962.
Elmer Rice, *The Iron Cross,* Proscenium, 1965.
(With M. J. O'Neill) *Joseph Holloway's Abbey Theatre,* Southern Illinois University Press, 1967.
Seven Irish Plays, 1946-1964, University of Minnesota Press, 1967.
(With H. Bogart) *The Plain Style,* American Book Co., 1967.
(With O'Neill) *Joseph Holloway's Irish Theatre,* 3 volumes, Proscenium, 1968-70.
The Crows of Mephistopheles and Other Stories by George Fitzmaurice, Dolmen Press, 1968.
Towards a National Theatre: The Theatrical Criticism of Frank J. Fay, Dolmen Press, 1969.
(With James Kilroy) *Lost Plays of the Irish Renaissance,* Proscenium, 1970.
Dictionary of Irish Literature, Greenwood Press, 1979.

(With Molin) *The Shaughraun,* Proscenium, Volume 1: *The Early Years,* 1979, Volume 2: *Up and Down in Paris and London,* 1982, Volume 3: *Three Early Plays,* 1985, Volume 4: *Three Early Potboilers,* 1989, Volume 5: *The American Debut,* 1991.

(With Jerry Beasley) *The Plays of Frances Sheridan,* University of Delaware Press, 1984.

(With Edward A. Nickerson) *Guarini's "The Faithful Shepherd,"* University of Delaware Press, 1989.

Jonathan, Jack, and GBS: Four Plays by John O'Donovan, University of Delaware Press, 1993.

NONFICTION

The Experiments of Sean O'Casey, St. Martin's, 1960.

Arthur Miller, University of Minnesota Press, 1964.

The Independence of Elmer Rice, Southern Illinois University Press, 1965.

After the Irish Renaissance, University of Minnesota Press, 1967.

Dion Boucicault, Twayne, 1969.

Mervyn Wall, Bucknell University Press, 1971.

Eimar O'Duffy, Bucknell University Press, 1971.

(With Kilroy) *The Modern Irish Drama: A Documentary History,* Volume 1: *The Irish Literary Theatre,* Dolmen Press, 1975, Volume 2: *Laying the Foundations,* Dolmen Press, 1976, Volume 3: *The Abbey Theatre, 1905-1909,* Dolmen Press, 1978, Volume 4 (with others): *The Rise of the Realists, 1910-1915,* Dolmen Press, 1979, Volume 5: *The Art of the Amateur,* Dolmen Press, 1984, Volume 6: *The Years of O'Casey,* University of Delaware Press, 1992.

Since O'Casey, Colin Smythe, 1984.

PLAYS

Saint Jane, Proscenium, 1966.

Betty and the Beast, Proscenium, 1968.

The Fan Club (produced in New York at American Theatre Co., 1971), Proscenium, 1969.

The Old Man Says Yes!, produced in New York at Clark Center for the Performing Arts, 1971.

Happy Hour, produced in New York at Provincetown Playhouse, 1974.

An Unsocial Socialist (produced in Wilmington, DE, at Wilmington Drama League, 1973), Proscenium, 1975.

(With James Douglas) *The Painting of Babbi Joe,* produced in New York at Nameless Theatre, 1978.

Meg and Mick, produced in New York at Cubiculo Theatre, 1982.

(With Douglas) *The Wild Turkey,* produced in Dublin, Ireland, at Academy Theatre, 1984.

A Better Place (produced in New York at American Theatre Co., 1972), published in *Journal of Irish Literature,* 1993.

FICTION

(With Douglas) *Murder at the Abbey Theatre,* Moytura, 1993.

OTHER

Editor of *Journal of Irish Literature,* 1972-93.

WORK IN PROGRESS: A study of Presidential rhetoric.

BIOGRAPHICAL/CRITICAL SOURCES:

PERIODICALS

Times Literary Supplement, April 27, 1984.

*   *   *

HORNER, Winifred Bryan   1922-

PERSONAL: Born August 31, 1922, in St. Louis, MO; daughter of Walter (an engineer) and Winifred (Kinealy) Bryan; married David Horner (a meteorologist), June 15, 1943; children: Winifred, Richard, Elizabeth, David. *Education:* Washington University, St. Louis, MO, A.B., 1943; University of Missouri—Columbia, M.A., 1960; University of Michigan, Ph.D., 1975.

ADDRESSES: Home—1904 Tremont Ct., Columbia, MO 65203. *Office*—Department of English, Texas Christian University, Fort Worth, TX 76129.

CAREER: University of Missouri—Columbia, instructor, 1961-74, assistant professor, 1975-80, associate professor, 1980-84, professor of English, 1984-85; Texas Christian University, Fort Worth, Radford Chair of Rhetoric, 1985—. Director of Missouri Writers Project, 1977; visiting lecturer at University of Iowa, 1979, 1980, and Beaver College, 1980.

MEMBER: International Society for the History of Rhetoric (member of executive council), National Council of Writing Program Directors (president, 1985-87), National Council of Teachers of English (executive council), Modern Language Association of America, Rhetoric Society of America (president, 1987-89).

AWARDS, HONORS: Fellow of National Endowment for the Humanities, 1982; award for University of Missouri, 1983, for contributions to the education of women; National Endowment for the Humanities research fellowship, 1989; fellow, University of Edinburgh, 1990.

WRITINGS:

(Contributor) Jasper P. Neel, editor, *Options for Teaching of English,* Modern Language Association of America, 1978.

Historical Rhetoric: An Annotated Bibliography of Selected Sources in English, G. K. Hall, 1980, revised edition, 1992.

(Contributor) James J. Murphy, editor, *The Rhetorical Tradition and Modern Writing,* Modern Language Association of America, 1982.

Composition and Literature: Bridging the Gap, University of Chicago Press, 1983.

The Present State of Scholarship in Historical and Contemporary Rhetoric, University of Missouri Press, 1983, revised edition, 1990.

Rhetoric in the Classical Tradition, St. Martin's, 1985.

Nineteenth-Century Scottish Rhetoric: The American Connection, Southern Illinois University Press, 1992.

SIDELIGHTS: Winifred Bryan Horner told *CA:* "Language is the one thing that separates human beings from other animals, and in studying language I feel that I am studying the human mind. I am concerned with historical rhetoric from Aristotle to the present, and by doing research in this area I hope to understand better how language functions in our society. In the twentieth century, we are in a language revolution, and I am interested in literacy as it affects individuals and cultures. I am deeply concerned with how we use language and are used by language."

*   *   *

HOUSE, Gloria 1941-
(Aneb Kgositsile)

PERSONAL: Born February 14, 1941, in Tampa, FL; daughter of Fred and Rubye (Robinson) Larry; married William Stuart House, 1966 (divorced, 1974); children: Uri Stuart. *Education:* American River College, A.A. (with highest honors), 1959; Monterey Institute of Foreign Studies (now Monterey Institute of International Studies), Diploma in French Studies, 1959; University of California, Berkeley, B.A., 1961, M.A., 1969; University of Michigan, Ph.D., 1986. *Avocational interests:* Travel (France, the Netherlands, Sweden, Denmark, Mexico, England, Italy, Egypt, Kenya, Tanzania, Ethiopia, Algeria, Bermuda, Cuba, Grenada, and Barbados), the arts, modern dance, architecture, politics, and international affairs.

ADDRESSES: Home—2822 Ewald Circle, Detroit, MI 48238. *Office*—Weekend College Program, Wayne State University, 5950 Cass Ave., Detroit, MI 48202.

CAREER: French teacher at school in Cambridge, England, 1961; San Francisco State College (now University), San Francisco, CA, instructor in French, spring, 1965; Cass Technical High School, Detroit, MI, high school teacher of French and English, 1967-68; free-lance television broadcaster in Detroit, 1969; *Detroit Free Press,* Detroit, news and editorial copy editor, 1969-71; Wayne State University, Detroit, instructor, 1971-74, associate professor of humanities, 1974—, co-producer and instructor of record for university-produced television series *An American Mosaic,* 1977, curriculum developer of Module at Jackson Prison Program, 1974-77. Instructor in Afro-American literature, Wayne State University, spring, 1969. Co-producer and interviewer for television series *Take the Black,* 1970. Field secretary for Lowndes County, AL, Student Non-Violent Coordinating Committee, 1965-67; member of board of directors of Interfaith Centers for Racial Justice, 1973-74, and Detroit Council of the Arts, 1980-88; member of Michigan Alliance Against Political and Racist Repression, 1973-74, and Michigan Council for the Humanities, 1974-75. Volunteer editor and coordinator of cultural presentations for Broadside/Crummell Press, 1977—; guest on radio and television programs; featured poet at poetry series and other cultural events; lecturer and consultant; poet-in-residence at Detroit public high schools, spring, 1980, and Richard Branch, Detroit Public Library, summer, 1992.

MEMBER: Progressive Artist and Educators Association (member of board of directors), Weekend Alumni Association (faculty founder).

AWARDS, HONORS: Rackham graduate fellow at University of Michigan, 1978-79, 1980-86; Center for Continuing Education of Women scholar, 1979-80; grant from Detroit Council of the Arts, 1981, for *Cinders Smoldering: Detroit since '67;* National Endowment for the Humanities fellowship, 1983; award for community service, Black Medical Association, 1984; award from the Michigan Labor Committee for Democracy and Human Rights in Central America, 1987; Distinguished Award for Pioneering in the Arts, United Black Artists, 1988.

WRITINGS:

(Under name Aneb Kgositsile) *Blood River: Poems, 1964-1983,* Broadside Press, 1983.

(Editor) *Cinders Smoldering: Detroit since '67* (anthology), Broadside Press, 1986.

Three Who Believed in Freedom: The Historical Contributions of Ella Baker, Septima Clark, and Fannie Lou Hamer (video documentary), Council on Interracial Books for Children, 1989.

(Under name Aneb Kgositsile) *Rainrituals,* Broadside Press, 1990.

Tower and Dungeon: A Study of Place and Power in American Culture, Casade Unidad, 1991.

Work represented in anthologies, including *Black Arts Anthology,* edited by Ahmed Alhanuisi, Broadside Press, 1969; *The Black Aesthetic,* edited by Addison Gayle,

Doubleday, 1971; *Moving to Antarctica,* edited by Margaret Kaminski, Dustbooks, 1975. Contributor of poems to periodicals, including *Negro Digest, Essence, Metro Times, Against the Current, Michigan Poetry Sampler, Moving Out,* and *Solid Ground: A New World Journal,* and of articles and book reviews to numerous periodicals, including *History Teacher, City Arts Quarterly,* and *Detroit News.* Poetry editor, *The Witness.*

* * *

HUBBARD, Ruth   1924-

PERSONAL: Born March 3, 1924, in Vienna, Austria; immigrated to United States, 1938; naturalized citizen, 1943; daughter of Richard (a physician) and Helene (a physician; maiden name, Ehrlich) Hoffman; married Frank Hubbard (a harpsichord maker), 1942 (divorced, 1951); married George Wald (an educator), June 11, 1958; children: Elijah, Deborah Hannah Wald. *Education:* Radcliffe College, B.A., 1944, Ph.D., 1950. *Politics:* Socialist. *Religion:* Jewish. *Avocational interests:* Travel, music, politics, physical fitness.

CAREER: Tennessee Public Health Service, Chattanooga, technician, 1945-46; University of London, University College Hospital Medical School, London, England, U.S. Public Health Service fellow, 1948-49; Harvard University, Cambridge, MA, research fellow, 1951-58, research associate, 1958-73, lecturer, 1969-73, professor of biology, 1974-90, professor emerita, 1990—. John Simon Guggenheim fellow, Carlsberg Laboratory, University of Copenhagen, 1952-53. Visiting professor at Massachusetts Institute of Technology, 1972. Marine Biology Laboratory, Woods Hole, MA, member of corporation, 1971—, trustee, 1973-78. Member of advisory board, Boston Woman's Fund, 1983—.

MEMBER: American Association for the Advancement of Science, American Society of Biological Chemists, American Civil Liberties Union, National Women's Health Network, Committee for Responsible Genetics, Emergency Civil Liberties Committee, Science for People, Cambridge Civic Association.

AWARDS, HONORS: Paul Karrer Medal from Swiss Chemical Society, 1967, for work on the photochemistry of vision; honorary degrees from Macalester College, Southern Illinois University at Edwardsville, and University of Toronto.

WRITINGS:

(Editor with Marian Lowe) *Genes and Gender II: Pitfalls in Research on Sex and Gender,* Gordian, 1979.

(Editor with Mary Sue Henifin and Barbara Fried) *Women Look at Biology Looking at Women: A Collection of Feminist Critiques,* Schenkman, 1979.

(With Henifin and Fried) *Biological Woman: The Convenient Myth,* Schenkman, 1982.

(With Low) *Woman's Nature: Rationalization of Inequality,* Pergamon, 1983.

(With Margaret Randall) *The Shape of Red: Insider/ Outsider Reflections,* Cleis, 1988.

The Politics of Women's Biology, Rutgers University Press, 1990.

Contributor to periodicals.

WORK IN PROGRESS: "Several articles on the new reproductive technologies and their effects on women's choices in childbearing; a collection of my writings from the past decade; an edited journal of a return trip to Vienna, Austria, in the mid-1970s."

SIDELIGHTS: Ruth Hubbard, with Marian Lowe, co-edited the 1979 work *Pitfalls in Research on Sex and Gender,* which appeared as the second volume of *Genes and Gender: A Series on Hereditarianism and Women.* The book "provides," according to a *Ms.* reviewer, "an analytical framework for understanding constraints and errors in research in the area of the biological basis of sex differences." In *Women Look at Biology Looking at Women: A Collection of Feminist Critiques,* Hubbard and co-editors Mary Sue Henifin and Barbara Fried investigate stereotypes of women in biology. This "excellent collection of essays," a *Harvard Educational Review* critic revealed, "carefully analyzes the ways in which biological theory and practice have been shaped by underlying stereotypical views of women as physically and mentally inferior." Describing the book as an "attempt to divest the field of sociobiology of its Victorianism in explanations of human behavior," a *Choice* reviewer praised *Women Look at Biology Looking at Women* as "a unique, well-written contribution to social science literature which may direct researchers' interests in designing and analyzing new research projects."

Hubbard told *CA:* "My main interest is to explore and explain the ways in which scientific ideas, discoveries, and applications are shaped by political and social forces, and to make information about scientific and health issues accessible to people who are not themselves scientists and think that they might not be able to understand those issues. I also want very much to contribute to improving people's lives, and especially the lives of women."

BIOGRAPHICAL/CRITICAL SOURCES:

PERIODICALS

Choice, March, 1980.
Harvard Educational Review, November, 1979.

Ms., September, 1981.

*   *   *

HUDDLESTON, Eugene L(ee) 1931-

PERSONAL: Born January 29, 1931, in Ironton, OH; son of James Earl (a railroad brakeman and conductor) and Bernice (McClave) Huddleston; married Mary Lou Fishbeck, June 17, 1961; children: John R. *Education:* Marshall University, A.B., 1953; Ohio University, M.A., 1956; additional study, Indiana University, 1956-57; Michigan State University, Ph.D., 1965. *Politics:* Democrat. *Avocational interests:* Railroad photography.

ADDRESSES: Home—3926 Raleigh Dr., Okemos, MI 48864. *Office*—Department of American Thought and Language, Michigan State University, East Lansing, MI 48824.

CAREER: Tri-State College, Angola, IN, instructor in technical writing, 1957-60; Kellogg Community College, Battle Creek, MI, instructor in English, 1960-61; Indiana State University, Terre Haute, assistant professor of English, 1962-66; Michigan State University, East Lansing, assistant professor, 1966-70, associate professor, 1970-77, professor of American thought and language, 1977-93.

MEMBER: National Railway Historical Society, Railway and Locomotive Historical Society, Chesapeake and Ohio Historical Society.

AWARDS, HONORS: Norman Foerster Award from American literature section of Modern Language Association of America, 1966, for article, "Topographical Poetry of the Early National Period."

WRITINGS:

(With Philip Shuster and Alvin Staufer) *C & O Power: Steam and Diesel Locomotives of the Chesapeake and Ohio Railway, 1900-1965,* privately printed, 1965.
(Contributor) Marshall Fishwick, editor, *The World of Ronald McDonald,* Bowling Green Popular Press, 1978.
(With Douglas A. Noverr) *The Relationship of Painting and Literature: A Guide to Information Sources,* Gale, 1978.
Thomas Jefferson: A Reference Guide, G. K. Hall, 1982.
(Contributor) W. H. Robinson, editor, *Critical Essays on Phyllis Wheatley,* G. K. Hall, 1982.
(Contributor) J. A. Levernier and D. R. Wilmes, editors, *American Writers before 1800: A Biographical and Critical Dictionary,* three volumes, Greenwood Press, 1983.
(With T. W. Dixon, Jr.) *The Allegheny: Lima's Finest,* Hundman Publishing, 1984.

(With R. A. LeMassena) *Norfolk and Western Railway, Vanishing Vistas,* 1985.
The Van Sweringen Berkshires, N. J. International, 1986.
The World's Greatest Mallets: C & O H-8 vs. N & W Class A, Chesapeake and Ohio Historical Society, 1986.
(Contributor) *The Book of Days 1988: An Encyclopedia of Information Sources on Historical Figures and Events,* Pierian, 1988.
Riding that New River Train, Chesapeake and Ohio Historical Society, 1989.
Appalachian Crossing: The Pocahontas Roads, TLC Publishers, 1989.

Contributor of more than forty articles to periodicals, including *English Record, Western Folklore,* and *New England Quarterly.*

WORK IN PROGRESS: A History of Locomotives of the United States Railroad Administration; Role of the Virginia Central in the North Anna Campaign of May, 1864.

SIDELIGHTS: Eugene L. Huddleston told *CA:* "As a railroad photographer I try mainly to please myself by giving the world as I know it some permanence. As a scholar of American thought and writing, I try to make some sense out of people and events as I perceive them, whether historian or contemporary. Gratification for the former activity comes from my seeing the finished photograph or color slide; for the latter, only in seeing my work in print or having an audience for it."

Huddleston adds, "I am gratified that there are so many opportunities and outlets for publishing today, especially on railroad and locomotive history, my avocation."

BIOGRAPHICAL/CRITICAL SOURCES:

BOOKS

Doering, Henry, editor, *The World Almanac Book of Buffs, Masters, Mavens, and Uncommon Experts,* World Almanac, 1980.

*   *   *

HUDSON, Henry T(homas) 1932-

PERSONAL: Born January 13, 1932, in County Durham, England; came to the United States in 1951, naturalized citizen, 1957; son of Henry Thomas (a marine) and Isabella (a housewife; maiden name, Hearst) Hudson; married Shirley Louise Smit (a teacher), June 2, 1955; children: Bruce T., Joan Carol Hudson Gauze, Linda Joy Hudson Lower. *Education:* Malone College, B.A., 1964; Kent State University, M.A., 1968; Chicago Graduate School of Theology, M.Div., 1970. *Religion:* Nondenominational.

ADDRESSES: Home—4574 Rohrway N. W., Massillon, OH 44646.

CAREER: Ordained by Grace Gospel Fellowship, 1957, and by the Conservative Congregational Christian Conference, 1975. Minister of nondenominational churches in Alton, IL, 1957-59; involved with Christian work in Europe, 1960-64; Calvary Chapel, Massillon, OH, pastor, 1964-92; church growth consultant to churches in Ohio, 1982—. History professor at Malone College, 1970-74. Chairman of local mission board, 1978-81; vice-chairman of local Young Men's Christian Association, 1976-80; consultant to European Christian organizations. *Military service:* British Army, Royal Military Police, AntiVice Squad, 1949-50; served in Italy.

AWARDS, HONORS: National recognition from Religious Heritage of America, 1978, for written work and community service; D.D. from American Christian College, 1978.

WRITINGS:

Christianity and the American Revolution, Calvary Chapel Publications, 1975.
The Magna Carta of Kingdom, Calvary Chapel Publications, 1976.
The Mystery and Ministry of Suffering, Calvary Chapel Publications, 1977.
Journey Into Truth, Berean Bible Society, 1978.
Rightly Dividing the Word, Grace Press, 1980.
Papal Power, Evangelical Press (UK), 1980, Presbyterian and Reformed, 1981.

Also author of *Baptism in the Bible,* 1986, *Filled Unto All the Fullness of God,* 1991, *What Did Jesus Preach,* 1992, and *Toward a Better Understanding of the Bible.* Contributor to magazines.

WORK IN PROGRESS: A novel about terrorism and police work in Italy.

SIDELIGHTS: Henry T. Hudson told *CA:* "My main research interest has been in the areas of theology that provoke controversy and division between professing Christians."

*   *   *

HUMPHRY, Derek   1930-

PERSONAL: Born April 29, 1930, in Bath, Somerset, England; came to United States, 1978; son of Royston Martin and Bettine (Duggan) Humphry; married Jean Edna Crane, May 5, 1953 (deceased March, 1975, in a suicide assisted by her husband); married Ann Wickett Kooman, February 16, 1976 (divorced, 1990); married Gretchen

Crocker, 1991; children: (first marriage) Edgar, Clive, Stephen. *Education:* Attended secondary school in England. *Politics:* Liberal. *Religion:* None.

ADDRESSES: Office—P. O. Box 10603, Eugene, OR 97440-2603. *Agent*—Robert I. Ducas, 350 Hudson St., New York, NY 10014.

CAREER: Association executive and writer. Reporter in England for *Yorkshire Post,* Yorkshire, 1945-46, *Bristol Evening World,* Bristol, 1946-51, *Manchester Evening News,* Manchester, 1951-55, and *Daily Mail,* London, 1955-61; *Havering Recorder,* Essex, England, editor, 1963-67; *Sunday Times,* London, race relations, immigration, and civil liberties reporter, 1967-78; *Los Angeles Times,* Los Angeles, CA, feature writer, 1978-79; Hemlock Society (a euthanasia advocacy group), Eugene, OR, founder and national director, 1980-92, president, 1988-90. Deputy editor of *Luton News,* 1961-63. *Military service:* Served with British Army, 1948-50.

MEMBER: World Federation of the Society for the Right To Die (newsletter editor, 1979-84; secretary and treasurer, 1983-84; president, 1988-90; director, 1992-94), Americans Against Human Suffering (director, 1986-88 and 1993-95).

AWARDS, HONORS: Martin Luther King Memorial Prize (co-winner with Gus John), 1972, for *Because They're Black.*

WRITINGS:

(With Gus John) *Because They're Black,* Penguin, 1971.
Police Power and Black People, Panther, 1972.
(With Michael Ward) *Passports and Politics,* Penguin, 1974.
The Cricket Conspiracy, NCCL, 1976.
(With David Tindall) *False Messiah: The Story of Michael X,* Hart-Davis, McGibbon, 1977.
(With wife, Ann Wickett) *Jean's Way,* Quartet Books, 1978.
(With Peter Hain and Brian Rose-Smith) *Policing the Police,* Calder, 1979.
Let Me Die Before I Wake: Hemlock's Book of Self-Deliverance for the Dying, Hemlock Society, 1981, revised edition, 1991.
(Editor and author of introduction) *Assisted Suicide: The Compassionate Crime,* Hemlock Society, 1982.
(With A. Wickett) *The Right to Die: Understanding Euthanasia,* Harper, 1986.
(Editor) *Compassionate Crimes, Broken Taboos: Mercy Killing, Assisted Suicide, Double Suicide, Euthanasia,* Hemlock Society, 1986.
Euthanasia: Help with a Good Death: Essays and Briefings, Hemlock Society, 1991.

Final Exit: The Practicalities of Self-Deliverance and Assisted Suicide for the Dying, Hemlock Society, 1991.

Dying with Dignity: Understanding Euthanasia, Carol Publishing Group, 1992.

Deliverance: Framing a Better Law for Physician-Assisted Dying, Euthansia Research and Guidance Organization, 1993.

Final Exit has been translated into eleven languages.

ADAPTATIONS: Is This the Day?, a play by Vilma Hollingberry and Michael Napier Brown, was inspired by *Jean's Way* and published by Hemlock Society, 1990, and performed in England, Germany, and the United States, 1991 and 1992.

WORK IN PROGRESS: Casualties of Age: An Investigation Into Elder Suicide and *Seesaw: An Autobiography.*

SIDELIGHTS: Euthanasia rights advocate Derek Humphry is the author of the controversial book *Final Exit: The Practicalities of Self-Deliverance and Assisted Suicide for the Dying.* Described by William A. Henry III in *Time* as "a manual for committing suicide or helping someone else to do so," *Final Exit* sparked debate among euthanasia activists, physicians, medical ethicists, and legalists about right-to-die issues. Humphry became a focal point of the controversy as well, serving as an object of both admiration and scorn for his pro-euthanasia beliefs.

A former journalist who earlier in his career examined race relations in books such as *Because They're Black* and *Police Power and Black People,* Humphry joined the euthanasia movement after his wife Jean contracted incurable cancer. Humphry assisted with her suicide by administering a drink laced with barbiturates. He later chronicled his wife's story in *Jean's Way,* a work which moved Humphry to the forefront of the right-to-die campaign. Humphry later founded the Hemlock Society, which derives its name from the poisonous herb that the ancient philosopher Socrates used to commit suicide. The Hemlock Society, whose motto is "Death with Dignity," claims tens of thousands of dues-paying members.

During the early 1980s, the Hemlock Society published several books intended to educate the public about the group's philosophy. These works, written primarily by Humphry, included *Let Me Die Before I Wake: Hemlock's Book of Self-Deliverance for the Dying* and *Assisted Suicide: The Compassionate Crime.* A later book, *The Right to Die: Understanding Euthanasia,* asked the question: should human life be prolonged at all costs? In *The Right to Die,* Humphry and his second wife Ann Wickett argue that there are instances where medical science, with its ability to sustain indefinitely the lives of terminally ill patients, unnecessarily prolongs their suffering. Euthanasia, the authors continue, is a merciful alternative to that suf-

fering and should therefore be available to those who choose it. In support of their arguments, Humphry and Wickett profile several people who chose euthanasia. To Earl E. Shelp, writing in the *New York Times Book Review,* the book's strength "lies in the numerous accounts of the conditions and circumstances of terminally ill people who elected to avoid some of the suffering of dying. These stories are sensitively told, eliciting in the reader an identification with the actors and a sympathy for their travail."

Despite the authors' compassionate handling of these stories, some critics felt that Humphry and Wickett fail to address some of the important moral and legal issues surrounding euthanasia. In the *Los Angeles Times Book Review,* Gerald R. Winslow commented that *The Right to Die* "is long on details but short on careful analysis and argument." Shelp agreed, adding that the book is "interesting to read but not intellectually convincing. . . . *The Right to Die: Understanding Euthanasia* may help sway public opinion on an emotional level, but is of limited value as a philosophical and moral approach to these issues."

In the early 1990s, Humphry's friends urged him to take a less philosophical, more pragmatic stance toward euthanasia in his writings. Humphry's response was *Final Exit,* which leaped to the top of the best-seller lists after reports about it were aired on national television and published in national newspapers. According to some health professionals, the public's acceptance of *Final Exit* signaled a change in the way euthanasia was viewed in America. Alan Meisel, a professor of law and director of the Center for Medical Ethics at the University of Pittsburgh, was quoted in *Time* as saying, "People are very worried that their dying is going to be prolonged and painful. With this book, it's clear we have entered a new phase of the right to die."

Final Exit instructs readers about euthanasia by discussing the merits of different suicide methods and then offering practical advice on how to accomplish those methods. The book includes charts of the toxicity of various prescription drugs, lists the potential consequences of failed suicide attempts, and describes legal measures that can help those who assist in a suicide avoid prosecution. Throughout the work, Humphry encourages doctors and nurses to become active participants in the euthanasia of their terminally ill patients. "Part of good medicine is to help you out of this life as well as help you in," Humphry told *Time.* "When cure is no longer possible and the patient seeks relief through euthanasia, the help of physicians is most appropriate."

For the most part, reviewers of *Final Exit* ignored its more sensational aspects to concentrate on the legitimacy of

Humphry's arguments. In the *New York Review of Books,* David J. Rothman asserted that "if one believes that doctors and hospitals will go too far in caring for the terminally ill . . . or that a person's autonomy includes the right to decide when life is not worth living, then *Final Exit* is a straightforward and practical guide." *Spectator'*s Peter Black offered a different view, suggesting that Humphry wrote the book more to encourage the involvement of medical professionals in assisted suicides than to outline suicide methods. "On the whole," Black wrote, "Humphry's compilation is discouraging, which may have been his intention. His message is: only the cooperation of physicians can give the patient a dignified and loving farewell."

Since the publication of *Final Exit,* Humphry has continued fighting for the rights of the terminally ill to choose their own deaths; he has also worked in California for the passage of laws that would protect doctors from liability when they assist a suicide. Humphry's latest books, *Dying With Dignity: Understanding Euthanasia* and *Deliverance: Framing a Better Law for Physician-Assisted Dying,* again attempt to raise public awareness about his cause. A controversy arose in 1990 when Humphry separated from Wickett after it was discovered that she had contracted cancer. The couple provided differing versions of what caused the separation, and their dispute created a power struggle within the Hemlock Society which gained national attention. In 1992 Humphry retired after twelve years as Hem-

lock's national director, and in 1993 he started a euthanasia "think-tank" named Euthansia Research and Guidance Organization (E.R.G.O.) Discussing the impact of his work, specifically the value of *Final Exit,* Humphry told *Newsweek,* "People want to take control of their dying. My book is a sort of insurance, a comforter there on the bookshelf that they could make their escape from this world if they were suffering unbearably."

BIOGRAPHICAL/CRITICAL SOURCES:

BOOKS

Humphry, Derek, *Jean's Way,* Quartet Books, 1978.
Newsmakers, Issue 2, Gale, 1992, pp. 58-61.

PERIODICALS

Los Angeles Times Book Review, August 17, 1986, p. 6.
Newsweek, August 26, 1991, pp. 40-41.
New York Review of Books, March 5, 1992, p. 37.
New York Times, February 8, 1990, p. A26; August 14, 1991, p. A19; August 22, 1991, p. A27.
New York Times Book Review, September 14, 1986, p. 32.
People, March 12, 1990, pp. 76-78.
Spectator, January 11, 1992, p. 26.
Time, August 19, 1991, p. 55.
U.S. News and World Report, September 30, 1991, pp. 38-39.

I

ISAACS, Susan 1943-

PERSONAL: Born December 7, 1943, in Brooklyn, NY; daughter of Morton (an electrical engineer) and Helen (a homemaker; maiden name, Asher) Isaacs; married Elkan Abramowitz (an attorney), August 11, 1968; children: Andrew, Elizabeth. *Education:* Attended Queens College (now Queens College of the City University of New York). *Politics:* Democratic. *Religion:* Jewish.

ADDRESSES: Agent—Owen Laster, William Morris Agency, 1350 Avenue of the Americas, New York, NY 10019.

CAREER: Novelist and screenwriter. *Seventeen* magazine, New York City, 1966-70, began as assistant editor, became senior editor; political speech writer for Democratic candidates in Brooklyn and Queens, New York, and for the president of the borough of Queens, New York City; movie producer.

MEMBER: International Association of Crime Writers, PEN, Mystery Writers of America, National Book Critics Circle, Poets & Writers, Queens College Foundation (trustee), North Shore Child and Family Guidance Association (trustee).

WRITINGS:

NOVELS

Compromising Positions (also see below), Times Books, 1978.
Close Relations, Lippincott & Crowell, 1980.
Almost Paradise, Harper, 1984.
Shining Through, Harper, 1988.
Magic Hour, HarperCollins, 1991.
After All These Years, HarperCollins, 1993.

OTHER

Compromising Positions (screenplay; based on her novel of the same name), Paramount, 1985.
Hello Again (screenplay), Buena Vista, 1987.

Also contributor of reviews to newspapers, including *New York Times, New York Newsday, Washington Post,* and *Los Angeles Times.*

ADAPTATIONS: Shining Through was adapted for film by David Seltzer and released by Twentieth Century-Fox, 1992.

SIDELIGHTS: Susan Isaacs's popular and critically acclaimed novels feature a distinctive type of heroine. In her books, a *Time* magazine reviewer summarized, "secretaries, housewives, the faceless masses of womanhood, all run into phone booths, change clothes, and come out like Cleopatra with the rectitude of Eleanor Roosevelt." This transformation begins when common people come in contact with uncommon events. Her characters confront murder, political intrigue, even World War II espionage. In spite of such daunting circumstances, the typical Isaacs protagonist displays an engaging sense of humor and a "can-do" attitude which ultimately prevails.

Isaacs achieved notoriety with her first novel, 1978's *Compromising Positions,* a book *Chicago Tribune* contributor Clarence Petersen described as "the seeming result of an Erica Jong-Joan Rivers collaboration on a Nancy Drew mystery." The hero of the book is Judith Singer, a bored housewife who seeks an outlet for her underemployed intelligence by playing detective when her periodontist is found murdered. Judith's list of suspects grows as she discovers that several of her neighbors—the attractive, upwardly mobile wives of successful men—had not only been seduced by the dentist, but were photographed in pornographic poses. While investigating the murder, Ju-

224

dith is romanced by a police officer, then confronted by her dull but dutiful husband. In the end, she discovers a vital clue in the photographs that resolves the mystery. *Compromising Positions'* blend of humor, mystery, and a generous dash of sexual situations made it a best-seller. Critical response was also encouraging, though more reserved. *New York Times Book Review* contributor Jack Sullivan praised the novel's direction and humor, but criticized its lack of consistency. "What begins as a brilliant parody of suburban potboilers," Sullivan wrote, "ends by becoming one itself." A *Publishers Weekly* review was more positive, noting that "the dialogue is ribald and wise-cracking, the action fast and furious every step of the way."

Isaacs used her experience as a political speech writer in creating her second novel, *Close Relations.* The protagonist, Marcia Green, is a divorced woman working for a New York Gubernatorial candidate. Against the backdrop of the campaign, Marcia becomes involved with two men—one Jewish and one Catholic—and her sexual encounters with each are treated in graphic detail. *Washington Post Book World* reviewer Susan Cheever noted Isaacs's refreshing portrayal of a female character who possesses "the kind of sexual appetites that have traditionally been a male prerogative—at least in literature." *Publishers Weekly*'s Barbara A. Bannon was also impressed with *Close Relations,* emphasizing the book's "snappy dialogue yielding up laughs on every page, the love story tender and satisfying, the plot pulsing with adrenalin."

Isaacs's next effort, *Almost Paradise,* also turned on a love story, this one between Nick Cobleigh, a member of a wealthy family and a successful actor, and Jane Heissenhuber, a lower class woman who was raised by abusive parents. In a contemporary twist on the Cinderella story, poor Jane marries rich Nick, but they do not live happily ever after. Jane suffers from frigidity and agoraphobia; Nick has several extramarital affairs. The couple eventually separates, but are about to be reconciled when a sudden death brings the story to a close. *Almost Paradise* received a cooler critical reaction than its predecessors. *Los Angeles Times Book Review* contributor Kenneth Atchity was particularly critical of the novel's conclusion, terming it a "shockingly happenstance, tragic ending." *New York Times* reviewer Michiko Kakutani also found fault with the book. "The characters not only speak in cliches," Kakutani wrote, "most of them *are* cliches." Other reviews were more favorable. Anna Shapiro, writing in *New York Times Book Review,* found flaws in the novel, but suggested that "one is reading too absorbedly to notice." Shapiro also praised Isaacs' pacing, emphasizing the author's ability to "keep the plot boiling."

For 1988's *Shining Through,* Isaacs moved away from her contemporary settings. Instead, she wrote a story of World War II intrigue that revolves around a secretary who becomes an American spy. This new subject matter challenged Isaacs, causing her to struggle with her portrayal of Linda Voss, the novel's protagonist. "She's not that easy to capture," Isaacs once told *CA.* "There are enormous changes in the character; she goes from being a rather ordinary legal secretary to be something of a hero, having gotten involved in the war." In the course of her adventure, Linda, a Jew, puts herself at risk by posing as a cook in Nazi Germany; romance also figures in the saga as Linda tries to win the affections of her married boss. *New York Times Book Review* contributor Anne Tolstoi Wallach compared the book to movies from the 1940s, "in which someone pretty much like us takes incredible risks for unimpeachable motives and wins just what *we* wanted." Wallach also applauded Isaacs's successful exploration of new subjects: "like her girl-next-door heroines, she takes risks and her readers reap the rewards."

Having begun her literary career with the mystery *Compromising Positions,* Isaacs returned to familiar ground with her next effort, *Magic Hour.* Here the sleuth is Steve Brady, a Bridgehampton, Long Island homicide detective and one of few male protagonists to be found in Isaacs's work. Brady is a Vietnam veteran with a past record of abusing drugs and alcohol. Though he is engaged to be married, his plans undergo a sudden change when a movie producer is found murdered. In the course of the investigation, Brady falls for Bonnie, the victim's ex-wife and one of several suspects in the case. When the facts point to Bonnie as the murderer, Brady is forced to choose between his heart and his duty as a detective.

New York Times Book Review contributor Helen Dudar found that "it takes a while for the story to develop the kind of narrative drive a light novel of this sort wants." Despite this shortcoming, Dudar complimented Isaacs's "wicked eye for small, telling detail," and was impressed by the author's satiric portraits of affluent Long Island residents. Ultimately, Dudar found that reading *Magic Hour* "is like polishing off an entire box of chocolates. You know it can't be nourishing, but it *is* fun." Carolyn Banks, writing in the *Washington Post Book World,* was more enthusiastic, noting that "the plot is streamlined and the time-frame is short and the voice we hear is witty, and coming-right-at-us-real. . . . Susan Isaacs never writes a *mere* mystery . . . but something more."

In addition to the success of her novels, Isaacs's tales have found favor among moviegoers. Her first exposure to the film industry came when she wrote the screenplay for *Compromising Positions.* Since that time she has written and coproduced a second movie, *Hello Again,* and has seen *Shining Through* adapted for the big screen. Whatever genre she is working in, Isaacs finds the writing process to be demanding but rewarding. She once told *CA:*

"There are always those days that you think you'd have been better off as a computer programmer, that you say to yourself, why am I doing this? I have no talent for it. Days when the prose is leaden, the work is lonely. . . . But most of the time, I enjoy it. It seems to me it's a legitimized way of telling yourself stories, and I guess very often I get that same thumb-sucking pleasure that a child gets from daydreaming. That part of it I like a lot."

BIOGRAPHICAL/CRITICAL SOURCES:

BOOKS

Contemporary Literary Criticism, Volume 32, Gale, 1985.

PERIODICALS

Chicago Tribune, September 1, 1985; September 4, 1985.
Chicago Tribune Book World, March 25, 1984.
Detroit News, November 9, 1980; March 18, 1984.
Los Angeles Times, September 1, 1980; August 30, 1985.
Los Angeles Times Book Review, March 4, 1984.
Newsweek, May 1, 1978.
New Yorker, May 15, 1978.
New York Times, February 1, 1984; August 30, 1985.
New York Times Book Review, April 30, 1978; February 12, 1984; September 11, 1988, p. 13; January 20, 1991, p. 12.
People, April 24, 1978; April 30, 1984.
Publishers Weekly, January 9, 1978; January 23, 1978; July 25, 1980; September 12, 1980; January 4, 1985.
Time, October 3, 1988.
Times Literary Supplement, November 3, 1978.
Washington Post, September 3, 1985.
Washington Post Book World, August 31, 1980; February 12, 1984; January 27, 1991, p. 1.

J

JACOBS, Vernon K(enneth) 1936-

PERSONAL: Born June 25, 1936, in Chicago, IL; son of Jerome (a stockbroker) and Marguerite (a homemaker; maiden name, Brown) Jacobs; married Marcia Lynn Mountain (a city councilman), July 2, 1960; children: Deanne Lynne Jacobs Letoumeau, Laura Ruth. *Education:* University of Wichita (now Wichita State University), B.B.A., 1962; American College, C.L.U., 1972. *Politics:* "Free market libertarian." *Religion:* Protestant.

ADDRESSES: Home—4500 West 72nd Ter., Prairie Village, KS 66208. *Office*—Research Press, Inc., Box 8137, Prairie Village, KS 66208.

CAREER: Deloitte, Haskins & Sells, Kansas City, MO, auditor, 1962-66; Old American Insurance Co., Kansas City, accounting manager, 1966-72, vice-president and controller, 1972-79; private practice as financial consultant in Prairie Village, KS, 1979—; Research Press, Inc. (publishing company), president, 1981—. President of Syntax Corp., 1978-89, and Jacobs, Ferrari & Co. Partner of Heartland Management Co., 1992—. Lecturer at colleges, seminars, and conferences. *Military service:* U.S. Navy, 1954-58.

MEMBER: International Association of Financial Planners (director, 1980-82), American College of Chartered Life Underwriters, American Institute of Certified Public Accountants, Rotary International Club.

WRITINGS:

(With Charles Schoeneman) *The Taxpayer's Audit Survival Manual,* Enterprise Publishing, 1980.
The Taxpayer's Counterattack, Alexandria House, 1980.
Computer Systems for Financial Planners, College for Financial Planning, 1983.
Taxwise Investing, Enterprise Publishing, 1985.

Tax Factors in Selecting a Form of Business, Research Press, 1989.
The Zero Tax Portfolio Manual, Research Press, 1990, 2nd edition, 1991.
How to Legally Beat the Pension Estate Tax, Research Press, 1992.

Author of column on taxes published in *Private Practice,* 1979-92. Also author of micro computer programs. Contributor of articles to periodicals, including *Free Enterprise, Computer Retailing, Investment Alert,* and *Financial Services Times.* Editor of newsletters, *Tax Angles,* 1977-84, *The Financial Systems Report,* 1980-82, *Small Business Tax Saver,* 1984-85, and *The Jacobs Report,* 1989—. Consulting editor, *Journal of Accounting,* 1988-91.

SIDELIGHTS: Vernon K. Jacobs told *CA:* "Although I have written seven books, more than 1,000 articles and more than two dozen computer programs, I am no longer an author, per se. I also work as an editor and self-publisher. I'm now devoting more of my time to the publishing aspects of my business, Research Press, Inc.

"I am essentially an entrepreneur who perceived an opportunity to convert information about taxes into a business. My first successful venture was a self-published newsletter that I later sold to a much larger publisher who wanted me to be the author/editor of their tax information newsletter. For eight years, I worked as a salaried editor and author, producing newsletters, articles, booklets, and three books. I also did a lot of public speaking at seminars and conferences regarding taxes and tax planning. As the editor of a very large newsletter (60,000 subscribers), I received many invitations to write articles about taxes.

"While I was working as a tax newsletter editor, I began another entrepreneurial venture to design and market tax analysis software for personal computers. That led to my second self-published newsletter, *The Financial Systems Report.* The computer software newsletter eventually led to a number of other writing opportunities, books, and public speaking engagements.

"In 1989, I began my third newsletter, *The Jacobs Report,* which has led to a number of new writing opportunities. However, I'm now devoting more of my time to the marketing aspects of selling my newsletter, books, and reports and less time in trying to constantly create more and more new information."

Jacobs continued to explain: "My writings are generally intended for upper income rather than middle income readers. The middle income family has an income of about $35,000 and an income tax bill of about $3,000. My target readers have an income of $50,000 or more. How can the average taxpayer protect his assets? The *average* taxpayer doesn't have any significant assets other than a home and a company pension plan. But if the average taxpayer wants to accumulate some wealth, I could describe more than two hundred different ways to legally pay less taxes and explain how to profit from inflation.

"*The Zero Tax Portfolio Manual* was intended to explain how the government is confiscating our savings through taxation and inflation, and how the informed reader can take steps to legally pay less income tax and to build an inflation-resistant portfolio."

*   *   *

JANOVY, John, Jr. 1937-

PERSONAL: Born December 27, 1937, in Houma, LA; son of John (a geologist) and Lillian Bernice (Locke) Janovy; married Karen Anne Oneth (an executive secretary), August 7, 1961; children: Cynthia Anne, Jenifer Lynn, John III. *Education:* University of Oklahoma, B.S., 1959, M.S., 1962, Ph.D.,1965; postdoctoral study at Rutgers University, 1965-66.

ADDRESSES: Home—Lincoln, NE. *Office*—School of Biological Sciences, University of Nebraska, Lincoln, NE 68588-0118. *Agent*—Jane Dystel, Acton & Dystel, 928 Broadway, New York, NY 10010.

CAREER: University of Nebraska, School of Biological Sciences, Lincoln, associate professor, 1966-74, Varner Professor of Biological Sciences, 1974—, assistant dean of College of Arts and Sciences, 1966—. *Military service:* U.S. Army Reserve, 1959-66; became captain.

MEMBER: American Society of Parasitologists, American Society of Tropical Medicine and Hygiene, Society of Protozoologists.

WRITINGS:

Keith County Journal (essays), St. Martin's, 1978.
Yellowlegs, St. Martin's, 1980.
Back in Keith County (essays), St. Martin's, 1981.
On Becoming a Biologist, Harper, 1985.
Fields of Friendly Strife, Viking, 1987.
Vermillion Sea: A Naturalist's Journey in Baja California, Houghton, 1992.

Contributor to scientific journals.

WORK IN PROGRESS: Another set of essays on western Nebraska natural history.

SIDELIGHTS: John Janovy, Jr.'s essays celebrate nature at all levels, from the smallest and most obscure parasite to the most complex of all species, the human being. Janovy's essays, many of which originate from field studies he conducts as a life sciences professor at the University of Nebraska, have been ranked with the writings of such renowned essayists as E. B. White and Lewis Thomas.

Reviewing Janovy's first book, *Keith County Journal,* in *Time,* Peter Stoler writes, "Like Blake seeing a world in a grain of sand, Professor Janovy discerns universes in the creeks, bogs and fields of the Sandhills country." Comments Paul T. Hornak in the *National Review:* "Certain of [Janovy's] analogies fall flat; certain ideas, though clothed respectably, are silly. But also like them, he speaks in a narrative voice both youthful and wise. He elucidates small wonders with abundant charm."

After the publication of *Keith County Journal,* Janovy took a year's leave from the university to follow the migration of a single sandpiper, a journey he chronicles in *Yellowlegs.* Janovy returned to the familiar terrain of Nebraska, however, in his third book, *Back to Keith County.* In a *Washington Post* review of *Back to Keith County,* Matthew Schudel writes that Janovy, "far from going to the same well once too often, has produced his best book. He has reined in his previous excesses of tone and occasional wantonness with language and developed instead a more controlled voice and a surer grasp of his subject." Concludes Schudel: "All in all, Janovy has given us a superb example of nature-writing and of life in the Great Plains. . . . [He] takes us on a journey of intellectual serendipity, deriving extraordinary thoughts from ordinary circumstances."

Janovy once told *CA:* "I feel a major responsibility to communicate the biological, scientific information in such a way that the average citizen can understand and appreciate the complexity of Earth. This is basically why I write, although that writing is really only an extension of the communication I've been doing in freshman classes for years. We live in the most technological society ever to have evolved, and the average citizen must be educated enough biologically to make decisions appropriate for the technological age. That's my responsibility as a scientist. As a writer, however, I feel that the major themes of literature, themes such as 'good' versus 'evil,' must eventually give way to literary themes such as humanity's ultimate peace with the planet that supports us. Literature must begin to express, consider, and analyze the values that allow that peace. I am making now, and will continue to make, an effort to do just that in my writing."

BIOGRAPHICAL/CRITICAL SOURCES:

PERIODICALS

American Health Magazine, December, 1987.
Audubon, January/February, 1992.
Best Sellers, April, 1979.
Christian Science Monitor, February 7, 1992.
Kirkus Reviews, November 1, 1978.
Lincoln Star, December 27, 1978.
National Review, September 18, 1979.
Omaha World-Herald, September 2, 1979; June 14, 1987.
Psychology Today, June, 1987.
Smithsonian, September, 1992.
Time, February 5, 1979.
Washington Post, December 4, 1981.

*   *   *

JAY, M(argaret) Ellen 1946-

PERSONAL: Born March 23, 1946, in Bridgeport, CT.; daughter of John (in government sales) and Hilda (a media specialist; maiden name, Lease) Jay. *Education:* Indiana University—Bloomington, B.S., 1968, M.S., 1969; Kent State University, Ph.D., 1981. *Avocational interests:* Travel (China, Africa, South America, Europe), playing french horn in community groups, outdoor activities, needlepoint.

ADDRESSES: Home—12754 Turquoise Ter., Silver Spring, MD 20904. *Office*—Damascus Elementary School, 10201 Bethesda Church Rd., Damascus, MD 20872.

CAREER: Montgomery County Public Schools, Silver Spring, MD, classroom teacher, 1969-70, elementary school media specialist, 1970-78; W. T. Page Elementary School, media specialist, 1981-92; Damascus Elementary School, Damascus, MD, media specialist, 1992—. Adjunct professor at Catholic University of America, 1988—. Consultant to Learning Unlimited, Invent America, 1983-86, Department of Education, Washington, DC, 1990—, and Discovery Channel, 1991—. Member of re-

view Panel for Schools of Excellence, Department of Education, 1987 and 1989.

MEMBER: American Library Association, American Association of School Librarians (member of board of directors 1989-94), Association Collaborative for Teaching Thinking, Association for Educational Communication and Technology, Association for Supervision and Curriculum Development, Outdoor Education Association, Maryland Educational Media Organization, Montgomery County Educational Media Specialists Association.

AWARDS, HONORS: Broome Award, National Education Association affiliate, 1984, for *Library Media Projects for the Gifted;* Teamwork Award for instructional design, 1984, and a publishing award for contribution to the school library media field, 1986, both from Association for Educational Communication and Technology.

WRITINGS:

Involvement Bulletin Boards and Other Motivational Reading Activities, Shoe String, 1976.
Library Media Projects for the Gifted, Shoe String, 1982.
(With mother, Hilda Jay) *Developing Library Museum Partnerships,* Shoe String, 1984.
(With H. Jay) *Building Reference Skills in Elementary School,* Shoe String, 1986.
(With H. Jay) *Motivation and the School Library Media Teacher,* Shoe String, 1988.
(With H. Jay) *Designing Instruction for Diverse Abilities and the Library Media Teacher's Role,* Shoe String, 1991.

WORK IN PROGRESS: Suggestions for integrating writing and thinking activities through computer lab media center program cooperation, for Neal Schyman, 1994.

SIDELIGHTS: M. Ellen Jay once told *CA:* "A major motivation for my books is the reaction of colleagues to oral presentation of the same material at various conventions. The motivation for the activities themselves is the need to get students involved with their own education. As a late bloomer myself, I can relate to these students, and I find that I have an ability to design activities that spark their interest and teach necessary concepts and lifelong skills."

*   *   *

JOHNSON, Arthur W(illiam) 1920-

PERSONAL: Born April 22, 1920, in London, England; son of Arthur Albert (a builder) and Florence (a housewife; maiden name, Jeffreys) Johnson; married second wife, Pamela Emily Nottingham (a teacher), August 8, 1974; children: Susan Johnson Baillie, Nicholas, David. *Education:* South East Essex Technical College, National

Diploma in Design (calligraphy), 1947; Hornsey College of Art, National Diploma in Design (bookbinding), 1948, Art Teachers Diploma, 1950, further study, 1955-56; attended Chiswick Polytechnic, 1948-49; City and Guilds London Institute, final examination in bookbinding, 1956.

ADDRESSES: Home—74 Mansfield Ave., East Barnet, Hertfordshire EN4 8QF, England.

CAREER: Hornsey College of Art, London, England, lecturer in calligraphy and bookbinding, 1950-65; London College of Printing, London, lecturer in bookbinding, 1965-82. Part-time member of faculty at West Dean College of Crafts and Hoger Institut voor de Conservatie van het Boek, Ghent, Belgium. *Military service:* British Army, Royal Armoured Corps, 1940-46; became sergeant.

MEMBER: Designer Bookbinders (founder, 1950; past president).

AWARDS, HONORS: Licentiate of College of Craft Education, 1980; honorary fellow of Designer Bookbinders, 1989.

WRITINGS:

The Thames Hudson Manual of Bookbinding, Thames & Hudson, 1978.
Practical Guide to Bookbinding, Thames & Hudson, 1985.
Book Repair and Conservation, Thames & Hudson, 1988.
(Translator) *Il Restauro del Libro,* Gruppo Editoriale Muzzio, 1989.
(Translator) *Manual de Encuadernacion,* Herman Blume, 1989.
(Translator from the Russian) *The Practical Guide to Craft Bookbinding,* Mockba, 1992.
Lettering of Books, Puriri Press (New Zealand), 1993.

SIDELIGHTS: Arthur W. Johnson's bookbindings have been exhibited in all the major cities of Europe and the United States, and his works are displayed in public and private collections, including those at the British Museum and the University of Texas. He has also executed numerous rolls of honor and illuminated scrolls. Now, in retirement, the author travels around the world to study bookbinding methods in other countries.

Johnson once told *CA:* "Foremost I am an art teacher, and my aims have been to train people who will be better craftsmen and more accomplished designers than myself. In this way, I believe, crafts will have a sound future.

"My sympathies are with books. I love to read the thoughts of the author, to follow the illustrations, and to appreciate the printed page. The feel of paper and bindings gives me much delight. I chose a career in binding and calligraphy because I believed that the coordination of hand and brain would, in my case, be best utilized in that way. Creativity, too, would be expressed by designing book covers in a nontraditional way. Calligraphy is a part of book production, and I was attracted to the simplicity and dignity of painted letters and to the perfection of letter forms written with a broad-nibbed pen. My goal is to raise the standard of design and construction in fine hand-bookbinding and to encourage recognition that the craft should be based on scientific principles.

"When creating a binding, one must first read the book and understand the author. Typography and illustrations must also be considered, and then a design (or a number of designs) are made in character with the book. I subject my own personality to that of the contents of the book and, with color, texture, and line, endeavor to make an original and suitable decoration for the cover.

"I believe my best work was the binding I did for Rothchild's *Extinct Birds.* I bound it in brown levant Morocco leather and light brown marbled Spanish leather with an onlay of impossible bird shapes in colored leathers across the covers."

*   *   *

JONES, Gareth (Elwyn) 1939-

PERSONAL: Born January 30, 1939, in Abergavenny, Wales; son of Henry Haydn (a minister) and Nellie Muriel (Morgan) Jones; married Katherine Scourse (a university tutor), August 16, 1963; children: Bethan Mari, Matthew Owain. *Education:* University College of Swansea, University of Wales, B.A., 1960, M.A., 1963, Ph.D., 1979; University College, Cardiff, University of Wales, M.Ed., 1972. *Religion:* United Reformed.

ADDRESSES: Home—130 Pennard Dr., Pennard, Gower, West Glamorganshire, Wales. *Office*— Department of Education, University of Wales, Old College, King Street, Aberystwyth, Dyfed, Wales.

CAREER: Second history master at grammar school in Croydon, England, 1963-65; Cardiff College of Education, Cardiff, Wales, lecturer in history, 1965-69; Swansea College of Education, Swansea, Wales, senior lecturer in history, 1969-72; University of Wales, University College of Swansea, lecturer, 1972-82, senior lecturer, 1982-87, reader in history of education, 1987-90; University of Wales, Aberystwyth, research professor of education, 1990—. Director of Welsh Office Education Department research project, 1984-86; senior visiting fellow of Welsh Office Education Department Open University in Wales, 1985-88.

MEMBER: Royal Historical Society (fellow), Glamorgan History Society (member of council), British Association for Local History (vice-chairman, 1982-85).

WRITINGS:

The Gentry and the Elizabethan State, Christopher Davies, 1977.

(Editor with Lionel Ward) *New History, Old Problems: Studies in History Teaching,* Faculty of Education, University College of Swansea, University of Wales, 1978.

Controls and Conflicts in Welsh Secondary Education, 1889-1944, University of Wales Press, 1982.

Modern Wales: A Concise History c. 1485-1979, Cambridge University Press, 1984.

Fifty Years of Secondary Education in Wales, 1934-1984, National Union of Teachers, 1985.

(Editor, with Trevor Herbert) *Edward I and Wales,* University of Wales Press, 1988.

(Editor, with Herbert) *Tudor Wales,* University of Wales Press, 1988.

(Editor, with Herbert) *Wales in the Eighteenth Century,* University of Wales Press, 1988.

(Editor, with Herbert) *Wales 1880-1914,* University of Wales Press, 1988.

(Editor, with Herbert) *People and Protest 1815-1880,* University of Wales Press, 1988.

(Editor, with Herbert) *Wales between the Wars,* University of Wales Press, 1988.

Which Nation's Schools?, University of Wales Press, 1990.

(Editor) *Education, Culture and Society,* University of Wales Press, 1991.

Contributor to education and history journals. Co-editor, *Morgannwg: Journal of Glamorgan History;* reviews editor, *Welsh Historian.*

WORK IN PROGRESS: Crises of Identity for Macmillan; *Welsh History and Its Sources.*

SIDELIGHTS: Gareth Jones once told *CA:* "As a Welshman and a historian I have been singularly fortunate to have spent most of my career teaching in Wales and writing about its history. My first interest was in the history of the Tudor period, and *The Gentry and the Elizabethan State* deals with the politics and government of Wales in the sixteenth century. I found it easy to be dispassionate on this subject—not so with my recent work on twentieth-century Welsh education.

"It is impossible for any Welsh person to be unaffected by the human consequences of, at best, inadequate British government policies as they affected Wales in the depressed twenties and thirties. Paradoxically, depopulation of industrial areas, particularly, greatly increased the percentage of secondary/grammar school attendance and contributed to the idealized picture of Welsh devotion to education. I nearly wrote 'myth,' yet throughout the century the Welsh secondary system has been more egalitarian, more open to talent, than the English. As a result it

has helped create and cement class differences in Wales. And that is only one of those paradoxes of Welsh education which consolidate the schizophrenia of being Welsh in Great Britain.

"History may not repeat itself, but since 1979 government policy towards state education has resulted in morale in schools and universities being at its lowest since the years of the Depression. Again in 1979 the Welsh voted against even limited self-government within the United Kingdom. Yet recent developments in the teaching of Welsh history are more exciting than at any time this century. In my country of Wales, Janus would rank as a low-achiever."

BIOGRAPHICAL/CRITICAL SOURCES:

PERIODICALS

Times Literary Supplement, March 1, 1985.

*   *   *

JOSEPH, William A(llen) 1947-

PERSONAL: Born June 10, 1947, in Chicago, IL; son of Howard Roy (a furniture merchant) and Myra (Joffe) Joseph; married Sigrid K. Bergenstein (a researcher and writer), September 10, 1977; children: Abigail Katherine, Hannah, Rebecca. *Education:* Cornell University, B.A. (with distinction), 1969; Stanford University, M.A., 1971, Ph.D., 1981.

ADDRESSES: Home—18 Lovewell Rd., Wellesley, MA 02181. *Office*—Department of Political Science, Wellesley College, Wellesley, MA 02181.

CAREER: Instructor, University of California at Berkeley, 1973, Dominican College, San Rafael, CA, 1974, and University of California at Santa Cruz, 1975; Stanford University, Stanford, CA, assistant director of Center for East Asian Studies, 1974-76; York University, Downsview, Ontario, lecturer in political science, 1978-80; Wellesley College, Wellesley, MA, assistant professor, 1980-86, associate professor of political science, 1986—. Boston-Hangzhou Sister City Program, academic consultant, 1980-84, Board of Trustees, 1986-89; grant evaluator, American Council of Learned Societies, National Endowment for the Humanities, Bunting Institute.

MEMBER: American Political Science Association, Association for Asian Studies (secretary-treasurer, New England Conference, 1986-90), American Association of University Professors (member of executive committee, Wellesley chapter, 1983-84).

AWARDS, HONORS: National Defense Foreign Language fellowship (Chinese), Stanford University, 1969-70, 1976-77; Mellon fellowship, Aspen Institute for Humanistic Studies, 1983-84.

WRITINGS:

(Contributor) *Perspectives on United States History,* Field Publications, 1975.

(Contributor) *People in Change: East Asia,* Addison-Wesley, 1975.

The Critique of Ultra-Leftism in China, 1958-1981, Stanford University Press, 1984.

(Editor) *Global Studies: China, Taiwan, and Hong Kong* (annual series), Dushkin, 2nd edition (Joseph not associated with previous editions), 1987, 3rd edition, 1989.

(Author of foreword) Gao Yuan, *Born Red: A Chronicle of the Cultural Revolution,* Stanford University Press, 1987.

(Editor) *China Briefing, 1991,* Westview Press, 1991.

(Editor with Christine Wong and David Zweig) *New Perspectives on the Cultural Revolution,* Harvard University Council on East Asian Studies, 1991.

(Editor) *China Briefing, 1992,* Westview Press, 1992.

(Section editor and contributor) Joel Krieger, editor-in-chief, *The Oxford Companion to Politics of the World,* Oxford University Press, 1993.

(Contributor) James L. Huffman, Fujiya Kawashima, and Ke-wen Wang, editors, *East Asian Nationalism: An Encyclopedia of Modern History and Culture in China, Japan, and Korea,* Garland Publishing, in press.

Contributor of articles and essays to *Harvard International Review, Modern China,* and *Studies in Comparative Communism.* Book review editor and member of editorial board, *Journal of Asian Studies,* 1987-90. Contributing editor, *Current History,* 1993—.

WORK IN PROGRESS: Editing *China Briefing, 1993-94* and *Comparative Politics in Transition;* research project: "The Thought of Deng Xioping: Ideological Revivalism in Late Twentieth Century China."

K

KAMM, Antony 1931-

PERSONAL: Born March 2, 1931, in London, England; son of George Emile (a publisher) and Josephine (an author; maiden name, Hart) Kamm; married Anthea Bell, July, 1957 (divorced, 1973); married Eileen Dunlop (a children's novelist), October 27, 1979; children: (first marriage) Richard, Oliver. *Education:* Worcester College, Oxford, B.A., 1955, M.A., 1960.

ADDRESSES: Home—46 Tarmangie Dr., Dollar, Clackmannanshire FK14 7BP, Scotland.

CAREER: National Book League, London, England, education officer, 1955-58; Bodley Head (publishers), London, senior children's editor, 1958-59; The Book Society, London, general manager, 1959-60; Brockhampton Press, Leicester, England, editor in chief, 1960-72; Commonwealth Secretariat, London, senior education officer, 1972-74; free-lance editor and publishing consultant, 1974-76; Oxford University Press, Oxford, England, Caribbean regional manager and development manager in Africa, 1976-77, managing editor of children's books, 1977-79; writer and free-lance editor, 1979—. Part-time lecturer in publishing studies, University of Stirling, 1988—. Has served as a UNESCO consultant on short-term assignments in India, Iran, Pakistan, Sri Lanka, Gambia, Lesotho, and Mauritius.

MEMBER: Children's Book Circle (chairman, 1965-67).

WRITINGS:

FOR ADULTS

(With Boswell Taylor) *Books and the Teacher,* University of London Press, 1966.
Choosing Books for Younger Children, Thornhill Press, 1977.

(With Charles Schofield) *Lager Lovelies,* Richard Drew, 1984.
(With Rennie McOwan) *Kilchurn Heritage: The History,* Kilchurn Heritage, 1986.
York Notes on Willis Hall's "The Long and the Short and the Tall," Longman, 1988.
Scotland, Colour Library Books, 1989.
York Notes on R. C. Sherriff's "Journey's End," Longman, 1990.
A Dictionary of British and Irish Authors, Longman, 1990.
(With Claude Poulet) *Britain and Her People,* Colour Library Books, 1990.
Collins Biographical Dictionary of English Literature, HarperCollins, 1993.

FOR CHILDREN

The Story of Islam, Cambridge University Press, 1976.
(With wife, Eileen Dunlop) *Edinburgh,* Cambridge University Press, 1982.
(With Dunlop) *The Story of Glasgow,* Richard Drew, 1983.
(With Dunlop) *Scottish Heroes and Heroines of Long Ago,* Richard Drew, 1984.
(With Dunlop) *Kings and Queens of Scotland,* Richard Drew, 1984, new edition, 1991.
(With Dunlop) *Scottish Homes through the Ages,* Richard Drew, 1985.

EDITOR

(With Dunlop) *A Book of Old Edinburgh,* Macdonald Publishers, 1984.
(With Dunlop) *Scottish Traditional Rhymes,* Richard Drew, 1985, new edition, 1991.
(With Dunlop) *The Scottish Collection of Verse to 1800,* Richard Drew, 1985.
(With Anne Lean) *A Scottish Childhood,* Collins, 1985.

(With A. Norman Jeffares) *An Irish Childhood,* Collins, 1987, new edition published as *Irish Childhoods,* Gill & Macmillan, 1992.

(With Jeffares) *A Jewish Childhood,* Boxtree, 1988.

OTHER

Also author of radio scripts for Scottish Educational Service of British Broadcasting Corp. (BBC), 1984-86. Book reviewer for *Scotland on Sunday,* 1988-90.

WORK IN PROGRESS: The Romans; History of John Smith and Son, Booksellers.

SIDELIGHTS: Antony Kamm told *CA,* "In writing information books for adults or for children I have aimed to use the formula which I have learned as an editor is the most effective way of keeping the reader's attention: to assume that they know nothing of the subject; to select the salient facts, arrange them in an interesting way, and present them enthusiastically."

*   *   *

KASLOW, Florence (Whiteman) 1930-

PERSONAL: Born January 6, 1930, in Philadelphia, PA; daughter of Irving and Rose (Tarin) Whiteman; married Solis Kaslow (a stockbroker), November 21, 1954; children: Nadine Joy, Howard Ian. *Education:* Temple University, A.B., 1952; Ohio State University, M.A.S.A., 1954; Bryn Mawr College, Ph.D., 1969. *Religion:* Jewish.

ADDRESSES: Home—1900 Consulate Pl., Apt. 1903, West Palm Beach, FL 33401. *Office*—Northwood Center, 2601 N. Flagler Dr., Suite 103, West Palm Beach, FL 33407.

CAREER: Temple University, Philadelphia, PA, instructor in sociology, 1961-62; Pennsylvania State University, Ogontz Campus, Abington, instructor in sociology, 1962-65, 1968-69; University of Pennsylvania, Philadelphia, assistant professor of social work, 1969-72, associate in psychiatry, 1972-73; Hahnemann Medical University, Department of Mental Health Sciences, Philadelphia, associate professor, 1973-78, professor, 1979-80; Duke University Medical School, adjunct professor of medical psychology, department of psychiatry, 1982—; currently president of Kaslow Associates, West Palm Beach. Therapist in private practice, 1964—. Diplomate, Forensic Psychology, 1979, Clinical Psychology, 1981, and Family Psychology, 1981, all from American Board of Professional Psychology. Licensed psychologist, Pennsylvania, 1973—, and Florida, 1982—. Director, Florida Couples and Family Institute, 1982—. Principal workshop leader, Psychological Seminars, Inc., 1980—; Allied Health Staff, Glenbeigh Hospital, West Palm Beach, Kennedy Hospi-

tal, Atlantis, FL, and Fair Oaks Hospital, Boca/Delray, FL. Member of faculty, Congregation Keneseth Israel, Elkins Park, 1967-68, 1969-70, 1972-73; special lecturer in family therapy, Family Institute of Philadelphia, 1972-80; visiting professor, Southwest Family Institute, Dallas, 1979—; Chair, American Board of Forensic Psychology Diplomate Examination Committee, Florida Region, 1980—. Supervisor of adoptive homes, Association for Jewish Children, Philadelphia, 1954; B'nai Brith Youth Organization, Philadelphia, assistant director, 1954-57, director of girls' division, 1959-60; staff specialist, Abington Hospital Community Mental Health Center, 1972-73, Moss Rehabilitation Hospital Social Service Department, 1973, Catholic Social Services of Philadelphia, 1973, Jewish Y's and Centers of Philadelphia, 1973—; staff training specialist, Bureau of Corrections, Harrisburg, PA, 1973-75. Marriage and family counselor, Camden Family Counsel, Camden, NJ, 1958-59; caseworker, Montgomery County Mental Health Clinics, summer, 1965, and Family Service of Montgomery County, summer, 1966. Member of board, Jewish Y's and Centers, Neighborhood Center Branch, 1972—. Public speaker.

Also consultant to business and industry, mental health and social agencies, and educational institutions, including U.S. Navy Department of Psychiatry Residency Training Programs, 1976—, Forensic Psychology Associates, Inc., Tampa, 1981—; senior consultant, Samaritan Center, Fort Lauderdale, 1981-84; member of consulting staff, Lake Hospital, Lake Worth, FL, 1983-91, and Palm Beach Institute, 1983-92; member of advisory board, Palm Beach Junior College Mental Health Program, 1984-88.

MEMBER: International Council of Psychologists, International Family Therapy Association (founder and first president, 1987-90), International Academy of Family Psychologists (American representative, 1990-94), American Association for the Advancement of Science, American Academy of Forensic Psychologists (president, 1979-80), Academy of Family Psychologists, Academy of Family Mediators, American Family Therapy Association, American Psychological Association (president, Division of Family Psychology, 1987; president-elect, Division of Media Psychology, 1992), American Board of Forensic Psychology (former president), American Association of Sex Educators, Counselors, and Therapists, American Association for Marital and Family Therapy (fellow), American Psychology-Law Society (chairman of certification committee, 1977-78), Pennsylvania Association of Marriage and Family Counselors (treasurer, 1974-75; chairman of licensing committee, 1974-76; vice-president, 1976-77), Pennsylvania Psychological Association (fellow; chairman of awards committee, 1976; president of academic division, 1978-79), Florida Psychological Association, Florida Association of Professional

Family Mediators (president, 1984-85), Palm Beach County Professional Mediation Association (president, 1982-83), Philadelphia Society of Clinical Psychologists (fellow; program chairman, 1975-78; member of executive board, 1975-78), Family Institute of Philadelphia, Temple University Liberal Arts Alumni (president of board, 1960-62), Temple University Alumni Association (member of board, 1964; member of executive committee, 1971—), Phi Alpha Theta, Pi Gamma Mu, Jewish Federation of Palm Beach Business and Professional Womens Group, Executive Women of Palm Beach.

WRITINGS:

Issues in Human Services: A Sourcebook in Supervisions and Staff Development, Jossey-Bass, 1972.
(With Lita L. Schwartz) *Personality* (instructor's manual for test by Elaine Donelson), Appleton-Century-Crofts, 1973.
(With L. L. Schwartz) *The Dynamics of Divorce: A Life Cycle Perspective,* Brunner, 1986.

EDITOR

Supervision, Staff Training and Consultation in the Helping Professions, Jossey-Bass, 1977.
(With R. Ridenour and contributor) *The Military Family: Dynamics, Structure, and Treatment,* Guilford, 1984.
(And contributor) *Psychotherapy with Psychotherapists,* Haworth Press, 1984.
(And contributor) *The Clinical Supervisor,* Haworth Press, 1985.
(And contributor) *Supervision and Training: Models, Dilemmas and Challenges,* Haworth Press, 1986.
(And contributor) *Journal of Psychotherapy and the Family,* Haworth Press, 1987.
Couples Therapy in a Family Context: Perspective and Retrospective, Aspen Publications, 1988.
(And contributor) *Voices in Family Psychology,* Sage Publications, 1990.

Also contributor to books, including *Handbook of Family Therapy,* edited by A. Gurman and D. Kniskern, Brunner, 1980; *The Family Therapist as Consultant,* edited by L. Wynne, T. Weber, and S. McDaniel, Guilford, 1985; *Work and Families* (with S. Kaslow), edited by S. Zedeck, Jossey-Bass, 1992; *Gender Issues Across the Life Cycle,* edited by B. R. Wainrib, Springer, 1992; *Readings in Forensic Psychology,* edited by G. Cooke, C. C. Thomas; and *Cults,* Haworth Press. Contributor to *Proceedings of South African Association for Learning and Educational Disabilities,* Johannesburg, South Africa.

OTHER

Contributor of more than 110 articles and reviews to professional journals, including *Growth and Change, Academic Therapy Quarterly, Public Welfare, Family Therapy Today,* and *Clinical Social Work Journal,* 1972. Editor, *Journal of Marital and Family Therapy,* 1976-81. Member of editorial board, *Conciliation Courts Review, Mediation Quarterly, Journal of Marital and Family Therapy, Journal of Divorce, Marriage and Family Review, Italian Journal of Family Therapy, Argentinian Journal of Family Therapy, Brazilian Journal of Family Therapy, Psychotherapy, Journal of Child Clinical Psychology* and *Journal of Family Psychology.*

Kaslow's work has been translated into Japanese, German, Polish, and Spanish.

*   *   *

KAYE, Marvin (Nathan) 1938-
(Eugene D. Goodwin, Joseph Lavinson, Saralee Terry)

PERSONAL: Born March 10, 1938, in Philadelphia, PA; son of Morris (a television and radio repairman) and Theresa (Buroski) Kaye; married Saralee Bransdorf, August 4, 1963; children: Terry Ellen. *Education:* Pennsylvania State University, B.A., 1960, M.A., 1962; University of Denver, graduate study, 1960.

ADDRESSES: Home—525 West End Avenue, 12-E, New York, NY 10024. *Agent*—Mel Berger, William Morris Agency, 1350 Avenue of the Americas, New York, NY 10019.

CAREER: Grit (newspaper), Williamsport, PA, reporter, 1963-65, then New York correspondent, 1966—; *Business Travel* (magazine), New York City, assistant managing editor, 1965; *Toys* (magazine), New York City, senior editor, 1966-70; full-time writer, 1970—. Faculty member, New School for Social Research, 1974-75; adjunct associate professor of creative writing, New York University, 1976—. Public relations director, Light Opera of Manhattan, 1973; co-founder and artistic director, The Open Book (theatre company), 1976—.

MEMBER: Authors Guild, Authors League of America, Mystery Writers of America (member of awards committee, 1977), Sons of the Desert (treasurer, 1973-75; president, 1977—), Illustrious Order of Dragon Killers, The Wolfe Pack (chairman, awards committee, 1991—).

WRITINGS:

The Histrionic Holmes, Luther Norris, 1971.
A Lively Game of Death, Saturday Review Press, 1972.
A Toy Is Born, Stein & Day, 1973, revised edition published as *The Story of Monopoly, Silly Putty, Bingo, Twister, Frisbee, Scrabble, Et Cetera,* 1977.
The Stein & Day Handbook of Magic, Stein & Day, 1973.
The Grand Ole Opry Murders, Saturday Review Press, 1974.

The Handbook of Mental Magic, Stein & Day, 1975.
Bullets for Macbeth, Dutton, 1976.
The Laurel and Hardy Murders, Dutton, 1977.
My Son, the Druggist, Doubleday, 1977.
Catalog of Magic, Dolphin Books, 1977.
(With Parke Godwin) *The Masters of Solitude,* Doubleday, 1978.
My Brother, the Druggist, Doubleday, 1979.
The Incredible Umbrella, Doubleday, 1980.
The Possession of Immanuel Wolf, and Other Improbable Tales, Doubleday, 1981.
The Amorous Umbrella, Doubleday, 1981.
The Soap Opera Slaughters, Doubleday, 1982.
(With Godwin) *Wintermind,* Doubleday, 1982.
(With Godwin) *A Cold Blue Light* (novel; also see below), Berkley Publishing, 1983.
Fantastique, St. Martin's, 1992.

EDITOR

Fiends and Creatures (anthology), Popular Library, 1975.
(And contributor) *Brother Theodor's Chamber of Horrors* (anthology), Pinnacle Books, 1975.
Ghosts, Doubleday, 1981.
Masterpieces of Terror and the Supernatural, Doubleday, 1985.
Devils and Demons, Doubleday, 1987.
"Weird Tales," the Magazine that Never Dies, Doubleday, 1988.
Witches and Warlocks, Doubleday, 1989.
Thirteen Plays of Ghosts and the Supernatural, Fireside Theatre, 1990.
Haunted America, Doubleday, 1990.
Lovers and Other Monsters, Doubleday, 1992.
Sweet Revenge: Ten Plays of Bloody Murder, Fireside Theatre, 1992.
Frantic Comedy, Fireside Theatre, in press.
The Best of "Weird Tales," 1923, Bleak House, in press.

Also the author of plays, including "Bertrand Russell's Guided Tour of Intellectual Rubbish" and "A Cold Blue Light" (based on his novel of the same name). Contributor of short stories, under pseudonyms Eugene D. Goodwin and Joseph Lavinson, and verse, under pseudonym Saralee Terry, to periodicals, including *Amazing/Fantastic Stories, Fantasy Macabre, Fantasy Tales, Playthings,* and *Thrust Science Fiction.* Author of column, "Marvin Kaye's Nth Dimension," *Science Fiction Chronicle;* guest-columnist, *Long Life.* Contributing editor of *Mass Retailing Merchandiser, Galileo,* and business publications in the toy-hobby field.

Kaye's books have been published in Canada, France, Great Britain, Germany, Holland, and Spain.

SIDELIGHTS: Writer Marvin Kaye once told *CA:* "A thorough training in theatre as an actor, director, and playwright is my principal background and passion. My chief interests in writing are drama and philosophy.

"As a writing instructor, I am constantly appalled by the professional writers who spread the noxious doctrine that *all* you need do is sit in a book-lined chamber and write, write, write and someday someone will find you, a doctrine postulated on the mystique of 'talent.' I maintain that writing is mostly disciplined, thoughtful hard work, training oneself to hew to a regular schedule, and finding out ways to sell and bring one's work before the public. Writing is a profession and it is a business.

"Instead of talent, I look for a psychological need in my students. If they cannot conceive of themselves as successful writers, they will probably not become so. I have constantly encountered sensitive souls who handle the language with intuitive brilliance. But they are so stultified with fear of defining themselves as creative people that they never set goals and work purposefully to achieve them. Those who do may not have as much 'talent,' but if they want to express themselves in this agonizing business, there is probably much more in their psyches than the run-of-the-mill writing professor ever sees.

"Dare people to fly in the face of criticism, and stick to it, and chances are they will eventually succeed—not without pain, but that's part of the dues we pay when we overexcite our brains, as all creators do. Once a famous New York writing teacher told one of my students her book-in-progress showed no talent for novel writing. She was decimated, crucified on the 'talent' mystery altar. I told her to keep at it, and the hell with adverse criticism that doesn't show how to improve one's technique. A month later she sold the same book to Simon & Schuster for more money than I've ever earned—a Literary Guild alternate!"

*   *   *

KELLETT, Arnold 1926-

PERSONAL: Born May 13, 1926, in Wibsey, Bradford, West Yorkshire, England; son of Horace and Gladys (Denton) Kellett; married Patricia Horsfall (a library assistant), July 25, 1953; children: Ruth, Rachel, Ann, Timothy. *Education:* University of Liverpool, B.A. (with first class honors), 1952; attended Sorbonne, University of Paris; University of Leeds, Ph.D., 1986. *Politics:* Independent.

ADDRESSES: Home—22 Aspin Oval, Knaresborough, North Yorkshire, England.

CAREER: Teacher of chemistry and modern languages at Methodist school in Harrogate, England, 1952-56; King

James's School, Knaresborough, North Yorkshire, England, teacher of French, German, and religion, 1956-64, head of modern languages department, 1964-83; writer and lecturer. Methodist lay preacher, 1953—. Town of Knaresborough, member of council, 1976—, mayor, 1979-80 and 1984-85. *Military service:* British Army, Intelligence Corps, 1944-48.

MEMBER: Yorkshire Dialect Society, Knaresborough Historical Society (honorary life member), Claro Sword and Morris Men (president).

AWARDS, HONORS: Yorkshire History Prize, 1988, for research establishing that Knaresborough had first known Royal Maundy in 1210; Bramley History Prize, 1992, for research on prophetess Mother Shipton.

WRITINGS:

(Editor) *Prayers for Patients,* Arthur James, 1964.
Isms and Ologies, Epworth, 1965.
(Editor) Guy de Maupassant, *Maupassant: Contes du surnaturel* (title means "Maupassant: Tales of the Supernatural"), Pergamon, 1969.
The Knaresborough Story, Advertiser Press, 1972, revised and enlarged edition, Lofthouse Publications, 1990.
Heros de France (title means "Heroes of France"), Dent, 1973.
(Editor and translator) de Maupassant, *Tales of Supernatural Terror,* Pan Books, 1973.
Le Prisonnier en pyjama (title means "Prisoner in Pajamas"), Dent, 1974.
(Translator) *A Night of Terror* (de Maupassant stories in simplified English), Oxford University Press, 1976, revised edition, 1992.
(Editor and translator) de Maupassant, *Diary of a Madman and Other Tales of Horror,* Pan Books, 1976.
French for Science Students, Macdonald & Evans, 1976.
Basic French, Macdonald & Evans, 1977, 2nd edition, 1978.
Harrogate, Dalesman Press, 1978, 3rd edition, 1991.
The Queen's Church, Friends of Knaresborough Parish Church, 1978.
Know Your Yorkshire, Dalesman Press, 1980.
Knaresborough in Old Picture Postcards, European Library, 1984.
Countryside Walks around Harrogate, Dalesman Press, 1984.
Exploring Knaresborough, Meridian Group, 1985.
(With foreword by the Princess Royal) *Kellett's Christmas* (poems), Methodist Publishing House, 1988.
The Dark Side (translation of de Maupassant tales), Xanadu Publications, 1989, Cardinal, 1990.
Historic Knaresborough, Smith Settle, 1991.
Basic Broad Yorkshire, Smith Settle, 1991.

Writer for local radio programs. Contributor of articles and poems to periodicals, including *Dalesman, Methodist Recorder, History Today,* and *Yorkshire Archaeological Journal.* Editor of *Transactions* (Yorkshire Dialect Society).

WORK IN PROGRESS: Preparing *The Yorkshire Dictionary* of dialect, tradition, and folklore; research on local history.

SIDELIGHTS: Arnold Kellett once told *CA:* "My principal interests are local history and religion, but I am fascinated by a great variety of subjects. My heroes are universal and wide-ranging men, especially Blaise Pascal and John Wesley.

"This is the age of the narrow specialist and the typecast writer. I would like to try all kinds of writing—fiction as well as nonfiction."

Kellett added: "Now that I am retired I have more time for research. In 1985 I discovered that the first known Royal Maundy took place in Knaresborough in 1210, when King John clothed and fed the poor of the town. It was a pleasure to describe the discovery in television interviews and magazine articles. I have also completed a doctoral thesis for Leeds University—a biographical and critical study of Eugene Aram—and have just finished a definitive study of Mother Shipton."

*   *   *

KENT, Katie
See GREEN, Kay

*   *   *

KERSHAW, Alister (Nasmyth) 1921-

PERSONAL: Born December 19, 1921, in Melbourne, Australia; son of Alton and Frances (Thomson) Kershaw; married Sheila Sanders, October 18, 1957 (marriage ended); married Helena Kozmus, March 10, 1987; children: (first marriage) Sylvain, Solange. *Education:* Attended Wesley College, Melbourne, Australia.

ADDRESSES: Home—Maison Salle, Sury-en-Vaux, Cher, France.

CAREER: Affiliated with Australian Broadcasting Commission, Melbourne, 1941-47; private secretary to author Richard Aldington in the south of France, 1947-51; U.S. Information Service, Paris, France, head of western press analysis, 1951-53; Paris correspondent, Australian Broadcasting Commission.

WRITINGS:

The Lonely Verge, Warlock Press, 1943.
Excellent Stranger, Reed & Harris, 1944.
Bibliography of the Works of Richard Aldington, Quadrant Press, 1950.
Accent and Hazard, Stramur Presse, 1951.
Murder in France, Constable, 1955.
A History of the Guillotine, J. Calder, 1958.
(Editor with Jacques Temple) *Richard Aldington: An Intimate Portrait,* Southern Illinois University Press, 1965.
No-Man's-Land, La Murene, 1969.
(Editor) *Critical Writings of Richard Aldington,* Southern Illinois University Press, 1970.
Opera Comique, La Murene, 1979.
Adrian Lawlor: A Memoir, Typographeum, 1981.
The Beginning and the End: Collected Poems, Typographeum, 1983.
(Editor) *Salute to Roy Campbell,* Typographeum, 1984.
The Pleasure of Their Company, University of Queensland Press, 1986.
Heydays, Collins/Angus & Robertson, 1991.
A Word from Paris, Collins/Angus & Robertson, 1991.
Collected Poems, Collins/Angus & Robertson, 1992.
From a Village to a Village, Collins/Angus & Robertson, 1993.

*   *   *

KESTELOOT, Lilyan   1931-

PERSONAL: Born February 15, 1931, in Brussels, Belgium; daughter of Medard (a captain in the marine corps) and Marguerite (a teacher; maiden name, De Ladriere) Kesteloot; married Simeon Fongang (a physicist), 1972; children: Georges, Frantz-Tenguela. *Education:* University of Brussels, Ph.D., 1961; Sorbonne, University of Paris, Ph.D., 1975. *Politics:* "Who cares?" *Religion:* "Who cares?"

ADDRESSES: Home—Ifan, B.P. 206, Dakar, Senegal; and 11 rue Guy de la Brosse, 75005 Paris, France.

CAREER: Professor of literature at various African universities (in Cameroon, Mali, Niger, and Ivory Coast), 1961-70; professor of literature at various French universities, including Vincennes, St. Denis, and the Sorbonne, 1971-72; University of Dakar, Dakar, Senegal, professor of oral literature, 1972-89; University of Paris, Sorbonne, Paris, professor of comparative literature, 1990-93.

MEMBER: Society of Africanists (Paris).

WRITINGS:

Les Ecrivains noirs de langue francaise: naissance d'une litterature, Universite Libre de Bruxelles, 1961, 8th edition, 1971, translation by Ellen C. Kennedy published as *Black Writers in French: A Literary History of Negritude,* Temple University Press, 1974.
Aime Cesaire, Seghers (Paris), 1963.
Anthologie negro-africaine (title means "Anthology of Black African Writers"), Editions Gerard & Cie, 1967, 2nd revised edition, Edicef Hachette, 1992.
Negritude et situation coloniale, Editions Cle, 1968, translation published as *Intellectual Origins of the African Revolution,* Black Orpheus Press, 1971.
(With Amadou-Hampate Ba) *Kaidara, recit initiatique peul,* Armand Colin, 1968.
(With Barthelemy Kotchy) *Aime Cesaire, l'homme et l'oeuvre* (title means "Aime Cesaire: The Man and His Works"), Presence Africaine (Paris), 1973.
(With Ba, Alpha Sow, and Christiane Seydou) *L'Eclat de l'etoile, recit initiatique peul* (title means "Starburst"), Armand Colin, 1974.
(With Gerard Dumestre and Jean Baptiste Traore) *La Prise de Dionkoloni,* Armand Colin, 1976.
Biton Koulibaly, fondateur de l'empire de Segou, Collection des grandes figures de l'histoire africaine, 1978.
Comprendre le Cahier d'un retour au pays natal d'Aime Cesaire, Classiques africains, 1982, 2nd edition, 1992.
Comprendre les Poemes de L. S. Senghor, Classiques africains, 1987.

EDITOR

(And contributor) *Neuf Poetes camerounais, anthologie* (title means "An Anthology of Nine Cameroonian Poets"), Editions Cle, 1965, 2nd edition, 1971.
(And translator) *La Poesie traditionnelle* (title means "Traditional Poetry"), Nathan, 1971.
(And translator) *L'Epopee traditionnelle* (title means "The Traditional Epic"), Nathan, 1971.
(And translator with J. B. Traore, Amadou Traore, and Ba) *Da Monzon de Segou, epopee bambara,* Nathan, 1972.
(With Thomas Hale) *Cahiers cesairiens,* Three Continents, 1977.
Contes et mythes wolof, Nouvelles Editions Africaines (Dakar), 1983.
Contes et mythes wolof II: Du Tieoldo au Talibe, Presence Africaine, 1989.

OTHER

Contributor of articles to *L'Homme, Presence Africaine, Etudes Francaises, Notes Africaines, Revues Ethiopiques, Research in African Literature, African Literature Today, Contemporary French Civilization,* and other journals in her field. Editor of special editions of *Notes Africaines,* 1986, *L'esprit createur,* 1992, and *Research in African Literature,* 1992.

WORK IN PROGRESS: Research in Dakar, Senegal, on the African epic, and on African myth and history.

SIDELIGHTS: Lilyan Kesteloot sums up her philosophy of life as: "Only truth is revolutionary."

* * *

KGOSITSILE, Aneb
   See HOUSE, Gloria

* * *

KING, Bruce (Alvin) 1933-

PERSONAL: Born January 1, 1933, in Philadelphia, PA; son of Joseph and Lillian (Gilbert) King; married Adele Cockshoot (a professor of French), December 28, 1955; children: Nicole. *Education:* Columbia University, B.A., 1954; studied at University of Minnesota, 1955-56; University of Leeds, Ph.D., 1960.

ADDRESSES: Home—411 South College Ave., Muncie, IN 47303.

CAREER: University of Ibadan, Ibadan, Nigeria, lecturer in English, 1962-65; University of Bristol, Bristol, England, lecturer in English, 1965-67; University of Lagos, Lagos, Nigeria, professor of English and head of department, 1967-69; University of Windsor, Windsor, Ontario, professor of English, 1970-73; Ahmadu Bello University, Zaria, Nigeria, professor of English and head of department, 1973-77; University of Paris III, Paris, France, visiting professor of English, 1977-78; University of Canterbury, Christchurch, New Zealand, professor of English, 1979-83; University of North Alabama, Florence, Alberta S. Johnston Visiting Professor of Literature, 1983-86; Ben Gurion University of the Negev, Israel, visiting professor of English, 1987-89; University of Paris VII, Paris, visiting professor of English, 1990-91; adjunct professor, University of Guelph, 1992—. Visiting professor of English at University of Stirling, 1979, and University of Bayreuth, 1984. Killam Visiting Scholar, University of Calgary, 1987.

AWARDS, HONORS: William Andrews Clark Library short term fellow, summer, 1977; Rockefeller Foundation humanities fellow, 1977-78; American Institute of Indian Studies research fellow, 1984; Rockefeller Foundation scholar in residence, Bellagio, Italy, 1984; National Endowment for the Humanities, fellowship, 1985, grant, 1990-93; Fulbright research fellowship, India, 1988.

WRITINGS:

Dryden's Major Plays, Barnes & Noble, 1966.
Marvell's Allegorical Poetry, Oleander, 1977.

The New English Literatures: Cultural Nationalism in a Changing World, St. Martin's, 1980.
G. B. Shaw's "Arms and the Man," Longman, 1980.
Ibsen's "A Doll's House," Longman, 1980.
Fielding's "Joseph Andrews," Longman, 1981.
History of Seventeenth-Century English Literature, Schocken, 1982.
Modern Indian Poetry in English, Oxford University Press, 1987, revised edition, 1992.
Coriolanus, Humanities, 1989.
Three Indian Poets: Ezekiel, Ramanujan, and Moraes, Oxford University Press, 1991.
V. S. Naipaul, St. Martin's, 1993.

EDITOR

Twentieth-Century Interpretations of "All for Love": A Collection of Critical Essays, Prentice-Hall, 1968.
(And contributor) *Dryden's Mind and Art,* Oliver & Boyd, 1969.
Introduction to Nigerian Literature, Africana Publishing, 1971.
(And contributor) *Literatures of the World in English,* Routledge & Kegan Paul, 1974.
A Celebration of Black and African Writing, Oxford University Press, 1976.
(And contributor) *West Indian Literature,* Archon Books, 1979.
The Commonwealth Novel since 1960, Macmillan, 1991.
Contemporary American Theatre, Macmillan, 1991.
The Later Fiction of Nadine Gordimer, Macmillan, 1992.
Post-Colonial English Drama: Commonwealth Drama since 1960, Macmillan, 1992.

OTHER

Contributor to many books, including *Centenary Essays on the Art of W. B. Yeats,* Ibadan University Press, 1965; *Critics on Dryden,* Allen & Unwin, 1973; *Individual and Community in Commonwealth Literature,* Malta, 1979; *Theory and Practice in Comparative Studies,* ANZACS, 1983.

General co-editor of the "Modern Dramatists" series, published by Grove, 1982—; editor of "English Dramatists" series, published by Macmillan, 1990—. Contributor of more than one hundred articles, poems, and reviews to periodicals, including *Concerning Poetry, Sewanee Review, Southern Review, English Studies, World Literature Today, Chelsea, Journal of Literature and Aesthetics, College English,* and *Modern Language Review.* Guest editor of Achebe issue of *Literary Half-Yearly,* January, 1980; guest co-editor of T. S. Eliot issue of *Literary Half-Yearly,* July, 1988.

WORK IN PROGRESS: Editing the "English Dramatists" series; *Derek Walcott and the Trinidad Theatre*

Workshop; editing *New Literature in English: An Introduction* and a revised and expanded version of *West Indian Literature.*

*   *   *

KING, Florence   1936-
(Laura Buchanan, Cynthia, Veronica King, Emmett X. Reed, Niko Stavros, Mike Winston)

PERSONAL: Born January 5, 1936, in Washington, DC; daughter of Herbert Frederick (a musician) and Louise (Ruding) King. *Education:* American University, B.A., 1957; graduate study at University of Mississippi, 1958-59. *Politics:* "Royalist (I'm serious)." *Religion:* Episcopalian. *Avocational interests:* Gay Nineties and turn-of-the-century popular songs, horseback riding, collecting guns.

ADDRESSES: Home—Fredericksburg, VA.

CAREER: Writer. History teacher in Suitland, MD, mid-1950s; file clerk, National Association of Realtors, late 1950s; *Raleigh News and Observer*, Raleigh, NC, feature writer, 1964-67; assistant editor, *Uncensored Confessions* (magazine), 1967-68; former book reviewer, *Newsday.*

MEMBER: Phi Alpha Theta.

AWARDS, HONORS: North Carolina Press Women Award, 1965, for reporting.

WRITINGS:

Southern Ladies and Gentlemen, Stein & Day, 1975.
WASP, Where Is Thy Sting?, Stein & Day, 1976.
(Under pseudonym Laura Buchanan) *The Barbarian Princess,* Berkley Publishing, 1977.
He: An Irreverent Look at the American Male, Stein & Day, 1978.
When Sisterhood Was in Flower, Viking, 1982.
Confessions of a Failed Southern Lady, St. Martin's, 1985.
Reflections in a Jaundiced Eye (Literary Guild and Doubleday Book Club selection), St. Martin's, 1989.
Lump It or Leave It, St. Martin's, 1991.
With Charity Toward None: A Fond Look at Misanthropy, St. Martin's, 1992.

Also author, under pseudonyms Cynthia, Veronica King, Emmett X. Reed, Niko Stavros, and Mike Winston, of thirty-seven erotic novels, including *Moby's Dick,* Midwood-Tower. Contributor of reviews and articles to *American Spectator, National Review, Redbook, Playgirl, Viva, Penthouse, Ms., Cosmopolitan,* and *Harper's;* contributor of stories to *True Story, Modern Romances,* and *Uncensored Confessions.* Member of usage panel, *American Heritage Dictionary,* 1986.

SIDELIGHTS: Florence King, according to Sam Staggs in *Publishers Weekly,* is "an equal-opportunity provocateuse with a bad word for everybody." Her witty essays skewering the absurdities of American society—written from the perspective of a politically-conservative former lesbian—have brought King critical acclaim as well as a wide readership. Speaking to Alanna Nash in *Writer's Digest,* King explains her popularity: "I say what I think, and that's so refreshing nowadays. So many writers are fence-straddling, state-of-the-art wimps. . . . And too, the novelty of a *woman* who rips the teats off sacred cows probably has something to do with it. We're supposed to be nurturing, and I come through as Medea."

While pursuing a graduate degree at the University of Mississippi in the late 1950s, King first began writing "true confessions" stories to earn extra money. "All it took," Tim Menees notes in the *Seattle Post-Intelligencer,* "was the prospect of $250 per confession, and Ms. King was down at the drugstore reviewing the pulps. Four hours and 5,000 words of typing, and she had 'My God, I'm Too Passionate for My Own Good!' They bought it, and some 100 more." Ten years later, with the demise of high-paying confessions magazines, King turned to writing what Menees describes as "el cheapo pornographic novels, one a month, to the not-so-cheap tune of about $1,600 per book. Thirty-seven volumes in all. . . ." King now regrets writing pornography. "I wish I hadn't written it," she tells Staggs. "But it was nothing like porn as we know it today; it was very soft. I couldn't write the stuff they sell now." The experience did teach her a valuable lesson: "How to apply the seat of the pants to the seat of the chair, which was good discipline."

While living in Seattle during the 1970s, King began writing for a variety of magazines. One of her articles for *Harper's* led to a book contract for *Southern Ladies and Gentlemen,* a guide to Southern types for those not from the South. In the process of explaining Southerners, Lynn Felder notes in the *Dictionary of Literary Biography Yearbook,* King "destroys, perpetuates, and invents myths about the South." She takes a similar approach in *When Sisterhood Was in Flower,* aiming her satirical guns at feminists this time. Calling it "one of the funniest books I have read all year," Barbara Mertz of the *Washington Post Book World* finds that *When Sisterhood Was in Flower* "is not so much a satire as a Marx Brothers burlesque of certain radical fringe elements of the Women's Movement."

With *Confessions of a Failed Southern Lady,* King turned to a fictional recounting of her own life story, albeit still from a humorous perspective. It marks, Felder comments, "a slight change of tone in King's work. . . . She discards her repertoire of stereotypes, and Granny, Herb, Louise, and Jensy . . . expand into their touching, funny, powerful, subtle selves." The book, Carolyn See notes in the *Los*

Angeles Times, "is so original, so odd, so wonderful, so bizarre and finally so heart-wrenching that it can't easily be summed up. . . . This is a stunning book, a masterpiece, a book that should be read 50 times and then put carefully away in case you ever have cancer and care to try the Norman Cousins cure-by-laughter."

Southern Lady drew a large audience to King's writings; so large, in fact, that her next essay collection, *Reflections in a Jaundiced Eye,* was chosen by two prominent book clubs. In this collection, King focuses on what she calls "Helpism," the American mania for expert problem-solvers to make our personal lives better. As she explains, "Self-esteem does not come from Self-Esteem Workshops, Self-Esteem Resources Centers or Self-Esteem Crisis Hot Lines. Like all of life, self-esteem begins with one tiny seed." She also takes aim at the American need to be "nice" to others. Watching television one evening, King notes that three commercials in a row "assured me that Eastern Air Lines, Allied Van Lines and Ex-Lax—movers and shakers all—were my friends. Moreover, Ex-Lax was my *family* friend because it's gentle." In his review of *Reflections in a Jaundiced Eye* for the *Los Angeles Times Book Review,* Pratapaditya Pal concludes that "more than any of her male competitors, [King] is the Will Rogers of our day," while Jonathan Yardley of the *Washington Post* calls King "one of the few contemporary American essayists of sufficient pungency and wit as to be almost always worth reading."

Among the targets in *Lump It or Leave It* are democracy (which King defines as "the crude leading the crud"), America's educational system, and race relations. "With the mouth of a truck driver . . . and the mind of a Jesuit, she can write a mean tour de force," Diane McWhorter admits in the *New York Times Book Review.* Alex Heard in the *Washington Post* allows that King "says what others are afraid to; her insights will cause your liberal orbs to bulge; love her or hate her, you'll be impressed by her merciless pungency."

In *With Charity Toward None: A Fond Look at Misanthropy* King argues on behalf of being a curmudgeon, particularly in a society where, she notes, "our feminized niceness has mired us in a soft, sickly, helpless tolerance of everything." As Joseph Sobran comments in his review of the book for the *National Review, With Charity Toward None* "is a sort of assertiveness-training course for victims of niceness. . . . She wittily offers frank misanthropy as a valid alternative lifestyle for those who have had it with perpetually aiming to please." "For us grumpy folks who already share her philosophical viewpoint," Larry Wallberg writes in the *Los Angeles Times Book Review,* "this Survey of Scurrility contains plenty of astutely phrased—if also comfortably familiar—political observations." Wallberg concludes that "there's a lot of meat in

this lean volume, and I savored much of it; not only that, but I think its creator is delicious."

Speaking to Nash, King explains that she enjoys being called a curmudgeon. "I consider it a compliment," she states. "How often does a woman get called a curmudgeon? Usually she's called a bitch." Speaking to Staggs, King notes that to be a good wit, "You must have a dismal outlook on life and human nature. You have to be a misanthrope, a loner, an introvert—all the things Americans don't want to be and don't think people should be." In an interview with Felder, King describes her political leanings: "My royalism is actually desperation for some escape from America's worship of the Average Person—formerly the Common Man. Politically I am a Hamiltonian elitist. I believe in a Republic of Merit in which water is allowed to find its own level, where voters, like drivers, are tested before being turned loose. Intelligence is my god. I don't care what else people are as long as they're intelligent." Summing herself up for Nash, King comments: "I don't suffer fools, and I like to see fools suffer."

BIOGRAPHICAL/CRITICAL SOURCES:

BOOKS

Authors in the News, Volume 1, Gale, 1976.
Dictionary of Literary Biography Yearbook, 1985, Gale, 1986.

PERIODICALS

American Spectator, August, 1989, p. 48.
Atlantic Monthly, December, 1982, p. 106.
Belles Lettres, fall, 1988, p. 6.
Best Sellers, May, 1985, p. 61.
Booklist, June 1, 1990, p. 1871; February 1, 1992, p. 1003.
Books, March, 1990, p. 21.
Lambda Book Report, May, 1992, p. 47.
Library Journal, October 1, 1982, p. 1904.
London Review of Books, February 20, 1986, p. 19.
Los Angeles Times, February 4, 1985.
Los Angeles Times Book Review, February 11, 1979; February 20, 1983, p. 9; April 30, 1989, p. 2; March 25, 1990, p. 10; September 22, 1991, p. 10; April 26, 1992, p. 1.
National Review, May 11, 1992, pp. 50-51.
New Statesman, September 6, 1985, p. 29.
Newsweek, June 30, 1975.
New York Times, June 30, 1977; October 29, 1982, p. 21; April 9, 1992.
New York Times Book Review, February 10, 1985, p. 27; January 26, 1986, p. 38; April 9, 1989, p. 11; July 8, 1990, p. 17; May 10, 1992, p. 16.
Observer, March 8, 1987, p. 27.
Publishers Weekly, June 22, 1990, pp. 38-39.
Seattle Post-Intelligencer, May 12, 1974.

Southern Living, February, 1983, p. 111.
Times (London), August 22, 1985.
Times Literary Supplement, October 18, 1985, p. 1191; July 6, 1990, p. 723.
Virginia Quarterly Review, autumn, 1983, p. 128.
Washington Post, March 29, 1989; July 10, 1990.
Washington Post Book World, January 2, 1983, p. 4; December 29, 1985, p. 12; September 22, 1991, p. 12.
West Coast Review of Books, January, 1983, p. 26.
Women's Review of Books, April, 1986, p. 8.
Writer's Digest, July, 1990, pp. 40-43, 51.

—Sketch by Thomas Wiloch

*   *   *

KING, Veronica
See KING, Florence

*   *   *

KNIGHT, Arthur Winfield   1937-

PERSONAL: Born December 29, 1937, in San Francisco, CA; son of Walter Arthur (a park supervisor) and Irja (Blomquist) Knight; married Veronica Joyce, 1960 (annulled, 1961); married Carole Gail Smith, August 10, 1963 (divorced September 26, 1966); married Glee Marquardt (a writer and publisher), September 27, 1966 (died October 30, 1975); married Kathleen Duell, August 25, 1976; children: (fourth marriage) Tiffany Carolyn. *Education:* Santa Rosa Junior College, A.A., 1958; San Francisco State College (now University), B.A., 1960, M.A. (with honors), 1962.

CAREER: Free-lance writer, 1962—; California University of Pennsylvania, California, PA, director of creative writing program, 1966-93; TUVOTI ("the unspeakable visions of the individual"; publisher), California, editor with wife, Glee Knight, 1971-75, editor with wife, Kathleen Knight, 1976-88. Free-lance photographer, 1953—.

WRITINGS:

All Together, Shift, Horizon Press, 1972.
Extracts, Sceptre Press, 1974.
(Editor with Glee Knight) *The Beat Book,* TUVOTI, 1974.
Who Moved among the Others as They Walked, Hilltop Press, 1974.
Our Summer Made Her Light Escape (fiction), Realit, 1974.
What You Do with Your Aloneness (chapbook), New York Culture Review, 1977.
Forty (chapbook), Tailings Press, 1979.
Angst (chapbook), Wolfsong Press, 1980.

(With wife, Kathleen Knight) *Interior Geographies: An Interview with John Clellon Holmes,* Literary Denim, 1981.
The First Time (autobiography), Dramatika, 1982.
The Mushroom Nightshirt (chapbook), Quick Books, 1984.
(With K. Knight) *A Marriage of Poets,* Spoon River Press, 1984.
The Golden Land (nonfiction), Ellis Press, 1985.
Wanted, Trout Creek Press, 1988.
Tell Me an Erotic Story, Tempus Fugit, 1988.
Basically Tender, Esoterica Press, 1991.

EDITOR; WITH K. KNIGHT

The Beat Journey, TUVOTI, 1978.
the unspeakable visions of the individual: Tenth Anniversary Issue, TUVOTI, 1980.
Beat Angels, TUVOTI, 1982.
Jack Kerouac, *Dear Carolyn* (letters to Carolyn Cassady), TUVOTI, 1983.
The Beat Road, TUVOTI, 1984.
The Beat Vision, Paragon House, 1987.
Kerouac and the Beats, Paragon House, 1988.

PLAYS

King of the Beatniks (three-act), Water Row Press, 1986.
The Abused (one-act), Norton Coker Press, 1986.

Also author of play *The Bones of Prehistoric Animals.*

OTHER

Contributor to numerous books, including *Writing: Fact and Imagination,* edited by Eleanor C. Hibbs, Prentice-Hall, 1971; *Quality American Poetry,* edited by William Lloyd Griffin, Valley Publications, 1974; *The Montanans,* edited by Martin H. Greenberg and Bill Pronzini, Fawcett, 1991; and *Cat Crimes III,* edited by Greenberg and Ed Gorman, Donald I. Fine, 1992.

Redwood Rancher, European correspondent, 1962-63, columnist, 1963. Film critic, *Anderson Valley Advertiser,* 1992—. Contributor of fiction, poetry, and articles to journals, including *Massachusetts Review, New York Quarterly, Poet Lore, Wisconsin Review, New York Culture Review, Great Speckled Bird, Poetry View, Poetry Now, College English, Rockbottom, Second Coming,* and *Panache.* Guest editor, with K. Knight, of the *Beats,* a review journal.

WORK IN PROGRESS: A novel about Jesse James; *The Erotic Life of Billy the Kid.*

SIDELIGHTS: Arthur Winfield Knight told *CA:* "I write because writing helps me to find out what I think; it helps me to define things. It is almost a compulsive act. If I knew exactly what I was going to say when I began writing something, there would be no need for the process. If I go too long without writing, I don't feel whole; I begin to get restless, unhappy, as if some part of me weren't there—or weren't functioning properly. Something in my system breaks down when I stop trying to discover myself and the world around me."

Knight has traveled in Europe, Mexico, Canada, and the United States and resided in Sussex, England in 1962. Among his published writings are an interview with Stan Laurel in 1963 and an account of a whaling expedition he made. His work has appeared in England, Canada, Australia, Sweden, Germany, France, Holland, India, Brazil, Yugoslavia, Mexico, Belgium, and Japan.

*   *   *

KNIGHT, Gareth
See WILBY, Basil Leslie

*   *   *

KOCKELMANS, Joseph J(ohn) 1923-

PERSONAL: Born December 1, 1923, in Meerssen, Netherlands; immigrated to the United States, 1964, naturalized citizen, 1968; son of Alphons Hubert and Philomena (Raeven) Kockelmans; married Dorothy H. Greiner, October 26, 1964; children: Joseph Martin. *Education:* Institute of Medieval Philosophy, Angelico, Rome, Baccalaureate, 1949, Ph.D., 1951; private postdoctoral studies in mathematics, physics, and phenomenology, 1951-63.

ADDRESSES: Home—903 Willard Circle, State College, PA 16803. *Office*—Department of Philosophy, 240 Sparks Building, Pennsylvania State University, University Park, PA 16802.

CAREER: Agricultural University, Wageningen, Netherlands, professor of philosophy, 1963-64; New School for Social Research, New York City, professor of philosophy, 1964-65; University of Pittsburgh, Pittsburgh, PA, professor of philosophy, 1965-68; Pennsylvania State University, University Park, professor of philosophy, 1968—, director of Interdisciplinary Graduate Program in the Humanities, 1972—.

MEMBER: American Philosophical Association, American Association for the Advancement of Science, Society of Phenomenology and Existential Philosophy, Philosophy of Science Association.

AWARDS, HONORS: Gold Medal, Teyler's Tweede Genootschap, 1958, for *On Time and Space: The Meaning of the Special Theory of Relativity for a Phenomenological Philosophy of Nature.*

WRITINGS:

On Time and Space: The Meaning of the Special Theory of Relativity for a Phenomenological Philosophy of Nature, Erven F. Bohn, 1958.
Martin Heidegger: Een inleiding in zijn denken, Lanoo (The Hague), 1962, translation by Therese Schrynemakers published as *Martin Heidegger: A First Introduction to His Philosophy,* Duquesne University Press, 1965.
Phaenomenologie en natuurwetenschap: Een inleiding in de wijsbegeerte der natuurwetenschappen, Erven F. Bohn, 1962, translation published as *Phenomenology and Physical Science: An Introduction to the Philosophy of Physical Science,* Duquesne University Press, 1966.
A First Introduction to Husserl's Phenomenology, Duquesne University Press, 1967.
Edmund Husserl's Phenomenological Psychology: A Historico-Critical Study, Duquesne University Press, 1967.
The World in Science and Philosophy, Bruce, 1969.
What Is Philosophy?, Lanoo, 1970.
Heidegger's Letter on Humanism, Lanoo, 1973.
On the Truth of Being: Reflections on Heidegger's Later Philosophy, Indiana University Press, 1984.
Heidegger and Science, University Press of America, 1985.
Heidegger on Art and Art Works, Nijhoff, 1985.
Heidegger's "Being and Time": The Analytic of Dasein as Fundamental Ontology, Center for Advanced Research in Phenomenology/University Press of America, 1989.

EDITOR

Phenomenology: The Philosophy of Edmund Husserl and Its Interpretation, Anchor Books, 1967.
Philosophy of Science: The Historical Background, Free Press, 1968.
(With Theodore J. Kisiel) *Phenomenology and the Natural Sciences: Essays and Translations,* Northwestern University Press, 1970.
(And translator and author of introduction) *Contemporary European Ethics: Selected Readings,* Anchor Books, 1972.
(And translator) *On Heidegger and Language,* Northwestern University Press, 1972.
Interdisciplinary and Higher Education, Pennsylvania State University Press, 1979.
(With Frederick Ferre and John E. Smith) *The Challenge of Religion,* Seabury Press, 1982.
(With Thomas M. Seebohm) *Kant and Phenomenology,* University Press of America, 1984.
A Companion to Martin Heidegger's "Being and Time," Center for Advanced Research in Phenomenology and University Press of America, 1986.

Phenomenological Psychology: The Dutch School, Nijhoff, 1987.

Hermeneutic Phenomenology: Lectures and Essays, Center for Advanced Research in Phenomenology and University Press of America, 1988.

OTHER

Co-editor of "Dutch Heidegger Library," 1970. Contributor to philosophy journals. Co-editor, *Man and World: An International Philosophical Review,* 1968.

SIDELIGHTS: Joseph J. Kockelmans once told *CA:* "For many years I have made an effort to promote some of the basic ideas developed by the leading phenomenologists of this century—Edmund Husserl, Martin Heidegger, Jean-Paul Sartre, Maurice Merleau-Ponty, and others. I have written books on aspects of the philosophies of Husserl and Heidegger and also edited some anthologies of essays on the philosophies of these thinkers.

"Most of my own work in philosophy has been in the area of the philosophy of science. I have tried to apply phenomenological and hermeneutical methods and insights to the study of the philosophy of science. In that area I am not so much concerned with logical or methodological issues, although I have developed some original ideas on the methods of the human sciences; rather, my main concern has always been with the regional ontologies underlying the natural and the human sciences. In other words, in my own publications I try to focus on the ontological or metaphysical assumptions which scientists must make, in order to make these assumptions explicit and examine them critically.

"My intention to specialize in philosophy of science explains why I devoted twelve years of my life to postdoctoral studies in mathematics (with H. Busard), physics (with A. Fokker), and phenomenology (with H. Van Breda). In mathematics I centered my studies around those mathematical ideas and procedures which are actually used in relativity theory and quantum mechanics. In physics I made a careful study of contemporary theoretical physics. In my own work I am influenced by the philosophies of both Husserl and Heidegger. Part of my philosophical perspective was inspired by Alphonse De Waelhens."

*   *   *

KOTIN, Armine Avakian
  See MORTIMER, Armine Kotin

KRUTZCH, Gus
  See ELIOT, T(homas) S(tearns)

*   *   *

KUNZ, Phillip Ray   1936-

PERSONAL: Born July 19, 1936, in Bern, ID; son of Parley Peter (a farmer) and Hilda I. (Stoor) Kunz; married Joyce Sheffield, March 18, 1960; children: Jay Phillip, Jenifer, Jody, Johnathan, Jana. *Education:* Brigham Young University, B.S. (cum laude), 1961, M.S., 1962; University of Michigan, Ph.D., 1967. *Politics:* Democrat. *Religion:* Church of Jesus Christ of Latter-day Saints (Mormon).

ADDRESSES: *Home*—3040 Navajo, Provo, UT 84601. *Office*—Department of Sociology, Brigham Young University, Provo, UT 84601.

CAREER: Lyman Latter-day Saints Seminary, Lyman, WY, principal, 1962-63; Eastern Michigan University, Ypsilanti, instructor in sociology, 1964; University of Michigan, Ann Arbor, instructor, 1965-67; University of Wyoming, Laramie, assistant professor of sociology, 1967-68; Brigham Young University, Provo, UT, professor of sociology, 1968—, acting department chairman, 1973, director of Institute of Genealogical Studies, 1972-74. Has read numerous papers at professional meetings. Member of executive council, Brigham Young University Family Research Center, 1972-77; Charles Redd Center of Western Studies, lecturer, 1978; member of advisory board, Demographic and Family Research Institute, 1980—. Member of advisory committee, Utah Center for Health Statistics, 1979, and Family Living Center, 1982; mission president, Louisiana Baton Rouge Mission, 1991—. Consultant to numerous public, industrial, and academic organizations. *Military service:* U.S. Army, 1954-56.

MEMBER: International Union for the Scientific Study of Population, International Platform Association, American Sociological Association, American Council on Family Relations, Society for the Scientific Study of Religion, Religious Research Association (member of membership committee, 1969), American Society of Criminology, Rural Sociological Society, Groves Conference of Marriage and the Family, Rocky Mountain Social Science Association (member of nominating committee), Utah Sociological Society (secretary-treasurer, 1977-78), Phi Kappa Phi, Sigma Xi, Alpha Kappa Delta.

AWARDS, HONORS: National Science Foundation fellow, 1962; National Institute of Mental Health fellow, 1963; Karl G. Maeser Research Award, 1977; various grants from Brigham Young University.

WRITINGS:

(With Merlin Brinkerhoff) *Utah in Numbers, Comparisons, Discussion, and Trends,* Brigham Young University Press, 1969.

(With Spencer Condie) *Man in His Social Environment,* Simon & Schuster, 1970.

(With Brinkerhoff) *Complex Organizations and Their Environments,* W. C. Brown, 1972.

Court Records Indexed in the Library of the Genealogical Society, Institute of Genealogical Studies, 1974.

(With Eric Jaehne) *Sociological Perspectives of Moral Development,* Lilly Foundation, 1975.

(Editor) *The Mormon Family: Proceedings of the Annual Family Research Conference, Brigham Young University, 1975,* Family Research Institute, 1977.

(With William Dyer) *Effective Mormon Families,* Deseret Book Co., 1987.

CONTRIBUTOR

Lincoln B. Young, editor, *Cavalcade of Poetry: Best Poems of 1963,* Young Publications, 1964.

Young, editor, *Melody of the Muse,* Young Publications, 1964.

Howard M. Bahr, Bruce A. Chadwick, and Darwin L. Thomas, editors, *Population, Resources and the Future: Non-Malthusian Perspectives,* Brigham Young University Press, 1972.

(And editor) *Selected Papers in Genealogical Research: Papers 1 through 12,* Institute of Genealogical Studies, 1973.

Glenn M. Vernon, editor, *Research in Mormonism,* Association for the Study of Religion, 1974.

Progress in Cybernetics and Systems Research, Volume IV: *Cybernetics of Cognition and Learning, Structure and Dynamics of Socio-Economic Systems, Health Care Systems, Engineering Systems Methodology,* Hemisphere Publishing, 1978.

Richard F. Ericson, editor, *Improving the Human Condition: Quality and Stability in Social Systems,* [London], 1979.

Thomas G. Alexander, editor, *The Mormon People: Their Character and Traditions,* Brigham Young University Press, 1980.

Also contributor, Norman A. Chigier and Edward A. Stem, editors, *Collective Phenomena and the Application of Physics to Other Fields of Science,* Brain Research. Contributor of reviews to periodicals, including *Review of Religious Research, Contemporary Sociology,* and *Rocky Mountain Social Science Journal.*

WORK IN PROGRESS: Writing on family topics, including polygamy, divorce, and the family through four generations.

SIDELIGHTS: In a sideline from his writing and research efforts, Phillip Ray Kunz is listed in the *Guinness Book of World Records* as the world record-holder in kite-flying at altitude.

*   *   *

KUSKIN, Karla (Seidman) 1932-
(Nicholas J. Charles)

PERSONAL: Born July 17, 1932, in New York, NY; daughter of Sidney T. (in advertising) and Mitzi (Salzman) Seidman; married Charles M. Kuskin (a musician), December 4, 1955 (divorced, August, 1987); married William L. Bell, July 24, 1989; children: (first marriage) Nicholas, Julia. *Education:* Attended Antioch College, 1950-53; Yale University, B.F.A., 1955.

ADDRESSES: Home—96 Joralemon St., Brooklyn, NY 11201. *Agent*—Harriet Wasserman, Harriet Wasserman Literary Agency, Inc., 137 East 36th St., New York, NY 10016.

CAREER: Writer and illustrator. Has done illustrating for Harper & Row Publishing, Inc., Macmillan Publishing Co., Inc., Seabury Press, Inc., Atlantic Monthly Press, Putnam Publishing Group, P. F. Collier, Inc., and Atheneum Publishers. Worked variously as an assistant to a fashion photographer, a design underling, and in advertising. Conducts poetry and writing workshops.

AWARDS, HONORS: American Institute of Graphic Arts Book Show awards, 1955-57, for *Roar and More,* 1958, for *In the Middle of Trees,* and 1958-60, for *Square as a House;* Children's Book Award, International Reading Association, 1976, for *Near the Window Tree: Poems and Notes;* Children's Book Showcase selection, Children's Book Council, 1976, for *Near the Window Tree: Poems and Notes,* and 1977, for *A Boy Had a Mother Who Bought Him a Hat;* award for excellence in poetry for children, National Council of Teachers of English, 1979; Children's Science Book Award, New York Academy of Sciences, 1980, for *A Space Story;* American Library Association Award, 1980, for *Dogs & Dragons, Trees & Dreams: A Collection of Poems;* named Outstanding Brooklyn Author, 1981; *The Philharmonic Gets Dressed* was named a best illustrated book by the *New York Times,* 1982; American Library Association Award, 1982, and National Book Award nomination, 1983, both for *The Philharmonic Gets Dressed.*

WRITINGS:

CHILDREN'S BOOKS

A Space Story, illustrated by Marc Simont, Harper, 1978.

The Philharmonic Gets Dressed, illustrated by Simont, Harper, 1982.

The Dallas Titans Get Ready for Bed, illustrated by Simont, Harper, 1986.

Jerusalem, Shining Still, illustrated by David Frampton, Harper, 1987.

SELF-ILLUSTRATED CHILDREN'S BOOKS

Roar and More, Harper, 1956, revised edition, HarperCollins, 1990.

James and the Rain, Harper, 1957.

In the Middle of the Trees (poems), Harper, 1958.

The Animals and the Ark, Harper, 1958.

Just Like Everyone Else, Harper, 1959.

Which Horse Is William?, Harper, 1959.

Square as a House, Harper, 1960.

The Bear Who Saw the Spring, Harper, 1961.

All Sizes of Noises, Harper, 1962.

Alexander Soames: His Poems, Harper, 1962.

(Under pseudonym Nicholas J. Charles) *How Do You Get from Here to There?,* Macmillan, 1962.

ABCDEFGHIJKLMNOPQRSTUVWXYZ, Harper, 1963.

The Rose on My Cake (poems), Harper, 1964.

Sand and Snow, Harper, 1965.

(Under pseudonym Nicholas J. Charles) *Jane Anne June Spoon and Her Very Adventurous Search for the Moon,* Norton, 1966.

The Walk the Mouse Girls Took, Harper, 1967.

Watson, the Smartest Dog in the U.S.A., Harper, 1968.

In the Flaky Frosty Morning, Harper, 1969.

Any Me I Want to Be: Poems, Harper, 1972.

What Did You Bring Me?, Harper, 1973.

Near the Window Tree: Poems and Notes, Harper, 1975.

A Boy Had a Mother Who Bought Him a Hat, Houghton, 1976.

Herbert Hated Being Small, Houghton, 1979.

Dogs & Dragons, Trees & Dreams: A Collection of Poems, Harper, 1980.

Night Again, Little, Brown, 1981.

Something Sleeping in the Hall, Harper, 1985.

Soap Soup, HarperCollins, 1992.

A Great Miracle Happened Here: A Chanukah Story, HarperCollins, 1993.

Patchwork Island, HarperCollins, 1994.

OTHER

Illustrator of many books, including Violette Viertel and John Viertel, *Xingu,* Macmillan, 1959; Margaret Mealy and Norman Mealy, *Sing for Joy,* Seabury, 1961; Virginia Cary Hudson, *Credos & Quips,* Macmillan, 1964; Marguerita Rudolph, *Look at Me,* McGraw, 1967; Sherry Kafka, *Big Enough,* Putnam, 1970; and Marcia Brown, *Stone Soup,* Great Books Foundation, 1984.

Author of screenplays, including *What Do You Mean by Design?* and *An Electric Talking Picture,* both 1973. Also author and narrator of filmstrip *Poetry Explained by Karla Kuskin,* Weston Woods, 1980. Contributor of essays and reviews to books and periodicals, including *Saturday Review, House and Garden, Parents, Choice,* and *Village Voice.*

Jerusalem, Shining Still has been recorded on audio cassette. An interview with the author entitled *A Talk with Karla Kuskin* has been produced by Tim Podell Productions.

ADAPTATIONS: The Philharmonic Gets Dressed was adapted for film by Sarson Productions.

WORK IN PROGRESS: The City Dog, for HarperCollins.

SIDELIGHTS: Award-winning author and illustrator Karla Kuskin, who first achieved popularity with the 1956 publication of *Roar and More,* has written and illustrated more than twenty-five children's books. Noted for their short, rhythmic verse and neatly designed drawings, Kuskin's works reflect her unique insight into the world of the young and her understanding of a child's sense of humor. "The children who hear my verses, or read them to themselves," the author commented in *Somebody Turned on a Tap in These Kids: Poetry and Young People Today,* "will, hopefully, recognize a familiar feeling or thought. Or possibly an unfamiliar feeling or thought will intrigue them. If that spark is lit, then my verse may encourage its individual audience to add his own thought or maybe even a poem of his own, to try his own voice in some new way."

Kuskin began writing poetry very early in her childhood and received much encouragement from her parents. Kuskin was raised in New York City except for a short period between the ages of three and five when she lived in Connecticut. "My first verifiable memories begin in that fieldstone house [in Connecticut] with hydrangea bushes on either side of the front door," she once said. "I made up a poem about that spot and my mother wrote it down for me because I was four and could not write yet." As the only child of Mitzi and Sidney Seidman "I was the focus of a lot of approving attention and scrutiny," Kuskin continued. "I preferred the attention. But my mother, a dry cleaner's daughter, has always had the ability to spot an imperfection in the material at fifty feet. While I was often highly praised I was also continually judged by that eye and have inherited the same sharp vision."

Kuskin's loves of poetry, reading books, and writing—interests she believes to be instrumental in her choice of career—were fostered by her parents as well as her teachers once she entered school. "My parents and my teachers were my best audience," Kuskin related in *Language Arts.* "Beginning when I was very young, both my parents and teachers read poetry to me and listened to me read aloud. I had wonderful teachers."

"I was not really sure, in those days, how I could best express myself," she once explained. "I knew that I enjoyed writing, drawing, painting; but when I graduated from high school in 1950 I had no idea what work I was really suited for and what work was really suited to me." Kuskin entered a work-study program at Antioch College where she was assigned a position as a salesperson at a Chicago department store. A vice-president of the store read a job report Kuskin had written for Antioch and, impressed by Kuskin's creativity, gave her a job writing promotional material for the store and designing such things as Christmas wrapping paper. Through her work she gradually developed an interest in the field of graphic arts and, in 1953, transferred to Yale University's School of Fine Arts.

Kuskin's final requirement before receiving her bachelor's degree from Yale was to create and print a book using a small motor-driven Vandercook press that had recently been purchased by the university. "The subject of my slim book, *Roar and More,* was animals and their noises," she once explained, "a subject well-suited to typographical illustration. The overall design was simple. On the left-hand page was a verse about an animal set in 14 point Bell Roman [type]. On the opposite right-hand page was a picture of the animal made from a linoleum cut. The cut fitted easily on the bed of the press. Turn the page and the animal's noise took up the next doublepage spread. It was a straightforward layout that worked smoothly." *Roar and More* was soon accepted for publication, though in a slightly different form than the original; a number of colors were eliminated and the linoleum cuts were changed to drawings. Despite the alterations the book fared well with critics and young readers, won an award from the American Institute of Graphic Arts, and was reprinted in a much more colorful edition in 1990.

Kuskin worked a series of not very satisfying jobs after graduating from college, including one in her father's small advertising agency. She often wondered if she could write and illustrate another children's book even though she no longer had use of the printing facilities at Yale University. In the summer of 1956 Kuskin contracted hepatitis and was told by her doctor that she had to stop working. "I didn't object," she wrote. "I had a number of book ideas in my head and I was anxious to pursue one." She and her husband Charles Kuskin traveled to Cape Cod, Massachusetts, to vacation at a friend's house. The stormy weather that persisted throughout the couple's stay inspired Kuskin to create a second book titled *James and the Rain,* the story of a young boy who sets out to discover what various animals do when it rains.

James and the Rain, like most of her following books, are based on Kuskin's personal experiences. For instance, Kuskin's experiences as a parent became a source of topics for a number of her books. *The Bear Who Saw the Spring,* for example, was written when Kuskin was pregnant and contemplating motherhood. The story focuses on a knowledgeable, older bear who teaches a young dog about the seasons of the year; the relationship of the two characters is similar to that of a parent and child. *Sand and Snow,* about a boy who loves the winter and a girl who loves the summer, was dedicated to Kuskin's infant daughter, Julia. And *Alexander Soames: His Poems,* a book Kuskin acknowledges was partly inspired by her children, recounts a conversation between a mother and her son Alex, who will only speak in verse despite his mother's repeated requests that he express himself in prose.

Kuskin also draws upon vivid memories of her own youth as themes for her books. Growing up in New York City, Kuskin reflected, "there was . . . the sense of being a small child in big places that was very much a part of my childhood. And I was determined to remember those places and those feelings. I vowed to myself that I would never forget what it was like to be a child as I grew older. Frustration, pleasure, what I saw as injustices, all made me promise this to myself." Kuskin has been lauded for knowing "what is worth saving and what is important to children," according to Alvina Treut Burrows in *Language Arts.* "Her pictures and her verse and poetry," the reviewer continued, "are brimming over with the experiences of children growing up in a big city."

Kuskin's great respect for education and her love of poetry have motivated her to visit schools and instruct children in writing their own verse. She stresses a different approach in the way she writes for children and the way children should write poetry themselves. "When I write I rhyme," Kuskin remarked in *Language Arts,* "I'm very much concerned with rhythm because children love the sound and swing of both. But when children write, I try to discourage them from rhyming because I think it's such a hurdle. It freezes all the originality they have, and they use someone else's rhymes. It's too hard. And yet their images are so original." The author encourages children to write verses by visualizing objects, concentrating on descriptions and experiences, and writing what they have imagined in short, easy lines rather than worrying about perfect sentences and paragraphs.

Kuskin has also employed an educational technique in some of her poetry collections. In *Dogs and Dragons, Trees and Dreams: A Collection of Poems,* for example, Kuskin adds notes to each poem, explaining her inspiration for the particular verse and encouraging the reader to write his own poetry. Critics lauded the author for including her commentary. *Washington Post Book World* contributor

Rose Styron thought that *Dogs and Dragons, Trees and Dreams* "works nicely" and praised Kuskin's "variety, wit and unfailing sensitivity" in addressing children.

In addition to teaching children to read, write, and appreciate poetry, Kuskin's self-illustrated books contain appealing pictures that serve to emphasize her themes. Her early books, such as *All Sizes of Noises*—an assortment of everyday sounds translated into visual representations—display Kuskin's belief that "the best picture book is a unity, a good marriage in which pictures and words love, honor, and obey each other," she wrote in *CA*. "For many years," Kuskin continued, "I assumed that I would illustrate whatever I wrote." In the late 1970s, however, the author asked Marc Simont to illustrate *A Space Story*, a book about the solar system that won an award from the New York Academy of Sciences. Her later collaborations with Simont and then David Frampton are among her most popular and acclaimed books.

After *A Space Story* Simont illustrated the well-received *The Philharmonic Gets Dressed*, which earned Kuskin several awards, including one from the American Library Association. The book, which *New York Times Book Review* contributor George A. Woods called "a marvelous idea," describes the pre-performance activities of 105 orchestra members. Their preparations include bathing, shaving, powdering, hair drying, and dressing. Woods declared that Kuskin and Simont "are in perfect tune with each other and, most important, with their audience." The reviewer termed *The Philharmonic Gets Dressed* a "symphony in words and pictures."

A similar topic is addressed in Kuskin's and Simont's third collaboration, *The Dallas Titans Get Ready for Bed*. After a difficult game, forty-five members of a victorious football team retreat to the locker room until the coach tells them they must go home and rest for practice the next morning. As reluctantly as a child who wishes to avoid an early bedtime, each player removes layers of football gear, takes a shower, dresses in street clothes, and leaves for home. Though Molly Ivins commented in the *New York Times Book Review* that *The Dallas Titans Get Ready for Bed* is "a much better book for boys than for girls," she described it as "neat" and "funny." And *Horn Book* contributor Hanna B. Zeiger found the story "a totally origi-

nal and very funny behind-the-scenes look at a large organization."

For *Jerusalem, Shining Still,* a book she wrote after a 1982 trip to the city, Kuskin chose a woodcut artist named David Frampton to provide illustrations. Recounting three thousand years of the history of Jerusalem, Israel, was a challenging task for the author. She spent a considerable amount of time thinking about her visit there and deciding what elements of the city and its past she would include in her book. "I wrote and cut and cut and wrote and condensed that long history into seven and a half pages," she related. Kuskin eventually chose Jerusalem's survival and growth despite frequent attacks by foreigners as the theme of *Jerusalem, Shining Still,* and she was praised for making the city's complex history more accessible to children.

Though many of Kuskin's works have earned her acclaim and awards, the author believes, as she wrote in *CA*, that "basically one works for oneself. It is the process that keeps you going much more than the little patches of appreciation you may have the good fortune to stumble into here and there. . . . Anyone can succeed gracefully. The trick is learning how to fail. I find failure as frightening, discouraging, and unpleasant as everyone else does, but I am quite sure that the ability to survive it, to get up and begin again, is as necessary as a good idea, a reasonable portion of talent, and a disciplined mind."

BIOGRAPHICAL/CRITICAL SOURCES:

BOOKS

Children's Literature Review, Volume 4, Gale, 1982.
Hopkins, Lee Bennett, *Pass the Poetry Please,* Citation Press, 1976.
Larrick, Nancy, editor, *Somebody Turned on a Tap in These Kids: Poetry and Young People Today,* Delacorte, 1971, pp. 38-48.

PERIODICALS

Horn Book, November-December, 1986, pp. 737-738.
Language Arts, November-December, 1979, pp. 934-940.
New York Times Book Review, November 9, 1986, p. 40; August 17, 1986.
Washington Post Book World, March 8, 1981, pp. 10-11.
Young Readers Review, March, 1965.

L

La FOUNTAINE, George 1934-

PERSONAL: Born November 10, 1934, in Attleboro, MA. *Education:* Attended high school in Seattle, WA; attended classes at Pasadena Playhouse, 1955-57.

ADDRESSES: Office—c/o Putnam Berkley Group Inc., 200 Madison Ave., New York, NY 10016.

CAREER: KCET-TV (educational station), Hollywood, CA, lighting director, 1964-65; Hollywood Video Center, Hollywood, lighting director, 1965-68; Academy Lighting Consultants, Hollywood, partner, 1968-72; writer. *Military service:* U.S. Marine Corps, 1952-55; became sergeant.

WRITINGS:

Two Minute Warning, Coward, 1975.
Flashpoint, Coward, 1976.
The Scott-Dunlap Ring, Coward, 1978.
The Killing Seed, Granada, 1980.
The Long Walk, Putnam, 1986.

ADAPTATIONS: Two Minute Warning was adapted for film and released by Universal, and *Flashpoint* was adapted for film and released by Tri-Star, both 1976.

SIDELIGHTS: George La Fountaine presents the suspenseful world of assassins and the painful recovery of former prisoners of war (POWs) in his various novels. His writing career began with his first two novels being adapted into movies shortly after their publication—his first novel, *Two Minute Warning,* was released by Universal a year after its publication. This suspense thriller relates the story of the Los Angeles coliseum security team's efforts to protect the crowd at a packed Super Bowl game from a crazed assassin out to kill some celebrities attending the game. *Two Minute Warning* "made enough of an impression to be picked up for the films," Newgate Callen-

dar commented in the *New York Times Book Review,* adding: "But it really was a pretty conventional suspense novel. *Flashpoint* is much better—more original, written with more security, and with a chilling impact in its last pages."

Flashpoint, La Fountaine's second novel, was published in 1976 and adapted and released by Tri-Star the same year. In this book La Fountaine tells the story of two border patrolmen who find $850,000 and a skeleton in a Jeep with 1963 license plates. The pair decide to investigate the source of the money before making a decision to keep it. During their investigation, they uncover a connection to the John F. Kennedy assassination and a great deal of unanticipated trouble. Callendar pointed out, "[La] Fountaine reserves the really heavy stuff for the very end, and it will bring most readers up sharp." According to Gene Siskel's observation in the *Chicago Tribune,* the movie is "worth watching because of its full portrait of two working-class characters," and is "a tight, well-told thriller."

La Fountaine's 1986 novel, *The Long Walk,* departs from the suspense genre to depict a Green Beret POW's return to the United States and his long recovery process after years of torture by the Vietcong during the Vietnam War. The POW is assisted in his journey back to physical and mental health by a half-Navajo medic who befriends him and takes him to his reservation to heal. The POW's recovery is likened to the return of the Navajos in 1868 to their homeland, a journey of courage and endurance called the "Long Walk." Tom Clark noted in the *Los Angeles Times Book Review,* "The novel's real characters are cultural values: Baker's adoption of the wary prisoner as a brother figure represents a nursing back to health of the white man's sad, crazy, spiritually displaced society by the gentle application of a saner, prior Native American value system." In conclusion, Clark especially praised the "novel's first hundred pages, which contain some of the more compelling prose yet written about the consequences for this country of its involvement in Vietnam."

BIOGRAPHICAL/CRITICAL SOURCES:

PERIODICALS

Chicago Tribune, August 31, 1984.
Los Angeles Times, August 31, 1984.
Los Angeles Times Book Review, August 3, 1986, p. 1.
New York Times Book Review, February 9, 1975, p. 16; September 19, 1976, p. 48; August 17, 1986, p. 22.
Publishers Weekly, November 4, 1974, p. 62; May 17, 1976, p. 46; May 9, 1986, p. 247.
West Coast Review of Books, May, 1978, p. 32.*

*   *   *

LAKE, David J. 1929-

PERSONAL: Born March 26, 1929, in Bangalore, India; naturalized Australian citizen; son of William George (a merchant) and Norah (Babington) Lake; married Marguerite Ferris, December 30, 1964; children: Sarah; stepchildren: Margarita, Anne, David. *Education:* Cambridge University, B.A., 1952, M.A., 1956; University College of North Wales, diploma in linguistics, 1965; University of Queensland, Ph.D., 1974. *Politics:* "Liberal/ environmentalist." *Religion:* "Taoist/agnostic."

ADDRESSES: Home—7 Eighth Ave., St. Lucia, Brisbane, Queensland 4067, Australia. *Office*—Department of English, University of Queensland, St. Lucia, Brisbane, Queensland 4067, Australia. *Agent*—Valerie Smith, 538 East Harford St., Milford, PA 18337.

CAREER: Assistant master, Sherrardswood School, Welwyn Garden City, Hertfordshire, England, 1953-58, and St. Albans Boys Grammar School, Hertfordshire, 1958-59; teacher of English, Saigon University, Vietnam, 1959-61, for Thai Government, Bangkok, Thailand, 1961-63, and Chiswick Polytechnic, London, England, 1963-64; Jadavpore University, Calcutta, India, reader in English and teacher, 1965-67; University of Queensland, Brisbane, Australia, lecturer, 1967-72, senior lecturer, 1973-76, reader in English, 1977—. *Military service:* British Army, gunner in Royal Artillery, 1948-49.

MEMBER: Anti-Slavery and Aboriginals Protection Society of London (life member).

AWARDS, HONORS: Ditmar Award for best Australian science fiction, 1977, for *Walkers on the Sky,* and 1982, for *The Man Who Loved Morlocks: A Sequel to the Time Machine as Narrated by the Time Traveller.*

WRITINGS:

John Milton: Paradise Lost, Mukhopadhyay, 1967.

Greek Tragedy, Excelsus Academy, 1969.
Hornpipes and Funerals (poems), University of Queensland Press, 1973.
The Canon of Thomas Middleton's Plays: Internal Evidence for the Major Problems of Authorship, Cambridge University Press, 1975.

SCIENCE FICTION NOVELS

Walkers on the Sky, DAW, 1976, revised edition, John M. Fontana, 1978.
The Right Hand of Dextra, DAW, 1977.
The Wildings of Westron, DAW, 1977.
The Gods of Xuma; or, Barsoom Revisited, DAW, 1978.
The Fourth Hemisphere, Void, 1980.
The Man Who Loved Morlocks: A Sequel to the Time Machine as Narrated by the Time Traveller, illustrated by Steph Campbell, Hyland House, 1981.
The Ring of Truth, Cory & Collins, 1982.
Warlords of Xuma, DAW, 1983.

FANTASY NOVELS

The Changelings of Chaan, Hyland House, 1985.
West of the Moon, Hyland House, 1988.

OTHER

Contributor to books, including *Rooms of Paradise,* edited by Lee Harding, Quartet Books, 1978; *Envisaged Worlds,* edited by Paul Collins, Void, 1978; *Alien Worlds,* edited by Collins, Void, 1979; *Transmutations,* edited by Rob Gerrand, Outback Press, 1979; and *Distant Worlds,* edited by Collins, Cory & Collins, 1981. Also contributor to *Notes and Queries, Extrapolation, Science Fiction Studies,* and *Wellsian.*

WORK IN PROGRESS: Critical edition of H. G. Wells's *The First Men in the Moon.*

SIDELIGHTS: David J. Lake once wrote that the most important influences on his writings are "my early life in India as the son of an imperialist family and a victim of Christian sexual ethics and metaphysics; also, the writings of C. S. Lewis, the Perennial Philosophy of the mystics, and William Blake; and all the sciences, especially astronomy and biology. In my novels my main preoccupations are beauty, sex, and religion, and in general the predicament of being a rational animal."

*   *   *

LAMB, G(eoffrey) F(rederick) (Balaam)

PERSONAL: Born in London, England; son of Frederick William (an accountant) and Elizabeth (Kendall) Lamb; married Olga Heckman, July 10, 1943; children: Christopher John, Anthony Stuart. *Education:* King's College, London, B.A., 1932, M.A., 1939.

ADDRESSES: Home—Penfold, Legion Lane, Kingsworthy, Winchester, Hampshire, England.

CAREER: Writer, 1950—. Teacher of English in schools in England, 1933-45; Camden Training College, London, England, lecturer in English, 1946-50.

MEMBER: Society of Authors, Children's Writer's Group (honorary secretary, 1963-68), National Book League, Magic Circle (London).

WRITINGS:

(Editor) *Valiant Deeds in Life and Literature,* Harrap, 1942.
(Editor) *United States and United Kingdom,* Harrap, 1944.
Tales of Human Endeavour, Harrap, 1946.
Six Good Samaritans, Oxford University Press, 1947.
(With C. C. Fitz-Hugh) *Precis and Comprehension,* Harrap, 1947.
Commentaries on Galsworthy's Plays, Pitman, 1948.
Questions Answered about Teaching, Jordan, 1949.
(Editor) *The English at School,* Allen & Unwin, 1950.
(Editor) *Other People's Lives,* Harrap, 1951.
(Editor) *All over the World,* Harrap, 1951.
Modern Action and Adventure, Harrap, 1952.
(With Fitz-Hugh) *Introductory Precis and Comprehension,* Harrap, 1952.
(Editor) *All Kinds of Adventure,* Harrap, 1952.
Your Child at School, F. Watts, 1953.
(Editor) *Essays of Action,* Macmillan, 1953.
(Under pseudonym Balaam) *Chalk in My Hair* (autobiography), Benn, 1953.
English for General Certificate, Harrap, 1954.
The Spirit of Modern Adventure, Harrap, 1955.
(Editor) *Short Stories of Action,* Allen & Unwin, 1955.
(Under pseudonym Balaam) *Chalk Gets in Your Eyes,* Benn, 1955.
English for Middle Forms, Harrap, Volume 1, 1956, Volume 2, 1963.
Franklin—Happy Voyager, Benn, 1956.
English for Lower Forms, Harrap, Volume 1, 1957, Volume 2, 1960, revised edition of both volumes (with D. R. Hughes) published in one volume as *English for Secondary Schools,* 1962.
Thrilling Exploits of Modern Adventure, Harrap, 1957.
The South Pole, Muller, 1957.
(Under pseudonym Balaam) *Come out to Play,* M. Joseph, 1958.
(Editor) *Living Dangerously,* Allen & Unwin, 1958.
(Editor) *Stirring Deeds,* Harrap, 1958.
The Happiest Days, M. Joseph, 1959.
Great Exploits of World War II, Harrap, 1959.

Thrilling Journeys of Modern Times, Harrap, 1962.
Punctuation for Schools, Harrap, 1962.
Modern Adventures in Air and Space, Harrap, 1964.
Look at Schools, Hamish Hamilton, 1964.
(Editor) *Story and Rhythm,* Harrap, 1966.
Composition and Comprehension for CSE, Harrap, 1968.
Magicians, International Publications Service, 1968, published in England as *The Pegasus Book of Magicians,* Dobson, 1968.
Practical Work in Precis and Comprehension, Harrap, 1969.
One Hundred Good Stories, Wheaton, Books 1-4, 1969, Books 5-6, 1970.
Modern Adventures at Sea, Harrap, 1970.
Wonder Book of the Seashore, Harrap, 1970.
Your Book of Card Tricks, Faber, 1972, published as *Card Tricks,* Elsevier-Nelson, 1973.
Your Book of Mental Magic, Faber, 1973.
Your Book of Table Tricks, Faber, 1974, published as *Table Tricks,* Elsevier-Nelson, 1975.
Discovering Magic Charms and Talismans, Shire Publications, 1974.
Secret Writing Tricks, Elsevier-Nelson, 1975, published in England as *Your Book of Secret Writing,* Faber, 1976.
More Good Stories, Wheaton, Books 1-4, 1976, Books 5-8, 1978.
Victorian Magic, Routledge & Kegan Paul, 1976.
Pencil and Paper Tricks, Elsevier-Nelson, 1977.
Magic, Witchcraft, and the Occult, Hippocrene, 1977.
Illustrated Magic Dictionary, Elsevier-Nelson, 1980, published in England as *Magic: Illustrated Dictionary,* Kaye & Ward, 1980.
Magic Tricks, Cornerstone, 1980.
Book of Magic Stories, Wheaton, 1981.
Pocket Companion Quotation Guide, Longman, 1983.
Fishermen's Doctor: The Story of Wilfred Grenfell, Religious & Moral Education Press, 1984.
Animal Quotations, Longman, 1985.
Apt and Amusing Quotations, Elliot Rightway Books, 1986.
Magic for All the Family, Elliot Rightway Books, 1987.
Funny Quotes for Numerous Occasions, David & Charles, 1988.
Harrap's Book of Humorous Quotations, Harrap, 1990.
Shakespeare Quotations, Chambers, 1992.

BIOGRAPHICAL/CRITICAL SOURCES:

BOOKS

Balaam, *Chalk in My Hair,* Benn, 1953.
Balaam, *Chalk Gets in Your Eyes,* Benn, 1955.

LANDOW, George P(aul) 1940-

PERSONAL: Born August 25, 1940, in White Plains, NY; son of Herman Irving (a psychiatrist) and Elizabeth Lilian (Driver) Landow (died, 1941); reared by Florence Strasmich Landow; married Ruth Macktez (a college teacher), May 22, 1966; children: Shoshona Macktez, Noah Macktez. *Education:* Princeton University, A.B., 1961, M.A., 1963, Ph.D., 1966; Brandeis University, M.A., 1962; Brown University, postdoctoral studies in art history, methodology, and exhibition sequence, 1975-76. *Religion:* Jewish.

ADDRESSES: Home—9 University Ave., Providence, RI 02906. *Office*—Department of English, Brown University, Providence, RI 02912.

CAREER: Columbia University, New York City, instructor, 1965-68, assistant professor of English, 1969-70, visiting associate professor, summer, 1971; Brown University, Providence, RI, associate professor, 1971-77, professor of English, 1978-83, professor of English and art, 1983—. University of Chicago, visiting associate professor of English, 1970-71; Oxford University, visiting fellow of Brasenose College, 1977; Brown University, fellow of Institute for Research in Information and Scholarship, 1989—. Consulting editor, UMI Research Press, 1985-87. Has evaluated manuscripts for various publishers and various literary, art history, and computing periodicals.

MEMBER: Ruskin Association, Tennyson Society, Pater Society, Phi Beta Kappa.

AWARDS, HONORS: Woodrow Wilson fellowship, 1961-62; Class of 1873 fellowship, Princeton University, 1962-64; Fulbright scholar at Birkbeck College, University of London, 1964-65; Society for the Humanities fellowship, 1968-69; Chamberlain fellowship, Columbia University, summer, 1969; honorary M.A., Brown University, 1972; Gustave O. Arldt Award, Council of Graduate Schools in the United States, 1972, for *The Aesthetic and Critical Theories of John Ruskin;* Guggenheim fellowships, 1974 and 1978; National Endowment for the Humanities grants, 1976, 1977-79, and 1984; National Endowment for the Arts grant, 1984-85; Annenburg/Corporation for Public Broadcasting project grant, 1985-88; Summer Institute for College Teachers at Yale University, National Endowment for the Humanities, 1988, 1991; Educom/Encriptal Award for Best Curriculum Innovation—Humanities, 1990, for *The Dickens Web.*

WRITINGS:

The Aesthetic and Critical Theories of John Ruskin, Princeton University Press, 1971.
"Your Good Influence on Me": The Correspondence of John Ruskin and William Holman Hunt (mono-graph), John Rylands Library, University of Manchester, 1977.
William Holman Hunt and Typological Symbolism, Yale University Press, 1979.
(Editor and author of introduction) *Approaches to Victorian Autobiography,* Ohio University Press, 1979.
(With Diana L. Johnson) *Fantastic Illustration and Design in Britain, 1850-1930,* Museum of Art, Rhode Island School of Design, 1979.
Victorian Types, Victorian Shadows: Typological Symbolism in Victorian Art, Literature, and Thought, Routledge & Kegan Paul, 1980.
Images of Crisis: Literary Iconology, 1750 to the Present, Routledge & Kegan Paul, 1981.
Ruskin, Oxford University Press, 1985.
Elegant Jeremiahs: The Sage from Carlyle to Mailer, Cornell University Press, 1986.
(Editor with J. Coombs and others) *A Pre-Raphaelite Friendship: The Correspondence of William Holman Hunt and John Lucas Topper,* UMI Research Press, 1986.
(With Paul Delaney) *Hypermedia and Literary Studies,* MIT Press, 1991.
Hypertext: The Convergence of Contemporary Critical Theory and Technology, Johns Hopkins University Press, 1992.
(With Delaney) *The Digital Word: Text-Based Computing in the Humanities,* MIT Press, 1993.

Contributor to books, including *The Mind and Art of Victorian England,* edited by Joseph P. Altholz, University of Minnesota Press, 1976; *D. H. Lawrence and Tradition,* edited by Jeffrey Meyers, University of Massachusetts Press, 1985; and *Literary Online: The Promise (and Peril) of Reading and Writing with Computers,* edited by Myron Tuman, University of Pittsburgh Press, 1992. Contributor of more than one hundred papers to conferences and proceedings in the United States and Europe. Contributor of over eighty-five articles and reviews to literature, art history, and computing journals. Associate editor, *Journal of Computing in Higher Education,* 1991—; member of editorial board, *Journal of Pre-Raphaelite and Aesthetic Studies,* 1987-89. Author of "electronic books" *The Dickens Web* and *The In Memoriam Web,* both Eastgate Systems, 1992.

Hypertext: The Convergence of Contemporary Critical Theory and Technology has been published in Japanese.

BIOGRAPHICAL/CRITICAL SOURCES:

PERIODICALS

Times Literary Supplement, June 14, 1985.

LANE, Roumelia
See GREEN, Kay

*   *   *

LANGER, Lawrence L(ee) 1929-

PERSONAL: Born June 20, 1929, in New York, NY; son of Irving and Esther (Strauss) Langer; married Sondra Weinstein (an educator), February 21, 1951; children: Andrew, Ellen. *Education:* City College (now City University of New York), B.A., 1951; Harvard University, A.M., 1952, Ph.D., 1961.

ADDRESSES: Home—249 Adams Ave., West Newton, MA 02165. *Office*—Department of English, Simmons College, 300 Fenway, Boston, MA 02115.

CAREER: University of Connecticut, Storrs, instructor in English, 1957-58; Simmons College, Boston, MA, instructor, 1958-61, assistant professor, 1961-66, associate professor, 1966-72, professor, 1972-76, alumnae professor of English, 1976-92, professor emeritus, 1992—. Fulbright lecturer at University of Graz, Austria, 1963-64.

MEMBER: PEN American Center, Modern Language Association of America, American Association of University Professors, Phi Beta Kappa.

AWARDS, HONORS: Howard M. Jones English prize, Harvard University, 1961; National Endowment for the Humanities fellowship for independent study and research, 1978-79, 1989-90; National Book Critics Circle Award for Criticism, Eugene M. Kayden University Press Prize, and *New York Times Book Review* Ten Best Books of the Year citation, all 1991, all for *Holocaust Testimonies: The Ruins of Memory.*

WRITINGS:

The Holocaust and the Literary Imagination, Yale University Press, 1975.
The Age of Atrocity: Death in Modern Literature, Beacon Press, 1978.
Versions of Survival: The Holocaust and the Human Spirit, State University of New York Press, 1982.
Holocaust Testimonies: The Ruins of Memory, Yale University Press, 1991.

Also contributor to *Confronting the Holocaust: The Impact of Elie Wiesel,* edited by Alvin Rosenfeld and Irving Greenberg, Indiana University Press, 1978; *The Holocaust: Ideology, Bureaucracy, and Genocide,* edited by Henry Friedlander and Sybil Milton, Kraus International Publications, 1981; *From Hester Street to Hollywood: The Jewish-American Stage and Screen,* edited by Sarah Blacher Cohen, University of Indiana Press, 1983; *Writing*

and the Holocaust, edited by Berel Lang, Holmes & Meier, 1988; *Reflections of the Holocaust in Art and Literature,* edited by Randolph L. Braham, Csengeri Institute for Holocaust Studies of CUNY, 1990; *Lessons and Legacies: The Meaning of the Holocaust in a Changing World,* edited by Peter Hayes, Northwestern University Press, 1991; and *Shapes of Memory,* edited by Geoffrey Hartman, Blackwell, 1993.

WORK IN PROGRESS: Art from the Ashes: A Holocaust Anthology, Oxford University Press, 1994; *Injured Merit: The Vindictive Spirit in Milton, Melville, and Dostoevsky.*

SIDELIGHTS: "If Elie Wiesel can be identified as the major literary figure of the Holocaust, then Lawrence Langer deserves the title Critic of the Holocaust," a *Choice* reviewer proclaimed. Langer's critical studies of Holocaust writing, *The Holocaust and Literary Imagination, The Age of Atrocity: Death in Modern Literature,* and *Versions of Survival: The Holocaust and the Human Spirit,* explore the impact of authors, including Wiesel, Bruno Bettelheim, and Viktor Frankl, on modern perceptions of the Holocaust experience. Langer focuses on the linguistic and semantic aspects of the retellings, asserting that the language used often produces an insufficient, skewed representation of the events.

Barbara Foley, writing in *Comparative Literature,* found that in *Versions of Survival* Langer has "sharpened our perception of the ethical and philosophical issues that divide scholars who examine the literature of the ghettos and the camps." Foley emphasized the value of Langer's critique of the various theories of survival put forth in Holocaust literature, noting his argument that metaphorical presentations have "the effect of trivializing—indeed, of distorting—the essential qualities of life and death in the camps." Examples include Frankl's use of an "alphabet and a vocabulary of transcendence," fraught with religious implications which serve to "[deflect] our response from protest, outrage and the need for reorientation in an outmoded or discredited moral universe to a stoic determination to transmute the gas chamber into an aftermath of Calvary," Langer wrote in *Versions of Survival.* Foley also noted Langer's dispute with some writers' belief in the exercise of choice or determination as the saving grace of Holocaust survivors, relegating such discussions to the realm of traditional moralism.

Langer continued his pursuit to present Holocaust experiences unencumbered by the writing process in *Holocaust Testimonies: The Ruins of Memory,* an interpretation of survivor testimonies gleaned from the Fortunoff Video Archive for Holocaust Testimonies housed at Yale University. *Commonweal* contributor Madeleine Marget noted of Langer's finding that "though the [written testimonies] convey the truth, the very fact that they have a structure and coherence means they don't accurately portray the Holocaust, because, as oral testimony shows, there was no shape or meaning to what happened." Bryan Cheyette in *Times Literary Supplement* interpreted Langer's view as a contention that "unlike written testimony, the fragmentary, incomplete, vulnerable nature of oral testimony—with its palpable silences and hesitations, its unresolved tension between 'consequential living' and 'inconsequential dying'—is most able to represent this irredeemable loss."

Langer's assertion of the merits of oral testimony over written accounts proved controversial among reviewers. While some found his distinctions convincing, others, including Cheyette, argued that by labeling written testimony as inferior due to its inherent processes of editing and organization Langer rejected nonetheless valuable memories. David G. Roskies, writing in *Commentary*, remarked, "Anyone who has communicated his thoughts in both writing and in live interviews knows that writing demands precision and accountability, while a person fielding questions tends to use cliches, to play for effect and affect."

As in his earlier works, in *Holocaust Testimonies* Langer challenges attempts to "impose a narrative of redemption or moral triumph onto the bleak reality" of the Holocaust experience, a *Virginia Quarterly Review* contributor noted. The author emphasizes the inappropriateness of describing those who lived through the Holocaust as "survivors." "Langer says that the survivors didn't, in a sense, survive, because that word has a moral resonance that doesn't represent the truth," Marget noted. "Instead, they remained alive, with the living death of what had happened to them within them." The use of words such as "nobility," "victory," and "dignity" to describe the victims, Marget added, "falsifies and thus diminishes the suffering of actual, decent people."

BIOGRAPHICAL/CRITICAL SOURCES:

BOOKS

Langer, Lawrence, *Versions of Survival: The Holocaust and the Human Spirit,* State University of New York Press, 1982.

PERIODICALS

Booklist, February 1, 1991, p. 1112.
Choice, July-August, 1982, p. 1554; September, 1991, p. 179; July, 1992, p. 1641.
Chronicle of Higher Education, May 15, 1991, p. A6.
Commentary, November, 1991, pp. 57-59.
Commonweal, September 27, 1991, p. 552.
Comparative Literature, summer, 1984, pp. 282-284.
Kirkus Reviews, February 15, 1991, p. 230.
Library Journal, February 1, 1991, p. 87.

Los Angeles Times Book Review, March 7, 1982.
New York Times Book Review, April 21, 1991, p. 7; May 5, 1991, p. 30; June 9, 1991, p. 34.
Publishers Weekly, February 8, 1991, p. 42.
Times Literary Supplement, March 6, 1992, p. 6.
Virginia Quarterly Review, summer, 1991, p. 98.

*   *   *

LANGLEY, Lester D(anny)   1940-

PERSONAL: Born August 7, 1940, in Clarksville, TX; son of Lester L. (a carpenter) and Lona J. (Clements) Langley; married Wanda Dickson (a teacher), August 19, 1962; children: Charles, Jonathan. *Education:* West Texas State College (now University), B.A., 1961, M.A., 1962; University of Kansas, Ph.D., 1965.

ADDRESSES: Office—Department of History, University of Georgia, Athens, GA 30603.

CAREER: Texas A & M University, College Station, assistant professor of history, 1965-67; Central Washington State College, Ellensburg, assistant professor of history, 1967-70; University of Georgia, Athens, associate professor, 1970-81, professor of history, 1981—, research professor, 1988—.

MEMBER: American Historical Association, Society of Historians of American Foreign Relations, Conference on Latin American History.

WRITINGS:

The Cuban Policy of the United States: A Brief History, Wiley, 1968.
(Editor) *The United States, Cuba, and the Cold War: American Failure or Communist Conspiracy,* Heath, 1970.
(Co-editor) *The United States and Latin America,* Addison-Wesley, 1971.
Struggle for the American Mediterranean: United States-European Rivalry in the Gulf Caribbean, University of Georgia Press, 1976.
The United States and the Caribbean, 1900-1970, University of Georgia Press, 1980, fourth edition published as *The United States and the Caribbean in the Twentieth Century,* 1989.
The Banana Wars: An Inner History of American Empire, 1900-1934, University Press of Kentucky, 1983.
Central America: The Real Stakes, Crown, 1985.
MexAmerica: Two Countries, One Future, Crown, 1988.
America and the Americas: The United States in the Western Hemisphere, University of Georgia Press, 1989.
Mexico and the United States: The Fragile Relationship, Twayne, 1991.

SIDELIGHTS: In *Central America: The Real Stakes,* Lester D. Langley guides his readers through the maze of Central American political and social life. Andrew Nikiforuk of the Toronto *Globe and Mail* believes that Langley's first-hand experience of his subject makes this book "a major find," observing that the author "has the good sense of a historian and the common touch of a reporter." In the *Los Angeles Times Book Review,* Doyle McManus describes the work as "leisurely, chatty and impressionistic, a travel book as much as a political primer." He adds that *Central America* "meanders around the issues and misses one or two entirely. But in the end, it radiates a [rich] sense of the flavor of Central American political life."

Langley's knowledge of the region's history as well as his personal experience—he has visited both the cities and the countryside on several occasions—offer him insight into the current attitudes of Central Americans. The anti-Americanism of the Nicaraguan people, he reveals, stems from their experience of United States intervention rather than differences in ideology. Because of the nature of the region's problems, as Nikiforuk notes, "Langley believes that there is no American solution to Central America's convulsions."

BIOGRAPHICAL/CRITICAL SOURCES:

PERIODICALS

Globe and Mail (Toronto), October 19, 1985.
Los Angeles Times Book Review, June 16, 1985.

*   *   *

LANGNER, Nola
   See MALONE, Nola Langner

*   *   *

LARKIN, Amy
   See BURNS, Olive Ann

*   *   *

LARKIN, Maia
   See WOJCIECHOWSKA, Maia (Teresa)

*   *   *

LARSON, Gary   1950-

PERSONAL: Born August 14, 1950, in Tacoma, WA; son of Vern (an automobile dealer) and Doris (a secretary) Larson; married, September, 1988. *Education:* Washington State University, graduated, 1972. *Avocational interests:* Basketball, playing guitar, visiting zoos.

ADDRESSES: Office—c/o Universal Press Syndicate, 4900 Main St., Kansas City, MO 64112.

CAREER: Cartoonist. Performed as a musician in a jazz duo, 1973-76; worked at a music store in Seattle, WA, 1976-77; *Seattle Times,* Seattle, cartoonist for weekly feature "Nature's Way," 1978-79; Humane Society, Seattle, animal abuse investigator, 1978-80; cartoonist for daily feature "The Far Side," syndicated by Chronicle Features, San Francisco, CA, 1979-80, syndicated by Universal Press Syndicate, Kansas City, MO, 1984—. Exhibitions include "The Far Side of Science," California Academy of Sciences, 1985, with subsequent tour.

AWARDS, HONORS: National Cartoonists Society Award for best humor panel, 1986.

WRITINGS:

CARTOON ANTHOLOGIES

The Far Side, Andrews & McMeel, 1982.
Beyond the Far Side, Andrews & McMeel, 1983.
In Search of the Far Side, Andrews, McMeel & Parker, 1984.
The Far Side Gallery, Andrews, McMeel & Parker, 1984.
Bride of the Far Side, Andrews, McMeel & Parker, 1985.
Valley of the Far Side, Andrews, McMeel & Parker, 1985.
It Came from the Far Side, Andrews, McMeel & Parker, 1986.
The Far Side Gallery 2, Andrews, McMeel & Parker, 1986.
The Far Side Observer, Andrews, McMeel & Parker, 1987.
Hound of the Far Side, Andrews, McMeel & Parker, 1987.
Night of the Crash-Test Dummies, Andrews & McMeel, 1988.
The Far Side Gallery 3, Andrews & McMeel, 1988.
The Prehistory of the Far Side: A Tenth Anniversary Exhibit, Andrews & McMeel, 1989.
Wildlife Preserves: A Far Side Collection, Andrews & McMeel, 1989.
Wiener Dog Art: A Far Side Collection, Andrews & McMeel, 1990.
Unnatural Selections: A Far Side Collection, Andrews & McMeel, 1991.
Cows of Our Planet: A Far Side Collection, Andrews & McMeel, 1992.

ILLUSTRATOR

(With B. Rodgers) Dee Scarr, *The Gentle Sea,* PADI, 1990.

(With others) Joel M. DeLuca, *Political Savvy: Systematic Approaches to Leadership Behind-the-Scenes,* LRP Publications, 1992.

John M. Berecz, *Understanding Tourette Syndrome, Obsessive-Compulsive Disorder and Related Problems: A Developmental and Catastrophe Theory Perspective,* Springer Publishing, 1992.

ADAPTATIONS: "The Far Side" has been optioned for a film based on the cartoon panel by writer-director Alan Rudolph and producer David Blocker, 1985; Larson's cartoons are featured on a line of merchandise that includes clothing, greeting cards, and gift items.

SIDELIGHTS: Cartoonist Gary Larson presents an unconventional and surreal world in his daily one-panel comic feature "The Far Side"; animals are always smarter than humans and the humans themselves are always very strange. Syndicated in more than three hundred newspapers throughout the United States, "The Far Side" has also been collected into numerous bestselling cartoon anthologies. In "The Far Side," observes Nancy Shute in the *Smithsonian,* "the simple line drawings—doodles, almost—get [Larson's] point across, hooking deeply into the psyches of the susceptible. The natural order of things goes seriously awry, with hilarious results." James Kelly, writing in *Time,* asserts that "if a single theme animates [Larson's] work, it is that man, for all his achievements, is just one species on earth, and not always the wisest or strongest one. His prehistoric cave dwellers and chunky matrons with beehive hairdos and sequined glasses are vulnerable and foolish, while his cows and bears are wise and resourceful." Larson relates to Kelly: "It's wonderful that we live in a world in which there are things that can eat us. It keeps us from getting too cocky."

This attitude is reflected in Larson's creations, which present such odd juxtapositions as a movie theater crowded with insects waiting to watch *Return of the Killer Windshield;* campers slumbering in sleeping bags while bears examining them exclaim, "Sandwiches!"; and a pilot mildly puzzling over the appearance of a mountain goat in the cloud bank directly ahead. Commenting on this brand of humor, *Detroit News* book critic Beaufort Cranford declares that "The Far Side" is "radically dependent on twists of perception," adding that Larson's humor is "so black that it can only have come from the eerie corridors of a very bizarre mind. . . . Clearly it is also the stuff of a demented imagination." Other reactions to Larson's work include *Washington Post* contributor Richard Harrington's announcement that "The Far Side" is nothing short of "macabre, weird, zany, twisted, whimsical, fiendish, bizarre, odd, strange."

Larson began cartooning in an offhand way while working at a series of diverse jobs. After performing as a jazz gui-

tarist in a duo called "Tom and Gary," he worked at a music store in Seattle, Washington. Larson recounts that in the late 1970s, while working at the music store, he drew several cartoons and offered them to *Pacific Search,* a nature magazine. "They bought all six," he relates in his interview with Harrington. "I was shocked." This sale, explains Larson, encouraged him to continue cartooning after he began working for the Humane Society in 1978. During an investigation of animal abuse, Larson met a *Seattle Times* reporter who saw his cartoons and urged him to submit them to her paper. Soon the *Seattle Times* was running a weekly cartoon, "Nature's Way," that the cartoonist referred to as his "training ground." Shute relates that "Nature's Way" was cancelled within a year "after complaints about the unnatural selection of the subject matter." Heeding a suggestion, Larson submitted his material to the *San Francisco Chronicle* and eventually signed a five-year contract with Chronicle Features syndicate, which nationally introduced Larson's daily cartoon as "The Far Side." The subject matter of the strip remained under fire, however. "I lived in terror of cancellation," reveals Larson in an interview with Tim Appelo for *Pacific Northwest.* "I was always being cancelled by newspapers, and I was horrified every time. All these 'Nancy' readers would see this hideous thing and cry out. But the people on the news staffs enjoyed the strip. I think that's the single thing that saved me."

"The Far Side," syndicated by Universal Press Syndicate since 1984, came in its first seven years to appear as a regular feature in more than three hundred American dailies. Larson's "weirdly inverted depictions of life in the food chain have snared him . . . a swift . . . fame," observes Lisa Kinoshita in *Saturday Review.* In addition to his highly successful cartoon, Larson has also had a number of bestselling anthologies of his work, including *The Far Side, In Search of the Far Side, Valley of the Far Side, Night of the Crash-Test Dummies, Wildlife Preserves,* and *Cows of Our Planet.* Discussing the success of "The Far Side" with Harrington, Larson observes, "It's a continual surprise to me that it's done as well as it has, because I do recognize that it's a little . . . *different.*"

Although he sees his work as being "different," Larson also explains to Cranford that he believes his strip "touches a sense of humor that's always been out there somewhere. Television and other media have reflected that kind of humor, but it had never found its way into the newspapers. I think there was an oddness out there that made people ready to accept and enjoy it." Fans delight, for example, in a panel depicting a boat full of headhunters staring incredulously at two tourists with enormously large heads as they paddle by. In another "Far Side" cartoon, one praying mantis responds to the accusations of another: "I don't know what you're insinuating, Jane, but

I haven't seen your Harold all day—besides, surely you know I would only devour my *own* husband!" And another favorite has a pack of dogs disguised as humans sneaking into a post office and attacking the workers.

In his interview with Cranford, Larson explains that for "Far Side" readers "a sort of vicarious release . . . takes place with this kind of humor. It's much akin to slapstick comedy. You laugh when someone gets a pie thrown in their face or takes a pratfall, but when you think about it, it's actually not funny at all—you're laughing at someone else's suffering. But it works because people know life's just like that." Larson continues: "I don't think it's sick, really. . . . There's a distinction between something that's sick and something that's morbid humor." "The Far Side," he concludes, is "morbid, maybe, but it keeps an innocent edge. I never try to analyze it, or to shock people. My focus is just to do something funny." This contention might be based on such "Far Side" scenes as a freeway-driving dog whose master, tongue lolling, projects his head through the car's open passenger window. Or one in which an astounded couple complains to a witch in whose care they had left their children, "We hired you to babysit the kids, and you cooked and ate them BOTH?" Larson admits to Carol Krucoff in the *Washington Post* that "people get the short end of the stick more often in my stuff"; but, the cartoonist tells Harrington, "I hope people see that it's just silliness."

Committed to the single-panel format, Larson describes his work in an interview for *People* as "basically sitting down at the drawing table and getting silly." He informs Harrington: "I think very visually and I think a single panel lends itself to that one instant visual image. . . . It all kind of comes to me at once, more or less simultaneous. Sometimes a caption will hit me first, but that's rare. Usually it's the image that will come first, this one hideous moment that just lands on me." Such moments result in cartoons like the one in which a lemming trailing a suicidal group at the water's edge glances furtively to determine if his life preserver will be detected; or one that depicts Reuben, the hospital worker, caught rubbing newborns on his clothes for static electricity and sticking them to the walls like balloons. For Larson, humor captured in single images like these depends on subtleties. "I really sweat over the nuances in a face or I try to think what is the focus of this cartoon," Larson tells Krucoff. This focus can sometimes be slightly blurred, however; not every reader always gets the joke. "I realize that some of my cartoons go over people's heads," admits Larson in an interview with Sheridan Warrick for *Pacific Discovery*. "But if out of ten people, I think that one will bellylaugh and the other nine will be dumbfounded, I'll go for it. The one thing I try not to do is condescend to people. If you start doing cartoons that are too universal, you end up with

something milked out and uninteresting. I'd rather be misunderstood."

A variety of characters fill Larson's subtle and sometimes "misunderstood" cartoons, but more often than not the starring roles are given to animals. "Mostly I think of animals as a vehicle for my own particular sense of humor," explains Larson in a *San Francisco Chronicle* interview with David Perlman. "A lot of the time I end up exploring the weird prejudices we humans have toward some animals. If a real animal starts adding too many legs or too many eyes, it seems to become too alien for most of us to stand." Among the many animals that are fodder for Larson's work are cows—one of his personal favorites. "I particularly enjoy drawing cows," Larson relates to Harrington. "I'm not exactly sure *why*. They seem to be some kind of absurd, almost non sequitur animal to put into certain situations. I even find humor in the *name*." Shute, who identifies scientists as among Larson's first and most appreciative fans, quotes a Smithsonian Institution National Zoo bird curator's admission that "if you have any knowledge of animals, the cartoon is ridiculous to the point that you laugh uncontrollably." Larson's use of other creatures includes kangaroos, dinosaurs, amoebas, warthogs, and a "Far Side" shark who approaches another with the line, "Say honey, didn't I meet you last night at the feeding frenzy?" And the menagerie continues to grow.

In "The Far Side" Larson's pursuit of fun and silliness has met with enormous success, a circumstance the cartoonist finds difficult to trust. He tells Krucoff: "Sometimes I have a hard time shaking the feeling that there's been a big mistake. It's taken me by surprise that things have happened the way they have. . . . I have a sense of not wanting to really give myself over to it entirely, a sense that it could all suddenly turn to smoke or I'm going to hear my mother's voice in the distance saying, '*Gaaaaary,* time for school!' and there I am, 12 years old." Larson echoes this skeptical outlook in an interview for *People*: "I keep thinking someone's gonna show up and say, 'There's been a mistake. The guy next door is supposed to be drawing the cartoon. Here's your shovel.'"

BIOGRAPHICAL/CRITICAL SOURCES:

PERIODICALS

Chicago Tribune, January 5, 1983; June 4, 1984; February 24, 1987; September 3, 1987; December 3, 1991, Section 14, pp. 11, 13.

Detroit News, November 20, 1984.

Los Angeles Times, December 1, 1984; December 9, 1985; November 19, 1986.

Los Angeles Times Book Review, December 4, 1983; December 9, 1984; November 26, 1989.

Newsweek, October 10, 1988.

New York Times Book Review, May 3, 1987; November 12, 1989, p. 54.

Pacific Discovery, October-December, 1985.

Pacific Northwest, September, 1987.

People, October 1, 1984; January 18, 1985; February 4, 1985; June 21, 1985.

Publishers Weekly, September 21, 1984.

Rolling Stone, September 24, 1987.

San Francisco Chronicle, February 3, 1982; October 11, 1983; May 13, 1985; December 1, 1985; August 20, 1987.

Saturday Review, November/December, 1984.

Smithsonian, April, 1984; April, 1987.

Time, December 1, 1986, p. 86.

Washington Post, June 16, 1983; June 10, 1984.

Washington Post Book World, September 2, 1984; October 19, 1986; November 12, 1989, p. 19.*

* * *

LATTA, Richard 1946-

PERSONAL: Born October 16, 1946, in East Chicago, IN; son of John (a welder) and Ann (Nastav) Latta; married Mary Tripodi (a teacher), August 24, 1968; children: Tena, Sara, Tara, Alyssa. *Education:* Illinois Benedictine College, B.S., 1968.

ADDRESSES: Home—126 Indiana Boundary Rd., Plainfield, IL 60544. *Office*—Forest Park Public Schools, 939 Beloit, Forest Park, IL 60130.

CAREER: Forest Park Public Schools, Forest Park, IL, teacher of junior high school science, 1968—. Free-lance writer, 1970—.

MEMBER: National Education Association, Illinois Education Association.

AWARDS, HONORS: Merit Award of Achievement from *Today's Catholic Teacher.*

WRITINGS:

PUZZLE AND QUIZ BOOKS

Science Puzzles, Business Stimulus, 1974.

Grammar Puzzles, Mafex Publishing, 1978.

Metric Puzzles, Mafex Publishing, 1978.

Word Find Puzzle Book, Q Publishing, 1980.

Mazes, Mazes, Mazes, Modern Promotions & Publishers, Nos. 1-6, 1982, Nos. 7-12, 1983.

This Little Pig Had a Riddle, Albert Whitman, 1984.

Puzzle Pick Search-a-Words (six volumes), Waldman Publishing, 1985.

Mother Goose Puzzles, Price, Stern, 1987.

More Mother Goose Puzzles, Price, Stern, 1990.

Dinosaur Mazes, Price, Stern, 1990.

State the Facts, Price, Stern, 1990.

The 40's Song Title Quiz Book, Price, Stern, 1990.

The 50's Song Title Quiz Book, Price, Stern, 1990.

The 60's Song Title Quiz Book, Price, Stern, 1990.

The 70's Song Title Quiz Book, Price, Stern, 1990.

1991 Word Find Calendar, Landmark Calendars, 1990.

The 50's TV Show Trivia Book, Price, Stern, 1991.

The 60's TV Show Trivia Book, Price, Stern, 1991.

The 70's TV Show Trivia Book, Price, Stern, 1991.

The 80's TV Show Trivia Book, Price, Stern, 1991.

1992 Word Find Calendar, Landmark Calendars, 1991.

212 Puzzles on Twenty-four Classic Children's Books, Alleyside Press, 1993.

Also author of four books in "Games for Travel" series, Price, Stern, 1976-81, revised editions, 1990; author of four grammar puzzle books published by Christopher Lee.

OTHER

Rain (poetry), Windless Orchard, 1970.

Concrete Poems, Cycle Press, 1972.

Creative Writing of Concrete Poetry for Schools, Mafex Publishing, 1974.

Letter Recognition, Mafex Publishing, 1975.

Art Activity Book, Gamco Publishing, 1979.

Also author of four supplementary curriculum books published by Christopher Lee. Contributor of poems, short stories, and articles to more than fifty-five journals. Advisor to *Current Science,* 1972-73.

ADAPTATIONS: Latta's poetry has been read on radio in the United States and Canada.

WORK IN PROGRESS: The Recycling Dictionary; The Environment Dictionary; The Rainforest Maze Book; The Rainforest Dot-to-Dot Book; 101 Recycling Questions; 101 Environmental Questions; The Baseball Card Dictionary; and *The Mother Goose Riddle Book.*

SIDELIGHTS: Richard Latta once told *CA:* "I have found that persistence is the key to successful writing. I write and create every day. Mornings see the height of my creativity; hence I rise at four-thirty in the morning. Most of my books are designed to get people to think or create for themselves.

"My advice to young writers is to write, write, write," Latta added, "and consider any rejection just a step up the ladder of success." He later told *CA:* "While education is important in writing, writing is not dependent on education. If you have a desire to write but have no education, then by all means write. We all learn how to be consumers in our society, but it is the producers who are reaping the profits. Writing is producing and it is the most satisfying thing you can do. 'Being gifted' becomes meaningless because the greatest gift you have is the ability to create. And this creativity is not exclusive to writing: You can paint, draw, sketch, design, carve, invent, sing, play music and compose. All creativity is a great gift that is created in itself—not necessarily something you *have*. All talent takes time to mature. Any great writer does not sit down for the first time and write his greatest novel. It might take him a lifetime, and each book or poem he creates is a small step to that great novel.''

*   *   *

LAVINE, Sigmund Arnold   1908-

PERSONAL: Born March 18, 1908, in Boston, MA; son of Phillip Henry and Etta (Bramson) Lavine; married Gertrude Kramer (a teacher), December 17, 1937; children: Maxine P. Lavine Rosenberg, Jerrold N. *Education:* Boston University, B.J., 1930, M.Ed., 1931. *Avocational interests:* Collecting Gilbert and Sullivan memorabilia, raising tropical fish, showing dogs, greenhouse gardening.

ADDRESSES: Home—9 Magnolia Rd., Milton, MA 02186.

CAREER: Free-lance author and book critic, 1926—; *Boston Transcript,* Boston, MA, literary critic, 1926-34; Associated Press, Boston, correspondent, 1926-31; *Boston Post,* Boston, feature writer, 1930-31; U.S. Indian Service, Belcourt, ND, teacher, 1931-34; *Boston Herald-American,* Boston, literary critic and columnist, 1934—; *Worcester Telegram,* Worcester, MA, critic, 1956—; Dennis C. Haley School, Roslindale, MA, assistant administrative principal, 1963-80. Trustee, Milton (MA) Public Library, 1970.

MEMBER: Massachusetts School Master's Club, Phi Gamma Mu.

AWARDS, HONORS: Joint Committee of the National Science Teachers Association and the Children's Book Council named several titles "outstanding science books for children"; Schoolman's Medal, Freedom Foundation at Valley Forge, 1973.

WRITINGS:

Wandering Minstrels We: The Story of Gilbert and Sullivan, Dodd, 1954.
Steinmetz, Maker of Lightning, Dodd, 1956.
Wonders of the Aquarium, Dodd, 1957.
Wonders of the Hive, Dodd, 1958.
Strange Partners, Little, Brown, 1959, published in England as *Animal Partners,* Phoenix House, 1959.
Wonders of the Ant Hill, Dodd, 1960.
Kettering, Master Inventor, Dodd, 1960.
Wonders of the Wasps' Nest, Dodd, 1961.
Strange Travelers (Junior Literary Guild selection), Little, Brown, 1961.

Famous Industrialists, Dodd, 1962.
Wonders of Animal Disguises, Dodd, 1962.
Wonders of the Beetle World, Dodd, 1962.
Allan Pinkerton, America's First Private Eye, Dodd, 1963.
Wonders of Animal Architecture, Dodd, 1964.
Famous Merchants, Dodd, 1965.
(With Mart Casey and Rosemary Casey) *Water since the World Began,* Dodd, 1965.
Handmade in America: The Colonial Craftsmen, Dodd, 1966.
Wonders of the Spider World, Dodd, 1966.
Famous American Architects, Dodd, 1967.
Handmade in England, Dodd, 1968.
Wonders of the World of Bats, Dodd, 1969.
Evangeline Booth: Daughter of Salvation, Dodd, 1970.
Wonders of the Fly World, Dodd, 1970.
Wonders of the Owl World, Dodd, 1971.
Wonders of the Hawk World, Dodd, 1972.
(With Brigid Casey) *Wonders of the World of Horses,* Dodd, 1972.
Wonders of the World of Eagles, Dodd, 1974.
Horses the Indians Rode, Dodd, 1974.
Indian Corn and Other Gifts, Dodd, 1974.
Wonders of the World of Cactus, Dodd, 1974.
Games the Indians Played, Dodd, 1974.
(With V. Scuro) *Wonders of the Bison World,* Dodd, 1975.
Ghosts the Indians Feared, Dodd, 1975.
Wonders of Herbs, Dodd, 1976.
Beginner's Book of Gardening, Dodd, 1977.
Wonders of Terrariums, Dodd, 1977.
Wonders of Marsupials, Dodd, 1978.
(With Scuro) *Wonders of the Donkey World,* Dodd, 1978.
Wonders of the Camel World, Dodd, 1979.
Wonders of Mice, Dodd, 1979.
(With Scuro) *Wonders of Elephants,* Dodd, 1979.
(With B. Casey) *Wonders of Ponies,* Dodd, 1980.
(With Scuro) *Wonders of Goats,* Dodd, 1980.
(With Scuro) *Wonders of Pigs,* Dodd, 1981.
Wonders of Peacocks, Dodd, 1982.
Wonders of Rhinos, Dodd, 1982.
Wonders of Hippos, Dodd, 1983.
(With B. Casey) *Wonders of Draft Horses,* Dodd, 1983.
Wonders of Coyotes, Dodd, 1984.
Wonders of Badgers, Dodd, 1985.
Wonders of Giraffes, Dodd, 1986.
Wonders of Tigers, Dodd, 1987.

Contributor of book reviews to several newspapers. Member of editorial board, *World in Books.*

WORK IN PROGRESS: Books on frontier folklore and rediscovered species.

SIDELIGHTS: Various works by Sigmund Arnold Lavine have been selected for overseas translation by the U.S. Information Agency.

BIOGRAPHICAL/CRITICAL SOURCES:

PERIODICALS

Detroit News, November 28, 1971.

* * *

LAVINSON, Joseph
    See KAYE, Marvin (Nathan)

* * *

LAYCOCK, George (Edwin) 1921-
    (Jeff Marshall)

PERSONAL: Born May 29, 1921, in Zanesville, OH; son of William D. and Hazel D. (Heim) Laycock; married Ellen M. Van Auken, February 14, 1943; children: Elaine, Michael, Steven. *Education:* Ohio State University, B.S., 1947.

ADDRESSES: Home and office—5944 Crittenden Dr., Cincinnati, OH 45244.

CAREER: Farm Quarterly, Cincinnati, OH, associate editor, 1947-51; free-lance writer, 1951—. Photographer, illustrating many of his own writings. Former member of Ohio Wildlife Council and of Ohio Governor's Task Force on the Environment. *Military service:* U.S. Army, World War II; served in European Theater.

MEMBER: Authors Guild, American Society of Journalists and Authors, Outdoor Writers Association of America, National Audubon Society, Sierra Club, Nature Conservancy, Wilderness Society, Wildlife Society, Outdoor Writers of Ohio (former president).

AWARDS, HONORS: Boys' Clubs of America Junior Book Award, 1966, for *Never Pet a Porcupine;* National Book Award nomination in sciences, 1974, for *Autumn of the Eagle;* Excellence in Craft Award, Outdoor Writers Association of America, 1983; Johnson Award for writings on water sports; Jade of Chiefs Award, Outdoor Writers of America; Boys' Clubs of America awards for best-liked books; five Science Teachers of America awards for outstanding books for young people.

WRITINGS:

Deer Hunters' Bible, Doubleday, 1963, 4th edition, 1986.
The Sign of the Flying Goose: The Story of the National Wildlife Refuges, Doubleday, 1965.
Never Pet a Porcupine, Norton, 1965.
Never Trust a Cowbird, Norton, 1966.
Whitetail, Norton, 1966.
The Alien Animals, Doubleday, 1966.
Big Nick: The Story of a Remarkable Black Bear, Norton, 1967.

King Gator, Norton, 1968.
America's Endangered Wildlife, Norton, 1969.
Wild Refuge, National History Press, 1969.
Shotgunner's Bible, Doubleday, 1969.
(With wife, Ellen Laycock) *The Flying Sea Otters,* Grosset, 1970.
The Diligent Destroyers, Doubleday, 1970.
Alaska: The Embattled Frontier, Houghton, 1971.
Animal Movers: A Collection of Ecological Surprises, Natural History Press, 1971.
The Pelicans, Doubleday, 1971.
Water Pollution, Grosset, 1972.
Air Pollution, Grosset, 1972.
Wingspread: A World of Birds, Four Winds, 1972.
Autumn of the Eagle, Scribner, 1973.
Strange Monsters and Great Searches, Doubleday, 1973.
Camels: Ships of the Desert, Doubleday, 1975.
People and Other Mammals, Doubleday, 1975.
Squirrels, Scholastic Book Services, 1975.
The Birdwatcher's Bible, Doubleday, 1976, 2nd edition, 1993.
Caves, Scholastic Book Services, 1976.
Death Valley, Scholastic Book Services, 1976.
Islands and Their Mysteries, Scholastic Book Services, 1977.
Beyond the Arctic Circle, Scholastic Book Services, 1978.
Exploring The Great Swamp, McKay, 1978.
How to Buy and Enjoy a Small Farm: Your Comprehensive Guide to the Country Life, McKay, 1978.
Mysteries, Monsters and Untold Secrets, Doubleday, 1978.
Wild Hunters: North America's Predators, McKay, 1978.
Beginner's Guide to Photography, Doubleday, 1979.
Tornados: Killer Storms, McKay, 1979.
Does Your Pet Have a Sixth Sense?, Doubleday, 1980.
(With E. Laycock) *How the Settlers Lived,* McKay, 1980.
(Under pseudonym Jeff Marshall) *The Bicycle Rider's Bible,* Doubleday, 1981.
(With E. Laycock) *The Ohio Valley: Your Guide to America's Heartland,* Doubleday, 1983.
North American Wildlife, Bison Books, 1983.
The Kroger Story, Kroger Co., 1983.
The Wild Bears, Times-Mirror Press, 1986.
The Young Naturalist's Guide to Wildlife, Simon & Schuster, 1986.
The Mountain Men, Grolier, 1988.
The Hunters and the Hunted, Meredith Press, 1990.

Former author of columns, including "Camping," *Sports Age,* and "Campfires," *Argosy.* Contributor to numerous periodicals, including *Popular Science, Boys' Life, Audubon, Outdoor Life, Reader's Digest, Field and Stream,* and *Sports Illustrated.* Field editor, *Audubon,* 1968-91.

WORK IN PROGRESS: John Ruthven's World, a book about wildlife artist John Ruthven, a modern day Audubon.

*   *   *

LAZARUS, Henry
See SLAVITT, David R(ytman)

*   *   *

LEAPMAN, Michael (Henry) 1938-

PERSONAL: Born April 24, 1938, in London, England; son of Nathan C. (a shopkeeper) and Leah (Isaacs) Leapman; married Olga Mason (a secretary), July 15, 1965; children: Benjamin. *Education:* Educated in England.

ADDRESSES: Home—13 Aldebert Terrace, London SW8 1BH, England. *Agent*—Felicity Bryan, 2A North Parade, Banbury Road, Oxford OX2 6PE, England.

CAREER: Scotsman, Edinburgh, Scotland, reporter, 1961-64; *London Sun,* London, England, reporter, 1964-69; *Times,* London, New York City bureau chief, 1969-72 and 1976-81, editor of *Times Diary,* 1972-76; *Daily Express,* London, columnist, 1981-83; free-lance writer, 1983—. *Military service:* Royal Navy, 1956-58.

MEMBER: National Union of Journalists, Society of Authors.

AWARDS, HONORS: Campaigning Journalist of the Year Award, British Press, 1968; Thomas Cook Travel Book Award, National Book League, 1983, for *The Companion Guide to New York.*

WRITINGS:

One Man and His Plot, J. Murray, 1976.
Yankee Doodles, Allen Lane, 1982.
The Companion Guide to New York, Prentice-Hall, 1983, revised edition, HarperCollins, 1991.
Barefaced Cheek: The Apotheosis of Rupert Murdoch, Hodder & Stoughton, 1983, published as *Arrogant Aussie: The Rupert Murdoch Story,* Lyle Stuart, 1985.
Treachery? The Power Struggle at TV-am, Allen & Unwin, 1984.
The Last Days of the Beeb, Allen & Unwin, 1986.
Kinnock, Unwin Hyman, 1987.
The U.S. Election: A Basic Guide, Coronet, 1988.
(Editor) *The Book of London,* Weidenfeld & Nicolson, 1989.
London's River: A History of the Thames, Pavilion, 1991.
Treacherous Estate: The Press after Fleet Street, Hodder & Stoughton, 1992.

Contributor of articles to periodicals, including *Connoisseur, Independent, New Statesman, New York Times,* and *British Journalism Review.*

SIDELIGHTS: "My books have all sprung from my journalism, more or less," British writer and humorist Michael Leapman once told *CA.* Involving his readers in subjects ranging from the English perspective on goings-on in Manhattan to the growing media empire of Australian publisher Rupert Murdoch, Leapman has cultivated his journalistic style to consistently entertain his audience while informing them on topics of current interest.

"I am primarily a journalist and suppose I shall remain so," Leapman explained. "My first book, *One Man and His Plot,* was about my London vegetable garden which I had written about in the *Times Diary.*" After being appointed New York bureau chief by the London *Times* in 1969, he was soon at work on his second book, *Yankee Doodles,* which Leapman published in 1982. A humorous collection of columns written for the *Times* during the three years he spent living in New York City, *Yankee Doodles* is described by reviewer John Lahr in the *Times Literary Supplement* as "a wry, well-written account of life in the USA, that is, the United States of Advertizing." A year later, Leapman wrote yet another book based on his experiences in the "Big Apple." *The Companion Guide to New York,* a travel guide organized around the evolution of the city, earned him the prestigious Thomas Cook Travel Book Award from Britain's National Book League. The revised edition, published in 1991, was included in reviewer Paul Graves' list of the one hundred best guide books in *New York* magazine. Leapman has continued actively writing for British newspapers, among them the *Independent.* He still finds inspiration in London life, gardening, and a continuing fascination with the United States that prompted him to write *The U.S. Election: A Basic Guide,* published in 1988.

However, the subjects he has chosen for more recent writing have been in the area of the British media: the press, the television industry, and the personalities that have risen and fallen from power in their various media empires. In 1983, Leapman published the biography of Australian newspaper tycoon Rupert Murdoch, whose purchase of the London *Times* caused Leapman to leave his position of New York bureau chief shortly thereafter. Chronicling the life of this enigmatic man from his early childhood—his father was Sir Keith Murdoch, head of a newspaper empire in his native Australia—*Arrogant Aussie* follows Murdoch's predestined path early in his career during the acquisition of small Australian and British newspapers and television stations, through his establishment of the *National Star* to compete with the *National Inquirer,* to his purchase of the London *Times,* the *Boston Herald American,* and the *Chicago Sun-Times.* Leapman followed *Arrogant Aussie* with *Treachery? The Power Struggle at TV-am,* published in 1984, and *The Last Days of the Beeb,* a study of the effects of deregulation upon the British Broadcasting Corporation that was published two years later. His 1992 book, *Treacherous Estate,* describes and comments on the British press from the 1960s to the death of Fleet Street. Leapman highlights the changes in both technology and industrial relations during the period and examines several threats to press freedom. In writing on such current topics, Leapman has adopted a somewhat dispassionate journalistic stance, which has caused some reviewers to fault him for maintaining a constrained relationship with his subjects. However, Leapman has been praised for his journalistic form: objectively approaching his topic and conscientiously reporting the facts.

BIOGRAPHICAL/CRITICAL SOURCES:

PERIODICALS

Chicago Tribune, May 12, 1985.
Daily Telegraph, September 19, 1992.
Economist, April 24, 1982; September 26, 1992.
Globe and Mail (Toronto), August 30, 1986.
Listener, July 29, 1976; April 15, 1982.
Literary Review (London), September, 1992.
Los Angeles Times Book Review, June 9, 1985, p. 4.
New Statesman, August 13, 1976.
New York, August 31, 1992.
New York Times Book Review, May 26, 1985, p. 13.
Punch, October 20, 1976.
Spectator, July 23, 1983, pp. 22-23; June 21, 1986, pp. 24-25.
Times (London), April 15, 1982; April 5, 1984; May 7, 1987; September 17, 1992.
Times Literary Supplement, July 30, 1982; July 22, 1983, p. 774; September 30, 1983, p. 1066; September 7, 1984, p. 993; September 12, 1986, p. 991; October 21, 1988, pp. 1169-71; November 13, 1992.
Washington Post Book World, July 28, 1985, p. 4.

*   *   *

Le BRETON, Auguste
See MONTFORT, Auguste

*   *   *

LEE, Wayne C. 1917-
(Lee Sheldon)

PERSONAL: Born July 2, 1917, in Lamar, NE; son of David Elmer (a farmer) and Rosa (Deselms) Lee; married Pearl Sheldon, March 17, 1948; children: Wayne Sheldon,

Charles Lester. *Religion:* Disciples of Christ. *Avocational interests:* Sports, especially community boys' sports, music, and singing.

ADDRESSES: Home—210 West 16th St., Imperial, NE 69033; (winter) Harlingen, TX.

CAREER: Farmer in Lamar, NE, 1935-51; rural mail carrier, 1951-77; full-time writer, 1977—. Teacher and board member, Disciples of Christ Church. *Military service:* U.S. Army, Signal Corps, 1945.

MEMBER: Western Writers of America (president, 1970-71), Nebraska State Historical Society (member of foundation board), Nebraska Writers Guild (president, 1974-76), Toastmasters Club (former president).

AWARDS, HONORS: Historian of the Year, High Plains Preservation of History Commission, 1981.

WRITINGS:

Prairie Vengeance, Arcadia House, 1954.
Broken Wheel Ranch, Arcadia House, 1956.
Slugging Backstop, Dodd, 1957.
His Brother's Guns, Arcadia House, 1958.
Killer's Ranger, Arcadia House, 1958.
Bat Masterson, Whitman Publishing, 1960.
Gun Brand, Arcadia House, 1961.
Blood on the Prairie, Arcadia House, 1962.
Thunder in the Backfield, F. Watts, 1962.
Stranger in Stirrup, Arcadia House, 1962.
The Gun Tamer, Arcadia House, 1963.
Devil Wire, Arcadia House, 1963.
The Hostile Land, Arcadia House, 1964.
Gun in His Hand, Arcadia House, 1964.
Warpath West, Ace Books, 1965.
Fast Gun, Avalon, 1965.
Mystery of Scorpion Creek, Abingdon, 1966.
Brand of a Man, Avalon, 1966.
Trail of the Skulls, Bouregy, 1966.
Showdown at Julesburg Station, Bouregy, 1967.
Return to Gunpoint, Ace Books, 1967.
Only the Brave, Bouregy, 1967.
(Under pseudonym Lee Sheldon) *Doomed Planet,* Bouregy, 1967.
Sudden Guns, Bouregy, 1968.
Trouble at the Flying H, Bouregy, 1969.
Stage to Lonesome Butte, Bouregy, 1969.
Showdown at Sunrise, Bouregy, 1971.
The Buffalo Hunter, Bouregy, 1972.
Suicide Trail, Lenox Hill, 1972.
Wind over Rimfire, Lenox Hill, 1973.
Son of a Gunman, Ace Books, 1973.
Law of the Prairie, Lenox Hill, 1974.
Scotty Philip: The Man Who Saved the Buffalo (biography), Caxton Printers, 1975.

Die Hard, Ace Books, 1975.
Law of the Lawless, Ace Books, 1977.
Skirmish at Fort Phil Kearny, Avalon, 1977.
Gun Country, Ace Books, 1978.
Petticoat Wagon Train, Ace Books, 1978.
The Violent Man, Ace Books, 1978.
Ghost of a Gun Fighter, Zebra Books, 1979.
McQuaid's Gun, Avalon, 1980.
Trails of the Smoky Hill (nonfiction), Caxton Printers, 1980.
Shadow of the Gun, Zebra Books, 1981.
Guns at Genesis, Leisure Books, 1981.
Putnam's Ranch War, Avalon, 1982.
Barbed Wire War, Avalon, 1983.
The Violent Trail, Avalon, 1984.
White Butte Guns, Avalon, 1984.
War at Nugget Creek, Avalon, 1985.
Massacre Creek, Avalon, 1985.
The Waiting Gun, Avalon, 1986.
Hawks of Autumn, Avalon, 1986.
Wild Towns of Nebraska (nonfiction), Caxton Printers, 1988.

PLAYS

Bachelor Bait, Eldridge Publishing, 1951.
Lightly Turn toward Love, Schubert, 1952.
Poor Willie, Denison, 1954.
Hold the Phone, Denison, 1955.
Deadwood, Denison, 1956.
For Evans Sake, Denison, 1957.
Big News, Denison, 1957.

Also author of numerous other plays.

OTHER

Short stories represented in numerous anthologies. Contributor of over six hundred short stories to more than thirty periodicals.

WORK IN PROGRESS: A historical novel, *Arickaree War Cry;* a work of nonfiction, *Bad Men and Bad Towns.*

SIDELIGHTS: Wayne C. Lee once told *CA:* "My writing day begins at 5 a.m. and runs until noon with time out for breakfast and news, weather, and sports. Being a sport nut, I have to hear how the leagues in all sports are doing. I find that, by starting my day while the house and the world around me are quiet, I can become submerged in my writing before outside activity has an opportunity to encroach on my thinking. Once 'into' my story, it is not difficult to hold my concentration. The result is twice as much work done as when, years ago, I waited until 7 a.m. to begin.

Lee recently explained to *CA:* "Since moving from the farm to town, I keep my same writing schedule—5 a.m.

till noon. We spend our winters in south Texas at Harlingen where I keep my same schedule. In Texas, I have organized and am in charge of the 'Men's Gospel Singers'— twelve men—and we sing many times throughout the winter around the valley. In Imperial, I have organized a male quartet and we sing at various functions around town. I love music and singing and these groups are a relaxing diversion from my writing."

*   *   *

LEFKOWITZ, Mary Rosenthal 1935-

PERSONAL: Born April 30, 1935, in New York, NY; daughter of Harold L. and Mena G. (Weil) Rosenthal; married Alan L. Lefkowitz, July 1, 1956 (divorced, 1981); married Hugh Lloyd-Jones (a professor), March 26, 1982; children: (first marriage) Rachel Greil, Hannah Weil. *Education:* Wellesley College, B.A. (summa cum laude), 1957; Radcliffe College, M.A., 1959, Ph.D., 1961.

ADDRESSES: Home—15 West Riding, Wellesley, MA 02181. *Office*—Departments of Greek and Latin, Wellesley College, Wellesley, MA 02181.

CAREER: Wellesley College, Wellesley, MA, instructor, 1960-63, assistant professor, 1963-69, associate professor, 1969-75, professor of Greek and Latin, 1975-79, chairman of department, 1970-72, 1975-78, 1981-87, 1991—, director of educational research, 1978-79, Andrew W. Mellon Professor in the Humanities, 1979—. Visiting professor at University of California, Berkeley, 1978; visiting fellow at St. Hilda's College, Oxford, 1979-80, Pembroke College, Oxford, 1986-87, and Corpus Christi College, Oxford, 1990-91. Director, National Endowment for the Humanities seminars for college teachers, 1984, 1985, and Pew Foundation Grant, 1986-91.

MEMBER: American Philological Association (member of national board of directors, 1974-77), Phi Beta Kappa.

AWARDS, HONORS: Woodrow Wilson fellow, 1957-58; Radcliffe Institute fellow, 1966-67, 1972-73; American Council of Learned Societies fellow, 1972-73; National Endowment for the Humanities fellow, 1979-80, 1990-91; Mellon Grant, Wellesley Center for Research on Women, 1980-81.

WRITINGS:

The Victory Ode: An Introduction, Noyes Press, 1976.
(Editor with Maureen B. Fant) *Women in Greece and Rome,* Samuel Stevens, 1977, revised edition published as *Women's Life in Greece and Rome,* Johns Hopkins University Press, 1982, 2nd edition, 1992.
Heroines and Hysterics, St. Martin's, 1981.
The Lives of the Greek Poets, Johns Hopkins University Press, 1981.

Women in Greek Myth, Johns Hopkins University Press, 1986, German translation by Holger Fliessbach and Axel Haase published as *Die Toechter des Zeus: Frauen im alten Griechenland,* C. H. Beck Verlag, 1992.

First Person Fictions: Pindar's Poetic "I", Clarendon Press, 1991.

Contributor of articles and reviews to periodicals, including *Times Literary Supplement, New York Times Book Review, New Republic, Partisan Review,* and *American Scholar.* New England editor, *Classical Journal,* 1977-83; editorial board member, *American Journal of Philology,* 1986-89; editorial board member, *American Scholar,* 1988—.

SIDELIGHTS: In *The Lives of the Greek Poets,* Mary Lefkowitz reexamines the traditional biographies of some of the major Greek poets, including Homer, Hesiod, Archilochus, Pindar, Aristophanes, and Callimachus. *Times Literary Supplement* contributor Oliver Taplin explains that the life-stories of these poets have been greatly distorted over the years; Lefkowitz's "sensible little book" attempts to restore historical accuracy to these biographies. "It is a careful, searching look," assesses Taplin, "and the [traditional] 'Lives' crumble before it."

BIOGRAPHICAL/CRITICAL SOURCES:

PERIODICALS

Observer, November 30, 1986, p. 21.
Sunday Times, December 17, 1981, p. 42.
Times Literary Supplement, March 5, 1982; May 21, 1982; December 10, 1982, p. 33.

*   *   *

LENSKI, Lois 1893-1974

PERSONAL: Born October 14, 1893, in Springfield, OH; died September 11, 1974, in Tarpon Springs, FL; daughter of Richard Charles Henry (a Lutheran minister) and Marietta (Young) Lenski; married Arthur S. Covey (an artist), 1921 (died, 1960); children: Stephen; (stepchildren) Margaret and Laird. *Education:* Ohio State University, B.S., 1915; additional study at Art Students' League, 1915-20, and Westminster School of Art, London, 1920-21. *Avocational interests:* Gardening, collecting old juvenile books.

CAREER: Artist, author, and illustrator.

AWARDS, HONORS: Newbery Honor Book, American Library Association (ALA), 1937, for *Phebe Fairchild: Her Book;* Newbery Honor Book, 1942, for *Indian Captive: The Story of Mary Jemison;* Martha Kinney Cooper Ohioana Medal, 1944, for *Bayou Suzette;* John Newbery

Medal, 1946, for *Strawberry Girl;* ALA Notable Book citation, for *The Little Fire Engine;* Child Study Association of America/Wel-Met Children's Book Award, 1947, for *Judy's Journey;* Litt.D., Wartburg College, 1959; L.H.D., University of North Carolina at Greensboro, 1962; D.Litt., Capital University, 1966, and Southwestern College, 1968; Regina Medal, Catholic Library Association, 1969, for lifetime work in the field of children's literature; University of Southern Mississippi Special Children's Collection Medallion, 1969.

WRITINGS:

JUVENILE FICTION; SELF-ILLUSTRATED

Skipping Village, Stokes, 1927.
A Little Girl of Nineteen Hundred, Stokes, 1928.
Two Brothers and Their Animal Friends, Stokes, 1929.
Two Brothers and Their Baby Sister, Stokes, 1930.
Spinach Boy, Stokes, 1930.
Benny and His Penny, Knopf, 1931.
Grandmother Tippytoe, Stokes, 1931.
Arabella and Her Aunts, Stokes, 1932.
Johnny Goes to the Fair, Minton, Balch, 1932.
The Little Family, Doubleday, Doran, 1932.
Gooseberry Garden, Harper, 1934.
The Little Auto (also see below), Oxford University Press, 1934, published in England as *The Baby Car,* 1937.
Surprise for Mother, Stokes, 1934.
Little Baby Ann, Oxford University Press, 1935.
Sugarplum House, Harper, 1935.
The Easter Rabbit's Parade, Oxford University Press, 1936.
Phebe Fairchild: Her Book, Stokes, 1936.
A-Going to the Westward, Stokes, 1937.
The Little Sail Boat (also see below), Oxford University Press, 1937, published in England as *The Little Sailing Boat,* 1938.
Bound Girl of Cobble Hill, Lippincott, 1938.
The Little Airplane (also see below), Oxford University Press, 1938.
Ocean-Born Mary, Stokes, 1939.
Blueberry Corners, Stokes, 1940.
The Little Train, Oxford University Press, 1940.
Indian Captive: The Story of Mary Jemison, Stokes, 1941.
The Little Farm (also see below), Oxford University Press, 1942.
Bayou Suzette, Stokes, 1943.
Davy's Day, Oxford University Press, 1943.
Let's Play House, Oxford University Press, 1944.
Puritan Adventure, Lippincott, 1944.
Strawberry Girl, Lippincott, 1945.
Blue Ridge Billy, Lippincott, 1946.
The Little Fire Engine, Oxford University Press, 1946.
Judy's Journey, Lippincott, 1947.
A Surprise for Davy, Oxford University Press, 1947.

Boom Town Boy, Lippincott, 1948.
Mr. and Mrs. Noah, Crowell, 1948.
Cotton in My Sack, Lippincott, 1949.
Cowboy Small (also see below), Oxford University Press, 1949.
Texas Tomboy, Lippincott, 1950.
Papa Small, Oxford University Press, 1951.
Prairie School, Lippincott, 1951.
Peanuts for Billy Ben, Lippincott, 1952.
We Live in the South (short stories), Lippincott, 1952.
Mama Hattie's Girl, Lippincott, 1953.
Corn-Farm Boy, Lippincott, 1954.
Project Boy, Lippincott, 1954.
We Live in the City (short stories), Lippincott, 1954.
A Dog Came to School, Oxford University Press, 1955.
San Francisco Boy, Lippincott, 1955.
Berries in the Scoop, Lippincott, 1956.
Big Little Davy, Oxford University Press, 1956.
Flood Friday, Lippincott, 1956.
We Live by the River (short stories), Lippincott, 1956.
Davy and His Dog, Oxford University Press, 1957.
Houseboat Girl, Lippincott, 1957.
Little Sioux Girl, Lippincott, 1958.
Coal Camp Girl, Lippincott, 1959.
We Live in the Country (short stories), Lippincott, 1960.
Davy Goes Places, Walck, 1961.
Policeman Small (also see below), Walck, 1962.
We Live in the Southwest (short stories), Lippincott, 1962.
Shoo-Fly Girl, Lippincott, 1963.
We Live in the North (short stories), Lippincott, 1965.
High-Rise Secret, Lippincott, 1966.
Debbie and Her Grandma, Walck, 1967.
To Be a Logger, Lippincott, 1967.
Deer Valley Girl, Lippincott, 1968.
Lois Lenski's Christmas Stories, Lippincott, 1968.
Debbie and Her Family, Walck, 1969.
Debbie Herself, Walck, 1969.
Debbie and Her Dolls, Walck, 1970.
Debbie Goes to Nursery School, Walck, 1970.
Debbie and Her Pets, Walck, 1971.
Lois Lenski's Big Book of Mr. Small (contains *Policeman Small, Cowboy Small,* and *The Little Farm*), McKay, 1979.
More Mr. Small (contains *The Little Auto, The Little Sail Boat,* and *The Little Airplane*), McKay, 1979.

ILLUSTRATOR

Children's Frieze-Book, Platt & Munk, 1918.
Kenneth Grahame, *The Golden Age,* John Lane, 1921.
Vera B. Birch, *The Green-Faced Toad,* John Lane, 1921.
Grahame, *Dream Days,* John Lane, 1922.
Padraic Colum, *The Peep-Show Man,* Macmillan, 1924.
Veronica S. Hutchinson, editor, *Chimney Corner Stories,* Putnam, 1925.

Henry Drummond, *The Monkey Who Would Not Kill,* Dodd, 1925.
Hutchinson, editor, *Chimney Corner Fairy Tales,* Putnam, 1926.
Kathleen Adams and Frances Atchinson, editors, *A Book of Princess Stories,* Dodd, 1927.
Hutchinson, editor, *Fireside Stories,* Putnam, 1927.
Caroline D. Emerson, *A Merry-Go-Round of Modern Tales,* Dutton, 1927.
Adams and Atchinson, editors, *A Book of Enchantments,* Dodd, 1928.
Hutchinson, editor, *Candle-Light Stories,* Putnam, 1928.
Emerson, *The Hat-Tub Tale; or, The Shores of the Bay of Fundy,* Dutton, 1928.
Elizabeth Robins and Octavia Wilberforce, *Prudence and Peter and Their Adventures with Pots and Pans,* Morrow, 1928.
May Lamberton Becker, editor, *Golden Tales of Our America,* Dodd, 1929.
Adams and Atchinson, editors, *There Were Giants,* Dodd, 1929.
Hutchinson, editor, *Chimney Corner Poems,* Putnam, 1930.
Hutchinson, editor, *Fireside Poems,* Putnam, 1930.
Ethel C. Phillips, *Little Rag Doll,* Houghton, 1930.
Emerson, *Mr. Nip and Mr. Tuck,* Dutton, 1930.
Alan Lake Chidsey, *Rustam, Lion of Persia,* Minton, 1930.
Sing a Song of Sixpence, Harper, 1930.
Hugh Lofting, *The Twilight of Magic,* Stokes, 1930.
Watty Piper, editor, *Mother Goose Rhymes,* Platt, 1931.
Chidsey, *Odysseus, Sage of Greece,* Minton, 1931.
Piper, editor, *Jolly Rhymes of Mother Goose,* Platt, 1932.
Tom Powers, *A Scotch Circus,* Houghton, 1934.
E. R. Mirrielees, editor, *Twenty-two Short Stories of America,* Heath, 1937.
Phil Stong, *Edgar, the 7:58,* Farrar, Straus, 1938.
Dorothy Thompson, *Once on a Christmas,* Oxford University Press, 1938.
Maud Hart Lovelace, *Betsy-Tacy,* Crowell, 1940.
Cornelia Meigs, *Mother Makes Christmas,* Grossett, 1940.
Lovelace, *Betsy-Tacy and Tib,* Crowell, 1941.
Phillips, *A Name for Obed,* Houghton, 1941.
Frances Rogers, *Indigo Treasure,* McClelland, 1941.
Lovelace, *Betsy and Tacy Go over the Big Hill,* Crowell, 1942.
Lena Barksdale, *The First Thanksgiving,* Knopf, 1942.
Mabel La Rue, *A Letter to Poppsey,* Grossett, 1942.
Lovelace, *Betsy and Tacy Go Downtown,* Crowell, 1943.
Roberta Whitehead, *Five and Ten,* Houghton, 1943.
Clara Ingram Judson, *They Came from France,* Houghton, 1943.
Piper, *The Little Engine That Could,* Platt, 1945.

Mary Graham Bonner, *The Surprise Place,* Ryerson Press, 1945.

Bulla, *The Donkey Cart,* Crowell, 1946.

Alan Chaffee, adapter, *Pinocchio,* by Carlo Collodi, Random House, 1946.

Read-to-Me Storybook, Child Study Association of America, 1947.

Also illustrator of *Dolls from the Land of Mother Goose,* 1918, *Cinderella* and *My ABC Book,* both 1922, and *Golden Tales of the Prairie States* (six volumes), 1932-41; illustrator of *Golden Tales of Canada,* edited by May Becker.

JUVENILE NONFICTION; SELF-ILLUSTRATED

The Wonder City: A Picture Book of New York, Coward, 1929.

The Washington Picture Book, Coward, 1930.

My Friend the Cow, National Dairy Council, 1946.

Ice Cream Is Good, National Dairy Council, 1948.

Living with Others, Hartford (CT) Council of Churches, 1952.

VERSE; SELF-ILLUSTRATED

(Editor) *Jack Horner's Pie: A Book of Nursery Rhymes,* Harper, 1927, also published as *Lois Lenski's Mother Goose.*

Alphabet People, Harper, 1928.

(Editor) *Susie Mariar* (folk rhyme), Oxford University Press, 1939.

Animals for Me, Oxford University Press, 1941.

Forgetful Tommy, Greenacres Press, 1943.

Spring Is Here, Oxford University Press, 1945.

Now It's Fall, Oxford University Press, 1948.

I Like Winter, Oxford University Press, 1950.

(With Clyde R. Bulla) *We Are Thy Children* (hymns), Crowell, 1952.

On a Summer Day, Oxford University Press, 1953.

(With Bulla) *Songs of Mr. Small,* Oxford University Press, 1954.

(With Bulla) *Songs of the City,* E. B. Marks, 1956.

(With Bulla) *Up to Six: Book I,* Hansen Music, 1956.

(With Bulla) *I Went for a Walk* (read-and-sing book), Walck, 1958.

(With Bulla) *At Our House* (read-and-sing book), Walck, 1959.

(With Bulla) *When I Grow Up* (read-and-sing book), Walck, 1960.

The Life I Live: Collected Poems, Walck, 1965.

City Poems, Walck, 1971.

Florida, My Florida: Poems (adult verse), Florida State University Press, 1971.

Sing a Song of People, with photographs by Giles Laroche, Little, Brown, 1987.

Sing for Peace, Herald Press, 1987.

PLAYS

The Bean Pickers: A Migrant Play, music by Clyde R. Bulla, National Council of Churches, 1952.

A Change of Heart: A Migrant Play, music by Bulla, National Council of Churches, 1952.

Strangers in a Strange Land: A Migrant Play, music by Bulla, National Council of Churches, 1952.

OTHER

Adventures in Understanding: Talks to Parents, Teachers, and Librarians, 1944-1966, Friends of Florida State University Library, 1968.

Journey into Childhood: Autobiography of Lois Lenski (adult), Lippincott, 1972.

Lenski's manuscripts are included in collections at University of Oklahoma Library; Florida State University Library; Amos Memorial Library, Sidney, OH; Capital University Library, Columbus, OH; Illinois State University Library; Kerlan Collection, University of Minnesota; State University of New York, Buffalo; and Syracuse University.

ADAPTATIONS: Cowboy Small was adapted into a motion-picture screenplay, NET Film Service, 1955; *Indian Captive: The Story of Mary Jemison* was adapted for the stage by Gertrude Breen, Coach House Press, 1961; *Strawberry Girl* was made into a filmstrip/record set, Miller-Brody Productions, 1973.

SIDELIGHTS: Writer and artist Lois Lenski was the author of more than ninety books for children during the many years she dedicated to her craft. Several of the books that she wrote and illustrated for preschool and early elementary school readers have become classics, a testament to her ability to relate to young people and capture the interest of youthful imaginations. Employing a writing style described by Anne Scott MacLeod in *Twentieth-Century Children's Writers* as "sober, realistic, and straightforward," Lenski created a methodical, familiar world wherein such characters as Policeman Small and The Little Fire Engine could provide children the comforts of a secure, known universe.

Lenski was born in Springfield, Ohio, in 1893, the fourth of five children. Her father, a Lutheran minister, and her mother, a former schoolteacher, moved their family to the nearby town of Anna in 1899. Lenski would later write in *Journey into Childhood: The Autobiography of Lois Lenski* that Anna "offered all a child could enjoy and comprehend. Commonplace and ordinary, it had no particular beauty or grace, but it soon became my own, a compound of sights and sounds and smells and buildings and people that became a part of me. . . . To have lived it and savored it and been a part of it, has given me great comfort through ensuing years."

Lenski attended Ohio State University and took classes in education as well as art courses to develop her drawing ability. After graduation, she continued her art study at both New York City's Art Students' League and the Westminster School of Art in London, England. In 1918, she was hired by Platt & Munk to illustrate the *Children's Frieze Book,* for which she was paid $100. From this starting point Lenski went on to illustrate works by a series of children's authors, including Veronica Hutchinson, Kenneth Grahame, and Henry Drummond. Finally, in 1927, Lenski published *Skipping Village,* the first of many books she would both write and illustrate. She later admitted in her autobiography that she had often "found it hard to be sympathetic to a story written by another person." In her own stories, Lenski would find "congenial material to illustrate," and finally her "writing and drawing dovetailed ideally."

Lenski was one of the most prolific children's writers of the twentieth century, not only because of her love of both writing and drawing, but also as a testament to her parents. "Learning was always our goal," she wrote. "My parents had a strong positive attitude toward learning and education. . . . They stressed, not so much in words, but by example, the importance of *work.* . . . They set the example and we children followed." Lenski's life embodied a strong work ethic: "Work to me is sacred," she wrote. "I have a strong urge to work, I am not happy unless I am at work. I believe this compulsion to work was not only a part of my conscious training, but also a part of my Polish inheritance." Her energies focused outward, through gaining and conveying knowledge and broadening the understanding of her young audience. As she herself believed, "Life is full of amazing drama if we have the awareness to see and understand it."

Lenski produced a wide variety of books for very young children, including such popular works as *Grandmother Tippytoe,* published in 1931, *The Little Auto,* published in 1934, and 1949's *Cowboy Small.* However, more representative of her works are those books written for an older audience, characterized by either an historical or regional focus. *Phebe Fairchild: Her Book, Bound Girl of Cobble Hill,* and *Indian Captive: The Story of Mary Jemison* were among the historical novels that Lenski meticulously researched. "All of Lenski's vigorous historical novels . . . depict events, customs, ways of making a living, and attitudes with authenticity because of Lenski's patient, time-consuming investigation of documentary sources," commented Taimi M. Ranta in *Dictionary of Literary Biography.* Well received by critics, *Phebe Fairchild,* published in 1936, and *Indian Captive,* which Lenski wrote five years later, each received a prestigious Newbery Honor Book designation.

In the early 1940s, Lenski's interest shifted away from recounting the history of another time and place. Believing that books for children were under a greater obligation than to merely entertain readers, Lenski noted in her autobiography that they "should illumine the whole adventure of living." In historical books she could research the factual details of everyday life, but had to develop both fictional characters and stories within which to convey such information. As a realist, Lenski was driven "to get out and see people and get to know them." *Bayou Suzette,* the first book to result from the author's shift from a historical to a contemporary regional focus, received the Ohioana Award in 1944. Lenski would go on to write seventeen more regional novels over the next twenty-four years: *Strawberry Girl,* the best known book of this category, received the Newbery Medal in 1946 and *Judy's Journey* received the Children's Book Award a year later.

Lenski shaped her regional novels around the lives and stories of ordinary people among whom she lived in order to learn their ways. It was in this respect that the author was a pioneer. "Unusual, particularly for the 1940's and 1950's, is her focus on the poorer levels of American society," noted MacLeod. "In all of [her regional works] Lenski presents patterns of life often invisible in children's books. For the most part, she does so with neither condescension nor sentimentality." While reviewers of the period were sometimes critical of her use of regional dialects to provide authenticity in her novels, with the passage of time children's literature has acknowledged a debt to Lenski. "In the development of realism in children's literature, Lenski's work is an important point of departure on the way to the stark realism of the late twentieth century," stated Ranta, adding that "it is her innovative use of regional speech that remains Lenski's most distinctive and enduring contribution to twentieth-century children's literature."

BIOGRAPHICAL/CRITICAL SOURCES:

BOOKS

Adams, Charles M., editor, *Lois Lenski: An Appreciation,* Friends of the Library of the Woman's College, University of North Carolina, 1963.
Bader, Barbara, *American Picturebooks from Noah's Ark to The Beast Within,* Macmillan, 1976.
Dictionary of Literary Biography, Volume 22: *American Writers for Children, 1900-1960,* Gale, 1983, pp. 241-252.
Lenski, Lois, *Journey into Childhood: The Autobiography of Lois Lenski,* Lippincott, 1972.
Newbery Medal Books, 1922-1955, Horn Book, 1957.
Reader's Encyclopedia of American Literature, Crowell, 1962.

Twentieth-Century Children's Writers, 3rd edition, St. Martin's, 1989, pp. 573-575.

PERIODICALS

Catholic Library World, February, 1969.
Horn Book, March-April, 1951.
Lutheran, March 28, 1956.
Lutheran Libraries, winter, 1969.
Ohioana Quarterly, spring, 1970.

OBITUARIES:

PERIODICALS

AB Bookman's Weekly, October 7, 1974.
Library Journal, November 15, 1974.
New York Times, September 14, 1974.
Publishers Weekly, September 30, 1974.
Time, September 23, 1974.*

*   *   *

LEVIN, Jack 1941-

PERSONAL: Born June 28, 1941, in New Orleans, LA; son of Max (a business executive) and Flory (Liebman) Levin; married Flora Lench, June 14, 1964; children: Michael Steven, Bonnie Lynn, Andrea Ilene. *Education:* American International College, B.A., 1963; Boston University, M.S., 1964, Ph.D., 1968.

ADDRESSES: Office—Department of Sociology, Northeastern University, Boston, MA 02115.

CAREER: Boston University, Boston, MA, assistant professor of sociology, 1968-70; Northeastern University, Boston, assistant professor, 1970-74, associate professor, 1974-80, professor of sociology and criminology, 1980—. Member of executive board, Understanding Aging, Inc., and Living Is for the Elderly. Consultant to President's Commission on Obscenity and Pornography, 1970, and to Columbia Point Nursery School Project, 1972.

MEMBER: American Sociological Association, Society for the Study of Social Problems, American Society of Criminology, Eastern Sociological Society, Massachusetts Sociological Association (president, 1973-74).

AWARDS, HONORS: Excellence in Teaching Award, Northeastern University, 1982; Pioneer Award, Massachusetts Sociological Association, 1988; Professor of the Year in Massachusetts, CASE, 1991.

WRITINGS:

Elementary Statistics in Social Research, Harper, 1973, 5th edition, 1991.
(With Gerald S. Ferman) *Social Science Research: A Handbook for Students,* Schenkman, 1974.

The Functions of Prejudice, Harper, 1975, 2nd edition, 1984.
(With James L. Spates) *Starting Sociology,* Harper, 1976, 4th edition, 1990.
(With W. Levin) *Ageism: Prejudice and Discrimination against the Elderly,* Wadsworth Publishing, 1980.
(With R. Bourne) *Social Problems and Social Policy,* West Publishing, 1983.
(With Ernie Anastos) *Twixt: Teens Yesterday and Today,* F. Watts, 1983.
(With J. Fox) *Mass Murder: America's Growing Menace,* Plenum, 1985.
(With A. Arluke) *Gossip: The Inside Scoop,* Plenum, 1987.
(With Levin) *The Human Puzzle,* Wadsworth Publishing, 1988.
(With Fox and S. Harkins) *Elementary Statistics in Behavioral Research,* HarperCollins, 1992.
Sociological Snapshots, Pine Forge Press, 1993.
(With J. McDevitt) *Hate Crimes: The Rising Tide of Bigotry and Bloodshed,* Plenum, 1993.
(With Fox) *Working with the Media: A Survival Guide for Scholars,* Sage Publications, 1993.

Contributor to professional journals.

WORK IN PROGRESS: Overkill, for Plenum, and *Killer on Campus: The Gainesville Murders,* for Avon, both with J. Fox.

*   *   *

LEVINSON, Richard (Leighton) 1934-1987

PERSONAL: Born August 7, 1934, in Philadelphia, PA; died of a heart attack, March 12, 1987, in Los Angeles, CA; son of William (a businessman) and Georgia (Harbert) Levinson; married Rosanna Huffman (an actress), April 12, 1969; children: Christine. *Education:* University of Pennsylvania, B.S., 1956.

ADDRESSES: Home—215 South Cliffwood, Los Angeles, CA. *Agent*—Creative Artists Agency, 9830 Wilshire Blvd., Beverly Hills, CA 90212.

CAREER: Writer of short stories and plays; writer and co-producer of teleplays. Columbia Broadcasting System, Inc. (CBS-TV), New York City, creator, with William Link, of *Mannix* television series, 1967-75; National Broadcasting Company, Inc. (NBC-TV), New York City, creator, with Link, of television series *The Bold Ones,* 1969-73, and *The Psychiatrist,* 1971, creator and producer, with Link, of television series *Tenafly,* 1971, and *Columbo,* 1971-76, developer and producer, with Link, of *Ellery Queen* television series, 1975-76, and, with Peter S. Fischer, *Murder, She Wrote,* 1983-87; Richard Levinson/ William Link Productions, Los Angeles, CA, co-president, 1978-87. *Military service:* Served during the 1950s.

MEMBER: Actors Studio West (chairperson of playwrights committee, 1965-68), Caucus for Writers, Producers, and Directors (member of steering committee, 1976-77).

AWARDS, HONORS: All with William Link—Emmy Award, 1970, for *My Sweet Charlie,* and 1972, for *Columbo* script; Image Award, National Association for the Advancement of Colored People (NAACP), 1970, for *My Sweet Charlie;* Golden Globe Award, Hollywood Foreign Press Association, 1972, for *Columbo* and *That Certain Summer;* Silver Nymph Award, Monte Carlo Film Festival, 1973, for *That Certain Summer;* George Foster Peabody Award, University of Georgia, 1974, for *The Execution of Private Slovik;* Edgar Awards, Mystery Writers of America, 1979, 1980, 1983; Christopher Award, 1981, for *Crisis at Central High;* Tony Award nomination, 1983, for *Merlin;* Paddy Chayefsky Laurel Award, Writers Guild of America, 1986, for advancing literature of television; Ellery Queen Award, Mystery Writers of America, 1989, for lifetime contribution to the art of the mystery.

WRITINGS:

WITH WILLIAM LINK

Prescription: Murder (three-act play; also see below), Samuel French, 1963.
Fineman (novel), Laddin Press, 1972.
Stay Tuned: An Inside Look at the Making of Prime-Time Television, St. Martin's, 1981.
(Authors of book) *Merlin* (two-act musical play), produced on Broadway, 1983.
The Playhouse (novel), Berkeley, 1984.
Guilty Conscience: A Play of Suspense in Two Acts, Samuel French, 1985.
Off-Camera: Conversations with the Makers of Prime-Time Television, New American Library, 1986.

TELEPLAYS; WITH LINK

Prescription: Murder, National Broadcasting Company, Inc. (NBC-TV), 1968.
My Sweet Charlie, NBC-TV, 1970.
That Certain Summer, American Broadcasting Companies, Inc. (ABC-TV), 1972.
(And executive producers) *The Execution of Private Slovik,* NBC-TV, 1974.
(And executive producers) *The Gun,* ABC-TV, 1974.
(And executive producers) *Murder by Natural Causes,* Columbia Broadcasting System, Inc. (CBS-TV), 1979.
(And executive producers with David Susskind) *Crisis at Central High* (based on book of same title by Elizabeth Huckaby), CBS-TV, 1981.

(And executive producers) *Rehearsal for Murder,* CBS-TV, 1982.
(And executive producers) *Take Your Best Shot,* CBS-TV, 1982.
Prototype, CBS-TV, 1983.
Blacke's Magic, NBC-TV, 1986.
The United States of America vs. Salim Ajami (posthumous), CBS-TV, 1988.
For the Boys, ABC-TV, 1990.

OTHER

Also author, with Link, of teleplay for movie *Vanishing Act.* Also contributor, with Link, of more than one hundred scripts for television series developed by others as well as themselves, including *General Motors Presents, Westinghouse Desilu Playhouse, Dr. Kildare, The Fugitive, The Rogues, Mannix, Columbo, Murder, She Wrote, Blacke's Magic,* and *The Alfred Hitchcock Hour.* Contributor of more than thirty short stories and book reviews to periodicals, including *Playboy.*

ADAPTATIONS: Rehearsal for Murder was adapted as *Rehearsal for Murder: A Full-Length Play* by D. D. Brooke, and as the play *Killing Jessica* by David Rodgers; *Murder by Natural Causes* was adapted as *Murder by Natural Causes: A Full-Length Play* by Tim Kelly.

SIDELIGHTS: Richard Levinson, who died on March 12, 1987, formed one-half of a prolific writing duo that specialized in television. Levinson and his partner, William Link, worked together for forty years on numerous writing projects, including television series, a Broadway play, short stories, novels, and memoirs. Levinson's ebullient energy contrasted with Link's more reserved personality, together creating one of Hollywood's most successful creative partnerships. Their best-known television series, *Columbo,* which ran for seven successful seasons, features Peter Falk as the rumpled, affable, seemingly inept, yet incredibly ingenious detective, Lieutenant Columbo. The show became something of a cult classic in the television industry.

Discussing the development of their Columbo character, Levinson once told an *American Film* interviewer: "We did a short story in Alfred Hitchcock's magazine many, many years ago, which in 1960 we reworked for the 'Chevrolet Mystery Show.' That's where Columbo first appeared. We derived the character basically from Petrovich in [Dostoevski's] *Crime and Punishment,* who was always clawing away at the student who killed the landlady. He was already very unassuming; we added the raincoat and cigar. That, along with G. K. Chesterton's Father Brown, is the genesis of Columbo. About a year later, we turned it into a play [*Prescription: Murder*] that toured with Thomas Mitchell as Columbo. We were not happy with that production, but we noticed that the character of

Columbo always got the biggest hand at curtain calls. We bought the rights back from the producer for about five hundred dollars. Which is probably the best deal we've ever made."

Upon Levinson's death, Link reflected in the *Hollywood Reporter* that "his real love was the TV movie. . . . Each time out we tried to do something that hadn't been seen before, something that would touch an emotional or social chord." In addition to their television series, the duo created several ground-breaking television movies which address controversial social issues, including the Emmy-winning *My Sweet Charlie*, which deals with an interracial relationship, *That Certain Summer*, a Golden Globe winner that presents television's first serious treatment of homosexual characters, and *The Gun*, which explores the real dangers of handgun abuse.

Throughout their working relationship, Levinson and Link, who met their first day of junior high school in Philadelphia, followed their projects from inception to completion. From the plays they co-authored in junior high school to their made-for-television movies to their novels, they collaborated on every aspect of their projects. As Marc Gunther of the *Detroit News* observed: "Each is involved in creating characters and stories, writing dialog, dealing with the networks and following the movies through the production process. . . . Typically, they work at one or the other's home, with one man at the typewriter and the other pacing and speaking lines." Their first important sale came after both had completed their military service; they sold an Army script, *Chain of Command*, to Desilu Playhouse. Their career in television expanded as they became more involved in the myriad aspects of writing and producing.

Describing the duo's hands-on approach to their career, Gunther noted that "Levinson and Link decided in the early 1970s to produce as well as write their movies so they could influence the choice of director, casting, filming and editing." Levinson explained to Gunther in the same article, "We became enamored of the television movie, because we realized that if we produced, we could have what very few writers of feature films can have, which is control—creative control over the work." Levinson added, "We are among the few writers in the public arts who get to see our work made as it was written so we know that it's our fault if it's bad and, maybe if it's good, we can take some credit for it."

Their penchant for the murder mystery characterizes their final television series together—*Murder, She Wrote*. Levinson was quoted by Lisa Belkin in a *New York Times* obituary as describing the renewed public interest in mysteries, and hence, the success of their series: " 'It is definitely a time for mysteries again,' he said. 'There is a the-

ory that during a time of chaos, the orderly procedures of the classic mystery have renewed appeal. I'm not sure I subscribe to that theory. I just think the form has a lot of juice to it. People keep rediscovering it.' "

Although Levinson's death ended his active collaboration with William Link, much of the pair's material lives on, entrancing a new generation of television viewers. Link continues in the entertainment industry, commenting to Stephen Farber in the *New York Times*, "The good thing is, I know how Dick thought about everything. . . . So it's not like I'm just one person. I've still got Dick in my head." About Levinson's approach to his long career, *Murder, She Wrote* co-creator Peter S. Fischer told Belkin in the *New York Times*, "He felt if it was worth doing it was worth doing well."

For more information on Richard Levinson, see the *CA* entry for his partner, William Link, in this volume.

BIOGRAPHICAL/CRITICAL SOURCES:

BOOKS

Levinson, Richard, and William Link, *Stay Tuned: An Inside Look at the Making of Prime-Time Television*, St. Martin's, 1981.
Levinson, Richard, and William Link, *Off-Camera: Conversations with the Makers of Prime-Time Television*, New American Library, 1986.

PERIODICALS

American Film, December, 1983.
Detroit News, January 5, 1986.
Los Angeles Times, March 24, 1986.
New York Daily News, October 24, 1972.
New York Post, October 25, 1974.
New York Times, November 3, 1972; January 31, 1983; July 13, 1987.
Time, November 26, 1973.
Times (London), November 21, 1986.
Washington Post, July 7, 1981; February 22, 1983.

OBITUARIES:

PERIODICALS

Chicago Tribune, March 15, 1987.
Hollywood Reporter, March 16, 1987.
Los Angeles Times, March 13, 1987.
New York Times, March 13, 1987.
Time, March 23, 1987.
Times (London), March 18, 1987.
Washington Post, March 14, 1987.

—*Sketch by Michaela Swart Wilson*

[Sketch reviewed by partner, William Link]

LEWIS-WILLIAMS, J(ames) David 1934-

PERSONAL: Born August 5, 1934, in Cape Town, South Africa. *Education:* University of Cape Town, B.A., 1955, S.T.D., 1956; University of South Africa, B.A. (with honors), 1964; University of Natal, Ph.D., 1978.

ADDRESSES: Home—P.O. Box 1892, Rivonia 2128, South Africa. *Office*—Department of Archaeology, University of the Witwatersrand, Johannesburg 2050, South Africa.

CAREER: Teacher of English at secondary school, East London, South Africa, 1958-63; head of English department at secondary school, Botha's Hill, South Africa, 1964-78; University of the Witwatersrand, Johannesburg, South Africa, lecturer, 1978-80, senior lecturer, 1981-84, reader in cognitive archaeology, 1984-87, professor of cognitive archaeology, 1987—. President of South African Archaeological Society; director of Rock Art Research Unit.

WRITINGS:

Believing and Seeing: Symbolic Meanings in Southern San Rock Paintings, Academic Press, 1981.
The Rock Art of Southern Africa, Cambridge University Press, 1983.
(Editor) *New Approaches to Southern African Rock Art,* South African Archaeological Society, 1983.
(With T. A. Dowson) *Images of Power: Understanding Southern African Rock Art,* Southern Book Publishers, 1989.
Discovering Southern African Rock Art, David Philip, 1990.

Contributor to professional publications, including *Current Anthropology, Proceedings of the Prehistoric Society,* and *L'Anthropologie.*

WORK IN PROGRESS: Research on the nineteenth-century Bleek manuscript of San (Bushman) life and belief, and on Southern African and West European rock art.

SIDELIGHTS: J. David Lewis-Williams once told *CA:* "My interest in archaeology dates back to my undergraduate days, with rock art always being a special interest. Since then I have conducted intensive field research in a number of areas in southern Africa and have studied San beliefs and rituals. It now seems clear that rock art was closely associated with the symbols, power, and hallucinations of San medicine men, or shamans, who entered trances to control game, cure the sick, and make rain. I'm glad to say the work has been well received, though much remains to be done. We are only beginning to understand the complexities of this breathtaking art."

LING, Roger (John) 1942-

PERSONAL: Born November 13, 1942, in Watford, England; son of Leslie James (a laboratory technician) and Kathleen Clara (Childs) Ling; married Lesley Ann Steer (a lecturer), December 30, 1967. *Education:* St. John's College, Cambridge, B.A., 1964, M.A., 1968, Ph.D., 1969. *Politics:* "Indeterminate." *Religion:* "Non-existent." *Avocational interests:* Sports, popular music, cinema, Watford Football Club.

ADDRESSES: Office—Department of History of Art, Victoria University of Manchester, Manchester M13 9PL, England.

CAREER: University of Wales, University College, Swansea, lecturer in classics, 1967-71; Victoria University of Manchester, Manchester, England, senior lecturer in classical art and archaeology, 1971-83, reader, 1983—, professor, 1992—, head of Department of History of Art, 1988-91. Member, Faculty of Archaeology, History, and Letters at British School at Rome, 1974-78, 1981-85.

MEMBER: Association Internationale pour la Peinture Murale Antique (secretary), Society for the Promotion of Roman Studies (member of council, 1978-82), Royal Archaeological Institute, Society of Antiquaries (fellow; member of council, 1988-91), British Pompeii Research Committee, Cambrian Archaeological Association, Derbyshire Archaeological Society (member of council, 1982—), North Derbyshire Archaeological Trust.

AWARDS, HONORS: Rome scholar at British School at Rome, 1965-67; Leverhulm senior research fellow, 1986-87; British Academy research reader, 1991-93.

WRITINGS:

The Greek World, Phaidon, 1976, revised edition published as *Classical Greece,* Phaidon, 1988.
(Editor with T. C. B. Rasmussen) Axel Boethius, *Etruscan and Early Roman Architecture,* Penguin, 1978.
(With Norman Davey) *Wall Painting in Roman Britain,* Society for the Promotion of Roman Studies, 1982.
The Hellenistic World to the Coming of the Romans: Cambridge Ancient History, Part 1, Cambridge University Press, 1984.
Romano-British Wall Painting, Shire Publications, 1985.
(Editor) Donald E. Strong, *Roman Art,* Penguin, 1986.
Roman Painting, Cambridge University Press, 1991.

Contributor to numerous books, including *Roman Crafts,* edited by Strong and David Brown, Duckworth, 1976; *Papers in Italian Archaeology,* edited by H. M. Blake, T. W. Potter, and D. B. Whitehouse, British Archaeological Reports, 1978; *Roman Urban Topography in Britain and the Western Empire,* edited by Francis Grew and Brian Hobley, Council for British Archaeology, 1985; *The Oxford*

History of the Classical World, edited by J. Broadman, J. Griffin, and O. Murray, Oxford University Press, 1986; *Civilization of the Ancient Mediterranean,* edited by Michael Cerant and Rachel Kitzinger, Scribner, 1988; and *Architecture and Architectural Sculpture in the Roman Empire,* edited by Martin Henig, Oxford University Committee for Archaeology, 1990.

Also contributor of articles and reviews to archaeology and classical studies journals.

WORK IN PROGRESS: The Iusula of the Menander at Pompeii, Volume 1.

SIDELIGHTS: Roger Ling told *CA:* "Though brought up in the traditional school of classical archaeology, which concentrates on classical art to the exclusion of the other material remains of antiquity, I find this an unduly blinded and restrictive approach. I am interested in all the material evidence of life in the past, in the various techniques by which that evidence is collected, and in the social and economic conclusions that can be drawn from it. Art is only one aspect of the evidence, and to focus solely on the aesthetic and stylistic development of art is a sterile exercise. Yet for too long excavations of classical sites have been entrusted to people trained in art history rather than in archaeological techniques, and for too long publications have concentrated on spectacular and artistic discoveries rather than on the anonymous bric-a-brac of everyday life. Only in recent years has there come a greater awareness of the value of, say, statistical studies of animal and human bones or distribution patterns of coarse pottery fabrics. But this, in my opinion, is the stuff from which history can be reconstructed."

*   *   *

LINK, William 1933-

PERSONAL: Born December 15, 1933, in Philadelphia, PA; son of William (a textile broker) and Elsie (Roerecke) Link; married Margery Nelson (a producer), 1980. *Education:* University of Pennsylvania, B.S.

ADDRESSES: Office—Universal Studios, Universal City, CA 91608. *Agent*—Bill Haber, Creative Artists Agency, 9830 Wilshire Blvd., Beverly Hills, CA 90212.

CAREER: Writer of short stories and plays; writer and co-producer of teleplays. Columbia Broadcasting System, Inc. (CBS-TV), New York City, creator, with Richard Levinson, of *Mannix* television series, 1967-75; National Broadcasting Company, Inc. (NBC-TV), New York City, creator, with Levinson, of television series *The Bold Ones,* 1969-73, and *The Psychiatrist,* 1971, creator and producer, with Levinson, of television series *Tenafly,* 1971, and

Columbo, 1971-76, developer and producer, with Levinson, of television series *Ellery Queen,* 1975-76, and, with Peter S. Fischer, *Murder, She Wrote,* 1983-89; Richard Levinson/William Link Productions, Los Angeles, CA, co-president, beginning 1978. Supervising producer, "ABC Mystery Movie." *Military service:* U.S. Army, 1956-58.

MEMBER: National Academy of Television Arts and Sciences (member of board of governors), Writers Guild of America, Caucus for Writers, Producers, and Directors.

AWARDS, HONORS: All with Richard Levinson— Emmy Award, 1970, for *My Sweet Charlie,* and 1972, for *Columbo* script; Image Award, National Association for the Advancement of Colored People (NAACP), 1970, for *My Sweet Charlie;* Golden Globe Award, Hollywood Foreign Press Association, 1972, for *Columbo* and *That Certain Summer;* Silver Nymph Award, Monte Carlo Film Festival, 1973, for *That Certain Summer;* George Foster Peabody Award, University of Georgia, 1974, for *The Execution of Private Slovik;* Edgar Awards, Mystery Writers of America, 1979, 1980, 1983; Christopher Award, 1981, for *Crisis at Central High;* Tony Award nomination, 1983, for *Merlin;* Paddy Chayefsky Laurel Award, Writers Guild of America, 1986, for advancing literature of television; Ellery Queen Award, Mystery Writers of America, 1989, for lifetime contribution to the art of the mystery.

WRITINGS:

WITH RICHARD LEVINSON

Prescription: Murder (three-act play; also see below), Samuel French, 1963.
Fineman (novel), Laddin Press, 1972.
Stay Tuned: An Inside Look at the Making of Prime-Time Television, St. Martin's, 1981.
(Authors of book) *Merlin* (two-act musical play), produced on Broadway, 1983.
The Playhouse (novel), Berkeley, 1984.
Guilty Conscience: A Play of Suspense in Two Acts, Samuel French, 1985.
Off-Camera: Conversations with the Makers of Prime-Time Television, New American Library, 1986.

TELEPLAYS; WITH LEVINSON

Prescription: Murder, National Broadcasting Company, Inc. (NBC-TV), 1968.
My Sweet Charlie, NBC-TV, 1970.
That Certain Summer, American Broadcasting Companies, Inc. (ABC-TV), 1972.
(And executive producers) *The Execution of Private Slovik,* NBC-TV, 1974.
(And executive producers) *The Gun,* ABC-TV, 1974.

(And executive producers) *Murder by Natural Causes,*
Columbia Broadcasting System, Inc. (CBS-TV),
1979.

(And executive producers with David Susskind) *Crisis at
Central High* (based on book of same title by Elizabeth Huckaby), CBS-TV, 1981.

(And executive producers) *Rehearsal for Murder,*
CBS-TV, 1982.

(And executive producers) *Take Your Best Shot,* CBS-TV,
1982.

Prototype, CBS-TV, 1983.

Blacke's Magic, NBC-TV, 1986.

The United States of America vs. Salim Ajami, CBS-TV,
1988.

For the Boys, ABC-TV, 1990.

OTHER

Also author, with Levinson, of teleplay for movie *Vanishing Act.* Also contributor, with Levinson, of more than one
hundred scripts for television series developed by others
as well as themselves, including *General Motors Presents,
Westinghouse Desilu Playhouse, Dr. Kildare, The Fugitive,
The Rogues, Mannix, Columbo, Murder, She Wrote,
Blacke's Magic,* and *The Alfred Hitchcock Hour.* Contributor of more than thirty short stories to periodicals, including *Playboy.*

ADAPTATIONS: Rehearsal for Murder was adapted as
Rehearsal for Murder: A Full-Length Play by D. D.
Brooke, and as the play *Killing Jessica* by David Rodgers;
Murder by Natural Causes was adapted as *Murder by Nat-
ural Causes: A Full-Length Play* by Tim Kelly.

WORK IN PROGRESS: Clive Barker's Devil's Night, for
ABC-TV; *The Courtmartial of Johnson Whitaker,* for
Showtime; *Penn and Teller's "Hocus Pocus,"* a television
series, for ABC-TV; *Shooting Script,* a novel.

SIDELIGHTS: William Link and Richard Levinson,
writing partners for forty years prior to Levinson's death
in March, 1987, met in school in Philadelphia and began
creating plays and short stories together as teens. In an interview with Stephen Farber for the *New York Times,*
Link commented, "I think we were the oldest team in Hollywood. . . . We met the first day of junior high school.
I saw Dick almost every day of my life since then." Their
lifelong writing association went from writing plays in junior high school to college journalism assignments, and
shortly thereafter, to military service together. After their
individual discharges from the service, they collaborated
on their first "big" break, a television Army script entitled
Chain of Command, which they sold to Desilu Playhouse.

Their subsequent writing/producing career focused on
television, where they became best known as the creators
of the bumbling-yet-astute cigar-chomping Lieutenant

Columbo. The show, which stars Peter Falk in the title
role as the resourceful, unassuming detective, ran for
seven seasons. In addition to their success with the series
Columbo, Link and Levinson were also responsible for
writing and producing some of the most highly-regarded
television movies ever made. Their scripts often tackled
controversial social issues, including *My Sweet Charlie,*
which focuses on an interracial romance, *That Certain
Summer,* acknowledged as the first serious television
treatment of homosexual characters, and *The Gun,* which
graphically details the dangers of handgun abuse. They
have received numerous prestigious entertainment awards
for their television work, including two Emmys, two Golden Globes, an unprecedented number of Edgar Awards,
and the George Foster Peabody Award.

The process of creating and producing network television,
a highly collaborative venture, can often prove equally
frustrating. In their book *Stay Tuned: An Inside Look at
the Making of Prime-Time Television,* Link and Levinson
explore their career as "hyphenates" (an entertainment industry term for an individual who performs two or more
jobs, such as writer/producer) and describe some of their
conflicts with network executives and others who would
alter the writers' work. "The most amusing and revealing
story in the book," asserts Don Shirley in a *Washington
Post* review of *Stay Tuned,* "relates a confrontation between the authors and two academics who were called in
by ABC to make sure all bases were covered in the network's presentation of 'That Certain Summer'. . . . The
professional watchdogs applauded [such aspects of the
script as] the 'oral sex symbolism . . .'—features the authors did not realize they had written. But the professors
also strongly urged the addition of a homophobic character as a nod toward 'balance.' For the most part, Levinson
and Link resisted. But they did add a line in which the father told his son that he would not have chosen homosexuality had he been given a choice—a concession that [the
authors] later deeply regretted."

Link and Levinson shared their project responsibilities
equally, with each contributing elements of plot and dialogue; they also worked jointly with networks and personnel. Over the years, they learned the secrets of successful
collaboration to avoid offending each other. In an interview with Marc Gunther in the *Detroit News,* Link remarked, "We don't get hurt anymore because we know it
(criticism) has nothing to do with one of us personally."
But, after some three decades concentrating on television
writing prior to Levinson's death, the creative duo saw
their share of compromise. As they described in an *American Film* interview: (Levinson) "If somebody should say,
'I'm going to direct [your script] just the way you write
it, and I love it, it's wonderful, we're going to make it, and

you guys go home and relax . . . ' " (Link) "We'll have him committed."

The quieter, more reserved half of the pair, Link complemented Levinson's extroverted enthusiasm. While they specialized in television series and made-for-TV movies, the pair also co-wrote novels, feature films, stage plays, a Broadway musical, and memoirs. Since Levinson's death, Link has continued in the same vein. At the time Levinson died, the pair was working on the three-hour television movie *The United States of America vs. Salim Ajami.* Link told Stephen Farber in the *New York Times* that although he wondered initially if he could face completion of the film alone, he "hurled himself into the project. I found myself doing the same things Dick and I had always done—making a little change here and there, watching dailies, working with the actors. . . . I've got energy and my health. I still have ideas. Why would I retire?" Link added: "I've still got Dick in my head. . . . I'm never going to lose Dick."

For more information on William Link, see the *CA* entry for his partner, Richard Levinson, in this volume.

BIOGRAPHICAL/CRITICAL SOURCES:

BOOKS

Link, William, and Richard Levinson, *Stay Tuned: An Inside Look at the Making of Prime-Time Television,* St. Martin's, 1981.
Link, William, and Richard Levinson, *Off-Camera: Conversations with the Makers of Prime-Time Television,* New American Library, 1986.

PERIODICALS

American Film, December, 1983.
Detroit News, January 5, 1986.
Los Angeles Times, March 24, 1986.
New York Daily News, October 24, 1972.
New York Post, October 25, 1974.
New York Times, November 3, 1972; January 31, 1983; July 13, 1987.
Time, November 26, 1973.
Times (London), November 21, 1986.
Washington Post, July 7, 1981; February 22, 1983.

—*Sketch by Michaela Swart Wilson*

*   *   *

LOCKWOOD, C. C. 1949-

PERSONAL: Born June 26, 1949, in Kansas City, MO; son of Franklin Markquis (a doctor) and Mary Spring (a homemaker; maiden name, Crafts) Lockwood. *Education:* Louisiana State University, B.S., 1971, graduate study,

1972; attended East Texas State University, 1972. *Religion:* Episcopalian.

ADDRESSES: Office—P.O. Box 14876, Baton Rouge, LA 70898.

CAREER: Free-lance wildlife photographer and writer, 1971—. Lecturer at national, state, and local conventions, seminars, workshops, and conferences relating to wildlife, photography, and the environment. Photographs displayed in exhibitions.

MEMBER: National Audubon Society (past president and founder of Baton Rouge, LA, chapter).

AWARDS, HONORS: San Francisco International Film Festival award, Columbus International Film Festival award, Virgin Islands International Film Festival award, Cindy Award from Information Film Producers of America, AV Learning Award, and Golden Eagle Award from Council on International Nontheatrical Events, all 1977, all for film *Atchafalaya: America's Largest River Basin Swamp;* Ansel Adams Award, Sierra Club, 1978, for conservation photography; Louisiana Literary Award for Book of the Year, Louisiana Library Association, 1981, for book *Atchafalaya: America's Largest River Basin Swamp; The Gulf Coast* was named a notable book of 1984, American Library Association.

WRITINGS:

(Self-illustrated with photographs) *Atchafalaya: America's Largest River Basin Swamp,* Beauregard Press, 1982.
(Self-illustrated with photographs) *The Gulf Coast: Where Land Meets Sea,* Louisiana State University Press, 1984.
Louisiana, Louisiana State University Press, 1986.
(Self-illustrated with photographs) *Discovering Louisiana,* Louisiana State University Press, 1986.
(Self-illustrated with photographs) *The Yucatan Peninsula,* Louisiana State University Press, 1989.

Contributor to books. Author and director of film *Atchafalaya: America's Largest River Basin Swamp,* released by Cactus Clyde Productions in 1977. Photographer and author of text for annual calendars "Skywatch," 1992, "Skywatch," 1993, and "Skywatch," 1994, all for Fulcrum Press. Contributor to more than one hundred periodicals, including *National Geographic.*

WORK IN PROGRESS: Louisiana Nature Guide for Kids, for Louisiana State University Press; "Skywatch" calendar for 1995.

SIDELIGHTS: C. C. Lockwood once told *CA:* "It started as a labor of love. My favorite place was the Atchafalaya Swamp, a massive wetland, beautiful but in great peril. I'd glide quietly through its silt-laden waters in my brown and green camouflage canoe, experiencing the peacefulness and noticing the encroaching development. With my paddle, my pen, and my camera, I studied the swamp for three years. Then, while living on a houseboat, I compiled my first book, *Atchafalaya: America's Largest River Basin Swamp*. I've always hoped that *Atchafalaya* would do more good than paying my grocery bills, for I felt a book would be the best way to educate the city folks on the life cycle of the swamp and its creatures great and small. Now I find the medium of books as the most natural way to get my photographs and meager writings displayed."

BIOGRAPHICAL/CRITICAL SOURCES:

PERIODICALS

American Photographer, November, 1984.
Louisiana Life, May/June, 1981.

* * *

LOCKWOOD, Margo 1939-

PERSONAL: Born January 16, 1939, in Boston, MA; daughter of Charles D. (a tunnel worker) and Margaret (a clerk-typist; maiden name, McCormick) Nyhan; married George F. Lockwood (a painter), May 22, 1960 (died, 1969); children: James, Jennifer, Juliet, Jonathan. *Education:* University of Massachusetts at Boston, B.A., 1973. *Politics:* Democrat. *Religion:* Roman Catholic.

ADDRESSES: Home—11 Goodwin Place, Brookline, MA 02146. *Office*—Alice James Books, 138 Mount Auburn St., Cambridge, MA 02138.

CAREER: Cricket Press, Boston, MA, co-founder and -owner, 1960-68; Horse in the Attic Bookshop, Brookline, MA, owner, 1975-86; associated with Alice James Books, Cambridge, MA, 1979—; secretary to the Catholic Chaplain, Massachusetts Institute of Technology, 1989-1993. Founder, Horse in the Attic Press, 1990—; co-founder, Impressions Workshop, 1960.

MEMBER: International PEN, New England Poetry Society.

WRITINGS:

POETRY

Three Poems Written in Ireland, Menhaden Press, 1977.
Temper (bound with *Openers* by Nina Nyhart), Alice James Books, 1979.
Bare Elegy, illustrated by Ray Metzger, Janus Press, 1981.
Eight Poems, illustrated by son, James Lockwood, Menhaden Press, 1982.
Black Dog, Alice James Books, 1986.
Left-Handed Happiness, Dirty Dish Press (Stanford, CA), 1987.

SIDELIGHTS: Poet Margo Lockwood once described her work to *CA* as "the Irish-American experience cast into high relief (and comic relief)." Widowed at the age of 30, Lockwood found herself suddenly a single parent with four children to support. "Before that I ran a fine arts atelier and letterpress printing business and arts gallery in Boston during the 1960s. Since then I have been writing books and selling secondhand and occasional rare books. This description makes me hyperventilate and wonder how it all happened." Lockwood sold her bookshop in 1986, and several years later founded Horse in the Attic Press, where she was able to publish the posthumous poetry of Ross Urquhart, one of her former students.

* * *

LORD, Bette Bao 1938-

PERSONAL: Born November 3, 1938, in Shanghai, China; immigrated to United States, 1946; naturalized U.S. citizen, 1964; daughter of Sandys (a Nationalist Chinese government official) and Dora (Fang) Bao; married Winston Lord (assistant secretary for Asian and Pacific affairs; former U.S. ambassador to People's Republic of China), May 4, 1963; children: Elizabeth Pillsbury, Winston Bao. *Education:* Tufts University, B.A., 1959; Fletcher School of Law and Diplomacy, M.A., 1960. *Avocational interests:* Dancing, photography.

ADDRESSES: Home—740 Park Ave. #2A, New York, NY 10021. *Agent*—Irving Paul Lazar Agency, 120 El Camino, Suite 216, Beverly Hills, CA 90212.

CAREER: Writer and lecturer. University of Hawaii, East-West Cultural Center, Honolulu, assistant to director, 1961-62; Fulbright Exchange Program, Washington, DC, program officer, 1962-63. Taught and performed modern dance in Geneva, Switzerland, and Washington, DC, 1964-73; conference director, National Conference for the Associated Councils of the Arts, 1970-71. Member of selection committee, White House Fellows, 1979-81; has served on the board of trustees for the Asia Foundation and the Committee of 100; member of board of trustees, Freedom House (and chair), Asia Society, Aspen Institute, and Freedom Forum (and member selection committee for Free Spirit Awards); National Committee on United States-China Relations, Inc., served as a special consultant to CBS News, 1989.

MEMBER: Council on Foreign Relations, PEN, Authors Guild, Organization of Chinese Americans.

AWARDS, HONORS: National Graphic Arts prize, 1974, for photographic essay on China; American Book Award nomination (first novel), 1982, for *Spring Moon;* honorary LL.D., Tufts University, 1982, Bryant College, 1990, Dominican College, 1990, Marymount College, 1992, and Skidmore College, 1992; named Woman of the Year, Chinatown Planning Council, 1982; Distinguished Americans of Foreign Birth Award, 1984; Distinguished American Award, International Center, 1984; honorary doctorate, University of Notre Dame, 1985; Jefferson Cup Award, American Library Association, 1985, and Book of the Year citation, Child Study Association of America, 1987, both for *In the Year of the Boar and Jackie Robinson;* American Women for International Understanding Award, 1988; U.S.I.A. Award for Outstanding Contributions, 1988; inducted into International Women's Hall of Fame, 1989; *Legacies: A Chinese Mosaic* was named one of *Time* magazine's ten best nonfiction books of 1990; Exceptional Achievement Award, Women's Project and Productions, 1992; Literary Lion citation, New York Public Library, 1992.

WRITINGS:

(With sister, Sansan Bao) *Eighth Moon: The True Story of a Young Girl's Life in Communist China,* Harper, 1964.

Spring Moon: A Novel of China, Harper, 1981.

In the Year of the Boar and Jackie Robinson (children's book), illustrated by Marc Simont, Harper, 1984.

Legacies: A Chinese Mosaic (nonfiction), Knopf, 1990.

Spring Moon has been translated into eighteen languages, *Eighth Moon* into fifteen languages, and *Legacies: A Chinese Mosaic* into ten languages.

WORK IN PROGRESS: The Middle Heart, a novel of China.

SIDELIGHTS: The writings of Bette Bao Lord, a chronicler of modern Chinese life and the experiences of Chinese in the United States, have proved popular with both critics and readers. Born in Shanghai, Lord moved with her family to the United States when she was eight years old. Her infant sister, Sansan, remained in China and was forced to stay with foster parents when the Communist revolution broke out. Lord had no contact with her sister until Sansan finally rejoined her family in 1962. Because she thought that Sansan's experiences in China—years of hard manual labor and waiting in long food ration lines— would provide readers with stories and insights they might never encounter otherwise, Lord tried to find someone to write her sister's biography; when she was unable to, she chose to write Sansan's story herself rather than let the idea fade. In the *New York Times Book Review,* Peggy Durdin wrote that the resulting work, *Eighth Moon,* "tells volumes about what is happening in Communist China through the little human details of how Sansan lived and worked and thought."

Lord's next book—her first novel—was originally planned as a nonfiction account of a trip she took to China in 1973. Fearing that her relatives might be punished by the oppressive Communist government because of certain biographical aspects of the book, Lord decided to write a historical novel instead. *Spring Moon,* set against the backdrop of the cultural and political upheavals that have troubled China during the past century, traces the destruction of the country's upper-middle-class structure and the traditional family system by concentrating on five generations of the aristocratic Chang family. Spring Moon Chang, an inquisitive nine-year-old when the novel begins, spends her childhood within her family's walled compound and is taught, according to Merryl Maleska in *Chicago Tribune Book World,* that "at all costs, the family and its honor must be preserved" and to view "yielding as a strength, not a weakness." Though Chinese history informs the plot of the novel, Charlotte Curtis noted in the *New York Times Book Review* that "the author's chief concern is with the Changs themselves, and how they feel, think and change through the years." This transformation is best reflected in the contrast between Spring Moon, who remains true to her Confucian ideals, and Lustrous Jade, her daughter, who becomes a Communist revolutionary. (In one example of this contrast, Lustrous Jade participates in Mao Tse-tung's Long March, something Spring Moon could not have done because the old social ritual of binding the feet of young girls had rendered her unable to do more than hobble.) "The interest of Mrs. Lord's novel lies precisely here," explained Joey Bonner in *New Republic,* "in her depiction of the clashes between Spring Moon and her daughter, old values and new, which constitute a principal motif of modern Chinese history." And, in *Saturday Review,* Ronal Nevans admired *Spring Moon*'s poignancy and restraint, praising the book as "one of the most remarkable novels ever to explain the East to the West."

"If the heroine of [*Spring Moon*] had been transferred to America as a little girl . . . she would have managed, I think, in much the same way as Shirley Temple Wong," wrote Jean Fritz in the *New York Times Book Review* of Lord's children's novel, *In the Year of the Boar and Jackie Robinson.* A semiautobiographical story, *In the Year of the Boar* relates the experiences of a ten-year-old Chinese girl whose family immigrates to New York in 1947. At first, Shirley, who speaks only Chinese and finds it difficult to absorb the American culture suddenly surrounding her, is ignored by her classmates. But once she begins speaking English and learning to play baseball, she is accepted and eventually honored by being chosen to present Jackie Robinson, her hero, with a key to the school. Critics praised Lord's portrayal of Shirley and the difficulties she has fitting into her new environment. Fritz wrote that "the story is warm and pleasant, and young readers will love Shirley."

Lord returned to nonfiction for her next book, *Legacies: A Chinese Mosaic,* a selection of oral histories culled from 600 audio tapes that the author collected while in Beijing with her husband, the U.S. ambassador to China from 1985 to 1989. The narratives, some told by Lord's close relatives, describe the cruel repression many Chinese citizens experienced under the Great Proletarian Cultural Revolution of the 1960s and 1970s. As Lord was collecting the stories in the spring of 1989, Chinese students piled into Tiananmen Square in protest of the still-oppressive government. A million fellow citizens joined in the demonstration, but the square was emptied on June 4—just days after Lord's return to the U.S.—when the Communist Party ordered the people's army to open fire on the protesters.

"When Americans saw the people in Tiananmen Square last year, they saw just a sea of black-haired people," Lord told Catharine Reeve in the *Chicago Tribune.* "I felt that I had to write *Legacies* because I wanted to put faces and stories with what happened there." The oral histories are often horrific. Lord's aunt, a teacher, is made to stand in an awkward "takeoff" position for hours a day on a stage before her Red Guard students. A young girl whose father has been branded a "rightist" ignores him and only realizes that the state, not her father, is corrupt after she collects his ashes from the prison in which he spent the Cultural Revolution. A scholar shunned by his family after having spent eight years in a labor camp experiences several breakdowns and is placed in a nursing home where he writes a 400,000 word study on ancient poetry which he has to conceal in a quilt.

Lord deliberately organized *Legacies* so that readers would draw parallels between China's current situation and the horrors of the Cultural Revolution. Each chapter opens with a description of events in 1989, which is then followed by one of the oral histories Lord gathered. The accounts hold no foreshadowing of the uprising that was just about to occur though they were told in the hope that readers of Lord's book would remember the political struggles of the past and then bar similar occurrences from happening in the future. *New York Times* contributor Christopher Lehmann-Haupt quoted one of Lord's friends, who spoke to the author hours after shots were fired in Tiananmen Square: "Warn Americans not to be fooled. Warn them not to judge by what will be said and what will be seen. Those men [the Chinese leaders] are masters at orchestrating a misery all the more insidious because it is silent and invisible."

Legacies was warmly received by critics. "Evocatively written, laced with wit and bitter humor, terrifying in

their candor," wrote *Los Angeles Times Book Review* contributor Carolyn Wakeman, "[Lord's] stories of broken lives reveal the human consequences of China's once glorious effort to usher in a bright socialist future." Sandra Burton, writing in *Time,* identified *Legacies* as "a vivid and startling mosaic of the political struggles that foreshadowed the Tiananmen Square uprising." And in the *New York Times Book Review,* Linda Mathews called *Legacies'* stories "stunning" and the book itself "franker, more penetrating and infinitely sadder than most journalistic accounts of the brave and tragic uprising at Tiananmen Square."

Though a successful writer of both fiction and nonfiction based on Chinese culture and politics, Lord recognizes and appreciates the gift that coming to the U.S. was for her. "I have often thought," she told Reeve, "that if I had not left China, any one of these people in [*Legacies*] could have been me."

BIOGRAPHICAL/CRITICAL SOURCES:

BOOKS

Bestsellers 90, Issue 3, Gale, 1990.
Contemporary Literary Criticism, Volume 23, Gale, 1983.

PERIODICALS

Best Sellers, September 15, 1964.
Chicago Tribune, July 10, 1986; April 1, 1990, p. 5; June 3, 1990, section 6, pp. 1, 8.
Chicago Tribune Book World, November 22, 1981.
Christian Science Monitor, November 9, 1981.
Globe and Mail (Toronto), June 9, 1990.
Los Angeles Times, September 7, 1987; November 24, 1988.
Los Angeles Times Book Review, October 18, 1981; April 29, 1990, pp. 2, 9.
New York, March 26, 1990, p. 84.
New Yorker, November 23, 1981.
New York Times, August 30, 1981; December 2, 1981; October 14, 1986; March 26, 1990.
New York Times Book Review, September 27, 1964; October 25, 1981; November 11, 1984, p. 47; April 15, 1990, p. 9.
People, November 23, 1981.
Publishers Weekly, October 20, 1981.
Saturday Review, October, 1981.
Time, March 12, 1990, p. 75.
Washington Post, September 2, 1987.
Washington Post Book World, October 11, 1981; January 13, 1988, p. 9; April 22, 1990, p. 1, 14.*

—Sketch by Roger M. Valade III

LORRAH, Jean

PERSONAL: Born in Canton, OH; daughter of Walter and Marie (Unger) Lorrah. *Education:* Western Reserve University (now Case Western Reserve University), B.A., 1962, M.A., 1963; Florida State University, Ph.D., 1968.

ADDRESSES: Home—P.O. Box 625, Murray, KY 42071. *Office*—Department of English, Murray State University, Murray, KY 42071.

CAREER: English teacher at private school, Montverde, FL, 1963-66, department head, 1964-66; Murray State University, Murray, KY, assistant professor, 1968-72, associate professor, 1972-80, professor of English, 1980—. Judge for the Andre Norton Fantasy/SF Short Story Award, 1993.

MEMBER: International Association for the Fantastic in the Arts, Modern Language Association of America, National Writers Club, Science Fiction Writers of America, American Name Society, South Atlantic Modern Language Association.

WRITINGS:

NOVELS

(With Jacqueline Lichtenberg) *First Channel,* Doubleday, 1980.
Savage Empire, Playboy Press, 1981.
Channel's Destiny, Doubleday, 1982.
Dragon Lord of the Savage Empire, Playboy Press, 1982.
Captives of the Savage Empire, Berkley Publishing, 1984.
The Vulcan Academy Murders, Pocket Books, 1984.
Ambrov Keon, DAW Books, 1986.
(With Winston A. Howlett) *Flight to the Savage Empire,* Signet Books, 1986.
Sorcerers of Frozen Isles, Signet Books, 1986.
(With Lichtenberg) *Zelerod's Doom,* DAW Books, 1986.
(With Howlett) *Wulfston's Odyssey,* Signet Books, 1987.
Empress Unborn, Signet Books, 1988.
The IDIC Epidemic, Pocket Books, 1988.
Survivors, Pocket Books, 1989.
Metamorphosis, Pocket Books, 1990.

OTHER

Contributor to books, including *The Keeper's Price,* edited by Marion Zimmer Bradley, DAW Books, 1980; *The Scope of the Fantastic,* edited by Collins and Pearce, Greenwood Press, 1981; and *Hecate's Cauldron,* edited by Susan Shwartz, DAW Books, 1981. Contributor to magazines, including *Dragon.* Associate editor, *Pandora,* 1981-88.

WORK IN PROGRESS: Blood Will Tell and *Snow Job.*

SIDELIGHTS: Jean Lorrah once commented: "I have had the incredible good fortune to have the field of litera-ture that I love, science fiction, open to me both creatively and academically in the past few years. I have been reading and writing science fiction since my teens; in the 1970s, pioneering women authors broke through the subject-theme barrier against the *kind* of science fiction I write, and opened the field to me. Meanwhile, via popular culture, the world of academe was becoming responsive to research in a field now called 'the fantastic.' Suddenly I can write what I want and be published, and research what I want and be published. Could anyone be more fortunate? I particularly owe a debt to Jacqueline Lichtenberg, whose allowing me to collaborate with her in a universe she created helped me to my first creative publication."

*   *   *

LOUISE, Heidi
See ERDRICH, Louise

*   *   *

LOVELACE, Earl 1935-

PERSONAL: Born July 13, 1935, in Toco, Trinidad; married; children: three. *Education:* Studied at Howard University, 1966-67, and Johns Hopkins University, 1974.

CAREER: Novelist, journalist, playwright, and short story writer; lecturer at University of the West Indies, 1982—. Has also worked as proofreader for Trinidad Publishing Co., a forest ranger, and an agricultural assistant for the Jamaican Civil Service. Instructor at Federal City College, Washington, DC, 1971-73, and Johns Hopkins University. Writer in residence, University of Iowa's Writers Program.

AWARDS, HONORS: British Petroleum Independence Award, 1965, for *While Gods Are Falling;* Guggenheim fellowship, 1980.

WRITINGS:

While Gods Are Falling (novel), Collins, 1965, Regnery, 1966.
The Schoolmaster (novel), Regnery, 1968.
The Dragon Can't Dance (novel), Deutsch, 1979, Three Continents Press, 1981.
The Wine of Astonishment (novel), Heinemann, 1982.
Jestina's Calypso and Other Plays (plays; also see below; includes "The New Hardware Store," "My Name Is Village," and "Jestina's Calypso"), Heinemann, 1984.
The New Hardware Store, produced in London, 1985.
Brief Conversion and Other Stories, Heinemann, 1988.

SIDELIGHTS: Born in Toco, Trinidad, Earl Lovelace has been hailed by numerous critics as one of the Caribbean's more gifted and talented writers. "Earl Lovelace is primarily a wonderful storyteller," states John J. Figueroa in *Contemporary Novelists.* "He holds one's interest whether through exciting dialogue which rings true, or by his descriptive ability and his portrayal of the inner conflicts which puzzle his characters."

According to Daryl Cumber Dance in his book, *Fifty Caribbean Writers: A Bio-Bibliographical Critical Sourcebook:* "The major theme in Earl Lovelace's work is the quest for personhood, a term which he prefers to *manhood* or *identity* and which he describes as 'man's view of himself, the search as it were for his integrity.' . . . Frequently, however, this quest is threatened as his characters encounter the impersonal, dehumanizing urban world."

For the most part, Lovelace sets his writings in his homeland of Trinidad or in one of the neighboring Caribbean islands. Julius Lester comments in the *New York Times Book Review* that Lovelace is "a writer of consummate skill. A native of Trinidad, Mr. Lovelace writes about his homeland from the inside, creating characters with whom the reader quickly identifies despite differences of race, place and time."

Lovelace's *The Schoolmaster* is a novel about the building of a school in the remote Trinidad village of Kumaca. "Lovelace's *The Schoolmaster* is set in Trinidad and is a real story-teller's novel, moving with grace from a gently sentimental beginning to a tragic climax," declares A. S. Byatt in the *New Statesman.* Martin Levin remarks in the *New York Times Book Review* that "*The Schoolmaster* is a folk fable with the clean, elemental structure of Steinbeck's *The Pearl.* But unlike *The Pearl,* Mr. Lovelace tells his story from the inside looking out, using the unsophisticated accents of everyday speech to lead to a Homeric conclusion." Levin added that Lovelace is a "writer of elegant skills, with an infectious sensitivity to the heady Caribbean atmosphere."

The Dragon Can't Dance tells the story of the poor and discouraged people of Calvary Hill as they attempt to renew their heritage, culture, and sense of community by participating in Carnival, an annual celebration commemorating the crucifixion and resurrection of Jesus Christ. Daryl Cumber Dance suggests that "Lovelace's most successful treatment of the quest for personhood comes in *The Dragon Can't Dance.*" Dance goes on to note that Lovelace "has powerfully revealed the folk of Calvary Hill and involved us in their lives in such a meaningful and moving manner that we appreciate their traditions, applaud their victories, suffer their defeats, rejoice in their growth, and acknowledge their personhood. Here too, as in all of his previous works, he has successfully captured the sights and sounds and rhythms of Trinidad in a captivating tale, often tragic, but also often relieved by the comic tone, style, language, and interludes that are vintage Lovelace."

Lovelace's next novel, *The Wine of Astonishment,* is perhaps the most well-known work to readers living outside the Caribbean. This novel follows a Bonasse peasant woman as she witnesses the repercussions that result after the government denies members of the Spiritual Baptists the right to worship their religion.

"The novel's basic theme is the clash between the tradition and the modern, between cultural integrity and assimilation, in the village of Bonasse," explains Julius Lester in the *New York Times Book Review.* "In *The Wine of Astonishment*—written entirely in the soft sibilance of Trinidadian speech—Mr. Lovelace sensitively and perceptively explores ancient conflicts, both personal and political."

Writing in the *Washington Post Book World,* Donald McCaig notes that *The Wine of Astonishment* "is written in patois, a musical dialect, full of sweet metaphors. It's lovely stuff to read aloud. And it can put the reader where he's never been before." McCaig also remarks that "Lovelace's idiomatic prose forces his reader to understand another people from the inside out. That's a good trick, and only the best novelists can do it."

BIOGRAPHICAL/CRITICAL SOURCES:

BOOKS

Contemporary Literary Criticism, Volume 51, Gale, 1989, pp. 266-272.
Contemporary Novelists, St. James Press, 1986, pp. 545-546.
Dance, Daryl Cumber, editor, *Fifty Caribbean Writers: A Bio-Bibliographical Critical Sourcebook,* Greenwood Press, 1986, pp. 276-283.

PERIODICALS

New Statesman, January 5, 1968, p. 15.
New York Times Book Review, October 30, 1966, p. 76; November 24, 1968, pp. 68-69; January 6, 1985, p. 9.
Times (London), March 12, 1985.
Washington Post Book World, March 6, 1988, p. 7.*

*   *   *

LOVELL, Ann 1933-

PERSONAL: Born December 11, 1933, in Bristol, England; daughter of Claude Lascelles (a theatre company manager) and Elsie (an actress; maiden name, Hewett) Scott-Buccleuch; married August 8, 1959 (divorced, 1975); children: Frank, Sara, Simon, Stephen (adopted). *Education:* University of Leeds, B.A. (with first class honors), 1955; graduate study at Cambridge University,

1955-58. *Politics:* "Mildly socialist." *Religion:* Church of England. *Avocational interests:* Opera, books, good food, good discussion, France, Somerset.

ADDRESSES: Home—3 Victoria Villas, St. Thomas Street, Wells, Somerset BA5 2UZ, England. *Agent*—Juliet Burton, Laurence Pollinger Ltd., 18 Maddox Street, London W1R OEU, England.

CAREER: J. Walter Thompson Co., Ltd., London, England, copywriter, 1958-61; chairperson of National Childbirth Trust, Chiltern branch, 1964-65.

AWARDS, HONORS: Lost and Found: The Story of a Family after Divorce was runner-up for the Delta Kappa Gamma Society's International Educator's Award, 1985.

WRITINGS:

In a Summer Garment: The Experience of an Autistic Child, Secker & Warburg, 1978, published as *Simple Simon,* Lion Publishing, 1983.
Lost and Found: The Story of a Family after Divorce, Gollancz, 1985.
Flying Time (novel), Gollancz, 1988.
Sun-Trap (novel), Gollancz, 1990.

Also author of documentary film, broadcast by Southern Television, and contributor of segments to series "Light of Experience" and "Light of Experience Revisited," British Broadcasting Co., both based on *In a Summer Garment;* contributor of segments based on *Lost and Found* to series "The Human Factor," Independent Television. Contributor of stories and articles to popular magazines and newspapers.

Lovell's works have been published in Finland, Denmark, Poland, Czechoslovakia, and Korea.

WORK IN PROGRESS: Simple Simon Grows Up, a sequel to *Simple Simon;* autobiography of war-time childhood, *The Big Ship Sailed;* a novel.

SIDELIGHTS: Ann Lovell once told *CA:* "I am intensely interested in all problems connected with handicapped or deprived children and in the social revolution which has brought about the existence of a new class of poor—the one-parent family. In Britain women rearing children on their own suffer immense, unjust handicaps. I want to help put this right. I am passionately interested in music, particularly when it is used as a therapy for children with problems.

"The outbreak of war in 1939 meant for me, at the age of five, a childhood deprived of security and continuity of affection, but led directly to an overwhelming love of the safer world of books and to writing as a means of coming to terms with an often unbearable reality. I began to write when I was eight and never wanted to be anything other

than a writer, although I seem nowadays to do a lot of public speaking as well, on the subject of autism for the most part.

"I only reached maturity both as an individual and as a writer in my early thirties when my beautiful and much-loved eldest child, then four years old, was diagnosed as autistic. The struggle to come to terms with this, the harshest blow I had yet been dealt, involved a total change of values and way of life. I found, by chance, the key to describing this modern 'Pilgrim's Progress' in a beautiful passage in William Langland's fourteenth-century poem, 'The Vision of Piers Plowman.' In it, the poet sees the vulnerability of the mentally handicapped and bids mankind love them." After her children had grown and left home, Lovell moved to Somerset, which she has loved since first evacuated there as a child during the war. "And with much more time for writing, which is heaven," she told *CA.* "I now live close to one of the most beautiful and historic cathedrals in England—a daily inspiration."

In a Summer Garment: The Experience of an Autistic Child is an account of Lovell's struggle to accept her child's autism. She describes "the impact of the diagnosis on her life, her other children, and her marriage," observes Anthony Clare in *Listener,* who adds that the tale "is told simply and economically and with great effect." And Nesta Roberts, writing in the *Times Literary Supplement,* calls *In a Summer Garment* "a rare book, brave, honest, poignant, as compelling for the reader as it must have been therapeutic for the writer."

"In middle age, writing remains a therapy for me," Lovell once commented to *CA.* "As a lone mother with four children, I know a great deal about isolation. I find that in coming to terms with myself and my own life, I can often help other people. Montaigne gave me that prescription—Connais-toi, toi meme—perhaps it is the prerequisite for any writer who has something to say. My own favorite modern writers are Paul Scott, Iris Murdoch, Angela Carter, Margaret Atwood, Alice Thomas Ellis, and Sara Paretski, all of whom I feel are in touch essentially with their own humanity, though in differing ways. The qualities I most admire are profundity of emotion held in apparent utter simplicity of style—like a slow movement from Mozart."

BIOGRAPHICAL/CRITICAL SOURCES:

PERIODICALS

British Book News, May, 1978; March, 1985.
Listener, February 23, 1978.
Times (London), March 2, 1978.
Times Literary Supplement, November 9, 1984.

LOWENTHAL, David 1923-

PERSONAL: Born April 26, 1923, in New York, NY; son of Max (a lawyer) and Eleanor (Mack) Lowenthal; married Mary Alice Lamberty (an editor), 1970; children: Eleanor. *Education:* Harvard University, B.S., 1943; University of California, Berkeley, M.A., 1950; University of Wisconsin—Madison, Ph.D., 1953.

ADDRESSES: Home—56 Crown St., Harrow-on-the-Hill, Middlesex, England. *Office*—Department of Geography, University College, University of London, 26 Bedford Way, London WC1H 0AP, England.

CAREER: U.S. Department of State, Washington, DC, research analyst, 1945; Vassar College, Poughkeepsie, NY, assistant professor of geography and chairman of department, 1952-56; American Geographical Society, New York City, research associate, 1956-72; University of London, London, England, professor of geography, 1972-85. Columbia University, seminars associate, 1957-72, chairman of Seminar on American Civilization, 1960-61; visiting professor at Massachusetts Institute of Technology, 1966, Clark University, 1966 and 1969, University of California, Berkeley, 1969 and 1977, Syracuse University and City University of New York, both 1971, University of Minnesota—Twin Cities, 1972, and University of Washington, Seattle; associate research professor at Harvard University, 1966-68; Regents' Lecturer at University of California, Davis, 1973; Katz Distinguished Professor of Humanities, University of Washington, 1988. Maconochie Foundation, member, 1962—, president, 1973; Caribbean consultant to U.S. Peace Corps, 1958-67; consultant to Institute for Race Relations, London, England, and Resources for the Future. *Military service:* U.S. Army, 1943-45.

MEMBER: American Geographical Society (fellow; secretary, 1967-72), American Association for the Advancement of Science (member of council, 1964-71), Association of American Geographers (member of council, 1964-71), American Historical Association, American Studies Association, Society for Caribbean Studies (chairman, 1977-79), English Heritage Historic Landscape (member of advisory committee, 1989—), Landscape Research Group (chairperson, 1984-89).

AWARDS, HONORS: Fulbright fellow at University College of the West Indies (now University of the West Indies), 1956-57; Herfurth Award from University of Wisconsin—Madison, 1959, award from Geographical Society of Chicago, 1960, and meritorious contribution award from Association of American Geographers, 1960, all for *George Perkins Marsh: Versatile Vermonter;* Guggenheim fellow, 1965-66; Historic Preservation Book Prize, 1989, for *The Past Is a Foreign Country.*

WRITINGS:

George Perkins Marsh: Versatile Vermonter (biography), Columbia University Press, 1958.

The Vermont Heritage of George Perkins Marsh, Woodstock Historical Society, 1960.

West Indian Societies, Oxford University Press, 1972.

Publications in Environmental Perception, eight volumes, American Geographical Society, 1972.

The Past Is a Foreign Country, Cambridge University Press, 1985.

EDITOR

The West Indies Federation: Perspectives on a New Nation, Columbia University Press, 1961.

George P. Marsh, *Man and Nature,* Harvard University Press, 1965.

Environmental Perception and Behavior, Department of Geography, University of Chicago, 1967.

(With Lambros Comitas) *West Indian Perspectives,* four volumes, Doubleday/Anchor Press, 1973.

(With Martyn J. Bowden) *Geographies of the Mind,* Oxford University Press, 1975.

(With wife, Mary Alice Lamberty, and Bowden) *Geography in Honor of John Kirtland Wright,* Oxford University Press, 1976.

(With Marcus Binney) *Our Past Before Us: Why Do We Save It?,* Temple Smith, 1981.

(With E. C. Penning-Rowsell) *Landscape Meanings and Values,* Allen & Unwin, 1986.

(With Peter Gatherdole) *The Politics of the Past,* Unwin Hyman, 1989.

OTHER

Contributor to numerous books, including *The Expanding City,* edited by J. Patten, Academic Press, 1983; *Earth as Transformed by Human Action,* B. L. Turner, editor, Cambridge University Press, 1990; *Museum Collecting Policies in Modern Science and Technology,* edited by Francesca Riccini, London Science Museum, 1991; and *The Political Economy of Small Tropical Islands,* edited by Helen Hintjens and Malyn Newitt, University of Exeter Press, 1992.

Also contributor to many journals, including *Apollo, Journal of American History, Perspecta, Pacific Viewpoint,* and *Anthropology and the Future.* Co-editor of *International Journal of Cultural Property.*

WORK IN PROGRESS: Heritage.

SIDELIGHTS: The author of a biography of George Perkins Marsh, David Lowenthal told *CA:* "George Perkins Marsh was the pioneer conservationist in America. As a nineteenth-century Vermont congressman and later U.S. ambassador to Turkey and to Italy, he was the first to see the consequences of human impact on the face of the earth and the need for restoration of a harmonious balance. I became interested in Marsh for that reason and also because he early advocated an understanding of history, from the ground up, through the analysis of everyday artifacts and the life stories of ordinary people."

Also the author of works on the West Indies, Lowenthal added: "The West Indies seemed a remarkable laboratory for understanding how life takes different social and cultural forms among people in islands quite similar in their terrain, resources, and histories and differentiated mainly by accidents of European settlement and language. I still believe that islands provide unique chances for understanding of this and other kinds.

"*Geographies of the Mind* reflects the awareness that we all inhabit a world not to be understood in terms of its physical characteristics alone, but of the perceptions and attitudes we form about environments, places, and peoples."

*   *   *

LOYN, H(enry) R(oyston) 1922-
(Henry Loyn, Henry R. Loyn)

PERSONAL: Born June 16, 1922, in Cardiff, Wales; son of Henry George and Violet Monica Loyn; married Patricia Beatrice Haskew, 1950; children: Richard, John, Christopher. *Education:* University College, Cardiff, University of Wales, M.A., 1949, D.Litt., 1968.

ADDRESSES: Home—25 Cunningham Hill Rd., St. Albans, Hertfordshire, England AL1 5BX.

CAREER: University of Wales, University College, Cardiff, assistant lecturer, 1946-49, lecturer, 1949-61, senior lecturer, 1961-66, reader, 1966-69, professor of medieval history, 1969-77, dean of students, 1968-70, 1975-76; University of London, London, England, professor of history, 1977-87, vice-principal of Westfield College, 1980-86. Member of Ancient Monuments Board for England, 1982-84.

MEMBER: Society of Antiquaries (fellow, vice-president), Royal Historical Society (fellow, vice president, 1983-87), British Academy (fellow), Historical Association (president, 1975-79), Society for Medieval Archaeology (president, 1983-86), Glamorganshire Historical Society (president, 1975-77), Cardiff Naturalists Society (president, 1975-76), St. Albans Archaeologists and Archaeological Society (president, 1989-92), Athenaeum Club.

WRITINGS:

Anglo-Saxon England and the Norman Conquest, Longmans, Green, 1962, revised edition, 1991.
The Norman Conquest, Hutchinson, 1965, 3rd edition, 1982.
(Under name Henry Loyn) *Norman Britain,* illustrations by Alan Sorrell, Lutterworth, 1966.
Alfred the Great, Oxford University Press, 1967.
(Editor under name Henry R. Loyn) *A Wuljstan Manuscript Containing Institutes, Laws, and Homilies,* Rosenkilde & Bagger, 1971.
(Editor with Harry Hearder) *British Government and Administration,* University of Wales Press, 1974.
(With John Percival) *The Reign of Charlemagne,* Edward Arnold, 1975.
The Vikings in Britain, Batsford, 1977, revised edition, Basil Blackwell, 1993.
(With Sorrell and Richard Sorrell) *Medieval Britain,* Lutterworth, 1977.
The Governance of Anglo-Saxon England, 500-1087, Edward Arnold, 1984.
(Author of introduction) *Domesday Book* (facsimile), Alecto Press, 1986.
(Editor) *The Concise Encyclopedia of the Middle Ages,* Thames & Hudson, 1989.
The Making of the English Nation, Thames & Hudson, 1991.
Society and Peoples: Studies in the History of England and Wales, c. 600-1200, Queen Mary and Westfield College, University of London, 1992.

Contributor to history journals.

SIDELIGHTS: H. R. Loyn once told *CA:* "My interest in medieval social history stemmed initially from a deep interest in the development of language, particularly Anglo-Saxon and Old Norse. As a historian my prime concern was and remains with the development of Western European society. It is hard to say how my studies differ from those of other people. Concern with archaeological evidence, numismatic evidence, and linguistic evidence is a feature of all of them.

"My main concern in *The Vikings in Britain* was to place the Viking movement of the West in a full British context—that is to say, to bring fully into the picture the Viking impact on the Celtic communities as well as on the Anglo-Saxon. Generally, my picture of European and British societies tends to stress the continuous development towards more ordered structures in Western Europe."

BIOGRAPHICAL/CRITICAL SOURCES:

PERIODICALS

Times Literary Supplement, August 31, 1984.

LOYN, Henry
   See LOYN, H(enry) R(oyston)

*   *   *

LOYN, Henry R.
   See LOYN, H(enry) R(oyston)

*   *   *

LUCKLESS, John
   See BURKHOLZ, Herbert

*   *   *

LUDLUM, Robert 1927-
   (Jonathan Ryder, Michael Shepherd)

PERSONAL: Born May 25, 1927, in New York, NY; son of George Hartford (a businessman) and Margaret (Wadsworth) Ludlum; married Mary Ryducha (an actress), March 31, 1951; children: Michael, Jonathan, Glynis. *Education:* Wesleyan University, B.A., 1951. *Politics:* Independent.

ADDRESSES: Home—Naples, FL. *Agent*—Henry Morrison, Box 235, Bedford Hills, NY 10507.

CAREER: Writer, 1971—. Actor on Broadway and on television, 1952-60; North Jersey Playhouse, Fort Lee, NJ, producer, 1957-60; producer in New York City, 1960-69; Playhouse-on-the-Mall, Paramus, NJ, producer, 1960-70. *Military service:* U.S. Marine Corps, 1944-46.

MEMBER: Authors Guild, Authors League of America, American Federation of Television and Radio Artists, Screen Actors Guild.

AWARDS, HONORS: New England Professor of Drama Award, 1951; awards and grants from American National Theatre and Academy, 1959, and from Actors' Equity Association and William C. Whitney Foundation, 1960; Scroll of Achievement, American National Theatre and Academy, 1960.

WRITINGS:

The Scarlatti Inheritance, World Publishing, 1971.
The Osterman Weekend, World Publishing, 1972.
The Matlock Paper, Dial, 1973.
(Under pseudonym Jonathan Ryder) *Trevayne,* Delacorte, 1973.
(Under pseudonym Jonathan Ryder) *The Cry of the Halidon,* Delacorte, 1974.
The Rhinemann Exchange, Dial, 1974.
(Under pseudonym Michael Shepherd) *The Road to Gandolfo,* Dial, 1975, reprinted under name Robert Ludlum, Bantam, 1982.

The Gemini Contenders, Dial, 1976.
The Chancellor Manuscript, Dial, 1977.
The Holcroft Covenant, Richard Marek, 1978.
The Matarese Circle, Richard Marek, 1979.
The Bourne Identity, Richard Marek, 1980.
The Parsifal Mosaic, Random House, 1982.
The Aquitaine Progression, Random House, 1984.
The Bourne Supremacy, Random House, 1986.
The Icarus Agenda, Random House, 1988.
The Bourne Ultimatum, Random House, 1990.
The Road to Omaha, Random House, 1992.

ADAPTATIONS: The Rhinemann Exchange was adapted as a television miniseries by NBC, 1977; *The Osterman Weekend* was filmed by EMI, 1980; *The Bourne Supremacy,* read by Michael Prichard, was released on cassette tape by Books on Tape, 1986; an abridged version of *The Bourne Identity,* read by Darren McGavin, was released on cassette tape by Bantam, 1987, and is also being adapted for television; *The Icarus Agenda,* read by Prichard, was released on cassette by Books on Tape, 1988; *The Bourne Identity* was adapted for television, c. 1989; *The Bourne Ultimatum,* read by Prichard, was released on cassette by Books on Tape, 1990; *The Road to Omaha,* read by Joseph Campanella, was released by Random House, 1992; *The Scarlatti Inheritance* was filmed by Universal Pictures.

SIDELIGHTS: Suspense novelist Robert Ludlum "has his share of unkind critics who complain of implausible plots, leaden prose, and, as a caustic reviewer once sneered, an absence of 'redeeming literary values to balance the vulgar sensationalism,' " Susan Baxter and Mark Nichols noted in *Maclean's.* "But harsh critical words have not prevented Robert Ludlum . . . from becoming one of the most widely read and wealthiest authors in the world." In fact, with sales of his books averaging 5.5 million copies each, Ludlum is "one of the most popular living authors [writing] in the English language," Baxter and Nichols concluded.

Authorship came as a second career for Ludlum, who worked in the theater and found success as a producer before writing his first novel at age forty-two. His most notable production, Bill Manhoff's *The Owl and the Pussycat,* featured then unknown actor Alan Alda, who later gained fame for his role in the television series, *M*A*S*H.* The play was performed at Playhouse-on-the-Mall in Paramus, New Jersey, the country's first theater in a shopping center, which Ludlum opened in 1960. After serving as producer at the Playhouse for ten years, Ludlum found himself bored and frustrated with the pressures of theater work. Finally, he gave in to his wife's admonition to try his hand at writing.

The Scarlatti Inheritance, Ludlum's first novel, was written around an old story idea and outline, drafted years earlier and finally fleshed out when he left the theater. Based on Ludlum's curiosity at the wealth of one group of Germans during that country's economic collapse and skyrocketing inflation following World War I, *The Scarlatti Inheritance* follows several financiers, including some Americans, who fund Hitler's Third Reich. The book set the pattern for Ludlum's career: the story of espionage and corruption became a best-seller. Criticism of *The Scarlatti Inheritance* also foreshadowed that of future works. The book was described by Patricia L. Skarda in *Dictionary of Literary Biography Yearbook: 1982* as having a "somewhat erratic pace and occasionally melodramatic characterizations" but was nonetheless "a thrilling, compelling tale"—pronouncements typical of each of Ludlum's novels.

In his next work, *The Osterman Weekend,* a television reporter is convinced by the CIA that his friends are involved in a conspiracy to control the world economy and agrees to gather evidence against them, but finds himself in over his head when his wife and children are threatened. Though the book's ending is considered disappointing by several reviewers, William B. Hill, writing in *Best Sellers,* noted, "If the ending is a bit weak, it is chiefly because it lets the rider down off a very high horse." Skarda pointed out that the story "exposes the inadequacies of American intelligence operations and our deepest fears that our friends cannot be trusted." Government agents again use a civilian as an investigator in a situation beyond his expertise in *The Matlock Paper.* Professor Matlock is pushed "into an untenable and dangerous situation" while snooping around campus for information on a group of crime bosses, Kelly J. Fitzpatrick related in *Best Sellers.* "The climax is effective and leaves the reader wondering, 'Can it be so?' " Yet Newgate Callendar countered in the *New York Times Book Review,* "The basic situation is unreal—indeed, it's unbelievable—but a good writer can make the reader suspend his disbelief, and Ludlum is a good writer."

Trevayne and *The Cry of the Halidon,* both written under the pseudonym Jonathan Ryder, feature protagonists who discover they were hired not for their skills, but in hopes that they would be unable to uncover the truth about their employers. Andrew Trevayne, appointed to investigate spending by the U.S. Defense Department, uncovers a company so powerful that even the president of the United States is controlled by it. "There is no doubt that big business exerts an inordinate amount of pressure," Callendar contended in a *New York Times Book Review.* "But how much pressure? Who is really running the country?" Reviewing *The Cry of the Halidon,* in which a young geologist is sent to Jamaica to conduct an industrial survey and

winds up in the crossfire of British Intelligence, the corporation that hired him, and various underground factions, Callendar disparaged Ludlum's "rather crude and obvious writing style," and commented, "[Ludlum] is not very good at suggesting real characters, and his hero is a cutout composite of a number of sources." A reviewer for *Publishers Weekly* found that, early on in *The Cry of the Halidon,* "cleverness ceases to look like a virtue and becomes an irritant. If the writing were as rich or subtle as the plot is involved the reader might more happily stay the course . . . , but the writing is in fact rather bare." Ludlum's final pseudonymous offering (this time writing as Michael Shepherd), *The Road to Gandolfo* is "a strange, lurching amalgam of thriller and fantasy," Henri C. Veit contended in *Library Journal.* Involving the Pope, the Mafia, and the U.S. Army, the book is intended to be funny, but falls short, Veit continued. A *Publishers Weekly* reviewer similarly noted that the book "comes crammed with zaniness and playful characters, but, unhappily, neither asset produces comedy or the black humor indictment of the military mind the author intended."

The Rhinemann Exchange contains "one extremely ingenious plot gimmick," according to Callendar in *New York Times Book Review,* in which the United States and Germany arrange a trade—industrial diamonds for Germany, a weapons guidance system for the United States. Despite the author's "commonplace and vulgar style apparently much relished by his vast audience," Veit predicted in a *Library Journal* review that the book would be a success. In a review of the audio version of *The Rhinemann Exchange,* a *Publishers Weekly* contributor believed Ludlum fans "will find exactly what they're looking for—in a format already quite familiar." A secret with devastating consequences, described by Irma Pascal Heldman in *New York Times Book Review* as "absolutely within the realms of authenticity and fascinating to contemplate," is the key to *The Gemini Contenders.* Twin brothers, compelled by their father's deathbed wish to find a hidden vault containing a volatile document, unleash the secret on the world. Despite criticizing the plot, characters, and period detail of *The Gemini Contenders,* reviewer T. J. Binyon commented in the *Times Literary Supplement* that Ludlum "has the ability to tell a story in such a way as to keep even the fastidious reader unwillingly absorbed."

In *The Chancellor Manuscript* Ludlum returned to remaking history as he had in *The Scarlatti Inheritance.* J. Edgar Hoover's death is found to be an assassination, not the result of natural causes as was previously believed. The murder was carried out to prevent Hoover from releasing his secret files, which, *Christian Science Monitor*'s Barbara Phillips noted, "contain enough damaging information to ruin the lives of every man, woman and child in the nation." A group of prominent citizens join forces to retrieve the files but find half have already been stolen. An unsuspecting decoy is deployed, as in many other Ludlum stories, to lead the group to the thieves. The message of *The Chancellor Manuscript* is familiar to Ludlum fans, as the book "seems to justify our worst nightmares of what really goes on in the so-called Intelligence Community in Washington," Richard Freedman maintained in the *New York Times Book Review.*

The Bourne Identity, which introduced a trilogy of books, follows Bourne, a spy who awakens in a doctor's office with amnesia; the story is played out as a remarkable number of killers and organizations attempt to finish Bourne off before he realizes his true identity. "Some of Mr. Ludlum's previous novels were so convoluted they should have been packaged with bags of bread crumbs to help readers keep track of the plot lines," Peter Andrews mused in the *New York Times Book Review.* "But *The Bourne Identity* is a Ludlum story at its most severely plotted, and for me its most effective." The second volume, *The Bourne Supremacy,* forces Bourne to face his past when his wife is kidnapped. The final story in the "Bourne" trilogy, *The Bourne Ultimatum,* finds Bourne drawn into one last battle with his arch-enemy, the Jackal. The *Los Angeles Times Book Review*'s Don G. Campbell praised the third "Bourne" book as an example of "how it *should* be done," concluding that "in the pulse-tingling style that began so many years ago with *The Scarlatti Inheritance,* we are caught up irretrievably."

A woman comes back from the dead and a spy in the White House threatens humanity's continued existence in *The Parsifal Mosaic.* "Certainly, millions of entranced readers tap their feet in time to his fiction, and I'm positive this new adventure will send his legions of fans dancing out into the streets," Evan Hunter remarked in the *New York Times Book Review.* "Me? I must be tone-deaf." A world takeover is again imminent in *The Aquitaine Progression,* this time at the hands of five military figures. "Ludlum's hero, Joel Converse, learns of a plot by generals in the United States, Germany, France, Israel and South Africa to spawn violent demonstrations. Once the violence bursts out of hand, the generals plan to step in and take over," Charles P. Wallace wrote in the *Los Angeles Times Book Review. The Icarus Agenda* features a similar plot. This time, five wealthy, powerful figures arrange the election of the next United States president. "There is a sufficient amount of energy and suspense present in *The Icarus Agenda* to remind the reader why Mr. Ludlum's novels are best sellers," Julie Johnson commented in the *New York Times Book Review.* "Ludlum is light-years beyond his literary competition in piling plot twist upon plot twist," Peter L. Robertson commented in the *Tribune Books,* "until the mesmerized reader is held captive, willing to accept any wayward, if occasionally implausible,

plotting device." In a more recent offering, *The Road to Omaha,* Ludlum departs from the seriousness of his espionage thrillers with a follow-up to *The Road to Gandolfo* that continues that novel's farcical tone. The Hawk and Sam, Ludlum's heroes in *Gandolfo,* return to fight the government for a plot of land legally belonging to an Indian tribe. In a review of the audio version of *The Road to Omaha,* a *Publishers Weekly* reviewer noted, "Hardcore Ludlum fans may be taken aback at first, but they stand to be won over in the listening."

The key elements of Ludlum's books—corruption in high places, elaborate secret plans, and unsuspecting civilians drawn into the fray—are what keep Ludlum fans waiting for his next offering. His writing, characterized by the liberal use of exclamation points, italics, sentence fragments, and rhetorical questions, has been described by some critics as crude, but others acknowledge that the style is popular with millions of readers and has proven difficult to duplicate, leaving Ludlum with little copycat competition. Still, reviewers often point to Ludlum's use of mixed metaphors and illogical statements as serious flaws in his books. Horror novelist Stephen King, in a somewhat tongue-in-cheek review of *The Parsifal Mosaic* for the *Washington Post Book World,* highlighted some of Ludlum's "strange, wonderful, and almost Zen-like thoughts: 'We've got . . . a confluence of beneficial prerogatives.' 'What I know is still very operative.' 'I'll get you your cover. But not two men. I think a couple would be better.'"

Journalist Bob Woodward, writing in the *Washington Post Book World,* summarized the media's view of Ludlum in a review of *The Icarus Agenda:* "Ludlum justifiably has a loyal following. Reviews of most of his previous books are critical but conclude, grudgingly, that he has another inevitable bestseller." In a review of *The Bourne Identity* for *Washington Post Book World,* Richard Harwood opined, "Whether reviewers are universally savage or effusive seems irrelevant: the book is bound to be a best seller. *The Bourne Identity* . . . is already on both the national and *Washington Post* best-seller lists and the damned thing won't officially be published [for three more days]. So much for the power of the press." Despite reviewers' advice, readers have voiced their approval of Ludlum in sales figures. As Baxter and Nichols noted in *Maclean's,* "For all his imperfections, Ludlum manages—by pumping suspense into every twist and turn in his tangled plots and by demanding sympathy for well-meaning protagonists afflicted by outrageous adversity—to keep millions of readers frantically turning his pages."

BIOGRAPHICAL/CRITICAL SOURCES:

BOOKS

Dictionary of Literary Biography Yearbook: 1982, edited by Richard Ziegfeld, Gale, 1983, pp. 305-316.
Ludlum, Robert, *The Matlock Paper,* Dial, 1973.

PERIODICALS

Best Sellers, April 15, 1973, p. 41; April, 1972, p. 5.
Christian Science Monitor, March 31, 1977, p. 31.
Library Journal, October 1, 1974, p. 2504; April 1, 1975, pp. 694-695.
Los Angeles Times Book Review, March 11, 1984, p. 3; March 23, 1986, p. 3; March 18, 1990, p. 8.
Maclean's, April 9, 1984, pp. 50-52.
New Republic, November 25, 1981, p. 38; September 20, 1982, p. 43.
New York, May 9, 1988, pp. 74-75.

New Yorker, June 20, 1988, pp. 90-92.
New York Review of Books, May 8, 1986, pp. 12-13.
New York Times, March 13, 1978, p. C19.
New York Times Book Review, January 28, 1973, p. 20; May 6, 1973, p. 41; August 4, 1974, p. 26; October 27, 1974, p. 56; March 28, 1976, p. 18; March 27, 1977, p. 8; April 8, 1979, p. 14; March 30, 1980, p. 7; March 21, 1982, p. 11; April 22, 1984, p. 14; March 9, 1986, p. 12; March 27, 1988, p. 16.
Publishers Weekly, April 8, 1974, p. 76; February 10, 1975, p. 52; March 1, 1991, pp. 49-50; March 2, 1992.
Times Literary Supplement, October 1, 1976, p. 1260.
Tribune Books (Chicago), February 28, 1988, Section 14, p. 7.
Washington Post Book World, March 23, 1980, p. 3; March 7, 1982, p. 1; February 21, 1988, p. 1.*

—*Sketch by Deborah A. Stanley*

M

MALCOLM, John
See ANDREWS, John Malcolm

* * *

MALONE, Nola Langner 1930-
(Nola Langner)

PERSONAL: Born September 24, 1930, in New York, NY; daughter of Gerald B. (the owner of an advertising agency) and Elsie (Feigenbaum) Spiero; married Thomas S. Langner (a research professor of sociology at Columbia University), February 21, 1953 (divorced, 1979); remarried; children: (first marriage) Lisa, Josh, Eli, Gretchen and Belinda (twins). *Education:* Attended Vassar College, 1948-50; Bennington College, B.A., 1952.

ADDRESSES: Home and studio—39 East 12th St., New York, NY 10003. *Agent*—Jane Feder, 39 East 12th St., New York, NY 10003.

CAREER: After college worked briefly doing paste-ups for movie magazines published by Ideal Publishing Co., New York City; TV Art Studio, New York City, New York City, illustrator, 1953-54; writer and illustrator of children's books. One-woman show of original art from books at Berkeley (CA) Gallery, 1984.

MEMBER: Author's Guild, PEN, Artist Equity Association.

AWARDS, HONORS: Miss Lucy was named by the *New York Times* as one of the outstanding picture books of 1969; Horn Book Award for illustrations, *Boston Globe,* 1975, for *Scram Kid!;* has also received several awards for her illustrations.

WRITINGS:

SELF-ILLUSTRATED JUVENILES; UNDER NAME NOLA LANGNER

Miss Lucy, Macmillan, 1969.
Go and Shut the Door, Dial, 1971.
Joseph and the Wonderful Tree, Addison-Wesley, 1972.
(Adapter) *Cinderella,* Scholastic Book Services, 1972.
Dusty, Coward, 1976.
Rafiki, Viking, 1977.
Freddy, My Grandfather, Four Winds Press, 1979.
By the Light of the Silvery Moon, Lothrop, 1983.

SELF-ILLUSTRATED JUVENILE BOOKS; UNDER NAME NOLA LANGNER MALONE

A Home, Macmillan, 1988.

OTHER

Also illustrator under name Nola Langner of many juvenile books, including Flora Fifield, *Pictures for the Palace,* Vanguard, 1958; Ann McGovern, *Who Has a Secret?,* Houghton, 1963; McGovern, *Scram Kid!,* Viking, 1974; McGovern, *Half a Kingdom,* Houghton, 1977; and Beverly Keller, *A Small Elderly Dragon,* Lothrop, 1984. Illustrator under name Nola Langner Malone of many juvenile books, including Judith Viorst, *Earrings,* Atheneum, 1990. Also designer and illustrator of pamphlet for Bureau of Child Heath Care, 1984.

SIDELIGHTS: Nola Langner Malone told *CA:* "I think of a book as a small, very condensed movie. I'm very influenced both by my childhood feelings and the child in me and also the way a camera moves, but character of the child—hero (or heroine) is always first for me. The expression on the face, the posture of the body. My books have had foreign editions—*Half a Kingdom* (written by Ann McGovern) had a Zulu edition."

Malone continued: "I think my early gorgeous German children's books influenced me a lot. Somehow, I always knew I wanted to do this. I do painting, printmaking (I love graphics), and drawing whenever I can."

BIOGRAPHICAL/CRITICAL SOURCES:

PERIODICALS

New York Times Book Review, April 10, 1983.

* * *

MAMET, David (Alan) 1947-

PERSONAL: Surname is pronounced "*Mam*-it"; born November 30, 1947, in Chicago, IL; son of Bernard Morris (an attorney) and Lenore June (a teacher; maiden name, Silver) Mamet; married Lindsay Crouse (an actress), December 21, 1977; children: Willa. *Education:* Attended Neighborhood Playhouse School of the Theater, 1968-69; Goddard College, B.A., 1969. *Politics:* "The last refuge of the unimaginative." *Religion:* "The second-to-last."

ADDRESSES: Home—Chicago, IL. *Agent*—Howard Rosenstone, Rosenstone/Wender, 3 East 48th St., New York, NY 10017.

CAREER: Playwright, screenwriter, and director. St. Nicholas Theater Company, Chicago, IL, founder, 1973, artistic director, 1973-76, member of board of directors, beginning 1973; Goodman Theater, Chicago, associate artistic director, 1978-79. Special lecturer in drama, Marlboro College, 1970; artist in residence in drama, Goddard College, 1971-73; faculty member, Illinois Arts Council, 1974; visiting lecturer in drama, University of Chicago, 1975-76 and 1979; teaching fellow, School of Drama, Yale University, 1976-77; guest lecturer, New York University, 1981; associate professor of film, Columbia University, 1988. Has also worked in a canning plant, a truck factory, at a real estate agency, and as a window washer, office cleaner, and taxi driver.

MEMBER: Dramatists Guild, Writers Guild of America, Actors Equity Association, PEN, United Steelworkers of America, Randolph A. Hollister Association.

AWARDS, HONORS: Joseph Jefferson Award, 1975, for *Sexual Perversity in Chicago,* and 1976, for *American Buffalo;* Obie Award, *Village Voice,* for best new playwright, 1976, for *Sexual Perversity in Chicago* and *American Buffalo,* and for best American play, 1983, for *Edmond;* Children's Theater grant, New York State Council on the Arts, 1976; Rockefeller grant, 1976; Columbia Broadcasting System fellowship in creative writing, 1976; New York Drama Critics Circle Award for best American play,

1977, for *American Buffalo,* and 1984, for *Glengarry Glen Ross;* Outer Critics Circle Award, 1978, for contributions to the American theater; Academy Award nomination for best adapted screenplay, Academy of Motion Picture Arts and Sciences, 1983, for *The Verdict;* Pulitzer Prize and Joseph Dintenfass Award, both 1984, for *Glengarry Glen Ross;* Hull-Warriner Award, Dramatists Guild, 1984; Antoinette Perry Award nominations, American Theater Wing, for best play, for *Glengarry Glen Ross,* and for re-production of a play, for *American Buffalo,* both 1984, and for best play, 1988, for *Speed-the-Plow;* American Academy and Institute of Arts and Letters Award for Literature, 1986; Golden Globe Award nomination for best screenplay, 1988, for *House of Games;* Writers Guild Award nomination for best screenplay based on material from another medium, 1988, for *The Untouchables.*

WRITINGS:

PLAYS

Lakeboat (one-act; also see below; produced in Marlboro, VT, 1970; revised version produced in Milwaukee, WI, 1980), Grove, 1981.

Sexual Perversity in Chicago and Duck Variations: Two Plays ("Duck Variations" [one-act], produced in Plainfield, VT, 1972; produced Off-Off-Broadway, 1975; produced with "Sexual Perversity in Chicago" in Louisville, KT, 1976; "Sexual Perversity in Chicago" [one-act; also see below], produced in Chicago, 1974; produced Off-Off-Broadway, 1975), Grove, 1978.

Squirrels (one-act), produced in Chicago, 1974.

The Poet and the Rent: A Play for Kids from Seven to 8:15 (also see below; produced in Chicago, 1974), published in *Three Children's Plays,* Grove, 1986.

American Buffalo (two-act; produced in Chicago, 1975; produced on Broadway, 1977), Grove, 1977.

Reunion [and] *Dark Pony* ("Reunion" [one-act], produced with "Sexual Perversity in Chicago" in Louisville, 1976; "Dark Pony" [one-act], produced with "Reunion" in New Haven, 1977; both produced Off-Broadway with "The Sanctity of Marriage" [also see below], 1979), Grove, 1979.

All Men Are Whores (produced in New Haven, 1977), published in *Short Plays and Monologues,* Dramatists Play Service, 1981.

A Life in the Theatre (one-act; produced in Chicago, 1977; produced Off-Broadway, 1977), Grove, 1978.

The Revenge of the Space Pandas, or Binky Rudich and the Two Speed-Clock (produced in Queens, NY, 1977), Sergel, 1978.

The Water Engine: An American Fable and Mr. Happiness ("The Water Engine" [two-act], produced as a radio play on the program "Earplay" by Minnesota Public Radio, 1977; stage adaptation produced in Chicago,

1977; produced Off-Broadway, 1977; "Mr. Happiness," produced with "The Water Engine" on Broadway, 1978), Grove, 1978.

(And director) *The Woods* (two-act; also see below; produced in Chicago, 1977; produced Off-Broadway, 1979), Grove, 1979.

Lone Canoe, or The Explorer (musical), music and lyrics by Alaric Jans, produced in Chicago, 1979.

The Sanctity of Marriage (one-act), produced Off-Broadway with "Reunion" and "Dark Pony," 1979.

Shoeshine (one-act; produced Off-Off-Broadway, 1979), published in *Short Plays and Monologues,* Dramatist Play Service, 1981.

A Sermon (one-act), produced Off-Off-Broadway, 1981.

Donny March, produced, 1981.

Litko (produced in New York City, 1984), published in *Short Plays and Monologues,* Dramatist Play Service, 1981.

Edmond (also see below; produced in Chicago, 1982; produced Off-Broadway, 1982), Grove, 1983.

Five Unrelated Pieces (includes *Two Conversations, Two Scenes,* and *Yes, But So What*; produced Off-Off-Broadway, 1983), published in *Dramatic Sketches and Monologues,* Samuel French, 1985.

The Disappearance of the Jews (one-act), produced in Chicago, 1983.

The Dog, produced, 1983.

Film Crew, produced, 1983.

4 A.M., produced, 1983.

Glengarry Glen Ross (two-act; produced on the West End, 1983; produced on Broadway, 1984), Grove, 1984.

Vermont Sketches (contains *Pint's a Pound the World Around, Deer Dogs, Conversations with the Spirit World,* and *Dowsing*; produced in New York City, 1984), published in *Dramatic Sketches and Monologues,* Samuel French, 1985.

The Shawl [and] *Prairie du Chien* (one-act plays; produced together at the Lincoln Center, 1985), Grove, 1985.

Vint (one-act; based on Anton Chekov's short story of the same name; produced in New York City with six other one-act plays based on Chekov's short works, under the collective title "Orchards", 1985), also published under same collective title, *Orchards,* Grove, 1986.

Three Children's Plays (includes *The Poet and the Rent: A Play for Kids from Seven to 8:15, The Revenge of the Space Pandas, or Binky Rudich and the Two Speed-Clock,* and *The Frog Prince*), Grove, 1986.

The Woods, Lakeboat, Edmond, Grove, 1987.

(Adaptor) Chekov, *The Cherry Orchard* (produced at Goodman Theatre, 1985), Grove, 1987.

Speed-the-Plow (produced on Broadway, 1988), Grove, 1988.

Where Were You When It Went Down?, produced in New York City, 1988.

(Adaptor) Chekov, *Uncle Vanya,* Grove, 1989.

Goldberg Street, Grove, 1989.

Bobby Gould in Hell, produced in New York with *The Devil and Billy Markham,* by Shel Silverstein, 1989.

Five Television Plays: A Waitress in Yellowstone; Bradford; The Museum of Science and Industry Story; A Wasted Weekend; We Will Take You There, Grove, 1990.

SCREENPLAYS

The Postman Always Rings Twice (adaptation of novel of the same title by James M. Cain), Paramount, 1981.

The Verdict (adaptation of novel of the same title by Barry Reed), Columbia, 1982.

(And director) *House of Games* (produced by Orion, 1987), Grove, 1987.

The Untouchables, Paramount, 1987.

(With Shel Silverstein; and director) *Things Change* (produced by Columbia Pictures, 1988), Grove, 1988.

We're No Angels (produced by Paramount, 1989), Grove, 1990.

OTHER

Warm and Cold (juvenile), illustrations by Donald Sultan, Solo Press, 1984.

(With wife, Lindsay Crouse) *The Owl,* Kipling Press, 1987.

Writing in Restaurants (essays, speeches, and articles), Penguin, 1987.

Some Freaks (essays), Viking, 1989.

On Directing Film, Viking Penguin, 1992.

Cabin, Random House, 1992.

Homicide, Grove, 1992.

Also author of episodes of *Hill Street Blues,* NBC, 1987, and *L.A. Law,* NBC. Contributing editor, *Oui,* 1975-76.

ADAPTATIONS: The film *About Last Night . . . ,* released by Tri-Star Pictures in 1986, was based on Mamet's *Sexual Perversity in Chicago; Glengarry Glen Ross* was adapted for film by New Line, 1992.

SIDELIGHTS: David Mamet has acquired a great deal of critical recognition for his plays, each a microcosmic view of the American experience. "He's that rarity, a pure writer," noted Jack Kroll in *Newsweek,* "and the synthesis he appears to be making, with echoes from voices as diverse as Beckett, Pinter, and Hemingway, is unique and exciting." Since 1976, Mamet's plays have been widely produced in regional theaters and in New York City. His most successful play, *Glengarry Glen Ross,* earned the New York Drama Critics' Circle Award for best American play and the Pulitzer Prize in drama, both in 1984. Critics have also praised Mamet's screenwriting; his adapted screenplay for the film *The Verdict* was nominated for an Academy Award in 1983.

Mamet "has carved out a career as one of America's most creative young playwrights," observed Mel Gussow in the *New York Times,* "with a particular affinity for working-class characters." These characters and their language give Mamet's work its distinct flavor. Mamet is, according to Kroll, "that rare bird, an American playwright who's a language playwright." "Playwriting is simply showing how words influence actions and vice versa," Mamet explained to *People* contributor Linda Witt. "All my plays attempt to bring out the poetry in the plain, everyday language people use. That's the only way to put art back into the theater." Mamet has been accused of eavesdropping, simply recording the insignificant conversations of which everyone is aware; yet, many reviewers recognize the playwright's artistic intent. Jean M. White commented in the *Washington Post,* "Mamet has an ear for vernacular speech and uses cliche with telling effect." Furthermore, added Jack Kroll, "Mamet is the first playwright to create a formal and moral shape out of the undeleted expletives of our foul-mouthed time."

In his personal and creative life, Mamet resists the lure of Broadway, its establishment, and its formulas for success. Chicago, where he was born and grew up and still lives part of the year, serves not only as inspiration for much of his work, but it also provides an accepting audience for Mamet's brand of drama. "Regional theaters are where the life is," he told Robin Reeves in *Us.* "They're the only new force in American theater since the 30s." He added, "Artistically and now commercially, regional theaters are taking over." Yet, despite Mamet's seeming indifference to Broadway and the fact that the language and subject matter of his plays make them of questionable commercial value, several of his plays have been featured on Broadway.

The first of David Mamet's plays to be commercially produced were *Sexual Perversity in Chicago* and *Duck Variations. Sexual Perversity in Chicago* portrays the failed love affair of a young man and woman, each trying to leave behind a relationship with a homosexual roommate. The dialogue between the lovers and their same-sex roommates reveals how each gender can brutally characterize the other. Yet, "the play, itself is not another aspect of the so-called battle of the sexes," observed C. Gerald Fraser in the *New York Times.* "It concerns the confusion and emptiness of human relationships on a purely physical level." Edith Oliver continued, "The piece is written with grace," and she called it "one of the saddest comedies I can remember." In *Duck Variations,* two old Jewish men sit on a bench in Chicago looking out on Lake Michigan. Their observation of the nearby ducks leads them into discussions of several topics. "There is a marvelous ring of truth in the meandering, speculative talk of these old men," maintained Oliver, "the comic, obsessive talk of men who spend most of their time alone, nurturing and indulging their preposterous notions." In the conversation of these men, wrote T. E. Kalem in *Time,* "[Mamet] displays the Pinter trait of wearing word masks to shield feelings and of defying communication in the act of communicating." *Duck Variations* reveals, according to Oliver, that David Mamet is an "original writer, who cherishes words and, on the evidence at hand, cherishes character even more." "What emerges is a vivid sense of [the old men's] friendship, the fear of solitude, the inexorable toll of expiring lives," concluded Kalem.

Mamet emerged as a nationally acclaimed playwright with his two-act *American Buffalo.* "America has few comedies in its repertory as ironic or as audacious as *American Buffalo,*" proclaimed John Lahr in the *Nation.* Set in a junk shop, the play features the shop's owner, an employee, and a friend engaged in plotting a theft; they hope to steal the coin collection of a customer who, earlier in the week, had bought an old nickel at the shop. When the employee fails to tail the mark to his home, the plot falls into disarray and "the play ends in confused weariness," explained Elizabeth Kastor in the *Washington Post.* Although little takes place, Oliver commented in the *New Yorker,* "What makes [the play] fascinating are its characters and the sudden spurts of feeling and shifts of mood—the mounting tension under the seemingly aimless surface, which gives the play its momentum."

American Buffalo confirmed Mamet's standing as a language playwright. Reviewing the play in the *Nation,* Lahr observed, "Mamet's use of the sludge in American language is completely original. He hears panic and poetry in the convoluted syntax of his beleaguered characters." And, even though the language is uncultivated, David Richards contended in the *Washington Post,* "the dialogue [is] ripe with unsettling resonance." As Frank Rich of the *New York Times* remarked, "Working with the tiniest imaginable vocabulary . . . Mr. Mamet creates a subterranean world with its own nonliterate comic beat, life-and-death struggles, pathos and even affection."

In this play, critics also see Mamet's vision of America, "a restless, rootless, insecure society which has no faith in the peace it seeks or the pleasure it finds," interpreted Lahr. "*American Buffalo* superbly evokes this anxious and impoverished world." Its characters, though seemingly insignificant, reflect the inhabitants of this world and their way of life. "In these bumbling and inarticulate meatheads," believed Lahr, "Mamet has found a metaphor for the spiritual failure of entrepreneurial capitalism."

Since its first Chicago production in 1975, *American Buffalo* has been produced in several regional theaters and has had three New York productions. In Mamet's management of the elements of this play, *New York Times* reviewer Benedict Nightingale highlighted the key to its success: "Its idiom is precise enough to evoke a city, a class, a subculture; it is imprecise enough to allow variation of mood and feeling from production to production." Nightingale added in another article, "[American] *Buffalo* is as accomplished as anything written for the American stage over . . . the last 20 years."

In 1979, Mamet was given his first opportunity to write a screenplay. As he told Don Shewey in the *New York Times,* working on the screenplay for the 1981 film version of James M. Cain's novel *The Postman Always Rings Twice* was a learning experience. "[Director Bob Rafelson] taught me that the purpose of a screenplay is to tell the story so the audience wants to know what happens next," Mamet maintained, "and to tell it in pictures." He elaborated, "I always thought I had a talent for dialogue and not for plot, but it's a skill that can be learned. Writing for the movies is teaching me not to be so scared about plots." Mamet's screenplay for *The Postman Always Rings Twice* has received mixed reviews. Its critics often point to, as Gene Siskel did in the *Chicago Tribune,* Mamet's "ill-conceived editing of the book's original ending." Yet, except for the ending, suggested Vincent Canby in the *New York Times,* "Mr. Mamet's screenplay is far more faithful to the novel than was the screenplay for Tay Garnett's 1946 version." Thus, Robert Hatch noted in the *Nation,* "Mamet and Rafelson recapture the prevailing insanity of the Depression, when steadiness of gaze was paying no bills and double or nothing was the game in vogue."

In the 1982 film *The Verdict,* screenwriter Mamet and director Sydney Lumet "have dealt powerfully and unsentimentally with the shadowy state that ideas like good and evil find themselves in today," observed Jack Kroll in *Newsweek.* The film stars Paul Newman as a washed-up lawyer caught in a personal, legal, and moral battle. "David Mamet's terse screenplay for *The Verdict* is . . . full of surprises," contended Janet Maslin in the *New York Times;* "Mamet has supplied twists and obstacles of all sorts." "Except for a few lapses of logic and some melodramatic moments in the courtroom," proclaimed a *People* reviewer, "[this] script from Barry Reed's novel is unusually incisive." Kroll detailed the screenplay's strong points, calling it "strong on character, on sharp and edgy dialogue, on the detective-story suspense of a potent narrative." In a *New Republic* article, Stanley Kauffmann concluded, "It comes through when it absolutely must deliver: Newman's summation to the jury. This speech is terse and pungent: the powerful have the power to convert all the rest of us into victims and that condition probably cannot be changed, but must it always prevail?"

After writing *The Verdict* Mamet began working on his next play, *Glengarry Glen Ross.* Mamet's Pulitzer Prize-winning play is "so precise in its realism that it transcends itself," observed Robert Brustein in the *New Republic,* "and takes on reverberant ethical meanings. It is biting, . . . showing life stripped of all idealistic pretenses and liberal pieties." The play is set in and around a Chicago real estate office whose agents are embroiled in a competition to sell the most parcels in the Florida developments Glengarry Highlands and Glen Ross Farms. "Craftily constructed, so that there is laughter, as well as rage, in its dialogue, the play has a payoff in each scene and a cleverly plotted mystery that kicks in with a surprise hook at its ending," wrote Richard Christiansen in the *Chicago Tribune.*

As in Mamet's earlier plays, the characters and their language are very important to *Glengarry Glen Ross.* In the *Nation,* Stephen Harvey commented on Mamet's ability to create characters who take on a life of their own within the framework of the play: "In *Glengarry,* . . . he adjusts his angle of vision to suit the contours of his characters, rather than using them to illustrate an idea." Mamet told Elizabeth Kastor of the *Washington Post,* "I think that people are generally more happy with a mystery than with an explanation. So the less that you say about a character the more interesting he becomes." Mamet uses language in a similar manner. Harvey noted, "The pungency of Glengarry's language comes from economy: if these characters have fifty-word vocabularies, Mamet makes sure that every monosyllable counts." And, Jack Kroll remarked, "His antiphonal exchanges, which dwindle to single words or even fragments of words and then explode into a crossfire of scatological buckshot, make him the Aristophanes of the inarticulate." Mamet is, according to *New York Times* reviewer Benedict Nightingale, "the bard of modern-day barbarism, the laureate of the four-letter word."

For the real estate agents in *Glengarry Glen Ross,* the bottom line is sales. And, as Robert Brustein noted, "Without a single tendentious line, without any polemical intention, without a trace of pity or sentiment, Mamet has launched an assault on the American way of making a living." Nightingale called the play "as scathing a study of unscrupulous dealing as the American theater has ever produced." The Pulitzer Prize awarded to Mamet for *Glengarry Glen Ross* not only helped increase its critical standing, but it also helped to make the play a commercial success. However, unlike his real estate agents, Mamet is driven by more than money. He told Kastor, "In our interaction in our daily lives we tell stories to each other, we gossip, we complain to each other, we exhort. These are means of defining what our life is. The theater is a way of doing it continually, of sharing that experience, and it's absolutely essential."

In the latter half of the 1980s, Mamet published two collections of essays, *Writing in Restaurants* and *Some Freaks.* Both books are packed with Mamet's fascinating thoughts, opinions, recollections, musings, and reports on a variety of topics such as friendship, religion, politics, morals, society, and of course, the American theater. "The 30 pieces collected in David Mamet's first book of essays contain everything from random thoughts to firmly held convictions," stated Richard Christiansen in his review of *Writing in Restaurants* published in Chicago *Tribune Books,* "but they all exhibit the author's singular insights and moral bearing." Christiansen pointed out that "many of the essays have to do with drama, naturally, but whether he is talking to a group of critics or to fellow workers in the theater, Mamet is always urging his audience to go beyond craft and into a proud, dignified, loving commitment to their art and to the people with whom they work."

Writing for the *Times Literary Supplement,* Andrew Hislop declared that "Mamet has been rightly acclaimed as a great dialoguist and a dramatist who most effectively expresses the rhythms of modern urban American (though the poetic rather than mimetic qualities of his dialogue are often underestimated). The best writing in [*Writing in Restaurants*] comes when he muses on the details of America—and his own life." Hislop continued, "Running through the book is the idea that the purpose of theatre is truth but that the decadence of American society, television and the materialism of Broadway are undermining not just the economic basis but the disciplines and dedication necessary for true theatre."

Some Freaks, Mamet's second collection of essays, was described by Gerald Weales in the *Chicago Tribune* as "a happy encounter." "Freak pieces or life pieces," noted Weales, "what we have here are ruminations on politics, aesthetics, society; recollections of other times; personalized journalistic reports. . . . A grab bag like *Some Freaks* cannot be expected to have the power of *Glengarry Glen Ross* or even *House of Games,* but it provides nice, small pleasures."

A man with numerous creative talents, Mamet has also written stage adaptations for several fictional works by Anton Chekov; made his directorial debut with the 1987 film *House of Games* (for which he also wrote the screenplay), about a psychiatrist's involvement with a con man; penned popstress Madonna's Broadway debut *Speed-the-Plow*; and produced the script for director Brian De Palma's blockbuster gangster epic *The Untouchables.*

BIOGRAPHICAL/CRITICAL SOURCES:

BOOKS

Bock, Hedwig, and Albert Wertheim, editors, *Essays on Contemporary American Drama,* 1981, Max Hueber, pp. 207-223.
Contemporary Authors Bibliographical Series, Volume 3, Gale, 1986.
Contemporary Literary Criticism, Gale, Volume 9, 1978, pp. 360-361, Volume 15, 1980, pp. 355-358, Volume 34, 1985, pp. 217-224, Volume 46, 1988, pp. 245-256.
Dictionary of Literary Biography, Volume 7: *Twentieth-Century American Dramatists,* Gale, 1981, pp. 63-70.

PERIODICALS

Chicago Tribune, October 11, 1987; May 4, 1988; February 19, 1989; December 10, 1989.
Harper's, May, 1978, pp. 79-80, 83-87.
Los Angeles Times, November 27, 1979; June 25, 1984; July 7, 1987; October 11, 1987.
Nation, May 19, 1979, pp. 581-582; April 14, 1981; October 10, 1981; April 28, 1984, pp. 522-523; June 27, 1987, pp. 900-902.
New Republic, July 12, 1982, pp. 23-24; February 10, 1986, pp. 25-26, 28.
Newsweek, February 28, 1977, p. 79; March 23, 1981; November 8, 1982; December 6, 1982; April 9, 1984, p. 109; October 19, 1987.
New York, December 20, 1982, pp. 62, 64; June 8, 1987, pp. 68-69.
New Yorker, November 10, 1975; October 31, 1977, pp. 115-116; January 16, 1978; October 29, 1979, p. 81; June 15, 1981; November 7, 1983; June 29, 1987, pp. 70-72.
New York Times, July 5, 1976; March 18, 1979; April 26, 1979; May 26, 1979; June 3, 1979; October 19, 1979; March 20, 1981; May 29, 1981; June 5, 1981; February 17, 1982; May 17, 1982; June 17, 1982; October 24, 1982; October 28, 1982, p. C20; December 8, 1982; May 13, 1983; October 9, 1983, pp. 6, 19; November 6, 1983; March 26, 1984, p. C17; March 28, 1984; April 1, 1984; April 18, 1984; April 24, 1984; September 30, 1984; February 9, 1986; April 23, 1986; January 1, 1987; March 15, 1987; June 3, 1987; October 11, 1987; May 4, 1988; December 4, 1989.
New York Times Book Review, December 17, 1989.
People, November 12, 1979; December 20, 1982; May 4, 1987.
Saturday Review, April 2, 1977, p. 37.
Time, July 12, 1976; April 9, 1984, p. 105.
Times Literary Supplement, January 29, 1988.
Tribune Books (Chicago), January 18, 1987.
Us, January 10, 1978.
Village Voice, July, 1976, pp. 101, 103-104.

Washington Post, May 4, 1988.*

* * *

MANNING-SANDERS, Ruth 1895(?)-1988

PERSONAL: Born in 1895 (some sources say 1888), in Swansea, Wales; died October 12, 1988, in Penzance, Cornwall, England; daughter of a minister; married George Manning-Sanders (an artist and writer; died, 1952); children: Joan, David. *Education:* Attended Manchester University.

ADDRESSES: Home—1 Morrab Terrace, Penzance, Cornwall, England.

CAREER: Poet and novelist prior to World War II, and author of books for children, 1948-88. Worked for two years with Rosaire's Circus, England.

AWARDS, HONORS: Blindman International Poetry Prize, 1926, for *The City.*

WRITINGS:

POETRY

The Pedlar and Other Poems, Selwyn & Blount, 1919.
Karn, Leonard and Virginia Woolf, 1922.
Pages from the History of Zachy Trenoy, Christophers, 1923.
The City, Dial Press, 1927.

ADULT BOOKS

The Twelve Saints, E. J. Clode, 1926.
Selina Pennaluna, Christophers, 1927.
Waste Corner, Christophers, 1927, E. J. Clode, 1928.
Hucca's Moor, Faber & Gwyer, 1929.
The Crochet Woman, Coward-McCann, 1930.
The Growing Trees, Morrow, 1931.
She Was Sophia, Cobden-Sanderson, 1932.
Run Away, Cassell, 1934.
Mermaid's Mirror, Cassell, 1935.
The Girl Who Made an Angel, Cassell, 1936.
Elephant: The Romance of Laura (short stories), F. A. Stokes, 1938.
Children by the Sea, illustrated by Mary Shepard, Collins, 1938, published in United States as *Adventure May Be Anywhere,* F. A. Stokes, 1939.
Luke's Circus, Collins, 1939, Little, Brown, 1940.
Mystery at Penmarth, illustrated by Susanne Suba, McBride, 1941.
Circus Book (nonfiction), Collins, 1947, published in United States as *The Circus,* Chanticleer Press, 1948.
The West of England (nonfiction), Batsford, 1949.
The River Dart (nonfiction), Westaway Books, 1951.
Seaside England (nonfiction), Batsford, 1951.
Mr. Portal's Little Lions, Hale, 1952.

The Golden Ball, Hale, 1954.
Melissa, Hale, 1957.

JUVENILE BOOKS

Swan of Denmark: The Story of Hans Christian Andersen, illustrated by Astrid Walford, Heinemann, 1949, McBride, 1950, published as *The Story of Hans Andersen, Swan of Denmark,* Dutton, 1966.
The English Circus, Laurie, 1952.
Peter and the Piskies: Cornish Folk and Fairy Tales, illustrated by Raymond Briggs, Oxford University Press, 1958, Roy, 1966.
Circus Boy, illustrated by Annette Macarthur-Onslow, Oxford University Press, 1960.
Red Indian Folk and Fairy Tales, illustrated by C. Walter Hodges, Oxford University Press, 1960, Roy, 1962.
Animal Stories, illustrated by Macarthur-Onslow, Oxford University Press, 1961, Roy, 1962.
A Book of Giants, illustrated by Robin Jacques, Methuen, 1962, Dutton, 1963.
The Smugglers, illustrated by William Stobbs, Oxford University Press, 1962.
A Book of Dwarfs, illustrated by Jacques, Methuen, 1963, Dutton, 1964.
A Book of Dragons, illustrated by Jacques, Methuen, 1964, Dutton, 1965.
Damian and the Dragon: Modern Greek Folk-Tales, illustrated by William Papas, Roy, 1965.
The Crow's Nest, illustrated by Lynette Hemmant, Hamish Hamilton, 1965.
Slippery Shiney, illustrated by Constance Marshall, Hamish Hamilton, 1965.
The Extraordinary Margaret Catchpole, Heinemann, 1966.
A Book of Wizards, illustrated by Jacques, Methuen, 1966, Dutton, 1967.
A Book of Mermaids, illustrated by Jacques, Methuen, 1967, Dutton, 1968.
The Magic Squid, illustrated by Eileen Armitage, Methuen, 1968.
Stories from the English and Scottish Ballads, illustrated by Trevor Ridley, Dutton, 1968.
A Book of Ghosts and Goblins, illustrated by Jacques, Methuen, 1968, Dutton, 1969.
The Glass Man and the Golden Bird: Hungarian Folk and Fairy Tales, illustrated by Victor G. Ambrus, Roy, 1968.
The Spaniards Are Coming!, illustrated by Jacqueline Rizvi, Heinemann, 1969, Watts, 1970.
Jonnikin and the Flying Basket: French Folk and Fairy Tales, illustrated by Ambrus, Dutton, 1969.
A Book of Princes and Princesses, illustrated by Jacques, Methuen, 1969, Dutton, 1970.

Gianni and the Ogre, illustrated by Stobbs, Methuen, 1970, Dutton, 1971.

A Book of Devils and Demons, illustrated by Jacques, Dutton, 1970.

A Book of Charms and Changelings, illustrated by Jacques, Methuen, 1971, Dutton, 1972.

A Choice of Magic, illustrated by Jacques, Dutton, 1971.

A Book of Ogres and Trolls, illustrated by Jacques, Methuen, 1972, Dutton, 1973.

A Book of Sorcerers and Spells, illustrated by Jacques, Methuen, 1973, Dutton, 1974.

A Book of Magic Animals, illustrated by Jacques, Methuen, 1974, Dutton, 1975.

Stumpy: A Russian Tale, illustrated by Leon Shtainmets, Methuen, 1974.

Grandad and the Magic Barrel, illustrated by Jacques, Methuen, 1974.

Old Dog Sirko: A Ukrainian Tale, illustrated by Shtainmets, Methuen, 1974.

Sir Green Hat and the Wizard, illustrated by Stobbs, Methuen, 1974.

Tortoise Tales, illustrated by Donald Chaffin, Nelson, 1974.

Ram and Goat, illustrated by Jacques, Methuen, 1974.

A Book of Monsters, illustrated by Jacques, Methuen, 1975, Dutton, 1976.

Young Gabby Goose, illustrated by J. Hodgson, Methuen, 1975.

Scottish Folk Tales, illustrated by Stobbs, Methuen, 1976.

Fox Tales, illustrated by Hodgson, Methuen, 1976.

The Town Mouse and the Country Mouse: Aesop's Fable Retold, illustrated by Harold Jones, Angus & Robertson, 1977.

Robin Hood and Little John, illustrated by Jo Chesterman, Methuen, 1977.

Old Witch Boneyleg, illustrated by Kilmeny Niland, Angus & Robertson, 1978.

The Cock and the Fox, illustrated by Jenny Williams, Angus & Robertson, 1978.

Boastful Rabbit, illustrated by Hodgson, Methuen, 1978.

Folk and Fairy Tales, illustrated by Jacques, Methuen, 1978.

A Book of Marvels and Magic, illustrated by Jacques, Methuen, 1978.

The Haunted Castle, illustrated by Niland, Angus & Robertson, 1979.

A Book of Spooks and Spectres, illustrated by Jacques, Dutton, 1979.

Robin Hood and the Gold Arrow, illustrated by Chesterman, Methuen, 1979.

Oh Really, Rabbit!, illustrated by Hodgson, Methuen, 1980.

A Book of Cats and Creatures, illustrated by Jacques, Dutton, 1981.

Hedgehog and Puppy Dog Tales, Methuen, 1982.

Tales of Magic and Mystery, illustrated by Christopher Quaile, Methuen, 1985.

EDITOR

A Bundle of Ballads, illustrated by Stobbs, Oxford University Press, 1959, Lippincott, 1961.

Birds, Beasts, and Fishes, illustrated by Rita Parsons, Oxford University Press, 1962.

The Red King and the Witch, illustrated by Ambrus, Oxford University Press, 1964, Roy, 1965.

The Hamish Hamilton Book of Magical Beasts, illustrated by Briggs, Hamish Hamilton, 1965, published in United States as *A Book of Magical Beasts,* T. Nelson, 1970.

A Book of Witches, illustrated by Jacques, Methuen, 1965, Dutton, 1966.

Festivals, illustrated by Briggs, Heinemann, 1972, Dutton, 1973.

A Cauldron of Witches, illustrated by Scoular Anderson, Methuen, 1988.

SIDELIGHTS: Ruth Manning-Sanders began publishing verse and fiction in her early years and continued right up until her death in 1988. Much of her beginning work is aimed at adults, but after her artist husband's untimely death in 1952 she turned to books for children, publishing some sixty titles over thirty years. She is best known for her tales of circus life, as well as for her re-tellings of folktales from all over the world.

Manning-Sanders attended Manchester University, specializing in English literature and Shakespearean studies. While still a student she met and married George Manning-Sanders, an artist and writer from Cornwall. From the outset theirs was an unusual union—they spent the early years of their married life touring Great Britain in a horse-drawn caravan. While her husband painted, Manning-Sanders worked with a circus and wrote poetry. Many of her experiences as an employee of Rosaire's Circus found their way into her books, including *The Circus, The English Circus,* and *Circus Boy.* In a review of *The English Circus,* a *Saturday Review* critic wrote: "No one even faintly interested in the circus—its history, traditions, and bizarre personalities—can fail to be interested in this detailed tribute. . . . [Manning-Sanders] more often than not manages to bring to life the glories of 'the art that eternally contemplates the proud enchantment of its own perfection.' "

After the birth of their two children, Manning-Sanders settled down a bit; she earned a significant reputation as a poet and novelist for adults. World War II and the death of her husband soon thereafter brought a change to Manning-Sanders's career. Before the war she had written almost exclusively for adults. After the war she turned to writing for children, and a great number of works flowed from her pen. Beginning with an autobiography of Hans Christian Andersen, Manning-Sanders went on to collect and re-write folk and fairy tales from every part of the world, taking great care to preserve each story's original flavor and tone. In a series with titles beginning *A Book of. . .* , she introduces English-speaking readers to dragons, dwarfs, witches, magicians, giants, sorcerers, and magic animals from every imaginable culture. *Junior Bookshelf* correspondent M. S. Crouch noted of Manning-Sanders: "Her personal preference seems to have been for the humorously bizarre, and she had a liking for dragons, ogres and other grotesques. She liked humble, unheroic heroes, simple people keeping their end up by means of cunning and persistence."

At the time of her death, Manning-Sanders had just released a collection of witch stories, and more than twenty-five of her books were still in print. Crouch claimed that the author never lost her touch for poetry, producing work with subtle rhythms and melodies. "Every present-day story-teller must be in her debt," the critic continued. "Her work is peculiarly suited to the domestic, one-to-one story-telling session. It forges a link between speaker and hearer whose strength is best appreciated in the home rather than the hall and the classroom." Crouch concluded: "For many long-lived writers, death is followed by eclipse. I hope that publishers will [continue to re-release Manning-Sanders's] priceless treasury of folk-tales. We would all be the poorer for their loss."

BIOGRAPHICAL/CRITICAL SOURCES:

BOOKS

Twentieth-Century Children's Writers, 3rd edition, St. Martin's, 1989.

PERIODICALS

Junior Bookshelf, February, 1989, pp. 7-9.
Saturday Review, April 3, 1954.
Times Literary Supplement, November 14, 1952; September 28, 1973; July 23, 1982.

OBITUARIES:

PERIODICALS

Times (London), October 13, 1988.*

* * *

MANSFIELD, Elizabeth
See SCHWARTZ, Paula

MANSFIELD, Libby
See SCHWARTZ, Paula

* * *

MARIANI, John Francis 1945-

PERSONAL: Born August 27, 1945, in New York, NY; son of Eligio A. (a podiatrist) and Renee T. (a housewife) Mariani; married Galina Stephanoff-Dargery (an artist), May 28, 1984. *Education:* Iona College, B.A., 1967; Columbia University, M.A., 1968, Ph.D., 1973.

ADDRESSES: Home and office—8 Henry St., Tuckahoe, NY 10707. *Agent*—Diane Cleaver, Inc., 55 Fifth Ave., New York, NY 10003.

CAREER: College of New Rochelle, New Rochelle, NY, instructor in film, 1974—. Instructor at Mercy College, Dobbs Ferry, NY, and Marymount College, Tarrytown, NY, both 1973—, and Iona College, 1973-75; academic humanist for National Project Center for Film and Humanities, 1973. Restaurant expert for Prodigy computer service.

MEMBER: Modern Language Association of America, Authors Guild, New York Wine Writers Circle (member of executive committee).

AWARDS, HONORS: Best reference book of the year in the food category, *Library Journal,* 1983, for *The Dictionary of American Food and Drink;* best reference/history book, International Association of Cooking Professionals, 1992, for *America Eats Out.*

WRITINGS:

The Dictionary of American Food and Drink, Ticknor & Fields, 1983.
Eating Out: Fearless Dining in Ethnic Restaurants, Morrow, 1985.
Editor, *Mariani's Coast-to-Coast Dining Guide,* Times Books, 1986.
America Eats Out, Morrow, 1991.
The Four Seasons, Crown, in press.

Food and travel correspondent for *Esquire,* food writer for *MD,* restaurant columnist for *Travel and Leisure,* and columnist for *Worth.*

SIDELIGHTS: John Francis Mariani once told *CA:* "The dictionary was written because nothing like it existed on American food and drink because too many myths and too much misinformation abounds. Only when a cuisine is taken seriously as part of the language of a country is it taken seriously at all.

"I like to think of myself as a writer who happens to write about food, rather than as a food expert who types out recipes. Food writing is generally abysmal, filled with superlatives that the subject in no way justifies and undertaken with every intention of pleasing advertisers. Recipes are more important than text, and a barrage of adjectives is generally preferred to insight or wit.

"As a result I have tried in my food writing to approach the subject both with respect and affection, but never with the outrageous seriousness of some. My *Dictionary of American Food and Drink* grew out of my own journalistic need to look up something authoritative on American cooking rather than rely on assumptions and hearsay. I hope my book pins down much definite detail, but I welcome—as does any scholar—the same kind of corrections and revisions from readers that H. L. Mencken received over his lifetime after publishing *The American Language.*

"American food is a wide-ranging subject and one I continue to be fascinated by, but it must be written about with the same aplomb as any writer on a good subject, and mere reveries of bygone meals and little restaurants in France are not all there is to it. There is far too much preciousness and nonsensical attempts at sensual style in food writing, and this is aggravated by a pedantry on the subject that is akin to a travel writer doing a chemical breakdown on the grains of sand in Aruba.

"I am completely against the notion that a chef can ever be an 'artist,' simply because a chef is in the business of serving hundreds of customers a day the same dish, with responsibility for that dish doled out to assistants and subordinates. When, in fact, personal ego steps into the kitchen, common sense is generally thrown out the window.

"In its traditional home character American food has thus far avoided being haughty, and I hate more than anything the attempt by some ignorant writers to exalt the greasiest taco in San Antonio, Texas, to the gastronomic sublime. American food is what Americans eat, but my definition of those dishes that make up the American dinner is based on those dishes that one will not find readily in other countries: these range from hamburgers to chili, from fettuccine Alfredo to goatcheese pizzas, from white chocolate mousse to negimaki. For although most of these have ethnic corollaries in other countries, they are rarely found in those countries except as an American transplant. In its diversity and regionality, American cooking is the most exciting in the world.

"As for my own career as a writer, I rather drifted into it at the same time that I began teaching college. Teaching I found constricting (remedial reading was not what I was trained to teach), while writing I found a key to life's diversity. I began writing magazine articles for *New York Magazine,* mainly on entertainment and arts; then, as I traveled more, my interest in food grew until I was writing

more about that subject than any other. My dictionary is, I hope, a starting point for more studies of American gastronomy—garlic and all—but I hope the tone will be germane to the subject."

*   *   *

MARSH, Dave 1950-

PERSONAL: Born March 1, 1950, in Pontiac, MI; son of O. K. (a railroad worker) and Mary (Evon) Marsh; married Barbara Carr (a recording executive), July 21, 1979; stepchildren: Sasha, Kristen. *Education:* Attended Wayne State University, 1968-69.

ADDRESSES: Office—Rock & Roll Confidential, P.O. Box 1073, Maywood, NJ 07607.

CAREER: Creem (magazine), Birmingham, MI, editor, 1969-73; *Real Paper,* Boston, MA, music editor, 1974; *Newsday,* Garden City, NY, staff member, 1974-75; *Rolling Stone,* New York City, record reviews editor and writer, 1975-78; free-lance writer, 1978—; *Rock & Roll Confidential,* Maywood, NJ, editor and publisher, 1983—; *Playboy,* music critic, 1984—; *Entertainment Weekly,* contributing editor, 1991—.

AWARDS, HONORS: Born to Run: The Bruce Springsteen Story was listed among the Best Books for Young Adults, American Library Association, 1979.

WRITINGS:

Born to Run: The Bruce Springsteen Story, Doubleday, 1979.
(Editor with John Swenson) *Rolling Stone Record Guide: Reviews and Ratings of Almost Ten Thousand Currently Available Pop, Rock, Soul, Country, Blues, Jazz, and Gospel Albums,* Random House, 1980, revised edition published as *The New Rolling Stone Record Guide,* 1984.
(With Kevin Stein) *The Book of Rock Lists,* Dell, 1980.
Elvis, Times Books, 1981.
Before I Get Old: The Story of the Who, St. Martin's, 1982.
(With Sandra Charon and Deborah Geller) *Rocktopicon,* Contemporary, 1984.
Fortunate Son: The Best of Dave Marsh, Random House, 1985.
The First Rock & Roll Confidential Report: Inside the World of Rock & Roll, Pantheon, 1985.
Sun City: The Struggle for Freedom in South Africa, Penguin, 1985.
Trapped: Michael Jackson and the Crossover Dream, Bantam, 1986.
Glory Days: Bruce Springsteen in the 1980s, Random House, 1987.

The Heart of Rock and Soul: The 1001 Greatest Singles Ever Made, New American Library, 1989.

(Editor with Harold Leventhal) Woody Guthrie, *Pastures of Plenty: A Self-Portrait by Woody Guthrie,* Harper, 1990.

50 Ways to Fight Censorship, Thunder's Mouth Press, 1991.

(Editor with Don Henley) *Heaven Is under Our Feet: A Book for Walden Woods,* Longmeadow Press, 1991.

Author of column "American Grandstand" for *Rolling Stone,* 1976-79. Contributor to periodicals, including *Boston Phoenix, Film Comment, Look, Los Angeles Times, New York Daily News,* and *Village Voice.*

WORK IN PROGRESS: Louie Louie, for Hyperion, spring, 1993; *Distant Lover: The Life of Marvin Gaye; Merry Christmas Baby,* with Steve Propes.

SIDELIGHTS: "Rock and roll is not just music," Dave Marsh once told *Publishers Weekly.* "It's one of the most important things that's ever happened in American culture." It has also been an important influence on Marsh's life, beginning with his childhood in a blue-collar suburb of Detroit, continuing through his first experience with writing, and culminating in his current status as "America's best-known rock critic."

Growing up in Pontiac, Michigan, an automobile manufacturing town like many of those around Detroit, "was pretty grim," Marsh told *Publishers Weekly.* "You were surrounded. If you walked a block and a half, you were at Assembly Line 16, where they made Bonnevilles and later GTOs. It was just a fact of life; you were going to go to work at the plant or, maybe, for the phone company." Marsh explained the importance of rock and roll music to such a community: "Where I came from, there were no writers. . . . Nothing and nobody that I knew about told their stories. Except for the songs on the radio. If I was blessed early with a calling to write, it came about very much as a response to this gap in our culture. And for me, that's why it was worthwhile to write about rock and roll music, which is made and listened to by all sorts of people but especially by the kind of people who didn't have writers to tell their stories."

Marsh discovered the power of the written word early on. "When I wrote, people displayed their emotions," he said. "Sometimes they even laughed when I wanted them to. Just as important, my own confused thoughts and feelings seemed clear. Writing for me has always been a way of disentangling the conflicting impressions of events and people and experiences, the basic circumstances of living in the world."

After graduating from high school Marsh attended Wayne State University in Detroit and began writing for small publications. It was at Wayne that Marsh met Barry Kramer, a fellow student and publisher of *Creem.* Marsh took over as editor of the rock tabloid, a position he maintained for four years. He made a name for himself at *Rolling Stone,* writing music reviews and a column from 1975 to 1978, then contributed on a free-lance basis. He created *Rock & Roll Confidential* in 1983, and serves as its editor and publisher. Marsh's first book, *Born to Run: The Bruce Springsteen Story,* led to more books on popular musicians, including The Who, Michael Jackson, Elvis, and Woody Guthrie, and a second book on Springsteen entitled *Glory Days: Bruce Springsteen in the 1980s.*

In his writing, Marsh's enthusiasm for his subject and his opinions of its artists are clear. He has made plain, for example, his admiration of Springsteen, with whom he has become friends. Often this subjective approach has brought Marsh disapproval among fellow writers, who question his ability to remain impartial in his criticism. Paula Span, writing in the *Washington Post,* noted, "His is a circle in which the distinctions between business and friendship are blurry, the conventions of journalistic detachment largely disregarded." Marsh, however, notes that impartiality has never been his goal. "I've never written an objective sentence in my life, on purpose," he told Susan Whitall of the *Detroit News.* "Objective criticism is an oxymoron to me."

BIOGRAPHICAL/CRITICAL SOURCES:

PERIODICALS

Chicago Tribune, February 12, 1989.

Choice, June, 1980.

Detroit News, May 17, 1987.

Globe and Mail (Toronto), March 2, 1991.

Los Angeles Times, May 15, 1983; December 11, 1983; February 5, 1984.

Los Angeles Times Book Review, December 2, 1990.

New Statesman, September 24, 1982.

Newsweek, October 31, 1983; April 13, 1987.

New York Times, November 16, 1979.

New York Times Book Review, December 30, 1979; November 28, 1982; July 28, 1985; July 5, 1987; October 8, 1989.

People, July 13, 1987.

Publishers Weekly, October 21, 1983, pp. 69-70.

Time, January 7, 1980; June 22, 1987.

Times Educational Supplement, December 24, 1982.

Tribune Books (Chicago), November 5, 1989.

Washington Post, April 26, 1987; June 15, 1987.

Washington Post Book World, September 11, 1982.

MARSHALL, Jeff
See LAYCOCK, George (Edwin)

*   *   *

MARSHALL, John David 1928-

PERSONAL: Born September 7, 1928, in McKenzie, TN; son of Maxwell Cole (a merchant) and Emma (Walpole) Marshall. *Education:* Bethel College, B.A., 1950; Florida State University, M.A., 1951, additional graduate study, 1951-52; attended Oxford University, 1989. *Politics:* Democrat. *Religion:* Cumberland Presbyterian.

ADDRESSES: Home—802 East Main, Apt. 38, Murfreesboro, TN 37130; and P.O. Box 2506, Murfreesboro, TN 37133. *Office*—Andrew L. Todd Library, Middle Tennessee State University, Murfreesboro, TN 37132.

CAREER: Florida State University, Library School, Tallahassee, administrative assistant, Office of Library School Dean, 1951-52; Clemson College (now University) Library, Clemson, SC, reference librarian, 1952-55; Auburn University Library, Auburn, AL, head of reference department, 1955-57; University of Georgia Libraries, Athens, head of Acquisitions Division and assistant professor of libraries, 1957-67; Middle Tennessee State University, Murfreesboro, university librarian and associate professor, 1967-76, professor of library science, 1980—, university bibliographer, 1976—. Chairman of jury, 1980 Mid-Western Books Competition, 1981. Consultant, Churchill Memorial and Library, summer, 1979. Member of Murfreesboro City Library Board, 1985—, and Highland Rim Regional Library Board, 1989—; member of board of Governors, Churchill Memorial and Library, 1989—.

MEMBER: International Churchill Society (life member), American Library Association (life member), American Society of Bookplate Collectors and Designers, Friends of the Churchill Memorial and Library (life member), Southeastern Library Association (chairman or member of numerous committees, 1966-86), Tennessee Library Association (life member; chairman or member of various committees), Tennessee Historical Society (life member), Association of Churchill Fellows of Westminster College (life member; library committee member, 1982—), Phi Kappa Phi, Beta Phi Mu (publications committee member, Gamma Chapter, 1963-64).

AWARDS, HONORS: Churchill fellow, Westminster College, Fulton, MO, 1982; Frances Neel Cheney Award, Tennessee Library Association, 1984, for "outstanding contributions to the world of books and librarianship"; Distinguished Alumni Award, Florida State University School of Library and Information Studies, 1989; elected honorary life member, Southeastern Library Association, 1990, for "significant and lasting contributions to the association and to the library profession"; Tennessee Library Association Honor Award, 1992, for "significant contributions to the improvement of library service in Tennessee"; Distinguished Service Award, Bethel College, 1992.

WRITINGS:

Books in Your Life, Bethel College, 1959.
Louis Shores: A Bibliography, Gamma Chapter, Beta Phi Mu, 1964.
A Fable of Tomorrow's Library, Peacock Press, 1965.
Of, By, and For Librarians: Second Series, Shoe String, 1974.
(Contributor) J. B. Howell, editor, *Special Collections in Libraries of the Southeast,* Southeastern Library Association/Howick House, 1978.
Louis Shoes, Author-Librarian: A Bibliography, Gamma Chapter, Beta Phi Mu, 1979.
The Southern Books Competition at Twenty-Five, Howick House, 1980.
(Contributor) Ellis Eugene Tucker, editor, *The Southeastern Library Association: Its History and Its Honorary Members, 1920-1980,* Southeastern Library Association, 1980.
(Contributor) Edwin S. Gleaves and John Mark Tucker, editors, *Reference Services and Library Education: Essays in Honor of Frances Neel Cheney,* Lexington Books, 1983.
One Librarian's Credo (miniature book), Tabula Rasa Press, 1986.
Lizzie Borden and The Library Connection, Florida State University School of Library and Information Studies, 1990.

EDITOR

(With Wayne Shirley and Louis Shores) *Books, Libraries, Librarians: Contributions to Library Literature,* Shoe String, 1955.
Of, By, and For Librarians: First Series, Shoe String, 1960.
An American Library History Reader, Shoe String, 1961.
In Pursuit of Library History, Florida State University Library School, 1961.
Louis Shores, Mark Hopkins' Log and Other Essays, Shoe String, 1965.
Approaches to Library History, Florida State University Library School, 1966.
The Library in the University, Shoe String, 1967.
Books Are Basic: The Essential Lawrence Clark Powell, University of Arizona Press, 1985.

OTHER

Also general editor, "Contributions to Library Literature" series, Shoe String, 1963-78. *Southern Observer,* contributing editor, 1953-66, contributor of column, "Bibliophile's Notebook," 1954-66; *Library Journal,* book reviewer, 1953-64; *Journal of Library History,* book review editor and member of editorial board, both 1966-76; *Southeastern Librarian,* book review editor and member of editorial board, both 1979-82.

WORK IN PROGRESS: Research on Winston S. Churchill's lecture in Fall River, Massachusetts, on December 21, 1900.

SIDELIGHTS: John David Marshall told *CA:* "In 1974 I suggested to Richard Armour's publisher (McGraw-Hill) that he write a light-Armoured history of libraries for publication sometime in 1976 which would be the hundredth anniversary of the founding of the American Library Association and the hundredth anniversary of the publication of the Dewey Decimal Classification System. [Armour's] publisher sent my letter to him. He wrote me that he liked my suggestion. *The Happy Bookers: A Playful History of Librarians and Their World from the Stone Age to the Distant Future* was published in 1976 with a dedication to 'librarian-scholar-author John David Marshall, who insisted that I write this book, and . . . to all librarians, since they are my favorite people.' Having Richard Armour dedicate this book to me is a highlight in my career. He also made me a footnote and an op. cit. on page 129!

"For more than forty years, I have collected works by and about Sir Winston S. Churchill. My collection includes more than 700 items, among which is a first edition of *Savrola* (Longmans, Green, 1900), [Churchill's] only novel. I was in the audience which heard Mr. Churchill (as he then was) deliver the famous 'iron curtain' speech at Westminster College, Fulton, Missouri, on March 5, 1946. I have never quite recovered from seeing and hearing Mr. Churchill, and I really don't want to! On May 6, 1992, I was in the audience that heard Mikhail Gorbachev speak at Westminster College. Gorbachev is no Churchill!"

BIOGRAPHICAL/CRITICAL SOURCES:

PERIODICALS

College and Research Libraries, December, 1967.
Los Angeles Times Book Review, February 2, 1986.
New York Times Book Review, May 6, 1956.
Southern Observer, April, 1960.
Tennessee Librarian, fall, 1984.

*   *   *

MARSHALL, Rosalind Kay

PERSONAL: Born in Dysart, Scotland; daughter of Arthur Frederick Kay Robertson (a school teacher) and Nan

(Duncan) Marshall. *Education:* University of Edinburgh, M.A., 1959, Dip.Ed., 1960, M.A. (with honors), 1966, Ph.D., 1970. *Avocational interests:* Concerts, cathedrals, needlepoint, reading, gardening.

ADDRESSES: Office—Scottish National Portrait Gallery, 1 Queen St., Edinburgh, Scotland.

CAREER: Dictionary of the Older Scottish Tongue, Edinburgh, Scotland, assistant editor, 1970-71; Scottish Record Office, Edinburgh, outside editor, 1971-73; Scottish National Portrait Gallery, Edinburgh, assistant keeper, 1973—. Member, London Library, Friends of the Scottish Dictionaries, Friends of the Royal Museum of Scotland, and Friends of Lambeth Palace Library.

MEMBER: Scottish History Society, Royal Society of Literature (fellow), Scottish Record Society, Costume Society of Scotland, Costume Society of England, Scottish Records Association, Scots Ancestry Research Society (member of council), Company of Scottish History (member of council).

AWARDS, HONORS: New Writing Award, Scottish Arts Council, 1974, for *The Days of Duchess Anne.*

WRITINGS:

The Days of Duchess Anne: Life in the Household of the Duchess of Hamilton, 1656-1716, St. Martin's, 1973.
Childhood in Seventeenth-Century Scotland (exhibition catalogue), Scottish National Portrait Gallery, 1976.
Mary of Guise, Collins, 1977.
Women in Scotland, National Galleries of Scotland, 1979.
Virgins and Viragos: A History of Women in Scotland 1080-1980, Collins, 1983.
Costume in Scottish Portraits 1080-1980, National Galleries of Scotland, 1986.
Mary, Queen of Scots (biography), H.M.S.O., 1986.
Sir John Medina (booklet), National Galleries of Scotland, 1986.
Bonnie Prince Charlie, H.M.S.O., 1988.
Henrietta Maria, the Intrepid Queen, H.M.S.O., 1990, Stemmer House, 1991.
(Editor and contributor) *Dynasty: The Royal House of Stewart,* National Galleries of Scotland, 1990.
Elizabeth I, Stemmer House, 1991.
(Editor and contributor) *The Art of Jewellery in Scotland,* National Galleries of Scotland, 1991.
Mary I, H.M.S.O., 1993.

Contributor of material to British Broadcasting Corp. (BBC)-Scotland. Contributor of articles and reviews to periodicals, including *Bulletin of the Scottish Costume Society, Local Historian, Scottish Historical Review, Scottish American, Nursing Mirror, Connoisseur,* and *Scotsman.* Associate editor, *Review of Scottish Culture,* 1984—.

BIOGRAPHICAL/CRITICAL SOURCES:

PERIODICALS

Times Literary Supplement, August 26, 1983.

* * *

MARTIN, William C. 1937-

PERSONAL: Born December 31, 1937, in San Antonio, TX; son of Lowell Curtis (an agricultural broker) and Joe Bailey Brite (a teacher) Martin; married Patricia Summerlin (a university administrator), December 31, 1957; children: Rex, Jeff, Elisabeth Dale. Education: Abilene Christian University, B.A., 1958, M.A., 1960; Harvard Divinity School, B.D., 1963; Harvard University, Ph.D., 1969. Politics: Independent. Religion: Protestant.

ADDRESSES: Home—2148 Addison, Houston, TX 77030. Office—Rice University, 6100 South Main St., Houston, TX 77005; (also) P.O. Box 1892, Houston, TX 77251. Agent—Gerald McCauley, P.O. Box AE, Outpost Rd., Katonah, NY 10536.

CAREER: Dana Hall School, Wellesley, MA, instructor in history, 1965-68, chaplain, 1967-68; Rice University, Houston, TX, instructor, 1968-69, assistant professor, 1969-73, associate professor, 1973-79, professor of sociology, 1979—, master of Sid W. Richardson College, 1976-81, chair of department, 1983-86, 1989—; writer. Houston Police Academy, instructor, 1971-77; Women's Institute, instructor, 1971-76; occasional referee for professional journals, university presses, and research grants; consultant to several film and television documentaries. President, board of directors, Fellowship for Racial and Economic Equality, 1970-71, and House of Carpenters, Inc. (non-profit housing corporations); member of many civic and university committees and advisory boards.

MEMBER: American Sociological Association, Society for the Scientific Study of Religion, Religious Research Association, Popular Culture Association, Texas Institute of Letters.

AWARDS, HONORS: Nicholas Salgo Outstanding Teacher Award, 1971; research grants from the American Council of Learned Societies and the American Philosophical Society, 1974; George R. Brown Award, 1974-77, 1982, 1984; George R. Brown Award for Teaching Excellence in Humanities, 1974, 1976; George R. Brown Life Honor Award for Teaching, 1985; J. Frank Dobi/Paisano Fellowship, 1980; National Headliner Award for "Consistently Outstanding Magazine Column," 1982.

WRITINGS:

The Layman's Bible Encyclopedia, Southwestern Co., 1964.

These Were God's People: A Layman's Bible History, Southwestern Co., 1966.
Christians in Conflict, Center for the Scientific Study of Religion, 1972.
(Author of text) Geoff Winningham, Going Texan, Kelsey, 1972.
(Contributor) Reed Geertsen and Richard A. Sundeen, editors, Eighty-One Techniques for Teaching Sociological Concepts, American Sociological Association, 1979.
A Prophet with Honor: The Billy Graham Story, Morrow, 1991.

Work appears in many anthologies, including Unsecular Man, edited by Andrew M. Greeley, Schocken, 1972; American Oblique, edited by Joseph R. Trimmer, Houghton-Mifflin, 1975; Modern Sociological Issues, edited by Louis C. Reichman and Barry J. Wishart, Macmillan, 1979; Society as It Is, 2nd edition, edited by Glen Gavligio and David Ray, Macmillan, 1980; Growing Old at Willie Nelson's Picnic, and Other Sketches of Life in the Southwest, edited by Ronald B. Querry, Texas A & M Press, 1983.

Contributor of articles, essays, and reviews to numerous periodicals including Texas Monthly, Atlantic, and Esquire. Contributor to Dictionary of Southern Religion and Encyclopedia of Religion in the South.

* * *

MARVICK, Elizabeth Wirth 1925-

PERSONAL: Born September 4, 1925, in Chicago, IL; daughter of Louis and Mary B. Wirth; married Dwaine Marvick, 1948; children: Louis Wirth, Andrew B. Education: University of Chicago, Ph.B., 1944, M.A., 1946; Columbia University, Ph.D., 1968.

ADDRESSES: Office: Department of Political Science, University of California, Los Angeles, CA 90024.

CAREER: Writer. Lecturer in political science in New York City, 1948-51, and at colleges and universities in Southern California, 1957-68; California Institute of Technology, Pasadena, lecturer in political science, 1968-72; Claremont Graduate School, Claremont, CA, lecturer and adjunct professor of government, 1972-75; University of Bordeaux, Bordeaux, France, senior Fulbright lecturer in American studies, 1975-76; University of California, Los Angeles, visiting lecturer in political science, 1976-83.

MEMBER: International Society of Political Psychology, American Historical Association, American Political Science Association, Western Society for French History.

AWARDS, HONORS: Fellowship, American Council of Learned Societies, 1972, 1973; Fulbright fellowship, 1975-76; fellow, Virginia Foundation for the Humanities, 1988-89; fellow, Virginia Historical Society, 1992.

WRITINGS:

(Contributor) Lloyd DeMause, editor, *History of Childhood,* Harper, 1975.
(Editor) *Psychopolitical Analysis: Selected Writings of Nathan Leites,* Halsted, 1977.
(Editor) *Case Studies in Psychopolitics,* Halsted, 1979.
The Young Richelieu: A Psychoanalytic Approach to Leadership, University of Chicago Press, 1983.
Louis XIII, the Making of A King, Yale University Press, 1986.

WORK IN PROGRESS: Founding Fathers of Virginia: Family Experience in Politics.

*   *   *

MASSMAN, Patti 1945-

PERSONAL: Born April 22, 1945, in Los Angeles, CA; children: Michael, Brent. *Education:* Boston University, B.A., 1967.

ADDRESSES: Home—Beverly Hills, CA.

CAREER: Jay Bernstein Public Relations, Los Angeles, CA, assistant publicist in theatrical public relations, 1967-68; Jerry Pam Public Relations, Los Angeles, assistant publicist in theatrical public relations, 1968-71; Ashley Famous Agency, Los Angeles, script reader, 1979—; B & P International (real estate investment firm), Beverly Hills, CA, general partner, 1979—.

WRITINGS:

(With Pamela Beck) *Fling* (novel), M. Evans, 1983.
(With Beck) *Rich Men, Single Women* (novel), Delacorte, 1986.
(With Susan Rosser) *Just Desserts* (novel), Crown, 1991.

ADAPTATIONS: Rich Men, Single Women was presented as an Aaron Spelling "ABC Movie of the Week" on television.

WORK IN PROGRESS: Lights and Shadows, a novel with Susan Rosser.

*   *   *

MATHIAS, Roland (Glyn) 1915-

PERSONAL: Born September 4, 1915, in Talybont-on-Usk, Wales; son of Evan (a chaplain to the Forces) and Muriel (Morgan) Mathias; married Molly Hawes, April 4, 1944; children: Jonathan Glyn and Mary Olwen (twins), Ceinwen Florence. *Education:* Jesus College, Oxford, B.A., 1936, B.Litt., 1939, M.A., 1944. *Politics:* Radical. *Religion:* United Reformed Church.

ADDRESSES: Home—Deffrobani, 5 Maescelyn, Brecon, Powys LD3 7NL, Wales.

CAREER: History master at schools in St. Helens, Lancashire, 1938-41, Reading, Berkshire, 1941-45, Carlisle, Cumberland, 1945-46, and London, England, 1946-48; Pembroke Grammar School, Pembrokeshire, Wales, headmaster, 1948-58; Herbert Strutt School, Belper, Derbyshire, England, headmaster, 1958-64; King Edward's Five Ways School, Birmingham, England, headmaster, 1964-69; full-time writer, 1969—. Part-time lecturer at University College, Cardiff, 1970-77; visiting lecturer at University of Alabama, 1971. Schoolmaster fellowship, Balliol College, Oxford, 1961, and Swansea University, 1967.

MEMBER: Academy of Welsh Writers (chairman of English section, 1975-78).

AWARDS, HONORS: Welsh Arts Council, grant, 1968, writers award, 1969, and prizes for poetry, 1972, for *Absalom in the Tree,* and 1980, for *Snipe's Castle;* Doctor of Humane Letters honoris causa, Georgetown University, 1985, for services to the literature of Wales in English.

WRITINGS:

The Eleven Men of Eppynt and Other Stories, Dock Leaves Press, 1956.
Whitsun Riot: An Account of a Commotion amongst Catholics in Herefordshire and Monmouthshire in 1605, Bowes, 1963.
Vernon Watkins, University of Wales Press, 1974.
The Hollowed-Out Elder Stalk: John Cowper Powys as Poet, Enitharmon Press, 1979.
A Ride through the Woods: Studies in Anglo-Welsh Writers, Poetry Wales Press, 1985.
Anglo-Welsh Literature: An Illustrated History, Poetry Wales Press, 1987.

POETRY

Days Enduring and Other Poems, Stockwell, 1943.
Break in Harvest and Other Poems, Routledge & Kegan Paul, 1946.
The Roses of Tretower, Dock Leaves Press, 1952.
The Flooded Valley, Putnam, 1960.
Absalom in the Tree, Gomer Press, 1971.
Snipe's Castle, Gomer Press, 1979.
Burning Brambles: Selected Poems 1944-1979, Gomer Press, 1983.

EDITOR

(With Sam Adams) *The Shining Pyramid and Other Stories by Welsh Authors*, Gomer Press, 1970.

(With Adams) *The Collected Short Stories of Geraint Goodwin*, H. G. Walters, 1976.

David Jones: Eight Essays on His Work as Writer and Artist, Gomer Press, 1976.

(With Raymond Garlick) *Anglo-Welsh Poetry: 1480-1980* (anthology), Poetry Wales Press, 1984, 2nd edition, 1992.

OTHER

Contributor to *Vernon Watkins, 1906-1967*, Faber, 1970. Contributor to numerous anthologies, including *Modern Welsh Poetry*, Faber, 1944; *New Poems*, M. Joseph, 1955; *Welsh Voices*, Dent, 1967; *The Welsh Language and the English Language*, Gomer Press, 1973; and *Poets in a Welsh Landscape*, Poetry Wales Press, 1985. Contributor to periodicals, including *Poetry Wales, London Welshman, Poetry Review*, and *Poetry Australia*. Editor, *Anglo-Welsh Review*, 1961-76.

SIDELIGHTS: Roland Mathias once told *CA:* "My interest, always devoted to a Wales whose culture is continuously in danger of being annihilated either by the pro-English snobbery of an older generation or by the mindless mid-Atlantic attitudes which seize the young, has been channelled more and more into the examination and support of contemporary writing in English from Wales, which a conservative university system has until recently ignored. This has sometimes seemed a parlous, even a hopeless, enterprise, so few are the people involved. But progress has been made, if slowly.

"My education in England and my inability to speak Welsh, as my father did, made my search for Wales slow and long drawn-out. My early inability to handle in poetry the emotion I felt (I was always very self-critical and had no time for either sentimentality or the confessional mode) made me concentrate on landscape, though I now feel that only landscape with humans interests me. *Place,* in a sense more exact than Wales, was always the more important because a wandering childhood had left me with none of the boyhood companions or settled memories that most people grow up with. Knowledge of place was something I had to fight for and valued accordingly.

"My writing method, influenced originally by the Dylan Thomas sound-association school, was to begin with a doodle and seek to make it grow. But for decades now I have been far away from that: poems do not come easily—I have to wait for my creative energy to top up, so to speak, and the poem that is waiting often has to signal for some time before it gets itself written. My mind is an intensely political and social caldron, the more obviously be-

cause it is impossible to live in Wales and be concerned with its future without being committed in one way or another. My poetry is always about *me,* in a sense, because I am the medium of feeling, but I have not the smallest wish to draw attention to myself as 'special.' I do not believe that the poet feels more deeply than the common man, merely that he knows how to create an artifact of his feeling by distancing it and making it as objective as possible."

BIOGRAPHICAL/CRITICAL SOURCES:

PERIODICALS

Times Literary Supplement, March 4, 1977; July 25, 1980.
World Literature Today, summer, 1984.

*　　*　　*

MATTHEWS, John (Pengwerne) 1927-

PERSONAL: Born October 22, 1927, in Sydney, Australia; son of George Pengwerne (a physician) and Rosalie (Pulsford) Matthews; married Jean Gilchrist, June 11, 1955; children: Peter, Rosalie, Christopher. *Education:* University of Melbourne, B.A. (with honors), 1951, Diploma in Education, 1952, M.A., 1953; University of London, LL.B., 1954; University of Toronto, Ph.D., 1957. *Politics:* Conservative. *Religion:* Anglican.

ADDRESSES: Home—55 Watts Cres., Kingston, Ontario, Canada K7M 2P4. *Office*—Department of English, Queen's University, Kingston, Ontario, Canada K7L 3N6.

CAREER: University of Toronto, Toronto, Ontario, instructor in English, 1955-56; University of Manitoba, Winnipeg, assistant professor, 1956-57, associate professor, 1957, professor of English and dean of arts and sciences, 1957-62; Queen's University, Kingston, Ontario, professor of English, 1962—, director of Commonwealth Institute, 1962-67. National president of Canadian Federation for the Humanities, 1984-86. Visiting fellow at Oriel College, Oxford University, 1972-73. *Military service:* Royal Canadian Air Force, 1958-61; became flight lieutenant.

MEMBER: International Association of University Professors of English, Humanities Association of Canada (national president, 1971-73), Association of Canadian University Teachers of English, Kingston Symphony Association (vice-president, 1967-71).

AWARDS, HONORS: Nuffield fellow, 1972-73; visiting fellow of Oriel College, Oxford.

WRITINGS:

Tradition in Exile, University of Toronto Press, 1962.

(Senior editor) *The Collected Letters of Benjamin Disraeli,* University of Toronto Press, Volume 1: *1815-1834,* 1982, Volume 2: *1835-1837,* 1982, Volume 3: *1841-1841,* 1987, Volume 4: *1842-1847,* 1989.

(Editor with Ellen Henderson) Sarah Disraeli and Benjamin Disraeli, *A Year at Hartlebury; or, The Election,* University of Toronto Press, 1983.

Contributor to periodicals, including *Mosaic, Humanities Review, Journal of Commonwealth Literature,* and *Our Living Tradition.*

WORK IN PROGRESS: Principal investigator for volumes 5 and 6 of *The Collected Letters of Benjamin Disraeli;* comparative research on Victorian and commonwealth literature.

SIDELIGHTS: John Matthews told *CA:* "I was born in Australia and spent my childhood in the United States and the United Kingdom. I returned to Australia and lived there until 1953, when I moved to Canada. My interest in comparative commonwealth literature developed from my observations of the similarities and differences in Australian and Canadian imaginative ways of looking at the world. I compared these with my own experiences in the United States and expanded my interest to all commonwealth countries, including the Caribbean, Africa, and India.

"My interest in Benjamin Disraeli arose almost by accident, when I was looking for a good focus for a sabbatical project in 1972. His letters, witty and frank, were supposed to number some twenty–four hundred. When I searched, I found more than ten thousand, and the number is still rising. I look at Disraeli as a principal founder of the commonwealth, so this interest seems consistent with my other studies."

*   *   *

MAY, Charles E(dward)   1941-

PERSONAL: Born February 18, 1941, in Paintsville, KY; son of Howard E. (a truck driver) and Kathleen (a housewife; maiden name, Newsom) May; married Patricia Treadway (a college instructor), March 29, 1980; children: Hillary, Hayden, Jordan. *Education:* Morehead State College (now University), B.A., 1963; Ohio University, M.A., 1964, Ph.D., 1966. *Politics:* Democrat. *Religion:* Presbyterian.

ADDRESSES: Home—5441 Ludlow Ave., Garden Grove, CA 92645. *Office*—Department of English, California State University, Long Beach, CA 90840.

CAREER: Ohio University, Athens, assistant professor of English, 1966-67; California State University, Long Beach, assistant professor, 1967-71, associate professor, 1971-77, professor of English, 1977—, chairman of department, 1980-83, president of English council, 1981-83.

AWARDS, HONORS: Long Beach Foundation grants, 1973, 1976, 1983, 1989, 1990, 1991; California State Department of Education grant, 1988; California State University Chancellors grants, 1989, 1991; first prize, Liberal Arts Zenith Masters of Innovation Contest, 1989, for computer software.

WRITINGS:

(Editor) *Short Story Theories,* Ohio University Press, 1976.
Twentieth Century European Short Story, Salem Press, 1989.
Edgar Allan Poe: A Study of the Short Fiction, Twayne, 1991.
(Editor) *Fiction's Many Worlds,* Heath, 1993.

Contributor to books, including *The Practice of Psychoanalytic Criticism,* edited by Wayne Tennehouse, Wayne State University Press, 1976; *Tennessee Williams: A Tribute,* edited by Jac Tharpe, University Press of Mississippi, 1977; *Critical Survey of Short Fiction,* edited by Walton Beacham, Salem Press, 1981; *Critical Survey of Long Fiction,* edited by Beacham, Salem Press, 1983; *A Chekhov Companion,* edited by Toby Clyman, Greenwood Press, 1985; and *Short Story Theory at a Crossroads,* edited by Lohafer and Clarey, Louisiana State University Press, 1989. Also contributor of over 100 articles to magazines, journals, and reference works.

WORK IN PROGRESS: The Theory and History of Short Fiction, six volumes, a study of short fiction of Europe, England, and America in the nineteenth and twentieth centuries; *The Short Story: Study of the Genre,* for Twayne; editing *New Approaches to Short Fiction;* editing *Interacting with Essays,* for Heath.

SIDELIGHTS: Charles E. May once told *CA:* "I grew up in a tiny Appalachian town of four thousand people. As a child, I liked to surround myself with books, which I read during the long, cold winters. Now I still find myself surrounded with books, and I wouldn't have it any other way. My teaching and writing are closely bound up together, with ideas developed in the classroom spilling over into print and research in the library and my study, hopefully enriching my classes. I wouldn't trade professions with anyone.

"My particular scholarly interest is the genre of short fiction. Although the form is primarily an American literary innovation, it has never been taken very seriously by academic critics. After reading practically everything that has been written about the form, I chose what I considered to be the best essays and edited them together in 1976 in

Short Story Theories, a book which I hoped would be a stimulus to other critics. And indeed, I am gratified to find that since the book was published, more critics are considering the particular characteristics of the short story. A new addition of the book will appear in 1994."

May recently added: "In a new book aimed at the college classroom, *Fiction's Many Worlds,* I have tried to integrate many of my ideas on the short story. I have also developed a software package for this book. Making use of hypertext techniques, I have created interactive versions of a number of short stories to help students transform mere temporal readings to discover 'what happens next' into spatial readings that reveal *what* the stories mean and *how* they mean what they do.

"My new book on the short story as a genre summarizes many of my theories about the form. My recent book on Edgar Allan Poe tries to account for his significant influence on the form. I am pleased that my writings on the short story have been so well received and that I may have played a role in the revival of critical interest in the form in the 1980s and 1990s."

BIOGRAPHICAL/CRITICAL SOURCES:

BOOKS

Lohafer and Clarey, *Short Story Theory at a Crossroads,* Louisiana State University Press, 1989.

PERIODICALS

College Composition and Communication, February, 1978.
Southern Quarterly, April, 1977.
Studies in Short Fiction, spring, 1992.

*   *   *

MAY, Florissa
  See GREEN, Kay

*   *   *

McCABE, Cameron
  See BORNEMAN, Ernest

*   *   *

McCARRY, Charles   1930-

PERSONAL: Born June 14, 1930, in Pittsfield, MA; son of Albert (a farmer) and Madeleine (Rees) McCarry; mar-

ried Nancy Neill, September 12, 1953; children: four sons. *Avocational interests:* Cooking.

ADDRESSES: Agent—Owen Laster, William Morris Agency, 1350 Avenue of the Americas, New York, NY 10019.

CAREER: Lisbon Evening Journal, Lisbon, OH, editor and reporter, 1952-55; *Youngstown Vindicator,* Youngstown, OH, reporter and columnist, 1955-56; assistant to Secretary of Labor, Washington, DC, 1956-57; worked for Central Intelligence Agency, 1958-67; free-lance writer and journalist, 1967-83; *National Geographic,* editor-at-large, 1983-90.

MEMBER: The Cosmos Club (Washington, DC).

WRITINGS:

NOVELS

The Miernik Dossier, Saturday Review Press, 1973.
The Tears of Autumn, Saturday Review Press, 1975.
The Secret Lovers, Dutton, 1977.
The Better Angels, Dutton, 1979.
The Last Supper, Dutton, 1983.
The Bride of the Wilderness, New American Library, 1988.
Second Sight, Dutton, 1991.

NONFICTION

Citizen Nader (biography), Saturday Review Press, 1972.
(With Ben Abruzzo, Maxie Anderson, and Larry Newman) *Double Eagle,* Little, Brown, 1979.
(Coauthor) *Isles of the Caribbean,* National Geographic Society, 1979.
The Great Southwest, National Geographic Society, 1980.
Caveat, Macmillan, 1983.
(With Donald T. Regan) *For the Record,* Harcourt, 1988.
(With Alexander M. Haig, Jr.) *Inner Circles: How America Changed the World,* Warner Books, 1992.

OTHER

Contributor of about one hundred stories and articles to magazines, including *Saturday Evening Post, Life, National Geographic, Esquire, Saturday Review,* and *True.*

WORK IN PROGRESS: A novel to be published by Random House in 1994.

SIDELIGHTS: Charles McCarry draws on both his experience as a reporter and his experience with the Central Intelligence Agency (CIA) to create insightful nonfiction accounts and suspenseful espionage novels. Among McCarry's works of nonfiction are his biography of government watchdog Ralph Nader, *Citizen Nader,* and his account of the voyage of the first three men to cross the Atlantic in a free balloon, *Double Eagle.* McCarry, however, is perhaps best known for his intricately plotted spy novels featuring CIA agent Paul Christopher. Praising McCarry's novels in *Armchair Detective,* Otto Penzler maintains: "For technical brilliance of plotting, combined with the brilliant achievements of characterization in a poetic composition of style that can wrench gasps of amazement from the reader, the work of Charles McCarry stands alone among the myriad American practitioners of that most difficult category of storytelling—the believable spy novel."

Despite his subsequent success in the fiction genre, McCarry began his writing career with the biography *Citizen Nader.* Nader, one of the best known public reformers of this century, has been expected to falter from the minute he burst on the Washington scene. This prophecy has yet to come true, and in *Citizen Nader* McCarry puts "together an interesting narrative of Nader's background, his rise to prominence, his forays into various issues, and the evolution of his thinking," according to Elizabeth Drew in the *New York Times Book Review.* "McCarry catches a good bit about Nader the human being that seems to have eluded many who write about him: the sense of humor, the somewhat childlike quality that arouses affection and protectiveness in his friends and associates, the intensity, the insatiable appetite for sheer information." A *Times Literary Supplement* contributor finds McCarry's account to be a bit shapeless because of its journalistic style, but concedes that "he has painted a vivid picture of Ralph Nader, his career and his associates, which provides a very good basis for consideration of an extraordinary phenomenon."

Another of McCarry's forays into nonfiction, *Double Eagle* tells the tale of three men who became the first to cross the Atlantic in a balloon. Based on tapes recorded by the participants during the flight, interviews, library research, and technical data, the narrative manages to be suspenseful even though the result of the adventure is already known. "This description of the first successful balloon-crossing of the Atlantic Ocean is a riveting affair—a remarkable achievement considering that we know the outcome before we begin," observes Jeff Greenfield in the *New York Times Book Review.* Macdonald Harris, writing in the *Times Literary Supplement,* points out that the personalities of all involved in the accomplishment are well depicted, and asserts: "*Double Eagle* does tell a beautiful story."

The stories McCarry has told since *Double Eagle* are also riveting and suspenseful, but the endings are far from being known. These are the novels that feature CIA agent and poet Paul Christopher, as well as many other spies and government officials. Christopher is introduced in McCarry's 1979 *The Miernik Dossier,* a story which is told in the form of a dossier, including reports, intercepted let-

ters, written communication, and bugged telephone conversations. Newgate Callendar, writing in the *New York Times Book Review,* calls *The Miernik Dossier* "a fast-moving tale of Byzantine intrigue," and Penzler finds it to be "an innovative novel."

The Tears of Autumn, McCarry's second thriller, has Christopher delving into the events surrounding Kennedy's assassination. A specialist in Vietnamese affairs, Christopher discovers a link between the killings of Ngo Dinh Diem and Ngo Dinh Nhu in Saigon and Kennedy's subsequent death. The assassination is portrayed as a revenge killing—blood for blood. "It is a clever idea, and McCarry makes the most of it," asserts Callendar in his review of *The Tears of Autumn.* Once Christopher realizes that the most prominent members of the Administration were inadvertently responsible for Kennedy's death, he is forbidden to continue his investigation. He resigns, only to become hunted by both the assassins and his own government. "This absolutely first-rate thriller is an irresistibly plausible speculation into the real motives for Kennedy's murder," maintains a *Library Journal* contributor.

In his third adventure, *The Secret Lovers,* Christopher is a witness to the killing of a Russian courier who is carrying what may be a very damaging piece of literature for the regime. Now that they have the book in their possession, the American agents must decide whether to follow the author's request of holding off the publishing until after his death, or print it regardless of the consequences. Also attempting to discover who tried to stop the operation, the agents find themselves following a plot that twists and turns all the way back to the Spanish Civil War. And in addition to this complex case, Christopher is also struggling to hold his unraveling marriage together. *The Secret Lovers* "is well written, well observed and warmed by attractive characters," points out Anatole Broyard in the *New York Times Book Review.* And *Publishers Weekly* contributor Barbara A. Bannon observes that McCarry "writes about the innermost workings of American intelligence operations with a cool expertise."

The Last Supper, published in 1983, and *Second Sight,* published in 1991, also center around the activities of Paul Christopher. *Last Supper* contains the ingredients of McCarry's usual spy thriller, but adds elements of family saga as Christopher traces the history of a secret American intelligence group calling themselves the Outfit. The trail leads all the way from Nazi Germany to the present time. "*The Last Supper* is a giant maze through which the reader is led by a guide who knows every inch of the apparently hostile and shifting territory," describes Penzler. In what McCarry deems to be Christopher's last adventure, *Second Sight,* the agent is brought out of retirement to stop an attempt by outsiders to learn vital agency secrets. Zarah, Christopher's long-lost daughter, is along for this adventure—the same organization threatening the Outfit's security is also threatening the band of Jewish nomads that raised her. "A marvelously drawn cast of characters join forces against evil in this compulsive page turner," relates Bettie Spivey Cormier in *Library Journal.* Sybil Steinberg, summing up McCarry's "Christopher" books in *Publishers Weekly,* states: "There is no denying McCarry's remarkable narrative gifts, his imaginative use of little-known information and his insider's knowledge of the CIA."

McCarry's 1988 novel *The Bride of the Wilderness* greatly deviates from his spy thrillers. The various settings of this saga include 18th Century London and New England, and there is a heroine instead of the usual hero. Fanny Harding, who manages to master anything she is exposed to, leaves England behind for an epic adventure in America. Surrounded by many other heroic figures, she constantly moves into new and alien worlds, including that of the Abenaki Indians—a seemingly savage tribe. "Skillfully using an omniscient narrative voice, McCarry moves us cleanly back and forth in time," explains Orson Scott Card in the *Washington Post Book World,* adding that "there are more stories told in this one book than most writers tell in a career." Also pointing out McCarry's shameless use of romance archetypes, Card concludes: "I never believed the characters for a moment—but I loved them, I lived their lives with them, and I will never forget the time I spent in their world."

BIOGRAPHICAL/CRITICAL SOURCES:

PERIODICALS

Armchair Detective, summer, 1989, pp. 272-73.
Library Journal, January 1, 1975, p. 67; June 1, 1991.
Los Angeles Times Book Review, May 8, 1983.
New Republic, August 4, 1979, pp. 42-44.
New York Times Book Review, March 19, 1972, pp. 7, 10, 12; July 8, 1973; March 23, 1975; May 1, 1977; July 29, 1979; September 16, 1979; April 23, 1989, p. 34.
Publishers Weekly, March 7, 1977, p. 90; April 16, 1979, p. 69; May 3, 1991, p. 65.
Times Literary Supplement, April 27, 1973, p. 463; June 13, 1980.
Village Voice, July 3, 1984.
Washington Post Book World, August 7, 1988, pp. 1-2.

—Sketch by Susan M. Reicha

*　　　*　　　*

McCONKEY, James (Rodney) 1921-

PERSONAL: Born September 2, 1921, in Lakewood, OH; son of Clayton Delano and Grace (Baird) McConkey; married Gladys Voorhees, 1944; children: Lawrence Clark, John Crispin, James Clayton. *Education:* Cleveland College, B.A., 1943; Western Reserve University (now Case Western Reserve University), M.A., 1946; State University of Iowa, Ph.D., 1953.

ADDRESSES: Home—402 Aiken Rd., Trumansburg, NY 14886. *Office*—Department of English, Cornell University, Goldwin Smith Hall, Ithaca, NY 14853.

CAREER: Cleveland College, Cleveland, OH, teaching fellow, 1945-46; State University of Iowa, Iowa City, teaching assistant, 1949-50; Morehead State College (now Morehead State University), Morehead, KY, began as assistant professor, associate professor, 1950-56; Cornell University, Ithaca, NY, began as assistant professor, associate professor, 1956-62, professor of English, 1962-87, Goldwin Smith Professor of English Literature, 1987-92, Goldwin Smith Professor of English Literature Emeritus, 1992—. Morehead Writer's Workshop, director, 1951-56; Antioch Seminar in Writing and Publishing, Yellow Springs, OH, director, 1957-60. *Military service:* U.S. Army Infantry, 1943-45; became corporal.

MEMBER: PEN.

AWARDS, HONORS: Eugene Saxton Literary Fellow, 1962-63; National Endowment for the Arts Essay Award, 1967; Ohioana Book Award, 1969, for *Crossroads;* Guggenheim fellow, 1969-70; American Academy and Institute of Arts and Letters Award in Literature, 1979, for *The Tree House Confessions.*

WRITINGS:

The Novels of E. M. Forster, Cornell University Press, 1957.
(Editor) *The Structure of Prose,* Harcourt, 1963.
Night Stand, Cornell University Press, 1965.
Crossroads: An Autobiographical Novel, Dutton, 1968.
A Journey to Sahalin (novel), Coward, 1971.
The Tree House Confessions (novel), Dutton, 1979.
Court of Memory, Dutton, 1983.
To a Distant Island (novel), Dutton, 1984.
(Editor) *Chekhov and Our Age: Responses to Chekhov by American Writers and Scholars,* Center for International Studies, Council of the Creative and Performing Arts, Cornell University, 1984.
Kayo: The Authentic and Annotated Autobiographical Novel from Outer Space (novel), Dutton, 1987.
Rowan's Progress, Pantheon, 1992.
Stories from My Life with the Other Animals, David Godine, 1993.

Also editor of *Kentucky Writing, I and II,* Morehead State College, 1954, 1956. Contributor of stories and essays to *Atlantic, Western Review, Yale Review, New Yorker,* and other periodicals.

WORK IN PROGRESS: Editing *The Oxford Book of Memories,* an anthology of works dealing with memory, for Oxford University Press.

SIDELIGHTS: James McConkey has proven himself as a skilled writer in many genres: literary criticism, short stories, novels, and memoirs. His first publications were scholarly works, little read by the general public; Mc-Conkey's first widely-reviewed book was *The Tree House Confessions.* In this novel, the protagonist, Peter Warden, has a visionary experience at his mother's deathbed. He feels absolute freedom from all the constraints of daily life. An urgent need to hold on to that revelation and examine it sends him away from his wife and into a treehouse he once built for his son, who is now dead. The body of the book is the writing that Warden does that summer—a love letter to his wife, reminiscences of his childhood, an exploration of his parents and their relationship, and finally a set of musings on his college years, marriages, and career. Through these writings, Warden attempts to come to terms with his life. *New York Times* reviewer Christopher Lehmann-Haupt reserves high praise for the childhood section of the novel, stating that it is "a haunting Wordsworthian evocation" of youth. He is less enthusiastic about the later sections, however, believing that "the gradual deterioration of Peter's (and Mr. McConkey's?) prose . . . suggests that he is getting farther from an understanding of himself rather than nearer. And given the wealth of clues betraying Peter's psychological problems, I can't help feeling that his experience is neurotic rather than spiritual." London *Times* contributor Stuart Evans has no such reservations, and finds the book as a whole to be remarkably fine. He writes: "Towards the end of the novel, Warden says that there has been nothing extraordinary in the story so far. No: Except that it has been told with perception, moral authority and a truly sensitive consideration for other people, in beautiful, well-considered prose."

Just as *The Tree House Confessions* begins with a religious experience of sorts, so too does *Court of Memory,* a collection of nonfiction, autobiographical pieces. McConkey describes how, at the height of the Cold War anxieties, he suddenly became aware of the precious nature of every commonplace moment. A side effect of this realization was feelings of impatience and dissatisfaction with fiction: it seemed to him to be a way of distancing the self from the realities of life that now seemed almost holy. The twenty-one essays in the book cover a wide range of human experience, from wartime experiences to child-rearing. Whatever the subject, "the author respects his opportunities, grasping that the least of them allows him— and those of us who see ourselves in him—precious glimpses of our possibilities as serious persons," writes Benjamin De Mott in the *New York Times Book Review.*

"The beauty and exceptional worth—now and then, yes, the awkward humorlessness—of 'Court of Memory,' . . . is that it never ducks and runs" from moments of emotion or self-examination.

In his next book, *To a Distant Island,* McConkey mingles fiction and memoir in a way that many reviewers judge uncommonly skillful. The book had its origins in a sabbatical McConkey spent in Florence, after a period of campus violence at his school left him emotionally drained. During his time abroad, the author became absorbed in the works of Anton Chekhov, developing a particular fascination with a strange trip that the Russian author took in 1890. Thirty years old, already famous and well respected, Chekhov nevertheless fell into a peculiar depression. He amazed and alarmed his friends when he announced his intention to travel 6,500 miles across Siberia to the desolate prison colony of Sakhalin. McConkey surmised that Chekhov's motivations for the journey were similar to his own reasons for coming to Florence. *To a Distant Island* is both an imaginative recreation of Chekhov's expedition and the story of McConkey's modern spiritual search. Jay Parini writes in the *Washington Post Book World:* "This new novel, which is and isn't a novel by conventional standards, shows off McConkey's talents at their best; its clear-eyed, lyrical style is marvelously sustained, and the author's voice remains as familiar, intelligent, and idiosyncratic as ever." Parini finds that McConkey's best writing is in the sections concerning Chekhov's journey; his "vivid language is well suited to landscape descriptions, and one gets a full sense of what it might have been like to travel across Russia in 1890. The account of Chekhov's stay on Sakhalin island itself is equally vivid, and nightmarish. One moves with Chekhov through this nether world of the living dead, an inferno of tormented and tormenting souls. . . . McConkey's own stay in Florence seems rather pale beside Chekhov's sojourn in Sakhalin. . . . But *To a Distant Island* is, on the whole, remarkably successful—a deeply moving, exquisitely written book." *New York Times* reviewer Harvey Shapiro notes similarly that "Mr. McConkey describes [Chekhov's] journey brilliantly—the scenes, the people, their probable impact on his subject. It is only in the later parts of the book, when he begins mechanically to alternate the account of his minor journey to Florence with Chekhov's major journey to Sakhalin that his book stalls; the connections he wants to make seem tenuous." However, Shapiro concludes that "Mr. McConkey's achievement in this fictionalized account of one chapter of Chekhov's life is to send the reader back to the Russian master with renewed wonder."

McConkey returned to pure fiction with *Kayo: The Authentic and Annotated Autobiographical Novel from Outer Space.* Reviews were mixed on this offering, which was described by *Los Angeles Times Book Review* writer John

Clute as an "intensely academic, self-referential 'postmodern' spoof of the satirical utopias more often found in European than in American science fiction." Clute expresses impatience with the intellectual wordplay and symbolism in the satire, writing that "games of this sort collapse into tedium and nullity if they are not infused with some overriding passion—for life, for the act of fabrication, for words themselves. McConkey's obvious models for 'Kayo' are books like Vladimir Nabokov's deeply elegiac 'Pale Fire' or John Barth's 'Giles Goat-Boy.' Both of these texts are self-conscious, arch, and self-referential; but both are energetic and full of love for the act of storytelling. 'Kayo' on the other hand lacks energy, lacks love. Because it is only a game, it crumbles into dust." Michael Anania differs strongly in the *New York Times Book Review.* He also notes McConkey's debt to Nabokov, Cervantes, and other master writers, but in his opinion, McConkey does justice to his models. Anania concludes: "Kayo's story is a wonderful satire on contemporary American life. Like the best satirists, Mr. McConkey uses the exaggeration of this otherworld to magnify and examine the inanities of our own. . . . In the midst of all the argument and counterargument, Mr. McConkey also gives us a wonderfully comic tale."

McConkey once again demonstrated his versatility by following the high intellectual satire of *Kayo* with a down-to-earth, real-life story of social development in the town where he spent his early years as a professor—Morehead, Kentucky. During the late nineteenth century, this small town in Rowan County was the setting for some very bloody, whiskey-inspired feuding between the Martin and Tolliver clans. The violence was such that more than half of the residents of the county eventually moved away. The first part of *Rowan's Progress* chronicles the feud; the second begins in 1950, when the author and his young family came to Morehead to live. It follows the lives of two remarkable women, a doctor and an educator, who did much to bring social progress to the county. The story is in itself fascinating, according to reviewers, but Louis D. Rubin, Jr. emphasizes in the *New York Times Book Review* that "what makes James McConkey's book so appealing, of course, is not simply the story of a small town's civic progress, or even the compelling role that one remarkable woman played in that success, but the way in which his own literary imagination has involved itself in the nature of this particular community's flowering. . . . It is not often that one gets to read a book like 'Rowan's Progress,' so well written, so sensible—not only heartening but enthralling."

McConkey's most recent work, *Stories from My Life with the Other Animals,* is the last volume of his autobiographical writings. He explains why he wrote these works, and why he is now finished with them in the foreword to the book: "*Stories from My Life with the Other Animals* is the third and concluding volume of *Court of Memory,* a more than thirty-year exploration of an ever-expanding personal past. When I embarked upon this autobiographical journey in 1960, I had no idea that it would go very far. It began out of personal need—from a desire that came to me late on a winter night, as nuclear war seemed an imminent possibility, to acknowledge my love for my family and the sacredness I felt in everything about me, and to communicate my truths, however subjective they might be, to anybody who would listen. The period covered by the three volumes approximates that of the Cold War. Though humanity faces problems of such urgency that they must be solved if we are to endure through the next millennium, the Cold War, at least, has become history. The reasons I am ending my account are only tangentially related to the ending of the Cold War, but I suppose *Stories from My Life with the Other Animals* and the two volumes that precede it can be read as the story of an American—a representative one, I hope—who was led to consider the possible meanings and the value of his life against the threat of mass extinction in the epoch that fortunately has come to a close."

BIOGRAPHICAL/CRITICAL SOURCES:

BOOKS

McConkey, James, *Stories from My Life with the Other Animals,* David Godine, 1993.

PERIODICALS

Los Angeles Times Book Review, February 6, 1983, p. 1; August 19, 1984, p. 2; May 17, 1987, p. 10.
New York Times, April 13, 1979; January 19, 1983; June 25, 1984.
New York Times Book Review, January 28, 1968; April 8, 1979, p. 7; January 16, 1983, pp. 3, 25; July 22, 1984, p. 25; June 28, 1987, p. 31; February 16, 1992, p. 11.
Saturday Review, January 20, 1968.
Times (London), March 20, 1980.
Times Literary Supplement, March 28, 1980, p. 368.
Washington Post Book World, June 3, 1979, p. E4; February 13, 1983, p. 6; June 17, 1984, pp. 4, 11; December 14, 1986, p. 12; February 16, 1992, p. 6.

—*Sketch by Joan Goldsworthy*

*   *   *

McEWAN, Ian (Russell) 1948-

PERSONAL: Born June 21, 1948, in Aldershot, England; son of David (an army officer) and Rose Lilian Violet (Moore) McEwan; married Penny Allen (a healer and astrologer), 1982; children: two sons, two daughters. *Educa-*

tion: University of Sussex, B.A. (with honors), 1970; University of East Anglia, M.A., 1971. *Avocational interests:* Hiking, tennis.

CAREER: Writer, beginning 1970.

AWARDS, HONORS: Somerset Maugham Award, 1976, for *First Love, Last Rites;* shortlisted for Booker Prize, 1981, for *The Comfort of Strangers; Evening Standard* award for best screenplay, 1983, for *The Ploughman's Lunch;* Whitbread Award, 1987, for *The Child in Time;* honorary D.Litt., University of Sussex, 1989.

WRITINGS:

SHORT STORIES

First Love, Last Rites (contains "Last Day of Summer" and "Conversations with a Cupboardman"; also see below), Random House, 1975.
In Between the Sheets, and Other Stories, Simon & Schuster, 1978.

NOVELS

The Cement Garden, Simon & Schuster, 1978.
The Comfort of Strangers (also see below), Simon & Schuster, 1981.
The Child in Time, Houghton, 1987.
The Innocent, Doubleday, 1990.
Black Dogs, J. Cape, 1992.

PLAYS

Conversations with a Cupboardman (radio play based on a story by McEwan), British Broadcasting Corporation (BBC), 1975.
The Imitation Game; Three Plays for Television (contains "Jack Flea's Celebration" [BBC-TV, 1976], "Solid Geometry," and "The Imitation Game" [BBC-TV, 1980]), J. Cape, 1981.
Or Shall We Die: An Oratorio (produced at Royal Festival Hall, 1983, produced at Carnegie Hall, 1985), score by Michael Berkeley, J. Cape, 1983.
The Ploughman's Lunch (screenplay, Samuel Goldwyn, 1983), Methuen, 1985.
Strangers (adapted from *The Comfort of Strangers*), produced in London, 1989.

Author of *Last Day of Summer* (screenplay based on a story by McEwan), 1984; and *The Innocent* (screenplay adapted from the novel by McEwan). Adaptor, with Mike Newell, of *Sour Sweet* (screenplay based on novel by Timothy Mo), 1989.

OTHER

Contributor to periodicals and literary journals, including the *Guardian, New American Review, New Review, Radio*

Times, Sunday Telegraph, Times Literary Supplement, Transatlantic Review, and *Tri-Quarterly.*

ADAPTATIONS: The Comfort of Strangers was adapted for film by Harold Pinter, 1991.

WORK IN PROGRESS: A novel.

SIDELIGHTS: British author Ian McEwan is considered by some critics to be the most famous protege of British novelist Malcolm Bradbury, a noted professor of creative writing at the University of East Anglia. Within his fictional worlds, McEwan weaves a haunting perversity: Childhood collides with violence and power manifests itself in aberrant sexuality and political authoritarianism. The element of horror is that existing within mankind—it is not an abstract terror generated by some mysterious, supernatural force—and the author explores it in a style described by George Stade in the *New York Times Book Review* as "self-effacing rather than gaudy prose, as cold and transparent as a pane of ice, noticeable only in that things on the other side of it are clearer and brighter than they should be, a touch sinister in their dazzle."

The collection of stories McEwan wrote for his master's thesis at the age of twenty-two was published in 1975 as *First Love, Last Rites.* Writing in the *New York Review of Books,* Robert Towers praises the collection as "possibly the most brilliantly perverse and sinister batch of short stories to come out of England since Angus Wilson's *The Wrong Set.*" Towers describes the author's England as a "flat, rubble-strewn wasteland, populated by freaks and monsters, most of them articulate enough to tell their own stories with mesmerizing narrative power and an unfaltering instinct for the perfect sickening detail." The "freaks" that inhabit the stories in *First Love, Last Rites* include an incestuous brother and sister, a gentleman who lives in a cupboard, a child-slayer, and a man who keeps the penis of a nineteenth-century criminal preserved in a jar. "Such writing would be merely sensational if it were not, like Kafka's so pointed, so accurate, so incapable indeed of being appalled," writes John Fletcher in *Dictionary of Literary Biography.* "In contemporary writing one has to turn to French literature to encounter a similar contrast between the elegance of the language and the disturbing quality of the material; in writing in English McEwan is wholly unique. No one else combines in quite the same way exactness of notation with a comedy so black that many readers may fail to see the funny side at all."

McEwan's first novel, *The Cement Garden,* had been likened to William Golding's *Lord of the Flies.* The book depicts four children's regression into a feral state with "suspense and chilling impact but without the philosophy lesson," as William McPherson notes in *Washington Post Book World.* McEwan's children have been raised in an isolation similar to the protagonists of Golding's novel: a

Victorian house that stands alone among the abandoned ruins of a post-war housing subdivision. After their parents die in quick succession, the children hide their absence (and in one case, the corpse) while the eldest siblings unsuccessfully attempt to assume parental roles. The children eventually lapse into filth and apathy while the house decays until an outsider discovers the orphans' secret and summons the police to the scene. Towers describes *The Cement Garden* as "a shocking book, morbid, full of repellent imagery—and irresistibly readable, . . . the work of a writer in full control of his materials" and calls McEwan's approach "magic realism—a transfiguration of the ordinary that has a far stronger retinal and visceral impact than the flabby surrealism of so many 'experimental' novels. The settings and events reinforce one another symbolically, but the symbolism never seems contrived or obtrusive." Fletcher praises the author's "quiet, precise, and sensuous touch" but adds that "it is difficult to see how McEwan can develop much further this line in grotesque horror and black comedy, with a strong admixture of eroticism and perversion."

McEwan's second collection of short stories, *In Between the Sheets,* also attracted a great deal of critical attention when it was published three years later. While the cast includes such typically unsavory characters as a romantic ape who laments the end of his affair with a woman writer and a man who eats ground glass, washes it down with juice, and then hurls himself under a train, several critics praised what they saw as the author's more restrained approach to his subject matter. V. S. Pritchett notes in the *New York Review of Books* that "McEwan is experimenting more," but adds that the collection contains "two encouraging breaks with 'mean' writing." Reviewing *In Between the Sheets* in the *Washington Post Book World,* Terrence Winch notes that McEwan's prose "is as clear as a windowpane" and calls the author "a gifted story-teller and possibly the best British writer to appear in a decade or more."

In contrast to the protagonists in his earlier works, McEwan's 1981 novel, *The Comfort of Strangers,* features a well-groomed, respectable couple on holiday in Venice. However, the author gradually draws his unsuspecting characters into a web of horror that climaxes in sadomasochistic murder. Although continuing his praise for McEwan's gifts as a storyteller, John Leonard finds the novel's plot contrived and unbelievable in *The New York Times,* adding that "this novel, by a writer of enormous talent, is definitely diseased." Stephen Koch, too, faults the plot while praising McEwan's craftsmanship. "McEwan proceeds through most of this sickly tale with subtlety and promise," Koch writes in the *Washington Post Book World.* "The difficulty is that all this skill is directed toward a climax which, even though it is duly horrific, is

sapped by a certain thinness and plain banality at its core. After an impressive send-up, the sado-masochistic fantasy animating *The Comfort of Strangers* is revealed as . . . a sado-masochistic fantasy. And not much more." But Koch goes on to praise the novel: "In all his recent fiction, McEwan seems to be reaching toward some new imaginative accommodation to the sexual questions of innocence and adulthood, role and need that have defined, with such special intensity, his generation. . . . I honor him for his effort."

The focus of McEwan's fiction underwent a shift after the birth of his own children. He told Amanda Smith in an interview for *Publishers Weekly:* "It was both inevitable and desirable that my own range or preoccupation should change and that my emotional range should increase. Having children has been a major experience in my life in the past few years. It's extended me emotionally, personally, in ways that could never be guessed at. It's inevitable that that change would be reflected in my writing." His 1987 novel *The Child in Time* confronts the unconscious fears and insecurities universally felt by parents: That a child might be separated from them and come to harm. In the novel, a three-year-old girl is stolen from her father's shopping cart at the grocery store. Despite a massive search, the child's whereabouts are never discovered and her parents' relationship disintegrates due to guilt, anger, and each parent's personal grieving. The mother retreats to a country house, and the father is left to find solace in the mindlessness of television and alcohol, and in his friendship with a man who, ironically, soon divests himself of adult responsibility and retreats to a child-like state of madness. McEwan's plot is threaded through with political hazards: the threat of nuclear war combines with economic collapse to propel the political state towards authoritarianism. Some critics felt that the complexity of the subject made the novel uneven. "What McEwan clearly has in mind is to document the . . . timelessness of childhood, to show how the child is never fully dead within us," comments Jonathan Yardley, reviewing the book in the *Washington Post Book World.* But, Yardley adds, "theme and story never quite connect." Michiko Kakutani agrees in the *New York Times,* noting that "if these motifs were successfully woven together, they might have reinforced McEwan's reverent vision of childhood, endowed it with some sort of symphonic resonance. As it is, they feel like afterthoughts grafted onto [the] story and not fully assimilated into the text." However, R. Z. Sheppard praises the book in *Time:* "McEwan bridges the chasm between private anguish and public policy with a death-defying story, inventive, eventful and affirmative without being sentimental."

McEwan explores the espionage of a past epoch in his fourth novel, *The Innocent,* which critics have compared to the work of such masters of the spy genre as John Le Carre and Graham Greene. Within the cold-war tensions of mid-1950 Berlin, the author creates a fiction overlaying the joint effort by the American CIA and British MI6 to infiltrate Soviet phone conversations by tunneling underneath East German phone lines. McEwan uses metaphor and symbolism to transform the historic account into a lesson on the dangers of ignoring the Socratic counsel "Know thyself." His protagonist, a placid, naive electronics technician employed by the British post office, suddenly finds himself embroiled in international tensions and swept up in the complex lives of what George V. Higgins calls McEwan's "richly supporting cast" in a review for the *Chicago Tribune.*

Setting up the stereotypic rigid Englishman, the brash American, and a sensual German seductress in his plot, the author then proceeds to penetrate their surfaces, flesh them out, and reveal their individuality. Calling McEwan "an acute psychologist of the ordinary mind," Stade praises *The Innocent,* noting of its author that "he gets our mundane virtues and vices, our craziness and sanities, exactly right, without the distortions of cynicism or sentimentality. . . . [and demonstrates] how violence and horror can erupt from what that mind does not know about itself." Comparing the novel to *The Child in Time,* Michiko Kakutani deems *The Innocent* "bone tight: every detail of every event works as a time bomb, waiting to go off, while every image seems to pay off in terms of plot, atmosphere or theme" in his review in the *New York Times.* Richard Eder commends the entertaining quality of McEwan's novel in a review for the *Los Angeles Times Book Review,* but notes that the ending is jarred loose from the work by an interlude of violence he calls "all but unbearable to read." "*The Innocent* evokes a dark moral world in a highly entertaining fashion," writes Eder. "Unlike Greene's entertainments, however, McEwan's leaves not even the trace of a feeling behind it." Higgins disagrees. "The reader's reward for all this ambiguity and gore is a book about a spy-tunnel that is not about a tunnel at all," notes Higgins, "but about people whom you recognize; you see them every day. . . . This is the function of good novels: They enable us to snoop, undetected, unobserved, into the details of other people's lives."

Black Dogs, published in 1992, is a novel narrated by a man endeavoring to collect the pieces of his family's history to compose a memoir. The black dogs of the book's title refer to a vision that haunts one of the narrator's relatives, and they represent the evil that lurks within every man. "The book richly suggests our human potentialities for mere waste as well as sheer evil, and for a sort of imperilled happiness," notes Caroline Moore in the *Spectator;* "the dogs, which disappear into the foothills of Europe like 'black stains in a grey dawn,' could take any form to

reappear." As one of McEwan's characters explains: "When the conditions are right, in different countries, at different times, a terrible cruelty, a viciousness against life erupts, and everyone is surprised by the depth of hatred within himself." The metaphoric black dogs clearly echo the themes more subtly expressed in McEwan's previous fiction. As M. John Harrison notes in the *Times Literary Supplement,* "McEwan's retreat from the cement garden of his earlier books has been exemplary . . . [*Black Dogs* is] an undisguised novel of ideas which is also Ian McEwan's best work."

In addition to his novels and short stories, McEwan is the author of several motion picture screenplays, including *The Innocent,* based on his novel, and the original *The Ploughman's Lunch,* which *New York Times* film critic Vincent Canby praises as "immensely intelligent." He has also written several scripts for television, including *Solid Geometry,* notorious in his native Britain for having been banned by the BBC in 1979 at an advanced stage of production due to its "grotesque and bizarre sexual elements." Commenting on the violence that some critics perceive as his fictional trademark—and so deem him "Ian Macabre"—McEwan commented to Daniel Johnson in the *Times Saturday Review,* "I don't think I am particularly obsessed by violence, but at the same time I am very disturbed by it. I suppose many of the things that disturb me find their way into my fiction." Remarking on his preference for the novel over the screenplay or the short story as a fictional means of expressing his concerns, McEwan explained to *Publishers Weekly* interviewer Amanda Smith: "The reason the novel is such a powerful form is that it allows the examination of the private life better than any other art form. Our common sense gives us such a thin wedge of light on the world, and perhaps one task of the writer is to broaden the wedge."

BIOGRAPHICAL/CRITICAL SOURCES:

BOOKS

Contemporary Literary Criticism, Volume 13, Gale, 1980.
Dictionary of Literary Biography, Volume 14: *British Novelists since 1960,* Gale, 1983, pp. 495-500.
McEwan, Ian, *Black Dogs,* J. Cape, 1992.

PERIODICALS

Bomb, fall, 1990, pp. 14-16.
Chicago Tribune Book World, November 26, 1978; September 30, 1979; July 19, 1981; June 10, 1990, p. 7.
Encounter, June, 1975; January, 1979.
Globe & Mail (Toronto), April 16, 1988; June 2. 1990.
Listener, April 12, 1979, pp. 526-27.
London Magazine, August, 1975; February, 1979.
Los Angeles Times Book Review, June 24, 1990, p. 3.
Monthly Film Bulletin, June, 1983.

New Review, autumn, 1978, pp. 9-21.

New Statesman & Society, May 11, 1990, pp. 18-19, 35-36.

New York Review of Books, March 8, 1979; January 24, 1980.

New York Times, November 21, 1978; August 14, 1979; June 15, 1981; September 26, 1987; May 29, 1990.

New York Times Book Review, November 26, 1978; August 26, 1979; July 5, 1981; June 3, 1990, p. 1.

Publishers Weekly, September 11, 1987, pp. 68-69.

Spectator, June 27, 1992, p. 32.

Time, November 17, 1978; September 21, 1987.

Times (London), February 16, 1981; October 8, 1981; June 27, 1987; May 8, 1990.

Times Literary Supplement, January 20, 1978; September 19, 1978; October 9, 1981; June 19, 1992.

Times Saturday Review, December 8, 1990, pp. 16-17.

Virginia Quarterly Review, autumn, 1975.

Washington Post Book World, October 29, 1978; August 5, 1979; June 28, 1981; April 30, 1987; June 3, 1990, p. 10.*

Sketch by Pamela L. Shelton

*   *   *

McMULLEN, Lorraine 1926-

PERSONAL: Born July 27, 1926, in Ottawa, Ontario, Canada; daughter of John Edmund (a public servant) and Anna (a public servant; maiden name, Foley) McMullen. *Education:* Royal Victoria Hospital, R.N., 1947; University of Ottawa, B.Sc.N., 1948, B.A., 1963, M.A., 1967, Ph.D., 1970.

ADDRESSES: Office—Department of English, University of Ottawa, 550 Cumberland St., Ottawa, Ontario, Canada K1N 6N5.

CAREER: St. Catharines-Lincoln Health Unit, St. Catharines, Ontario, public health nurse, 1948-50; associated with Victorian Order of Nurses, Ottawa, Ontario, 1950-54; Bell Telephone Co. Occupational Health Center, Ottawa, head nurse, 1954-63; North Dundas District High School, Chesterfield, Ontario, teacher of English, 1965-67; Woodroffe High School, Ottawa, teacher of English, 1965-67; University of Ottawa, Ottawa, associated with Teachers' College, 1968-69, lecturer, 1969-72, assistant professor, 1972-74, associate professor, 1975-76, professor of English, 1980—. Visiting professor, Concordia University, Montreal, summers, 1975-76, University of British Columbia, 1988-89, 1991; visiting scholar, University of Edinburgh, 1982. Member of assessment committee for Canadian research tools, Social Sciences and Humanities Research Council of Canada.

MEMBER: Association for Canadian and Quebec Literature (vice-president, 1976-77; member of executive com-

mittee, 1978-80), Canadian Association for Commonwealth Literature and Language Studies (member of executive committee, 1980-83), Canadian Research Institute for the Advancement of Women, Association of Canadian University Teachers of English, Modern Language Association, American Society for 18th-Century Studies, Northeast Modern Language Association.

AWARDS, HONORS: Grants from Canada Council, 1976-77 and 1978-80; grants from Social Science and Humanities Research Council of Canada, 1980 and 1982-83.

WRITINGS:

An Introduction to the Aesthetic Movement, Bytown Press, 1971.

Sinclair Ross, G. K. Hall, 1979, 2nd edition, Tecumseh Press, 1990.

An Odd Attempt in a Woman: The Literary Life of Frances Brooke, University of British Columbia Press, 1983.

Ernest Thompson Seton and His Works (monograph), ECW Press, 1989.

(With Carrie MacMillan and Elizabeth Waterston) *Silenced Sextet: Six Nineteenth-Century Women Novelists,* McGill/Queen's University Press, 1993.

EDITOR AND AUTHOR OF INTRODUCTION

Selected Stories of E. W. Thomson, University of Ottawa Press, 1973.

Twentieth-Century Essays on Confederation Literature, Tecumseh Press, 1976.

The Lampman Symposium, University of Ottawa Press, 1976.

The Race, and Other Stories by Sinclair Ross, University of Ottawa Press, 1976.

The Ethel Wilson Symposium, University of Ottawa Press, 1982.

Re(Dis)covering our Foremothers: Nineteenth-Century Canadian Women Writers, University of Ottawa Press, 1989.

(Co-editor, with Sandra Campbell) *New Women: Stories by Canadian Women, 1900-1920,* University of Ottawa Press, 1991.

(Co-editor, with Campbell) *Pioneering Women: Short Stories by Canadian Women, 1880-1900,* University of Ottawa Press, 1993.

General editor, "Early Canadian Women Writers" series, Tecumseh Press.

OTHER

Contributor to books, including *Amazing Space: Canadian Women Writing, Dictionary of British and American Women Writers 1660-1800, New Canadian Encyclopedia, Profiles in Canadian Literature, Dictionary of Literary Bi-*

ography, Volumes 88 and 99, and *Oxford Companion to Canadian Literature.*

Contributor to literary journals, including *Canadian Children's Literature, Canadian Ethnic Studies, Canadian Fiction Magazine, Fiddlehead, Inscape, Studies in Canadian Literature,* and *World Literature Written in English .* Associate editor, *Journal of Canadian Fiction,* 1976—; guest editor, *Laurentian University Review,* November, 1976, and *Atlantis: A Women's Studies Journal,* Volume IV, number 1, 1978; member of editorial board, *Canadian Poetry* and *Atlantis.*

WORK IN PROGRESS: Co-editing *Pioneering Women: Short Stories by Canadian Women, 1800-1880* with Sandra Campbell for publication by University of Ottawa Press in 1994.

SIDELIGHTS: Lorraine McMullen once told *CA:* "At one time I was a public health nurse, but I was led by literary interests to my present profession. My main areas are Canadian literature, eighteenth- and nineteenth-century British literature, and images of women in literature. I also teach in the Women's Studies Program at the University of Ottawa."

McMullen later added: "In recent years I have been directing my research to recovering lost or neglected Canadian women authors. In 1988 I organized a symposium on nineteenth-century Canadian women writers, and the following year published the papers resulting from this symposium as *Re(Dis)covering Our Foremothers.* The volume of short fiction by earlier Canadian women and other recent publications are an outcome of this interest."

BIOGRAPHICAL/CRITICAL SOURCES:

PERIODICALS

Times Literary Supplement, December 21, 1984.

*   *   *

MEYER, Lynn
    See SLAVITT, David R(ytman)

*   *   *

MIKESELL, Raymond F(rech)   1913-

PERSONAL: Born February 13, 1913, in Eaton, OH; son of Otho Francis (a businessman) and Josephine (Frech) Mikesell; married Desyl De Lauder, July 6, 1937 (deceased); married Irene Langdoc, 1956; children: (first marriage) George D., Norman D. *Education:* Attended Carnegie Institute of Technology (now Carnegie-Mellon

University), 1931-33; Ohio State University, B.A., 1935, M.A., 1935, Ph.D., 1939. *Religion:* Non-sectarian. *Avocational interests:* Hiking, tennis, skiing.

ADDRESSES: Home—2290 Spring Blvd., Eugene, OR 97403. *Office*—Department of Economics, University of Oregon, Eugene, OR 97403.

CAREER: University of Washington, Seattle, assistant professor, 1937-41; U.S. Government, various appointments as economist, 1941-83, including U.S. Treasury Department, 1942-47, one year of that time as Treasury representative in Cairo, Egypt, President's Foreign Economic Policy Commission, 1953-54, Council of Economic Advisors, 1955-56; University of Virginia, Charlottesville, professor, 1946-57; University of Oregon, Eugene, acting director, Institute of International Studies and Overseas Administration, 1956-60, associate director, 1960-68, W. E. Miner Professor of Economics, 1957—. Visiting professor, Graduate Institute of International Studies, Geneva, Switzerland, 1964. Co-chairman of Research Council, Center for Strategic and International Studies, Georgetown University, 1976-81; member, National Materials Advisory Board, 1981-84; chair, National Economics Committee, Sierra Club, 1988—. Consultant to U.S. Department of State, 1947-53, 1963-67, 1971-83, Pan American Union, 1954-63, International Cooperation Administration, 1961, Ford Foundation, 1962, Organization of American States, 1963-73, and U.S. Department of Commerce, 1963-64. *Military service:* U.S. Naval Reserve, 1940-42.

MEMBER: American Economic Association, National Planning Association, Middle East Institute, Pi Kappa Alpha, Theta Tau, Alpha Kappa Psi.

WRITINGS:

(With Hollis Chenery) *Arabian Oil: America's Stake in the Middle East,* University of North Carolina Press, 1949.
U.S. Economic Policy and International Relations, McGraw, 1952.
Foreign Exchange in the Postwar World, Twentieth Century Fund, 1954.
The Emerging Pattern of International Payments, Princeton University Press, 1954.
(With M. N. Trued) *Postwar Bilateral Payments Agreements,* Princeton University Press, 1955.
Foreign Investments in Latin America, Pan American Union, 1955.
Liberalization of Inter-Latin American Trade, Pan American Union, 1957.
Promoting United States Private Investment Abroad, National Planning Association, 1957.
Agricultural Surpluses and Export Policy, American Enterprise Association, 1958.

(With Jack N. Behrman) *Financing Free World Trade with the Sino-Soviet Bloc,* Princeton University Press, 1958.

(With Robert Allen) *Economic Policies toward Less Developed Countries,* U.S. Government Printing Office, 1961.

(Editor) *U.S. Private and Government Investments Abroad,* University of Oregon Press, 1962.

Some Observations on the Operation of the Alliance for Progress: The First Six Months, Committee on Foreign Affairs, U.S. Senate, 1962.

(With Raymond L. Staepelaere) *Common Market Competition in Manufactures,* Stanford Research Institute, 1963.

Public International Lending for Development, Random House, 1965.

(With Robert Adler) *Public External Financing of Development Banks in Developing Countries,* University of Oregon Press, 1966.

The Economics of Foreign Aid, Aldine, 1968.

Financing World Trade, Crowell, 1969.

The U.S. Balance of Payments and the International Role of the Dollar, American Enterprise Institute of Public Policy Research, 1970.

(With others) *Foreign Investment in the Petroleum and Mineral Industries,* Johns Hopkins University Press, 1971.

(With J. Herbert Furth) *Foreign Dollar Balances and the International Role of the Dollar,* Columbia University Press, 1974.

Foreign Investment in Copper Mining, Johns Hopkins University Press, 1975.

Nonfuel Minerals—U.S. Investment Policies Abroad, Sage Publications, 1975.

The World Copper Industry, Johns Hopkins University Press, 1979.

(With M. G. Farah) *U.S. Export Competitiveness in Manufactures in Third World Markets,* Georgetown University Press, 1980.

(With Robert A. Kilmarx) *The Economics of Foreign Aid and Self-Sustaining Development,* Westview, 1983.

Foreign Investment in Mining Projects: Case Studies of Mines in Peru and Papua, New Guinea, Resources for the Future, 1983.

Petroleum Company Operations and Agreements in the Developing Countries, Resources for the Future, 1984.

National Defense Stockpile: Historical Review and Current Assessment, American Enterprise Institute, 1986.

Nonfuel Minerals: Foreign Dependence and National Security, University of Michigan Press, 1987.

(With John W. Whitney) *The World Mining Industry,* Allen & Unwin, 1987.

The Global Copper Industry, Croom Helm, 1988.

(With Lawrence W. Williams) *International Banks and the Environment,* Sierra Books, 1992.

Economic Development and the Environment, Mansell, 1992.

Member of editorial advisory board, *Middle East Journal,* 1947-58; member of board of editors, *American Economic Review,* 1953-55. Contributor to about twenty journals in United States, Canada, and South America.

*   *   *

MILLER, Joan I(rene) 1944-

PERSONAL: Born December 7, 1944, in Lima, OH; daughter of Myron Lee and Lucia Irene (a homemaker; maiden name, Murrow) Miller. *Education:* Greenville College, B.A., 1967; University of Georgia, M.S., 1970; Kent State University, Ph.D., 1978.

ADDRESSES: Office—2520 Windy Hill, Suite 106, Marietta, GA 30067.

CAREER: Teacher of mentally retarded students at junior high school in Acworth, GA, 1967-68; Kent State University, Tuscarawas Campus, New Philadelphia, OH, assistant professor of psychology, 1970-76, 1977-78; Institute for Rational Psychotherapy, New York, NY, psychologist, 1976-77; private practice of clinical psychology in Marietta, GA, 1979—.

MEMBER: American Psychological Association, Georgia Psychological Association.

WRITINGS:

Headaches: The Answer Book, Revell, 1983.

(With Bruce J. Taylor) *The Thesis Writer's Handbook: A Complete One-Source Guide for Writers of Research Papers,* Alcove Publishing, 1987.

(With Bruce J. Taylor) *The Punctuation Handbook,* Alcove Publishing, 1989.

Also author of cassette series "Taking the 'Ouch' Out of Headaches," J. Miller, 1983. Author of video cassettes, "Thinking Thin," "Stress Reduction," and "Stop Smoking."

SIDELIGHTS: From 1978 to 1979, Joan I. Miller backpacked around the world.

*   *   *

MITCHELL, Jay
See ROBERSON, Jennifer

MOLE, John 1941-

PERSONAL: Born October 12, 1941, in Taunton, Somerset, England; son of Edgar Douglas (a chartered accountant) and Lilian Joyce (Hook) Mole; married Mary Norman (a freelance artist), August 22, 1968; children: Simon, Benjamin. *Education:* Magdalene College, Cambridge, M.A., 1964. *Avocational interests:* Playing jazz clarinet and alto-sax, giving poetry readings in combination with jazz performances.

ADDRESSES: Home—11 Hill St., St. Albans, Hertfordshire AL3 4QS, England.

CAREER: Haberdashers' Aske's School, Elstree, Hertfordshire, England, English teacher, 1964-73; Verulam School, St. Albans, English teacher and department head, 1973-81; St. Albans School, St. Albans, English teacher and department head, 1981—. Exchange teacher in Riverdale, NY, 1969-70. Co-founder and editor of the Mandeville Press. Has made guest appearances on BBC-Radio programs, including *Poetry Now, Forget Tomorrow's Monday, Time for Verse, Pick of the Week,* and *Poetry Please;* has appeared as critic on *Kaleidoscope;* has written and presented several feature programs.

MEMBER: National Poetry Society (member of council), Eastern Arts Association, Ver Poets (vice-president, 1979—).

AWARDS, HONORS: Eric Gregory Award, Society of Authors, 1970; Signal Award, 1988, for outstanding contribution to children's poetry.

WRITINGS:

POETRY

A Feather for Memory, Outposts Publications, 1961.
The Instruments, Phoenix Pamphlet Poets Press, 1970.
Something about Love, Sycamore Press, 1972.
The Love Horse, Peterloo Poets, 1973.
A Partial Light, Dent, 1975.
Our Ship, Secker & Warburg, 1977.
The Mortal Room, Priapus Poets, 1977.
On the Set, Keepsake Poems, 1978.
From the House Opposite, Secker & Warburg, 1979.
Feeding the Lake, Secker & Warburg, 1981.
In and out of the Apple, Secker & Warburg, 1984.
Homing, Secker & Warburg, 1987.

JUVENILE

(With wife, Mary Norman) *Once There Were Dragons* (riddles), Deutsch, 1979.
Boo to a Goose, Peterloo, 1987.
The Mad Parrot's Countdown, Peterloo, 1990.
Catching the Spider, Blackie, 1990.

NONFICTION

Passing Judgements: Poetry in the Eighties, Bristol Press, 1989.

EDITOR

Poetry: A Selection, Dacorum College, 1974.
(With Anthony Thwaite) *British Poetry since 1945,* Longman, 1981.

Also author of *The Conjuror's Rabbit.* Contributor to books, including *All Sorts of Poems* (juvenile anthology), Methuen, 1980; *Over the Bridge* (juvenile anthology), Puffin Books, 1981; *Forty-Five Contemporary Poems: The Creative Process,* edited by Alberta Turner, Longman, 1985; and *Meet and Write,* edited by Alan Brownjohn and Sandy Brownjohn, Hodder & Stoughton, 1985.

OTHER

Author of numerous scripts for BBC-Radio. Poetry reviewer for *Encounter,* 1983-89. Contributor to newspapers and magazines, including *Times Literary Supplement, Spectator, Sunday Times, Observer,* and *Independent.*

SIDELIGHTS: British poet John Mole told *CA:* "Much of my work has been concerned with the experience of childhood—not in any blandly nostalgic sense, but in the attempt to dramatize the fascination and bewilderment of being young. I have also found myself moved by 'sacred' places—what the painter Paul Nash called 'charged landscapes.' This sense of the sacred is peculiarly personal, can be located anywhere but only realized in the making of poems.

"A firm believer in grace under pressure and the effectiveness of restraint in poetry, I feel nevertheless that the elegance of much of my earlier work was evasive, and that its polished surfaces were too often the be-all and end-all. When I read these poems now they seem to lack substance and to be rather wilfully oblique. An increasing political concern has, I think, resulted in my poetry becoming more declarative, more direct. Not that I value humour and lightness of touch less than I did. If anything I value it more. In the words of a character from Henry James, 'the increasing seriousness of things, that's the great opportunity of jokes,' or as the Chinese proverb runs, 'govern a country as you would cook a small fish.' Though my work has come, I hope, to take on larger, more overtly universal, themes, I should like to believe that it has done so without losing touch with the parochial. For me, the successful poem keeps the particular situation as its starting point and the individually human as its scale of reference."

In a review of *Homing,* a critic for *Poetry Review* comments that Mole "is a poet at the height of his powers, finding new strength with each volume and with a considerable body of work to his name. *Homing* will make it still more difficult to fail to see him as one of the most accomplished and salutary poets of the age." According to a contributor to *The Cambridge Review,* Mole's poetry is "skilful, approachable, often deeply moving," while a reviewer for *Encounter* asserts that Mole "is proof, if any were needed, that poetry is as necessary in ordinary circumstances as in times and places of crisis. His poems are light in the best sense—lucid, sharp, economical."

Describing Mole's critical writings, collected in his book of review-essays, *Passing Judgements,* Terry Eagleton of *The Times Literary Supplement* states: "Mole is a shrewd, easy-tempered, resourceful reviewer, striking just the right balance between high critical discourse and racy journalese, adept at the judicious epithet and capable of wearing his convictions lightly."

Mole's work for children has become of increasing importance to him in recent years. Reviewing Mole's efforts in *Boo to a Goose* in the *Times Educational Supplement,* Charles Causley writes that the author "demonstrated the rare ability to write poems that appeal simultaneously to the child and the adult." Indeed, Mole's underlying assumption when writing verse for children can be seen as taking its cue from a remark by W. H. Auden: "While there are some good poems that are only for adults, because they presuppose adult experience in their readers, there are no good poems which are only for children."

BIOGRAPHICAL/CRITICAL SOURCES:

PERIODICALS

Cambridge Review, December, 1987.
Encounter, September/October, 1984.
PN Review, Volume 16, number 5, 1990.
Poetry Review, June, 1987.
Signal 56, May, 1988.
Times Educational Supplement, March 6, 1988; August 6, 1990.
Times Literary Supplement, November 24, 1989.

*   *   *

MONEY, John (William) 1921-

PERSONAL: Born July 8, 1921, in Morrinsville, New Zealand; son of Frank (a builder) and Ruth (Read) Money. *Education:* Victoria University of Wellington, M.A., 1943, Diploma of Honors, 1944; University of Pittsburgh, graduate study, 1947-48; Harvard University, Ph.D., 1952. *Avocational interests:* Contemporary and ethnic art, especially improvisational art (three-dimensional and miniature graphics), international travel.

ADDRESSES: Home—2104 East Madison St., Baltimore, MD 21205. *Office*—Johns Hopkins Hospital, Baltimore, MD 21205.

CAREER: University of Otago, Dunedin, New Zealand, junior lecturer in philosophy and psychology, 1945-47; Johns Hopkins University, Baltimore, MD, instructor, 1951-55, assistant professor of medical psychology, 1955-57, assistant professor of medical psychology and pediatrics, 1957-59, associate professor of medical psychology, 1959-72, associate professor of pediatrics, 1959-86, professor of medical psychology, 1972-86, professor emeritus of pediatrics and medical psychology, 1986—, director of psychohormonal research unit, Johns Hopkins Hospital, 1951—, psychologist, 1955—, codirector of biosexual psychohormonal clinic, 1978—. Visiting professor at Albert Einstein College of Medicine, Yeshiva University, 1969, Harvard University, 1970, University of Nebraska, 1972, and University of Connecticut, 1975.

Visiting lecturer at Bryn Mawr College, 1952-53; Rachford Lecturer at Children's Hospital, Cincinnati, 1969; American Urological Association Lecturer, 1975; Master Lecturer on Physiological Psychology, American Psychological Association, 1975; Plenary Lecturer at University of Rochester School of Medicine, 1976, and at New York University's Sesquicentennial, 1981; Lindemann Distinguished Lecturer in pediatrics at Cornell University, 1983; Bernadin Distinguished Lecturer at University of Missouri—Kansas City, 1985; lecturer at hospitals and universities throughout the world. Member of board of directors of Sex Information and Education Council of the United States, 1965-68, Erickson Educational Foundation, 1967-77, and Neighborhood Family Planning Center, Inc., 1970-82; member of National Institute of Mental Health Task Force on Homosexuality, 1967-69.

MEMBER: International Academy of Sex Research (charter member), International Society of Psychoneuroendocrinology, Society for the Scientific Study of Sex (charter member; fellow; president-elect, 1972-74; president, 1974-76), Deutsche Gesellschaft fuer Sexualforschung, Royal Society of Medicine (England; affiliate member), American Association of Sex Educators, Counselors, and Therapists (honorary member), American Foundation for Gender and Genital Medicine and Science (president, 1978—), American Psychopathological Association, Society for Sex Therapy and Research, Lawson Wilkins Pediatric Endocrine Society (founding member), Society of Pediatric Psychology, European Society for Paediatric Endocrinology (corresponding member), Gesellschaft zur Forderung Sozialwissenschaftlicher Sexualforschuag (honorary member), Colombian Society of Sexology, Czechoslovak Sexological Society, New Zealand Society on Sexology (honorary life member), American Association for the Advancement of Science (fellow, 1975—), Federation of Parents and Friends of Gays and Lesbians (honorary director, 1983—), Maryland Society for Medical Research, Maryland Psychological Association, New York Academy of Sciences, Sigma Xi.

AWARDS, HONORS: Co-recipient of Hofheimer Prize, American Psychiatric Association, 1956; Gold Medal Award, Children's Hospital of Philadelphia, 1966; Society for the Scientific Study of Sex award, 1972; American Association for Sex Educators and Counselors award for pioneering research and distinguished service, 1976; Maryland Psychological Association award for outstanding contributions to psychology, 1976; honored by the Society for the Scientific Study of Sex for service, research, and education in the field of human sexuality, 1976; Harry Benjamin, M.D. Medal of Honor, Erickson Educational Foundation, 1976; American Psychological Association Distinguished Scientific Award for the applications of psychology, 1985; National Institute for Child Health and Human Development Award in recognition of outstanding research achievement, 1987; Masters and Johnson Fourth Annual Award, Society for Sex Therapy, 1988; Sexologist of the Year Award, Polish Academy of Sexological Science, 1988; award in recognition of distinguished contributions to sexology research, International Academy of Sex Research, 1991; Richard J. Cross Award, Department of Environmental and Community Medicine, University of Medicine and Dentistry of New Jersey, Robert Wood Johnson Medical School, 1991; Honorary Doctor of Humane Letters, Hofstra University, 1992.

WRITINGS:

The Psychological Study of Man, C.C Thomas, 1957.
(With Duane Alexander and H. Thomas Walker, Jr.) *A Standardized Road-Map Test of Direction Sense,* Johns Hopkins Press, 1965.
Sex Errors of the Body: Dilemmas, Education and Counseling, Johns Hopkins Press, 1968.
(With Anke A. Ehrhardt) *Man and Woman, Boy and Girl: Differentiation and Dimorphism of Gender Identity from Conception to Maturity,* Johns Hopkins University Press, 1972.
(With P. Tucker) *Sexual Signatures,* Little, Brown, 1975.
Love and Lovesickness: The Science of Sex, Gender Difference, and Pair-Bonding, Johns Hopkins University Press, 1980.
The Destroying Angel: Sex, Fitness, and Food in the Legacy of Degeneracy Theory, Graham Crackers, Kellogg's Cornflakes, and American Health History, Prometheus Books, 1985.
Lovemaps: Clinical Concepts of Sexual/Erotic Health and Pathology, Paraphilia, and Gender Transposition in Childhood, Adolescence and Maturity, Irvington, 1986.
Venuses Penuses: Sexology, Sexosophy, and Exigency Theory, Prometheus Books, 1986.

Gay, Straight, and In-Between: The Sexology of Erotic Orientation, Oxford University Press, 1988.
(With M. Lamacz) *Vandalized Lovemaps: Paraphilic Outcome in Seven Cases of Pediatric Sexology,* Prometheus Books, 1989.
Biographies of Gender and Hermaphroditism in Paired Comparisons: Clinical Supplement to the Handbook of Sexology, Elsevier, 1991.
(With G. Wainwright and D. Hingsburger) *The Breathless Orgasm: A Lovemap Biography of Asphyxiophilia,* Prometheus Books, 1991.
The Kaspar Hauser Syndrome of "Psychosocial Dwarfism": Deficient Statural, Intellectual, and Social Growth Induced by Child Abuse, Prometheus Books, 1992.
The Adam Principle: Genes, Genitals, Hormones, and Gender: Selected Readings in Sexology, Prometheus Books, 1993.

EDITOR AND CONTRIBUTOR

Reading Disability: Progress and Research Needs in Dyslexia, Johns Hopkins Press, 1962.
Sex Research: New Developments, Holt, 1965.
The Disabled Reader: Education of the Dyslexic Child, Johns Hopkins Press, 1966.
(Sections only) D. B. Cheek, editor, *Human Growth: Body Composition, Cell Growth, Energy and Intelligence,* Lea & Febiger, 1968.
(With Richard Green) *Transsexualism and Sex Reassignment,* Johns Hopkins Press, 1969.
Sexual Behavior—Readings V: Introduction to Psychiatry and the Behavioral Sciences, School of Medicine, Johns Hopkins University, 1970.
(With Joseph Zubin) *Contemporary Sexual Behavior: Critical Issues in the 1970s,* Johns Hopkins University Press, 1973.

EDITOR

(With W. K. Anderson and G. McClearn) *Developmental Human Behavior Genetics,* Heath, 1975.
(With H. Musaph) *Handbook of Sexology,* Excerpta Medica Foundation, 1977.
(With G. Williams) *Traumatic Abuse and Neglect of Children at Home,* Johns Hopkins University Press, 1980.
(With B. B. Wolman) *Handbook of Human Sexuality,* Prentice-Hall, 1980.
(With Musaph and J. M. Sitsen) *Handbook of Sexology,* Volume 6: *The Pharmacology and Endocrinology of Sexual Function,* Elsevier, 1988, (with Musaph and M. Perry) Volume 7: *Childhood and Adolescent Sexology,* 1990.

OTHER

Contributor to numerous books, including *Determinants of Human Sexual Behavior*, edited by George Winokur, C. C Thomas, 1963; *Endocrinology and Human Behavior*, edited by R. P. Michael, Oxford University Press, 1968; *The Sexual and Gender Development of Young Children*, edited by E. K. Oremland and J. D. Oremland, Ballinger, 1977; *Homosexual Behavior: A Modern Reappraisal*, edited J. Marmor, Basic Books, 1980; *Gynecologic Endocrinology*, edited by J. J. Gold and J. B. Josimovich, 3rd edition, Harper, 1980; and *Pedophilia: Biosocial Dimensions*, edited by J. R. Feierman, Springer-Verlag, 1990. Many of Money's articles, reprints, and translations have been included in a number of other books. Contributor to *Technical Report of the Commission on Obscenity and Pornography*, Volume 5, *Annual Review of Medicine, American Handbook of Psychiatry*, and various encyclopedias. Also contributor of more than 600 articles, reviews, abstracts, and editorials to medical journals and such periodicals as *Reading Teacher, Playboy, St. John's Law Review*, and *American Sociological Review*.

Member of editorial board, *Sexology*, 1961-83, *Journal of Learning Disabilities*, 1970—, *Journal of Autism and Childhood Schizophrenia*, 1972—, *Journal of Sex and Marital Therapy*, 1974—, *Behavioral Medicine*, 1974-76, *Psychoneuroendocrinology*, 1974-83, *Signs: Journal of Women in Culture and Society*, 1974-78, *Journal of Homosexuality*, 1975-77, *Journal of Sex Education and Therapy*, 1975—, *British Journal of Sexual Medicine*, 1977—, *Journal of Preventive Psychiatry*, 1980—, *Medicine and Law*, 1984—, and *Cuardernos de Sexologia y Medicina Conductual*, 1984—; associate editor, *Archives of Sexual Behavior*, 1970-82; consulting editor, *Sexualmedezin*, 1972—, *Journal of the Psychology of Women*, 1975—, *Sexual Insight*, 1975—, *Sexuality and Disability*, 1977—, and *Journal of Pediatric Psychology*, 1981—.

WORK IN PROGRESS: Journal articles.

SIDELIGHTS: John Money once wrote *CA:* "I have become internationally known for my work in both psychoendocrinology and the new and growing science of developmental sexology. In sexology, I am the person who, in 1955, first formulated and defined the concept of gender role, later expanded to include identity, as in gender-identity/role. I am by reputation an expert in gender science, research, and clinical care, ranging from neonatal sex assignment in cases of birth defect and ambiguity of the sex organs to the syndromes of erotosexual pathology in adulthood. My expertise covers also the theory of homosexuality, bisexuality, and heterosexuality. In 1961, I proposed the hypothesis that androgen is the libido hormone for both sexes. In 1966, I was a founding member of the Gender Identity Clinic for transsexualism and sex

reassignment at Johns Hopkins and, in the same year, the founder of the program for treating paraphilic sex offenders with combined antiandrogenic (hormonal) and counseling therapy.

"Not surprisingly, my research in sex attracts more public attention, and also more criticism, than does my research in the wider range of hormones and behavior in human beings. My sex research has related the differentiation and development of gender status to chromosomal genetics, prenatal hormones, postnatal sensory and social experience, and the hormones of puberty. Extending psychoendocrinology to include cognitive and intellectual development in many endocrine syndromes of infancy, childhood and adolescence, I have done research also on learning disability and dyslexia. Examining the effects of child abuse on failure to develop, I have published definitive papers on the psychoendocrinology of the syndrome of abuse dwarfism, which is characterized by child abuse, hormonal insufficiency, statural dwarfism, mental retardation, and social immaturity, all of which are reversible by the simple expedient of early rescue from abuse. In 1976, I formulated the concept of child abuse as Munchausen Syndrome by Proxy.

"I have always considered that the discovery of new knowledge is an obligation that all medical professionals owe to their patients, so as to avoid the perpetuation of ignorance and harmful treatment. In working on behalf of human beings, however, I have always held it an article of faith that research must be accompanied by the delivery of the best possible in health care—for me, psychological and sexological health care—regardless of people's ability to pay. Since, one way or another, the public pays for research, I have accepted the obligation to pay back this investment by telling the public what I have discovered. Therefore, I have extended my teaching to the public via the popular media, despite the contempt and attempted censorship of ultra-conservatives. I have also engaged actively in scholarly meetings and have published in both scientific and medical journals. In addition, I have followed a very active policy of training young people in research, on a person-to-person basis, and of rewarding their achievements by giving them the privilege of being first author when their research is published. Their greatest difficulty has been in learning the logic of scientific prose, free from banality and platitude.

"In the last few years, I have expanded my writing interest from the clinic to clinical history. I wrote about the eighteenth-century origins and present consequences of antisexualism in *The Destroying Angel*. My book *Lovemaps* presents the original concept of 'Lovemaps' in its title. It examines the adverse effects of antisexualism on child development.

"The combined demands of research, clinical care, and teaching are magnified by the demands of fund-raising, writing and finding a publisher. They require as much dedication as does a monastic career. Sometimes I say, jokingly, that I left the religion of my childhood in New Zealand to become a missionary of psychoendocrinology and sexology in the United States. The sacrifices of monastic life, as some perceive them, are rewards for others. It has been my fate to experience a career in research and authorship as rewarding—which, perhaps, is in itself an accident of fate, upon which the existence of my research unit has depended."

BIOGRAPHICAL/CRITICAL SOURCES:

BOOKS

Brecher, Edward M., *The Sex Researchers,* Little, Brown, 1969, revised edition, Specific Press, 1979.

PERIODICALS

Harper's Bazaar, May, 1984.
New York Times Book Review, February 25, 1973; August 10, 1980.
Playboy, February, 1980.

*   *   *

MONTFORT, Auguste 1913-
(Auguste Le Breton)

PERSONAL: Born February 18, 1913, in Lesneven, France; son of Eugene Montfort; married Marguerite Lecacheur; children: Maryvonne Le Breton Lederfajn. *Politics:* None. *Religion:* "Without *Francmacon.*"

ADDRESSES: Home and office—12 rue Pasteur, 78110 Le Vesinet, France.

CAREER: Worked as a construction worker, elevator repairman, and gambler. Writer, 1953—. *Military service:* Forces Francaises Combattantes, served in World War II; received Croix de Guerre.

WRITINGS:

UNDER PSEUDONYM AUGUSTE LE BRETON

Du Rififi chez les hommes, Gallimard, 1953.
Les Hauts Murs (novel), Denoel, 1954.
Le Rouge est mis, Gallimard, 1954, reprinted, 1976.
Razzia sur la chnouf, Gallimard, 1954.
La Loi des rues, Presses de la Cite, 1955, translation by Nigel Ryan published as *The Law of the Streets,* Collins, 1957.
Rafles sur la ville, Presses de la Cite, 1956.
Du Rififi chez les femmes, Presses de la Cite, 1957.
Les Tricards, Presses de la Cite, 1958.

L'Argot chez les vrais de vrais, Presses de la Cite, 1960.
Du Rififi a Hambourg: Les Racketteurs, Presses de la Cite, 1960.
Langue verte et noirs desseins, Presses de la Cite, 1960.
Priez pour nous, Presses de la Cite, 1961.
Du Rififi a New York, Presses de la Cite, 1962, translation by Peter Leslie published as *Rififi in New York,* Stein & Day, 1962.
Du Rififi au Mexique: Chez Cuanthemoc, empereur azteque, Presses de la Cite, 1963.
Du Rififi au Proche-Orient, Presses de la Cite, 1963.
Du Rififi a Paname: Face au syndicat du crime, Plon, 1964.
Du Rififi a Hong-Kong: Societes secretes criminelles, Plon, 1964.
Du Rififi a Barcelone: Toreros et truands, Presses de la Cite, 1964.
Brigade anti-gangs: Section de recherche et d'intervention, Plon, 1965.
Du Rififi au Cambodge: Opium sur Angkor-Vat, Plon, 1965.
Le Clan des Siciliens, Plon, 1967.
Les Jeunes Voyous: A Chacun son destin, Plon, 1967.
Du Rififi derriere le rideau de fer: Le Soleil du Prague, Plon, 1968.
Du vent (poems), Plon, 1968.
Les Maq's, Plon, 1968.
Du Rififi au Canada: Le Bouncer, Plon, 1969.
Le Tueur a la une, Plon, 1971.
Rouges etaient les emeraudes, Plon, 1971.
Malfrats and Co. (biography), R. Laffont, 1971.
Les Bourlingueurs, Plon, 1972.
Les Pegriots, R. Laffont, 1973.
Du Rififi en Argentine: Ou souffle le Pampero, Presses Pocket, 1973.
Monsieur Rififi (biography), Table Ronde, 1976.
L'As des antigangs, Plon, 1977.
L'As et belles chaussures, Plon, 1977.
L'As et le casse du siecle, Plon, 1977.
L'As et la marquise, Plon, 1977.
L'As et l'ennemi public, Plon, 1977.
L'As et les terroristes, Plon, 1978.
L'As au Senegal, Plon, 1978.
L'As et les Malfrats, Plon, 1978.
La Mome Piaf, Hachette, 1980.
Bontemps a New York, Presses de la Cite, 1981.
Fortifs, Hachette, 1982.
Bontemps et le jeune tueur, Presses de la Cite, 1982.
Bontemps et le sadique, Presses de la Cite, 1982.
Bontemps et les Caids, Presses de la Cite, 1982.
Bontemps a Hong Kong, Presses de la Cite, 1982.
Bontemps contre les anti-gangs, Presses de la Cite, 1983.
Bontemps et la chienne rouge, Presses de la Cite, 1983.
Bontemps et la mine d'El Papayo, Presses de la Cite, 1983.

Bontemps: Le juif et le criminel de guerre, Presses de la Cite, 1983.

Bontemps et les holdopeuses, Presses de la Cite, 1984.

Bontemps et les Indiens, Presses de la Cite, 1984.

Bontemps et les jack-pots, Presses de la Cite, 1984.

Also author of *Rififi en Bresil: Escadron de la mort,* Presses Pocket, *Adventures sous les tropiques,* Editions Pygmalion, *Deux Sous d'amour (presque pu l'Occupation),* 1986, *Rebecca chez les aristos,* 1991, and *Carrere front donne le Rififi* (memoirs), 1991.

ADAPTATIONS: Many of Auguste Montfort's books have been adapted for films, including *Rififi chez les hommes, Razzia sur la chnouf, Le Rouge est mis, Du Rififi chez les femmes, Du Rififi a Paname, Le Clan des Siciliens, Rafles sur la ville, Brigade anti-gangs,* and *La Loi des rues.*

SIDELIGHTS: Auguste Montfort told *CA* that he published his first book after struggling with life for nearly forty years. An orphan, he left a detention center at age eighteen to take a job as a construction worker. Economic conditions forced him out of his work, however, and onto the streets, where for nine months he slept in parks and subways, eating whatever scraps he could find. After surviving a bout with tuberculosis, Montfort found employment again as an elevator repairman. His hard luck continued, though, when he was fired for helping a fellow worker organize a strike.

A career as a clandestine gambler followed, he commented to *CA*. Montfort ran illegal poker and roulette games and worked as a bookie until called to do undercover work for France during World War II. He returned from service to become a full-time bookmaker.

Montfort had decided during one of his unemployment periods that if he were ever to have a child, he would want it to know about and understand his past. So when his daughter was born in 1947, he decided to write a book about his own childhood. The result was *Les Hauts Murs,* which was rejected by publisher after publisher until finally being accepted in 1954. The book became a bestseller. Montfort has continued to write and has also done a great deal of traveling in order to enrich his experiences and better understand mankind.

In a letter to *CA* detailing some of his thoughts on writing, Montfort mentioned that he most often works "early in the morning, dressed in a jogging suit, as for a fight." He lists Hemingway, Steinbeck, and Simeon among the authors who have most influenced him. In conclusion, he philosophized that the human race "will be over one day and the literary writers who want immortality by their writings make me smile. All of us should show humility."

MOORE, Geoffrey H(oyt) 1914-

PERSONAL: Born February 28, 1914, in Pequannock, NJ; son of Edward H. (a builder) and Marian (Leman) Moore; married Ella Goldschmid, July 12, 1938 (died June, 1975); married Melita Holly, September 28, 1975; children: Stephen, Peter, Kathleen Moore Holness, Pamela Moore Pelligrino. *Education:* Rutgers University, B.S., 1933, M.S., 1937; Harvard University, Ph.D., 1947. *Avocational interests:* Tennis, sailing, gardening.

ADDRESSES: Home—1171 Valley Rd., New Canaan, CT 06840. *Office*—Graduate School of Business, Columbia University, New York, NY 10027.

CAREER: Rutgers University, New Brunswick, NJ, instructor in agricultural economics, 1936-42; National Bureau of Economic Research, New York City, member of research staff, 1939-48, associate director of research, 1948-65, director of research, 1965-68, vice-president of research, 1968-69; U.S. Department of Labor, Washington, DC, commissioner of labor statistics, 1969-73; National Bureau of Economic Research, vice-president of research, 1973-75, director of business cycle research, 1975-79; Rutgers University, director of Center for International Business Cycle Research, 1979-83; Columbia University, New York City, director of Center for International Business Cycle Research, 1983—. New York University, associate professor, 1947-48; Columbia University, visiting lecturer, 1953-54. Hoover Institution on War, Revolution and Peace, senior research fellow, 1973-78; American Enterprise Institute for Public Policy Research, adjunct scholar, 1975—.

MEMBER: American Statistical Association (director, 1957-59; vice-president, 1961-63; president, 1968; fellow), American Economic Association, National Association of Business Economists (fellow), National Economists Club, Conference of Business Economists, Cosmos Club, Phi Beta Kappa, Alpha Zeta.

WRITINGS:

Business Cycle Indicators, Volume 1: *Contributions to the Analysis of Current Business Conditions,* Volume 2: *Basic Data on Cyclical Indicators,* Princeton University Press, 1961.

(With Philip A. Klein) *The Quality of Consumer Installment Credit,* National Bureau of Economic Research, 1967.

(With Julius Shiskin) *Indicators of Business Expansions and Contractions,* National Bureau of Economic Research, 1967.

The Cyclical Behavior of Prices, Bureau of Labor Statistics, 1971.

How Full Is Full Employment?, and Other Essays on Interpreting the Unemployment Statistics, American Enterprise Institute for Public Policy Research, 1973.

Improving the Presentation of Employment and Unemployment Statistics, National Commission on Employment and Unemployment Statistics, 1978.

(With Philip Cagan) *Consumer Price Index: Issues and Alternatives,* American Enterprise Institute for Public Policy Research, 1981.

Business Cycles, Inflation, and Forecasting, National Bureau of Economic Research, 1980, 2nd edition, 1983.

(With Klein) *Monitoring Business Cycles in Market-Oriented Economies,* National Bureau of Economic Research, 1985.

(With wife, Melita H. Moore) *International Economic Indicators: A Sourcebook,* Greenwood Press, 1985.

Leading Indicators for the 1990s, Dow Jones-Irwin, 1990.

(With Kajal Lahiri) *Leading Economic Indicators: New Approaches and Forecasting Records,* Cambridge University Press, 1991.

Contributor to *Contemporary Economic Problems,* American Enterprise Institute for Public Policy Research, 1976, 1977, 1978.

SIDELIGHTS: Geoffrey H. Moore once told *CA* that he believed that by 1979 the time had come "to establish a center for international business cycle research to investigate booms and recessions, inflation, and growth. Its objective would be to provide factual information and objective interpretations of these phenomena, presented in a simple straightforward style." Later that year the Center for International Business Cycle Research was established at Rutgers University, and in 1983 it moved to Columbia University, where Moore continues to direct its work.

*   *   *

MORRICE, J(ames) K(enneth) W(att) 1924-
(Ken Morrice)

PERSONAL: Born July 14, 1924, in Aberdeen, Scotland; son of James Watt and Elizabeth (Ogston) Morrice; married Norah Thompson (a schoolteacher), July 5, 1948; children: Iain, Julia, Lucy. *Education:* University of Aberdeen, M.B.Ch.B., 1946, M.D., 1954; University of London, D.P.M., 1951.

ADDRESSES: Home—30 Carnegie Cres., Aberdeen AB2 4AE, Scotland.

CAREER: Dingleton Hospital, Melrose, Scotland, consultant psychiatrist, 1956-66; Fort Logan Mental Health Center, Denver, CO, consultant psychiatrist, 1966-67; Grampian Area Health Board, Grampian, Scotland, consultant psychiatrist, 1968-85; private practice of psychia-

try, 1985-89; Hon. Fellow, University of Aberdeen, 1985—. Clinical senior lecturer at University of Aberdeen, 1968-85. *Military service:* Royal Naval Volunteer Reserve, 1947-49; became Surgeon Lieutenant.

MEMBER: Royal College of Psychiatrists (fellow).

AWARDS, HONORS: Book award from Scottish Arts Council, 1982, for *For All I Know.*

WRITINGS:

POETRY

Prototype, Macdonald & Co., 1965.

Relations, Rainbow Books, 1979.

(Under name Ken Morrice) *For All I Know,* Pergamon, 1981.

Twal Mile Roon, Rainbow Books, 1985.

(Under name Ken Morrice) *When Truth Is Known,* Aberdeen University Press, 1986.

The Scampering Marmoset, Aberdeen University Press, 1990.

Selected Poems, Keith Murray Publishing, 1991.

OTHER

Crisis Intervention, Pergamon, 1976.

Contributor to medical journals, including *British Journal of Psychiatry.* Contributor of articles, poems, and stories to Scottish newspapers and literary journals, under name Ken Morrice.

SIDELIGHTS: J. K. W. Morrice told *CA:* "I am a psychotherapist who writes poetry. Psychotherapy and poetry have something in common, and I find more and more that one activity is reflected in the other. I write mostly in English, but also in Scots.

"Just as a psychotherapist is concerned with people and their relationships, so this is my main subject matter as a poet. The two occupations have a common root, although the metaphors of psychotherapy are aimed directly at healing, while poetry—if it is therapeutic—is so as a by-product of the expression of emotion and its structuring. Both activities may be viewed as the conscious use of unconscious processes, engaging in creative play to achieve a sense of wholeness and freedom. Both are reaching toward an imaginative understanding of reality. Shakespeare talks of 'the lunatic, the lover and the poet' sharing the same field of imagination. It is certain that all three inhabit a dangerous transitional area, but each in his own way may prove to be creative.

"Sometimes in the past I have felt, writing poetry, that I was talking only to myself in a sort of sophisticated madness. Now, having gained more recognition, I know that I write from a deep compulsion in order to articulate important experience. Sometimes I try to offer a challenge to the plastic values of our society. At other times I rhyme for fun.

"My experiences with psychiatric patients have informed much of my recent verse. But my poetry these days can also be a celebration of a personal event, a woman, or a high mountain. Since returning to live in Aberdeen, my roots have become important also. W. H. Auden says it for me when he writes of a poet's hope 'to be like some valley cheese, local, but prized elsewhere.' "

*   *   *

MORRICE, Ken
See MORRICE, J(ames) K(enneth) W(att)

*   *   *

MORTIMER, Armine Kotin   1943-
(Armine Avakian Kotin)

PERSONAL: Born May 13, 1943, in Detroit, MI; daughter of Arra Steve (an engineer) and Georgia (a tax examiner; maiden name, Keosaian) Avakian; married Joel T. Kotin, September 1, 1962 (divorced July 14, 1970); married Rudolf G. Mortimer (a professor of safety and accident prevention), August 18, 1980; children: (first marriage) Daniel, Ilana. *Education:* Radcliffe College, B.A., 1964; University of California, Los Angeles, M.A., 1970; Yale University, M.Phil., 1973, Ph.D., 1974. *Religion:* None.

ADDRESSES: Home—3 Florida Court, Urbana, IL 61801. *Office*—Department of French, 2090 Foreign Languages Building, 707 South Mathews Ave., University of Illinois at Urbana-Champaign, Urbana, IL 61801.

CAREER: Yale University, New Haven, CT, teaching fellow, 1973-74; University of Illinois at Urbana-Champaign, Urbana, assistant professor, 1974-80, associate professor, 1980-88, professor of French literature, 1988—, professor of criticism and interpretive theory, 1981—, associate dean, college of liberal arts and sciences, 1990-92; fellow in French literature at Center for Advanced Study, 1977.

MEMBER: Modern Language Association of America, American Association of Teachers of French (secretary, 1977, president, 1978).

AWARDS, HONORS: Yale University fellowship, 1970-74; Danforth graduate fellowship for women, 1970-74; numerous research grants from University of Illinois and University of Illinois at Urbana-Champaign.

WRITINGS:

(Contributor) L. Sozzi, editor, *La nouvelle francaise a la Renaissance,* Slatkine, 1981.
La Cloture narrative (title means "Narrative Closure"), Jose Corti, 1985.
The Gentlest Law: Roland Barthes' The Pleasure of the Text, Peter Lang, 1989.
(Contributor) Susan Lohafer and Jo Ellyn Clarey, editors, *Short Story Theory at a Crossroads,* Louisiana State University Press, 1989.
Plotting to Kill, Peter Lang, 1991.
(Contributor) *Selected Proceedings of the Nineteenth Century French Studies Conference,* Rodopi, 1992.

UNDER NAME ARMINE AVAKIAN KOTIN

The Narrative Imagination: Comic Tales by Philippe de Vignuelles, University Press of Kentucky, 1977.

OTHER

Bibliographer, *Twentieth Century Literature,* 1970-1975; editor, *Journal of Practical Structuralism,* 1980. Contributor of articles and reviews to numerous periodicals including *L' Esprit Createur, Journal of Practical Structuralism, Bulletin du Cercle Francais de Poesie, Studies in Short Fiction, French Forum,* and *Genre.*

WORK IN PROGRESS: Second Stories, analysis of French, English, American, and German short stories.

SIDELIGHTS: Armine Kotin Mortimer told *CA:* "*Plotting to Kill* came into being when I discovered a curious similarity between several French novels from the 19th and 20th centuries: all autobiographical love stories, they end with the death of a female character based on a real-life woman who was still alive when the novel was written. The plots of these novels 'kill' real people; fiction brings to life a simple resolution. I combined literary with biographical analysis to show how the authors created plots that largely follow the life stories but deviate from them by ending with the woman's death. Writing this book was often entertaining—almost a voyeuristic pleasure. Most of all, I enjoyed demonstrating the power of fiction to reveal realities that the nonfiction texts by the same writers did their best to hide.

"I think the mimetic illusion is alive and well, and that its manifestation is a kind of magic."

BIOGRAPHICAL/CRITICAL SOURCES:

PERIODICALS

French Forum, September, 1987.
French Review, May, 1979, p. 925; October, 1988, p. 155; December, 1990, p. 362.
Modern Language Review, October, 1979, p. 937; July, 1991, p. 747.

Poetics Today, Volume 7, number 4, 1986, p. 785.
World Literature Today, autumn, 1986, p. 694.

* * *

MOSLEY, Nicholas 1923-

PERSONAL: Born June 25, 1923, in London, England; son of Oswald Ernald (a politician) and Cynthia (Curzon) Mosley; married Rosemary Salmond, November 14, 1967 (divorced 1974); married Verity Raymond, July 17, 1974; children: Shaun, Ivo, Robert, Clare, Marius. *Education:* Attended Balliol College, Oxford, 1946-47. *Politics:* Liberal. *Religion:* Church of England.

ADDRESSES: Home—2 Gloucester Crescent, London NW1 7DS, England. *Agent*—A. D. Peters, The Chambers, Chelsea Harbour, London SW10 0XE, England.

CAREER: Writer. Became third Baron Ravensdale, 1966; inherited his father's baronetcy, 1980. *Military service:* British Army, 1942-46; became captain.

AWARDS, HONORS: Whitbread Award, 1991, for *Hopeful Monsters.*

WRITINGS:

NOVELS

Spaces of the Dark, Hart Davis, 1951.
The Rainbearers, Weidenfeld & Nicolson, 1955.
Corruption, Weidenfeld & Nicolson, 1957, Little, Brown, 1958.
Meeting Place, Weidenfeld & Nicolson, 1962.
Accident, Hodder & Stoughton, 1965, Coward, 1966.
Assassins, Hodder & Stoughton, 1966, Coward, 1967.
Impossible Object (also see below), Hodder & Stoughton, 1968, Coward, 1969.
Natalie, Natalia, Coward, 1971.

"CATASTROPHE PRACTICE" SERIES

Catastrophe Practice: Plays for Not Acting, and Cypher, a Novel, Secker & Warburg, 1979, revised edition, Dalkey Archive Press, 1989.
Imago Bird, Secker & Warburg, 1980, revised edition, Dalkey Archive Press, 1989.
Serpent, Secker & Warburg, 1981, Dalkey Archive Press, 1990.
Judith, Secker & Warburg, 1986, revised edition, Dalkey Archive Press, 1991.
Hopeful Monsters, Dalkey Archive Press, 1990.

NONFICTION

African Switchback (travel), Weidenfeld & Nicolson, 1958.
The Life of Raymond Raynes, Faith Press, 1961.

Experience and Religion: A Lay Essay in Theology, Hodder & Stoughton, 1965, United Church Press, 1967.
The Assassination of Trotsky (also see below), M. Joseph, 1972.
Julian Grenfell: His Life and the Time of His Death, 1888-1915, Holt, 1976.
Rules of the Game: Sir Oswald and Lady Cynthia Mosley, 1896-1933 (also see below), Secker & Warburg, 1982.
Beyond the Pale: Sir Oswald Mosley and Family, 1933-1980 (also see below), Secker & Warburg, 1983.
Rules of the Game/Beyond the Pale: Memoirs of Sir Oswald Mosley and Family, Dalkey Archive Press, 1991.

OTHER

(Editor) Raymond Raynes, *The Faith: Instructions on the Christian Faith,* Faith Press/Community of the Resurrection, 1961.
(With Masolino d'Amico) *The Assassination of Trotsky* (screenplay), Josef Shastel Productions, 1972.
Impossible Object (screenplay), Franco-London Films, 1973.
(Author of introduction) Hugo Charteris, *The Tide Is Right,* Dalkey Archive Press, 1992.

Prism, joint editor, 1957-59, member of advisory board, 1960-65, and poetry editor, 1962-65.

ADAPTATIONS: Accident was adapted for the screen by Harold Pinter and directed by Joseph Losey in 1968.

SIDELIGHTS: Nicholas Mosley is regarded by many critics as one of the most innovative English novelists to emerge since World War II. According to Peter Lewis in the *Dictionary of Literary Biography,* Mosley is "one of the most individualistic and interesting of postwar English novelists." Lewis notes that Mosley has "followed his own path with artistic integrity, avoiding every kind of fashionable fiction during a period when modishness has been widespread." The novel *Hopeful Monsters* won Mosley the prestigious Whitbread Award in 1991. In addition to his novels Mosley has also published family memoirs in which he speaks of his controversial father, Oswald Mosley, founder of the British Union of Fascists.

Over the course of a forty-year writing career, Mosley has gone through several changes in writing style in an attempt "to invent fictional forms capable of dealing adequately with both the complexity of contemporary experience and the perplexing nature of reality," as Lewis explains it. Speaking to *Contemporary Literature Criticism,* Mosley allows: "I want to write of human beings, and the way they experience their lives, as creatures who think and who have some small areas of choice in their lives—not as the mindless and helpless creatures so often depicted in novels."

The first phase of Mosley's career saw the author publish three novels during the 1950s, *Spaces of the Dark, The Rainbearers,* and *Corruption.* From the beginning Mosley was concerned with the limits of what could be expressed through language. In *Spaces of the Dark,* for example, Mosley writes of a dying German soldier who speaks emphatically, and unintelligibly, to the British narrator who, despite not knowing the language, finds himself compelled to memorize the message he has received because of the force of its delivery. "Thus the speech achieves its point—a testament of faith . . . precisely because it was unintelligible," John Banks notes in *Review of Contemporary Fiction.* In *Experience and Religion,* Mosley outlines what Banks calls the "central paradox of the human condition," the importance of language to human society and its inability to meet "our higher purposes." This essentially spiritual outlook colors all of Mosley's later writings.

Intrigued by the Anglican religious magazine *Prism,* Mosley turned to writing nonfiction in the late 1950s. For a time he served as editor of *Prism,* writing a number of articles and reviews for the magazine until it was merged with another publication in 1965. At this time he also published *Experience and Religion,* a theological study, and *The Life of Raymond Raynes,* the biography of an Anglican monk, and edited *The Faith: Instructions on the Christian Faith.*

When Mosley returned to the novel in 1962 with *Meeting Place,* it marked a change in his writing. *Meeting Place* features a pared-down prose style and is told in an elliptical manner. The novel ends with an assertion of faith as an estranged married couple is reunited. This spiritual element is found in his next novel as well, *Accident,* published in 1965. It tells the story of a university don and a novelist who bear responsibility for a young man's death in a car crash. With this novel Mosley reached what Lewis calls "the first high point in his career, the vindication of his innovative techniques at this time. . . . Highly distinctive of *Accident* is the spare, compressed, and selective way in which this story . . . is told. There is an intense nervous edginess in the writing, with its verbal fragments and staccato rhythms." Writing in *New Statesman,* Adrian Mitchell states that Mosley "uses sentences like stepping-stones: the gaps between them may seem incredibly wide at first glance, but you can always get to the other side." The *Times Literary Supplement* critic finds that "the texture of the writing itself is deliberately simple; the complexity arises from the way in which the parts are put together." Although noting a comparison between Mosley's method and that of the French *nouvelle vague,* the critic explains that Mosley also uses an "unusual and paradoxical combination of a highly sophisticated, determinedly 'contemporary' and sympathetic awareness of atheistic despair,

something that is much in the air nowadays, with an evidently well developed, even doctrinal, Christianity."

With *Impossible Object* Mosley further developed his pared-down style, connecting eight seemingly-independent stories with brief interludes set in italics. These interludes highlight recurring themes in the stories, obliquely tying them into a single work. Robert Scholes, writing in *Saturday Review,* calls these interludes "brilliant prose constructions, combining images and perspectives with a vigor and control reminiscent of the later work of Picasso. . . . These little pieces frame the 'real' action, but the word 'frame' is too inactive to convey how they really operate. Mosley uses his perspectivist parables as a way of generating an emotionally charged field of ideas and attitudes which then cluster around the situations in the 'real' stories, illuminating them with a fabulous phosphorescence." In his review for the *New York Times Book Review,* Saul Maloff finds that "like Pinter, Mosley is most effective—which is to say first-rate—when he is most menacing, deadly; when, laconically, he proposes, surprising our expectations, the tense union of affective opposites—the excitement of fear, the exhilaration of terror, persistent hints of the nameless and uncaused in human conduct." Lewis concludes that *Impossible Object* is "individual and unmistakable."

The distinctive prose of *Impossible Object's* interludes is further developed in Mosley's next novel, *Natalie Natalia.* This novel tells the story of Anthony Greville, a member of parliament who sees his mistress as two contrasting people: Natalie, the ravenous side, and Natalia, the angelic side. "What Natalie said," he remarks at one point, "was often a code for what Natalia was meaning." "The disorder of Greville's private life mirrors the disorder of his public life," Lewis observes. Scholes, in his review of the novel, calls *Natalie Natalia* "a remarkable fusion of sex and politics." He finds that "the bizarre appropriateness of [Mosley's] prose to the actualities of political life is dazzling." Maloff, writing in *Commonweal,* finds the most impressive aspect of the novel to be Mosley's voice. "To sustain the sense of 'perpetual anxiety,' " Maloff writes, "is a difficult achievement; and to evolve a style that seems its natural voice is Mosley's impressive gift."

Just after completing *Natalie Natalia* Mosley was involved in a serious car accident which left him hospitalized for a year. He published no new fiction for some eight years, returning in 1979 with *Catastrophe Practice.* A collection of three plays and a novella, *Catastrophe Practice* presents a group of characters and several related plots which Mosley drew upon for a series of five further novels. Calling the series of novels "one of this country's more ambitious fictional enterprises," Jonathan Coe of the *London Review of Books* explains that it stressed "the need to devise new structures of thinking and language which would 'provide for both art and science an encompassing covenant'; the need for a new literature of self-consciousness . . . and the need for new literary forms which jettison the dishonesties of tragedy and comedy in favour of a more explicitly liberal, optimistic and humanist position."

The original collection from which the series evolved was unfortunately considered by many critics to be obscure in its intentions or deficient in fulfilling those intentions. As Tom LeClair writes in the *Washington Post Book World,* "What Mosley wants [in the three plays in this collection] is to force the audience to share the actors' self-consciousness. Watching himself watch the self-watching actors and imagining the responses of a theater audience, the reader should recognize his own self-limiting cognitive routines and understand how to discover them. . . . I didn't get this proposed meta-effect." "Despite three introductions and a postscript," Thomas Hinde remarks in the London *Times,* "almost everything else is challengingly obscure."

The obscurity of *Catastrophe Practice* is not found in the novels derived from that collection's characters and plots. *Imago Bird,* the first of these novels, is "a much clearer, more self-assured work than its predecessor," according to Craig Brown of the *Times Literary Supplement.* LeClair, too, sees the novel as being "eminently accessible." Telling the story of a young man who uncovers a sex scandal in his politically-prominent family, *Imago Bird* focuses on its protagonist's mode of thinking. "Mosley," Brown writes, "has an uncanny ability to remember and scrutinize the process of thought being transformed into external or internal speech and, like a scientist, he knows that the presence of observation alters the observed." Writing in the *Listener,* John Naughton calls *Imago Bird* "a skilful, sardonic work with some contemporary references which resonate."

Also derived from *Catastrophe Practice* is the novel *Serpent,* which Peter Lewis in the *Times Literary Supplement* calls "a more demanding book than *Imago Bird*" because of its "web of symbolism" and "pattern of elusive correspondences." Revolving around a film writer and his script about the ancient mass suicide of Jews at Masada, the story concerns the related themes of survival and self-sacrifice. When Mosley successfully weaves these themes together, James Ladsun writes in the *Spectator,* he creates "a scene of enormous power. Moments of such coherence are rare, but their existence at all suggests that this sequence [the 'Catastrophe Practice' series], while never likely to be entertaining, may prove to be genuinely innovatory."

In 1990 Mosley published the novel *Hopeful Monsters,* the last in the "Catastrophe Practice" series. In it, he expresses a sense of faith in the ability of mankind to con-

front and overcome its problems. Two characters—one a British scientist, the other a German anthropologist—recount the story of their lives, and thereby recount the story of the twentieth century as well. First as student friends and later as a married couple, Max and Eleanor meet many of the leading figures of their time, including philosophers, politicians, scientists, and artists. They also participate in its pivotal events: Max is a member of the team that develops the atomic bomb; Eleanor is a nurse in the Spanish Civil War. In the course of their lives, they experience much of the century's agony as well. *Hopeful Monsters,* Jennifer Potter writes in the *Independent,* "is a gigantic achievement that glows and grows long after it is put aside. In this anthology of our century, one may carp at the bits left out, and one longs for the earthy sound of laughter to puncture the high moral tone. But the final message is of hope."

The hope offered in *Hopeful Monsters* lies in one of Max's early experiments. As a boy he has raised salamanders in a miniature Garden of Eden, accidently proving that the creatures could successfully adapt to changes in their environment. The salamanders were, Eleanor explained, "creatures that were able perhaps naturally to watch themselves and their relation to the universe." As Potter expresses it, "if, like hopeful monsters, we adapt to our environment, then we, too, might find our way back to the Garden of Eden." Banks believes that Mosley's language is meant to push the reader toward liberation. The author's "allusive, reflexive language," Banks writes, "is intended to model, sometimes generate, the subtle processes of self-consciousness, thereby forcing recognition of our freedom to bring new patterns to bear upon existence."

Writing in the *Spectator,* Francis King finds Mosley's "intellectual energy and rigour and [his] gift . . . for summarizing extremely difficult ideas in an easily intelligible manner" to be "extremely impressive." A reviewer for the *Voice Literary Supplement* finds *Hopeful Monsters* to be "one of the grandest epistolary novels of ideas of our time," while Paul Binding of *New Statesman and Society* calls the novel "enormously ambitious and continuously fascinating. . . . Richly worked, this novel abounds in echoes, images taken up and translated, mutations indeed. The book is thus mimetic of its title, and one hopes that it too will beget a progeny—of other novels which do what the novel's business surely is, to try honestly to clarify what seems so terrifyingly dark and bewildering."

In *Rules of the Game* and *Beyond the Pale* Mosley presents a part biography/part memoir account of his father's long and controversial political career. Oswald Mosley first entered politics after the First World War, becoming a member of Parliament in 1919 at the age of 22. At that time he was a member of the Conservative Party. Two years later he became an Independent, then a member of the Labour Party, and finally formed the New Party, which became the British Union of Fascists in 1934. Known for his rousing speeches, good looks and distinctive black uniform (his followers were commonly called Black Shirts), Mosley argued for peace with Hitler and Mussolini, called for an authoritarian government, and attacked the Jews. His followers routinely provoked street fights and disrupted political meetings. Many prominent Englishmen, including poet Osbert Sitwell, who wrote the lyrics to the Black Shirts' theme song, were attracted to the movement. In 1940 Mosley was imprisoned without charges, only being released at the end of World War II. For the rest of his life he served as leader of the Union Movement, a group urging the consolidation of Europe into a single nation, the subjugation of Africa for its raw materials, and the planned breeding of a higher species of man. As Eve Auchincloss remarks in the *Washington Post Book World,* the younger Mosley "was naturally proud of his glamorous father and struggled to see him in the best light. It was to be many years before he could accept what was brilliant and perhaps lovable in him while questioning and rejecting much else."

Nicholas Mosley presents his father as a "willful dreamer," a man who never saw the potential danger of his pronouncements. Revealed, too, are the elder Mosley's many sexual conquests and his habitual derision of his wife, children and servants. Although the two men were not on speaking terms until shortly before his father's death, Nicholas received all of his father's papers. With these papers as his guide, Mosley reconstructs his father's career. He "seeks to be fair to his father and is unsparing of himself. . . .," Auchincloss admits. "[But] there is little left to admire, though Nicholas Mosley, whose life has been conducted in that appalling, charismatic shadow, heroically attempts a balanced assessment." The resulting two-volume biography is, Jon Manchip White concludes in the *Chicago Tribune,* "a magnificent achievement, immeasurably transcending the essential shallowness of its subject. It will take its place among the finest and most absorbing biographies of recent years."

Evaluations of Mosley's career stress the originality of his work. "Mosley," writes Samuel Hynes in the *Washington Post Book World,* "has brought out 13 novels—all very individual, all intelligent and challenging." Often classified as an experimental writer, Mosley more accurately tries "to invent fictional forms capable of dealing adequately with both the complexity of contemporary experience and the perplexing nature of reality," according to Lewis. Mosley, Hynes explains, endeavors "to find new ways of making words tell us the complicated truths of existence in a complicated modern world."

BIOGRAPHICAL/CRITICAL SOURCES:

BOOKS

Contemporary Literary Criticism, Gale, Volume 43, 1987, Volume 70, 1992.
Dictionary of Literary Biography, Volume 14: *British Novelists since 1960,* Gale, 1983.

PERIODICALS

American Book Review, April, 1992, p. 9.
Atlantic Monthly, February, 1958, pp. 85-86.
Books and Bookmen, August, 1979, p. 50; November, 1982, p. 6; October, 1983, p. 11.
Boston Review, December, 1989, p. 28.
British Book News, December, 1980, p. 760; April, 1982, p. 259; February, 1983, p. 130; December, 1983, p. 783; October, 1986, p. 600.
Chicago Tribune, June 30, 1991, p. 3.
Christian Science Monitor, January 29, 1992, p. 13.
Commonweal, December 17, 1971, pp. 283-284.
Contemporary Review, January, 1980, p. 48; December, 1982, p. 331; December, 1983, p. 331.
Economist, October 23, 1982, p. 98; December 3, 1983, p. 104.
Guardian Weekly, November 13, 1983, p. 21; August 25, 1991, p. 20.
History Today, December, 1983, p. 60; March, 1984, p. 60.
Illustrated London News, November, 1980, p. 102; December, 1982, p. 82.
Independent, June 3, 1990.
Listener, June 28, 1979, p. 895; October 16, 1980, p. 513; December 10, 1981, p. 728; October 14, 1982, p. 27; December 8, 1983, p. 28; August 21, 1986, p. 24.
London Review of Books, November 4, 1982, p. 3; December 1, 1983, p. 3; September 18, 1986, p. 22; July 12, 1990, p. 16.
Los Angeles Times Book Review, March 3, 1991, p. 6; December 15, 1991, p. 3.
New Statesman, January 15, 1965, p. 82; October 14, 1966, p. 553; August 3, 1979, p. 171.
New Statesman and Society, June 15, 1990, p. 34.
New Yorker, August 5, 1991, p. 80.
New York Herald Tribune Book Review, January 26, 1958, p. 5.
New York Review of Books, March 23, 1978, p. 49.
New York Times, December 26, 1991, p. C19.
New York Times Book Review, January 26, 1958, p. 5; February 2, 1969, p. 35; November 10, 1985, p. 56; February 9, 1992, p. 19.
Observer, September 14, 1980, p. 29; November 1, 1981, p. 34; December 5, 1982, p. 25; October 30, 1983, p. 33; November 6, 1983, p. 31; September 7, 1986, p. 26; March 31, 1991, p. 54.

Review of Contemporary Fiction, summer, 1982, pp. 118-123; spring, 1988, p. 187; spring, 1991, pp. 309-310.

Saturday Review, January 25, 1969, p. 31; November 6, 1971, p. 48.

Spectator, November 22, 1980, p. 25; January 9, 1982, p. 22; October 30, 1982, p. 22; October 29, 1983, p. 22; June 23, 1990, p. 30; February 2, 1991, p. 33.

Stand, winter, 1991, pp. 76-83.

Time, April 22, 1966, pp. 88-90; June 16, 1967, p. D10.

Times (London), October 6, 1955, p. 11; October 5, 1962, p. 16; July 1, 1979, p. 12; June 3, 1990, p. 2.

Times Literary Supplement, November 16, 1962, p. 869; January 14, 1965, p. 21; October 27, 1966, p. 974; October 17, 1968, p. 1171; September 19, 1980, p. 1012; October 16, 1981, p. 1192; October 22, 1982, p. 1149; August 15, 1986, p. 894.

Tribune Books (Chicago), April 30, 1989, p. 5; June 30, 1991, p. 3; December 22, 1991, p. 3.

Voice Literary Supplement, June, 1991, p. 30; December, 1991, p. 14.

Washington Post Book World, April 30, 1989, p. 6; July 7, 1991, p. 5; November 10, 1991, p. 12.

World and I, March, 1992, pp. 351-357.

—Sketch by Thomas Wiloch

* * *

MOYNIHAN, Ruth B(arnes) 1933-

PERSONAL: Born August 19, 1933, in Wallingford, CT; daughter of Russell Norris (a landscape architect) and Helen (a community leader; maiden name, MacKenzie) Barnes; married William Trumbull Moynihan (a professor, critic, and playwright), 1953; children: Robert B., Edward R., Elaine Moynihan Lisle, Neil T., Susan Moynihan Murray, Richard K., Benjamin. *Education:* Attended Smith College, 1951-53; University of Connecticut, B.A., 1973; Yale University, M.A., 1976, Ph.D., 1979.

ADDRESSES: Home—37 Farrell Rd., R.R.1, Storrs, CT 06268.

CAREER: Home manager, researcher, writer, and lecturer, 1956-77; University of Connecticut, Storrs, lecturer in history, 1977; University of Texas at Dallas, visiting professor of history, 1979-80; Yale University, New Haven, CT, visiting lecturer in history and women's studies, 1980-81; University of Connecticut, lecturer in history, 1982-83, 1984—; consulting historian, lecturer, and writer, 1984—. Visiting assistant professor of history, Lewis and Clark College, 1983-84, and St. Joseph College, 1991-92.

MEMBER: American Historical Association, Organization of American Historians, Council on Women in His-

torical Professions, Berkshire Conference of Women Historians, Pax Christi, Phi Beta Kappa.

AWARDS, HONORS: Danforth Graduate Fellowship for Women, 1973-77; Yale University, graduate fellowship, 1973-79, Beinecke Prize in Western History, 1979; grant from American Council of Learned Societies, 1980; honorable mention, Western Writers Association, 1984.

WRITINGS:

Rebel for Rights: Abigail Scott Duniway, Yale University Press, 1983.

(Editor with Susan Armitage and Christiane DiChamp) *So Much to Be Done: Women Settlers on the Mining and Ranching Frontier,* University of Nebraska Press, 1989.

Coming of Age: Four Centuries of Connecticut Women and Their Choices, Connecticut Historical Society, 1989.

Contributor to small magazines and to academic journals, including *Western Historical Quarterly.*

WORK IN PROGRESS: Editing, with Cynthia Russett and Laurie Crumpacker, *Voices of American Women: A Documentary History of American Women from the Sixteenth Century to the Present,* two volumes, for University of Nebraska Press.

SIDELIGHTS: Ruth B. Moynihan once told *CA:* "The subject of my 1983 book, Abigail Scott Duniway, was a brilliant, irascible, witty suffragist/orator/journalist; she is still an exciting and controversial figure in the Pacific Northwest. Her life exemplifies frontier and nineteenth-century womanhood, negates stereotypes, and provides another role model for women of every place and time. She opened up western and women's history for me, and she did that for her own generation, too.

"I have always been fascinated by books, by writing, and by history. Raising seven children, one adopted, has enriched my life and my perceptions, but kept me busy. Now I want to help others, especially women, understand and value their own past and accomplish as much as they can in the present. But I've only just begun to write the many books I have in mind. I can give no advice except that one must live with integrity and define oneself—and that's the hardest task of all. Writing a good book, or a good poem, is a great help."

* * *

MULLER, Marcia 1944-

PERSONAL: Born September 28, 1944, in Detroit, MI; daughter of Henry J. (a marketing executive) and Kathryn (Minke) Muller; married Frederick T. Guilson, Jr. (in sales), August 12, 1967. *Education:* University of Michigan, B.A., 1966, M.A., 1971.

ADDRESSES: Home—San Francisco, CA. *Agent*— Virginia Barber, 44 Greenwich Ave., New York, NY 10011.

CAREER: Sunset (magazine), Menlo Park, CA, merchandising supervisor, 1968-69; University of Michigan Institute for Social Research, Ann Arbor, field interviewer in the San Francisco Bay area, 1971-73; free lance writer and novelist, 1973—.

MEMBER: Mystery Writers of America, Sisters in Crime, Women in Communications.

WRITINGS:

NOVELS

Edwin of the Iron Shoes, McKay, 1977.
Ask the Cards a Question, St. Martin's, 1982.
Games to Keep the Dark Away, St. Martin's, 1984.
There's Nothing to Be Afraid Of, St. Martin's, 1985.
The Legend of Slain Soldiers: An Elena Oliverez Mystery,
    Walker & Company, 1985.
Beyond the Grave, Walker & Company, 1986.
(With Bill Pronzini) *The Lighthouse,* Methuen, 1987.
Eye of the Storm, Mysterious Press, 1988.
There Hangs the Knife, St. Martin's, 1988.
The Cavalier in White, Harlequin, 1988.
Dark Star, St. Martin's, 1989.
The Shape of Dread, Mysterious Press, 1989.
There's Something in a Sunday, Mysterious Press, 1989.
The Cheshire Cat's Eye, Mysterious Press, 1990.
Trophies And Dead Things, Mysterious Press, 1990.
Leave A Message for Willie, Mysterious Press, 1990.
Where Echoes Live, Mysterious Press, 1991.
Pennies on A Dead Woman's Eyes, Mysterious Press,
    1992.

COLLECTIONS; EDITED WITH PRONZINI

Witches' Brew, Macmillan, 1984.
Kill or Cure, Macmillan, 1985.
She Won the West: An Anthology of Western and Frontier
    Stories By Women, Morrow, 1985.
Dark Lessons: Crime and Detection on Campus, Macmillan, 1985.
The Wickedest Show on Earth, Morrow, 1986.

OTHER

(Author of preface) *Hard-Boiled Dames: A Brass-Knuckled Anthology of the Toughest Women from the Classic Pulps,* St. Martin's, 1986.

SIDELIGHTS: Novelist Marcia Muller has been credited with helping revolutionize the depiction of female private eyes in works such as *The Cheshire Cat's Eye* and *Trophies and Dead Things.* Muller's most popular character, ace

San Francisco legal investigator Sharon McCone, differs from some of her more hard-boiled counterparts in that she is more apt to use her wits than her gun. The author once described the genesis of her fictional sleuth by noting that, when entering the detective genre, her aim was "to use the classical puzzle form of the mystery to introduce a contemporary female sleuth, a figure with surprisingly few counterparts in the world of detective fiction." Since introducing McCone in *Edwin of the Iron Shoes,* Muller has been praised for both the realistic depiction of her heroine and for giving readers vivid descriptions of the series' Bay area locales. In a review of *There's Something In a Sunday* for the *Los Angeles Times Book Review,* Charles Champlin notes that "as before, Muller's strength is in her characters—McCone is likable and believable—and her ability to convey places and atmospheres."

Muller has also edited a number of short story collections with Bill Pronzini, including *Dark Lessons* (which offers murder and mayhem on school campuses) and *Kill or Cure* (an introduction to mysteries set in the medical world). "Pronzini and Muller have unearthed some genuine gems," Margaret Cannon writes of *Kill or Cure* for the *Globe and Mail,* "there are no turkeys in the collection." Cannon is also impressed by a Pronzini/Muller novel collaboration entitled *The Lighthouse.* The critic concludes that this tale of yuppies and murder in a small town on the Oregon coast "combines both authors' strengths . . . and avoids their weaknesses" in a setting that is "excellent."

BIOGRAPHICAL/CRITICAL SOURCES:

PERIODICALS

Globe and Mail (Toronto), December 7, 1985; April 11, 1987.
Library Journal, October 1, 1977.
Los Angeles Times, August 14, 1985; June 6, 1986.
Los Angeles Times Book Review, October 10, 1982, p. 7; February 12, 1989, p. 6.
New York Times Book Review, November 7, 1982, p. 39; October 6, 1985; March 12, 1989, p. 24; December 24, 1989, p. 23; November 4, 1990, p. 30.
USA Today, July 27, 1987.*

*   *   *

MUNSLOW, Barry 1950-

PERSONAL: Born June 2, 1950, in Derby, England; son of Thomas Eric (an insurance agent) Munslow and Joyce Mildred (a shopkeeper) Bartram; married Bie Nio Ong (a university senior lecturer); children: Karl. *Education:* Victoria University of Manchester, B.A. (with honors), 1971,

Ph.D., 1980. *Avocational interests:* Rugby, walking, squash.

ADDRESSES: Office—School of Politics and Communication Studies, University of Liverpool, Liverpool L69 3BX, England.

CAREER: Universidad Eduardo Mondlane, Maputo, Mozambique, lecturer at Center of African Studies, 1976-78; University of Leeds, Leeds, England, research fellow in politics, 1979-80; Victoria University of Manchester, Manchester, England, research fellow in government, 1980-81; University of Liverpool, Liverpool, England, senior lecturer in politics, 1981—. Senior policy advisor on environment and development to numerous organizations, including World Bank, and Scandinavian government.

MEMBER: Political Studies Association, Development Studies Association.

WRITINGS:

(Co-author) *A Questao Rodesiana* (title means "The Rhodesian Question"), Iniciativas Editorias, 1977.
(Editor) *Southern Africa: A Student Reader,* University of Bradford, 1981.
Mozambique: The Revolution and Its Origins, Longman, 1983.
(Editor with Phil O'Keefe, and contributor) *Energy and Development in Southern Asia,* Volume 1-2, Scandinavian Institute of African Studies, 1984.
(Editor with Henry Finch, and contributor) *Proletarianization in the Third World,* Croom Helm, 1984.
(Editor and author of introduction) *Samora Machel: An African Revolutionary, Selected Speeches and Writings,* Zed Press, 1985.
(Editor and author of introduction) *Africa's Problems in the Transition to Socialism,* Zed Press, 1986.
The Fuelwood Trap: A Study of the SADCC Region, Earthscan, 1988.
(With C. Pycroft) *Southern Africa: Annual Review 1987/88,* Hans Zell, Volume 1: *Country Events,* 1990, Volume 2: *Regional Events,* 1990.

Contributor to numerous books, including *Socialist Arguments,* edited by D. Coates and G. Johnson, Martin Robertson, 1983; *World Recession and the Food Crisis in Africa,* edited by P. Lawrence, James Curry, 1986; *World Government,* edited by P. J. Taylor, Oxford University Press, 1990; and *Rural Development and Planning in Zimbabwe,* edited by N. D. Mutizwa-Mangiza and A. H. J. Helmsing, Aldershot, 1991. Also contributor to political science and development journals and newspapers, including *Review of African Political Economy, Journal of Area Studies, Ambio,* and *Parliamentary Affairs.* Member of editorial boards of *Third World Planning Review* and *Review*

of African Political Economy. Past Third World politics editor of *Politics.*

WORK IN PROGRESS: Research on sustainable development.

SIDELIGHTS: Barry Munslow told *CA:* "How to combine the need for development with protection of the environment has been a major concern of mine for fifteen years or more. This takes shape in the form of my work in policy advice and in academic writing on the subject. The two activities are mutually reinforcing."

*   *   *

MURPHY, Lois Barclay   1902-

PERSONAL: Born March 23, 1902, in Lisbon, IA; daughter of Wade Crawford and May (Hartley) Barclay; married Gardner Murphy, 1926 (deceased); children: Alpen Gardner, Margaret Murphy Small. *Education:* Vassar College, A.B., 1923; Union Theological Seminary, B.D., 1928; Columbia University, Ph.D., 1937; Topeka Psychoanalytic Institute, graduate, 1962.

ADDRESSES: Home—(summer) R.F.D., Ashland, NH 03217; (winter) 3217 Connecticut Ave. S., Washington, DC 20008.

CAREER: Sarah Lawrence College, Bronxville, NY, member of faculty of psychology department, 1928-52, adviser to college nursery school, 1937-52; Menninger Foundation, Topeka, KS, research psychologist, 1952-69, director of Developmental Studies. Consultant to B. M. Institute, Ahmedabad, India, 1950—, and to research organizations in the United States.

MEMBER: National Association for Nursery Education, International Association of Child Psychoanalysis, New York Academy of Sciences, Topeka Psychoanalytical Society, Phi Beta Kappa.

AWARDS, HONORS: G. Stanley Hall Award in developmental psychology, American Psychological Association, 1981; Distinguished Alumna Award, Columbia University, 1984; Dolly Madison Award, National Center for Clinical Infant Programs, 1985.

WRITINGS:

(With husband, Gardner Murphy) *Experimental Social Psychology,* 1931, (with T. Newcomb) revised edition, Harper, 1937, reprinted, Greenwood Press, 1970.
Social Behavior and Child Personality: An Exploratory Study of Some Roots of Sympathy, Columbia University Press, 1937.
(With Eugene Lerner and others) *Methods for the Study of Personality in Young Children,* National Research

Council, 1941, reprinted, Kraus Reprint, 1966, published with *Colin, a Normal Child,* as *Personality in Young Children,* two volumes, Basic Books, 1956.

(With Henry Ladd) *Emotional Factors in Learning,* Columbia University Press, 1944, reprinted, Greenwood Press, 1970.

(With others) *Life and Ways of the Seven-to-Eight-Year-Old,* Basic Books, 1952.

(Editor with Esther Raushenbush) *Achievement in the College Years,* Harper, 1960.

(With others) *The Widening World of Childhood: Paths toward Mastery,* Basic Books, 1962.

(Editor with G. Murphy) *Asian Psychology,* Basic Books, 1968.

(Editor with G. Murphy) *Western Psychology: From the Greeks to William James,* Basic Books, 1969.

(Editor with L. Joseph Stone and Henrietta T. Smith) *The Competent Infant: Research and Commentary,* Basic Books, 1973.

Growing Up in Garden Court, Child Welfare League of America, 1974.

(With Alice E. Moriarty) *Vulnerability, Coping, and Growth: From Infancy to Adolescence,* Yale University Press, 1976.

(With Cotter Hirschberg) *Robin: Comprehensive Treatment of a Vulnerable Adolescent,* Basic Books, 1982.

The Home Hospital, Basic Books, 1982.

There Is More Beyond: Selected Papers of Gardner Murphy, McFarland & Co., 1989.

Gardner Murphy: Integrating, Expanding and Humanizing Psychology, McFarland & Co., 1990.

Contributor to books, including *Personality and the Behavior Disorders,* Ronald, 1944; *Prevention of Mental Disorders in Children,* Basic Books, 1961; *L'enfant dans la famille,* edited by James E. Anthony and C. Koupernik, Masson (Paris), 1970; *Coping and Adaptations,* edited by Coelho, Hamburg, and Adams, Basic Books, 1974; *The Psychologists,* Clinical Psychology Publishing, 1978; *Psychoanalytic Approach to Development,* U.S. Government Printing Office, 1980; *Models of Achievement: Reflections of Eminent Women in Psychology,* edited by Nancy F. Russo and Agnes N. O'Connell, Columbia University Press, 1983; *Invulnerable Children,* Guilford Press, 1986; *Emotions: Development and Research;* and *Psychoanalytic Views of Infancy in the Course of Life.* Contributor to periodicals, including *Zero to Three.* Also author of "Caring for Children" series (with Ethel Leeper), ten booklets, U.S. Government Printing Office, and of monographs and articles, including one of the studies published in *The Nation's Children* for the White House Conference on Children and Youth, 1960. Associate editor, *Journal of Projective Techniques,* 1951-62.

SIDELIGHTS: Lois Barclay Murphy once told *CA:* "Most of my work and my writing have evolved from a wish to help grownups understand children. My writing has nearly always grown out of work with and research on children and adolescents, including psychotherapy. In addition to books, I have written scores of articles, some of which have been translated into Norwegian, French, and Greek. I have found some of my books in libraries in India, Japan, and Europe.

"My writing has been appreciated for its readability, lack of jargon, and making children come alive for the reader. At the same time, some of my books have been used in teaching professionals working with children. I have never boarded a trendy bandwagon, [yet] I am considered a pioneer in the study of 'prosocial' behavior. With Ruth Horowitz I introduced the term 'projector techniques'; I undertook the study of children's ways of coping with everyday problems in 1952, before the term coping was in the index of psychological abstracts. I was always interested in undertaking the study of new problems, filling a gap. I learn most by *listening* to children."

*   *   *

MYERSON, Joel 1945-

PERSONAL: Born September 9, 1945, in Boston, MA; son of Edward Yale (a theatre manager) and Gwenne (Rubenstein) Myerson. *Education:* Attended Case Institute of Technology (now Case Western Reserve University), 1963-64; Tulane University, B.A., 1967; Northwestern University, M.A., 1968, Ph.D., 1971.

ADDRESSES: Home—5879 Woodvine Rd., Columbia, SC 29206. *Office*—Department of English, University of South Carolina, Columbia, SC 29208.

CAREER: University of South Carolina, Columbia, assistant professor, 1971-76, associate professor, 1976-80, professor of English, 1980-90; Carolina Research Professor of American Literature, 1990—.

MEMBER: Modern Language Association of America (member of advisory council, American literature section; secretary, Committee on Scholarly Editions), Association for Documentary Editing (president), Bibliographical Society of America, Society for Textual Scholarship (member of program committee), American Literature Association (member of executive board), Poe Society, Nathaniel Hawthorne Society, Melville Society, South Atlantic Modern Language Association (chairman of textual and bibliographical section), Northeast Modern Language Association (chairman, Transcendentalism discussion section), Philological Association of the Carolinas (president), Thoreau Society (president), Emerson Society (president).

AWARDS, HONORS: Endowment for the Humanities fellow, 1976, grant, 1978-81, 1988-92; outstanding academic book of the year citation, *Choice,* 1977, for *Margaret Fuller: An Annotated Secondary Bibliography,* 1979, for *The American Renaissance in New England, Brook Farm: An Annotated Bibliography and Resources Guide,* and *Margaret Fuller: A Descriptive Bibliography,* and 1984, for *The Transcendentalists: A Review of Research and Criticism;* outstanding reference book citation, *Library Journal,* 1979, for *The American Renaissance in New England;* Guggenheim fellow, 1981-82; South Carolina Committee for the Humanities fellow, 1984; Distinguished Service Award, Association for Documentary Editing, 1986; Children's Literature Association Book Award, 1990, for *The Journals of Louisa May Alcott.*

WRITINGS:

(With Arthur H. Miller, Jr.) *Melville Dissertations: An Annotated Directory,* Melville Society, 1972.

Margaret Fuller: An Exhibition from the Collection of Joel Myerson, University of South Carolina Press, 1973.

Margaret Fuller: An Annotated Secondary Bibliography, B. Franklin, 1977.

Brook Farm: An Annotated Bibliography and Resources Guide, Garland Publishing, 1978.

Margaret Fuller: A Descriptive Bibliography, University of Pittsburgh Press, 1978.

(Editor) *Margaret Fuller: Essays on American Life and Letters,* College & University Press, 1978.

(Editor) *Dictionary of Literary Biography,* Gale, Volume 1: *The American Renaissance in New England,* 1978, Volume 3: *Antebellum Writers in New York and the South,* 1979.

The New England Transcendentalists and the "Dial": A History of the Magazine and Its Contributors, Fairleigh Dickinson University Press, 1980.

(Editor) *Critical Essays on Margaret Fuller,* G. K. Hall, 1980.

Theodore Parker: A Descriptive Bibliography, Garland Publishing, 1981.

Ralph Waldo Emerson: A Descriptive Bibliography, University of Pittsburgh Press, 1982.

(Editor with Philip Gura) *Critical Essays on American Transcendentalism,* G. K. Hall, 1982.

(Editor) *Emerson Centenary Essays,* Southern Illinois University Press, 1982.

(Editor with Robert E. Burkholder) *Critical Essays on Ralph Waldo Emerson,* G. K. Hall, 1983.

Emily Dickinson: A Descriptive Bibliography, University of Pittsburgh Press, 1984.

(Editor) *The Transcendentalists: A Review of Research and Criticism,* Modern Language Association of America, 1984.

(With Burkholder) *Emerson: An Annotated Secondary Bibliography,* University of Pittsburgh Press, 1985.

(Editor) *The Brook Farm Book: A Collection of First-Hand Accounts of the Community,* Garland Publishing, 1987.

(Editor with Daniel Shealy and Madeleine B. Stern) *The Selected Letters of Louisa May Alcott,* Little, Brown, 1987.

(Editor) *The American Transcendentalists,* Gale, 1988.

(Editor) *Critical Essays on Henry David Thoreau's "Walden,"* G. K. Hall, 1988.

(Editor with Shealy and Stern) *A Double Life: Newly Discovered Thrillers of Louisa May Alcott,* Little, Brown, 1988.

(Editor with Shealy and Stern) *The Journals of Louisa May Alcott,* Little, Brown, 1989.

(Editor with Shealy and Stern) Louisa May Alcott, *Selected Fiction,* Little, Brown, 1990.

(Editor) *Whitman in His Own Time,* Omnigraphics, 1991.

(Editor) *Emerson and Thoreau: The Contemporary Reviews,* Cambridge University Press, 1992.

Walt Whitman: A Descriptive Bibliography, University of Pittsburgh Press, 1993.

(Editor with Greta D. Little) *Three Children's Novels by Christopher Pearse Cranch,* University of Georgia Press, 1993.

Editorial associate, "The Writings of Herman Melville," Northwestern University Press, 1970-77; editor, *Studies in the American Renaissance,* 1977—; member of editorial board, "Pittsburgh Series in Bibliography," University of Pittsburgh Press; member of editorial board, *Text, Resources for American Literacy Study, Concord Saunterer, American Literature,* and *American Periodicals.*

WORK IN PROGRESS: Editing *Walt Whitman: Poetry Manuscripts,* for Garland Publishing; editing *The Cambridge Companion to Henry David Thoreau,* for Cambridge University Press; editing, with Ronald A. Bosco, *The Later Lectures of Ralph Waldo Emerson,* for University of Georgia Press; editing, with Len Gougeon, *Emerson and Anti-Slavery;* with Burkholder, *Supplement to Emerson: An Annotated Secondary Bibliography.*

N

NANASSY, Louis C(harles) 1913-

PERSONAL: Born December 3, 1913, in Debrecen, Hungary; son of Kalman and Elizabeth (Olah) Nanassy; married Evelyn Horner Starkey, August 21, 1941; children: Richard Louis, Jean Evelyn (Mrs. Francis D. Harris). *Education:* Indiana University of Pennsylvania, B.S., 1936; Ohio State University, M.A., 1941; Harvard University, graduate study, 1942; Columbia University, Ed.D., 1952. *Religion:* Protestant.

ADDRESSES: Home—7 Cascade Ct., Brick Town, NJ 08724.

CAREER: Chairman of business education department at high schools in Rockwood, PA, 1936-37, and Manasquan, NJ, 1937-40; teacher in Irvington, NJ, 1940-46; New Jersey State Teachers College (now William Paterson College of New Jersey), Paterson, assistant professor, 1946-51, associate professor, 1951-55, professor of business education, 1955-57; Montclair State College, Upper Montclair, NJ, professor of business education, 1957-79, chairman of department, 1963-65, professor emeritus, 1980—.

Visiting professor or distinguished lecturer at numerous universities and colleges, 1946—, including Upsala College, fall, 1946, Western Michigan University, summer, 1953, University of Vermont, summer, 1956, University of Denver, summer, 1960, Syracuse University, summer, 1965, University of Wyoming, summer, 1973, California State University at Los Angeles, 1980, and Montclair State College, 1991. Vice-president and guidance consultant, Sherwood School of Business, Paterson, 1950-56. Business manager, *American Business Education Quarterly*, 1956-58.

MEMBER: International Society for Business Education, American Vocational Association, Association of Teacher Educators, National Association for Business Teacher Education (member of executive board, 1964-66), National Association of Supervisors of Business Education, National Business Education Association (member of executive board, 1956-59), National Education Association, Eastern Business Teachers Association, Association of New Jersey State College Faculties (member of executive board, 1949-52), New Jersey Business Education Association (president, 1956-57), New Jersey Education Association, Delta Pi Epsilon, Kappa Delta Pi, Phi Delta Kappa, Omicron Tau Theta, Phi Kappa Phi, Alpha Phi Gamma, Gamma Rho Tau, Phi Sigma Pi, Pi Omega Pi.

AWARDS, HONORS: Distinguished Service Award, Ohio State University, 1970; Outstanding Service Award, Delta Pi Epsilon, 1972; John Robert Gregg Award, 1978; Distinguished Alumni Award, Indiana University of Pennsylvania, 1990.

WRITINGS:

Clerical Payroll Project, Pitman, 1954.
Standard Payroll Project, Pitman, 1955, 9th edition, 1986.
(With Albert C. Fries) *Business Timed Writings,* Prentice-Hall, 1960, revised edition, Glencoe, 1974.
(Compiler with W. H. Selden) *Business Dictionary,* Prentice-Hall, 1960.
(With others) *College Typewriting,* Pitman, 1961.
(With Nathan Krevolin) *Junior High Timed Writings,* Pitman, 1962.
(With Krevolin) *Timed Writings for Teen-Agers,* Pitman, 1963.
(With Leonard J. Porter) *Managing Your Money,* American Bankers Association, 1967.
(With C. M. Fancher) *General Business and Economic Understandings,* 3rd edition (Nanassy was not associated with earlier editions), Prentice-Hall, 1968, 4th edition, 1973.

(With Krevolin and John E. Whitcraft) *Personal Typing,* Pitman, 1970.

(With Herbert A. Tonne) *Principles of Business Education,* 4th edition (Nanassy was not associated with earlier editions), Gregg, 1970.

(With Selden and Jo Ann Lee) *Reference Manual for Office Workers,* Glencoe, 1977, 2nd edition, 1986.

(With Tonne and Dean R. Malsbary) *Principles and Trends in Business Education,* Bobbs-Merrill, 1977.

Readings in Teaching Business Subjects, Fearon, 1980.

(With Selden and Lee) *Canadian Secretary's Handbook,* Collier Books, 1983.

(With Selden) *The Prentice-Hall Word Book,* Prentice-Hall, 1984.

(With Selden) *The Business Dictionary,* Prentice-Hall, 1984.

(With Krevolin and Whitcraft) *Keyboarding for Personal and Professional Use,* Prentice-Hall, 1986.

Associate editor, *American Business Education Yearbook,* 1947-48; editorial associate, *Eastern Business Teachers Association Yearbook,* 1948, 1949, and 1967. Contributor of more than eighty-five articles to business education and other professional journals. Editor, Delta Pi Epsilon's *Business Education Index,* 1947-77; editor and business manager, *Business Education Observer,* 1954-55; basic business editor, *Business Education Forum,* 1966-68; consulting editor, *Journal of Business Education,* 1977-84.

*   *   *

NEVINS, Albert J. 1915-

PERSONAL: Born September 11, 1915, in Yonkers, NY; son of Albert J. and Bessie L. (Corcoran) Nevins. *Education:* Attended Venard College, 1932-36, Maryknoll Noviate, Bedford, MA, 1936-37, and Maryknoll Seminary, Maryknoll, NY, 1937-42.

ADDRESSES: Home—Winter: 4606 West Loughman St., Tampa, FL 33616; summer: Box 154, Acra, NY 12405.

CAREER: Worked in editorial departments of Yonkers newspapers before studying for priesthood. Ordained Roman Catholic priest, 1942; director of World Horizon Films, 1945-68; editor, *Maryknoll Magazine,* 1955-69, and *World Campus Magazine,* 1958-67; director of social communications, Catholic Foreign Mission Society of America, 1960-69; editor-in-chief, Our Sunday Visitor, Inc., 1969-81, and The Priest, 1973-81; columnist, 1969—. Civil Air Patrol, became lieutenant colonel.

MEMBER: Inter-American Press Association (member of board of directors and Freedom of the Press committee; treasurer, technical center), Catholic Institute of the Press (founder; member of executive board), Catholic Press Association (former vice-president, treasurer, president, and member of board of directors), Catholic Association for International Peace, Gallery of Living Catholic Authors, Africa Studies Association, Overseas Press Club, Latin America Studies Association, Catholic Historical Society.

AWARDS, HONORS: Catholic Press Association certificates of outstanding achievement for editorials, 1955, 1957, 1960, and 1961, and Most Distinguished Contribution to Catholic Journalism Award, 1961; special citation, Catholic Institute of the Press, 1957; National Conference of Christians and Jews certificate of recognition for editorial writing, 1957, and National Brotherhood Award for editorial writing, 1958; International Film Festival, Lille, France, premier prix for films *The Story of Juan Mateo,* 1957, and *The Problem of People,* 1961; Maria Moors Cabot Prize, Columbia University, 1961, for interhemispheric journalism advancing friendship; St. Augustine Award, Villanova University, 1962; Golden Eagle Award, Committee on International Non-Theatrical Events, 1966, for film *The Gods of Todos Santos;* LL.D., St. Benedict's College, Atchinson, KS, and Catholic University, San Juan, PR; Benemerenti Medal, Holy See, 1981.

WRITINGS:

BOOKS

The Catholic Year, Essential Books, 1949.
Adventures of Wu Han of Korea, Dodd, 1951.
Adventures of Kenji of Japan, Dodd, 1952.
Adventures of Pancho of Peru, Dodd, 1953.
Adventures of Ramon of Bolivia, Dodd, 1954.
St. Francis of the Seven Seas, Farrar, Straus, 1955.
Adventures of Duc of Indochina, Dodd, 1955.
The Meaning of Maryknoll, McMullen Books, 1956.
(Editor) *The Maryknoll Golden Book: An Anthology of Mission Literature,* Book Treasures, 1956.
Adventures of Men of Maryknoll, Dodd, 1957.
The Making of a Priest, Newman, 1958.
Away to East Africa, Dodd, 1959.
The Maryknoll Book of Peoples, Crawley, 1959.
The Young Conquistador, Dodd, 1960.
Away to the Lands of the Andes, Dodd, 1962.
(Editor) *The Maryknoll Catholic Dictionary,* Grosset, 1964.
(With Donald J. Casey) *The Church in the Modern World,* Maryknoll Publications, 1965.
Away to Mexico, Dodd, 1965.
The Story of Pope John XXIII, Grosset, 1965.
Away to Central America, Dodd, 1967.
(Editor) *Maryknoll Book of Treasures,* Maryknoll Publications, 1968.
Away to Venezuela, Dodd, 1969.
The Prayer of the Faithful, Our Sunday Visitor, 1970.

Our American Catholic Heritage, Our Sunday Visitor, 1972.

The World Book of People, Our Sunday Visitor, 1973.

(Editor) John Francis Noll, *Father Smith Instructs Jackson,* revised edition, Our Sunday Visitor, 1975.

The Way, Tyndale, 1976.

General Intercessions, Our Sunday Visitor, 1978.

Questions Catholics Ask, Our Sunday Visitor, 1978.

A Saint for Your Name: Names for Boys, Our Sunday Visitor, 1980.

A Saint for Your Name: Names for Girls, Our Sunday Visitor, 1980.

Called to Serve, Our Sunday Visitor, 1981, revised edition, 1992.

Life after Death, Our Sunday Visitor, 1983.

The Sunday Readings, Our Sunday Visitor, 1984.

Builders of Catholic America, Our Sunday Visitor, 1985.

American Martyrs, Our Sunday Visitor, 1987.

The Life of Jesus Christ, Costello, 1987.

Strangers at Your Door, Our Sunday Visitor, 1988.

Ask Me a Question, Our Sunday Visitor, 1989.

Answering a Fundamentalist, Our Sunday Visitor, 1990.

Scriptures of Faith, Our Sunday Visitor, 1992.

SCREENPLAYS

Wrote and produced the films *The Miracle of Blue Cloud County, Kyoto Saturday Afternoon, The Kid Down the Block,* and *Indian Street.* Wrote, photographed, and produced the films *The Story of Juan Mateo, Adan of the Andes, Men of Tomorrow, School for Farmers, Light Up the Jungle, The Royal Road, A Boy of the Bakuria, Bride of Africa, Land of the Twelve Tribes, New Day in Africa, The Training of a Maryknoller, The Maryknoll Brother, The Problem of People, The Golden Kimono, Man with a Mission, Dateline Orient, The Gods of Todos Santos, Children of the Dust,* and *The Quiet Revolution.*

OTHER

Also author of pamphlets. Contributor of articles to periodicals. Editor, *The Pope Speaks,* 1981—, *Diaconate Magazine,* 1984-92, and *Nova,* 1989—.

WORK IN PROGRESS: The Faith of Our Fathers.

*   *   *

NORMAN, Marsha   1947-

PERSONAL: Born September 21, 1947, in Louisville, KY; daughter of Billie Lee (a realtor) and Bertha Mae (Conley) Williams; married Michael Norman (a teacher; divorced, 1974); married Dann C. Byck, Jr. (a theatrical producer), November, 1978 (divorced); married Timothy Dykman; children: (third marriage) Angus, Katherine. *Education:*

Agnes Scott College, B.A., 1969; University of Louisville, M.A.T., 1971.

ADDRESSES: Office—c/o The Tantleff Office, 375 Greenwich St., No. 700, New York, NY 10013.

CAREER: Playwright. Teacher, Kentucky Department of Health, 1969-70, Jefferson County Public Schools, 1970-72, and Kentucky Arts Commission, 1972-76; book reviewer and editor for the *Louisville Times,* 1974-79; worked with disturbed children at Kentucky Central State Hospital.

AWARDS, HONORS: American Theater Critics Association named *Getting Out* the best play produced in regional theatre during 1977-78; National Endowment for the Arts grant, 1978-79; John Gassner New Playwrights Medallion, Outer Critics Circle, and George Oppenheimer-Newsday Award, both 1979, both for *Getting Out;* Rockefeller playwright-in-residence grant, 1979-80, at the Mark Taper Forum; Susan Smith Blackburn prize, 1982, Tony award nomination, 1983, and Pulitzer Prize, 1983, all for *'Night, Mother;* Tony Award for Best Book of Musical, 1991, for *The Secret Garden.*

WRITINGS:

PLAYS

Getting Out, (two-act; first produced in Louisville, KY, 1977; produced Off-Broadway at Phoenix Theatre, 1978), Avon, 1977.

Third and Oak: The Laundromat [and] *The Pool Hall,* (two one-act plays; produced in Louisville, 1978), Dramatists Play Service, 1978.

It's the Willingness (teleplay), broadcast by Public Broadcasting Service (PBS), 1978.

Circus Valentine (two-act), produced in Louisville, 1979.

The Holdup (two-act), produced in workshop in Louisville, 1980.

In Trouble at Fifteen, broadcast on television program *Skag,* Lorimar Productions, 1980.

'Night, Mother (also see below), Hill & Wang, 1982.

Traveler in the Dark, produced at the Mark Taper Forum, 1984.

Four Plays by Marsha Norman (collection), Theatre Communications, 1988.

Sarah and Abraham, produced at Actors Theater of Louisville's Festival of New American Plays, 1988.

The Secret Garden (musical), book and lyrics, produced on Broadway, 1991.

D.Boone, produced at Actors Theatre of Louisville, 1992.

Author of book and lyrics for *The Secret Garden,* produced on Broadway, 1991-92.

SCREENPLAYS

'Night, Mother, Universal, 1986.

OTHER

The Fortune Teller (novel), Random House, 1987.

Also author of unproduced screenplays *The Children with Emerald Eyes,* for Columbia, *The Bridge,* for Joseph E. Levine, and *Thy Neighbor's Wife,* for United Artists. Work represented in anthology *The Best Plays of 1978-79: The Burns Mantle Yearbook of the Theatre,* edited by Otis L. Guernsey, Jr., Dodd, 1980.

SIDELIGHTS: From the astounding successes of her 1979 stage-writing debut, *Getting Out,* and her 1983 Pulitzer Prize-winning play, *'Night, Mother,* to her continued success as a playwright, screenwriter and novelist, Marsha Norman has established herself as an honest and intelligent writer with a powerful message about ordinary people confronting extraordinary circumstances. "I always write about the same thing: people having the nerve to go on," she once told *CA.* "The people I care about are those folks you wouldn't even notice in life—two women in a laundromat late at night as you drive by, a thin woman in an ugly scarf standing over the luncheon meat at the grocery, a tiny gray lady buying a big sack of chocolate covered raisins and a carton of Kools. Someday I'd love to write a piece about people who can talk. The problem is I know so few of them."

In 1979, Norman took the theater world by storm with her playwriting debut, *Getting Out.* A drama about a woman released from prison after an eight year sentence and a lifetime of trouble, the play concentrates on the psychological changes she undergoes as she is transformed from a hate-filled child named Arlie into the rehabilitated woman Arlene. To contrast the two sides of her protagonist's personality, Norman used two actresses on the stage simultaneously. Critics hailed the innovative drama for its powerful dialogue and emotional honesty. In *Newsweek,* Jack Kroll praised *Getting Out* as a "superb first play . . . we see one of those before and after diptychs living right before our eyes, but this one blazes in the uncompromising light of truth." John Simon of *New York* declared: "No gesture is arbitrary, no syllable rings false. The language is the play's greatest asset: coarse-grained, unvarnished, often hateful, sometimes fumbling for tenderness, funny yet beyond laughter (except the hysterical kind), heartbreaking yet a stranger to tears. And always frighteningly true."

In writing the play, Norman drew upon experiences she'd had while teaching disturbed children at a state hospital. "What we had there were children who never talked at all, as well as ones who would just as soon stab you in the back as talk to you," Norman once told *CA.* "There were lots of violent kids there, lots of Arlies there. But there was one girl in particular, a 13-year-old, who was absolutely terrifying. She's the kind of kid you would not for your life be locked up in a room with for 10 minutes. People got bruises when this kid walked in the room, she was so vicious. . . . Eight years later, when I began to think about writing my first play, I thought back to that experience, because it was so terrifying to me."

Norman's next two plays, *Third and Oak* (1978) and *Circus Valentine* (1979), were written while she was playwright-in-residence at Actors Theater in Louisville. *Third and Oak* consists of two one-act plays, "The Laundromat" and "The Pool Hall." The former features two women in a laundromat and the latter two men in a pool hall, both pairs brought together out of loneliness. "Neither has the power of *Getting Out,*" observed Mary Ellen Miller in the *Dictionary of Literary Biography Yearbook,* "but both show Norman's ability to dramatize the ordinary in extraordinary fashion." *Circus Valentine,* a romanticized account of a traveling circus on the small-town circuit, was panned by critics. Norman spoke with Allan Wallack of *Newsday* about its negative critical reception: "It was devastating. It took me about two years to recover from it and regain my confidence . . . . But the most wonderful result of failure was that ultimately I felt strengthened by it—that they [the critics] hated the play and I survived. That they had said everything awful that could be said. And I *still* wanted to write."

Norman's perseverance paid off in the form of a Pulitzer Prize in 1983 for her fifth play, *'Night, Mother.* A two-character drama, the play premiered at Harvard's American Repertory Theater starring Anne Pitoniak and Kathy Bates as Thelma and Jessie, a mother and daughter who spend a harrowing evening together in what turns out to be the last night of Jessie's life. "*'Night, Mother* reflects what I believe about the theater: Plays should deal with moments of crises," Norman commented in the *New York Times.* The crisis in *'Night, Mother* stems from Jessie's calm but determined announcement to her mother at the beginning of the play: "I'm going to kill myself." Her reasons are myriad: she's an overweight, plain woman who is afraid of going outside. She spends most of her time indoors caring for her self-indulgent, inept mother, gossiping about the neighbors, and eating junk food. Her husband has deserted her because she wouldn't quit smoking and her son is a petty thief. She was recently fired from her job in a hospital gift shop. In short, she neither enjoys nor controls her life and wants to end it. "I'm just not having a very good time, Mama," Jessie explains to Thelma. The rest of the play, Norman stated in the *New York Times,* "is the fight of their lives. We all know people who killed themselves. These suicides leave us hurt and wanting desperately to talk about it and understand." Norman has declined to elaborate on the incident in her own life that inspired the play, but she told Mel Gussow of the *New York Times Magazine,* "The play should not be seen as something from my life but as something from our lives. The best plays, the ones that last, are communal dreams."

Although Jessie spends the bulk of the play justifying her reasons for wanting to end her life, most critics contend that the drama is much more than simply a suicide story. "The play is about suicide only on its surface," observed Holly Hill of the *Times*. "Its subjects are perhaps the most difficult of all relationships—parent and child—and the definition of self." Miller sees the individual's right to choose as the drama's central concern. "It was not Norman's intention to judge the act of suicide in philosophical, religious, or social terms," Miller asserted. Instead, she wrote, the play is "about choice, about Jessie's decision to 'get off the bus,' because it is going nowhere she wants to be." Simon described the play's subjects as "suicide, love, and the meaning of life—as huge as they come; but they are treated with the specificity of threading a needle or choosing the right breakfast for your needs." Different interpretations of the play are to be expected, Simon added. "Believers and atheists, Freudians and anti-Freudians, rationalists and idealists, Marxists and capitalists, parents and children—everyone will have his or her interpretation of *'Night, Mother,*'" he wrote. "Miss Norman may not provide any answers, but anyone who can serve up questions so brilliantly—in language that is only slightly, but finally appositely and awesomely, heightened—has more than earned that right," Simon concluded.

When she learned that *'Night, Mother* had won the prestigious Pulitzer Prize, Norman was vacationing by herself in a secluded cabin four hours north of San Francisco. Later, she told Gussow of the *New York Times*: "The Pulitzer seems like these redwood trees I've been sitting in all week. Enormous but very still at the center. I am thrilled." She continued: "I feel like someone just came into my room in my mind where I work and embroidered a big 'P' on the back of my typing chair. It may not change my life, but it will feel good to know it's back there."

In 1985, Norman wrote another play about ordinary people in a crisis situation entitled *Traveler in the Dark*. The cast of four consists of Sam, a famous surgeon; his wife, Glory; his son, Stephen; and his father Everett, a preacher. The focus of the play is Sam's attempt to deal with the death of a childhood friend on whom he unsuccessfully operated. During the course of the play, Sam's despair at death comes in conflict with his father's faith and his son's questionings. "Sam tries to put his rationality against the face of death," explained Norman in the *Los Angeles Times*. "There's this section of the play when young Stephen asks his dad, 'Is there a center of everything?' Sam replies, 'There was one, the Big Bang theory, but it blew up.' Stephen says, 'Everett says God lit the fire. Did he? Is there a God?' Sam answers 'I think there is something

out there. I want there to be a God, but I don't want it to be me.' That's the play: the incredible longing for God, while saying 'I don't want it to be me,' " Norman summarized.

Critics gave the *Traveler in the Dark* a lukewarm reception, praising it for its thoughtfulness and seriousness but questioning its lack of direction and pat ending. The play "makes large, dark gestures, but its tone is oddly cozy," wrote Dan Sullivan in the *Los Angeles Times.* "It is getting at something that isn't platitudinous, but platitudes are all that seem to come out." Richard Christiansen of the *Chicago Tribune* pointed out that the play shared some of *'Night, Mother*'s faults: "a hortatory argumentation, a schematic working out of a carefully set up problem and an ending that's too neatly wrapped up. But it's also a play that sincerely tries to grapple with the basic issues of human life and death, and it does so with stretches of powerful and moving dialogue." In the *Chicago Tribune,* Norman blamed the play's negative reviews on poor production and a shaky opening night that was "little better than a staged reading." Critics, she added, "didn't think I should write a play about a man."

In order to "escape the brutality of the theater," Norman told Hilary DeVries of the *Chicago Tribune,* she decided to try her hand at writing a novel. *The Fortune Teller* centers around Fay Morgan, a clairvoyant who is helping police solve a mystery involving 27 kidnapped children. As she attempts to use her psychic powers to locate the missing youngsters, she becomes increasingly worried about her own 19-year-old daughter, whom she has envisioned running away with a rich but shallow boyfriend and leading a life of misery. While Fay tries to save her daughter from an unhappy future, she only succeeds in driving her further away. Despite her special gifts, Fay encounters the same obstacles as any mother who tries to spare her daughter the pain of making her own mistakes.

In the *New York Times Book Review,* Amy Hempel observed: "The mystic overlay is effective, and the feminist concerns that become key to the story are worth talking about. But the characters are rendered as just that—characters. Their ways and exchanges are so familiar that 'The Fortune Teller' ends up being a quick read that does not linger or make us think." Comparing the novel unfavorably to *'Night, Mother,* Michiko Kakutani of the *New York Times* wrote: "Clearly the exchanges between the two women provide some of the best, most fully realized scenes in the novel, but while they occasionally promise to open into the sort of painful, revelatory talks that lent *'Night, Mother* its power, Ms. Norman never lets them develop fully." The novel, Kakutani concludes, feels "contrived and heavy-handed." In the *Detroit News,* Liza Schwarzbaum also drew a comparison between *The Fortune Teller* and Norman's Pulitzer Prize-winning drama, and found that the author traded "dramatic tension for fullness, a roundness like a wheel of fortune. . . . There is a roundness to this plot, a symmetry to the actions and relationships that is itself a kind of fortune telling."

Speaking of *The Fortune Teller* in the *New York Times Book Review,* Norman, too, compared writing to fortune-telling: "You look into someone's life, read where they have been and predict what will happen to them. What Fay does for her clients . . . I've done for characters my whole writing life." The novel, she continued, originated as a play, but eventually Norman realized there were too many characters to fit onstage and she "wanted to be able to include things like fire engines and sex, things you can't do onstage."

During her hiatus from the theater, Norman found herself, like many other established playwrights, being courted by Hollywood studios. "There are lots of opportunities there now for playwrights, and people are usually willing to trust our judgment," she remarked to Michael Bloom of the *New York Times.* Writing for medium other than the theater provides an opportunity to reach the people she writes about, who Norman contends cannot always afford to go to the theater. "If I want to speak to them, I have to write in a different form," she told Bloom. One such opportunity Norman took advantage of was the chance to adapt her Pulitzer Prize-winning drama into a screenplay. The resulting movie garnered mixed reviews. "The structure of *'Night, Mother* is essentially a conceit built for the theater—two people talking in a room—and its power depends on the theater experience, the fact that you're watching flesh and blood and spittle and sweat 10 rows away," observed Paul Attanasio in the *Washington Post.* "Adapting it would have required the kind of imagination that, apparently, was sorely missing." Jay Scott of the *Globe and Mail* also found the play's believability diminished in the film version, which he found "packed with tiny esthetic intermissions that weaken Norman's premise irreparably. . . . the illusion of real time and space that gave the play the power to persuade its audience that these were real people is disrupted." Janet Maslin of the *New York Times* found that despite a camera that is "constantly, annoyingly, in motion," the movie's momentum is maintained by the "urgency of Miss Norman's writing" and the persuasive performances of actresses Anne Bancroft and Sissy Spacek.

In 1988, three years after her last playwriting effort, Norman decided to return to the theater with an experimental workshop piece entitled *Sarah and Abraham.* "That's been my pattern—to get mad at the theater and go away for a while," she told DeVries. "I seem to write better from the outside," she added. As a workshop production, *Sarah and Abraham* was unreviewable and thus allowed Norman to try her hand at something "quite risky and

bold" without fear of critical repercussions, she explained to DeVries. What was evident during the play's run, observed DeVries, was "the return of one of the country's most articulate and intelligent theatrical voices." *Sarah and Abraham,* she continued, "marks a new chapter in [Norman's] career."

Norman's stature in contemporary American theater puts her at "the crest of a wave of adventurous young women playwrights," declared Gussow. Throughout the highs and lows of her critical reception, the universality of Norman's themes continues to draw audiences from all over the world to her plays. By 1986, *'Night, Mother* had been produced in 32 foreign countries, including Italy, Scandinavia and New Guinea. In each country, the characters of Jessie and Mama were altered only slightly to suit the archetypes of the particular culture. The feelings stirred by the play, however, remained the same no matter which language the characters were speaking. Norman explained the play's applicability around the world to Aljean Harmentz in the *New York Times*: "We all lose our children. You can live for a lifetime and not know what their life is to them. You think for a lifetime they belong to you, but they are only on loan."

The role of the playwright is one that Norman takes very seriously. "I almost see us as this battalion, marching, valiant, soldiers on the front lines, and we must not step on the mines," she told Gussow. "We are trying as best we can to clear the path, to tell you what's out there." As a woman, Norman is pleased with the emergence of women as major playwrights during the 1980s, a movement she helped launch. "Now we can write plays and not have people put them in a little box labeled 'women's theater,' " she continued. "It's a time of great exploration of secret worlds, of worlds that have been kept very quiet."

BIOGRAPHICAL/CRITICAL SOURCES:

BOOKS

Dictionary of Literary Biography Yearbook: 1984, Gale, 1985.
Norman, Marsha, *'Night, Mother,* Hill & Wang, 1982.

PERIODICALS

Chicago Tribune, July 1, 1988; May 17, 1989; June 4, 1989.
Detroit News, May 17, 1987.
Globe and Mail (Toronto), September 20, 1986.
Los Angeles Times, January 17, 1985; January 25, 1985.
Newsday, May 8, 1983.
Newsweek, May 28, 1979.
New York, November 13, 1978; May 28, 1979.
New York Times, February 18, 1983; August 10, 1986; September 12, 1986; May 13, 1987; October 29, 1988.
New York Times Book Review, May 24, 1987, p. 10.

New York Times Magazine, May 1, 1983.
Saturday Review, September-October, 1983.
Times (London), May 5, 1983.
Washington Post, April 30, 1983; October 13, 1986.

—*Sketch by Cornelia A. Pernik*

*   *   *

NORTH, Milou
   See ERDRICH, Louise

O

O'BRIEN, Edna 1936-

PERSONAL: Born December 15, 1936, in Tuamgraney, County Clare, Ireland; daughter of Michael and Lena (Cleary) O'Brien; married Ernest Gebler (an author), 1952 (divorced, 1964); children: Sasha, Carlos (sons). *Education:* Attended Pharmaceutical College of Ireland. *Avocational interests:* Reading, remembering.

ADDRESSES: Home—England.

CAREER: Novelist, short story writer, playwright, and screenwriter. Teacher of creative writing at City College, New York City, 1986—.

AWARDS, HONORS: Kingsley Amis Award, 1962; *Yorkshire Post* Book of the Year award, 1970, for *A Pagan Place; Los Angeles Times* Book Prize, 1990, for *Lantern Slides.*

WRITINGS:

The Country Girls (novel; also see below), Knopf, 1960.
The Lonely Girl (novel; also see below), Random House, 1962, published as *The Girl with Green Eyes,* Penguin, 1964.
Girls in Their Married Bliss (novel; also see below), J. Cape, 1964.
August Is a Wicked Month (novel), Simon & Schuster, 1965.
Casualties of Peace (novel), J. Cape, 1966.
The Love Object, J. Cape, 1968.
A Pagan Place: A Novel (also see below), Weidenfeld & Nicolson, 1970.
Zee and Company (novel; also see below), Weidenfeld & Nicolson, 1971.
Night: A Novel, Knopf, 1972.
Mother Ireland (nonfiction), photographs by Fergus Bourke, Harcourt, 1976.

Arabian Days (nonfiction), photographs by Gerard Klijn, Quartet Books, 1977.
Johnny I Hardly Knew You: A Novel, Weidenfeld & Nicolson, 1977, published as *I Hardly Knew You,* Doubleday, 1978.
Seven Novels and Other Short Stories, Collins, 1978.
(Editor) *Some Irish Loving: A Selection,* Harper, 1979.
James and Nora: A Portrait of Joyce's Marriage (nonfiction), Lord John Publishers, 1981.
The Country Girls Trilogy and Epilogue (contains *The Country Girls, The Lonely Girl,* and *Girls in Their Married Bliss*), Farrar, Straus, 1986, published as *The Country Girls Trilogy: Second Epilogue,* Dutton, 1989.
Vanishing Ireland (nonfiction), photographs by Richard Fitzgerald, J. Cape, 1986.
The High Road (novel), Farrar, Straus, 1988.
On the Bone (poetry), Greville Press, 1989.
Time and Tide, Farrar, Straus, 1992.

SHORT STORIES

A Scandalous Woman, and Other Stories, Harcourt, 1974.
Mrs. Reinhardt, and Other Stories, Weidenfeld & Nicolson, 1978.
A Rose in the Heart, Doubleday, 1979.
Returning: Tales, Weidenfeld & Nicolson, 1982.
A Fanatic Heart: Selected Stories of Edna O'Brien, foreword by Philip Roth, Farrar, Straus, 1984.
Lantern Slides: Stories, Farrar, Straus, 1990.

Also author of *Stories of Joan of Arc,* 1984.

JUVENILES

The Dazzle, illustrated by Peter Stevenson, Hodder & Stoughton, 1981.
A Christmas Treat (sequel to *The Dazzle*), illustrated by Stevenson, Hodder & Stoughton, 1982.
The Expedition, Hodder & Stoughton, 1982.

The Rescue, illustrated by Stevenson, Hodder & Stoughton, 1983.

Tales for the Telling: Irish Folk and Fairy Stories, illustrated by Michael Foreman, Atheneum, 1986.

PLAYS

A Cheap Bunch of Nice Flowers (produced in London, England, 1962), Elek, 1963.

A Pagan Place: A Play (produced at the West End, 1972), Knopf, 1970.

The Gathering, first produced in Dublin, Ireland, 1974, then New York City at Manhattan Theatre Club, 1977.

Virginia: A Play (first produced in Stratford, Ontario, then New York City at the Public Theater, 1985), Harcourt, 1981, revised edition, 1985.

(Adaptor) *Madame Bovary* (based on the novel by Gustave Flaubert), produced at the Palace, Watford, England, 1987.

Also author of plays, including *The Keys of the Cafe* (also see below), *Home Sweet Home,* 1984, and *Flesh and Blood,* 1987.

SCREENPLAYS

The Girl with Green Eyes (based on O'Brien's novel *The Lonely Girl*), Lopert, 1964.

Three into Two Won't Go, Universal, 1969.

X Y and Zee (based on O'Brien's novel *Zee and Company*), Columbia, 1972.

Also author of screenplays, including *A Woman at the Seaside, I Was Happy Here, The Wicked Lady,* 1979, and *The Country Girls,* 1983.

OTHER

Also author of television plays, including *The Wedding Dress,* 1963, *The Keys of the Cafe,* 1965, *Give My Love to the Pilchards,* 1965, *Which of These Two Ladies Is He Married To?,* 1967, *Nothing's Ever Over,* 1968, and *The Hard Way,* 1980. Contributor to *Oh! Calcutta!,* compiled by Kenneth Tynan, Grove, 1969. Also contributor to magazines, including *New Yorker, Ladies' Home Journal,* and *Cosmopolitan,* and to various English journals.

SIDELIGHTS: Irish author Edna O'Brien is "renowned for her anguished female characters, lonely Catholic girls in search of adventure, or single, older women in wretched affairs with married men," wrote Richard B. Woodward in the *New York Times Magazine.* "A poet of heartbreak, she writes most tellingly about the hopeless, angry passion that courts self-ruin." Her women are loving, but frustrated, betrayed, lonely, and struggling to escape the role society has assigned them, while her male characters are cruel, cold, drunken, and irresponsible. The divorced mother of two, O'Brien knows about struggle, heartbreak,

and pain firsthand. She has used her personal experiences, especially her childhood in Ireland, as sources for many of her works, drawing on her memories to evoke the emotions of her readers. An author of novels, short stories, plays, and children's books, she is a prolific writer, often considered controversial, who appeals to many audiences.

O'Brien was born in Tuamgraney, County Clare, a small, rural, devoutly Catholic village of about two hundred people in the west of Ireland. Raised on a farm, she grew up in an area where everyone knew everyone else's secrets, business, and problems. She claims this has helped her in her writing, telling Amanda Smith in *Publishers Weekly,* "I had sort of a limitless access to everyone's life story. For a writer, it's a marvelous chance." Educated first at the local national school and then in a convent, she escaped rural life by attending Pharmaceutical College in Dublin. In 1952 she eloped with Czech-Irish author Ernest Gebler. They moved first to County Wicklow, and then to London, where O'Brien has remained. They divorced after twelve years of marriage, and she raised their two sons alone.

Books were scarce in O'Brien's childhood, and it wasn't until she was in Dublin that she began to take an interest in them. *Introducing James Joyce* by T. S. Eliot was among her first purchases, and she recalls in *Lear's* that "reading it was the most astonishing literary experience of my life. . . . What I learned from that brief extract from *A Portrait of the Artist as a Young Man* was that as a writer one must take one's material from life, from the simple, indisputable, and often painful world about one, and give it somehow its transfiguration, but at the same time shave all excess and untruth from it, like peeling a willow. What I did not know, although I must have sensed it, was that this would bring me into conflict with parents, friends, and indeed the Irish establishment."

Conflict and writing seemed to go hand in hand for O'Brien throughout her career. The birth of her first published novel, *The Country Girls,* heralded the death of her marriage. Written at the age of twenty-six and published in 1960, *The Country Girls* broke new ground in Irish literature, giving a frank speaking voice to women characters. The subject matter and especially the daringly graphic sexual scenes caused this book, and the six that followed, to be banned in Ireland. The first novel in what became a trilogy, *The Lonely Girl* and *Girls in Their Married Bliss* completed the set. The three novels were collected in *The Country Girls Trilogy and Epilogue,* published in 1986.

"It's a difficult trip, this coming of age," wrote Mary Rourke in the *Los Angeles Times Book Review* of *The Country Girls Trilogy and Epilogue.* "Two girls set adrift, misdirected, lost at sea. O'Brien tells it with love and outrage, compassion and contempt." The stories revolve around two young women, the "country girls" Kate and Baba, who search for love and sex in a series of tragicomic adventures after being expelled from their convent school. Kate Brady, the daughter of a drunken father, was raised in poverty. She is the shy, naive but pretty woman who begins her adventure by having an affair with an older, married man. Baba Brennan, the daughter of the village veterinarian, is the tough, sassy character willing to live as freely as a man. Through affairs, marriages, more affairs, children, and psychotherapy, Baba and Kate remain friends.

"Miss O'Brien's outlook is intemperate, like Irish weather. She's fond of blarney, but a bleak, literary kind, more in the mood of the later Yeats than of Celtic charm," commented Anatole Broyard, writing in the *New York Times Book Review.* "She has no patience with the ordinary, the soothing monotony of innocent small events." Feelings of loss, conflict, and disappointment in love pervade each novel of *The Country Girls Trilogy and Epilogue* as the girls try to reach their dreams. *Village Voice* contributor Terrence Rafferty declared that "the psychological insights are sharp, the descriptions graceful and resonant" in *The Country Girls Trilogy and Epilogue.* At the conclusion of the trilogy, both women are disillusioned, neither one having reached her dreams or found love or happiness. What began in *The Country Girls* ends far from "married bliss."

O'Brien added the epilogue to *The Country Girls Trilogy* when the stories were released in one volume. Rafferty explained that it "brings the story full circle, back to earth, in a tragedy that would be unbearable were it not for the exuberance of the writing, the hope engendered by language that goes on and on." The epilogue is presented as Baba's soliloquy, a retrospective view of both women's lives. Mourning the deceased Kate, raging against the men who took advantage or abused them in some way, blaming men for Kate's death, and remembering the happier times, Baba concludes the trilogy with emotional force. Broyard, commenting on the whole collection, declared: "Everyday scenes . . . are the truest and best parts of Miss O'Brien's work. Reading them, we wonder whether love and sex, for which she has become an ambivalent apologist, are her natural subject after all—or just a burlesque to keep the genuine terrors at bay."

Many of O'Brien's short stories have also been assembled and published as collections, including *A Fanatic Heart.* Covering two decades of her career, the twenty-nine stories in this collection explore the themes of childhood, love, and loss, all from a woman's perspective. "Most of the stories in *A Fanatic Heart* are set down in languorous, elegiac prose," declared Michiko Kakutani in the *New York Times,* adding that "they're enlivened by Miss O'Brien's earthy humor and her sense of place." She

writes of relationships, exile, and betrayal, drawing the reader in by seeming to reveal herself. Tales such as "My Mother's Mother," describing the "ghastly" death of her grandfather one night while saying the Rosary, evoke O'Brien's native Ireland. Others explore the temptations of the flesh in strictly-reared young women, as in "The Connor Girls," or contrast girls with carousing drunks, as in "Irish Revel." Still others concern affairs, mental breakdown, and entrapment in bad marriages. In the *Los Angeles Times Book Review* Charles Champlin commented, "She writes with a graceful, poetical simplicity, a soft and mesmerizing brogue audible in every cadence." *Washington Post Book World* contributor Jonathan Yardley concluded by saying, "It's all there: the violence, the superstition, the craziness, the drink, the brooding religion, the terrorized women. O'Brien's Ireland is as hard and unremitting a place as O'Connor's South. Yet longings her women feel for love and peace, for a kind connection with another human being, give these stories a tenderness that is both surprising and enriching."

O'Brien presents another side of Ireland in *Tales for the Telling: Irish Folk and Fairy Stories,* a book for children published in 1986. Twelve stories reveal a land of fairy folk, giants, castles, princes and princesses, magic, and heroes. A fierce wolf and a young boy dance to the magic tune of fife music in one tale, and another tells of a giant who betters an opponent with help from his cunning wife. O'Brien writes her stories in standard English, using the characters' conversations to express their Irish descent. "In the dialogue she revels in the glories of local dialect," declared Elizabeth MacCallum in the Toronto *Globe and Mail,* "and in her descriptive passages she evokes wondrous visions." Another critic, *Times Literary Supplement* contributor Patricia Craig, remarked that O'Brien's stories correspond rather closely to those published in *Donegal Fairy Stories* written by Seumas MacManus, but commented that O'Brien's "tales are notable for their decorativeness and sturdy vocabulary." E. F. Bleiler, writing in the *Washington Post Book World,* judged that while "O'Brien does convey the flavor of Ireland. . . . The book as a whole is pleasant to look at and into, but not very exciting." Illustrated by Michael Foreman, Diane Roback proclaimed in *Publishers Weekly* that the "color-rich, vigorous paintings" complement "a collection for the entire family [that] fires the imagination."

O'Brien examines more than Ireland in her various writings. In two stage plays she focuses on Virginia Woolf and Gustave Flaubert's Madame Bovary. "O'Brien . . . knows how to create climax, epiphany and incandescence by compression," declared Jack Kroll in *Newsweek,* discussing the play *Virginia.* The story of Virginia Woolf, one of the Bloomsbury group and a prominent literary figure, the play encompasses her life from her birth in 1882 to her suicide in 1942. Woolf's "intense subjective style" is echoed throughout the piece, often transcending "chronological narrative," wrote Lawrence Christon in the *Los Angeles Times.* "*Virginia* is virtually a monologue," Christon continued, noting that the play "is top-heavy with talk."

Madame Bovary is similar to *Virginia,* particularly in its use of time and narration. O'Brien claims the title character as her own creation rather than an adaptation of Flaubert's novel. The story of love, marriage, boredom, adultery, and death by suicide, O'Brien's work, however, closely follows Flaubert's piece. The drama takes place in Emma Bovary's mind, even juggling the events as if they were really memories happening in her head, giving the audience clear access to her thoughts and emotions. *Observer* contributor Michael Ratcliffe remarked, "Edna O'Brien has turned Flaubert's novel into a tasteful melodrama whose tragic ironies shine sharp and bright." But, Ratcliffe noted, the "dramatic narrative unfolds in a series of sketches and jerks. . . . Time-leaps and chronology are not always clear." Irving Wardle, writing in the London *Times,* proclaimed that "the action unrolls as if by flashes of lightning. . . . the effect is to present an ever-strengthening sequence of hopes and defeats in which grand emotions are brought tumbling down."

While continuing to publish books for children, short stories, and plays, O'Brien waited ten years after *Johnny I Hardly Knew You: A Novel* before publishing another novel. The long-awaited volume, *The High Road,* concerns Anna, a middle-aged, successful Irish writer recovering from the break-up of an affair. She escapes to an unidentified Spanish island, hoping to take time to write in her diary and repair her broken heart. But she becomes involved with the other inhabitants, eventually having an affair with another woman. The story ends in tragedy, with the death of Anna's lover. "This is a disorderly novel about the disorder of human needs and the grotesqueries of appetite, how unsuitable, how inappropriate our longings often are, how difficult it is to find even a moment of pure unspoiled happiness," claimed Carol Shields in the Toronto *Globe and Mail.* Many critics seemed to share this viewpoint, with *Publishers Weekly* contributor Sybil Steinberg calling *The High Road* "a disappointing narrative." "At its best O'Brien's prose is, as usual, eloquent and passionate, but it cannot disguise the fundamental confusion of this strange little book," wrote Jonathan Yardley in the *Washington Post.* "There are enough bright moments in it to reward O'Brien's most devoted followers, but few other readers are likely to take any pleasure in trying to make connections between characters that O'Brien herself never makes."

"Raise a jar to Edna O'Brien herself, back among us from foreign parts . . . the black mood of *The High Road* all but dispelled," proclaimed Elaine Kendall in the *Los An-*

geles Times in her discussion of *Lantern Slides: Stories.* "She is at her best again, telling of people and places close to her heart." Published in 1990, O'Brien returns to the short story with *Lantern Slides.* "Though she covers little new ground here, she also digs deeper into the old ground than ever before, unearthing a rich archeology," declared David Leavitt in the *New York Times Book Review.* The stories focus on women and their relationships—with lovers, fathers, husbands, and children. Insanity, jealousy, and fear are only some of the emotions O'Brien calls into play in her tales. In "Brother," an incestuous relationship causes one woman to plot the death of her new sister-in-law. Another story explores the feelings between a mother and her son during a Mediterranean vacation in the company of his girlfriend. The title story, "Lantern Slides," was highly praised by many critics, Leavitt labeling it the "collection's masterpiece." Describing a birthday party held for a woman whose husband has deserted her, the tale reveals the guests individually, discussing their problems as it moves along. Regarding the whole collection, Victoria Glendinning wrote in the London *Times* that "this is good writing; and good thinking." *Times Literary Supplement* contributor Louise Doughty praised *Lantern Slides,* writing: "The same precision with which she portrays landscape is applied to human emotions; there isn't a single character in these stories who is unconvincing. O'Brien continues to display acute powers of observation in a prose that is always neat and often immaculate."

O'Brien's confessional tone and use of the first person in many of her novels has led to speculation concerning the distance between her life and her fiction. In the *Dictionary of Literary Biography,* Patricia Boyle Haberstroh quotes an interview between Ludovic Kennedy and O'Brien wherein the author says her life and her work are "quite close, but they're not as close as they seem . . . . I think writing, especially semi-autobiographical writing, is the life you might have liked to have had." In an interview with Woodward, O'Brien concludes: "All I know is that I want to write about something that has no fashion and that does not pander to any period or to a journalistic point of view. I want to write about something that would apply to any time because it's a state of the soul." O'Brien also discusses her writing in *Lear's,* noting that "The need to write becomes as intrinsic as the need to breathe. I believe that the hidden reason is to do with time and emotion and the retrieval of both. It is as if the life lived has not been lived until it is set down in this unconscious sequence of words."

BIOGRAPHICAL/CRITICAL SOURCES:

BOOKS

Contemporary Literary Criticism, Gale, Volume 3, 1975,
    Volume 5, 1976, Volume 8, 1978, Volume 13, 1980,
    Volume 36, 1986, Volume 65, 1991.
Dictionary of Literary Biography, Volume 14: *British Nov-
    elists since 1960,* Gale, 1983.
Eckley, Grace, *Edna O'Brien,* Bucknell University Press,
    1974.

PERIODICALS

Atlantic Monthly, July, 1965.
Books, June, 1965.
Books and Bookmen, December, 1964.
Chicago Tribune Book World, December 9, 1984, p. 31.
Globe and Mail (Toronto), December 17, 1988; December
    31, 1988.
Lear's July, 1992, pp. 62-65.
Los Angeles Times, April 3, 1979; May 1, 1986; December
    16, 1988; June 8, 1990.
Los Angeles Times Book Review, June 30, 1985, p. 1; Janu-
    ary 19, 1986, p. 4; April 27, 1986, p. 4; September 2,
    1990, p. 9.
Ms., November, 1988, pp. 76, 78.
National Observer, June 21, 1965.
Newsweek, March 18, 1985, p. 72.
New York Review of Books, June 3, 1965; August 24, 1967;
    January 31, 1985, p. 17.
New York Times, November 12, 1984; March 1, 1985;
    May 30, 1990.
New York Times Book Review, March 26, 1967; February
    9, 1969; September 22, 1974; June 27, 1978; February
    11, 1979; November 18, 1984, pp. 1, 38; May 11,
    1986, p. 12; March 1, 1987, p. 31; November 20, 1988,
    p. 11; June 25, 1990, p. 9.
New York Times Magazine, March 12, 1989.
Observer, February 8, 1987.
People, April 17, 1978.
Publishers Weekly, November 28, 1986, p. 71; December
    26, 1986, p. 30; September 9, 1988, p. 122.
Saturday Review, June 5, 1965; March 25, 1967.
Times (London), February 6, 1987; October 14, 1988; Oc-
    tober 27, 1988; June 7, 1990.
Times Literary Supplement, April 23, 1982, p. 456; Janu-
    ary 9, 1987, p. 46; October 28, 1988, p. 1212; June 8,
    1990, p. 616.
Tribune Books, November 20, 1988, p. 6; May 27, 1990,
    p. 1.
Village Voice, July 1, 1985, p. 61.
Vogue, September 1, 1971.
Washington Post, November 2, 1988.

Washington Post Book World, January 7, 1973; November
    25, 1984, p. 3; November 9, 1986, p. 19; April 8, 1987;
    November 2, 1988; June 24, 1990, p. 9.

—*Sketch By Terrie M. Rooney*

*   *   *

O'CONNOR, (Mary) Flannery   1925-1964

PERSONAL: Born March 25, 1925, in Savannah, GA;
died August 3, 1964, in Milledgeville, GA, of lupus;
daughter of Edward Francis and Regina (Cline)
O'Connor. *Education:* Women's College of Georgia (now
Georgia College), A.B., 1945; State University of Iowa,
M.F.A., 1947. *Religion:* Roman Catholic.

CAREER: Author.

AWARDS, HONORS: Kenyon Review fellowship in fiction, 1953; National Institute of Arts and Letters grant in
literature, 1957; first prize, O. Henry Memorial Awards,
1957, for "Greenleaf," 1963, for "Everything That Rises
Must Converge," and 1965, for "Revelation"; Ford Foundation grant, 1959; Litt.D. from St. Mary's College, 1962,
and Smith College, 1963; Henry H. Bellaman Foundation
special award, 1964; an annual, *The Flannery O'Connor
Bulletin,* was established in 1972; National Book Award,
1972, for *The Complete Short Stories;* Board Award, National Book Critics Circle, "Notable Book" citation, *Library Journal,* Bowdoin College Award, and Christopher
Award, all 1980, all for *The Habit of Being: Letters.*

WRITINGS:

Wise Blood (also see below; novel), Harcourt, 1952.
A Good Man Is Hard to Find (also see below; stories; con-
    tains "A Good Man Is Hard to Find," "The River,"
    "The Life You Save May Be Your Own," "A Stroke
    of Good Fortune," "A Temple of the Holy Ghost,"
    "The Artificial Nigger," "A Circle in the Fire," "A
    Late Encounter with the Enemy," "Good Country
    People," and "The Displaced Person"), Harcourt,
    1955 (published in England as *The Artificial Nigger,*
    Neville Spearman, 1957).
(Contributor) Granville Hicks, editor, *The Living Novel,*
    Macmillan, 1957.
The Violent Bear It Away (also see below; novel), Farrar,
    Straus, 1960.
(Editor and author of introduction) *A Memoir of Mary
    Ann,* Farrar, Straus, 1961, reprinted, Beil, 1989 (pub-
    lished in England as *Death of a Child,* Burns & Oates,
    1961).
Three by Flannery O'Connor (contains *Wise Blood,* "A
    Good Man Is Hard to Find," and *The Violent Bear
    It Away*), Signet, 1964, reprinted, New American Li-
    brary, 1986.

Everything That Rises Must Converge (also see below; stories; contains "Everything That Rises Must Converge," "Greenleaf," "A View of the Woods," "The Enduring Chill," "The Comforts of Home," "The Lame Shall Enter First," "Revelation," "Parker's Back," and "Judgment Day"), Farrar, Straus, 1965.

Mystery and Manners: Occasional Prose, edited by Sally Fitzgerald and Robert Fitzgerald, Farrar, Straus, 1969.

The Complete Short Stories, Farrar, Straus, 1971.

The Habit of Being: Letters, edited by S. Fitzgerald, Farrar, Straus, 1979.

The Presence of Grace and Other Book Reviews, edited by Carter W. Martin, University of Georgia Press, 1983.

(With others) *The Language of Grace,* Cowley, 1983.

Collected Works (contains *Wise Blood, A Good Man Is Hard to Find, The Violent Bear It Away,* and *Everything That Rises Must Converge*) edited by S. Fitzgerald, Library of America, 1988.

Work represented in many anthologies. Contributor to periodicals, including *Accent, Mademoiselle, Critic,* and *Esquire.* O'Connor's papers are part of the permanent collection of the Georgia College Library.

O'Connor's writings have been translated into French, Italian, Portuguese, Spanish, Greek, Danish, and Japanese.

ADAPTATIONS: A two-act play, *The Displaced Person,* by Cecil Dawkins (first produced in New York at American Place Theatre, 1966) was based on five stories by Flannery O'Connor; *The Displaced Person* was adapted for television by Horton Foote and broadcast on *American Short Story Series,* Public Broadcasting System, 1979; a film adaptation of *Wise Blood* was directed by John Huston and released by New Line Cinema in 1980.

SIDELIGHTS: Among the leading short-story writers of American literature, Flannery O'Connor has been compared with Nathaniel Hawthorne, Nathanael West, and Fyodor Dostoevsky. A Catholic from the Bible-belt South, O'Connor wrote of the power of God's grace in a fallen world. Often classified as examples of the Southern Gothic because of their grotesque characters and bizarre incidents, O'Connor's fiction is her own, set apart from any genre or school. She once explained that her stories were purposely shocking because "to the hard of hearing you shout and for the almost blind you draw large and startling figures." As John R. May explained in the *Dictionary of Literary Biography,* the strong response to O'Connor's fiction was due to "the fact that in an age of existential angst and the eclipse of traditional belief, Flannery O'Connor wrote brilliant stories that brought the issue of religious faith into dramatic focus." "Despite the small body of her work and the narrowness of its range,"

Robert Towers wrote in the *New York Review of Books,* "[she] seems as permanently seated among the American immortals as Emily Dickinson or Hawthorne."

Speaking of her work, O'Connor once explained: "I see from the standpoint of Christian orthodoxy. This means that for me the meaning of life is centered in our Redemption by Christ and that what I see in the world I see in relation to that." In O'Connor's fiction, characters attain redemption only in the midst of turmoil. O'Connor's God is one whose "grace hits the characters in [her] stories with the force of a mugging," Josephine Hendin wrote in *The World of Flannery O'Connor.* The climactic moments of grace in her stories and in her characters' lives have been described by Preston M. Browning, Jr., in his book *Flannery O'Connor* as "those moments when her characters undergo a traumatic collapse of their illusions of righteousness and self-sufficiency." As *Washington Post* critic William McPherson put it, "the question behind Miss O'Connor's stories is not whether God exists—he's there, all right—but whether men can bear it."

O'Connor's characters are often the familiar misanthropes found in Southern Gothic fiction. As Ted R. Spivey explained in *Studies in Short Fiction,* O'Connor depicted violent and grotesque people because "man has in his soul a powerful destructive element, which often makes him behave in a violent and grotesque manner." This violence is combined with a human arrogance as well. As Claire Katz summarized in *American Literature,* "it is the impulse toward secular autonomy, the smug confidence that human nature is perfectible by its own efforts, that [O'Connor] sets out to destroy, through an act of violence so intense that the character is rendered helpless, . . . [thus establishing] the need for absolute submission to the power of Christ." Hermione Lee of *New Statesman* echoed this view: "Essentially, O'Connor's subject is acceptance: the point at which her sinners become aware of the awful unavoidability of Grace. All the stories drive towards an appointed end, often of horrifying violence. . . . The power of the work lies in its suppression of this severely orthodox subject beneath a brilliantly commonplace surface. . . . Its masterly realism springs from the life in Georgia, but its intellectual energy, and its penetration of grotesque extremes, derives from the faith."

In addition to a strong religious sense, O'Connor's fiction is colored by her life-long ill health. Diagnosed with lupus at the age of twenty-five, she was crippled by and ultimately died from the hereditary disease at the age of thirty-nine. She spent much of her life in rural Georgia, where she lived with her mother. "I have never been anywhere but sick," she explained in *Mystery and Manners.* "In a sense sickness is a place, more instructive than a long trip to Europe, and it's always a place where there's no company, where nobody can follow." Although O'Connor at first believed that her illness would end her writing, Lee observed that O'Connor's "work was shaped by it, and is much occupied with an orthodox stoicism modelled on Teilhard de Chardin's notion of 'passive diminishment'. . . . Some of the finest stories used handicapped figures . . . not, Carson McCullers-like, for baroque effect, but in order to contemplate, often ironically, the discipline of suffering." Similarly, Gilbert H. Muller in his *Nightmares and Visions: Flannery O'Connor and the Catholic Grotesque* found that O'Connor's illness "forced a certain austerity upon her fiction; inevitably she transferred personal agony and suffering to her work. Yet in dealing with her characters' agonies, and is sustaining her own, Flannery O'Connor was sardonic rather than sentimental. She wielded a literary hatchet rather than a handkerchief; she realized that only a stern intellect, and an accretion of humor which usually shaded into the grotesque could confront suffering, violence, and evil in this world."

In all of her fiction, O'Connor expressed her vision of the world through a small set of recurring symbols. "A few simple images recur so strikingly," Stanley Edgar Hyman recounted in his *Flannery O'Connor,* "that every reader notices them: the flaming suns, the mutilated eyes, the 'Jesus-seeing' hats, the colorful shirts. These images may be obsessive with the author, but they are used organically in the fiction." Jonathan Baumbach, writing in *The Landscape of Nightmare: Studies in the Contemporary American Novel,* found that O'Connor "explored in all her fiction the same private world, a world of corrosion and decay, invested with evil, apparently God-forsaken, but finally redeemed by God. . . . Her world lacks breadth and texture; it hangs gloomily in space, revolving on its axis, but it manages—and this is its achievement as art—to create its own claustrophobic reality." Writing in his book *Flannery O'Connor: A Critical Essay,* Robert Drake allowed that O'Connor's "range was narrow, and perhaps she had only one story to tell. (But then didn't Hemingway?) But each time she told it, she told it with renewed imagination and cogency. . . . She remains absolutely unique in American fiction. . . . Her vision and her methods were distinctively her own; and her rage for the *holy*—and the *whole*—has left its indelible mark on our literature and our literary consciousness."

Writing in the *Southern Literary Journal,* Andre Bleikasten described the primary quality of O'Connor's fiction to be a unique blend of the ordinary and the extraordinary. "O'Connor's novels and stories are not all of equal merit," he explained, "yet each of them has its moments of eerie intensity, each of them at some point verges on what Freud, in one of his essays, termed 'the uncanny,' . . . that disquieting strangeness apt to arise at every turn out of the most intimately familiar, and through which our everyday sense of reality is made to yield to the troubling awareness

of the world's otherness. Much of the impact and lasting resonance of O'Connor's work proceeds from its ability to *bewilder* the reader, to take him out of his depths and jolt him into a fictional environment which is both homely . . . and uncannily estranged."

The violence, shock endings, and grotesque events in O'Connor's fiction are meant, Diane Tolomeo wrote in *Studies in Short Fiction,* to "announce moments of recognition for a character and perhaps more importantly for the reader." As Joyce Carol Oates remarked in her *New Heaven, New Earth: The Visionary Experience in Literature,* O'Connor "is a primitive; she insists that only through an initiation by violence does man 'see.' " In O'Connor's fiction, this violence shocks rational, secular man out of his smug complacency to a realization that a higher power is operating. Much of O'Connor's work, Jane Carter Keller wrote in the *Arizona Quarterly,* is satire directed against the "secular notion that men can define moral absolutes for themselves. Man's reliance upon reason to define such absolutes as goodness and compassion leads only to Auschwitz, [O'Connor] believed, for reason in men is by definition corrupt and can only be depended upon to lead to self-deception." By satirizing rational men in her stories, O'Connor meant to spur the reader "into an examination of his own state of being," Keller explained. *Hollins Critic* reviewer Walter Sullivan stated, "what she did well, she did with exquisite competence: her ear for dialogue, her eye for human gestures were as good as anybody's ever were; and her vision was as clear and direct and as annoyingly precious as that of an Old Testament prophet or one of the more irascible Christian saints."

O'Connor's posthumously nonfiction and collected letters have made her personal observations on literature available to many critics for the first time. *The Habit of Being,* a collection of her correspondence, clarified some of the author's artistic motivations and revealed her dedication to the writing life. She wrote for two hours every day, no matter how she felt. "Sometimes I work for months," she stated in one letter, "and have to throw everything away, but I don't think any of that was time wasted. Something goes on that makes it easier when it does come well." Granville Hicks in the *Saturday Review* wrote of *Mystery and Manners: Occasional Prose,* "I had read some of these lectures in one form or another, but until they were brought together I had not realized what an impressive body of literary criticism they constituted." John Leonard of the *New York Times* wrote that *Mystery and Manners* "should be read by every writer and would-be writer and lover of writing. . . . [O'Connor] ranks with Mark Twain and Scott Fitzgerald among our finest prose-stylists."

Critical evaluations of O'Connor place her among the top ranks of American fiction writers, while her posthumous collections have been awarded the National Book Award and Christopher Award, among others. "I am sure [O'Connor's] few books will live on and on in American literature," Elizabeth Bishop commented in the *New York Review of Books.* "They are narrow, possibly, but they are clear, hard, vivid, and full of bits of description, phrases, and odd insights that contain more real poetry than a dozen books of poems." Writing in the *Times Literary Supplement,* Harold Beaver ranked O'Connor "among the outstanding writers of American fiction of the twentieth century." May concluded that "O'Connor's modest bequest to American Letters has been enough to assure her a permanent place among our greatest writers of fiction."

BIOGRAPHICAL/CRITICAL SOURCES:

BOOKS

Allen, Walter, *The Modern Novel,* Dutton, 1964, p. 308.

Asals, Frederick, *Flannery O'Connor: The Imagination of Extremity,* University of Georgia Press, 1982.

Baumbach, Jonathan, *The Landscape of Nightmare: Studies in the Contemporary American Novel,* New York University Press, 1965, pp. 87-100.

Browning, Preston M., Jr., *Flannery O'Connor,* Southern Illinois University Press, 1974.

Bryant, Jerry, *The Open Decision,* Free Press, 1970, pp. 263-264.

Coles, Robert, *Flannery O'Connor's South,* Louisiana State University Press, 1980.

Contemporary Literary Criticism, Gale, Volume 1, 1973, Volume 2, 1974, Volume 3, 1975, Volume 6, 1976, Volume 10, 1979, Volume 13, 1980, Volume 15, 1980, Volume 21, 1982.

Desmond, John F., *Risen Sons: Flannery O'Connor's Vision of History,* University of Georgia Press, 1987.

Dictionary of Literary Biography, Volume 2: *American Novelists since World War II,* Gale, 1978.

Dictionary of Literary Biography Yearbook 1980, Gale, 1981.

Drake, Robert, *Flannery O'Connor: A Critical Essay,* Eerdmans, 1966.

Driskell, Leon V., and Joan T. Brittain, *The Eternal Crossroads: The Art of Flannery O'Connor,* University Press of Kentucky, 1971.

Eggenschwiler, David, *The Christian Humanism of Flannery O'Connor,* Wayne State University Press, 1972.

Farmer, David, *Flannery O'Connor: A Descriptive Bibliography,* Garland, 1981.

Feeley, Kathleen, *Flannery O'Connor: Voice of the Peacock,* Rutgers University Press, 1972.

Fickett, Harold and Douglas R. Gilbert, *Flannery O'Connor: Images of Grace,* Eerdmans, 1986.

French, Warren, editor, *The Fifties: Fiction, Poetry, Drama,* Everett/Edwards, 1970, pp. 111-120.

Friedman, Melvin J., and Lewis A. Lawson, *The Added Dimension: The Art and Mind of Flannery O'Connor,* Fordham University Press, 1966.

Friedman, Melvin J., and Beverly Lyon Clark, editors, *Critical Essays on Flannery O'Connor,* G. K. Hall, 1985.

Gentry, Marshall Bruce, *Flannery O'Connor's Religion of the Grotesque,* University Press of Mississippi, 1986.

Getz, Lorine M., *Nature and Grace in Flannery O'Connor's Fiction,* Edwin Mellen Press, 1982.

Golden, Robert E., and Mary C. Sullivan, *Flannery O'Connor and Caroline Gordon: A Reference Guide,* G. K. Hall, 1977.

Gossett, Louise Y., *Violence in Recent Southern Fiction,* Duke University Press, 1965, pp. 75-97.

Grimshaw, James A., Jr., *The Flannery O'Connor Companion,* Greenwood, 1981.

Hendin, Josephine, *The World of Flannery O'Connor,* Indiana University Press, 1970.

Hicks, Granville, editor, *The Living Novel: A Symposium,* Macmillan, 1957.

Hicks, Granville, and Jack Alan Robbins, *Literary Horizons: A Quarter Century of American Fiction,* New York University Press, 1970, pp. 135-136.

Hoffman, Frederick J., *The Art of Southern Fiction: A Study of Some Modern Novelists,* Southern Illinois University Press, 1967, pp. 74-95.

Hyman, Stanley Edgar, *Flannery O'Connor,* University of Minnesota Press, 1966.

Johnson, Ira D., and Cristiane Johnson, editors, *Les Americanistes: New French Criticism on Modern American Fiction,* Kennikat, 1978.

Kazin, Alfred, *Bright Book of Life: American Novelists and Storytellers from Hemingway to Mailer,* Atlantic-Little, Brown, 1973, pp. 57-60.

Kellogg, Gene, *The Vital Tradition: The Catholic Novel in a Period of Convergence,* Loyola University Press, 1970, pp. 180-205.

Kunkel, Francis L., *Passion and the Passion: Sex and Religion in Modern Literature,* Westminster Press, 1975, pp. 129-156.

Magee, Rosemary M., editor, *Conversations with Flannery O'Connor,* University Press of Mississippi, 1987.

Malin, Irvin, *New American Gothic,* Southern Illinois University Press, 1962.

Martin, Carter W., *The True Country: Themes in the Fiction of Flannery O'Connor,* Vanderbilt University Press, 1969.

May, John R., *The Pruning Word: The Parables of Flannery O'Connor,* University of Notre Dame Press, 1976.

McFarland, Dorothy Tuck, *Flannery O'Connor,* Ungar, 1976.

Montgomery, Marion, *Why Flannery O'Connor Stayed Home,* Sherwood Sugden, 1981.

Muller, Gilbert H., *Nightmares and Visions: Flannery O'Connor and the Catholic Grotesque,* University of Georgia Press, 1972.

Oates, Joyce Carol, *New Heaven, New Earth: The Visionary Experience in Literature,* Vanguard Press, 1974, pp. 141-176.

O'Connor, Flannery, *Everything That Rises Must Converge,* introduction by Robert Fitzgerald, Farrar, Straus, 1965.

O'Donnell, Patrick, *Passionate Doubts: Designs of Interpretation in Contemporary American Fiction,* University of Iowa Press, 1986, pp. 95-115.

Orvell, Miles, *Invisible Parade: The Fiction of Flannery O'Connor,* Temple University Press, 1972.

Reiter, Robert E., editor, *Flannery O'Connor,* Herder, 1968.

The Shaken Realist: Essays in Modern Literature in Honor of Frederick J. Hoffman, Louisiana State University Press, 1970, pp. 287-299.

Shloss, Carol, *Flannery O'Connor's Dark Comedies: The Limits of Inference,* Louisiana State University Press, 1980.

Short Story Criticism, Volume 1, Gale, 1988.

Solotaroff, Theodore, *The Red Hot Vacuum and Other Pieces on the Writing of the Sixties,* Atheneum, 1970, pp. 171-177.

Stephens, Martha, *The Question of Flannery O'Connor,* Louisiana State University Press, 1973.

Waldmier, Joseph J., editor, *Recent American Fiction: Some Critical Views,* Houghton, 1963.

Walters, Dorothy, *Flannery O'Connor,* Twayne, 1973.

Westling, Louise, *Sacred Groves and Ravaged Gardens: The Fiction of Eudora Welty, Carson McCullers, and Flannery O'Connor,* University of Georgia Press, 1985.

World Literature Criticism, Gale, 1992.

Young, Thomas Daniel, editor, *Modern American Fiction: Form and Function,* Louisiana State University Press, 1989, pp. 198-212.

PERIODICALS

America, March 30, 1957; October 17, 1964; September 8, 1979, pp. 86-88.

American Literature, March, 1974, pp. 54-67; May, 1974; May, 1986, pp. 256-270.

Arizona Quarterly, autumn, 1972, pp. 263-273; autumn, 1973, pp. 266-276; autumn, 1976, pp. 245-259.

Books and Bookmen, May, 1972, pp. 38-39.

Book World, February 11, 1979.

Bulletin of Bibliography, Number 25, 1968.

Catholic Library World, November, 1967.

Catholic World, January, 1959, pp. 285-291; February, 1960, pp. 280-285.

Censer, fall, 1960.

Chicago Tribune, April 15, 1979.

Christian Century, September 30, 1964; May 19, 1965; July 9, 1969.

Chronicle Review, April 16, 1979, p. R6.

College English, December, 1965, pp. 235-239.

College Literature, Volume 11, number 3, 1984, pp. 276-279.

Columbia Forum, spring, 1970, pp. 38-41.

Commentary, November, 1965, pp. 93-99.

Commonweal, March 7, 1958, pp. 586-588; July 9, 1965; December 3, 1965; August 8, 1969, pp. 490-491; April 13, 1979, pp. 216-220.

Comparative Literature Studies, Volume 3, number 2, 1966, pp. 183-196, 235-245.

Contemporary Literature, winter, 1968, pp. 58-73.

Critic, August-September, 1962, pp. 4-5; October-November, 1965.

Critique: Studies in Modern Fiction, Volume II, number 2, 1958, pp. 3-10; Volume III, number 2, 1960, pp. 11-19; Volume X, number 2, 1968, pp. 69-80; Volume XI, number 3, 1969, pp. 5-10.

Detroit News, March 25, 1979.

English Journal, April, 1962, pp. 233-243.

Esprit, winter, 1964 (entire issue).

Esquire, May, 1965.

Explicator, fall, 1978, pp. 19-20.

Flannery O'Connor Bulletin (annual), 1972—.

Georgia Review, summer, 1958; fall, 1965, pp. 310-316; summer, 1968, pp. 188-193; summer, 1977, pp. 404-426.

Hollins Critic, September, 1965, pp. 1-9.

Hudson Review, spring, 1953, pp. 144-150.

Journal and Constitution (Atlanta), May 29, 1960, p. G2.

Journal and Constitution Magazine (Atlanta), November 1, 1959, pp. 38-40.

Jubilee, June, 1963, pp. 32-35.

Kansas Quarterly, spring, 1977, pp. 61-63.

Massachusetts Review, summer, 1962, pp. 784-788; spring, 1978, pp. 183-198.

Mediterranean Review, spring, 1972, pp. 56-57.

Mississippi Quarterly, spring, 1975, pp. 171-179; spring, 1976, pp. 197-205.

Modern Age, fall, 1960.

Modern Fiction Studies, summer, 1970, pp. 147-162; spring, 1973, pp. 29-41.

Ms., December, 1975, p. 77.

Nation, April 28, 1979, pp. 472-474.

National Review, March 16, 1979, pp. 364-368.

New Leader, June 23, 1952, p. 23-24.

New Orleans Review, Number 6, 1979, pp. 336-356.

New Republic, July 7, 1952, pp. 19-20; July 5, 1975; March 10, 1979.

New Statesman, April 1, 1966, p. 469; December 7, 1979, pp. 895-896.

Newsweek, May 19, 1952; November 8, 1971, pp. 115-117.

New Yorker, September 11, 1965, pp. 220-221.

New York Herald Tribune Book Week, May 30, 1965.

New York Review of Books, October 8, 1964, p. 21; May 3, 1979, pp. 3-6.

New York Times, May 18, 1952, p. 4; May 13, 1969; March 9, 1979.

New York Times Book Review, June 12, 1955, p. 5; February 24, 1960; May 30, 1965; November 28, 1971, p. 1; March 18, 1979; August 7, 1983, p. 31; August 21, 1988, p. 1.

Papers on Language and Literature, winter, 1969, pp. 209-223.

Quarterly Journal of Speech, May, 1989, pp. 198-211.

Renascence, spring, 1961, pp. 147-152; summer, 1963, pp. 195-199; spring, 1964, pp. 126-132; spring, 1965, pp. 137-147; autumn, 1969, pp. 3-16; spring, 1978, pp. 163-166.

Saturday Review, May 12, 1962, pp. 22-23; December 16, 1962; May 29, 1965; May 10, 1969; November 13, 1971, pp. 63-64; April 14, 1979, pp. 42-45.

Sewanee Review, summer, 1962, pp. 395-407; autumn, 1962, pp. 380-394; autumn, 1963, pp. 644-652; autumn, 1964, pp. 555-558; spring, 1968 (entire issue).

Shenandoah, winter, 1965, pp. 5-10.

Southern Humanities Review, summer, 1968, pp. 303-309; winter, 1968, pp. 14-32; spring, 1973, pp. 210-214.

Southern Literary Journal, spring, 1970, pp. 3-25; spring, 1972, pp. 41-54; spring, 1975, pp. 33-49; spring, 1982, pp. 8-18.

Southern Quarterly, winter, 1979, pp. 104-122.

Southern Review, summer, 1968, pp. 665-672; winter, 1971, pp. 295-313; autumn, 1975, pp. 802-819; July, 1978, pp. 438-448.

Southwest Review, summer, 1965, pp. 286-299.

Spectator, August 30, 1968.

Studies in American Fiction, spring, 1989, pp. 33-50.

Studies in Short Fiction, winter, 1964, pp. 85-92; spring, 1964, pp. 200-206; summer, 1969, pp. 433-442; winter, 1973, pp. 103-104; spring, 1973, pp. 199-204; summer, 1973, pp. 294-295; spring, 1975, pp. 139-144; winter, 1976, pp. 31-36; summer, 1979, pp. 233-235; summer, 1980, pp. 335-341; summer, 1984, pp. 251-258; fall, 1985, pp. 475-479.

Thought, autumn, 1962, pp. 410-426; winter, 1966, pp. 545-560; December, 1984, pp. 483-503.

Time, June 6, 1955, p. 114; May 30, 1969; February 14, 1972; March 5, 1979.

Times Literary Supplement, September 12, 1968; November 21, 1980, p. 1336.

University Review, summer, 1968, pp. 295-297.

Vagabond, February, 1960, pp. 9-17.

Washington Post, December 1, 1971.

Western Humanities Review, autumn, 1968, pp. 325-338.

World and I, January, 1987, pp. 429-433.

Xavier University Studies, summer, 1969, pp. 32-43.*

—*Sketch by Thomas Wiloch*

*   *   *

O'GREEN, Jennifer
See ROBERSON, Jennifer

*   *   *

O'GREEN, Jennifer Roberson
See ROBERSON, Jennifer

*   *   *

OLDS, Sharon 1942-

PERSONAL: Born November 19, 1942, in San Francisco, CA. *Education:* Stanford University, B.A. (with distinction), 1964; Columbia University, Ph.D., 1972.

ADDRESSES: Agent—c/o Alfred A. Knopf, 201 East 50th St., New York, NY 10022.

CAREER: Poet. Lecturer-in-residence on poetry at Theodor Herzl Institute, 1976-80; visiting teacher of poetry at Manhattan Theater Club, 1982, Nathan Mayhew Seminars of Martha's Vineyard, 1982, Poetry Center, Young Men's Christian Association of New York City, 1982, Poetry Society of America, 1983, New York University, 1983 and 1985, Sarah Lawrence College, 1984, Goldwater Hospital, Roosevelt Island, NY, 1985-90, Columbia University, 1985-86, and State University of New York College at Purchase, 1986. Holder of Fanny Hurst Chair, Brandeis University, 1986-87; New York University, associate professor of English, 1992—.

MEMBER: Poetry Society of America, PEN, Author's Guild.

AWARDS, HONORS: Grants from Creative Artists Public Service, 1978, Guggenheim fellowship Foundation, 1981-82, and National Endowment for the Arts, 1982-83; Madeline Sadin Award, *New York Quarterly,* 1978; younger poets award from *Poetry Miscellany,* 1979; San Francisco Poetry Center Award, 1981, for *Satan Says;* Lamont Poetry Selection of the Academy of American Poets, 1984, and National Book Critics Circle Award, 1985, both for *The Dead and the Living.*

WRITINGS:

POETRY

Satan Says, University of Pittsburgh Press, 1980.
The Dead and the Living, Knopf, 1984.
The Gold Cell, Knopf, 1987.
The Matter of This World, Slow Dancer Press, 1987.
The Sign of Saturn, Secker and Warburg, 1991.
The Father, Knopf, 1992.

Also contributor to numerous anthologies and textbooks, including *The Norton Introduction to Poetry,* 2nd edition, Norton, 1981; *The Bread Loaf Anthology of Contemporary American Poetry,* edited by Robert Pack, Sydney Lea, and Jay Parini, University Press of New England, 1985; *Three Genres, The Writing of Poetry, Fiction, and Drama,* edited by Stephen Minot, Prentice-Hall, 1988; *The Pushcart Prize, VIII: Best of the Small Presses,* Wainscott, 1989; *Read to Write,* Donald M. Murray, Holt, 1990; and *The Longman Anthology of American Poetry: Colonial to Contemporary,* edited by Hilary Russell, Longman, 1992.

Contributor to literary journals and magazines, including *New Yorker, Poetry, Atlantic Monthly, American Poetry Review, Nation, New Republic, Paris Review, Kayak, Massachusetts Review, Iowa Review, Poetry Northwest, Prairie Schooner, Ploughshares, Ms., Kenyon Review, Pequod, Mississippi Review, Yale Review,* and *Antioch Review.*

Olds's works have been translated into Italian, Chinese, French, and Russian.

WORK IN PROGRESS: Several books of poems.

SIDELIGHTS: Sharon Olds's poetry, which graphically depicts personal family life as well as global political events, has won several prestigious awards and has established her as a poet of great promise. "Sharon Olds is enormously self-aware," writes David Leavitt in the *Voice Literary Supplement.* "Her poetry is remarkable for its candor, its eroticism, and its power to move." Discussing Olds's work in *Poetry,* Lisel Mueller notes: "By far the greater number of her poems are believable and touching, and their intensity does not interfere with craftsmanship. Listening to Olds, we hear a proud, urgent, human voice."

Satan Says, Olds's first collection, explores "the roles in which she experiences herself, 'Daughter,' 'Woman,' and 'Mother,'" according to Mueller. In an article for the *American Book Review,* Joyce Peseroff claims: "Throughout *Satan Says,* the language often does 'turn neatly about.' In Olds's vocabulary ordinary objects, landscapes—even whole planets—are in constant motion. Using verbs which might seem, at first, almost grotesque, she manages to describe a violent, changing universe. . . . In a way, these poems describe a psychic world as turbulent, sensual, and strange as a world seen under

water. . . . Sharon Olds convincingly, and with astonishing vigor, presents a world which, if not always hostile, is never clear about which face it will show her."

In a review for the *Nation,* Richard Tillinghast comments on Olds's National Book Critics Circle Award-winner, *The Dead and the Living:* "While *Satan Says* was impossible to ignore because of its raw power, *The Dead and the Living* is a considerable step forward. . . . Olds is a keen and accurate observer of people." "I admire Sharon Olds's courage . . .," writes Elizabeth Gaffney in *America.* "Out of private revelations she makes poems of universal truth, of sex, death, fear, love. Her poems are sometimes jarring, unexpected, bold, but always loving and deeply rewarding." Tillinghast finds, however, that Olds's attempts "to establish political analogies to private brutalization . . . are not very convincing. . . . This becomes a mannerism, representing political thinking only at the superficial level." Nevertheless, Tillinghast concedes that the book "has the chastening impact of a powerful documentary."

Olds's works are described by Sara Plath in *Booklist* as "poems of extreme emotions." Critics have found intense feelings of many sorts—humor, anger, pain, terror, and love. "Her poetry focuses on the primacy of the image rather than the 'issues' which surround it," writes Leavitt, "and her best work exhibits a lyrical acuity which is both purifying and redemptive."

BIOGRAPHICAL/CRITICAL SOURCES:

BOOKS

Contemporary Literary Criticism, Volume 32, Gale, 1985.
Contemporary Poets, 5th edition, St. James Press, 1991.

PERIODICALS

America, June 30, 1984.
American Book Review, February, 1982.
American Poetry Review, September, 1984; November/ December, 1989.
Nation, October 13, 1984.
New York Times Book Review, March 18, 1984.
Poetry, June, 1981.
Voice Literary Supplement, May, 1984.

*   *   *

OLENDORF, Bill
See OLENDORF, William

OLENDORF, William 1924-
(Bill Olendorf)

PERSONAL: Born April 18, 1924, in Deerfield, IL; son of Harry A. and Beatrice (Carr) Olendorf; married Mary Gillies (a theatre president), June 1, 1943; children: William, Jr., Donald. *Education:* Attended Washington and Lee University, 1941-42, and Harvard University, 1942. *Politics:* Republican.

ADDRESSES: Home and office—9 East Ontario St., Chicago, IL 60611.

CAREER: Associated with *Better Homes and Gardens,* 1946-55; Leo Burnett Co., Chicago, IL, account executive, 1955-58; Tobias & Olendorf, Chicago, president, 1958-62; Foote, Cone & Belding, Chicago, account executive, 1962-68; Promotion Network, Chicago, president, 1968-74; Olendorf Art Promotions, Chicago, principal, 1974—. *Military service:* U.S. Navy, 1942-46.

MEMBER: Sigma Alpha Epsilon.

AWARDS, HONORS: Rockefeller Foundation grant, 1963.

WRITINGS:

ALL AS BILL OLENDORF

(With Robert Tolf) *Discover Florida,* Gale, 1982.
(With Tolf) *Addison Mizner: Architect to the Affluent,* Gale, 1984.
(With Tolf) *Chicago Sketchbook,* Olendorf International Publications, 1986.
(With Tolf) *Palm Beach Sketchbook,* Gale, 1989.
(With Tolf) *Paris Sketchbook: An American Retrospective of a Beautiful City,* Gale, 1990.

WORK IN PROGRESS: London Sketchbook, Russian Sketchbook, and *Bermuda Sketchbook,* all for Gale; *Pen and Ink Sketching.*

SIDELIGHTS: Bill Olendorf once told *CA,* "As a working artist, I am illustrating travel articles in national magazines and trade magazines."

*   *   *

OLIVER, Robert T(arbell) 1909-

PERSONAL: Born July 7, 1909, in Sweet Home, OR; son of Harry Orville and Iris (Tarbell) Oliver; married Mary W. Laack (a college professor), June 10, 1932; married second wife, Margaret K. Spangler (a librarian), 1965; children: (first marriage) Robert W., Dennis M. *Education:* Pacific University, A.B., 1932; University of Oregon, M.A., 1932; University of Wisconsin, Ph.D., 1937. *Politics:* Democrat. *Religion:* Unitarian Universalist. *Avoca-*

tional interests: "Above all, travel, and gardening, and bridge, and reading, and conversation, and trying to know people as they really are."

ADDRESSES: Home—10 Byford Ct., Chestertown, MD 21620.

CAREER: Clark Junior College, Vancouver, WA, dean, 1933-35; member of faculty at Bradley University, Peoria, IL, 1937, and Bucknell University, Lewisburg, PA, 1937-42; U.S. Government, Washington, DC, administrative assistant, Victory Speakers Bureau, 1942, administrative head of food conservation program, War Foods Administration, 1943-44; Syracuse University, Syracuse, NY, associate professor and head of division of rhetoric and public address, 1944-47; Pennsylvania State University, University Park, professor and head of department of speech, 1949-65, research professor of international speech, 1965-70, professor emeritus, 1970—. Adviser to Korean delegation to United Nations, 1945-60; consultant to President Syngman Rhee and Republic of Korea, 1947-60; manager of Korean Research and Information Office, Washington, DC, 1947-60. American-Korean Foundation, member of board of directors, 1953-65, member of advisory council, 1964—. Professional lecturer.

MEMBER: Speech Association of America (vice-president, 1960-64; president, 1964), Speech Association of the Eastern States (president, 1965-66), Pennsylvania Speech Association (president, 1940, 1957), Phi Kappa Phi, Pi Gamma Mu, Delta Sigma Rho, Torch Club.

AWARDS, HONORS: L.L.D., Pacific University, 1949; Presidential Medal of Republic of Korea, 1959; named speaker of the year, Pennsylvania Speech Association, 1964; Korean Federation of Education Association special award.

WRITINGS:

Training for Effective Speech, Cordon, 1939, 4th edition (with Rupert L. Cortright) published as *Effective Speech,* Holt, 1961, 5th edition, 1970.
Effective Speech Notebook, 1940, 2nd revised edition (with Virgil Anderson, T. Earle Johnson, Earl W. Wells, and Agnes Allardyce), Syracuse University Press, 1958.
The Psychology of Persuasive Speech, Longmans, Green, 1942, revised edition, 1957.
(With Harry W. Robbins) *Developing Ideas for Essays and Speeches,* Longmans, Green, 1943.
Korea: Forgotten Nation, Public Affairs, 1944.
(With Cortright and Cyril F. Hager) *The New Training for Effective Speech,* Dryden Press, 1946.
Four Who Spoke Out: Burke, Fox, Sheridan, and Pitt, Syracuse University Press, 1946.

(With Dallas C. Dickey and Harold P. Zelko) *Essentials of Communicative Speech,* Dryden Press, 1949, 2nd revised edition (with Paul D. Holtzman and Zelko), Holt, 1962, 4th edition published as *Communicative Speaking and Listening,* 1968.

Persuasive Speaking: Principles and Methods, Longmans, Green, 1950.

Why War Came in Korea, Fordham University Press, 1950.

The Truth about Korea, Putnam, 1951.

Verdict in Korea, Bald Eagle, 1952.

(Editor) Y. T. Pyun, *Korea My Country,* Korean Pacific Press, 1953.

Syngman Rhee: The Man behind the Myth, Dodd, 1954.

Effective Speech for Democratic Living, [Seoul, Korea], 1956, revised edition, Prentice-Hall, 1957.

(Editor with Marvin G. Bauer) *Re-Establishing the Speech Profession: The First Fifty Years,* Speech Association of the Eastern States, 1959.

Conversation: The Development and Expression of Personality, C. C Thomas, 1961.

(With Dominick A. Barbara) *The Healthy Mind in Communion and Communication,* C. C Thomas, 1962.

Culture and Communication: The Problem of Penetrating National and Cultural Boundaries, C. C Thomas, 1962.

Becoming an Informed Citizen, Holt, 1964.

(With Carroll C. Arnold and Eugene White) *Speech Preparation Sourcebook,* Allyn & Bacon, 1965.

History of Public Speaking in America, Allyn & Bacon, 1965.

(Editor with Eugene White) *Selected Speeches from American History,* Allyn & Bacon, 1966.

Leadership in 20th Century Asia, Center for Continuing Liberal Education, Pennsylvania State University, 1966.

Communication and Culture in Ancient India and China, Syracuse University Press, 1971.

Making Your Meaning Effective, Holbrook, 1971.

(Editor with DeWitt Talmadge Holland) *A History of Public Speaking in Pennsylvania,* Pennsylvania Speech Association, 1971.

Syngman Rhee and American Involvement in Korea, 1942-60: A Personal Narrative, Panmun Press, 1978.

The Influence of Rhetoric in the Shaping of Great Britain: From the Roman Invasion to the Early Nineteenth Century, University of Delaware Press and Associated University Presses, 1986.

Public Speaking in the Reshaping of Great Britain, Associated University Presses, 1987.

Leadership in Asia: Persuasive Communication in the Making of Nations, 1850-1950, Associated University Presses, 1989.

The History of Modern Korea, 1800 to the Present, Associated University Presses, 1993.

Contributor to magazines and journals, including *Reader's Digest, True, American Mercury,* and *Sewanee Review.* Editor of *Korean Survey,* 1951-60, and *Today's Speech,* 1953-60.

SIDELIGHTS: Robert T. Oliver writes: "Aspiring but not yet productive writers should pay less attention to their style and more to the substance of topics they discuss. Force is the first stylistic quality you want—to make your ideas penetrate and stick. Clarity is the next. As for the writing, the first rule is to know what you are writing about—to really know it—and be sure that it is worth knowing. Rule two is to be clear about purpose—what it is that you wish to accomplish. Rule three is to aim your writing precisely at a particular type of reader and to do so in terms of [the reader's] interest, knowledge, [and] needs. Rule four is to write regularly, on schedule, like doing any other kind of work, and to rewrite again and again until what you mean to say is phrased precisely as you wish it to be, in terms so simple and direct that it can be read without difficulty. If you wait till you feel like writing, or until you have time, or until inspiration strikes, or until the words pile up and pour forth effortlessly, you will have a long wait—probably forever."

Oliver has travelled extensively in Europe, Asia, Latin America, and the South Pacific.

*   *   *

O'ROURKE, P(atrick) J(ake)   1947-

PERSONAL: Born November 14, 1947, in Toledo, OH; son of Clifford Bronson (an auto salesman) and Delphine (a school administrator; maiden name, Loy) O'Rourke; married, wife's name Amy Lumet. *Education:* Miami University, B.A., 1969; Johns Hopkins University, M.A., 1970. *Politics:* Republican. *Religion:* None. *Avocational interests:* Art, architecture, history.

ADDRESSES: Home—Washington, DC, and Shannon, NH.

CAREER: Writer and editor with underground newspapers, including *Baltimore Harry,* in Baltimore, MD, and New York City, 1968-71; *New York Herald,* New York City, feature editor, 1971-72; free-lance writer, 1972-73; *National Lampoon,* New York City, executive editor and managing editor, 1973-77, editor-in-chief, 1978-81; *Rolling Stone,* New York City, head of international affairs desk, 1981—. Speaker, Hillsdale College, 1992.

AWARDS, HONORS: Woodrow Wilson fellow, 1969-70; Merit Award, Art Directors Club, 1973; Gold Award,

1975; Merit Award, Society of Publication Designers, 1976; received other awards for visual excellence for *National Lampoon.*

WRITINGS:

(Editor with Douglas C. Kenney, and contributor) *The 1964 High School Yearbook,* National Lampoon, 1974.

Our Friend the Vowel (poems), Stone House, 1975.

(Editor and contributor) *Sunday Newspaper Parody,* National Lampoon, 1978.

(With Rodney Dangerfield, Michael Endler, and David Blain) *Easy Money* (screenplay), Orion Pictures, 1983.

Modern Manners: An Etiquette Book for Rude People, Dell, 1983, revised edition, Atlantic Monthly Press, 1989.

Republican Party Reptile, Atlantic Monthly Press, 1987.

The Bachelor Home Companion, Pocket Books, 1987, revised edition, Atlantic Monthly Press, 1993.

Holidays in Hell, Atlantic Monthly Press, 1988.

Parliament of Whores: A Lone Humorist Attempts to Explain the Entire U.S. Government, Atlantic Monthly Press, 1991.

Give War a Chance: Eyewitness Accounts of Mankind's Struggle against Tyranny, Injustice and Alcohol-Free Beer, Atlantic Monthly Press, 1992.

Also author of *Nancy Adler Poems,* 1970. Contributor of articles to *Harper's, Playboy, Vanity Fair, American Spectator, House and Garden, Wall Street Journal, Esquire, Car and Driver,* and *Automobile.* Member of editorial board, *American Spectator.*

SIDELIGHTS: Humorist P. J. O'Rourke follows in the tradition of the New Journalism practiced by Tom Wolfe and Hunter Thompson, a journalism in which objectivity gives way to an unabashed subjectivity and the story is colored by the emotions and beliefs of the writer himself. Whether writing of the world's trouble spots or of life in the United States, O'Rourke serves up a humorous mixture of rock-and-roll wildness and libertarian conservativism which makes even his political opponents laugh out loud. Jeffrey Abbott of the London *Times* calls him "the gunslinger of the eminently respectable school of American right-wing libertarian philosophers." Michael Riley of *Time* finds O'Rourke to be "an acerbic master of gonzo journalism and one of America's most hilarious and provocative writers." One-time editor-in-chief of the satirical *National Lampoon* magazine, O'Rourke now serves as head of the international affairs desk at *Rolling Stone* and as a member of the editorial board for the *American Spectator.* His books *Parliament of Whores* and *Give War a Chance* have taken him to the top of the nation's bestseller lists.

O'Rourke began his career with an underground, "anti-war, anti-capitalist" newspaper in Baltimore. One day the Balto-Cong, a group of Baltimore radicals named after the Vietcong, invaded the newspaper's office with knives and clubs. "They had come, you know, to liberate us," O'Rourke explains to Chris Peachment in the London *Times.* "This involved taking each of us upstairs and screaming at us that we were all running dog lackeys of capitalist pigs and so on. . . . After they had all gone, it fell to me and the staff photographer to guard the office each night, simply because we had a pistol each. He, it turned out, was an undercover cop who had been planted on us. The trouble was that when we discovered this, we realized that we all liked him a lot better than the Balto-Cong. And he liked us too. So he quit the cops and we all cut our hair and got jobs."

The job search soon landed O'Rourke at the *National Lampoon,* where he rose through the ranks to become editor-in-chief. Being editor, O'Rourke tells David Streitfeld of the *Washington Post,* was "sort of like being the guy who feeds the animals and cleans the cages in a small and not very select zoo." While with *Lampoon* O'Rourke turned out humorous articles and two books, *The 1964 High School Yearbook,* a bestselling parody he edited with Douglas C. Kenney, and *Sunday Newspaper Parody,* a similar spoof of the Sunday papers.

Following up on the success of his bestselling parodies for the *National Lampoon,* O'Rourke published two tongue-in-cheek guidebooks, *Modern Manners: An Etiquette Book for Rude People* and *The Bachelor Home Companion,* after he left the magazine in 1981. The books serve as parodies of stuffy guides to "proper behavior" while deploring the lack of civilized standards in modern society. *Modern Manners,* Kerry Luft writes in the *Chicago Tribune,* is "a book of outrageous etiquette that's likely to leave you howling. . . . O'Rourke's writing has a cutting edge behind it, which makes a reader's laughter just a bit thought-provoking, and just a bit rueful." Under the surface of O'Rourke's humor, too, is a strong sense of outrage. Speaking of correct conduct in *Modern Manners,* O'Rourke opines: "It may be years before anyone knows if what you are doing is right. But if what you are doing is nice, it will be immediately evident. . . . When Miss Kopechne seemed to be in trouble, Senator Kennedy swam all the way to Edgartown rather than run up a stranger's phone bill calling for help."

In *The Bachelor Home Companion,* O'Rourke argues on behalf of bad housekeeping. "People who put a slipcover on the furniture are probably not ones who would confront the deep inner truths in their soul," O'Rourke claims. "They'd probably put a slipcover over that, too." Written at a time when he was still a bachelor himself, much of the book rationalizes his own disheveled apartment. As O'Rourke admits to Streitfeld, "Okay, it's horrible by a girlfriend's standards. But if I were a Hell's Angel, I would be thought of as obsessive-compulsive." When bringing someone over to your apartment, O'Rourke advises, "get creative and explain you were robbed earlier in the day by an unusual burglar, who drank all your beer and put the cans under the couch."

With *Republican Party Reptile,* a gathering of twenty-one magazine essays and articles, O'Rourke first presented his persona of a hip conservative libertarian. Arguing that an outrageous sensibility naturally leads to support for individualism and a limited government, O'Rourke claims that many younger people are therefore "Republican Party Reptiles." "We look like Republicans, and think like conservatives," O'Rourke explains, "but we drive a lot faster and keep vibrators and baby oil and a video camera behind the stack of sweaters on the bedroom closet shelf." As William French summarizes in the Toronto *Globe and Mail,* Republican Party Reptiles "oppose government spending, seat-belt laws, the United Nations, aerobics and taxation without loopholes, among other things. They favor guns, drugs, free love, a sound dollar, Star Wars and the right to drive a red Ferrari at 130 miles per hour."

Called "sometimes a bit too rude" by Susan Avallone of *Library Journal, Republican Party Reptile* ranges over a wide variety of topics, including peacenik tourists in Soviet Russia, cocaine smuggling in the Caribbean, and driving fast on drugs without spilling your drink. The usual flamboyant style is evident here. Describing former Philippines president Ferdinand Marcos, O'Rourke claims he was "a vicious lying dirtball who ought to have been dragged through the streets of Manila with his ears nailed to a truck bumper." Expressing a warm fondness for President Roosevelt, O'Rourke clarifies: "Not the one in the wheelchair, the good one who killed bears."

"O'Rourke blasts the liberal agenda with a shower of ridicule," Jack Shafer writes in the *American Spectator,* "proclaiming that if liberty means anything, it means that we should be able to smoke, shoot guns, drive Corvairs, swallow sacharin, get in fistfights, and start barbecue fires with gasoline without interference from mom or OSHA." "The main point about his writing," Peachment notes, "is that it tells the truth. His account of a trip to Russia is the most accurate description I have ever read. . . . Few foreign correspondents seem brave enough to tell you that the Russians are a manic depressive race, born three vodkas under par, who live in a country of staggering imaginative poverty, but who are yet more interesting than the witless lefties from the West who go there and ask questions about their Gross National Product and praise hydroelectric dam schemes." Edward H. Crane, speaking of *Republican Party Reptile* in the *American Spectator,* calls O'Rourke

"a closet libertarian who shares not only Mencken's wit, but his hatred of the state as well." "Beneath a flippant surface and a frequently vulgar brand of humor," Bob Mack writes in *National Review,* "O'Rourke is remarkably concerned with mores and morals."

Since his appointment in 1981 as head of the international affairs desk at *Rolling Stone* magazine, O'Rourke has globe-trotted to Korea, Lebanon, the Phillipines, South Africa, Nicaragua, and the Soviet Union. *Holidays in Hell* gathers together his reports from these trouble spots. "Armed with cynicism and the obligatory apparel," as Jonathan Yardley puts it in the *Washington Post,* O'Rourke provides acidic sketches of tyranny, war, and corruption around the world. He plays, Henry Jaworski explains in the Toronto *Globe and Mail,* "the cynical innocent abroad." Throughout, O'Rourke keeps in mind that "so-called Western civilization . . . is better than anything else available. Western civilization not only provides a bit of life, a pinch of liberty and the occasional pursuit of a happiness, it's also the only thing that's ever tried to." Although the book is humorous, Mark Cunningham admits in *National Review,* when O'Rourke departs from his humorous voice, his prose achieves a "tremendous power."

The moral outrage O'Rourke has expressed in previous books is a major ingredient in *Parliament of Whores: A Lone Humorist Attempts to Explain the Entire U.S. Government,* his bestselling attack on modern American politics. O'Rourke begins with a libertarian conservative's statement of purpose: "The government is huge, stupid, greedy, and makes nosy, officious, and dangerous intrusions into the smallest corners of life." He explains that government doesn't understand it's proper relationship to its citizens: "To shut up and get out of our faces." He then proceeds to such chapters as "The Three Branches of Government: Money, Television and Bullshit" and "Our Government: What the F--- Do They Do All Day and Why Does It Cost So Goddamned Much Money?" Along the way, O'Rourke mixes insightful political jabs with the humor. In the chapter "Why God Is a Republican and Santa Claus Is a Democrat," he explains that God is "a stern fellow, patriarchal rather than paternal and a great believer in rules and regulations. He holds men strictly accountable for their actions." In contrast, Santa Claus "may know who's been naughty and who's been nice, but he never does anything about it. He gives everyone everything they want. . . . Santa Claus is preferable to God in every way but one: There is no such thing as Santa Claus."

"*Parliament of Whores,*" Allen Randolph writes in the *National Review,* "is being touted as a belly-aching good time. . . . But don't expect brain candy. The author has asked too many questions and seen too much of the world to be shrugged off as a mere entertainer. The fizzing cynicism is as much a reflection of experience as a literary style." O'Rourke concludes the book by observing: "The whole idea of our government is: if enough people get together and act in concert, they can take something and not pay for it. . . . Every government is a parliament of whores. The trouble is, in a democracy, the whores are us." Daniel Wattenberg in the *American Spectator* finds that O'Rourke makes a single point time and again throughout the book: "Limited government depends on self-government. We have only ourselves to blame if government is too big. We demand way too much from our leaders and do way too little for ourselves." Calling O'Rourke "a bit of a smart-assed jerk," David Olive of the Toronto *Globe and Mail* nonetheless concludes that "he has some valid points to make, and never fails to entertain." Signe Wilkinson in the *New York Times Book Review* claims that "for anyone majoring in or teaching political science, P. J. O'Rourke's latest should be required reading."

In *Give War a Chance: Eyewitness Accounts of Mankind's Struggle against Tyranny, Injustice and Alcohol-Free Beer* O'Rourke collects articles on a variety of topics, including his "Notes Toward a Blacklist for the 1990s," a satirical call for a new McCarthyism aimed at a wide range of irritating liberal types, and his coverage of the Persian Gulf War. Chris Goodrich in *Publishers Weekly* notes that O'Rourke uses his humor to "write about subjects that border on the unspeakable." "When I'm doing these stories where people are getting hurt . . . ," O'Rourke explains, "it's important to have comic relief, and a fool is very useful for that. And I use myself as that fool—not that I'm not a fool, it's certainly an accurate persona in that respect—by making myself seem a little more ignorant of the situation than I actually am." "Rare is the writer who can make his readers laugh out loud in the privacy of their living rooms, much less in the middle of a crowded railroad car," Terry Teachout notes in the *New York Times Book Review*. "P. J. O'Rourke is one of those fortunate souls. I read 'Give War a Chance' . . . on a train from New York to Baltimore, and it made me laugh so hard that my fellow passengers started pointing and whispering. . . . It's the gift of a Kingsley Amis or an H. L. Mencken, and you either have it or you don't."

O'Rourke's writing persona is a slightly exaggerated version of himself. "I take a very conventional, middle-aged, Midwestern sensibility to very peculiar places," he explains to Goodrich. According to Wilkinson, O'Rourke "just arrives in some odd place, wanders around (never far from a bar) and then describes what he sees." Writing in the *World and I*, Lauren Weiner describes O'Rourke as "a fundamentally decent midwesterner who hypes his hippie past and supposedly boorish playboy present, and who writes political travelogues and essays in a New Journalis-

tic style of satire that sometimes hits and sometimes misses." "Humor is just what I'm good at," O'Rourke tells Goodrich, "and I'm not even that good at it." But Riley finds that "O'Rourke's writing is driven by a practiced wit, a brilliant use of analogy, and a hard edge capable of offending almost anyone."

After years of covering the world's hotspots, O'Rourke has lately found events moving in the right direction: the Soviet Union has collapsed, Nicaragua has gone democratic, and the Cold War has been won. He has even greeted Bill Clinton's election as president with favor. As O'Rourke remarked at the *American Spectator*'s twenty-fifth anniversary celebration, "Clinton may be a disaster for the rest of the nation, but he is meat on our table." Speaking of the task ahead for conservatives now that the liberals run both Congress and the White House, O'Rourke opines: "Welcome to the 1990s. Let us all salute (and be sensitive to the needs of) the shiftless, the feckless, the senseless, the worthwhileness-impaired, the decency-challenged, and the differently-moraled. And hello to their leaders—progressive, committed, and filled to the nose holes with enormous esteem for themselves."

BIOGRAPHICAL/CRITICAL SOURCES:

PERIODICALS

American Spectator, September, 1987, p. 45; December, 1987, p. 42; December, 1988, p. 20; September, 1991, pp. 36-38; December, 1991, pp. 13-14; February, 1993, pp. 20-21.
Business Week, June 29, 1992, p. 14.
Chicago Tribune, January 29, 1984; July 10, 1989.
Commentary, October, 1991, p. 57.
Economist, August 10, 1991, p. 78.
Esquire, August, 1990, p. 126.
Fortune, December 30, 1991, p. 138.
Globe and Mail (Toronto), May 2, 1987; September 3, 1988; June 22, 1991.
Human Events, April 15, 1989, p. 13; May 2, 1992, p. 11.
Library Journal, June 15, 1987, p. 70.
Listener, February 11, 1988, p. 23; December 15, 1988, p. 32.
Los Angeles Times, August 19, 1983; November 16, 1988.
Los Angeles Times Book Review, October 29, 1989, p. 12; May 24, 1992, p. 14.
National Review, June 5, 1987, p. 47; September 30, 1988, p. 60; July 14, 1989, p. 58; August 26, 1991, p. 41; April 13, 1992, p. 58.
New York, May 4, 1992, p. 78.
New York Times, August 19, 1983.
New York Times Book Review, May 3, 1987, p. 30; January 29, 1989, p. 32; June 30, 1991, p. 15; April 19, 1992, p. 6.
Observer, January 10, 1988, p. 20; January 22, 1989, p. 49.

People, June 8, 1987; July 3, 1989, p. 47.

Publishers Weekly, March 16, 1992, pp. 60-61.

Punch, January 15, 1988, p. 46.

Reason, October, 1991, p. 62.

Spectator, January 21, 1989, p. 38; August 24, 1991, p. 22; November 30, 1991, p. 38.

Time, October 17, 1988, p. 82; June 12, 1989, p. 69; April 15, 1991, p. 58; July 8, 1991, p. 59.

Times (London), January 6, 1988; September 7, 1991, p. 36.

Times Literary Supplement, September 27, 1991, p. 31.

Tribune Books, May 10, 1987, p. 4; May 20, 1990, p. 8; May 10, 1992, p. 8.

Wall Street Journal, April 28, 1987, p. 32; November 4, 1988, p. A13; July 15, 1991, p. A9.

Washington Journalism Review, September, 1988, p. 22.

Washington Monthly, July, 1991, p. 54.

Washington Post, August 22, 1983; March 20, 1987; September 14, 1988; June 21, 1989.

World and I, August, 1992, pp. 350-55.

—*Sketch by Thomas Wiloch*

*　　　*　　　*

OSBECK, Kenneth W.　1924-

PERSONAL: Born December 13, 1924, in Grand Rapids, MI; son of Emil and Hilda Osbeck; married Elizabeth Mary Didier (an assistant professor of drama), August 26, 1950; children: Kathleen, Gregory, Mark, Lisa. *Education:* University of Michigan, B. of Music Ed., 1950, M. of Music Ed., 1956. *Politics:* Republican.

ADDRESSES: Home—107 Ivanhoe N.E., Grand Rapids, MI 49546.

CAREER: Grand Rapids School of the Bible and Music, Grand Rapids, MI, director of music, 1950-66; Grand Rapids Baptist College, Grand Rapids, associate professor of music and fine arts, 1966-84. Owner of custom music publishing company.

WRITINGS:

A Pocket Guide for the Church Choir Member, Zondervan, 1958, reprinted, Kregel, 1975.

A Junior's Praise, Kregel, 1959, reprinted, 1981.

Ministry of Music, Zondervan, 1961, reprinted, Kregel, 1975.

A Teen-Age Praise, Kregel, 1962.

Choir Responses, Kregel, 1962.

Choral Praises, Kregel, 1963.

My Music Workbook, Kregel, 1973.

Singing with Understanding: Including 101 Beloved Hymn Backgrounds, Kregel, 1978.

One Hundred One Hymn Stories, Kregel, 1978.

One Hundred One More Hymn Stories, Kregel, 1985.

Devotional Warm-ups for Church Choirs, Kregel, 1985.

Amazing Grace—366 Inspiring Hymn Stories for Daily Devotions, Kregel, 1990.

52 Hymn Stories Dramatized, Kregel, 1992.

WORK IN PROGRESS: Enter in to Worship, a manual/resource book for leaders of praise and worship, expected in 1993.

P

PALMER, Norman D(unbar) 1909-

PERSONAL: Born June 25, 1909, in Hinckley, ME; son of Walter Elmer (a merchant) and Gertrude (Dunbar) Palmer; married Evelyn Florence Kalal, October 28, 1944; married second wife, Gurina McIlrath, February 8, 1992; children: Patricia Lee (Mrs. Ron Baisch). *Education:* Colby College, B.A., 1930; Yale University, M.A., 1932, Ph.D., 1936. *Religion:* Protestant.

ADDRESSES: Home—485 Friday Ave., Friday Harbor, WA 98250.

CAREER: Colby College, Waterville, ME, 1933-42, 1946-47, began as instructor, became associate professor and chairman of department of history and government; University of Pennsylvania, Philadelphia, associate professor, 1947-51, professor of political science, 1951-79, professor emeritus, 1979, chairman of political science department, 1949-52, chairman of international relations department, 1957-65. Fulbright professor, University of Delhi, 1952-53. Visiting professor at Columbia University, 1950, School of Advanced International Studies, 1951, Swarthmore College, 1961, University of Hawaii, 1968, Bombay University, 1968, 1973, American University in Cairo, 1971, Duke University, 1974, U.S. Naval Postgraduate School, 1976, and Graduate Institute of Peace Studies, Kyung Hee University, 1984, 1989, and 1992. Senior associate, Foreign Policy Research Institute, 1955—; senior specialist, East-West Center (Honolulu), 1966-67. Member, Philadelphia Charter Commission, 1951-52; member of steering committee, Global Interdependence Center; director, Philadelphia Transnational Project; trustee, Princeton-in-Asia Program. Consultant, Foreign Operations Administration, 1954, and U.S. Department of State, 1954-76. *Military service:* U.S. Navy, Air Combat Intelligence, 1942-46; became lieutenant commander; received Bronze Star.

MEMBER: International Political Science Association, International Study and Research Institute (vice-president; director), International Studies Association (life member; national president, 1970-71), American Political Science Association, American Academy of Political and Social Science (secretary; director), Indian Political Science Association (life member), Association for Asian Studies, National Council of Asian Affairs (president), Friends of India Committee (chairman), American Society for Public Administration, Council on Foreign Relations, World Affairs Council of Philadelphia (director), Philadelphia Council for International Visitors (director).

AWARDS, HONORS: L.H.D., Colby College, 1955; Carnegie Endowment for International Peace fellow, 1959-60; American Council of Learned Societies fellow and Guggenheim fellow, both 1961-62; Council on Foreign Relations research fellow in South Asia, 1961-63; American Institute of Indian Studies research fellow in India, 1966-67 and 1971-72; Association of Indians in America honors award, 1988.

WRITINGS:

The Irish Land League Crisis, Yale University Press, 1940.

(Co-author) *Fundamentals of Political Science,* Prentice-Hall, 1942.

(With H. C. Perkins) *International Relations,* Houghton, 1953, 3rd edition, 1969.

(Co-author) *Major Governments of Asia,* Cornell University Press, 1958, 2nd edition, 1963.

(Co-author) *Leadership and Political Institutions in India,* Princeton University Press, 1959.

(With Shao Chuan Leng) *Sun Yat-sen and Communism,* Praeger, 1961.

The Indian Political System, Houghton, 1961, 2nd edition, 1971.

(Co-author) *The United States and the United Nations,* University of Oklahoma Press, 1964.

South Asia and United States Policy, Houghton, 1966.

Elections and Political Development: The South Asian Experience, Duke University Press, 1975.

(Co-author) *Pakistan: The Long View,* Duke University Press, 1978.

(Co-author) *Dynamics of Development,* Concept Publishing, 1978.

(Co-author) *The Subcontinent in World Politics,* Praeger, 1980, 2nd edition, 1982.

(Co-author) *Changing Patterns of Security and Stability in Asia,* Praeger, 1980.

(Co-author) *Great Power Relations, World Order, and the Third World,* Vikas (New Delhi), 1981.

The United States and India: The Dimensions of Influence, Praeger, 1984.

Contributor to professional journals. Contributing editor, *Current History;* book review editor, *Global Futures Digest;* former member of editorial boards, *Orbis* and *Asian Affairs.*

WORK IN PROGRESS: A New Agenda for International Relations in a Changing World.

SIDELIGHTS: Norman D. Palmer has traveled to four continents, including fifteen trips to South Asia. Palmer told *CA:* "Over a period of many years, I have been able to spend a great deal of time and thought both in 'the highlands of the mind' and in many parts of the world, especially South Asia. This opportunity has enabled me to live in several worlds, both literally and figuratively speaking. It has given added dimension to my own life, and has prompted me to write. I write (1) because I must, (2) because writing forces me to be more thorough in my investigations and to learn more about many things than I otherwise would, (3) because I want to contribute to my major fields of interest, and (4) because I want to project myself into the future."

*   *   *

PARGETER, Edith Mary 1913-
(Ellis Peters)

PERSONAL: Born September 28, 1913, in Horsehay, Shropshire, England; daughter of Edmund Valentine and Edith (Hordley) Pargeter. *Education:* Attended schools in England. *Avocational interests:* Music (especially opera and folk), reading, theatre, art.

ADDRESSES: Home—Parkville, 14 Park Lane, Madeley, Telford, Shropshire TF7 5HF, England. *Agent*—Deborah Owen Ltd., 78 Narrow St., Limehouse, London E14 8BP, England.

CAREER: Pharmacist's assistant and dispenser in Dawley, Shropshire, England, 1933-40; full-time novelist and translator of prose and poetry from the Czech and Slovak. *Military service:* Women's Royal Naval Service, 1940-45; became petty officer; received British Empire Medal.

MEMBER: International Institute of Arts and Letters, Society of Authors, Authors League of America, Authors Guild, Crime Writers Association.

AWARDS, HONORS: Edgar Allan Poe Award for best mystery novel, Mystery Writers of America, 1961, for *Death and the Joyful Woman;* Gold medal, Czechoslovak Society for International Relations, 1968; Silver Dagger, Crime Writers Association, 1981, for *Monk's-Hood.*

WRITINGS:

Hortensius, Friend of Nero, Dickson, 1936.

Iron-Bound, Dickson, 1936.

The City Lies Foursquare, Reynal & Hitchcock, 1939.

Ordinary People, Heinemann, 1941, published as *People of My Own,* Reynal, 1942.

She Goes to War (novel), Heinemann, 1942.

The Eighth Champion of Christendom, Heinemann, 1945.

Reluctant Odyssey (sequel to *The Eighth Champion of Christendom*), Heinemann, 1946.

Warfare Accomplished, Heinemann, 1947.

The Fair Young Phoenix, Heinemann, 1948.

By Firelight, Heinemann, 1948, published as *By This Strange Fire,* Reynal & Hitchcock, 1948.

The Coast of Bohemia (travel), Heinemann, 1950.

Lost Children (novel), Heinemann, 1950.

Holiday with Violence, Heinemann, 1952.

This Rough Magic (novel), Heinemann, 1953.

Most Loving Mere Folly (novel), Heinemann, 1953.

The Soldier at the Door (novel), Heinemann, 1954.

A Means of Grace (novel), Heinemann, 1956.

The Assize of the Dying: 2 Novelletes (contains "The Assize of the Dying" and "Aunt Helen"), Doubleday, 1958, published in England with an additional story, "The Seven Days of Monte Cervio," as *The Assize of the Dying: 3 Stories,* Heinemann, 1958.

The Heaven Tree, Doubleday, 1960.

The Green Branch, Heinemann, 1962.

The Scarlet Seed, Heinemann, 1963.

The Lily Hand and Other Stories, Heinemann, 1965.

A Bloody Field by Shrewsbury, Macmillan (London), 1972, published as *The Bloody Field,* Viking, 1973.

Sunrise in the West (first volume in "The Brothers of Gwynedd" sequence), Macmillan (London), 1974.

The Dragon at Noonday (second volume in "The Brothers of Gwynedd" sequence), Macmillan (London), 1975.

The Hounds of Sunset (third volume in "The Brothers of Gwynedd" sequence), Macmillan (London), 1976.

Afterglow and Nightfall (fourth volume in "The Brothers of Gwynedd" sequence), Macmillan (London), 1977.

The Marriage of Megotta, Viking, 1979.

UNDER PSEUDONYM ELLIS PETERS

Death Mask, Collins, 1959, Doubleday, 1960.

Where There's a Will, Doubleday, 1960, published in England as *The Will and the Deed,* Collins, 1960, published as *The Will and the Deed,* Avon, 1966.

Funeral of Figaro, Collins, 1962, Morrow, 1964.

The Horn of Roland, Morrow, 1974.

Never Pick up Hitch-Hikers!, Morrow, 1976, bound with *Catch a Falling Spy* by Len Deighton and *More Tales of the Black Widowers* by Isaac Asimov, W. J. Black, 1978.

"FELSE FAMILY" DETECTIVE NOVELS

Fallen into the Pit, Heinemann, 1951.

(Under pseudonym Ellis Peters) *Death and the Joyful Woman,* Collins, 1961, Doubleday, 1962.

(Under pseudonym Ellis Peters) *Flight of a Witch,* Collins, 1964.

(Under pseudonym Ellis Peters) *Who Lies Here?,* Morrow, 1965, published in England as *A Nice Derangement of Epitaphs,* Collins, 1965.

(Under pseudonym Ellis Peters) *The Piper on the Mountain,* Morrow, 1966.

(Under pseudonym Ellis Peters) *Black Is the Colour of My True-Love's Heart,* Morrow, 1967.

(Under pseudonym Ellis Peters) *The Grass Widow's Tale,* Morrow, 1968.

(Under pseudonym Ellis Peters) *The House of Green Turf,* Morrow, 1969.

(Under pseudonym Ellis Peters) *Mourning Raga,* Macmillan (London), 1969, Morrow, 1970.

(Under pseudonym Ellis Peters) *The Knocker on Death's Door,* Macmillan (London), 1970, Morrow, 1971.

(Under pseudonym Ellis Peters) *Death to the Landlords!,* Morrow, 1972.

(Under pseudonym Ellis Peters) *City of Gold and Shadows,* Macmillan (London), 1973, Morrow, 1974.

(Under pseudonym Ellis Peters) *Rainbow's End,* Macmillan (London), 1978, Morrow, 1979.

"CHRONICLES OF BROTHER CADFAEL" MYSTERIES; UNDER PSEUDONYM ELLIS PETERS

A Morbid Taste for Bones (also see below), Macmillan (London), 1977, Morrow, 1978.

One Corpse Too Many (also see below), Macmillan (London), 1979, Morrow, 1980.

Monk's-Hood, Macmillan (London), 1980, Morrow, 1981.

Saint Peter's Fair, Morrow, 1981.

The Leper of St. Giles, Macmillan (London), 1981, Morrow, 1982.

The Virgin in the Ice, Macmillan (London), 1982, Morrow, 1983.

The Sanctuary Sparrow, Morrow, 1983.

The Devil's Novice, Macmillan (London), 1983, Morrow, 1984.

Dead Man's Ransom, Morrow, 1984.

The Pilgrim of Hate, Macmillan (London), 1984, Morrow, 1985.

An Excellent Mystery, Morrow, 1985.

The Raven in the Foregate, Morrow, 1986.

The Rose Rent, Morrow, 1987.

The Hermit of Eyton Forest, Headline, 1987, Mysterious Press, 1988.

The Confession of Brother Haluin, Headline, 1988, Mysterious Press, 1989.

A Rare Benedictine (short stories), Headline, 1988, Mysterious Press, 1989.

The Heretic's Apprentice, Headline, 1989, Mysterious Press, 1990.

The Potter's Field, Headline, 1990, Mysterious Press, 1991.

The Summer of the Danes, Mysterious Press, 1991.

The Benediction of Brother Cadfael (contains *A Morbid Taste for Bones* and *One Corpse Too Many,* and *Cadfael Country: Shropshire and the Welsh Border*), Mysterious Press, 1992.

The Holy Thief, Headline, 1992, Mysterious Press, 1993.

TRANSLATIONS FROM THE CZECH

Jan Neruda, *Tales of the Little Quarter* (short stories), Heinemann, 1957, reprinted, Greenwood, 1977.

Frantisek Kosik, *The Sorrowful and Heroic Life of John Amos Comenius,* State Educational Publishing House (Prague), 1958.

A Handful of Linden Leaves: An Anthology of Czech Poetry, Artia (Prague), 1958.

Joseph Toman, *Don Juan,* Knopf, 1958.

Valja Styblova, *The Abortionists,* Secker & Warburg, 1961.

(With others) Mojmir Otruba and Zdenek Pesat, editors, *The Linden Tree: An Anthology of Czech and Slovak Literature, 1890-1960,* Artia (Prague), 1962.

Bozena Nemcova, *Granny: Scenes from Country Life,* Artia (Prague), 1962, reprinted, Greenwood, 1977.

Joseph Bor, *The Terezin Requiem,* Knopf, 1963.

Alois Jirasek, *Legends of Old Bohemia,* Hamlyn, 1963.

Karel Hynek Macha, *May,* Artia (Prague), 1965.

Vladislav Vancura, *The End of the Old Times,* Artia (Prague), 1965.

Bohumil Hrabel, *A Close Watch on the Trains,* J. Cape, 1968.

Josefa Slanska, *Report on My Husband,* Macmillan (London), 1969.

Ivan Klima, *A Ship Named Hope: Two Novels,* Gollancz, 1970.

Jaroslav Seifert, *Mozart in Prague,* Artia (Prague), 1970.

CONTRIBUTOR

Alfred Hitchcock Presents: Stories Not for the Nervous, Random House, 1965.

Alfred Hitchcock Presents: Stories That Scared Even Me, Random House, 1967.

George Hardinge, editor, *Winter's Crimes 1,* St. Martin's, 1969.

A. S. Burack, editor, *Techniques of Novel Writing,* The Writer, 1973.

Hilary Watson, editor, *Winter's Crimes 8,* St. Martin's, 1976.

Hardinge, editor, *Winter's Crimes 11,* St. Martin's, 1979.

Hardinge, editor, *Winter's Crimes 13,* St. Martin's, 1981.

OTHER

Also author of *The Horn of Roland,* bound with *Danger Money* by Mignon G. Eberhart and *The Romanov Succession* by Brian Garfield, for the Detective Book Club by W. J. Black. Contributor of short stories to magazines, including *The Saint* and *This Week.*

ADAPTATIONS: The Assize of the Dying was filmed under the title *The Spaniard's Curse; Death and the Joyful Woman* was presented on "The Alfred Hitchcock Hour"; *Mourning Raga* and *The Heaven Tree* were adapted for radio in 1971 and 1975, respectively; Pargeter's short story "The Purple Children" was produced on television in Canada and Australia.

SIDELIGHTS: Edith Pargeter, writing as Ellis Peters, has "recreated the world of England in the first years of the High Middle Ages" in her chronicles of Brother Cadfael, according to Andrew M. Greeley in the *Armchair Detective.* A twelfth-century crusader turned monk and herbalist, Brother Cadfael is the protagonist of a series of novels and stories that mix historical background, romance, and detection, and which Greeley describes as "a fascinating reconstruction of the religion, the history, the social structure, the culture, the politics, and the lifestyle of England in the twelfth century." Set on the Welsh border near Shrewsbury, where Peters lives today, the books take place during the tumultuous reign of Stephen of England, when fighting between the king and his cousin the Empress Matilda (or Maud) wracked the realm.

"I was born and bred in Shropshire," states Peters in her introduction to *The Benediction of Brother Cadfael,* "and have never yet found any sound reason for leaving it, except perhaps for the pleasure of coming back to it again, after forays into regions otherwise delightful in themselves but no substitute for home." Shropshire and the Marches of Wales, especially Shrewsbury, are central to much of the author's work. The "Brothers of Gwynedd" sequence, set in a different time, takes place in Wales, across the bor-

der. Her historical novel *The Bloody Field* is set near Shrewsbury in the early 15th century, where Harry Percy (the "Hotspur" of Shakespeare's *Henry IV*) led a rebellion against Henry Bolingbroke, who had seized the English throne from Richard II.

Peters's evocation of Shropshire in the Brother Cadfael chronicles is so strong, Greeley states, that "one feels that one has become part of a little section of England around Shrewsbury between 1137 and 1140, and that one knows the monks and the townsfolk and the squires and the nobility almost as though they were friends and neighbors." "Even after eight centuries," Peters states in *The Benediction of Brother Cadfael,* "you may find yourself, now and then, seeing the Marches very much as Cadfael saw them, perhaps thinking the same thoughts and experiencing the same contemplative pleasures that illuminated his chosen lot in life." Greeley continues, "Perhaps the greatest achievement of the Cadfael chronicles is Peters's ability to help us feel and accept the common humanity which links us to these inhabitants' world, so very different from our own."

Cadfael himself, Peters states in her introduction to *A Rare Benedictine,* is a product of the Welsh borders. He "sprang to life suddenly and unexpectedly when he was already approaching sixty, mature, experienced, fully armed and seventeen years tonsured." Unlike another famous ecclesiastical sleuth, G. K. Chesterton's Father Brown, Cadfael is not a priest; he is only a monk, holding no offices within the community. While Father Brown makes his deductions based on his knowledge of the dark recesses of his own soul, Cadfael draws on his many years as a crusader, warrior, and sailor, which gives him a vast amount of experience with men and women of all types. As a herbalist who doctors the sick, he has special access to the world outside the cloister, enabling him to apply his experience and his curiosity to the mysterious events he encounters.

Cadfael is truly a product of his times, involved in many of the major crises of his day. He was born in Wales in 1080, only fourteen years after William of Normandy seized the crown of England. He joined the First Crusade and served with Godfrey de Bouillon, participating in the sieges of Antioch, Ascalon and Jerusalem. He returned to England in November of 1120—as related in the story "A Light on the Road to Woodstock" in *A Rare Benedictine*—shortly before the death by drowning of Prince William, Henry I's only legitimate son and heir. He was a member of Prior Robert Pennant's expedition into Wales in 1137 to acquire the relics of St. Winifred from the village of Gwytherin. "Although the *First Chronicle of Brother Cadfael (A Morbid Taste for Bones)* is based on this historical journey," write Talbot and Whiteman in "Cadfael Country: Shropshire and the Welsh Border" (contained in *The Benediction of Brother Cadfael*), "the events and monastic characters depicted in it—except Prior Robert Pennant and Abbot Heribert—are entirely fictional." The Second Chronicle, *One Corpse Too Many,* also has a historical basis; it is set shortly after King Stephen's seige and capture of Shrewsbury in 1138. Most of Cadfael's adventures take place in these turbulent middle years of 12th-century England, and they reflect the unrest and violence of the times.

Peters's Cadfael novels have been compared with Umberto Eco's best-seller *The Name of the Rose,* which tells the story of another crime-solving monk in fourteenth-century Italy. The resemblence, however, is only superficial; seven Cadfael chronicles preceeded Eco's book, and Peters does not expound a theory of semiotics as Eco does. As Greeley points out, "Eco undoubtedly describes truth in his book. Ellis Peters, for her part, has only verisimilitude; and, as any storyteller knows, verisimilitude makes for a better story than truth and may, finally, at the level of myth and symbol, be even more true." Peters lists Rudyard Kipling, Thomas Mallory and Helen Waddell among her literary influences, and she described herself to *CA* as "essentially a storyteller, and in my view no one who can't make that statement can possibly be a novelist, the novel being by definition an extended narrative reflecting the human condition, with the accent on the word 'narrative.'"

Pargeter once told *CA:* "Streams of consciousness and probings of the solitary, and usually uninteresting, human-soul-at-the-end-of-its-tether are not for me. Nor do I find vice and evil more interesting than virtue, and I hope my books go some way to defy and disprove that too-easily accepted judgement. It gives me great satisfaction that many times people have written to me to tell me, in varying terms, that I have made them feel better, not worse, about being human. That's all the acknowledgment I need."

BIOGRAPHICAL/CRITICAL SOURCES:

BOOKS

Peters, Ellis, *A Rare Benedictine: The Advent of Brother Cadfael,* Mysterious Press, 1989.
Peters, Ellis, *The Benediction of Brother Cadfael,* Mysterious Press, 1993.

PERIODICALS

Armchair Detective, summer, 1985, pp. 238-45.
Best Sellers, October 1, 1966; August 1, 1967; June 1, 1968; April 15, 1969; March 15, 1970; February, 1984; July, 1984; March, 1986; August, 1986; February, 1987.
Books and Bookmen, April, 1965; December, 1967; June, 1968; June, 1969; August, 1970.

Globe and Mail (Toronto), May 5, 1984; July 5, 1986; December 13, 1986.
Listener, May 19, 1983.
Los Angeles Times Book Review, January 31, 1982; February 26, 1984; October 27, 1985.
National Review, December 5, 1986.
New Yorker, November 5, 1984.
New York Times Book Review, May 9, 1965; November 6, 1966; August 13, 1967; May 26, 1968; September 26, 1982.
Observer, February 14, 1965; May 15, 1966; September 17, 1967; April 21, 1968; January 23, 1983; August 4, 1985.
Publishers Weekly, February 8, 1985.
Punch, May 29, 1968.
Spectator, March 5, 1965; June 3, 1966.
Time, August 17, 1987.
Times (London), January 21, 1983; July 11, 1985.
Times Literary Supplement, February 25, 1965; June 2, 1966; September 21, 1967; July 18, 1968; October 3, 1980; February 18, 1983; July 13, 1984; January 11, 1985; October 3, 1986; January 30, 1987.
Village Voice, July 16, 1985.
Washington Post Book World, January 31, 1981; June 21, 1981; May 16, 1982.
Wilson Library Bulletin, October, 1983.

*   *   *

PARKER, John Thomas   1950-
(Tom Parker)

PERSONAL: Born June 10, 1950, in Kingston, NY; son of John Hunter (an engineer) and Mary Ellen (a teacher; maiden name, Ayer) Parker; married Cheryl A. Russell, October 11, 1975 (divorced, 1983); married Cheryl A. Baudendistle, August 9, 1989. *Education:* Earlham College, B.A., 1972.

ADDRESSES: Home—Alpine, NY. *Office*—P.O. Box 6680, Ithaca, NY 19851. *Agent*—Van der Leun Associates, 464 Mill Hill Dr., Southport, CT 06490.

CAREER: Full-time writer, illustrator, designer, and book producer, 1974—.

AWARDS, HONORS: Book design award from American Institute of Graphic Arts, 1984, for *In One Day.*

WRITINGS:

UNDER NAME TOM PARKER

Rules of Thumb, self-illustrated, Houghton, 1983.
In One Day: The Things Americans Do in a Day, self-illustrated, Houghton, 1984.
Rules of Thumb 2, Houghton, 1987.

Never Trust a Calm Dog, self-illustrated, HarperCollins, 1990.

Also designer and illustrator of *Abcedar,* by George Ella Lyon, Orchard Books, 1989.

OTHER

Cover photographer and editor for *American Demographics,* monthly magazine published by Dow Jones, Inc., 1980—.

Rules of Thumb has been translated into French.

WORK IN PROGRESS: Mousetrap, a history of American invention and the Industrial Revolution "as reflected in mousetraps and the invention of the mousetrap"; *The Lincoln Sample,* a photo essay "as serialized in *American Demographics*—I drove across the U.S, and stopped exactly every nine miles and took a photo facing west"; *B is for Buttzville,* a photo essay and alphabet book of "strange towns across the U.S."; and *Encyclopedia Titanica,* "a history of the world—for those who failed [history] the first time."

SIDELIGHTS: Tom Parker told *CA:* "Free-lance editorial illustration can be a thankless and mindbending job. After ten years, I would have to say I am more interested in using my illustration skills as a personal tool than I am in embellishing other people's work. For one thing, why let other people kick you around when you can sit at home and torture yourself?"

*   *   *

PARKER, Tom
   See PARKER, John Thomas

*   *   *

PATTERSON, Charles 1935-

PERSONAL: Born August 5, 1935, in New Britain, CT; son of Robert Fenton and Ann Janet (Wilson) Patterson. *Education:* Amherst College, B.A., 1958; Columbia University, M.A., 1960, Ph.D., 1970; Episcopal Theological School, Cambridge, MA, B.D., 1963.

ADDRESSES: Home—545 West End Ave., New York, NY 10024.

CAREER: St. Stephen's School, Rome, Italy, teacher of ancient and biblical history, 1964-65; American Universities Field Staff, New York City, editor and compiler, 1967-69; Trinity School, New York City, part-time English and comparative religions teacher, 1972-74; Hunter College of the City University of New York, New York

City, adjunct assistant professor of literature of the Bible, 1974-75; New Lincoln School, New York City, teacher of history and writing, 1978-80; free-lance editor and writer, 1980-81, 1984—; Calhoun School, New York City, history and English teacher, 1981-84; Charles Scribners & Sons (publisher), New York City, associate editor and copy editor, 1985-87. New School for Social Research, part-time teacher of history, religion, and literature, 1971-82; Adelphi University, adjunct faculty member, 1985-86.

MEMBER: Authors Guild, National Writers Union, P.E.N.

AWARDS, HONORS: Carter G. Woodson Book Award, National Council for the Social Studies, 1989, for *Marian Anderson.*

WRITINGS:

Anti-Semitism: The Road to the Holocaust and Beyond, Walker & Co., 1982.
Thomas Jefferson, F. Watts, 1987.
Marian Anderson, F. Watts, 1988.
Hafiz al-Asad of Syria, Messner, 1991.
Animal Rights, Enslow Publishers, 1993.

WORK IN PROGRESS: A book on the United Nations, in conjunction with the U.N.'s fiftieth anniversary in 1995, for Oxford University Press; a book about the civil rights movement.

SIDELIGHTS: Charles Patterson told *CA:* "After I finished my fifth book, *Animal Rights* (published in July, 1993), I realized that the books that have engaged me the most have been about injustice. My first book was about anti-Semitism and the climate in Europe that led to the Holocaust. My third book was a biography of Marian Anderson, the black concert singer who overcame so much (it won the 1989 Carter G. Woodson Book Award given by the National Council for the Social Studies). My most recent book is about injustice against animals and people who are working to defend them. Clearly, those who move me the most are those who stand up for the weak and defenseless against the strong and mighty. I am now at work on two new books—one about the civil rights movement and the other about the United Nations, which will be fifty years old in 1995.

"The research I did for my book on animal rights changed my point of view as well as my diet (I've become a total vegetarian, which means no meat or dairy products). I agree completely with the writer and Nobel laureate, Isaac Bashevis Singer: 'The longer I am a vegetarian the more I feel how wrong it is to kill animals and eat them. I think that eating meat or fish is a denial of all ideals, even of all religions. . . . As long as people will shed the blood of innocent creatures there can be no peace, no liberty, no harmony between people. Slaughter and justice cannot dwell together.' "

*   *   *

PATTERSON, Richard North 1947-

PERSONAL: Born February 22, 1947, in Berkeley, CA; son of Richard W. (a business executive) and Marjorie Frances (North) Patterson; married Judith Anne Riggs (a teacher and editor), January 12, 1974; children: Shannon Heath, Brooke North. *Education:* Ohio Wesleyan University, B.A., 1968; Case Western Reserve University, J.D., 1971. *Politics:* Independent. *Avocational interests:* Tennis, racquetball, jogging, film, reading, theatre, ballet, and "most music, particularly contemporary rock."

ADDRESSES: Home—4758 Tarton Dr., Santa Rosa, CA 95405. *Office*—U.S. Securities and Exchange Commission, 450 Golden Gate Ave., San Francisco, CA 94102. *Agent*—Hy Cohen Literary Agency, Ltd., 111 West 57th St., New York, NY 10019.

CAREER: Admitted to Ohio State Bar, 1971, District of Columbia Bar, 1973, and Alabama State Bar, 1975; Office of the Attorney General, Columbus, OH, assistant attorney general, 1971-73; U.S. Securities and Exchange Commission, Washington, DC, trial attorney, 1973-75; Berkowitz, Lefkovits & Patrick (law firm), Birmingham, AL, partner in firm, 1975-78; U.S. Securities and Exchange Commission, San Francisco, CA, attorney, 1978—. Writer.

MEMBER: Mystery Writers of America.

AWARDS, HONORS: Edgar Award, Mystery Writers of America, 1979, for *The Lasko Tangent.*

WRITINGS:

NOVELS

The Lasko Tangent, Norton, 1979.
The Outside Man, Little, Brown, 1981.
Escape the Night, Random House, 1983.
Private Screening, Villard, 1985.
Degree of Guilt, Knopf, 1993.

Also contributor of a short story, "The Client," to *Atlantic Monthly.*

SIDELIGHTS: Richard North Patterson had already established a successful career in law including work as a prosecutor on the Watergate case when he decided to try his hand at writing a mystery novel. The idea came from reading the work of Ross Macdonald, creator of the Lew Archer series. As he once told *CA,* Patterson began "to realize that Macdonald had crystalized a vague impulse to

write that I'd felt for several years. I admired his conciseness, his gift for mood and setting, his eye for detail. More than that, it seemed Macdonald had made the detective novel humane and compassionate, with the insight of psychology. Clearly, Macdonald cared about his characters and their situations, and that inspired me to try."

Patterson began with a creative writing course at the University of Alabama, and completed the first draft for *The Lasko Tangent* in six months. He then spent another six months revising, "tightening and complicating the plot to make it more effective. This effort—at times quite discouraging—concluded with astonishing good luck: the sale of my final version to W. W. Norton & Co. as an unsolicited submission, the first such sale at Norton in about five years." The story follows Christopher Kenyon Paget, a lawyer in the Special Investigations Section of the Washington Economic Crimes Commission, and his investigation of a possible stock scam involving a friend of the President. T. J. Binyon, in a review for *Times Literary Supplement,* noted that Patterson's teachers could be proud of his first novel, "fast-moving, neatly put together, with an ingenious plot."

After the sale of *The Lasko Tangent,* Patterson continued his pursuit of "learning the craft of writing," studying for a year with Jesse Hill Ford, "a truly great writer who was more generous with his time and talents than his students had any right to expect," Patterson once remarked to *CA.* "Because of Ford's comprehensive understanding of the writer's work, I gained a much deeper appreciation of what writing is about." Patterson completed a short story, "The Client," during that time, which he sold to *Atlantic Monthly.* Patterson's second novel, *The Outside Man,* traces a northerner's search for the murderer of his best friend's wife in an Alabama town. "The air hangs heavy with old secrets and the prose is as lush as overgrown magnolia as Patterson recounts his story of the intertwined lives of three generations of Southern families," Jean M. White commented in *Washington Post Book World.* *New Republic* reviewer Robin Winks described the book as "rich, complex, [and] beautifully written," and commented, "One might see it as Ross Macdonald transplanted to Alabama, though it is far more than that."

Patterson left behind the world of law in his third novel, *Escape the Night,* focusing instead on a powerful publishing family and the heir to its fortune. Peter Carey is haunted by nightmares of his parents' gruesome death, which he witnessed but is unable to remember. On the eve of his inheritance of the firm, Peter realizes that someone is following him, monitoring his every word. "This novel keeps the reader rapt and the secrets wrapped right up to the end," *West Coast Review of Books*'s Dorothy H. Rochmis declared. In *Private Screening* Patterson returned to the courtroom with San Francisco trial attorney Tony

Lord, who successfully defends a Vietnam vet charged with assassinating a senator, then finds himself involved in a terrorist kidnapping. The kidnapper makes use of a satellite link to telecast his actions across the country and invites viewers to vote on whether or not he should kill his hostages. "A measure of *Private Screening*'s merit is that one can guess its outcome early on and still find it a compelling read," *Washington Post Book World* reviewer Dennis Drabelle remarked. Several critics applauded Patterson's handling of modern issues including the dangers of technology in the hands of criminals. "This book reverberates with intensive concern for some of the important issues confronting us today," a *West Coast Review of Books* contributor noted. "Engaging and intelligent," Barbara Conaty commented in *Library Journal*, "this complex story puts a new gloss on the terror and troubles of our times."

"To some degree," Patterson once told *CA*, "my work seems to reflect the individual's necessary effort to make sense of his situation in a world which is often absurd and hostile, and which may lack any ultimate meaning."

BIOGRAPHICAL/CRITICAL SOURCES:

PERIODICALS

Armchair Detective, fall, 1987, p. 385.
Best Sellers, August, 1983, p. 166; April, 1986, p. 8.
Birmingham Post Herald, May 9, 1978.
Kirkus Reviews, February 1, 1981, p. 168; April 1, 1983, p. 398; August 15, 1985, p. 813.
Library Journal, February 1, 1979; May 1, 1981, p. 995; June 1, 1983, p. 1159; October 15, 1985, p. 103.
Los Angeles Times Book Review, May 25, 1986, p. 4.
New Republic, May 30, 1981, p. 38.
New Statesman, June 27, 1980, p. 973.
New York Times Book Review, June 8, 1980, p. 51; May 10, 1981, p. 45; March 7, 1982, p. 35.
Publishers Weekly, February 27, 1981, p. 142; April 15, 1983, p. 44; September 20, 1985, p. 104; May 16, 1986, p. 77.
Times Literary Supplement, September 5, 1980, p. 948.
Washington Post Book World, May 17, 1981, p. 11; November 17, 1985, p. 9; July 20, 1986, p. 12.
West Coast Review of Books, September, 1983, p. 38; November, 1985, p. 22.*

*   *   *

PEASE, (Clarence) Howard   1894-1974

PERSONAL: Born September 6, 1894, in Stockton, CA; died April 14, 1974, in Mill Valley, CA; son of Newton and Stella (Cooley) Pease; married Pauline Nott, November 4, 1927 (deceased); married Rossie Ferrier, September,

1956; children: Philip H. *Education:* Stanford University, A.B., 1924; graduate study. *Politics:* Democrat. *Religion:* Unitarian Universalist.

CAREER: Merchant seaman; writer. Teacher in California, 1924-25, 1928-34; Vassar College, Poughkeepsie, NY, instructor in English, 1926-27. *Military service:* U.S. Army, World War I; served for two years, one year with ambulance unit in France.

MEMBER: PEN.

AWARDS, HONORS: Commonwealth Club of California silver medal, 1945, for *Mystery at Thunderbolt House;* Child Study Association children's book award, 1946, and Boys' Clubs of America junior book award, 1949, both for *Heart of Danger.*

WRITINGS:

TOD MORAN MYSTERIES

The Tattooed Man, Doubleday, 1926.
The Jinx Ship, Doubleday, 1927.
Shanghai Passage, Doubleday, 1929.
The Ship without a Crew, Doubleday, 1934.
Hurricane Weather, Doubleday, 1936.
Foghorns, Doubleday, 1937.
The Black Tanker, Doubleday, 1941.
Night Boat, and Other Tod Moran Mysteries, Doubleday, 1942.
Heart of Danger, Doubleday, 1946.
Captain of the "Araby," Doubleday, 1953.
Mystery on Telegraph Hill, Doubleday, 1961.

OTHER

The Gypsy Caravan, Doubleday, 1930.
Secret Cargo, Doubleday, 1931.
Wind in the Rigging, Doubleday, 1935.
Captain Binnacle (for beginning readers), Dodd, 1938.
Jungle River, Doubleday, 1938.
The Long Wharf, Doubleday, 1938.
High Road to Adventure, Doubleday, 1939.
Mystery at Thunderbolt House, Doubleday, 1944.
Bound for Singapore, Doubleday, 1948.
The Dark Adventure, Doubleday, 1950.
Shipwreck, Doubleday, 1957.

Contributor to books and journals. Pease's novels were translated and published in Denmark, Belgium, Germany, France, Spain, and Italy.

SIDELIGHTS: Howard Pease turned a fascination for the sea into a profitable writing career. A former merchant seaman who gathered first-hand research for his novels in exotic ports of call, Pease wrote more than a dozen seafaring adventures for teens, including the popular "Tod Moran" mystery series. Pease offered children heroes who act independently in order to right wrongs. His plots often hinged upon lost treasure or unsolved murders in settings as close as New Orleans and as far removed as New Guinea.

"Even as a small child the sea always attracted me," Pease told the *Junior Book of Authors*. "Probably because I lived on inland soil, out of sight of the fogs of the coast yet on a river that flowed into San Francisco Bay." Pease's grandparents had crossed the Great Plains in a covered wagon and settled in Northern California. He grew up there and called the state home for most of his life.

Pease's interest in books began as a child when his parents read aloud to him every evening before bedtime. His interest in writing came from his sixth-grade teacher. "One day," he remembered in the second edition of the *Junior Book of Authors*, "my sixth grade teacher said, 'This is Friday afternoon, our free period. How would you like to write short stories? All those in favor? Hands swung aloft. One girl pupil remarked, 'That might be fun, Mrs. Gaines; but how in the world would you do it?' Our teacher had come prepared; she had forty pictures clipped from magazines, many of them advertisements. She held up a picture of a camel caravan crossing the desert. 'Who would like to write a story about this?' she asked. A boy held up his hand and received the picture. My hand did not go up until I saw a picture of a steamer heading into a storm at sea. . . . At the end of the term we printed a little magazine filled with our work, and that is how I still happen to have a copy of my first short story—'Turn Back, Never!' " One of his novels, *Foghorns*, is dedicated to Mrs. Gaines.

While a freshman at Stanford University, Pease was sent to fight in the First World War. After two years of service, some of which was spent with a French ambulance corps, he returned to Stanford. The war had made him determined to become a writer. After taking a teaching degree, he began teaching in public schools in California, writing stories in his spare time. Pease's first sale was an adventure story, published in *American Boy* magazine.

That initial success spurred Pease to further writing. To find material for his fiction, he shipped out of San Francisco as a wiper on a freighter bound for Panama. In the years that followed the young author visited Tahiti, Mexico, France, and seaports throughout the Caribbean, gathering impressions of foreign landscapes, seascapes, and the people who pilot ships of all kinds. All of these experiences found their way into his novels for boys.

Besides his books based on his own experiences at sea, Pease drew on his travels on the Pan-American Highway, a walking tour of Europe, and auto traveling with his wife in the United States for some of his adventures. Pease eventually settled in Palo Alto, California, where he

turned out numerous adventure tales. The most popular of these featured Tod Moran, a third mate on trading vessels in the Pacific. His adventures take him to Hong Kong, Manila, and other distant ports. Only a teen himself, Tod is able to solve mysteries and endure deadly typhoons without losing his cool. Moran, Pease once explained, is based on his own younger self, and on every other young man who ever went to sea.

In Pease's study, lined with original paintings from his book jackets, the author worked at his typewriter six hours a day. He often revised each chapter as many as five times, and spent an average of ten months on each of his books. Although his books were adventure stories filled with the usual twists of plot common to the genre, Pease's stories featured realistic characters from many cultures, all of whom were shown to be human beings despite their differing backgrounds. C. J. Finger, writing in *Books*, believed that "there is no one quite like [Pease] writing adventure books today. He has the Fenimore Cooper and Captain Marryat knowledge of the sea, and masculinity of Jack London, [and] the mystery cleverness of that forgotten romanticist, Charles Brockden Brown."

Moran once told *CA* that he wrote stories with many different kinds of readers in mind—serious works for scholarly students and escapist adventure fiction for those with learning difficulties. "I've written some escape fiction. *Jungle River* and *Hurricane Weather* are just stories. In state industrial schools where most of the delinquent boys are so ill-adjusted they cannot face the world, such books are eagerly read. So we need, you see, all kinds of books for all kinds of readers. Still, if you are to become a reader of our better novels instead of a reader only of popular magazines with their romantic serials and murder tales, you must learn while young *how* to read."

BIOGRAPHICAL/CRITICAL SOURCES:

BOOKS

Carlsen, G. Robert, *Books and the Teen-Age Reader,* Harper, 1967.
The Children's Bookshelf, Child Study Association of America/Bantam, 1965.
Junior Book of Authors, Wilson, 1934, pp. 292-293, second edition, 1951, pp. 239-240.
Twentieth-Century Children's Writers, 3rd edition, St. James Press, 1989.

PERIODICALS

Books, April 26, 1931, p. 8.

OBITUARIES:

PERIODICALS

Elementary English, September, 1974.*

PELIKAN, Jaroslav Jan 1923-

PERSONAL: Born December 17, 1923, in Akron, OH; son of Jaroslav Jan, Sr. (a minister) and Anna (Buzek) Pelikan; married Sylvia Burica, June 9, 1946; children: Martin John, Michael Paul, Miriam Ruth. *Education:* Concordia Junior College, diploma (summa cum laude), 1942; Concordia Theological Seminary, B.D., 1946; University of Chicago, Ph.D., 1946.

ADDRESSES: Home—156 Chestnut Lane, Hamden, CT 06518. *Office*—Department of History, Yale University, New Haven, CT 06520.

CAREER: Ordained minister of the Lutheran Church; Valparaiso University, Valparaiso, IN, professor, 1946-49; Concordia Theological Seminary, St. Louis, MO, professor, 1949-53; University of Chicago, IL, professor, 1953-62; Yale University, New Haven, CT, Titus Street Professor of Ecclesiastical History, 1962-72, Sterling Professor of History and Religious Studies, 1972—, acting dean of Graduate School, 1973-74, dean, 1975-78. President, Fourth International Congress for Luther Research, 1971; president, New England Conference on Graduate Education, 1976-77. Member of commission on faith and order, World Council of Churches. Lecturer at numerous universities, including Duke University, Harvard University, Princeton University, University of Toronto, University of Virginia, and Rutgers University.

MEMBER: American Society for Reformation Research, American Society of Church History (member of council, 1961—; president, 1965), American Academy of Arts and Sciences (fellow; councillor, 1974; vice-president, 1976—), Medieval Academy of America (fellow), Americans for Democratic Action, National Academic Council of Valparaiso University (president, 1963—), Phi Beta Kappa.

AWARDS, HONORS: Abingdon Award, 1959, for *The Riddle of Roman Catholicism;* Pax Christi Award, Saint John's University, 1966; National Endowment for the Humanities senior fellow, 1967-68; John Gilamry Shea Prize, American Catholic Historical Association, 1971; National Award, World Slovak Congress, 1973; Religious Book Award, Catholic Press Association, 1974; Christian Unity Award, Atonement Friars, 1975; American Philosophical Society award, 1978; Jefferson Award, National Endowment for the Humanities, 1983; Shaw Medal, Medieval Academy of America, 1985; award of excellence, American Academy of Religion, 1989; has received many honorary degrees from colleges and universities, including Concordia College, 1960, Gettysburg College, 1967, Concordia Seminary, 1967, Albertus Magnus College, 1973, Coe College, 1976, St. Anselm College, 1983, LaSalle University, 1987, Jewish Theological Seminary of America, 1991, and Comenius University, 1992.

WRITINGS:

From Luther to Kierkegaard, Concordia, 1950.
Fools for Christ, Muhlenberg, 1955.
The Riddle of Roman Catholicism, Abingdon, 1959.
Luther the Expositor, Concordia, 1959.
The Shape of Death: Life, Death, and Immortality in the Early Fathers, Abingdon, 1961.
The Light of the World: A Basic Image in Early Christian Thought, Harper, 1962.
Obedient Rebels: Catholic Substance and Protestant Principle in Luther's Reformation, Harper, 1964.
The Finality of Jesus Christ in an Age of Universal History: A Dilemma of the Third Century, Lutterworth, 1965.
The Christian Intellectual, Harper, 1966.
Spirit Versus Structure: Luther and the Institutions of the Church, Harper, 1968.
Development of Christian Doctrine: Some Historical Prolegomena, Yale University Press, 1969.
The Christian Tradition, University of Chicago Press, Volume 1: *The Emergence of the Catholic Tradition,* 1971, Volume 2: *The Spirit of Eastern Christendom,* 1974, Volume 3: *The Growth of Medieval Theology,* 1978, Volume 4: *Reformation of Church and Dogma,* 1984, *Christian Doctrine and Modern Culture,* 1989.
Historical Theology: Continuity and Change in Christian Doctrine, Westminster, 1971.
Scholarship and Its Survival: Questions on the Idea of Graduate Education, Carnegie Fund, 1983.
The Vindication of Tradition, Yale University Press, 1984.
Jesus through the Centuries, Harper, 1985.
The Mystery of Continuity: Time and History, Memory, and Eternity, University Press of Virginia, 1986.
Bach among the Theologians, Augsburg, 1986.
The Excellent Empire: The Fall of Rome and the Triumph of the Church, Harper, 1987.
The Melody of Theology, Harvard University Press, 1988.
Confessor between East and West, Eerdmans, 1990.
Imago Dei, Princeton University Press, 1990.
Eternal Feminines: Three Theological Allegories in Dante's Paridiso, Rutgers University Press, 1990.
The Idea of the University: A Reexamination, Yale University Press, 1992.

EDITOR

(With others) Theodore Tappert, *Book of Concord: The Confessions of the Evangelical Lutheran Church,* Fortress, 1959.
The Preaching of Chrysostom: Homilies on the Sermon on the Mount, Fortress, 1967.
Interpreters of Luther: Essays in Honor of Wilhelm Pauck, Fortress, 1968.
Twentieth Century Theology in the Making, Collins, Volume 1: *The Themes of Biblical Theology,* 1969, Volume 2: *The Theological Dialogue: Issues and Re-*

sources, 1970, Volume 3: *Ecumenicity and Renewal,*
1971.
The Preaching of Augustine, Fortress, 1973.
The World Treasury of Modern Religious Thought, Little,
Brown, 1990.

OTHER

Editor and translator with others of *Luther's Works,* twenty-two volumes, 1955-70; also editor of *Makers of Modern
Theology,* five volumes, 1966-68; occasional department
editor for religion, *Encyclopaedia Britannica.* Member of
editorial board, *Collected Works of Erasmus, Classics of
Western Spirituality,* and *Evangelisches Kirchenlexikon;*
member of advisory board, *Cross Currents,* 1990—.

SIDELIGHTS: Clark M. Williamson calls *The Christian
Intellectual* "another in a list of highly instructive books
which [Jaroslav Pelikan] has written for the theological
public. Professor Pelikan long ago demonstrated his ability to bring his rich knowledge of the history of Christian
thought decisively to bear on the issues and problems facing people in their immediate situations. . . . *The Christian Intellectual* brings the same helpful and resourceful
approach to a new problem, the one stated in the title."
Williamson concludes that the book, "is written in an in-
viting style, and quietly stresses the importance of a grasp
of the history of Christian thought if one is properly to
comprehend what is involved in speaking meaningfully to
the contemporary world."

In *Spirit Versus Structure,* Pelikan deals with the issue of
institutional structure and the problems which faced Martin Luther, who, according to Thomas Tredway, during
the heat of the early Reformation, "tended to view the extant institutions of the church as inhibiting grace. But in
the crises of the 1520s and 1530s he came increasingly to
realize the inevitability of structure and even to admit with
characteristic candor that the institutions being erected in
the name of Reformation were not necessarily better than
those of the Roman church which they replaced." Tredway, however, finds that "a cursory reading of this book
may . . . produce impatience and even disappointment in
some quarters, for Pelikan is as cautious as Luther himself. Those wanting a moratorium on criticism of the
church will find little comfort in Luther's commitment to
ecclesia semper reformanda. And those wanting to wipe
clean the churchly slate and start all over will be equally
frustrated by the respect which he considered the extant
institutions of Christianity."

In a review of *The Christian Tradition,* Robert L. Wilken
says that Jaroslav Pelikan "stands in a grand line extending back to the great period of Christian historiography
in nineteenth-century Germany, the time of Ferdinand
Christian Baur, Albrecht Ritschl, and Adolf von
Harnack. As such, his work can and could be seen as the

first major attempt by an American historian to answer
the chief question that has dominated the study of early
Christian thought, namely the problem of 'hellenization'
of the gospel. How did a movement which began with the
preaching of a Jewish rabbi in Palestine become the dog-
matic religion that we know from Christian history? . . .
Though this inquiry is historical in its conception and execution, it clearly bears a message for contemporary Christian thinkers. The author has no patience with those shrill
voices that, proclaiming their liberation from the past, de-
spise the Christian intellectual tradition in the name of
modernity. Indeed, he is convinced that the Christian intellectual tradition is worth taking seriously even—
perhaps particularly—in the late twentieth century."

BIOGRAPHICAL/CRITICAL SOURCES:

PERIODICALS

Christian Century, November 6, 1968; July 16, 1969.
Encounter, winter, 1967.
Saturday Review, August 7, 1971.
Times Literary Supplement, October 12, 1967.
Yale Review, spring, 1969.

*   *   *

PENE du BOIS, William (Sherman)   1916-1993

PERSONAL: Surname is pronounced "*pen*-due-*bwah*";
born May 9, 1916, in Nutley, NJ; died February 5, 1993,
after suffering a stroke, in Nice, France; son of Guy (a
painter and art critic) and Florence (a children's clothes
designer; maiden name, Sherman) Pene du Bois; married
Jane Bouche, 1943 (marriage ended); married Willa Kim
(a theatrical designer), March 26, 1955. *Education:* Attended Lycee Hoche, Versailles, France, 1924-28, Lycee
de Nice, Nice, France, 1928-29, and Morristown School,
1930-34. *Politics:* Democrat. *Religion:* Protestant. *Avocational interests:* Tennis, raising dogs.

ADDRESSES: Home—60 boulevard Franck Pilatte,
06300 Nice, France. *Agent*—Watkins/Loomis Agency,
150 East 35th St., New York, NY 10016.

CAREER: Author and illustrator of children's books.
Paris Review, Flushing, NY, art editor and designer,
1956-66. *Military service:* U.S. Army, 1941-45, served in
coast artillery in Bermuda; correspondent for *Yank.*

AWARDS, HONORS: Spring Book Festival Younger
Honor Award, *New York Herald Tribune,* 1940, for *The
Great Geppy;* Spring Book Festival Middle Honor Award,
New York Herald Tribune, 1946, for *Harriet,* and 1954, for
My Brother Bird; Spring Book Festival Older Award, *New
York Herald Tribune,* 1947, and Newbery Medal, Ameri-
can Library Association, 1948, both for *The Twenty-one*

Balloons; Spring Book Festival Picture Book Honor Award, *New York Herald Tribune,* 1951, for *The Mousewife;* Caldecott Honor Award, American Library Association, 1952, for *Bear Party;* Child Study Award, 1952, for *Twenty and Ten;* Spring Book Festival Prize, *New York Herald Tribune,* 1956, and Caldecott Honor Award, American Library Association, 1957, both for *Lion;* awards from New Jersey Institute of Technology, 1961, for *Otto in Africa* and *The Three Policemen,* 1965, for *The Alligator Case,* 1967, for *The Horse in the Camel Suit,* and 1969, for *Porko von Popbutton;* Clara Ingram Judson Award, 1966, for *A Certain Small Shepherd; New York Times* Best Illustrated Book citation, 1971, Children's Book Showcase Title, 1972, and Lewis Carroll Shelf Award, 1972, all for *Bear Circus;* Art Books for Children Award, 1974, for *The Hare and the Tortoise and the Tortoise and the Hare: La Liebre y la tortuga & la tortuga y la liebre;* Christopher Award, 1975, for *My Grandson Lew;* Children's Book Showcase Award, 1975, for *Where's Gomer?; New York Times* Best Illustrated Book citation, 1978, for *The Forbidden Forest;* award from *Redbook,* 1985, for *William's Doll.*

WRITINGS:

SELF-ILLUSTRATED BOOKS FOR CHILDREN

Elizabeth, the Cow Ghost, Nelson, 1936, published with new illustrations, Viking, 1964.

Giant Otto, Viking, 1936, revised edition with new illustrations published as *Otto in Africa,* 1961.

Otto at Sea, Viking, 1936, published with new illustrations, 1958.

The Three Policemen; or, Young Bottsford of Farbe Island, Viking, 1938, published with new illustrations, 1960.

The Great Geppy, Viking, 1940.

The Flying Locomotive, Viking, 1941.

The Twenty-one Balloons, Viking, 1947.

Peter Graves, Viking, 1950.

Bear Party, Viking, 1951.

Squirrel Hotel, Viking, 1952, revised edition, G. K. Hall, 1979.

The Giant, Viking, 1954.

Lion, Viking, 1956.

Otto in Texas, Viking, 1959.

The Alligator Case, Harper, 1965.

Lazy Tommy Pumpkinhead, Harper, 1966.

The Horse in the Camel Suit, Harper, 1967.

Pretty Pretty Peggy Moffitt, Harper, 1968.

Porko von Popbutton, Harper, 1969.

Call Me Bandicoot, Harper, 1970.

Otto and the Magic Potatoes, Viking, 1970.

Bear Circus, Viking, 1971.

(With Lee Po) *The Hare and the Tortoise and the Tortoise and the Hare: La Liebre y la tortuga & la tortuga y la liebre* (text in Spanish and English), Doubleday, 1972.

Mother Goose for Christmas, Viking, 1973.

The Forbidden Forest, Harper, 1978.

Gentleman Bear, Farrar, Straus, 1985.

OTHER

Illustrator of over twenty-five additional books, including Richard Plant and Oskar Seidlin, *S.O.S. Geneva,* Viking, 1939; Charles McKinley, *Harriet,* Viking, 1946; Rumer Godden, *The Mousewife,* Viking, 1951; Claire Huchet Bishop, *Twenty and Ten,* Viking, 1952; Evelyn Ames, *My Brother Bird,* Dodd, Mead, 1954; Edward Lear, *The Owl and the Pussycat,* Doubleday, 1961; Rebecca, Caudill, *A Certain Small Shepherd,* Holt, 1965; Roald Dahl, *The Magic Finger,* Harper, 1966; Isaac Bashevis Singer, *The Topsy-Turvy Emperor of China,* Harper, 1971; Charlotte Shapiro Zolotow, *My Grandson Lew,* Harper, 1974; Norma Farber, *Where's Gomer?,* Dutton, 1974; Mark Strand, *The Planet of Lost Things,* C. N. Potter, 1982; Zolotow, *William's Doll,* Harper, 1985; Strand, *The Night Book,* Crown, 1985; May Garelick, *Just My Size,* Harper-Collins, 1990. Also illustrator of *Castles and Dragons,* edited by Child Study Association, 1958, and *The Poison Belt,* by Arthur Conan Doyle, 1964.

Pene du Bois's manuscripts are housed in the May Massee Collection at Emporia State University, Kansas.

WORK IN PROGRESS: "A book with just one word, which is also the title, *Surprise.* It will be profusely illustrated."

SIDELIGHTS: William Pene du Bois was a widely recognized author and illustrator of children's books. Throughout a prolific career that has spanned five decades, he has illustrated more than fifty books—half of those his own—and garnered several distinguished awards, including the Newbery Medal and two Caldecott Honor Awards. As evidenced by such popular works as *The Twenty-one Balloons* and his "Otto" books, he is best known for artfully combining adventure, fantasy, and humor. His characters are essentially good, though frequently eccentric and absurd, and even his villains are more foolish than evil. His illustrations, too, are acclaimed for their detail, inventiveness, and technical skill.

Pene du Bois was born to a family already well established in the art world. His father, Guy Pene du Bois, was a distinguished American painter and art critic, and his mother, Florence, was a children's clothes designer. As early as the 1700s, his forebears had distinguished themselves as painters, stage designers, and architects, many of whom were known throughout the United States and Europe.

As a child, Pene du Bois developed a strong interest in the circus. After he moved to France with his family at the age of eight, he spent so much time at one French circus that he could name each performer and act by heart. Much of his time, too, was spent poring over the books of Jules Verne, who wrote colorful science-fiction and adventure novels. Pene du Bois, however, admitted that he was fascinated more by the illustrations in Verne's books—especially those depicting mechanical devices—than by the actual texts. "As a child I hardly read at all, although I loved to look at books," he later said in his Newbery Award acceptance speech reprinted in *Horn Book.* "I was the sort of fellow who just looks at the pictures. I try to keep such impatient children in mind in making my books."

During his childhood, Pene du Bois learned much about drawing from his father. Yet he also credited the strict discipline of the Lycee Hoche, one of two French schools he attended, for instilling neatness, clarity, and order in his work habits and artistic style. At the school, for example, meticulousness was of paramount importance to Pene du Bois's arithmetic teacher, who refused any work that failed to meet his strict standards for neatness. "I remember doing a magnificent page of arithmetic," Pene du Bois recalled, "in which I neglected to rule one short line under a subtraction of two one-digit figures. . . . 'What have we here,' [my teacher] said, 'an artist? Monsieur [Pene] du Bois is drawing free hand.' He neatly tore my work in four pieces." Later, Pene du Bois would employ a similar strategy in his own work—if he felt any of his drawings was not his best, he tore it up.

At age fourteen, Pene du Bois moved with his family back to the United States, and two years later, in 1933, he announced his decision to enter Carnegie Technical School of Architecture. "I was awarded a scholarship to that institution," he explained "but to my amazement, I sold a children's book I wrote and illustrated as a divertissement during vacation. It was *The Great Geppy.*" So instead of attending Carnegie, Pene du Bois embarked on a new career: writing and illustrating books for children. By age nineteen, he completed and saw the publication of his first book, and by the time he entered the armed forces at age twenty-five, he had written and illustrated five more books for children.

Pene du Bois continued to write and illustrate children's books at a steady, though unhurried, pace. He worked on only one drawing per day, and he often wrote the text for his books only after the illustrations were complete. In this way, his story ideas were almost fully developed by the time he actually composed on paper.

Among Pene du Bois's earliest self-illustrated works is *Giant Otto,* the first in a comical series that features a gigantic hound and his owner, Duke. In *Giant,* Otto joins the French Foreign Legion and successfully wards off an Arab invasion by wagging his tail to create a huge sand-

storm. In *Otto at Sea* he bravely saves all the passengers of a sinking ship. Other "Otto" books include *Otto in Texas,* where Otto unmasks oil thieves, and *Otto and the Magic Potatoes,* where Otto and Duke discover that an evil baron is actually a humanitarian who wants to feed the hungry. The "Otto" stories were well received by reviewers, who especially praised Pene du Bois's imaginative and vivid illustrations. A reviewer for *Virginia Kirkus Service* wrote that Pene du Bois's "boldly colored illustrations vividly illustrate the madcap continental atmosphere in which the unusual but always dignified Otto performs."

Pene du Bois drew upon his love of the circus for his 1940 book, *Great Geppy.* The title character is a horse that is hired to solve a robbery at a circus. To investigate the crime, Geppy poses as a variety of circus entertainers, including a freak, a tightrope walker, and a lion tamer. In the end he discovers that there never was a theft; the culprit broke into the safe to *donate* money to the struggling circus, not steal any. For his success Geppy is honored as a hero and is even appointed the circus's newest star—he gives an extraordinary performance when shot from a cannon.

During World War II, Pene du Bois served in the U.S. Army, but he didn't stop writing and illustrating. In addition to working as a correspondent for *Yank,* he also edited the camp newspaper, painted portraits, and illustrated strategic maps. And, according to Susan Garness in the *Dictionary of Literary Biography,* he also may have been working on his next children's book, for two years after his discharge, he completed what is perhaps his best known work, *The Twenty-one Balloons.*

Winner of the 1948 Newbery Medal, *The Twenty-one Balloons* relates the fantastic adventures of Professor William Waterman Sherman, a retired mathematics teacher who embarks on a cross-Pacific journey in a hot-air balloon. Unfortunately his balloon is punctured, and he crashes on the island of Krakatoa, whose inhabitants live in luxury atop a volcano filled with diamonds. One day, though, the volcano erupts, and everyone escapes on a platform held aloft by twenty-one balloons. Equipped with parachutes, the Krakatoans later jump to safety, but the professor is left to crash-land in the ocean. Eventually, he is rescued by a freighter and welcomed home as a hero.

In *Books: A Guide for the Middle Grades,* John Gillespie and Diane Lembo remarked that *The Twenty-one Balloons* is "a mixture of fantasy and science" that demonstrated Pene du Bois's "skill in combining literary style and creative imagination." Gillespie and Lembo went on to comment that "reminiscent of H. G. Well's science fiction tales, it will appeal to many beginning science fiction fans. In addition, [Pene] du Bois's superb artistic craftsmanship conveys both the imaginative and scientific quality of his story in numerous and detailed drawings." And in another review of *The Twenty-one Balloons,* a critic for the *Junior Bookshelf* wrote: "The numerous illustrations are not only most beautiful in themselves but also exact and illuminating interpretations of the story. The production is worthy of the quality of this remarkable book, in which fantasy, invention and high adventure are so happily blended."

During the 1950s Pene du Bois won the Caldecott Honor Award for each of two self-illustrated books, *Bear Party* and *Lion.* The former relates the simple tale of a masquerade party given by "real" teddy bears. Told with little text, the story relies on Pene du Bois's colorful and elaborate drawings, which depict bears dressed in costumes ranging from clowns, to angels, to bullfighters, to knights. The latter story is an original fable that reveals how the Artist Foreman created the Lion at the beginning of the universe. With detailed illustrations, Pene du Bois fills the factory—where angels invent the animals—with charts of ears, tails, and tongues. He also depicts the angels' drawing instruments, which include white paper and gold brushes. The book is "graceful and charming," judged Nancy Ekholm Burkert in *Horn Book,* and added that "the delight of *Lion* in both art and text lies in its celebration of the creation of uniqueness and in the uniqueness of creation."

Throughout Pene du Bois's career, he also illustrated numerous works of other notable children's authors, including Verne, Isaac Bashevis Singer, and Charlotte Shapiro Zolotow. He especially enjoyed the challenge of illustrating books entirely different from his own, such as Patricia Gordon's *Witch of Scrapfaggot Green,* which features an evil sorceress. Undoubtedly, though, many of the books he illustrated contained characters and elements familiar to him. In Charles McKinley's *Harriet,* for example, he drew the title character, a horse, much like his own *Geppy.* And in Leslie Greener's *Moon Ahead,* a science fiction story, he indulged his love for precisely drawn illustrations of machinery—a love first inspired by Verne's books. Moreover, fussy characters greatly resembling those in his *Twenty-one Balloons* appeared in Daisy Ashford's *Young Visitors.*

Pene du Bois continued to add to his already lengthy list of children's books. And he also continued to attract widespread recognition for his humorous fantasies, amusing characters, and detailed drawings. But he wished to dispel the myth that creating books for children is a simple task. In a lecture at the New York Public Library, as quoted in the *Dictionary of Literary Biography,* he addressed the point: "I have the feeling that when I'm asked 'How did you ever think of such a crazy idea?' the person who asked the question felt that the book was thought of in a moment, illustrated in a week, and printed in a day. There is a widespread feeling that doing children's books is a diver-

tissement or a hobby, never a full-time job, and that it's quick and easy. I don't want to discourage people who want to dash off a children's book, but I would like to slow them down a bit."

BIOGRAPHICAL/CRITICAL SOURCES:

BOOKS

Children's Literature Review, Volume 1, Gale, 1976, pp. 62-67.
Dictionary of Literary Biography, Volume 61: *American Writers for Children since 1960: Poets, Illustrators, and Nonfiction Authors,* Gale, 1987, pp. 27-37.
Gillespie, John, and Diana Lembo, *Introducing Books: A Guide for the Middle Grade,* Bowker, 1970, pp. 266, 268.
Klemin, Diana, *The Art of Art for Children's Books,* C. N Potter, 1966.

PERIODICALS

Horn Book, July, 1948, pp. 245-250; December, 1980, pp. 671-676.
Junior Bookshelf, October, 1950, pp. 130-131.
Virginia Kirkus Service, July 1, 1958, p. 377.

OBITUARIES:

PERIODICALS

Publishers Weekly, March 22, 1993.

*   *   *

PERETZ, Don 1922-

PERSONAL: Born October 31, 1922, in Baltimore, MD; son of Haym Victor (a social worker) and Josephine (a teacher; maiden name, Lasser) Peretz; married Janet Bentson, August, 1962 (divorced, 1978); married Maya Wesolowska, May, 1979; children: (first marriage) Debora Dawn, Jonathan Lief; (second marriage) Ervin. *Education:* University of Minnesota, B.A., 1944; Columbia University, M.A., 1952, Ph.D., 1955.

ADDRESSES: Home—1602A Belmont St. N.W., Washington, DC 20009.

CAREER: National Broadcasting Co., New York City, foreign correspondent, 1947-48; American Friends Service Committee, New York City, representative in Israel for relief program for Palestinian refugees, 1949, foreign correspondent for *United Nations World,* 1949-50; U.S. Department of State, New York City, Middle East media evaluator for Voice of America, 1952, regional research analyst, 1954-56; consultant on Middle East, American Jewish Committee, 1956-58; lecturer on Middle East, Long Island University, Brooklyn, NY, and Vassar College, Poughkeepsie, NY, 1959-62; New York State Education Department, Albany, NY, associate director of Office of Foreign Area Studies, 1962-67; State University of New York at Binghamton, professor of political science and director of South West Asia/North Africa Program, 1967-92. Lecturer, Williams College, 1964-65; Fulbright professor, Haifa University, 1979; visiting fellow, U.S. Institute of Peace, 1992. Member of Middle East advisory panel, American Friends Service Committee and U.S. Department of State, 1967-69. *Military service:* U.S. Army, 1943-46.

MEMBER: Middle East Studies Association of North America (member of board of directors, 1970-74), Council on Foreign Relations, Middle East Institute, Institute for Strategic Studies, American Friends Service Committee (member of Middle East panel), National Press Club.

AWARDS, HONORS: Ford Foundation grant, 1952-54; Rockefeller Foundation grant, 1962-63.

WRITINGS:

Egyptian Jews Today, American Jewish Committee, 1956.
Israel and the Palestine Arabs, Middle East Institute, 1958.
Education in the Middle East: A Selected and Annotated Reading Guide, Office of Foreign Area Studies, New York State Education Department, 1963.
The Middle East Today, Holt, 1963, 6th edition, 1993.
(With Hugo Jaeckel) *The Middle East,* Scholastic Book Services, 1964, revised edition, 1967.
(Editor) *The Middle East: Selected Readings,* Houghton, 1968.
(With E. Wilson and R. Ward) *A Palestine Entity: Special Study Number One,* Middle East Institute, 1970.
The Middle East: Regional Study (textbook for grades seven through twelve), Houghton, 1972.
(With Wilson and Ward) *The Palestine State: A Rational Approach,* Kennikat, 1977.
Government and Politics of Israel, Westview, 1979, 2nd edition, 1983.
(With R. D. McLaurin and M. Mughisuddin) *Foreign Policy Making in the Middle East,* Praeger, 1981.
(With Richard U. Moench and Safia K. Mohsen) *Islam: Legacy of the Past, Challenge of the Future,* North River Press, 1984.
The West Bank: History, Politics, Society, and Economy, Westview, 1986.
Intifada: The Palestinian Uprising, Westview, 1991.

Also contributor to numerous books, including *The Contemporary Middle East: Tradition and Innovation,* edited by Benjamin Revlin and J. S. Szyliowicz, Random House, 1965; *Modernization of the Arab World,* edited by Jack Howell Thompson and R. D. Reischauer, Van Nostrand, 1966; *Search for Peace in the Middle East,* edited by Lan-

drum Bolling, Fawcett, 1970; *Arab-Israeli Conflict,* edited by John Norton More, Princeton University Press, 1977; *The Palestinians and the Middle East Conflict,* edited by Gabriel Ben-Dor, Turtledove Press, 1978; *The Arab-Israeli Conflict: Two Decades of Change,* edited by Y. Lukacs and A. M. Battah, Westview, 1988; *Bi-national Israel the Second Republic in the Making,* edited by I. Peleg and O. Seliktar, Westview, 1989; and *New Perspectives on Israeli History,* New York University Press, 1991.

Also contributor of articles to *Reporter, New Republic, Foreign Affairs, United Nations World, Middle East Journal, Christian Century, Commonweal, New Leader, Jewish Social Studies, International Journal, Vital Issues, Orbis, Journal of Palestine Studies, Progressive, Saturday Review, Wilson Quarterly, Journal of Conflict Resolution, Nation,* and other periodicals. Member of board of advisory editors, *Middle East Journal,* 1976—. Member of editorial board, *The Mid-East Annual,* 1981.

*   *   *

PETERS, Ellis
See PARGETER, Edith Mary

*   *   *

POMPER, Gerald M(arvin) 1935-

PERSONAL: Born April 2, 1935, in New York, NY; son of Moe Joseph (a storekeeper) and Celia (Cohen) Pomper; married Marlene Michels (an English professor), January 20, 1957; children: Marc, David, Miles. *Education:* Columbia University, A.B., 1955; Princeton University, M.A., 1957, Ph.D., 1959.

ADDRESSES: Office—Eagleton Institute of Politics, Rutgers University, New Brunswick, NJ 08903.

CAREER: City College (now City College of the City University of New York), New York City, assistant professor of political science, 1959-62; Rutgers University, New Brunswick, NJ, assistant professor, 1962-64, associate professor, 1964-69, professor of political science, 1969—, chairman of political science department, 1974-81. Visiting professor, Nuffield College, Oxford University, and Australian National University; lecturer, United States Information Agency. President of Highland Park, NJ, board of education.

MEMBER: American Political Science Association (president of section on political organizations and parties), American Association of University Professors, New Jersey Political Science Association, Phi Beta Kappa, Kappa Delta Phi.

AWARDS, HONORS: National Convention Faculty fellowship; Fulbright fellowship; distinguished service award, New Jersey Political Science Association; Fulbright professor at Tel-Aviv University.

WRITINGS:

Cases in State and Local Government, Prentice-Hall, 1961.

Nominating the President: The Politics of Convention Choice, Northwestern University Press, 1963, revised edition, 1966.

(Editor with Donald G. Herzberg) *American Party Politics: Essays and Readings,* Holt, 1966.

Elections in America: Control and Influence in Democratic Politics, Dodd, 1968, 2nd edition, 1980.

(Editor and contributor) *Performance of American Government,* Free Press, 1972.

Voters' Choice, Harper, 1975.

(Editor and contributor) *The Election of 1976,* Longman, 1977.

Party Renewal in America, Praeger, 1980.

(With others) *The Election of 1980,* Chatham House, 1981.

American Government, Macmillan, 1983.

(With others) *The Election of 1984,* Chatham House, 1985.

(With others) *The Political State of New Jersey,* Rutgers University Press, 1986.

Voters, Elections and Parties: The Practice of Democratic Theory, Transaction Books, 1988.

(With others) *The Election of 1988,* Chatham House, 1989.

Passions and Interests: Political Party Concepts of American Democracy, University Press of Kansas, 1992.

(With others) *The Election of 1992,* Chatham House, 1993.

Editor, "Praeger Special Studies in American Parties and Elections" series. Contributor of articles to professional journals.

WORK IN PROGRESS: Research on political parties and American biographies.

*   *   *

POPOVSKY, Mark   1922-

PERSONAL: Born July 8, 1922, in Odessa, Ukraine; came to the United States, 1978; naturalized citizen, 1983; son of Alexander (a writer) and Eugene (a biologist; maiden name, Lubarsky) Popovsky; married Vasilevskaya Tatiana, 1948 (divorced, 1968); married Lilya Grinberg (a clerk), November 4, 1969; children: Konstantin, Anna. *Education:* Moscow State University, B.A., 1950, M.A., 1952.

ADDRESSES: Home—65 Hillside Ave., Apt. 5H, New York, NY 10040.

CAREER: Free-lance writer and journalist in Moscow, Russia, 1946-77; free-lance writer in New York, NY, 1978—. Founder of news agency, Mark Popovsky Press, 1977. Fellow of Kennan Institute for Advanced Russian Studies, Woodrow Wilson International Center for Scholars, 1980. Deputy to the editor in chief of Russian language quarterly *Grany* (title means "Facets"), 1984-86. Lecturer on scientific subjects. *Military service:* Soviet Union Army, Medical Science, 1941-45; became lieutenant.

MEMBER: International PEN, Writers-in-Exile.

WRITINGS:

IN ENGLISH TRANSLATION

The Manipulated Science, translated from Russian by Paul Falla, Doubleday, 1979.

The Vavilov Affair, translated by David Floyd, Doubleday, 1981, reprinted with a foreword by Andrei Sakharov, 1984.

IN RUSSIAN

Kogda vrach mechtaet (essays on physicians; title means "When a Doctor Dreams"), Trudovye Rezervy Publishing House, 1957.

Put k serdtzu (on military medicine; title means "The Road to the Heart"), U.S.S.R. Ministry of Defense Publishing House, 1960.

Khozyain solnechnogo zvetka (essays about agriculturists; title means "The Master of the Sunflower"), Molodaya Gvardia Publishing House, 1960.

Razorvannaya pautina (about the helminthologist, Skryabin; title means "The Torn Spider's Web"), Soverskaya Rossia Publishing House, 1962.

Sudba Doktora Khavkina (biography; title means "The Fate of Doctor Khavkin"), Vostochnaya Literatura Publishing House, 1963.

Po sledam otstupaushikh (about epidemiologists; title means "Following in the Tracks of Retreat"), Molodaya Gvardia Publishing House, 1963.

Kormittsy planeti (about agronomists; title means "Food Suppliers of the Planet"), Znaniye Publishing House, 1964.

Pyat dnei odnoi zhizni (novel about Russian Jewish bacteriologist, Khavkin; title means "Five Days of a Life"), Detskaya Literatura Publishing House, 1964.

Dorozhe zolota (on plant breeders; title means "More Precious than Gold"), Detskaya Literatura Publishing House, 1966.

Tisyacha dnei akademika Nikolaya Vavilova (title means "A Thousand Days of the Academician Nikolai Vavilov"), Prostor Journal, 1966.

Nado speshit (biography of geneticist, Nikolai Vavilov; title means "Let Us Hurry!"), Detskaya Literatura Publishing House, 1968.

Nad kartoi chelovecheskikh stradanii (on infectious diseases and epidemiologists; title means "A Map of Human Suffering"), Detskaya Literatura Publishing House, 1971.

Ludi sredi ludei (on Vavilov, Khavkin, and Isayev; title means "Men among Men"), Detskaya Literatura Publishing House, 1972.

Panatzeya, doch Eskulapa (on pharmacologists; title means "Panacea, Daughter of Aesculapius"), Detskaya Literatura Publishing House, 1973.

Russkie muzhiki rasskazyvaiut (title means "Russian Peasants Speak Out"), Overseas Publications Interchange, 1983.

Tretii lishnii: On vona i Sovetskii rezhim (title means "The Superfluous Third: He, She, and the Soviet Regime"), Overseas Publications Interchange, 1985.

Tri zhizni doktora Havkina (title means "Three Lifes of Doctor Havkin"), Jews in the World Culture, 1990.

Delo Akademika Vavilova (title means "The Vavilov Affair"), Kniga Publishing House, 1991.

OTHER

Also author of books written in Russian, *June News: Notes of a Nonaccredited Correspondent,* Posev-Verlag, 1978, and *The Blessed Life of Professor Voino-Yasenetzki, Archbishop and Surgeon,* Young Men's Christian Association Press, 1979. Contributor of about five hundred articles to scientific journals in Russia and to *Samizdat.* Editor of Russian language, *Our Country and the World,* 1986-90.

SIDELIGHTS: Mark Popovsky, a former Soviet journalist and author of books on Russian scientists and their achievements left his native Russia in 1977, after his articles exposing the government's treatment of Soviet botanist Nikolai Vavilov alienated the Soviet government authorities. The text for Popovsky's biography of Vavilov, published in English as *The Vavilov Affair,* was smuggled out of the Soviet Union, together with notes Popovsky had been allowed to take from official KGB files. Popovsky wrote three other books that were scheduled to be published in the Soviet Union and were canceled just before his immigration to the United States—one on the ethics of Soviet scientists, another about the surgeon Seppo, geneticist Khadzhinov, and agronomist Mazlumov, and a third on discoveries of the twentieth century.

Popovsky wrote *CA:* "I left medicine because I had a special interest in literature. For the last twenty-five years my major interest has fallen in the area of ethics of the Russian intelligentsia, particularly Russian scientists. I write nonfiction about those scientists. Unfortunately, I write only Russian."

BIOGRAPHICAL/CRITICAL SOURCES:

PERIODICALS

New York Times, August 20, 1979.
Times Literary Supplement, April 12, 1985.

*   *   *

POWELSON, John Palen 1920-

PERSONAL: Born September 3, 1920, in New York, NY; son of John Abrum (an accountant) and Mary (a nurse; maiden name, Stephen) Powelson; married Alice Roberts, May 31, 1953; children: Cynthia Louise (died, 1992), Judith Carol, Kenneth Byron, Carolyn Rennie, Lawrence Howard. *Education:* Harvard University, A.B., 1941, A.M., 1947, Ph.D., 1950; University of Pennsylvania, M.B.A., 1942. *Religion:* Society of Friends (Quaker).

ADDRESSES: Home—45 Bellvue Dr., Boulder, CO 80302. *Office*—Department of Economics, Campus Box 256, University of Colorado, Boulder, CO 80309.

CAREER: Haskins & Sells (certified public accountants), New York, NY, junior assistant accountant, 1942-44, senior assistant accountant, 1944; University of Pennsylvania, Wharton School of Finance and Commerce, Philadelphia, instructor in accounting, 1944-45; Harvard University, Cambridge, MA, teaching fellow in economics, 1946-48; Price Waterhouse & Co. (certified public accountants), Paris, France, senior accountant, 1948-49; University of Buffalo (now State University of New York at Buffalo), Buffalo, NY, assistant professor of accounting, 1949-50; International Monetary Fund, Washington, DC, economist, 1951-55, assistant chief of training, 1955-58; Johns Hopkins University, School of Advanced International Studies, Washington, DC, professor of economic development, 1958-64; University of Pittsburgh, Graduate School of Public and International Affairs, Pittsburgh, PA, professor of economic development, 1964-66; University of Colorado, Boulder, professor of economics, 1966-91 (retired), research associate, Institute of Behavioral Science, 1968-88.

Certified public accountant, State of New York, 1950. Lecturer in economics, George Washington University, 1953-55; visiting professor, University of La Paz, Bolivia, 1960. Lecturer in Foreign Service Institute, Washington, DC, 1958-64; lecturer in Peace Corps training programs, Putney, VT, 1962-63, and Puerto Rico, 1966; lecturer at numerous universities in Latin America and Africa. Director of Program of National Accounts, Latin American Monetary Studies Center, Mexico, 1963-64; director of economics and lecturer, Inter-American University of the Air (economics radio course in Spanish), 1965-66. Participant in and director of seminars on Latin America and U.S.-Latin American relations, U.S. Department of State, 1964-70. Economic adviser, Minister of Finance, Bolivia, 1959-60; consultant, Inter-American Development Bank, Washington, DC, 1967-68; senior economic adviser, Ministry of Finance and Planning, Kenya, 1972-74; economic consultant, International Institute for Rural Reconstruction, Philippines, 1978.

WRITINGS:

Economic Accounting, McGraw, 1955.

A Survey of Economic Accounting, American Accounting Association, 1958.

National Income and Flow of Funds Analysis, McGraw, 1960.

Latin America: Today's Economic and Social Revolution, McGraw, 1964.

Institutions of Economic Growth: A Theory of Conflict Management in Developing Countries, Princeton University Press, 1972.

(Editor with Philip Ndegwa) *Employment in Africa,* International Labor Office (Geneva), 1973.

(Co-editor) *Economic Development, Poverty, and Income Distribution,* Westview, 1977.

A Select Bibliography of Economic Development, Westview, 1979.

(Co-author) *The Economics of Development and Distribution,* Harcourt, 1981.

(Co-author) *Threat to Development: Pitfalls of the NIEO,* Westview, 1983.

(Co-author) *The Peasant Betrayed: Agriculture and Land Reform in the Third World,* Oelgeschlager, 1986.

Facing Social Revolution: The Personal Journey of a Quaker Economist, Horizon Society Publications, 1987.

Dialogue with Friends, Horizon Society Publications, 1988.

Also author of *The Story of Land: A World History of Land Tenure and Agrarian Reform,* for Oelgeschlager, and of various limited-distribution economic reports.

Also contributor to Piper and Cole, editors, *Post-Primary Education and Political and Economic Development,* Duke University Press, 1964; Cole Blasier, editor, *Constructive Change in Latin America,* University of Pittsburgh Press, 1968; Nicholas Rescher and Kurt Baier, editors, *Values and the Future,* Macmillan, 1969; John H. Adler, editor, *International Development, 1968,* Oceana, 1969; Luis Eugenio di Marco, editor, *International Economics and Development: Essays in Honor of Raul Prebisch,* Academic Press, 1972; Daniel A. Sharp, editor, *U.S. Foreign Policy and Peru,* University of Texas Press, 1972; Barry Poulson and Noel T. Osborn, editors, *U.S.-Mexico Economic Relations,* Westview, 1979; Etelberto Ortiz, Carlos Rozo, Poul-

son, and Osborn, editors, *El Dilema de dos Naciones: Relaciones Economicas entre Mexico y Estados Unidos,* Editorial Trillas, 1981; Ragaei el Mallakh, editor, *OPEC: Twenty Years and Beyond,* Westview, 1981; (With Grace Goodell) Raymond D. Gastil, editor, *Freedom in the World, 1982,* Greenwood, 1982; John D. Montgomery, editor, *The International Dimensions of Land Reform,* Westview, 1984. Contributor of articles and reviews to professional journals.

WORK IN PROGRESS: Our World of Rich and Poor; The Historical Causes of Economic Development.

SIDELIGHTS: Many of John Palen Powelson's works have been translated into Spanish and Portuguese.

*   *   *

PUTNAM, Robert E. 1933-

PERSONAL: Born September 13, 1933, in Mt. Sterling, IL; son of John Harold and Florence Pauline (Curran) Putnam; married Linda Jane Wiant, August 30, 1960; children: Justine, Robbie, Dylan. *Education:* Attended University of Missouri, 1951-52, and Eastern Illinois State College (now Eastern Illinois University), 1955-56; University of Illinois, B.A., 1959; Roosevelt University, M.A., 1969. *Avocational interests:* Hiking, backpacking, cross country skiing, Middle Eastern travel, human rights.

ADDRESSES: Home and office—256 Lester Rd., Park Forest, IL 60446.

CAREER: Western Electric Co., Chicago, IL, associate engineer, 1960-62; American Technical Society, Chicago, technical editor, 1964-69, senior editor, 1969-71, managing editor, 1971-73, editor-in-chief, 1973-80, vice-president, 1980-82. Employees Profit Sharing Plan, American Technical Publishers, trustee, 1980-82. *Military service:* U.S. Army Engineers, 1953-55.

MEMBER: American Vocational Association, American Welding Society, American Society for Training and Development, Illinois Vocational Association.

WRITINGS:

(Editor with Peter Hutchinson) *Young Poets of Illinois,* privately printed, 1959.

Basic Blueprint Reading: Residential, American Technical Society, 1980.

Blueprint Reading and Sketching, American Technical Society, 1980.

Builder's Comprehensive Dictionary, Reston, 1984.

(Co-author) *Intermediate Construction,* Dow Jones-Irwin, 1984.

Construction Blueprint Reading, Reston, 1985.

Building Trades Blueprint Reading, Reston, 1986.

Welding Print Reading, Reston, 1986.

(With Jay Webster) *Motorcycle Operation and Service,* Reston, 1986.

Masonry, Technology Publications, 1988.

Builder's Comprehensive Dictionary, Craftsman, 1989.

REVISER OF EDITIONS

Walter E. Durbahn, *Fundamentals of Carpentry,* Volume 1, American Technical Society, 4th edition, 1967, 5th edition, 1977.

(With John Burnett) *Concrete Block Construction,* American Technical Society, 3rd edition, 1973.

Bricklaying Skill and Practice, American Technical Society, 3rd edition, 1974.

(With G. E. Carlson) *Architectural and Building Trades Dictionary,* American Technical Society, 3rd edition, 1974.

Building Trades Blueprint Reading, Part 3, American Technical Society, revised edition, 1981.

EDITOR

Architectural Drafting, American Technical Society, 1965.

Engineering Drafting Problems, American Technical Society, 1965.

The Instructor and His Job, American Technical Society, 1966.

Machine Trades Blueprint Reading, American Technical Society, 1966.

Building Trades Blueprint Reading, Volume 1, American Technical Society, 1967.

Food Preparation for Hotels, Restaurants and Cafeterias, American Technical Society, 1968.

Fundamentals of Carpentry, Volume 2, American Technical Society, 1969.

Heavy Timber Construction, American Technical Society, 1969.

The Performance-Demonstration Lesson, Part 1 and Part 2, American Technical Society, 1969.

Printing Estimating, American Technical Society, 1970.

Electrical Construction Wiring, American Technical Society, 1970.

Plastering Skill and Practice, American Technical Society, 1971.

OTHER

Contributor of poems and articles to periodicals, including *Road Apple, Northeast, Wild Onion, Sou'wester, Back Roads, School Shop,* and *Industrial Education.*

R

RABIN, A(lbert) I(srael) 1912-

PERSONAL: Surname is pronounced *Ray*-bin; born June 20, 1912, in Merkine, Lithuania; naturalized U.S. citizen; son of David J. (a businessman) and Sarah (Syman) Rabin; married Beatrice Marceau (a laboratory assistant), May 4, 1949; children: Sarah. *Education:* Boston University, B.S., 1935, M.A., 1939, Ph.D., 1939; attended Harvard University, 1937-38. *Religion:* Jewish.

ADDRESSES: Home—2472 Hawthorne Ln., Okemos, MI 48864. *Office*—Department of Psychology, Michigan State University, 334 Baker Hall, East Lansing, MI 48824.

CAREER: Boston State Hospital, Boston, MA, psychologist, 1938-39; New Hampshire State Hospitals and Clinics, Concord, chief psychologist, 1939-47; Michael Reese Hospital, Chicago, IL, research psychologist, 1947-48; Michigan State University, East Lansing, associate professor, 1948-53, professor of psychology, 1953—, Centennial Review Lecturer, 1973. Lecturer at Boston University, 1941, and Harvard Extension of Boston University, 1944; guest professor at Hebrew University (Jerusalem) and Bar-Ilan University, both 1962; professor at City University of New York, 1964-65, and Wright Institute, Berkeley, CA, 1987-90; Fulbright professor at Aarhus University, 1970-71; adjunct professor of psychology at U.S. International University, San Diego. Member of Michigan Governor's Commission on Criminally Sexual Deviates, 1949-53.

MEMBER: American Psychological Association, American Orthopsychiatric Association, American Association for the Advancement of Science, Society for Projective Techniques (president), Midwest Psychological Association.

AWARDS, HONORS: Distinguished contribution award, Society of Personality Assessment, 1977; distinguished faculty award, Michigan State University, 1979.

WRITINGS:

(Editor with M. R. Haworth) *Projective Techniques with Children,* Grune, 1960.
Growing Up in the Kibbutz, Springer Publishing, 1965.
(Editor) *Projective Techniques in Personality Assessment,* Springer Publishing, 1968.
Kibbutz Studies, Michigan State University Press, 1971.
(Editor with Bertha Hazan) *Collective Education in the Kibbutz,* Springer Publishing, 1973.
(Editor) *Clinical Psychology: Issues of the Seventies,* Michigan State University Press, 1974.
(Editor with J. Aronoff, A. Barcley, and R. A. Zucker) *Further Explorations in Personality,* Wiley, 1981.
(Editor) *Assessment with Projective Techniques: A Concise Introduction,* Springer Publishing, 1981.
(With B. Beit Hallahmi) *Twenty Years Later: Kibbutz Children Grown Up,* Springer Publishing, 1982.
(Editor with Aronoff and Zucker) *Personality and the Prediction of Behavior,* Academic Press, 1984.
(Editor) *Projective Techniques for Adolescents and Children,* Springer Publishing, 1986.
(Editor with Aronoff and Zucker) *The Emergence of Personality,* Springer Publishing, 1987.
(Editor with Zucker, R. Emmors, and S. Frank) *Studying Persons and Lives,* Springer Publishing, 1990.

Also contributor to books, including *Personality and the Behavior Disorders,* edited by N. S. Endler and J. McV. Hunt, Wiley, 1984; and *Encyclopedia of Time,* edited by Samuel Macey, 1993. Contributor of more than one hundred articles to psychology journals, including *Journal of Psychology.* Consulting editor, *Journal of Personality As-*

sessment and *Journal of Consulting and Clinical Psychology.*

Growing Up in the Kibbutz has been translated into Japanese, and *Projective Techniques with Children* has been translated into Spanish.

WORK IN PROGRESS: Biblical Psychology, for Springer Publishing; *Temporal Experience.*

SIDELIGHTS: A. I. Rabin once explained his thoughts on writing to *CA* readers: "Actually, I am not a writer by profession. I am an 'academic,' a university professor whose writing is a natural extension of his teaching and his research. As a teacher I have felt that certain areas of information have not been well represented in the available literature. So, to fill the gap, I edited several volumes and contributed to many more. In addition to the intriguing aspect about research—the gratification of one's curiosity—is the communication stage involved in the process. Research is to a considerable extent a social activity; private knowledge does not qualify as research."

He added: "In general, writing helps you clarify your ideas even to yourself, in addition to fulfilling some narcissistic needs. I found it especially pleasing when one of my books (*Growing Up in the Kibbutz*) was translated into Japanese, and another that I edited (*Projective Techniques with Children*) was translated into Spanish."

*   *   *

REDWOOD, John (Alan) 1951-

PERSONAL: Born June 15, 1951, in Dover, England; son of William Charles and Amy (Champion) Redwood; married Gail Felicity Chippington (a barrister), April 12, 1974; children: Catherine Gail Acott. *Education:* Magdalen College, Oxford, B.A. (with honors), 1971; St. Antony's College, Oxford, D.Phil., 1975, M.A., 1975. *Politics:* Conservative. *Religion:* Church of England.

ADDRESSES: Office—House of Commons, London SW1, England.

CAREER: Oxford College, Oxford, England, fellow of All Souls College, 1972—; Member of Parliament for Wokingham, 1987—, parliamentary Under Secretary of State for Corporate Affairs, 1989-90, minister of state for trade and industry, 1990-92, minister of state for local government and inner cities, 1992—. Merchant banker, 1973-87. Member of Oxfordshire County Council, 1973-77, and Centre for Policy Studies; head of Prime Minister's Policy Unit, 1983-85. Member of board of governors of Oxford Polytechnic, 1974-77, and Silverthorne School, 1980-83; director of Norcros PLC, 1985, and N. M. Rothschild & Sons, 1986.

WRITINGS:

Reason, Ridicule, and Religion: The Age of Enlightenment in England, Thames & Hudson, 1976.
Public Enterprise in Crisis, Basil Blackwell, 1980.
(With Michael Grylls) *National Enterprise Board: A Case for Euthanasia,* Centre for Policy Studies, 1980.
(With John V. Hatch) *Value for Money Audits: New Thinking on the Nationalized Industries,* Centre for Policy Studies, 1981.
(With Hatch) *Controlling Public Industries,* Basil Blackwell, 1982.
Going for Broke: Gambling with Taxpayers' Money, Basil Blackwell, 1983.
Rolling Back the Frontiers of the State, Selsdon Group, 1986.
Popular Capitalism, Routledge & Kegan Paul, 1987.
Can Growth and Greenery Be Reconciled?, CPC, 1989.
Conservative Philosophy in Action, CPC, 1992.
New Life for Old Cities, CPC, 1993.

Also author of *Popular Capitalist Manifesto,* 1988. Contributor to *The Conservative Opportunity,* edited by Lord Blake and John Patten, Macmillan, 1976. Contributor of articles to periodicals, including London *Times, Spectator,* and *Daily Telegraph.*

WORK IN PROGRESS: Research on economic and political change: *Global Capitalism and Local Identity.*

SIDELIGHTS: In his book *Going for Broke: Gambling with Taxpayers' Money,* John Redwood examines the British government's intervention in industry. He once told *CA:* "My work on public enterprise in the United Kingdom is related to my political activities within the Conservative party and involves me in a number of policy questions concerning the future of government involvement in industry." About the book, Jeremy Hardie notes in the *Times Literary Supplement,* "His case studies, mostly taken from the 1970s, recall an era of muddled accountancy, false optimism, and terror in the face of change which nobody would want to bring back." Citing the British shipbuilders, DeLorean Motors, and British Rail ventures, Redwood concludes that government measures have proven ineffective at sparking recoveries in ailing industries and claims that "it would be better if [the government] did not intervene at all." In Hardie's judgment, Redwood's "excellent and stimulating book would have been even better had he had the time and space to deal more explicitly with how the private sector manages industrial change." Hardie contends finally that "we have certainly learned a great deal since the 1970s; but the lesson is not, in the end, quite the self-denial which Mr. Redwood advocates."

BIOGRAPHICAL/CRITICAL SOURCES:

PERIODICALS

Times Literary Supplement, May 4, 1984.

* * *

REED, Emmett X.
See KING, Florence

* * *

REIBEL, Paula
See SCHWARTZ, Paula

* * *

REID, John Phillip 1930-

PERSONAL: Born May 17, 1930, in Weehawken, NJ; son of Thomas Francis (a physician) and Teresa (Murphy) Reid. *Education:* Georgetown University, B.S.S., 1952; Harvard University, LL.B., 1955; University of New Hampshire, M.A., 1957; New York University, LL.M., 1960, J.S.D., 1962. *Politics:* Republican. *Religion:* Roman Catholic.

ADDRESSES: Home—23 Newmarket Rd., Durham, NH 03824. *Office*—School of Law, New York University, 40 Washington Sq., New York, NY 10012.

CAREER: United States District Court, Concord, NH, law clerk, 1956-57; New York University, School of Law, New York City, instructor, 1960-62, assistant professor, 1962-64, associate professor, 1964-66, professor of legal history, 1966—.

MEMBER: American Society of Legal History (treasurer and director), New Hampshire Bar Association.

AWARDS, HONORS: Guggenheim Foundation fellow, 1980; Huntington Library fellow, 1980; National Endowment for the Humanities fellow, 1984.

WRITINGS:

Chief Justice: The Judicial World of Charles Doe, Harvard University Press, 1967.
An American Judge: Marmaduke Dent of West Virginia, New York University Press, 1968.
A Law of Blood: The Primitive Laws of the Cherokee Nation, New York University Press, 1969.
A Better Kind of Hatchet: Law, Trade, and Diplomacy in the Cherokee Nation during the Early Years of Euro-

pean Contact, Pennsylvania State University Press, 1976.
In a Defiant Stance: The Conditions of Law in Massachusetts Bay, the Irish Comparison, and the Coining of the American Revolution, Pennsylvania State University Press, 1977.
In a Rebellious Spirit: The Argument of Facts, the Liberty Riot, and the Coming of the American Revolution, Pennsylvania State University Press, 1979.
Law for the Elephant: Property and Social Behavior on the Overland Trail, Huntington Library, 1980.
In Defiance of the Law: The Standing-Army Controversy, the Two Constitutions, and the Coming of the American Revolution, University of North Carolina Press, 1981.
(Editor) *The Briefs of the American Revolution: Constitutional Arguments between Thomas Hutchinson, Governor of Massachusetts Bay, and James Bowdoin for the Council and John Adams for the House of Representatives,* New York University Press, 1981.
(With William E. Nelson) *The Literature of American Legal History,* Oceana, 1985.
Constitutional History of the American Revolution, University of Wisconsin Press, Volume 1: *The Authority of Rights,* 1986, Volume 2: *The Authority to Tap,* 1987, Volume 3: *The Authority to Legislate,* 1991.
The Concept of Liberty in the Age of the American Revolution, University of Chicago Press, 1988.
The Concept of Representation in the Age of the American Revolution, University of Chicago Press, 1989.

Contributor to books, including *Studies in Comparative Criminal Law,* edited by Edward M. Wise and Gerhard O. W. Mueller, C. C. Thomas, 1975; and *The Cherokee Indian Nation: A Troubled History,* edited by Duane King, University of Tennessee Press, 1979. Also contributor of numerous articles to law journals. Editor, *Annual Survey of American Law,* 1963, 1964.

WORK IN PROGRESS: Volume four of *Constitutional History of the American Revolution.*

BIOGRAPHICAL/CRITICAL SOURCES:

PERIODICALS

American Historical Review, April, 1980; October, 1981.
Journal of American History, March, 1982.
New England Quarterly, June, 1982.

* * *

RICE, C(harles) David 1941-

PERSONAL: Born December 4, 1941, in Atlanta, GA; son of Thomas L. (a laborer) and Mary Lou (a laborer;

maiden name, Powell) Rice; married Judith Kay Wammack (a homemaker), December 15, 1972; children: Maggie, Whitney, Merideth, Virginia, Kathleen. *Education:* Georgia State College (now University), B.A., 1966; Vanderbilt University, M.A., 1968; Emory University, Ph.D., 1973. *Politics:* Democrat. *Religion:* Episcopal.

ADDRESSES: Home—525 Southeast Brentwood Dr., Lee's Summit, MO 64063. *Office*—Department of History, Central Missouri State University, Warrensburg, MO 64093.

CAREER: West Georgia College, Carrollton, instructor in history, 1967-68; high school social studies teacher in College Park, GA, 1968-69; Central Missouri State University, Warrensburg, assistant professor, 1973-80, associate professor, 1980-84, professor of history, 1984—. *Military service:* U.S. Army, 1959-62.

MEMBER: American Historical Association, Southern Historical Association, Phi Alpha Theta.

AWARDS, HONORS: Author's Award from Missouri State Historical Society, 1978, for "Pierre Chouteau: Entrepreneur as Indian Agent"; Vivian Paladin Writer's Award from *Montana*, 1979, for "The Return of the Mandan Chief"; honorable mention, Thorpe Menn Writer's Award for *The First Chouteaus;* Byler Distinguished Faculty Award, Central Missouri State University, 1988.

WRITINGS:

(With William E. Foley) *The First Chouteaus: River Barons of Early St. Louis,* University of Illinois Press, 1983.

(With Arthur McClure) *Ronald Reagan: A Bibliography of the Movie Years,* Mellen Press, 1988.

(With McClure) *A Bibliographical Guide to the Works of William Inge,* Mellen Press, 1991.

Contributor to history journals.

WORK IN PROGRESS: Pierre Chouteau, Jr.: A Life, with William E. Foley, for University of Missouri Press, 1994; *The King's Defender: A Life of Jacques Cazales.*

SIDELIGHTS: C. David Rice told *CA:* "The study of history is a liberation. It frees the mind from the shackles of the present. It lifts the imagination from the daily. It also expands the possible by recreating what has been done and inspiring us to what must be done. At the same time it liberates, however, it reminds us that we are duty bound—to God, to humanity, to the wisdom of submission to God's will.

"My selection of topics is related to my education and training. I am interested in France because of the years I spent there in the military and later in research. My principal interest, historically, is the French Revolution, and

the proposed work on Cazales goes back to my dissertation days. He was an exceptional French royalist, an outstanding speaker for the royalist cause in the National Constituent Assembly and, later, after emigrating to England, one of the few sensible counter-revolutionaries in the royalist underground. He has been neglected, perhaps because he was on the losing side. His capacities and his forceful articulation of the opposition view, however, warrant him a place in the history of the French Revolution.

"I came to the Chouteaus by way of William Foley, a friend and colleague, who asked me to do the biography with him. The amount of research was formidable, and we complemented one another by his knowledge of Spanish and my smattering of French. It was a good project for me, as European research was far away and very expensive, and because I was fortunate to work with an accomplished historian on an important work. The Chouteaus were the founding family of St. Louis, the pioneers of commerce in the trans-Mississippi West, and the undisputed leaders of the French frontier community between 1764 and 1803. More than most, their careers illustrate the connection between commerce and frontier settlement and expansion. The second Chouteau book will complete the saga of a remarkable family whose mercantile and political career helped to shape early America.

"The Reagan bibliography was designed as a research tool for future biographers of President Reagan and for students of Mr. Reagan in general. It deals with Reagan's first career, his years in show business. Dr. McClure, a film historian of national prominence, asked me to work on the project with him, and, once again, I think we proved to be a good team. We include thousands of references, obvious and obscure, and we believe it to be as complete a record of publications, films, statements, and other references to Ronald Reagan before his political career as can presently be compiled. In the future when scholars undertake studies of the president's early days, we hope this work will be available to them. It will be an invaluable asset.

"The William Inge work was a joyful undertaking for both McClure and me. I grew up watching movie versions of Inge's plays. His was an honest and genuine voice of America at mid-century. Indeed, there is still much to experience in his creations.

"My work is rather eclectic, but it is so by both choice and necessity. On the one hand, I am interested in many things and not afraid to follow my interests where they take me. On the other, my research and writing may be typical of historians teaching in regional state universities in these times. We must make do with the circumstances in which we find ourselves in a time of declining interest in and support of the humanities. Good scholarship is not dependent upon a choice academic position; it is dependent upon the love of research and composition and the belief that such things still matter."

*   *   *

RIPLEY, Randall B(utler) 1938-

PERSONAL: Born January 24, 1938, in Des Moines, IA; son of Henry Dayton and Aletha (Butler) Ripley; married Grace Anne Franklin, October 15, 1974; children: Frederick Joseph, Vanessa Gail. *Education:* DePauw University, B.A., 1959; Harvard University, M.A., 1961, Ph.D., 1963.

ADDRESSES: Home—2685 Berwyn Rd., Columbus, OH 43221. *Office*—Department of Political Science, Ohio State University, Columbus, OH 43210.

CAREER: Brookings Institution, Washington, DC, research fellow, 1962-63; U.S. House of Representatives, Office of the Democratic Whip, Washington, DC, intern, 1963; Brookings Institution, research assistant, 1963-64, research associate, 1964-67; Ohio State University, Columbus, associate professor, 1967-69, professor of political science, 1969—, chairperson of department, 1969-91, acting dean, College of Social and Behavioral Sciences, 1992—.

Consultant to Department of Housing and Urban Development, Senate Committee on Rules and Administration, House Select Committee on Committees, Commission on Population Growth and the American Future, Commission on the Organization of the Government for the Conduct of Foreign Policy, Employment and Training Administration, National Council on Employment Policy, Commission on the Operation of the Senate, IMPACT, Inc., Manpower Demonstration Research Corp., Urban Systems Research and Engineering, Inc., MDC, Inc., Mathematics Policy Research, Ohio Management Training Institute, National Alliance of Business, Michigan Employment Training Institute, and Illinois Management Training Institute.

MEMBER: American Political Science Association (secretary, 1978; president of public policy section, 1991-92), Midwest Political Science Association, Southern Political Science Association, Policy Studies Organization (member of council, 1977-79), Phi Beta Kappa.

AWARDS, HONORS: Woodrow Wilson fellow, 1959-60; Danforth Foundation fellow, 1959-63; Brookings Research fellow, 1962-63.

WRITINGS:

(Editor) *Public Policies and Their Politics,* Norton, 1966.

(With Charles O. Jones) *The Role of Political Parties in Congress: A Bibliography and Research Guide,* University of Arizona Press, 1966.

Party Leaders in the House of Representatives, Brookings Institution, 1967.

Majority Party Leadership in Congress, Little, Brown, 1969.

Power in the Senate, St. Martin's, 1969.

The Politics of Economic and Human Resource Development, Bobbs-Merrill, 1972.

Kennedy and Congress, General Learning Press, 1972.

(Editor with Theodore J. Lowi) *Legislative Politics, U.S.A.,* 3rd edition (Ripley was not associated with earlier editions), Little, Brown, 1973.

American National Government and Public Policy, Free Press, 1974.

Congress: Process and Policy, Norton, 1975, 4th edition, 1988.

(Editor with wife, Grace A. Franklin, and contributor) *Policy Making in the Federal Executive Branch,* Free Press, 1975.

(With G. A. Franklin) *Congress, the Bureaucracy, and Policy in the United States,* Dorsey, 1976, 5th edition, 1991.

(Editor with G. A. Franklin) *National Government and Policy in the United States,* F. E. Peacock, 1977.

(With Samuel C. Patterson and Roger H. Davidson) *A More Perfect Union,* Dorsey, 1979, 4th edition, 1989.

(With G. A. Franklin) *Policy Implementation and Bureaucracy,* Dorsey, 1982, 2nd edition, 1986.

(With G. A. Franklin) *CETA: Politics and Policy, 1973-1982,* University of Tennessee Press, 1984.

Policy Analysis in Political Science, Nelson-Hall, 1985.

(Editor with Elliot E. Slotnick) *Readings in American Government and Politics,* McGraw, 1989, 2nd edition, Wadsworth, 1993.

(Editor with James M. Lindsay, and contributor) *Congress Resurgent: Foreign and Defense Policy on Capitol Hill,* University of Michigan Press, 1993.

Also author of monographs on CETA for U.S. Department of Labor, Employment and Training Administration, 1977-79. Contributor to books, including *Congress and Urban Problems,* edited by Frederick N. Cleaveland and others, Brookings Institution, 1969; and *The Presidency: Studies in Public Policy,* edited by Steven A. Shull and Lance T. LeLoup, King's Court, 1979. Editor of "Sage Professional Papers in American Politics," 1973-77. Contributor of articles and book reviews to political science journals, including *Midwest Journal of Political Science, American Political Science Review, Political Science Quarterly, Review of Politics, Legislative Studies Quarterly,* and *Western Political Quarterly.* Former member of editorial board, *Journal of Politics, American Politics Quarterly,* and *Policy Studies Journal.*

ROBERSON, Jennifer 1953-
(Jennifer O'Green, Jennifer Roberson O'Green; Jay Mitchell, a pseudonym)

PERSONAL: Surname is pronounced "*robb*-erson"; born October 26, 1953, in Kansas City, MO; daughter of Donald and Shera (a literary agent's reader) Roberson; married Mark O'Green (a designer-manager in computer games systems), February 16, 1985. *Education:* Northern Arizona University, B.S., 1982. *Religion:* Christian. *Avocational interests:* Professional dog obedience trainer, exhibitor of Labrador retrievers and Cardigan Welsh corgis in conformation and obedience.

ADDRESSES: Home—Chandler, AZ. *Agent*—Russ Galen, Scott Meredith Literary Agency, 845 Third Ave., New York, NY 10022.

CAREER: Wyoming Eagle, Cheyenne, WY, investigative reporter, 1976; Farnam Companies, Phoenix, AZ, advertising copywriter, 1977; writer, 1982—. Speaker at schools, colleges, professional writers' organizations, and science fiction conferences.

MEMBER: Science Fiction and Fantasy Writers of America, Novelists, Inc., Cardigan Welsh Corgi Club of America, Southern California Cardigan Welsh Corgi Club, Bluebonnet Cardigan Welsh Corgi Club.

AWARDS, HONORS: Selected best new fantasy author, *Romantic Times* (magazine), 1984, for *Shapechangers;* Junior Alumni Achievement Award, Northern Arizona University, 1985; selected best new historical author, *Romantic Times,* 1987; outstanding young woman of America, 1988; selected as reviewer's choice annual top fantasy novel, *Science Fiction Chronicle,* 1989, for *Sword-Dancer* and *Sword-Singer,* and 1990, for *Sword-Maker;* certificate of appreciation, city of Tempe, 1990, for outstanding volunteer service to the community; Jubilee Year Distinguished Alumnus Award, Northern Arizona University, 1990.

WRITINGS:

Smoketree, (romantic suspense), Walker & Co., 1985.
(Under pseudonym Jay Mitchell) *Kansas Blood,* Zebra Books, 1986.
(Under name Jennifer O'Green) *Royal Captive,* Dell, 1987.
Lady of the Forest, Zebra Books, 1992.
Glen of Sorrows, Bantam, in press.

"CHRONICLES OF THE CHEYSULI" FANTASY SERIES

Shapechangers, DAW, 1984.
The Song of Homana, DAW, 1985.
Legacy of the Sword, DAW, 1986.
Track of the White Wolf, DAW, 1987.
A Pride of Princes, DAW, 1988.

Daughter of the Lion, DAW, 1989.
Flight of the Raven, DAW, 1990.
A Tapestry of Lions, DAW, 1992.

"SWORD-DANCER SAGA" FANTASY SERIES

Sword-Dancer, DAW, 1986.
Sword-Singer, DAW, 1988.
Sword-Maker, DAW, 1989.
Sword-Breaker, DAW, 1991.

OTHER

Work represented in several anthologies, including *Sword and Sorceress,* volumes 1-8, edited by Marion Zimmer Bradley, DAW, 1984-91; *Spell Singers,* edited by A. B. Newcomer, DAW, 1988; *Herds of Thunder, Manes of Gold,* edited by Bruce Coville, Doubleday, 1989; *Horse Fantastic,* edited by Martin Greenberg and Rosalind Greenberg, DAW, 1991; and *Christmas Bestiary,* edited by M. Greenberg and R. Greenberg, DAW, 1992. Also columnist (as Jennifer Roberson O'Green) for *Corgi Quarterly* and *AKC Gazette.* Contributor to periodicals, including *Fantasy, Writer,* and *Aboriginal Science Fiction.*

WORK IN PROGRESS: Prince of Night, Queen of Sleep, and *King of Dreams,* all for DAW; two untitled historical novels for Bantam.

SIDELIGHTS: Jennifer Roberson commented to *CA:* "I was fortunate to grow up in a family of readers; our genealogical chart is filled with bookaholics, including the renowned English author Thomas Hardy. An only child of divorced parents, I discovered very young that siblings and best friends were available at all times between the pages of favorite novels. It was not at all unusual for three generations—grandfather, mother, and daughter—to gather in the living room and while away the hours engrossed in our books of the moment."

This environment also helped foster Roberson's enjoyment of writing. By age fourteen she had already completed her first novel and received her first rejection slip. Even though she was hurt by the rejection, she did not allow it to quell her desire to be published. During the next fourteen years, she wrote three more unpublished novels before settling into the fantasy genre. Her first fantasy series "Chronicles of Cheysuli" was begun while in college; it was during her final semester that she received notice of the sale of her first book, *Shapechangers.*

After completing several more published novels, Roberson began another series, creating characters who would help break the traditional, sexist role females had often been assigned by other fantasy authors. Roberson explained: " . . .I wanted to write about a man who, in meeting up with a strong, competent woman in the same line of work, has his consciousness raised during a dangerous journey that taxes them physically as well as emotionally. My personal description was 'Conan the Barbarian meets Gloria Steinem'; the true title was *Sword-Dancer,* and it was published in 1986. It became the first of four novels featuring my Tracy/Hepburn-like duo."

Roberson expanded her work into other genres by writing a western novel from a woman's viewpoint and a contemporary romantic suspense novel. She added: "But one thing I'd always wanted to try—another 'someday' dream—was a big, sprawling, mainstream historical epic. Russ [Galen, Roberson's agent] won me the chance when I submitted an outline/sample chapter package to him in which I proposed to write a reinterpretation of the Robin Hood legend, but with a twist—I wanted to emphasize Marian's point of view and contribution to the legend. Russ auctioned the manuscript and secured me an outstanding mainstream deal. I then spent the next year of my life researching and writing *my* version of the story; in actuality, a 'prequel' to the familiar legend. I wanted very much to write the story of how the legend came to be; the tale of how seven very different people from a rigidly stratified social structure came to join together to fight the inequities of medieval England. To me, the key was *logic*—I interwove historical fact with the fantasy of the classic legend, and developed my own interpretation of how things came to be. I wanted to come to know all of these people; to climb inside their heads and learn what motivated them to do what they did."

Roberson pointed out: "One thing I have learned along the way that a writer, to be successful, must *write;* she cannot be satisfied with what she has already done, but must look ahead to what she will do. A writer completely satisfied with her work ceases to grow, and stunts her talent. It is far more important to *write* than it is *to have written.*"

BIOGRAPHICAL/CRITICAL SOURCES:

PERIODICALS

Fantasy Review, August, 1984, p. 22; October, 1985, p. 19; September, 1986, p. 30; June, 1987, p.40.
Locus, November, 1989, p. 57; July, 1990, p. 55; June, 1991, p. 50.
Science Fiction Chronicle, March, 1986, p. 36; December, 1986, p. 50; January, 1987, p. 40; October, 1987, p. 27; March, 1989, p. 39; December, 1989, p. 39.
Voice of Youth Advocates, October, 1988, p. 196; August, 1989, p. 167; December, 1990, p. 301.

*   *   *

RODMAN, Maia
See WOJCIECHOWSKA, Maia (Teresa)

ROOTHAM, Jasper (St. John) 1910-1990

PERSONAL: Born November 21, 1910, in Cambridge, England; died May 30, 1990; son of Cyril Bradley (a composer) and Rosamond (Lucas) Rootham; married Joan McClelland (a dancer and ballet teacher), September 25, 1944; children: John Daniel, Catherine Virginia. *Education:* St. John's College, Cambridge, M.A. *Religion:* Church of England. *Avocational interests:* Farming, travel, music, ornithology.

ADDRESSES: Home—30 West St., Wimborne Minster, Dorset BH21 1JS, England.

CAREER: British civil servant, serving with Ministry of Agriculture, Colonial Office, and Treasury, 1933-40; employee at Bank of England, London, England, 1946-67; Lazard Brothers & Co. Ltd., London, managing director, 1967-75. Member of general advisory council, British Broadcasting Corp. *Military service:* British Army, 1940-46; became colonel; mentioned in dispatches.

MEMBER: International PEN.

WRITINGS:

Miss Fire, Chatto & Windus, 1946.
Demi-Paradise, Chatto & Windus, 1960.

POETRY

Verses 1928-72, Rampant Lions Press, 1973.
The Celestial City, Two Jays Press, 1975.
Reflections from a Crag, Unit Offset Press, 1978.
Selected Poems, Weybrook Press, 1980.
Stand Fixed in Steadfast Gaze, The Lomond Press, 1981.
Affirmation (long narrative poem), The Lomond Press, 1982.
Lament for a Dead Sculptor and Other Poems, The Wimborne Bookshop, 1985.
Saluting the Colours: Religion and Race, The Conclusion, Unit Offset Press, 1990.

SIDELIGHTS: Jasper Rootham once told *CA:* "I have now been writing poetry for sixty years and more. I do so because I must, in order to record ideas and observations which have come my way during a life of varied experience. I try in my poetic writing to develop my native tongue—English—to describe developing events and emotions in language which can be understood but remains essentially poetical, rhythmic, and musical. The task is to distinguish the ugly from the beautiful and having done that, to assert the beautiful which, unlike the ugly, is eternal."

[Date of death provided by wife, Joan Rootham.]

ROSENBERG, Maxine B(erta) 1939-

PERSONAL: Born August 6, 1939, in New York, NY; daughter of Stanley (in sales) and Martha (Kleinman) Schick; married Paul A. Rosenberg (a dentist), June 5, 1960; children: Mark, David, Seth, Karin. *Education:* Hunter College of the City University of New York, A.B., 1961, M.S., 1969; attended Columbia University, 1963. *Religion:* Jewish. *Avocational interests:* Jazz, gourmet cooking, sewing, aerobics, travel (Europe, Israel, Mexico, and the Caribbean).

ADDRESSES: Home—1 Washington Square Village, Apt. 9B, New York, NY 10012. *Agent*—Gina MacCoby, 1123 Broadway, Suite 1010, New York, NY 10010.

CAREER: Elementary school teacher in New York, NY, 1961-64; special education teacher in Peekskill, NY, 1977; free-lance writer, 1977—.

AWARDS, HONORS: My Friend, Leslie was named a notable book by American Library Association, 1984; *Being Adopted* was named a notable book by the American Library Association, 1985.

WRITINGS:

JUVENILES

My Friend, Leslie: The Story of a Handicapped Child, Lothrop, 1983.
Being Adopted, Lothrop, 1984.
Being a Twin, Having a Twin, Lothrop, 1985.
Making a New Home in America, Lothrop, 1986.
Living in Two Worlds, Lothrop, 1986.
Artists of Handcrafted Furniture, Lothrop, 1988.
Finding a Way: Living with Exceptional Brothers and Sisters, Lothrop, 1988.
Not My Family: Sharing the Truth about Alcoholism, Bradbury, 1988.
Growing Up Adopted, Bradbury, 1989.
Talking about Stepfamilies, Bradbury, 1990.
On the Mend: Getting Away from Drugs, Bradbury, 1991.
Brothers and Sisters, Clarion, 1991.
Living with a Single Parent, Bradbury, 1992.

Contributor to magazines and newspapers.

SIDELIGHTS: Maxine B. Rosenberg informed *CA:* "My education centered on teaching the visually handicapped and emotionally disturbed. I have also taught the non-handicapped.

"I am most interested in the feelings and experiences of people, of people dealing with difficult situations in life and how they have learned to cope and move on.

"A handicapped child, an adopted one, a twin, a child emigrating from another country, a Holocaust survivor, all have joys and pains they want to share. By putting their feelings in books, I offer people in special situations the comfort of knowing there are others like them with the same or similar agonies and ecstasies.

"One of my greatest joys is visiting schools and talking to children about my books—how they came to be written and the 'behind-the-scenes' cover-ups and near crises. I love speaking to adult groups too, but when I can get a child to feel comfortable enough to express his feelings before others, I've achieved what I've hoped for in my writing.

"Before I begin writing any of my books, I do extensive reading on the subject. Usually I focus on the areas of psychology and sociology to gain further understanding about people I intend to interview. Before I actually interview subjects, I meet with a psychologist to go over the questions I propose to ask. Since many of my books deal with sensitive issues, I want to be careful not to offend people or be intrusive in their private lives.

"Through my readings, interviewing, and writing, I am the one who grows most in the understanding of children. Often what I hypothesized does not hold true. Children in all types of situations are resilient. If given love, care, warmth, and a secure home, with time they are able to overcome handicaps and discrimination—and often with a sense of humor.

"Sometimes before I investigate a subject, I hold a notion that children in a particular stressful situation will be scarred and not be able to develop positive feelings about themselves. Over and over again, I am proven wrong—happily! I love hearing the laughter and joy of kids who with patience, time, and hard work have found happiness where they never dreamed it existed."

BIOGRAPHICAL/CRITICAL SOURCES:

PERIODICALS

New York Times, March 16, 1984.

* * *

ROSSI, Peter Henry 1921-

PERSONAL: Born December 27, 1921, in New York, NY; son of Peter M. (a truck driver) and Elizabeth (Porcelli) Rossi; married Norma Westen, October 4, 1942 (divorced, 1951); married Alice Schaerr, September 29, 1951; children: Peter Eric, Kristin Alice, Nina Alexis. *Education:* City College (now City College of the City University of New York), B.S., 1943; Columbia University, Ph.D., 1951. *Politics:* Democratic Socialist.

ADDRESSES: Home—34 Stagecoach Rd., Amherst, MA 01002. *Office*—Department of Sociology, University of Massachusetts, Amherst, MA 01003.

CAREER: Columbia University, New York City, instructor in sociology and research associate, 1950-51; Harvard University, Cambridge, MA, assistant professor of sociology, 1951-55; University of Chicago, Chicago, IL, professor of sociology, 1955-67, National Opinion Research Center, director, beginning 1960; Johns Hopkins University, Baltimore, MD, professor of sociology, 1967-74; University of Massachusetts at Amherst, professor of sociology, 1974-92, professor emeritus, 1992—, director of Social and Demographic Research Institute. *Military service:* U.S. Army, 1942-45; became technical sergeant.

MEMBER: American Sociological Association (president, 1979-80), American Association for the Advancement of Science (fellow), American Academy of Arts and Sciences (fellow).

AWARDS, HONORS: Awards from political behavior committee, Social Science Research Council, 1957, 1958; Reflective Year Fellowship, Carnegie Corp., 1965; Myrdal Award, Evaluation Research Society, 1980; Common Wealth Award, 1985; Campbell Award, Policy Studies Association, 1985.

WRITINGS:

Why Families Move, Free Press, 1956, 2nd edition, Sage Publications, 1980.

(With Robert A. Dentler) *The Politics of Urban Renewal,* Free Press, 1962.

(With Andrew M. Greeley) *The Education of Catholic Americans,* Aldine, 1966.

(With Bruce J. Biddle) *New Media and Education,* Aldine, 1967.

(Editor) *Ghetto Revolts,* Transaction Books, 1972, 2nd edition, 1973.

(Editor with Walter Williams) *Evaluating Social Programs,* Academic Press, 1972.

(With others) *The Roots of Urban Discontent,* Wiley, 1974.

(With Katharine C. Lyall) *Reforming Public Welfare,* Russell Sage, 1976.

(With Richard A. Berk) *State Elites and Prison Reform,* Ballinger, 1977.

(With Howard G. Freeman and Sonia Wright) *Evaluation: A Systematic Approach,* Sage Publications, 1979.

(With James D. Wright) *After the Cleanup,* Sage Publications, 1979.

(With Berk and Kenneth J. Lenihan) *Money, Work, and Crime,* Academic Press, 1980.

(With Wright) *Social Science and Natural Hazards,* ABT Books, 1981.

(With S. Mork) *Measuring Social Judgments,* Sage Publications, 1982.

Natural Hazards and Public Choice, Academic Press, 1982.

Applied Sociology, Jossey-Bass, 1983.

Victims of the Environment, Plenum, 1983.

Handbook of Survey Research, Academic Press, 1983.

Under the Gun, Aldine, 1983.

Collecting Evaluation Data, Sage Publications, 1985.

(With Wright) *The Armed Criminal in America: A Survey of Incarcerated Felons,* National Institute of Justice, U.S. Department of Justice, 1985.

(With Wright) *Armed and Considered Dangerous: A Survey of Felons and Their Firearms,* Aldine, 1986.

(With G. A. Fisher and G. Willis) *The Condition of the Homeless of Chicago,* SADRI and National Opinion Research Center, 1986.

Without Shelter: Homelessness in the 1980s, Priority Press Publications, 1989.

Down and Out in America: The Origins of Homelessness, University of Chicago Press, 1989.

(With Jeffry A. Will) *Public Opinion on Environmental Problems and Programs in Massachusetts,* Environmental Institute and Social and Demographic Research Institute, University of Massachusetts at Amherst, 1989.

(With wife, Alice S. Rossi) *Of Human Bonding: Parent-Child Relations across the Life Span,* Aldine, 1990.

(With Berk) *Thinking about Evaluation,* Sage Publications, 1990.

Evaluating Family Preservation Services, Edna McConnell Clark Foundation, 1991.

(Editor with Huey-tsyh Chen) *Using Theory to Improve Program and Policy Evaluations,* Greenwood Press, 1992.

Co-editor with William F. Whyte of Dorsey Press series in anthropology and sociology, 1959-61; editor of "Quantitative Studies in Social Relations," Academic Press, 1974-83. Contributor of nearly two hundred articles to professional journals. Editor, *American Journal of Sociology,* 1957-58, and *Social Science Research,* 1974—; associate editor, *American Sociological Review,* 1957-60, and *American Sociologist,* 1965-68.

Evaluation: A Systematic Approach has been published in German and Spanish.

*   *   *

RUBIA BARCIA, Jose 1914-
(Juan Bartolome de Roxas)

PERSONAL: Born July 31, 1914, in Galicia, Spain; became American citizen, 1957; married Eva Lopez, 1945; children: Elena, Adela. *Education:* University of Granada, Lic. Fil. y Let. (with honors), 1934; International University of Santander, graduate study, 1935.

ADDRESSES: Office—Department of Spanish and Portuguese, University of California, 5303 Rolfe Bldg., Los Angeles, CA 90024.

CAREER: University of Granada, Granada, Spain, lecturer in Spanish literature, 1935-36; affiliated with University of Havana, Havana, Cuba, 1939-43; Princeton University, Princeton, NJ, lecturer in Spanish literature, 1943-44; University of California, Los Angeles, lecturer, 1947-49, professor of contemporary Spanish literature, 1949-85, professor emeritus, 1985—, chairman of department of Spanish and Portuguese, 1963-69.

AWARDS, HONORS: Research fellow at Escuela de Estudios Arabes, 1933-36; Guggenheim fellow, 1961; National Book Award for translation, 1978; elected member of Real Academia Galega, 1983; "Liceo Rubia Barcia" was created in his native city, El Ferrol, Spain, 1988.

WRITINGS:

A Bibliography and Iconography of Valle Inclan, 1866-1936, University of California Press, 1960.
(Editor and contributor, with M. A. Zeitlin) *Unamuno: Creator and Creation,* University of California Press, 1967.
(Translator, with Clayton Eshleman) *Vallejo's Spain: Take This Cup from Me,* Grove, 1974.
(Editor, with Selma Margaretten, and contributor) *Americo Castro and the Meaning of Spanish Civilization,* University of California Press, 1976.
Studies in Honor of Jose Rubia Barcia, edited by Roberta Johnson and Paul C. Smith, University of Nebraska Press, 1982.

IN SPANISH

(Under pseudonym Juan Bartolome de Roxas, except for epilogue) *Tres en Uno: Auto Sacramental a la Usanza Antigua,* La Veronica, 1940, 2nd edition, Do Castro, 1992.
Umbral de Suenos, Orbe Publications, 1961, 2nd edition, Anthropos (Barcelona), 1989.
Lengua y Cultura (three volumes), Holt, 1967.
Prosas de Razon y Hiel, Casuz, 1976.
A Aza Enraizada: Cantigas de Bendizer (poems), Do Castro, 1981.
Mascaron de Proa, Do Castro, 1983.
Memoria de Espana (essays), Pre-Textos, Volume 1, 1989, Volume 2, 1991.
Con Luis Bunuel en Hollywood y despues, Do Castro, 1992.

OTHER

Contributor to books, including *Valle Inclan: Centennial Studies,* edited by R. Gullon, University of Texas, 1968; *Homenaje a Gabriel Miro,* edited by Roman del Cerro,

Caja de Ahorros, 1979; and *Al Amor de Larrea,* edited by Diaz de Guerenu, Pre-Textos, 1985. Contributor to language journals.

*   *   *

RUBIN, Dorothy   1932-

PERSONAL: Born February 11, 1932, in New York, NY; daughter of Harry and Clara (Schweller) Schleimer; married Arthur I. Rubin, August 24, 1950; children: Carol Anne (Mrs. Smith), Sharon Anne (Mrs. Seth Johnson). *Education:* Rutgers University, B.A., 1959, M.Ed., 1961; Johns Hopkins University, Ph.D., 1968.

ADDRESSES: Home—917 Stuart Rd., Princeton, NJ 08540. *Office*—Department of Reading and Language Arts, Trenton State College, Hillwood Lakes, CN 4700, Trenton, NJ 08650.

CAREER: Teacher at public schools in New Jersey, 1959-62; Coppin State College, Baltimore, MD, assistant professor of education, 1962-63; Towson State College (now University), Baltimore, assistant professor of education, 1963-66; Rollins College, Winter Park, FL, adjunct professor of education, 1968-69; Trenton State College, Trenton, NJ, associate professor, 1969-73, professor, 1973—. Lecturer and conductor of workshops; producer and host of "Quest," broadcast on Cable Television Network of New Jersey. Speaker at conferences and workshops. Consultant to Study Group on Textbooks, Commission on Excellence, U.S. Department of Education, 1984, and to many schools systems.

MEMBER: International Reading Association, National Council of Teachers of English, Kappa Delta Pi, Phi Kappa Phi.

AWARDS, HONORS: CAPE Awards for best educational program, 1989, 1991, and 1992.

WRITINGS:

Teaching Elementary Language Arts, Holt, 1975, 5th edition, in press.
Gaining Word Power, Macmillan, 1978, 3rd edition, 1993.
The Vital Arts: Reading and Writing, Macmillan, 1979, 2nd edition published as *Writing and Reading: The Vital Arts,* 1983.
Reading and Learning Power, Macmillan, 1980, 3rd edition, 1990.
The Teacher's Handbook of Reading-Thinking Exercises, Holt, 1980.
The Primary Grade Teacher's Language Arts Handbook, Holt, 1980.
The Intermediate Grade Teacher's Language Arts Handbook, Holt, 1980.
Gaining Sentence Power, Macmillan, 1981.

The Teacher's Handbook of Writing-Thinking Exercises, Holt, 1981.

The Teacher's Handbook of Primary Grade Reading-Thinking Exercises, Holt, 1982.

Vocabulary Expansion I, Macmillan, 1982, 2nd edition, 1991.

Vocabulary Expansion II, Macmillan, 1982.

A Practical Approach to Teaching Reading, Holt, 1982, 2nd edition, Allyn & Bacon, 1993.

Diagnosis and Correction in Reading Instruction, Holt, 1982, Allyn & Bacon, 2nd edition, 1991.

Teaching Reading and Study Skills in Content Areas, Holt, 1983, Allyn & Bacon, 2nd edition published as *Reading and Study Skills in Content Areas,* 1992.

(Contributor) *Harper & Row English* (for kindergarten through eighth grade), Harper, 1983.

(Contributor) *Holt English* (teacher's guide; for grades nine through twelve), Holt, 1983.

"Basic Language Skills for Adults Power English" series, ten books, Prentice Hall, 1989-90.

"Power Vocabulary: A Basic Vocabulary Book for Adults" series, five books, Prentice Hall, 1992.

Also author and recorder of audio cassette tape program "Power English"; author of several audio cassette tapes. Originator and author of educational video games, "Mind Bind," "Moon Master," and "Quick Scramble." Contributor of articles to education and psychology journals, including *Psychological Reports, Journal of Social Psychology, English Record, Journal of Reading,* and *Audiovisual Instruction;* also contributor of Opinion/Editorial and comment articles to *USA Today.*

WORK IN PROGRESS: Comprehension Power: A Basic Comprehension Book for Adults; textbook revisions; tradebooks; in-depth articles for *USA Today.*

SIDELIGHTS: Dorothy Rubin told *CA:* "What can be more gratifying than to have someone write to tell you how helpful your books are? I try to write substantive textbooks that are readable and enjoyable, and one of my greatest joys is when students say that they can't believe that they are reading a textbook. I also feel that I have staying power because I am not an extremist."

Gaining Word Power has been translated into Korean.

*   *   *

RUNTE, Alfred 1947-

PERSONAL: Born April 16, 1947, in Binghamton, NY; son of Paul and Erika (Brinkman) Runte; married Christine Ann Salo, 1984. *Education:* State University of New York at Binghamton, B.A., 1969; Illinois State University, M.A., 1971; University of California, Santa Barbara,

Ph.D., 1976. *Avocational interests:* Public speaking, media commentary, and activism on behalf of rail and environmental projects nationwide, with specific interest in the reestablishment of rail passenger service to the national parks.

ADDRESSES: Home and office—7716 34th Ave. N.E., Seattle, WA 98115.

CAREER: University of California, Santa Barbara, lecturer in history and environmental studies, 1973-78; Smithsonian Institution, Washington, DC, fellowship specialist at Woodrow Wilson International Center for Scholars, 1978-79; Baylor University, Waco, TX, assistant professor of environmental studies and assistant director of Institute of Environmental Studies, 1979-80; University of Washington, Seattle, assistant professor of history and adjunct assistant professor of environmental studies, 1980-87; seasonal ranger, naturalist, and historian, Yosemite National Park, 1980-83; full-time writer, public historian, and environmental consultant, 1987—. Member of editorial board, University of Alaska Press, 1991—. Consultant to California Department of Transportation and Burlington Northern, Inc.

MEMBER: National Parks and Conservation Association (member of board of trustees, 1992—), Organization of American Historians, Forest History Society, Western History Association, National Association of Railroad Passengers (member of board of directors, 1974-80), Phi Alpha Theta.

AWARDS, HONORS: Frederick K. Weyerhauser Award from *Journal of Forest History,* 1978, for article, "The National Park Idea: Origins and Paradox of the American Experience."

WRITINGS:

National Parks: The American Experience, University of Nebraska Press, 1979, 2nd edition, 1987.

Trains of Discovery: Western Railroads and the National Parks, Northland Press, 1984, revised edition, Roberts Rinehart, 1990.

Yosemite: The Embattled Wilderness, University of Nebraska Press, 1990.

Public Lands, Public Heritage: The National Forest Idea, Roberts Rinehart, 1991.

(Co-editor and contributor) *Yosemite and Sequoia: A Century of California National Parks,* University of California Press, 1993.

Author of numerous monographs, pamphlets, and government reports. Also contributor to numerous books, including *The American Environment: Perceptions and Policies,* edited by J. Wreford Watson and Timothy O'Riordan, Wiley, 1976; *The American Land,* Smithsonian Books, 1979; *That Awesome Space: Human Interac-*

tion with the Intermountain Landscape, edited by Richard E. Hart, Westwater Press, 1981; and *Niagara: Two Centuries of Changing Attitudes, 1697-1901,* edited by Jeremy Elwell Adamson, Corcoran Gallery of Art, 1985. Contributor of articles to scholarly journals, popular magazines, and newspapers including *California History, Journal of the West, National Parks, Montana, Journal of Forest History, Los Angeles Times, Washington Post,* and *Pacific Northwest Quarterly.*

WORK IN PROGRESS: National Park Railroad Guide; Following the Great Frontier: Reflections on Western History; California: An Environmental History; The Romantic Terminus: The Railroad as Image-Maker in the American West.

SIDELIGHTS: Alfred Runte told *CA:* "As an academic historian, my ability to influence public opinion was rarely appreciated. In coming years, however, I doubt if the general public will accept—or fully support—the writing of history for its own sake. The public wants results from its universities, and I subscribe to that mission. Meanwhile, I am enjoying my new life and career as a private historian, specializing in contracts for government agencies, corporations, and other public clients. Public history has rejuvenated my interest and enthusiasm—reawakening the excitement I initially discovered back in 1959, when my mother took my brother and me on a summer camping trip through Yellowstone, Grand Teton, Crater Lake, Yosemite, and Grand Canyon national parks.

"I simply cannot turn my back on the professional outgrowth—and obligations—of that experience. If the parks, indeed the environment, are to survive, critical scholars must never forget who supports their work in the first place."

BIOGRAPHICAL/CRITICAL SOURCES:

PERIODICALS

American Historical Review, December, 1991.
Forest and Conservation History, October, 1992.

*   *   *

RYDER, Jonathan
   See LUDLUM, Robert

S

SABINE, Gordon Arthur 1917-

PERSONAL: Surname is pronounced Say-bine; born February 10, 1917, in Brockton, MA; son of Charles Arthur (a manufacturer) and Esther (Carey) Sabine; married Lois Eleanor Freiburg, June 26, 1941 (divorced, 1973); married Patricia Lundblade Williams (a writer), May 15, 1980; children: (first marriage) Ellen Jean, Gordon Arthur, Robert Allan, Roger Malcolm. *Education:* University of Wisconsin—Madison, A.B., 1939, M.A., 1941; University of Minnesota—Twin Cities, Ph.D., 1949.

ADDRESSES: Home—2625 East Southern Ave., C-102, Tempe, AZ 85282. *Office*—113 Hayden Library, Arizona State University, Tempe, AZ 85282-1006.

CAREER: Lynchburg News, Lynchburg, VA, reporter, 1931-35; *Wisconsin State Journal,* Madison, reporter and copy editor, 1939-42; University of Kansas, Lawrence, instructor in journalism, 1945-47; University of Oregon, Eugene, assistant professor of journalism, 1948-50, dean of School of Journalism, 1950-55; Michigan State University, East Lansing, dean of College of Communication Arts, 1955-60, vice-president for special projects, 1960-71; Illinois State University, Normal, special assistant to the president, 1971-72; University of Iowa, Iowa City, director of School of Journalism, 1972-75; Virginia Polytechnic Institute and State University, Blacksburg, professor of journalism, 1975-84; Arizona State University, Tempe, professor of journalism, 1985, special assistant to the dean for Arizona State University Libraries, 1986—. *Military service:* U.S. Army, 1942-45; became first lieutenant.

MEMBER: American Political Science Association, Association for Education in Journalism, Association of Accredited Schools and Departments of Journalism (president, 1954-55), Sigma Delta Chi, Omicron Delta Kappa.

AWARDS, HONORS: Fellow of Carnegie Corp., 1953.

WRITINGS:

Quiz for College Presidents, American College Testing Program, 1969.

If You Listen This Is What You Can Hear, American College Testing Program, 1970.

Teachers Tell It: Like It Is, Like It Should Be, American College Testing Program, 1970.

The Folks in the Newsroom, Virginia Polytechnic Institute/State University, 1977.

The Newspaper in Society, Virginia Polytechnic Institute/State University, 1977.

(With John Eure) *Do You or Don't You? A Casebook in Journalism Ethics,* Virginia Polytechnic Institute/State University, 1977.

Broadcasting in Virginia, Virginia Polytechnic Institute/State University, 1979.

(With wife, Patricia L. Sabine) *Books That Made the Difference: What People Told Us,* Library Professional Publications, 1983.

Monsignor Donohoe: A Memoir, Arizona State University, 1988.

(With Donald Riggs) *Libraries in the '90s,* Oryx, 1988.

Tom Chauncey: A Memoir, Arizona State University, 1989.

Dean Ellis Smith: A Memoir, Arizona State University, 1990.

Rabbi Plotkin: A Memoir, Arizona State University, 1992.

G. Homer: A Biography of the President of Arizona State University, 1960-1969, Arizona State University, 1992.

Culver "Bill" Nelson: A Memoir, Arizona State University, 1993.

Phyllis Steckler and the Oryx Press, Arizona State University, 1993.

Nan Pyle: Payson's Unhappy Millionaire, Arizona State University, 1993.

Father Burkhardt: A Memoir, Arizona State University, 1993.

Also author of *Advanced Tennis Tactics,* 1946. Author of "Youthpoll America," a column for Chicago Tribune-New York News Syndicate, 1976-77. Contributor to *Media Studies Journal.*

WORK IN PROGRESS: The Norton Reader: A Memoir of a Book.

*   *   *

SANDS, Kathleen M.
See SANDS, Kathleen Mullen

*   *   *

SANDS, Kathleen Mullen
(Kathleen M. Sands)

PERSONAL: Born in Portland, OR. *Education:* Fort Wright College, B.A., 1961; University of Arizona, M.A., 1974, Ph.D., 1977.

ADDRESSES: Office—Department of English, Arizona State University, Tempe, AZ 85281.

CAREER: Arizona State University, Tempe, assistant professor, 1977-81, associate professor, 1981-85, professor of English, 1985—; Fulbright professor in Salonika, Greece, 1985-86. Editorial assistant for Rocky Mountain Review, 1979-80; visiting professor at University of Arizona, summer, 1981, and Portland State University, 1989-90; member of Arizona Humanities Council, 1984-86.

MEMBER: Modern Language Association of America, American Folklore Society, Society for American Indian Studies and Research.

WRITINGS:

(With Gretchen M. Bataille) *American Indian Women: Telling Their Lives,* University of Nebraska Press, 1984.
Chameria Mexicana: An Equestrian Folk Tradition, University of Arizona Press, 1993.

EDITOR

(And author of background material under name Kathleen M. Sands) *Refugio Savala, The Autobiography of a Yaqui Poet,* University of Arizona Press, 1980.
Circle of Motion: Contemporary Indian Literature of Arizona, Arizona Historical Foundation, 1990.
(With Bataille) *American Indian Women: A Research Guide,* Garland Publishing, 1991.

Also senior editor of *People of Pascua,* by Edward H. Spicer, University of Arizona Press, 1988.

OTHER

Contributor to scholarly journals, including *American Indian Quarterly, American Indian Culture and Research Journal,* and *Telescope.*

SIDELIGHTS: American Indian Women: Telling Their Lives, which Kathleen Mullen Sands wrote with Gretchen M. Bataille, "marks a turning point in developing literature on American Indian women," praised Roxanne Dunbar Ortiz in a review for *Western American Literature.* An analytical study of autobiographies and biographies of American Indian women, the book examines the methods of recording the women's life histories as well as the role of women in Native American culture. The authors earned recognition from Ortiz for establishing a guide for future studies on the subject while a critic for *Booklist* lauded their efforts to dispel stereotypical images of American Indians.

As editor of Refugio Savala's *The Autobiography of a Yaqui Poet,* Sands was commended by reviewer Geary Hobson in the *American Book Review* for the "long and extremely helpful" background information and interpretations she contributed. The critic likewise praised Sands's comprehensive bibliography of Savala's writings, both published and unpublished, as an "invaluable aid" and ranked the book among other distinguished works of Native American literature. In conclusion Hobson deemed *The Autobiography of a Yaqui Poet* "a remarkable addition . . . that Refugio Savala and the Yaqui people can be proud of."

BIOGRAPHICAL/CRITICAL SOURCES:

PERIODICALS

American Book Review, July, 1982.
Booklist, October 1, 1984.
Western American Literature, fall, 1984.

*   *   *

SARGENT, Pamela 1948-

PERSONAL: Born March 20, 1948, in Ithaca, NY. *Education:* State University of New York at Binghamton, B.A., 1968, M.A., 1970.

ADDRESSES: Home—Box 486, Johnson City, NY 13790. *Agent*—Joseph Elder Agency, P.O. Box 298, Warwick, NY 10990.

CAREER: Honigsbaum's, Albany, NY, sales clerk and model, 1964-65; Endicott Coil Co., Inc., Binghamton,

NY, solderer on assembly line, 1965; Towne Distributors, Binghamton, sales clerk, 1965; State University of New York at Binghamton, typist in library cataloging department, 1965-66, teaching assistant in philosophy, 1969-71; Webster Paper Co., Albany, office worker, 1969; freelance writer and editor, 1971—.

MEMBER: Fiction Writers of America, Authors Guild, Authors League of America, Science Fiction Writers of America, Amnesty International U.S.A., National Wildlife Federation.

AWARDS, HONORS: Best book for young adults designation, American Library Association (ALA), 1983, for *Earthseed;* finalist, Nebula Award, 1992, for novelette "Danny Goes to Mars."

WRITINGS:

SCIENCE FICTION; FOR ADULTS

Cloned Lives, Fawcett, 1976.
Starshadows (short stories), introduction by Terry Carr, Ace Books, 1977.
The Sudden Star, Fawcett, 1979, published in England as *The White Death,* Futura, 1980.
Watchstar, Pocket Books, 1980.
The Golden Space, Timescape, 1982.
The Alien Upstairs, Doubleday, 1983.
The Mountain Cage (chapbook), Cheap Street, 1983.
Venus of Dreams, Bantam, 1986.
The Shore of Women, Crown, 1986.
The Best of Pamela Sargent (short stories), edited by Martin H. Greenberg with a foreword by Michael Bishop, Academy Chicago, 1987.
Alien Child, Harper, 1988.
Venus of Shadows (sequel to *Venus of Dreams*), Doubleday, 1988.
Ruler of the Sky, Crown, 1993.

SCIENCE FICTION; FOR CHILDREN AND YOUNG ADULTS

Earthseed, Harper, 1983.
Eye of the Comet, Harper, 1984.
Homesmind, Harper, 1984.

Also contributor of stories for young readers to anthologies, including "A Friend from the Stars," in *The Missing World, and Other Stories;* "The Invisible Girl," in *The Killer Plants, and Other Stories;* and "Aunt Elvira's Zoo," in *Night of the Sphinx, and Other Stories,* all edited by Roger Elwood, Lerner, 1974.

EDITOR

Women of Wonder: Science Fiction Stories by Women about Women, Vintage, 1975.
Bio-Futures: Science Fiction Stories about Biological Metamorphosis, Vintage, 1976.
More Women of Wonder: Science Fiction Novelettes by Women about Women, Vintage, 1976.
The New Women of Wonder: Recent Science Fiction Stories by Women about Women, Vintage, 1978.
(With Ian Watson) *Afterlives: Stories about Life after Death,* Vintage Book, 1986.

OTHER

Contributor to numerous science-fiction and fantasy anthologies, including *Wandering Stars,* edited by Jack Dann, Harper, 1972; *Two Views of Wonder,* edited by Thomas N. Scortia and Chelsea Quinn Yarbro, Ballantine, 1973; and *Ten Tomorrows,* edited by Roger Elwood, Fawcett, 1973. Contributor to *Twentieth-Century Science-Fiction Writers,* St. James Press, 1986. Contributor to science-fiction and fantasy magazines, including *Amazing Stories, Futures, Fantasy and Science Fiction, Isaac Asimov's Science Fiction Magazine, Science-Fiction Studies,* and *Twilight Zone;* contributor to *Washington Post Book World.* Author of afterword to *The Fifth Head of Cerberus,* by Gene Wolfe, Ace Books, 1976; *Fantasy Annual V,* edited by Terry Carr, Timescape, 1982; and *The Road to Science Fiction: From Here to Forever,* Volume IV, edited by James Gunn, Signet, 1982.

Sargent's works have been translated into several foreign languages, including Dutch, French, German, Japanese, and Spanish.

Sargent's manuscripts are included in the David Paskow Science Fiction Collection at Temple University, Philadelphia, PA.

ADAPTATIONS: "The Shrine" (short story) was adapted for an episode of *Tales from the Darkside,* 1986.

SIDELIGHTS: "Although I write science fiction, my primary interest is in characters—people," short-story writer, editor, and novelist Pamela Sargent once told *CA.* "Through them I try to explore possible future societies." Although she never intended to write science fiction (SF) exclusively, Sargent has found the genre to be an effective medium through which to examine aspects of human experience and emotion, as well as a way to challenge the long-held stereotypical portrayal of women as passive components rather than active participants of change. From the time her first short story "Landed Minority" was published in 1970, Sargent has continuously written and edited works through which she has acquired a position of significance in her chosen genre. She has earned the respect of critics for both bringing to light and attempting to counteract sexual stereotypes within the field of science fiction literature.

As Jeffrey M. Elliot noted of her shorter works in *Twentieth-Century Science Fiction Writers,* "Sargent eschews prediction; she *does,* however, seek plausibility. The imaginary settings of her stories are typified by an underlying reality and possess a solid grounding in what we know of science (and people) today. In that sense, Sargent resembles several of the 'hard' science-fiction writers who ground their work solidly in science, but, unlike many such writers, she also emphasizes characterization." Fourteen of her short stories from the period 1972 to 1984 are collected in *The Best of Pamela Sargent*. John Gregory Betancourt commented in the *Washington Post Book World* that "there are enough gems here to keep anyone reading, and together they provide a good preview of one of the genre's best—and most overlooked—writers."

Sargent's concern with characterization has at its roots her feminist perspective on what she considers a genre dominated by men. "Most science fiction has been written by men, and they still form a majority of the writers today," she stated in her introduction to *Women of Wonder: Science Fiction Stories by Women about Women*. Noting that the readership of SF has traditionally been composed to a great extent by "young men or boys who stop reading SF regularly when they get older," she added: "We can perhaps understand why the writers of science fiction took for granted certain presumptions, as did almost everyone else in the society around them. Women, and racial minorities as well, suffered under these assumptions. If science was the province of males, it was also the province of white males. It is more common now to find black people and other minorities represented as characters in SF stories, although the number of black SF writers can be counted on the fingers of one hand. Women characters have been around longer but usually in unimportant roles."

The first of her anthologies to directly address this issue, *Women of Wonder* exhibits a "broadening perspective" according to a critic in the *Washington Post Book World;* Sargent's introduction contains "some acute observations about sex roles in traditional science fiction." Several reviewers, however, felt that the anthology fell short of its goal. While noting that *Women of Wonder* "contains few clinkers and many stories well worth reading," Algis Budrys commented in a series of reviews for the *Magazine of Fantasy and Science Fiction* that "Sargent's editorial motive is to be polemical, rather than entertaining. The stories [in *Women of Wonder*] are only incidentally to divert, empathize with, or parade before the reader. They are blows against the masculine SF establishment [and Sargent] uses the sledgehammer approach as basic to her method of argument." Critics responded more positively in their reviews of succeeding "Women of Wonder" volumes. *More Women of Wonder*, noted Budrys, is "everything [*Women of Wonder*] claimed to be. . . . Its selections, while not always excellent, are exactly representative of what has been available in the field." The critic

praised the work as "a good book, a valuable book, and in the bargain a very nice collection of reading." And an *English Journal* reviewer commented positively on the "realistic" characters in 1978's *New Women of Wonder*.

In addition to writing short stories for both adults and young people, Sargent is the author of several well-received novels. *Cloned Lives,* published in 1976 and her first long work of fiction, was based on "Clone Sister" and "A Sense of Difference," two short stories she had previously written. The novel examines the consequences of cloning as a possible way to achieve immortality, and explores the self-perception of both the clones and the person undergoing genetic duplication. Novels *The Sudden Star,* written three years later, *Watchstar,* and *The Golden Space* each deal with the unique perspective that children might bring to the future. According to Elliot, "for Sargent, youthful experiences somehow seem more vivid, passionate, and exciting than what happens to many people later in life, when the decisions they made while young have overtaken them and set their lives along a certain path." Sargent's three novels specifically written for children, *Eye of the Comet, Homesmind,* and *Earthseed*—listed as an ALA 1983 Best Book for Young Adults—also reflect her interest in directing science fiction to a youthful audience. As she wrote in *Women of Wonder,* "Science fiction novels for young adults and children can also offer role models for younger readers. This has happened often enough in the past for boys." Sargent believes that the genre has the ability and obligation to address young women equally.

In a departure from her usual writing in the science fiction genre, Sargent's 1993 novel, *Ruler of the Sky,* has a historical focus. Taking as its subject the life of the Mongol leader Genghis Khan, Sargent's novelization of Khan's early life necessitated a search into a number of scholarly works as well as contemporary sources in an attempt to piece together the early history of one of history's most renown villains. "To enter Mongol minds and to tell their stories, the women's in particular, was still an act of imagination," Sargent told *CA,* describing the process of writing historical fiction, "and when the story required that I take some liberties with the facts, I took them. But the tale I told is rooted in what some of those Mongols remembered and believed about their great leader."

"Sargent creates enough complex, convincing, layered societies and strong, believable characters to keep a dozen lesser novelists stocked up for years," Orson Scott Card commented in his review of *The Shore of Women* in *The Magazine of Fantasy and Science Fiction.* "Other SF writers might consider enacting sumptuary laws to keep writers with so much intelligent imagination from displaying it so ostentatiously." In a series of topics that include genetic engineering, the psychological effects of cloning and immortality, facing a society and ecology declining into oblivion, space colonization; in short, the effects of technology on the individual, Sargent positions her characters and lets them evolve. In *Venus of Shadows,* a sequel to her 1986 novel *Venus of Dreams,* the Venus Project is reaching fruition: the planetary surface is becoming habitable due to a device which has cloaked it from the sun to reduce Venus's temperature and the addition of hydrogen molecules to the oxygen-rich Venusian atmosphere to form water. Pioneers must now create a society on this new world: establishing a political framework, religions, and a new social order. Gerald Jonas criticized the work in the *New York Times Book Review,* remarking that although the plot addressed many thought-provoking questions, "the answers to these . . . are buried between layer after layer of stiff, unyielding prose. . . . Characters keep lecturing one another about current and past events in a manner clearly designed to inform not one another but eavesdropping readers." Other reviewers, however, have praised the work, particularly the humanity of its characters. "This is the generational saga writ large indeed," Greg Benford commented in the *Los Angeles Times Book Review.* "Yet the ponderous sway of worlds and human masses does not cloak the personal tales that Sargent follows with a patient, insightful eye."

Sargent believes that the responsibility for change in the science-fiction genre lies in large part with the reading public. "If more women begin to take an interest in SF and the scientific and futurological ideas involved, publishers will have an interest in publishing and writers in writing novels exploring such ideas from different perspectives," she noted in the introduction to *Women of Wonder.* "If, however, publishers and writers can do better with the old stereotypes and have little reason to believe that readers want anything else, women will remain minor characters, and familiar roles and prejudices will be a major part of the literature." "It is up to us, both as writers and readers," she added, "to begin exploring the unfamiliar, to acquaint ourselves with scientific and futurological concerns, and give serious thought to what we are and what we would like to become."

BIOGRAPHICAL/CRITICAL SOURCES:

BOOKS

Elliot, Jeffrey M., and R. Reginald, *The Work of Pamela Sargent: An Annotated Bibliography and Guide,* Borgo Press, 1988.
Elliot, Jeffrey M., "Pamela Sargent," in *Twentieth-Century Science-Fiction Writers,* edited by Curtis C. Smith, St. James Press, 1986, pp. 626-27.
Rubens, Philip M., "Pamela Sargent," in *Dictionary of Literary Biography,* Volume 8: *Twentieth-Century*

American Science-Fiction Writers, Gale, 1981, pp. 96-99.
Sargent, Pamela, editor, *Women of Wonder: Science Fiction Stories by Women about Women,* Vintage, 1975.

PERIODICALS

Analog Science Fiction/Science Fact, October, 1979.
English Journal, May, 1978.
Fantasy Newsletter, October, 1982.
Horn Book, June, 1984.
Los Angeles Times Book Review, January 29, 1989.
Magazine of Fantasy and Science Fiction, November, 1975; November, 1976; June, 1977; June, 1987, pp. 53-54.
New York Times Book Review, May 4, 1975; May 11, 1980; January 18, 1987; February 26, 1989.
Psychology Today, April, 1975.
Publishers Weekly, April 26, 1976; January 3, 1986; September 26, 1986.
Washington Post Book World, February 16, 1975; November 23, 1986; November 29, 1987.

*   *   *

SAYLES, John (Thomas) 1950-

PERSONAL: Born September 28, 1950, in Schenectady, NY; son of Donald John (a school administrator) and Mary (a teacher; maiden name, Rausch) Sayles. *Education:* Williams College, B.A., 1972. *Politics:* "Survivalist." *Religion:* "Roman Catholic Atheist."

ADDRESSES: Home—Hoboken, NJ. *Agent*—Robinson, Weintraub, Gross and Associates, Inc., 8428 Melrose Place, Suite C, Los Angeles, CA 90069.

CAREER: Writer, director, actor, playwright, and film editor. Director of films, including *The Return of the Secaucus Seven,* Libra, 1980; and *Eight Men Out,* Orion, 1988. Director of plays, including *New Hope for the Dead* and *Turnbuckle,* both 1981. Actor in films and on TV, including *Something Wild,* Orion, 1986; *Hard Choices,* Lorimar, 1986; and *Unnatural Causes,* NBC, 1986. Writer and creative consultant for *Shannon's Deal,* NBC, 1990-91. Director of music videos. Has also worked as hospital orderly, plastic molder, meat worker, and day laborer.

AWARDS, HONORS: MacArthur Foundation Fellow, 1983-88; Academy Award nomination, best original screenplay, 1993, for *Passion Fish;* National Book Award and National Book Critics Circle nominations, both for *Union Dues;* O. Henry Award for short story.

WRITINGS:

SCREENPLAYS

Piranah, New World, 1978.

The Lady in Red (also known as *Guns, Sin, and Bathtub Gin*), New World, 1979.

Battle Beyond the Stars, New World, 1980.

(And actor, editor, and director) *The Return of the Secaucus Seven,* Libra, 1980.

Alligator (adapted from story by Sayles with Frank Ray Perilli), BLC, 1981.

(With Terence H. Winkless) *The Howling* (adapted from novel by Gary Brandner), AVCO-Embassy Pictures Corporation, 1981.

(With Richard Maxwell) *The Challenge,* CBS, 1982.

(And director) *Baby, It's You* (adapted from story by Amy Robinson), Paramount, 1983.

(And actor, editor, and director) *Lianna,* United Artists Classics, 1983.

(And actor, editor, and director) *The Brother from Another Planet,* Cinecom International, 1984.

The Clan of the Cave Bear (adapted from novel by Jean Auel), Warner Brothers, 1986.

(And actor and director) *Matewan,* Cinecom International, 1987.

Wild Thing (adapted from story by Sayles with Larry Stamper), Atlantic, 1987.

(And actor and director) *Eight Men Out* (adapted from book by Eliot Asinof), Orion, 1988.

Breaking In, Samuel Goldwyn, 1989.

(And director) *City of Hope,* Samuel Goldwyn, 1991.

(And director) *Passion Fish,* Miramax, 1992.

TELEPLAYS

A Perfect Match, CBS, 1980.

(With Susan Rice, based on stories by Grace Paley) *Enormous Changes at the Last Minute,* PBS, 1983.

Unnatural Causes, NBC, 1986.

PLAYS

New Hope for the Dead, produced Off-Off-Broadway, 1981.

Turnbuckle, produced Off-Off-Broadway, 1981.

NOVELS

Pride of the Bimbos, Little, Brown, 1975.

Union Dues, Little, Brown, 1977.

Los Gusanos, HarperCollins, 1991.

OTHER

The Anarchists' Convention & Other Stories (short stories), Little, Brown, 1979.

Thinking in Pictures: The Making of the Movie Matewan (non-fiction), Houghton, 1987.

Also contributor to *New Republic, New York Times Book Review,* and *Film Comment.*

SIDELIGHTS: John Sayles "has carved out a reputation as one of the country's best independent filmmakers," according to David Streitfeld of the *Washington Post Book World.* A noted screenwriter and director, Sayles has also acted in and edited several of his features. Though many of his movies are considered somewhat out-of-the-mainstream, Sayles has developed a loyal following for what *Los Angeles Times* film writer Dale Pollock termed "a series of highly personal, idiosyncratic films."

Interestingly, Sayles first made his mark on the literary, not cinematic, scene, with the publication of an O. Henry Award-winning short story and the critically acclaimed *Union Dues,* a novel that examines the social and political climate of the United States in the late 1960s. The story concerns widower and West Virginia miner Hunter McNatt, who follows his runaway son Hobie to Boston during the height of the hippie movement in that city. Hunter's prolonged search for Hobie, who has sought refuge in a commune, forces him to take a factory job, and Hunter's interactions with characters at both locations serve to illustrate the social divisiveness that existed at that time. "In a way," wrote John Leonard in a *New York Times* review, "this ambitious, textured novel is about two cities: the city of children, playing at revolution in 1969, and the city of workers, blue-collar workers, trying to survive in spite of their own, corrupt unions. . . . 'Disunion,' rather than union, is the subject matter of *Union Dues.*" In his profile of Sayles, Streitfeld added: "It's one of the best novels about that impassioned era, achieving a rare balance between sympathy for all sorts of political persuasions while simultaneously keeping some critical distance."

Following the publication of *Union Dues,* Sayles went to work as a screenwriter, penning scripts for low-budget action pictures like *Piranha, The Lady in Red,* and *Battle Beyond the Stars.* He then used the profits from those projects to bankroll his first film, *The Return of the Secaucus Seven.* Like *Union Dues, The Return of the Secaucus Seven* examines characters whose lives have been shaped by the Sixties. The film depicts the reunion of a group of East Coast friends who, as college students, had attempted to join a protest at the Pentagon. The seven students only got as far as Secaucus, New Jersey, however, where they were arrested on trumped-up charges. Ten years after the event, the friends have come together to reminisce about the past and reflect on the changes that have taken place in their lives.

Made for a mere $60,000, the picture earned many times that and enjoyed some critical success. Vincent Canby of the *New York Times* found *The Return of the Secaucus Seven* to be "an honest, fully realized movie," and Gene Siskel of the *Chicago Tribune* remarked that "in its best moments *Secaucus Seven* comes across with a documentary-like force." Siskel added that a particular strength of

Secaucus Seven was its nonjudgemental tone: "The film's only position is a wise recognition that the young men and women who were of . . . college age in the '60's, lived in a very exciting time, a time of enormous questioning. That is their legacy, and this little film about a 10-year reunion honors that legacy."

After the release of *Secaucus Seven,* Sayles returned to his initial source of income—writing screenplays for other directors. While some of those projects, like *The Challenge,* met with critical resistance, they contributed needed dollars for Sayles' directorial efforts. Described by Pollock as a "typewriter for hire," Sayles admitted, "My motive for doing as many [screenplays] as I do is to get money for my own pictures." Due to his scriptwriting efforts during this period, Sayles was able to finance and direct several films. They included: *Lianna,* the story of a faculty wife's lesbian affair; *Baby, It's You,* Sayles's first big-studio venture, a tale of an ill-fated teenage romance; and the much-admired *The Brother from Another Planet,* about a fugitive black slave from outer space who lands in Harlem and is adopted by the inhabitants of a local bar. The alien, who is unable to speak but possesses extraordinary healing powers, earns the trust and loyalty of the bar's patrons. When a pair of intergalactic bounty hunters appear, intent on recapturing the runaway slave, they instantly arouse the suspicions of the neighborhood's residents because of their clumsy tracking methods and white skin. Reviewing *Brother* in the *Los Angeles Times,* Patrick Goldstein noted that "the film uses its mute, pensive hero to give us a fresh look at our society, with all its harsh divisions." He added that Sayles "reminds us that most science-fiction focuses not on faraway places but on the troubled corners of our own planet."

Sayles eventually earned enough money from those movies to fund his "dream project," the film *Matewan.* The idea for *Matewan* stemmed from stories Sayles had heard years earlier while researching *Union Dues.* Based on the 1920 Matewan massacre—a bloody shootout between striking mineworkers and company-hired security guards that incited the West Virginia mine wars—the film follows union organizer Joe Kenehan's efforts to unite disparate black, Italian, and mountaineer miners into one union. Attempting to sabotage Kenehan's work, the mining company sends out hired thugs whose intimidation tactics eventually lead to a tragic outburst of violence.

Some reviewers saw definite political leanings to *Matewan,* leanings that reflect Sayles's pro-labor politics. One critic who believed that this stance weakened the film was Rita Kempley of the *Washington Post.* "Riddled with labor rhetoric," she argued, "this coal-dusted tragedy wavers between well-acted propaganda and historical burlesque." Another reviewer felt that the director gave a more balanced presentation of union activity. "Mr. Sayles

understands that there *is* strength in unity," remarked Canby, "but his film is seen in the context of more than 60 years of labor history, which had included the growth of giant unions vulnerable to corruption. . . . He recognizes that good intentions sometimes leave as many victims dead on the street as greed." Michael Wilmington of the *Los Angeles Times* saw the film as something altogether different, regarding *Matewan* as "not so much a celebration of the labor movement as an attempt to reinvoke the idealism that once infused it—and, by extension, make that idealism valid again."

Sayles came out that same year with a book documenting his experiences with *Matewan.* Written during the film's editing stage, *Thinking in Pictures: The Making of the Movie Matewan* is "a primer, a 'Dick and Jane' that takes you step by step through the [filmmaking] process," opined *Los Angeles Times Book Review* contributor John Boorman. *Thinking in Pictures* includes the director's thoughts on Matewan's financing, screenwriting, casting, filming, editing—in short, every aspect of the movie's production. Boorman complimented Sayles for his clear explanations of moviemaking's technical elements, but he also criticized the author for the book's clinical tone, stating that Sayles "found it necessary to leave out just about everything—the magic, the poetry and . . . the glamour—that makes movies so compelling, fascinating and vital." A more positive assessment came from Caryn James, who suggested in the *New York Times Book Review* that "for the curious movie viewer this is a lively tale of how some of the smarter movies get made."

Sayles followed *Matewan* with another period piece that examines conflicts between labor and management. *Eight Men Out* chronicles one of America's greatest sports scandals: the notorious 1919 World Series in which eight members of the Chicago White Sox baseball team, (or "Black Sox" as they came to be known), conspired with gamblers to intentionally lose the championship. Sayles presents the players sympathetically, portraying them as victims of both their miserly owner, Charles Comiskey, and their own lack of business savvy. Sayles explained his feelings about the players' decision to accept bribes to a *Los Angeles Times* writer: "It's a labor situation. . . . If you got hurt, there was no pension, no nothing. There was no Social Security. You were just gone. You were in Pawtucket [playing minor league baseball] the next week. So everybody else was just trying to make what they could when they could."

Several reviewers judged *Eight Men Out* to be more than simply a movie about baseball. Film critic Sheila Benson of the *Los Angeles Times* found it an important work, declaring that Sayles had "woven each of the story's complex strands—moral, psychological, political, journalistic, personal—into a watershed American drama that's rich and clear." She also noted the similarities in the director's style and themes between *Eight Men Out* and his other movies, writing: "Sayles' irony is inherent; it's been there since *Return of the Secaucus Seven.* His curiosity about interlocking groups of characters, his blue-collar sympathies are by now his signature." Less enthusiastic about the film was the *Chicago Tribune*'s Dave Kehr, who felt the director lacked vision: "Sayles is just too prosaic and literal a filmmaker to launch the romantic swell his material needs . . . Sayles wants to deal in myths, but as a moviemaker he can never rise above glum facts."

Since *Eight Men Out,* Sayles has made the independent features *City of Hope,* which depicts corruption in an eastern city, and *Passion Fish,* about a paraplegic's struggles to come to terms with her disability. In a review of *Passion Fish, Time*'s Richard Corliss remarked that the woman's search for inner peace was at the core of the movie: "[*Passion Fish*] suggests that heroism is found not in the public victories we achieve but in the intimate truths we learn to accept." Corliss also praised Sayles's low-key approach to storytelling, mentioning the film's "leisurely tempo" and the director's ability to "get at the way real people behave, without the hysterics of Hollywood melodrama."

In an interview with George Vecsey of the *New York Times,* Sayles offered his reasons for remaining an independent: "I can take a lot of risks that studios won't talk about. I can talk about things in depth. I can make the audience uneasy." Sayles then discussed his goals as a filmmaker, telling Vecsey: "I always want people to leave the theater thinking about their own lives, not about other movies. When I write a genre movie like *The Howling,* that's fine, it reminds people of other werewolf movies. But in my movies, I want them to say, 'This is something I see in my life, not in the movies.' "

BIOGRAPHICAL/CRITICAL SOURCES:

BOOKS

Sayles, John, *Thinking in Pictures: The Making of the Movie Matewan,* Houghton, 1987.

PERIODICALS

Chicago Tribune, March 2, 1981; August 20, 1985; September 2, 1988.
Globe and Mail (Toronto), June 15, 1991.
Los Angeles Times, October 11, 1984; October 20, 1984; January 24, 1986; September 11, 1987, pp. 1, 26; October 25, 1987, pp. 3-5, 99-100; September 2, 1988.
Los Angeles Times Book Review, November 1, 1987, p. 2; June 2, 1991.
New York Times, August 9, 1977; September 3, 1979, p. C12; April 11, 1980; April 11, 1985; January 17, 1986; August 23, 1987; August 28, 1987; October 9, 1989.

New York Times Book Review, September 6, 1981, p. 3; November 29, 1987, p. 21; June 16, 1991.
Time, January 25, 1993, p. 69.
Washington Post, November 16, 1984, pp. C1, C4; February 25, 1986; October 15, 1987; October 16, 1987; September 2, 1988.
Washington Post Book World, April 29, 1979, p. M5; May 26, 1991.*

*   *   *

SCHAAP, James C(alvin) 1948-

PERSONAL: Surname is pronounced "Skop"; born February 17, 1948, in Sheboygan, WI; son of Calvin (a loan adviser) and Jean H. (a piano teacher; maiden name, Dirkse) Schaap; married Barbara Kaye Van Gelder (a teacher and housewife), June 27, 1972; children: Andrea Jane, David Michael. *Education:* Dordt College, B.A., 1970; Arizona State University, M.A., 1974; University of Wisconsin—Milwaukee, Ph.D., 1986. *Religion:* Christian Reformed.

ADDRESSES: Home—347 Third Ave. N.E., Sioux Center, IA 51250. *Office*—Department of English, Dordt College, Sioux Center, IA 51250.

CAREER: Dordt College, Sioux Center, IA, instructor, 1976-78, assistant professor, 1978-82, professor of English, 1982—.

AWARDS, HONORS: Scholar at Bread Loaf Writers' Conference, 1980; Country Playhouse One-Act Play Contest winner, 1984, for *Virginia Is for Lovers;* first prize for fiction, Iowa Arts Council, 1985 and 1991; first prize for fiction, Evangelical Press Association, 1991 and 1992.

WRITINGS:

Sign of a Promise and Other Stories, Dordt College Press, 1979.
Family Portrait, CRC Publications, 1983.
Intermission: Breaking away with God, CRC Publications, 1985.
Home Free (novel), Crossway, 1985.
Thirty-Five and Counting (essays/stories), Dordt College Press, 1985.
Someone's Singing, Lord, CRC Publications, 1988.
No Kidding, God, CRC Publications, 1989.
The Privacy of Storm (short stories), Dordt College Press, 1990.
Take It from a Wise Guy, CRC Publications, 1990.
One Hundred Percent Chance of Frogs, CRC Publications, 1992.

PLAYS

Maggie's Song (three-act), produced in Sioux Center, IA, 1983.

Virginia Is for Lovers (one-act), produced in Houston, TX, 1984.

The House of the Lord (three-act), produced in Chattanooga, TN, 1985.

WORK IN PROGRESS: In the Silence There Are Ghosts, a novel; *The Secrets of Neukirk,* short stories; research on the war years of Diet Eman.

SIDELIGHTS: James C. Schaap told *CA:* "For better or worse, I am the recipient of an ethos that is small-town, Midwestern, and steeply protestant. As a consequence, as well as choice, this is the culture from which both my characters and myself spring, the world where I live today, and the corner of creation where someday, I suppose, I'll be buried.

"Men here wear seed caps. Otherwise, I find people beneath this prairie sky no more barren than the plains landscape they inhabit, their lives as full of sin and salvation as mortals anywhere.

"That's why I'm staying put, at least for now."

*   *   *

SCHICK, Eleanor 1942-

PERSONAL: Born April 15, 1942, in New York, NY; daughter of William (a psychiatrist) and Bessie (a social worker; maiden name, Grossman) Schick; children: Laura, David. *Education:* Attended high school in New York City; studied modern dance with Martha Graham, Alvin Ailey, and others.

ADDRESSES: Home—207 Aliso NE, Albuquerque, NM 87108.

CAREER: Author and illustrator of children's books. Writer in Residence, Rio Grande Writing Project (a New Mexico site of The National Writing Project), 1986—. Speaker at public schools.

WRITINGS:

JUVENILES; SELF-ILLUSTRATED, EXCEPT WHERE INDICATED

A Surprise in the Forest, Harper, 1964.
The Little School at Cottonwood Corners, Harper, 1965.
The Dancing School, Harper, 1966.
I'm Going to the Ocean!, Macmillan, 1966.
5A and 7B, Macmillan, 1967.
Katie Goes to Camp, Macmillan, 1968.
Jeanie Goes Riding, Macmillan, 1968.
City in the Summer, Macmillan, 1969.

Making Friends, Macmillan, 1969.
Peggy's New Brother, Macmillan, 1970.
City in the Winter, Macmillan, 1970.
Andy, Macmillan, 1971.
Student's Encounter Book for When a Jew Celebrates, Behrman House, 1973.
Peter and Mr. Brandon, illustrated by Donald Carrick, Macmillan, 1973.
City Green, Macmillan, 1974.
City Sun, Macmillan, 1974.
Neighborhood Knight, Greenwillow, 1976.
One Summer Night, Greenwillow, 1977.
Summer at the Sea, Greenwillow, 1979.
Home Alone, Dial, 1980.
Rainy Sunday, Dial, 1981.
Joey on His Own, Dial, 1981.
A Piano for Julie, Greenwillow, 1983.
My Album, Greenwillow, 1984.
Art Lessons, Greenwillow, 1987.
I Have Another Language: The Language Is Dance, Macmillan, 1992.

ILLUSTRATOR

Jan Wahl, *Christmas in the Forest,* Macmillan, 1967.
Jeanne Whitehouse Peterson, *Sometimes I Dream Horses,* Harper, 1987.
Sheldon Zimmerman, *The Family Prayerbook: Holidays and Festivals,* Rossel Books, 1988.
Zimmerman, *The Family Prayerbook: The Fall Holidays,* Rossel Books, 1989.
Zimmerman, *The Family Prayerbook: Shabbot,* Rossel Books, 1989.

ADAPTATIONS: City in the Winter and *City in the Summer* have been made into filmstrips.

WORK IN PROGRESS: "Two books, each under contract with Macmillan. One, a collaboration with Luci Taphanaso, addressing Navajo themes; the second, tentatively titled *My Navajo Sister.*"

SIDELIGHTS: Eleanor Schick told *CA:* "Children always excite me. They are always reachable. They are always responsive when an adult makes it clear to them that he or she is interested in listening to them speak, or write, about what really happens in their lives, and how they feel about it.

"It is gratifying to me, today, that we listen to children more. We write with more sensitivity to what children really do think, and see, and feel. There is a true literature developing which speaks to children. It speaks to their thoughts, dreams, and yearnings. It addresses some of the experiences that they do have, which were not dealt with some fifteen or twenty years ago. I have witnessed, and surely been a part of, the development of 'children's books' from being vehicles or didactic adult teaching to a true literature which includes very deep and poetic expression of childhood experience. This is very meaningful to me, and I feel deeply gratified to have been a part of this growth."

*   *   *

SCHRADER, Paul (Joseph) 1946-

PERSONAL: Born July 22, 1946, in Grand Rapids, MI; son of Charles A. (an executive) and Joan (Fisher) Schrader; married second wife, Mary Beth Hurt (an actress), August 6, 1983; children: (second marriage) two. *Education:* Calvin College, B.A., 1969; University of California, Los Angeles, M.A., 1970. *Religion:* Episcopalian.

ADDRESSES: Office—9696 Culva Blvd., Suite 203, Culver City, CA 90232. *Agent*—c/o Jeff Berg, International Creative Management, 8899 Beverly Blvd., Los Angeles, CA 90048.

CAREER: Screenwriter and director. *Free Press,* Los Angeles, CA, film critic, 1968-69; *Coast,* Beverly Hills, CA, film critic, 1970; *Cinema,* Beverly Hills, editor, beginning 1970. Director of films, including *Cat People,* Universal, 1981, *Patty Hearst,* Atlantic-Zenith, 1988, and *The Comfort of Strangers,* 1990. Executive producer of *Old Boyfriends,* AVCO-Embassy, 1978.

MEMBER: Writers Guild of America, West.

AWARDS, HONORS: First place essays, 1968, for contests in *Atlantic* and *Story: The Magazine of Discovery.*

WRITINGS:

Transcendental Style in Film: Ozu, Bresson, Dreyer, University of California Press, 1972.

SCREENPLAYS

(With Robert Towne) *The Yakuza,* Warner Brothers, 1974.
Taxi Driver, Columbia, 1976.
(With Brian DePalma) *Obsession,* Columbia, 1976.
(With Leonard Schrader; and director) *Blue Collar,* Universal, 1977.
(With Heywood Gould) *Rolling Thunder,* American-International, 1977.
(And director) *Hardcore,* Columbia, 1978.
(With L. Schrader) *Old Boyfriends,* AVCO-Embassy, 1978.
(And director) *American Gigolo,* Paramount, 1979.
(With Mardik Martin) *Raging Bull,* United Artists, 1980.
(With L. Schrader; and director) *Mishima: A Life in Four Chapters,* Warner Brothers, 1985.
The Mosquito Coast (adapted from the novel by Paul Theroux), Orion, 1986.

(And director) *Light of Day,* Tri-Star, 1987.
The Last Temptation of Christ (adapted from the novel by Nikos Kazantzakis), Universal, 1988.
(And director) *Light Sleeper,* Seven Arts/New Line Cinema, 1992.

OTHER

Contributor to periodicals, including *Cinema, Film Comment,* and *Film Quarterly.*

SIDELIGHTS: The films of screenwriter and director Paul Schrader explore redemption, violence, and sexuality. In the process, they frequently stir up considerable controversy among both seasoned film critics and the general public. "Schrader has always had a fascination for decadence and corruption and how they can lead, via violence, to spiritual release," described Gavin Smith in *Film Comment.* "His films are at once rigorously considered and robustly sensual—lurid yet somehow chaste spectacles that enact the moral friction of the worldly and the metaphysical." Schrader himself acknowledges that his preoccupation with these themes had its genesis in his strict religious upbringing. He was raised as a member of the Calvinist Christian Reform Church, and in his youth, members of that church were not allowed to listen to music, dance, drink, smoke—or see motion pictures. Thus, Schrader, who has become one of the best-known figures on the American film scene, did not see his first film until he was seventeen years old. He is quoted by Joel Bellman in the *Dictionary of Literary Biography* as saying that his lack of exposure to movies is "probably the greatest thing that ever happened to me—because I have no adolescent memories of movies. I have no desire to make the movies I saw when I was a child because I never saw movies as a child. So I can approach movies as an adult, and make movies for adults. I don't have to make . . . all the kid's movies my peers are making now."

Schrader entered the seminary at Calvin College after completing high school, but it was not long before he traveled to New York and began making contacts within the world of film. Though he did graduate from Calvin, he never became a minister; instead, he enrolled in the University of California Film School. After completing his master's degree there, he remained in California and worked as a writer, reviewer, and editor for several film publications. His first screenplay, *Pipeliner,* failed to win any financial backing, and his first book, *Transcendental Style in Film: Ozu, Bresson, Dreyer,* attracted scant attention. His first marriage failed during this same period, and Schrader plunged into a deep depression. He is quoted by Samuel G. Freedman in the *New York Times* as saying: "I was very enamored of guns, I was very suicidal, I was drinking heavily, I was obsessed with pornography in the way a lonely person is." Ironically, this state of mind gave rise to the screenplay that would make Schrader a hot property in Hollywood: *Taxi Driver.*

The unlikely protagonist of *Taxi Driver,* a New York cabbie named Travis Bickle, reflects Schrader's state of mind at the time he wrote the screenplay. In the film, which was directed by Martin Scorsese, Bickle is at once fascinated and enraged by the seamy world he inhabits. After following his attempted relationships with two women, an upper-class campaign worker and a teenage prostitute, the film reaches its climax when Travis attempts to purge the world of its corruption in a bloody shooting spree. Upon its release in 1976, *Taxi Driver* divided film critics into two camps. Many felt that there was simply too much violence and sordidness in the movie, while others believed that the film showed the reality of New York City and the people who inhabit its streets at night. David Sterrit, writing in the *Christian Science Monitor,* accorded the film high praise, stating: "*Taxi Driver* is one of those rare films that use visual discoveries of the adventurous 'experimental' cinema in narrating a full-fledged story. For its blend of rapid-fire story-telling and artful visual insight, *Taxi Driver* deserves its own niche in recent film history."

Patricia Patterson and Manny Farber, writing in *Film Comment,* on the other hand, praised the film's use of humor, but pointed out that it lacked direction: "*Taxi Driver* is a half-half movie: half of it is a skimpy story line with muddled motivation about the way an undereducated misfit would act, and the other half is a clever, confusing, hypnotic sell." *Film Quarterly* contributor Michael Dempsey expressed dissatisfaction with the script's ending, maintaining that "if *Taxi Driver* had unleashed its firestorm, say halfway through its running time and then had gone on to show Travis dealing with the changes in his life brought on by this catharsis and the resulting fame, it might have become an analysis of contemporary confusion rather than an example of it. . . . It fails to transcend because its makers are caught in too many contradictions."

Despite such negative comment, *Taxi Driver* was an enormous success, assuring Schrader a place of high standing among the Hollywood establishment. By 1978 he had realized his dream to direct as well as write, with the film *Blue Collar,* which is a complex look at corruption in labor unions and the life of the factory worker. *Village Voice* writer Terry Curtis Fox commented favorably on it, and also pointed out the startling differences between it and *Taxi Driver:* "*Blue Collar* is the single most overtly political movie made for a major Hollywood studio since Abe Polonsky's *Tell Them Willie Boy Was Here* a decade ago. . . . The entire film is constructed to propound the notion that race is used in place of class to keep workers on the line. That Schrader, intellectual and theologian manqué, should make a schematic movie is not surprising.

That the man who wrote *Taxi Driver,* a textbook example of existential plotting, where not a single action has an exterior motivation, should make a movie [*Blue Collar*] in which every moment is motivated, in which every action of every character can be explained by a specific emotional moment that is also an economic and social fact is, well, astonishing."

Schrader again acted as writer and director for the film *Hardcore.* His Calvinist background was strongly in evidence in this story, which concerns a father and daughter from Schrader's home town, Grand Rapids, Michigan. When the daughter disappears during a religious convention in California, the father sets off in search of her, only to find that she has entered the world of prostitution and pornography. The clash between the stern, rigidly religious father and the amoral world where he searches for his child forms the basis of the film. Some critics saw the father's unbending nature as a major flaw in the script, finding it unbelievable that he could be unchanged by his experiences in the sexual underworld. But Gene Siskel, film critic for the *Chicago Tribune,* approved of the way in which *Hardcore* showed the human sides of both the father and the prostitutes and porn stars he encountered. The film "neither allows the nonbeliever to scorn the religious man, nor does it allow the sexual thrill-seeker to ignore the object of his or her fixation," wrote Siskel. "*Hardcore* thus is both a rich film of ideas and of strikingly real characters."

Schrader's next major film also examines the world of sex for money, but its tone is vastly different from that of *Hardcore.* Whereas *Hardcore* presents the gritty world of sex shops and peep shows as seen through the eyes of a puritanical man, *American Gigolo* is a sympathetic character study of an expensive male prostitute working in the glamorous setting of Beverly Hills. The title character, Julian Kay, is shown as a man adept at giving pleasure but incapable of receiving love. Although the plot involves his being framed for murder, the story turns on Julian's developing ability to truly experience love. Bellman quoted Schrader as saying that *American Gigolo* represents "the flip side of *Taxi Driver.* It's very light, where *Taxi Driver* was dark. It's a story of redemption by blood. [*American Gigolo* is] a movie about grace."

Numerous critics remarked favorably on the stylish look of the film, but some also pointed out that it was difficult to care about Julian, and that the plot took too many unrelated turns. Vincent Canby wrote in the *New York Times* that "*American Gigolo* is a laughable movie but it's not without interest. . . . The major difficulty . . . is that Mr. Schrader has too effectively established Julian as high-priced sex-machine to make the character work as the consciousness-raised hero he's supposed to be in the murder-mystery that takes over the second half of the movie. . . . Julian is a trivial character. . . . When [his] soul is salvaged, it's salvaged not by God or by some breakthrough in understanding but by a plot device." Andrew Sarris commented in the *Village Voice* that *American Gigolo* is "the most elegant of Schrader's directorial exercises, and there are never any lapses of tone. What's lacking . . . are narrative flow, dramatic development, and psychological coherence." Nevertheless, he concluded that the film is "an honorable and fascinating work by an American artist." Siskel praised the film without reservation, calling it "another uncompromising and absolutely fascinating yarn told by Paul Schrader. . . . *American Gigolo* is not a pleasant film. In mood, if not graphic detail, it's almost as kinky as *Hard Core*. . . . But it also is an honest, compelling drama that sheds a little light in some beguilingly dark places." Notwithstanding the mixed critical reaction to the film, it was a great success with the moviegoing public.

All the controversy generated by *Taxi Driver, Hardcore, American Gigolo,* and Schrader's many other films faded in comparison to the furor that erupted over his adaptation of Nikos Kazantzakis's novel *The Last Temptation of Christ,* which was directed by Schrader's frequent collaborator, Martin Scorsese. Kazantzakis's novel, which Schrader followed closely in his script, presents the human side of Christ—a Jesus who sometimes doubted and feared his own divinity. His "last temptation," referred to in the title, was to come down off the cross, reject his destiny, and live as an ordinary man. This option is portrayed in both book and film as a hallucination experienced by the crucified Christ before he ultimately regains consciousness and accepts his martyrdom.

Months before the film's release, fundamentalist religious groups began protesting against it, claiming that it was a blasphemous depiction of Christ as a deranged, lust-driven creature. As the publicity increased, so did the force of the protests. A Baptist minister offered to pay millions to the movie's distributor, Universal Studios, in exchange for all existing prints of the film, which he intended to burn. Numerous other Christian denominations eventually joined the fundamentalist protestors, as did members of the Jewish and Islamic faiths. A boycott was called for against all theaters showing the film and all business interests of MCA, the parent company of Universal Studios. In an effort to cut short the negative publicity, Universal rushed *Last Temptation* into theaters in major cities nearly a month ahead of schedule.

Both sold-out houses and shouting, angry mobs greeted the film. Critics were less excited by the event. Stripping away the hysteria that had grown up around the picture, they generally reviewed *The Last Temptation of Christ* as a sincere, deeply-felt religious epic, flawed perhaps by an overly-conventional approach. Sheila Benson noted in the

Los Angeles Times that *Last Temptation* is "an intense, utterly sincere, frequently fascinating piece of art. . . . The film's greatest virtue may be its vision of Jesus' time; its biggest drawback is the deliberate flatness and banality of the words used to convey it." *Chicago Tribune* contributor Dave Kehr evaluated it as "an admirably serious, accomplished movie," but added that it is "actually less bold than most historical novels in its attempt to imagine the inner life of a historical figure." Siskel found *Last Temptation* to be thought-provoking and "a great recruiting film for Christianity."

"If *Last Temptation* errs on the side of making Jesus too human," Schrader told Siskel, "that's a small step toward correcting the 2000 years in which the church has ignored his humanity, treating him only as a god." The screenwriter found the controversy sparked by his screenplay to be startling in its intensity. Toronto *Globe & Mail* contributor Rick Groen quoted him as saying: "I was raised in a very conservative Christian community, but one where it wasn't considered wrong to read the books of Kazantzakis. . . . Such religious discussions were pretty much a staple of my childhood, all part of a Christian education. So it always takes me aback when people suggest that this kind of questioning isn't allowed, particularly within Protestantism, which, after all, was founded on the notion that each person must confront the scriptures individually. . . . What we're seeing here is the non-intellectual wing of Christianity trying to drag the moderate middle into the fray with florid descriptions of a film they haven't seen. Descriptions like, 'The Jesus Sex Film.' I think that phrase says more about the imagination of the evangelical right than about my or [Scorsese's] imagination. . . . It *is* possible for an intelligent, thinking person to have faith. I don't have much tolerance or understanding of those who see Christianity as a simple, childlike acceptance. Because you need the faith of a child to enter the kingdom of heaven doesn't mean you have to have the mind of a child."

One of Schrader's recent films, 1992's *Light Sleeper,* reverts to his earlier examinations of crime and redemption. The main character, drug-dealing John LeTour, is a loner along the lines of Travis Bickle in *Taxi Driver* and Julian Kay in *American Gigolo*. Having reached middle age, LeTour is going through a crisis, which is set off when his upscale dealer boss, Ann, decides she is going to leave drug dealing behind and move into the field of herbal cosmetics. LeTour sees this as a chance to change his life, and this goal is further heightened when he runs into an ex-lover and aspires to win her back. Such a change doesn't come easily, though, especially as LeTour makes his way through the mean streets of New York—violence erupts before things settle down. "Like all of Schrader's anti-heroes, John LeTour embodies his creator's fascination with the individual's struggle for cleanliness in a hopelessly besmirched world," described John Powers in *New York*. John Simon, writing in *National Review*, found *Light Sleeper* to be lacking motivation, and asserted that "as usual with Schrader, dark moods and lurking evil preempt psychological credibility and sound dramatic structure." *Rolling Stone* contributor Peter Travers, however, saw the film as "a boldly resonant thriller," adding: "Schrader is out there again, testing the limits of audience tolerance. Good for him. Buoyed by his questing spirit . . . *Light Sleeper* might just keep you up nights."

One of the reasons why Schrader is sometimes seen as "testing" the audience is because he makes movies for himself and not for them. In an interview with Peter Biskind for *Premiere* he related: "I never think about what people want to see. I think about what I need to say. Because they want to see what they just saw. But you can't make what they just saw; you have to work with an evangelical fervor that simply says, 'I need to make a movie about a drug dealer.' Then I have to believe that other people need to see it. Some filmmakers are much more plugged in to what other people really want than I am; they're inspired by making money, but I can't think that way." This approach has not always been a commercially successful one for Schrader. "It's no fun being 45 years old and having to struggle like I just arrived on the scene," he explained to Biskind. "But finally, it's the work that makes the struggle worthwhile. You live with your filmography. . . . Maybe it's because of my religious background, but how do you explain at the end of the day, when you meet your maker—you say, 'Well, I made a bunch of shitty pictures. People wanted me to make them.' I'm proud of the fact that I never did shit in order to do good stuff. I never did stuff that I was really embarrassed by. Never."

BIOGRAPHICAL/CRITICAL SOURCES:

BOOKS

Contemporary Literary Criticism, Volume 26, Gale, 1983.
Dictionary of Literary Biography, Volume 44: *American Screenwriters, Second Series*, Gale, 1986.
Jackson, Kevin, editor, *Schrader on Schrader and Other Writings*, Faber & Faber, 1990.

PERIODICALS

American Film, April, 1982, pp. 38-45.
Chicago Tribune, February 23, 1979; May 2, 1979; February 1, 1980, p. 16; May 9, 1982; October 23, 1985; January 7, 1987; February 4, 1987; August 12, 1988; August 13, 1988; August 14, 1988; August 21, 1988; September 11, 1988.
Christian Science Monitor, February 19, 1976.
Cineaste, winter, 1978, pp. 34-37, 59.
Cinefantastique, winter, 1978, p. 36.
Commonweal, January 16, 1981, pp. 20-21.
Film Comment, July, 1973; March-April, 1976, pp. 6-19; May-June, 1976; July-August, 1978, p. 45; March-April, 1992, pp. 50-59.
Film Information, March, 1976.
Film Quarterly, summer, 1976.
Globe & Mail (Toronto), August 13, 1988; August 27, 1988.
Los Angeles Times, March 12, 1978; April 15, 1979; October 3, 1985; November 26, 1986; December 16, 1986; February 6, 1987; May 16, 1988; July 12, 1988; July 13, 1988; July 14, 1988; July 15, 1988; July 16, 1988; July 20, 1988; July 22, 1988; July 27, 1988; July 29, 1988; July 30, 1988; July 31, 1988; August 5, 1988; August 6, 1988; August 10, 1988; August 11, 1988; August 12, 1988; August 13, 1988; August 14, 1988; August 15, 1988; August 16, 1988; August 21, 1988; August 26, 1988; August 27, 1988; August 30, 1988; September 3, 1988; September 6, 1988; September 9, 1988; September 18, 1988; September 23, 1988; October 22, 1988.
Maclean's, April 12, 1982, pp. 62-63.
Millimeter, February, 1979, pp. 60-72.
Monthly Film Bulletin, May, 1980, pp. 87-88; August, 1982, pp. 156-157.
National Review, October 5, 1992, p. 62.
New Republic, March 6, 1976; February 11, 1978.
Newsweek, February 13, 1978.
New York, February 12, 1979, p. 84; December 1, 1980, pp. 61-63; April 12, 1982, pp. 60-61; August 31, 1992, p. 47.
New Yorker, February 27, 1978; February 19, 1979; March 22, 1979; February 4, 1980; May 3, 1982, pp. 124, 126, 128, 130-131.
New York Times, February 5, 1978; February 9, 1979, p. C5; February 11, 1979, p. 15; February 1, 1980, p. C14; February 3, 1980, pp. D15, D42; November 14, 1980; February 26, 1984; November 26, 1986; February 6, 1987; February 15, 1987; August 12, 1988; August 13, 1988; July 28, 1989, p. C8; August 25, 1991, p. H9.
Premiere, April, 1992, pp. 98-106.
Rolling Stone, March 19, 1992, pp. 102, 104.
Saturday Review, April 15, 1978, p. 65.
Sight and Sound, winter, 1977-78, pp. 58-59.
Times (London), November 1, 1985; February 6, 1987; August 1, 1988; September 17, 1990.
Variety, May 17, 1978.
Village Voice, February 16, 1976; February 27, 1978, pp. 32-33; February 12, 1979, p. 51; February 4, 1980, p. 43.
Voice Literary Supplement, November, 1989, p. 28.

Washington Post, February 1, 1980, pp. C1, C8; February 8, 1980, p. 20; October 15, 1985; December 19, 1986; February 6, 1987; July 22, 1988; September 23, 1988.

—*Sketch by Joan Goldsworthy*

*   *   *

SCHWARTZ, Muriel A.
See ELIOT, T(homas) S(tearns)

*   *   *

SCHWARTZ, Paula 1925-
(Paula Reibel; pseudonyms: Elizabeth Mansfield, Libby Mansfield)

PERSONAL: Born March 13, 1925, in New York, NY; daughter of Samuel and Hilda (Horowitz) Reibel; married Ira A. Schwartz (a metallurgical engineer), May 29, 1956; children: Wendy Elizabeth, David Saul. *Education:* Hunter College (now Hunter College of the City University of New York), B.A., 1945; City College (now City College of the City University of New York), M.A., 1950; American University, further graduate study, 1969-70.

ADDRESSES: Home—8303 The Midway Dr., Annandale, VA 22003. *Agent*—Victoria Pryor, Arcadia Ltd., 221 West 82nd St., Suite 7D, New York, NY 10024.

CAREER: High school English teacher in New York City, 1947-65; George Washington University, Washington, DC, lecturer in English, 1966-67; Dunbarton College, Washington, DC, assistant professor of English, 1967-73; Northern Virginia Community College, Annandale, part-time lecturer in English, beginning 1974; writer. New York University, lecturer, 1963-64; guest lecturer at other colleges. Theater director for college and community productions.

MEMBER: Authors Guild, Authors League of America, Dramatists Guild.

AWARDS, HONORS: Pauline Eaton Oak Award, District of Columbia Recreation Department, 1971, for direction and production of *You're a Good Man, Charlie Brown;* Sallie Shepherd Prize, Irene Leache Memorial, 1974, for light verse, "Fragmented"; first prize, *Dramatics* one-act play contest, 1974, for *Parcel Pick-Up;* first prize, Delaware Theater Association bicentennial play contest, 1975, for *The Tory Spinster;* Fanny Rogers Curd Prize, Irene Leache Memorial, 1976, for essay "The Last Secret Vice," and 1978, for essay "To the One Who Ripped Off My Purse"; first prize, Wilmette Children's Theater national children's play competition, 1978, for *Sensible Sam and the Noodleheads;* *Romantic Times*-Waldenbooks award, Romance Writers Convention, 1983, for best Regency writer.

WRITINGS:

Parcel Pick-Up (one-act comedy; produced in 1976), published in *Dramatics* magazine, 1974.
The Tory Spinster (two-act musical), produced in Dover, DE, by the Kent County Theatre Guild, 1976.
Afterwords (three one-act plays), produced in Abingdon, VA, at Barter Theater, 1977.
(With N. Moyer) *Sensible Sam and the Noodleheads* (one-act children's musical), produced in Wilmette, IL, at Wilmette Children's Theater, 1979.
(Under name Paula Reibel) *A Morning Moon* (novel), Morrow, 1984.

UNDER PSEUDONYM ELIZABETH MANSFIELD; ROMANCE NOVELS

Unexpected Holiday, Dell, 1978, published as *Christmas Kiss,* Berkley Publishing, 1990.
My Lord Murderer, Berkley Publishing, 1978.
The Phantom Lover, Berkley Publishing, 1979.
A Very Dutiful Daughter, Berkley Publishing, 1979.
A Regency Sting, Berkley Publishing, 1980.
Her Man of Affairs, Berkley Publishing, 1980.
A Regency Match, Berkley Publishing, 1980.
Duel of Hearts, Berkley Publishing, 1980.
A Regency Charade, Berkley Publishing, 1981.
The Fifth Kiss, Berkley Publishing, 1981.
The Reluctant Flirt, Berkley Publishing, 1981.
Regency Wager, Berkley Publishing, 1981.
The Counterfeit Husband, Berkley Publishing, 1982.
The Frost Fair, Berkley Publishing, 1982.
Mama's Choice, Berkley Publishing, 1982.
The Second Best Lady, Berkley Publishing, 1983.
Her Heart's Captain, Berkley Publishing, 1983.
Love Lessons, Berkley Publishing, 1983.
Passing Fancies (sequel to *The Counterfeit Husband*), Berkley Publishing, 1983.
A Marriage of Inconvenience, Berkley Publishing, 1984.
A Splendid Indiscretion, Berkley Publishing, 1985.
A Grand Passion, Berkley Publishing, 1986.
The Magnificent Masquerade, Berkley Publishing, 1987.
The Grand Deception, Berkley Publishing, 1987.
An Accidental Romance, Berkley Publishing, 1988.
The Lady Disguised, Berkley Publishing, 1989.
The Bartered Bride, Berkley Publishing, 1989.
A Prior Engagement, Berkley Publishing, 1990.
A Brilliant Mismatch, Berkley Publishing, 1991.

OTHER

Also author of plays, *A Savage Mother* (one-act drama), 1977; (with Moyer) *An Accident at Lyme,* (musical), 1985; *Second Thoughts* (full-length comedy), 1986; (with H. Levitsky) *A Personnel Affair* (one-act musical), 1990; (with Moyer) *Elinor and Marianne* (musical), 1990; (with Levitsky) *Four Star Quartet* (musical), 1991; and (with

Levitsky) *Justice Con Brio* (musical), 1992. Also author of a musical based on Jane Austen's novel *Persuasion;* also author of a screenplay, *Where's Eleanor,* 1990. Contributor to *A Regency Holiday,* Berkley Publishing, 1991; and *A Christmas Treasure,* Berkley Publishing, 1992. Contributor to periodicals, including *Good Housekeeping, Seventeen, Reader's Digest,* and *Today's Family.*

WORK IN PROGRESS: A Minor Quartet, a contemporary novel; *To Spite the Devil,* a novel of the American Revolution.

SIDELIGHTS: Writing under the pseudonym Elizabeth Mansfield, Paula Schwartz has established herself in the crowded company of romance novelists, choosing to specialize in the Regency genre. Novelist Georgette Heyer, who wrote from 1921 to 1974, popularized the Regency period, which consists of the waning years of George III's reign, during which his eldest son served as regent. Now "readers of Regency novels say that Elizabeth Mansfield is the heiress to the literary crown of Georgette Heyer, the high priestess of Regency novels," notes Kathryn Falk in *Love's Leading Ladies.*

A former full-time professor of English, Schwartz has studied and taught the works of major authors. For some time, her knowledge of these authors inhibited her from pursuing her own writing career. As she once explained to *CA:* "As a teacher of literature, I viewed writers with a respect bordering on awe, and I was able to try my hand at it only when it dawned on me that I didn't have to be Tolstoy to make a living at writing." An award-winning essay on Georgette Heyer provided Schwartz the confidence to attempt her own Regency novel. Her agent quickly found publishers for her first two books, and her continued success in romance novels has allowed her to venture into mainstream fiction.

BIOGRAPHICAL/CRITICAL SOURCES:

BOOKS

Falk, Kathryn, *Love's Leading Ladies,* Pinnacle Books, 1982.

PERIODICALS

Publishers Weekly, January 29, 1979; October 5, 1984.

*   *   *

SCOPPETTONE, Sandra 1936-
(Jack Early)

PERSONAL: Born June 1, 1936, in Morristown, NJ; daughter of Casimiro Radames and Helen Katherine (Greis) Scoppettone; partner of Linda Crawford (a writer). *Avocational interests:* Old movies, reading, gambling (in moderation), computers and on-line connections with bulletin boards, tennis.

ADDRESSES: Home—131 Prince St., New York, NY 10012. *Agent*—Charlotte Sheedy, Charlotte Sheedy Literary Agency, 611 Broadway, New York, NY 10012.

CAREER: Full-time professional writer.

AWARDS, HONORS: Eugene O'Neill Memorial Theatre Award, 1972, for *Stuck;* Ludwig Vogelstein Foundation grant, 1974; American Library Association best young adult book citation, 1975, and New Jersey Institute of Technology, New Jersey Authors Award, 1976, both for *Trying Hard to Hear You;* California Young Readers Medal (high school), California Reading Association, 1979, for *The Late Great Me;* (as Jack Early) Shamus Award, Private Eye Writers of America, and Edgar Allan Poe Award nomination, Mystery Writers of America, both 1985, both for *A Creative Kind of Killer;* Edgar Allan Poe Award nomination, 1986, for *Playing Murder.*

WRITINGS:

PICTURE BOOKS

Suzuki Beane, illustrated by Louise Fitzhugh, Doubleday, 1961.
Bang Bang You're Dead, illustrated by Fitzhugh, Harper, 1968.

YOUNG ADULT NOVELS

Trying Hard to Hear You, Harper, 1974.
The Late Great Me, Putnam, 1976.
Happy Endings Are All Alike, Harper, 1978.
Long Time between Kisses, Harper, 1982.
Playing Murder, Harper, 1985.

NOVELS

Some Unknown Person, Putnam, 1977.
Such Nice People, Putnam, 1980.
Innocent Bystanders, New American Library, 1983.
Everything You Have Is Mine ("Lauren Laurano" mystery), Little, Brown, 1991.
I'll Be Leaving You Always ("Lauren Laurano" mystery), Little, Brown, 1993.

NOVELS UNDER PSEUDONYM JACK EARLY

A Creative Kind of Killer, F. Watts, 1984.
Razzamatazz, F. Watts, 1985.
Donato and Daughter, Dutton, 1988.

PLAYS

Home Again, Home Again Jiggity Jig, produced at Cubiculo Theatre, 1969.
Something for Kitty Genovese (one-act), performed by Valerie Bettis Repertory Company, 1971.

Stuck, produced at Eugene O'Neill Memorial Theatre, Waterford, CT, 1972, produced at Open Space Theatre, New York City, 1976.

SCREENPLAYS

Scarecrow in a Garden of Cucumbers, Maron-New Line, 1972.
The Inspector of Stairs, Independent, 1975.

TELEPLAYS

Love of Life, Columbia Broadcasting System, Inc. (CBS-TV), 1972.
A Little Bit Like Murder, American Broadcasting Companies, Inc. (ABC-TV), 1973.

OTHER

Scoppettone's manuscripts are housed in the Kerlan Collection at the University of Minnesota.

WORK IN PROGRESS: A third "Lauren Laurano" mystery; a new mystery under the pseudonym Jack Early.

ADAPTATIONS: The Late Great Me was adapted into a film directed by Anthony Lover, Daniel Wilson Productions, 1982; *Donato and Daughter* was adapted into a television movie starring Charles Bronson and Dana Delany, CBS-TV, 1993.

SIDELIGHTS: "One thing I would like to say is that I'm a lesbian," proclaims Sandra Scoppettone in an interview with Susan M. Reicha for *Authors and Artists for Young Adults (AAYA).* "I mean, that should be clear. I also want to say that I've been with the same person for twenty years—I think it's important for people to know that it can be done." Author of both young adult novels that deal with homosexuality, alcoholism, and murder, and adult novels that depict a hallucinatory seventeen-year-old, a single-parent male detective, and a witty lesbian private investigator, Scoppettone has been accused of writing about such controversial topics merely for the money. "But it isn't true," she asserts in *Speaking for Ourselves.* "The books I've written have been about important issues in my own life or in the lives of people I've known."

Growing up in South Orange, New Jersey, Scoppettone knew as early as the age of five that she wanted to be a writer. And right from the start, her parents encouraged this ambition. "They gave me the feeling that I could do this," recalls Scoppettone in her interview. "They certainly encouraged it and said I could do whatever I wanted and were very supportive the whole time." In addition to being supportive, Scoppettone's parents were also very overprotective of her, especially her father. "I wasn't allowed to do a lot of physical stuff that other kids were allowed to do, like riding bikes or going down our hill all the way on a sled. It was hard, so it made me feel a little

different." To compensate for these feelings, Scoppettone would escape into her imagination and write stories when she was alone. One of her favorite activities took place at her grandparent's house when she was about five or six and the only grandchild. "It was a fairly big family, and I would get under the table and listen to everything and spy," relates Scoppettone in her *AAYA* interview. "I loved to listen and loved to hear adults tell stories and talk. I made up my own stories a lot. I remember playing with marbles, not playing regular marble games, but making a marble a person, giving them a name and moving them around."

By the time she finished high school, Scoppettone had no interest in attending college; she wanted to move to New York City and write. Her parents supported her in her endeavors, and she took on various jobs within the city. "I really began to support myself with my writing around the age of thirty," observes Scoppettone in her interview with Reicha. Children's author and illustrator Louise Fitzhugh collaborated with Scoppettone on her first published work—the picture book *Suzuki Beane.* "Louise came over one day with all these little drawings, dumped them all over my bed, and said we should do a book," Scoppettone tells *AAYA.* "When she left I started to lay them out. I remember sitting on my bed and putting them around, and then putting them into notebook form. In some places I wrote under her pictures, others I left blank. She then took it back and we sold it practically overnight."

Scoppettone's next book was another picture book with Fitzhugh. In the meantime, she also wrote for other media, including television, film, and stage. "Writing for television, film, or theater is a cooperative thing, and I don't like it much because you usually don't have the final word like you do with books," points out Scoppettone in her interview. And because of the lack of control a writer has in these media, she doesn't plan on writing for them again. "I've had productions and it's very exciting to hear your words on one hand," relates Scoppettone in her *AAYA* interview. "On the other hand, it's horrifying when you know they've skipped three pages of an act and they don't know it. It's a very out of control situation. Something I like about writing books is that you have control."

It was Scoppettone's ability to handle and control a touchy situation that inspired the subject matter for her first young adult novel. "I was living on the North Fork off Long Island where there was a thing called 'Youth on Stage,' " she remembers in her interview. "They needed someone to direct the summer musical and I had directed adult things, so I volunteered. There were two high school boys who were obviously having an affair, and the kids were being awful to them. I stepped in and didn't let all the awful things that happen in the book happen, but that was the basis for *Trying Hard to Hear You.*"

Published in 1974, *Trying Hard to Hear You* tells a similar tale. Set in the summer of 1973 on the North Fork of Long Island, the story is told by sixteen-year-old Camilla Crawford. A summer production of the musical *Anything Goes* is under way, and Camilla and her group of friends are all participating in one way or another. During the course of rehearsals, Camilla falls for one of the actors, Phil Chrystie. The two go out on a couple of dates, but Camilla is confused when Phil asks more than a few questions about her best friend and next-door neighbor Jeff Grathwohl. Things come to a head when Jeff and Phil are caught kissing during a Fourth of July party. The group then proceeds to ostracize the two boys and violence ensues. "The confrontation between the gentle sincerity of the lovers and the tittering shock of the 'straights' is . . . the most emotionally genuine and moving thing in the book," maintains Annie Gottlieb in the *New York Times Book Review.* A *Booklist* reviewer asserts that "plot threads are credibly interwoven" and "adult as well as teenage characters are well developed and interrelated" in *Trying Hard To Hear You* to create "a teenage story of unusual depth for mature readers."

Scoppettone's next young adult novel, *The Late Great Me,* also has somewhat personal origins. "*The Late Great Me* deals with alcoholism," she tells Reicha. "I had done my research because I'm a recovered alcoholic. When I wrote it I was sober, but I have had years of being an active alcoholic. This was not my story, however—I didn't write about myself. Things such as hangovers and blackouts are the same, but this is not my story. I do think I was a teenage alcoholic, though, in the sense that I think I was an alcoholic the first time I picked up a drink. I didn't get sober until I was in my thirties."

Geri Peters, the young alcoholic in *The Late Great Me,* is able to overcome her drinking problem approximately a year after it starts. Considering herself one of the "freaks" in her high school, Geri is thrilled at the beginning of her junior year when Dave Townsend, a handsome new student, picks her to befriend. The two start dating, and Dave introduces Geri to drinking the first time they go out. As time goes by, Geri's drinking escalates until she has bottles stashed in her school locker and in her closet at home. Nothing can make Geri realize she has a problem, not even the death of Dave's mother—another alcoholic. It is finally one of her teachers, a member of Alcoholics Anonymous (AA) herself, who spots the signs, and Geri grudgingly accepts her help. Scoppettone "has a swift, engaging style but the story is centered on a problem rather than on empathetic characters," asserts a *Publishers Weekly* contributor. Karen McGinley, however, concludes in *Best Sellers* that "*The Late Great Me* is a book which will make us all more aware of a problem that is growing around us.

It will help us to grow in our own awareness and understanding."

Scoppettone deals with another "controversial" issue in *Happy Endings Are All Alike,* a book which has been banned in several areas. "That's the one that got the least attention when I wrote it, the least reviews, the least anything. It sold the least because it's about girls," relates Scoppettone in her interview with Reicha. The novel, published in 1978, focuses on the lesbian relationship between two teenage girls in a small American town. Jaret and Peggy are spending a loving summer together when Peggy decides to test her sexual orientation by dating a young man. In the meantime, a jealous youth who has been spying on the two girls savagely beats and rapes Jaret, threatening to reveal her lesbianism if she tells anyone. With the support of her family, Jaret bravely brings charges against the boy. Although many critics found the rape scene unnecessarily brutal, Lenore Gordon writes in the *Interracial Books for Children Bulletin* that Scoppettone's "intent is not to shock, but to leave the reader with no illusions about the violence inherent in the act." Geraldine De-Luca, writing in the *Lion and the Unicorn,* sees *Happy Endings Are All Alike* as successfully exposing the prejudice against homosexuals, and maintains that "it is a book that challenges many of our conventional assumptions about life, particularly the belief that certain patterns lead to happiness and that they are the same for all of us. And it encourages the individual to stand for what he or she needs and believes."

Scoppettone's most recent young adult novel, *Playing Murder,* is similar to many of her adult novels—it concerns a murder and the solving of a crime. Anna Parker has just moved to Blue Haven Island, Maine, with her mother and father, her twin brother Bill, and her younger sister. Upon arriving in Maine, the entire Parker family starts to work at the restaurant they've bought. Despite the fact that she still has a boyfriend, Tony, in her old hometown, Anna falls for handsome Kirk Cunningham and begins to see him. The action reaches a turning point one night when the group is playing an after dark game called murder and Kirk, who is playing the "victim," is actually killed. In an attempt to clear her brother, who's been arrested for the crime, Anna learns that Kirk wasn't what he appeared to be, and eventually discovers the true murderer. Finding "several . . . questionable bits in the whodunit," a *Publishers Weekly* reviewer, however, goes on to add that *Playing Murder* "is nevertheless fine escape reading." Susan Levine, writing in *Voice of Youth Advocates,* finds Anna's narrative to be a bit repetitive at times, but asserts that "the book is interesting" and that "its suspense holds it together well."

In addition to her young adult novels, Scoppettone has written several novels for adults, under both her own name and the pseudonym Jack Early. The first, written under her own name, combines fact with fiction in a tale of sex and scandal. *Some Unknown Person* concerns the events leading up to and surrounding the actual death of twenty-five-year-old playgirl Starr Faithfull. A drug addict and alcoholic, Faithfull had been seduced at the age of eleven by her forty-five-year-old uncle—Andrew J. Peters, then Mayor of Boston. The details of their nine-year affair made the Faithfull murder case infamous. "Scoppettone has blended fact and fiction in this novel, creating her own conjecture of who the 'Unknown Person' responsible for Starr Faithfull's death might be," notes a *New York Times Book Review* contributor. The book introduces most of the people who were important in Faithfull's life, alternating back and forth in time between 1906 and 1977. *Some Unknown Person* "is an entertaining [and] interesting idea presented in an interesting way," concludes the *New York Times Book Review* contributor.

After publishing two more novels under her own name, *Such Nice People* and *Innocent Bystanders,* Scoppettone next turned to detective and mystery writing for adults under the pseudonym Jack Early. "One day this voice came to me in first person male, and I thought this is a private eye and his name is Fortune Fanelli," she explains in her *AAYA* interview. "He started talking to me, this sounds crazy, but that's what happened. I started writing in that voice and it was a forty-two-year-old man and in first person. I thought it would be very jarring to put a woman's name on the book, so I just picked the name Jack Early. Jack got prizes and all kinds of reviews that Sandra had never gotten and so I just sort of stuck with the name for a while. It was very nice to be anonymous—people didn't know until the third book who Jack Early was."

Scoppettone's first Jack Early book, *A Creative Kind of Killer,* was published in 1984 to favorable reviews. The book features Fortune Fanelli, an ex-cop and long-divorced single parent whose good investments have enabled him to become a part-time private detective. When the body of teenager Jennifer Baker is found in New York's SoHo district, Fanelli is hired by her uncle to find both Baker's killer and her younger runaway brother. During the investigation Fanelli is threatened, another body is found, and a kiddie porn ring is uncovered. "Early has filled his book with well-drawn characters and believable dialogue," writes a *Library Journal* contributor. And *Washington Post Book World* reviewer Jean M. White concludes that *A Creative Kind of Killer* is "a solid, well-crafted mystery, although not without flaws. But Fortune himself is a refreshingly different narrator-shamus."

Scoppettone's most recent Early novel was made into a television movie starring Charles Bronson and Dana Delany. *Donato and Daughter* concerns both the alienated members of the Donato family and a psychopath on the loose in New York City who is killing nuns. Lt. Dina Donato is in charge of the detective team, and appoints Sgt. Mike Donato, her father, as her partner, despite the difficulties the two have been having relating to each other since her brother's suicide. "Events move at a breakneck pace," relates a *Publishers Weekly* contributor, adding that the "suspense is unremitting" and that "numerous side plots and intriguing characters enliven" *Donato and Daughter.*

"I had three years after I finished *Donato and Daughter* where I couldn't write at all," reveals Scoppettone in her interview with Reicha. "When I was able to write again it was under my own name and it was *Everything You Have Is Mine.*" The first installment of a three book contract, *Everything You Have Is Mine* introduces the character Lauren Laurano and is "the first book I've ever written directly about myself," adds Scoppettone in her interview. "Meet Lauren Laurano," invites Michael Lassell in the *Advocate.* "She's short, Italian, and 42 (although she looks younger). She's a witty, articulate feminist, a lesbian chocoholic who gets queasy at the sight of blood. She's a wisecracking sweetheart of a pistol-packing private eye and the protagonist of one of the summer's hottest novels."

Published in 1991, *Everything You Have Is Mine* details Laurano's attempts to solve a rape case that quickly turns into a murder investigation. Laurano resides in Greenwich Village with her long-time lover Kip, a psychologist who has a large family that is very accepting of the couple's relationship. The young victim, who is date-raped and then murdered a short time later, is called Lake Huron and was born during the 1960s to a very complicated family. To find first the rapist, and then the murderer, Laurano must overcome her fear of computers and untangle Huron's family ties from amid lies that have been told over the years. In her review of *Everything You Have Is Mine,* White finds the plot to be overcomplicated, but concedes that Scoppettone "is a sharply observant writer and captures the flavor of the Greenwich Village scene with its quirky characters and sassy-smart talk." A *Publishers Weekly* contributor concludes that "a lively pace, convincing characterization, colorful scene setting and sensitive observations about complications among families ordinary and unusual far outweigh the overwrought elements of the plot; readers will want to follow Lauren on her next case."

The next novel featuring Laurano, *I'll Be Leaving You Always,* has the detective dealing with the death of a close friend and solving the murder at the same time. Scoppettone hopes that the books featuring Laurano will help women "feel prouder and have more self-esteem as lesbians. I think it's already happening," she explains in her *AAYA* interview. "*Everything You Have Is Mine* is the first mainstream lesbian private eye book and it took a courageous publisher to print it. I got my first daily *New York Times* review for that book—I don't know if you know what that means. After writing for all these years, to finally be reviewed in the daily *Times* was really exciting. I had gotten other reviews in the Sunday *Times,* but that's not quite as prestigious. It was this book, and it was reviewed very well without making a big number about the lesbianism either. It is what it is and that's the way the reviewer took it and it was really great."

Although she has written for both young adult and adult audiences, Scoppettone now chooses to write for the older group. "I do prefer writing for adults now only because I feel I've said everything I have to say to young adults," she tells Reicha. "However, if something should come to mind that I feel would be best in that form I would do it. I think my young adult books have been fairly successful because I don't write down, I pretty much write the same." The several young adult novels that Scoppettone has written deal with issues not normally presented to teens and have had a greater impact on them because of it. "My young adult books have had a tremendous effect," asserts Scoppettone in her interview. "I've known people who have gotten sober after reading *The Late Great Me;* it ticked off something in their head. Certainly the gay and lesbian books have affected people's lives. I wish that I'd had such books when I was a kid. What I really hoped was that the books would let them know it was okay. It was amazing, because when I was doing readings for *Everything You Have Is Mine* a number of people came up to me and said, 'I was a fan of yours when I was a little girl and your books changed my life.' It's very thrilling. So I guess I hope these books change people's lives in a positive way."

BIOGRAPHICAL/CRITICAL SOURCES:

BOOKS

Contemporary Literary Criticism, Volume 26, Gale, 1983.
Scoppettone, Sandra, in an essay for *Speaking for Ourselves,* compiled and edited by Donald R. Gallo, National Council of Teachers of English, 1990, pp. 186-87.
Scoppettone, in an interview with Susan M. Reicha for *Authors and Artists for Young Adults,* Volume 11, Gale, 1993.

PERIODICALS

Advocate, July 2, 1991, p. 93.
Best Sellers, May, 1976, p. 40; June, 1982, p. 123.
Booklist, November 15, 1974, p. 340.
Interracial Books for Children Bulletin, Volume 10, number 6, 1979, p. 16.

Library Journal, September 15, 1974, pp. 2297-298; April 15, 1980, p. 1005; April 1, 1984, p. 736; May 1, 1985, p. 81.
Lion and the Unicorn, winter, 1979-80, pp. 125-48.
New York Times Book Review, January 12, 1975, p. 8; February 22, 1976, p. 38; September 25, 1977, p. 22; April 25, 1982, p. 44; October 13, 1985, p. 29; April 14, 1991, p. 25.
Publishers Weekly, November 10, 1975, p. 47; June 20, 1977, p. 66; July 24, 1978, p. 100; February 22, 1980, p. 92; December 3, 1982, p. 50; February 17, 1984, p. 73; March 22, 1985, p. 54; August 16, 1985, p. 71; January 15, 1988, p. 79; February 22, 1991, p. 213.
School Library Journal, January, 1976, p. 58; February, 1979, p. 65; May, 1980, p. 92.
Village Voice, December 16, 1974, pp. 51-52.
Voice of Youth Advocates, August, 1982, p. 37; June, 1985, p. 135.
Washington Post Book World, May 20, 1984, pp. 8-9; April 21, 1991, p. 10.
Wilson Library Bulletin, December, 1978, p. 341.

—Sketch by Susan M. Reicha

*   *   *

SCOTT, Arthur Finley 1907-

PERSONAL: Born November 30, 1907, in Kronstadt, Orange Free State (now part of Union of South Africa); son of Ernest Finley (a physician) and Mary (Edwards) Scott; married Margaret Clare Smith (died May 16, 1969); children: Jennifer Ann (Mrs. Michael Green), Christine Margaret (Mrs. Peter Pearce). *Education:* Emmanuel College, Cambridge, B.A. (with honors), 1930, M.A. (with honors), 1934; Oxford University, graduate study, 1930. *Religion:* "Methodist nonconformist." *Avocational interests:* Rugby football, cricket, swimming, painting, gardening.

ADDRESSES: Home—59 Syon Park Gardens, Osterley, Isleworth TW7 5NE, Middlesex, England.

CAREER: Oakham School, Oakham, Rutland, England, senior English master, 1930-33; Taunton School, Taunton, Somerset, England, senior English master, 1933-43; Grammar School, Kettering, Northants, England, headmaster, 1943-51; Borough Road Training College, Isleworth, Middlesex, England, senior lecturer, 1951-73. Lecturer for British Council at Cambridge University, 1951; University of London, examiner in English, 1955-58. Reader in English for Cambridge University Press, Macmillan Co., and George C. Harrap & Co. Ltd. Member, Kettering Youth Employment Committee, 1947-51, Kettering Film Society (chairman, 1947-51), and Kettering Three Arts Society (chairman, 1948-51). *Military service:* Royal Navy, Volunteer Reserve; became sub-lieutenant.

MEMBER: International Biographical Association (life fellow), International Platform Association, Society of Authors, Royal Society of Literature, Institute of Education (University of London).

WRITINGS:

Meaning and Style, Macmillan, 1938.
Poetry and Appreciation, Macmillan, 1939.
A Year's Work in Precis, Cambridge University Press, 1939.
From Paragraph to Essay, two books, Cambridge University Press, 1941.
Country Life, Macmillan, 1947.
English Composition, four books, Cambridge University Press, 1951-52.
English Literature: The Younger Children's Encyclopaedia, Odhams, 1956.
New Reading, fourteen books, Reader's Digest, 1956-60.
Illustrated English, four books, Parrish, 1957.
The Poet's Craft, Cambridge University Press, 1957.
Odhams Young People's Encyclopaedia, four volumes, Odhams, 1958.
(With Kathleen Box) *A Bridge to English,* two books, Parrish, 1958.
Plain English, five books, Cambridge University Press, 1960-62.
Thought and Expression, Cambridge University Press, 1962.
(With D. M. Mukherjee) *English Composition and Translation,* Macmillan, 1962.
New English Readers, sixteen books, Mellifont Press, 1962-63.
The Craft of Prose, Macmillan, 1963.
Poems of the Piper, four books, Ward, Lock, 1963-64.
Current Literary Terms: A Concise Dictionary of Their Origin and Use, Macmillan, 1965.
Close Readings: A Course in the Critical Appreciation of Poetry, Heinemann, 1968.
The Savage King of the Seven Seas, Geoffrey Chapman, 1968.
The Vixen, the Bear and the Blacksmith, Geoffrey Chapman, 1968.
The Devil's Hat, Geoffrey Chapman, 1968.
Clet and the Sound of the Sea, Geoffrey Chapman, 1968.
The Gardener's Daughter, Geoffrey Chapman, 1968.
The Jealous Lioness, Geoffrey Chapman, 1968.
(With N. K. Aggarwala) *New Horizons,* ten books, Macmillan (India), 1968-71.
Who's Who in Chaucer, Hamish Hamilton, 1974.
America Grows, Vantage, 1982.
What Fire Kindles Genius?, Vantage, 1982.
What Makes a Prose Genius?, Vantage, 1983.
Five Hundred Special Places in Britain, Allborough Press, 1990.

"EVERY ONE A WITNESS" SERIES

The Georgian Age, Martins Publishers, 1970.
The Stuart Age, White Lion, 1974, Crowell, 1975.
The Plantagenet Age, White Lion, 1975, Crowell, 1976.
The Tudor Age, White Lion, 1975.
The Norman Age, White Lion, 1976.
The Roman Age, White Lion, 1977.
The Saxon Age, Croom Helm, 1979.
The Early Hanoverian Age, Croom Helm, 1980.

Also author of *The Early Victorian Age* and *The Late Victorian Age.*

EDITOR OR COMPILER

Modern Essays, three books, Macmillan, 1941-52.
Poems for Pleasure, Cambridge University Press, Books 1 and 2, 1955, Book 3 (teacher's guide and critical commentary), 1957.
Topics and Opinions, Macmillan (London), 1956, St. Martin's, 1962, 2nd series, Macmillan, 1963, 3rd series, 1964.
Selected Modern Reading, Parrish, 1956.
Blue Skies, Parrish, 1958.
Yellow Sands, Parrish, 1958.
Green Fields, Parrish, 1959.
Red Sails, Parrish, 1959.
Sing to the Sun, Parrish, 1959.
The Spoken Word, Macmillan, 1961.
New Paths to Poetry, four books, Parrish, 1961.
Speaking of the Famous, Macmillan, 1963.
Days of Adventure, Macmillan, 1963.
Tales Far and Near, Macmillan, 1963.
Thrills and Action, Macmillan, 1964.
Vital Themes Today, Macmillan, 1967.
Witch, Spirit, Devil, White Lion, 1974.

Also editor of other books.

OTHER

Contributor of literary critical articles and short stories to periodicals.

SIDELIGHTS: Arthur Finley Scott once told *CA:* "English literature is a splendid heritage and deserves special critical appreciation. My teaching and the best of my writing come from the way my tutor, Dr. F. R. Leavis, at Cambridge University, established true respect for creative writing, creative minds in English literature, a respect without which literary criticism can have no validity and no life."

SELBY, Bettina 1934-

PERSONAL: Born August 25, 1934, in Southsea, Hampshire, England; daughter of Sydney Thomas St. Clair (an insurance agent) and Emma Cecilia (a homemaker; maiden name, Woodhead) Desmonde; married Peter Max Selby (a film producer), September 1, 1958; children: Jonathan St. Clair, Catherine St. Clair, Anna St. Clair Baillie. *Education:* University of London, B.Ed. (with honors), 1974. *Politics:* "None." *Religion:* Anglican. *Avocational interests:* "I'm very interested in all religions, other cultures, ancient civilizations, classical music (especially high baroque), and the theatre, as well as children, mountains, bicycles and quiet country lanes to ride them on, good food, wine, and conversation. I value freedom more than money, which is probably why I can afford to be a writer."

ADDRESSES: Home and office—13 Tristan Sq., London SE3 9UB, England. *Agent*—Peter Selby, 13 Tristan Sq., London SE3 9UB, England.

CAREER: Free-lance photographer, 1954-70; teacher at primary schools in London, 1974-81; writer, 1981—. Gives frequent lectures and appears periodically on radio and television broadcasts. *Military service:* Women's Royal Army Corps, 1952-54.

WRITINGS:

Riding the Mountains Down, Gollancz, 1984.
Riding to Jerusalem, Sidgwick & Jackson, 1985.
Riding the Desert trail, Chatto & Windus, 1988.
The Fragile Islands, Richard Drew Publishing, 1989.
Riding North One Summer, Chatto & Windus, 1990.
Frail Dream of Timbuktu, John Murray, 1991.
Beyond Ararat, John Murray, 1993.

Contributor of articles to periodicals, including *Cyclists Monthly, Independent Times, Sunday Times,* and *Telegraph.*

About half of Selby's books have been translated into German, Dutch, and Japanese.

ADAPTATIONS: Riding the Desert Trail was the featured subject of a half-hour program in the "Art of Travel" series.

WORK IN PROGRESS: A television documentary about the medieval pilgrimage route through France and northern Spain to Santiago de Compostela, to be followed by a book on the same subject; a semi-autobiographical work about a young wartime evacuee's experience in a remote coal-mining village.

SIDELIGHTS: Bettina Selby's *Riding the Mountains Down* describes a four-thousand-mile solo bicycle trip the British author made across the Himalayas from Karachi to Kathmandu. Having become "addicted to cycling on holiday in Ireland," Selby undertook the adventure at age forty-seven without ever before visiting the Indian subcontinent. In a *Times Literary Supplement* review, Dervla Murphy observes, "*Riding the Mountains Down* conveys the everyday feel of Pakistan, Northern India and Nepal through an accumulation of the sort of detail that no one travelling by motor vehicle would be likely to observe."

Among other daunting trials of endurance, Selby voyaged across a thousand miles of the Sind desert and the Punjab at a pace of one hundred miles a day against a constant wind and temperatures in the high nineties. Negotiating the steep mountain grades sometimes required sidestepping avalanches and rock slides, and Selby describes once having to stuff a flat tire with clothing to make her way along a dried river-bed in a desolate region near the border of Himachal Pradesh and Uttar Pradesh in northern India.

Selby told *CA,* "I seem to have become a 'role model' for women at that medial stage of life, when their children are just leaving home, and they face a future of suddenly (and often frighteningly) increased freedom."

BIOGRAPHICAL/CRITICAL SOURCES:

PERIODICALS

Times Literary Supplement, June 22, 1984.

* * *

SHAW, Bob 1931-

PERSONAL: Born December 31, 1931, in Belfast, Northern Ireland; son of Robert William (a policeman) and Elizabeth (Megaw) Shaw; married Sarah Gourley, July 3, 1954 (died March, 1991); children: Alisa Claire, Robert Ian, Elizabeth Denise. *Education:* Attended Technical High School, Belfast, 1945-47. *Religion:* None.

ADDRESSES: Home—66 Knutsford Rd., Grappenhall, Warrington, Cheshire, England. *Agent*—Carnell Literary Agency, "Danescroft," Goose Lane, Little Hallingbury, Bishops Stortford, Herts CM22 7RG, England.

CAREER: Short Brothers and Harland Ltd. (aircraft manufacturers), Belfast, Northern Ireland, public relations officer, 1960-66; Belfast Telegraph Newspapers Ltd., Belfast, journalist, 1966-69; freelance writer in Belfast, 1969-70; Short Brother and Harland Ltd., public relations officer, 1970-73; Vickers Shipbuilding Group, Barrow-in-Furness, England, public relations officer, 1973-75; freelance writer, 1975—.

AWARDS, HONORS: Hugo Award, 1978 and 1979, for best science fiction small press writer.

WRITINGS:

NOVELS

Night Walk, Avon, 1967.
The Two-Timers, Ace Books, 1968.
The Palace of Eternity, Ace Books, 1969.
The Shadow of Heaven, Avon, 1969.
One Million Tomorrows, Ace Books, 1971.
The Ground Zero Man, Avon, 1971, revised version published as *The Peace Machine,* Gollancz, 1985.
Other Days, Other Eyes, Ace Books, 1972.
Orbitsville, Ace Books, 1975.
A Wreath of Stars, Doubleday, 1977.
Who Goes Here?, Ace Books, 1978.
Medusa's Children, Doubleday, 1979.
Ship of Strangers, Ace Books, 1979.
Vertigo, Ace Books, 1979, expanded version published as *Terminal Velocity,* Gollancz, 1991.
Dagger of the Mind, Gollancz, 1979.
The Ceres Solution, Gollancz, 1981.
Orbitsville Departure, Gollancz, 1983.
Fire Patteni, Gollancz, 1984.
The Ragged Astronauts, Gollancz, 1986.
The Wooden Spaceships, Gollancz, 1988.
The Fugitive Worlds, Gollancz, 1989.
Killer Planet (juvenile), Gollancz, 1989.
Orbitsville Judgement, Gollancz, 1991.
Warren Peace, Gollancz, 1993.

SHORT STORIES

Tomorrow Lies in Ambush, Ace Books, 1973.
Cosmic Kaleidoscope, Doubleday, 1977.
A Better Mantrap, Gollancz, 1982.
Dark Night in Toyland, Gollancz, 1989.

Also contributor of numerous short stories to American and British science fiction magazines.

NONFICTION

How to Write Science Fiction, Allison and Busby, 1993.

WORK IN PROGRESS: A humorous novel for Gollancz.

SIDELIGHTS: Bob Shaw's *The Ceres Solution* is "outstanding; unusually well-written, well-paced, economically and stylishly constructed," declared Galen Strawson in the *Times Literary Supplement.* In *The Ceres Solution,* Shaw ponders the mysteries of human longevity, proposing a future universe in which humans live to an average of seven hundred years on the multitude of planets they inhabit, except on Earth, where a longevity-reducing agent introduced into the atmosphere has shortened lifespans to seventy years. Tom Hutchinson of the *London Times* noted that Shaw's treatment of the premise is "delineated with care and precision, converting our disbelief

to an understanding of the way life might be in the early twenty-first century."

BIOGRAPHICAL/CRITICAL SOURCES:

PERIODICALS

Times (London), August 27, 1981; April 18, 1985.
Times Literary Supplement, August 7, 1981; March 12, 1982; January 13, 1984.

*   *   *

SHAY, Lacey
    See SHEBAR, Sharon Sigmond

*   *   *

SHEBAR, Sharon Sigmond   1945-
    (Lacey Shay, a joint pseudonym)

PERSONAL: Born July 24, 1945, in Brooklyn, NY; daughter of Joseph and Sara Libby (Stein) Sigmond; married Jonathan Shebar (a teacher), December 16, 1967; children: Tom, Joseph Franklin, Susan Ethel, Amy Johanna. *Education:* Hofstra University, B.Sc., 1966; Fairleigh Dickinson University, Montessori Society certificate, 1968; graduate study at Queens College of the City University of New York and at C. W. Post College of Long Island University.

ADDRESSES: Home—15 Connecticut Ave., Freeport, NY 11520. *Agent*—Denise Marcil Literary Agency, 316 West 82nd St., New York, NY 10024.

CAREER: Elementary school teacher in Amityville, NY, 1966-68; William Mount School, Rego Park, NY, teacher of Montessori education, 1969-74, director of Montessori education, 1972-74; author, 1977—. Special education teacher for New York school system, 1980—.

WRITINGS:

JUVENILES

(With Judith Schoder) *Groundhog Day,* illustrated by Bob Reese, Aro Publishing, 1977.
Whaling for Glory!, illustrated by Paul Frame, Messner, 1978.
The Mysterious World of Honeybees, illustrated with photographs by Steve Orlando and drawings by Jacqueline Seitz, Messner, 1979.
Milk, illustrated by Reese, Aro Publishing, 1979.
The Night Monsters, illustrated by Reese, Aro Publishing, 1979.
(With husband, Jonathan Shebar) *Animal Dads Take Over,* illustrated by Lino Saffioti, Simon & Schuster, 1981.

(With Schoder) *Blood Suckers* (nonfiction), Messner, 1981.
The Cardiff Giant, Messner, 1981.
The Bell Witch, Messner, 1983.

FOR ADULTS

The Montessori Enrichment Program, privately printed, 1970.
(With Schoder) *How to Make Money at Home,* Wallaby Books, 1983.
(With Schoder under joint pseudonym Lacey Shay) *Loving Enemy* (romance novel), Wallaby Books, 1983.
Franklin D. Roosevelt and the New Deal, Barron's, 1987.
Bats, F. Watts, 1990.

OTHER

Also author, with daughter, Susan E. Shebar, of *Pennsylvania,* F. Watts. Author of column "Our Kids" in *Freeport Leader.* Contributor to periodicals, including *Weight Watchers, Animals, Catholic Digest, Young Judean, Dog Fancy, Cat Fancy,* and *Rainbow.*

WORK IN PROGRESS: Cape George Mouse, "a child's book about how a mouse and a ten-year-old girl befriend each other and escape their mutual loneliness."

SIDELIGHTS: Sharon Sigmond Shebar once told *CA:* "I write because I have to write; my nature will not allow me to do otherwise. For me, writing is an obsession and a passion. And when that passion is combined with talent and an interesting topic it brings both financial reward and a sense of accomplishment that is hard to equal in other areas of life."

*   *   *

SHELDON, Lee
   See LEE, Wayne C.

*   *   *

SHEPHERD, Michael
   See LUDLUM, Robert

*   *   *

SHERIDAN, Jane
   See WINSLOW, Pauline Glen

SHERRY, James (Terence) 1946-

PERSONAL: Born December 30, 1946, in Philadelphia, PA; son of Fred (a businessman) and Shirley (a yoga teacher; maiden name, Socolof) Sherry; married Lee Sahlins (a painter), 1968 (marriage ended); married Deborah Thomas, 1990. *Education:* Reed College, A.B., 1968.

ADDRESSES: Home—300 Bowery, New York, NY 10012.

CAREER: Poet. Roof Books, New York City, editor, 1976—; independant management consultant, 1977—. President of Segue Foundation, 1977—; member of the board of Igor Foundation.

MEMBER: Poets and Writers, PEN, Academy of American Poets.

WRITINGS:

Lazy Sonnets (poems), Gibralter, 1974.
Part Songs (poems), Segue Books, 1978.
In Case (prose), Sun and Moon Press, 1980.
Integers (poems), Dance Theatre Workshop, 1980.
Converses (poems), Awede Press, 1982.
Popular Fiction, Roof Books, 1985.
The Word I Like White Paint Considered (poems), Awede Press, 1987.
Our Nuclear Heritage, Sun and Moon Press, 1991.
Dos Capade (poems), Hot Bird Mfg., 1991.

SIDELIGHTS: James Sherry told *CA:* "Writing should entertain the brain."

*   *   *

SLAVIN, Morris 1913-

PERSONAL: Born June 28, 1913, in Kiev, Russia; came to the United States, 1923; naturalized U.S. citizen, 1929; son of Lazar (in business) and Vera (a dentist; maiden name, Hansburg) Slavin; married Sophie S. Lockshin, December 31, 1940; children: Jeanne Slavin Kaplan. *Education:* Ohio State University, B.S., 1938; University of Pittsburgh, M.A., 1952; Western Reserve University (now Case Western Reserve University), Ph.D., 1961.

ADDRESSES: Home—262 Outlook Ave., Youngstown, OH 44504. *Office*—Department of History, Youngstown State University, 410 Wick Ave., Youngstown, OH 44555.

CAREER: Youngstown State University, Youngstown, OH, assistant professor, 1961-63, associate professor, 1963-71, professor, 1971-81, emeritus professor of history, 1981—. Visiting associate professor at State University of New York at Stony Brook, 1966-67; fellow, Princeton Institute for Advanced Study, 1987-88. Active participant in

American Civil Liberties Union and Peace Council of Youngstown. *Military service:* U.S. Army, Field Artillery, 1942-43; became sergeant.

MEMBER: Wester Society for French History, American Historical Association, American Society for Eighteenth-Century Studies, Society for French Historical Studies, Societe des Etudes Robespierristes, Societe Francaise d'Etude du 18e Siecle, East Central Society for Eighteenth-Century Studies, Amnesty International, Ohio Academy of History.

AWARDS, HONORS: Distinguished professor award, Youngstown State University, 1976; *The French Revolution in Miniature: Section Droits-de-l'Homme, 1789-1795,* was named an outstanding book of 1984 by *Choice* and selected by the Ohio Academy of History as "the outstanding historical publication" of 1984; Heritage Award, Youngstown State University, 1988; Doctor of Humane Letters, Youngstown State University, 1989.

WRITINGS:

The French Revolution in Miniature: Section Droits-de-l'Homme, 1789-1795, Princeton University Press, 1984.
The Making of an Insurrection: Parisian Sections and the Gironde, Harvard University Press, 1986.
The End of the Popular Movement: The French Revolution and the Hebertistes, Louisiana State University Press, 1993.
The Left and the French Revolution, Humanities Press, 1994.

CONTRIBUTOR

(And editor with Agnes M. Smith) *Bourgeois, Sans-Culottes, and Other Frenchmen,* Wilfrid-Laurier University, 1981.
Eine Jury fur Jacques Roux, Akademie Verlag, 1981.
Samuel F. Scott and Barry Rothaus, editors, *Historical Dictionary of the French Revolution, 1789-1799,* Greenwood Press, 1984.
Louis Patsouras and William O. Reichert, editors, *The Crucible of Socialism,* Humanities Press, 1987.
Women in History, Literature and the Arts, Youngstown State University Press, 1989.
Patsouras and Jack Ray Thomas, editors, *Essays on Socialism,* Mellen Research University Press, 1992.

Contributor to periodicals, including *Annales Historiques de la Revolution Francaise, Historian, Cahiers Leon Trotsky,* and *Journal of Modern History.*

SIDELIGHTS: Morris Slavin told *CA:* "I became interested in the French Revolution during my teens, while still reading the Merriwell novels, Sinclair Lewis, and Leo Tolstoy. As a child of the Depression I also became aware of the many problems arising from social injustice. My interest in the Sans-Culottes may be traced to this early experience. Both of my parents had been members of the Jewish Bund in its struggle against Czarism. Later, they opposed the monopoly of political power enjoyed by the Bolsheviks."

BIOGRAPHICAL/CRITICAL SOURCES:

PERIODICALS

American Historical Review, June, 1985; December, 1987, p. 1218.
Eighteenth Century Studies, winter, 1985, p. 296.
English History Review, January, 1990, p. 216.
Historian, August, 1986, p. 588; August, 1988, p. 586.
History: Reviews of New Books, November, 1986, p. 47.
History Today, August, 1984.
Journal of Modern History, June, 1989, p. 386.
Times Literary Supplement, August 3, 1984; March 11, 1988, p. 287.

*   *   *

SLAVITT, David R(ytman) 1935-
(David Benjamin, Henry Lazarus, Lynn Meyer, Henry Sutton)

PERSONAL: Born March 23, 1935, in White Plains, NY; son of Samuel Saul (a lawyer) and Adele Beatrice (Rytman) Slavitt; married Lynn Nita Meyer, August 27, 1956 (divorced December 20, 1977); married Janet Lee Abrahm (a physician), April 16, 1978; children: (first marriage) Evan Meyer, Sarah Rebecca, Joshua Rytman. *Education:* Yale University, A.B. (magna cum laude), 1956; Columbia University, M.A., 1957. *Politics:* Independent. *Religion:* Jewish.

ADDRESSES: Home—523 South 41st St., Philadelphia, PA 19104. *Agent*—William Morris Agency, 1350 Avenue of the Americas, New York, NY 10019.

CAREER: Georgia Institute of Technology, Atlanta, instructor in English, 1957-58; *Newsweek,* New York City, began as mailroom clerk, became book and film critic and associate editor, 1958-63, movie editor, 1963-65; freelance writer, 1965—. Assistant professor at the University of Maryland at College Park, 1977; associate professor of English at Temple University, 1978-80; lecturer in English at Columbia University, 1985-86; lecturer at Rutgers University, 1987—; lecturer in English and classics at University of Pennsylvania, 1991—. Visiting professor at the University of Texas at El Paso, University of Maryland, and Temple University. Has read his poetry at numerous colleges and universities and at the Folger Shakespeare Library and the Library of Congress.

AWARDS, HONORS: Pennsylvania Council on Arts award, 1985; National Endowment for the Arts fellowship in translation, 1988; Award in literature, American Academy and Institute of Arts and Letters, 1989; Rockefeller Foundation Artist's Residence, 1989.

WRITINGS:

POETRY

Suits for the Dead (Volume 8 of "Poets of Today" series), Scribner, 1961.
The Carnivore, University of North Carolina Press, 1965.
Day Sailing and Other Poems, University of North Carolina Press, 1969.
Child's Play, Louisiana State University Press, 1972.
Vital Signs: New and Selected Poems, Doubleday, 1975.
Rounding the Horn, Louisiana State University Press, 1978.
Dozens, Louisiana State University Press, 1981.
Big Nose, Louisiana State University Press, 1983.
The Elegies to Delia of Albius Tibullus, Bits Press, 1985.
The Walls of Thebes, Louisiana State University Press, 1986.
Equinox and Other Poems, Louisiana State University Press, 1989.
Eight Longer Poems, Louisiana State University Press, 1990.
Crossroads, Louisiana State University Press, 1993.

NOVELS

Rochelle; or Virtue Rewarded, Chapman & Hall, 1966, Delacorte, 1967.
Feel Free, Delacorte, 1968.
Anagrams, Hodder & Stoughton, 1970, Doubleday, 1971.
ABCD, Doubleday, 1972.
The Outer Mongolian, Doubleday, 1973.
The Killing of the King, Doubleday, 1974.
(Under pseudonym Lynn Meyer) *Paperback Thriller,* Random House, 1975.
King of Hearts, Arbor House, 1976.
(Under pseudonym Henry Lazarus) *That Golden Woman,* Fawcett, 1976.
Jo Stern, Harper, 1978.
(Under pseudonym David Benjamin) *The Idol,* Putnam, 1979.
Cold Comfort, Methuen, 1980.
Ringer, Dutton, 1982.
Alice at 80, Doubleday, 1984.
The Agent (created by Bill Adler), Doubleday, 1986.
The Hussar, Louisiana State University Press, 1987.
Salazar Blinks, Atheneum, 1988.
Lives of the Saints, Atheneum, 1989.
Turkish Delights, Louisiana State University Press, 1993.
The Cliff, Louisiana State University Press, 1994.

NOVELS UNDER PSEUDONYM HENRY SUTTON

The Exhibitionist, Geis, 1967.
The Voyeur, Geis, 1969.
Vector, Geis, 1970.
The Liberated, Doubleday, 1973.
The Sacrifice: A Novel of the Occult, Grosset & Dunlap, 1978.
The Proposal, Charter, 1980.

TRANSLATOR

(And adapter) *The Eclogues of Virgil,* illustrated by Raymond Davidson, Doubleday, 1971.
(And adapter) *The Eclogues and the Georgics of Virgil,* illustrated by Davidson, Doubleday, 1972.
(And adapter) *The Tristia of Ovid,* illustrated by Davidson, Bellflower Press, 1986.
(And adapter) *Ovid's Poetry of Exile,* Johns Hopkins University Press, 1990.
(And editor) *Seneca,* Volume 1: *The Tragedies,* Johns Hopkins University Press, 1992.
(And adapter) *The Fables of Avianus,* Johns Hopkins University Press, 1993.
(And adapter) *The Metamorphoses of Ovid,* Johns Hopkins University Press, 1994.

OTHER

King Saul (play), produced in New York City, 1967.
The Cardinal Sins (two-act play; produced in New York City, 1969), Gardner, Pimm & Blackman, 1972.
(With Paul F. Secord and Carl W. Backman) *Understanding Social Life: An Introduction to Social Psychology,* McGraw-Hill, 1976.
(Editor) Adrien Stoutenburg, *Land of Superior Mirages: New and Selected Poems,* Johns Hopkins University Press, 1986.
Physicians Observed (nonfiction), Doubleday, 1987.
Short Stories Are Not Real Life: Short Fiction, Louisiana State University Press, 1991.
Virgil (criticism and interpretation), Yale University Press, 1991.

Contributor to books, including *The Girl in the Black Raincoat,* edited by George Garrett, Duell, Sloan & Pearce, 1966; *Man and the Movies,* edited by W. R. Robinson, Louisiana State University Press, 1967; *The Writer's Voice,* edited by Garrett, Morrow, 1973; *Contemporary Poetry in America,* edited by Miller Williams, Random House, 1973; *Poetry: Points of Departure,* edited by Henry Taylor, Winthrop, 1974; *Sexuality in the Movies,* edited by Thomas R. Atkins, Indiana University Press, 1975; *The Brand-X Anthology of Poetry,* edited by William Zaranka, Apple-Wood Books, 1981; and *Tygers of Wrath: Poems of Hate, Anger, and Invective,* edited by X. J. Kennedy, University of Georgia Press, 1981. Also contributor to periodicals, including *Kenyon Review, Sewanee Review, Yale Review, New Republic,* and *Esquire.* Occasional contributor of book reviews to the *New York Times, Newsday, Chicago Tribune,* and *Philadelphia Inquirer.*

ADAPTATIONS: Film rights to *The Hussar* have been sold.

SIDELIGHTS: David R. Slavitt has "lived three lives," writes Margo Jefferson in the *New York Times Book Review:* "as a scrupulously genteel poet, as a serious minor novelist and as an exuberantly crass pseudonymous writer of potboilers." Despite his ventures into numerous literary genres, though, Slavitt considers himself a poet first and foremost—a poet who in fact writes novels only to support his habit of writing poetry. "Slavitt may well be unique in the contemporary American literary scene," maintains George Garrett in the *Dictionary of Literary Biography: American Novelists since World War II,* "being able to write 'public' and 'private' novels (a distinction he now uses instead of the earlier and widely used division between 'popular' and 'serious' fiction) with apparent ease, with certainly no fall-off of energy, and, at one and the same time, to continue to be one of our most productive and independent poets."

Born in White Plains, New York, in 1935, Slavitt soon realized that he was part of "a grand scheme" of his father's to right an old wrong. At the end of his sophomore year in college, Slavitt's father was forced to withdraw from Yale because his father had died and the family could no longer afford to pay the tuition. His hopes and dreams dashed, he was forced to finish his education through night classes at New York University, but he vowed to have a son one day and send him first to Andover and then to Yale. "Depending on how this story is told, it is either sad or else absurd and therefore funny. (Or maybe just plain nuts?)," reflects Slavitt in an essay for *Contemporary Authors Autobiography Series (CAAS).* "It is Faulknerian, if on a somewhat smaller scale. As far as I was concerned, though, it was grand enough to surround me and dictate the terms of much of my life."

Making his way through the public schools in White Plains, Slavitt reflects that he was, and still is, "bright, quick, and also easily bored." Constantly told that he was not applying himself and he would never get into Yale if he did not, Slavitt explains in *CAAS* how this tempered his view of himself: "I was . . . aware of my enormous *importance.* Even in these elementary grades, I was getting double messages from my parents about how proud they were of my obvious abilities, and at the same time how distressed—or furious—they often were at my indifferent performance." Finishing up at the local schools, Slavitt continued on to Andover at the age of fifteen and experienced one of his first great disappointments. "What I dis-

covered after a while was that it was just a huge, rich, rather picky high school that looked pretty good in comparison with most public high schools where the physical safety of the students can't be guaranteed," recalls Slavitt in his autobiographical essay. "My life was again divided between a set of arbitrary external demands—whether my father's or Andover's hardly made much difference—and an inner life, the expression, or at least the fantasy, of that specialness I'd been taught I bore. What I needed to prove, both to myself and to the world, was that I was as good as my parents had always thought, but on my terms and for my reasons rather than theirs."

It was while he was at Andover that Slavitt first began to write poetry, and for a while he even thought of applying to Harvard because he thought it would provide a better atmosphere for a would-be writer. Slavitt's father would not even discuss such an idea—his son would go to Yale, and then to Harvard Law School. Going along with his father, Slavitt did attend Yale and had a much better time than anticipated; Andover had prepared him well. In his *CAAS* essay Slavitt recalls that he viewed "Yale's general indifference to artists and intellectuals [as] appropriate preparation for the great world where nobody gives much of a damn whether you're a writer or not, or, if you're a writer, whether you finish the book you're working on or not, or do today's stint or just bag it."

Graduating magna cum laude in 1956, Slavitt disappointed his father by not going on to law school, and instead got his first job in the personnel office of *Reader's Digest.* After earning enough money to buy two spots on the *Queen Elizabeth* for himself and his bride to be, Slavitt married Lynn Meyer and the two sailed for Europe. Only a week after their arrival, however, the couple learned that Lynn's mother had died and they had to return home. Slavitt then decided to go back to school for his master's, which he earned from Columbia in 1957. His son was born a month later, and Slavitt resolved to give teaching a try before going on to earn his doctorate. The best offer he received was from Georgia Tech, but the experience was so unpleasant that Slavitt lasted for just less than a year. "It was just dreadful," he explains in *CAAS.* "The students weren't stupid, or most of them weren't. But they were badly educated in rural secondary schools in Georgia. They were ambitious kids who wanted to escape the farms and get jobs where they'd wear suits and ties and do drafting for Lockheed at Marietta. But there were no English majors at Tech, and the department was a service department, was made up of hopefuls like me and desperate has-beens who, to assuage the wounds to their pride, were teaching high-class stuff—Homer, Shakespeare, and all the classy authors. Fundamentally, there were two courses, remedial writing, and remedial reading, although they were called Composition and Literature."

When his wife came down with mononucleosis and required a significant amount of bed rest, Slavitt was able to escape back to his parents' house in White Plains. Soon after, he began his seven years at *Newsweek,* eventually becoming the film critic. "I look back on those . . . years at *Newsweek* as a valuable part of my training as a writer, both for the writing itself and for the observation of the world of show biz and the arts," relates Slavitt in *CAAS.* It was near the beginning of his career at *Newsweek* that he had his first volume of poetry published in the "Poets of Today" series. "I was a published poet, but I didn't feel like one. I felt like a guy who works at *Newsweek,*" says Slavitt in *CAAS.* It wasn't until he had published a novel and completed another volume of poetry that Slavitt finally decided to leave the magazine behind and become a full-time writer.

"Since the appearance of his first collection of poems, *Suits for the Dead* (1961), in the distinguished Scribners *Poets of Today* series, Slavitt has proved himself to be one of the most adroitly versatile and productive writers in America," notes Garrett in his essay in the *Dictionary of Literary Biography: American Poets since World War II.* Garrett continues on to proclaim that "by most definitions and standards he would have to be regarded . . . as a major poet." In one of his principal collections, *Vital Signs: New and Selected Poems,* Slavitt collects all of his previously published poetry along with eighty-eight new pieces to create a volume of poems which "seem to be equally well crafted, equally finished, and thus for all practical purposes, to be virtually simultaneous in the making rather than the result of a steady and discernable development," describes Garrett. The poems in this collection, which are arranged by theme and subject, combine classical figures, "lively humor," and "wry truths," asserts *Library Journal* contributor James McKenzie; and the subjects they encompass range from Slavitt's own everyday experience to the experience of ancient civilizations. Although Helen Vendler suggests in the *New York Times Book Review* that the poems are frequently flat and didactic, *Poetry* contributor Robert Holland considers *Vital Signs* to be "the kind of book one should not just read, but live with."

"Slavitt has always conceived of poetry as, essentially and by definition, an elite and hermetic art," relates Garrett. His 1978 collection *Rounding the Horn,* which contains "poems of statement and meditation, each built around a central image or metaphor, each related to all the others thematically and in sequence," says Garrett, deals with many of the same topics found in Slavitt's earlier works. Although Peter Stitt declares in *Poetry* that Slavitt "takes no artistic chances" and that the poems are "just a kind of mindless opinionizing," William H. Pritchard maintains in the *Hudson Review* that *Rounding the Horn* "is a

thoroughly satisfactory book, always alive in its language, sometimes poignant and touching."

Slavitt's "special quality" in *The Walls of Thebes* is his "comic vision," remarks J. Hafley in *Choice,* adding that it is the poet's "finest volume thus far." Life and art are the themes of this book, and there is a "pervasive melancholy" which is warranted by the "personal horror" found in the poems, observes *Booklist* contributor Joseph Parisi. *Eight Longer Poems* also examines these themes, suggests a *Publishers Weekly* contributor, adding that Slavitt is able to transform "personal tragedy and individual suffering into universal circumstance." Slavitt is "a poet of almost brutally ironic contradictions," writes Garrett. "He is a learned and gifted metricist and an elegant formalist, whose use of many and various verse forms, both traditional and oddly and newly designed, book by book, could easily be taken as a textbook for the use of forms in contemporary American poetry."

Aside from writing his own poetry, Slavitt also translated and interpreted the poetry of Virgil in *The Eclogues of Virgil* and *The Eclogues and the Georgics of Virgil.* "Borrowing from the ways of Medieval and Renaissance translators, Slavitt developed a method involving sections of summary, critical interpretation, and commentary; and dramatically, and with deliberate anachronism, introducing himself, the living poet and translator, speaking directly to the present-day reader," describes Garrett. In the preface to the first volume, Slavitt justifies the liberties he takes in his translation: "My hope, in these renditions of Virgil's exciting poems, is that by taking certain liberties, I shall have been able to convey something of the experience of the originals, the exhilarating whipsaw feeling Virgil's readers must have experienced as they translated back from the bucolic pastures and fields of Meliboeus and Menalcas and Moeris to the elegant drawing rooms of Roman literary life, and then, feeling the brittleness, the sophistication, the suffocation of Rome, yearned for something else, something better—and by that yearning made the cardboard shepherds suddenly real as only the objects of profound desire can be." Philip Murray, writing in *Poetry,* believes Slavitt is successful in his translations, creating "a bright and clever book." Murray also asserts: "The qualities Mr. Slavitt projects best are not always those most in evidence in the original although they are at times admirable in themselves. This is a 'fun' book, a funny and sad book, and eminently readable."

In addition to his poetry and his translations, Slavitt has also written a number of novels. Garrett asserts in his essay on Slavitt's novels that "if we turn back to his poetry as a kind of touchstone for all his work, we shall see that one major characteristic of his poetry has not yet appeared in his fiction. And that quality is his profound interest in history." Among the characteristics that do appear

Slavitt's novels are humor and satire. "He brings to his fiction a great deal of practical knowledge of and experience in the craft of writing, ranging from poetry to reportage and made richer and complex by his educational background with its emphasis on the classics," comments Garrett.

One of Slavitt's earlier novels, *Anagrams,* published in 1970, "offers a satirical insight into the Quality Lit Biz as conducted on American campuses," explains Michael Mewshaw in the *New York Times Book Review.* The novel centers on Jerome Carpenter, a young poet who writes phony doctoral theses on the side to support his struggle as a poet. "As a display of verbal pyrotechnics, the book is unbeatable," states Mewshaw. "Each page pulses with provocative opinions, puns, jokes and the sort of throwaway lines most authors parcel out for maximum mileage." Throughout the novel, the process of writing a long poem is described as Carpenter goes through it. Although a *Publishers Weekly* contributor finds *Anagrams* "dry and stifling," Thomas Lask writes in the *New York Times* that the novel "races along with comic inventiveness, like the last reel of a silent movie."

With another novel, *Alice at 80,* Slavitt blends fact and fiction. The book begins in 1932 with eighty-year-old Alice Liddell Hargreaves—the inspiration for Lewis Carroll's *Alice in Wonderland*—receiving an honorary doctorate from Columbia University. Realizing that it is really Carroll who is being honored, Liddell begins to look back at how he influenced both her life and those of other young girls. *Alice at 80* "has a hint of the dreamy magic of 'Alice,' " asserts *Los Angeles Times Book Review* contributor Richard Eder; "at the same time, it is a dangerously unsettling hypothesis about Dodgson's shy proclivities and their effect on three children that he photographed, sometimes nude." The other two girls are Isa Bowman, an actress who played Alice on stage, and Glenda Fenwick, who Carroll befriended on a beach in England. "Slavitt arranges their crossed paths and purposes in order to examine sex, fantasy and power as well as the emotional ties that bind them, the rules of age, gender and class that govern them," writes Jefferson. "*Alice at 80* is an original, an ingenious mixture of rumination and fantasy. . . . Slavitt writes with subtlety and a piercing indirection," concludes Eder.

The plot from a novel by an obscure German author is interpreted and rewritten by Slavitt in *The Hussar.* The protagonist is Stefan, a young new lieutenant in the Austro-Hungarian Empire just prior to the Seven Weeks' War. His regiment is billeted in a small, insignificant border town, and Stefan must lodge with a sophisticated widow, Sonja, and her lame, beautiful daughter Eugenie. Fantasizing about the women before he arrives, Stefan becomes involved with both of them, and is astonished when they

want the relationships to continue. After impregnating and marrying Eugenie, Stefan becomes morally confused and he shoots himself. The novel "is brought to life by the characters who engage our emotions" and "its esoteric source and intent" will appeal to "more scholarly audiences," maintains *Library Journal* contributor Lawrence Rungren. Pointing to the "witty and eruditious verve" in Slavitt's writing, Christopher Zenowich adds in the *Chicago Tribune Book World* that "*The Hussar* is a curiously charming and bittersweet meditation."

The narrator of *Lives of the Saints,* published in 1989, is a journalist who writes for a trashy Florida tabloid. Working on a story about the victims of a mass murder at the local Piggly-Wiggly, he focuses on the things they left behind, using the objects to get a sense of who the victims were. Throughout the novel the narrator routinely quotes Nicolas Malebranche, a French writer who did not believe in cause and effect, only random and illogical events. This is accounted for when it is explained that the narrator's wife and daughter were recently killed by a drunk driver; by spouting the philosophy of Malebranche, the journalist is saying he can find no logical explanation for the accident. "Slavitt is an original and ingenious writer," remarks Eder in the *Los Angeles Times,* adding: "*Lives of the Saints* juggles with a lovely selection of paradoxes and speculations and with the silliness, comedy and grief that lie in its characters' lives." And according to Michael Upchurch in the *Washington Post,* the novel "is angelically written, devilishly constructed and all too peculiarly human. Here's some impressive and entertaining fiction by a writer who deserves to be better known."

Although Slavitt suffers from anonymity under his own name, he did gain fame and recognition with his writings under the pseudonym Henry Sutton. Slavitt entered the popular literary business after publisher Bernard Geis was amused by one of his book reviews in the *New York Herald Tribune* and suggested what financial gains Slavitt could realize by writing a bestseller. "I replied," recalls Slavitt in his *CAAS* essay, "thanking him for his interest but letting him know that he had the wrong fellow. I was a highbrow low-revenue kind of author." Geis was insistent, though, and Slavitt met with him during his next trip to New York; and under the pseudonym of Henry Sutton, *The Exhibitionist* catapulted Slavitt into the world of popular fiction. The only reason for the pseudonym, explains Slavitt in his essay, was to sustain his first novel written under his own name, *Rochelle; or Virtue Rewarded,* which was to be published in the same month *The Exhibitionist* was slated to appear. In this way, book stores could carry a substantial number of both works.

Discussing the pseudonym in relation to his other work, Slavitt told *CA:* "I have had to struggle with Sutton for years. It seemed to me at the time a simple enough indication of what I was doing. No one criticizes the Chrysler for manufacturing Plymouths under a different name, or the Omega company for putting out Tissot watches. But my assumption of a second name for a different kind of writing seemed to offend a certain middle-brow sensibility. Most newspapers dismissed any Sutton book as slumming, and also dismissed anything I did under my own name as high-brow and low-revenue and, paradoxically, just as proper to be ignored. Now that I've paid for the educations of my children, I think it extremely unlikely that I'll ever write a pseudonymous book again."

Slavitt also commented to *CA* on his relative anonymity since his Sutton books. "Even as a poet, I have been more or less ignored," he explains. "The old snobbishness about poets who wrote any fiction at all seems to have faded away. But it is not yet permissible to have written successful commercial fiction. I say this without any particular complaint. I rather like being ignored, having by now become accustomed to the freedom and the privacy that are the handmaidens to obscurity. I've come to understand that the lit biz is a silly waste of time. Literature, on the other hand, is not." And in his autobiographical essay Slavitt explains that this obscurity has enabled him "to return to a kind of amateur status as a writer, by which I mean that from here on I'm unlikely to write anything strictly or even primarily for money. It has to be a book I'd do for the fun of it. And if it doesn't get published, too bad."

BIOGRAPHICAL/CRITICAL SOURCES:

BOOKS

Contemporary Authors Autobiography Series, Volume 3, Gale, 1986.
Contemporary Literary Criticism, Gale, Volume 5, 1976, Volume 14, 1980.
Dictionary of Literary Biography, Gale, Volume 5: *American Poets since World War II,* 1980, Volume 6: *American Novelists since World War II, Second Series,* 1980.
Garrett, George, editor, *The Writer's Voice: Conversations with Contemporary Writers,* Morrow, 1973.
Garrett, *My Silk Purse and Yours,* University of Missouri Press, 1992.
Slavitt, David, translator and adapter, *The Eclogues of Virgil,* illustrated by Raymond Davidson, Doubleday, 1971.

PERIODICALS

Booklist, October 15, 1986.
Chicago Tribune, January 2, 1990.
Chicago Tribune Book World, August 10, 1980; May 31, 1987.
Choice, October, 1986.
Hollins Critic, June, 1971.

Hudson Review, winter, 1975-76; summer, 1979.
Library Journal, May 15, 1975; February 15, 1981; May 15, 1987; April 15, 1990.
Life, January 26, 1968.
Los Angeles Times, December 21, 1989.
Los Angeles Times Book Review, July 15, 1984.
New Republic, August 20, 1990.
New Yorker, January 29, 1990.
New York Times, November 3, 1967; July 26, 1971.
New York Times Book Review, September 17, 1967; May 5, 1968; February 16, 1969; June 14, 1970; September 5, 1971; January 14, 1973; July 8, 1973; October 27, 1974; September 7, 1975; January 2, 1977; March 18, 1979; August 19, 1984; February 15, 1987; August 2, 1987; September 13, 1987; February 26, 1989; February 11, 1990; June 3, 1990; January 19, 1992.
Poetry, August, 1972; February, 1977; January, 1980.
Publishers Weekly, September 4, 1967; May 10, 1971; March 30, 1990.
Spectator, May 4, 1974.
Times Literary Supplement, August 11, 1966; November 6, 1970; May 3, 1974.
Tribune Books (Chicago), May 31, 1987; October 8, 1987.
Virginia Quarterly Review, winter, 1972; spring, 1973; spring, 1975; autumn, 1979.
Washington Post, January 25, 1990.
Washington Post Book World, August 22, 1971; March 18, 1973; August 26, 1984; October 25, 1987.
West Coast Review of Books, July, 1978; November, 1978.

—*Sketch by Susan M. Reicha*

*   *   *

SLOTKIN, Richard S(idney) 1942-

PERSONAL: Born November 8, 1942, in Brooklyn, NY; son of Herman and Roselyn B. (Seplowitz) Slotkin; married Iris F. Shupack (a clinical social worker), June 23, 1963; children: Joel Elliot. *Education:* Brooklyn College of the City University of New York, B.A., 1963; Brown University, Ph.D., 1967. *Religion:* Jewish.

ADDRESSES: Home—708 Ridge Rd., Middletown, CT 06457. *Office*—American Studies Program, Wesleyan University, Middletown, CT 06459. *Agent*—Carl D. Brandt, Brandt & Brandt Literary Agents, Inc., 1501 Broadway, New York, NY 10036.

CAREER: Wesleyan University, Middletown, CT, assistant professor, 1966-73, associate professor, 1973-76, professor, 1976-82, Olin Professor of English, 1982—, director of American studies, 1976—.

MEMBER: American Studies Association, American Association of University Professors (chapter president,

1979-80), Modern Language Association of America, Western History Association, Organization of American Historians, American Historical Association, Authors Guild, Authors League of America, American Film Institute, Popular Culture Association, PEN, Society of American Historians (fellow).

AWARDS, HONORS: Albert Beveridge Award, American Historical Association, 1973, and National Book Award nomination, both for *Regeneration through Violence: The Mythology of the American Frontier, 1600-1860;* National Endowment for the Humanities fellow, 1973-74; honorary M.A., Wesleyan University, 1976; Rockefeller Foundation fellow, 1977-78; Little Big Horn Associates literature award, 1986; Don D. Walker Prize.

WRITINGS:

Regeneration through Violence: The Mythology of the American Frontier, 1600-1860 (first of trilogy; also see below), Wesleyan University Press, 1973.

(Editor with James L. Folsom) *So Dreadfull a Judgment: Puritan Responses to King Philip's War, 1675-1677,* Wesleyan University Press, 1978.

The Crater: A Novel of the Civil War, Atheneum, 1980.

The Fatal Environment: The Myth of the Frontier in the Age of Industrialization, 1800-1890 (second of trilogy; also see below), Atheneum, 1985.

(Editor) James Fenimore Cooper, *The Last of the Mohicans,* Viking, 1986.

The Return of Henry Starr (novel), Atheneum, 1988.

Gunfighter Nation: The Myth of the Frontier in Twentieth-Century America (third of trilogy), Atheneum, 1992.

Contributor of articles and reviews to periodicals, including *American Quarterly, Popular Culture, Journal of the West, New York Times Book Review, Newsday, Life,* and *Saturday Review.*

SIDELIGHTS: Richard S. Slotkin's childhood fascination with the "Wild West" led him to examine the popular theories of its effect on society's development. In *Regeneration through Violence: The Mythology of the American Frontier, 1600-1860,* which began as his doctoral thesis at Brown University, Slotkin challenged the prevailing views of Henry Nash Smith, whose work is considered integral to American studies. "Smith was right when he said the frontier was a key myth in shaping the American culture," Slotkin told *Publishers Weekly* interviewer Robert Dahlin, "but he also got things wrong." Slotkin identified the issues of race and violence, not addressed by Smith, as significant to winning the West. "Ignoring the pursuit of white supremacy allows Americans to feel more democratic than they are," Slotkin remarked to Dahlin, "and in the era of Vietnam and the civil rights movement, that struck me as very interesting. I decided that I would fill in the blanks."

Regeneration through Violence, a finalist for the National Book Award, was the first in a trilogy of works exploring the frontier. The second book, *The Fatal Environment: The Myth of the Frontier in the Age of Industrialization, 1800-1890,* focuses on "the social and historical settings that influenced and were influenced by the U.S. population's inexorable and often ruthless move west," Dahlin summarized. In the *New York Times Book Review,* Roger D. McGrath found that *The Fatal Environment* encourages readers to ask, "In what way are today's complex issues reduced to the most inane and oversimplified terms—terrorists, freedom fighters, savages, heroes—in an effort to evoke unthinking reactions that are rooted in a culturally ingrained myth?" While McGrath determined, "Some may argue with the author's conclusions or even with his assumptions," the reviewer added, "Most will have to admit that Mr. Slotkin makes a very important contribution."

In *Gunfighter Nation: The Myth of the Frontier in Twentieth-Century America,* the final work in the trilogy, Slotkin examines the old cowboys-and-Indians movies he first saw as a child, discussing their impact on Americans and drawing parallels between the perception of the lawless West and modern U.S. foreign policy. "Westerns from 1939 to 1950 portrayed heroes who acted within the law," Slotkin told Dahlin, "but after 1950, with the Cold War under way, lawmakers lost confidence in the people who voted for them. And just like the movies, we got the vigilante ethic, which has been a critical ideology motivating political leaders." Those political leaders, Slotkin noted, "think through scenarios. To imagine a solution, they draw on the heritage of available stories." The solutions that those stories provide have influenced U.S. behavior in conflicts including Vietnam and the Persian Gulf War, Slotkin asserts.

Slotkin began his first frontier novel as a break from his nonfiction work. *The Crater* explores the racially motivated destruction of a black battalion during the Civil War. His second novel, *The Return of Henry Starr,* chronicles the life and death of bank robber Henry Starr, nephew of the notorious outlaw Belle Starr. *Los Angeles Times's* James Kaufmann suggested that Slotkin "has researched too thoroughly, served history too well" in *The Crater,* evidence of the difficulty of switching from historical nonfiction to fiction, and described Slotkin in his first endeavor into fiction as "an author who found the siren song of history too seductive." John Byrne Cooke, however, writing in *Washington Post Book World,* saw no such difficulty in *The Return of Henry Starr.* "Perhaps Slotkin found that mastering academic prose was necessary to his university career," Cooke remarked, but "as he makes dramatically clear [in *Henry Starr*], the poetic voice is the one that comes from the heart. . . . This is no eastern intellectual describing a time and place he has read about in books. This is the work of a man who has the rhythms of the American language and untold chapters of the American story in the marrow of his bones."

BIOGRAPHICAL/CRITICAL SOURCES:

PERIODICALS

American Scholar, spring, 1987, p. 266.
Best Sellers, February, 1981, p. 391; July, 1985, p. 146.
Booklist, April 1, 1985, p. 1097.
Chicago Tribune Book World, June 14, 1981, sec. 7, p. 13.
Choice, September, 1985, p. 193.
Christian Century, February 5, 1986, p. 149.
Journal of American History, December, 1985, p. 695.
Kirkus Reviews, April 1, 1985, p. 330; March 1, 1988, p. 321.
Library Journal, October, 1980; April 15, 1985, p. 72; May 1, 1988, p. 93.
Los Angeles Times, November 10, 1980.
New York Review of Books, November 21, 1985; October 27, 1988, p. 74.
New York Times Book Review, July 7, 1974; January 4, 1981; May 5, 1985, p. 14; September 27, 1987, p. 50.
Publishers Weekly, December 28, 1992, pp. 49-50.
Tribune Books (Chicago), March 27, 1988, p. 6.
Village Voice, January 28, 1981, p. 40.
Virginia Quarterly Review, autumn, 1981, p. 136.
Washington Post Book World, March 22, 1981; August 7, 1988, p. 10.
West Coast Review of Books, Volume 14, Number 1, 1988, p. 28.
Western Historical Quarterly, April, 1986, p. 202; November, 1988, p. 475.
Yale Review, summer, 1986, p. 619.

*   *   *

SMITH, E(ric) D(avid)   1923-

PERSONAL: Born August 19, 1923, in Cupar, Scotland; son of William C. and Jessica L. (Bartram) Smith; married Jill Waycott (a homemaker and councillor), May 1, 1957; children: Joanna Smith Davis, Beverly. *Education:* British Army Staff College, Camberly, Surrey, "Qualified," 1957. *Politics:* "Patriot!" *Religion:* Christian.

ADDRESSES: Home and office—Dharmsala, 2 Balfour Mews, Station Rd., Sidmouth EX10 8XL, England. *Agent*—S. Watson, 26 Charing Cross Rd., London WC2, England.

CAREER: British Army, career officer, 1942-78; majority of service with Brigade of Gurkhas in Southeast Asia, with active duty in Italy, Greece, Malaya, and Borneo territo-

ries (now East Malaysia); retired as brigadier. Professional reader for Robert Hale & Co. (publishers). Bursar and part-time instructor at St. John's Preparatory School, Sidmouth; town councillor; governor of local schools.

MEMBER: Society of Authors, Royal British Legion.

AWARDS, HONORS: Distinguished Service Order, 1944; Member of the Order of the British Empire, 1954; Commander of the Order of the British Empire, 1974.

WRITINGS:

The Story of the Sirmoor Rifles, Birch, 1968.
Britain's Brigade of Gurkhas, Leo Cooper, 1973.
Battles for Cassino, Ian Allan, 1975.
East of Kathmandu, Leo Cooper, 1976.
Even the Brave Falter, R. Hale, 1978.
Battle for Burma, Batsford, 1979.
Johnny Gurkha, Leo Cooper, 1985.
Counter-Insurgency Far East, Ian Allan, 1985.
Victory of a Sort, R. Hale, 1988.
Wars Bring Scars, R. J. Leach, 1993.

WORK IN PROGRESS: Book reviews.

SIDELIGHTS: In a London *Times* review Cyril Jarvis described E. D. Smith's *Britain's Brigade of Gurkhas* as "an excellent account of the history and achievements since 1815 of the four regiments of Gurkhas who were transferred from the Indian to the British Army in 1948." The critic added that the book is "easy to read and well produced, with excellent illustrations."

Smith told *CA:* "I always intended to be a journalist, but after joining the Gurkhas for the duration of World War II, I stayed on for a further thirty-six years! I am a keen sportsman and mountaineer. I lost my right arm (plus suffering other injuries) in a helicopter crash in Sarawak while on 'active service' in 1964. As a consequence, I began writing professionally, on a part-time basis. I began writing full-time in 1983."

BIOGRAPHICAL/CRITICAL SOURCES:

PERIODICALS

Times (London), February 17, 1983.

*   *   *

SMITH, Hedrick (Laurence)   1933-

PERSONAL: Born July 9, 1933, in Kilmacolm, Scotland; son of Sterling L. (in management) and Phebe (an artist; maiden name, Hedrick) Smith; married Ann Bickford (an educator), June 29, 1957 (divorced December, 1985); married Susan Zox, March 7, 1987; children: (first marriage) Laurel Ann, Jennifer Laurence, Sterling Scott, Lesley

Roberts. *Education:* Williams College, B.A., 1955; graduate study at Balliol College, Oxford, 1955-56, and Harvard University, 1969-70. *Avocational interests:* Foreign travel, skiing, sailing, tennis, wine.

ADDRESSES: Home—Chevy Chase, MD. *Agent*—Julian Bach Literary Agency, Inc., 747 Third Ave., New York, NY 10017.

CAREER: United Press International, New York City, reporter in Tennessee, 1959-61, Georgia, 1961-62, and at Cape Canaveral, 1962; *New York Times,* New York City, reporter in Washington, DC, 1962-63, Saigon (now Ho Chi Minh City), South Vietnam, 1963-64, Cairo, Egypt, 1964-66, diplomatic correspondent in Washington, DC, 1966-71, bureau chief in Moscow, Russia (then part of U.S.S.R.), 1971-74, deputy national editor in New York City, 1975-76, bureau chief, 1976-79, and chief correspondent, 1979-85, in Washington, DC; American Enterprise Institute, visiting journalist, 1985-86; *New York Times Magazine,* Washington correspondent, 1987-88. Anchor panelist on Public Broadcasting Service (PBS-TV) program *Washington Week in Review,* 1969—; host of television documentaries, including *Star Wars,* 1985, *Moscow Jews,* 1986, *Space Bridge,* 1987, and *Chernobyl/Three Mile Island,* 1987; creator of television documentaries, including *Power Game* (four part series), PBS-TV, 1989, *Countdown to White House: The Bush Transition,* 1989, *After Gorbachev's U.S.S.R.,* 1990, and *Inside Gorbachev's U.S.S.R.* (series), PBS-TV, 1990. *Military service:* U.S. Air Force, 1956-59.

MEMBER: White House Correspondents Association, Gridiron Club, Washington Press Club, Phi Beta Kappa.

AWARDS, HONORS: Fulbright scholar, 1955-56; Nieman Fellow at Harvard University, 1969-70; member of Pulitzer Prize-winning reporting team, 1972; Pulitzer Prize for International Reporting, 1974; Litt.D., Williams College, 1975, Wittenburg University, 1985, and Amherst College, 1992; Overseas Press Club Book Award, 1976, for *The Russians;* fellow, Foreign Policy Center, School of Advanced International Studies, Johns Hopkins University, 1989—; D.H.L., University of South Carolina and Columbia College, both 1992.

WRITINGS:

(With Neil Sheehan, E. W. Kenworthy, and others) *The Pentagon Papers,* Quadrangle, 1971.
The Russians, New York Times, 1976, revised edition, Ballantine, 1984.
(With Leonard Silk, Adam Clymer, Richard Burt, and Robert Lindsey) *Reagan: The Man, the President,* Macmillan, 1980.
(With others) *Counterattack: The U.S. Response to Japan,* Times Books, 1983.

(With others) *Washington Week in Review,* Warner Books, 1986.
(With others) *Beyond Reagan: The Politics of Upheaval,* Warner Books, 1987.
The Power Game: How Washington Works, Random House, 1988.
The New Russians, Random House, 1990.

Contributor to books, including *Fodor's Soviet Union, 1974-75: A Definitive Handbook of the U.S.S.R. for Foreign Visitors,* by Eugene Fodor, McKay, 1974. Also contributor to magazines, including *Atlantic, Saturday Review,* and *Reader's Digest.*

SIDELIGHTS: Hedrick Smith is one of the foremost authorities in the Western world on the Russian people and their country's history. During the era of Leonid Brezhnev, when the Soviet Union was still locked behind the Iron Curtain, Smith served as Moscow bureau chief for the *New York Times.* His experiences and research during that time formed the foundation for his bestselling book *The Russians,* published in 1976. The book quickly established itself as indispensable reading for any serious student of the Soviet Union. In 1985, after Mikhail Gorbachev began instituting the sweeping reforms that eventually led to the fall of the Communist regime, Smith returned to the U.S.S.R. to work on a Public Broadcasting System (PBS-TV) television series about the dramatic changes that were underway. That visit resulted in a 600-page volume, *The New Russians,* which was immediately recognized as an essential companion to his earlier book.

During his years as a resident of Moscow, Smith lived as close to the Russians as an American journalist possibly could. Determined to explore the lives of Soviet citizens, he enrolled his children in Russian schools, shopped where average families bought their limited supplies of goods and produce, and actively sought both Russians' and Westerners' reactions to events and conditions in the U.S.S.R. In writing *The Russians,* he sought to portray the human story of the Soviet Union—to give his readers a sense of the texture and fabric of the lives of the common people there. The personal tone he struck gave his work a vitality that similar accounts lacked, in the opinion of many reviewers. "Smith's greatest appeal is his ability to weave together a colorful and persuasive portrait of Russians as people, rich in detail and sensitive to nuance," asserted Allen H. Kassof in *New Republic.* "His warm and sympathetic accounts of family life, of love and friendship in an imposing social and political environment, and of patience and endurance in the face of perennial shortages and mismanagement are among the best I have seen." Commenting in *Newsweek,* Paul D. Zimmerman similarly stated that Smith writes "vividly and with a greater feel for the texture of everyday life" than other commentators on contemporary Russia.

Smith's book ended on a pessimistic note. Based on his observations of the Communist government and the psychology of the Russian people—in particular, their need for order and their so-called "culture of envy" that led them to reject anyone who succeeded in reaching a higher standard of living than his neighbors—Smith stated his belief that fundamental change within the U.S.S.R. was impossible. Less than ten years later, he was forced to admit that he had underestimated the power of millions of Soviet citizens who, while going quietly through their daily routines, were seething inwardly with resentment toward the totalitarian regime that controlled their country. Mikhail Gorbachev had come to power and was in the process of dismantling the very government of which he was in charge.

While *The New Russians,* like *The Russians,* has a personal flavor to it and includes many interviews with average citizens—who were now much more willing to speak freely with a reporter—the book is dominated by the figure of Gorbachev. *Time* contributor Bruce W. Nelan wrote, "Smith deftly presents a biography of Gorbachev that puts him into the context of national malaise: clever enough to advance through the mediocrities of the party, honest enough to recognize the need for change." Speaking to *Publishers Weekly* interviewer Sam Staggs, Smith said of Gorbachev: "He's probably more like Franklin D. Roosevelt than like any other American politician, in the sense of having a strategy and yet not having worked it out, and also in having a capacity to communicate with people but somewhat overdoing it. FDR didn't have a clear concept of the New Deal in his mind when he came into office; he devised it as he went along. He knew roughly the direction he wanted to go. That's also true of Gorbachev and *perestroika.*"

Even with the swift course of events in the Soviet Union, Smith told *CA* that many of the insights about change set out in *The New Russians* "remain timely in today's chaotic picture. But political changes, including Gorbachev's ouster and the breakup of the U.S.S.R., necessitated an update and several new chapters in late 1991." According to many reviewers, the book remains invaluable reading. "Smith drives the potentially confusing narrative with such clarity that it all reads like an eyewitness account," noted Nelan. " 'The New Russians' is rich in experience and huge in scope," asserted Colin Thubron in the *Los Angeles Times Book Review.* "It charts a kaleidoscope of different movements and beliefs, and ranges from the early roots of Soviet reform to a cautious prognosis for the future. In particular, Smith's comprehensive picture of the workings of Soviet power politics during the past half-decade is shaped by an incipient understanding of the divergent roots and allegiances of its players. This political narrative is enriched by studies of Soviet life where *per-*

estroika has changed or challenged it. . . . And his survey is bolstered by a host of biting interviews."

Smith delved into the mysteries of his own country's government in *The Power Game: How Washington Works,* written in the years between his two books on Russia. He had gained fame—and notoriety—in the U.S. capitol years before, as one of the Pulitzer Prize-winning team of reporters that brought the Pentagon's secret papers on the Vietnam War to light. While many of the anecdotes related in *The Power Game* are already well known to the public, the insight Smith brings to them drew praise from reviewers. *Los Angeles Times Book Review* contributor Mary Anne Dolan called the book "reporting at its best. . . . It is extensive (729 pages), it is careful (25 pages of footnotes) and up to the minute. Most significantly, it is thoughtful. As a working person's guide to the strange and evanescent nature of our national government, I doubt that it could be topped." Dolan went on to conclude: "This will be a classic text for years to come."

The focus of *The Power Game* is the story of how the political system was changed by the Watergate scandal and the reforms that followed, including limits on executive power, changes in the congressional seniority system, and the rise of political action committees. Smith describes in detail the elaborate games engaged in by legislators, including "the access game, the turf game, the image game, the coalition game, the opposition game or the porcupine power game, which is where you keep anything from happening by being prickly and being difficult," *Los Angeles Times* writer Betty Cuniberti quoted him as saying.

Some reviewers saw Smith's status as a Washington insider as bringing invaluable authority to his book, but Robert Sherrill, writing in the *Washington Post Book World,* stated that Smith's "Inside-the-Beltway" outlook was also a weakness. Acknowledging that the author is "a superb writer" and urging the public to read the book, Sherrill nevertheless added: "My appreciation of this brilliant power primer was considerably diminished by three things. First, there's serious history here, much of it unpleasant history, and I got tired of being asked to think about it as games. Second, the subtitle is so misleading that if it were on a bottle of medicine the FDA would ban it. And third, sometimes the book seems gutless." Declaring that *The Power Game* seems to prove that Washington does *not* work, Sherrill went on to fault Smith for failing to come up with solutions to the problems of government. "What hope does Smith offer? None for the reform of structural maladies, 'short of a national calamity.' " "Although citing a thousand wrongs," continues Sherrill, "Smith, a voice of the establishment press, limply concludes that 'from all of us, what is required is a tolerance for the untidiness of democracy, even genuine enjoyment in a democracy's untidiness.' "

Sherrill's concerns were by no means universal, however. Michael R. Beschloss, writing in *Tribune Books,* claimed that "the book's most vital contribution is to show where the system fails and how it might be improved. . . . [Smith] calls for reforms that would allow presidents to run for a third term, send them to Capitol Hill for a regular 'Question Time,' help them to form Congressional coalitions, toughen criminal penalties for lying to Congress, keep the CIA out of policy-making, increase the power of parties." Beschloss summarized: "No one has done a better or more comprehensive job of explaining how Washington operates at this moment in history." And Alan Brinkley expressed similar enthusiasm in the *New York Times Book Review:* " 'The Power Game' may be the most sweeping and in many ways the most impressive portrait of the culture of the Federal Government to appear in a single work in many decades. It is knowledgeable and informative. And it is often highly entertaining, filled with enough inside information and spicy anecdotes to satisfy even the most jaded political junkie. . . . No one, I suspect, will read this book without learning something new."

BIOGRAPHICAL/CRITICAL SOURCES:

BOOKS

Smith, Hedrick, *The Russians,* New York Times, 1976, revised edition, Ballantine, 1984.

PERIODICALS

America, June 12, 1976; January 29, 1977.
Business Week, January 21, 1991, pp. 12-13.
Christian Science Monitor, January 28, 1976.
Commonweal, June 18, 1976.
Detroit Free Press, December 9, 1990, p. 11P.
Globe & Mail (Toronto), April 27, 1991, p. C6.
Harper's, March, 1976.
Los Angeles Times, April 4, 1988.
Los Angeles Times Book Review, March 20, 1988, pp. 1, 15; December 16, 1990, pp. 1, 11.
New Review, May 1, 1976.
New Statesman, December 9, 1977.
Newsweek, January 19, 1976.
New Yorker, April 26, 1976.
New York Review of Books, April 1, 1976.
New York Times, January 8, 1976; January 9, 1976; July 30, 1976; March 24, 1988.
New York Times Book Review, January 25, 1976; April 14, 1985, p. 42; March 27, 1988, pp. 1, 20-21; December 9, 1990, p. 9.
Publishers Weekly, November 2, 1990, p. 62; November 23, 1990, pp. 48-49.
Saturday Review, February 7, 1976.
Spectator, June 5, 1976.
Time, May 10, 1976; December 10, 1990, p. 99.

Times Literary Supplement, January 4, 1991, p. 8.
Tribune Books (Chicago), April 3, 1988.
Virginia Quarterly Review, summer, 1976.
Wall Street Journal, January 19, 1976; December 8, 1976.
Washington Post, April 19, 1988.
Washington Post Book World, April 3, 1988, pp. 1-2; December 9, 1990, pp. 1, 11.*

—*Sketch by Joan Goldsworthy*

*   *   *

SPENCE, J. A. D.
See ELIOT, T(homas) S(tearns)

*   *   *

SPIEGELMAN, Art 1948-

PERSONAL: Born February 15, 1948, in Stockholm, Sweden; immigrated to United States; naturalized citizen; son of Vladek (in sales) and Anja (Zylberberg) Spiegelman; married Francoise Mouly (a publisher), July 12, 1977; children: Nadja Rachel, Dashiel Alan. *Education:* Attended Harpur College (now State University of New York at Binghamton), 1965-68.

ADDRESSES: Home—New York, NY. *Office*—Raw Books and Graphics, 27 Greene St., New York, NY 10013; Galerie St. Etienne, 24 West 57th St., New York, NY 10019. *Agent*—Wylie, Aitken, & Stone, 250 West 57th St., Suite 2106, New York, NY 10107.

CAREER: Free-lance artist and writer, 1965—; Topps Chewing Gum, Inc., Brooklyn, NY, creative consultant, artist, designer, editor, and writer for novelty packaging and bubble gum cards and stickers, including "Wacky Packages" and "Garbage Pail Kids," 1966-89. Instructor in studio class on comics, San Francisco Academy of Art, 1974-75; instructor in history and aesthetics of comics at New York School of Visual Arts, 1979-87. Advisory board member of the Swann Foundation.

MEMBER: PEN.

AWARDS, HONORS: Annual *Playboy* Editorial Award for best comic strip and Yellow Kid Award (Italy) for best comic strip author, both 1982; Regional Design Award, *Print* magazine, 1983, 1984, and 1985; Joel M. Cavior Award for Jewish Writing, and National Book Critics Circle nomination, both 1986, both for *Maus: A Survivor's Tale, My Father Bleeds History;* Inkpot Award, San Diego Comics Convention, and Stripschappenning Award (Netherlands) for best foreign comics album, both 1987; Special Pulitzer Prize, National Book Critics Circle award, *Los Angeles Times* book prize, and Before Columbus Foundation Award, all 1992, all for *Maus: A Survivor's Tale II, and Here My Troubles Began;* Spiegelman also received a Guggenheim fellowship for his work on *Maus.*

WRITINGS:

COMICS

The Complete Mr. Infinity, S. F. Book Co., 1970.
The Viper Vicar of Vice, Villainy, and Vickedness, privately printed, 1972.
Zip-a-Tune and More Melodies, S. F. Book Co., 1972.
(Compiling editor with Bob Schneider) *Whole Grains: A Book of Quotations,* D. Links, 1972.
Ace Hole, Midget Detective, Apex Novelties, 1974.
Language of Comics, State University of New York at Binghamton, 1974.
(Contributor) Don Donahue and Susan Goodrich, editors, *The Apex Treasury of Underground Comics,* D. Links, 1974.
Breakdowns: From Maus to Now, an Anthology of Strips, Belier Press, 1977.
Work and Turn, Raw Books, 1979.
Every Day Has Its Dog, Raw Books, 1979.
Two-Fisted Painters Action Adventure, Raw Books, 1980.
(Contributor) Nicole Hollander, Skip Morrow, and Ron Wolin, editors, *Drawn Together: Relationships Lampooned, Harpooned, and Cartooned,* Crown, 1983.
Maus: A Survivor's Tale, My Father Bleeds History, Pantheon, 1986.
(Editor with wife, Francoise Mouly, and contributor) *Read Yourself Raw: Comix Anthology for Damned Intellectuals,* Pantheon, 1987.
Maus: A Survivor's Tale II, and Here My Troubles Began, Pantheon, 1991.

Also contributor to numerous underground comics. Editor of *Douglas Comix,* 1972; editor, with Bill Griffith, and contributor, *Arcade, the Comics Revue,* 1975-76; founding editor, with Mouly, and contributor, *Raw,* 1980—.

Maus has been translated into sixteen languages, including Japanese and Hungarian.

WORK IN PROGRESS: "Profusely illustrating" *The Wild Party* by Joseph March; editing *The Raw and the Restless.*

SIDELIGHTS: "Art Spiegelman's *Maus* is among the remarkable achievements in comics," wrote Dale Luciano in *The Comics Journal.* The comic, an epic parable of the Holocaust that substitutes mice and cats for human Jews and Nazis, marks a zenith in Spiegelman's artistic career. Prior to the *Maus* books, Spiegelman made a name for himself on the underground comics scene. He has been a significant presence in graphic art since his teen years, when he wrote, printed, and distributed his own comics

magazine. In the early 1980s Spiegelman and his wife, Francoise Mouly, produced the first issue of *Raw,* an underground comics (or as Spiegelman and Mouly refer to them, "comix") anthology that grew into a highly respected alternative press by the middle of the decade. It was not until the publication of the first *Maus* collection in 1986, however, that a wide range of readers became aware of Spiegelman's visionary talent and his considerable impact on the realm of comics.

Spiegelman has described *Maus* as "the point where my work starts." As he told Joey Cavalieri in *Comics Journal:* "Up to that point, I feel like I'd been floundering. . . . All of a sudden, I found my own voice, my own needs, things that I wanted to do in comics." Although his work on *Maus* began in earnest in the 1980s, the comic actually had its genesis as a three page strip back in 1972. In that year Spiegelman was approached to contribute to a compilation titled *Funny Aminals* (sic), whose only dictum required the strips to feature animals exhibiting human characteristics. Spiegelman contemplated several ideas and finally hit upon his theme while watching old cartoons. Viewing cartoons that featured cats and mice, Spiegelman related to Cavalieri that he was struck with the epiphany that "this cat and mouse thing was just a metaphor for some kind of oppression." Initially he thought of using cats and mice for a strip dealing with slavery, but being a white Jewish man, he reasoned that he could not be true to what was, regardless of the form, a black man's story. He decided to explore a theme that was much closer to him: his mother and father's experience in, and survival of, a Nazi concentration camp.

Maus starts with Spiegelman, representing himself as a humanoid mouse, going to his father, Vladek, for information about the Holocaust. As Vladek's tale begins, he and his wife, Anja, are living in Poland with their young child, Richieu, at the outset of World War II. The Nazis, as cats, have overrun much of Eastern Europe, and their oppression is felt by everyone, especially the Jews/mice. The story recalls Vladek's service in the Polish army and subsequent incarceration in a German war prison. As he returns to Anja and his home, the Nazi "Final Solution"—to exterminate the entire Jewish race—is well under way. There is much talk of Jews being rounded up and shipped off to the camps, where they are either put to strenuous work or put to death. Vladek and Anja's attempt to flee is thwarted and they are sent to Auschwitz, Poland, site of one of the most notorious camps. As the first book of *Maus* concludes, Richieu has been taken from his parents by the Nazis—never to be seen again—and Vladek and Anja are separated and put in crowded train cars for shipment to Auschwitz.

As the second volume, *And Here My Troubles Began,* opens, Art and his wife, Francoise, are visiting Vladek at his summer home in the Catskills. During the visit Art and his father resume their discussion. Vladek recounts how he and Anja were put in separate camps, he in the Auschwitz facility, she in the neighboring Birkenau. The horrors and inhumanity of concentration camp life are related in graphic detail. Vladek recalls the discomfort of cramming three or four men into a bunk that is only a few feet wide and the ignominy of scrounging for any scrap of food to sate his unending hunger. His existence at Auschwitz is marked by agonizing physical labor, severe abuse from the Nazis, and the ever present fear that he—or Anja—may be among the next Jews sent to the gas chambers. Despite these overwhelming incentives to abandon hope, Vladek is bolstered by his clandestine meetings with Anja and the discovery of supportive allies among his fellow prisoners. In an encounter with a former priest, Vladek is told that the numerals in his serial identification, which the Nazis tattooed upon their victims, add up to eighteen, a number signifying life.

Vladek manages to hold on through several harrowing incidents, including a bout with typhus. As the war ends and the Allied troops make their way toward Auschwitz, Vladek and some fellow prisoners flee the camp and eventually make their way to safety. In the haste of his escape, however, Vladek loses contact with Anja and does not know if she is alive. Their reunion marks a happy point in Vladek's tale. As the book continues Vladek and Anja desperately search orphanages in Europe for Richieu, to no avail. They eventually immigrate to Sweden where Art is born, and from there the family moves to America. However, the horrors of the war have scarred Anja permanently, and in 1968 she commits suicide. The book concludes with Art visiting Vladek just before his death in 1982.

Although *Maus* is essentially the story of Vladek and Anja's ordeal, Spiegelman has stated that *Maus* is, in part, a meditation on "my own awareness of myself as a Jew." There are deeply personal passages depicting conversations between Art and his psychiatrist, Pavel, who, like Vladek, survived the Nazi's attempted purge. Their conversation ranges from Anja's suicide to the guilt that Art feels for being successful in light of his father's tribulation. As much as *Maus* serves as a piece of edifying literature, it also provided its creator with an opportunity to confront his personal demons. As Spiegelman wrote in an article in the *Voice, Maus* was motivated "by an impulse to look dead-on at the root cause of my own deepest fears and nightmares."

A good deal of discussion has arisen since the publication of the *Maus* books, much of it regarding Spiegelman's use of animals in the place of humans. When the story originated in *Funny Aminals,* Spiegelman made no mention of Jews or Nazis. The protagonists were mice, persecuted because they were "Maus." Likewise, the antagonists were cats, or "Die Katzen," and they chased the mice, although "chasing" the mice meant rounding them up in camps for work, torture, and extermination. The closest the strip comes to an outright identification with the Holocaust is in the name of the concentration camp, "Mauschwitz." As Spiegelman began the expanded version however, he found that he had to write in terms of "Jews" and "Nazis" when going into detail. Spiegelman decided to maintain his characters as animals, however, citing a fear that using human characters would turn the work into a "corny" plea for sympathy. He explained to Cavalieri, "To use these ciphers, the cats and mice, is actually a way to allow you past the cipher at the people who are experiencing it. So it's really a much more direct way of dealing with the material." Luciano agreed with Spiegelman's reasoning in his description of *Maus:* "By making the characters cats and mice, the result is that the characters' *human* qualities are highlighted all the more, to an inexplicably poignant effect." Luciano continued, "The situations recalled and acted-out in *Maus* place the characters in a variety of delicate situations: they express themselves with a simplicity and candor that is unsettling because it is so accurately *human.*"

Prior to *Maus,* the idea of a comic book that dealt with serious, realistic issues was considered a commercially unsound project. Comic books were not viewed as an outlet for sober or reflective writing. Spiegelman began to change that perception with *Raw,* and with the first collection of *Maus* in 1986, he demonstrated the height to which comics literature could be taken. Both volumes of *Maus* became bestsellers and firmly established their author in the pantheon of great graphic artists. In addition, *Maus* made readers aware of other graphic works that forsook superheroes and wackiness for realistic situations. Books like the Hernandez brothers' *Love and Rockets* and Harvey Pekar's *American Splendor* received greater recognition due to *Maus*'s popularity. Luciano summed up the book's impact, stating that "after *Maus,* nobody will ever be able to say that the graphic story medium isn't well-suited to convey the complexity and delicacy of human emotion. The Goddamn thing is brilliant."

Spiegelman stated in *Comics Journal,* "There's something that I like about the fact that comics are such a gritty medium. That they're so ignored. There's something to be said for that." While some might disagree that comics are ignored, Spiegelman's implication that the format is sufficiently removed from mainstream literature to serve as a proving ground for new techniques is evident in his work. Critics such as Luciano have commented on the artist's groundbreaking work, citing *Maus* as a defining plateau for comics. In graphic art, Spiegelman not only sees a potential for exploration, but also a medium through which ideas can be disseminated.

BIOGRAPHICAL/CRITICAL SOURCES:

PERIODICALS

Cavalier, April, 1969.
Comics Journal, August, 1981, pp. 98-125; December, 1986, pp. 43-45; April, 1989, pp. 110-117.
New York Times Book Review, November 3, 1991, pp. 1, 35-36.
Publishers Weekly, April 26, 1991.
Reform Judaism, spring, 1987, pp. 22-23, 32.
Rolling Stone, November 20, 1986, pp. 103-106, 146-148.
Voice, June 6, 1989, pp. 21-22.

* * *

SPIER, Peter (Edward) 1927-

PERSONAL: Born June 6, 1927, in Amsterdam, Netherlands; came to the United States, 1951; became U.S. citizen, 1958; son of Joseph Eduard A. (a journalist and illustrator) and Albertine Sophie (van Raalte) Spier; married Kathryn M. Pallister, July 12, 1958; children: Thomas Pallister, Kathryn Elizabeth. *Education:* Attended Ryksacademie voor beeldende kunsten, Amsterdam, 1945-47; attended Willems Park School, Amsterdams Lyceum. *Religion:* Reformed Church of America. *Avocational interests:* Sailing, history, model ship building.

ADDRESSES: Home—Warden Cliff Rd., P.O. Box 210, Shoreham, Long Island, NY 11786.

CAREER: Elsevier's Weekblad (a newspaper), Paris, France, junior editor, 1949-51; Elsevier Publishing, Houston, TX, junior editor, 1951-52; author and illustrator, 1952—. *Military service:* Royal Netherlands Navy, 1947-51; became lieutenant.

MEMBER: Netherlands Club.

AWARDS, HONORS: Diploma de Triennale de Milano, 1956; Caldecott Honor Book, American Library Association (ALA), 1962, for *The Fox Went Out on a Chilly Night; Boston Globe-Horn Book* Award (illustration), 1967, for *London Bridge Is Falling Down!,* and *Boston Globe-Horn Book* Honor Book Award, 1967, for *To Market! To Market!;* Child Study Association of America's Children's Books of the Year citation, 1968, for *Hurrah, We're Outward Bound!,* 1969, for *And So My Garden Grows,* 1970, for *The Erie Canal,* 1972, for *Crash! Bang! Boom!,* 1975, for *Tin Lizzie,* 1979, for *The Legend of New Amsterdam,* and 1987, for *Dreams;* Christopher Award, 1971, for *The Erie Canal,* 1978, for *Noah's Ark,* and 1981, for *People;* Outstanding Books of the Year citation, New

York Times, 1971, for *Gobble, Growl, Grunt,* 1973, for *The Star-Spangled Banner,* and 1978, for *Bored—Nothing to Do!;* Children's Science Book Award, New York Academy of Science, 1972, for *Gobble, Growl, Grunt;* Best Illustrated Children's Books of the Year citation, *New York Times,* 1977, Caldecott Medal, Lewis Carroll Shelf Award, and National Religious Book Award, all 1978, Art Books for Children award, 1979, International Board on Books for Young People Honor List (illustration), 1980, and American Book Award (picturebook paperback), 1982, all for *Noah's Ark;* Little Archer Award, University of Wisconsin-Oshkosh, 1978, and Prix Belgique de Famille, 1980, both for *Oh, Were They Ever Happy;* Golden Archer Award, 1978, for *Bored—Nothing to Do!;* American Book Award finalist (children's hardcover nonfiction) and Mass Media Award from the Conference of Christians and Jews, both 1980, both for *People;* Silver Medallion in recognition of his distinguished career as author/illustrator of books for children, University of Southern Mississippi School of Library Service, 1984; Association of Logos Bookstores Award, 1986, for *The Book of Jonah;* David McCord award, 1989; many of Spier's books have been designated ALA Notable Books.

WRITINGS:

SELF-ILLUSTRATED; ALL PUBLISHED BY DOUBLEDAY, EXCEPT AS INDICATED

The Fox Went Out on a Chilly Night: An Old Song, 1961.
Of Dikes and Windmills, 1970.
The Erie Canal, 1970.
Gobble, Growl, Grunt, 1971.
Crash! Bang! Boom!, 1972.
Fast-Slow, High-Low: A Book of Opposites, 1972.
The Star-Spangled Banner, 1973.
Tin Lizzie, 1975.
Noah's Ark, 1977.
Bored—Nothing to Do!, 1978.
Oh, Were They Ever Happy!, 1978.
The Legend of New Amsterdam, 1979.
People, 1980.
The Pet Store, 1981.
My School, 1981.
The Fire House, 1981.
The Food Market, 1981.
The Toy Shop, 1981.
Bill's Service Station, 1981, published in England as *Bill's Garage,* Collins, 1981.
Rain, 1982.
Peter Spier's Christmas!, 1983.
Peter Spier's Little Bible Storybooks, 1983.
Peter Spier's Little Cats, 1984.
Peter Spier's Little Dogs, 1984.
Peter Spier's Little Ducks, 1984.
Peter Spier's Little Rabbits, 1984.

(Adapter) *The Book of Jonah,* 1985.
Dreams, 1986.
Peter Spier's Advent Calendar: Silent Night, Holy Night, 1987.
We the People: The Story of the U.S. Constitution, 1987.
Peter Spier's Little Animal Books, 1987.
Pop-Up Peter Spier's Birthday Cake, 1990.
Peter Spier's Circus, 1991.
Father, May I Come?, Lemniscaat (Rotterdam), 1992, Doubleday, 1993.

"MOTHER GOOSE LIBRARY" SERIES

London Bridge Is Falling Down!, Doubleday, 1967.
To Market! To Market!, Doubleday, 1967.
Hurrah, We're Outward Bound!, Doubleday, 1968.
And So My Garden Grows, Doubleday, 1969.

ILLUSTRATOR

Nikolai Gogol, *De Mantel* (title means "The Goat"), [Holland], 1946.
P. Bakker, *Logboek van de Gratias* (title means "Logbook of the Gratias"), Elsevier, 1948.
E. Elias, *Op Reis Met Prins Bernhard* (title means "On a Journey with Prince Bernhard"), Bezige Bij, 1951.
Steussy, *Straten Schrijven Historie* (title means "Streets Write History"), Schoonderbeek, 1951.
Elmer Reynolds, *Thunder Hill,* Doubleday, 1953.
Louis Untermeyer, *Adventures All,* Golden Press, 1953.
Ruth Langland Holberg, *Tam Morgan, the Liveliest Girl in Salem,* Doubleday, 1953.
Margaret G. Otto, *Cocoa,* Holt, 1953.
H. J. Berkhard, *Wonders of the World,* Simon & Schuster, 1953.
Frieda K. Brown, *Last Hurdle,* Crowell, 1953.
Marjorie Vetter, *Cargo for Jennifer,* Longmans, 1954.
Frances H. Burnett, *Little Lord Fauntleroy,* Doubleday, 1954.
Mark Twain, *Prince and the Pauper,* Doubleday, 1954.
(With Emil Lowenstein) Paul Friedlander and Joseph Brooks, *Italy,* Simon & Schuster, 1955.
Michel Rouze, *Mystery of Mont Saint-Michel,* translated by George Libaire, Holt, 1955.
Vera A. Amrein, *Cabin for the Mary Christmas,* Harcourt, 1955.
Science and Living in Today's World series, Volumes 6-8, Doubleday, 1955-56.
Joy Anderson, *Hippolyte: Crab King,* Harcourt, 1956.
Jennie Darlington and Jane McIlvaine, *My Antarctic Honeymoon: A Year at the Bottom of the World,* Doubleday, 1956.
Phyllis Krasilovsky, *The Cow Who Fell in the Canal,* Doubleday, 1957.
Margaret Hubbard, *Boss Chombale,* Crowell, 1957.
England, Ginn, 1957.

Ruth Strang and others, *Teenage Tales,* Volume 4, Heath, 1957.
Margaret B. Boni, *Favorite Christmas Carols: Fifty-nine Yuletide Songs Both Old and New,* arranged by Norman Lloyd, Simon & Schuster, 1957.
Mary Mapes Dodge, *Hans Brinker; or, the Silver Skates,* Scribner, 1958.
Jessica Reynolds, *Jessica's Journal,* Holt, 1958.
Douglas Angus, *Lions Fed the Tigers,* Houghton, 1958.
Kenneth Dodson, *Hector the Stowaway Dog: A True Story,* Little, Brown, 1958.
Elizabeth Fairholme and Pamela Powell, *Esmeralda Ahoy!,* Doubleday, 1959.
Ann Frank, *Works of Ann Frank,* Doubleday, 1959.
Betty Crocker's Guide to Easy Entertaining, Golden Press, 1959.
Richard Watkins, *Mystery of Willet,* T. Nelson, 1959.
Frances Carpenter, *Wonder Tales of Ships and Seas,* Doubleday, 1959.
John L. Strohm, *Golden Garden Guide: A Practical Handbook of Gardening and Outdoor Living,* Golden Press, 1960.
Ardo Flakkeberg, *The Sea Broke Through,* Knopf, 1960.
Elinor Parker, editor, *One Hundred More Story Poems,* Crowell, 1960.
J. L. Strohm, *Golden Guide to Lawns, Shrubs, and Trees,* Golden Press, 1961.
Lavinia Davis, *Island City: Adventures in Old New York,* Doubleday, 1961.
George H. Grant, *Boy Overboard!,* Little, Brown, 1961.
Dola De Jong, *The Level Land,* Scribner, 1961.
Strohm and others, *Golden Guide to Flowers: Annuals, Perennials, Bulbs, and a Special Section on Roses,* Golden Press, 1962.
Margaretha Shemin, *The Little Riders,* Coward, 1963.
C. W. Ceram (pseudonym of Kurt Marek), *Archaeology,* Odyssey, 1964.
Jan de Hartog, *Sailing Ship,* Odyssey, 1964.
K. Marek, *The History of the Theater,* Odyssey, 1964.
R. Butterfield, *Ancient Rome,* Odyssey, 1964.
M. Valmarana, *Architecture,* Odyssey, 1965.
Anthony West, *Elizabethan England,* Odyssey, 1965.
Donald D. MacMillan, *Great Furniture Styles, 1660-1830,* Odyssey, 1965.
World of Michelangelo, Time-Life, 1966.
E. Parker, editor, *Here and There: One Hundred Poems about Places,* Crowell, 1967.
Animals You Will Never Forget, Reader's Digest, 1969.
M. Shemin, *Empty Moat,* Coward, 1969.
T. R. Reese, *Frederica: Colonial Fort and Town,* United States National Park Service, 1969.
Golden Book Encyclopedia, Volume 1, Golden Press, 1970.
Traveler's Tale of Tikal, National Geographic, 1975.

Elmer Bendiner, *Virgin Diplomats,* Knopf, 1975.
Peter Lippman, *Trucks, Trucks, Trucks,* Doubleday, 1984.

Contributor to periodicals, including *Reader's Digest* and *National Geographic.* Contributor of illustrations to periodicals, including *Collier's, Ford Almanac, Look,* and *Saturday Evening Post.* Spier's manuscript collections are housed at the de Grummond Collection at the University of Southern Mississippi, the Kerlan Collection at the University of Minnesota, and the Port Washington Public Library in New York.

Spier's works have been translated into twenty-four languages, including Japanese and Chinese.

ADAPTATIONS: Many of Spier's works have been released in cassette, sound filmstrip, or feature film formats by Weston Woods, including *The Cow Who Fell in the Canal,* cassette and filmstrip, 1965, film, 1970, *The Fox Went Out on a Chilly Night,* cassette and filmstrip, 1965, *London Bridge Is Falling Down,* film, 1969, cassette and filmstrip, 1971, *The Erie Canal,* cassette and filmstrip, 1974, film, 1976, *The Star-Spangled Banner,* cassette, filmstrip, and film, 1975, and *Noah's Ark,* cassette and filmstrip; *Noah's Ark* was released as a video, "Stories to Remember," by Lightyear Entertainment in 1990; *Oh, Were They Ever Happy!* was released as a filmstrip by Random House.

SIDELIGHTS: Peter Spier, a prolific author and illustrator of children's books, has been lauded for the realistic, meticulous, accurate detail and charming sense of humor found in his pictures. Spier began his career illustrating books for other authors, but found a greater sense of satisfaction in working on his own. His later books, almost all of which he wrote and illustrated himself, have won him critical and popular admiration. Bible stories, individuality, natural phenomena, and American history have all been subjects of Spier's pen. Spier filled his wordless picture book, *Noah's Ark,* with realistic details in order to differentiate it from less specific versions of the tale. "None of [the other retellings of the story] shows Noah shoveling manure or even hinted at the stench and the mess inside," Spier said in his 1978 Caldecott acceptance speech. "It was then that I knew that there was room for one more *Noah's Ark.*" Spier's adaptation was recognized for its beauty, message, and unique sense of humor. A *Washington Post Book World* critic called *Noah's Ark* "the ideal introduction to a classic Bible story."

Spier's picture book celebrating the great diversity of shapes, sizes, and colors the citizens of the world come in, simply titled *People,* was praised for its ambition and for the range of its material. Comprehensive pictures depict the distinct clothing, homes, languages, and religions that exist in particular nations; half of one page, for example, is filled with fifty-four kinds of noses. George A. Woods wrote in the *New York Times Book Review* that Spier's drawings exhibit "a charming, colorful 'lookability' to which children as well as adults respond."

Another of Spier's wordless books, *Rain,* describes the adventures a young brother and sister have during a downpour as Spier attempts to capture the mood of the storm itself in the pictures. In the *Los Angeles Times Book Review,* Barbara Karlin called the book "a perfect evocation of rain," and a *New York Times Book Review* contributor wrote that Spier's "pictures conjure up rain you can almost feel and hear."

With the two-hundredth anniversary of the U.S. Constitution approaching, Spier wrote *We the People: The Story of the U.S. Constitution* in 1987. In the book, Spier focuses on the fifty-two word preamble and represents each phrase pictorially. He also details how the Constitution came into being and illustrates how people today continue the work of the Constitution, drawing together the past and present through the power of the document. In *Washington Post Book World,* Selma G. Lanes called the book "an exhilarating visual appreciation of the document and of its living meaning."

With an admired body of work including illustrations for over 150 books, Peter Spier has established himself as one of America's most popular children's book authors. Joan Hess Michel summed up Spier and his work in *American Artist:* "Peter Spier sets high standards for himself, demanding his best. He is exact and thorough in his research. His work is careful, detailed, and precise, yet has spontaneity, humor, and charm. His fine illustrations possess a joyous quality; they delight as well as teach."

BIOGRAPHICAL/CRITICAL SOURCES:

BOOKS

Children's Literature Review, Volume 5, Gale, 1983.
De Montreville, Doris, and Donna Hill, editors, *Third Book of Junior Authors,* H. W. Wilson, 1972.
Dictionary of Literary Biography, Volume 61: *American Writers for Children since 1960: Poets, Illustrators, and Nonfiction Authors,* Gale, 1987, pp. 282-296.
Hopkins, Lee Bennett, *Books Are by People,* Citation Press, 1969.
Illustrators of Books for Young People, 2nd edition, Scarecrow, 1975.
Kingman, Lee and others, compilers, *Illustrator's of Children's Books: 1957-1966,* Horn Book, 1968.
Kingman and others, compilers, *Illustrators of Children's Books: 1967-1976,* Horn Book, 1978.
Kingman, editor, *Newbery and Caldecott Medal Books: 1976-1985,* Horn Book, 1986.

Miller, Bertha M. and others, compilers, *Illustrator's of Children's Books: 1946-1956,* Horn Book, 1958.

Roginski, Jim, compiler, *Newbery and Caldecott Medalists and Honor Book Winners,* Libraries Unlimited, 1982.

Ward, Martha E., and Dorothy A. Marquardt, *Illustrators of Books for Young People,* second edition, Scarecrow, 1975.

PERIODICALS

American Artist, October, 1969, pp. 49-55, 82-86.

Horn Book, October, 1970; August, 1978, pp. 379-81.

Junior Literary Guild Catalogue, March, 1972; September, 1972.

Los Angeles Times Book Review, October 5, 1980, p. 12; May 2, 1982, p. 7.

New York Times, April 8, 1973.

New York Times Book Review, February 1, 1970; January 23, 1972; December 7, 1980, p. 41; April 25, 1982, p. 35; March 16, 1986; June 29, 1986; October 4, 1987, p. 49.

Publishers Weekly, July 25, 1980, pp. 93-94.

Times Literary Supplement, March 27, 1981.

Washington Post Book World, July 12, 1981, p. 12; December 13, 1981, p. 8; May 9, 1982; November 8, 1987.

Wilson Library Bulletin, October, 1974.

Writer, August, 1982.

*   *   *

SPINK, Reginald (William) 1905-

PERSONAL: Born December 9, 1905, in York, England; son of William and Lilian Annie (Newbold) Spink; married Else Marie Buus, 1932; children: Allan Olaf, Karen Margaret Ann. *Education:* Educated in England.

ADDRESSES: Home and office—6 Deane Way, Eastcote, Ruislip, Middlesex HA4 8SU, England.

CAREER: Journalist, editor, translator, and author of books for both children and adults. Worked as office worker; English teacher in Copenhagen, Denmark, 1928-39; Copenhagen correspondent for *New Leader,* 1935-39, 1945-50, and for *Financial Times* and *Shipping World,* both London, England, 1946-49. Has taken part in many radio broadcasts in Britain and Denmark; has appeared on television in Britain and Denmark. *Wartime service:* Special Operations Executive, senior member of Danish section, 1940-45; Political Warfare Executive, 1943-44.

MEMBER: Society of Authors, Translators Association (member of executive committee, 1965-67, 1972-74), Special Forces Club (founding member), Danish Club (London).

AWARDS, HONORS: Freedom Medal from King Christian X, 1945; Knight's Cross of the Order of the Dannebrog, 1966; Ebbe Munck Memorial Award, 1982.

WRITINGS:

(With Jens Otto Krag) *England bygger op* (title means "Britain Rebuilds"), Det danske Forlag (Copenhagen), 1947.

The Land and People of Denmark (juvenile), Macmillan, 1953.

Fairy Tales of Denmark (juvenile), Dutton, 1961.

The Young Hans Andersen (juvenile), Roy, 1962.

Hans Christian Andersen and His World, Thames & Hudson, 1972.

Hans Christian Andersen: The Man and His Work, Hoest (Copenhagen), 1972, Arthur Vanous, 1975.

DBC: The Story of the Danish Bacon Company, Danish Bacon Company (London), 1977.

40 aar efter (memoirs), Odense University Press, 1983.

Alexander and the Golden Bird and other Danish Folk Tales (retelling of folk tales), Floris Books, 1991.

TRANSLATOR

Carl Nielsen, *My Childhood,* Hutchinson, 1953.

Nielsen, *Living Music,* Hutchinson, 1953.

Palle Lauring, *The Roman,* Museum Press, 1956.

Anton Bruun and others, *The Galathea Deep Sea Expedition,* Allen & Unwin, 1956.

Lauring, *Land of the Tollund Man,* Lutterworth, 1957.

Ludvig Holberg, *Three Comedies,* Theatre Arts, 1957.

Poul Borchsenius, *Behind the Wall,* Simon & Schuster, 1957.

Hans Christian Andersen, *Fairy Tales,* Dutton, 1958.

Prince George of Greece and Denmark, *The Cretan Drama: Memoirs,* Robert Speller, 1959.

Frank Wenzel, *The Buzzard,* Allen & Unwin, 1959.

Henry Harald Hansen, *Daughters of Allah,* Allen & Unwin, 1960.

Andersen, *Fairy Tales and Stories,* Dutton, 1960.

Rolf Blomberg, *Chavante,* Allen & Unwin, 1960.

Bengt Danielsson, *Terry in the South Seas,* Allen & Unwin, 1960.

Danielsson, *Terry in Australia,* Allen & Unwin, 1961.

Joergen Bisch, *Ulu: The World's End,* Dutton, 1961.

Borchsenius, *And It Was Morning,* Simon & Schuster, 1962.

Bisch, *Behind the Veil of Arabia,* Dutton, 1962.

Bisch, *Mongolia: Unknown Land,* Dutton, 1963.

Einar Rud, *Vasari's Life and Lives,* Thames & Hudson, 1963.

Danielsson, *Gauguin in the South Seas,* Doubleday, 1965.

Andersen, *A Christmas Greeting,* Hoest, 1965.

G. Boesen, *Danish Museums,* Samvirkeraadet (Copenhagen), 1966.

Knud Soenderby, *The Blue Flashes,* Danish Ministry of Foreign Affairs, 1966.

Poul Abrahamsen, *Royal Wedding,* Danish Ministry of Foreign Affairs, 1967.

Andersen, *New Tales, 1843,* Hoest, 1973.

K. Heltoft, *Hans Christian Andersen as an Artist,* Danish Ministry of Foreign Affairs, 1977.

Sven Tito Achen, *Symbols around Us,* Van Nostrand Reinhold, 1978.

Svend Erik Stybe, *Copenhagen University: Five Hundred Years of Science and Scholarship,* Danish Ministry of Foreign Affairs, 1979.

Hanne Westergaard, *Hans Christian Andersen's Flowers,* Danish Ministry of Foreign Affairs, 1979.

Ludwig Albertsen, *On the Threshold of a Golden Age: Denmark around 1800,* Danish Ministry of Foreign Affairs, 1979.

Asiatisk Plads: Danish Foreign Service's New Headquarters in Copenhagen, Danish Ministry of Foreign Affairs, 1980.

Bent Rying, *Denmark: Introduction, Prehistory,* Danish Ministry of Foreign Affairs, 1981.

Erling Nielsen, *Hans Christian Andersen,* Danish Ministry of Foreign Affairs, 1983.

Peter P. Rohde, *Soeren Kierkegaard,* Danish Ministry of Foreign Affairs, 1983.

Poul Dam, *N. F. S. Grundtvig,* Danish Ministry of Foreign Affairs, 1983.

Gustav Scherz, *Niels Steengen and Nicolaus Stent,* Danish Ministry of Foreign Affairs, 1988.

Bent Rying, *Denmark's History,* Danish Ministry of Foreign Affairs, 1988.

August Bournonville, *La Sylphide* (ballet libretto), Dance Books, 1990.

Mogens Kofod-Hansen, *Andy: Anders Lassen, V.C.,* Freedom Museum, 1991.

Translator or editor of several editions of *Denmark: An Official Handbook,* Danish Ministry of Foreign Affairs, 1946-74.

OTHER

Contributor to American, British, Irish, South African, Canadian, Australian, New Zealand, and Danish journals. Translator and English text editor of *Danish Foreign Office Journal* (now *Danish Journal*), 1946-80; editor of *Denmark: A Quarterly Review of Anglo-Danish Relations,* 1961-74.

BIOGRAPHICAL/CRITICAL SOURCES:

BOOKS

Schroeder, Carol L., *A Biography of Danish Literature in English Translation,* Det danske Selsikab, 1982.

Spink, Reginald, *40 aar efter* (memoirs), Odense University Press, 1983.

*   *   *

SPRINGER, Nancy 1948-

PERSONAL: Born July 5, 1948, in Montclair, NJ; daughter of Harry E. (in business) and Helen (an artist; maiden name, Wheeler) Connor; married Joel Springer (a fine art photographer), September 13, 1969; children: Jonathan, Nora. *Education:* Gettysburg College, B.A. (cum laude), 1970.

ADDRESSES: Home—360 West Main St., Dallastown, PA 17313. *Agent*—Jean V. Naggar, 216 East 75th St., New York, NY 10021.

CAREER: Delone Catholic High School, McSherrystown, PA, teacher, 1970-71; writer, 1972—. University of Pittsburgh at Johnstown, personal development plan instructor, 1983-85; York College of Pennsylvania, personal and professional growth instructor, 1986—; Franklin and Marshall College, Et Cetera program instructor, 1987—; part-time communications instructor at Bradley Academy for the Visual Arts. Volunteer aide for York County Easter Seals 4-H Horseback Riding for the Handicapped. Violin player with the York College of Pennsylvania orchestra.

MEMBER: Society of Children's Book Writers, Pennwriters (president), Children's Literature Council of Pennsylvania (board member), Phi Beta Kappa.

AWARDS, HONORS: Iowa State Best Books for Young Adults citation, for *Chains of Gold;* International Reading Association Children's Book Council Children's Choice citation, 1988, Florida Master Reading List citation, 1988, and Georgia Master Reading List citation, 1989, all for *A Horse to Love;* New York Public Library Books for the Teen Age citation, Enoch Pratt Free Library Youth-to-Youth Books: A List for Imagination and Survival citation, and American Library Association Best Books for Young Adults citation, all for *The Hex Witch of Seldom;* Nebula Award nomination, for *Apocalypse;* Dorothy Canfield Fisher Award nomination, for *Red Wizard;* Joan Fassler Memorial Book Award, 1992, for *Colt.*

WRITINGS:

FANTASY NOVELS

The Book of Suns, Pocket Books, 1977.
The White Hart (Science Fiction Book Club selection), Pocket Books, 1979.
The Silver Sun (based on *The Book of Suns*), Pocket Books, 1980.
The Sable Moon, Pocket Books, 1981.

The Black Beast (also see below), Pocket Books, 1982.

The Golden Swan (also see below), Pocket Books, 1983.

The Book of Vale (Science Fiction Book Club edition; contains *The Black Beast* and *The Golden Swan*), Doubleday, 1983.

Wings of Flame, Tor Books, 1985.

Chains of Gold, Arbor House, 1986.

Madbond (Volume 1 of "The Sea King" trilogy), Tor Books, 1987.

Mindbond (Volume 2 of "The Sea King" trilogy), Tor Books, 1987.

Godbond (Volume 3 of "The Sea King" trilogy), Tor Books, 1988.

The Hex Witch of Seldom, Baen Books, 1988.

Apocalypse, Baen Books, 1989.

Larque on the Wing, Avon, in press.

Volos the Unholy, New American Library, in press.

CHILDREN'S BOOKS

A Horse to Love, Harper, 1987.

Not on a White Horse, Atheneum, 1988.

They're All Named Wildfire, Atheneum, 1989.

Red Wizard (Junior Library Guild selection), Atheneum, 1990.

Colt, Dial Books for Young Readers, 1991.

The Friendship Song, Atheneum, 1992.

The Great Pony Hassle, Dial Books for Young Readers, in press.

The Boy on a Black Horse, Atheneum, in press.

Music of Their Hooves (poetry), Boyds Mills Press, in press.

COLLECTIONS

Chance: And Other Gestures of the Hand of Fate (short stories, poetry, and novellas), Baen Books, 1987.

Stardark Songs (fantasy poetry), New Establishment Press, in press.

OTHER

Also author of novellas, including "Chance," in *Under the Wheel,* Baen Books, 1987; "Serenity," in the *Magazine of Fantasy and Science Fiction,* 1989; and "Damnbanna," in *Axolotl Press,* 1992. Contributor of short stories to periodicals, including *Fantasy Book* and the *Magazine of Fantasy and Science Fiction;* also contributor of short stories to anthologies, including *Magic in Ithkar,* edited by Andre Norton and Robert Adams, Tor Books, 1985; and *Moonsinger's Friends,* edited by Susan Shwartz, Bluejay Books, 1985.

WORK IN PROGRESS: Various children's novels; *Feather of a Dove,* a mainstream novel following through twenty years twin boys whose lives are warped by their abusive father.

SIDELIGHTS: Nancy Springer told *CA:* "People often ask me how I can write novels for both children and adults. I can't understand why this should be such a strange idea to them. The way any fiction writer works is to get inside the main character, to see through the character's eyes, to walk around in the character's skin awhile—and when writing a novel for children the main character is a child, that's all. Style, vocabulary, subject matter, everything else follows naturally once the fundamental act of imagination takes place. It's no big deal.

"I think the reason I perplex people is that they have notions about children's book writers, rather as they have notions about nuns. Aren't children's book writers supposed to be set apart, different, teacherly, idealistic, morally pure? Don't they write for children because they are incapable of dealing with adult interests? Um, gee, sorry to disappoint, but my contemporary fantasies such as *Larque on the Wing* are quite adult in content. I write for children because I like kids.

"The biggest real difference between writing for adults and writing for children is the distance between me and the audience. In order to get a book anywhere near a child, I as the writer must run a gauntlet of adults—editors, librarians, teachers, reviewers, parents—many of whom are eager to censor out any bit of subversive mischief that might actually be of interest to a child. This is frustrating for me as a writer, that do-gooders are interfering between me and my readers.

"I am spoiled, perhaps, be having written fantasy for many years. In the fantasy/science fiction/speculative fiction field, I enjoyed a remarkable amount of creative liberty. I still write fantasy—for adults and children—but am more and more interested in writing about the real world in a fantastic way, integrating what I have learned from writing fantasy into what I want to say about contemporary life."

BIOGRAPHICAL/CRITICAL SOURCES:

PERIODICALS

Gettysburg Times, November 2, 1977.

Library Journal, August, 1986.

Publishers Weekly, February 27, 1987; February 12, 1988.

Susquehanna, May, 1978; April, 1980.

Voice of Youth Advocates, December, 1986; April, 1990.

Washington Post Book World, May 10, 1992.

York Daily Record, January 8, 1980.

*   *   *

STAVROS, Niko
See KING, Florence

STEVENSON, William Henri   1924-

PERSONAL: Born June 1, 1924, in London, England; son of William (a master mariner) and Alida (Deleporte) Stevenson; married Glenys Rowe (an aviation draftswoman), July 28, 1945 (divorced, 1983); married Monika Jensen (a television producer), February, 1984; children: (first marriage) Andrew, Jacqueline, Kevin, Sally; (second marriage) Alexandra. *Education:* Attended Royal Navy College, 1942; Ruskin College, Oxford, B.A., 1948. *Religion:* Church of England.

ADDRESSES: Office—Office of the Principal Private Secretary to His Majesty the King of Thailand, Grand Palace, Bangkok, Thailand; also William Stevenson, Ltd., P. O. Box 1179, Hamilton-5, Bermuda. *Agent*—Tom Mori, President, Tuttle-Mori Agency, Inc., 2-15 Kanda Jimbocho, Chiyoda-Ku, Tokyo 101, Japan.

CAREER: Toronto Star, Toronto, Ontario, Canada, foreign correspondent, 1948-1958; *Toronto Globe and Mail,* Toronto, foreign correspondent, 1958-63; Independent Television News, London, England, editor, 1963-64; Near and Far East News (NAFEN), Malaya, Far East bureau chief, 1964-66; Canadian Broadcasting Corp. (CBC-TV), executive producer of television documentaries, 1966-77; independent writer, broadcaster, 1977—. Host of *Dateline* nightly newsmagazine and syndicated columnist. *Military service:* Royal Navy Air Service, 1942-45, carrier fighter pilot; became lieutenant commander. Advisor with Canadian contingent, International Truce Supervisory Commission, Vietnam, 1956.

MEMBER: Royal Overseas League (London), Royal Institute of Strategic Studies (Thailand), Association Naval Aviation U.S.A., Authors Guild, Boy Scouts of United Kingdom (King's Scout), Royal Bermuda Yacht Club, Bangkok Sports Club.

WRITINGS:

Saka the Seagull, Brockhampton Press, 1947.
The Yellow Wind: An Excursion in and Around Red China, Houghton, 1959.
Nehru's India, Toronto Globe and Mail Book Publishing Division, 1960.
Canada in the World, Toronto Globe and Mail Book Publishing Division, 1961.
After Nehru—What?, Toronto Globe Publishing Book Publishing Division, 1961.
The World's Most Rugged Frontier, Toronto Globe Publishing Book Publishing Division, 1962.
Revolution in Indonesia, Houghton, 1963.
Birds' Nests in Their Beards, Houghton, 1964.
The Bushbabies (juvenile), Houghton, 1965.
Strike Zion!, Bantam, 1967.
Zanek!: A Chronicle of the Israeli Air Force, Viking, 1971.

The Bormann Brotherhood, Harcourt, 1971.
A Man Called Intrepid: The Secret War, Macmillan, 1976.
Ninety Minutes at Entebbe, Bantam, 1976.
Intrepid's Last Case, Villard, 1983.
(Co-author with wife Monika Jensen) *Kiss the Boys Goodbye: How the United States Betrayed Its Own POWs in Vietnam,* Dutton, 1990.

Also author of screenplay for *The Bushbabies,* filmed under the title *The Bushbaby,* Metro-Goldwyn-Mayer, 1970.

NOVELS

Emperor Red, Bantam, 1970.
The Ghosts of Africa, Harcourt, 1980.
Eclipse, Doubleday, 1986.
Booby Trap, Doubleday, 1987.

ADAPTATIONS: Ninety Minutes at Entebbe was adapted for film, 1976; *A Man Called Intrepid* was broadcast as a mini-series for British Broadcasting Co., National Broadcasting Co. (NBC-TV), and CBC-TV, 1979, and was made into a feature film by Lorimar; *The Bushbabies* was adapted by Nippon animation for a forty-segment television series running through 1993.

WORK IN PROGRESS: A nonfiction book about the Cold War in Asia entitled *The Power of One.*

SIDELIGHTS: William Stevenson, described by *New York Times* critic Paul Grimes as "an expert reporter and raconteur," has written travel and adventure books, political studies, and children's fiction. His more popular nonfiction works document the efforts of British intelligence agents and Israeli commandos during wartime, and his semi-fictional spy thrillers investigate historical puzzles and rework past military events. According to Joseph McLellan of the *Washington Post,* Stevenson's work is marked by "an ambition that is . . . matched by his skill."

The bulk of Stevenson's efforts are tales of political intrigue and military adventure. The author's trio of books about Israel's armed forces, *Zanek!: A Chronicle of the Israeli Air Force, Strike Zion!,* and *90 Minutes at Entebbe,* illustrate the power and efficiency of that nation's combat forces. Each book examines a different aspect of Israeli military might: *Zanek!* looks at the achievements of the Air Force personnel, while *Strike Zion!* and *90 Minutes at Entebbe* describe famous, successful military missions.

Stevenson was granted access to the inner circles of the Israeli military for *Zanek!* Written in an anecdotal style, the book portrays the pilots and ground personnel of the IAF as courageous, dedicated individuals; it also discusses tactical and technical aspects of flight missions. *Publishers Weekly* reviewer Albert Johnston lauded Stevenson's effort, stating that the author "does manage vividly to give an inside picture of the Air Force through the eyes of the people involved." *Strike Zion!* and *90 Minutes at Entebbe* both fall under the category of "instant" books—works written about an event shortly after it occurs to capitalize on the public's heightened awareness of the incident. *Strike Zion!,* which chronicles the Six-Day War—the 1967 Israeli-Arab conflict that resulted in Israel's occupation of the Sinai peninsula—was published within two weeks of that military action. Reviewing *Strike Zion!* in the *New York Times,* Richard F. Shepard acknowledged that "what it covers, it covers well," but he also noted that "there are certain omissions," specifically citing unmentioned American involvement. *Saturday Review* critic Geoffrey Godsell commended Stevenson's decision to include first-person accounts from individuals involved in the hostilities, but he argued that because *Strike Zion!* lacks historical perspective, it remains "journalism rather than history."

90 Minutes at Entebbe was published two weeks after the daring Israeli rescue of 103 hostages from a hijacked airliner in Entebbe, Uganda. Stevenson anticipated the raid, and he interviewed Israeli ministers and military personnel before the rescue operation began. After the rescue, Stevenson remained with the participants to gather more information. Grimes congratulated Stevenson for the speed with which he wrote the book, though he suggested that *90 Minutes at Entebbe* "was perhaps published too quickly to be easily readable and completely credible." Michael Twaddle of the *Times Literary Supplement* disagreed, writing: "Inevitably there are errors in accounts composed at such speed . . . . But overall the authenticity of the descriptive sections . . . together with the extracts from hostages' testimonies . . . more than compensate for such minor errors."

Stevenson continued his behind-the-scenes look at military ventures with a pair of books about British spy activities during and after World War II. The bestseller *A Man Called Intrepid: The Secret War* is perhaps Stevenson's most widely-known work. The book concerns Canadian industrialist William Stephenson, who acted as liaison between Winston Churchill and Franklin Roosevelt and headed British intelligence operations in the Western Hemisphere. Stephenson, whose code name was "Intrepid," directed the British Security Coordination, or BSC, an organization responsible for coordinating several branches of British intelligence, as well as the training of undercover agents. Stephenson's mission was twofold: to enlist the United States's aid against the Axis powers and to use every means at his disposal to help defeat the enemy. He performed these tasks brilliantly with the assistance of the BSC staff, a group of amateur spies skilled at forging documents, tapping communication lines, and inventing devices like cyanide-filled fountain pens. The

agents also resorted to theft, blackmail and murder when they deemed it necessary.

Critical response to *A Man Called Intrepid* was mixed. Several reviewers felt that the author's assessment of Stephenson's role in British intelligence circles was overblown and distorted, amounting to little more than heroworship. *Times Literary Supplement* critic David Hunt chided the work for its "two main faults: inaccuracy and a tendency to magnify the ubiquity and omnicompetence of Sir William Stephenson . . . Mr. Stevenson is at pains to show that almost everything done in the fields of intelligence in the broadest sense, and of subversive operations, is to be attributed to Sir William Stephenson." And Hanson W. Baldwin, writing in *Saturday Review,* argued that "the book's case for Intrepid as a mover and shaker is greatly weakened by inaccuracies and overstatements, the lack of supporting data, and the author's propensity for verbatim quotation of unrecorded conversations that took place 30 years ago."

Other critics, while expressing reservations about Stevenson's technique, saw the book in a more positive light. Novelist John le Carre, reviewing in the *New York Times Book Review,* complimented *A Man Called Intrepid* for its richness of detail, but he also admitted that the reader "must put up with muddled organization, mawkishly 'reconstructed' dialogues," and "a provocative, not to say patronizing habit of self-censorship at crucial points. . . . Nevertheless," he added, "my advice is to persevere. It's worth it." Harry Rositzke of the *Washington Post Book World* referred to the work as "detailed and precisely documented. . . . For the action buff there is a generous quota of spy stories and tales of derring-do." Stevenson also earned praise for his revealing insights into the murky world of counterintelligence. "Stevenson's book adds to our knowledge of the underground war," remarked Baldwin, and *Spectator* contributor Maurice Buckmaster, the wartime chief of British underground resistance in Europe, stated: "*A Man called Intrepid* reveals much background information which was unknown before its publication, even to those who were engaged in carrying out the Chief's policy down the chain of command."

Stevenson continued the saga of BSC director Stephenson with *Intrepid's Last Case.* The book details the efforts of Intrepid to clear his wartime deputy, the late Col. Charles H. Ellis, of allegations that he had served as a double agent for both Germany and the Soviet Union. The author surmises that another high-ranking British intelligence worker, not Ellis, suppressed evidence of Soviet counterintelligence activity in British, U.S., and Canadian military centers. With the aid of Stevenson, Sir William attempts to uncover the worker's name, but as *New York Times Book Review* critic James Bamford noted, "in the end, Intrepid and Mr. Stevenson are no closer to discovering the identity of the mysterious [Englishman] than they were more than 300 pages earlier.'' Nonetheless, *National Review* critic Curtis Carroll Davis found *Intrepid's Last Case* worthwhile as a commentary on the role of espionage agents in the escalating Cold War, calling the work a "horror story . . . a cautionary tale brought up to the present.''

In addition to his true-life spy adventures, Stevenson has written novels that fictionalize historical events. In *Eclipse,* Stevenson raises anew questions about Nazi deputy Rudolph Hess's 1941 solo flight into Scotland and possible Allied complicity with Hitler's Germany. An earlier work, *The Ghosts of Africa,* was based on the military exploits of Col. Paul von Lettow-Vorbeck, a German commander in East Africa whose tiny band of German officers and native soldiers rebelled against occupying British forces during World War I. Considered a victory for Germany, this little-known part of the war foreshadowed the end of British colonialism in Africa. In McLellan's view, *The Ghosts of Africa* "mixes historic fact with fiction in a rich texture . . . it should give readers an eye-opening glimpse of a relatively unknown but significant corner of 20th-century history."

Stevenson's strength is that he writes about what he knows best. Reviewers cite his knowledge about international espionage and exhaustive research as the keys to his most successful works. As for his most recent efforts, Stevenson says that he has been "working toward a narrative style in fiction that allows him to weave into fantasy those realities not easily documented."

Stevenson told *CA:* "My books have been based on first-hand experience: I was first among non-communist correspondents to enter Maoist China and film Chairman Mao Tse-Tung, producing a television documentary for CBC-TV and NBC-TV, and as a correspondent I interviewed some of the Cold War's leading devils like Ho Chi Minh, Zhou Enlai, Nikita Khrushchev, and Marshal Tito. My father had been with the French Resistance in World War II and then joined the Bletchley Park ULTRA teams, chiefly keeping contact with underground anti-Nazis, and this resulted in my own decision to fly Hellcats in the Royal Navy for behind-the-lines 'spy plane' operations over Japanese-occupied territory, after being launched from British carriers offshore.

"I have been working in East Asia with my wife, Monika Jensen, for the past three years to reconstruct Cold War secret warfare in the region with the cooperation of Asian leaders. That book will be accompanied by a separate book by Jensen on a related true adventure. Our daughter Alexandra attends the palace school founded by the present King Rama VII of Thailand. A book about the only girl from abroad to attend the palace school, and become a friend of the twelve sacred white elephants stabled under her classroom, is also in the works.''

BIOGRAPHICAL/CRITICAL SOURCES:

PERIODICALS

Globe and Mail (Toronto), April 29, 1989.
Los Angeles Times Book Review, December 7, 1980.
National Review, May 18, 1984.
New York Times, August 26, 1967; July 30, 1976.
New York Times Book Review, February 29, 1976, pp. 1-2; January 22, 1984, p. 20; March 16, 1986.
Publishers Weekly, December 28, 1970, p. 57.
Saturday Review, August 26, 1967, pp. 29, 36; March 6, 1976, pp.26-28.
Spectator, April 10, 1976, p. 20.
Times Literary Supplement, May 28, 1976, p. 643; October 29, 1976, p. 1366; June 28, 1991.
Washington Post, October 16, 1980, p. F4; May 1, 1987.
Washington Post Book World, March 14, 1976; February 5, 1984.

*   *   *

STILLER, Brian C(arl) 1942-

PERSONAL: Born August 10, 1942, in Naicam, Saskatchewan, Canada; son of Carl H. (a clergyman) and Mildred (a housewife; maiden name, Parsons) Stiller; married Lily Rogers (a music teacher), August 31, 1963; children: Murray, Murriel. *Education:* Central Pentecostal College, B.Th., 1963; University of Toronto, B.A., 1966, M.Rel., 1975. *Religion:* Protestant.

ADDRESSES: Home—50 Howlett Ave., Newmarket, Ontario, Canada L3Y 5S5. *Office*—Box 8800, Station B, Willowdale, Ontario, Canada M2K 2R6.

CAREER: Ordained Pentecostal minister, 1968; Youth for Christ/Canada, president, 1967-83; Evangelical Fellowship of Canada, Willowdale, Ontario, executive director, 1983—. Host of *The Stiller Report,* a weekly television program aired nationally.

WRITINGS:

A Generation Under Siege, Victor Books, 1983.
Life Gifts, Stoddart, 1990.
Critical Option, FT Publications, 1991.

FILMS

The Pearl, released by International Child Care, 1972.
Guns of Love, released by World Vision, Inc., 1975.
Beyond the Mountains, released by International Child Care, 1978.
Agents of Change, released by Youth for Christ, 1978.
The Promise, released by Roundtable, 1983.

OTHER

Editor-in-chief, *Faith Today.*

WORK IN PROGRESS: From the Tower of Babel to Parliament Hill, expected 1994.

SIDELIGHTS: Brian Stiller told *CA:* "Because I was raised in a minister's home, I was fascinated with religious ideas and phenomena from an early age. Sixteen years in youth ministry heightened not only my concern but my interest in people and their environment. In publishing *Faith Today* and hosting a weekly show on current issues, my interest in the relation of faith to life has increased."

*   *   *

STOLZ, Mary (Slattery) 1920-

PERSONAL: Born March 24, 1920, in Boston, MA; daughter of Thomas Francis and Mary Margaret (a nurse; maiden name, Burgey) Slattery; married Stanley Burr Stolz (a civil engineer), January, 1940 (divorced, 1956); married Thomas C. Jaleski (a doctor), June, 1965; children: (first marriage) William. *Education:* Attended Columbia University, 1936-38, and Katharine Gibbs School, NY, 1938-39. *Politics:* "Liberal Northern Democrat." *Avocational interests:* "Writing letters to editors as to the many matters in society that infuriate me—neglect of the sick, the poor, the jobless, the homeless, and the helpless by the last two administrations, and also about the indifference to the environment, to the creatures of the earth, to children, to the future of this poor little planet. I love ballet, baseball, and cats. I like to play hard games of Scrabble. And, of course, I read constantly."

ADDRESSES: Home—P.O. Box 82, Longboat Key, FL 34228. *Agent*—Roslyn Targ Literary Agency, Inc., 105 West Thirteenth St., Suite 15E, New York, NY 10011.

CAREER: Writer of books for children and young adults. Worked at various jobs, including R. H. Macy's (department store), book salesperson, 1938, and Columbia University, secretary at Teachers College, 1938.

MEMBER: Authors League.

AWARDS, HONORS: Child Study Children's Book Award, Child Study Children's Book Committee at Bank Street College, 1953, for *In a Mirror;* Spring Book Festival Older Honor Award, *New York Herald Tribune,* 1953, for *Ready or Not,* and 1956, for *The Day and the Way We Met;* Spring Book Festival Older Award, *New York Herald Tribune,* 1957, for *Because of Madeline;* Newbery Award Honor Books, American Library Association (ALA), 1962, for *Belling the Tiger,* and 1966, for *The Noonday Friends;* Junior Book Award, Boys' Club of America,

1964, for *The Bully of Barkham Street; Horn Book* Honor List citation, and National Book Award nomination, Association of American Publishers, 1975, both for *The Edge of Next Year;* Recognition of Merit Award, George G. Stone Center for Children's Books, 1982, for entire body of work; Children's Science Book Younger Honor Award, New York Academy of Sciences, 1986, for *Night of Ghosts and Hermits;* German Youth Festival Award; ALA Notable Book citation, for *The Sea Gulls Woke Me, Belling the Tiger, Quentin Corn,* and other books.

WRITINGS:

YOUNG ADULT

To Tell Your Love, Harper, 1950.
The Organdy Cupcakes, Harper, 1951.
The Sea Gulls Woke Me, Harper, 1951.
In a Mirror, Harper, 1953.
Ready or Not, Harper, 1953.
Pray Love, Remember, Harper, 1954.
Two by Two, Houghton, 1954, revised edition published as *A Love, or a Season,* Harper, 1964.
Rosemary, Harper, 1955.
Hospital Zone, Harper, 1956.
The Day and the Way We Met, Harper, 1956.
Good-by My Shadow, Harper, 1957.
Because of Madeline, Harper, 1957.
And Love Replied, Harper, 1958.
Second Nature, Harper, 1958.
Some Merry-Go-Round Music, Harper, 1959.
The Beautiful Friend and Other Stories, Harper, 1960.
Wait for Me, Michael, Harper, 1961.
Who Wants Music on Monday?, Harper, 1963.
By the Highway Home, Harper, 1971.
Leap before You Look, Harper, 1972.
The Edge of Next Year, Harper, 1974.
Go and Catch a Flying Fish, Harper, 1979.
What Time of Night Is It?, Harper, 1981.

JUVENILE

The Leftover Elf, illustrated by Peggy Bacon, Harper, 1952.
Emmett's Pig, illustrated by Garth Williams, Harper, 1959.
A Dog on Barkham Street (also see below), illustrated by Leonard Shortall, Harper, 1960.
Belling the Tiger, illustrated by Beni Montresor, Harper, 1961.
The Great Rebellion (also see below), illustrated by Montresor, Harper, 1961.
Fredou, illustrated by Tomi Ungerer, Harper, 1962.
Pigeon Flight, illustrated by Murray Tinkelman, Harper, 1962.
Siri, the Conquistador (also see below), illustrated by Montresor, Harper, 1963.

The Bully of Barkham Street (also see below), illustrated by Shortall, Harper, 1963.

The Mystery of the Woods, illustrated by Uri Shulevitz, Harper, 1964.

The Noonday Friends, illustrated by Louis S. Glanzman, Harper, 1965.

Maximilian's World (also see below), illustrated by Shulevitz, Harper, 1966.

A Wonderful, Terrible Time, illustrated by Glanzman, Harper, 1967.

Say Something, illustrated by Edward Frascino, Harper, 1968.

The Story of a Singular Hen and Her Peculiar Children, illustrated by Frascino, Harper, 1969.

The Dragons of the Queen, illustrated by Frascino, Harper, 1969.

Juan, illustrated by Glanzman, Harper, 1970.

Land's End, illustrated by Dennis Hermanson, Harper, 1973.

Cat in the Mirror, Harper, 1975.

Ferris Wheel, Harper, 1977.

Cider Days, Harper, 1978.

Cat Walk, illustrated by Erik Blegvad, Harper, 1983.

Quentin Corn, illustrated by Pamela Johnson, David Godine, 1985.

The Explorer of Barkham Street (also see below), illustrated by Emily Arnold McCully, Harper, 1985.

Night of Ghosts and Hermits: Nocturnal Life on the Seashore, illustrated by Susan Gallagher, Harcourt, 1985.

The Cuckoo Clock, illustrated by Johnson, David Godine, 1986.

Ivy Larkin, Harcourt, 1986.

The Scarecrows and Their Child, illustrated by Amy Schwartz, Harper, 1987.

Zekmet, the Stone Carver: A Tale of Ancient Egypt, illustrated by Deborah Nourse Lattimore, Harcourt, 1988.

Storm in the Night, illustrated by Pat Cummings, Harper, 1988.

Pangur Ban, illustrated by Johnson, Harper, 1988.

Barkham Street Trilogy (contains *A Dog on Barkham Street, The Bully of Barkham Street,* and *The Explorer of Barkham Street*), Harper, 1989.

Bartholomew Fair, Greenwillow, 1990.

Tales at the Mousehole (characters' names have been changed; contains *The Great Rebellion, Siri, the Conquistador,* and *Maximilian's World*), illustrated by Johnson, David Godine, 1990.

Deputy Shep, illustrated by Johnson, Harper, 1991.

King Emmett the Second, illustrated by Williams, Greenwillow, 1991.

Go Fish, illustrated by Cummings, Harper, 1991.

OTHER

Truth and Consequence (adult), Harper, 1953.

Contributor of fiction to periodicals, including *Seventeen, Ladies' Home Journal, Woman's Day, Good Housekeeping, McCall's, Redbook,* and *Cricket.*

Stolz's works have been published in nearly thirty languages, and some have been issued in Braille. Her manuscripts are housed in the Kerlan collection at the University of Minnesota, Minneapolis.

ADAPTATIONS: "Baby Blue Expression" (short story; first published in *McCall's*) was adapted for television by Alfred Hitchcock.

WORK IN PROGRESS: A book that features Thomas, a black child who appears in both *Storm in the Night* and *Go Fish,* publication expected by HarperCollins; *Cezanne Pinto, Cowboy,* a book "about Thomas's ancestor, who was a runaway slave who eventually became a cowboy. Not many people know there were any."

SIDELIGHTS: Mary Stolz is well known to young readers ranging in age from children just learning to read to teenagers on the brink of adulthood. As evidenced by such popular works as *To Tell Your Love* and *The Edge of Next Year,* she has achieved success among her older readers, who enjoy her candid examinations of such topics as young love, family conflicts, death, and maturity. And she has also gained a wide following among her younger readers, who favor award-winning works like *Belling the Tiger* and her tales about growing up, such as her "Barkham Street" stories. In 1982 Stolz was recognized for her entire body of work with the George G. Stone Recognition of Merit Award, and in her acceptance speech, she summed up the reasons she writes for young people: "From my mail, I know that there are many children still looking for answers in books. I used to, as a child. I still think something reassuring is to be found in them. If we read hard enough they can offer us at least part of a perspective to *What are we going to do about it?* With even that part of a perspective we could, possibly, still save our world. . . . The children are, at present, all we can hope through. Which is why I write for them."

Stolz wrote her initial novel, *To Tell Your Love,* about a young girl who is abandoned by her first boyfriend. Since the publication of *To Tell Your Love,* Stolz has alternated between writing for children and writing for teenagers. Among the earliest of these is *In a Mirror.* Revolving around Bessie, a college junior, the story unfolds through journal entries, which reveal her innermost thoughts about college life, dates, and parties. The entries also reveal her emerging sense of self-understanding. When Bessie finally admits that she has a weight problem, for example, she recognizes that she overeats to compensate for other problems in her life. The story "is a work of art," wrote a reviewer in *Horn Book*.

In *Because of Madeline* and *Who Wants Music on Monday?*, Stolz portrays heroines whose appeal lies in their intellect and ambition, not their physical beauty or popularity. In the former story, the title character is an underprivileged student who earns a scholarship to an exclusive, private school. With no desire to be accepted by the school's "in" crowd, she instead concentrates on her strong academic abilities, which enable her to achieve scholastic success. In the latter story, Cassie is an intelligent but awkward fourteen-year old who resents the charm and grace of her attractive sister, Lotta. As the narrative develops, however, Lotta's shallowness and arrogance are revealed, and she is rejected by the man she loves. The same man, though, welcomes a new friendship with Cassie. *Who Wants Music on Monday?* is a "wonderful book," judged Mary K. Ealin in *Good Books for Children*. She added that the characters "are drawn with sharp perception; relationships between characters are described with the rarely found combination of deep and intelligent insight and that seemingly easy flow of prose that marks the craftsman."

During the 1960s Stolz concentrated on writing for children, not completing her next young adult novel, *By the Highway Home,* until 1971. *By the Highway Home* features the Reed family, whose young son has been killed more than a year earlier while fighting in the Vietnam War. Throughout the course of the narrative the Reeds deal with economic misfortune—Mr. Reed loses his job—and an unsettling move to Vermont. But the sorrow they continually suffer over their son's tragic death overshadows all their daily events. In *By the Highway Home,* "Stolz [exhibits] remarkable insight into that long, aching grief that settles down to live with a family," concluded Jean Fritz in the *New York Times Book Review*.

In *The Edge of Next Year,* Stolz again focuses on a family that has suffered an immediate death. In the story, fourteen-year-old Orin Woodward lives a serene and almost idyllic life on a rustic farm. Days are happily spent both with his parents, who read poetry aloud and gaze at the moon, and his younger brother, Victor, who collects bugs and snakes. Orin's security is shattered, though, the day his mother is struck by a motorist. Her death plummets Orin's father into alcoholism and forces Orin to assume sole responsibility for not only Victor but for the management of the entire household. As the story progresses, Orin increasingly becomes not only emotionally isolated but also terrified that his father is abandoning him forever. "The shock and numbness of sudden tragedy are sharply drawn," noted a critic in *Kirkus Review*.

Following *The Edge of Next Year,* Stolz wrote two other young adult novels, *Go and Catch a Flying Fish* and its sequel, *What Time of Night Is It?*. Then she again turned her talents to composing children's books. Among Stolz's most popular works for children are her "Barkham Street" books, which include *The Dog on Barkham Street, The Bully of Barkham Street,* and *The Explorer of Barkham Street*. The first of these revolves around ten-year-old Edward Frost, who is terrified of Martin Hastings, the bully who lives next door. As the story evolves, Edward continually flees from Martin's abuse—until Martin dares to insult Edward's favorite uncle. *Bully* and *Explorer,* on the other hand, focus on Martin. In the second, Martin retells the events of *Dog* from his own point of view and gradually exposes his loneliness and unhappiness. In *Explorer,* set a few years later, Martin resolves to make amends with Edward and redeem himself in the eyes of his neighbors. Through a successful baby-sitting venture and a memorable vacation to the country, he slowly gains self-confidence. The "sensitivity to the feelings which may lie beneath the armor of a young ruffian mark a fine book," declared a reviewer in *Horn Book*.

Stolz also wrote the highly-regarded *Belling the Tiger* and *The Noonday Friends*. The first begins a series of adventures about Asa and Rambo, two timid cellar mice who are selected to fasten a belled collar on a cat. During the course of the story, they find themselves transported to a tropical island, where they not only ward off an elephant, but ultimately bell a tiger. *The Noonday Friends* features Franny and Simone, two schoolmates so burdened with after school chores that they only see each other during lunch. Although the narrative also chronicles the events of their individual families—Franny's family deals with her father's unemployment, for example—the story focuses primarily on Franny and her determination to maintain her new friendship. *The Noonday Friends* "is warm, convincing," stated a reviewer in the *Bulletin of the Center for Children's Books*.

In other children's books Stolz delves into such topics as animal fantasies and historical fiction. In *Quentin Corn,* for instance, a smart pig escapes a butchering by disguising himself as human. Since he has learned to speak "people," he secures a job and becomes friends with the neighborhood children, the only ones who know his true identity. In *Bartholomew Fair,* set in sixteenth-century London, six people ranging from a town orphan to the Queen of England attend the final day of the Bartholomew Fair. The story is "a compelling tale brimming with . . . traditions [and] pageantry," asserted a reviewer in *Publishers Weekly*.

Throughout the years, as evidenced by *Storm in the Night* and *Go Fish,* Stolz has decided to write stories that are for and about black children. "It is my opinion that black children do not have enough books written for them," she once remarked. "They don't have enough of anything done for them, of course." Stolz also added that she "car-e[s], deeply, about the future of this earth, about all that part of it that cannot speak to us or defend itself—the creatures we term the 'lower animals,' the rivers and forests, the oceans, the *land.* I do not think we will save ourselves, or the planet, and aside from sending as much money as I can to organizations trying to balance out the kinds of human beings who can't see beyond the next lottery ticket, my aim until I am out of all this is to write for young children, specifically black children."

BIOGRAPHICAL/CRITICAL SOURCES:

BOOKS

Authors in the News, Volume 1, Gale, 1976.
Contemporary Literary Criticism, Volume 12, Gale, 1980.
Ealin, Mary K., *Good Books for Children,* 3rd edition, University of Chicago Press, 1966.
Hopkins, Lee Bennett, *More Books by More People: Interviews with Sixty-five Authors of Books for Children,* Citation, 1974.
Something about the Author Autobiography Series, Volume 3, Gale, 1986.

PERIODICALS

Atlantic Monthly, December, 1953.
Booklist, September 15, 1974; January 1, 1976; November 1, 1988.
Bulletin of the Center for Children's Books, November, 1965; May, 1969; December, 1969; July, 1979; July, 1981; July, 1983; October, 1985; May, 1988.
Chicago Sunday Tribune, August 23, 1953; November 6, 1960.
English Journal, September, 1952; September, 1955.
Hartford Courant, June 2, 1974.
Horn Book, December, 1953; April, 1957; October, 1957; October, 1965; December, 1975; April, 1981; November, 1985; January, 1986.
Kirkus Review, October 15, 1974.
Los Angeles Times Book Review, July 28, 1985; April 20, 1986; May 3, 1987.
New York Herald Tribune Book Review, October 28, 1951; December 13, 1953; November 14, 1954; November 28, 1954; November 13, 1955; December 30, 1956.
New York Times Book Review, May 13, 1951; August 30, 1953; September 26, 1954; April 22, 1956; May 18, 1958; November 13, 1960; May 14, 1961; November 12, 1961; October 24, 1971.
Publishers Weekly, July 12, 1985; August 9, 1985; September 20, 1985; September 26, 1986; October 9, 1987; January 15, 1988; February 12, 1988; August 26, 1988; August 31, 1990.

School Library Journal, April, 1964; September, 1985; November, 1985; January, 1986; December, 1986; April, 1987; January, 1988; November, 1990.
Times Literary Supplement, November 26, 1954.
Washington Post Book World, May 10, 1987; February 10, 1991.
Writer, October, 1980.

*   *   *

STORR, Anthony 1920-

PERSONAL: Born May 18, 1920, in Bentley, England; son of Vernon Faithfull (a Subdean of Westminster) and Katherine Cecilia (Storr) Storr; married Catherine Cole, February 6, 1942 (divorced); married Catherine Peters (a writer), October 9, 1970; children: (first marriage) Sophia, Polly, Emma. *Education:* Attended Winchester College and Westminster Hospital Medical School; Christ's College, Cambridge, Bachelor of Medicine and Bachelor of Surgery, 1944; Maudsley Hospital, diploma in psychological medicine, 1950. *Avocational interests:* Music, broadcasting, journalism.

ADDRESSES: Home—45 Chalfont Rd., Oxford OX2 6TJ, England. *Agent*—Peters, Fraser, Dunlop, The Chambers, Chelsea Harbour, London SW10 0XF, England.

CAREER: Private practice of psychiatry, 1950-74; University of Oxford, Oxford, England, Faculty of Medicine, clinical lecturer in psychiatry, 1974-84; Oxford Area Health Authority, Oxford, consultant psychotherapist, 1974-1984; writer and lecturer, 1984—; Oxford Health Authority, Honorary Consulting Psychiatrist, 1986—. Fellow of Green College, Oxford, 1979-84, now Emeritus. Member of parole board, 1976-77; member of Committee on Obscenity and Film Censorship, 1977-79.

MEMBER: Royal College of Physicians (fellow), Royal College of Psychiatrists (fellow), Royal Society of Literature (fellow), New York Academy of Sciences.

WRITINGS:

The Integrity of the Personality, Atheneum, 1961.
Sexual Deviation, Penguin, 1964.
Human Aggression, Atheneum, 1968.
Human Destructiveness, Basic Books, 1972, revised edition, Grove Weidenfeld, 1991.
The Dynamics of Creation, Secker & Warburg, 1972, Atheneum, 1973.
C. G. Jung, Viking, 1973, published in England as *Jung,* Fontana, 1973.
The Art of Psychotherapy, Methuen, 1980, 2nd edition, Routledge, 1990.

(Editor and author of introduction) *The Essential Jung,* Princeton University Press, 1983.

Solitude: A Return to the Self, Free Press, 1988, published in England as *The School of Genius,* Deutsch, 1988.

Churchill's Black Dog, Kafka's Mice, and Other Phenomena of the Human Mind, Grove Press, 1988, published in England as *Churchill's Black Dog and Other Phenomena of the Human Mind,* Collins, 1989.

Freud, Oxford University Press, 1989.

Music and the Mind, Free Press, 1992.

Also contributor to books, including *Asthma: The Facts,* by Donald J. Lane, Oxford University Press, 1979, 2nd edition, 1987; *Paths and Labyrinths,* Institute of Germanic Studies, University of London, 1985; *Freud and the Humanities,* Duckworth, 1985; and *William Golding: A Tribute on His 75th Birthday,* Faber, 1986. Contributor to newspapers and journals.

SIDELIGHTS: Anthony Storr once wrote: "In 1974 I gave up private practice to become a full-time employee of the National Health Service, in which my job was to teach postgraduate doctors who are becoming psychiatrists the elements of psychotherapy." Storr's book *The Art of Psychotherapy* is intended as a manual for would-be psychotherapists, but Howard Gardner, writing for the *New York Times Book Review,* feels that it "provides an accessible overview of psychotherapeutic practice. Seldom have 'outsiders' had the opportunity to peer over the therapist's shoulder and into his mind." The book suggests that psychotherapy is not a science, but rather an art, based as it is upon empathy and interest in people, but at the same time emphatically demanding professional training. According to Gardner, Storr's goal for individuals involved in this type of therapy is simply "insight into . . . problems and how to cope with them." While Gardner disagrees with Storr's definition of psychotherapy as more art than science, he nevertheless states: "I expect I will not be alone among Dr. Storr's readers in concluding that he would be an excellent minister to my 'problems in living.' "

Storr continues to delve into the mysteries of psychotherapy and genius with *Solitude: A Return to the Self.* The volume represents Storr's position that "psychoanalytic thinkers underrate solitude and overrate relationships in gauging the ingredients of contentment," as Daniel Goleman writes in the *New York Times Book Review.* Storr notes that additional interests are necessary to reach personal fulfillment—a balance between solitude and social activity. He explores the isolation of fantasy life in the exceptionally creative, using biographical essays of a diverse group of people, such as Kafka and Edward Lear, to illustrate "the enriching possibilities of solitude, and . . . suggest that the wish for it does not necessarily indicate maladjustment but may be a sign of emotional maturity," as

Richard Davenport-Hines explains in the *Times Literary Supplement.*

Often neglected as children or faced with personal trauma at a young age, genius learns how to cope, to strive for material success and recognition that will fill the void left by their childhood. Michiko Kakutani in the *New York Times* explains that Storr argues in *Solitude* "that play, fantasy and dreaming are not necessarily escapist activities, that they may equally be regarded as 'adaptive' mechanisms, used 'to come to terms with reality.' " That "reality" may be one of despair or even acute depression, and the solitude of fantasy is a survival technique, a route to personal happiness. *Spectator* contributor Anita Brookner writes that "it is precisely as a sign or confession of diminished status that solitude is often read, or misread. It is that error that Dr. Storr's excellent and lucid book seeks to correct." Paul Roazen in the Toronto *Globe and Mail* concludes: "[Storr] has written a lucid and well-organized book, and gently drives his central point home with balance and sophistication."

In *Churchill's Black Dog, Kafka's Mice, and Other Phenomena of the Human Mind,* Storr takes an in-depth look at the theory of isolation and fantasy as a coping technique that he proposed in *Solitude: A Return to the Self.* He writes a series of essays that present his ideas on the link between creativity and solitude, often using famous people, such as Churchill, as models of his theory. While this method is nothing new, writes Kakutani, Storr "illuminates the mysterious transactions that occur between life and art, between personality and accomplishment, and in doing so, helps to shed light on the creative process." Lee Dembart in the *Los Angeles Times* has a similar view: "The sources of creativity and their relationship to genius and madness remain enigmatic, but Storr has lifted one of the veils." *Chicago Tribune* writer Ron Grossman asserts, "In *Churchill's Black Dog,* Storr illustrates that theory [of creativity as a survival mechanism] with a literary grace that compliments the subjects of his analyses." Nicola Murphy, writing in the *London Times,* calls Storr's book an "inspiring, challenging collection of essays; psychology made properly and truly popular." And Herbert concludes: "Storr's range is extraordinary and his analyses of human creativity are penetrating."

BIOGRAPHICAL/CRITICAL SOURCES:

PERIODICALS

Atlantic, February, 1989, p. 83.

Best Sellers, November 15, 1972.

Chicago Tribune, January 4, 1989, Section 2, p. 3.

Globe and Mail (Toronto), December 17, 1988.

Los Angeles Times, February 21, 1989.

Los Angeles Times Book Review, August 28, 1988, pp. 2, 6, 11.

New Republic, October 14, 1972.

New Statesman, September 22, 1972.

New York Review of Books, December 14, 1972; February 23, 1973.

New York Times, August 5, 1980; March 14, 1989.

New York Times Book Review, February 25, 1973; June 27, 1976; October 5, 1980; November 8, 1981; October 2, 1988, p. 12; March 5, 1989, p. 23.

Observer, January 10, 1971; September 3, 1972; November 5, 1972.

Spectator, June 25, 1988, p. 39; July 29, 1989, pp. 33-34.

Times (London), July 29, 1989.

Times Literary Supplement, September 22, 1972; September 14, 1973; May 9, 1980; August 5, 1988, p. 852; September 7, 1989, p. 942.

Washington Post Book World, July 17, 1988, pp. 4-5; February 5, 1989, p. 9; June 25, 1989.

* * *

SUTTON, Henry
See SLAVITT, David R(ytman)

* * *

SWAIN, Roger (Bartlett) 1949-

PERSONAL: Born February 5, 1949, in Cambridge, MA; son of C. Gardner and Marguerite (Stay) Swain; married Elisabeth Ward, July, 1979. *Education:* Harvard University, A.B., 1971, M.A., 1972, Ph.D., 1977.

ADDRESSES: Office—c/o Horticulture, 98 North Washington St., Boston, MA 02114.

CAREER: Horticulture, Boston, MA, science editor, 1978—; WGBH-TV, Public Broadcasting Service, host of *The Victory Garden,* 1987—.

WRITINGS:

Earthly Pleasures: Tales from a Biologist's Garden, illustrated by Laszlo Kubinyi, Scribner, 1981.

Field Days: Journal of an Itinerant Biologist, Scribner, 1983.

The Practical Gardener: A Guide to Breaking New Ground, illustrated by Frank Fretz, Little, Brown, 1989, published as *The Practical Gardener: Understanding the Elements of Good Growing,* Holt, 1991.

Saving Graces: Sojourns of a Backyard Biologist, illustrated by Abigail Rorer, Little, Brown, 1991.

SIDELIGHTS: In addition to books on practical gardening tips, Roger Swain also writes about the often overlooked and little known facts of the natural world that are encountered daily in gardens, backyards, and even the land beside the railroad tracks. Swain explains the purpose of these writings in his first book, *Earthly Pleasures:* "By closely examining familiar events, everyday life is enriched. Knowing how honeybees perceive a flower or how tomatoes ripen means that whenever we encounter bees or tomatoes we are reminded of the information, and both the bees and the tomatoes are suddenly more interesting." Beaufort Cranford, writing in the *Detroit News,* describes Swain as a "splendid rarity, a professional naturalist who writes as precisely as he thinks."

According to *Washington Post* reviewer Peggy Thomson, *Earthly Pleasures* "is a nice mix of observation, glimpses into current research and snippets of history." The book is a compilation of Swain's essays from *Horticulture* magazine, where he has been the science editor since 1978. It contains tips and tidbits of information covering a variety of subjects, including environmentally safe techniques for collecting maple syrup and obscure facts about the night activities of plants and animals. Bayard Webster observes in the *New York Times,* "In . . . Dr. Swain's first [book], he has presented new insights into the mysteries and science of nature while revealing his admiration for the homely details of human life."

In *Field Days,* Swain's next compilation, the essays range from uncovering the wonder and joy of nature in backyards to examining the impact human behavior has on the earth. Cranford points out that Swain "sets out—abetted by humor and a thoroughly accessible style—to explore the wonders waiting in commonplace events and phenomena." Cranford goes on to relate that the book reflects more on conservation practices than *Earthly Pleasures,* but also asserts that Swain does not proselytize. He contends that Swain maintains a positive outlook while discussing how certain behavior aids in the destruction of the South American rain forest, explaining eutrophication, and lauding Costa Rica for setting aside seven percent of its land mass for national parks in contrast to one percent set aside by the United States. Linda Yang similarly suggests in the *New York Times* that "Mr. Swain is much too clever—and much too optimistic—to race about on a roaring doomsday machine." And Cranford concludes: "It is a grand thing indeed to have writers like Roger Swain, with diplomas on their walls and mud on their shoes, to edify and entertain us with eloquent tales of creation's lovely intricacy."

More technical information is found in Swain's 1989 work *The Practical Gardeners's Guide.* Good advice for beginning and experienced gardeners abounds, observes Allen Lacy in the *New York Times Book Review.* "Mr. Swain's good-humored and engaging voice, with its unmistakable New England accent, is the main attraction. He writes of common things like strawberries and tomatoes and squash in an uncommonly appealing manner, and he explains such matters as microclimates and plant hardiness zones with economy and authority." Swain covers the usual fare of composting, watering, and mulching, plus more advanced material like constructing benches in the garden areas for rest periods. Lacy applauds the material for its freshness and concludes that gardeners "will feel, by the time they finish reading, that they have become friends with Mr. Swain."

BIOGRAPHICAL/CRITICAL SOURCES:

BOOKS

Swain, Roger, *Earthly Pleasures: Tales from a Biologist's Garden,* illustrated by Laszlo Kubinyi, Scribner, 1981.

PERIODICALS

Detroit News, October 23, 1983.
New Yorker, March 19, 1984, p. 148.
New York Times, April 7, 1981; April 16, 1987.
New York Times Book Review, February 15, 1981, p. 16; March 28, 1982, p. 35; February 19, 1984, p. 23; June 11, 1989, p. 30.
Washington Post, March 23, 1981.
Washington Post Book World, May 19, 1985, p. 12; May 21, 1989, p. 13.

*   *   *

SWANN, Donald (Ibrahim) 1923-
(Hilda Tablet)

PERSONAL: Born September 30, 1923, in Llanelli, Wales; son of Herbert (a doctor) and Naguime Sultan (a nurse; maiden name, Piszova) Swann; married Janet Mary Oxborrow, August 7, 1955 (marriage dissolved); children: Rachel, Natasha. *Education:* Christ Church, Oxford, M.A. (honors), 1948. *Politics:* Liberal pacifist. *Religion:* Quaker.

ADDRESSES: Home—13 Albert Bridge Rd., London SW11 4PX, England.

CAREER: Composer, singer, pianist, and entertainer, 1948—. Has performed on the English television shows "Festival of the Performing Arts," 1962, 1967, "Strike That Rock," 1975, and on American television on the "Jack Paar," "Ed Sullivan," and "Dave Garroway" shows. *Wartime service:* Served with a Quaker ambulance unit and with United Nations Relief and Rehabilitation Administration in Greece and the Middle East for four years during World War II.

MEMBER: British Musicians Union, Composers Guild, Actors Equity.

WRITINGS:

(Contributor) *Oranges and Lemons* (revue), produced in London, 1950.
(Contributor) *Penny Plain* (revue), produced in London, 1951.
(With Michael Flanders and others) *Airs on a Shoestring* (revue; first produced in London at the Royal Court Theatre, April 22, 1953), Samuel French, 1957.
(Contributor) *Pay the Piper* (revue), produced in London, 1954.
(With Henry Reed and others, under pseudonym Hilda Tablet) *Emily Butter* (radio script), British Broadcasting Corp., 1950s.
(With Philip Guard) *Wild Thyme* (musical), first produced on the West End at the Duke of York's Theatre, July 4, 1955.
(With Flanders) *Fresh Airs* (revue), first produced in London, January, 1956.
(Composer, and performer with Flanders) *At the Drop of a Hat* (also see below), first produced in London at the New Lindsey Theatre, December 31, 1956; produced on the West End at the Fortune Theatre, 1957-59; produced on Broadway at the John Golden Theatre, October 8, 1959.
(Composer, and performer with Flanders) *At the Drop of Another Hat* (also see below), first produced on the West End at the Haymarket Theatre, October 2, 1963; produced in New York at the Booth Theatre, Christmas, 1966-April 1, 1967.
(Librettist) *The Man with a Thousand Faces,* Colin Wilson, 1964.
Setting of John Betjeman Poems (songs), Chappell & Co., 1964.
(With David Marsh) *Perelandra* (musical drama based on the novel by C. S. Lewis), first produced in London at the Mermaid Theatre, June 21, 1964; produced in Haverford, PA, at Haverford College, 1970.
Sing Round the Year: Songs of Praise (children's carols), Bodley Head, 1964, D. White, 1966.
The Space between the Bars: A Book of Reflections, Hodder & Stoughton, 1968, Simon & Schuster, 1969.
(With C. Day Lewis) *Requiem for the Living* (cantata; also see below), E. C. Schirmer, 1970.
(With J. R. R. Tolkien) *The Road Goes Ever On* (song cycle), Allen & Unwin, 1970, 2nd edition, Houghton, 1978.
(With Arthur Scholey) *The Song of Caedmon* (narration with song), Bodley Head, 1970.
The Rope of Love (anthology of carols), Bodley Head, 1973.
Swann's Way Out, Weidenfeld & Nicolson, 1975.
(With Flanders) *The Songs of Michael Flanders and Donald Swann,* St. Martin's, 1977.
(With Scholey) *Singalive* (songs), Collins, 1978.

Wacky and His Fuddlejig (children's play), Universal Edition, 1978.

(With Alec Davison) *The Yeast Factory; or, The Letting Go of Andor Seelig,* Leaveners' Press, 1978.

(With Scholey) *Baboushka,* Collins, 1980.

The Poetic Image (11 new settings of Victorian poets), with images by Alison Smith, Albert Howe Press, 1991.

Swann's Way: A Life in Song (autobiography), William Heinemann, 1991, Arthur James, 1993.

(With Flanders) *The Hippopotamus Song: A Muddy Love Story,* Little, Brown, 1991.

Also author of *London Sketches* with Sebastian Shaw, 1958, *Festival Matins,* 1962, *The Five Scrolls* with Albert Friedlander, 1975, *Alphabetaphon: 26 Essays, A-Z,* 1978, *Round the Piano with Donald Swann,* 1979, *Lucy and the Hunter* with Sydney Carter, *Brendan A-hoy!, Candle Tree* (an opera), and *The Visitors* (an opera) with Schuler. Composer of *Minehaha* (musical), words by Evelyn and Mary Morgan, 1984.

RECORDINGS

At the Drop of a Hat: An After Dinner Farrago (performance of the revue of the same title; also see below), Angel Records, 1960.

The Bestiary of Flanders and Swann: Songs and Verses about Animals (also see below), Angel Records, 1961.

At the Drop of Another Hat (performance of the revue of the same title; also see below), Angel Records, 1964.

The Complete Flanders and Swann (3 compact disks; contains reissues of *The Bestiary of Flanders and Swann, At the Drop of a Hat,* and *At the Drop of Another Hat,* with additional material), EMI Records, 1991.

Donald Swann has also recorded his cantata *Requiem for the Living. Alphabetaphon* (A-Z of personal repertoire at the piano; 80 songs) is available on three cassettes from Albert Howe Press.

OTHER

The Only Flanders and Swann Video (recording of television performance), ETN, 1983.

SIDELIGHTS: Composer Donald Swann has written songs for the British theater for more than forty years. Among his best-known works are the songs that he created and performed with the late Michael Flanders in the Broadway and West End revues *At the Drop of a Hat* and *At the Drop of Another Hat.* The gentle satire and charming melodies of songs like *The Hippopotamus* and *The Gnu* captivated audiences. Opening night for *At the Drop of a Hat* in January, 1957, explains John Amis in the sleeve notes to *The Complete Flanders and Swann,* was "full; second and third nights [were] . . . somewhat sparse; after that, a sell-out for over two years. One night almost the

entire Royal Family was there, singing 'Mud, mud, glorious mud' with the commoners. In fact the 'Hippopotamus' soon achieved the status of folk music; another almost universal adoption is that 'gnu' is nowadays pronounced like a two-syllable word: g-nu." The two shows together ran for more than a decade, playing in London, New York, Scotland, Canada, Australia, New Zealand, and Hong Kong during the 1950s and 1960s.

Although Donald Swann was born in Llanelli, Wales, in 1923, his roots lie in Europe and Asia. "The Swanns," Amis explains, "migrated to St. Petersburg in the 18th century and they became russified; Donald's father was a doctor, born and bred in Russia where he married a Moslem nurse of nomad stock from Transcaspia. They escaped from the Revolution and Dr. Herbert Swann had a practice in Wales when Donald made his debut in the world." Donald Swann was raised in London, and first met Michael Flanders in 1940, when they both attended the Westminster School. After serving as an ambulance driver in World War II, Swann reunited with Flanders to write songs for the impresario Laurier Lister.

Lister was responsible for producing such post-war entertainments as *Oranges and Lemons, Penny Plain, Airs on a Shoestring, Pay the Piper,* and *Fresh Airs*—small theater pieces consisting of skits, dances, and songs (often satirical). "During the preparations for these shows," writes Amis, Swann and Flanders " . . . would often run-through their numbers to the artists who were going to perform them on the stage. They also quite often sang to friends at parties; in fact they used to say that they were ready to perform their material 'at the drop of a hat.' " This was the title the pair adopted when they started to perform their own work on stage early in 1957.

At the Drop of a Hat was, in the words of critic Charles Fox, writing the sleeve notes of *The Bestiary of Flanders and Swann,* "a rip-roaring success." In that show, its sequel, and the recordings made of the songs they performed, Flanders and Swann exercised their gentle wit and humor to capture something of the spirit of the times in which they performed. Songs such as *The Warthog*—where the title lady, although "kiss-proofed/and prettily dressed," cannot find a partner at the jungle party until she meets someone who can appreciate her for what she is—and *The Ostrich,* who refuses to think about the world's problems even when caught in the middle of a mine field, (alternatively, in the midst of a nuclear testing ground), provide examples of the tasteful satire that characterized their work together. "Both men," declares Fox, "think of these songs as 'the kind that any animal would sing if he could and—in his own language—probably does.' " Many of these works were published years later in *The Songs of Michael Flanders and Donald Swann.*

Flanders and Swann parted company as a team in 1967 in New York, reuniting only once for a television program broadcast once in the United States and once in Great Britain. Flanders died in 1975; Swann continues to work as a composer and performer. "Writing a tune is a rare gift," declares Amis; "Swann not only has that, he has passion and supreme craftsmanship. There is also passion in his playing, a terrific vitality and nervous energy; he is never bland; he may have played these songs hundreds of times but there is a total absence of routine, it's now-or-never all the time."

Summing up, Donald Swann told *CA*: "My career as listed in titles and tentative dates is better understood if seen as the career of a songwriter, i.e., using words as the spur to nearly all music, but often losing the music and resorting to words to explain the motivations (i.e., a paradox). I try to explain the paradox in the word books *The Space between the Bars, Swann's Way Out,* and most comprehensively in *Swann's Way.* The long-running *At the Drop of a Hat* revues, satirical and often humorous, have been followed by many songs, song cycles, cantatas and chamber operas, usually accompanied by piano (but fully scored). The musical idiom is on a rainbow spectrum from folk to classical."

BIOGRAPHICAL/CRITICAL SOURCES:

BOOKS

Amis, John, album notes to *The Complete Flanders and Swann,* EMI Records, 1991.
Fox, Charles, album notes to *The Bestiary of Flanders and Swann: Songs and Verses about Animals,* Angel Records, 1961.
Swann, Donald, *Swann's Way: A Life in Song* (autobiography), William Heinemann, 1991, Arthur James, 1993.

*   *   *

SWARTLEY, Willard M(yers) 1936-

PERSONAL: Born August 6, 1936, in Doylestown, PA; son of William Henry G. (a farmer) and Ida (a homemaker; maiden name, Myers) Swartley; married Mary Louise Lapp (a teacher), August 16, 1958; children: Louisa Renee, Kenton Eugene. *Education:* Eastern Mennonite College, B.A., 1959, graduate study, 1959-60; Goshen Biblical Seminary, B.D., 1962; Princeton Theological Seminary, Ph.D., 1973; also attended Fuller Theological Seminary at Winona Lake School of Theology, Garrett Theological Seminary (now Garrett-Evangelical Theological Seminary), Union Theological Seminary (New York, NY), University of Heidelberg, University of Goettingen, University of Tuebingen, and Yale Divinity School.

ADDRESSES: Office—Associated Mennonite Biblical Seminaries, 3003 Benham Ave., Elkhart, IN 46517.

CAREER: Ordained Mennonite minister, 1961; pastor of Mennonite church in Elkhart, IN, 1961-65; Eastern Mennonite College, Harrisonburg, VA, instructor, 1965-68, associate professor, 1971-74, professor of biblical studies and chairman of department of Bible, 1975-78; Associated Mennonite Biblical Seminaries, Elkhart, professor of New Testament, 1978—, director of Institute of Mennonite Studies, 1979—. Instructor at Goshen College, 1962-63, 1964-65; visiting professor at Conrad Grebel College and University of Waterloo, 1975-76; Bible teacher at Keystone Institutes and Mennonite seminars and retreats in Swaziland, Kenya, Botswana, and Egypt. Mennonite Publication Board, member of board, 1971-80, chairman of publishing committee, 1973-77; executive secretary of Conrad Grebel Projects Committee, 1972-80; member of Mennonite Church Committee for Women in Leadership Ministries, 1980-88.

MEMBER: Society of Biblical Literature, Chicago Society of Biblical Research.

WRITINGS:

Mark: The Way for All Nations, Herald Press, 1979, revised edition, 1981.
Slavery, Sabbath, War, and Women: Case Issues in Biblical Interpretation, Herald Press, 1983.
(Editor and contributor) *Essays on Biblical Interpretation: Anabaptist-Mennonite Perspectives,* Institute of Mennonite Studies, Associated Mennonite Biblical Seminaries, 1984.
(Editor with C. J. Dyck) *Annotated Bibliography of Mennonite Writings on War and Peace: 1930-1980,* Herald Press, 1987.
(Editor) Henry Swartley, *Living on the Fault Line: Portrait and Journals of a Church Planter-Pastor,* Evangel, 1992.
(Editor) *The Love of Enemies and Nonretaliation in the New Testament,* Westminster/John Knox, 1992.
(Editor with Perry Yoder) *The Meaning of Peace: Biblical Essays,* Westminster/John Knox, 1992.
Story Shaping Story: Israel's Faith Traditions and the Synoptic Gospels, Hendrickson Press, 1993.

Contributor to books, including *Peacemakers in a Broken World,* edited by John A. Lapp, Herald Press, 1969; *The Earth Is the Lord's,* edited by Evelyn Jegen and Bruno Manno, Paulist Press, 1978; and *War and Pacifism: When Christians Disagree,* edited by Oliver Barclay, Inter-Varsity Press (London, England), 1984. Herald Press, curriculum writer for "Youth Bible Studies" series, 1962-68, and New Testament editor for "Believers Church Bible Commentary" series, 1988; editor of "Occasional Papers" series, Associated Mennonite Biblical Seminaries, 1981—; New Testament editor for "Studies in Peace and Scripture" series, WJK Press. Contributor to periodicals, including *Sojourners, Seeds,* and *Peace Section Newsletter.*

SIDELIGHTS: Willard M. Swartley once told *CA:* "I write primarily in response to current needs and issues in the life of the Mennonite Church and the larger Christian context. My book on the Gospel of Mark grew out of a series of Bible studies presented at a church-wide Mennonite assembly at Estes Park in 1977. My book *Slavery, Sabbath, War, and Women* was developed at the request of a church-wide committee asking for case studies as an approach to resolve current differences in biblical interpretation. Overall, my writings are inspired by a vision for human justice and the reign of God in the human community."

Swartley added, "My motivation for writing has focused on the peace emphases of the Christian scriptures, in an effort to bring these emphases into prominent light for biblical scholarship as well as promotion at a more popular level."

T

TABLET, Hilda
See SWANN, David (Ibrahim)

* * *

TAMBASCO, Anthony J(oseph) 1939-

PERSONAL: Born May 23, 1939, in Brooklyn, NY; son of Montana (a salesman) and Filomena (a homemaker; maiden name, Nofi) Tambasco; married Joan McNeil (a teacher), August 9, 1980. *Education:* Catholic Institute of Paris, S.T.L. (magna cum laude), 1968; Pontifical Biblical Institute, Rome, S.S.B. (magna cum laude), 1969, S.S.L. (magna cum laude), 1970; Union Theological Seminary, New York, NY, Ph.D., 1981. *Religion:* Roman Catholic.

ADDRESSES: Office—Department of Theology, Georgetown University, 37th and O Sts. N.W., Washington, DC 20057.

CAREER: St. Louis University, St. Louis, MO, assistant professor of theology, 1970-73; Maryknoll Seminary (now Maryknoll School of Theology), Maryknoll, NY, assistant professor of theology, 1975-79; Georgetown University, Washington, D.C., associate professor, 1979-92, professor of theology, 1992—.

MEMBER: Catholic Biblical Association of America, American Academy of Religion, Society of Biblical Literature, College Theological Society, Society of Christian Ethics.

WRITINGS:

The Bible for Ethics: Juan Luis Segundo and First-World Ethics, University Press of America, 1981.
In the Days of Jesus: The Jewish Background and Unique Teachings of Jesus, Paulist Press, 1983.
What Are They Saying about Mary?, Paulist Press, 1984.

(Editor and contributor) *Blessed Are the Peacemakers: Biblical Perspectives on Peace and Its Social Foundations,* Paulist Press, 1989.
A Theology of Atonement and Paul's Vision of Christianity, Liturgical Press, 1991.
In the Days of Paul: The Social World and Teaching of the Apostle, Paulist Press, 1991.

Contributor to *Christian Biblical Ethics: From Biblical Revelation to Contemporary Christian Praxis,* edited by Robert Daly, Paulist Press, 1984; and *The Deeper Meaning of Economic Life: Critical Essays on the U.S. Bishops' Pastoral Letter on the Economy,* edited by R. Bruce Douglass, Georgetown University Press, 1986. Contributor to theology journals.

WORK IN PROGRESS: In the Days of Paul, for Paulist Press; research on the relationship of the Bible to ethics and on liberation theology.

SIDELIGHTS: Anthony J. Tambasco told *CA:* "I bring a special approach to theological scholarship, namely, the combining of expertise in both biblical studies and Christian ethics. The relationship of these areas has been and continues to be the major interest of my scholarship. Several lecture trips to Latin America have focused my interest on the way Bible and ethics have been joined in the Latin American context of liberation theology.

"As a result of these combined interests, I wrote a study of Juan Luis Segundo because he is one of the more prolific authors of liberation theology and also one who is more self-conscious of methodology. He afforded me the opportunity to study not only liberation theology, but the specific methodological questions concerning the relationship of the Bible to the ethical concerns of social justice. The focus of my book is on this biblical methodology of Segundo and how it compares with the use of the Bible by first-world Christian ethicists, i.e., ethical scholars in the North American and Western European tradition.

"Over the past fifteen years or so I have been active in three ongoing seminars at the annual conventions of the Catholic Biblical Association of America, which centered on the use of the Bible in Christian ethics. The first seminar resulted in a book, to which I was a contributor, dealing with the general methodological questions of how the Bible is normative for Christian ethics. I organized the second seminar, which took the general methodological observations of the first seminar and made application to the ethical considerations of war and peace. I am chairing the third seminar which is following the same methodology applied to the problem of suffering. We hope it will lead to publication.

"Extensive travel in the United States and Canada has also involved me in abundant work in adult education, a project to which I show partiality and preference. The needs of adult education prompted me to write a book on the Jesus of history and on the social world of Paul.

"From my studies overseas I have benefitted from travel throughout Europe and the Holy Land and have learned to speak French and Italian and to read German, Spanish, Portuguese, Latin, Greek, and Hebrew."

He adds, "Present interest continues in using the Bible for ethics, and I am beginning a major work on an introduction to the New Testament from a liberation perspective."

*   *   *

TAPPLY, William G(eorge) 1940-

PERSONAL: Born July 16, 1940, in Waltham, MA; son of H. G. (an outdoor writer) and Muriel (a registered nurse; maiden name, Morgridge) Tapply; married Cynthia Ehrgott (a secretary), March 7, 1970; children: Michael, Melissa, Sarah. *Education:* Amherst College, B.A., 1962; Harvard University, M.A.T., 1963; attended Tufts University, 1965-67.

ADDRESSES: Home and office—187 Great Rd., # C-1, Acton, MA 01720.

CAREER: High school history teacher, Lexington, MA, 1963-65; Tufts University, Medford, MA, director of economic education, 1967-68; Lexington High School, housemaster and teacher, 1969-90. Writer's Digest School, editorial associate, 1992—.

MEMBER: Mystery Writers of America, Authors Guild, Private Eye Writers of America.

AWARDS, HONORS: Scribner Crime Novel award, 1984, for *Death at Charity's Point.*

WRITINGS:

CRIME NOVELS

Death at Charity's Point, Scribner, 1984.

MYSTERY NOVELS

The Dutch Blue Error, Scribner, 1985.
Follow the Sharks, Scribner, 1985.
The Marine Corpse, Scribner, 1986.
Dead Meat, Scribner, 1987.
The Vulgar Boatman, Scribner, 1987.
A Void in Hearts, Scribner, 1988.
Dead Winter, Delacorte, 1989.
Client Privilege, Delacorte, 1989.
The Spotted Cats, Delacorte, 1991.
Tight Lines, Delacorte, 1992.
The Snake Eater, Otto Penzler Books, 1993.

NONFICTION

Those Hours Spent Outdoors, Scribner, 1988.
Opening Day and Other Neuroses, Lyons and Burford, 1990.
Home Water Near and Far, Lyons and Burford, 1992.

Also contributing editor to *Field and Stream.* Contributor of numerous articles and stories to magazines, including *Sports Illustrated, Better Homes and Gardens, Organic Gardening, Scholastic Coach, The Drummer, The Writer, Fins and Feathers, Worcester,* and *Outdoor Life.*

WORK IN PROGRESS: A mystery novel, tentatively titled *The Seventh Enemy.*

SIDELIGHTS: William G. Tapply's series of mysteries featuring Brady Coyne, fictional Boston attorney to the rich, has met with good reviews. Lauding Tapply for writing "quietly and perceptively" in *Death at Charity's Point,* the story of Coyne's investigation of an apparent suicide, *London Times* contributor Marcel Berlins assessed the book a "superior" thriller, and *New York Times Book Review* critic Newgate Callender judged *Follow the Sharks,* in which Coyne is hired as a liaison in a kidnapping case, as "well-wrought" and "one of the best" in Tapply's series.

William G. Tapply told *CA:* "I didn't begin writing seriously until I turned forty. Maybe it was my own way of coping with midlife crisis. Part-time free-lance writing was good to me—not in fame or fortune, but in new friends and in an engrossing, exciting avocation. Since I retired from teaching to write full-time, it has continued to reward me (although I'm still waiting for some of that fame and fortune).

"I write what are classified as 'mystery novels.' I accept the classification reluctantly. I write novels that, like most worthwhile novels, contain mysteries. I try to avoid formulas, although I suppose with a series character like my attorney Brady Coyne I have conceded that much. I place great emphasis in my writing on characterization, motivation, suspense, and humor—all of which seem to me important in all fiction. I try to tell stories rather than truths, but I think my stories convey some small truths now and then. I have been asked on occasion when I intend to write a 'real novel.' I reply, of course, that I already have.''

BIOGRAPHICAL/CRITICAL SOURCES:

PERIODICALS

Chicago Tribune, September 25, 1988.
New York Times Book Review, April 18, 1984; December 8, 1985.
Times (London), January 31, 1985.

*   *   *

TARRANT, John J(oseph) 1924-

PERSONAL: Surname is accented on the first syllable; born July 5, 1924, in New York, NY; son of John J. and Margaret Tarrant; married Dorothy Kuusela (the executive director of Westport-Weston Community Council), November 8, 1948; children: Cathy, Patricia, John. *Education:* University of Missouri, B.J., 1948. *Politics:* Democrat.

ADDRESSES: Home—167 South Compo Rd., Westport, CT 06880. *Agent*—Arthur Pine Associates, Inc., 1780 Broadway, New York, NY 10019.

CAREER: Free-lance writer and newspaperman, 1948-54; Research Institute of America, New York City, editorial director, 1954-65; Benton & Bowles (advertising agency), New York City, vice-president for training and development, 1964-67; free-lance writer, 1967—. Member of Westport Democratic Town Committee. *Military service:* U.S. Naval Reserve, 1943-45, 1950-52; became lieutenant senior grade.

WRITINGS:

Tomorrow's Techniques for Today's Salesmen, Hawthorn, 1970.
The Corporate Eunuch, Crowell, 1973.
(With Auren Uris) *How to Win Your Boss's Love, Approval, and Job,* Van Nostrand, 1974.
Getting Fired, Van Nostrand, 1974.
How to Negotiate for More Money, Van Nostrand, 1975.
(With Henry Voegeli) *Survival 2001,* Van Nostrand, 1975.
(With Mortimer Feinberg and Robert Tanofsky) *New Psychology for Managing People,* Prentice-Hall, 1975.
The End of Exurbia, Stein & Day, 1976.
Drucker: The Man Who Invented the Corporate Society, CBI Publishing, 1977.

Leavetaking, Simon & Schuster, 1978.
Playboy's Small Business Guide, Playboy Press, 1981.
Career Stages, Putnam, 1983.
Perks and Parachutes, Linden Press, 1985.
Stalking the Headhunter, Bantam, 1986.
Business Writing with Style, Wiley, 1991.
Power Public Relations, NTC, 1992.

SIDELIGHTS: John J. Tarrant told *CA:* "Writing this sketch for *Contemporary Authors* makes my whole life pass before me—a misspent youth, middle and old age, staring at the keyboard, waiting for inspiration. Well, maybe not altogether misspent: What I do is transmute complex ideas into simple English. There is a great satisfaction when you do it reasonably well."

*   *   *

TAYLOR-GOOBY, Peter 1947-

PERSONAL: Born March 5, 1947, in Watford, England; son of John (a tax inspector) and Irene (a teacher; maiden name, Bootle) Taylor-Gooby; married Susan Irene Langman (a social worker); children: Joseph, Gabriel, Alice. *Education:* University of Bristol, B.A. (with honors), 1969; University of York, Diploma in Social Administration (with distinction), 1972, M.Phil., 1974; University of Kent at Canterbury, Ph.D., 1985. *Politics:* Labour. *Religion:* None.

ADDRESSES: Home—99 Old Dover Rd., Canterbury CT1 3PG, England. *Office*—Darwin College, University of Kent at Canterbury, Canterbury CT2 7NY, England.

CAREER: Victoria University of Manchester, Manchester, England, lecturer in social administration, 1974-79; University of Kent at Canterbury, Canterbury, England, lecturer, 1979-85, senior lecturer, 1985-89, professor of social policy, 1989—, chairman of Social Policy Group, 1982-84, joint organizer of Seminar on Social Policy for Members of Parliament, 1985. Civil Service College, organizer of Civil Service/Joint University Council for Social and Public Policy, 1983, organizer of Conference on New Directions in Welfare, 1984; consultant to London Weekend Television.

MEMBER: Social Administration Association.

WRITINGS:

(With Raymond Plant and Harry Lesser) *Political Philosophy and Social Welfare,* Routledge & Kegan Paul, 1980.
(Contributor) Noel Timms and David Watson, editors, *Social Welfare: Why and How?,* Routledge & Kegan Paul, 1980.
(With Jen Dale) *Social Theory and Social Welfare,* Edward Arnold, 1981.

(Contributor) Krishman Kumar and Andrew Ellis, editors, *Economy and Society,* Tavistock Publications, 1983.

Public Opinion: Ideology and the Welfare State, Routledge & Kegan Paul, 1985.

(Contributor) Rudolf Klein and Michael O'Higgins, editors, *The Future of Welfare,* Basil Blackwell, 1985.

(With Elim Papadakis) *The Private Provision of Public Welfare: Market, State, and Family,* Wheatsheaf Books, 1987, St. Martin's, 1988.

Social Change, Social Welfare, and Social Science, Wheatsheaf Books, 1991.

(With Hartley Dean) *Dependency Culture,* Wheatsheaf, 1992.

(Editor with Robyn Lawson) *Markets and Managers,* Open University Press, 1993.

Contributor of more than fifty articles and reviews to journals in the social sciences. Member of editorial collective of *Journal of Critical Social Policy,* 1980—; member of editorial board of *Journal of Social Policy,* 1983—.

SIDELIGHTS: Peter Taylor-Gooby told *CA:* "The major influence on my thinking in recent years has been my anger at the policies of the Conservative British government—led by Mrs. Thatcher from 1979 onward and then by John Major—against the poor. The policies of this government constitute a radical change in British social policy, shattering the consensus that has existed on the welfare state during the postwar period. Previously, there had been a high level of political agreement between political parties on the desirability of universal health care, education, and social security provided by the state. The Thatcher government has cut state welfare spending drastically and has encouraged the growth of private services. It is those who are too poor to afford these services who lose out."

*   *   *

TERRY, Saralee
   See KAYE, Marvin (Nathan)

*   *   *

THEISSEN, Gerd 1943-

PERSONAL: Born April 24, 1943, in Rheydt, Germany; son of Albert (a teacher) and Else (a social worker; maiden name, Finken) Theissen; married Christa Schaible (a psychologist), August 30, 1968; children: Oliver, Gunnar. *Education:* University of Bonn, D.Theol., 1968, D.Habil.Theol., 1972. *Religion:* Protestant.

ADDRESSES: Home—Max-Josef-Strasse 54/1, 69 Heidelberg, Germany. *Office*—Wissenschaftlich-Theolog-isches Seminar, University of Heidelberg, Kisselgasse 1, 69 Heidelberg, Germany.

CAREER: University of Copenhagen, Copenhagen, Denmark, professor of New Testament, 1978-80; University of Heidelberg, Heidelberg, Germany, professor of New Testament, 1980—.

AWARDS, HONORS: Honorary doctorate from University of Neuchatel, 1989, and University of Glasgow, 1990.

WRITINGS:

Untersuchungen zum Hebraeerbrief (title means "Studies on the Letter to the Hebrews"), Mohn, 1969.

Urchristliche Wundergeschichten, Mohn, 1974, translation published as *The Miracle Stories of the Early Christian Tradition,* Fortress, 1982.

Soziologie der Jesusbewegung, Kaiser, 1977, translation published as *The First Followers of Jesus,* SCM (London), 1978, and as *The Sociology of Early Palestinian Christianity,* Fortress, 1978.

Argumente fuer einen kritischen Glauben oder: Was haelt der Religionskritik stand?, Kaiser, 1978, translation published as *A Critical Faith: A Case for Religion,* Fortress, 1979, and as *On Having a Critical Faith,* SCM, 1979.

Studien zur Soziologie des Urchristentums (essays; also see below; title means "Studies on the Sociology of Early Christianity"), Mohn, 1979.

The Social Setting of Pauline Christianity: Essays on Corinth (contains essays originally published in *Studien zur Soziologie des Urchristentums*), translated by John H. Schutz, Fortress, 1982.

Psychologische aspekte Paulinischer theologie, Vandenhoeck & Ruprecht, 1983, translation published as *Psychological Aspects of Pauline Theology,* Fortress, 1987.

Biblischer Glaube in evolutionaerer Sicht, Kaiser, 1984, translation published as *Biblical Faith: An Evolutionary Approach,* Fortress, 1984.

Der Schatten des Galilaers: Historische Jesusforschung in erzaehlender Form, Kaiser, 1986, translation published as *The Shadow of the Galilean,* Fortress, 1987.

Lokalkolorit und Zeitgeschichte in den Evangelien: Eim Beitrag zur Geschichte der synoptischen Tradition, Fribourg University Press, 1989, translation published as *The Gospel in Context: Social and Political History in the Synoptic Tradition,* Fortress, 1991.

Die offene Tuer: Biblische Variationen zu Predigttexten, Kaiser, 1990, translation published as *The Open Door: Variations on Biblical Themes,* SCM, 1991.

WORK IN PROGRESS: A book on changes in value and early Christianity.

SIDELIGHTS: Gerd Theissen once told *CA:* "Three intellectual problems have influenced my writings: On the one side it is the conflict between the analyses of religious beliefs by the means of modern thought like sociology and psychology and the theological interpretation; on the other side it is the conflict between the belief that developed in a preindustrial society and the ethical problems of our modern world, and last but not least, the gap between academic theology and the religious life and thoughts of ordinary people. In my writings I try to show that early Christian belief is something like a 'mutation' in cultural evolution that anticipates new possibilities of human life. It is above all a rebellion against the principle of selection that is dominating in all hitherto existing periods of evolution. This interpretation opens a new way of adapting to the central reality called God by the religious tradition. An adaptation to this reality includes a change in personal motivations and social structures. Historical research investigates the tendencies these changes had in early Christianity. The 'itinerant charismatics' who abandoned home and family in order to follow Jesus are a good example."

Theissen recently told *CA:* "To bridge the gap between academic theology and life I wrote about Jesus in the form of a novel and thus tried to make biblical scholarship meaningful to laymen in *The Shadow of the Galilean.*"

*   *   *

THOMAS, D(avid) O(swald) 1924-

PERSONAL: Born March 4, 1924, in Ruthin, Denbighshire, Wales; son of Oswald (a local government official) and Martha Hannah (James) Thomas; married Beryl Irene Evans Jones (a medical doctor), December 18, 1965; children: Janet Mary, Isobel (deceased). *Education:* University of Wales, University College of North Wales, Bangor, B.A., 1950, M.A., 1952; Bedford College, London, Ph.D., 1956.

ADDRESSES: Home—Orlandon, 31 North Parade, Aberystwyth, Dyfed SY23 2JN, Wales.

CAREER: Coleg Harlech, Harlech, Wales, tutor in philosophy and psychology, 1955-60; University of Wales, Aberystwyth, lecturer, 1960-65, senior lecturer, 1965-78, reader in philosophy, 1978-85. *Military service:* Royal Air Force, 1943-46.

MEMBER: Royal Historical Society (fellow), Royal Institute of Philosophy, Mind Association, British Society for Eighteenth-Century Studies, Friends of National Library of Wales, Denbighshire Historical Society, Friends of Dr. Williams's Library, Society of Cymmrodorion.

WRITINGS:

Richard Price and America, privately printed, 1975.

Richard Price, University of Wales Press, 1976.

The Honest Mind: The Thought and Work of Richard Price, Clarendon Press, 1977.

(Editor with W. Bernard Peach) *The Correspondence of Richard Price,* Duke University Press, Volume 1: *July 1748-March 1778,* 1983, Volume 2: *March 1778-February 1786,* 1989.

Yhatebi Chanldor: Response to Revolution, University of Wales Press, 1989.

Co-editor of *Price-Priestley Newsletter,* 1977-80, and *Enlightenment and Dissent,* 1982—.

WORK IN PROGRESS: Editing with P. P. L. Jones and John Stephens, *A Bibliography of Richard Price,* Scolar Press.

SIDELIGHTS: D. O. Thomas informed *CA:* "I am and have been, throughout my academic career, principally concerned with the work of the leaders of rational dissent in the eighteenth century: Richard Price (1723-1791) and Joseph Priestley (1733-1804). I believe that it is vitally important to investigate and to publicize their ideas, particularly their conception of the need for the development of rational enquiry in all fields, especially in matters of religious belief, and in strengthening the appeal to individual conscience. The leaders of rational dissent also made important contributions to the development of the idea of self-government in political matters, in particular to the development of representative institutions, and to the growth of national autonomy.

"The Rational Dissenters laid great stress on the duty each one of us has to think for himself, to subject his own beliefs to rational criticism, and to act in accordance with his own convictions. I believe that in the twentieth century it remains extremely important to maintain the emphasis they placed upon the importance of these duties.

"In an age of abundant scientific enquiry this may seem to be a strange claim to make. Do we not already suffer a surfeit of investigations, of all kinds? The claim the Rational Dissenters made is that the responsibility to think for oneself is a responsibility that each *individual* has. One only has to reflect upon the appeals to prejudice made by so many institutions in Western society to see how much we need more—not less—active criticism and positive action by individual men and women. Take, for example, the role of advertising in Western society—how often the advertiser relies upon false assumptions and how often he directs the attention of the consumer to trivial ends and unworthy pursuits. Or, again, consider the quality of the material offered to the public by the bulk of our newspapers and media men who treat their readers, viewers, and listeners as though they were incapable of thinking for themselves. The Rational Dissenters stressed the contribution that each one could make to defeating prejudice, eliminating superstition, and directing activity towards worthwhile intellectual, cultural, and spiritual goals. They stressed the need for each individual to *dare* to think for himself or herself. But not only this: they also stressed the need for everyone to be active in promoting the welfare of the community. Individualism is often thought to be a selfish creed—that the individual only claims liberty to further his self-interest—but such a misunderstanding belies the intentions of the Rational Dissenters, for they wanted the individual to assume responsibility not only for his own welfare but also for the well-being of those around him and for the community at large. That this was so is evidenced by the emphasis they placed upon the need for benevolence and philanthropy. Now the duty to think for oneself and to act for the greater good of the community has important implications for the defense of liberty and democracy. Since every man and every woman has the duties I have just referred to, so do they need to enjoy the liberty, as a matter of right, to think for themselves, to express their opinions, and to persuade their fellow human beings. The Rational Dissenters were optimistic—some might say too optimistic—that given such freedom the majority of mankind would use it to better the lot of every member of society. But even if we have come to believe that their extreme optimism was not entirely well-founded, we have to recognize that they had a faith and a trust in the virtues of people, without which no civilization can hope to survive. The liberties they defended were not just the civil liberties I have mentioned, but the liberties to participate to the full in the life of the community. The responsibility that we each have for the well-being of the other extends into politics. We need to be able to participate in some measure at least—in the decision-making processes that relate to society if we are to discharge our basic responsibilities.

"The Rational Dissenters constructed a coherent political philosophy upon the basic moral duties of every man and woman. Their work will always remain of interest because it concerns the promotion and the defense of those values that are essential to Western civilization. If we ignore the teachings of the defenders of liberty, swift will be our descent into barbarism."

*   *   *

THOMAS, Graham Stuart 1909-

PERSONAL: Born April 3, 1909, in Cambridge, England; son of William Richard and Lilian (Hays) Thomas. *Education:* Horticultural and botanical training, Cambridge University Botanic Garden, 1926-29. *Avocational interests:* Music, painting, and drawing plants.

ADDRESSES: Home—21 Kettlewell Close, Horsell, Woking, Surrey, England.

CAREER: Writer, illustrator, photographer, and lecturer on horticulture. Employed by Six Hills Nursery, Stevenage, England, 1930; T. Hilling & Co., Chobham, England, foreman, then manager, 1931-55; Sunningdale Nurseries, Windlesham, Surrey, manager, 1956-68, associate director, 1968-73; gardens consultant, 1973—. Gardens advisor, National Trust, 1955-73.

MEMBER: Royal Horticultural Society (vice-president), Royal National Rose Society (vice-patron), Garden History Society (vice-president), National Council for the Conservation of Plants and Gardens, British Hosta and Hemerocalis Society, Irish Garden Plant Society (honorary member).

AWARDS, HONORS: Veitch Memorial Medal, 1966, and Victoria Medal of Honour, 1968, both from Royal Horticultural Society; Order of the British Empire (OBE), 1975; Dean Hole Medal, Royal National Rose Society, 1976.

WRITINGS:

SELF-ILLUSTRATED

The Old Shrub Roses, Phoenix House, 1955, 5th edition, Dent, 1979.
The Manual of Shrub Roses: A Concise Account of the Wild Species, the Old French, and New Hybrid Roses, Sunningdale Nurseries, 1957, 3rd edition, 1962.
Colour in the Winter Garden, Branford, 1957, 3rd edition, Dent, 1984.
The Modern Florilegium, Sunningdale Nurseries, 1958.
Shrub Roses of Today, Phoenix House, 1962, St. Martin's, 1963, revised edition, Dent, 1980.
Climbing Roses Old and New, Phoenix House, 1965, St. Martin's, 1966, revised edition, 1983.
Plants for Ground Cover, Dent, 1970, revised edition, 1989.
Perennial Garden Plants; or, The Modern Florilegium: A Concise Account of Herbaceous Plants, Including Bulbs, for General Garden Use, Dent, 1976, 3rd edition, 1990.
Three Gardens of Pleasant Flowers, Collingridge, 1983.
The Art of Planting, or, The Planter's Handbook, Dent, 1984.
(With forward by Sir George Taylor) *The Complete Flower Paintings and Drawings of Graham Stuart Thomas,* Abrams, 1987.
The Rock Garden and Its Plants: From Grotto to Alpine House, Dent, 1989.
The Art of Gardening with Roses, Timber Press, 1991, published as *An English Rose Garden,* M. Joseph, 1991.
Ornamental Shrubs, Climbers, and Bamboos, Timber Press, 1992.

OTHER

Great Gardens of Britain, Mayflower, 1979.

Gardens of the National Trust, Weidenfeld & Nicolson, 1979.

Trees in the Landscape, J. Cape, 1983.

(Editor) *Recreating the Period Garden,* Collins, 1984.

A Garden of Roses, illustrations by Alfred Parsons, Salem House, 1987.

Contributor to books, including *Shell Gardens Book,* Phoenix House, 1964, and *The Book of Garden Ornament,* Dent, 1974, both edited by Peter Hunt. Contributor of illustrated articles to horticultural journals. Author of numerous pamphlets on historic garden properties owned by the National Trust.

WORK IN PROGRESS: The Graham Thomas Rose Book, to be published by Timber Press.

SIDELIGHTS: The name Graham Stuart Thomas is well-known among horticulturalists, gardeners, and readers of gardening books. Noted as a rosarian and garden designer both in his native England and abroad, Thomas has spent much of his time propagating and naming varieties of roses which, due to lack of widespread interest, would most likely have been lost to cultivation. The term "shrub rose" originated in Thomas's efforts to document one of the many varieties of old garden roses that have lost their place to hybrid teas, their less-fragrant but more disease-resistant cousins in the modern flowerbed—indeed, one variety of shrub rose now bears his name. In addition to his work with rose cultivars, Thomas has served as designer in the restoration of almost one hundred historic gardens, including those at Hidecote Manor and Cliveden.

Thomas began his writing career with an article on the oak-leaved hydrangea and has, since then, produced a series of highly-regarded books on horticultural topics. A trained botanist, Thomas has illustrated many of his texts with the botanically correct drawings that once won him a medal from the Royal Horticultural Society. Many of his more noteworthy illustrations have been collected in *The Complete Flower Paintings and Drawings of Graham Stuart Thomas,* described by Allen Lacy of the *New York Times Book Review* as "a book to be treasured by all who love gardening and painting—not to mention intelligence and style as manifested in the written word."

BIOGRAPHICAL/CRITICAL SOURCES:

PERIODICALS

New York Times Book Review, December 6, 1987, p. 32; December 3, 1989, p. 74.

Times Literary Supplement, September 16, 1983; June 22, 1984.

Washington Post Book World, December 6, 1987, pp. 14-15.*

THORNTON, W. B.
See BURGESS, Thornton Waldo

*   *   *

THWAITE, Ann (Barbara Harrop) 1932-

PERSONAL: Born October 4, 1932, in Hampstead, London, England; daughter of Angus John (a journalist and historian) and Hilda (Valentine) Harrop; married Anthony Thwaite (a writer), August 4, 1955; children: Emily, Caroline, Lucy, Alice. *Education:* St. Hilda's College, Oxford University, B.A. (honors), 1955, M.A., 1959. *Religion:* Church of England.

ADDRESSES: Home—The Mill House, Low Tharston, Norfolk NR15 2YN, England. *Agent*—Michael Shaw, Curtis Brown, 162-168 Regent Street, London W1R 5TB, England.

CAREER: Children's book author and biographer. Tokyo Joshi Daigaku (Women's University), Tokyo, Japan, part-time lecturer in English literature, 1956-57, visiting professor, 1985-86.

AWARDS, HONORS: Duff Cooper Memorial Prize for nonfiction, 1986, for *Edmund Gosse: A Literary Landscape, 1849-1928;* Whitbread Biography of the Year Award, 1990, for *A. A. Milne: His Life.*

WRITINGS:

Waiting for the Party: The Life of Frances Hodgson Burnett, 1849-1924, Scribner, 1974.

(Editor) *My Oxford* (bound with *My Cambridge,* edited by Ronald Hayman), Taplinger, 1977, published as *My Oxford, My Cambridge: Memories of University Life by Twenty-Four Distinguished Graduates,* edited and introduced by Thwaite and Hayman, 1979, revised edition published as *My Oxford,* edited and introduced by Thwaite, Robson Books, 1986.

Edmund Gosse: A Literary Landscape, 1849-1928, University of Chicago Press, 1984.

A. A. Milne: The Man behind Winnie-the-Pooh, Random House, 1990, published in England as *A. A. Milne: His Life,* Faber & Faber, 1990.

(Editor and author of introduction) Edmund Gosse, *Portraits from Life,* Gower, 1991.

The Brilliant Career of Winnie-the-Pooh, Methuen, 1992.

CHILDREN'S BOOKS

The Young Traveller in Japan, Phoenix House, 1958.

The House in Turner Square, illustrated by Robin Jacques, Constable, 1960, Harcourt, 1961.

Toby Stays with Jane, illustrated by Janet Martin, Constable, 1962.

A Seaside Holiday for Jane and Toby, illustrated by Martin, Constable, 1962.

Toby Moves House, illustrated by Martin, Constable, 1965.

Jane and Toby Start School, illustrated by Martin, Constable, 1965.

Home and Away, illustrated by Shirley Hughes, Brockhampton, 1967, published in the United States as *The Holiday Map,* Follett, 1969.

The Travelling Tooth, illustrated by George Thompson, Brockhampton, 1968.

(Editor) *Allsorts, 1-5,* Macmillan, 1968-72.

The Camelthorn Papers, Macmillan, 1969.

The Day with the Duke, illustrated by George Him, World, 1969.

The Only Treasure, illustrated by Glenys Ambrus, Brockhampton, 1970.

(Editor) *Allsorts, 6-7,* Methuen, 1974-75.

The Poor Pigeon, illustrated by Ambrus, Brockhampton, 1974, Childrens Press, 1976.

Rose in the River, illustrated by John Dyke, Brockhampton, 1974, Childrens Press, 1976.

Horrible Boy, illustrated by Ambrus, Brockhampton, 1975, Childrens Press, 1976.

The Chatterbox, illustrated by Ambrus, Deutsch, 1978.

Tracks, illustrated by Gavin Rowe, Methuen, 1978.

A Piece of Parkin: A True Story from the Autobiography of Frances Hodgson Burnett, illustrated by Ambrus, Deutsch, 1980.

My Hat, illustrated by Anna Hancock, Macmillan, 1983.

Pennies for the Dog, illustrated by Margery Gill, Deutsch, 1985.

Gilbert and the Birthday Cake, illustrated by Jack Harvey, Hutchinson, 1986.

Amy and the Night-Time Visit, illustrated by J. C. Skinner, Deutsch, 1987.

OTHER

Compiler of *Frances Hodgson Burnett: Exhibition Guide,* [London], 1974. Regular reviewer for *Times Literary Supplement,* London, and other publications, 1963-84. Contributing editor to *Cricket,* 1974—, member of editorial board, 1977—.

SIDELIGHTS: Ann Thwaite is both an author and anthologizer of children's fiction and a biographer of such literary figures as Frances Hodgson Burnett, Edmund Gosse, and A. A. Milne. What marks her children's works "is her acute understanding of contemporary sensibilities," maintains Lissa Paul in *Twentieth-Century Children's Writers.* "Her eye unerringly selects the stories of daily life that are the stuff of fiction. Her ear is tuned to the rhythms of everyday speech, and to the finer diction of contemporary poetry." Working with children's books for over twenty-five years, it was Thwaite's interest in other children's writers that led her to write her first biog-

raphy—*Waiting for the Party: The Life of Frances Hodgson Burnett, 1849-1924.* And from there, Thwaite went on to outline the lives of the English critic Edmund Gosse, and the creator of Winnie-the-Pooh, A. A. Milne.

"From her picture books to her juvenile novels," explains Paul, "Thwaite chooses stories that apparently play within conventional forms of children's literature but ultimately subvert them." *The Chatterbox,* for example, cautions teachers instead of children. Miss Walters, a young English teacher, comes to the conclusion that children talk entirely too much. In an attempt to stop the incessant chatter, she has a wooden box erected in the school yard and calls it the Chatterbox—any child talking too much will be sent to it. A few days later, Miss Walters finds herself facing an empty room and decides to turn the Chatterbox into a playhouse. "The vignettes of school life will be recognized by students and teachers everywhere," asserts Caroline S. Parr in the *School Library Journal.* And Elizabeth Weir concludes in *School Librarian* that *The Chatterbox* is a "humorous and lively" tale.

One of Thwaite's books for older children, *The Camelthorn Papers,* also appears to be something that it is not—a traditional adventure story. Set in Libya, *The Camelthorn Papers* follows the adventures of two English sisters, Jessica and Kate, and their half-Egyptian friend Gamal. In the beginning of the book, Kate promises one of her father's friends, Derek Lister, to look for a box of poems and journals that he buried near Benghazi during World War II. Instead of finding the treasure she is looking for, however, Kate finds Derek's lost youth and lost dreams of being a poet. By the time Kate actually finds his tin box of writings, it is not a surprise that they have disintegrated into dust. "The story Thwaite tells is not one of happily-ever-after fairytales," relates Paul, "but a contemporary story of choices and possibilities, coded in the refrain that runs through the book: 'He who does not keep moving is lost.' "

Among Thwaite's more recent works for children is her 1987 *Amy and the Night-Time Visit.* This picture book deals with a quandary common to many parents—can a child be left alone in an empty house for a short period of time? Amy's mother decides the answer is yes, and leaves her sleeping daughter a note as she visits her own mother. When Amy awakes, she senses the emptiness of the house, wandering around a bit before deciding she needs some human contact. Her mother arrives home to find her gone, and visits a neighbor's house for help, only to find her daughter there. The relationship between Amy and her mother is portrayed as "warm and honest," describes Sue Davis in *School Librarian,* adding that *Amy and the Night-Time Visit* is a perfect book for "sharing one-to-one."

In addition to her own writing for children, Thwaite has also collected the writings of other children's authors in a series of annuals entitled *Allsorts*. Published from 1969 until 1975, these collections contain poems, stories, and puzzles, and are similar to the popular annuals of the nineteenth century. Unlike other annuals, though, *Allsorts* is full of new material that Thwaite commissioned from such writers as X. J. Kennedy, Philip Larkin, Ted Hughes, and Penelope Lively. "It is the literary content, together with the quality of illustration, that distinguishes *Allsorts* from its slapdash and sometimes barely literate competitors," points out a *Times Literary Supplement* contributor. Thwaite "demonstrates that a miscellany-annual of new material for eight-year-olds can be not only easy, absorbing, delicious (like trifle), but also good," sums up an *Observer* reviewer.

Thwaite remains in the world of children's literature with her first adult biography. *Waiting for the Party: The Life of Frances Hodgson Burnett, 1849-1924* provides a close examination of the creator of the children's classics *Little Lord Fauntleroy* and *The Secret Garden*. Burnett spent most of her life writing sentimental magazine stories and romantic novels for adults, but "twice in over half a century of constant and often exhausting commercial productivity she happened to tell one of those stories that turn out to be the externalized dreams of a whole society, which pass beyond ordinary commercial success to become part of popular culture," contends Alison Lurie in the *New York Review of Books*. In *Waiting for the Party* Thwaite covers everything from Burnett's American adolescence to her thirty-three visits to her native England and her unsuccessful search for happiness. "The Frances Hodgson Burnett who emerges from [Thwaite's] biography is an interesting and sympathetic if not a completely lovable character," observes Lurie, concluding: "*Waiting for the Party* is a good book: intelligent, moderate, thoughtful, well documented, well organized, and well written."

Thwaite's next biography takes on the English critic and author of *Father and Son*, Edmund Gosse. In *Edmund Gosse: A Literary Landscape, 1849-1928*, Thwaite begins with Gosse's religious Islington childhood, which Gosse himself describes in his famous novel *Father and Son*. From this background, Gosse ventured to London in the 1870s, hoping to make a name for himself as a poet. Unsuccessful in this endeavor, Gosse found that he did have a future as a man of letters, and wrote on numerous literary subjects during his career. He suffered a severe setback, however, when a literary history he wrote was found to be full of inexcusable inaccuracies. Gosse was never able to shake off this reputation for sloppiness, but he was still very successful—he was a lively conversationalist, a graceful prose writer, and was friends with a number of literary figures, including Thomas Hardy and Henry James. Thwaite's "version of [Gosse's] life is more complicated, and more credible, than any summing of opinions about him could be; she acknowledges his follies and limitations, but she also notes what was good, and what was interesting, about him," relates Samuel Hynes in the *New York Times Book Review*. Thwaite's "portrait of this touchy, feline, ambitious, cautious, snobbish, self-stroking, vivacious, generous, warm-hearted, and *interesting* man is an authoritative and just one," concludes *New York Review of Books* contributor Janet Malcolm.

A. A. Milne: The Man behind Winnie-the-Pooh, published in 1990, is one of Thwaite's more recent biographies. Milne was a humorist, playwright, and novelist who took a short trip into children's literature and found fame and fortune. He then spent the rest of his days hating the fact that his four children's books would be his immortality. Milne was a remote person throughout his life, moving from the academic world to the offices of *Punch*, and finally becoming a popular playwright and children's author. He based his two Winnie-the-Pooh books on stories he told his son Christopher Robin, and the shadow this cast over Christopher's life eventually drove father and son apart. "Thwaite tries to establish Milne's profile by a slow, careful, skilfully deployed accumulation of detail, based on free access to family papers and interviews with surviving friends and relatives," describes Peter Green in the *Washington Post Book World*. "I doubt whether we will ever learn more *facts* about Milne than are gathered in this biography." Chris Goodrich, writing in the *Los Angeles Times Book Review*, explains that "Thwaite argues . . . that A. A. Milne was 'a mass of contradictions,' being shy yet confident, modest yet proud, warm yet judgmental." Goodrich goes on to state that *A. A. Milne* is "a sympathetic, understanding portrait, and Pooh fans will savor it."

BIOGRAPHICAL/CRITICAL SOURCES:

BOOKS

Chevalier, Tracy, editor, *Twentieth-Century Children's Writers*, 3rd edition, St. James Press, 1989.

PERIODICALS

Books and Bookmen, July, 1969.
Chicago Tribune, August 26, 1990.
Horn Book, February, 1975, pp. 65-66.
Junior Bookshelf, April, 1988, p. 87.
Library Journal, September 15, 1970, p. 3054.
Los Angeles Times Book Review, September 16, 1990.
New York Review of Books, November 28, 1974, pp. 39-41; March 14, 1985, pp. 7-12.
New York Times Book Review, September 9, 1984, pp. 14-15.

Observer, December 7, 1969; December 6, 1970.
Publishers Weekly, July 29, 1974, pp. 41-42; July 16, 1979, p. 70.
School Librarian, March, 1979, p. 29; May, 1988, p. 59.
School Library Journal, October, 1979, pp. 145-146.
Times (London), May 10, 1984; November 8, 1985; June 9, 1990.
Times Literary Supplement, October 16, 1969; April 27, 1984, p. 468; March 29, 1985; June 8, 1990.
Washington Post Book World, August 5, 1984; September 9, 1990, pp. 5, 11.

—*Sketch by Susan M. Reicha*

*   *   *

THWAITE, Anthony (Simon) 1930-

PERSONAL: Born June 23, 1930, in Chester, England; son of Hartley (in banking) and Alice Evelyn (Mallinson) Thwaite; married Ann Harrop (a writer), August 4, 1955; children: Emily, Caroline, Lucy, Alice. *Education:* Christ Church, Oxford, B.A. (with honours), 1955, M.A., 1959. *Avocational interests:* Antiquarian beachcombing, collecting a variety of things.

ADDRESSES: Home—The Mill House, Low Tharston, Norfolk NR15 2YN, England.

CAREER: Tokyo University, Tokyo, Japan, visiting lecturer in English literature, 1955-57; British Broadcasting Corporation, London, England, radio producer, 1957-62; *The Listener,* London, literary editor, 1962-65; University of Libya, Benghazi, assistant professor of English literature, 1965-67; *New Statesman,* London, literary editor, 1968-72; *Encounter,* London, co-editor, 1973-85; Kuwait University, visiting professor, 1974; Vanderbilt University, Nashville, TN, poet in residence, 1992. *Military service:* British Army, 1949-51; became sergeant.

AWARDS, HONORS: Richard Hillary Memorial Prize, 1967, for *The Stones of Emptiness: Poems 1963-66;* University of East Anglia Henfield Writing Fellow, 1972; Royal Society of Literature fellow, 1977; Cholmondeley Award, Society of Authors (Great Britain), 1984; Japan Foundation fellow, Tokyo University, 1985-86; Honorary D.Litt., University of Hull, 1989; Order of the British Empire, 1990.

WRITINGS:

POETRY

(*Poems*), Fantasy Press, 1953.
Home Truths, Marvell Press, 1957.
The Owl in the Tree: Poems, Oxford University Press, 1963.
The Stones of Emptiness: Poems 1963-66, Oxford University Press, 1967.

Points (limited edition), Turret, 1972.
Inscriptions: Poems 1967-72, Oxford University Press, 1973.
Jack, Cellar Press, 1973.
New Confessions, Oxford University Press, 1974.
A Portion for Foxes, Oxford University Press, 1977.
Victorian Voices, Oxford University Press, 1980.
Telling Tales (limited edition), wood engraving by Simon Brett, Gruffyground Press, 1983.
Poems, 1953-1983, Secker & Warburg, 1984, expanded and published as *Poems, 1953-1988,* Hutchinson, 1989.
Letter from Tokyo, Hutchinson, 1987.

EDITOR

(With Hilary Corke and William Plomer) *New Poems 1961: A PEN Anthology of Contemporary Poetry,* Hutchinson, 1961.
(And translator with Geoffrey Bownas) *The Penguin Book of Japanese Verse,* Penguin, 1964.
(With A. Alvarez and Roy Fuller) *Penguin Modern Poets 18,* Penguin, 1970.
(With Peter Porter) *The English Poets: From Chaucer to Edward Thomas,* Secker and Warburg, 1974.
Poems for Shakespeare 3, Globe Playhouse, 1974.
(With Dannie Abse, D. J. Enright, and Michael Longley) *Penguin Modern Poets 26,* Penguin, 1975.
(With Fleur Adock) *New Poetry 4,* Hutchinson, 1978.
Larkin at Sixty, Faber & Faber, 1982.
(With John Mole) *Poetry 1945 to 1980,* Longman, 1983.
(And author of introduction) *Collected Poems of Philip Larkin,* Faber & Faber, 1988.
(And author of introduction) *Selected Letters of Philip Larkin,* Faber & Faber, 1992.

OTHER

Essays on Contemporary English Poetry: Hopkins to the Present Day, Kenkyusha, 1957, revised as *Contemporary English Poetry: An Introduction,* Heinemann, 1959, Dufour, 1961, 3rd edition, 1964, revised and published as *Twentieth-Century English Poetry: An Introduction,* Barnes & Noble, 1978.
Japan in Colour, photographs by Roloff Beny, McGraw, 1967.
The Deserts of Hesperides: An Experience of Libya, Roy, 1969.
Poetry Today 1960-1973, Longman, 1973, revised and expanded as *Poetry Today: A Critical Guide to British Poetry, 1960-1984,* Longman, 1985.
(With Porter) *Roloff Beny in Italy,* photographs and design by Beny, Harper, 1974.
Beyond the Inhabited World: Roman Britain (juvenile), Deutsch, 1976, Seabury Press, 1977.

Odyssey: Mirror of the Mediterranean, photographs and design by Beny, Harper, 1981.

(With Howard Sergeant) *Gregory Awards Anthology, 1981 and 1982,* Carcanet New Press for the Society of Authors, 1982.

(Compiler and author of introduction) *Six Centuries of Verse* (companion to Thames TV/Channel 4 series), Thames Methuen, 1984.

Contributor of poems to British periodicals and to anthologies, including *Oxford Book of Twentieth Century English Verse, Penguin Book of Contemporary Verse, New Poets of England and America 2,* and *New Lines 2.* Collections of Thwaite's manuscripts are housed at the University of Hull, Yorkshire, in the Brynmor Jones Library, and at the University of Leeds, Yorkshire, in the Brotherton Library.

ADAPTATIONS: The English Poets: From Chaucer to Edward Thomas was adapted for audio cassette, Longman, 1980.

SIDELIGHTS: Anthony Thwaite, a noted contemporary British poet, is also an accomplished author and editor. Known for his reflective, detailed, and perceptive poetry, Thwaite's early works focus on domestic themes and everyday life, while his later volumes contain the thoughts and experiences of a well-travelled poet. Often compared to the late poet and novelist Philip Larkin, mainly for the ability to subtly weave predicaments or stories into poetry, Thwaite edited two volumes concerning Larkin— *Collected Poems of Philip Larkin* and *Larkin at Sixty,* a book filled with anecdotes provided by those who knew him. Thwaite also includes prose works in his literary stable, from textbooks about contemporary poetry to historical surveys. A varied interest, a wide literary range, and broad experience allow Thwaite to excel at expressing himself and to reach many audiences.

Thwaite was born in Chester, England, although he considers himself a Yorkshireman due to his parents' lineage—both can trace their ancestors as far back as records go. Born June 23, 1930, Thwaite has had a life filled with travel. His father, employed by Lloyds Bank, was often promoted to positions throughout England, and as a result, Thwaite spent a childhood living in various British locations. At the age of ten, he was evacuated to the United States to live with relatives from 1940 until 1944, during World War II. Returning to England at fourteen, Thwaite was enrolled at the school his father had attended—Kingswood School, an educational institution founded by John Wesley for the sons of itinerant preachers. It was there that Thwaite's interests in archaeology and poetry were encouraged; he intended to be a professional archeologist even through his army days. Eventually, poetry won out and Thwaite graduated from Christ

Church, Oxford, in 1955 with a bachelor of arts. His first professional position was teaching English at Tokyo University, and his first titled volume of poetry, *Home Truths,* was published soon after in 1957. Thwaite has continued to travel and incorporate his experiences into his writings throughout his adult life.

Places, objects, and historical times have evolved into the basis for Thwaite's poetry. In *New Confessions* (1974), he reworks St. Augustine of Hippo's *Confessions* to create his own personal volume of meditation and reflection, while revealing his interpretation of the saint's life and thought. A sequence written in both prose and verse, set in an exotic North Africa, *New Confessions* drew the attention of many critics. A reviewer in *Choice* commented that "many lines are memorable," and another, writing in the *Times Literary Supplement,* noted "a new, fragmentary intensity, and a new breadth" in the poems. Andrew Crozier, on the other hand, declared in the *Spectator* that "the reflections are unmotivated," but later went on to praise Thwaite's "classy personal eloquence." Crozier felt that the Augustinian text was detrimental to the poet's breadth, limiting Thwaite and resulting in a "load of pseudo-significance" poorly hidden behind an "Augustinian mask." *New Statesman* contributor Alan Brownjohn also asserted that the poet restricted himself with his topic, in spite of the "versatile variety of forms," and that his tone was a bit too "deferentially appropriate."

In Thwaite's next volume of poetry, *A Portion for Foxes* (1977), he turned from historic figures to historical objects and ancient places. England, Yugoslavia, and the Arabian Gulf, as well as a Victorian stereoscope and Romano-British altars are a few of the starting points for poems in this volume, many of which had previously been published in newspapers and magazines. While a reviewer in *Choice* contended that Thwaite "has changed little as a poet" since *Home Truths* was published in 1957, other critics reacted more favorably to *A Portion for Foxes.* Russell Davies, writing in the *New Statesman,* noted Thwaite's "fine instinct for matching textures" within poems and within the book. *Spectator* contributor Anthony Burgess labeled the volume "very intelligent . . . witty, with a wide stretch of subject-matter and a great boldness." Roy Fuller, in the *Times Literary Supplement,* also noted the "critical intelligence," and praised the "verbal power" of Thwaite's technique, commenting that "Thwaite is a poet who cares about interesting (and, often, amusing) his readers, as well as delineating the poignant histories of cultures, creatures and human beings."

Interested in both history and poetic voices, Thwaite explores the past age with *Victorian Voices,* published in 1980, in a series of fourteen dramatic monologues. Based on twelve actual, lesser-known Victorians, such as Philip Henry Gosse who knew Darwin and was the father of critic Edmund Gosse, the volume also includes two representational characters, one a malicious Oxford don recording his colleagues' foibles. George Meredith's first wife, Mary Ellen, is also one of the voices, sounding as if she's responding to Meredith's poem of marital breakup, *Modern Love,* even mimicking his stanza form. While Richard Tobias, writing in *World Literature Today,* panned *Victorian Voices* as containing fourteen monologues in "blank-verse lines that seem alike," regardless of who is speaking, other critics were more enthusiastic. London *Observer* contributor Hilary Spurling called the volume "part history, part impersonation," and Andrew Motion in the *New Statesman* praised the monologues as "earnest and absorbing." Several critics commented on Thwaite's emotional input into each piece, with Dick Davis noting in the *Listener* the poet's "aim . . . to awaken sympathy for the varieties of loneliness he charts." *Times Literary Supplement* contributor Robert Bernard Martin praised the effects of "Thwaite's warm vein of compassion for the also-rans," and concluded: "In its easy maturity, its generous understanding of character, and its deliberate neglect of flashy effects or attempts to startle, *Victorian Voices* seems to me the best of Anthony Thwaite's fine volumes of poetry. It is a book that invites rereading and rewards it thoroughly."

Thwaite has also published several collections of his verse culled from both previously printed and new poems, including *Poems, 1953-1983.* Published in 1984, this volume contains works from the preceding thirty years, and was expanded and re-released in 1989 as *Poems, 1953-1988.* The original release was given generally good reviews, most of which centered on Thwaite's poetic style. "Technical virtuosity combined with a keen observant eye" place Thwaite amongst the finest of the same generation of poets, declared Thom Tammaro in the *Library Journal.* John Bayley commented in the *Times Literary Supplement* that Thwaite "is an excellent poet, even an original one, his originality having about it a deliberate sort of blankness which comes from the contrasts he makes between efficiency and mastery of conventional form." John Lucas, writing in the *New Statesman,* was with the minority of critics in lamenting, "Writing like this is the . . . death of art," specifically referring to the poem "Mr. Cooper." The second release, *Poems, 1953-1988,* received much the same response, with *Times Literary Supplement* contributor Simon Rae concluding: "And looking back over 270 pages of poems written over thirty-odd years, one is struck by the integrity of purpose with which Thwaite has pursued his often pained, but sometimes funny and always compassionate exploration of human existence."

Looking closely at one human in particular, poet and novelist Philip Larkin, Thwaite uses his skills as editor and as prose author to examine another's life and work. In 1982,

Thwaite edited a collection of essays written in honor of Larkin, entitled *Larkin at Sixty.* These glimpses of the man behind the verse, written by his friends and associates, explore his achievements and put them in perspective. "The reminiscences and anecdotes both amuse and inform," wrote D. J. Enright in the London *Observer.* A reviewer in *Choice* noted that while the book does not reveal any new information, it helps to "flesh out" Larkin as a professional poet. "All the friends who write about him seem anxious to stress the anti-literary side of his character," remarked Derwent May in the *Listener.* Several critics, however, commented that the book might infringe on Larkin's sense of privacy, with *Spectator* contributor Peter Levi labeling the stories as an "invasion," and noting that Eliot and Tennyson were not treated in the same manner. "All this in a collection of thin essays, without those advantages of slow pace or serious analysis or nourishing drabness which a full biography might offer," Levi contended, going on to add, "Outsiders owe a debt to Anthony Thwaite all the same." After Larkin's death, Thwaite edited, wrote an introduction, and published an encompassing collection of the late poet's poems in 1988—*Collected Poems of Philip Larkin.*

Thwaite has also collected and published several volumes of others' poetry, not exclusively Philip Larkin's verse. *Six Centuries of Verse* (1984), selected and introduced by Thwaite, was written as a companion book to a British television series. From early English poetry to poems of the twentieth century up until 1984, including some American authors like Emily Dickinson and Walt Whitman, Thwaite attempts to encompass centuries of thought, change, and language all written in verse. Reviews of the volume were favorable, with many critics commending his poetic selections. *British Book News* contributor R. B. Kennedy lauded Thwaite's "shrewdness of choice," and another critic, writing in *Washington Post Book World,* praised both the poetry selection and the prose commentaries, noting that "Thwaite's text never gets in the way of the verse," and yet somehow illustrates the development of English poetry.

Six centuries covers a great deal of poetry, and in *Poetry Today: A Critical Guide to British Poetry, 1960-1984,* Thwaite narrows his field to more modern poets, those writing within twenty-five years of the publication date in 1985. This volume is a revised and expanded version of an essay, published in 1973 in conjunction with the British Council, entitled *Poetry Today 1960-1973.* Written with a historic perspective, Thwaite attempts to maintain continuity among the poets, both established and emerging, by delineating the period in which they wrote. While Claude Rawson, writing in the *Times Literary Supplement,* called *Poetry Today* "civilized, literate, and dull," he also noted that Thwaite "writes with real discrimination" about the "quieter, more decorous styles." *British Book News* contributor Raymond Tong concluded "*Poetry Today* is a remarkably comprehensive and stimulating survey."

Thwaite is adept at assembling and editing collections, whether they are poetry or prose, and also at creating his own. Thwaite's talents have been praised by numerous critics, with Christopher Levenson, writing in the *Dictionary of Literary Biography,* calling him "an heir apparent to the title of reigning [British] man of letters." Levenson also maintained: "While there are others who have produced a more obviously major body of work in poetry, or who have excelled in a number of genres, there is none who has combined both the scope and seriousness of Thwaite's own poetry with his breadth of experience and authority as an editor."

Commenting in 1968 on his writing and critical reception, Thwaite once wrote: "I have always felt—at any rate since I wrote most of the poems in my first book, *Home Truths*—that my best work comes from fairly definable personal impulses and observations. For this reason I seemed to have become typecast by reviewers (particularly of my second book, *The Owl in the Tree*) as a poet of domestic themes, and was even quoted in a jokey booklet (*The Bluffer's Guide to Literature*) as having styled myself 'the Yeats of the suburbs'—a remark neither true nor perceptive. In Libya the impulses and observations [had] been so different that I had to change; or rather, they changed me. The colours, the heat, the sense of it being 'a land where ruins flourish' . . . , the almost oppressive feeling of the past caught up in the blowing dust and sand, all gave me for the first time in my poems the chance to make clear my obsession with the ancient and the transient: an obsession which—in the pigeon-holing way I have—I trace back to my seventh birthday, when my favorite uncle gave me a Roman silver denarius. For me, every step and every breath is a constant apprehension of the physical past: everywhere, we touch and see what has been left behind."

BIOGRAPHICAL/CRITICAL SOURCES:

BOOKS

Dictionary of Literary Biography, Volume 40: *Poets of Great Britain and Ireland since 1960,* 2 parts, Gale, 1985.

PERIODICALS

Books and Bookmen, May, 1967; August, 1984, p. 31.
British Book News, September, 1984, p. 563; July, 1985, p. 435.
Choice, November, 1974, p. 1333; January, 1978, p. 1501; October, 1982, p. 266.
Library Journal, October 1, 1984, p. 1852.

Listener, September 7, 1967; January 29, 1981, p. 151; June 3, 1982.
London Magazine, August, 1967.
Los Angeles Times Book Review, July 30, 1989, p. 3.
New Statesman, June 7, 1974, p. 808; September 30, 1977, p. 448; December 5, 1980, p. 22; June 4, 1982, p. 20; June 22, 1984, p. 23; August 21, 1987, p. 22.
New York Times, December 22, 1963.
New York Times Book Review, May 21, 1989, p. 24.
Observer (London), June 18, 1967; December 7, 1980; May 30, 1982; April 5, 1987, p. 24.
Poetry, December, 1973.
Spectator, September 21, 1974; August 6, 1977, p. 29; June 12, 1982, p. 22.
Times (London), October 22, 1988.
Times Educational Supplement, August 17, 1987, p. 22.
Times Literary Supplement, June 21, 1974, p. 667; July 15, 1977, p. 848; January 23, 1981, p. 81; November 18, 1983; June 22, 1984, p. 705; February 7, 1986, p. 137; November 10, 1989, p. 1245.
Washington Post Book World, September 1, 1985, p. 13; May 7, 1989, p. 1.
World Literature Today, winter, 1982, p. 115.

—*Sketch by Terrie M. Rooney*

*   *   *

TOWNSEND, John Rowe 1922-

PERSONAL: Born May 10, 1922, in Leeds, Yorkshire, England; son of George Edmund Rowe (a chief clerk) and Gladys (a secretary; maiden name, Page) Townsend; married Vera Lancaster, July 3, 1948 (died May 9, 1973); children: Alethea Mary, Nicholas John, Penelope Anne. *Education:* Emmanuel College, Cambridge, B.A., 1949, M.A., 1954.

ADDRESSES: Home—72 Water Lane, Histon, Cambridge CB4 4LR, England.

CAREER: Employed by British civil service, 1939-42. Journalist for *Yorkshire Post,* 1946, and *Evening Standard,* 1949; *Manchester Guardian,* Manchester, England, subeditor, 1949-54, art editor, 1954-55, editor of *Manchester Guardian Weekly* (international edition), 1955-59, children's book editor (part-time), 1968-78, columnist, 1968-81; writer and lecturer, 1969—. Adjunct board member for United Kingdom, Children's Literature New England, 1990—. Permanent visiting faculty member, Center for Children's Literature, Simmons College, 1978-84. Visiting lecturer, University of Pennsylvania, 1965, and University of Washington, 1969 and 1971; May Hill Arbuthnot Honor lecturer, New York Public Library, 1971; Whittall lecturer, Library of Congress, 1976.

Military service: Royal Air Force, 1942-46; became flight sergeant.

MEMBER: British Society of Authors (member of management committee, 1982-85), Children's Writers Group (chairman, 1975-76, 1990-91).

AWARDS, HONORS: Participant in Harvard International Seminar, 1956; Carnegie Medal Honours list, British Library Association, 1963, for *Hell's Edge;* Carnegie Medal Honours list, and Edgar Allen Poe Award, Mystery Writers of America, both 1969, *Boston Globe/Horn Book* Award, and Silver Pen Award, English Centre of International PEN, both 1970, all for *The Intruder;* Christopher Award, 1982, for *The Islanders;* many of author's works have been named to both the American Library Association Notable Book list and the *Horn Book* Honor list.

WRITINGS:

FOR CHILDREN

Gumble's Yard, illustrated by Dick Hart, Hutchinson, 1961, published as *Trouble in the Jungle,* illustrated by W. T. Mars, Lippincott, 1969.

Widdershins Crescent, Hutchinson, 1966, published as *Good-bye to the Jungle,* Lippincott, 1967.

Pirate's Island, illustrated by Douglas Hall, Lippincott, 1968.

A Wish for Wings, illustrated by Philip Gough, Heinemann, 1972.

Top of the World, illustrated by Nikki Jones, Oxford University Press, 1976, illustrated by John Wallner, Lippincott, 1977.

Clever Dick: The Diary of a Dreadful Child, illustrated by Nick Ward, Oxford University Press, 1982.

Dan Alone, Lippincott, 1983.

Gone to the Dogs, illustrated by Andy Bylo, Oxford University Press, 1984.

Tom Tiddler's Ground, illustrated by Mark Peppe, Kestrel, 1985, Lippincott, 1986.

The Persuading Stick, Viking Kestrel, 1986, Lothrop, 1987.

FOR YOUNG ADULTS

Hell's Edge, Hutchinson, 1963, Lothrop, 1969.

The Hallersage Sound, Hutchinson, 1966.

The Intruder, illustrated by Graham Humphreys, Oxford University Press, 1969, illustrated by Joseph A. Phelan, Lippincott, 1970.

Goodnight, Prof, Love, illustrated by Peter Farmer, Oxford University Press, 1970, published as *Goodnight, Prof, Dear,* Lippincott, 1971, published as *The Runaways,* edited by David Fickling, Oxford University Press, 1979.

(Editor) *Modern Poetry: A Selection for Young People,* with photographs by Barbara Pfeffer, Oxford University Press, 1971, Lippincott, 1974.

The Summer People, illustrated by Robert Micklewright, Lippincott, 1972.

Forest of the Night, illustrated by Farmer, Oxford University Press, 1974, illustrated by Beverly Brodsky McDermott, Lippincott, 1975.

Noah's Castle, Oxford University Press, 1975, Lippincott, 1976.

The Xanadu Manuscript, illustrated by Paul Ritchie, Oxford University Press, 1977, published as *The Visitors,* Lippincott, 1977.

King Creature, Come, Oxford University Press, 1980, published as *The Creatures,* Lippincott, 1980.

The Islanders, Lippincott, 1981.

A Foreign Affair, Kestrel, 1982, published as *Kate and the Revolution,* Lippincott, 1983.

Cloudy-Bright: A Novel, Lippincott, 1984, published as *Sam and Jenny,* Random Century, 1992.

Downstream: A Novel, Lippincott, 1987.

Rob's Place, Kestrel, 1987, Lothrop, 1988.

The Golden Journey, Viking, 1989, published as *The Fortunate Isles: A Novel,* Lippincott, 1989.

The Invaders, Oxford University Press, 1992.

OTHER

Written for Children: An Outline of English-Language Children's Literature, J. Garnet Miller, 1965, Lothrop, 1967, 4th revised edition, HarperCollins, 1992.

A Sense of Story: Essays on Contemporary Writers for Children, Lippincott, 1971.

A Sounding of Storytellers: New and Revised Essays on Contemporary Children's Writers, Lippincott, 1979.

Also the author of *Cranford Revisited,* 1990. Contributor to books, including *The Openhearted Audience: Ten Authors Talk about Writing for Children,* edited by Virginia Haviland, Library of Congress, 1980. Contributor of articles and reviews to numerous periodicals, including *Horn Book, Manchester Guardian* and *Times Educational Supplement.*

ADAPTATIONS: Several of Townsend's works have been adapted for television, including *The Intruder* (series), ITV, 1972, *Noah's Castle* (series), ITV, 1980, and *Gumble's Yard.*

SIDELIGHTS: British writer John Rowe Townsend is the author of numerous novels for both children and young adults. Early in his career as a children's author, Townsend was praised by reviewers for his innovative technique of interspersing elements of social realism among the fictional realities of the young characters in his novels. In marked contrast to the predominately "comfortable" children's literature produced in the early 1960s, the characteristic Townsend style exemplified in such early books as *Hell's Edge,* published in 1963, and 1969's *The Intruder,* resulted in critic Rosemary Stone lauding the author as a "social pioneer" in a review for the London *Times.* In addition to acclaim from critics, Townsend's work has garnered many awards, including the *Boston Globe-Horn Book* Award, Christopher Award, and Edgar Allen Poe Award, as well as being named to the British Library Association's prestigious Carnegie Medal Honours list in both 1963 and 1969.

Originally employed as a journalist for the *Manchester Guardian,* Townsend did not embark upon a career as a full-time children's author until 1960, when he was in his late thirties. Once he started to write his first novel, Townsend found he enjoyed his new audience of younger readers: "I'd rather write for children than anyone else," Townsend once told *CA.* "They're a responsive audience: eager, unsated, ready to live the story. They won't put up with longwindedness or pomposity, they won't go on reading if they're not enjoying the book, but that's a healthy discipline."

One of the concerns that prompted his first novel, *Gumble's Yard,* was Townsend's belief that there was a need for books that depicted children facing such realities of life as economic and family hardships. He noted in *Something about the Author Autobiography Series* (*SAAS*): "As a reviewer of books for children [for the *Manchester Guardian*], I'd come to the conclusion, rightly or wrongly, that British children's books . . . were altogether too harmless, hygienic, and middle-class, with little in them of the flavor of life as it was known to a large part of the population." In conjunction with research he was currently undertaking for the British Society for the Prevention of Cruelty to Children, Townsend found himself spending a good deal of his time in the industrialized areas of Manchester, a major British commercial center. It was against that urban backdrop, supplemented with memories of his own upbringing in the nearby city of Leeds, that his imagination went to work creating the characters and plot of *Gumble's Yard.* "The real world I knew as a child would seem to many people to be a grim one," Townsend wrote in *SAAS.* "It was a small, urban world—a maze of narrow streets and alleyways, a world of little cramped dwellings and corner shops." This inner-city landscape would find itself replicated in many of Townsend's later books, including *Pirate's Island* and *Dan Alone.*

In addition to what he saw as a dearth of books for and about children from lower-class families, Townsend also perceived a need for more books for teenage readers. In *Written for Children: An Outline of English-Language Children's Literature,* which he published in 1965, Townsend stated what he then saw as the status quo: "Young

people who read at all . . . will be reading adult books before they are far into their teens. So they will and so they should. But I do not think we can safely assume that adult books will meet all their needs, any more than adult recreations meet all their needs. There are matters . . . that are of the utmost interest to adolescents but that are not often dealt with in adult fiction, or at least not often looked at from a 'young' point of view." In his young adult novels, Townsend deals with things of specific interest to adolescent readers: first loves, relationships between parents and children, leaving school to start work. In many of his books for teenagers he takes the approach characteristic of his work for younger readers, focusing on young protagonists who find themselves victims of financial deprivation and social class discrimination, which has caused critic Patricia Craig to wonder in the *Times Literary Supplement* whether "this gifted children's author has become fatally under-ambitious."

Overall, the novels of Townsend have found increasing popularity among both critics and young readers. That he possesses "an uncanny sensitivity to the deepest yearnings of children who have inadequate parents or are orphaned," is an aspect of his prose noted by Bryna J. Fireside in the *New York Times Book Review.* Describing the author's "heroes" as young people who "live on the edge of poverty, but are not themselves impoverished," Fireside explains: "Rather, they are endowed with a tenaciousness that helps them survive situations that would crush those more protected." Whether writing a novel for young adult readers, a story for younger children, or an article discussing the craft of children's fiction, Townsend's enthusiasm for his work is apparent. "I like writing for adults about children's books and trying to get them interested in the books for their own sake," he told *CA:* "That way we can all share with children, and maybe recapture a little of childhood's excitement."

BIOGRAPHICAL/CRITICAL SOURCES:

BOOKS

Blishen, Edward, *The Thorny Paradise,* Kestrel, 1975, pp. 146-156.
Children's Literature Review, Volume 2, Gale, 1976.
Something about the Author, Volume 68, Gale, 1991, pp. 228-231.
Something about the Author Autobiography Series, Volume 2, Gale, 1986.
Townsend, John Rowe, *Written for Children: An Outline of English Children's Literature,* revised edition, Lippincott, 1975.
Wintle, Justin, and Emma Fisher, *Pied Pipers,* Paddington Press, 1975, pp. 236-248.

PERIODICALS

Best Sellers, May 1, 1967; June 1, 1969.

Books and Bookmen, July, 1968.

Book World, December 3, 1967; May 5, 1968; May 17, 1970; May 9, 1971.

Canadian Children's Literature, Volume 48, 1987, pp. 29-42.

Children's Literature in Education, winter, 1975.

Christian Science Monitor, May 4, 1967.

Cricket, September, 1983.

English Journal, March, 1974, pp. 89-90.

Horn Book, April, 1967; June, 1967; August, 1968; August, 1970; June, 1971; August, 1971; October, 1971; April, 1973; June, 1973, pp. 241-247; April, 1975; October, 1975; August, 1977; December, 1977; October, 1982; January, 1985; January, 1987; July, 1987; March, 1988; March, 1990.

New Society (London), December 7, 1967.

New Yorker, December 16, 1967; December 14, 1968.

New York Times Book Review, May 7, 1967; November 5, 1967; May 26, 1968; August 31, 1969; April 26, 1970; May 2, 1971; November 5, 1972; November 19, 1972; December 29, 1974; April 11, 1976; April 3, 1977; November 6, 1977; February 19, 1984, p. 29.

Times (London), August 25, 1983.

Times Literary Supplement, May 25, 1967; October 16, 1969; July 18, 1980, p. 812; September 18, 1981, p. 1069; September 17, 1982, p. 1001; September 30, 1983, 1049; July 27, 1984, p. 854; October 11, 1985, p. 1154; November 28, 1986, p. 1344.

Young Reader's Review, May, 1967; April, 1968.

*   *   *

TRUNDLETT, Helen B.
  See ELIOT, T(homas) S(tearns)

U-V

USHERWOOD, Stephen Dean 1907-

PERSONAL: Born September 14, 1907, in London, England; son of John Frederick (a school headmaster) and Grace Ellen (a college headmistress; maiden name, Crush) Usherwood; married Hazel Doreen Weston (teacher of crafts and author of children's books), July 27, 1935 (died, 1968); married Elizabeth Ada Beavington (a bank official), October 24, 1970; children: (first marriage) Susan Clare, Nicholas John. *Education:* Oriel College, Oxford, M.A. (with honors in classics), 1928, M.A. in modern history, 1930, diploma in education, 1931. *Politics:* Conservative. *Religion:* Roman Catholic.

ADDRESSES: Home and office—24 St. Mary's Grove, London N1 2NT, England.

CAREER: Teacher of history and religion at various schools, Hampshire and Surrey, England, 1931-41; British Broadcasting Corp., London, England, foreign news reporter, 1946-55, liaison officer with U.S. Intelligence units in United States, Japan, and Okinawa, 1951-52, producer, school broadcasting department, 1955-68. Lecturer and broadcaster on history, religion, and travel. Producer of Festival of Britain Pageant, Basingstoke, Hampshire, England, 1951. *Military service:* Royal Air Force, Air Sea Rescue Service, 1941-42; became flight lieutenant; staff intelligence duties attached to Foreign Office, 1943-46.

MEMBER: Oxford Union, Oriel Society.

WRITINGS:

Reign by Reign, Norton, 1960.
The Bible: Book by Book, Norton, 1962.
Shakespeare: Play by Play, Hill & Wang, 1968.
History from Familiar Things, five volumes, Ginn, 1968-72.
Britain: Century by Century, David & Charles, 1972.
Food, Drink and History, David & Charles, 1972.

Europe: Century by Century, David & Charles, 1972.
The Great Enterprise, Folio Society, 1979.
(With wife, Elizabeth Usherwood) *Visit Some London Catholic Churches,* Mayhew-McCrimmon, 1981.
(With E. Usherwood) *The Counter-Armada, 1596: The Journal of the "Mary Rose,"* Bodley Head, 1983.
(With E. Usherwood) *We Die for the Old Religion: The Story of the 85 Martyrs of England and Wales Beatified 22 November 1987,* Sheed & Ward, 1987.
(With E. Usherwood) *A Saint in the Family,* St. Paul, 1992.

Contributor of articles on Soviet radio propaganda to *World Today,* on lacrosse to *Country Life* and *Oxford Junior Encyclopedia,* on history to *History Today, International History, Port of London Authority,* and other publications. Writer of radio scripts on history, art, religion, and sports, and of historical teaching notes accompanying forty-two educational filmstrips, issued by the Rank Organisation Film Library and Drake International.

SIDELIGHTS: Stephen Dean Usherwood's book *The Counter Armada, 1596: The Journal of the "Mary Rose"* (written with his wife, Elizabeth Usherwood) concerns the sacking of the Spanish port of Cadiz by British privateers in the year 1596. The *Mary Rose* was one of the ships in that expedition, and the journal of her captain, Sir George Carew, "has long been known to authorities on the Anglo-Spanish war," notes *Times Literary Supplement* contributor K. R. Andrews. "The authors have done a service to students of this subject by making it more accessible in what appears to be a fairly reliable transcription." Besides the manuscript of Carew's journal, the Usherwoods' book includes a narrative and running commentary on the events related therein. Andrews criticizes the Usherwoods' book as "a rather limited and superficial treatment" because they have not attempted an analysis of the Cadiz venture, but concludes, "The graceful style of this amateur history will charm many a reader as the professional product seldom can."

BIOGRAPHICAL/CRITICAL SOURCES:

PERIODICALS

Times Literary Supplement, December 30, 1983.

*   *   *

VALLENTINE, John F(ranklin)   1931-

PERSONAL: Born August 1, 1931, in Clark County, KS; son of John Fillmore (a farmer-stockman) and Venna Irene (Wilson) Vallentine; married Bonnie Blanche Clawson, August 10, 1950; children: Dixie Lee (Mrs. Michael Davis), Cinda Grace (Mrs. Richard Richins), John Michael. *Education:* Kansas State University, B.S., 1952; Utah State University, M.S., 1953; Texas A & M University, Ph.D., 1959. *Religion:* Church of Jesus Christ of Latter-day Saints (Mormon).

ADDRESSES: Home—1081 South 700 E., Springville, UT 84663. *Office*—Department of Botany and Range Science, Brigham Young University, 425 WIDB, Provo, UT 84602.

CAREER: Utah State University, Logan, assistant professor of range science, 1958-62; University of Nebraska, North Platte, associate professor of range science, 1962-68; Brigham Young University, Provo, UT, associate professor, 1968-71, professor of range science, 1971—. Certified and accredited genealogist. *Military service:* U.S. Air Force, 1953–55; became first lieutenant.

MEMBER: Society for Range Management, American Society of Animal Science, Utah Genealogical Association (member of board of directors, 1972-78), Alpha Zeta, Sigma Xi, Xi Sigma Pi.

AWARDS, HONORS: Vocational Agriculture Service Award; Society for Range Management, Utah Section Rangeman of the Year Award, 1985, Outstanding Achievement Award, 1987.

WRITINGS:

(Editor) *Handbook for Genealogical Correspondence,* Bookcraft, 1962, 2nd edition, Everton, 1974.
Range Development and Improvements, Brigham Young University Press, 1971, 3rd edition, Academic Press, 1989.
Livelys of America, National Association of Lively Families, 1971.
Fox Family History, privately printed, 1976.
(Editor) *U.S.-Canadian Range Management, 1935-1977: A Selected Bibliography on Ranges, Pastures, Wildlife, Livestock, and Ranching,* Oryx, 1978.

Grazing Systems as a Management Tool, Utah State University, 1979.
(Co-editor) *Range Science: A Guide to Information Sources,* Gale, 1980.
Vallentine Family History, privately printed, 1980.
U.S.-Canadian Range Management, 1978-80, Oryx, 1981.
(With R. Phil Shumway and Sydney C. James) *Cattle Ranch Planning Manual,* Brigham Young University Press, 1984.
Lexington, 1884-1984: The History of a Kansas Community, Lexington Centennial Commission, 1984.
Grazing Management, Academic Press, 1990.

Contributor of chapters to *Encyclopedia of Environmental Biology;* also contributor to numerous journals, including *Journal of Range Management, Rangelands, American Genealogist, Ecology, Genealogical Journal, Genealogical Society of Pennsylvania Publications, American Hereford Journal,* and *Nebraska Quarterly.* Editor of *Genealogical Journal,* 1972-78.

*   *   *

VARDY, Steven Bela   1936-

PERSONAL: Born July 3, 1936, in Bercel, Hungary; naturalized U.S. citizen; son of Alexander (an architect) and Elizabeth (Kiss) Vardy; married Agnes M. Huszar (a professor of comparative literature), July 14, 1962; children: Attila Nicholas, Zoltan Alexander, Laura Agnes. *Education:* Attended Western Reserve University (now Case Western Reserve University), 1953-55; John Carroll University, B.S., 1959; Indiana University, M.A., 1961, Ph.D., 1967; graduate study at Kent State University, 1961, and University of Vienna, 1962-63. *Politics:* Independent. *Religion:* Roman Catholic.

ADDRESSES: Home—5740 Aylesboro Ave., Pittsburgh, PA 15217. *Office*—Department of History, Duquesne University, Pittsburgh, PA 15282.

CAREER: Washburn University, Topeka, KA, instructor in history, 1963-64; Duquesne University, Pittsburgh, PA, assistant professor, 1964-67, associate professor, 1967-71, professor of East European history, 1971—, director of history forum, 1979-83, 1990—, chairman of department of history, 1985-89. Visiting scholar at Hungarian Academy of Sciences and University of Budapest, 1969-70 and 1975-76; adjunct professor at University of Pittsburgh, 1979—; visiting professor, Institute of Shipboard Education, Semester-at-Sea program, S.S. *Universe,* 1990. Founding member of Inter-University Program on Comparative Communism, Pittsburgh, 1967—, and of Pittsburgh Center for Social History, 1985—; member of planning committee, ethnic heritage studies of western Pennsylvania, 1971—. *Military service:* Ohio National Guard, 1953-56; U.S. Army Reserve, 1956-61.

MEMBER: International Association of Southeast European Studies, International Association of Hungarian Studies (charter member), World Federation of Hungarian Historians (member of board of directors), International PEN, PEN American Branch, American Historical Association, American Association for the Advancement of Slavic Studies, American Association for the Study of Hungarian History (founding member; vice-president, 1980-81; president, 1981-83, 1993—; member of board of directors, 1983—), Hungarian Professional Association (president, 1973-75), Hungarian Cultural Foundation (vice-president, 1973-75, 1985-86; president, 1986—), American Hungarian Foundation (member of advisory council, 1974—), Arpad Academy of Arts and Sciences.

AWARDS, HONORS: Carnegie Foundation institutional grant, 1967-70; International Research and Exchanges Board (IREX) faculty fellowship, 1969-70, 1975-76, and 1982; American Hungarian Studies Foundation research grant, 1973-74; Hillman Foundation institutional grant, 1973-75; Uralic and Altaic research grant, 1979; William Penn Association grant, 1980; Hunkele Foundation grant, 1980, 1983-84, 1984-85, and 1991; two International Research and Exchanges Board (IREX) conference grants, 1980; Inner Asian and Uralic Nation Research fellowship, 1982; Duquesne University Presidential Award for excellence in scholarship, 1984; Nobel J. Dick research grant, 1984-85 and 1986-87; German American National Congress research grant, 1989; IREX cooperative research grant, 1989; joint National Endowment for the Humanities-Duquesne University research grant, 1991-92; recipient of Berzsenyi Prize, one of the most respected literary prizes of Hungary.

WRITINGS:

(With D. G. Kosary) *History of the Hungarian Nation,* Danubian Press, 1969.

Magyarsagtudomany az eszak-amerikai egyetemeken es fois kolakon (title means "Hungarian Studies at North American Colleges and Universities"), Arpad Publishers (Cleveland), 1973.

Hungarian Historiography and the "Geistesgeschichte" School, Arpad Academy (Cleveland), 1974.

Modern Hungarian Historiography, Columbia University Press, 1976.

The Development of East European Historical Studies in Hungary, Balkan Institute (Greece), 1977.

(With wife, Agnes H. Vardy) *Society in Change,* Columbia University Press, 1983.

The Hungarian-Americans, Twayne, 1985.

(With Agnes H. Vardy) *Clio's Art in Hungary and in Hungarian America,* Columbia University Press, 1985.

(With G. Grosschmid and L. S. Domonkos) *Louis the Great: King of Hungary and Poland,* Columbia University Press, 1986.

Baron Joseph Eotvos: A Literary Biography, Columbia University Press, 1987.

(With Agnes H. Vardy) *Triumph in Adversity: Studies in Hungarian Civilization,* Columbia University Press, 1988.

The Hungarian Americans: The Hungarian Experience in North America, Chelsea House, 1989.

(With Agnes H. Vardy) *The Austro-Hungarian Mind: At Home and Abroad,* Columbia University Press, 1989.

Attila, Chelsea House, 1990.

Hungarians in the New World, Kapu Publishers (Budapest), 1993.

Contributor to *Encyclopedia of World Biography, World Book Encyclopedia, Academic American Encyclopedia, Encyclopedia Americana, Grolier International Encyclopedia,* and to many international journals and newspapers in Europe and North America. Member of editorial board, *Hungarian Historical Review,* 1970-73, *Turkish Review,* 1972-73, and *Canadian-American Review of Hungarian Studies,* 1974—; editor of *Duquesne University Studies in History,* 1976—, and *Regio: Journal of Minority Studies* (Budapest), 1990—.

ADAPTATIONS: Hungarians in the New World is being filmed as a 10 to 12-part series by the Hungarian National Television.

WORK IN PROGRESS: Modern Hungarian Historiography, volume 2; *History of East Central Europe; Ottoman Turkish Impact on European Civilization; Historical Dictionary of Hungary.*

SIDELIGHTS: Steven Bela Vardy speaks German, in addition to Hungarian and English, and has reading competence in French, Turkish, Russian, classical Greek, Italian and Latin. He devotes whatever time he has left from his obligations to traveling throughout the world with his family, with the hope of writing about their experiences.

*   *   *

VAUGHN, Lewis 1950-

PERSONAL: Born December 30, 1950, in Greenville, SC; son of Lewis Avery (a carpenter) and Edith (Massengill) Vaughn; married Kathleen Patrick, August 25, 1973; children: Erin Leah; Patrick Lee. *Education:* Attended Wright State University, 1969-70; University of Dayton, B.A., 1973; Miami University, Oxford, OH, M.A., 1978.

ADDRESSES: Office—Prevention, 33 East Minor St., Emmaus, PA 18049.

CAREER: TAB Books, Blue Ridge Summit, PA, copy editor and staff writer, 1976-79; National Liberty Marketing, Frazer, PA, senior copywriter, 1979-82; *Prevention,* Emmaus, PA, senior editor, 1982-88, managing editor, 1988—.

WRITINGS:

(With Don Geary) *The How-To Book of Interior Walls,* TAB Books, 1978.

(With Geary) *The How-To Book of Floors and Ceilings,* TAB Books, 1978.

Chilton's Guide to Home Energy Savings, Chilton, 1982.

(Contributor) Debora Tkac, editor, *Exercises for Everyone,* Rodale Press, 1984.

(Contributor) Sharon Faelten, editor, *A Lifetime of Beauty,* Rodale Press, 1985.

(Editor) *Medical Care Yearbook, 1988,* Rodale Press, 1988.

(Editor) John H. Renner, *Healthsmarts: How to Spot the Quacks, Avoid the Nonsense and Get the Facts That Affect Your Health,* Health Facts Publishing, 1990.

(With Theodore Schick) *How to Think About Weird Things* (textbook), in press.

Contributor to *Prevention.*

SIDELIGHTS: Lewis Vaughn told *CA:* "Medical and health writing has got to be some of the toughest nonfiction that a writer could tackle. Being crystal clear, mastering an effective style, sidestepping the deadly hazard of dullness—this is only half the job. The harder part (which separates the stylistic whiz kids from real journalists) is getting the facts straight. And not just straight, but balanced to fulfill your responsibility to the reader and your own conscience. Maybe the whole enterprise is so difficult because health information is so complicated, so tentative, so subject to change. Whatever the reason, I have encountered precious few writers who handle the genre well."

*   *   *

VEDRAL, Joyce L(auretta) 1943-

PERSONAL: Born July 23, 1943, in Bronx, NY; daughter of David (a boxer, wrestler, and mathematician) and Martha (a communications technician; maiden name, Dash) Yellin; married Charles J. Vedral (divorced April 11, 1976); children: Marthe Simone. *Education:* City College of the City University of New York, B.S., 1970, M.A., 1973; New York University, Ph.D., 1980. *Politics:* Republican. *Religion:* Protestant.

ADDRESSES: Home—P.O. Box A 433, Wantagh, NY 11793-0433. *Office*—Department of English, Pace University—New York, Pace Plaza, New York, NY 10038.

Agent—Mel Berger, William Morris Agency, 1350 Avenue of the Americas, New York, NY 10019.

CAREER: Pace University—New York, New York City, member of faculty, 1980—; writer and lecturer.

MEMBER: National Council of Teachers of English, New York City Council of Teachers of English.

WRITINGS:

I Dare You!: How to Use Psychology to Get What You Want Out of Life, Holt, 1983.

(With Bill Reynolds, Jr.) *Supercut: Nutrition for the Ultimate Physique,* Ballantine, 1985.

(With Gladys Portugues) *Hard Bodies,* Dell, 1985.

Now or Never, Warner Books, 1986.

My Parents Are Driving Me Crazy, Ballantine, 1986.

My Teenager Is Driving Me Crazy, Ballantine, 1987.

I Can't Take It Anymore, Ballantine, 1987.

The Opposite Sex Is Driving Me Crazy, Ballantine, 1988.

The Twelve-Minute Total-Body Workout, Warner Books, 1989.

Boyfriends: Getting Them, Keeping Them, Living without Them, Ballantine, 1990.

The Fat-Burning Workout, Warner Books, 1991.

Gut Busters, Warner Books, 1992.

My Teacher Is Driving Me Crazy, Ballantine, 1992.

Get Rid of Him, Warner Books, 1993.

Teens Are Talking: The Question Game for Teens, Ballantine, 1993.

Contributor to magazines, including *Muscle and Fitness, Shape, Self, Guideposts, Christian Herald,* and *Parent Connections.*

WORK IN PROGRESS: Top Shape, a fitness guide for men who have only thirty to forty minutes, three days a week—and want to achieve the physique of athletically perfectly shaped muscles in twenty-four hour workouts—at home or in the gym.

SIDELIGHTS: Joyce L. Vedral told *CA:* "I write about fitness—physical and mental. All of my books are about empowering—the mind affects the body and the body affects the mind. I approach the problem from both directions—whichever helps first—it doesn't matter. Get in shape first and then your mind will follow, or get your mind in shape, and then your body will follow. In this sense, all roads lead to Rome!!

"My book *Get Rid of Him* is a book addressed to women who are in relationships that are draining their energy and are more trouble than they're worth. It is an inspirational book that helps to shine a light on a woman's negative relationship and to build her self-esteem so that she can leave and enjoy and respect her life alone for a while. There are chapters for every situation—from leaving a man who bores you to death to getting out of it if you're staying in it just for the money, the security or the children. The chapter, 'Fifteen ways to leave your lover' tells you how, and the chapter, 'Oh what a catch,' warns you when to throw back that 'DOGFISH,' CHAMELEON, CRAB AND BLOWFISH before you get burned. Not a man-bashing book, the book encourages women to stop blaming men and take responsibility for their own lives.

"My two bestselling bodybuilding books originated with my taking up bodybuilding. *Supercut* is a bodybuilders diet book, showing professional and amateur bodybuilders how to diet in order to achieve the best possible competitive form. More than two hundred low-fat, low-sodium recipes are included. *Hard Bodies* is a book that shows women how to sculpt their bodies through the use of weights into the most sensual possible form.

"My two latest bodyshaping books provide a solution for women, *The Fat-Burning Workout,* and men, *Gut Busters,* who want to get in shape but have only fifteen to twenty minutes four to six days a week to spare. Combined, they have sold over 3/4 million copies—my files are replete with before and after photos of men and women who rejoice that they were able to do it in twelve weeks time!!"

*   *   *

VESTLY, Anne-Cath(arina) 1920-

PERSONAL: Born February 15, 1920, in Rena, Norway; daughter of Aagot and Mentz Schulerud; married Johan Vestly. *Education:* Studied acting at Studioteatret, Oslo.

ADDRESSES: Home—Noeklesvingen 30, 0689 Oslo 6, Norway.

CAREER: Actress and writer.

CAREER: Norwegian Authors' Association, Norwegian Dramatists' Association, Association of Authors of Children's Books.

AWARDS, HONORS: Awards from Norwegian Ministry of Education, 1955, for *Ole Aleksander faar skjorte,* 1957, for *Aatte smaa, to store og en lastebil,* and 1958, for *Mormor og de aatte ungene i skogen;* Peer Gynt Prize, 1980; award from Norwegian Cultural Department, 1982; Teskjekjerring honour prize, 1986; Sofus Media Prize, 1987; Save the Children—Rainbow Prize, 1989; Culture Prize, Oslo, 1990; Paul Robeson Prize, Anti-Racist Center, 1990; knight of honour order, Artists Association, 1991; Spelemann Prize, 1992, for tape recording; knight of first class, St. Olav Order, 1992; has received numerous other Norwegian prizes and awards.

WRITINGS:

BOOKS FOR CHILDREN

Barnas store sangbok (title means "Children's Big Songbook"), J. W. Cappelen, 1962.

Lillebror og knerten (title means "Lillebror and 'Rooty' "), Tiden Norsk Forlag, 1962.

Lilla Olaug og Lubben (title means "Lilla Olaug and Lubben"), Tiden Norsk Forlag, 1982.

Lappeteppe fra en barndom (title means "Patchwork from a Childhood"), Tiden Norsk Forlag, 1990.

Ellen Andrea og Mormor (title means "Ellen Andrea and Grandma"), Tiden Norsk Forlag, 1992.

"OLE ALEKSANDER" SERIES

Ole Aleksander Fili-bom-bom-bom, Tiden Norsk Forlag, 1953.

Ole Aleksander paa farten (title means "Ole Aleksander on the Run"), Tiden Norsk Forlag, 1954.

Ole Aleksander far skjorte (title means "Ole Aleksander Has a Shirt"), Tiden Norsk Forlag, 1955.

Ole Aleksander og Bestemor til vaers (title means "Ole Aleksander and Grandmother in the Air"), Tiden Norsk Forlag, 1956.

Ole Aleksander paa flyttefot (title means "Ole Aleksander Moves the House"), Tiden Norsk Forlag, 1958.

"EIGHT CHILDREN" SERIES

Aatte smaa, to store og en lastebil, Tiden Norsk Forlag, 1957, translation published as *Eight Children and a Truck,* Methuen, 1973.

Mormor og de atte ungene i skogen, Tiden Norsk Forlag, 1958, translation by Patricia Crampton published as *Eight Children in the House,* Methuen, 1974.

Marte og mormor og mormor og Morten, Tiden Norsk Forlag, 1959, translation published as *Eight Children in Winter,* Methuen, 1975.

En liten takk fra Anton, Tiden Norsk Forlag, 1960, translation published as *Eight Children and Rosie,* Methuen, 1977.

Mormors promenade, Tiden Norsk Forlag, 1961, translation published as *Eight Children and a Bulldozer,* Methuen, 1979.

"KNERTEN" SERIES

Trofaste Knerten (title means "Faithful Knerten"), Tiden Norsk Forlag, 1963.

Knerten gifter seg (title means "Knerten Marries"), Tiden Norsk Forlag, 1964.

Knerten i Bessby (title means "Knerten in Bessby"), Tiden Norsk Forlag, 1965.

Knerten og Forundringskpakken (title means "Knerten and the Surprise Packet"), Tiden Norsk Forlag, 1973.

Knerten paa sykkeltur (title means "Knerten on the Bicycle Tour"), Tiden Norsk Forlag, 1974.

"AURORA" SERIES

Aurora i blokk z, Tiden Norsk Forlag, 1966, translation by Eileen Amos published as *Hallo Aurora!,* Longman Young Books, 1973, adaptation by Jane Fairfax published as *Hello, Aurora,* Crowell, 1974.

Aurora og pappa (title means "Aurora and Daddy"), Tiden Norsk Forlag, 1967.

Aurora og den vesle blaa bilen, Tiden Norsk Forlag, 1968, translation published as *Aurora and the Little Blue Car,* Longman, 1974.

Aurora og Sokrates, Tiden Norsk Forlag, 1969, translation published as *Aurora and Socrates,* Crowell, 1973.

Aurora i Holland, Tiden Norsk Forlag, 1970, translation published as *Aurora in Holland,* Kestrel, 1976.

Aurora paa burtigruten (title means "Aurora on the Express Liner"), Tiden Norsk Forlag, 1971.

Aurora fra Fabelvik (title means "Aurora from Fabelvik"), Tiden Norsk Forlag, 1972.

"GURO" SERIES

Guro, Tiden Norsk Forlag, 1975.

Guro og nokkerosene (title means "Guro and the Water Lilies"), Tiden Norsk Forlag, 1976.

Guro alene hjemme (title means "Guro Alone at Home"), Tiden Norsk Forlag, 1977.

Guro og fiolinen (title means "Guro and the Violin"), Tiden Norsk Forlag, 1978.

Guro og Lille-Bjorn (title means "Guro and Little Bjorn"), Tiden Norsk Forlag, 1979.

Guro pa Tirilltoppen (title means "Guro on the Tirillhill"), Tiden Norsk Forlag, 1980.

Guro og Frydefoniorkestret (title means "Guro and the Joy/Delight Orchestra"), Tiden Norsk Forlag, 1981.

"KAOS" SERIES

Kaos og Bjornar (title means "Chaos and Bjoernar"), Tiden Norsk Forlag, 1982.

Kaos-gutten i Vetleby og verden (title means "Chaos-boy in Little-village and the World"), Tiden Norsk Forlag, 1984.

Kaos foerskolegutt (title means "Chaos in Nursery School"), Tiden Norsk Forlag, 1985.

Kaos og hemmeligheten (title means "Chaos and the Secret"), Tiden Norsk Forlag, 1987.

PLAYS

Huset i skogen (title means "The House in the Woods"), 1960.

Ut av Trolldommen (title means "Out of the Witchery"), 1965.

Den vesle kloden (title means "The Little Globe"), 1969.

Heksen Innmaria og Frankogfri (title means "The Wish Nasty and Frankandfree"), 1990.

OTHER

Also author of puppet shows, *Nyfoedt-Andersen, Rampegutt,* and *Rabbleboy,* 1970.

ADAPTATIONS: Several books in the "Eight Children" series have been adapted for film, with Vestly in the role of Grandma.

SIDELIGHTS: Anne-Cath Vestly's books have been translated and published in the United States, England, Denmark, Finland, Iceland, Sweden, Germany, Switzerland, France, Holland, Poland, and the Soviet Union. She told *CA:* "After [working] five years at a theatre, Studioteatret, I discovered that I wanted to write about people instead of playing them. But I still like the combination of writing and performing my own manuscripts as I can do in radio and television.

"Many people ask me why I write for children. Well, I like to write for all people as long as I can get my thoughts down on paper. I take it as a compliment when [children] identify themselves with the persons I write about. It seems to me, however, that people at all ages are receptive and enjoy reading what is called books for children. To be sure, they are welcome! Because in this way, children and grown-up people can get something in common."

*   *   *

von BAEYER, Hans Christian   1938-

PERSONAL: Born April 6, 1938, in Berlin, Germany; son of Hans Jakob (an engineer) and Renate (a social worker; maiden name, Freudenberg) von Baeyer; married Beatrice Beutel, February 22, 1961 (divorced, 1981); married Barbara Ann Watkinson (an art historian), January 8, 1983; children: (first marriage) Hans Christopher, Melissa Andrea; (second marriage) Madelynn, Lili. *Education:* Columbia University, A.B., 1958; University of Miami, Coral Gables, FL, M.Sc., 1961; Vanderbilt University, Ph.D., 1964. *Religion:* Unitarian/Universalist. *Avocational interests:* Running (especially ten-kilometer races).

ADDRESSES: Home—802 Jamestown Rd., Williamsburg, VA 23185. *Office*—Department of Physics, College of William and Mary, Williamsburg, VA 23185. *Agent*—Beth Vesel, Sanford J. Greenburger Associates, Inc., 55 Fifth Ave., New York, NY 10003.

CAREER: McGill University, Montreal, Quebec, assistant professor of physics, 1964-68; College of William and Mary, Williamsburg, VA, assistant professor, 1971-75, professor of physics, 1975—, chairman of department,

1972-78, director of Virginia Associated Research Campus, 1979-85. Visiting scientist at Deutsches Elektronen-Synchrotron, Hamburg, Germany, 1966, and Simon Fraser University, 1978-79.

MEMBER: American Physical Society (fellow; chairman of executive committee of southeastern section), Federation of American Scientists, American Association of University Professors, American Association of Physics Teachers, Southern Universities Research Association (fellow), Phi Beta Kappa.

AWARDS, HONORS: Science writing award from American Institute of Physics, 1979, for "The Wonder of Gravity," a birthday tribute to Albert Einstein; honorable mention from New York Academy of Sciences, 1985, for *Rainbows, Snowflakes, and Quarks: Physics and the World Around Us;* science writing award, American Association for the Advancement of Science, 1990; Emmy Award, 1991, for *The Quantum Universe.*

WRITINGS:

Rainbows, Snowflakes, and Quarks: Physics and the World Around Us, McGraw, 1984.
The Quantum Universe (television documentary), Public Broadcasting System, 1991.

Taming the Atom: The Emergence of the Visible Microworld, Random House, 1992.
The Fermi Solution: Essays in Science, Random House, 1993.

Author of "Physika," a column in the *Sciences,* a bimonthly publication of the New York Academy of Sciences. Contributor of articles to *Discover* and *Readers Digest.* Contributing editor of the *Sciences.*

SIDELIGHTS: Hans Christian von Baeyer wrote *CA:* "Communicating science to the public is my responsibility as a scientist, as well as my avocation. In return for the privilege of pursuing scientific research without the imposition of any direction, I believe that we scientists have a serious and universal obligation to society to translate what we are doing into common language, but I think most scientists disagree with me. The problem I am wrestling with is how to make science into a STORY—not a story about scientists, not a history, not science fiction, but a scientific STORY, with all the trappings of that genre. It can be done with nature study, it can be done with medicine, it can be done with paleontology, because those have human interest at their cores. But can it be done with physics? I don't know."

W

WAGNER, Ray(mond) David 1924-

PERSONAL: Born February 29, 1924, in Philadelphia, PA; son of James and Ethel (Shreiber) Wagner; married Beatrice Walsh, 1952 (divorced, 1965); married Mary Davidson, 1967; children: (first marriage) Roger; (second marriage) Wendy, David. *Education:* University of Pennsylvania, B.S., 1953, M.S., 1955; San Diego State College (now University), additional study.

ADDRESSES: Home—5865 Estelle St., San Diego, CA 92115. *Office*—San Diego Aerospace Museum, 2001 Pan American Plaza, San Diego, CA 92101.

CAREER: Crawford High School, San Diego, CA, history teacher, 1957-84; San Diego Aerospace Museum, San Diego, archivist, 1985—.

MEMBER: American Aviation Historical Society, San Diego Teachers Association.

WRITINGS:

American Combat Planes, Hanover House, 1960, revised edition, Doubleday, 1968.
North American Sabre, Macdonald & Co., 1963.
(With Heinz Nowarra) *German Combat Planes,* Doubleday, 1971.
(Editor) *Soviet Air Force in World War II,* Doubleday, 1973.
American Combat Planes since 1917, Doubleday, 1980, enlarged edition published as *American Combat Planes,* 1982.
(With Meyers Jacobsen) *B-36 in Action,* Squadron Signal, 1980.
(Co-author) *The History of U.S. Naval Air Power,* Military Press, 1984.
Liberator: 50th Anniversary of the B-24, San Diego Aerospace Museum, 1989.

Mustang Designer: Edgar Schmued and the Development of the P-51, Orion, 1990.

WORK IN PROGRESS: Research on military aircraft history in America and abroad.

BIOGRAPHICAL/CRITICAL SOURCES:

PERIODICALS

San Diego Evening Tribune, February 21, 1961.

*   *   *

WALDROP, Howard 1946-

PERSONAL: Born September 15, 1946, in Houston, MS; son of Raymond Evans (an aircraft worker) and Zora Vee (a waitress; maiden name, Morris) Waldrop. *Education:* Attended University of Texas at Arlington, 1965-70 and 1972-74.

ADDRESSES: Home and office—P.O. Box 49335, Austin, TX 78765. *Agent*—Joseph Elder, Joseph Elder Agency, P.O. Box 298, Warwick, NY 10990.

CAREER: Free-lance writer, 1972—. Dynastat, Inc., Austin, TX, auditory researcher, 1975-80. *Military service:* U.S. Army, 1970-72.

MEMBER: Science Fiction Writers of America, Trout Unlimited.

AWARDS, HONORS: Nebula Award from Science Fiction Writers of America, 1980, and World Fantasy Award from World Fantasy Society, 1981, both for "The Ugly Chickens."

WRITINGS:

(With Jake Saunders) *The Texas-Israeli War: 1999* (science fiction novel), Ballantine, 1974.

Them Bones (science fiction novel), Ace Books, 1984, re-printed in hardcover by Zeising Books, 1989.

Howard Who? (stories; includes "The Ugly Chickens;" also see below), Doubleday, 1986.

All about Strange Monsters of the Recent Past (stories; also see below), Ursus, 1987.

Strange Things in Close-Up (contains *Howard Who?* and *All about Strange Monsters of the Recent Past*), Legends, 1989.

A Dozen Tough Jobs (novella; also see below), Zeising Books, 1989.

Night of the Cooters (stories), Ursus/Zeising Books, 1991, revised edition (includes *A Dozen Tough Jobs*), Ace Books, 1993.

You Could Go Home Again (novella) Cheap Street, 1993.

WORK IN PROGRESS: Two novels: *I, John Mandeville* and *The Moon World.*

SIDELIGHTS: Though he is characterized as an author of science fiction, Howard Waldrop is more likely to explore the possible past than the distant future. Many of Waldrop's most popular stories are tales of what would have happened if history had turned out differently. In his Nebula- and World Fantasy award-winning "The Ugly Chickens," for example, a scientist discovers that dodo birds, long thought extinct, were being raised for food on a Mississippi farm. "Since recollection and science . . . are inevitably man-made distortions of the Truth," notes Richard Gehr in the *Voice Literary Supplement,* "Waldrop forces those alterations to the edges of believability, fabricating *better* alternate histories for his and our pleasure."

The believability of Waldrop's histories are a reflection of the exhaustive research the author puts into each story, enabling him to layer his fables with rich detail. This same detail, however, has made some of Waldrop's stories somewhat intimidating. For the reader to find the clues and get the jokes planted within the narrative, he often must have working knowledge of the time period. As Gehr points out: "Interdisciplinarianism isn't required, but it sure helps." "Waldrop's densely-imagined and erudite stories have rather oddly gotten the reputation of being caviar for the general. . . . ," says the *Washington Post Book World*'s Gregory Feeley. "In fact he is caviar for the masses, and deserves a wider audience than he has hitherto found."

It is not surprising that Waldrop's name goes largely unrecognized, even among science fiction enthusiasts—after all, he has produced only a handful of books since 1974, and most of those in limited editions. Still, Gehr explains that as "a free agent, Waldrop writes with the unconstricted pleasure of the nonaligned autodidact, and as such he steadily, weirdly, and affectionately breaks and remakes the promises inscribed in the history of ideas." This freedom has consistently paid off, for, as Karen Joy Fowler says in the *Washington Post Book World,* "Waldrop is one of sf's most dependably surprising writers."

Waldrop once told *CA:* "I fish and help my friends move to new apartments. I am interested in books, movies, dancing, rock and roll (what's left of it), and all the stuff my stories are about. If it were possible to make a living writing short stories, that's all I would do."

BIOGRAPHICAL/CRITICAL SOURCES:

BOOKS

Lane, Daryl, William Vernon, and David Carson, editors, *The Sounds of Wonder: Interviews from the Science Fiction Radio Show,* Volume I, Oryx, 1985.

PERIODICALS

Observer, December 17, 1989, p. 46.
Voice Literary Supplement, August, 1989, p. 19.
Washington Post Book World, February 24, 1991, p. 8; October 29, 1991, p. 8.

*   *   *

WALSH, Marcus 1947-

PERSONAL: Born October 28, 1947, in Leeds, England; son of Leslie (a physician) and Janie B. (Keidan) Walsh; married A. Wendy Perkins (a university lecturer), September 6, 1979. *Education:* University of Toronto, Ph.D., 1975.

ADDRESSES: Office—School of English, University of Birmingham, Birmingham B15 2TT, England.

CAREER: University of Birmingham, Birmingham, England, lecturer in English, 1975-89; senior lecturer, 1989—.

MEMBER: British Society for Eighteenth-Century Studies.

WRITINGS:

EDITOR

Christopher Smart: Selected Poems, Carcanet Press, 1979.
John Gay: Selected Poems, Carcanet Press, 1979.
The Poetical Works of Christopher Smart, Oxford University Press, Volume 2 (with Karina Williamson), 1983, Volume 3, 1987.
(With Ian Small) *The Theory and Practice of Test Editing,* Cambridge University Press, 1992.

OTHER

Also contributor of essays to scholarly journals, including *The Library, English Studies, Milton Quarterly, Modern*

Language Review, British Journal for Eighteenth-Century Studies, and *Essays in Criticism.*

WORK IN PROGRESS: Research on theories of meaning and literary editing in the seventeenth and eighteenth centuries.

SIDELIGHTS: Marcus Walsh told *CA:* "For most of my academic career I have been an editor, concerned in practice more with exegesis, annotation, and contextual research than with textual criticism. My interest in [Christopher] Smart began with a commission from Michael Schmidt to produce a brief *Selected Poems* for student use and has developed into a considerable involvement in the full Oxford English texts: *The Poetical Works of Christopher Smart.* My co-editor Karina Williamson and I hope that our work has made Smart's poetry more accessible and comprehensible to a much wider audience.

"I am currently working towards completion of a book on the early development of the practice and theory of literary editing, especially of Milton and Shakespeare, in the eighteenth century, with a special interest in the theories of text and meaning that underpin the work of the first editors.

"I am a convinced believer in the value of literature as a medium which communicates between people and between times, and I am persuaded that literary texts contain determinate meanings, the explication of which is the central task of the teacher and scholar.

"I feel most indebted to the published theory and scholarship of R. S. Crane, M. H. Abrams, Alastair Fowler, and, most especially, E. D. Hirsch, Jr."

*   *   *

WANG Zhongshu 1925-

PERSONAL: Given name also transliterated as "Chungshu"; born October 15, 1925, in Ningbo, Zhejiang Province, China; son of Xuanbing (a teacher) and Sujuan (Ling) Wang; married Chen Kai (a professor), July 15, 1960; children: Jianzhi. *Education:* Graduated from Beijing University, 1950. *Politics:* Member of Communist Party of China.

ADDRESSES: Home—1-2-602 Chang Yun Gong, Zi Zhu Yuan, Beijing 100044, China. *Office*—Institute of Archaeology, Chinese Academy of Social Sciences, 27 Wangfujing Dajie, Beijing 100710, China.

CAREER: Chinese Academy of Sciences, Institute of Archaeology, Beijing, China, training researcher, 1950-52, associate researcher, 1952-79; Chinese Academy of Social Sciences, Institute of Archaeology, Beijing, deputy direc-

tor, 1978-82, senior fellow, 1979—, vice-chairman of scientific committee, 1979-82, chairman of scientific committee, 1982-88, 1992—, director, 1982-88, professor and instructor in archaeology department of Graduate School, 1982—. National University of San Antonio Abad, Cuzco, Peru, honorary professor, May, 1973; German Archaeological Institute, correspondent fellow, March, 1988.

MEMBER: Chinese Society of Archaeology (general secretary, 1979-88), Japanese Society of Asian History (member of standing council, 1990—).

WRITINGS:

Han Civilization, translation by K. C. Chang and others, Yale University Press, 1982.
An Outline of Archaeology of the Han Period, Zhong Hua Book Co. (Beijing), 1984.
Triangular-Rimmed Bronze Mirrors with Mythical Figure and Animal Designs Unearthed from Japan, Gakuseisha Press (Tokyo), 1992.
Ancient Japan Seen from China, Gakuseisha Press, 1992.

Contributor of articles on archaeology to scholarly journals, including *Kaogu* (title means "Archaeology"), *Kaogu Xuebao,* and *Acta Archaeologica Sinica.*

WORK IN PROGRESS: Articles on Chinese and Japanese archaeology for archaeology journals.

SIDELIGHTS: Wang Zhongshu's book *Han Civilization* is an account of the Han dynasty of China which ruled from 202 B.C. to 220 A.D. From an archaeological perspective, the author examines developments in agriculture and city planning, relating them to excavation data and various artifacts. *Times Literary Supplement* critic William Watson describes the book as "beautifully illustrated" and written with "unswerving objectivity." He further applauds it as "the fullest one-volume account of the [Han] period superior to anything produced in the [People's] Republic [of China] itself."

Wang once told *CA:* "I have long engaged in the archaeology of the Han Dynasty of China and am interested in the archaeology of Japan as well. I would like to bring to light the close cultural relationships between China and Japan in ancient times, taking all available archaeological data as a basis of research."

BIOGRAPHICAL/CRITICAL SOURCES:

PERIODICALS

Times Literary Supplement, June 24, 1983.

WATSON, Jean 1936-

PERSONAL: Born March 18, 1936, in Tachu, Szechuan, China; daughter of William Hugh C. (a minister and missionary) and Lilian Alice (a missionary; maiden name, Wilden) Simmonds; married Michael John MacLaren Watson (in sales and engineering), June 8, 1963; children: Malcolm MacLaren, Rachel Joy, Esther Jean. *Education:* University of London, B.A., 1957; University of Birmingham, certificate in education, 1958. *Religion:* Church of England.

ADDRESSES: Home and office—33 Braeside Ave., Sevenoaks, Kent TN13 2JJ, England.

CAREER: High school teacher of English and history in Wolverhampton, England, 1958-61; Cassell & Co., London, England, educational editor, 1961-63; teacher at primary school in Kent, England, 1963-64; writer, 1965—; River Green Playgroup (for pre-schoolers), Kent, supervisor, 1967-75.

WRITINGS:

The Pilgrim's Progress: Retold in Modern English from the Original Story by John Bunyan, Scripture Union, 1978, published as *The Family Pilgrim's Progress: From the Original Story by John Bunyan,* Scripture Union/Tyndale, 1983.
See All the Things We Share (juvenile), Lion Publishing, 1979.
The Kingdom That God Builds, Lion Publishing, 1979.
The Princess and the Goblin [and] *The Princess and Curdie* (abridgements of stories by George Macdonald), Scripture Union, 1979.
The Day the Robbers Came, Lion Publishing, 1980.
Sounds, Sounds, All Around, Lion Publishing, 1981.
The Lost Princess, The Golden Key and Other Stories [and] *At the Back of the North Wind* (abridgements of stories by Macdonald), Scripture Union, 1981.
Corrie: Watchmaker's Daughter, Kingsway, 1982, published as *Watchmaker's Daughter,* Fleming Revell, 1982.
Through the Year with David Watson (devotional readings), Hodder & Stoughton, 1982, published as *Grow and Flourish: A Daily Guide to Personal Renewal,* Harold Shaw, 1982.
Happy Families: Bringing Up Children in a Christian Home, Hodder & Stoughton, 1983.
(With Rhona Prime) *Time of Trial: The Personal Story behind the Cheltenham Spy Scandal,* Hodder & Stoughton, 1984.
Play Is Great, Grandreams Ltd., 1984.
Through the Year with J. I. Packer (devotional readings), Hodder & Stoughton, 1986, published as *Your Father Loves You,* Harold Shaw, 1986.

The Prayer Adventure (devotional readings), Highland Books, 1989.
(With Jenny Davis) *Rescued by Love,* Hodder & Stoughton, 1991.
Our New Grandchild, Lion Publishing, 1993.

"IN TIMES OF" SERIES

In Times of Success, Scripture Union, 1979.
In Times of Sorrow, Scripture Union, 1979.
In Times of Need, Scripture Union, 1979.
In Times of Joy, Scripture Union, 1979.
In Times of Growth, Scripture Union, 1979.
In Times of Doubt, Scripture Union, 1979.
In Times of Courage, Scripture Union, 1979.
In Times of Change, Scripture Union, 1979.

"ALOT" SERIES

Fred Fear-Alot, Scripture Union, 1980.
Humphrey Hope-Alot, Scripture Union, 1980.
Magnus Think-Alot, Scripture Union, 1980.
Martha Do-Alot, Scripture Union, 1980.
Grant Grab-Alot, Scripture Union, 1980.
Desmond Dither-Alot, Scripture Union, 1980.
Harriet Help-Alot, Scripture Union, 1980.
Lucy Laugh-Alot, Scripture Union, 1980.
Kitty Cry-Alot, Scripture Union, 1980.
Lottie Lie-Alot, Scripture Union, 1980.

"MEET THE SAMUEL FAMILY" SERIES

Meet the Samuel Family: Martha's Busy Morning, Lion Publishing, 1980.
Meet the Samuel Family: Dan the Shepherd, Lion Publishing, 1980.
Meet the Samuel Family: Martha Is Afraid of the Dark, Lion Publishing, 1980.
Meet the Samuel Family: Matthew Goes to Market, Lion Publishing, 1980.

"I WONDER ABOUT" SERIES

I Wonder about Me, Lion Publishing, 1983.
I Wonder about Plants, Lion Publishing, 1983.
I Wonder about Farm Animals, Lion Publishing, 1983.
I Wonder about Zoo Animals, Lion Publishing, 1983.

OTHER

Also author of stories for *Listen with Mother,* BBC Radio, 1967—, of script outlines and ideas for *Playschool,* BBC-TV, 1970—, *The Sunday Gang,* BBC-TV, 1977, and *Playaway,* BBC-TV, 1981, and of sixty installments of a fictional story for weekly newspaper *Christian Herald,* 1988. Author of worship and teaching material for use in churches, including songs, cassettes, coloring book stories, and services, 1970-88. Contributor to books, including *A Way with Words: A Handbook for Christian Writers,* edited by Edward England, Highland Books, 1984. Also contributor of stories to books, including "A Goose Called Fred," published in *Storytime from Playschool,* BBC/Piccolo, 1974; "The Junk Shop," published in *Stories for Bedtime,* Collins, 1975; "Play Is Great," published in *More Stories for Playschool,* BBC/Piccolo, 1976; "May Queen" and "The Angry Giant," published in *All the Year Round,* Evans, 1980; and "Kindhearted Jack" and "Where Can I Sleep?," published in *Playschool Stories,* BBC/Knight, 1982. Contributor to newspapers and magazines, including *Church of England Newspaper* and *Christian Woman* (now *Woman Alive*).

WORK IN PROGRESS: Children's stories and other fiction.

SIDELIGHTS: Jean Watson once told *CA:* "I regard writing as a calling and myself as apprenticed to the craft. This involves working hard on my raw materials, which are *myself* (who I am and all the experiences, thoughts, feelings and ideas which have helped to shape me), *life* (where I am—my circumstances, what I do and the people I meet each day), and *words* (what I say/write and how I say/write it). Keeping personal journals which record events, conversations (actual or imaginary), thoughts, feelings, ideas and description/character sketches of actual or imagined places/people helps to develop awareness, imagination, ideas and writing skills.

"I believe that writing which brings healing and sheds light, must be characterized by truth and love. As far as I am concerned, true love and the truth about the human situation impinge on the truth about God—his character, ways, and plans. I would like to avoid what J. B. Phillips accuses the modern writer of doing: though having 'few reticences' and being 'sometimes almost morbidly analytical of his character's actions,' he frequently uses 'the bypass road round the whole sphere of man's relations with God.' "

*   *   *

WATTS, Thomas D(ale) 1941-

PERSONAL: Born September 19, 1941, in Hattiesburg, MS; son of D. (a paint contractor) and Martina C. (in sales; maiden name, Landwehr) Watts; married Ilene M. Peters, November 28, 1970; children: Rebecca, Jeanine. *Education:* Wichita State University, B.A., 1963; Arizona State University, M.S.W., 1970; Tulane University, D.S.W., 1976. *Politics:* Democrat. *Religion:* Roman Catholic.

ADDRESSES: Home—1108 Briarwood Blvd., Arlington, TX 76013-1509. *Office*—School of Social Work, University of Texas at Arlington, Arlington, TX 76019-0129.

CAREER: Associated with St. Vincent School for Boys, San Rafael, CA, 1966-67; Arizona State Department of Public Welfare, Phoenix, medical social work supervisor and consultant, 1970-72; member of faculty of University of Texas at Arlington School of Social Work, 1974—, chairperson of Social Welfare Policy and Service Sequence, 1979-88. Member of Council on Social Work Education. Chairperson of Texas voting precinct 2181, 1978—.

MEMBER: International Association of Schools of Social Work, Council on Social Work Education, Bread for the World.

WRITINGS:

The Societal Learning Approach: A New Approach to Social Welfare Policy and Planning in America, Century Twenty One, 1981.
(With Roosevelt Wright, Jr., Dennis Saleebey, and Pedro J. Lecca) *Transcultural Perspectives in the Human Services,* C. C Thomas, 1983.
(With Lecca) *Pathways for Minorities into the Health Professions,* University Press of America, 1989.
(With Lecca) *Preschoolers and Substance Abuse: Strategies for Prevention and Intervention,* Haworth Press, 1993.

EDITOR

(With Wright) *Black Alcoholism: Toward a Comprehensive Understanding,* C. C Thomas, 1983.
(With Wright) *Prevention of Black Alcoholism: Issues and Strategies,* C. C Thomas, 1985.
Social Thought on Alcoholism: A Comprehensive Review, Robert E. Krieger, 1986.
(With Wright) *Black Alcohol Abuse and Alcoholism: An Annotated Bibliography,* Praeger, 1986.
(With Michael L. Lobb) *Native American Youth and Alcohol: An Annotated Bibliography,* Greenwood Press, 1989.
(With Wright) *Alcoholism in Minority Populations,* C. C Thomas, 1989.
(With Wright) *Alcohol Problems of Minority Youth in America,* Edwin Mellen, 1989.
(With Doreen Elliott and Nazneen S. Mayadas) *The World of Social Welfare: Social Welfare and Services in an International Context,* C. C Thomas, 1990.
(With Raymond Sanchez Mayers and Barbara L. Kail) *Hispanic Substance Abuse,* C. C Thomas, in press.

OTHER

Contributor to numerous books, including *Training in the Human Services,* Volume 2, edited by Richard L. Edwards and Thomas D. Morton, Office of Continuing Social Work Education, School of Social Work, University of Tennessee at Knoxville, 1980; *Guidelines for Developing Mental Health and Minority Aging Curriculum with a*

Focus on Self-Help Groups, edited by John S. McNeil and Shirley Wesley King, Graduate School of Social Work, University of Texas at Arlington, 1984; and *Proceedings of the First Annual Ethnic Minorities and Gender Conference: Implications for Social Practitioners,* edited by Alfred A. Jarrett and King, Graduate School of Social Work, University of Texas at Arlington, 1990. Contributor to numerous periodicals, including *International Quarterly of Community Health Education, International Journal of the Addictions, Social Justice Review, New Studies in Athletics, Journal of Social Welfare, Journal of Drug Issues,* and *Journal of Religious Thought.*

SIDELIGHTS: Thomas D. Watts once told *CA:* "I have a long-term interest in social thought and social welfare. This interest gets translated in most all of the work I have done. My interest in social thought on alcohol and on alcoholism centers on the important role that social thinking on alcohol and alcoholism has played in the history of social thought, and its impact on society and social welfare.

"I have been interested in recent years in social thought on the welfare state. One particular aspect of this topic that interests me is the growing challenge to the welfare state of an increasing number of people (the aged and others) who do need the support of the welfare state in various ways. The welfare state as we have understood it faces a present and future challenge that is enormous and complex. How do people feel or think about this? What should be done? Ultimately, we must come to grips with what it is we want in a welfare state (or whether we even want a welfare state), with what the welfare state is and is not capable of doing, and how society will be caring for the numerous large (and ever-growing) number of people who need such care."

* * *

WEARING, J. P.

PERSONAL: Born in Birmingham, England; came to the United States in 1974, naturalized citizen. *Education:* University of Wales, B.A., 1967, Ph.D., 1971; University of Saskatchewan, M.A., 1968.

ADDRESSES: Office—Department of English, University of Arizona, Tucson, AZ 85721.

CAREER: University of Alberta, Edmonton, lecturer in English, 1971-74; University of Arizona, Tucson, assistant professor, 1974-77, associate professor, 1977-84, professor of English, 1984—. Theatre critic on CKUA-Radio, 1973-74.

MEMBER: Society for Theatre Research (England).

AWARDS, HONORS: Izaac Walton Killam Memorial Fellowship, University of Alberta, 1971-73; Guggenheim fellowship, 1978-79; National Endowment for the Humanities grant, 1987-91.

WRITINGS:

(Editor) *Collected Letters of Sir Arthur Pinero,* University of Minnesota Press, 1974.
(With L. W. Connolly) *English Drama and Theatre, 1800-1900,* Gale, 1978.
American and British Theatrical Biography: A Directory, Scarecrow, 1979.
G. B. Shaw: An Annotated Bibliography of Writings about Him, Volume 1: *1871-1930,* Northern Illinois University Press, 1986.

"THE LONDON STAGE" SERIES

The London Stage, 1890-1899: A Calendar of Plays and Players, two volumes and index, Scarecrow, 1976.
The London Stage, 1900-1909: A Calendar of Plays and Players, two volumes, Scarecrow, 1981.
The London Stage, 1910-1919: A Calendar of Plays and Players, two volumes, Scarecrow, 1982.
The London Stage, 1920-1929: A Calendar of Plays and Players, three volumes and index, Scarecrow, 1984.
The London Stage, 1930-1939: A Calendar of Plays and Players, three volumes and index, Scarecrow, 1990.
The London Stage, 1940-1949: A Calendar of Plays and Players, two volumes, Scarecrow, 1991.

OTHER

Contributor to literature and theatre journals. Editor of *Nineteenth-Century Theatre Research,* 1973-86.

WORK IN PROGRESS: The London Stage, 1950-1959.

SIDELIGHTS: J. P. Wearing once told *CA,* "My main ambition is to complete the calendar of plays and players on the London stage from 1890 to the end of 1999, which I hope will rank as one of the major scholarly works in English theatre history."

BIOGRAPHICAL/CRITICAL SOURCES:

PERIODICALS

Times Literary Supplement, September 2, 1983.

* * *

WHITE, Jude Gilliam 1947-
(Jude Deveraux)

PERSONAL: Born September 20, 1947, in Louisville, KY; daughter of Harold J. (an electrician) and Virginia (Berry) Gilliam; married Richard G. Sides, February 4, 1967 (divorced February, 1969); married Claude B. White (a contractor), June 3, 1970. *Education:* Murray State University, B.S., 1970; College of Santa Fe, teaching certificate, 1973; University of New Mexico, remedial reading certificate, 1976. *Avocational interests:* Body building, costume history.

ADDRESSES: Home—Route 9, Box 53JW, Santa Fe, NM 87505.

CAREER: Writer. Worked as an elementary school teacher, Santa Fe, NM, 1973-77.

MEMBER: Romance Writers of America, Costume Society of America.

WRITINGS:

ROMANCE NOVELS; AS JUDE DEVERAUX

The Enchanted Land, Avon, 1978.
The Black Lyon, Avon, 1980.
The Velvet Promise, Pocket Books, 1981.
Casa Grande, Avon, 1982.
Highland Velvet, Pocket Books, 1982.
Velvet Song, Pocket Books, 1983.
Velvet Angel, Pocket Books, 1983.
Sweetbriar, Pocket Books, 1983.
Counterfeit Lady (first book of "James River" trilogy), Pocket Books, 1984.
Lost Lady (second book of "James River" trilogy), Pocket Books, 1985.
River Lady (third book of "James River" trilogy), Pocket Books, 1985.
Twin of Ice, Pocket Books, 1985.
Twin of Fire, Pocket Books, 1985.
The Temptress, Pocket Books, 1986.
The Raider, Pocket Books, 1987.
The Princess, Pocket Books, 1987.
The Maiden, Pocket Books, 1988.
The Awakening, Pocket Books, 1988.
The Taming, Pocket Books, 1989.
A Knight in Shining Armor, Simon & Schuster, 1990.
Wishes, Pocket Books, 1990.
Mountain Laurel, Pocket Books, 1990.
The Conquest, Pocket Books, 1991.
The Duchess, Pocket Books, 1991.
Eternity, Pocket Books, 1992.
Sweet Liar, Pocket Books, 1992.
The Invitation, Pocket Books, 1993.

WORK IN PROGRESS: A romance novel.

SIDELIGHTS: Jude Deveraux is the pseudonym for Jude Gilliam White, a prolific author who has seen several of her popular romance novels on the *New York Times* best seller list. White once told *CA* that she started writing because she was tired of reading what she terms "rape sagas." "I was tired of women who hid behind some granite-cheeked, taciturn man who fought off villains and later threw her on a bed," explained White. "I wanted to write about women who had some power, who could create things, could make things happen.

"I consider myself a feminist, a believer in equality between men and women," she continued. "Although some people say it's a contradiction in terms to be a feminist and a romantic, I am both. I believe in the family, in love between men and women but not in a love where the man gives all the orders and the woman meekly stands by and obeys. It must be a relationship of give and take."

Within the realm of fantasy fiction, White feels strongly that writers of the romance genre are treated with relatively little respect. "Depending on the section of the country, romance novels comprise forty-five to fifty-five percent of all sales. In spite of romances being the backbone and most of the muscle of the publishing industry, romance writers are not respected, either by the media or the public," she contends. "Personally, I've had many people say, 'I thought you were a *real* writer.' The media seems to think romances are easier than other novels, do not require the discipline other novelists must have, or the work. . . . All the romance writers I have met are hard-working women, with a firm grasp of what goes into making a good story, and above all, a strong sense of self discipline. In other words, they have all the qualities that go into making a good writer."

BIOGRAPHICAL/CRITICAL SOURCES:

PERIODICALS

Washington Post Book World, August 6, 1989.

*   *   *

WILBUR, James B(enjamin) III 1924-

PERSONAL: Born February 21, 1924, in Hartford, CT; son of James Benjamin (an industrialist) and Martha (Shekosky) Wilbur; married Margie Ann Mattmiller (an educator), July 9, 1949; children: James Benjamin IV, Ann Elizabeth. *Education:* University of Kentucky, A.B., 1948; graduate study at Harvard University, 1948-49; Columbia University, M.A., 1951, Ph.D., 1954. *Avocational interests:* Golf.

CAREER: Adelphi University, Long Island, NY, assistant professor, 1954-59, associate professor of philosophy, 1959-64, head of department, 1954-64; University of Akron, Akron, OH, professor of philosophy and head of department, 1964-68; State University of New York College at Geneseo, professor of philosophy, 1968-90, chairman of department, 1968-78. Visiting professor at University of Kent, 1971. Member of board of advisors, Empire State College of the State University of New York, 1971-75. Founder and director of Conferences on Value Inquiry, 1967—. *Military service:* U.S. Army, 1942-45.

MEMBER: American Philosophical Association, American Metaphysics Society, American Association of University Professors, American Society of Value-Inquiry (secretary-treasurer, 1970-72; president, 1973), Long Island Philosophy Society (founder, 1964), Creighton Club (president, 1970-72), Rochester Oratorio Society.

AWARDS, HONORS: State University of New York grant, 1969-70; National Endowment for the Humanities grant, 1981-82; Western Electric Fund award, American Assembly of Collegiate Schools of Business, 1983.

WRITINGS:

(With Harold Allen) *The Worlds of Plato and Aristotle,* American Book Co., 1962, revised edition, Prometheus Books, 1979.
(With Allen) *The Worlds of Hume and Kant,* American Book Co., 1965, revised edition, Prometheus Books, 1982.
(Editor and contributor with B. Magnus) *Cartesian Essays,* Nijhoff, 1969.
(Editor with Erwin Laszlo) *Value in Philosophy and Social Science,* Gordon & Breach, 1970.
(Editor with Laszlo) *Human Values and Natural Science,* Gordon & Breach, 1970.
(Editor with Laszlo) *Human Values and the Mind of Man,* Gordon & Breach, 1971.
(Editor and contributor) *Spinoza's Metaphysics,* Van Gorcum, 1976.
(With Allen) *The Worlds of the Early Greek Philosophers,* Prometheus Books, 1979.
The Moral Foundations of Business Practice, University Press of America, 1992.

Also author, with E. E. Young, of *Modern Drama and the Modern World,* 1991.

EDITOR OF MONOGRAPHS

(With Laszlo) *The Dynamics of Value Change,* State University of New York at Geneseo, 1978.
Human Values and Economic Activity, State University of New York at Geneseo, 1978.
(With Laszlo) *Value and the Arts,* State University of New York at Geneseo, 1979.
The Life Sciences and Human Value, State University of New York at Geneseo, 1979.
Human Value and the Law, State University of New York at Geneseo, 1980.
Ethics and Management, State University of New York at Geneseo, 1981.

Ethics and the Market Place: An Exercise in Bridge-Building; or, On the Slopes of the Interface, State University of New York at Geneseo, 1982.
Integrating Ethics into Business Education, State University of New York at Geneseo, 1984.
(And contributor) *The Integration of Ethics into Business Education: Essays on the S.U.N.Y. College at Geneseo Experience,* State University of New York at Geneseo, 1984.
The Bishop's Pastoral Letter on Catholic Social Teaching and the U.S. Economy: Critique and Discussion, State University of New York at Geneseo, 1985.
The Federalist Papers: An Explanation and Defense of Ideas and Issues in the U.S. Constitution, State University of New York at Geneseo, 1988.

Contributor to *Proceedings of the Second Conference on Business Ethics,* 1982, and to *Proceedings of the Seventh Conference on Business Ethics.* Founder and executive editor of *Journal of Value Inquiry,* 1967—; guest editor of *Journal of Business Ethics,* 1982, 1984, and 1988.

WORK IN PROGRESS: Studies in Kant's ethics.*

*   *   *

WILBY, Basil Leslie 1930-
(Gareth Knight)

PERSONAL: Born in 1930, in Colchester, England; son of Leslie Bernard (a postal telegraphist) and Constance Mabel (a postal telegraphist; maiden name, Sutherland) Wilby; married Roma Buckley Berryman (a teacher), March 12, 1960; children: Richard Duncan, Rebecca Julia. *Education:* Attended grammar school in Colchester. *Politics:* "Romantic *laissez faire* liberal." *Religion:* "Non-denominational Christian with mystical and ritualistic tendencies." *Avocational interests:* Visiting historical sites, walking, playing piano, chess, Indian coins, "omnivorous reading."

ADDRESSES: Home—8 Acorn Ave., Braintree, Essex, England.

CAREER: Free-lance writer, 1960-65; Longman Group Ltd., Harlow, England, educational representative, 1965-70, university sales manager, 1970-76, further education publisher, 1976-91; free-lance publishing consultant, 1991—. Director, Helios Book Service Ltd., 1963-82; former consultant to C. G. Jung Foundation. *Military Service:* Royal Air Force, 1948-56; became sergeant.

AWARDS, HONORS: D. Hum. from Sangreal Foundation, 1976.

WRITINGS:

(Editor) *The New Dimensions Red Book,* Helios, 1969.

Meeting the Occult, Lutterworth, 1974.

UNDER PSEUDONYM GARETH KNIGHT

A Practical Guide to Cabalistic Symbolism, Samuel
Weiser, 1965.
The Practice of Ritual Magic, Aquarian, 1969.
Occult Exercises and Practices, Aquarian, 1969.
The Pigeon Fancier (three-act play), produced in Leices-
ter, England at Phoenix Theatre, 1969.
Experience of the Inner Worlds, Helios, 1975.
The Occult: An Introduction, Kahn & Averill, 1975, re-
vised, 1990.
A History of White Magic, Samuel Weiser, 1979, revised
as *Magic and the Western Mind,* Llewellyn, 1992.
The Secret Tradition in Arthurian Legend, Aquarian,
1983.
The Rose Cross and the Goddess, Aquarian, 1985, as *Evok-
ing the Goddess,* Destiny Books, 1993.
The Treasure House of Images, Aquarian, 1986, as *Tarot
and Magic,* Destiny Books, 1991.
The Magical World of the Inklings, Element, 1990.

Author's works have been translated into French, Portuguese, Spanish, and Greek.

CONTRIBUTOR; AS GARETH KNIGHT

John Matthews, editor, *At the Table of the Grail,* Rout-
ledge & Kegan Paul, 1984.
McLean, editor, *Commentary on the Chymical Wedding
of Christian Rosenkreutz,* Magnum Opus Hermetic
Sourceworks, 1984.
R. S. Stewart, editor, *The Book of Merlin,* Blanford, 1987.
Stewart, editor, *Merlin and Woman,* Blanford, 1988.
Stewart, editor, *Psychology and the Spiritual Traditions,*
Element, 1990.
Matthews, editor, *The Household of the Grail,* Aquarian,
1990.
Matthew and Cheska Potter, editors, *Aquarian Guide to
Legendary London,* Aquarian, 1990.
Button and Bloom, editors, *The Seeker's Guide,* Aquarian,
1992.

Contributor to magazines, including *Light, Atlantean,
Sangreal, Fate, Quest, Gnostica News,* and *Hermetic Jour-
nal.* Editor of *New Dimensions,* 1962-65 and 1973-76, and
Quadriga, 1977-82.

WORK IN PROGRESS: A book on the principles and
practices of high magic, summarizing a lifetime experience
of the subject; as yet untitled.

SIDELIGHTS: Basil Leslie Wilby once told *CA:* "My
main aim in literary works is to rescue the word 'magic'
from its sinister and sensational associations and to present it as a world-view of important practical applications
that give great insights into modern religious and scientific

thinking—which took a turn for the worse, particularly in
the seventeenth century, landing us in the mess we are in
today.

"Briefly, when science broke away from the domination
of the authoritarian religious establishment that had hitherto prevailed, it received, because of its struggle for intellectual freedom, a considerable materialistic bias. This
was compounded by the Cartesian assumption that there
is a great divide between 'subjective consciousness' and the
'objective world' and that they are two discrete realities
acting somehow in parallel. As a result we have misunderstood great scientific thinkers of the past such as Francis
Bacon and Isaac Newton. Bacon, commonly regarded as
being the father of the scientific method, was in fact more
of a Platonist than is nowadays admitted. Similarly, Newton was, besides being perhaps the greatest scientific and
mathematical genius of all time, a profound theologian
and researcher of alchemy. These facts are either conve-
niently forgotten nowadays or dismissed as quaint pecca-
dillos.

"With the passage of time, a threatening chasm has developed in human thought and practice. The inadequacy of
the Cartesian assumptions, which are now so ingrained in
our thinking that they appear to be 'common sense,' is
being revealed by scientific experiment in the realms of
atomic physics, where it is now realized that the observer
is an intrinsic part of the phenomena observed. At the
same time, the new science of ecology shows an awareness
that the mechanistic view of the world, resulting in the
rape of the world by technological parasites, cannot be
much longer countenanced if we are to survive.

"The link between the two polarities of 'objective' and
'subjective' reality lies in a proper understanding of the
function of the imagination as a means of perception and
'participative creation.' . . . Before the mid-seventeenth
century, which was the great divide, the linking ground
was in 'natural magic'—hence my interest in the subject.
Properly understood, it is a 'technology of the imagination' which builds the bridge between spirit and matter.
It illuminates, rather than contradicts, both science and
religious beliefs."

*   *   *

WILLIAMS, Denis (Joseph Ivan)   1923-

PERSONAL: Born February 1, 1923, in Georgetown,
Guyana; son of Joseph Alexander (a merchant) and Isabel
(Adonis) Williams; married Catherine Hughes, 1949 (di-
vorced, 1974); married Toni Dixon (a poultry farmer),
August 21, 1975 (separated, 1982); children: (first mar-
riage) Janice, Evelyn, Isabel, Charlotte; (second marriage)

Miles, Morag, Everard, Rachael, Denis; Kibileri Wishart Williams. *Education:* Attended Camberwell School of Art, 1946-48; University of Guyana, M.A., 1979. *Politics:* None. *Religion:* Christian.

ADDRESSES: Home—13, Thorne's Dr., D'Urban Backlands, Botanic Gardens, Georgetown, Guyana. *Office*—Department of Culture, Ministry of Education, 15 Carifesta Ave., Georgetown, Guyana; and Walter Roth Museum of Anthropology, 65 Main St., P.O. Box 10187, Georgetown, Guyana. *Agent*—John Wolfers, 42 Russel Sq., London W.C. 1, England.

CAREER: Central School of Art, London, England, lecturer in art, 1950-57; Khartoum School of Art, Khartoum, Sudan, lecturer in art, 1957-62; University of Ife, Ife, Nigeria, lecturer in African studies, 1962-66; University of Lagos, Lagos, Nigeria, lecturer in African studies, 1966-68; National History and Arts Council, Georgetown, Guyana, art consultant, 1968-74; Ministry of Education, Georgetown, director of art and department of culture, 1974—. Founder and director of Walter Roth Museum. Artist, exhibiting work at numerous art shows and in many one-man exhibitions. Visiting tutor at Slade School of Fine Art, University of London, 1950-52; visiting professor at Makerere University, 1966; visiting research scholar, Smithsonian Institution, 1980. Chairman of National Trust, Georgetown, 1978-88. Member of International Visitor Program, United States Information Agency, 1985.

MEMBER: National Commissions for the Acquisition, Preservation, Republication of Research Materials on Guyana.

AWARDS, HONORS: Second prize from *London Daily Express* "Artists under Thirty-five" competition, 1955; Golden Arrow of Achievement, government of Guyana, 1973; first prize in National Theatre's mural competition, 1976; awarded Cacique's Crown of Honour, 1989; D.Litt., University of West Indies, 1989; received numerous grants from University of Ife, International African Institute, University of Lagos, Smithsonian Institution, and UNESCO.

WRITINGS:

Other Leopards (novel), Hutchinson, 1963.
The Third Temptation (novel), Calder & Boyars, 1968.
Giglioli in Guyana, 1922-1972 (biography), National History and Arts Council (Georgetown, Guyana), 1970.
Image and Idea in the Arts of the Caribbean, National History and Arts Council, 1970.
Icon and Image: A Study of Sacred and Secular Forms of African Classical Art, New York University Press, 1974.

The Amerindian Heritage, Walter Roth Museum (Georgetown, Guyana), 1984.
Habitat and Culture in Ancient Guyana, Edgar Mittelholzer Memorial Lectures, 1984.
Ancient Guyana, Guyana Department of Culture, 1985.
Pages in Guyanese Prehistory, Walter Roth Museum of Anthropology, 1988.

Contributor to several books, including *Africa in the Nineteenth and Twentieth Centuries*, edited by Joseph C. Anene and Godfrey N. Brown, Thomas Nelson, 1966; *Sources of Yoruba History*, edited by S. O. Biobaku, Clarendon Press, 1973; *Advances in World Archaeology*, Volume 4, Academic Press, 1985; *Americans Before Columbus*, Smithsonian Institution, in press; and *Handbook of Caribbean Prehistory*, Island Archaeological Museum, in press.

Contributor to *The Dictionary of World Art*, Macmillan; contributor of numerous articles to African studies and anthropology journals, including *Africa: Journal of the International African Institute London, Lagos Notes and Records, Carifesta Forum, Archaeology and Anthropology*, and *Odu: University of Ife Journal of African Studies*. Editor of *Odu*, 1964, *Lagos Notes and Records*, 1967, and *Archaeology and Anthropology*, 1978—.

WORK IN PROGRESS: A novel, *The Sperm of God.*

SIDELIGHTS: Denis Williams told *CA:* "A Colonial artist or writer who has received his professional education in Britain and made his first home there is not likely easily to forget that experience. I find that in my own case the experience has proven not only formative, but to a degree even determinative. It seems to have shaped the entire course of my subsequent development. Thus, to me, it is impossible to imagine a career built other than upon the solid foundation of early recognition and acceptance which was accorded to me during the first half of the fifties in London. Paradoxically, however, as Fanon has so perceptively shown, given the circumstances and the day, acceptance on this level was in fact far the most unacceptable, indeed probably the most humiliating, of choices open to the Colonial artist.

"This may explain the rapid and apparently permanent darkness which followed the explosion of Caribbean writing in Britain during the time I was there. Colonial territories were all becoming independent, which was quickly to render the Colonial artist or writer obsolete; for just as national independence seems to have pulled the rug from under the feet of the Colonial writer, new national writers were arising in English-and French-speaking West Africa and in the Caribbean.

"By this time I was myself in Africa writing *Other Leopards,* or trying to resolve some of the problems of identity which provided the theme for that novel. By the time of its completion it was becoming evident that even though the new African literature was being written all around me, and by familiar hands, Africa did not represent the uttermost swing of the pendulum in my reaction from an unwilling acceptance in Europe. Indeed, the African experience tended to reveal to me deeply ingrained attitudes to various aspects of European art, life, and literature that had remained so far undetected. Odd as it may seem, it was very easy to write *The Third Temptation* (in an experimental French idiom) simultaneously with my study of African classical art, which in itself represented an intellectual search for African roots.

"I have since returned to Guyana, and see clearly that such a thing could never take place against my rediscovered background. However, if this means that the pendulum has at last reached its ultimate distance of travel, it is no comfort to realize that my first true Caribbean novel, *The Sperm of God,* has remained unfinished now for over thirteen years."

BIOGRAPHICAL/CRITICAL SOURCES:

BOOKS

Cartey, Wilfred, *Whispers from the Caribbean: I Going Away, I Going Home,* University of California, Los Angeles, 1991.
Dathorne, O. R., *The Black Mind: A History of African Literature,* University of Minnesota Press, 1974.
Fox, C. J., and Walter Michel, *Wyndham Lewis on Art: Collected Writings, 1913-1956,* Thames & Hudson, 1969.
Moore, Gerald, *The Chosen Tongue,* Longman, 1969.
Ramchand, Kenneth, *The West Indian Novel and Its Background,* Faber, 1974.

PERIODICALS

Daily Express, April 28, 1955.
Geo, May, 1981.
Science Digest, November, 1981.
Science News, January 24, 1981.

*   *   *

WILLIAMS, Howard L(loyd) 1950-

PERSONAL: Born March 23, 1950, in Aberystwyth, Wales; son of Mervin Owen (a headmaster) and Joan (a nurse; maiden name, Haig) Williams; married Jennifer Amos (a language teacher), July, 1970; children: Ceri John, David Wyn, Huw Lloyd. *Education:* University of London, B.Sc., 1971; University of Durham, Ph.D., 1974; attended University of Heidelberg, 1974. *Politics:* "Left of center." *Avocational interests:* Good music, great art,

travel, bringing up children, swimming, broadcasting, film, golf, reading, good conversation.

ADDRESSES: Home—Swn yr Awel, Dole, Bow St., Aberystwyth, Dyfed, Wales. *Office*—Department of International Politics, University College of Wales, Penglais, Aberystwyth, Wales.

CAREER: University of Wales, University College of North Wales, Bangor, research officer in education, 1974-76, lecturer in extra-mural studies, 1976-78; University of Wales, University College of Wales, Aberystwyth, lecturer, 1979-88, senior lecturer in political science, 1988, reader, 1989-92, professor of political theory, 1992—, dean of Faculty of Economic and Social Studies, 1987-89. Chairperson of local Labour Party, 1983—.

MEMBER: British Political Studies Association, Hegel Society of Great Britain (executive member), Association of University Professors (local president, 1984-85).

AWARDS, HONORS: International Relations in Political Theory was named outstanding academic book, *Choice,* 1993.

WRITINGS:

Marx, Gee, 1980.
Kant's Political Philosophy, Basil Blackwell, 1983.
Concepts of Ideology, St. Martin's, 1988.
Hegel, Heraclitus and Marx's Dialectic, St. Martin's, 1989.
International Relations in Political Theory, Open University Press, 1991.
(Editor) *Essays on Kant's Political Philosophy,* University of Chicago Press, 1992.
(Editor with A. Evans and P. Moorhead Wright) *Reader in Political Philosophy and International Relations,* Open University Press, 1992.

Contributor to numerous books, including *Hegel's Critique of Kant,* edited by S. Priest, Oxford University Press, 1986; *Political Thinkers and Political Ideas since 1945,* edited by L. Tivey and A. Wright, Edward Elgar, 1992. Also contributor of articles and book reviews to philosophy, political science, and history journals, including *Philosophical Quarterly, Political Studies, Journal of the History of Political Studies, Journal of the History of Political Thought,* and *Idealistic Studies.*

WORK IN PROGRESS: Kant and World Politics; a research project on political theory and the reunification of Germany.

SIDELIGHTS: Howard L. Williams once told *CA:* "Writing extensively in two languages makes one particularly conscious of the problems of style and presentation. Conveying the precise meaning one wants depends on choosing the right phrase current in the speech and writing of the day. This entails a sound knowledge of the cultural and literary activity taking place in the languages in which the author writes. To extend oneself over two cultures requires a great deal more of the author but brings rewards in greater sensitivity to the standpoint of others.

"I take one of the most important aspects of my literary activity to be my reviewing work. This is particularly important for an academic author. To be asked to undertake a review for a learned journal is distinction in itself; however, to complete a review which is not only of value to the author of a work, but also to the interested reader, requires both knowledge and insight. Reviewing extends an academic writer's knowledge of his own field and brings home to him the pitfalls to be avoided in his own writing."

Williams recently told *CA:* "My emphasis in the next decade will be upon reconciling the relation between political theory and international relations and looking at in greater detail the principal concepts of political philosophy. I am particularly interested in the concepts of justice, democracy, equality, freedom, and rights. I think political theory can help us get to the heart of a rapidly developing world."

*   *   *

WILLIAMSON, David (Keith) 1942-

PERSONAL: Born February 24, 1942, in Melbourne, Australia; son of Edwin Keith David (a bank official) and Elvie May (Armstrong) Williamson; married Carol Ann Cranby, 1965 (divorced, 1972); married Kristin Ingrid Lofven (a journalist), May 29, 1974; children: Rebecca, Matthew, Rory. *Education:* Monash University, B.E., 1964.

ADDRESSES: Home—85 Louisa Road, Birchgrove, New South Wales 2041, Australia. *Agent*—Anthony Williams Management Pty. Ltd., The Basement, 55 Victoria Street, Potts Point, New South Wales 2011, Australia.

CAREER: General Motors, Melbourne, Australia, design engineer, 1965; Swinburne College of Technology, lecturer in mechanical engineering, 1966-72; writer, 1972—. Chairman, Australian National Playwrights Conference, 1979-80.

MEMBER: Australian Writers Guild (president, 1979-86).

AWARDS, HONORS: Australian Writers Guild Award, 1972, for *The Removalists,* 1973, for *Don's Party,* 1978, for *The Club,* and 1980, for *Travelling North;* George Devine Award (with others), Royal Court Theatre, 1972, and Most Promising Playwright Award, *London Evening Standard,* 1973, both for *The Removalists;* Best Screenplay Award, Australian Film Institute, 1973, for *Petersen,*

1976, for *Don's Party,* and 1981, for *Gallipoli;* Eric Award, Melbourne Critics, 1974, for *Jugglers Three;* nominated for screenwriting achievement award, Writer's Guild of America, 1983, for *The Year of Living Dangerously;* Sydney Critics Award, 1983, for *Phar Lap;* Penguin Award for best mini-series, 1985, for *The Last Bastion;* Best Screenplay Award, Oxford Film Festival, for *Don's Party;* Christopher Award for *Gallipoli.*

WRITINGS:

PLAYS

The Removalists (two-act play; produced in Melbourne, Australia, 1971, produced in London at Royal Court Theatre, 1973, produced Off-Broadway at Actors Playhouse, 1973), Currency Press, 1972.

Don's Party (two-act play; also see below; produced in Melbourne, 1971, produced at Royal Court Theatre, 1975), Currency/Methuen, 1973.

Three Plays (contains *The Coming of Stork,* produced in Melbourne, 1970; *Jugglers Three,* produced in Melbourne, 1972; *What If You Died Tomorrow* [two-act play], produced in Melbourne, 1973, produced in London, 1974), Eyre/Methuen, 1974.

The Department (two-act play; produced in Adelaide, Australia, 1974), Currency Press, 1975.

A Handful of Friends (two-act play; produced in Adelaide, 1976), Currency Press, 1976.

The Club (two-act play; produced in Washington D.C., at Kennedy Center, 1978, produced on Broadway, 1978), Currency Press, 1977.

Travelling North (two-act play; also see below; produced in London, 1980), Currency Press, 1980.

The Perfectionist (produced in Sydney, Australia, 1982, produced in London, 1983), Currency Press, 1983.

Sons of Cain, produced in Melbourne, 1985, produced in London, 1986.

Emerald City (also see below), produced in Sydney, 1986; produced in London, 1987.

Top Silk, produced in Sydney, 1988.

Siren, produced in Sydney, 1990.

Money and Friends, produced in Sydney, 1992.

SCREENPLAYS

Stork, Tim Burstall and Roadshow, 1971.

The Removalists, Margaret Fink Productions, 1974.

Petersen, Tim Burstall and Roadshow, 1974.

Don's Party, Satori Productions, 1976.

Eliza Frazer, Tim Burstall and Roadshow, 1976.

The Club, South Australian Film Corp., 1980.

Partners, Tim Burstall and Associates, 1981.

Gallipoli (adapted from a story by Peter Weir), Paramount, 1981, published in *The Story of Gallipoli* by Bill Gammage, Penguin, 1981.

Phar Lap, Twentieth Century-Fox, 1983.

(With C. J. Koch and Peter Weir) *The Year of Living Dangerously* (based on the novel by Koch), Metro-Goldwyn-Mayer, 1983.

(Principal screenwriter and co-producer) *The Last Bastion* (six-hour television series), Channel 10 Network, Australia, 1985.

Travelling North, View Pictures, 1986.

Also author of screenplays *Emerald City,* 1988; *The Four Minute Mile* (two-part television series), 1988; and *The Four Day Revolution* (six-hour television series), 1988.

SIDELIGHTS: Writer David Williamson is one of Australia's most highly-regarded contemporary playwrights. Recognized not only in his own country but also throughout Britain and the United States for his critically acclaimed stage plays, Williamson includes such theatrical dramas as *The Removalists, The Coming of Stork,* and *The Perfectionist* among his ouvre. Beginning his writing career as a playwright, Williamson has gone on to supplement his work for the stage by teaming with such notable directors as fellow-Australian Peter Weir to translate both his own works and those of other writers for the screen. The screenplays to his credit include those for such major films as *Emerald City, Gallipoli,* and *The Year of Living Dangerously.*

A former psychology instructor, Williamson first turned to the writing of drama as a means of examining the intricacies of human relationships. *The Coming of Stork,* his first play, was written in 1969, when its author was twenty-seven years old, and produced in Melbourne, Australia the following year. Critic Lawrence Christon noted in the *Los Angeles Times* that the work is "very much the play of a young man writing about his generation starting out." The drama's plot centers around the young occupants of a bachelor flat and highlights the attempts of each of the main characters as they choose the path they will follow in making their way in the world. Christon commented of Williamson that "we already can see his knowledge of competing self-interests that pull at each other like strands in a social net. And he's able to show us several levels operating at once."

The Coming of Stork was followed by such successful stage plays as *What If You Died Tomorrow* (1973), *The Department* (1974), and *A Handful of Friends* (1976). Williamson's 1982 play, *The Perfectionist* is a dramatic portrayal of the relationship between father and son; of the striving of young people to achieve the aspirations of their parents and the destructive consequences of the drive to attain extraneous goals on family relationships. Theatre critic Mel Gussow praised Williamson in the *New York Times* as "an astute, economical observer of those universal subjects, husbands and wives, parents and children, in shared discord."

Williamson has adapted many of the works he originally wrote for the theatre into motion picture screenplays. The success of the 1974 filming of *The Removalists* was followed by film versions of *Don's Party, The Club, Travelling North,* and *Emerald City,* the latter a satiric look at the movie and publishing business released as a motion picture two years after the play's initial 1986 stage run in Sydney. With many successful original films also to his credit, Williamson has gone on to adapt the works of other authors for the screen. In 1981 he wrote the screenplay for the first of several films he would author for noted director Peter Weir; *Gallipoli,* based on a story by Weir, garnered Williamson that year's Best Screenplay Award from the Australian Film Institute, one of several he has received during his career as a writer. Williamson's original screenplay for *Phar Lap,* an old-fashioned, sentimentally-told tale of the New Zealand racehorse who rose from a gangly "cross between a kangaroo and a sheep dog" to become a nationally-known champion racehorse during Australia's depression-era, was directed by Simon Wincer in 1983. That year also marked the second Weir-Williamson triumph when the film *The Year of Living Dangerously* was released to international critical acclaim. The praise it has received as "a film of rich textures, density, and nuance . . . a film of many levels and implications" by Kevin Thomas in the *Los Angeles Times* is a testament not only to its artistic direction but also to the ambitious screenplay on which Williamson served as primary author—with the assistance of director Weir and author C.J. Koch, on whose novel the film is based.

Regarding the advantages of writing in more than one format, Williamson once told *CA:* "I'm spending approximately equal amounts of time on stage and film writing—very different types of writing that don't really complement each other; they provide two distinct types of experience. By the time I've had a gutful of one I can thankfully turn to the other."

BIOGRAPHICAL/CRITICAL SOURCES:

BOOKS

Williamson, David, *Phar Lap* (screenplay), Twentieth Century–Fox, 1983.

PERIODICALS

Los Angeles Times, February 17, 1983, pp. 1, 9; February 1, 1984, pp. 1, 4.
New York Times, June 5, 1984.
Times (London), May 9, 1988.*

WILMETH, Don B(urton) 1939-

PERSONAL: Born December 15, 1939, in Houston, TX; son of Perry D. (a minister and editor) and Pauline M. (Goodrum) Wilmeth; married Judy Eslie Hansgen (a secretary), June 10, 1966; children: Michael Tyler. *Education:* Abilene Christian University, B.A., 1961; University of Arkansas, M.A., 1962; University of Illinois, Ph.D., 1964.

ADDRESSES: Home—525 Hope St., Providence, RI 02906. *Office*—Department of Theatre, Speech and Dance, Brown University, Box 1897, Providence, RI 02912.

CAREER: Eastern New Mexico University, Portales, assistant professor of drama and head of department, 1964-67; Brown University, Providence, RI, assistant professor, 1967-70, associate professor, 1970-76, professor of theatre and English, 1976—, chairman of department of theatre arts, 1979-87, associate director of theatre, 1967-70, acting director, 1970, executive officer of theatre arts, 1973-78. Curator of H. Adrian Smith Collection of Conjuring Books and Magicana, 1988—.

Member of board of directors of local Players, 1972-74, 1978-80, and of Institute for American Theatre Studies, 1981-85; member of advisory board, East Lynne Theatre Co., NJ, 1981—, and Langston Hughes Center for the Performing Arts, 1982-92; member of discipline committee in theatre, Fulbright International Exchange of Scholars, 1982-84. Member of College of Fellows of the American Theatre, 1985, and of National Theatre Conference, 1991; corporation member of Providence Public Library, 1983—. Consultant to Library of Congress, 1992—.

MEMBER: International Federation for Theater Research, American Society for Theatre Research (member of board of directors, 1976-78, 1980-83, and 1985-88; president, 1991—), American Theatre Association (fellow; chairman of publications committee, 1974-79), Society for the Advancement of Education (member of board of trustees, 1977-91), Theatre Library Association (member of board of directors, 1978-83; vice-president, 1981-84), Theatre Historical Society, National Collegiate Players, American Association of University Professors, Circus Historical Society, Society for Theatre Research (England), New England Theater Conference, Providence Shakespeare Society, Phi Beta Kappa, Alpha Chi, Phi Kappa Phi, Alpha Psi Omega.

AWARDS, HONORS: Honorary M.A., Brown University, 1970; Henry Wriston grant, Brown University, 1981, 1988; Barnard Hewitt Award for Excellence in Theatre History, American Theatre Association, 1981, for *George Frederick Cooke: Machiavel of the Stage;* John Simon Guggenheim fellow, 1982.

WRITINGS:

(Editor) *The American Stage to World War I,* Gale, 1978.

George Frederick Cooke: Machiavel of the Stage, Greenwood Press, 1980.

(Editor) *American and English Popular Entertainment,* Gale, 1980.

The Language of Popular Entertainment: A Glossary of Argot, Slang, and Terminology, Greenwood Press, 1981.

Variety Entertainment and Outdoor Amusements, Greenwood Press, 1982.

(Co-editor) *Plays by William Hooker Gillette,* Cambridge University Press, 1983.

(Co-editor) *Plays by Augustin Daly,* Cambridge University Press, 1984.

(Author of text) *Mud Show: American Tent Circus Life,* University of New Mexico Press, 1988.

(Co-editor and contributor) *The Cambridge Guide to World Theatre,* Cambridge University Press, 1988.

(Co-editor and contributor) *The Cambridge Guide to American Theatre,* Cambridge University Press, 1993.

Documents in American Theatre History, Cambridge University Press, in press.

Contributor to books, including *Theatrical Touring and Founding in North America,* edited by L. W. Conolly, Greenwood Press, 1982; *American Playwrights since 1945,* edited by Philip Kolin, Greenwood Press, 1989; and *American Theatre Studies,* Cambridge University Press, 1993. Also contributor to *World Book Encyclopedia,* 1985—, and to *Dictionary of American Biography,* 1986-93. Editor of "Studies in American Theatre and Drama" series, Cambridge University Press. Author of "Theatre Today" column in *U.S.A. Today,* 1974-80. Contributor of more than one hundred articles and reviews to periodicals, including *Choice.* Advisory editor for six journals; book review editor, *Theatre Journal,* 1977-80.

WORK IN PROGRESS: Co-editing *History of American Theatre,* a multi-volume project for Cambridge University Press.

SIDELIGHTS: Don B. Wilmeth told *CA:* "I have long been a lover of books and have consequently collected large numbers in the area of theatre. I consider myself a theatre historian, director, and actor as well as an educator and writer. For over a decade I have served as juror or chairman of two prestigious book awards given by the Theatre Library Association. Within the last ten years, my focus has turned to popular entertainments, and my writing has begun to turn in that direction."

He adds, "A good deal of energy has gone into editing, and a recent initiative has been the editing of a new series on American theatre and drama."

WILSON, Bryan R(onald) 1926-

PERSONAL: Born June 25, 1926, in Leeds, England. *Education:* University College of Leicester, B.Sc., 1952; London School of Economics, Ph.D., 1955. *Avocational interests:* Music, graphic arts, oriental porcelain, herbaceous borders.

ADDRESSES: Office—All Souls College, Oxford University, Oxford OX1 4AL, England.

CAREER: University of Leeds, Leeds, England, lecturer in sociology, 1955-62, warden of Sadler Hall, 1959-62; Oxford University, Oxford, England, reader in sociology, 1962—, fellow of All Souls College, 1963—. Visiting professor at University of Ghana, 1964, University of Leuven, 1976, 1982, and 1986, University of Toronto, 1978, Ormond College, University of Melbourne, 1981, and University of East Asia, 1981-82. Distinguished professor, University of California, Santa Barbara, 1987, and Abo University, 1990. *Military service:* British Army, 1944-47.

MEMBER: Societe international de sociologie des religions (president, 1971-75; member of council, 1975-89; honorary president, 1991—), Society for the Scientific Study of Religion (member of council, 1977-80).

AWARDS, HONORS: Commonwealth Fund fellow at University of California, Berkeley, 1957-58; American Council of Learned Societies fellow at University of California, Berkeley, 1966-67; Japan Society fellow, 1975; D.Litt., Oxford University, 1984, and Soka University, Japan, 1985; Dr. Hon. Causa, University of Louvain, Belgium, 1992.

WRITINGS:

Sects and Society, University of California Press, 1961.
Religion in Secular Society, F. Watts, 1966.
The Youth Culture and the Universities, Faber, 1970.
Religious Sects, McGraw, 1970.
Magic and the Millennium, Harper, 1973.
The Noble Savages, University of California Press, 1975.
Contemporary Transformations of Religion, Oxford University Press, 1976.
Religion in Sociological Perspective, Oxford University Press, 1982.
(With Daisaku Ikeda) *Human Values in a Changing World,* Macdonald & Co., 1984.
The Social Dimensions of Sectarianism, Clarendon Press, 1990.

EDITOR AND CONTRIBUTOR

Patterns of Sectarianism, Heinemann, 1967.
Rationality, Harper, 1970.
Education, Equality, and Society, Allen & Unwin, 1975.
The Social Impact of New Religious Movements, Rose of Sharon Press, 1981.

Values: A Symposium, Humanities, 1988.
Religion: Contemporary Issues, Bellew, 1992.

OTHER

Contributor to numerous books, including *Society: Problems and Methods of Study,* edited by A. T. Welford, Routledge & Kegan Paul, 1962; *The Sacred in a Secular Age,* edited by Phillip E. Hammond, University of California Press, 1985; *Religion and Modernization,* edited by Steve Bruce, Clarendon Press, 1992. Also contributor to *Encyclopaedia Britannica, Encyclopedia of the Social Sciences,* and *Encyclopedia of Religion;* contributor to numerous periodicals, including *Twentieth Century, Sunday Times, Observer, Spectator, Texas Quarterly, Archives de Sociologie des Religions, Criminal Law Review, Education Today,* and to sociology journals in England and America. Joint founding editor, *Annual Review of the Social Sciences of Religion,* 1977—; associate European editor, *Journal for the Scientific Study of Religion,* 1977—.

WORK IN PROGRESS: Comparative studies of sectarianism; new religious movements; the Soka Gakkai movement in Britain.

SIDELIGHTS: Bryan Wilson's 1966 book, *Religion in Secular Society,* "has been read by more people than has any other British book on the sociology of religion," according to *Times Literary Supplement* reviewer Robert Towler. Wilson has produced several other books that pertain to religion. In his work *Religious Sects,* the author "has usefully categorized those sects predominantly within or at the fringe of Christian tradition, about which most is known, and recorded the more significant of their similarities and diversities," another *Times Literary Supplement* reviewer reports. The critic believes that the "special strength of his careful, splendidly organized book is the way in which it situates each sect in its social context and where appropriate, brings out its beneficial effects."

Wilson's 1982 work *Religion in Sociological Perspective* is based on lectures he gave in Tokyo in 1979. Towler writes that because these lectures are addressed to Japanese audiences, Wilson "has produced a general statement of his view of Western society and Western religion, and one which is exceptionally clear and uncluttered." In Towler's opinion, "the book is an important one, therefore, for those who have benefitted from his perspective in the past."

BIOGRAPHICAL/CRITICAL SOURCES:

PERIODICALS

Spectator, April 11, 1970.
Times Literary Supplement, August 27, 1971; November 16, 1973; September 24, 1982.

WILSON, Robert M. 1944-

PERSONAL: Born October 4, 1944, in Waco, TX; son of D. M. (a lawyer) and Loree (Hamilton) Wilson. *Education:* Attended University of Texas, 1959-62; studied painting with George McNeil in Paris, 1962; Pratt Institute, B.F.A., 1965; apprentice to architect Paolo Soleri in Phoenix, AZ, 1966.

ADDRESSES: Home—67 Vestry St., New York, NY 10013. *Office*—Byrd Hoffman Foundation, Inc., 325 Spring St., New York, NY 10013.

CAREER: Playwright, director, designer, painter, teacher, and architect. Artistic director, Byrd Hoffman Foundation, Inc., New York City. Has conducted seminars and workshops at various institutions, including University of California, Berkeley, Newark State College (now Keane College of New Jersey), University of California, Los Angeles, New York University, Harvard University, and Centre de Development du Potential Humain, Paris; lecturer at University of Iowa Center for New Performing Arts, Ohio State University, International School, Paris, University of Torino, Italy, UNESCO International Theater Institute, Durdan, France, and at European theatre festivals; teacher and consultant in body movement and body awareness with numerous colleges, universities, schools, community groups, and government agencies.

Solo exhibitions of work at Paula Cooper Gallery (New York City), Marian Goodman Gallery, (New York City), Galerie le Dessin (Paris), Galerie Annemarie Verna (Zurich), Pavillion des Arts (Paris), Galerie Brinkman (Amsterdam), Gallery Ueda (Tokyo), Otis Art Institute/ Parsons School of Design (Los Angeles), Museo di Folklore (Rome), Kolnishcer Kunstverein (Koln), Galleria Franca Mancini (Pesaro, Italy), and Institute of Contemporary Art (Boston); work displayed in group exhibitions, including "Biennal Exhibition," Whitney Museum of American Art (New York City), "The Next Wave Artists," Paula Cooper Gallery (New York City), "Der Hang zum Gesamtkunstwerk," Museum Moderner Kunst (Vienna) and Kunsthaus (Zurich), "Survey of Contemporary Painting and Sculpture," "New Works on Paper 3" and "Spatial Relationships in Video," all Museum of Modern Art (New York City), "Highlights: Selections from the BankAmerica Corporation Art Collection," Giannini Gallery (San Francisco), and "Large Drawings," a traveling exhibit organized by Independent Curators, Inc. (New York City); public collections of work at Australian National Gallery (Canberra), Museum of Modern Art (New York City), Museum of Modern Art (Paris), Rhode Island School of Design (Providence), Bank of America (San Francisco), and Museum of Fine Arts (Boston). Has directed 16-mm films, including *Slant,* for NET-TV, 1963,

The House, 1963, and adaptation of own play *Overture for a Deafman,* 1971.

MEMBER: Societe des Auteurs et Compositeurs Dramatiques (Paris), PEN American Center, Dramatists Guild.

AWARDS, HONORS: Critics Award for best foreign play, Syndicat de la Critique Musicale (Paris), 1970, for *Deafman Glance;* Vernon Rice Drama Desk Award, 1971, for direction of *Deafman Glance;* Guggenheim fellowship, 1971; Off-Broadway Award (OBIE) special citation for direction, 1974, for *The Life and Times of Joseph Stalin;* Antoinette Perry Award (Tony) nomination for best score and lyrics, and Joseph Maharam Foundation Award for best set design, both 1975, both for *A Letter for Queen Victoria;* Rockefeller Foundation fellowship, 1975 and 1981; Grand Prize, International Festival of Nations (Belgrade), Critics Award for best musical theatre, Le Syndicat de la Critique Musicale, and Lumen Award for design, all 1977, all for *Einstein on the Beach;* citation in "Top Ten Plays," German Critics Award (Berlin) and first prize in playwright category, German Press Award (Berlin), both 1979, both for *Death, Destruction and Detroit;* Der Rosenstrauss Award (Munich) for best play of the year, 1982, for *The Golden Windows;* San Sebastian Film and Video Festival award (San Sebastian, Spain), 1984, for *Stations;* Berlin Festspiele Theatertreffen, 1984, for *the CIVIL warS: a tree is best measured when it is down*/German Section; Picasso Award, Malaga Theatre Festival, 1986; Circle Award, Boston Theatre Critics, 1986.

WRITINGS:

THEATER WORKS; AND DIRECTOR

Dance Event, produced in New York City, 1965.
Solo Performance, produced in New York City at Byrd Hoffman Studio, 1966.
Theater Activity (one-act), first produced in New York City at Bleecker Street Cinema, 1967.
Byrd-woMAN (two-act), first produced in New York City at Byrd Hoffman Studio, 1968.
Alley Cats, produced in New York City at New York University, 1968.
The Life and Times of Sigmund Freud (three-act), first produced Off-Broadway at Brooklyn Academy of Music, 1969.
The King of Spain (also see below; one-act), first produced Off-Broadway at Anderson Theater, January 30, 1969.
Deafman Glance (also see below; one-act), first produced in Iowa City, IA at University Theater, 1970, produced Off-Broadway at Brooklyn Academy of Music, 1971.
Program Prologue Now, Overture for a Deafman (three-act), first produced in Paris, France, at Espace Pierre

Cardin, 1971, produced in New York City at Byrd Hoffman Studio, 1972.

Overture (two-act), first produced in New York City at Byrd Hoffman Studio, 1972, produced as one-act play in Shiraz, Iran, at Khaneh-e Zinatolmolk, 1972, produced as *twenty-four hour continuous one-act* in Paris at Musee Galliera and Opera Comique, 1972.

KA MOUNTAIN AND GUARDenia TERRACE: A Story about a Family and Some People Changing ("seven-day continuous one-act"), produced in Shiraz at Haft Tan Mountain, 1972.

king lyre and lady in the wasteland (one-act), first produced in New York City at Byrd Hoffman Studio, 1973.

The Life and Times of Joseph Stalin (seven-act), first produced in Copenhagen, Denmark, at Det Ny Teater, 1973, produced Off-Broadway at Brooklyn Academy of Music, December 15, 1973, produced in Sao Paulo, Brazil, as *The Life and Times of Dave Clark,* 1974.

A Letter for Queen Victoria (produced in Spoleto, Italy, at Spoleto Festival, June, 1974, produced on Broadway at ANTA Theatre, March 22, 1975), privately printed, 1974.

A Mad Man a Mad Giant a Mad Dog a Mad Urge a Mad Face, produced in Washington, DC, 1974.

'Prologue' to a Letter for Queen Victoria, produced in Spoleto, 1974.

To Street, produced in Bonn, Germany, 1975.

The $ Value of Man, produced Off-Broadway at Brooklyn Academy of Music, 1975.

(With Christopher Knowles) *Dia Log,* produced Off-Broadway at Public Theatre, 1975, produced as *Dia Log/Curious George,* in New York City at Mitzi E. Newhouse Theater, 1980.

(With Philip Glass) *Einstein on the Beach* (opera; produced in New York City at Metropolitan Opera House, 1976, produced Off-Broadway at Brooklyn Academy of Music, 1984), EOS Enterprises, 1976.

(With Ralph Hilton) *Spaceman* (also see below), produced in New York City, 1976.

I Was Sitting on My Patio This Guy Appeared I Thought I Was Hallucinating (first produced Off-Broadway at Cherry Lane Theatre, May 22, 1977), privately printed, 1978.

Death, Destruction and Detroit (also see below; first produced in Berlin, West Germany, at Schaubuehne Theatre, 1979), Schaubuehne am Halleschen Ufer, 1979.

Edison, first produced in Lyon, France, 1979, produced in New York City at Lion Theatre, 1979.

The Man in the Raincoat, produced in Koln, West Germany, at Theater der Welt, 1981.

(Adaptor with Gavin Bryars) *Medea* (from the opera *Medee* by Marc Antoine Charpentier), produced in Washington, D.C., at Kennedy Center for the Per-

forming Arts, 1981, produced in New York City at City College of New York, 1982, produced in Paris at Theatre des Champs-Elysees, October 23, 1984.

The Golden Windows (produced in Munich at Kammerspiele, 1982, produced Off-Broadway at Brooklyn Academy of Music, October, 1985), Carl Hanser Verlag (Munich), 1982.

(With Jessye Norman) *Great Day in the Morning,* produced in Paris at Theatre des Champs-Elysees, 1982.

the CIVIL warS: a tree is best measured when it is down/ Dutch Section (produced in Rotterdam, Holland, at Schouwburg Theater, 1983, with subsequent productions throughout France), Meulenhoff/Landshoff (Amsterdam), 1983.

the CIVIL warS: a tree is best measured when it is down/ Japan, produced in Tokyo, February 10, 1984.

the CIVIL warS: a tree is best measured when it is down/ Marseille, produced in Marseille, France, at Office Regionale de la Culture de Provence-Alpe-Cote d'Azur, 1984.

the CIVIL warS: a tree is best measured when it is down/ Rome Section (produced in Rome, Italy, at Teatro dell'Opera di Roma, March 25-31, 1984, concert version [with music by Glass] produced Off-Broadway at Brooklyn Academy of Music, December, 1986), Edizioni del Teatro dell'Opera (Rome), 1984.

(With music by David Byrne) *the CIVIL warS: a tree is best measured when it is down/*American Section, or *The Knee Plays,* first produced in Minneapolis, MN, at Guthrie Theater, Walker Art Center, April 26-28, 1984, produced in New York City at Alice Tully Hall, December, 1986.

the CIVIL warS: a tree is best measured when it is down/ German Section (first produced in Koln, West Germany, at Schauspiel Koln, January 19, 1984), Suhrkamp Verlag (Frankfurt), 1984.

(With Heiner Mueller) *the CIVIL warS: a tree is best measured when it is down/*Act III, Scene E, and Act IV, Scene A and Epilogue (produced in Cambridge, MA, at American Repertory Theatre, February 27, 1985), American Repertory Theatre, 1985.

(Adaptor) *King Lear* (from the play by William Shakespeare), produced as work in progress in Hollywood, CA, at Stage One by UCLA Extension, Metromedia Square, May, 1985.

(Adaptor with Mueller) *Hamletmachine* (from the play by Mueller), produced in New York City at Mainstage II by New York University Theatre Department, May, 1986.

(Adaptor) *Alcestis* (from the opera by Christoph Willibald Gluck), produced in Stuttgart, West Germany, by Stuttgart Opera Company, December, 1986; produced in Cambridge, MA, 1986.

(Adaptor) *Salome* (from the opera by Richard Strauss), produced in Milan, Italy, at Teatro alla Scala, January, 1987.

Death Destruction & Detroit II (sequel), produced in Berlin at Schaubuehne Theatre, May, 1987.

(With Byrne) *The Forest* (includes parts of *The Knee Plays*), produced Off-Broadway at Brooklyn Academy of Music, December, 1988.

The Black Rider, produced in Paris, 1990.

OTHER

(Contributor) William Hoffman, editor, *New American Plays,* Volume 3 (contains *The King of Spain*), Hill & Wang, 1970.

the CIVIL warS: Drawings, Models and Documentation, Otis Institute/Parsons School of Design, 1984.

Also author of video works *Spaceman,* 1976, *Video 50,* 1978, *Deafman Glance,* 1981, and *Stations,* 1982. Contributor of articles to *Drama Review* and *Performance Art.*

ADAPTATIONS: Audio recordings of Wilson's plays include *The Life and Times of Joseph Stalin,* Byrd Hoffman Foundation, 1973, *Einstein on the Beach* (originally released by Tomato Records), CBS Masterworks, 1979, and *the CIVIL warS: Knee Plays,* ECM/Warner Brothers, 1985.

SIDELIGHTS: One of the most innovative figures in American theatre, playwright, director, and designer Robert M. Wilson is credited with developing a new kind of theatre that combines surrealistic sets and images, music, dance, and what Jack Kroll of *Newsweek* terms "psychodrama." The outcome and effect of this combination, as well as the large-scale productions and length of his plays, are often compared to that of a spectacle. Leo Bersani explains, "The dozens of players in each work, the dizzying number of things going on, the elaborate sets, the hundreds of costumes, the rich colors and symphonies of variegated sounds make Wilson the Cecil B. De Mille of the avant-garde."

Wilson's plays are composed of what Kroll describes as a "shifting collage of images and actions." Frequently taking five or more hours to perform, his work relies on visual elements and experimental "uses of space, silence and sound," according to Judith Searle in the *New York Times.* That is, rather than the conventional theatrical means of plot, language, and character interaction, Wilson employs a variety of acts and scenes that are simultaneously performed on different sets, changing backdrops, pantomime, and little, if any, dialogue. In her article on the performance of *KA MOUNTAIN AND GUARDenia TERRACE* (a seven-day-and-night event that began at the base of Iran's Haf Tan Mountain and concluded at its summit), Searle comments: "Actors—some on platforms, some in

side rooms, some on a kind of low stage at one end—began to perform very slowly actions related to the stated theme of the piece—'a family and some people changing.' But the actors never related to each other in the conventional theatrical way. Their actions took place simultaneously, but with no apparent effect on each other." The *Village Voice*'s Michael Smith offers a similar description of *The Life and Times of Joseph Stalin,* Wilson's twelve-hour, seven-act play: "There is always so much going on that . . . the eye never catches up with it. Some of it is always changing, some of it always stays the same. You get interested in watching something on the left side of the stage . . . and when you look back over on the right, everything is different. Or a new backdrop will suddenly slowly fly in and the whole reality be changed."

Time and movement are of major concern to Wilson; his plays frequently explore the effects of slowing down body movements. For example, a character will take hours to peel and slice an onion or to walk from one end of the stage to the other. Searle states that through these methods Wilson is "attempting . . . to explore the gradualness and imperceptibility of change." Stanley Kauffmann notes that the use of slow motion is a basic point of difference between Wilson's theatre and Surrealist theatre: "Wilson's tempo is *largo.* His intent is not the surrealist fracture of our 'defenses' with speedy sequences of illogic. He wants us to savor pictures."

Reviewers have commented that the length, slow motion, and spectacle of Wilson's plays produce a dream or trance-like state. To look for meanings or to form conclusions during a performance, they contend, ruins the intent of his work. In a *New Yorker* profile of Wilson and his work, the playwright tells Calvin Tomkins the "ideal" effect he is striving for: "When you have a group of people together for twelve hours or twenty-four hours, all sorts of things happen. The brain begins to operate on a slower frequency. Ideally, in our work, someone in the audience might reach a point of consciousness where he is on the same frequency as one of the performers—where he receives communications directly."

Because Wilson's chief interests lie in visual imagery and non-verbal communication, his plays contain a minimum of dialogue. Moreover, what little dialogue there is usually amounts to "verbal anarchy," according to T. E. Kalem of *Time.* In a review of "A Letter for Queen Victoria," he writes: "In a typical scene, characters shoutingly reiterate the following word-sounds contrapuntally: 'HAP-HATH-HAP-HAP-HATH—O.K., O.K., A-O.K., O.K., O.K.—SKY-SKY.' This sort of thing is punctuated by screams of primal therapy." And a writer for the *New York Times* reports that the dialogue in *Death, Destruction and Detroit* is made up of "fragmentary snatches of conversation, frequently repeated, and used as a kind of acoustic back-drop."

Tomkins suggests that "language is something [Wilson] uses as another theatrical material, like movement or light; the sense of the words is of minor importance." In the same article, Wilson tells Tomkins that "most of the important things never get communicated in words anyway"; and he outlines the motive behind his experimental approach to language and movement: "The object of a lot of the work we're doing with movement is to break movements down into very small units. Like Balinese dancers, who have something like a hundred and seventy-five eye movements alone. The question becomes 'Can we break down the phrasing of sounds in the same way and work with that?' "

Critical reaction to Wilson's methods and theories has been mixed. While some reviewers consider Wilson's plays truly innovative works of art, others find them boring, sometimes tasteless, exhibitions. As Kroll states, "[His] tactics enrage many critics, but others place Wilson among such modern masters as Beckett." Kauffmann, for example, praises Wilson's skill in presenting a "flowing gallery of pictures," but remarks, "This does not keep the performance from frequently being boring." *New York Magazine*'s John Simon holds a somewhat harsher opinion of Wilson's work. He claims that *A Letter for Queen Victoria* is a "scandal . . . that deadens you with its boredom more surely than Novacain could." He adds that "though the work calls itself an opera, it is merely *tableaux vivants* done to monotonous nonmusic and accompanied by meaningless verbalizing and gyrations." And *The $ Value of Man,* according to Simon in a later review, is no more than "a farrago of meaningless stage images, nonsensical verbal fragments, and purposeless actions endlessly repeated and dribbling into numbing inertia."

Response to one of Wilson's better-known plays, the multimedia stage epic *the CIVIL warS: a tree is best measured when it is down,* is likewise divided. Wilson has been quoted that the play—staged in sections around the world and not yet in its entirety—is meant to depict "a civil struggle that has gone on through all times" and provides a "comment on man's long journey to brotherhood." The effect of the work, according to John Rockwell in the *New York Times,* is one of "a sequence of dreamy stage-pictures without overt plot but interweaving a variety of world myths and historical personages." Some of the more striking elements of Wilson's assemblage, as Alan M. Kriegsman recounts in a *Washington Post* review of the play's "Rome Section," include "a giant Abraham Lincoln [which] floats across the stage like a dirigible; a pounding choric dance styled after Hopi rituals . . . ; a vision of Robert E. Lee gyrating in the porthole of a spaceship . . . ; and the descent of Hercules from the stage ceil-

ing on a golden ladder." Kriegsman finds "throughout the opera, sounds, images and choreographed movements of stunning originality and imaginative reach." Frank Rich of the *New York Times* complains, however, that such elements are "intermingled . . . to the self-aggrandizement of the author rather than the invigoration of the audience," adding that "not even Mr. Wilson's levitating tableaux of figurative or literal trees could prevent a potentially towering theater piece from falling with a thud." The Pulitzer Prize committee was also divided on *the CIVIL warS.* While the prize jury unanimously chose the play for the 1986 Pulitzer Prize in drama, the board overruled their decision in light of the fact that the work had never been staged in its entirety, "queasy about honoring work so few had seen or could see," reports Kriegsman.

Most critics—although they may not be able to understand or interpret his work—agree that Wilson is exploring important new concepts in the theatre and arts. Smith believes that Wilson is "reaching back to a deeper level of theatre," and gives this account of his reaction to *The Life and Times of Joseph Stalin:* "What is performed and witnessed doesn't translate into anything. . . . I didn't know what to follow; I didn't know if there was anything to follow. I didn't even try to make sense of it. It's in another language, one that has its meaning on another level. . . . It's a slow, heady language, its content accumulated through years of work and elusive as any esoteric communication." And Tomkins offers a similar assessment of Wilson's theatre. He notes that these experimental plays are not "susceptible to rational interpretation. All Wilson's plays," he continues, "come out of his own inner imagery, or that of people who are close to him, and they must be experienced rather than understood."

BIOGRAPHICAL/CRITICAL SOURCES:

BOOKS

Arrabal, Fernando, editor, *Le Theatre,* 1972, Volume 1, Christian Bourgeois, 1972.

Bersani, Leo, *A Future for Astyanax: Character and Desire in Literature,* Little, Brown, 1976.

Bourgeois, Araball Christian, editor, *Le Theatre,* [Paris], 1972.

Brecht, Stephan, *The Theater of Visions: Robert Wilson,* Suhrkamp Verlag (Frankfurt), 1979, Methuen, 1982.

Contemporary Literary Criticism, Gale, Volume 7, 1977, Volume 9, 1978.

Denby, Edwin, *Two Conversations with Edwin Denby,* Byrd Hoffman Foundation, 1973.

Kauffmann, Stanley, *Persons of the Drama,* Harper, 1976.

Nelson, Craig, editor, *Robert Wilson: The Theater of Images,* Contemporary Arts Center, Cincinnati, 1980, 2nd edition, Harper, 1984.

Quadri, Franco, *Il teatro di Robert Wilson,* Edizioni de La Biennale di Venizia, 1976.

Rose, Bernice, *New Works on Paper 3,* Museum of Modern Art, New York, 1985.

Shank, Theodore, *American Alternative Theater,* Grove Press, 1982.

Tomkins, Calvins, *The Scene,* Viking, 1976.

PERIODICALS

Artforum, February, 1977; February, 1978; October, 1984.

Art in America, November, 1980.

Boston Phoenix, July 18, 1978.

Die Buehne, summer, 1991, p. 30.

Cahiers, Numbers 81-82, 1972.

Connoisseur, April, 1984; June, 1991, p. 28.

Dallas Morning News, May 20, 1984.

Diapason-Harmonie, November, 1990, p. 32; June, 1991, p. 22.

Drama Review, June, 1973; June, 1974; September, 1975; March, 1976; December, 1976.

Ear: Magazine of New Music, Volume 13, number 8, 1988, pp. 18-21.

Kansas Quarterly, Volume 12, number 4, 1980.

Le Monde, October 24, 1984.

Los Angeles Times, December 23, 1984; December 21, 1986.

Mes en melodie, January, 1977, pp. 12-14.

Neue Zeitschrift fuer Musik, July-August, 1990, p. 61.

Newsweek, December 6, 1976; April 9, 1984; December 31, 1984.

New York Arts Journal, spring, 1977.

New Yorker, March 27, 1971; January 13, 1975.

New York Magazine, April 7, 1975; May 26, 1975.

New York Post, May 23, 1977.

New York Times, March 7, 1971; July 5, 1971; November 12, 1972; May 23, 1977; February 18, 1979; October 30, 1979; November 1, 1984; December 2, 1984; December 17, 1984; December 23, 1984; October 20, 1985; October 28, 1985,; November 3, 1985; May 25, 1986; December 4, 1986; December 11, 1986; December 16, 1986; December 23, 1986; January 8, 1987; January 10, 1987; May 2, 1987; May 20, 1990; June 20, 1990.

Oesterreichische Musikzeitschrift, May, 1990, pp. 260-261.

Opera News, September, 1990, p. 24.

Performance Art, Volume 1, number 1, 1979.

Der Spiegel, July 4, 1983.

Theater, summer/fall, 1981; fall/winter, 1984.

Theater Heute, September, 1980; July, 1982.

Time, December 31, 1973; April 7, 1975; May 21, 1984.

Times (London), June 10, 1978.

Vanity Fair, June, 1984, pp. 94-97.

Variety, March 3, 1971.

Village Voice, December 20, 1973; November 22, 1976; December 6, 1983, p. 95.

Wall Street Journal, December 21, 1984.

Washington Post, December 17, 1984; November 16, 1986; December 16, 1986; December 5, 1988.

* * *

WINSLOW, Pauline Glen (Jane Sheridan)

PERSONAL: Born in London, England; daughter of Stanley Glen (a boxer); married Raymond Winslow (a trombonist). *Education:* Attended Hunter College of the City University of New York, New School for Social Research, and Columbia University; studied fiction writing with Caroline Gordon.

ADDRESSES: Home—New York, NY.

CAREER: Free-lance court reporter in New York City; writer.

AWARDS, HONORS: Fellowships from Yaddo Foundation and Huntington Hartford Foundation.

WRITINGS:

NOVELS

The Strawberry Marten, Macmillan (London), 1973, published as *Gallows Child,* St. Martin's, 1978.

The Windsor Plot, Arlington Books, 1981, St. Martin's, 1985.

I, Martha Adams, Arlington Books, 1982, St. Martin's, 1984.

The Kindness of Strangers, Arlington Books, 1983.

Judgement Day, Arlington Books, 1984.

A Cry in the City, St. Martin's, 1990.

Judy Piatkus, St. Martin's, 1991.

NOVELS; AS JANE SHERIDAN

Damaris: A Romantic Historical Novel, St. Martin's, 1981.

My Lady Hoyden, St. Martin's, 1981.

Love at Sunset, St. Martin's, 1982.

NOVELS; "MERLE CAPRICORN" SERIES

Death of an Angel, St. Martin's, 1975.

The Brandenburg Hotel, St. Martin's, 1976.

The Witch Hill Murder, St. Martin's, 1977.

Copper Gold, St. Martin's, 1978.

The Counsellor Heart, St. Martin's, 1980, published as *Sister Death,* Fontana, 1982.

The Rockefeller Gift, St. Martin's, 1981.

Contributor to *Murderess Ink,* edited by Dilys Winn, Workman Publishing, 1981.

SIDELIGHTS: Unnamed gothic horrors, religious cultism, the threat of military destruction: Author Pauline Glen Winslow uses such classic subjects to craft her popular crime and mystery novels. While in some cases drawing on political and historical fact to create "what if " stories of thought-provoking proportions, Winslow also composes works of full fiction sometimes including her character Merle Capricorn, the British detective whom she has featured in a successful series of crime novels.

Winslow's first book, *The Strawberry Marten,* published in 1973, calls to mind Ruth Ellis, the London model who shot and killed her wealthy lover in 1950. In an account closely paralleling the actual events of the Ellis case, the book's quasi-fictional protagonist, Garnett Moore, is proclaimed to be the last woman hanged in England. Reviewing the novel in the London *Journal,* Phillip Crawley noted that Winslow "exploits to the maximum every irony of the story, so that it becomes a penetrating and moving study of the destruction of a human being."

"My first novel was not a mystery," Winslow told *CA,* "but it dealt with a murder and a hanging and led to my editor looking for more. Death has become a familiar theme: *The Strawberry Marten, Gallows Child,* the 'Capricorn' series, *Judgement Day, The Kindness of Strangers,* and *A Cry in the City.*" Describing 1990's *A Cry in the City* as "fast-paced and energetic . . . with its labyrinth plot and subtle details, involving old money families, Nazis, and a devoted loving young mother—or is she?," John Roux of the *New York City Tribune* praised the work as a "fine, engrossing new mystery novel, satisfying until the last page."

Winslow's detective creation, Superintendent Capricorn of Scotland Yard, is featured in a series of mystery novels, including *Death of an Angel, The Brandenburg Hotel, The Witch Hill Murder,* and *Copper Gold. Death of an Angel,* published in 1975, finds the British detective investigating the aftereffects of the death of a New York clairvoyant known as "Smoky Angel." Reviewers found the first "Capricorn" novel entertaining, as they did *The Brandenburg Hotel,* which followed a year later. A classic murder mystery set in a British country hotel at the close of World War II, Winslow's story involves German ex-prisoners of war: a beautiful model is found dead and her handsome older mentor and suspected lover is the prime suspect when Detective Sergeant Capricorn is called in to investigate. Capricorn is called into service again in *The Witch Hill Murder,* which *Publishers Weekly* called "a winner on all counts." This time the plot revolves around a religious cult as its activities intrude upon the quiet of a small English village and it succeeds in recruiting several local young people into its ranks.

Not all Winslow's books have been set in her native England. As she commented to *CA:* "My work has been translated in Europe and Japan, but my settings are mostly in the countries where I have lived—England and America." *I, Martha Adams,* first published in 1982, is set squarely on American soil—which is occupied by Soviet troops in this futuristic novel. The title character, a widow whose late husband had been involved in the construction of secret weaponry, attempts to locate the only weapon that has the chance to save democracy. Michael J. Bonafield, reviewing the novel for the *Washington Times Magazine,* called *I, Martha Adams* "a real spellbinder, a book with an intricate plot and clever political allusions."

I, Martha Adams is one of two books by Winslow that deal with "the possible death of a nation," she noted. "*I, Martha Adams,* written during the Cold War, shows the U.S. under occupation by the U.S.S.R., to be saved by an American Joan-of-Arc," she explained. "The other, *The Windsor Plot,* based in World War II, depicts an attempted coup d'etat." A thoughtful portrayal of what could have resulted if the late Duke of Windsor had been a collaborator with Nazi Germany, *The Windsor Plot* was praised by critics. *Publishers Weekly* proclaimed that the novel's author had "sorted the confusion of wartime international intricacies into an emotional, convincing novel that leaves the reader breathless at its conclusion."

Although residing for many years in New York City, Winslow often visits her native England to undertake the hours of research that gives her novels their realism. "I work every day, except when I am travelling, always under the eye of a cat," Winslow told *CA.* "The first was a black cat named Dinah, a tyrannical beast; and now there is Miss Jane, prim, grey-and-white, who loves to get a paw into a pile of manuscript."

BIOGRAPHICAL/CRITICAL SOURCES:

PERIODICALS

Journal (London), October 20, 1973.
Library Journal, August, 1977, p. 1682.
New York City Tribune, October 12, 1990.
New York Times Book Review, August 6, 1978, p. 33.
Publishers Weekly, June 20, 1977, p. 68; February 15, 1985.
Sunday Times (London), November 25, 1973.
Time, April 17, 1978, p. 98.
Times Literary Supplement, November 16, 1973, p. 1407.
Washington Times, October 23, 1984.

*   *   *

WINSTON, Mike
See KING, Florence

WODEHOUSE, Lawrence 1934-

PERSONAL: Surname is pronounced Wood-house; born June 14, 1934, in Norwich, England; son of Walter G. and Flora (Parsons) Wodehouse. *Education:* University of Durham, diploma in architecture, 1959; University of London, diploma in town planning, 1962; Cornell University, M.Arch., 1963; University of St. Andrews, Ph.D., 1980.

ADDRESSES: Office—University of Tennessee, Knoxville, TN 37996-2400.

CAREER: North Carolina State University at Raleigh, assistant professor of architectural history, 1964-69; Pratt Institute, Brooklyn, NY, associate professor, 1969-73, professor of architectural history, 1973-74; University of Dundee, Jordanstone College, Dundee, Scotland, lecturer in architecture, 1974-79; University of Tennessee, Knoxville, professor of architectural history, 1979—.

MEMBER: Royal Institute of British Architects (associate).

WRITINGS:

(Editor) *American Architecture from the Civil War to the First World War,* Gale, 1975.
(Editor) *American Architecture from the First World War to the Present,* Gale, 1975.
(Editor) *British Architects: 1840-1940,* Gale, 1978.
(Editor) *Indigenous Architecture Worldwide,* Gale, 1980.
Ada Louise Huxtable: A Bibliography, Garland Publishing, 1981.
(With Marian Moffett) *Built for the People of the United States: Fifty Years of TVA Architecture,* Art and Architecture Gallery, University of Tennessee, 1983.
(With Moffett) *The Cantilever Barn in East Tennessee,* School of Architecture, University of Tennessee, 1984.
White of McKim, Mead and White, Garland Publishing, 1986.
(With Moffett) *A History of Western Architecture,* Mayfield Publishing, 1989.
The Roots of International Style Architecture, Lotus Hill Press, 1991.
(With Moffett) *East Tennessee Cantilever Barns,* University of Tennessee Press, 1993.

Contributor of more than two dozen articles to professional journals, including *Art Journal, Antiques, Historic Preservation, Journal of the Society of Architectural Historians,* and *Old Time New England.*

WOJCIECHOWSKA, Maia (Teresa) 1927- (Maia Larkin, Maia Rodman)

PERSONAL: Surname pronounced "Voi-che-*hov*-skah"; born August 7, 1927, in Warsaw, Poland; immigrated to United States, 1942, naturalized citizen, 1950; daughter of Zygmunt (wartime chief-of-staff, Polish Air Force) and Zofia (Rudakowska) Wojciechowski; married Selden Rodman (a writer), December 8, 1950 (divorced, 1957); married Richard Larkin (a poet and antique restorer), January 9, 1972 (divorced, 1981); children: (first marriage) Oriana (daughter); Leonora (adopted daughter). *Education:* Attended schools in Poland, France, and England; attended Immaculate Heart College, 1945-46. *Politics:* "Jeffersonian Christian Anarchist." *Religion:* Roman Catholic.

ADDRESSES: Home—122 North Railroad Ave., Mahwah, NJ 07430. *Agent*— Gunther Stuhlmann, P.O. Box 276, Becket, MA 01223.

CAREER: Poet, translator, and children's fiction writer. Has worked at a variety of jobs (seventy-two in one year), including undercover detective, poll taker, and ghost writer. Translator for Radio Free Europe, 1949-51; *Retail Wholesale and Department Store Union Record,* New York City, assistant editor, 1953-55; *Newsweek,* New York City, copy girl, 1956; *RWDSU Record* (labor newspaper), New York City, assistant editor, 1957; *American Hairdresser* (trade publication), New York City, assistant editor, 1958-60; Kurt Hellmer, New York City, literary agent, 1960-61; independent literary agent, 1960-61; Hawthorn Books, Inc., New York City, publicity manager, 1961-65. Professional tennis player and instructor, 1949—. Founder and president of Maia Productions, Inc., Independent Books, 1975—, and ENOUGH!!!, 1986—.

AWARDS, HONORS: New York Herald Tribune Children's Spring Book Festival Awards honor book, 1964, and John Newbery Medal, 1965, both for *Shadow of a Bull;* Deutscher Jugendbuchpries, 1968; named to New Jersey Literary Hall of Fame, 1985.

WRITINGS:

Shadow of a Bull, Atheneum, 1964.
Odyssey of Courage: The Adventure of Alvar Nunez Cabeza de Vaca (juvenile biography), Atheneum, 1965.
A Kingdom in a Horse, Harper, 1966.
The Hollywood Kid, Harper, 1967.
A Single Light, Harper, 1968.
Tuned Out, Harper, 1968.
Hey, What's Wrong with This One?, Harper, 1969.
Don't Play Dead Before You Have To, Harper, 1970.
(Translator) Monika Kotowska, *The Bridge to the Other Side,* Doubleday, 1971.
The Rotten Years, Doubleday, 1971.

The Life and Death of a Brave Bull, Harcourt, 1972.

Through the Broken Mirror with Alice (includes parts of *Through the Looking Glass* by Lewis Carroll), Harcourt, 1972.

Winter Tales from Poland, Doubleday, 1972.

Till the Break of Day: Memories, 1939-1942, Harcourt, 1973.

How God Got Christian into Trouble, Westminster/John Knox, 1984.

UNDER NAME MAIA RODMAN

Market Day for Ti Andre (juvenile), Viking, 1952.

The Loved Look: International Hairstyling Guide, American Hairdresser, 1960.

The People in His Life (novel; Book-of-the-Month Club alternate selection), Stein & Day, 1980.

OTHER

Contributor of poetry to anthologies; writer of humorous pieces for *Sports Illustrated.* Contributor of articles and reviews to numerous periodicals. Translator from the Polish of a play by Slawomir Mrozek, performed Off-Broadway, 1962, and on British Broadcasting Corp. Radio, 1963 and 1964.

ADAPTATIONS: Tuned Out was adapted for film and released as *Stoned: An Anti-Drug Film* by Learning Corp. of America, 1981; *A Single Light* was adapted for film and released by Learning Corp. of America, 1986; the movie rights to *The People in His Life* and *Shadow of a Bull* have been optioned.

SIDELIGHTS: Maia Wojciechowska is a Polish-born novelist, biographer, poet, and translator who has long been considered an influential and respected figure in young adult and juvenile literature. Once described by John R. Tunis in the *New York Times Book Review* as "a magnificent writer," Wojciechowska's skill for accurately writing with sensitivity about the various problems confronting young people today in their search to find their own identity is admired and appreciated by her many readers. Awarded the prestigious Newbery Medal in 1965 for *Shadow of a Bull,* Wojciechowska has created many unique and unforgettable characters who courageously confront and resolve their problems.

One has only to look at Wojciechowska's interesting and adventurous life to understand the inspiration behind many of her popular works of fiction. Born in Warsaw, the capital of Poland, in 1927, Wojciechowska was a middle child—a resourceful and capable girl sandwiched between her two energetic brothers and surrounded by many colorful relatives. Wojciechowska's father was a pilot in the Polish Air Force and her mother often raised the family alone for the periods of time her father was stationed away from home. Definitely a daredevil, Wojciechowska was

constantly challenging herself with some dangerous feat. "I liked to do things I could feel were individualistic or strange," Wojciechowska told Justin Wintle in *The Pied Pipers.* For example, before her eleventh birthday, Wojciechowska had already parachuted three times from an airplane.

But all her childhood adventures paled when compared to Wojciechowska's dangerous escape from her homeland following the Nazi invasion of Poland at the outbreak of World War II in 1939. This historic event would dramatically change her life and force Wojciechowska to grow up quickly and face unimaginable challenges. Witnessing the horrible and vicious behavior of the Nazi invading troops towards the Polish people, especially those of Jewish descent, and fearing for her family's safety, Wojciechowska's mother decided to leave their home and join her husband who was stationed in France. She bravely guided Wojciechowska and her two brothers out of war-torn Poland. Often travelling on foot and desperately trying to avoid both the German and Soviet invaders, the Wojciechowska family made their way through Rumania and Italy, finally reaching France.

In 1940, when the French government surrendered to the power of the German occupation forces, Colonel Wojciechowski left for England while his family remained in France. The family would later seek refuge in Spain, Portugal, and England before deciding that the United States would make the safest and best home. At the end of 1942, Colonel Wojciechowski, who had been chief-of-staff of the Polish Air Force in Great Britain, accepted an assignment as air attache to the Polish Embassy in Los Angeles and the family started their new life in America.

Wojciechowska discusses this intriguing and fascinating time of her life in her autobiographical work, *Till the Break of Day.* Mary M. Burns writes in *Horn Book* of Wojciechowska's book in this manner: "Confession may be good for the soul, but confessional writing may not be good reading unless the penitent is blessed, as is the author of this remarkable document, with an understanding of life's absurdities, a sense of the dramatic, and a felicitous talent for precise, vivid description. Because of these qualities, her reminiscences of a turbulent adolescence during the Second World War are both intensely personal and yet recognizable as a universal statement on the tragicomic conditions which are a necessary part of maturation. . . . The book is a dazzling blend of emotional pyrotechnics and disciplined structure." In her *Best Sellers* review of *Till the Break of Day,* Shirley Weinstein remarks: "With great candor, humor, and vividness, Maia Wojciechowska gives an autobiographical account of how she lived through the years 1939-1942." Weinstein goes on to note that "many of Maia's escapades and lucky breaks will make the reader gasp. In describing herself Maia gives a true picture of the adolescent. Her obsession with ideals, death, love, self-hatred will strike a responsive chord. This is a book for everyone."

After graduation from high school in Los Angeles, Wojciechowska attended Immaculate Heart College for a year before leaving school in 1946. Although she always wanted to write for a living, Wojciechowska's first novel was rejected by over thirty publishers. Unable to survive as a writer and unsure of what other career she wanted to pursue, Wojciechowska tried her hand at a myriad of professions and amused herself with numerous adventures, such as motorcycle racing and downhill skiing. In one year, Wojciechowska worked at an unbelievable seventy-two jobs—ranging from waitress, masseuse, and undercover detective. During this time Wojciechowska also maintained a career as a professional tennis player and instructor.

In 1952, Wojciechowska finally discovered a vent for her sense of adventure and her passion for the unorthodox—writing. With the help and encouragement of her then husband, Selden Rodman, Wojciechowska wrote a story to accompany the artwork of a Haitian artist whose work she admired. Wojciechowska's first book, *Market Day for Ti Andre,* was published, launching what would become a very successful and rewarding writing career for her. Although never really losing her daredevil ways and her thirst for excitement, writing brought more stability to Wojciechowska's life. "Becoming a full-time writer 'for a living' was my way, I think, of growing up," explains Wojciechowska in her essay for *Something about the Author Autobiography Series.* "That I began to write children's books was perhaps my way of not cutting away from the childhood too drastically."

It is perhaps Wojciechowska's childlike spirit of adventure as well as her still vivid memories of her own adolescence that have made her stories for young people so appealing and popular. Her award-winning book, *Shadow of a Bull,* for example, is an exciting tale involving bullfighting set in a colorful city located in Spain. Manolo, the son of a famous bullfighter who lost his life in a bullfight, feels immense pressure to follow in his father's footsteps. Manolo is unhappy and confused and does not understand why he is feeling these emotions. Manolo finally realizes that he is training to be a bullfighter out of loyalty to his late father and not because it is what he really wants. For the first time in his life, Manolo is free to look within himself to discover what he wants to do with his life. "In this somber tale, the author captures the rhythm of the Spanish people and the personal conflict of a young boy," write John Gillespie and Diane Lembo in *Juniorplots: A Book Talk Manual for Teachers and Librarians.* "Wojciechowska's style reflects the austere grandeur of the Andalusian countryside. It is reminiscent of Hemingway, both

in the knowledge of bullfighting and in the deceptively spare construction."

Ruth Hill Viguers explains in *Horn Book* that this book is "no manifesto for or against bullfighting. [*Shadow of a Bull*] is a perceptive story, with a perfectly realized setting, of a boy torn between loyalty and the need to be himself. Rarely in a book for any age does one find such understanding of bullfighting background and the symbolic role of the *torero* (the 'killer of death'), of the agonies of an adolescent boy longing to be understood and recognized for himself, and of the phenomenon of the oneness of viewpoint of all the people of a village."

Wojciechowska shared her thoughts on writing *Shadow of a Bull* in her acceptance speech upon receiving the Newbery Medal in 1965. She told the audience attending the awards ceremony that "*Shadow [of a Bull]* was mostly about pride and being locked in. I say pride rather than self-respect, because in Spain the word *pride* encompasses so much—honor and dignity and self-esteem. You'll find that sort of pride in others, more often in the poor than in the rich, and you'll find it in yourself. Because you are you, you'll respect it wherever you find it in spite of what others may say about it. That sort of pride, sometimes—most of the time—makes life harder than it needs to be. But without pride, life is less.

"About being locked in. Sometimes one lives in a prison without a key, without hope of a pardon. Sometimes one never gets out. And sometimes, when one gets out, it is at a cost in pride, and sometimes at a cost in success. It all depends on who built the prison. If you've built the prison yourself, you should never pay in pride. If others have built it, I hope you'll pay them in success. So, you see, *Shadow of a Bull* is not a book about bullfighting after all." Wojciechowska's entire speech was also printed in *Newbery and Caldecott Medal Books: 1956-1965.*

This philosophy of self-respect or self-realization or searching for identity is a favorite theme of Wojciechowska's and is the focal point of most of her books. Wojciechowska believes in order to find happiness with themselves young people must first develop their own sense of self or identity. Critics often point to such Wojciechowska books as *The Hollywood Kid, A Single Light,* and *Tuned Out* as examples of how gifted Wojciechowska is at portraying the emotions experienced by many of today's youths as they move closer to adulthood.

For example, in *The Hollywood Kid,* fifteen-year-old Bryan finds himself lonely, emotionally empty, and confused. As the only son of a famous Hollywood movie star, Bryan was given all the material advantages money could buy, but none of the good things a stable, supportive family would provide. After several failed attempts to find happiness, Bryan finally discovers that what really matters in life is learning to accept and be content with who he is. Bryan rejects his old, shallow lifestyle and works hard to find his true self and achieve inner peace and fulfillment. "[In *The Hollywood Kid*] Bryan must choose between psychic independence or a relationship in which he is his mother's prop," explains Zena Sutherland in the *Bulletin of the Center for Children's Books.* "This is a problem faced by many adolescents, a problem not always recognized by the parental instigator; for this reason, the book has value."

In *A Single Light,* Wojciechowska once again draws on the starkly beautiful countryside of Spain to set her story of a deaf and nonverbal girl who was abandoned by her family and ostracized by the villagers confused by her handicap. Treated meanly and called a witch because of her inability to communicate and to hear properly, the young child takes a priceless religious statue she has grown attached to and hides in the nearby woods. The townspeople finally come to their senses and accept the girl for who she is and give her the love and understanding she has desired for so long. "I wanted to see whether I was any good as a writer," Wojciechowska once wrote, "so I picked the most difficult character, a mute-deaf girl. I am strongest at dialogue, you see, so it was working uphill. But it's probably my best book."

John R. Tunis states in the *New York Times Book Review* that *A Single Light* "is a short book, not more than 30,000 words. (How often good books are short!) I read it twice, to see whether it was as fine as it seemed. It was even better. . . . The unnamed girl's story is told in the simplest terms. As it moves to its climax, we see how her presence changes the lives of those around her. . . . The overtones in Maia Wojciechowska's book defy synopsis. The finale, in the hands of a less skillful craftsman, could have seemed overdone, even spurious. Here, it is both austere and moving. The whole tale moves and flows, like life. Hope for the future of man is its essence."

Three other books that contain the same themes of self-realization and the need for love as Wojciechowska's earlier works are *Tuned Out, Don't Play Dead Before You Have To,* and *The Rotten Years.* However, these novels for young people are different because they deal with very modern and serious problems—such as drug abuse in *Tuned Out,* depression and suicide in *Don't Play Dead Before You Have To,* and passionate political activism in *The Rotten Years.* In general, these books have been praised for their realistic and straightforward treatment of their sensitive subject matter. In her *New York Times Book Review* article discussing Wojciechowska's *Tuned Out,* Anita Macrae Feagles writes, "A hopeful trend in teen-age fiction is the increase in titles dealing with current, serious and often unpleasant situations." Feagles goes on to state that she believes *Tuned Out* "is certainly worthwhile read-

ing for young people, for whom fictionalized material is likely to be more meaningful." Zena Sutherland remarks in the *Bulletin of the Center for Children's Books* that *Tuned Out* is "a story of intensity and bleak honesty. . . . At times the writing slows, but this seems curiously appropriate in a story in which the stunned protagonist is fighting against time. [The book is candid], with no melodrama except the terrible melodrama of what is happening, and with a lack of didacticism that makes the message all the more effective."

Of Wojciechowska's novel dealing with suicide, *Don't Play Dead Before You Have To,* John Neufeld comments in the *New York Times Book Review* that there are several good things in this book: "Here is an attempt to write about the kid in-between—neither college nor slumbound, neither bright nor deadeningly dumb, not ambitious but aware—the middle achiever who is too frequently ignored. There is an honest, moving, yet oddly oblique look at the depression and attempted suicide of a very bright child whose parents are separating. And there is a lovely *coup de theatre* as an old man, a once-famous philosopher, allows a television interview knowing he will die on camera." Reviewing Wojciechowska's book about political activism, *The Rotten Years,* Benjamin DeMott remarks in the *New York Times Book Review* that "the strength of the book . . . is the author's fine enthusiasm for great moral and political undertakings. *The Rotten Years* doesn't stand back from 'causes' and commitment: it embraces them with a quickness and force that's the best kind of answer to the question, Does injustice matter?"

Summing up Wojciechowska's work for young adults, I. V. Hansen states in *Children's Literature in Education* that "Wojciechowska moralizes to a point where we as older readers become impatient. Classroom experience suggests to me that this impatience is an adult phenomenon. . . . In the affairs of people, animals and even things, the young teenager is still attracted by the bald contrast between good and evil, beauty and ugliness, calm and convulsion, courage and fear, all part of [Wojciechowska's] novels. For these novels breathe a myth-quality that makes some sense of a violent world of pain, uncertainty and rejection. Young readers want to feel that, after all, people are just. All too soon they will learn bitterly that this is not so."

In her acceptance speech at the Newbery Awards ceremony, Wojciechowska directed the following statement of her purpose as a writer to her readers: "I want to give you a glimpse of the choices you have before you, of the price that will be asked of you. . . . When you know what life has to sell, for how much, and what it can give away free, you will not live in darkness. I hope that in books you'll find your light, and that by this light you may cross from one shore of love to another, from your childhood into your adulthood. I hope that some of the light will come from my books and that, because of this light, life will lose its power to frighten you."

Wojciechowska went on to share some of her thoughts on what she feels makes a good writer of books for young people in *Writer*. She notes: "First of all, you must be a natural *admirer* of children. You must be one of those people who *instinctively* knows that children are the truly beautiful people. You must be aware of the magnificent beginning that is the lot of every human being, a beginning that is invariably loused up by people who don't recognize children as a superior breed. Children are more intelligent than adults. The directness of their thought processes must be the delight of logicians. They can write any adult under the table as readily as they can put to shame any painter. So you owe them *respect*."

BIOGRAPHICAL/CRITICAL SOURCES:

BOOKS

Children's Literature Review, Volume 1, Gale, 1976.
Contemporary Literary Criticism, Volume 26, Gale, 1983.
Gillespie, John, and Diane Lembo, *Juniorplots: A Book Talk Manual for Teachers and Librarians*, Bowker, 1967, p. 54.
Hopkins, Lee Bennett, *More Books by More People*, Citation, 1974.
Kingman, Lee, editor, *Newbery and Caldecott Medal Books: 1956-1965*, Horn Book, 1965, pp. 140-52.
Wintle, Justin, and Emma Fisher, *The Pied Pipers*, Paddington Press, 1975.
Wojciechowska, Maia, *Till the Break of Day: Memories 1939-1942*, Harcourt, 1973.
Wojciechowska, essay in *Something about the Author Autobiography Series*, Volume 1, Gale, 1986.

PERIODICALS

Best Sellers, April 15, 1973, p. 47.
Bulletin of the Center for Children's Books, March, 1967, p. 116; February, 1969, p. 104.
Children's Literature in Education, winter, 1981, pp. 186-91.
Horn Book, June, 1964, pp. 293-94; December, 1972, p. 609.
Kirkus Service, August 1, 1966, pp. 757-58.
Library Journal, July, 1968, p. 2738.
National Observer, December, 1968.
New York Times Book Review, November 6, 1966 (Part 2), p. 8; May 5, 1968 (Part 2), p. 3; November 24, 1968, p. 42; August 16, 1970, p. 22; November 7, 1971, pp. 3, 22; November 5, 1972.
Saturday Review, March 27, 1965.
Writer, April, 1971, p. 3; July, 1987; September, 1990.

OTHER

Wojciechowska, Maia, acceptance speech at the Newbery and Caldecott Awards Ceremony, 1965.

*   *   *

WOOD, Donna (Marie) 1949-

PERSONAL: Born June 6, 1949, in Detroit, MI; daughter of Eugene (in retailing) and Dolores (Zuchowski) Stickel; married Gregory Wood (an auditor), November 12, 1971. *Education:* Wayne State University, B.A., 1971. *Politics:* Democrat. *Religion:* Roman Catholic.

ADDRESSES: Home—41795 Alden Dr., Clinton Township, MI 48038. *Office*—Gale Research Inc., 835 Penobscot Bldg., Detroit, MI 48226.

CAREER: National Bank of Detroit, Detroit, MI, proof machine operator, 1968-69; *New Center News*, Detroit, reporter, 1969-71; Gale Research Inc., Detroit, editorial assistant, 1972-73, assistant editor, 1973-77, associate editor, 1977-79, editor, 1979-85, senior editor, 1985—.

WRITINGS:

(Editor) *Business Firms Master Index: A Guide to Sources of Information about Companies in the United States and Canada and Foreign Firms with Offices in the United States*, Gale, 1985.
(Editor) *International Trade Names Dictionary*, Gale, 1988.
(Editor) *International Brands and Their Companies: International Consumer Products and Their Manufacturers, Importers, and Distributors with Addresses*, Gale, 1990.
(Editor) *International Companies and Their Brands: International Manufacturers, Importers, and Distributors, Their Addresses and Consumer Products*, Gale, 1990.

SIDELIGHTS: Donna Wood once told *CA:* "Nearing completion of my college days, majoring in journalism, I was unsure of the course to follow. I was not fond of the constant deadlines involved in newspaper reporting. Upon the advice of a professor, who apparently knew me better than I thought, I contemplated a career in publishing and found employment at Gale Research. It has proven to be exactly what I wanted."

*   *   *

WOODIWISS, Kathleen E(rin) 1939-

PERSONAL: Born June 3, 1939, in Alexandria, LA; daughter of Charles Wingrove, Sr., and Gladys (Coker)

Hogg; married Ross Woodiwiss (a U.S. Air Force major), July 20, 1956 (divorced); children: Sean Alan, Dorren James, Heath Alexander. *Education:* Attended schools in Alexandria, LA. *Politics:* Republican.

ADDRESSES: Home—Princeton, MN. *Office*—c/o Avon Books, 105 Madison Ave., New York, NY 10016.

CAREER: Writer. Worked as a model in fashion shows in Tokyo, Japan.

WRITINGS:

NOVELS

The Flame and the Flower, Avon, 1972.
The Wolf and the Dove, Avon, 1974.
Shanna, Avon, 1977.
Ashes in the Wind, Avon, 1979.
A Rose in Winter, Avon, 1982.
Come Love a Stranger, Avon, 1984.
So Worthy My Love, Avon, 1989.
Forever in Your Embrace, Avon, 1992.

ADAPTATIONS: So Worthy My Love has been adapted for audio cassette.

SIDELIGHTS: A pioneering writer of romance fiction, Kathleen E. Woodiwiss's first novel is generally credited with creating the subgenre known as "erotic historical" romance. When *The Flame and the Flower* was published in 1972 the field of romance writing was dominated by "contemporary gothics" produced by writers such as Mary Stewart, Victoria Holt, and Phyllis Whitney. *The Flame and the Flower* differed from its predecessors in that it was substantially longer, but also because it contained lengthy, often detailed passages describing the sexual encounters of the hero and heroine. The immediate success of *The Flame and the Flower* cleared the way for writers like Rosemary Rogers and Laura McBain, authors who, along with Woodiwiss, have helped make the historical romance an enormously popular form.

The novels following *The Flame and the Flower* continued to be ground-breakers and assured Woodiwiss a large and loyal readership. *Shanna,* Woodiwiss's third book, made publishing history by becoming the first historical romance released in a trade paperback edition, and went on to sell over three million copies and spend a full year on the *New York Times* bestseller list. And in 1979 Avon published *Ashes in the Wind* with a first printing of 1.5 million copies and backed the book with a huge promotional campaign, including full-page advertisements in national women's magazines and commercials on network television. The publicity paid off almost immediately as *Ashes in the Wind* sold over two million copies and went into a third printing within a month of its release. All told, Woodiwiss's books have sold over ten million copies.

In spite of her remarkable success, Woodiwiss's initial motives for writing were rather simple. "I couldn't find anything good to read, a good romantic book to pass a few hours away, so I decided to write one myself," she explains in an interview with Judy Klemesrud for the *New York Times Book Review.* "I just started pecking away at this story set during the American Revolution. It wasn't anything I could get completely absorbed in. I had three boys at home, and there were always dishes to be put in the dishwasher." Woodiwiss finished the book and, following the advice of her husband and friends, submitted it to half a dozen publishers. After they had all rejected it, she sent the book to Avon where an editor, Nancy Coffey, picked it out of a group of submitted manuscripts known as the "slush pile." The book became *The Flame and the Flower* and went on to launch Woodiwiss into a successful writing career.

Historical romances vary in some respects but share fundamental similarities. Settings are typically exotic and frequently change from continent to continent. Heroes are characteristically handsome and commanding while heroines are beautiful and sensitive. Often innocent, the heroine is usually introduced to the hero with whom she falls in love, only to be parted from him for much of the story. The book inevitably ends with the heroine being united with her true love. *The Flame and the Flower* clearly embodies the traditions of its genre. The heroine, Heather, is a teenager throughout the narrative, which begins in England around 1800 and eventually moves to the American Carolinas. A beautiful and decorous girl who becomes the ward of a cruel aunt, Heather is raped by an attractive Yankee who in turn is forced to marry her. After many adventures, the pair reunite and their initial hatred for each other turns to love. *The Flame and the Flower* also maintains the traditional structural relationship of males as dominant to and protective of females.

Where *The Flame and the Flower* and other Woodiwiss novels break with tradition is in their frank depiction of the sexual relationship between the hero and the heroine. While her books contain occasional sexual passages, Woodiwiss objects to charges that her books are "erotic." "I'm insulted when my books are called erotic," she maintains in a *Cosmopolitan* interview. "I don't think people who say that have read my books. I believe I write love stories. With a little spice. Some of the other current romances are a bit savage, though. They make sex dirty. It's embarrassing to read them. But women are looking for the love story. I get a lot of fan mail, and they tell me that." Janice Radway, writing in *Twentieth-Century Romance and Historical Writers,* sees the erotic passages in Woodiwiss's novels as being integral parts of "complex plots which all focus on the *gradual* development of love between the two principal characters. Unlike many writers of this subgenre who keep the heroine and the hero apart until the final pages of the novel, Woodiwiss brings them into contact early in the tale. Having established their initial attraction for each other, she then shows how love develops between two extraordinary individuals, emphasizes that the relationship must be cultivated carefully, and demonstrates that compromise, tenderness, and generosity are necessary to maintain it."

Just such a relationship is presented in Woodiwiss's 1979 novel *Ashes in the Wind*. This tale features the heroine Alaina MacGaren, a seventeen-year-old orphan who must leave her home in Virginia for New Orleans when a rumor is started that she is a traitor. In order to keep her identity a secret, Alaina assumes a number of disguises, including that of a street urchin, a penniless widow, and a hospital volunteer. In the midst of these many identities, the life of surgeon Captain Cole Lattimer becomes entangled with Alaina's, and the two overcome adversity to find a deep and lasting love. Although *Washington Post Book World* contributor Maude McDaniel finds *Ashes in the Wind* to be filled with silly characters, a formulaic plot, and awful writing, she goes on to conclude: "Actually, I rather enjoyed." And a *Publishers Weekly* contributor maintains that Woodiwiss "has fashioned her heroine in a picaresque tradition. Readers will find Alaina's spunky ingenuity refreshing."

In Woodiwiss's 1989 romance *So Worthy My Love*, Maxim Seymour, another alleged traitor, this time to Queen Elizabeth, is thought to be dead. The young man, hated by the noble Radborne family, is actually hiding in Germany, desperately wanting his beloved, Arabella Radborne, to be with him. Sending his men to kidnap her, Maxim is surprised when they bring back Arabella's beautiful cousin Elise by mistake. Unable to let Elise go, the two battle each other defiantly until they realize that they are actually in love. Woodiwiss "provides ripe descriptions" in *So Worthy My Love*, states a *Publishers Weekly* contributor, adding: "This long romance by a veteran of the genre delivers well-paced, well-structured diversion."

Although *So Worthy My Love*, and most of Woodiwiss's other novels, are enormously successful with the public, they are generally ignored by "serious" reviewers. This situation does not seem to bother Woodiwiss, however, nor does it make her wish to change her approach to writing. "I never started out to win any prizes for my writing," she relates in her interview with Klemesrud. "I wanted to appease a hunger for romantic novels, and that is what I shall continue to do." Woodiwiss similarly points out in an interview with Jean W. Ross for *CA* that her books are only an attempt to give readers "enjoyment. Escape. I would like to be able to give the reader a time period of relaxation and pleasure, a time of being able to put the worries and everything aside and just enjoy and relax."

BIOGRAPHICAL/CRITICAL SOURCES:

BOOKS

Bestsellers 90, Issue 1, Gale, 1990.
Falk, Kathryn, *Love's Leading Ladies,* Pinnacle Books, 1982.
Henderson, Lesley, editor, *Twentieth-Century Romance and Historical Writers,* 2nd edition, St. James Press, 1990.
Woodiwiss, Kathleen, in an interview with Jean W. Ross for *Contemporary Authors New Revisions Series,* Volume 23, Gale, 1988, pp. 461-63.

PERIODICALS

Cosmopolitan, February, 1978.
Library Journal, May 15, 1974, p. 1410.
New York Times Book Review, November 4, 1979.
Publishers Weekly, January 21, 1974, p. 88; January 31, 1977; May 30, 1977; September 3, 1979, p. 94; October 22, 1982, p. 51; August 25, 1989, p. 57.
Village Voice, May 9, 1977.
Washington Post Book World, April 9, 1972, p. 9; October 7, 1979, pp. 9, 14.
WB, September-October, 1989.
West Coast Review of Books, January, 1983, p. 42.

*   *   *

WRIGHT, Cynthia Challed 1953-

PERSONAL: Born April 1, 1953, in Cedar Rapids, IA; daughter of Eugene Frank (a pharmacist) and Priscilla (Patterson) Challed; married Richard Wright (a naval officer), April 1, 1972; children: Jennifer Rae. *Education:* Attended University of Iowa, 1971-72. *Avocational interests:* Reading, exploring New England, European travel.

CAREER: Writer, 1975—.

WRITINGS:

Caroline, Ballantine, 1977.
Touch the Sun, Ballantine, 1978.
Brighter Than Gold, Ballantine, 1990.
Natalya, Ballantine, 1991.
Fireblossom, Ballantine, 1992.

SIDELIGHTS: Cynthia Challed Wright once told *CA:* "My career . . . is a dream come true for me. *Caroline* was my hobby. I knew the odds and had little hope of being published, yet I had to try. Now I believe in pursuing one's dreams, no matter how elusive they may seem.

"I chose historical romance. I enjoy writing love stories, and I also feel that they can have an impact on readers' lives. I avoid the violent, degrading aspects of the current genre, instead emphasizing women's strengths and capabilities. I try to leave the reader feeling positive about herself and her ability to deal with life."

Y-Z

YAMAUCHI, Edwin M(asao) 1937-

PERSONAL: Surname is pronounced Ya-ma-*u*-chi; born February 1, 1937, in Hilo, HI; son of Shokyo and Haruko (Owan) Yamauchi; married Kimie Honda (a secretary), August 31, 1962; children: Brian, Gail. *Education:* Attended Columbia Bible College, 1955-56, and University of Hawaii, 1957-58; Shelton College, B.A., 1960; Harvard University, additional study, 1962; Brandeis University, M.A., 1962, Ph.D., 1964. *Politics:* Independent. *Religion:* Evangelical.

ADDRESSES: Home—807 Erin Dr., Oxford, OH 5056. *Office*—Department of History, Miami University, Oxford, OH 5056.

CAREER: Shelton College, Ringwood (now in Cape May), NJ, instructor in Greek, 1960-61; Rutgers University, New Brunswick, NJ, assistant professor of history, 1964-69; Miami University, Oxford, OH, associate professor, 1969-73, professor of history, 1973—, director of graduate studies, 1978-82. Has participated in archaeological excavations in Jerusalem and Tel Anafa, Israel.

MEMBER: American Oriental Society, Association of Ancient Historians, Evangelical Theological Society (chairman of Eastern section, 1965-66), Society of Biblical Literature, Near East Archaeological Society (member of board of directors, 1973—; vice-president, 1978-79), Archaeological Institute of America (president of Oxford chapter, 1973-74), Conference on Faith and History (president, 1974-76), American Scientific Affiliation (fellow; president, 1983), Institute for Biblical Research (chairman, 1984-86; president, 1987-89), Ohio Academy of History, Ohio Classical Conference, Society of Biblical Literature.

AWARDS, HONORS: National Endowment for the Humanities fellow, 1968; American Institute of Holy Land Studies research fellow, 1968; American Philosophical Society grant for research in England, 1970; Institute for Advanced Christian Studies fellow, 1974-75.

WRITINGS:

Composition and Corroboration in Classical and Biblical Studies, Presbyterian & Reformed, 1966.
Greece and Babylon: Early Contacts between the Aegean and the Near East, Baker Book, 1967.
Mandaic Incantation Texts, American Oriental Society, 1967.
Gnostic Ethics and Mandaean Origins, Harvard University Press, 1970.
The Stones and the Scriptures, Lippincott, 1972, revised edition, Inter-Varsity Press, 1973.
Pre-Christian Gnosticism, Eerdmans, 1973, 2nd edition, Baker Book, 1983.
(With D. J. Wiseman) *Archaeology and the Bible,* Zondervan, 1979.
The Archaeology of New Testament Cities in Western Asia Minor, Baker Book, 1980, published as *New Testament Cities in Western Asia Minor,* 1987.
The Scriptures and Archaeology, Western Conservative Baptist Seminary, 1980.
The World of the First Christians, Lion, 1981, published as *Harper's World of the New Testament,* Harper, 1981.
Foes from the Northern Frontier, Baker Book, 1982.
(Editor with Jerry Vardaman and contributor) *Chronos, Kairos, Christos,* Eisenbrauns, 1989.
Persia and the Bible, Baker Book, 1990.

Contributor of chapters to books, including *New Perspectives on the Old Testament,* edited by Payne, Word Books, 1970; *The New Testament Student and His Field,* edited by Skilton and Ladley, Presbyterian and Reformed, 1982; and *The Miracles of Jesus,* edited by Wenham and Blomberg, JSOT Press, 1986. Contributor to dictionaries and encyclopedias, including *Biblical World: A Dictionary of Biblical Archaeology, New Illustrated Bible Encyclopaedia, Pictorial Encyclopedia of the Bible, Dictionary of Christian Ethics, Dictionary of Biblical Archaeology, Handbook of Christian History, Theological Wordbook of the Old Testament, Interpreter's Dictionary of the Bible* (Supplementary Volume), *Expositor's Bible Commentary, The World's Religions, New Dictionary of Christian Theology, Great Leaders of the Christian Church, Baker Encyclopedia of the Bible, Layman's Bible Dictionary, Dictionary of Jesus and the Gospels, The Anchor Bible Dictionary,* and *International Standard Bible Encyclopedia,* and to festschrifts and journals. *Christianity Today,* editor-at-large, 1972-80, senior editor, 1992—; consulting editor in history, *Journal of the American Scientific Affiliation;* member of editorial boards, *Fides et Historia, Bulletin for Biblical Research,* and *Perspectives on Science and Christian Faith;* member of editorial committee, *Journal of the Evangelical Theological Society.*

WORK IN PROGRESS: Editor with Mattingly and Hoerth, *Peoples of the Old Testament World,* for Baker Book; co-author with Clause and Pierard, *Christians and Culture: The Church in the World,* for Moody Press; editor, *Africa and Africans in Antiquity; Africa and the Bible;* editor and contributor, *Dictionary of Biblical Customs and Manners,* for Zondervan.

*   *   *

YOUNG, Ahdele Carrine   1923-
(Carrie Young)

PERSONAL: Born May 29, 1923, in Alamo, ND; daughter of Sever K. (a farmer) and Carrine (a pioneer homesteader; maiden name, Gafkjen) Berg; married Gerald W. Young (in public relations), May 10, 1949; children: Lee, Felicia. *Education:* University of Minnesota, B.A., 1944. *Religion:* Lutheran.

ADDRESSES: Office—Rte. 2, Tipp City, OH 45371.

CAREER: Blue Earth Post and Faribault County Register, Blue Earth, MN, reporter, 1946; Rike's Department Store, Dayton, OH, advertising copywriter, 1948-50; raising Welsh ponies on Ohio farm, 1957—; writer, 1981—. Member of Troy-Tipp Book Review Club.

MEMBER: Authors Guild, Authors League of America.

AWARDS, HONORS: Florence Roberts Head Memorial Award, Ohioana Library Association, 1982, for *Green Broke; Nothing to Do But Stay: My Pioneer Mother* was named a Best Book of 1991, *School Library Journal.*

WRITINGS:

UNDER NAME CARRIE YOUNG

Green Broke (autobiographical account), Dodd, 1981.
Nothing to Do But Stay: My Pioneer Mother, University of Iowa Press, 1991.
The Wedding Dress: Stories from the Dakota Plains, University of Iowa Press, 1992.
(With daughter, Felicia Young) *Prairie Cooks: Glorified Rice, Three-Day Buns, and Other Reminiscences,* University of Iowa Press, 1993.

Contributor to periodicals.

WORK IN PROGRESS: Research for a contemporary Ohio novel.

SIDELIGHTS: Carrie Young told *CA:* "I had always wanted to write a book about my pioneer mother, who homesteaded on the North Dakota plains in the early 1900s, and whose entire life was an example of vision and courage. I began several times, but could never seem to get a spark. So I wrote *Green Broke* instead, the story of my life on a Welsh pony farm in Ohio—a story that I was at that moment living. I used the essay form, taking just one subject at a time, and it worked very well for me.

"After *Green Broke* was published, having sharpened my wits, my teeth, and my writing skills on the Ohio farm, I decided to use the essay form to write about the North Dakota farm and my pioneer mother.

"I sold the first two essays to *Gourmet,* and when the *Missouri Review* enthusiastically accepted the third, I knew I had found my form, so I kept going. I collected the essays in the book entitled *Nothing to Do But Stay: My Pioneer Mother.* In describing the essays, [reviewer Ben Logan of] the *New York Times Book Review* said, 'Each, like a single block in an old-fashioned quilt, add up to a whole that shows us a way of physical and psychic survival.'

"After *Nothing to Do But Stay* was published, my mind was still teeming with the North Dakota experience; I wasn't yet ready to leave it. The act of writing the book had reactivated in my memory all sorts of dormant emotions and impressions from my childhood, which I could only do justice to in the short story form. So I began for the first time to write fiction. One story opened up the flood gates to another, and when I had seven I collected them into the book *The Wedding Dress: Stories from the Dakota Plains.*

"But I still am not through with the Dakota experience. I received so many letters from persons who had read *Nothing to Do But Stay* and wanted specific recipes for dishes mentioned in the book that I have written a food memoir about prairie cooking. One remembered taste led to another until I was dreaming about food I hadn't eaten in half a century. Written with my daughter, Felicia Young, *Prairie Books: Glorified Rice, Three-Day Buns, and Other Reminiscences* [was] published by the University of Iowa Press in the fall of 1993."

BIOGRAPHICAL/CRITICAL SOURCES:

BOOKS

Young, Carrie, *Green Broke* (autobiographical account), Dodd, 1981.

PERIODICALS

Columbus Dispatch, September 20, 1981; October 4, 1981.
New York Times Book Review, September 22, 1991, p. 53.
Orion Nature Book Review, October, 1981.
Piqua Daily Call, October 6, 1981.
Tipp City Herald, May 26, 1981.
Troy Daily News, May 6, 1981.
Welsh Roundabout, November-December, 1981.
Western Horseman, September, 1981.
West Milton Record, May 12, 1981.
Williston Daily Herald, June 14, 1981.

*   *   *

YOUNG, Carrie
  See YOUNG, Ahdele Carrine

*   *   *

ZISTEL, Era

PERSONAL: Born in Cleveland, OH; daughter of Herman and Mary (Rodecker) Zistel; married Eric Posselt, 1942 (deceased). *Education:* Western Reserve University (now Case Western Reserve University), B.A. *Politics:* Variable.

ADDRESSES: Home—Haines Falls, NY. *Agent*—Larry Sternig, 742 Robertson St., Milwaukee, WI 53213.

CAREER: Writer.

WRITINGS:

(Editor) *A Treasury of Cat Stories,* Greenberg, 1944.
(Editor) *Golden Book of Cat Stories,* Ziff-Davis, 1946.
(Editor) *Golden Book of Dog Stories,* Ziff-Davis, 1947.
Haesel und Gretel, Kosmos, 1956.
Orphan, a Raccoon, Rand McNally, 1958, revised edition, Townsend, 1990.
Good Year, Crowell, 1959.
Wintertime Cat, Holt, 1963.
The Gentle People, Holt, 1964.
Thistle, Random House, 1967.
The Dangerous Year, Random House, 1967.
Hi Fella, Lippincott, 1977.
Good Companions, Little, Brown, 1980.
(And photographer) *Thistle & Co.,* Little, Brown, 1982.
A Cat Called Christopher, Townsend, 1991.

Contributor of articles to *Down East, Everywoman, Defenders of Wildlife, Reader's Digest, Catholic Digest, Saturday Evening Post, Christian Science Monitor, McCall's,* and other periodicals.

SIDELIGHTS: Era Zistel told *CA:* "Turning against the tide, I strive for simplicity in writing, my belief being that the straining for unusual metaphors and similes and other squirmings to produce something 'original'—perhaps to compensate for lack of subject matter—[is] getting quite out of bounds."

BIOGRAPHICAL/CRITICAL SOURCES:

PERIODICALS

Audubon, March, 1969.
Chicago Tribune, February 11, 1968.
New York Times Book Review, November 15, 1967.
Washington Post, March 15, 1980.